THIRD EDITION

Programming iOS 6

Matt Neuburg

Beijing · Cambridge · Farnham · Köln · Sebastopol · Tokyo

Programming iOS 6, Third Edition

by Matt Neuburg

Published by O'Reilly Media, Inc., 1005 Gravenstein Highway North, Sebastopol, CA 95472.

O'Reilly books may be purchased for educational, business, or sales promotional use. Online editions are also available for most titles (*http://my.safaribooksonline.com*). For more information, contact our corporate/institutional sales department: (800) 998-9938 or *corporate@oreilly.com*.

Editor: Rachel Roumeliotis		**Cover Designer:** Randy Comer
Production Editor: Kristen Borg		**Interior Designer:** David Futato
Proofreader: O'Reilly Production Services		**Illustrator:** Matt Neuburg
Indexer: Matt Neuburg		

March 2013:   Third Edition

Revision History for the Third Edition:

2013-02-27:   First release

See *http://oreilly.com/catalog/errata.csp?isbn=9781449365769* for release details.

ISBN: 978-1-449-36576-9

[LSI]

Table of Contents

Part II.   IDE

Part III. Cocoa

Part V.   Interface

Part VI.   Some Frameworks

Part VII.   Final Topics

Preface

Aut lego vel scribo; doceo scrutorve sophian.

—Sedulius Scottus

With the advent of version 2 of the iPhone system, Apple proved they could do a remarkable thing — adapt their existing Cocoa computer application programming framework to make applications for a touch-based device with limited memory and speed and a dauntingly tiny display. The resulting Cocoa Touch framework, in fact, turned out to be in many ways better than the original Cocoa.

A programming framework has a kind of personality, an overall flavor that provides an insight into the goals and mindset of those who created it. When I first encountered Cocoa Touch, my assessment of its personality was: "Wow, the people who wrote this are really clever!" On the one hand, the number of built-in interface widgets was severely and deliberately limited; on the other hand, the power and flexibility of some of those widgets, especially such things as UITableView, was greatly enhanced over their Mac OS X counterparts. Even more important, Apple created a particularly brilliant way (UIViewController) to help the programmer make entire blocks of interface come and go and supplant one another in a controlled, hierarchical manner, thus allowing that tiny iPhone display to unfold virtually into multiple interface worlds within a single app without the user becoming lost or confused.

Even more impressive, Apple took the opportunity to recreate and rationalize Cocoa from the ground up as Cocoa Touch. Cocoa itself is very old, having begun life as NeXTStep before Mac OS X even existed. It has grown by accretion and with a certain conservatism in order to maintain something like backward compatibility. With Cocoa Touch, on the other hand, Apple had the opportunity to throw out the baby with the bath water, and they seized this opportunity with both hands.

So, although Cocoa Touch is conceptually based on Mac OS X Cocoa, it is very clearly *not* Mac OS X Cocoa, nor is it limited or defined by Mac OS X Cocoa. It's an independent creature, a leaner, meaner, smarter Cocoa. I could praise Cocoa Touch's deliberate use of systematization (and its healthy respect for Occam's Razor) through numerous examples. Where Mac OS X's animation layers are glommed onto views as a kind of afterthought, a Cocoa Touch view always has an animation layer counterpart. Memory management policies, such as how top-level objects are managed when a nib loads, are simplified and clarified. And so on.

At the same time, Cocoa Touch is still a form of Cocoa. It still requires a knowledge of Objective-C. It is not a scripting language; it is certainly not aimed at nonprogrammers, like HyperCard's HyperTalk or Apple's AppleScript. It is still huge and complicated. In fact, it's rather difficult.

The popularity of the iPhone, with its largely free or very inexpensive apps, and the subsequent popularity of the iPad, have brought and will continue to bring into the fold many new programmers who see programming for these devices as worthwhile and doable, even though they may not have felt the same way about Mac OS X. Apple's own annual WWDC developer conventions have reflected this trend, with their emphasis shifted from Mac OS X to iOS instruction.

The widespread eagerness to program iOS, however, though delightful on the one hand, has also fostered a certain tendency to try to run without first learning to walk. iOS gives the programmer mighty powers that can seem as limitless as imagination itself, but it also has fundamentals. I often see questions online from programmers who are evidently deep into the creation of some interesting app, but who are stymied in a way that reveals quite clearly that they are unfamiliar with the basics of the very world in which they are so happily cavorting.

It is this state of affairs that has motivated me to write this book, which is intended to ground the reader in the fundamentals of iOS. I love Cocoa and have long wished to write about it, but it is iOS and its popularity that has given me a proximate excuse to do so. Indeed, my working title was "Fundamentals of Cocoa Touch Programming." Here I have attempted to marshal and expound, in what I hope is a pedagogically helpful and instructive yet ruthlessly Euclidean and logical order, the principles on which sound iOS programming rests, including a good basic knowledge of Objective-C (starting with C itself) and the nature of object-oriented programming, advice on the use of the tools, the full story on how Cocoa objects are instantiated, referred to, put in communication with one another, and managed over their lifetimes, and a survey of the primary interface widgets and other common tasks. My hope, as with my previous books, is that you will both read this book cover to cover (learning something new often enough to keep you turning the pages) and keep it by you as a handy reference.

This book is not intended to disparage Apple's own documentation and example projects. They are wonderful resources and have become more wonderful as time goes on. I have depended heavily on them in the preparation of this book. But I also find that they don't fulfill the same function as a reasoned, ordered presentation of the facts. The online documentation must make assumptions as to how much you already know; it can't guarantee that you'll approach it in a given order. And online documentation is more suitable to reference than to instruction. A fully written example, no matter how well commented, is difficult to follow; it demonstrates, but it does not teach.

A book, on the other hand, has numbered chapters and sequential pages; I can assume you know C before you know Objective-C for the simple reason that Chapter 1 precedes Chapter 2. And along with facts, I also bring to the table a degree of experience, which I try to communicate to you. Throughout this book you'll see me referring to "common beginner mistakes"; in most cases, these are mistakes that I have made myself, in addition to seeing others make them. I try to tell you what the pitfalls are because I assume that, in the course of things, you will otherwise fall into them just as naturally as I did as I was learning. You'll also see me construct many examples piece by piece or extract and explain just one tiny portion of a larger app. It is not a massive finished program that teaches programming, but an exposition of the thought process that developed that program. It is this thought process, more than anything else, that I hope you will gain from reading this book.

iOS is huge, massive, immense. It's far too big to be encompassed in a book even of this size. And in any case, that would be inappropriate and unnecessary. There are entire areas of Cocoa Touch that I have ruthlessly avoided discussing. Some of them would require an entire book of their own. Others you can pick up well enough, when the time comes, from the documentation. This book is only a beginning — the fundamentals. But I hope that it will be the firm foundation that will make it easier for you to tackle whatever lies beyond, in your own fun and rewarding iOS programming future.

Conventions Used in This Book

The following typographical conventions are used in this book:

Italic
> Indicates new terms, URLs, email addresses, filenames, and file extensions.

`Constant width`
> Used for program listings, as well as within paragraphs to refer to program elements such as variable or function names, databases, data types, environment variables, statements, and keywords.

`Constant width bold`
> Shows commands or other text that should be typed literally by the user.

`Constant width italic`
> Shows text that should be replaced with user-supplied values or by values determined by context.

This icon signifies a tip, suggestion, or general note.

 This icon indicates a warning or caution.

Using Code Examples

This book is here to help you get your job done. In general, you may use the code in this book in your programs and documentation. You do not need to contact us for permission unless you're reproducing a significant portion of the code. For example, writing a program that uses several chunks of code from this book does not require permission. Selling or distributing a CD-ROM of examples from O'Reilly books does require permission. Answering a question by citing this book and quoting example code does not require permission. Incorporating a significant amount of example code from this book into your product's documentation does require permission.

We appreciate, but do not require, attribution. An attribution usually includes the title, author, publisher, and ISBN. For example: "*Programming iOS 6* by Matt Neuburg (O'Reilly). Copyright 2013 Matt Neuburg, 978-1-449-36576-9."

If you feel your use of code examples falls outside fair use or the permission given above, feel free to contact us at *permissions@oreilly.com*.

Safari® Books Online

 Safari Books Online is an on-demand digital library that lets you easily search over 7,500 technology and creative reference books and videos to find the answers you need quickly.

With a subscription, you can read any page and watch any video from our library online. Read books on your cell phone and mobile devices. Access new titles before they are available for print, and get exclusive access to manuscripts in development and post feedback for the authors. Copy and paste code samples, organize your favorites, download chapters, bookmark key sections, create notes, print out pages, and benefit from tons of other time-saving features.

O'Reilly Media has uploaded this book to the Safari Books Online service. To have full digital access to this book and others on similar topics from O'Reilly and other publishers, sign up for free at *http://my.safaribooksonline.com*.

How to Contact Us

Please address comments and questions concerning this book to the publisher:

O'Reilly Media, Inc.
1005 Gravenstein Highway North
Sebastopol, CA 95472
800-998-9938 (in the United States or Canada)
707-829-0515 (international or local)
707-829-0104 (fax)

We have a web page for this book, where we list errata, examples, and any additional information. You can access this page at:

http://oreil.ly/programming_ios_6_3e

To comment or ask technical questions about this book, send email to:

bookquestions@oreilly.com

For more information about our books, courses, conferences, and news, see our website at *http://www.oreilly.com*.

Find us on Facebook: *http://facebook.com/oreilly*

Follow us on Twitter: *http://twitter.com/oreillymedia*

Watch us on YouTube: *http://www.youtube.com/oreillymedia*

Acknowledgments for the First Edition

It's a poor craftsman who blames his tools. No blame attaches to the really great tools by which I have been assisted in the writing of this book. I am particularly grateful to the Unicomp Model M keyboard (*http://pckeyboard.com*), without which I could not have produced so large a book so painlessly. I was also aided by wonderful software, including TextMate (*http://macromates.com*) and AsciiDoc (*http://www.methods.co.nz/asciidoc*). BBEdit (*http://www.barebones.com*) helped with its `diff` display. Screenshots were created with Snapz Pro X (*http://www.ambrosiasw.com*) and GraphicConverter (*http://www.lemkesoft.com*); diagrams were drawn with OmniGraffle (*http://www.omnigroup.com*).

The splendid O'Reilly production process converted my AsciiDoc text files into PDF while I worked, allowing me to proofread in simulated book format. Were it not for this, and the Early Release program that permitted me to provide my readers with periodic updates of the book as it grew, I would never have agreed to undertake this project in the first place. I would like particularly to thank Tools maven Abby Fox for her constant assistance.

I have taken advice from two tech reviewers, Dave Smith and David Rowland, and have been assisted materially and spiritually by many readers who submitted errata and encouragement. I was particularly fortunate in having Brian Jepson as editor; he provided enthusiasm for the O'Reilly tools and the electronic book formats, a watchful eye, and a trusting attitude; he also endured the role of communications pipeline when I needed to prod various parts of the O'Reilly machine. I have never written an O'Reilly book without the help of Nancy Kotary, and I didn't intend to start now; her sharp eye has smoothed the bristles of my punctuation-laden style. For errors that remain, I take responsibility, of course.

Notes on the Second Printing

For the second printing of this book, screenshots have been rendered more legible, and a major technical error in the presentation of key–value coding in Chapter 5 has been corrected. In addition, numerous small emendations have been made; many of these have resulted from errata submissions by my readers, whom I should like to thank once again for their continued assistance and kind support. Please note that these changes have altered the pagination of the printed and PDF editions of the book.

Acknowledgments for the Second Edition

Not surprisingly, I'd like to thank once again my editor, Brian Jepson, who made me write this new edition. You can put down the whip now, Brian. Thanks also to the O'Reilly team for their many-faceted assistance, and always to my readers for their enthusiasm, encouragement, loyalty, and suggestions.

Notes on the Second Edition

In order to describe the relationship of the second edition of this book with the first edition, it will help if I first recap the recent history of iOS and Xcode versions.

At the time I started writing the first edition this book, system versions 3.1.3 (on the iPhone) and 3.2 (on the iPad) were current. As I was working on the book, iOS 4 and the iPhone 4 came into being, but iOS 4 didn't yet run on the iPad. Subsequently iOS 4.2 emerged; this was the first system able to run on both the iPhone and the iPad. At the same time, Xcode was improved up to 3.2.5. iOS 4 was the first version of the system to support multitasking, which necessitated much scurrying about on the part of developers, to adapt their apps to the new world order.

Just in time for my final revisions of the first edition, Xcode 3.2.6 and iOS 4.3 were released, along with the first public version of the long-awaited Xcode 4. Xcode 4 was a thorough overhaul of the IDE: menus, windows, and preferences are quite different from Xcode 3.2.x. Both Xcode 4 and Xcode 3.2.x can coexist on the same machine (up through Snow Leopard) and can be used to work on the same project; moreover, Xcode

3.2.x has some specialized capabilities that Xcode 4 lacks, so some long-standing developers may well continue to use it. This situation presents a dilemma for an author describing the development process. However, for iOS programming, I recommend adoption of Xcode 4, and the first edition of this book assumed that the reader had adopted it.

Such was the situation in May 2011, when the first edition was formally released, describing how to program iOS 4.

Less than five months later, in October 2011, Apple released iOS 5. Some of the features that are new in iOS 5 are dramatic and pervasive, and it is this fact which has necessitated a full revision of this book. At the same time, Apple also released Xcode 4.2, and this book assumes that you are using that version of Xcode (or later), since it is the earliest version of Xcode on which iOS 5 development is officially possible. (It may be that, by deep trickery, one can develop for iOS 5 using an earlier version of Xcode, but that would constitute unsupported behavior.) The first edition had a few mentions of menu commands and other interface in Xcode 3.2.x, but they have been excised from this edition. Xcode 4.2 comes in two flavors, depending whether you're running Snow Leopard (Mac OS X 10.6) or Lion (Mac OS X 10.7) on your development machine; they are supposed to behave more or less identically, but in fact each has its own bugs, so feel free to try both.

As I was finishing the second edition, in February 2012, Xcode 4.3 was released (for Lion only). Its chief innovation has to do with the organization of files on disk: instead of arriving as an installer that creates a top-level Developer folder to hold its many ancillary files and folders, Xcode 4.3 *contains* the Developer folder inside its file package (you can see it with the Finder's Show Package Contents command). So when I speak of the Developer folder in this book, you would need to understand that I mean something like */Applications/Xcode.app/Contents/Developer*. I have not found any other major differences between Xcode 4.2 and Xcode 4.3, and in this book I will sometimes say "Xcode 4.2" to mean Xcode 4.2 or later.

The chief purpose of this new edition, then, is to bring the book up to date for iOS 5. You, the reader, might be coming to iOS programming for the first time, so this edition assumes no prior knowledge of iOS 4 or any previous version. On the other hand, you, like me, could be making the transition from iOS 4 to iOS 5, so this edition lays some special emphasis on features that are new in iOS 5. This emphasis could also be useful to new iOS programmers who are thinking of writing apps that can also run under iOS 4. My goal, however, is not to burden the reader with outdated information. The vast majority of devices that could run iOS 4 have probably been updated to iOS 5, and you will probably be right in assuming that there will plenty of iOS 5 users out there, without your having to bother to target earlier systems. And from a pedagogical point of view, it seems counterproductive to describe how things used to be — especially as, if you're really interested, you can always consult the previous edition of this book! For this reason, some references to the state of things before iOS 4.2 have been excised from this edition.

Here is a case in point, showing my attitude and pedagogical approach with regard to new iOS 5 features in this edition. iOS 5 introduces ARC (automatic reference counting), which changes the way in which Objective-C programmers manage object memory so profoundly as to render Objective-C a different language. Use of ARC is optional in programming iOS, but it is extraordinarily helpful to have it turned on, and in this book I therefore assume throughout that you do have it turned on. In Chapter 12, where I discuss memory management, I still describe what life is like without ARC, as I did in the previous edition; but, outside that chapter, all code examples, unless specifically stated otherwise, are supposed to be running under ARC. If you start a new Xcode project with File → New Project and pick any iOS application template, then if "Use Automatic Reference Counting" is checked in the second screen, you're using ARC.

iOS 5 also introduces storyboards. A storyboard file is similar to a nib file: it's a place where Xcode lets you "draw" parts of the interface. The main difference is that a single storyboard file can do the work of multiple nib files. Nib files and storyboard files are not identical, nor are they used identically, but because of their similarity, when I speak of a nib file generically, in this book, I mean a nib or storyboard file, indifferently. I'll try to indicate this at the time, but the reader will forgive me if I don't keep saying "nib or storyboard" all the time.

In closing, I should like to say a few words to the people who have, in my opinion, gratuitously criticized the previous edition of this book on one or more of the following grounds:

a. It isn't a "cookbook" (a book full of step-by-step instructions for creating full working applications).

b. It devotes hundreds of pages to fundamentals.

c. It doesn't get the reader started early on with hands-on programming; there isn't even a "Hello, World" tutorial.

All of that is perfectly true. It is also quite deliberate. As both the table of contents and this preface are at pains to make clear, this is not that type of book. To paraphrase Butler's Law, this book is the type of book it is, and not some other type. That's why I wrote this book in the first place. The books of the type that these critics seem to want this book to be exist by the score; books of the type that this book is, however, seemed to me not to exist at all. As with all my other books, so with this one: when I couldn't find the book I wanted, I wrote it myself. I expect this book to be useful to those who need this type of book. People who prefer some other type of book should get some other type of book, and not mar my book's web page by criticizing it for not being what it was never intended to be.

The purpose of this book is to proceed by focusing on the underlying knowledge needed for an actual understanding of iOS programming. That is precisely the opposite of a cookbook. This book has no simple recipes ready for you to drop into your own code and come up with an app. I don't give you some fish; I teach you what a fish is and what you need to know to obtain one. The number of books out there that skip blithely past the fundamentals, leaving the reader to pick up Objective-C somehow independently, is painfully huge. The result is that numerous learners are encouraged to try their hand at programming when, to judge from the nature of the questions they ask and the confusion they exhibit, they don't understand what they are doing.

This book acts as a corrective, which in turn requires that space be devoted to fundamentals. The book does not hold a gun to your head and force you to read all about all of those fundamentals; if *you* already know everything there is to know about C, about Objective-C, about Xcode, about Cocoa, about views and drawing or whatever (but *do* you? do you *really*?), then by all means, skip those opening chapters. But don't begrudge to the people who need them the explanations that this book contains, as those are the people at whom they are aimed.

That explains why there's no attempt, in this book, to rush the reader into hands-on programming. My book does not pander to a desire for the false, cheap gratification of making believe that one is a programmer merely because one can parrot some instructions. My book is about *knowledge* — hard-won, rigorously gained knowledge. It's about gaining an understanding of what you are doing when you program iOS 5. It calls for a substantial investment of time and thought, and many pages elapse before any practical programming is demonstrated.

Perhaps part of the misunderstanding here is that the critic has not noticed, or has not understood, the sentence earlier in this Preface stating that my book is written in "a pedagogically helpful and instructive yet ruthlessly Euclidean and logical order." Some people may not know or appreciate what "Euclidean" means. It means "in the manner of Euclid." Euclid wrote our first surviving mathematical textbook, and it is distinguished by the following remarkable characteristic, among others: if concept or assertion B depends upon concept or assertion A, A comes first. Nothing is postponed; Euclid never says, "I'll explain/prove/discuss this point later, but for now, just take my word for it." I have attempted to copy Euclid's model. So, to take an obvious example, all real iOS apps use view controllers. It's true, then, that the reader isn't told what's involved in constructing a real iOS app until Chapter 19 is reached and view controllers are discussed. But to understand view controllers, you need to know what's being controlled, namely, a view; hence Chapter 14 and the rest of Part IV. And to grasp the relationship between a view controller and its view, you need to know about Cocoa's architectural patterns, such as lifetime events and the responder chain; hence Chapter 11 and the rest of Part III. Moreover, a view controller's view is often loaded from a nib; hence Chapter 7. And all of that requires a knowledge of the programming language you'll be using,

Objective-C; hence Chapter 3. But Objective-C is C; hence Chapter 1. So to reach view controllers any sooner would have been impossible. I rest my case.

Anyway, the complaint that the reader of my book doesn't get to run any code is factually false. The book is crammed full of substantial code examples — all of which are available for download from my GitHub site (*https://github.com/mattneub*), so you can obtain them, run them in Xcode, and play with them to your heart's content. So you can and should, in fact, be running code right from the outset. Nevertheless, the purpose of the code in this book is not for the fun of running it. All of my code is to support your understanding of whatever *concepts* I'm explaining at that point in the book.

In any case, perfectly good hands-on "Hello, World" tutorials are a dime a dozen; they're plastered all over the Internet, including at Apple's own site (*http://developer.apple.com/library/ios/#documentation/iPhone/Conceptual/iPhone101/Articles/*). You don't need *me* to show you that the process of writing a trivial iPhone application is fun and easy.

Still, for those who feel strongly that I haven't done my job unless I supply a "Hello, World" example, here is one, complete with step-by-step instructions:

1. Install Xcode, and launch the Xcode application.
2. Choose File → New → Project.
3. In the "Choose a template" dialog, under "iOS" on the left (not "Mac OS X"), click Application. On the right, click Empty Application. Click Next.
4. For Product Name, type Hello. Enter a company identifier if there isn't one already, such as com.yourLastName.yourFirstName. Choose Device Family: iPhone. Un-check all three checkboxes. Click Next.
5. Navigate to the Desktop. Uncheck "Create local git repository." Click Create.
6. The project window opens. Press Command-1. At the left, click *AppDelegate.m*.
7. Work in the editor in the middle of the window. Look for the words "Override point for customization after application launch." Place the cursor to the right of those words and hit Return a few times, to make some white space. Click in that white space and type these lines of code:

   ```
   UILabel* label = [[UILabel alloc] init];
   label.text = @"Hello, world!";
   [label sizeToFit];
   CGRect f = label.frame;
   f.origin = CGPointMake(100,100);
   label.frame = f;
   [self.window addSubview:label];
   ```

8. Press Command-R. If you see a dialog asking whether you want to save, accept.
9. After a while, the iOS Simulator application appears, containing a white window with "Hello, world!" in it.

Congratulations. You've made a "Hello, world" example. Wasn't that easy? Wasn't it boring? Wasn't it pointless? And are you any the wiser as to what, in fact, you just did? To find out — and, even more important, to know enough to be able to progress further on your own — read this book.

Acknowledgments for the Third Edition

This edition was written in the full public gaze, and I'd like to thank, as always, my many sharp-eyed readers who assisted me by spotting mistakes and making suggestions. I would also like to say a word for wonderful, wonderful git (*http://git-scm.com*), as well as the extraordinary SourceTree (*http://www.sourcetreeapp.com*).

At O'Reilly Media, I am grateful to XSL and CSS wizard Sarah Schneider, who brilliantly and quickly tweaked the automated layout process to make this book look great in printed and PDF form.

Notes on the Third Edition

Shortly after the official release of iOS 6 and Xcode 4.5, I began revising the code examples in this book (available at *https://github.com/mattneub*) to use and demonstrate the new iOS features. When that was done, I proceeded to rewrite the book text; while I was doing so, iOS 6.1 and Xcode 4.6 were released, so those are the versions that the book now assumes you're using.

For this third edition, I have eliminated most references to previous iOS versions. Many iOS 6 features, of course, do not exist in iOS 5 or before; I usually mention that a new feature is new, but I have not generally addressed the problem of writing backwards-compatible code. The text would become confusing and bloated if everything had to be qualified with advice for different versions ("but if you're targeting iOS 5.1, do this; if you're targeting iOS 5.0, do that; if you're targeting iOS 4.3, do the other"). I believe I can justify such omission on the grounds that the previous editions of this book exist! If you're targeting iOS 5, I've already described what to do, in the second edition; there's no need to repeat myself here.

New iOS 6 features are, of course, both explained and adopted in this edition. For example, having described NSArray subscripting (in Chapter 10), I then use it consistently, in place of `objectAtIndex:`, throughout the rest of the book. Aside from this, the book's structure remains the same as in previous editions, growing where necessary to accommodate explanations of new features, such as autolayout (in Chapter 14), state restoration (in Chapter 19), and collection views (in Chapter 21). Also, in response to reader requests, I have inserted a short example of Core Data programming into Chapter 36.

PART I

Language

Apple has provided a vast toolbox for programming iOS to make an app come to life and behave the way you want it to. That toolbox is the *API* (application programming interface). To use the API, you must speak the API's language. That language, for the most part, is Objective-C, which itself is built on top of C; some pieces of the API use C itself. This part of the book instructs you in the basics of these languages:

- Chapter 1 explains C. In general, you will probably not need to know all the ins and outs of C, so this chapter restricts itself to those aspects of C that you need to know in order to use both Objective-C and the C-based areas of the API.

- Chapter 2 prepares the ground for Objective-C, by discussing object-based programming in general architectural terms. It also explains some extremely important words that will be used throughout the book, along with the concepts that lie behind them.

- Chapter 3 introduces the basic syntax of Objective-C.

- Chapter 4 continues the explanation of Objective-C, discussing the nature of Objective-C classes, with emphasis on how to create a class in code.

- Chapter 5 completes the introduction to Objective-C, discussing how instances are created and initialized, along with an explanation of such related topics as polymorphism, instance variables, accessors, `self` and `super`, key–value coding, and properties.

We'll return in Part III to a description of further aspects of the Objective-C language — those that are particularly bound up with the Cocoa frameworks.

CHAPTER 1

Just Enough C

*Do you believe in C? Do you believe in anything
that has to do with me?*

—Leonard Bernstein and Stephen Schwartz,
Mass

To program for iOS, you need to speak to iOS. Everything you say to iOS will be in accordance with the iOS API. (An API, for *application programming interface*, is a list or specification of things you are allowed to say when communicating.) Therefore, you will need some knowledge of the C programming language, for two reasons:

- Most of the iOS API involves the Objective-C language, and most of your iOS programming will be in the Objective-C language; and Objective-C is a superset of C. This means that Objective-C presupposes C; everything that is true of C trickles up to Objective-C. A common mistake is to forget that "Objective-C is C" and to neglect a basic understanding of C.

- Some of the iOS API involves C rather than Objective-C. Even in Objective-C code, you often need to use C data structures and C function calls. For example, a rectangle is represented as a CGRect, which is a C *struct*, and to create a CGRect from four numbers you call `CGRectMake`, which is a C *function*. The iOS API documentation will very often show you C expressions and expect you to understand them.

The best way to learn C is to read *The C Programming Language* (PTR Prentice Hall, 1988) by Brian W. Kernighan and Dennis M. Ritchie, commonly called K&R (Ritchie was the creator of C). It is one of the best computer books ever written: brief, dense, and stunningly precise and clear. K&R is so important for effective iOS (and Mac OS X) programming that I keep a physical copy beside me at all times while coding, and I recommend that you do the same. Another useful manual is *The C Book*, by Mike Banahan, Declan Brady and Mark Doran, available online at *http://publications.gbdir ect.co.uk/c_book/*.

It would be impossible, and unnecessary, for me to describe all of C in a single chapter. C is not a large or difficult language, but it has some tricky corners and can be extremely subtle, powerful, and low-level. Moreover, since C is described fully and correctly in the manuals I've just mentioned, it would be a mistake for me to repeat what they can tell you better than I.

You don't have to know *all* about C in order to use Objective-C effectively, though; so my purpose in this chapter is to outline those aspects of C that are important for you to understand at the outset, before you even start using Objective-C for iOS programming. That's why this chapter is "Just Enough C": it's just enough to get you going, comfortably and safely. Just keep in mind that this chapter is *not* a technical manual of C.

If you know no C at all, I suggest that, as an accompaniment to this chapter, you also read select parts of K&R (think of this as "C: The Good Parts Version"). Here's my proposed K&R syllabus:

- Quickly skim K&R Chapter 1, the tutorial.
- Carefully read K&R Chapters 2 through 4.
- Read the first three sections of K&R Chapter 5 on pointers and arrays. You don't need to read the rest of Chapter 5 because you won't typically be doing any pointer arithmetic, but you do need to understand clearly what a pointer is, as Objective-C is all about objects, and every reference to an object is a pointer; you'll be seeing and using that * character constantly.
- Read also the first section of K&R Chapter 6, on structures (structs); as a beginner, you probably won't define any structs, but you will use them quite a lot, so you'll need to know the notation (for example, as I've already said, a CGRect is a struct).
- Glance over K&R Appendix B, which covers the standard library, because you may find yourself making certain standard library calls, such as the mathematical functions; forgetting that the library exists is a typical beginner mistake.

Just to make things a little more confusing, the C defined in K&R is not precisely the C that forms the basis of Objective-C. Developments subsequent to K&R have resulted in further C standards (ANSI C, C89, C99), and the Xcode compiler extends the C language in its own ways. By default, Xcode projects are treated as GNU99, which is itself an extension of C99 (though you could specify another C standard if you really wanted to). Fortunately, the most important differences between K&R's C and Xcode's C are small, convenient improvements that are easily remembered, so K&R remains the best and most reliable C reference.

Compilation, Statements, and Comments

C is a compiled language. You write your program as text; to run the program, things proceed in two stages. First your text is compiled into machine instructions; then those machine instructions are executed. Thus, as with any compiled language, you can make two kinds of mistake:

- Any purely syntactic errors (meaning that you spoke the C language incorrectly) will be caught by the compiler, and the program won't even begin to run.

- If your program gets past the compiler, then it will run, but there is no guarantee that you haven't made some other sort of mistake, which can be detected only by noticing that the program doesn't behave as intended.

The C compiler is fussy, but you should accept its interference with good grace. The compiler is your friend: learn to love it. It may emit what looks like an irrelevant or incomprehensible error message, but when it does, the fact is that you've done something wrong and the compiler has helpfully caught it for you. Also, the compiler can warn you if something seems like a possible mistake, even though it isn't strictly illegal; these warnings, which differ from outright errors, are also helpful and should not be ignored.

I have said that running a program requires a preceding stage: compilation. But in fact there is a third stage that precedes compilation: preprocessing. (It doesn't really matter whether you think of preprocessing as a stage preceding compilation or as the first stage of compilation.) Preprocessing modifies your text, so when your text is handed to the compiler, it is not identical to the text you wrote. Preprocessing might sound tricky and intrusive, but in fact it proceeds only according to your instructions and is helpful for making your code clearer and more compact.

Xcode allows you to view the effects of preprocessing on your program text (choose Product → Generate Output → Preprocessed File), so if you think you've made a mistake in instructing the preprocessor, you can track it down. I'll talk more later about some of the things you're likely to say to the preprocessor.

C is a statement-based language; every statement ends in a semicolon. (Forgetting the semicolon is a common beginner's mistake.) For readability, programs are mostly written with one statement per line, but this is by no means a hard and fast rule: long statements (which, unfortunately, arise very often because of Objective-C's verbosity) are commonly split over multiple lines, and extremely short statements are sometimes written two or three to a line. You cannot split a line just anywhere, however; for example, a literal string can't contain a return character. Indentation is linguistically meaningless and is purely a matter of convention (and C programmers argue over those conventions with near-religious fervor); Xcode helps "intelligently" by indenting automatically, and

Choosing a Compiler

The compiler situation in Xcode is rather complicated. Originally, Xcode's compiler was the free open source GCC (*http://gcc.gnu.org*). More recently, Xcode has phased in use of another free open source compiler, LLVM (*http://llvm.org*). Changing compilers is scary, so Apple has proceeded in stages, as follows:

- A hybrid compiler, LLVM-GCC, provides the advantages of LLVM compilation, but the code is parsed with GCC for maximum backward compatibility.

- A pure LLVM compiler (also referred to as Clang) does its own parsing and provides more intelligent and helpful error messages and warnings.

As Xcode 3.2.x evolved, LLVM-GCC was eventually considered the best choice, but Apple was hesitant to make it the default compiler, so GCC remained the default. When Xcode 4 emerged, LLVM-GCC was the default compiler, but GCC remained available. Finally, in Xcode 4.2, LLVM 3.0 became the default compiler, and pure GCC was withdrawn; in Xcode 4.6, LLVM has advanced to version 4.2. (The choice of compiler is a project-level build setting; see Chapter 6.)

you can use its automatic indentation both to keep your code readable and to confirm that you're not making any basic syntactic mistakes.

Comments are delimited in K&R C by /* ... */; the material between the delimiters can consist of multiple lines (K&R 1.2). In modern versions of C, a comment also can be denoted by two slashes (//); the rule is that if two slashes appear, they and everything after them on the same line are ignored:

```
int lower = 0; // lower limit of temperature table
```

These are sometimes called C++-style comments and are much more convenient for brief comments than the K&R comment syntax.

Throughout the C language (and therefore, throughout Objective-C as well), capitalization matters. All names are case-sensitive. There is no such data type as Int; it's lowercase "int." If you declare an int called lower and then try to speak of the same variable as Lower, the compiler will complain. By convention, variable names tend to start with a lowercase letter.

Variable Declaration, Initialization, and Data Types

C is a strongly typed language. Every variable must be declared, indicating its data type, before it can be used. Declaration can also involve explicit initialization, giving the variable a value; a variable that is declared but not explicitly initialized is of uncertain value (and should be regarded as dangerous until it *is* initialized). In K&R C, declarations must precede all other statements, but in modern versions of C, this rule is relaxed so that you don't have to declare a variable until just before you start using it:

```
int height = 2;
int width = height * 2;
height = height + 1;
int area = height * width;
```

The basic built-in C data types are all numeric: char (one byte), int (four bytes), float and double (floating-point numbers), and varieties such as short (short integer), long (long integer), unsigned short, and so on. A numeric literal may optionally express its type through a suffixed letter or letters: for example, 4 is an int, but 4UL is an unsigned long; 4.0 is a double, but 4.0f is a float. Objective-C makes use of some further numeric types derived from the C numeric types (by way of the typedef statement, K&R 6.7) designed to respond to the question of whether the processor is 64-bit; the most important of these are NSInteger (along with NSUInteger) and CGFloat. You don't need to use them explicitly unless an API tells you to, and even when you do, just think of NSInteger as int and CGFloat as float, and you'll be fine.

To *cast* (or *typecast*) a variable's value explicitly to another type, precede the variable's name with the other type's name in parentheses:

```
int height = 2;
float fheight = (float)height;
```

In that particular example, the explicit cast is unnecessary because the integer value will be cast to a float implicitly as it is assigned to a float variable, but it illustrates the notation. You'll find yourself typecasting quite a bit in Objective-C, mostly to subdue the worries of the compiler (examples appear in Chapter 3).

Another form of numeric initialization is the enum (K&R 2.3). It's a way of assigning names to a sequence of numeric values and is useful when a value represents one of several possible options. The Cocoa API uses this device a lot. For example, the three possible types of status bar animation are defined like this:

```
typedef enum {
    UIStatusBarAnimationNone,
    UIStatusBarAnimationFade,
    UIStatusBarAnimationSlide,
} UIStatusBarAnimation;
```

That definition assigns the value 0 to the name UIStatusBarAnimationNone, the value 1 to the name UIStatusBarAnimationFade, and the value 2 to the name UIStatusBar-AnimationSlide. The upshot is that you can use the suggestively meaningful names without caring about, or even knowing, the arbitrary numeric values they represent. It's a useful idiom, and you may well have reason to define enums in your own code.

Modern Enum Notation

Starting with LLVM compiler version 4.0, which made its debut in Xcode 4.4, Objective-C extends the enum notation ever so slightly. The status bar animation types, for example, are now defined like this:

```
typedef NS_ENUM(NSInteger, UIStatusBarAnimation) {
    UIStatusBarAnimationNone,
    UIStatusBarAnimationFade,
    UIStatusBarAnimationSlide,
};
```

NS_ENUM is a macro, a form of preprocessor text substitution discussed at the end of this chapter; when the text substitution is performed, that code turns out to be shorthand for this:

```
typedef enum UIStatusBarAnimation : NSInteger UIStatusBarAnimation;
enum UIStatusBarAnimation : NSInteger {
    UIStatusBarAnimationNone,
    UIStatusBarAnimationFade,
    UIStatusBarAnimationSlide,
};
```

That looks almost exactly like the old way of expressing the same enum, but the new way involves some notation that isn't part of standard C, telling the compiler what variety of integer value is being used here (it's an NSInteger). This makes UIStatusBarAnimation a little more like a genuine data type. It also lets Xcode help you more intelligently — for example, when performing code completion, as discussed in Chapter 9. Another macro, NS_OPTIONS, evaluates in Objective-C as a synonym of NS_ENUM (they are distinct only in C++ code, which is not discussed in this book).

There appears to be a native text type (a string) in C, but this is something of an illusion; behind the scenes, it is actually a null-terminated array of char. For example, in C you can write a string literal like this:

```
"string"
```

But in fact this is stored as 7 bytes, the numeric (ASCII) equivalents of each letter followed by a byte consisting of 0 to signal the end of the string. This data structure, called a C string, is rarely encountered while programming iOS. In general, when working with strings, you'll use an Objective-C object type called NSString. An NSString is totally different from a C string; it happens, however, that Objective-C lets you write a literal NSString in a way that looks very like a C string:

```
@"string"
```

Notice the at-sign! This expression is actually a directive to the Objective-C compiler to form an NSString object. A common mistake is forgetting the at-sign, thus causing your expression to be interpreted as a C string, which is a completely different animal.

Because the notation for literal NSStrings is modeled on the notation for C strings, it is worth knowing something about C strings, even though you won't generally encounter them. For example, K&R lists a number of escaped characters (K&R 2.3), which you can also use in a literal NSString, including the following:

\n

A Unix newline character

\t

A tab character

\"

A quotation mark (escaped to show that this is not the end of the string literal)

\\

A backslash

 NSStrings are natively Unicode-based, but because Objective-C is C, including non-ASCII characters in a literal NSString was, until quite recently, remarkably tricky, and you needed to know about such things as the \x and \u escape sequences. Now, however, it is perfectly legal to type a non-ASCII character directly into an NSString literal, and you should ignore old Internet postings (and even an occasional sentence in Apple's own documentation) warning that it is not.

K&R also mention a notation for concatenating string literals, in which multiple string literals separated only by white space are automatically concatenated and treated as a single string literal. This notation is useful for splitting a long string into multiple lines for legibility, and Objective-C copies this convention for literal NSStrings as well, except that you have to remember the at-sign:

```
@"This is a big long literal string "
@"which I have broken over two lines of code.";
```

Structs

C offers few simple native data types, so how are more complex data types made? There are three ways: structures, pointers, and arrays. Both structures and pointers are going to be crucial when you're programming iOS. You're less likely to need a C array, because Objective-C has its own NSArray object type, but it will arise in a couple of examples later in this book.

A C structure, usually called a struct (K&R 6.1), is a compound data type: it combines multiple data types into a single type, which can be passed around as a single entity. Moreover, the elements constituting the compound entity have names and can be accessed by those names through the compound entity, using dot-notation. The iOS API has many commonly used structs, typically accompanied by convenience functions for working with them.

For example, the iOS documentation tells you that a CGPoint is defined as follows:

```
struct CGPoint {
    CGFloat x;
    CGFloat y;
};
typedef struct CGPoint CGPoint;
```

Recall that a CGFloat is basically a float, so this is a compound data type made up of two simple native data types; in effect, a CGPoint has two CGFloat parts, and their names are x and y. (The rather odd-looking last line merely asserts that one can use the term CGPoint instead of the more verbose `struct CGPoint`.) So we can write:

```
CGPoint myPoint;
myPoint.x = 4.3;
myPoint.y = 7.1;
```

Just as we can assign to `myPoint.x` to *set* this part of the struct, we can say `myPoint.x` to *get* this part of the struct. It's as if `myPoint.x` were the name of a variable. Moreover, an element of a struct can itself be a struct, and the dot-notation can be chained. To illustrate, first note the existence of another iOS struct, CGSize:

```
struct CGSize {
    CGFloat width;
    CGFloat height;
};
typedef struct CGSize CGSize;
```

Put a CGPoint and a CGSize together and you've got a CGRect:

```
struct CGRect {
    CGPoint origin;
    CGSize size;
};
typedef struct CGRect CGRect;
```

So suppose we've got a CGRect variable called `myRect`, already initialized. Then `myRect.origin` is a CGPoint, and `myRect.origin.x` is a CGFloat. Similarly, `myRect.size` is a CGSize, and `myRect.size.width` is a CGFloat. You could change just the width part of our CGRect directly, like this:

```
myRect.size.width = 8.6;
```

Instead of initializing a struct by assigning to each of its elements, you can initialize it at declaration time by assigning values for all its elements at once, in curly braces and separated by commas, like this:

```
CGPoint myPoint = { 4.3, 7.1 };
CGRect myRect = { myPoint, {10, 20} };
```

You don't actually have to be assigning to a struct-typed variable to use a struct initializer; you can use an initializer anywhere the given struct type is expected, but you might also have to cast to that struct type in order to explain to the compiler what your curly braces mean, like this:

```
CGContextFillRect(con, (CGRect){myPoint, {10, 20}});
```

In that example, CGContextFillRect is a function. I'll talk about functions later in this chapter, but the upshot of the example is that what comes after the first comma has to be a CGRect, and can therefore be a CGRect initializer provided this is accompanied by a CGRect cast.

Pointers

The other big way that C extends its range of data types is by means of pointers (K&R 5.1). A pointer is an integer (of some size or other) with a meaning: it designates the location in memory where the real data is to be found. Knowing the structure of that data and how to work with it, as well as allocating a block of memory of the required size beforehand and disposing of that block of memory when it's no longer needed, is a very complicated business. Luckily, this is exactly the sort of complicated business that Objective-C is going to take care of for us. So all you really have to know to use pointers is what they are and what notation is used to refer to them.

Let's start with a simple declaration. If we wanted to declare an integer in C, we could say:

```
int i;
```

That line says, "i is an integer." Now let's instead declare a *pointer* to an integer:

```
int* intPtr;
```

That line says, "intPtr is a pointer to an integer." Never mind how we know there really is going to be an integer at the address designated by this pointer; here, I'm concerned only with the notation. It is permitted to place the asterisk in the declaration before the name rather than after the type:

```
int *intPtr;
```

You could even put a space on both sides of the asterisk (though this is rarely done):

```
int * intPtr;
```

I prefer the first form, but I do occasionally use the second form, and Apple quite often uses it, so be sure you understand that these are all ways of saying the same thing. No matter how the spaces are inserted, the name of the type is still `int*`. If you are asked what type is `intPtr` is, the answer is `int*` (a pointer to an int); the asterisk is part of the name of the type of this variable. If you needed to cast a variable `p` to this type, you'd cast like this: `(int*)p`. Once again, it is possible that you'll see code where there's a space before the asterisk, like this: `(int *)p`.

Pointers are very important in Objective-C, because Objective-C is all about objects (Chapter 2), and every variable referring to an object is itself a pointer. For example, I've already mentioned that the Objective-C string type is called NSString. So the way to declare an NSString variable is as a pointer to an NSString:

```
NSString* s;
```

An NSString literal is an NSString value, so we can even declare and initialize this NSString object, thus writing a seriously useful line of Objective-C code:

```
NSString* s = @"Hello, world!";
```

In pure C, having declared a pointer-to-integer called `intPtr`, you are liable to speak later in your code of `*intPtr`. This notation, outside of a declaration, means "the thing pointed to by the pointer `intPtr`." You speak of `*intPtr` because you wish to access the integer at the far end of the pointer; this is called *dereferencing* the pointer.

But in Objective-C, this is generally *not* the case. In your code, you'll be treating the pointer to an object as the object; you'll never dereference it. So, for example, having declared `s` as a pointer to an NSString, you will *not* then proceed to speak of `*s`; rather, you will speak simply of `s`, as if it *were* the string. All the Objective-C stuff you'll want to do with an object will expect the pointer, not the object at the far end of the pointer; behind the scenes, Objective-C itself will take care of the messy business of following the pointer to its block of memory and doing whatever needs to be done in that block of memory. This fact is extremely convenient for you as a programmer, but it does cause Objective-C users to speak a little loosely; we tend to say that "`s` is an NSString," when of course it is actually a pointer to an NSString.

The logic of how pointers work, both in C and in Objective-C, is different from the logic of how simple data types work. The difference is particularly evident with assignment. Assignment to a simple data type changes the data value. Assignment to a pointer re-points the pointer. Suppose `ptr1` and `ptr2` are both pointers, and you say:

```
ptr1 = ptr2;
```

Now `ptr1` and `ptr2` are pointing at the same thing. Any change to the thing pointed to by `ptr1` will also change the thing pointed to by `ptr2`, because they are the same thing (Figure 1-1). Meanwhile, whatever `ptr1` was pointing to before the assignment is now not being pointed to by `ptr1`; it might, indeed, be pointed to by nothing (which could

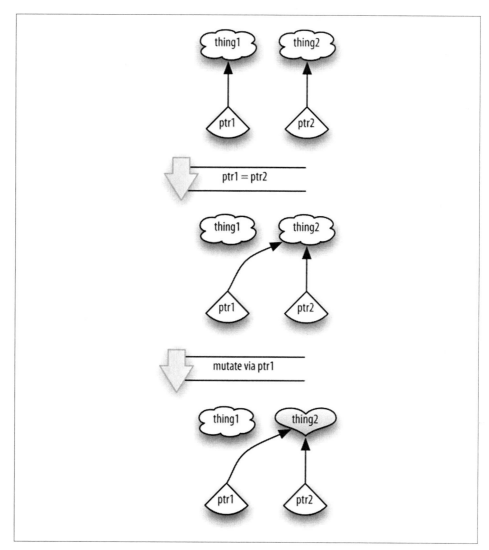

Figure 1-1. Pointers and assignment

be bad). A firm understanding of these facts is crucial when working in Objective-C, and I'll return to this topic in Chapter 3.

The most general type of pointer is *pointer-to-void* (void*), the *generic pointer*. It is legal to use a generic pointer wherever a specific type of pointer is expected. In effect, pointer-to-void casts away type checking as to what's at the far end of the pointer. Thus, the following is legal:

```
int* p1; // and pretend p1 has a value
void* p2;
p2 = p1;
p1 = p2;
```

Arrays

A C array (K&R 5.3) consists of multiple elements of the same data type. An array declaration states the data type of the elements, followed by the name of the array, along with square brackets containing the number of elements:

```
int arr[3]; // means: arr is an array consisting of 3 ints
```

To refer to an element of an array, use the array's name followed by the element number in square brackets. The first element of an array is numbered 0. So we can initialize an array by assigning values to each element in turn:

```
int arr[3];
arr[0] = 123;
arr[1] = 456;
arr[2] = 789;
```

Alternatively, you can initialize an array at declaration time by assigning a list of values in curly braces, just as with a struct. In this case, the size of the array can be omitted from the declaration, because it is implicit in the initialization (K&R 4.9):

```
int arr[] = {123, 456, 789};
```

Curiously, the name of an array is the name of a pointer (to the first element of the array). Thus, for example, having declared arr as in the preceding examples, you can use arr wherever a value of type int* (a pointer to an int) is expected. This fact is the basis of some highly sophisticated C idioms that you almost certainly won't need to know about (which is why I don't recommend that you read any of K&R Chapter 5 beyond section 3).

C arrays rarely arise in practice when programming iOS, because you'll work mostly with the NSArray object type instead. But here's a case where they do. The function CGContextStrokeLineSegments is declared like this:

```
void CGContextStrokeLineSegments (
    CGContextRef c,
    const CGPoint points[],
    size_t count
);
```

The second parameter is an array (meaning a C array) of CGPoints. That's what the square brackets tell you. So to call this function, you'd need to know at least how to make an array of CGPoints. You might do it like this:

```
CGPoint arr[] = {{4,5}, {6,7}, {8,9}, {10,11}};
```

Having done that, you can pass `arr` as the second argument in a call to `CGContextStroke-LineSegments`.

Also, a C string, as I've already mentioned, is actually an array. For example, the NSString method `stringWithUTF8String:` takes (according to the documentation) "a NULL-terminated C array of bytes in UTF8 encoding;" but the parameter is declared not as an array, but as a `char*`. Those are the same thing, and are both ways of saying that this method takes a C string.

(The colon at the end of the method name `stringWithUTF8String:` is not a misprint; many Objective-C method names end with a colon. I'll explain why in Chapter 3.)

Operators

Arithmetic operators are straightforward (K&R 2.5), but watch out for the rule that "integer division truncates any fractional part." This rule is the cause of much novice error in C. If you have two integers and you want to divide them in such a way as to get a fractional result, you must represent at least one of them as a float:

```
int i = 3;
float f = i/2; // beware! not 1.5
```

To get 1.5, you should have written `i/2.0` or `(float)i/2`.

The integer increment and decrement operators (K&R 2.8), ++ and - -, work differently depending on whether they precede or follow their variable. The expression ++i replaces the value of `i` by 1 more than its current value and then uses the resulting value; the expression i++ uses the current value of `i` and then replaces it with 1 more than its current value. This is one of C's coolest features.

C also provides bitwise operators (K&R 2.9), such as bitwise-and (&) and bitwise-or (|); they operate on the individual binary bits that constitute integers. Of these, the one you are most likely to need is bitwise-or, because the Cocoa API often uses bits as switches when multiple options are to be specified simultaneously. For example, there are various ways in which a UIView can be resized automatically as its superview is resized, and you're supposed to provide one or more of these when setting a UIView's `autoresizing-Mask` property. The autoresizing options are listed in the documentation as follows:

```
typedef NS_OPTIONS(NSUInteger, UIViewAutoresizing) {
    UIViewAutoresizingNone                 = 0,
    UIViewAutoresizingFlexibleLeftMargin   = 1 << 0,
    UIViewAutoresizingFlexibleWidth        = 1 << 1,
    UIViewAutoresizingFlexibleRightMargin  = 1 << 2,
    UIViewAutoresizingFlexibleTopMargin    = 1 << 3,
    UIViewAutoresizingFlexibleHeight       = 1 << 4,
    UIViewAutoresizingFlexibleBottomMargin = 1 << 5
};
```

The << symbol is the left shift operator; the right operand says how many bits to shift the left operand. So pretend that an NSUInteger is 8 bits (it isn't, but let's keep things simple and short). Then this enum means that the following name–value pairs are defined (using binary notation for the values):

UIViewAutoresizingNone
```
00000000
```

UIViewAutoresizingFlexibleLeftMargin
```
00000001
```

UIViewAutoresizingFlexibleWidth
```
00000010
```

UIViewAutoresizingFlexibleRightMargin
```
00000100
```

UIViewAutoresizingFlexibleTopMargin
```
00001000
```

and so on. The reason for this bit-based representation is that these values can be combined into a single value (a *bitmask*) that you pass to set the autoresizingMask. All Cocoa has to do to understand your intentions is to look to see which bits in the value that you pass are set to 1. So, for example, 00001010 would mean that UIView-AutoresizingFlexibleTopMargin and UIViewAutoresizingFlexibleWidth are true (and that the others, by implication, are all false).

The question is how to form the value 00001010 in order to pass it. You could just do the math, figure out that binary 00001010 is decimal 10, and set the autoresizing-Mask property to 10, but that's not what you're supposed to do, and it's not a very good idea, because it's error-prone and makes your code incomprehensible. Instead, use the bitwise-or operator to combine the desired options:

```
myView.autoresizingMask =
    UIViewAutoresizingFlexibleTopMargin | UIViewAutoresizingFlexibleWidth;
```

This notation works because the bitwise-or operator combines its operands by setting in the result any bits that are set in either of the operands, so 00001000 | 00000010 is 00001010, which is just the value we're trying to convey. (And how does the runtime parse the bitmask to discover whether a given bit is set? With the bitwise-and operator.)

Simple assignment (K&R 2.10) is by the equal sign. But there are also compound assignment operators that combine assignment with some other operation. For example:

```
height *= 2; // same as saying: height = height * 2;
```

The ternary operator (?:) is a way of specifying one of two values depending on a condition (K&R 2.11). The scheme is as follows:

```
(condition) ? exp1 : exp2
```

If the condition is true (see the next section for what that means), the expression *exp1* is evaluated and the result is used; otherwise, the expression *exp2* is evaluated and the result is used. For example, you might use the ternary operator while performing an assignment, using this schema:

```
myVariable = (condition) ? exp1 : exp2;
```

What gets assigned to myVariable depends on the truth value of the condition. There's nothing happening here that couldn't be accomplished more verbosely with flow control (see the next section), but the ternary operator can greatly improve clarity, and I use it a lot.

Flow Control and Conditions

Basic flow control is fairly simple and usually involves a condition in parentheses and a block of conditionally executed code in curly braces. These curly braces constitute a new scope, into which new variables can be introduced. So, for example:

```
if (x == 7) {
    int i = 0;
    i += 1;
}
```

After the closing curly brace in the fourth line, the i introduced in the second line has ceased to exist, because its scope is the inside of the curly braces. If the contents of the curly braces consist of a single statement, the curly braces can be omitted, but I would advise beginners against this shorthand, as you can confuse yourself. A common beginner mistake (which will be caught by the compiler) is forgetting the parentheses around the condition. The full set of flow control statements is given in K&R Chapter 3, and I'll just summarize them schematically here (Example 1-1).

Example 1-1. The C flow control constructs

```
if (condition) {
    statements;
}

if (condition) {
    statements;
} else {
    statements;
}

if (condition) {
    statements;
} else if (condition) {
    statements;
} else {
```

```
    statements;
}

while (condition) {
    statements;
}

do {
    statements;
} while (condition);

for (before-all; condition; after-each) {
    statements;
}
```

The if...else if...else structure can have as many else if blocks as needed, and the else block is optional. Instead of an extended if...else if...else if...else structure, when the conditions would consist of comparing various values against a single value, you can use the switch statement; be careful, though, as it is rather confusing and can easily go wrong (see K&R 3.4 for full details). The main trick is to remember to end every case with a break statement, unless you want it to "fall through" to the next case (Example 1-2).

Example 1-2. A switch statement

```
NSString* key;
switch (tag) {
    case 1: { // i.e., if tag is 1
        key = @"lesson";
        break;
    }
    case 2: { // i.e., if tag is 2
        key = @"lessonSection";
        break;
    }
    case 3: { // i.e., if tag is 3
        key = @"lessonSectionPartFirstWord";
        break;
    }
}
```

The C for loop needs some elaboration for beginners (Example 1-1). The *before-all* statement is executed once as the for loop is first encountered and is usually used for initialization of the counter. The condition is then tested, and if true, the block is executed; the condition is usually used to test whether the counter has reached its limit. The *after-each* statement is then executed, and is usually used to increment or decrement the counter; the condition is then immediately tested again. Thus, to execute a block using integer values 1, 2, 3, 4, and 5 for i, the notation is:

```
int i;
for (i = 1; i < 6; i++) {
    // ... statements ...
}
```

The need for a counter intended to exist solely within the for loop is so common that C99 permits the declaration of the counter as part of the *before-all* statement; the declared variable's scope is then inside the curly braces:

```
for (int i = 1; i < 6; i++) {
    // ... statements ...
}
```

The for loop is one of the few areas in which Objective-C extends C's flow-control syntax. Certain Objective-C objects represent enumerable collections of other objects; "enumerable" basically means that you can cycle through the collection, and cycling through a collection is called *enumerating* the collection. To make enumerating easy, Objective-C provides a for...in operator, which works like a for loop:

```
SomeType* oneItem;
for (oneItem in myCollection) {
    // ... statements ....
}
```

On each pass through the loop, the variable oneItem (or whatever you call it) takes on the next value from within the collection. As with the C99 for loop, oneItem can be declared in the for statement, limiting its scope to the curly braces:

```
for (SomeType* oneItem in myCollection) {
    // ... statements ....
}
```

To abort a loop from inside the curly braces, use the break statement. To abort the current iteration from within the curly braces and proceed to the next iteration, use the continue statement. In the case of while and do, continue means to perform immediately the conditional test; in the case of a for loop, continue means to perform immediately the *after-each* statement and then the conditional test.

C also has a goto statement that allows you to jump to a named (labeled) line in your code (K&R 3.8); even though goto is notoriously "considered harmful," there are situations in which it is pretty much necessary, especially because C's flow control is otherwise so primitive.

It is permissible for a C statement to be compounded of multiple statements, separated by commas, to be executed sequentially. The last of the multiple statements is the value of the compound statement as a whole. This construct, for instance, lets you perform some secondary action before each test of a condition or perform more than one *after-each* action (an example appears in Chapter 17).

We can now turn to the question of what a condition consists of. C has no separate boolean type; a condition either evaluates to 0, in which case it is considered false, or it doesn't, in which case it is true. Comparisons are performed using the equality and relational operators (K&R 2.6); for example, == compares for equality, and < compares for whether the first operand is less than the second. Logical expressions can be combined using the logical-and operator (&&) and the logical-or operator (||); using these along with parentheses and the not operator (!) you can form complex conditions. Evaluation of logical-and and logical-or expressions is short-circuited, meaning that if the left condition settles the question, the right condition is never even evaluated.

 Don't confuse the logical-and operator (&&) and the logical-or operator (||) with the bitwise-and operator (&) and the bitwise-or operator (|) discussed earlier. Writing & when you mean && (or *vice versa*) can result in surprising behavior.

The operator for testing basic equality, ==, is not a simple equal sign; forgetting the difference is a common novice mistake. The problem is that such code is legal: simple assignment, which is what the equal sign means, has a value, and any value is legal in a condition. So consider this piece of (nonsense) code:

```
int i = 0;
while (i = 1) {
    i = 0;
}
```

You might think that the while condition tests whether i is 1. You might then think: i is 0, so the while body will never be performed. Right? Wrong. The while condition does not test whether i is 1; it assigns 1 to i. The value of that assignment is also 1, so the condition evaluates to 1, which means true. So the while body *is* performed. Moreover, even though the while body assigns 0 to i, the condition is then evaluated again and assigns 1 to i a second time, which means true yet again. And so on, forever; we've written an endless loop, and the program will hang. (And, depending on what compiler and settings you're using, you might not even get a warning of trouble ahead.)

C programmers actually revel in the fact that testing for zero and testing for false are the same thing and use it to create compact conditional expressions, which are considered elegant and idiomatic. I don't recommend that you make use of such idioms, as they can be confusing, but I must admit that even I do occasionally resort to it, especially because in Objective-C it is so common to test an object reference to see whether it is nil (discussed further in Chapter 3). Since nil is a form of zero, I usually ask whether an object s is nil like this:

```
if (s) {
    // ...
}
```

Objective-C introduces a BOOL type, which you should use if you need to capture or maintain a condition's value as a variable, along with constants YES and NO (actually representing 1 and 0), which you should use when setting a boolean value. Don't compare anything against a BOOL, not even YES or NO, because a value like 2 is true in a condition but is not equal to YES or NO. Just use the BOOL directly as a condition, or as part of a complex condition, and all will be well. For example:

```
BOOL isnil = (nil == s);
if (isnil) { // not: if (isnil == YES)
    // ...
}
```

Functions

C is a function-based language (K&R 4.1). A *function* is a block of code defining what should happen; when other code *calls* (invokes) that function, the function's code does happen. A function returns a value, which is substituted for the call to that function.

Here's a definition of a function that accepts an integer and returns its square:

```
int square(int i) {
    return i * i;
}
```

Now I'll call that function:

```
int i = square(3);
```

Because of the way square is defined, that is exactly like saying:

```
int i = 9;
```

That example is extremely simple, but it illustrates many key aspects of functions.

Let's analyze how a function is defined:

```
int❶ square❷(❸int i) {❹
    return i * i;
}
```

❶   We start with the type of value that the function returns; here, it returns an int.

❷   Then we have the name of the function, which is `square`.

❸   Then we have parentheses, and here we place the data type and name of any values that this function expects to receive. Here, `square` expects to receive one value, an int, which we are calling `i`. The name `i` (along with its expected data type) is a *parameter*; when the function is called, its value will be supplied as an *argument*. If a function expects to receive more than one value, multiple parameters in its definition are separated by a comma (and when the function is called, the arguments supplied are likewise separated by a comma).

❹   Finally, we have curly braces containing the statements that are to be executed when the function is called.

Those curly braces constitute a scope; variables declared within them are local to the function. The names used for the parameters in the function definition are also local to the function; in other words, the `i` in the first line of the function definition is the same as the `i` in the second line of the function definition, but it has nothing to do with any `i` used outside the function definition (as when the result of the function call is assigned to a variable called `i`). The value of the `i` parameter in the function definition is assigned from the corresponding argument when the function is actually called; in the previous example, it is 3, which is why the function result is 9. Supplying a function call with arguments is thus a form of assignment. Suppose a function is defined like this:

```
int myfunction(int i, int j) { // ...
```

And suppose we call that function:

```
int result = myfunction(3, 4);
```

That function call effectively assigns 3 to the function's `i` parameter and 4 to the function's `j` parameter.

When a `return` statement is encountered, the value accompanying it is handed back as the result of the function call, and the function terminates. It is legal for a function to return no value; in such a case, the `return` statement has no accompanying value, and the definition states the type of value returned by the function as `void`. It is also legal to call a function and ignore its return value even if it has one. For example, we could say:

```
square(3);
```

That would be a somewhat silly thing to say, because we have gone to all the trouble of calling the function and having it generate the square of 3 — namely 9 — but we have done nothing to *capture* that 9. It is exactly as if we had said:

```
9;
```

You're allowed to say that, but it doesn't seem to serve much purpose. On the other hand, the point of a function might be not so much the value it returns as other things it does as it is executing, so then it might make perfect sense to ignore its result.

The parentheses in a function's syntax are crucial. Parentheses are how C knows there's a function. Parentheses after the function name in the function *definition* are how C knows this is a function definition, and they are needed even if this function takes no parameters. Parentheses after the function name in the function *call* are how C knows this is a function call, and they are needed even if this function call supplies no arguments. Using the bare name of a function is possible, because the name is the name of something, but it doesn't call the function. (I'll talk later about something it does do.)

Let's return to the simple C function definition and call that I used as my example earlier. Suppose we combine that function definition and the call to that function into a single program:

```
int square(int i) {
    return i * i;
}
int i = square(3);
```

That is a legal program, but only because the definition of the `square` function precedes the call to that function. If we wanted to place the definition of the `square` function elsewhere, such as after the call to it, we would need at least to precede the call with a declaration of the `square` function (Example 1-3). The declaration looks just like the first line of the definition, but it is a statement, ending with a semicolon, rather than a left curly brace.

Example 1-3. Declaring, calling, and defining a function

```
int square(int i);
int i = square(3);
int square(int i) {
    return i * i;
}
```

The parameter names in the declaration do not have to match the parameter names in the definition, but all the types (and, of course, the name of the function) must match. The types constitute the *signature* of this function. In other words, it does not matter if the first line, the declaration, is rewritten thus:

```
int square(int j);
```

What does matter is that, both in the declaration and in the definition, `square` is a function taking one int parameter and returning an int. (In a modern Objective-C program, though, the function declaration usually won't be necessary, even if the function call precedes its definition; see "Modern Objective-C Function Declarations" (page 29).)

In Objective-C, when you're sending a message to an object (Chapter 2), you won't use a function call; you'll use a method call (Chapter 3). But you will most definitely use plenty of C function calls as well. For example, earlier we initialized a CGPoint by setting its x element and its y element and by assigning its elements values in curly braces. But what you'll usually do to make a new CGPoint is to call `CGPointMake`, which is declared like this:

```
CGPoint CGPointMake (
    CGFloat x,
    CGFloat y
);
```

Despite its multiple lines and its indentations, this is indeed a C function declaration, just like the declaration for our simple `square` function. It says that `CGPointMake` is a C function that takes two CGFloat parameters and returns a CGPoint. So now you know (I hope) that it would be legal (and typical) to write this sort of thing:

```
CGPoint myPoint = CGPointMake(4.3, 7.1);
```

Pointer Parameters and the Address Operator

Objective-C is chock-a-block with pointers (and asterisks). Objective-C methods typically expect pointer parameters and return a pointer value. But this doesn't make things more complicated, because, as I've already mentioned, your variables referring to Objective-C objects *are* pointers. Pointers are what Objective-C expects, but pointers are also what Objective-C gives you. Pointers are exactly what you've got, so there's no problem.

For example, one way to concatenate two NSStrings is to call the NSString method `stringByAppendingString:`, which the documentation tells you is declared as follows:

```
- (NSString *)stringByAppendingString:(NSString *)aString
```

This declaration is telling you (after you allow for the Objective-C syntax) that this method expects one `NSString*` parameter and returns an `NSString*`. That sounds messy, but it isn't, because *every* NSString is really an `NSString*`. So nothing could be simpler than to obtain a new NSString consisting of two concatenated NSStrings:

```
NSString* s1 = @"Hello, ";
NSString* s2 = @"World!"
NSString* s3 = [s1 stringByAppendingString: s2];
```

Sometimes, however, a function or method expects as a parameter a pointer to a thing, but what you've got is not that pointer but the thing itself. Thus, you need a way to create a pointer to that thing. The solution is the address operator (K&R 5.1), which is an ampersand before the name of the thing.

For example, there's an NSString method for reading from a file into an NSString, which is declared like this:

```
+ (id)stringWithContentsOfFile:(NSString *)path
                      encoding:(NSStringEncoding)enc
                         error:(NSError **)error
```

Now, never mind what an id is, and don't worry about the Objective-C method declaration syntax. Just consider the types of the parameters. The first one is an NSString*; that's no problem, as every reference to an NSString is actually a pointer to an NSString. An NSStringEncoding turns out to be merely an alias to a primitive data type, an NSUInteger, so that's no problem either. But what on earth is an NSError**?

By all logic, it looks like an NSError** should be a pointer to a pointer to an NSError. And that's exactly what it is. This method is asking to be passed a pointer to a pointer to an NSError. Well, it's easy to declare a pointer to an NSError:

```
NSError* myError;
```

But how can we obtain a pointer to that? With the address operator! So our code might look, schematically, like this:

```
NSString* myPath = // something or other;
NSStringEncoding myEnc = // something or other;
NSError* myError = nil;
NSString* result = [NSString stringWithContentsOfFile: myPath
                                             encoding: myEnc
                                                error: &myError];
```

The important thing to notice is the ampersand. Because myError is a pointer to an NSError, &myError is a pointer to a pointer to an NSError, which is just what we're expected to provide. Thus, everything goes swimmingly.

This method effectively returns *two* results. It returns a real result, which we have captured by assigning it to the NSString pointer we're calling result. But if there's an error, it also wants to set the value of another object, an NSError object; the idea is that you can then study that NSError object to find out what went wrong. (Perhaps the file wasn't where you said it was, or it wasn't stored in the encoding you claimed it was.) By passing a pointer to a pointer to an NSError, you give the method free rein to do that. Before the call to stringWithContentsOfFile:, myError was initialized to nil; during the call to stringWithContentsOfFile:, if there's an error, the pointer is repointed, thus giving myError a meaningful NSError value describing that error. (Repointing a pointer in this way is sometimes called *indirection*.)

So the idea is that you first check result to see whether it's nil. If it isn't, fine; it's the string you asked for. If it is, you then study the NSError that myError is now pointing to, to learn what went wrong. This pattern is frequently used in Cocoa.

You can use the address operator to create a pointer to any named variable. A C function is technically a kind of named variable, so you can even create a pointer to a function! This is an example of when you'd use the name of the function without the parentheses: you aren't calling the function, you're talking about it. For example, &square is a pointer to the square function. Moreover, just as the bare name of an array is implicitly a pointer to its first element, the bare name of a function is implicitly a pointer to the function; the address operator is optional. In Chapter 3, I describe a situation in which specifying a pointer to a function is a useful thing to do.

Another operator used in connection with pointers, or when memory must be allocated dynamically, is sizeof. It may be followed by a type name in parentheses or by a variable name; a variable name needn't be in parentheses, but it *can* be, so most programmers ignore the distinction and use parentheses routinely, as if sizeof were a function.

For example, the documentation shows the declaration for the CTParagraphStyle-Setting struct like this:

```
typedef struct CTParagraphStyleSetting {
    CTParagraphStyleSpecifier spec;
    size_t valueSize;
    const void* value;
} CTParagraphStyleSetting;
```

A CTParagraphStyleSpecifier is just an enum, so concentrate on the second and third elements of this struct, valueSize and value. The value element is a pointer-to-void, meaning an anonymous pointer; it's a pointer to something-or-other. Since pointer-to-void casts away any concern for what data type the pointer is pointing to, it also casts away any knowledge of how big that data type is. The job of the second element of the struct is to provide that information. Here's an actual example of initializing a CTParagraphStyleSetting struct (from Chapter 23):

```
CTTextAlignment centerValue = kCTCenterTextAlignment;
CTParagraphStyleSetting center =
    {kCTParagraphStyleSpecifierAlignment, sizeof(centerValue), &centerValue};
```

Files

The little dance of declaring a function before calling it (Example 1-3) may seem rather absurd, but it is of tremendous importance in the C language, because it is what allows a C program to be arbitrarily large and complex.

As your program grows, you can divide and organize it into multiple files. This kind of organization can make a large program much more maintainable — easier to read, easier to understand, easier to change without accidentally breaking things. A large C program therefore usually consists of two kinds of file: code files, whose filename extension is *.c*, and header files, whose filename extension is *.h*. The build system will automatically "see" all the files and will know that together they constitute a single program, but there is also a rule in C that code inside one file cannot "see" another file unless it is explicitly told to do so. Thus, a file itself constitutes a scope; this is a deliberate and valuable feature of C, because it helps you keep things nicely pigeonholed.

The way you tell a C file to "see" another file is with the `#include` directive. The hash sign in the term `#include` is a signal that this line is an instruction to the preprocessor. In this case, the word `#include` is followed by the name of another file, and the directive means that the preprocessor should simply replace the directive by the entire contents of the file that's named.

So the strategy for constructing a large C program is something like this:

- In each *.c* file, put the code that only this file needs to know about; typically, each file's code consists of related functionality.

- In each *.h* file, put the function declarations that multiple *.c* files might need to know about.

- Have each *.c* file include those *.h* files containing the declarations it needs to know about.

So, for example, if `function1` is defined in *file1.c*, but *file2.c* might need to call `function1`, the declaration for `function1` can go in *file1.h*. Now *file1.c* can include *file1.h*, so all of its functions, regardless of order, can call `function1`, and *file2.c* can also include *file1.h*, so all of *its* functions can call `function1` (Figure 1-2). In short, header files are a way of letting code files share knowledge about one another without actually sharing code (because, if they did share code, that would violate the entire point of keeping the code in separate files).

But how does the compiler know where, among all these multiple *.c* files, to begin execution? Every real C program contains, somewhere, exactly one function called `main`, and this is always the entry point for the program as a whole: the compiler sets things up so that when the program executes, `main` is called.

The organization for large C programs that I've just described will also be, in effect, the organization for your iOS programs. (The chief difference will be that instead of *.c* files, you'll use *.m* files, because *.m* is the conventional filename extension for telling Xcode that your files are written in Objective-C, not pure C.) Moreover, if you look at any iOS Xcode project, you'll discover that it contains a file called *main.m*; and if you look at that file, you'll find that it contains a function called `main`. That's the entry point to your application's code when it runs.

The big difference between your Objective-C code files and the C code files I've been discussing is that instead of saying `#include`, your files will say `#import`. The `#import` preprocessor directive is not mentioned in K&R. It's an Objective-C addition to the

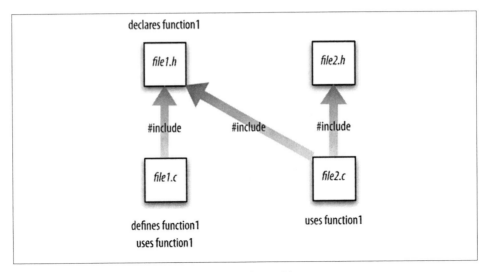

Figure 1-2. How a large C program is divided into files

language. It's based on #include, but it is used instead of #include because it (#import)
contains some logic for making sure that the same material is not included more than
once. Such repeated inclusion is a danger whenever there are many cross-dependent
header files; use of #import solves the problem neatly.

Furthermore, your iOS programs consist not only of *your* code files and their corresponding .h files, but also of Apple's code files and *their* corresponding .h files. The
difference is that Apple's code files (which are what constitutes Cocoa, see Part III) have
already been compiled. But your code must still #import Apple's .h files so as to be able
to see Apple's declarations. If you look at an iOS Xcode project, you'll find that any .h
files it contains by default, as well as its *main.m* file, contain a line of this form:

```
#import <UIKit/UIKit.h>
```

That line is essentially a single massive #import that copies into your program the declarations for the entire basic iOS API. Moreover, each of your *.m* files #imports its
corresponding .h file, including whatever the .h file #imports. Thus, all your code files
include the basic iOS declarations.

For example, earlier I said that CGPoint was defined like this:

```
struct CGPoint {
  CGFloat x;
  CGFloat y;
};
typedef struct CGPoint CGPoint;
```

Modern Objective-C Function Declarations

Starting with LLVM compiler version 3.1, which made its debut in Xcode 4.3, Objective-C no longer requires that a function declaration precede the use of that function, provided that the definition of that function follows in the same file. In other words, code inside an Objective-C class can call a function — or an Objective-C method — even if that call *precedes* the definition of that function or method, and even if there is no separate declaration of that function or method. Thus, in modern Objective-C, the order of functions and methods within a .*m* file doesn't matter, and it is not necessary to declare functions or methods within a .*m* file at all! The only place you'll ever need to declare functions or methods will be in a .*h* file, and only so that some .*m* file *other* than the file where they are defined can import that .*h* file and call the function (or method).

Bear in mind that this convenience is a feature of Objective-C, not of C. I'm talking about .*m* files, not .*c* files. I'll describe more precisely in Chapter 4 the region of a .*m* file in which this convenience applies — namely, a class's implementation section.

After the preprocessor operates on all your files, your .*m* files actually *contain* that definition of CGPoint. (You can even choose Product → Generate Output → Preprocessed File, as I mentioned earlier, to confirm that this is true.) And that is why your code is able to use a CGPoint!

The `#import` directive, like the `#include` directive (K&R 4.11), can specify a file in angle brackets or in quotation marks:

```
#import <UIKit/UIKit.h>
#import "MyHeader.h"
```

Here's what those two forms of syntax mean:

Quotation marks

Look for the named file in the same folder as this file (the .*m* file in which the `#import` line occurs).

Angle brackets

Look for the named file among the various header search paths supplied in the build settings. (These search paths are set for you automatically, and you normally won't need to modify them.)

In general, you'll use angle brackets to refer to a header file owned by the Cocoa API and quotation marks to refer to a header file that you wrote. If you're curious as to what an `#import` directive imports, select it (in Xcode) and choose File → Open Quickly to display the contents of the designated header file.

The Standard Library

You also have at your disposal a large collection of built-in C library files. A library file is a centrally located collection of C functions, along with a .*h* file that you can include so as to make those functions available to your code.

For example, suppose you want to round a float up to the next highest integer. The way to do this is to call some variety of the `ceil` function. You can read the `ceil` man page by typing `man ceil` in the Terminal. The documentation tells you what `#include` to use to incorporate the correct header and also shows you the function declarations and tells you what those functions do. A small pure C program might thus look like this:

```
#include <math.h>
float f = 4.5;
int i = ceilf(f); // now i is 5
```

In your iOS programs, *math.h* is included for you as part of the massive UIKit `#import`, so there's no need to include it again. But some library functions might require an explicit `#import`.

The standard library is discussed in K&R Appendix B. But the modern standard library has evolved since K&R; it is a superset of K&R's library. The `ceil` function, for example, is listed in K&R appendix B, but the `ceilf` function is not. Similarly, if you wanted to generate a random number (which is likely if you're writing a game program that needs to incorporate some unpredictable behavior), you probably wouldn't use the `rand` function listed in K&R; you'd use the `random` function, which supersedes it.

Forgetting that Objective-C is C and that the C library functions are available to your code is a common beginner mistake.

More Preprocessor Directives

Of the many other available preprocessor directives, the one you'll use most often is `#define`. It is followed by a name and a value; at preprocess time, the value is substituted for the name down through this code file. As K&R very well explain (K&R 1.4), this is a good way to prevent "magic numbers" from being hidden and hard-coded into your program in a way that makes the program difficult to understand and maintain.

For example, in an iOS app that lays out some text fields vertically, I might want them all to have the same space between them. Let's say this space is 3.0. I shouldn't write 3.0 repeatedly throughout my code as I calculate the layout; instead, I write:

```
#define MIDSPACE 3.0
```

Now instead of the "magic number" 3.0, my code uses a meaningful name, MIDSPACE; at preprocessor time, the text MIDSPACE is replaced with the text 3.0. So it amounts to the same thing, but if I decide to change this value and try a different one, all I have to change is the #define line, not every occurrence of the number 3.0.

A #define simply performs text substitution, so any expression can be used as the value. Sometimes you'll want that expression to be an NSString literal. Here's why. In Cocoa, NSString literals can be used as a key to a dictionary or the name of a notification. (Never mind for now what a dictionary or a notification is.) This situation is an invitation to error. If you have a dictionary containing a key @"mykey" and you mistype this elsewhere in your code as @"myKey" or @"mikey", the compiler won't complain, but your program will misbehave. The solution is to define a name for this literal string:

```
#define MYKEY @"mykey"
```

Now use MYKEY throughout your code instead of @"mykey", and if you mistype it (as MYKKEY or what have you), the preprocessor won't perform any substitution and the compiler *will* complain, catching the mistake for you.

The #define directive can also be used to create a macro (K&R 4.11.2), a more elaborate form of text substitution. You'll encounter a few Cocoa macros in the course of this book, but they will appear indistinguishable from functions; their secret identity as macros won't concern you.

The #warning directive deliberately triggers a warning in Xcode at compile time; this can be a way to remind yourself of some impending task or requirement:

```
#warning Don't forget to fix this bit of code
```

There is also a #pragma mark directive that's useful with Xcode; I talk about it when discussing the Xcode programming environment (Chapter 9).

Data Type Qualifiers

A variable's data type can be declared with a qualifier before the name of the type, modifying something about how that variable is to be used. For example, the declaration can be preceded by the term const, which means (K&R 2.4) that it is illegal to change the variable's value; the variable must be initialized in the same line as the declaration, and that's the only value it can ever have.

You can use a const variable as an alternative way (instead of #define) to prevent "magic numbers" and similar expressions. For example:

```
NSString* const MYKEY = @"Howdy";
```

The Cocoa API itself makes heavy use of this device. For example, in some circumstances Cocoa will pass a dictionary of information to your code. The documentation tells you what keys this dictionary contains. But instead of telling you a key as a string, the documentation tells you the key as a const NSString variable name:

```
UIKIT_EXTERN NSString *const UIApplicationStatusBarOrientationUserInfoKey;
```

(Never mind what UIKIT_EXTERN means.) This declaration tells you that UIApplication-StatusBarOrientationUserInfoKey is the name of an NSString, and you are to trust that its value is set for you. You are to go ahead and use this name whenever you want to speak of this particular key, secure in the knowledge that the actual string value will be substituted. You do not have to know what that actual string value is. In this way, if you make a mistake in typing the variable name, the compiler will catch the mistake because you'll be using the name of an undefined variable.

Another commonly used qualifier is static. This term is unfortunately used in two rather different ways in C; the way I commonly use it is inside a function. Inside a function, static indicates that the memory set aside for a variable should not be released after the function returns; rather, the variable remains and maintains its value for the next time the function is called. A static variable is useful, for example, when you want to call a function many times without the overhead of calculating the result each time (after the first time). First test to see whether the static value has already been calculated: if it hasn't, this must be the first time the function is being called, so you calculate it; if it has, you just return it. Here's a schematic version:

```
int myfunction() {
    static int result = 0; // 0 means we haven't done the calculation yet
    if (result == 0) {
        // calculate result and set it
    }
    return result;
}
```

A very common use of a static variable in Objective-C is to implement a singleton instance returned by a class factory method. If that sounds complicated, don't worry; it isn't. Here's an example from my own code, which you can grasp even though we haven't discussed Objective-C yet:

```
+ (CardPainter*) sharedPainter {
    static CardPainter* sp = nil;
    if (nil == sp)
        sp = [CardPainter new];
    return sp;
}
```

That code says: If the CardPainter instance sp has never been created, create it, and in any case, now return it. Thus, no matter how many times this method is called, the instance will be created just once and that same instance will be returned every time.

Static variables are a C language feature, not an Objective-C language feature. Therefore, a static variable knows nothing of classes and instances; even if it appears inside a function or a method, it is defined at the level of a file, which means, in effect, at the level of your program as a whole. That's fine when you're using it in a class factory method, because a class is unique to your program as a whole. But never use a static variable in an Objective-C instance method, because your program can have multiple such instances, and the value of this one static variable will apply across all of them. In other words, don't use a C static variable as a lazy substitute for an Objective-C instance variable (Chapter 2). I've made that mistake, and trust me, the results are not pretty.

CHAPTER 2

Object-Based Programming

My object all sublime.

—W. S. Gilbert, *The Mikado*

Objective-C, the native language for programming the Cocoa API, is an object-oriented language; to use it, the programmer must have an appreciation of the nature of objects and object-based programming. There's little point in learning the syntax of Objective-C message sending or instantiation without a clear understanding of what a message or an instance is. That is what this chapter is about.

Objects

An object, in programming, is based on the concept of an object in the real world. It's an independent, self-contained thing. These objects, unlike purely inert objects in the real world, have abilities. So an object in programming is more like a clock than a rock; it doesn't just sit there, but actually does something. Perhaps one could compare an object in programming more to the animate objects of the real world, as opposed to the inanimate objects, except that — unlike real-world animate things — a programming object is supposed to be predictable: in particular, it does what you tell it. In the real world, you tell a dog to sit and anything can happen; in the programming world, you tell a dog to sit and it sits. (This is why so many of us prefer programming to dealing with the real world.)

In object-based programming, a program is organized into many discrete objects. This organization can make life much easier for the programmer. Each object has abilities that are specialized for that object. You can think of this as being a little like how an automobile assembly line works. Each worker or station along the line does one thing (screw on the bumpers, or paint the door, or whatever) and does it well. You can see immediately how this organization helps the programmer. If the car is coming off the assembly line with the door badly painted, it is very likely that the blame lies with the door-painting object, so we know where to look for the bug in our code. Or, if we decide to change the color that the door is to be painted, we have but to make a small change in the door-painting object. Meanwhile, other objects just go on doing what they do. They neither know nor care what the door-painting object does or how it works.

Objects, then, are an organizational tool, a set of boxes for encapsulating the code that accomplishes a particular task. They are also a conceptual tool. The programmer, being forced to think in terms of discrete objects, must divide the goals and behaviors of the program into discrete tasks, each task being assigned to an appropriate object. Of course, objects can cooperate with one another, and the ways in which this cooperation can be arranged are innumerable. The assembly-line analogy illustrates one such arrangement — first, object 1 operates upon the end-product; then it hands it off to object 2, and object 2 operates upon the end-product, and so on — but that arrangement won't be appropriate to most tasks. Coming up with an appropriate arrangement — an *architecture* — for the cooperative and orderly relationship between objects is one of the most challenging aspects of object-based programming.

Messages and Methods

Nothing in a computer program happens unless it is instructed to happen. In a C program, all code belongs to a function and doesn't run unless that function is called. In an object-based program, all code belongs to an object, and doesn't run unless that object is told to run that code. All the action in an object-based program happens because an object was told to act. What does it mean to tell an object something?

An object, in object-based programming, has a well-defined set of abilities — things it knows how to do. For example, imagine an object that is to represent a dog. We can design a highly simplified, schematic dog that knows how to do an extremely limited range of things: eat, come for a walk, bark, sit, lie down, sleep. The purpose of these abilities is so that the object can be told, as appropriate, to exercise them. So, again, we can imagine our schematic dog, rather like some child's toy robot, responding to simple commands: Eat! Come for a walk! Bark!

In object-based programming, a command directed to an object is called a *message*. To make the dog object eat, we send the eat message to the dog object. This mechanism of message sending is the basis of all activity in the program. The program consists entirely of objects, so its activity consists entirely of objects sending messages to one another.

For objects to send messages to one another, objects must know about one another in some appropriate way at some appropriate time. Ensuring such mutual knowledge is part of the architectural design process I spoke of earlier. Returning for a moment to the assembly-line architecture, it's no use saying that object 1 operates on the end-product and then object 2 operates on the end-product; that isn't going to happen all by itself. It has to be arranged somehow. We can imagine various architectures for arranging it. Perhaps we will set things up so that object 1 knows about object 2, and as the last step in its own operation, sends a message to object 2, handing it the end-product and telling it to commence its own operation. Or perhaps we will have a conveyor-belt object, which will hand the end-product to object 1 and tell it to commence its operation, wait until object 1 finishes with it, and then hand the end-product to object 2 and tell *it* to commence its operation. Each of these is a perfectly reasonable architectural pattern, and many others are possible; it is the programmer's job to implement an architecture that not only makes the program work appropriately, but also makes the program itself clear and easy for the programmer to work on. But the problem of making sure that within that architecture, each object knows about — technically, has a *reference* to — any other object to which it might need to send a message can be quite tricky (so much so, indeed, that an entire chapter of this book, Chapter 13, is devoted to it).

A moment ago, I said that in a C program, all code belongs to a function. The object-based analogue to a function is called a *method*. So, for example, a dog object might have an `eat` method. When the dog object is sent the `eat` message, it responds by calling the `eat` method.

It may sound as if I'm not drawing any clear distinction between a message and a method. But there is a difference. A message is what one object says to another. A method is a bundle of code that gets called. The connection between the two is not perfectly direct. You might send a message to an object that corresponds to no method of that object. For example, you might tell the dog to recite the soliloquy from Hamlet. I'm not sure what will happen if you do that; the details are implementation-dependent. (The dog might just sit there silently. Or it might get annoyed and bite you. Or, I suppose, it might nip off, read Hamlet, memorize the soliloquy, and recite it.) But that implementation-dependence is exactly the point of the distinction between message and method.

Nevertheless, in general the distinction between sending a message and calling a method won't usually be important in real life. Most of the time, when you're using Objective-C, your reason for sending a message to an object will be that that object implements the corresponding method and you are expecting to call that method. So sending a message to an object and calling a method of an object will appear to be the same act.

Classes and Instances

We come now to an extremely characteristic and profound feature of object-based programming. Just like in the real world, every object in the object-based programming world is of some type. This type, called a *class*, is the object-based analogy to the data type in C. Just as a simple variable in C might be an int or a float, an object in the object-based programming world might be a Dog (or an NSString). In the object-based programming world, the idea of this arrangement is to ensure that more than one individual object can be relied upon to act the same way.

There can, for example, be more than one dog. You might have a dog called Fido and I might have a dog called Rover. But both dogs know how to eat, come for a walk, and bark. In object-based programming, they know this because they both belong to the Dog class. The knowledge of how to eat, come for a walk, and bark is part of the Dog class. Your dog Fido and my dog Rover possess this knowledge solely by virtue of being Dog objects.

From the programmer's point of view, what this means is simple: all the code you write is put into a class. All the methods you write will be part of some class or other. You don't program an individual dog object: you program the Dog class.

But I just got through saying that an object-based program works through the sending of messages to individual objects. So even though the programmer does not write the code for an individual dog object, there still needs to *be* an individual dog object in order for there to be something to send a message to. It is the Dog class that knows how to bark, but it is an individual dog object that is told to bark, and that actually does bark. So the question is: if all Dog code lives in a Dog class, where do individual dogs come from?

The answer is that they have to be created in the course of the program as it runs. When the program starts out, it contains code for a Dog class, but no individual dog objects. If any barking by any dogs is to be done, the program must first create an individual dog object. This object will belong to the Dog class, so it can be sent the bark message. An individual object belonging to the Dog class (or any class) is an *instance* of that class. To manufacture, from a class, an actual individual object that is an instance of that class, is to *instantiate* that class.

So every individual object, such as I talked about in the preceding sections — every individual object, that is, to which a message can be sent — is an instance of some class. Classes exist from the get-go, as part of the fact that the program exists in the first place; they are where the code is. Instances are manufactured, deliberately and individually, as the program runs. Each instance is manufactured *from* a class, it is an instance *of* that class, and it has methods by virtue of the fact that the class has those methods. The instance can then be sent a message; what it will do in response depends on what code the class contains in its methods. The instance is the individual thing that can be sent messages; the class, with its methods, is the locus of the thing's ability to respond to messages (Figure 2-1).

This relationship between instance and class begins to sound rather ethereal or metaphysical. Instances and classes seem to be programming-language analogies to what a philosopher would call particulars and universals. Indeed, the whole setup reminds one of nothing so much as Plato's theory of Forms. For Plato, this world of ours is the world of individual things, but those things derive their natures by virtue of archetypal Forms that live off in another world. I'm not the only person ever to make this comparison to Platonic Forms — it is, indeed, implicit in the design of object-based languages and has

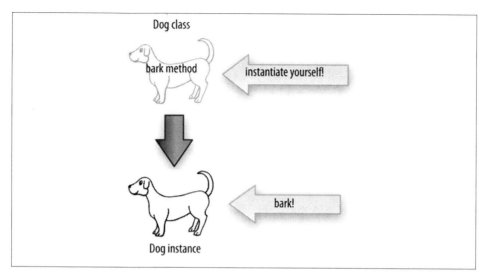

Figure 2-1. Class and instance

been evoked explicitly in discussions of such languages ever since Smalltalk. But the comparison is still an apt one. As I said many years ago in my book *REALbasic: The Definitive Guide*:

> Indeed, object-oriented programming seems to fulfill Plato's philosophical program announced in the *Euthyphro* (6e, my translation):
>
> SOCRATES. Now, you recall that I asked you to explain to me, not this or that particular pious thing, but that Form Itself through which all pious things are pious? You did say, I believe, that it was through one Form that impious things are impious and pious things are pious; don't you remember?
>
> EUTHYPHRO. Yes, I do.
>
> SOCRATES. All right, then; so, explain to me what is this Form Itself, so that by keeping my eyes upon it and using it as a model, I may declare that whatever you or anyone else does that is of this sort, is pious, and that whatever is not, is not.
>
> The problems with Plato's characterization are well known: the Form seems to be a "thing" separate from the particular things of the world around us, the notion "through" is crucial but slippery, and Plato seems to equivocate rather glibly between the Form's being responsible for a thing's being such and such and our ability to know that a thing is such and such; thus, his program is almost certainly doomed to failure as an explanation of how the world works. But he is perfectly accurate about how an object-oriented program works! If an instance is of the Pious type, there really is a separate Pious class that really is responsible for the instance being such as it is.

Because every individual object is an instance of a class, to know what messages you can officially send to that object, you need to know at least what methods its class has endowed it with. The public knowledge of this information is that class's API. (A class may also have methods that you're not really supposed to call from outside that object; these would not be public and other objects couldn't officially send those messages to an instance of that class.) That's why Apple's own Cocoa documentation consists largely of pages listing and describing the methods supplied by some class. For example, to know what messages you can send to an NSString object (instance), you'd start by studying the NSString class documentation. That page is really just a big list of methods, so it tells you what an NSString object can do. That isn't everything in the world there is to know about an NSString, but it's a big percentage of it.

Class Methods

Up to now I've been keeping something back, and if you've been paying close attention, you may have caught me at it, because it looks as though I've contradicted myself. I said that nothing happens in a program unless a message is sent to an object. But I also said that there are no instances until they are created as the program runs. The contradiction is that if messages can be sent only to instances, it appears that no instances can ever be created (because, when the program starts up, there are no instances to which you can send the message asking for an instance to be created).

The truth that I've been keeping back, which complicates things only a little, is that classes are themselves objects and can be sent messages. This revelation solves the contradiction completely. No instances exist as the program starts up, but the classes do. The classes may live off in a world of Platonic Forms, but they can still be sent messages. And one of the most important things you can ask a class to do by sending it a message is to instantiate itself.

You cannot, however, ask an instance to instantiate itself. It thus begins to look as if there must be two kinds of message: messages that you are allowed to send to a class (such as telling the Dog class to instantiate itself) and messages that you are allowed to send to an instance (such as telling an individual dog to bark). That is exactly true. More precisely, all code lives as a method in a class, but methods are of two kinds: class methods and instance methods. If a method is a class method, you can send that message to the class. If a method is an instance method, you can send that message to an instance of the class.

In Objective-C syntax, class methods and instance methods are distinguished by the use of a plus sign or a minus sign. For example, Apple's NSString class documentation page listing the methods of the NSString class starts out like this:

```
+ string
- init
```
(+)   (−)

The `string` method is a class method. The `init` method is an instance method.

In general, though not exclusively, class methods tend to be factory methods — that is, methods for generating an instance. This makes sense, because making an instance of itself is one of the main things you're likely to want to ask a class to do. You might think that a class really needs only *one* class method for generating an instance of itself, and that is rigorously true, but classes tend to provide multiple factory methods purely as a convenience to the programmer. For example, here are three NSString class methods:

```
+ string
+ stringWithFormat:
+ stringWithContentsOfFile:encoding:error:
```

They all make instances. The first class method, `string`, generates an empty NSString instance (a string with no text). The second class method, `stringWithFormat:`, generates an NSString instance based on text that you provide, which can include transforming other values into text; for example, you might use it to start with an integer 9 and generate an NSString instance @"9". The third class method reads the contents of a file and generates an NSString instance from those contents. When you come to write your own classes, you too might well create multiple class methods that act as instance factories for your own future programming convenience.

Instance Variables

Now that I've revealed that classes are objects and can be sent messages, you might be wondering why there need to be instances at all. Why doesn't the mere existence of classes as objects suffice for object-based programming? Why would you ever bother to instantiate any of the classes? Why wouldn't you write all your code as class methods, have the program send messages from one class object to another, and be done with it?

The answer is that instances have a feature that classes do not: instance variables. An instance variable is just what the name suggests: it's a variable belonging to an instance. Like instance methods, instance variables are defined as part of the class. But the *value* of an instance variable is set as the program runs and belongs to one instance alone. In other words, different instances can have different values for the same instance variable.

For example, suppose we have a Dog class and we decide that it might be a good idea for every dog to have a name. Just as you can learn a real-world dog's name by reading the tag on its collar, we want to be able to assign every dog instance a name and, subsequently, to learn what that name is. So, in designing the Dog class, we declare that this class has an instance variable called name, whose value is a string (probably an NSString, as we're using Objective-C). Now when our program runs we can instantiate Dog and assign the resulting dog instance a name (that is, we can assign its name instance variable a value). We can also instantiate Dog again and assign *that* resulting dog instance a name. Let's say these are two different names: one is @"Rover" and one is @"Fido". Then

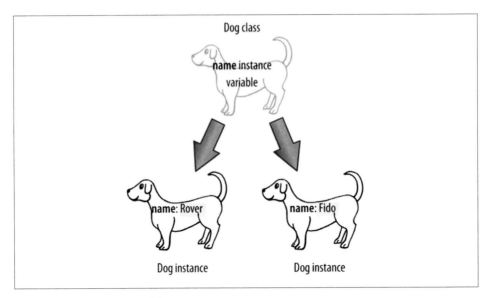

Figure 2-2. Instance variables

we've got two instances of Dog, and they are significantly different; they differ in the value of their name instance variables (Figure 2-2).

So an instance is a reflection of the instance methods of its class, but that isn't *all* it is; it's also a collection of instance variables. The class is responsible for what instance variables the instance has, but not for the values of those variables. The values can change as the program runs and apply only to a particular instance. An instance is a cluster of particular instance variable values.

In short, an instance is both code and data. The code it gets from its class and in a sense is shared with all other instances of that class, but the data belong to it alone. The data can persist as long as the instance persists. The instance has, at every moment, a state — the complete collection of its own personal instance variable values. An instance is a device for maintaining state. It's a box for storage of data.

The Object-Based Philosophy

In my REALbasic book, I summarized the nature of objects in two phrases: encapsulation of functionality, and maintenance of state:

Encapsulation of functionality

Each object does its own job, and presents to the rest of the world — to other objects, and indeed in a sense to the programmer — an opaque wall whose only entrances are the methods to which it promises to respond and the actions it promises to perform when the corresponding messages are sent to it. The details of how, behind the scenes, it actually implements those actions are secreted within itself; no other object needs to know them.

Maintenance of state

Each individual instance is a bundle of data that it maintains. Typically that data is private, which means that it's encapsulated as well; no other object knows what that data is or in what form it is kept. The only way to discover from outside what data an object is maintaining is if there's a method that reveals it.

As an example, imagine an object whose job is to implement a stack — it might be an instance of a Stack class. A *stack* is a data structure that maintains a set of data in LIFO order (last in, first out). It responds to just two messages: push and pop. Push means to add a given piece of data to the set. Pop means to remove from the set the piece of data that was most recently pushed and hand it out. It's like a stack of plates: plates are placed onto the top of the stack or removed from the top of the stack one by one, so the first plate to go onto the stack can't be retrieved until all other subsequently added plates have been removed (Figure 2-3).

The stack object illustrates encapsulation of functionality because the outside world knows nothing of how the stack is actually implemented. It might be an array, it might be a linked list, it might be any of a number of other implementations. But a client object — an object that actually sends a push or pop message to the stack object — knows nothing of this and cares less, provided the stack object adheres to its contract of behaving like a stack. This is also good for the programmer, who can, as the program develops, safely substitute one implementation for another without harming the vast machinery of the program as a whole. And just the other way round, the stack object knows nothing and cares less about who is telling it to push or to pop, and why. It just hums along and does its job in its reliable little way.

The stack object illustrates maintenance of state because it isn't just the gateway to the stack data — it *is* the stack data. Every object that has a reference to the stack object has the same access to its data, the same ability to push or to pop. (And that's all it can do. The stack data is effectively inside the stack object; no one else can see it. All that another object can do is push or pop.) If a certain object is at the top of our stack object's stack right now, then whatever object sends the pop message to this stack object will receive that object in return. If no object sends the pop message to this stack object, then the object at the top of the stack will just sit there, waiting.

As a second example of the philosophy and nature of object-based programming at work, I'll revert to another imaginary scenario I used in my REALbasic book. Pretend we're writing an arcade game where the user is to "shoot" at moving "targets," and the score increases every time a target is hit. We immediately have a sense of how we might organize our code using object-based programming and can see how object-based programming will fulfill its nature and purpose:

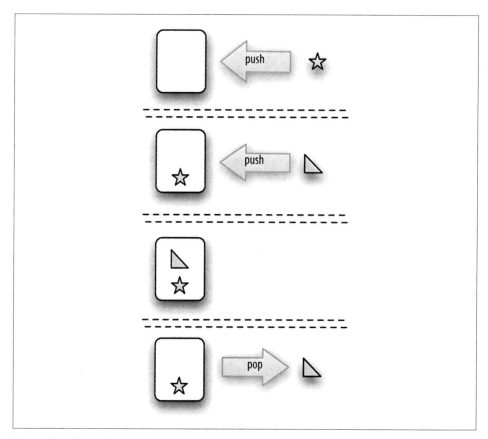

Figure 2-3. A stack

- There will be a Target class. Every target object will be an instance of this class. This decision makes sense because we want every target to behave the same way. A target will need to know how to draw itself; that knowledge will be part of the Target class, which makes sense because all targets will draw themselves in the same way. Thus we have the relationship between class and instance.

- Targets may draw themselves the same way, but they may also differ in appearance. Perhaps some targets are blue, others are red, and so on. This difference between individual targets can be expressed as an instance variable. Call it color. Every time we instantiate a target, we'll assign it a color. The Target class's code for drawing an individual target will look at that target's color instance variable and use it when filling in the target's shape. Clearly, we could extend this individualization as much as we like: targets could have different sizes, different shapes, and so on, and all of these parametric distinctions could be made on an individual basis through the use of instance variables. Thus we have both encapsulation of functionality and maintenance of state. A target has a state, the parameters that describe how it should look, and also has the ability to draw itself, expressing that state visually.

- When a target is hit by the user, it will explode. So perhaps the Target class will have an `explode` instance method; thus, every target knows how to explode. One thing that should happen whenever a target explodes is that the user's score should increase. So let's imagine a score object — an instance of the Score class. Give every target object a reference to this score object so that it can send a message to it. When a target explodes, one of the things its `explode` instance method will do is send an `increase` message to the score object. Thus we have both encapsulation of functionality and maintenance of state. The score object responds indifferently to any object that sends it the `increase` message; it doesn't need to know why it's being sent that message. Nor does the score object even need to know that targets exist, or indeed that it's part of a game. It just sits there maintaining the score, and when it receives the `increase` message, it increases it.

This chapter has described only the rudiments of object-based philosophy — enough to communicate the correct mind-set. Using object-based programming effectively to make a program clear and maintainable is something of an art; your abilities will improve with experience. Eventually, you may want to do some further reading on how to construct an object-based program most effectively. I recommend in particular two classic, favorite books. *Refactoring*, by Martin Fowler (Addison-Wesley, 1999), describes how you can get a sense that you might need to rearrange what methods belong to what classes (and how to conquer your fear of doing so). *Design Patterns*, by Erich Gamma, Richard Helm, Ralph Johnson, and John Vlissides (also known as "the Gang of Four"), is the bible on architecting object-based programs, listing all the ways you can arrange objects with the right powers and the right knowledge of one another (Addison-Wesley, 1994).

CHAPTER 3

Objective-C Objects and Messages

One of the first object-based programming languages to achieve maturity and wide-spread dissemination was Smalltalk. It was developed during the 1970s at Xerox PARC under the leadership of Alan Kay and started becoming widely known in 1980. The purpose of Objective-C, created by Brad Cox and Tom Love in 1986, was to build Smalltalk-like syntax and behavior on top of C. Objective-C was licensed by NeXT in 1988 and was the basis for its application framework API, NeXTStep. Eventually, NeXT and Apple merged, and the NeXT application framework evolved into Cocoa, the framework for Mac OS X applications, still revolving around Objective-C. That history explains why Objective-C is the base language for iOS programming. (It also explains why Cocoa class names often begin with "NS" — it stands for "NeXTStep.")

Having learned the basics of C (Chapter 1) and the nature of object-based programming (Chapter 2), you are ready to meet Objective-C. This chapter describes Objective-C structural fundamentals; the next two chapters provide more detail about how Objective-C classes and instances work. (A few additional features of the language are discussed in Chapter 10.) As with the C language, my intention is not to describe the Objective-C language completely, but to provide a practical linguistic grounding, founded on my own experience of those aspects of the language that need to be firmly understood as a basis for iOS programming.

An Instance Reference Is a Pointer

In C, every variable must be declared to be of some type. In an object-based language such as Objective-C, an instance's type is its class. The C language includes very few basic data types. To facilitate the multiplicity of class types required by its object-based nature, Objective-C takes advantage of C pointers. So, in Objective-C, if a variable is an instance of the class MyClass, that variable is of type `MyClass*` — a pointer to a MyClass. In general, in Objective-C, a reference to an instance is a pointer and the name of the data type of what's at the far end of that pointer is the name of the instance's class.

Note the convention for capitalization. Variable names tend to start with a lowercase letter; class names tend to start with an uppercase letter.

As I mentioned in Chapter 1, the fact that a reference to an instance is a pointer in Objective-C will generally not cause you any difficulties, because pointers are used consistently throughout the language. For example, a message to an instance is directed at the pointer, so there is no need to dereference the pointer. Indeed, having established that a variable representing an instance is a pointer, you're likely to forget that this variable even *is* a pointer and just work directly with that variable:

```
NSString* s = @"Hello, world!";
NSString* s2 = [s uppercaseString];
```

Having established that s is an NSString*, you would never dereference s (that is, you would never speak of *s) to access the "real" NSString. So it feels as if the pointer *is* the real NSString. Thus, in the previous example, once the variable s is declared as a pointer to an NSString, the uppercaseString message is sent directly to the variable s. (The uppercaseString message asks an NSString to generate and return an uppercase version of itself; so, after that code, s2 is @"HELLO, WORLD!")

The tie between a pointer, an instance, and the class of that instance is so close that it is natural to speak of an expression like MyClass* as meaning "a MyClass instance," and of a MyClass* value as "a MyClass." A Objective-C programmer will say simply that, in the previous example, s *is* an NSString, that uppercaseString returns "an NSString," and so forth. It is fine to speak like that, and I do it myself (and will do it in this book) — provided you remember that this is a shorthand. Such an expression means "an NSString instance," and because an instance is represented as a C pointer, it means an NSString*, a pointer to an NSString.

Although the fact that instance references in Objective-C are pointers does not cause any special difficulty, you must still be conscious of what pointers are and how they work. As I emphasized in Chapter 1, when you're working with pointers, you must keep in mind the special meaning of your actions. So here are some basic facts about pointers that you should keep in mind when working with instance references in Objective-C.

Forgetting the asterisk in an instance declaration is a common beginner mistake, and will net you a mysterious compiler error message, such as "Interface type cannot be statically allocated."

Instance References, Initialization, and nil

Merely declaring an instance reference's type doesn't bring any instance into existence. For example:

```
NSString* s; // only a declaration; no instance is pointed to
```

After that declaration, s is *typed* as a pointer to an NSString, but it is not *in fact* pointing to an NSString. You have created a pointer, but you haven't supplied an NSString for it to point to. It's just sitting there, waiting for you to point it at an NSString, typically by assignment (as we did with @"Hello, world!" earlier). Such assignment *initializes* the variable, giving it an actual meaningful value of the proper type.

You can declare a variable as an instance reference in one line of code and initialize it later, like this:

```
NSString* s;
// ... time passes ...
s = @"Hello, world!";
```

But this is not common. It is much more common, wherever possible, to declare and initialize a variable all in one line of code:

```
NSString* s = @"Hello, world!";
```

Declaration *without* initialization, before the advent of ARC in iOS 5 (Chapter 12), created a dangerous situation:

```
NSString* s;
```

What *is* s after a mere declaration like that? It could be anything. But it is *claiming* to be a pointer to an NSString, and so your code might proceed to *treat* it as a pointer to an NSString. But it is pointing at garbage. A pointer pointing at garbage is liable to cause serious trouble down the road when you accidentally try to use it as an instance. Sending a message to a garbage pointer, or otherwise treating it as a meaningful instance, can crash your program. Even worse, it might *not* crash your program: it might cause your program to behave very, very oddly instead — and figuring out why can be difficult.

For this reason, if you *aren't* going to initialize an instance reference pointer at the moment you declare it by assigning it a real value, it's a good idea to assign it nil:

```
NSString* s = nil;
```

A small but delightful bonus feature of using ARC is that this assignment is performed for you, implicitly and invisibly, as soon as you declare a variable without initializing it:

```
NSString* s; // under ARC, s is immediately set to nil for you
```

This prevents the existence of a garbage pointer, and could save you from yourself by preventing a crash when you accidentally use s as an instance without initializing it. Nevertheless, long years of habit have trained me to initialize or explicitly set to nil an instance pointer as soon as I declare it, and you'll see that I continue to do so in examples in this book.

What is nil? It's simply a form of zero — the form of zero appropriate to an instance reference. The nil value simply means: "This instance reference isn't pointing to any instance." Indeed, you can test an instance reference against nil as a way of finding out whether it is in fact pointing to a real instance. This is an extremely common thing to do:

```
if (nil == s) // ...
```

As I mentioned in Chapter 1, the explicit comparison with nil isn't strictly necessary; because nil is a form of zero, and because zero means false in a condition, you can perform the same test like this:

```
if (!s) // ...
```

I do in fact write nil tests in that second form all the time, but some programmers would take me to task for bad style. The first form has the advantage that its real meaning is made explicit, rather than relying on a cute implicit feature of C. The first form places nil first in the comparison so that if the programmer accidentally omits an equal sign, performing an assignment instead of a comparison, the compiler will catch the error (because assignment to nil is illegal).

Many Cocoa methods use a return value of nil, instead of an expected instance, to signify that something went wrong. You are supposed to capture this return value and test it for nil in order to discover whether something *did* go wrong. For example, the documentation for the NSString class method stringWithContentsOf-File:encoding:error: says that it returns "a string created by reading data from the file named by path using the encoding, enc. If the file can't be opened or there is an encoding error, returns nil." So, as I described in Chapter 1, your next move after calling this method and capturing the result should be to test that result against nil, just to make sure you've really got an instance now:

```
NSString* path = // ... whatever;
NSStringEncoding enc = // ... whatever;
NSError* err = nil;
NSString* s =
    [NSString stringWithContentsOfFile:path encoding:enc error:&err];
if (nil == s) // oops! something went wrong...
```

You should now be wondering about the implications of a nil-value pointer for sending a message to a noninstance. For example, you can send a message to an NSString instance like this:

```
NSString* s2 = [s uppercaseString];
```

That code sends the uppercaseString message to s. So s is supposedly an NSString instance. But what if s is nil? With some object-based programming languages, sending a message to nil constitutes a runtime error and will cause your program to terminate prematurely (REALbasic and Ruby are examples). But Objective-C doesn't work like that. In Objective-C, sending a message to nil is legal and does not interrupt execution. Moreover, if you capture the result of the method call, it will be a form of zero — which means that if you assign that result to an instance reference pointer, it too will be nil:

```
NSString* s = nil; // now s is nil
NSString* s2 = [s uppercaseString]; // now s2 is nil
```

Whether this behavior of Objective-C is a good thing is a quasi-religious issue and a subject of vociferous debate among programmers. It is useful, but it is also extremely easy to be tricked by it. The usual scenario is that you accidentally send a message to a nil reference without realizing it, and then later your program doesn't behave as expected. Because the point where the unexpected behavior occurs is later than the moment when the nil pointer arose in the first place, the genesis of the nil pointer can be difficult to track down (indeed, it often fails to occur to the programmer that a nil pointer is the cause of the trouble in the first place).

Short of peppering your code with tests to ascertain that your instance reference pointers are not accidentally nil, which is not generally a good idea, there isn't much you can do about this. This behavior is strongly built into the language and is not going to change. It's just something you need to be aware of.

If, on the other hand, a method call can return nil, be conscious of that fact. Don't assume that everything will go well and that it won't return nil. On the contrary, if something can go wrong, it probably will. For example, to omit the nil test after calling `stringWith-ContentsOfFile:encoding:error:` is just stupid. I don't care if you know perfectly well that the file exists and the encoding is what you say it is — test the result for nil!

 In pure C code, you will sometimes see a pointer-to-nothing expressed as NULL. NULL and nil are functionally equivalent nowadays, and I'll use nil exclusively in this book.

Instance References and Assignment

As I said in Chapter 1, assigning to a pointer does not mutate the value at the far end of the pointer; rather, it repoints the pointer. Moreover, assigning one pointer to another repoints the pointer in such a way that both pointers are now pointing to the very same thing. Failure to keep these simple facts firmly in mind can have results that range from surprising to disastrous.

For example, instances in general are usually mutable: they typically have instance variables that can change. If two references are pointing at one and the same instance, then when the instance is mutated by way of one reference, that mutation also affects the instance as seen through the other reference. To illustrate, pretend that we've implemented the Stack class described in the previous chapter:

```
Stack* myStack1 = // ... create Stack instance and initialize myStack1 ... ;
Stack* myStack2 = myStack1;
[myStack1 push: @"Hello"];
[myStack1 push: @"World"];
NSString* s = [myStack2 pop];
```

After we pop myStack2, s is @"World" even though nothing was ever pushed onto myStack2 (and the stack myStack1 contains only @"Hello" even though nothing was ever popped off of myStack1). That's because we did push two strings onto myStack1 and then pop one string off myStack2, and myStack1 *is* myStack2 — in the sense that they are both pointers to the very same stack instance. That's perfectly fine, as long as you understand and intend this behavior.

In real life, you're likely to pass an instance off to some other object, or to receive it from some other object:

```
Stack* myStack = // ... create Stack instance and initialize myStack ... ;
// ... more code might go here ...
[myObject doSomethingWithThis: myStack]; // pass myStack to myObject
```

After that code, myObject has a pointer to the very same instance we're already pointing to as myStack. So we must be careful and thoughtful. The object myObject might mutate myStack right under our very noses. Even more, the object myObject might *keep* its reference to the stack instance and mutate it *later* — possibly much later, in a way that could surprise us. This is possible because instances can have instance variables that point to other objects, and those pointers can persist as long as the instances themselves do. This kind of shared referent situation can be intentional, but it is also something to watch out for and be conscious of (Figure 3-1).

Another possible misunderstanding is to imagine that the assignment myStack2 = myStack1 somehow makes a new, separate instance that duplicates myStack1. That's not at all the case. It doesn't make a new instance; it just points myStack2 at the very same instance that myStack1 is pointing at. It may be possible to make a new instance that duplicates a given instance, but the ability to do so is not a given and it is not going to happen through mere assignment. (For how a separate duplicate instance might be generated, see the NSCopying protocol and the copy method mentioned in Chapter 10.)

Instance References and Memory Management

The pointer nature of instance references in Objective-C also has implications for management of memory. The scope, and in particular the lifetime, of variables in pure C is typically quite straightforward: if you bring a piece of variable storage into existence by declaring that variable within a certain scope, then when that scope ceases to exist, the

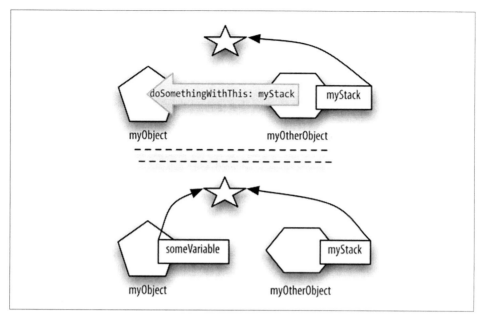

Figure 3-1. Two instances end up with pointers to the same third instance

variable storage ceases to exist. That sort of variable is called *automatic* (K&R 1.10). So, for example:

```
void myFunction() {
    int i; // storage for an int is set aside
    i = 7; // 7 is placed in that storage
} // the scope ends, so the int storage and its contents vanish
```

But in the case of a pointer, there are two pieces of memory to worry about: the pointer itself, which is an integer signifying an address in memory, and whatever is at that address, at the far end of that pointer. Nothing about the C language causes the destruction of what a pointer points to when the pointer itself is automatically destroyed as it goes out of scope:

```
void myFunction() {
    NSString* s = @"Hello, world!"; // pointer and NSString
    NSString* s2 = [s uppercaseString]; // pointer and NSString
} // the two pointers go out of existence...
// ... but what about the two NSStrings they point to?
```

Some object-based programming languages in which a reference to an instance is a pointer do manage automatically the memory pointed to by instance references (REALbasic and Ruby are examples). But Objective-C, at least the way it's implemented when you're programming for iOS, is not one of those languages. Because the C language has nothing to say about the automatic destruction of what is pointed to by a reference to an instance, Objective-C implements an explicit mechanism for the management of memory. I'll talk in a later chapter (Chapter 12) about what that mechanism is and what responsibilities for the programmer it entails. Fortunately, under ARC, those responsibilities are fewer than they used to be; but memory must still be managed, and you must still understand how memory management works.

Messages and Methods

An Objective-C method is defined as part of a class. It has three aspects:

Whether it's a class method or an instance method
> If it's a class method, you call it by sending a message to the class itself. If it's an instance method, you call it by sending a message to an instance of the class.

Its parameters and return value
> As with a C function, an Objective-C method takes some number of parameters; each parameter is of some specified type. And, as with a C function, it may return a value, which is also of some specified type; if the method returns nothing, its return type is declared as void.

Its name
> An Objective-C method's name must contain as many colons as it takes parameters. The name is split after each colon in a method call or declaration, so it is usual for the part of the name preceding each colon to describe the corresponding parameter.

Sending a Message

As you've doubtless gathered, the syntax for sending a message to an object involves square brackets. The first thing in the square brackets is the object to which the message is to be sent; this object is the message's *receiver*. Then follows the message:

```
NSString* s2 = [s uppercaseString]; // send "uppercaseString" message to s ...
// ... (and assign result to s2)
```

If the message is a method that takes parameters, each corresponding argument value comes after a colon:

```
[myStack1 push: @"Hello"]; // send "push:" message to myStack1 ...
// ...with one argument, the NSString @"Hello"
```

To send a message to a class (calling a class method), you can represent the class by the literal name of the class:

```
NSString* s = [NSString string]; // send "string" message to NSString class
```

To send a message to an instance (calling an instance method), you'll need a reference to an instance, which (as you know) is a pointer:

```
NSString* s = @"Hello, world!"; // s is initialized as an NSString instance
NSString* s2 = [s uppercaseString]; // send "uppercaseString" message to s
```

You can send a class method to a class, and an instance method to an instance, no matter how you got hold of and represent the class or the instance. For example, @"Hello, world!" is itself an NSString instance, so it's legal to say:

```
NSString* s2 = [@"Hello, world!" uppercaseString];
```

If a method takes no parameters, then its name contains no colons, like the NSString instance method uppercaseString. If a method takes one parameter, then its name contains one colon, which is the final character of the method name, like the hypothetical Stack instance method push:. If a method takes two or more parameters, its name contains that number of colons. In the minimal case, its name ends with that number of colons. For example, a method taking three parameters might be called hereAreThree-Strings:::. To call it, we split the name after each colon and follow each colon with an argument, which looks like this:

```
[someObject hereAreThreeStrings: @"string1" : @"string2" : @"string3"];
```

That's a legal way to name a method, but it isn't very common, mostly because it isn't very informative. Usually the name will have more text; in particular, the part before each colon will describe the parameter that follows that colon.

For example, there's a UIColor class method for generating an instance of a UIColor from four CGFloat numbers representing its red, green, blue, and alpha (transparency) components, and it's called colorWithRed:green:blue:alpha:. Notice the clever construction of this name. The colorWith part tells something about the method's purpose: it generates a *color*, starting *with* some set of information. All the rest of the name, Red:green:blue:alpha:, describes the meaning of each parameter. And you call it like this: THIS REMINDS ME OF NAMED PARAMETERS

```
UIColor* c = [UIColor colorWithRed: 0.0 green: 0.5 blue: 0.25 alpha: 1.0];
```

The space after each colon in the method call is optional. (Space before a colon is also legal, though in practice one rarely sees this.)

The rules for naming an Objective-C method, along with the conventions governing such names (like trying to make the name informative about the method's purpose and the meanings of its parameters), lead to some rather long and unwieldy method names, such as getBytes:maxLength:usedLength:encoding:options:range:remaining-Range:. Such verbosity of nomenclature is characteristic of Objective-C. Method calls, and even method declarations, are often split across multiple lines to prevent a single line of code from becoming so long that it wraps within the editor, as well as for clarity.

Declaring a Method

The declaration for a method has three parts:

- Either + or -, meaning that the method is a class method or an instance method, respectively.
- The data type of the return value, in parentheses.
- The name of the method, split after each colon. Following each colon is the corresponding parameter, expressed as the data type of the parameter, in parentheses, followed by a placeholder name for the parameter.

So, for example, Apple's documentation tells us that the declaration for the UIColor class method `colorWithRed:green:blue:alpha:` is:

```
+ (UIColor*) colorWithRed: (CGFloat) red green: (CGFloat) green
                  blue: (CGFloat) blue alpha: (CGFloat) alpha
```

(Note that I've split the declaration into two lines, for legibility and to fit onto this page. The documentation puts it all on a single line.)

 Make very sure you can read this declaration! You should be able to look at it and say to yourself instantly, "The name of this method is `colorWithRed:green:blue:alpha:`. It's a class method that takes four CGFloat parameters and returns a UIColor."

It is not uncommon, outside of code, to write a method's name along with the plus sign or the minus sign, to make it clear whether this is a class method or an instance method. So you might speak informally of "-uppercaseString," just as a way of reminding yourself or a reader that this is an instance method. Again outside of code, it is not uncommon, especially when communicating with other Objective-C programmers, to speak of a method's name along with the class in which this method is defined. So you might say "NSString's -uppercaseString," or even something like "-[NSString uppercaseString]." Notice that that isn't code, or even pseudo-code, because you are not actually speaking of a method call, and in any case you could never send the uppercaseString message to the NSString class; it's just a compact way of saying, "I'm talking about the uppercaseString that's an instance method of NSString."

Nesting Method Calls

Wherever in a method call an object of a certain type is supposed to appear, you can put another method call that returns that type. Thus you can nest method calls. A method call can appear as the message's receiver:

```
NSString* s = [[NSString string] uppercaseString]; // silly but legal
```

That's legal because NSString's class method `string` returns an NSString instance (formally, an `NSString*` value, remember), so we can send an NSString instance method to that result. Similarly, a method call can appear as an argument in a method call:

```
[myStack push: [NSString string]]; // ok if push: expects NSString* parameter
```

However, I must caution you against overdoing that sort of thing. Code with a lot of nested square brackets is very difficult to read (and to write). Furthermore, if one of the nested method calls happens to return nil unexpectedly, you have no way to detect this fact. It is often better, then, to be even more verbose and declare a temporary variable for each piece of the method call. Just to take an example from my own code, instead of writing this:

```
NSArray* arr = [[MPMediaQuery albumsQuery] collections];
```

I might write this:

```
MPMediaQuery* query = [MPMediaQuery albumsQuery];
NSArray* arr = [query collections];
```

Even though the first version is quite short and legible, and even though in the second version the variable query will never be used again — it exists solely in order to be the receiver of the collections message in the second line — it is worth creating it as a separate variable. For one thing, it makes this code far easier to step through in the debugger later on, when I want to pause after the albumsQuery call and see whether the expected sort of result is being returned.

 Incorrect number or pairing of nested square brackets can net you some curious messages from the compiler. For example, too many pairs of square brackets ([[query collections]]) or an unbalanced left square bracket ([[query collections]) is reported as "Expected identifier."

No Overloading

The data type returned by a method, together with the data types of each of its parameters in order, constitute that method's *signature*. It is illegal for two methods of the same type (class method or instance method) to exist in the same class with the same name but different signatures.

So, for example, you could not have two MyClass instance methods called myMethod, one of which returns void and one of which returns an NSString. Similarly, you could not have two MyClass instance methods called myMethod:, both returning void, one taking a CGFloat parameter and one taking an NSString parameter. An attempt to violate this rule will be stopped dead in its tracks by the compiler, which will announce a "duplicate declaration" error. The reason for this rule is that if two such conflicting methods were allowed to exist, there would be no way to determine from a method call to one of them which method was being called.

You might think that the issue could be decided by looking at the types involved in the call. If one myMethod: takes a CGFloat parameter and the other myMethod: takes an NSString parameter, you might think that when myMethod: is called, Objective-C could look at the actual argument and realize that the former method is meant if the argument is a CGFloat and the latter if the argument is an NSString. But Objective-C doesn't work that way. There are languages that permit this feature, called *overloading*, but Objective-C is not one of them.

Parameter Lists

It isn't uncommon for an Objective-C method to require an unknown number of parameters. A good example is the NSArray class method `arrayWithObjects:`, which looks from the name as if it takes one parameter but in fact takes any number of parameters, separated by comma. The parameters are the objects of which the NSArray is to consist. The trick here, however, which you must discover by reading the documentation, is that the list must end with nil. The nil is not one of the objects to go into the NSArray (nil isn't an object, so an NSArray can't contain nil); it's to show where the list ends.

So, here's a correct way to call the `arrayWithObjects:` method:

```
NSArray* pep = [NSArray arrayWithObjects:@"Manny", @"Moe", @"Jack", nil];
```

The declaration for `arrayWithObjects:` uses three dots to show that a comma-separated list is legal:

```
+ (id)arrayWithObjects:(id)firstObj, ... ;
```

Without the nil terminator, the program will not know where the list ends, and bad things will happen when the program runs, as it goes hunting off into the weeds of memory, incorporating all sorts of garbage into the NSArray that you never meant to have incorporated.

Forgetting the nil terminator is a common beginner error, but not as common as it used to be: by a bit of deep-C voodoo, the Objective-C compiler now notices if you've forgotten the nil, and warns you ("missing sentinel in method dispatch"). Even though it's just a warning, don't run that code! Another way to avoid forgetting the nil terminator is to avoid calling `arrayWithObjects:` altogether; this is now possible starting with LLVM compiler version 4.0 (Xcode 4.4 or later), which allows you to form a literal NSArray object directly, using `@[ ... ]` syntax, like this:

```
NSArray* pep = @[@"Manny", @"Moe", @"Jack"];
```

That's just a notation, a kind of syntactic sugar; behind the scenes, `arrayWithObjects:` is presumably still being called for you. But it's being called for you correctly, nil terminator and all, so this notation is much more bullet-proof than explicitly calling `arrayWithObjects:` yourself; plus it's a lot less typing. I'll be using this new Objective-C notation for literal arrays throughout this book.

Nevertheless, you will still encounter other Objective-C methods that do have a parameter that's a nil-terminated list of variable length. For example, there's the UIAppearance protocol class method `appearanceWhenContainedIn:` (Chapter 25), or UIAlertView's `initWithTitle:message:delegate:cancelButtonTitle:otherButtonTitles:` (Chapter 26). It's a pity that Apple hasn't somehow tweaked Objective-C or these methods to avoid the use of the nil terminator; for instance, they could have made the variable-length list parameter into an NSArray parameter instead. But until they do, knowing how to call such methods remains important.

The C language has explicit provision for argument lists of unspecified length, which Objective-C methods such as `arrayWithObjects:` are using behind the scenes. I'm not going to explain the C mechanism, because I don't expect you'll ever write a method or function that requires it; see K&R 7.3 if you need the gory details.

Unrecognized Selectors

Objective-C messaging is dynamic, meaning that the compiler takes no formal responsibility for whether a particular object is a legal recipient of a given message. That's because whether an object can deal with a message sent to it isn't decided until the program actually runs and the message actually arrives. Objective-C has various devices for dealing at runtime with a message that doesn't correspond directly to a method, and for all the compiler knows, one of them might come into play in this case. For example, at the time the program runs, the recipient of the message might be nil — and it's harmless to send *any* message to nil.

Thus, it is theoretically legal to direct a message at an object with no corresponding method. The only guardian against this possibility is the compiler. Before ARC, the compiler was not a very strong guardian in this respect. For example:

```
NSString* s = @"Hello, world!";
[s rockTheCasbah]; // without ARC, compiler warns
```

An NSString has no method `rockTheCasbah`. But the (non-ARC) compiler will not stop you from running a program containing this code; it's legal. The compiler will *warn* you, but it won't stop you. There are actually two possible warnings:

- If no `rockTheCasbah` method is defined *anywhere* in your code, the compiler will say: "Instance method '-rockTheCasbah' not found (return type defaults to 'id')." Without going into the details, what the compiler means is: "I know of no instance method `rockTheCasbah`, so I can't check its signature against the return type and arguments you're actually using, so I'll just make some loose assumptions and let it pass."

- If a `rockTheCasbah` method *is* defined somewhere in your code, the compiler will say: "'NSString' may not respond to 'rockTheCasbah'." This means: "There's a rock-

TheCasbah method, all right, but you seem to be sending the rockTheCasbah method to an instance of a class that doesn't have it as an instance method."

This is a good example of what I meant in Chapter 2 when I said that sending a message and calling a method were not the same thing. The compiler is saying that NSString has no rockTheCasbah instance method, but that it isn't going to stop you from sending an NSString a rockTheCasbah message. At runtime, the object that receives the rockTheCasbah message might be able to deal with it, for all the compiler knows.

With ARC, however, the compiler is much stricter. The example above won't compile at all under ARC! The compiler declares a fatal compilation error: "Receiver type 'NSString' for instance message does not declare a method with selector 'rockTheCasbah'." There is no NSString method rockTheCasbah, and by golly the compiler isn't going to let you send the rockTheCasbah message to an NSString, and that's final.

This is another of those delightful secondary benefits of using ARC. In order to do what it primarily does (manage memory), ARC must insist on more information about classes and their methods than the Objective-C standard calls for. Here, ARC is demanding that you *prove* that an NSString can respond to rockTheCasbah, or it won't let you run this code at all. (Nevertheless, if you really want to, you can slip past even ARC's stringent guardianship; I'll explain how in the next section.)

Let us assume for a moment that we are compiling without ARC, or that we have somehow tricked even ARC into letting us compile successfully. Warning or no warning, we are now ready to run a program that sends the rockTheCasbah message to an NSString, and damn the consequences. What might those consequences be? Quite simply, if you send a message to an object that can't deal with it, your program will crash at that instant. So, for example, our attempt to send an NSString the rockTheCasbah message will crash our program, with a message (in the console log) of this form: "-[NSCFConstantString rockTheCasbah]: unrecognized selector sent to instance 0x3048."

The important thing here is the phrase *unrecognized selector*. The term "selector" is roughly equivalent to "message," so this is a way of saying that a certain instance was sent a message it couldn't deal with. The console message also tries to tell us *what* instance this was. 0x3048 is the value of the instance pointer; it is the address in memory to which our NSString* variable s was actually pointing. (Never mind why the NSString is described as an NSCFConstantString; this has to do with NSString's implementation behind the scenes.)

(Strictly speaking, I should not say that a situation like this will "crash our program." What it will actually do is to generate an *exception*, an internal message as the program runs signifying that something bad has happened. It is possible for Objective-C code to "catch" an exception, in which case the program will not crash. The reason the program crashes, technically, is not that a message was sent to an object that couldn't handle it, but that the exception generated in response wasn't caught. That's why the crash log may also say, "Terminating app due to uncaught exception.")

Typecasting and the id Type

One way to silence the compiler when it warns in the way I've just described is by typecasting. A typecast, however, is not a viable way of fixing the problem unless it also tells the truth. It is perfectly possible to lie to the compiler by typecasting; this is not nice, and is not likely to yield nice consequences.

For example, suppose we've defined a class MyClass that does contain an instance method rockTheCasbah. As a result, it is fine with the compiler if you send the rockThe-Casbah message to a MyClass, although it is not fine to send the rockTheCasbah message to an NSString. So you can silence the compiler by claiming that an NSString instance *is* a MyClass instance:

```
NSString* s = @"Hello, world!";
[(MyClass*)s rockTheCasbah];
```

The typecast silences the compiler; there is no warning. Notice that the typecast is not a value conversion; it's merely a claim about what the type will turn out to be at runtime. You're saying that when the program runs, s will magically turn out to be a MyClass instance. Because MyClass has a rockTheCasbah instance method, that silences the compiler. Of course, you've lied to the compiler, so when the program runs it will crash anyway, in exactly the same way as before! You're still sending an NSString a message it can't deal with, so the very same exception about sending an unrecognized selector to an NSCFConstantString instance will result. So don't do that!

Sometimes, however, typecasting to silence the compiler is exactly what you do want to do. This situation quite often arises in connection with class inheritance. We haven't discussed class inheritance yet, but I'll give an example anyway. Let's take the built-in Cocoa class UINavigationController. Its topViewController method is declared to return a UIViewController instance. In real life, though, it is likely to return an instance of some class you've created. So in order to call a method of the class you've created on the instance returned by topViewController without upsetting the compiler, you have to reassure the compiler that this instance really will be an instance of the class you've created. That's what I'm doing in this line from one of my own apps:

```
[(RootViewController*)[navigationController topViewController] setAlbums: arr];
```

The expression (RootViewController*) is a typecast in which I'm assuring the compiler that at this moment in the program, the value returned by the topView-Controller method call will in fact be an instance of RootViewController, which is my own defined class. The typecast silences the compiler when I send this instance the set-Albums: message, because my RootViewController class has a setAlbums: instance method and the compiler knows this. And the program doesn't crash, because I'm not lying: this `topViewController` method call really *will* return a RootViewController instance.

Objective-C also provides a special type designed to silence the compiler's worries about object data types altogether. This is the `id` type. An `id` is a pointer, so you don't say `id*`. It is defined to mean "an object pointer," plain and simple, with no further specification. Thus, every instance reference is also an `id`.

Use of the `id` type causes the compiler to stop worrying about the relationship between object types and messages. The compiler can't know anything about what the object will really be, so it throws up its hands and doesn't warn about anything. Moreover, any object value can be assigned or typecast to an `id`, and a value typed as an `id` can be assigned where any object type is expected. The notion of assignment includes parameter passing. So you can pass a value typed as an `id` as an argument where a parameter of some particular object type is expected, and you can pass any object as an argument where a parameter of type `id` is expected. (I like to think of an `id` as analogous to both type AB blood and type O blood: it is both a universal recipient and a universal donor.) So, for example:

```
NSString* s = @"Hello, world!";
id unknown = s;
[unknown rockTheCasbah];
```

The second line is legal, because any object value can be assigned to an `id`. The third line doesn't generate any compiler warning, because any message can be sent to an `id`. (Of course the program will *still* crash when it actually runs and `unknown` turns out to be an NSString — which is incapable of receiving of the `rockTheCasbah` message!)

That trick works even under ARC, with one caveat. ARC is willing to let that code compile — but only if a matching `rockTheCasbah` method is defined *somewhere* in your code (even if it isn't an NSString method). If there's no such method, ARC will stop you with a different error: "No known instance method for selector 'rockTheCasbah.'" This is another way of saying the same thing the non-ARC compiler said earlier: "I know of no instance method `rockTheCasbah`, so I can't check its signature against the return type and arguments you're actually using." But instead of implicitly adding, "So I'll just make some loose assumptions and let it pass," ARC is stricter. After all, even without knowing what class `unknown` will turn out to be when the program runs, ARC can be pretty sure that that class won't have a `rockTheCasbah` method, because *no* known class has a `rockTheCasbah` method. So ARC, like a good guardian, continues to bar the way.

If, however, a matching `rockTheCasbah` method *is* defined somewhere in your code, even though it isn't an NSString method, ARC now takes its hands off the tiller entirely, and permits the program to compile and run without warning. You are now sending a message to an `id`, and an `id` can legally receive any message. If you crash at runtime, that's your problem; ARC can't save you from yourself.

If an `id`'s ability to receive any message reminds you of nil, it should. I have already said that nil is a form of zero; I can now specify what form of zero it is. It's zero cast as an `id`. Of course, it still makes a difference at runtime whether an `id` is nil or something else; sending a message to nil won't crash the program, but sending an unknown message to an actual object will.

Thus, `id` is a device for turning off the compiler's type checking altogether. Concerns about what type an object is are postponed until the program is actually running. All the compiler can do is intelligently analyze your code to see if you might be making a mistake that could matter at runtime. Using `id` turns off this part of the compiler's intelligence and leaves you to your own devices.

I do not recommend that you make extensive use of `id` to live in a world of pure dynamism. The compiler is your friend; you should let it use what intelligence it has to catch mistakes in your code. Thus, I almost never declare a variable or parameter as an `id`. I want my object types to be specific, so that the compiler can help check my code.

On the other hand, the Cocoa API does make frequent use of `id`, because it has to. For example, consider the NSArray class, which is the object-based version of an array. In pure C, you have to declare what type of thing lives in an array; for example, you could have "an array of int." In Objective-C, using an NSArray, you can't do that. Every NSArray is an array of `id`, meaning that each element of the array can be of any object type. You can put a specific type of object into an NSArray because any specific type of object can be assigned to an `id` (`id` is the universal recipient). You can get any specific type of object back out of an NSArray because an `id` can be assigned to any specific type of object (`id` is the universal donor).

So, for example, NSArray's `lastObject` method is defined as returning an `id`. So, given an NSArray `arr`, I can fetch its last element like this:

```
id unknown = [arr lastObject];
```

However, after that code, `unknown` can now be sent any message at all, and we are dispensing with the compiler's type checking. Therefore, if I happen to *know* what type of object an array element is, I always assign or cast it to that type. For example, let's say I happen to know that `arr` contains nothing but NSString instances (because I put them there in the first place). Then I will say:

```
NSString* s = [arr lastObject];
```

The compiler doesn't complain, because an `id` can be assigned to any specific type of object (`id` is the universal donor). Moreover, from here on in, the compiler regards s as an NSString, and uses its type checking abilities to make sure I don't send s any non-

NSString messages, which is just what I wanted. And I didn't lie to the compiler; at runtime, s really *is* an NSString, so everything is fine.

The compiler's type checking is called *static typing*, as opposed to the dynamic behavior that takes place when the program actually runs. What I'm saying here, then, is that I prefer to take advantage of static typing as much as possible.

The Cocoa API will sometimes return an id from a method call where you might not expect it. It's good to be conscious of this, because otherwise the compiler can mislead you into thinking you're doing something safe when you're not. For example, consider this code:

```
UIColor* c = [NSString string];
```

This is clearly a mistake — you're assigning an NSString to a UIColor variable, which is likely to lead to a crash later on — but the compiler is silent. Why doesn't the compiler warn here? It's because the NSString string class method is declared like this:

```
+ (id)string
```

The string method returns an NSString, but its return value is typed as an id. An id can be assigned where any object type is expected, so the compiler doesn't complain when it's assigned to a UIColor variable. This fact is a common source of programmer mistakes (especially if the programmer is me).

Earlier, I said that it is illegal for the same class to define methods of the same type (class method or instance method) with the same name but different signatures. But I did not say what happens when two *different* classes declare conflicting signatures for the same method name. This is another case in which it matters whether you're using static or dynamic typing. If you're using static typing — that is, the type of the object receiving the message is specified — there's no problem, because there's no doubt which method is being called (it's the one in that object's class). But if you're using dynamic typing, where the object receiving the message is an id, you might get a warning from the compiler; and if you're using ARC, you'll get a downright error: "Multiple methods named 'rockTheCasbah' found with mismatched result, parameter type or attributes." This is another reason why method names are so verbose: it's in order to make each method name unique, preventing two different classes from declaring conflicting signatures for the same method.

Accidentally defining your own method with the same name as an existing Cocoa method can cause mysterious problems. For example, in a recent online query, a programmer was confused because the compiler complained that his call to initWithObjects: lacked a nil terminator, even though his initWithObjects: didn't need a nil terminator. No, *his* initWithObjects: didn't, but *Cocoa's* did, and the compiler couldn't distinguish them because this message was being sent to an id. He should have picked a different name.

Messages as Data Type

Objective-C is so dynamic that it doesn't have to know until runtime what message to send to an object or what object to send it to. Certain important methods actually accept both pieces of information as parameters. For example, consider this method declaration from Cocoa's NSNotificationCenter class:

```
- (void)addObserver:(id)notificationObserver
        selector:(SEL)notificationSelector
            name:(NSString *)notificationName
          object:(id)notificationSender
```

We'll discuss later what this method does (when we talk about notifications in Chapter 11), but the important thing to understand here is that it constitutes an instruction to send a certain message to a certain object at some later, appropriate time. For example, our purpose in calling this method might be to arrange to have the message tickleMe-Elmo: sent at some later, appropriate time to the object myObject.

So let's consider how we might actually make this method call. The object to which the message will be sent is here called notificationObserver, and is typed as an id (making it possible to specify any type of object to send the message to). So, for the notification-Observer parameter, we're going to pass myObject. The message itself is the notificationSelector parameter, which has a special data type, SEL (for "selector," the technical term for a message name). The question now is how to express the message name tickleMeElmo:.

You can't just put tickleMeElmo: as a bare term; that doesn't work syntactically. You might think you could express it as an NSString, @"tickleMeElmo:", but surprisingly, that doesn't work either. It turns out that the correct way to do it is like this:

```
@selector(tickleMeElmo:)
```

The term @selector() is a directive to the compiler, telling it that what's in parentheses is a message name. Notice that what's in parentheses is not an NSString; it's the bare message name. And because it is the name, it must have no spaces and must include any colons that are part of the message name.

So the rule is extremely easy: when a SEL is expected, you'll usually pass a `@selector` expression. Failure to get this syntax right, however, is a common beginner error. Notice also that this syntax is an invitation to make a typing mistake, especially because there is no checking by the compiler. If `myObject` implements a `tickleMeElmo:` method and I accidentally type `@selector(tickleMeElmo)`, forgetting the colon or making any other mistake in specifying the message name, there is no compiler error; the problem won't be discovered until the program runs and something bad happens. (In this case, if the `tickleMeElmo` message without the colon is ever sent to `myObject`, the app will probably crash with an unrecognized selector exception.)

C Functions

Although your code will certainly call many Objective-C methods, it will also probably call quite a few C functions. For example, I mentioned in Chapter 1 that the usual way of initializing a CGPoint based on its x and y values is to call CGPointMake, which is declared like this:

```
CGPoint CGPointMake (
    CGFloat x,
    CGFloat y
);
```

Make certain that you can see at a glance that this *is* a C function, not an Objective-C method, and be sure you understand the difference in the calling syntax. To call an Objective-C method, you send a message to an object, in square brackets, with each argument following a colon in the method's name; to call a C function, you use the function's name followed by parentheses containing the arguments.

You might even have reason to write your own C functions as part of a class, instead of writing a method. A C function has lower overhead than a full-fledged method; so even though it lacks the object-oriented abilities of a method, it is sometimes useful to write one, as when some utility calculation must be called rapidly and frequently. Also, once in a while you might encounter a Cocoa method or function that requires you to supply a C function as a "callback."

An example is the NSArray method `sortedArrayUsingFunction:context:`. The first parameter is typed like this:

```
NSInteger (*)(id, id, void *)
```

That expression denotes, in the rather tricky C syntax used for these things, a pointer to a function that takes three parameters and returns an NSInteger. The three parameters of the function are an `id`, an `id`, and a pointer-to-void (which means any C pointer). The bare name of a function (see Chapter 1) can be used as a pointer to a C function. So to call `sortedArrayUsingFunction:context:` you'd need to write a C function that meets this description, and use its name as the first argument.

To illustrate, I'll write a "callback" function to sort an NSArray of NSStrings on the last character of each string. (This would be an odd thing to do, but it's only an example!) The NSInteger returned by the function has a special meaning: it indicates whether the first parameter is to be considered less than, equal to, or larger than the second. I'll obtain it by calling the NSString `compare:` method, which returns an NSInteger with that same meaning. Example 3-1 defines the function and shows how we'd call `sortedArrayUsingFunction:context:` with that function as our callback (assume that `arr` is an NSArray of strings).

Example 3-1. Using a pointer to a callback function

```
NSInteger sortByLastCharacter(id string1, id string2, void* context) {
    NSString* s1 = (NSString*) string1;
    NSString* s2 = (NSString*) string2;
    NSString* string1end = [s1 substringFromIndex:[s1 length] - 1];
    NSString* string2end = [s2 substringFromIndex:[s2 length] - 1];
    return [string1end compare:string2end];
}

NSArray* arr2 = [arr sortedArrayUsingFunction:sortByLastCharacter context:nil];
```

CFTypeRefs

Many Objective-C objects have lower-level C counterparts, along with C functions for manipulating them. For example, besides the Objective-C NSString, there is also something called a CFString; the "CF" stands for "Core Foundation," which is a lower-level C-based API. A CFString is an opaque C struct ("opaque" means that the elements constituting this struct are kept secret, and that you should operate on a CFString only by means of appropriate functions). As with an NSString or any other object, in your code you'll typically refer to a CFString by way of a C pointer; the pointer to a CFString has a type name, CFStringRef (a "reference to a CFString," evidently). You work with a CFString in pure C, by calling functions.

You might, on occasion, actually have to work with a Core Foundation type even when a corresponding object type exists. For example, you might find that NSString, for all its power, fails to implement a needed piece of functionality, which is in fact available for a CFString. Luckily, an NSString (a value typed as `NSString*`) and a CFString (a value typed as `CFStringRef`) are interchangeable: you can use one where the other is expected, though you will have to typecast in order to quiet the worries of the compiler. The documentation describes this interchangeability by saying that NSString and CFString are "toll-free bridged" to one another.

To illustrate, I'll use a CFString to convert an NSString representing an integer to that integer (this use of CFString is unnecessary, and is just by way of demonstrating the syntax; NSString has an `intValue` method):

```
NSString *answer = @"42";
CFStringRef stringRef = (CFStringRef)answer; // non-ARC
int ans = CFStringGetIntValue(stringRef);
```

The typecast prevents the compiler from complaining, and works because NSString is toll-free bridged to CFString — in effect, behind the scenes, an NSString *is* a CFString.

Under ARC, that code won't compile unless you supply a little more information. ARC, as we'll see in Chapter 12, is about memory management; but ARC manages only Objective-C objects, not their C counterparts. So although ARC manages the memory for an NSString, it leaves memory management for a CFStringRef up to you; and in order to compile that code, it needs you to show it that you understand the memory management status of this value as it crosses the toll-free bridge. You do so like this:

```
NSString *answer = @"42";
CFStringRef stringRef = (__bridge CFStringRef)answer;
int ans = CFStringGetIntValue(stringRef);
```

The extra qualifier __bridge means: "Don't worry, ARC, I know I'm crossing the toll-free bridge, and I assure you that this has no implications for memory management." On the other hand, there are situations where crossing the toll-free bridge *does* have implications for memory management, and you may rest assured that I'll discuss them in Chapter 12.

The pointer-to-struct C data types, whose name typically ends in "Ref", may be referred to collectively as CFTypeRef, which is actually just the generic pointer-to-void. Thus, crossing the toll-free bridge may usefully be thought of as a cast between an object pointer and a generic pointer — that is, in general terms, from id to void* or from void* to id. Even where there is no toll-free bridging between *specific* types (as there is with NSString and CFString), there is always bridging at the top of the hierarchy, so to speak, between NSObject (the base object class, as explained in Chapter 4) and CFType-Ref.

 It is sometimes necessary to assign a CFTypeRef to an id variable or parameter. For example, a CALayer's setContents: method (Chapter 16) expects an id parameter, but the actual value must be a CGImageRef. This is legal, because a pointer is just a pointer, but the compiler will complain unless you also typecast to an id, along with a __bridge qualifier if you're using ARC.

REVISH

✳ Blocks

A *block* is an extension to the C language, introduced in Mac OS X 10.6 and available in iOS 4.0 or later. It's a way of bundling up some code and handing off that entire bundle as an argument to a C function or Objective-C method. This is similar to what we did in Example 3-1, handing off a pointer to a function as an argument, but instead we're handing off the code *itself*. The latter has some major advantages over the former, which I'll discuss in a moment.

As an example, I'll rewrite Example 3-1 to use a block instead of a function pointer. Instead of calling `sortedArrayUsingFunction:context:`, I'll call `sortedArrayUsingComparator:`, which takes a block as its parameter. The block is typed like this:

```
NSComparisonResult (^)(id obj1, id obj2)
```

That's similar to the syntax for specifying the type of a pointer to a function, but a caret character is used instead of an asterisk character. So this means a block that takes two id parameters and returns an NSComparisonResult (which is merely an NSInteger, with just the same meaning as in Example 3-1). We can define the block and hand it off as the argument to `sortedArrayUsingComparator:` all in a single move, as in Example 3-2.

Example 3-2. Using a block instead of a callback function

```
NSArray* arr2 = [arr sortedArrayUsingComparator: ^(id obj1, id obj2) {
    NSString* s1 = (NSString*) obj1;
    NSString* s2 = (NSString*) obj2;
    NSString* string1end = [s1 substringFromIndex:[s1 length] - 1];
    NSString* string2end = [s2 substringFromIndex:[s2 length] - 1];
    return [string1end compare:string2end];
}];
```

The syntax of the inline block definition is:

```
^❶(id obj1, id obj2)❷ {❸
```

❶   First, the caret character.

❷   Then, parentheses containing the parameters.

❸   Finally, curly braces containing the block's content.

Thanks to the block, as you can see, we've combined the definition of the callback function with its use. You might object that this means the callback isn't reusable; if we had *two* calls to `sortedArrayUsingComparator:` using the same callback, we'd have to write out the callback in full twice. To avoid such repetition, or simply for clarity, a block can be assigned to a variable:

```
NSComparisonResult (^sortByLastCharacter)(id, id) = ^(id obj1, id obj2) {
    NSString* s1 = (NSString*) obj1;
    NSString* s2 = (NSString*) obj2;
    NSString* string1end = [s1 substringFromIndex:[s1 length] - 1];
    NSString* string2end = [s2 substringFromIndex:[s2 length] - 1];
    return [string1end compare:string2end];
};
NSArray* arr2 = [arr sortedArrayUsingComparator: sortByLastCharacter];
NSArray* arr4 = [arr3 sortedArrayUsingComparator: sortByLastCharacter];
```

The return type in an inline block definition is usually omitted. If included, it *follows* the caret character, *not* in parentheses. If omitted, you may have to use typecasting in the return line to make the returned type match the expected type. For a complete technical syntax specification for blocks, see *http://clang.llvm.org/docs/BlockLanguageSpec.html*.

The power of blocks really starts to emerge when they are used instead of a selector name. In an example earlier in this chapter, we talked about how you could pass @selector(tickleMeElmo:) as the second argument to addObserver:selector:name:object: as a way of saying, "When the time comes, please call my tickleMeElmo: method." We also talked about how error-prone this syntax was: make a typing error, and your tickleMeElmo: method mysteriously won't be called. Moreover, such code is hard to maintain; there's the tickleMeElmo: method sitting there, completely separate from the code that calls addObserver:selector:name:object:, yet existing only to specify what should happen at the later time when our message arrives. It might well be clearer and more compact to call addObserverForName:object:queue:usingBlock: and specify there and then as a block what should happen at message time, with no separate method callback. (I'll talk about this again, along with an example, in Chapter 11.)

Perhaps the most remarkable feature of blocks is this: variables in scope at the point where a block is defined keep their value within the block at that moment, even though the block may be executed at some later moment. (Technically, we say that a block is a *closure*.) It is this aspect of blocks that makes them useful for specifying functionality to be executed at some later time, or even, as we'll see in Chapter 38, in some other thread.

Here's an example that will appear in Chapter 17. It will make perfect sense to you in its proper context, so I won't explain it fully now; but the point is that *outside* any blocks we have a UIView object v in scope, along with a CGPoint p and another CGPoint pOrig, and we can use the two CGPoint values to mutate v *inside* two blocks (called anim and after), even though these blocks won't be executed until some indeterminate moment in the future, at the start and end of an animation:

```
CGPoint p = v.center;
CGPoint pOrig = p;
p.x += 100;
void (^anim) (void) = ^{
    v.center = p;
};
void (^after) (BOOL) = ^(BOOL f) {
    v.center = pOrig;
```

```
    };
    NSUInteger opts = UIViewAnimationOptionAutoreverse;
    [UIView animateWithDuration:1 delay:0 options:opts
                        animations:anim completion:after];
```

If a variable outside a block is in scope within the block, and if that variable is an object reference, messages can be sent to it and the object may be mutated, as we did with the UIView object v in that example. But if we try, inside a block, to assign *directly* to a variable outside the block, we can't do it; the variable is protected, and the compiler will stop us ("variable is not assignable"):

```
    CGPoint p;
    void (^aBlock) (void) = ^{
        p = CGPointMake(1,2); // error
    };
```

On rare occasions, you may need to turn off this protection; you can do so by declaring the variable using the __block qualifier. Here's an example that will appear in Chapter 35. We cycle through an array until we find the value we want; when we find it, we set a variable (dir) to that value. That variable is declared outside the block, because we intend to use its value after executing the block; therefore we qualify the variable's declaration with __block, so that we can assign to it from inside the block:

```
    CGFloat h = newHeading.magneticHeading;
    __block NSString* dir = @"N";
    NSArray* cards = @[@"N", @"NE", @"E", @"SE",
                       @"S", @"SW", @"W", @"NW"];
    [cards enumerateObjectsUsingBlock:^(id obj, NSUInteger idx, BOOL *stop) {
        if (h < 45.0/2.0 + 45*idx) {
            dir = obj;
            *stop = YES;
        }
    }];
    // now we can use dir
```

(Note also the assignment to a dereferenced pointer-to-BOOL. When the method to which we are submitting a block is going to call the block repeatedly as the equivalent of a for loop, we can't abort the loop with a break statement, because this isn't a *real* for loop. So the method will commonly specify that our block should take a pointer-to-BOOL parameter; the idea is that we can set this BOOL by indirection to YES, and the method will notice this as it prepares to call the block for the next iteration, and will stop instead. This is one of the few common situations in iOS programming where it is necessary to dereference a pointer.)

Another use of the __block qualifier is to allow a block to capture the value of a variable that is set by the very same method call that takes the block as an argument. Here's an example that will appear in Chapter 38:

```
__block UIBackgroundTaskIdentifier bti =
    [[UIApplication sharedApplication]
        beginBackgroundTaskWithExpirationHandler: ^{
            [[UIApplication sharedApplication] endBackgroundTask:bti];
    }];
```

The method `beginBackgroundTaskWithExpirationHandler:` takes a block and returns a `UIBackgroundTaskIdentifier`, which is really just an integer. We want to use that integer inside the block, which will actually be executed at some later time (if ever). If we don't declare the integer variable with the `__block` qualifier, the block will capture the variable's value *at the time the block is defined*, which is *before* the `beginBackground-TaskWithExpirationHandler:` method call is actually executed. After the method call is executed, the variable is set to its true value, the value we want to use inside the block; because we declared the variable with `__block`, the block has access to that true value.

Note that this trick works only because the block is being stored (by the receiver of the `beginBackgroundTaskWithExpirationHandler:` message) for later execution. If the block were to be executed right now, before returning from the `beginBackgroundTask-WithExpirationHandler:` call, the result of that call would not yet have been set.

At the same time that blocks were introduced into Objective-C, Apple introduced a system library of C functions called Grand Central Dispatch (GCD) that makes heavy use of them. GCD's most important use is for threading (Chapter 38), but it also comes in handy for expressing neatly and compactly certain notions about when code should be executed. For example, GCD can help us delay execution of our code (*delayed performance*). The following code (from Chapter 14) means, "change the bounds of `v1`, but not right this moment — wait two seconds and then do it":

```
dispatch_time_t popTime = dispatch_time(DISPATCH_TIME_NOW, 2 * NSEC_PER_SEC);
dispatch_after(popTime, dispatch_get_main_queue(), ^(void){
    CGRect f = v1.bounds;
    f.size.width += 40;
    f.size.height -= 50;
    v1.bounds = f;
});
```

This next example rewrites the code from the end of Chapter 1, where a class method vends a singleton object. GCD promises that the block creating the singleton object to begin with will execute only once in the entire life of our program, thus guaranteeing that the singleton *is* a singleton:

```
+ (CardPainter*) sharedPainter {
    static CardPainter* sp = nil;
    static dispatch_once_t onceToken;
    dispatch_once(&onceToken, ^{
        sp = [CardPainter new];
    });
    return sp;
}
```

Why is calling `dispatch_once` better, as a way of making sure we generate the singleton instance only once, than testing sp against nil, as in Chapter 1? Aside from being thread-safe, it isn't; it's just an example of GCD's elegant use of a block.

CHAPTER 4

Objective-C Classes

This chapter describes some linguistic and structural features of Objective-C having to do with classes; in the next chapter, we'll do the same for instances.

Class and Superclass

In Objective-C, as in many other object-oriented languages, a mechanism is provided for specifying a relationship between two classes: they can be *subclass* and *superclass* of one another. For example, we might have a class Quadruped and a class Dog and make Quadruped the superclass of Dog. A class may have many subclasses, but a class can have only one immediate superclass. I say "immediate" because that superclass might itself have a superclass, and so on in a rising chain, until we get to the ultimate superclass, called the *base class*, or *root class*.

Because a class can have many subclasses but only one superclass, there is a hierarchical tree of subclasses, each branching from its superclass, and so on, with a single class, the base class, at the top. Indeed, Cocoa itself consists of just such a tree (a huge tree!) of hierarchically arranged classes, even before you write a single line of code or create any classes of your own. We can imagine diagramming this tree as an outline, with a single ultimate superclass at the top, then all of its immediate subclasses in the next level below that, then each of *their* immediate subclasses in the next level below that, and so on. And in fact Xcode will show you this outline: choose View → Navigators → Show Symbol Navigator and click Hierarchical, with the first and third icons in the filter bar darkened (Figure 4-1).

The reason for the class–subclass relationship is to allow related classes to share functionality. Suppose, for example, we have a Dog class and a Cat class, and we are considering defining a walk method for both of them. We might reason that both a dog and a cat walk in pretty much the same way, by virtue of both being quadrupeds. So it might make sense to define walk as a method of the Quadruped class, and make both Dog and

Figure 4-1. Browsing the built-in class hierarchy in Xcode

Cat subclasses of Quadruped. The result is that both Dog and Cat can be sent the walk message, even if neither of them has a walk method, because each of them has a super-class that *does* have a walk method. We say that a subclass *inherits* the methods of its superclass.

The purpose of subclassing is not merely so that a class can inherit another class's meth-ods; it's so that it can define methods of its own. Typically, a subclass consists of the methods inherited from its superclass *and then some*. If Dog has no methods of its own, it's hard to see why it should exist separately from Quadruped. But if a Dog knows how to do something that not every Quadruped knows how to do — let's say, bark — then it makes sense as a separate class. If we define bark in the Dog class, and walk in the Quadruped class, and make Dog a subclass of Quadruped, then Dog inherits the ability to walk from the Quadruped class and also knows how to bark.

It is also permitted for a subclass to redefine a method inherited from its superclass. For example, perhaps some dogs bark differently from other dogs. We might have a class NoisyDog, for instance, that is a subclass of Dog. Dog defines bark, but NoisyDog also defines bark, and defines it differently from how Dog defines it. This is called *overrid-ing*. The very natural rule is that if a subclass overrides a method inherited from its superclass, then when the corresponding message is sent to an instance of that subclass, it is the subclass's version of that method that is called.

Interface and Implementation

As you already know from Chapter 2, all your code is going to go into some class or other. So the first thing we must do is specify what is meant by putting code "into a class" in Objective-C. How does Objective-C say, linguistically and structurally, "This is the code for such-and-such a class"?

To write the code for a class, you must provide two chunks or sections of code, called the *interface* and the *implementation*. Here's the complete minimum code required to define a class called MyClass. This class is so minimal that it doesn't even have any methods of its own:

```
@interface MyClass
@end
@implementation MyClass
@end
```

The @interface and @implementation compiler directives show the compiler where the interface and implementation sections begin for the class that's being defined, My-Class; the corresponding @end lines show where each of those sections end.

In real life, the implementation section is where any methods for MyClass would be defined. So here's a class that's actually defined to do something:

```
@interface MyClass
@end
@implementation MyClass
- (NSString*) sayGoodnightGracie {
    return @"Good night, Gracie!";
}
@end
```

Observe how a method is defined. The first line is just like a method declaration, stating the type of method (class or instance), the type of value returned, and the name of the method along with the types of any parameters and local names for those parameters (see Chapter 3). That's followed by curly braces containing the code to be executed when the method is called, just as with a C function (see Chapter 1).

Our minimal class is still pretty much useless, because it can't be instantiated. In Cocoa, knowledge of how to be instantiated, plus how to do a number of other things that any class should know how to do, resides in the base class, which is the NSObject class. Therefore, all Cocoa classes must be based ultimately on the NSObject class, by declaring as the superclass for your class either NSObject or some other class that inherits from NSObject (as just about any other Cocoa class does). The syntax for this declaration is a colon followed by the superclass name in the @interface line, like this:

```
@interface MyClass : NSObject
@end
@implementation MyClass
- (NSString*) sayGoodnightGracie {
    return @"Good night, Gracie!";
}
@end
```

 NSObject is not the only Cocoa base class. It used to be, but there is now another, NSProxy. NSProxy is used only in very special circumstances and is not discussed in this book. If you have no reason for your class to inherit from any other class, make it inherit from NSObject.

In its fullest form, the interface section might contain some more material. In particular, if we want to declare our methods, so that other classes can learn about them and call them, those method declarations go into the interface section. A method declaration in code matches the name and signature for the method definition and ends with a semicolon (required):

```
@interface MyClass : NSObject
- (NSString*) sayGoodnightGracie;
@end
@implementation MyClass
- (NSString*) sayGoodnightGracie {
    return @"Good night, Gracie!";
}
@end
```

(Actually, it's legal for a method definition to have a semicolon as well, before the curly braces. But that notation is rare, and I never use it in this book.)

There are also instance variables to be considered. If our class is to have any instance variables (other than those inherited from its superclass), they must be declared. In actual fact, in modern Objective-C, you will probably declare most of your instance variables implicitly, using a technique that I'll explain in Chapter 5 and Chapter 12. But you might still occasionally declare an instance variable explicitly; and in any case, you certainly need to know how to do so.

Before iOS 5.0, explicit declaration of instance variables had to take place in curly braces at the start of the interface section:

```
@interface MyClass : NSObject {
    // instance variable declarations go here
}
- (NSString*) sayGoodnightGracie;
@end
@implementation MyClass
```

```
- (NSString*) sayGoodnightGracie {
    return @"Good night, Gracie!";
}
@end
```

However, starting with LLVM compiler version 3.0 (Xcode 4.2 and later), it is permitted to put instance variable declarations in curly braces at the start of the implementation section instead. This is a more logical place for variable declarations to go, because, as I'll explain in the next section, the interface section is usually visible to other classes, but there is no reason why instance variables need to be visible to other classes, as they are usually private. Therefore, I prefer the new style, and will use it consistently throughout this book:

```
@interface MyClass : NSObject
- (NSString*) sayGoodnightGracie;
@end
@implementation MyClass {
    // instance variable declarations go here          THE "NEW" STYLE MAKES
}                                                        MORE SENSE.
- (NSString*) sayGoodnightGracie {
    return @"Good night, Gracie!";
}
@end
```

I'll go into more detail about instance variables in Chapter 5.

Header File and Implementation File

It's perfectly possible for the interface and implementation of a class to appear in the same file, or for multiple classes to be defined in a single file, but that isn't the usual convention. The usual convention is one class, two files: one file containing the interface section, the other file containing the implementation section. For example, let's suppose you are defining a class MyClass. Then you have two files, *MyClass.h* and *MyClass.m*. (The file naming is not magical or necessary; it's just part of the convention. The file extensions are pretty much necessary, though, because the build process and Xcode itself rely on them.) The interface section goes into *MyClass.h*, which is called the *header file*. The implementation section goes into *MyClass.m*, which is called the *implementation file*. The separation into two files is not inconvenient, because Xcode, expecting you to follow this convention, makes it easy to jump from editing a .h file to the corresponding .m file and *vice versa* (Navigate → Jump to Next Counterpart). Finally, the implementation file imports the header file (see Chapter 1 on the #import directive); this effectively unites the full class definition, making the definition legal even though it is split between two files.

With this arrangement in place, further imports become easy to configure. The header file imports the basic header file for the entire Cocoa framework; in the case of an iOS program, that's *UIKit.h* (again, see Chapter 1). There is no need for the implementation file to import *UIKit.h*, because the header file imports it, and the implementation file imports the header file. If a class needs to know about another class that isn't already imported in this way, its implementation file imports that class's header file. Example 4-1 summarizes this conventional schema.

Example 4-1. Conventional schema for defining a class

```
// MyClass.h:

#import <UIKit/UIKit.h>

@interface MyClass : NSObject
- (NSString*) sayGoodnightGracie;
@end

// MyClass.m:

#import "MyClass.h"
#import "OtherClass.h"

@implementation MyClass {
    // instance variable declarations go here
}
- (NSString*) sayGoodnightGracie {
    return @"Good night, Gracie!";
}
@end
```

The result of this arrangement is that everything has the right visibility. No file ever imports an implementation file; that way, what's inside a class's implementation file is private to that class. If something about a class needs to be public, such as a method that you want other classes to be able to call, it is declared in the header file, and other classes import that header file in their implementation files (as I do with *OtherClass.h* in Example 4-1); this keeps the chain of imports clear and simple.

A header file is also an appropriate place to define constants. In Chapter 1, for example, I talked about the problem of mistyping the name of a notification or dictionary key, which is a literal NSString, and how you could solve this problem by defining a name for such a string:

```
#define MYKEY @"mykey"
```

The question then arises of where to put that definition. If only one class needs to know about it, the definition can go near the start of its implementation file (it doesn't need to be inside the implementation section). But if multiple classes need to know about this name, then a header file is an appropriate location; every implementation file that imports this header file will acquire the definition, and you can use the name MYKEY in that implementation file.

The ultimate header file in an Xcode project is the *.pch* file. The suffix *.pch* stands for "precompiled header", and your project has exactly one such file, which is implicitly imported by all *.h* files. It isn't common to edit the *.pch* file, but sometimes it's the most convenient place to define a constant, or even to import a class interface section, that needs to be visible to pretty much every class in your program. I'll talk more about the *.pch* file in Chapter 6.

A slight problem arises when a header file needs to mention one of your other classes. Suppose, for example, that MyClass has a public method that takes or returns an instance of MyOtherClass. So *MyClass.h* needs to speak of `MyOtherClass*`. But *MyClass.h* does not import *MyOtherClass.h*, so *MyClass.h* doesn't know about MyOtherClass, and the compiler will complain. To silence the compiler without violating the arrangement of imports (by importing *MyOtherClass.h* in the header file *MyClass.h*), use the `@class` directive. The word `@class` is followed by a comma-separated list of class names, ending with a semicolon. So *MyClass.h* might start out like this:

```
#import <UIKit/UIKit.h>
@class MyOtherClass;
```

Then the interface section would follow, as before. The `@class` directive simply tells the compiler, "Don't worry, MyOtherClass really is the name of a class." That's all the compiler needs to know in order to permit the mention of the type `MyOtherClass*` in the header file.

If, on the other hand, MyClass is to be a subclass of some other class, then MyClass's header file must import that superclass's header file (or some other header file that imports that superclass's header file); otherwise, it would be unable to speak of that superclass. For instance, in Example 4-1, *MyClass.h* imports *UIKit.h*; thus it knows about NSObject, so that MyClass can declare NSObject as its superclass.

Cocoa's Own Header Files

The Cocoa classes themselves also follow the convention described in Example 4-1: each class is separated into a header file (containing the interface) and an implementation file. However, the Cocoa class implementation files are not visible to you. This is one of the major limitations of Cocoa; unlike many programming frameworks, you can't see the source code for Cocoa — it's secret. To figure out how Cocoa works, you have to rely purely on the documentation (and experimentation). You can, however, see the Cocoa header files, and indeed you are expected to look at them, as they can be a useful form of documentation (see Chapter 8).

The Global Namespace

When defining classes, choose your class names wisely to prevent name collisions. Objective-C has no namespaces; there's a single vast namespace containing all names. You don't want your own class name (or, for that matter, any other top-level constant name) to match a name defined in Cocoa. Instead of namespaces, there's a convention: each Cocoa framework prefixes its names with a particular pair of capital letters (NSString and NSArray, CGFloat and CGRect, and so on). Apple suggests that you use a prefix of your own as well; in fact, when you create a new project in Xcode, you're offered an opportunity to specify a prefix, which will appear before the automatically created class names. Don't use any of Apple's prefixes. Nothing limits your prefix to two letters, or requires that both letters be uppercase. In fact, because all of Apple's own prefixes *are* two uppercase letters, "My" as a prefix is safe.

Class Methods

Class methods are useful in general for two main purposes:

Factory methods

A factory method is a method that dispenses an instance of that class. For example, the UIFont class has a class method `fontWithName:size:`. You supply a name and a size, and the UIFont class hands you back a UIFont instance corresponding to a font with that name and size. A class method that vends a singleton instance, such as appears at the end of Chapter 1, is also a factory method.

Global utility methods

Classes are global (visible from all code, Chapter 13), so a class is a good place to put a utility method that anyone might need to call and that doesn't require the overhead of an instance. For example, the UIFont class has a class method `family-Names`. It returns an array of strings (that is, an NSArray of NSString instances) consisting of the names of the font families installed on this device. Because this method has to do with fonts, the UIFont class is as good a place as any to put it.

Most methods that you write will be instance methods, but now and then you might write a class method. When you do, your purpose will probably be similar to those examples.

The Secret Life of Classes

A class method may be called by sending a message directly to the name of a class. For example, the `familyNames` class method of UIFont that I mentioned a moment ago might be called like this:

```
NSArray* fams = [UIFont familyNames];
```

Clearly, this is possible because a class is an object (Chapter 2), and the name of the class here represents that object.

You don't have to do anything to create a class object. One class object for every class your program defines is created for you automatically as the program starts up. (This includes the classes your program imports, so there's a MyClass class object because you defined MyClass, and there's an NSString class object because you imported *UIKit.h* and the whole Cocoa framework.) It is to this class object that you're referring when you send a message to the name of the class.

Your ability to send a message directly to the bare name of a class is due to a kind of syntactic shorthand. You can use the bare class name only in two ways (and we already know about both of them):

To send a message to
> In the expression [UIFont familyNames], the bare name UIFont is sent the family-Names message.

To specify an instance type
> In the expression NSString*, the bare name NSString is followed by an asterisk to signify a pointer to an instance of this class.

Otherwise, to speak of a class object, you need to obtain that object formally. One way to do this is to send the `class` message to a class or instance. For example, [MyClass class] returns the actual class object. Some built-in Cocoa methods expect a class object parameter, whose type is described as Class. To supply this as an argument, you'd need to obtain a class object formally. Take, for example, introspection on an object to inquire what its class is. The `isKindOfClass:` instance method is declared like this:

```
- (BOOL)isKindOfClass:(Class)aClass
```

So that means you could call it like this:

```
if ([someObject isKindOfClass: [MyClass class]]) // ...
```

A class object is not an instance, but it is definitely a full-fledged object. Therefore, a class object can be used wherever an object can be used. For example, it can be assigned to a variable of type id:

```
id classObject = [MyClass class];
```

You could then call a class method by sending a message to that object, because it is the class object:

```
id classObject = [MyClass class];
[classObject someClassMethod];
```

All class objects are also members of the Class class, so you could say this:

```
Class classObject = [MyClass class];
[classObject someClassMethod];
```

CHAPTER 5

Objective-C Instances

Instances are the heart of the action in an Objective-C program. Most of the methods you'll define when creating your own classes will be instance methods; most of the messages you'll send in your code will call instance methods. This chapter describes how instances come into existence and how they work.

How Instances Are Created

Your class objects are created for you automatically as your program starts up, but instances must be created deliberately as the program runs. The entire question of where instances come from is thus crucial. Ultimately, every instance comes into existence in just one way: someone deliberately asks a class to instantiate itself. But there are three different ways in which this can occur: ready-made instances, instantiation from scratch, and nib-based instantiation.

Ready-Made Instances

One way to create an instance is indirectly, by calling code that does the instantiation for you. You can think of an instance obtained in this indirect manner as a "ready-made instance." (That's my made-up phrase, not an official technical term.) Consider this simple code:

✓ BUG - NEEDS TO BE INSTANTIATED FIRST, e.g.,

```
NSString* s2 = [s uppercaseString];
```
NSString s = @"The quick fox";

The documentation for the NSString instance method uppercaseString says that it returns "a string with each character from the receiver changed to its corresponding uppercase value." In other words, you send the uppercaseString message to an NSString, and you get back a *different*, newly created NSString. After that line of code, s2 points to an NSString instance that didn't exist beforehand.

The NSString produced by the `uppercaseString` method is a ready-made NSString instance. Your code didn't say anything about instantiation; it just sent the `uppercaseString` message. But clearly *someone* said something about instantiation, because instantiation took place; this is a newly minted NSString instance. That someone is presumably some code inside the NSString class. But we don't have to worry about the details. We are guaranteed of receiving a complete brand spanking new ready-to-roll NSString, and that's all we care about.

Similarly, any class factory method instantiates the class and dispenses the resulting instance as a ready-made instance. So, for example, the NSString class method `stringWithContentsOfFile:encoding:error:` reads a file and produces an NSString representing its contents. All the work of instantiation has been done for you. You just accept the resulting string and away you go.

 A Cocoa class factory method is likely to have its return value typed as `id`. As I mentioned in Chapter 3, this can lead to trouble if you mistakenly assign the resulting instance where a different class of object is expected; the compiler doesn't complain (because `id` is the universal donor) but you can mysteriously crash later when the wrong message is sent to the instance.

Not every method that returns an instance returns a new instance, of course. For example, this is how you ask an array (an NSArray) for its last element:

```
id last = [myArray lastObject];
```

The NSArray `myArray` didn't *create* the object that it hands you. That object already existed; `myArray` was merely containing it, as it were — it was holding the object, pointing to it. Now it's sharing that object with you, that's all.

Similarly, many classes dispense one particular object. For example, your app has exactly one instance of the UIApplication class (we call this the *singleton* UIApplication instance); to access it, you send the `sharedApplication` class method to the UIApplication class:

```
UIApplication* theApp = [UIApplication sharedApplication];
```

This singleton instance existed before you asked for it; indeed, it existed before any code of yours could possibly run. You don't care how it was brought into being; all you care is that you can get hold of it when you want it. I'll talk more about globally available singleton objects of this kind in Chapter 13.

Instantiation from Scratch

The alternative to requesting a ready-made instance is to tell a class, yourself, directly, to instantiate itself. There is basically one way to do this: you send a class the alloc message. The alloc class method is implemented by the NSObject class, the root class from which all other classes inherit. It causes memory to be set aside for the instance so that an instance pointer can point to it. (Management of that memory is a separate issue, discussed in Chapter 12.)

You must never, never, *never* call alloc by itself. You must *immediately* call another method, an instance method that *initializes* the newly created instance, placing it into a known valid state so that it can be sent other messages. Such a method is called an *initializer*. Moreover, an initializer returns an instance — usually the same instance, initialized. Therefore you can, and always should, call alloc and the initializer in the same line of code. The minimal initializer is init. So the basic pattern, known informally as "alloc-init," looks like Example 5-1.

Example 5-1. The basic pattern for instantiation from scratch

```
SomeClass* aVariable = [[SomeClass alloc] init];
```

You cannot instantiate from scratch if you do not also know how to initialize, so we turn immediately to a discussion of initialization.

Initialization

Every class defines or inherits at least one initializer. This is an instance method; the instance has just been created, by calling alloc on the class, and it is to this newly minted instance that the initializer message must be sent. An initialization message must be sent to an instance immediately after that instance is created by means of the alloc message, and it must not be sent to an instance at any other time.

The basic initialization pattern, as shown in Example 5-1, is to nest the alloc call in the initialization call, assigning the result of the *initialization* (not the alloc!) to a variable. One reason for this is that if something goes wrong and the instance can't be created or initialized, the initializer will return nil; therefore it's important to capture the result of the initializer and treat that, not the result of alloc, as the pointer to the instance.

To help you identify initializers, all initializers are named in a conventional manner. The convention is that all initializers, and only initializers, begin with the word init. The ultimate bare-bones initializer is called simply init, and takes no parameters. Other initializers do take parameters, and usually begin with the phrase initWith followed by descriptions of their parameters. For example, the NSArray class documentation lists these methods:

```
- initWithArray:
- initWithArray:copyItems:
- initWithContentsOfFile:
- initWithContentsOfURL:
- initWithObjects:
- initWithObjects:count:
```

Let's try a real example. A particularly easy and generally useful initializer for NSArray is `initWithObjects:`. It takes a list of objects; the list must be terminated by nil. In Chapter 3, we illustrated this by creating an NSArray from three strings, by means of a class factory method that returned a ready-made instance:

```
NSArray* pep =
    [NSArray arrayWithObjects:@"Manny", @"Moe", @"Jack", nil];
```

Now we'll do what amounts to exactly the same thing, except that we'll create the instance ourselves, from scratch:

```
NSArray* pep =
    [[NSArray alloc] initWithObjects:@"Manny", @"Moe", @"Jack", nil];
```

In that particular case, there exist both a factory method and an initializer that work from the same set of data. Ultimately, it makes no difference which you use; given the same arguments, both approaches result in NSArray instances that are indistinguishable from one another. It will turn out in the discussion of memory management (Chapter 12) that there might be a reason to choose instantiation from scratch over ready-made instances (though not, perhaps, under ARC).

In modern Objective-C, as I mentioned in Chapter 3, you are unlikely to call `arrayWithObjects:`, because there is now a convenient literal array syntax that calls it for you. For the same reason, you are unlikely to call `initWithObjects:`. So I'll give another example. Suppose that, one way or another, you now have an array `pep` containing the three strings @"Manny", @"Moe", and @"Jack", and that you want to instantiate a second array based on it and containing those same three strings. It is not sufficient to assign `pep` to another NSArray variable:

```
NSArray* pep2 = pep; // no, that isn't another array
```

Object references are pointers, and pointer assignment merely points two references at the same thing (Chapter 3). So `pep2` in that code isn't a second array; it's the same array, which isn't what we said we wanted. To make a new array instance based on the first, we can call the class method `arrayWithArray:`, like this:

```
NSArray* pep2 = [NSArray arrayWithArray: pep];
```

Now `pep2` is a newly minted instance, separate from `pep`. It's a ready-made instance, returned from a class factory method. To create the instance ourselves, from scratch, we call the corresponding initializer:

```
NSArray* pep2 = [[NSArray alloc] initWithArray: pep];
```

In looking through the documentation for an initializer, don't forget to look upward through the class hierarchy. For example, the class documentation for UIWebView lists no initializers, but UIWebView inherits from UIView, and in UIView's class documentation you'll discover initWithFrame:. Moreover, the init method is defined as an instance method of the NSObject class, so every class inherits it and every newly minted instance can be sent the init message. Thus it is a given that if a class defines no initializers of its own, you can initialize an instance of it with init. For example, the UIResponder class documentation lists no initializers at all (and no factory methods). So to create a UIResponder instance from scratch, you'd call alloc and init.

> In just the single case where init is the initializer you want to call, you can collapse the successive calls to alloc and init into a call to new. In other words, [MyClass new] is a synonym for [[MyClass alloc] init]. I used to avoid new as confusing, chiefly because it conceals the initialization that guarantees this is a proper instance (and, before ARC, the need for memory management). But recently I've reversed course; I now use new quite a bit, and I'll use it freely in this book.

The designated initializer

If a class does define initializers, one of them may be described in the documentation as the *designated initializer*. (There's nothing about a method's name that tells you it's the designated initializer; you must peruse the documentation to find out.) For example, in the UIView class documentation, the initWithFrame: method is described as the designated initializer. A class that does not define a designated initializer inherits its designated initializer; the ultimate designated initializer, inherited by all classes without any other designated initializer anywhere in their superclass chain, is init.

The designated initializer is the initializer on which any other initializers depend, in this class or any subclasses: ultimately, they *must* call it. The designated initializer might have the most parameters, allowing the most instance variables to be set explicitly, with the other initializers supplying default values for some instance variables, for convenience. Or it might just be the most basic form of initialization. But in any case, it is a bottleneck through which all other initializers pass. Here are some examples:

- The NSDate class documentation says that initWithTimeIntervalSinceReferenceDate: is the designated initializer, and that initWithTimeIntervalSinceNow: calls it.

- The UIView class documentation says that initWithFrame: is the designated initializer. UIView contains no other initializers, but some of its subclasses do. UIWebView, a UIView subclass, has no initializer, so initWithFrame: is its inherited designated initializer. UIImageView, a UIView subclass, has initializers such as init-

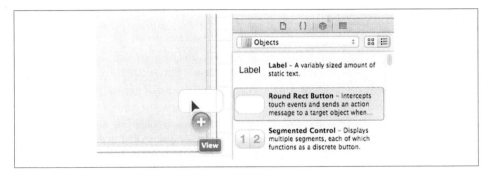

Figure 5-1. Dragging a button into a view

WithImage:, but none of them is a designated initializer; so initWithFrame: is its inherited designated initializer as well, and initWithImage: must call initWith-Frame:.

Moreover, a class that implements a designated initializer will override the designated initializer inherited from its superclass. The idea is typically that even the inherited designated initializer, if called, will be overridden so as to call this class's designated initializer. For example, UIView overrides the inherited init to call its own designated initializer, initWithFrame:, with a value of (CGRect){{0, 0}, {0, 0}}.

Nib-Based Instantiation

The third means of instantiation is through a nib file (or storyboard file). A nib file is where Xcode lets you "draw" parts of the user interface. Most Xcode projects will include at least one nib file, which will be built into the app bundle, and will then be loaded as the app runs. A nib file consists, in a sense, of the names of classes along with instructions for instantiating and initializing them. When the app runs and a nib file is loaded, those instructions are carried out — those classes *are* instantiated and initialized.

For example, suppose you'd like the user to be presented with a view containing a button whose title is "Howdy." Xcode lets you arrange this graphically by editing a nib file: you drag a button from the Object library into the view, place it at a certain position in the view, and then set its title to "Howdy" (Figure 5-1). In effect, you create a drawing of what you want the view and its contents to look like.

When the app runs, the nib file loads, and that drawing is turned into reality. To do this, the drawing is treated as a set of instructions for instantiating objects. The button that you dragged into the view is treated as a representative of the UIButton class. The UI-Button class is told to instantiate itself, and that instance is then initialized, giving it the same position you gave it in the drawing (the instance's frame), the same title you gave it in the drawing (the instance's title), and putting it into the window. In effect, the loading of your nib file is equivalent to this code (assuming that view is a reference to the view object):

```
UIButton* b =
    [UIButton buttonWithType:UIButtonTypeRoundedRect]; // instantiate
[b setTitle:@"Howdy!" forState:UIControlStateNormal]; // set up title
[b setFrame: CGRectMake(100,100,100,35)];             // set up frame
[view addSubview:b];                                  // place button in view
```

The fact that nib files are a source of instances, and that those instances are brought into existence as the nib file is loaded, is a source of confusion to beginners. I'll discuss nib files and how they are used to generate instances in much more detail in Chapter 7.

Polymorphism

The compiler, even in the world of static typing, is perfectly happy for you to supply a subclass instance where a superclass type is declared. To see this, let's start with the first line of the previous example:

```
UIButton* b = [UIButton buttonWithType:UIButtonTypeRoundedRect];
```

UIButton is a subclass of UIControl, which is a subclass of UIView. So it would be perfectly legal and acceptable to say this:

```
UIButton* b = [UIButton buttonWithType:UIButtonTypeRoundedRect];
UIView* v = b;
```

The variable b is a UIButton instance, but I'm assigning it to a variable declared as a UIView. That's legal and acceptable because UIView is an ancestor (up the superclass chain) of UIButton. Putting it another way, I'm behaving as if a UIButton were a UIView, and the compiler accepts this because a UIButton *is* a UIView.

What's important when the app runs, however, is not the declared class of a variable, but the actual class of the object to which that variable points. Even if I assign the UIButton instance b to a UIView variable v, the object to which the variable v points is still a UIButton. So I can send it messages appropriate to a UIButton. For example:

```
UIButton* b = [UIButton buttonWithType:UIButtonTypeRoundedRect];
UIView* v = b;
[v setTitle:@"Howdy!" forState:UIControlStateNormal];
```

That code will cause the compiler to complain, because UIView doesn't implement set-Title:forState:; under ARC, in fact, that code won't even compile. So I'll calm the compiler's fears by typecasting:

```
UIButton* b = [UIButton buttonWithType:UIButtonTypeRoundedRect];
UIView* v = b;
[(UIButton*)v setTitle:@"Howdy!" forState:UIControlStateNormal];
```

The typecast calms the compiler's fears, but the important thing is what happens when the program runs. What happens is that this code works just fine! It works fine not because I typecast v to a UIButton (typecasting doesn't magically convert anything to anything else; it's just a hint to the compiler), but because v really *is* a UIButton. So when the message setTitle:forState: arrives at the object pointed to by v, everything is fine. If v had been a UIView but *not* a UIButton, on the other hand, the program would have crashed at that instant.

An object, then, responds to a message sent to it on the basis of what it really is, not on the basis of anything said about what it is — and what it really is cannot be known until the program actually runs and the message is actually sent to that object.

Now let's turn the tables. We called a UIButton a UIView and sent it a UIButton message. Now we're going to call a UIButton a UIButton and send it a UIView message.

What an object really is depends not just upon its class but also upon that class's inheritance. A message is acceptable even if an object's own class doesn't implement a corresponding method, provided that the method is implemented somewhere up the superclass chain. For example, returning again to the same code:

```
UIButton* b = [UIButton buttonWithType:UIButtonTypeRoundedRect];
[b setFrame: CGRectMake(100,100,100,35)];
```

This code works fine. But you won't find setFrame: in the documentation for the UIButton class. That's because you're looking in the wrong place. A UIButton is a UIControl, and a UIControl is a UIView. To find out about setFrame:, look in the UIView class's documentation. (Okay, it's more complicated than that; you won't find setFrame: there either. But you will find a term frame which is called a "property," and this amounts to the same thing, as I'll explain later in this chapter.) So the setFrame: message is sent to a UIButton, but it corresponds to a method defined on a UIView. Yet it works fine, because a UIButton *is* a UIView.

 A common beginner mistake is to consult the documentation without following the superclass chain. If you want to know what you can say to a UIButton, don't just look in the UIButton class documentation: also look in the UIControl class documentation, the UIView class documentation, and so on.

To sum up: we treated a UIButton object as a UIView, yet we were still able to send it a UIButton message. We treated a UIButton as a UIButton, yet we were still able to send it a UIView message. What matters when a message is sent to an object is not how the variable pointing to that object is declared but what class the object really is. What an object really is depends upon its class, along with that class's inheritance from the superclass chain; these facts are innate to the object and are independent of how your code characterizes the variable pointing to the object. This independent maintenance of object type integrity is the basis of what is called *polymorphism*.

But it is not quite the whole of polymorphism. To understand the whole of polymorphism, we must go further into the dynamics of message sending.

The Keyword self

A common situation is that code in an instance method defined in a class must call another instance method defined within the same class. We have not yet discussed how to do this. A method is called by sending a message to an object; in this situation, what object would that be? The answer is supplied by a special keyword, self. Here's a simple example:

```
@implementation MyClass

- (NSString*) greeting {
    return @"Goodnight, Gracie!";
}

- (NSString*) sayGoodnightGracie {
    return [self greeting];
}

@end
```

When the sayGoodnightGracie message is sent to a MyClass instance, the say-GoodnightGracie method runs. It sends the greeting message to self. As a result, the greeting instance method is called; it returns the string @"Goodnight, Gracie!", and this same string is then returned from the sayGoodnightGracie method.

The example seems straightforward enough, and it is. In real life, your code when you define a class will sometimes consist of a few public instance methods along with lots of other instance methods on which they rely. The instance methods within this class will be calling each other constantly. They do this by sending messages to self.

Behind this simple example, though, is a subtle and important mechanism having to do with the real meaning of the keyword self. The keyword self does not actually mean "in the same class." It's an instance, after all, not a class. What instance? It's this same instance. The same as what? The same instance to which the message was sent that resulted in the keyword self being encountered in the first place.

So let's consider in more detail what happens when we instantiate MyClass and send the sayGoodnightGracie message to that instance:

```
MyClass* thing = [MyClass new];
NSString* s = [thing sayGoodnightGracie];
```

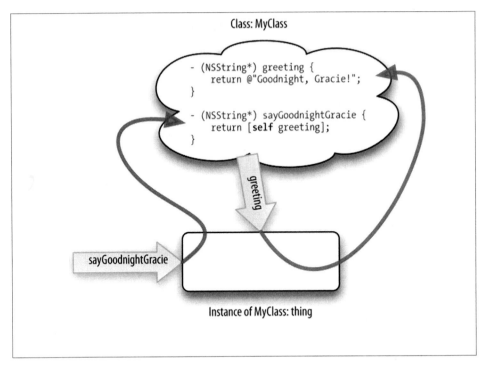

Figure 5-2. The meaning of self

We instantiate MyClass and assign the instance to a variable `thing`. We then send the `sayGoodnightGracie` message to `thing`, the instance we just created. The message arrives, and it turns out this instance is a MyClass. Sure enough, MyClass implements a `sayGoodnightGracie` instance method, and this method is called. As it runs, the keyword `self` is encountered. It means "the instance to which the original message was sent in the first place." That, as it happens, is the instance pointed to by the variable `thing`. So now the `greeting` message is sent to that instance (Figure 5-2).

This mechanism may seem rather elaborate, considering that the outcome is just what you'd intuitively expect. But the mechanism *needs* to be elaborate in order to get the right outcome. This is particularly evident when superclasses are involved and a class overrides a method of its superclass. To illustrate, suppose we have a class Dog with an instance method `bark`. And suppose Dog also has an instance method `speak`, which simply calls `bark`. Now suppose we subclass Dog with a class Basenji, which overrides `bark` (because Basenjis can't bark). What happens when we send the `speak` message to a Basenji instance, as in Example 5-2?

Example 5-2. Polymorphism in action

```
@implementation Dog

- (NSString*) bark {
    return @"Woof!";
}

- (NSString*) speak {
    return [self bark];
}

@end

@implementation Basenji : Dog

- (NSString*) bark {
    return @""; // empty string, Basenjis can't bark
}

@end

// So, in some other class:

Basenji* b = [Basenji new];
NSString* s = [b speak];
```

If the keyword self meant merely "the same class where this keyword appears," then when we send the speak message to a Basenji instance, we would arrive at the implementation of speak in the Dog class (because that's where speak is implemented), and the Dog class's bark method would be called. This would be terrible, because it would make nonsense of the notion of overriding; we'd return @"Woof!", which is wrong for a Basenji. But that is *not* what the keyword self means. It has to do with the instance, not the class.

So here's what happens. The speak message is sent to our Basenji instance, b. The Basenji class doesn't implement a speak method, so we look upward in the class hierarchy and discover that speak is implemented in the superclass, Dog. We call Dog's instance method speak, the speak method runs, and the keyword self is encountered. It means "the instance to which the original message was sent in the first place." That instance is still our Basenji instance b. So we send the bark message to the Basenji instance b. The Basenji class implements a bark instance method, so this method is found and called, and the empty string is returned (Figure 5-3).

Of course, if the Basenji class had *not* overridden bark, then when the bark message was sent to the Basenji instance, we would have looked upward in the class hierarchy *again* and found the bark method implemented in the Dog class and called that. Thus,

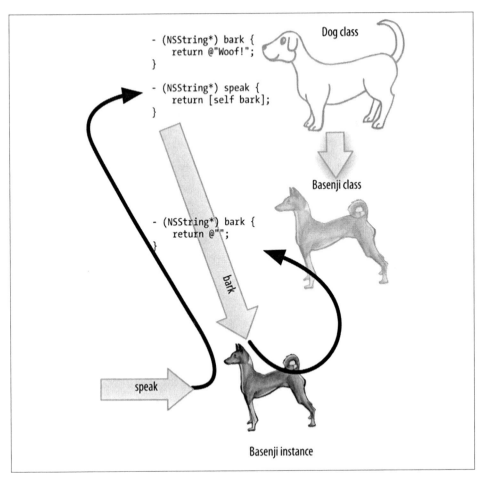

```objc
- (NSString*) bark {
    return @"Woof!";
}

- (NSString*) speak {
    return [self bark];
}
```

Dog class

Basenji class

```objc
- (NSString*) bark {
    return @"";
}
```

bark

speak

Basenji instance

Figure 5-3. Class inheritance, overriding, self, and polymorphism

thanks to the way the keyword self works, inheritance works correctly both when there is overriding and when there is not.

If you understand that example, you understand polymorphism. The mechanism I've just described is crucial to polymorphism and is the basis of object-oriented programming. (Observe that I now speak of object-oriented programming, not just object-based programming as in Chapter 2. That's because, in my view, the addition of polymorphism is what turns object-based programming into object-oriented programming.)

The Keyword super

Sometimes (quite often, in Cocoa programming) you want to override an inherited method but still access the overridden functionality. To do so, you'll use the keyword super. Like self, the keyword super is something you send a message to. But its meaning has nothing to do with "this instance" or any other instance. The keyword super is class-based, and it means: "Start the search for messages I receive in the superclass of this class" (where "this class" is the class where the keyword super appears).

You can do anything you like with super, but its primary purpose, as I've already said, is to access overridden functionality — typically from within the very functionality that does the overriding, so as to get both the overridden functionality and some additional functionality.

For example, suppose we define a class NoisyDog, a subclass of Dog. When told to bark, it barks twice:

```
@implementation NoisyDog : Dog

- (NSString*) bark {
    return [NSString stringWithFormat: @"%@ %@", [super bark], [super bark]];
}

@end
```

That code calls super's implementation of bark, twice; it assembles the two resulting strings into a single string with a space between, and returns that (using the stringWith-Format: method). Because Dog's bark method returns @"Woof!", NoisyDog's bark method returns @"Woof! Woof!". Notice that there is no circularity or recursion here: NoisyDog's bark method will never call itself.

A nice feature of this architecture is that by sending a message to the keyword super, rather than hard-coding @"Woof!" into NoisyDog's bark method, we ensure maintainability: if Dog's bark method is changed, the result of NoisyDog's bark method will change to match. For example, if we later go back and change Dog's bark method to return @"Arf!", NoisyDog's bark method will return @"Arf! Arf!" with no further change on our part.

In real Cocoa programming, it will very often be Cocoa's own methods that you're overriding. For example, the UIViewController class, which is built into Cocoa, implements a method viewDidAppear:, defined as follows:

```
- (void)viewDidAppear:(BOOL)animated
```

The documentation says that UIViewController is a class for which you are very likely to define a subclass (so as to get all of UIViewController's mighty powers — we'll find out what they are in Chapter 19 — along with your own custom behavior). The documentation proceeds to suggest that in your subclass of UIViewController you might want to override this method, but cautions that if you do, "you must call super at some point in your implementation." The phrase "call super" is a kind of shorthand, meaning "pass on to super the very same call and arguments that were sent to you." So your own implementation might look like this:

```
@implementation MyViewController : UIViewController
// ...
- (void) viewDidAppear: (BOOL) animated {
    [super viewDidAppear: animated];
    // ... do more stuff here ...
}
```

The result is that when viewDidAppear: is called in a MyViewController instance, we do both the standard stuff that its superclass UIViewController does in response to viewDidAppear: and the custom stuff pertaining to our own class MyViewController. In this particular case, we don't even know exactly what the UIViewController stuff is, and we don't care. When the documentation tells you to call super when overriding, call super when overriding!

Instance Variables and Accessors

In Chapter 3, I explained that one of the main reasons there are instances and not just classes is that instances can have instance variables. Instance variables, you remember, are declared when you define the class, and in Chapter 4 I said that these declarations go into curly braces at the start of the class's interface section or, in modern Objective-C, its implementation section. But the value of an instance variable differs for each instance.

 The term "instance variable" arises so often that it is often abbreviated to *ivar*. I'll use both terms indiscriminately from now on.

Let's write a class that uses an instance variable. Suppose we have a Dog class and we want every Dog instance to have a number, which should be an int. (For example, this number might correspond to the dog's license number, or something like that.) In modern Objective-C, we would probably declare number in the implementation section for the Dog class, like this:

```
@implementation Dog {
    int number;
}
// method implementations go here
@end
```

(You might ask why, for this example, I don't use instead the concept of giving the dog a name. The reason is that a name would be an NSString instance, which is an object; instance variables that are pointers to objects raise some additional issues I don't want to discuss just now. But instance variables that are simple C data types raise no such issues. We'll return to this matter in Chapter 12.)

By default, instance variables are *protected*, meaning that other classes (except for subclasses) can't see them. So if, somewhere else, I instantiate a Dog, I won't be able to access that Dog instance's number instance variable. This is a deliberate feature of Objective-C; you can work around it if you like, but in general you should not. Instead, if you want to provide public access to an instance variable, write an accessor method and make the method declaration public.

Within a class, on the other hand, that class's own instance variables are global. Any Dog method can just use the variable name number and access this instance variable, just like any other variable. But code that does this can be confusing when you're reading it; suddenly there's a variable called number and you don't understand what it is, because there's no nearby declaration for it. So I often use a different notation, like this: self->ivarName. The "arrow" operator, formed by a minus sign and a greater-than sign, is called the *structure pointer* operator, because of its original use in C (K&R 6.2).

So let's write, in Dog's implementation section, a method that allows setting a value for the number ivar:

```
- (void) setNumber: (int) n {
    self->number = n;
}
```

Of course, to make setNumber: public to any other class that imports Dog's interface file, we must also declare it in Dog's interface section:

```
@interface Dog : NSObject
- (void) setNumber: (int) n;
@end
```

We can now instantiate a Dog and assign that instance a number:

```
Dog* fido = [Dog new];
[fido setNumber: 42];
```

We can now set a Dog's number, but we can't get it (from outside that Dog instance). To correct this problem, we'll write a second accessor method, one that allows for getting the value of the number ivar:

```
- (int) number {
    return self->number;
}
```

Again, we declare the number method in Dog's interface section. Now we can both set and get a Dog instance's number:

```
Dog* fido = [Dog new];
[fido setNumber: 42];
int n = [fido number];
// sure enough, n is now 42!
```

This architecture is very typical. Your class can have as many ivars as you like, but if you want them to be publicly accessible, you must provide accessor methods. Luckily, Objective-C 2.0 — which is what you're using to program for iOS — provides a mechanism for generating accessor methods automatically (discussed in Chapter 12), so you won't have to go through the tedium of writing them by hand every time you want to make an ivar publicly accessible. (Though, to be honest, I don't see why you shouldn't have to go through that tedium; before Objective-C 2.0, we all had to, so why shouldn't you? We also had to clean the roads with our tongues on the way to school. And we liked it! You kids today, you don't know what real programming is.)

You've probably noticed that Dog now has both a number method and a number instance variable. This fact should not confuse you. It doesn't confuse the compiler, because the method name and the instance variable name are used in completely different ways in code. If the compiler can tell the difference, so can you. Nevertheless, a convention that is becoming increasingly common, for reasons that I'll explain in Chapter 12, is to begin ivar names with an underscore: _number, not number. If we follow this convention and rename our ivar, we'll also have to rewrite (but not rename) the methods that access it:

```
@implementation Dog {
    int _number;
}

- (void) setNumber: (int) n {
    self->_number = n;
}

- (int) number {
    return self->_number;
}

@end
```

Key–Value Coding

Objective-C provides a means for translating from a string to an instance variable accessor, called *key–value coding*. Such translation is useful, for example, when the name of the desired instance variable will not be known until runtime. So instead of calling [fido number], we might have a string @"number" that tells us what accessor to call. This string is the "key." The key–value coding equivalent of calling a getter is valueForKey:; the equivalent of calling a setter is setValue:forKey:.

Thus, for example, suppose we wish to get the value of the `number` instance variable from the `fido` instance. We can do this by sending `valueForKey:` to `fido`. However, even though the `number` instance variable is an int, the value returned by `valueFor-Key:` is an object — in this case, an NSNumber, the object equivalent of a number (see Chapter 10). If we want the actual int, NSNumber provides an instance method, `int-Value`, that lets us extract it:

```
NSNumber* num = [fido valueForKey: @"number"];
int n = [num intValue];
```

Similarly, to use key–value coding to set the value of the `number` instance variable in the `fido` instance, we would say:

```
NSNumber* num = [NSNumber numberWithInt:42];
[fido setValue: num forKey: @"number"];
```

Before handing off the number 42 as the `value` argument in `setValue:forKey:`, we had to wrap it up as an object — in this case, an NSNumber object. Starting with LLVM compiler version 4.0 (Xcode 4.4), there's a syntactic shorthand for doing that; just as we can create an NSString by wrapping text in a compiler directive `@"..."`, we can create an NSNumber by wrapping a numeric expression in a compiler directive `@(...)` — or, if the numeric expression is just a literal number, by preceding that literal number with `@`. So we can rewrite the previous example like this:

```
NSNumber* num = @42;
[fido setValue: num forKey: @"number"];
```

In real life, you'd probably omit the intermediate variable `num` and write the whole thing as a single line of code:

```
[fido setValue: @42 forKey: @"number"];
```

In these examples there is no advantage to using key–value coding over just calling the accessors. But suppose we had received the value `@"number"` in a variable (as the result of a method call, perhaps). Suppose that variable is called `something`. Then we could say:

```
id result = [fido valueForKey: something];
```

Thus we could access a different instance variable under different circumstances. This powerful flexibility is possible because Objective-C is such a dynamic language that a message to be sent to an object does not have to be formed until the program is already running.

When you call `valueForKey:` or `setValue:forKey:`, the correct accessor method is called if there is one. Thus, when we use `@"number"` as the key, a `number` method and a `setNumber:` method are called if they exist. (This is one reason why your accessors should be properly named.) On the other hand, if there isn't an accessor method, the instance variable is accessed directly. Such direct access violates the privacy of instance variables, so there's a way to turn off this feature for a particular class if you don't like it. (I'll explain what it is, with more about key–value coding, in Chapter 12.)

Properties

A *property* is a syntactic feature of Objective-C 2.0 designed to provide an alternative to the standard syntax for calling an accessor method. As syntactic sugar for formally calling a method, you can append the property name to an instance reference using dot-notation. You can use the resulting expression either on the left side of an equal sign (to call the corresponding setter) or elsewhere (to call the corresponding getter). The name of the property relies, by default, on the accessor naming conventions.

I'll use the Dog class as an example. If the Dog class has a public getter method called number and a public setter method called setNumber:, then the Dog class also has a number property. This means that, instead of saying things like this:

```
[fido setNumber: 42];
int n = [fido number];
```

You can talk like this:

```
fido.number = 42;
int n = fido.number;
```

Your use of property syntax is entirely optional. The existence of a property is equivalent to the existence of the corresponding getter and setter methods, and you're free to call those methods by either syntax. When you use property syntax in code, it is translated behind the scenes into a call to the corresponding getter or setter method, so it's all the same if you call the corresponding getter or setter method explicitly. In the case of Dog, you can use number as a property, or you can call the getter and setter methods number and setNumber:.

(Naturally, there are verbal quasi-religious wars on this topic, with one side claiming that property syntax is convenient and compact, and makes Objective-C more like other languages that use dot-notation, and the other side retorting that it does no such thing, because it is so limited. For example, property syntax opponents would argue, a UIScrollView has a contentView property, but when *setting* it you are most likely to want to animate the scroll view at the same time, which you do by calling setContentView:animated:. That's a kind of setter, but it takes two parameters; property syntax can't express that, so we're back to using an explicit method call, and property syntax has saved us nothing, and in fact is more likely to mislead us into forgetting to add the animation. Another objection to property notation is that the compiler restricts its use; for example, you can use a formal method call to send the number message to a Dog instance typed as an id, but you can't append the number property with dot-notation to such an instance.)

To use a property within the class that has that property, you must use self explicitly. So, for example:

```
self.number = 42;
```

 Do not confuse a property with an instance variable. An expression like self->number = n, or even simply number = n, sets the instance variable directly (and is possible only within the class, because instance variables are protected by default). An expression like fido.number or self.number involves a property and is equivalent to calling a getter or setter method. That getter or setter method may access an instance variable, and that instance variable may even have the same name as the property, but that doesn't make them the same thing.

Properties will be taken up again in Chapter 12, where it will turn out that they are much more powerful and interesting beasts than I'm suggesting here. But I'm telling you about properties now because they are so widely used in Cocoa and because you'll encounter them so frequently in the documentation. For example, in Chapter 1, I talked about setting a UIView's autoresizingMask property:

```
myView.autoresizingMask =
    UIViewAutoresizingFlexibleTopMargin | UIViewAutoresizingFlexibleWidth;
```

How did I know I could talk that way? Because the UIView documentation says that UIView has an autoresizingMask property. Near the top of the documentation page, we see this line:

autoresizingMask *property*

And further down, we get the details:

autoresizingMask

An integer bit mask that determines how the receiver resizes itself when its superview's bounds change.

```
@property(nonatomic) UIViewAutoresizing autoresizingMask
```

That last line is a *property declaration*. From the point of view of the UIView class's client — in this case, that's you — the property declaration is simply a shorthand, telling you that such a property exists, rather than bothering to tell you about the two accessor methods autoresizingMask and setAutoresizingMask:. (Never mind for now what nonatomic means.) That's how I knew there was a setter setAutoresizingMask:. In my code, I used property syntax as a way of calling that setter method; alternatively, I could have called setAutoresizingMask: explicitly.

Similarly, earlier in this chapter I called UIView's `setFrame:` method, even though no such method is mentioned in the UIView documentation. What the UIView documentation does say is this:

frame

The frame rectangle, which describes the view's location and size in its superview's coordinate system.

```
@property(nonatomic) CGRect frame
```

The documentation is telling me about the UIView property name `frame`, but that's the same thing as telling me about the existence of UIView instance methods `frame` and `setFrame:`; I can use these methods either through the `frame` property and dot-notation or by calling them explicitly.

Objective-C uses dot-notation for properties, and C uses dot-notation for structs; these can be chained. So, for example, UIView's `frame` is a property whose value is a struct (a CGRect); thus, you can say `myView.frame.size.height`, where `frame` is a property that returns a struct, `size` is an element of that struct, and `height` is an element of *that* struct. But there are limitations on this syntax; you cannot (for example) *set* a frame's height directly through a chain starting with the UIView, like this:

```
myView.frame.size.height = 36.0; // error, "Expression is not assignable"
```

Instead, if you want to change a component of a struct property, you must fetch the property value into a struct variable, change the struct variable's value, and set the entire property value from the struct variable:

```
CGRect f = myView.frame;
f.size.height = 0;
myView.frame = f;
```

How to Write an Initializer

Now that you know about `self` and `super` and instance variables, we can return to a topic that I blithely skipped over earlier. I described how to initialize a newly minted instance by calling an initializer, and emphasized that you must always do so, but I said nothing about how to write an initializer in your own classes. You will wish to do so only when you want your class to provide a convenient initializer that goes beyond the functionality of the inherited initializers. Often your purpose will be to accept some parameters and use them to set the initial values of some instance variables.

For example, in the case of a Dog with a number, let's say we don't want any Dog instances to come into existence without a number; every Dog *must* have one. So having a value for its number ivar is a *sine qua non* of a Dog being instantiated in the first place. An initializer publicizes this rule and helps to enforce it — especially if it is the class's designated initializer. So let's decide that this initializer will be Dog's designated initializer.

Moreover, let's say that a Dog's number should not be changed. Once the Dog has come into existence, along with a number, that number should remain attached to that Dog instance for as long as that Dog instance persists.

So delete the setNumber: method and its declaration, thus destroying any ability of other classes to set a Dog instance's number after it has been initialized. Instead, we're going to set a Dog's number as it is initialized, using a method we'll declare like this:

```
- (id) initWithNumber: (int) n
```

Our return value is typed as id, not as a pointer to a Dog, even though in fact we will return a Dog object. This is a convention that we should obey. The name is conventional as well; as you know, the init beginning tells the world this is an initializer.

Now I'm just going to show you the actual code for the initializer (Example 5-3). Much of this code is conventional — a dance you are required to do. You should not question this dance: just do it. I'll describe the meaning of the code, but I'm not going to try to justify all the parts of the convention.

Example 5-3. Conventional schema for an initializer

```
- (id) initWithNumber: (int) n {
    self = [super init]; ❶ ❷
    if (self) {
        self->_number = n; ❸
    }
    return self; ❹
}
```

The parts of the convention are:

❶ We send some sort of initialization message, calling a designated initializer. If the method we are writing is our class's designated initializer, this message is sent to super and calls the superclass's designated initializer. Otherwise, it is sent to self and calls either this class's designated initializer or another initializer that calls this class's designated initializer. In this case, the method we are writing is our class's designated initializer, and the superclass's designated initializer is init.

❷ We capture the result of the initialization message to super, and assign that result to self. It comes as a surprise to many beginners (and not-so-beginners) that one can assign to self at all or that it would make sense to do so. But one can assign to self (because of how Objective-C messaging works behind the scenes), and it makes sense to do so because in certain cases the instance returned from the call to super might not be same as the self we started with.

❸ If self is not nil, we initialize any instance variables we care to. This part of the code is typically the only part you'll customize; the rest will be according to the pattern. Observe that I don't use any setter methods (or properties); in initializing an instance variable not inherited from the superclass, you should assign directly to the instance variable.

❹ We return self.

All instance variables are set to a form of zero by alloc. Therefore, any instance variables not initialized explicitly in an initializer remain 0. This means, among other things, that by default a BOOL instance variable is NO and an object reference instance variable is nil. It is common practice to take advantage of these defaults in your program; if the default values are satisfactory initial values, you won't bother to set them in your designated initializer.

But we are not finished. Recall from earlier in this chapter that a class that defines a designated initializer should also override the inherited designated initializer (in this case, init). And you can see why: if we don't, someone could say [[Dog alloc] init] (or [Dog new]) and create a dog without a number — the very thing our initializer is trying to prevent. Just for the sake of the example, I'll make the overridden init assign a negative number as a signal that there's a problem. Notice that we're still obeying the rules: this initializer is not the designated initializer, so it calls this class's designated initializer.

```
- (id) init {
    return [self initWithNumber: -9999];
}
```

Just to complete the story, here's some code showing how we now would instantiate a Dog:

```
Dog* fido = [[Dog alloc] initWithNumber:42];
int n = [fido number];
// n is now 42; our initialization worked!
```

PART II

IDE

By now, you're doubtless anxious to jump in and start writing an app. To do that, you need a solid grounding in the tools you'll be using. The heart and soul of those tools can be summed up in one word: Xcode. In this part of the book we explore Xcode, the *IDE* (integrated development environment) in which you'll be programming iOS. Xcode is a big program, and writing an app involves coordinating a lot of pieces; this part of the book will help you become comfortable with Xcode. Along the way, we'll generate a simple working app through some hands-on tutorials.

- Chapter 6 tours Xcode and explains the architecture of the *project*, the collection of files from which an app is generated.

- Chapter 7 is about nibs. A *nib* is a file containing a drawing of your interface. Understanding nibs — knowing how they work and how they relate to your code — is crucial to your use of Xcode and to proper development of just about any app.

- Chapter 8 pauses to discuss the Xcode documentation and other sources of information on the API.

- Chapter 9 explains editing your code, testing and debugging your code, and the various steps you'll take on the way to submitting your app to the App Store. You'll probably want to skim this chapter quickly at first, returning to it as a detailed reference later while developing and submitting an actual app.

CHAPTER 6

Anatomy of an Xcode Project

Xcode is the application used to develop an iOS app. An Xcode *project* is the source for an app; it's the entire collection of files and settings needed to construct the app. To create, develop, and maintain an app, you must know how to manipulate and navigate an Xcode project. So you must know something about Xcode, and you must know something about the nature and structure of Xcode projects and how Xcode shows them to you. That's the subject of this chapter.

The term "Xcode" is actually used in two ways. It's the name for the entire suite of developer tools — the Xcode tools — and it's the name of one application within that suite, the application in which you edit and build your app. This ambiguity should generally present little difficulty.

Xcode is a powerful, complex, and extremely large program. My approach in introducing Xcode is to suggest that you adopt a kind of deliberate tunnel vision: if you don't understand something, don't worry about it — don't even look at it, and don't touch it, because you might change something important. Our survey of Xcode will chart a safe, restricted, and essential path, focusing on aspects of Xcode that you most need to understand immediately, and resolutely ignoring everything else.

For full information, study Apple's own documentation (choose Help → Xcode Help); it may seem overwhelming at first, but what you need to know is probably in there somewhere. There are also entire books devoted to describing and explaining Xcode.

The structure of the Xcode installation changed starting with Xcode 4.3. The Developer folder in Xcode 4.2 and before was a top-level install folder. In Xcode 4.3 and later, the Developer folder is inside the Xcode application bundle itself, *Xcode.app/Contents/Developer*. When I say */Developer*, this is the folder I'm referring to.

New Project

Even before you've written any code, an Xcode project is quite elaborate. To see this, let's make a new, essentially "empty" project; you'll see instantly that it isn't empty at all.

1. Start up Xcode and choose File → New → Project.

2. The "Choose a template" dialog appears. The template is your project's initial set of files and settings. When you pick a template, you're really picking an existing folder full of files; basically, it will be one of the folders inside */Developer/Platforms/ iPhoneOS.platform/Developer/Library/Xcode/Templates/Project Templates/Application*. This template folder will essentially be copied, and a few values will be filled in, in order to create your project.

   So, in this case, on the left, under iOS (not Mac OS X!), choose Application. On the right, select Single View Application. Click Next.

3. You are now asked to provide a name for your project (Product Name). Let's call our new project *Empty Window*.

   In a real project, you should give some thought to the project's name, as you're going to be living in close quarters with it. As Xcode copies the template folder, it's going to use the project's name to "fill in the blank" in several places, including some filenames and some settings, such as the name of the app. Thus, whatever you type at this moment is something you'll be seeing in a lot of places throughout your project. I'll talk at the end of this chapter about how to change an existing project's name.

   It's fine to use spaces in a project name. Spaces are legal in the folder name, the project name, the app name, and the various names of files that Xcode will generate automatically; and in the few places where spaces are problematic (such as the bundle identifier, discussed in the next paragraph), the name you type as the Product Name will have its spaces converted to hyphens.

4. Note the Company Identifier field. The first time you create a project, this field will be blank, and you should fill it in. The goal here is to create a unique string (unique to you personally); your app's bundle identifier, which is shown in gray below the company identifier, will consist of the company identifier plus a version of the project's name, and because every project should have a unique name, the bundle

identifier will also be unique and will thus uniquely identify this project along with the app that it produces and everything else connected with it. The convention is to start the company identifier with com. and to follow it with a string (possibly with multiple dot-components) that no one else is likely to use. For example, I use com.neuburg.matt.

5. Make sure the Devices pop-up menu is set to iPhone. Make sure that Use Automatic Reference Counting is checked but that the other two checkboxes are unchecked. (Ignore the Class Prefix field for now; it should be empty, with its default value "XYZ" shown in gray.) Click Next.

6. You've now told Xcode how to construct your project. Basically, it's going to copy the *Single View Application.xctemplate* folder from within the *Project Templates/ Application* folder I mentioned earlier. But you need to tell it where to copy this template folder to. That's why Xcode is now presenting a Save dialog. You are to specify the location of a folder that is about to be created — a folder that will be the *project folder* for this project.

   The project folder can go just about anywhere, and you can move it after creating it. I usually create new projects on the Desktop.

7. Xcode also offers to create a git repository for your project. In real life, this can be a great convenience (see Chapter 9), but for now, uncheck that checkbox. Click Create.

8. The *Empty Window* project folder is created on disk (on the Desktop, if that's the location you just specified), and the project window for the Empty Window project opens in Xcode.

The project we've just created is a working project; it really does build an iOS app called Empty Window. To see this, make sure that the Scheme pop-up menu in the project window's toolbar reads Empty Window → iPhone 6.0 Simulator (though the exact system version number might be different), and choose Product → Run. After some delay, the iOS Simulator application eventually opens and displays your app running — an empty gray screen.

 To *build* a project is to compile its code and assemble the compiled code, together with various resources, into the actual app. Typically, if you want to know whether your code compiles and your project is consistently and correctly constructed, you'll build the project (Product → Build). To *run* a project is to launch the built app, in the Simulator or on a connected device; if you want to know whether your code works as expected, you'll run the project (Product → Run), which automatically builds first if necessary.

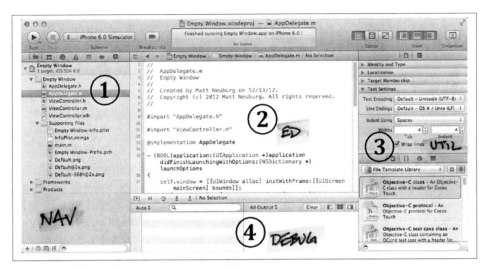

Figure 6-1. The project window, on steroids

The Project Window

An Xcode project embodies a lot of information about what files constitute the project and how they are to be used when building the app, such as:

- The source files (your code) that are to be compiled

- Any resources, such as icons, images, or sound files, as well as nib and storyboard files, that are to be part of the app

- Any frameworks to which the code must be linked as the app is built

- All settings (instructions to the compiler, to the linker, and so on) that are to be obeyed as the app is built

Xcode presents this information in graphical form, and this is one reason why a project window is so elaborate, and why learning to navigate and understand it takes time. Also, this single window must let you access, edit, and navigate your code, as well as reporting the progress and results of such procedures as building or debugging an app. In short, the single project window displays a lot of information and embodies a lot of functionality. You won't lose your way, however, if you just take a moment to explore this window and see how it is constructed.

Figure 6-1 shows the project window, configured in rather an extreme manner, so as to display as many parts of the window as possible. In real life, you'd probably never show all these parts of the window at the same time, except very briefly, unless you had a really big monitor.

1. On the left is the Navigator pane. Show and hide it with View → Navigators → Show/Hide Navigator (Command-0) or with the first button in the View segmented control in the toolbar.

2. In the middle is the Editor pane (or simply "editor"). This is the main area of a project window. A project window nearly always displays at least one Editor pane. I could have made this window display multiple Editor panes, but I was afraid that might make you run screaming from the room.

3. On the right is the Utilities pane. Show and hide it with View → Utilities → Show/Hide Utilities (Command-Option-0) or with the third button in the View segmented control in the toolbar.

4. At the bottom is the Debugger pane. Show and hide it with View → Show/Hide Debug Area (Shift-Command-Y) or with the second button in the View segmented control in the toolbar.

 All Xcode keyboard shortcuts can be customized; see the Key Bindings pane of the Preferences window. Keyboard shortcuts that I cite are the defaults.

The Navigator Pane

The Navigator pane is the column of information at the left of the window. Among other things, it's your primary mechanism for controlling what you see in the main area of the project window. An important general use pattern for Xcode is: you select something in the Navigator pane, and that thing is displayed in the main area (the editor) of the project window.

It is possible to toggle the visibility of the Navigator pane (View → Navigators → Hide/Show Navigator, or Command-0); for example, once you've used the Navigator pane to reach the item you want to see or work on in the editor, you might hide the Navigator pane temporarily to maximize your screen real estate (especially on a smaller monitor). You can change the Navigator pane's width by dragging the vertical line at its right edge.

The Navigator pane itself can display seven different sets of information; thus, there are actually seven navigators. These are represented by the seven icons across its top; to switch among them, use these icons or their keyboard shortcuts (Command-1, Command-2, and so on). You will quickly become adept at switching to the navigator you want; their keyboard shortcuts will become second nature. If the Navigator pane is hidden, pressing a navigator's keyboard shortcut both shows the Navigator pane and switches to that navigator.

Depending on your settings in the Behaviors pane of Xcode's preferences, a navigator might show itself automatically when you perform a certain action. For example, by default, when you build your project, if warning messages or error messages are generated, the Issue navigator will appear. This automatic behavior will not prove troublesome, because it is generally precisely the behavior you want, and if it isn't, you can change it; plus you can easily switch to a different navigator at any time.

Let's begin experimenting immediately with the various navigators:

Project navigator (Command-1)

Click here for basic navigation through the files that constitute your project. For example, in the Empty Window folder (these folder-like things in the Project navigator are actually called *groups*), click *AppDelegate.m* to view its code in the editor (Figure 6-2).

At the top level of the Project navigator, with a blue Xcode icon, is the Empty Window project itself; click it to view the settings associated with your project and its targets. Don't change anything here without knowing what you're doing! I'll talk later in this chapter about what these settings are for.

The filter bar at the bottom of the Project navigator lets you limit what files are shown; when there are many files, this is great for quickly reaching a file with a known name. For example, try typing "delegate" in the filter bar search field. Don't forget to remove your filter when you're done experimenting.

 Once you've filtered a navigator, it stays filtered until you remove the filter — even if you close the project! A common mistake is to filter a navigator, forget that you've done so, fail to notice the filter (because you're looking at the navigator itself, not down at the bottom where the filter bar is), and wonder, "Hey, where did all my files go?"

Symbol navigator (Command-2)

A *symbol* is a name, typically the name of a class or method. Depending on which of the three icons in the filter bar at the bottom of the Symbol navigator you highlight, you can view Cocoa's built-in symbols or the symbols defined in your project. The former can be a useful form of documentation; the latter can be helpful for navigating your code. For example, highlight the first two icons in the filter bar (the first two are dark-colored, the third is light), and see how quickly you can reach the definition of AppDelegate's `applicationDidBecomeActive:` method.

Try highlighting the filter bar icons in various ways to see how the contents of the Symbol navigator change. Type in the search field in the filter bar to limit what appears in the Symbol navigator; for example, try typing "active" in the search field, and see what happens.

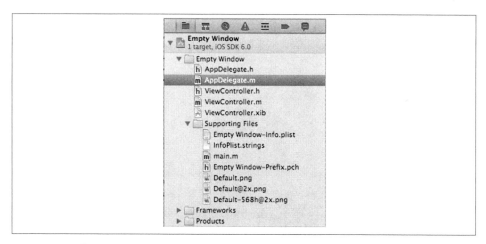

Figure 6-2. The Project navigator

Search navigator (Command-3)

This is a powerful search facility for finding text globally in your project, and even in the headers of Cocoa frameworks. You can also summon the Search navigator with Edit → Find → Find in Workspace (Shift-Command-F). To access the full set of options, click the magnifying glass and choose Show Find Options. For example, try searching for "delegate" (Figure 6-3). Click a search result to jump to it in your code.

You can type in the other search field, the one in the filter bar at the bottom, to limit further which search results are displayed. (I'm going to stop calling your attention to the filter bar now, but every navigator has it in some form.)

Issue navigator (Command-4)

You'll need this navigator primarily when your code has issues. This doesn't refer to emotional instability; it's Xcode's term for warning and error messages emitted when you build your project.

To see the Issue navigator in action, you'll need to give your code an issue. For example, navigate (as you already know how to do, in at least three different ways) to the file *AppDelegate.m*, and in the blank line after the last comment at the top of the file's contents, above the #import line, type howdy. Build (Command-B), saving if you're prompted to. The Issue navigator will display numerous error messages, showing that the compiler is totally unable to cope with this illegal word appearing in an illegal place. Click an issue to see it within its file. In your code, issue "balloons" may appear to the right of lines containing issues; if you're distracted or hampered by these, toggle their visibility with Editor → Issues → Hide/Show All Issues (Control-Command-M).

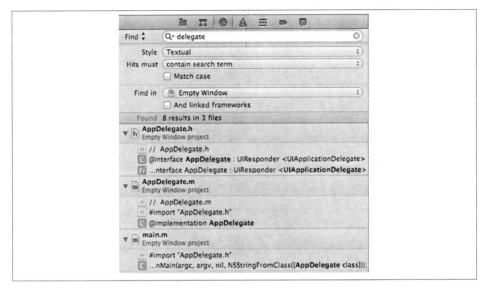

Figure 6-3. The Search navigator

Now that you've made Xcode miserable, select "howdy" and delete it; build again, and your issues will be gone. If only real life were this easy!

Debug navigator (Command-5)

By default, this navigator will appear when your code is paused while you're debugging it. There is not a strong distinction in Xcode between running and debugging; the milieu is the same. The difference is mostly a matter of whether breakpoints are obeyed (more about that, and about debugging in general, in Chapter 9). If your code runs and doesn't pause, the Debug navigator by default won't come into play.

To see the Debug navigator in action, you'll need to give your code a breakpoint. Navigate once more to the file *AppDelegate.m*, select in the line that says `return YES`, and choose Product → Debug → Add Breakpoint at Current Line to make a blue breakpoint arrow appear on that line. Run the project. (If the project is already running, the Stop dialog may appear; click Stop to terminate the current run and begin a new one.) By default, as the breakpoint is encountered, the Navigator pane switches to the Debug navigator, and the Debug pane appears at the bottom of the window.

This overall layout (Figure 6-4) will rapidly become familiar as you debug your projects. The Debug navigator displays the call stack, with the names of the nested methods in which the pause occurs; as you would expect, you can click on a method name to navigate to it. You can shorten or lengthen the list with the slider at the

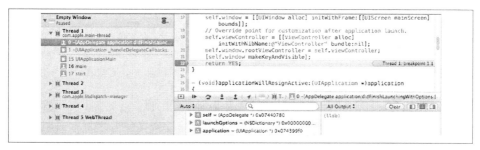

Figure 6-4. The Debug layout

bottom of the navigator. The Debug pane, which can be shown or hidden at will (View → Debug Area → Hide/Show Debug Area, or Shift-Command-Y), consists of two subpanes — the variables list and the console. Either of these can be hidden using the segmented control at the top right of the pane. The console can also be summoned by choosing View → Debug Area → Activate Console.

- On the left, the variables list is populated with the variables in scope for the selected method in the call stack (and you can optionally display processor registers as well).

- On the right is the console, where the debugger displays text messages; that's how you learn of exceptions thrown by your running app. Exceptions are extremely important to know about, and this is your only way to know about them, so keep an eye on the console as your app runs. You can also use the console to communicate via text with the debugger. This can often be a better way to explore variable values during a pause than the variables list.

Breakpoint navigator (Command-6)
This navigator lists all your breakpoints. At the moment you've only one, but when you're actively debugging a large project with many breakpoints, you'll be glad of this navigator. Also, this is where you create special breakpoints (such as symbolic breakpoints), and in general it's your center for managing existing breakpoints. We'll return to this topic in Chapter 9.

Log navigator (Command-7)
This navigator lists your recent major actions, such as building or running (debugging) your project. Click on a listing to see the log file generated when you performed that action. The log file might contain information that isn't displayed in any other way, and also it lets you dredge up messages from the recent past ("What was that exception I got while debugging a moment ago?").

For example, by clicking on the listing for a successful build, and by choosing to display All and All Messages using the filter switches at the top of the log, we can

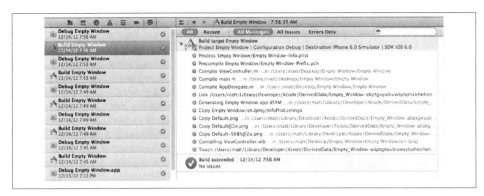

Figure 6-5. Viewing a log

see the steps by which a build takes place (Figure 6-5). To reveal the full text of a step, click on that step and then click the Expand Transcript button that appears at the far right (and see also the menu items in the Editor menu).

When navigating by clicking in the Navigator pane, modifications to your click can determine where navigation takes place. By default, Option-click navigates in an assistant pane (discussed later in this chapter), double-click navigates by opening a new window, and Shift-Option-click summons the navigation window, a little heads-up pane where you can specify where to navigate (a new window, a new tab, or a new assistant pane). For the settings that govern these click modifications, see the General pane of Xcode's preferences.

The Utilities Pane

The Utilities pane is the column at the right of the project window. It contains inspectors that provide information about the current selection or its settings; in some cases, these inspectors let you change those settings. It also contains libraries that function as a source of objects you may need while editing your project. The Utilities pane's importance emerges mostly when you're working in the nib editor (Chapter 7). But it can also be useful while editing code, because Quick Help, a form of documentation (Chapter 8), is displayed here as well, plus the Utilities pane is the source of code snippets (Chapter 9). To toggle the visibility of the Utilities pane, choose View → Utilities → Hide/Show Utilities (Command-Option-0). You can change the Utilities pane's width by dragging the vertical line at its left edge.

Many individual inspectors and libraries are discussed in subsequent chapters. Here, I'll just describe the overall physical characteristics of the Utilities pane.

The Utilities pane consists of a set of palettes. Actually, there are so many of these palettes that they are clumped into multiple sets, divided into two major groups: the top half of the pane and the bottom half of the pane. You can change the relative heights of these two halves by dragging the horizontal line that separates them.

The top half

What appears in the top half of the Utilities pane depends on what's selected in the current editor. There are two main cases:

A code file is being edited

The top half of the Utilities pane shows either the File inspector or Quick Help. Toggle between them with the icons at the top of this half of the Utilities pane, or with their keyboard shortcuts (Command-Option-1, Command-Option-2). The File inspector is rarely needed, but Quick Help can be useful as documentation. The File inspector consists of multiple sections, each of which can be expanded or collapsed by clicking its header.

A nib or storyboard file is being edited

The top half of the Utilities pane shows, in addition to the File inspector and Quick Help, the Identity inspector (Command-Option-3), the Attributes inspector (Command-Option-4), the Size inspector (Command-Option-5), and the Connections inspector (Command-Option-6). Like the File inspector, these can consist of multiple sections, each of which can be expanded or collapsed by clicking its header.

The bottom half

The bottom half of the Utilities pane shows one of four libraries. Toggle between them with the icons at the top of this half of the Utilities pane, or with their keyboard shortcuts. They are the File Template library (Command-Option-Control-1), the Code Snippet library (Command-Option-Control-2), the Object library (Command-Option-Control-3), and the Media library (Command-Option-Control-4). The Object library is the most important; you'll use it heavily when editing a nib or storyboard.

To see a help pop-up describing the currently selected item in a library, press Spacebar.

The Editor

In the middle of the project window is the *editor*. This is where you get actual work done, reading and writing your code (Chapter 9), or designing your interface in a nib or storyboard file (Chapter 7). The editor is the core of the project window. You can eliminate the Navigator pane, the Utilities pane, and the Debug pane, but there is no such thing as a project window without an editor (though you can cover the editor completely with the Debug pane).

The editor provides its own form of navigation, the *jump bar* across the top. Not only does the jump bar show you hierarchically what file is currently being edited, but also it allows you to switch to a different file. In particular, each path component in the jump bar is also a pop-up menu. These pop-up menus can be summoned by clicking on a path component, or by using keyboard shortcuts (shown in the second section of the View → Standard Editor submenu). For example, Control-4 summons a hierarchical pop-up menu, which can be navigated entirely with the keyboard, allowing you to choose a different file in your project to edit. Moreover, each pop-up menu in the jump bar also has a filter field; to see it, summon a pop-up menu from the jump bar and start typing. Thus you can navigate your project even if the Project navigator isn't showing.

It is extremely likely, as you develop a project, that you'll want to edit more than one file simultaneously, or obtain multiple views of a single file so that you can edit two areas of it simultaneously. This can be achieved in three ways: assistants, tabs, and secondary windows.

Assistants

You can split the editor into multiple editors by summoning an *assistant* pane. To do so, click the second button in the Editor segmented control in the toolbar, or choose View → Assistant Editor → Show Assistant Editor (Command-Option-Return). Also, by default, adding the Option key to navigation opens an assistant pane; for example, Option-click in the Navigator pane, or Option-choose in the jump bar, to navigate by opening an assistant pane (or to navigate in an existing assistant pane if there is one). To remove the assistant pane, click the first button in the Editor segmented control in the toolbar, or choose View → Standard Editor → Show Standard Editor (Command-Return), or click the X button at the assistant pane's top right.

Your first task will be to decide how you want multiple editor panes arranged with respect to one another. To do so, choose from the View → Assistant Editor submenu. I usually prefer All Editors Stacked Vertically, but it's purely a matter of personal taste and convenience.

Once you've summoned an assistant pane, you can split it further into additional assistant panes. To do so, click the Plus button at the top right of an assistant pane. To dismiss an assistant pane, click the X button at its top right.

What makes an assistant pane an assistant, and not just a form of split-pane editing, is that it can bear a special relationship to the primary editor pane. The primary editor pane is the one whose contents, by default, are determined by what you click on in the Navigator pane; an assistant pane, meanwhile, can respond to what file is being edited in the primary editor pane by changing intelligently what file it (the assistant pane) is editing. This is called *tracking*.

To see tracking in action, open a single assistant pane and set the first component in its jump bar to Counterparts (Figure 6-6). Now use the Project navigator to select *AppDelegate.m*; the primary editor pane displays this file, and the assistant automatically displays *AppDelegate.h*. Next, use the Project navigator to select *App-*

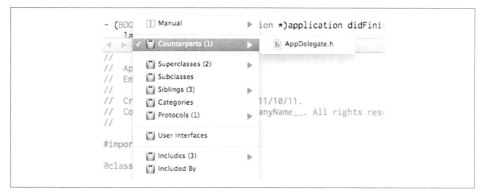

Figure 6-6. Telling an assistant pane to display counterparts

Delegate.h; the primary editor pane displays this file, and the assistant automatically displays *AppDelegate.m*. There's a lot of convenience and power lurking here, which you'll explore as you need it.

Tabs

You can embody the entire project window interface as a tab. To do so, choose File → New → Tab (Command-T), revealing the tab bar (just below the toolbar) if it wasn't showing already. Use of a tabbed interface will likely be familiar from applications such as Safari. You can switch between tabs by clicking on a tab, or with Command-Shift-}. At first, your new tab will look largely identical to the original window from which it was spawned. But now you can make changes in a tab — change what panes are showing or what file is being edited, for example — without affecting any other tabs. Thus you can get multiple views of your project. You can assign a descriptive name to a tab: double-click on a tab name to make it editable.

Secondary windows

A secondary project window is similar to a tab, but it appears as a separate window instead of a tab in the same window. To create one, choose File → New → Window (Command-Shift-T). Alternatively, you can promote a tab to be a window by dragging it right out of its current window. Or choose Navigate → Open In and navigate left in the resulting dialog until the dialog offers to make a new window.

There isn't a strong difference between a tab and a secondary window; which you use, and for what, will be a matter of taste and convenience. I find that the advantage of a secondary window is that you can see it at the same time as the main window, and that it can be small. Thus, when I have a file I frequently want to refer to, I often spawn off a secondary window displaying that file, sized fairly small and without any panes other than the editor.

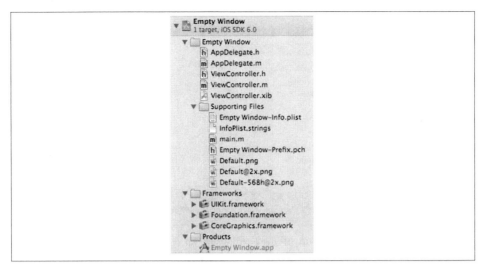

Figure 6-7. The Project navigator again

The Project File and Its Dependents

Now that you're comfortable with the Xcode project window, you're ready to explore the project and its constituents.

The first item in the Project navigator (Command-1) represents the project file on disk (in our new project, this is called Empty Window). Hierarchically dependent upon it are items that contribute to the building of the project (Figure 6-7).

Many of these items, including the project file itself, correspond to items on disk in the project folder. To survey this correspondence, let's examine the project folder in the Finder simultaneously with the Xcode project window. Select the project file listing in the Project navigator and choose File → Show in Finder.

The Finder displays the contents of your project folder (Figure 6-8). The most important of these is *Empty Window.xcodeproj*. This is the project file. All Xcode's knowledge about your project — what files it consists of and how to build the project — is stored in this file.

To open a project from the Finder, double-click the project file. This will launch Xcode if it isn't already running.

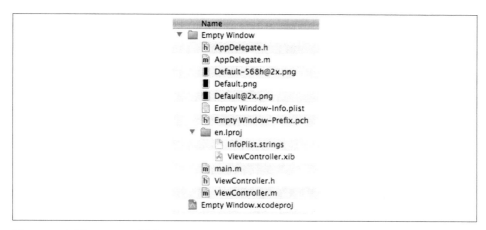

Name
▼ 📁 Empty Window
ⓗ AppDelegate.h
ⓜ AppDelegate.m
▮ Default-568h@2x.png
▮ Default.png
▮ Default@2x.png
📄 Empty Window-Info.plist
ⓗ Empty Window-Prefix.pch
▼ 📁 en.lproj
📄 InfoPlist.strings
📄 ViewController.xib
ⓜ main.m
ⓗ ViewController.h
ⓜ ViewController.m
📘 Empty Window.xcodeproj

Figure 6-8. The project folder

Never, never, *never* touch anything in a project folder by way of the Finder, except for double-clicking the project file to open the project. Don't put anything directly into a project folder. Don't remove anything from a project folder. Don't rename anything in a project folder. Don't touch anything in a project folder! Do all your interaction with the project through the project window in Xcode. (When you're an Xcode power user, you'll know when you can disobey this rule. Until then, just obey it blindly and rigorously.)

The reason is that the project expects things in the project folder to be a certain way. If you make any alterations to the project folder directly in the Finder, behind the project's back, you can upset those expectations and break the project. When you work in the project window, it is Xcode itself that makes any necessary changes in the project folder, and all will be well.

Consider now the groups and files shown in the Project navigator (Figure 6-7) as hierarchically dependent upon the project file, and how they correspond to reality on disk as portrayed in the Finder (Figure 6-8). (Recall that *group* is the technical term for the folder-like objects shown in the Project navigator.)

Observe that groups in the Project navigator don't necessarily correspond to folders on disk in the Finder, and folders on disk in the Finder don't necessarily correspond to groups in the Project navigator.

- The Empty Window group is, to some extent, real; it corresponds directly to the *Empty Window* folder on disk. If you were to create additional files (which, in real life, you would almost certainly do in the course of developing your project), you would likely put them in the Empty Window group in the Project navigator so that they'd be in the *Empty Window* folder on disk. (Doing so, however, is not a requirement; your files can live anywhere and your project will still work fine.)

- The Supporting Files group, on the other hand, corresponds to nothing on disk; it's just a way of clumping some items together in the Project navigator, so that they can be located easily and can be shown or hidden together. The things *inside* this group are real, however; you can see that the four files *Empty Window-Info.plist*, *InfoPlist.strings*, *Empty Window-Prefix.pch*, and *main.m*, along with the three *Default.png* files, do exist on disk — they're just not inside anything called *Supporting Files*. Rather, they're at the top level of the *Empty Window* folder.

- Two files, *InfoPlist.strings* and *ViewController.xib*, appear in the Finder inside a folder called *en.lproj*, which doesn't appear in the Project navigator. The folder *en.lproj* has to do with *localization*, which I'll discuss in Chapter 9.

You may be tempted to find all this confusing. Don't! Remember what I said about not involving yourself with the project folder on disk in the Finder. Keep your attention on the Project navigator, make your modifications to the project there, and all will be well.

By convention, as you add other files to your project that are not code but need to be copied into the app as it is built, such as sound and image files, you would usually put them into yet another group — probably, though not necessarily, a group inside the Empty Window group. You might call this group Resources. (I usually do.) And as your project grows further, you should feel free to create even more groups to help organize your files. To make a new group, choose File → New → Group. To rename a group, select it in the Project navigator and press Return to make the name editable.

When I say "feel free," I mean it. You want navigating your project to be easy and intuitive. That's what groups are for. They are just ways of making the Project navigator work well for you. As we've seen, they don't necessarily affect how the actual files are stored on disk. Even more important, they don't affect how the app is built. It is not the placement of files in groups or in the Finder that causes them to be built into the app; it's their inclusion in the appropriate target build phase, as I'll explain later in this chapter.

The things in the Frameworks group and the Products group don't correspond to anything in the project folder, but they do correspond to real things that the project needs to know about in order to build and run:

Frameworks

This group, by convention, lists frameworks (Cocoa code) on which your code depends. Frameworks exist on disk, but they are not built into your app when it is constructed; they don't have to be, because they are present also on the target device (an iPhone, iPod touch, or iPad). Instead, the frameworks are *linked* to the app, meaning that the app knows about them and expects to find them on the device when it runs. Thus, all the framework code is omitted from the app itself, saving considerable space.

Products
> This group, by convention, holds an automatically generated reference to the built app.

The Target

A *target* is a collection of parts along with rules and settings for how to build a product from them. It is a major determinant of how an app is built. Whenever you build, what you're really building is a target.

Select the Empty Window project at the top of the Project navigator, and you'll see two things on the left side of the editor: the project itself, and a list of your targets. In this case, there is only one target, called Empty Window (just like the project itself). But there could be more than one target, under certain circumstances. For example, you might want to write an app that can be built as an iPhone app or as an iPad app — two different apps that share a lot of the same code. So you might want one project containing two targets.

If you select the project in the left side of the editor, you *edit the project*. If you select the target in the left side of the editor, you *edit the target*. I'll use those expressions a lot in later instructions.

Build Phases

Edit the target and click Build Phases at the top of the editor (Figure 6-9). These are the stages by which your app is built. By default, there are three of them with content — Compile Sources, Link Binary With Libraries, and Copy Bundle Resources — and those are the only stages you'll usually need, though you can add others. The build phases are both a report to you on how the target will be built and a set of instructions to Xcode on how to build the target; if you change the build phases, you change the build process.

The meanings of the three build phases are pretty straightforward:

Compile Sources
> Certain files (your code) are compiled, and the resulting compiled code is copied into the app.

Link Binary With Libraries
> Certain libraries, usually frameworks, are linked to the compiled code (now referred to as the *binary*), so that it will expect them to be present on the device when the app runs.

Copy Bundle Resources
> Certain files are copied into the app, so that your code or the system can find them there when the app runs. For example, if your app had an icon, it would need to be copied into the app so the device could find and display it.

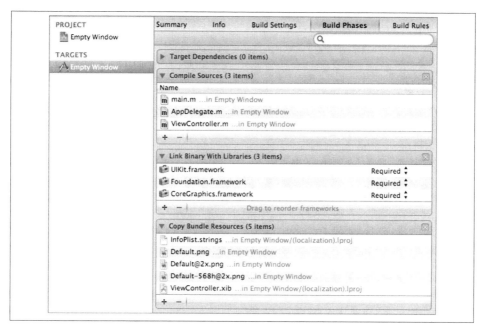

Figure 6-9. Build phases

By opening the build phases in the editor, you can see the files to which each phase applies. The first phase, Compile Sources, presently compiles three files (*main.m*, *App-Delegate.m*, and *ViewController.m*). The second phase, Link Binary With Libraries, presently links three libraries (frameworks). The third phase, Copy Bundle Resources, presently copies five files — *InfoPlist.strings*, *ViewController.xib* (a nib file), and three *.png* files that supply a default image of your app as it launches, as explained in Chapter 9.

You can alter these lists. If something in your project was not in Copy Bundle Resources and you wanted it copied into the app during the build process, you would drag it from the Project navigator into the Copy Bundle Resources list, or (easier) click the Plus button beneath the Copy Bundle Resources list to get a helpful dialog listing everything in your project. If something in your project was in Copy Bundle Resources and you didn't want it copied in the app, you would delete it from the list; this would not delete it from your project, from the Project navigator, or from the Finder, but only from the list of things to be copied into your app.

Build Settings

Build phases are only one aspect of how a target knows how to build the app. The other aspect is build settings. To see them, edit the target and click Build Settings at the top

Setting	Resolved	Empty Window	Empty Window	iOS Default
▼ Architectures				
Additional SDKs				
Architectures	Standard (armv7, armv7s) ⟂			Standard (armv7, armv7s) ~ $ ⟂
Base SDK	Latest iOS (iOS 6.0) ⟂		Latest iOS (iOS 6.0) ⟂	iOS 6.0 ⟂
▼ Build Active Architecture Only	<Multiple values> ⟂		<Multiple values> ⟂	No ⟂
Debug	Yes ⟂		Yes ⟂	No ⟂
Release	No ⟂			No ⟂
Supported Platforms	:OS ⟂			iOS ⟂
Valid Architectures	armv7 armv7s			armv7 armv7s

Figure 6-10. Target build settings

of the editor (Figure 6-10). Here you'll find a long list of settings, most of which you'll never touch. But Xcode examines this list in order to know what to do at various stages of the build process. Build settings are the reason your project compiles and builds the way it does.

You can determine what build settings are displayed by clicking Basic or All. The settings are combined into categories, and you can close or open each category heading to save room. If you know something about a setting you want to see, such as its name, you can use the search field at the top right to filter what settings are shown.

You can determine how build settings are displayed by clicking Combined or Levels; in Figure 6-10, I've clicked Levels, in order to discuss what levels are. It turns out that not only does a *target* contain values for the build settings, but the *project* also contains values for the same build settings; furthermore, Xcode has certain built-in default build setting values. The Levels display shows all of these levels at once, so you can understand the derivation of the actual values used for every build setting.

To understand the chart, read from right to left. For example, the iOS default for the Build Active Architecture Only setting's Debug configuration (far right) is No. But then the project comes along (second column from the right) and sets it to Yes. The target (third column from the right) doesn't change that setting, so the result (fourth column from the right) is that the setting resolves to Yes.

If you wanted to change this value, you could, here and now. You could change the value at the project level or at the target level. I'm not suggesting that you should do so; indeed, you will rarely have occasion to manipulate build settings directly, as the defaults are usually acceptable. Nevertheless, you *can* change build setting values, and this is where you would do so. For details on what the various build settings are, consult Apple's documentation, especially the *Xcode Build Setting Reference*. Also, you can select a build setting and show Quick Help in the Utilities pane to learn more about it.

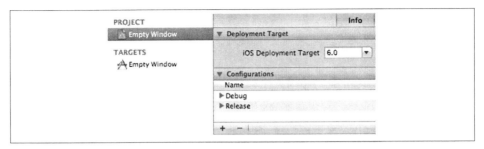

Figure 6-11. Configurations

Configurations

There are actually multiple lists of build setting values — though only one such list applies when a build is performed. Each such list is called a *configuration*. Multiple configurations are needed because you build in different ways at different times for different purposes, and thus you'll want certain build settings to take on different values under different circumstances.

By default, there are two configurations:

Debug
> This configuration is used throughout the development process, as you write and run your app.

Release
> This configuration is used for late-stage testing, when you want to check performance on a device.

Configurations exist at all because the project says so. To see where the project says so, edit the project and click Info at the top of the editor (Figure 6-11). Note that these configurations are just names. You can make additional configurations, and when you do, you're just adding to a list of names. The importance of configurations emerges only when those names are coupled with build setting values. Configurations can affect build setting values both at the project level and at the target level.

For example, return to the target build settings (Figure 6-10) and type "Optim" into the search field. Now you can look at the Optimization Level build setting. The Debug configuration value for Optimization Level is None: while you're developing your app, you build with the Debug configuration, so your code is just compiled line by line in a straightforward way. The Release configuration value for Optimization Level is Fastest, Smallest; when your app is ready to ship, you build it with the Release configuration, so the resulting binary is faster and smaller, which is great for your users installing and running the app on a device, but would be no good while you're developing the app because breakpoints and stepping in the debugger wouldn't work properly.

Schemes and Destinations

So far, I have said that there are configurations, and I have explained that you may need to switch between configurations in order to get the build setting values appropriate for your current purpose. But I have not said how the configuration is determined as you actually build. It's determined by a scheme.

A *scheme* unites a target (or multiple targets) with a build configuration, with respect to the purpose for which you're building. A new project comes by default with a single scheme, named after the project's single target. Thus the Empty Window project's single scheme is currently called Empty Window. To see it, choose Product → Edit Scheme. The scheme editor dialog opens. Make sure that Info at the top of the dialog is selected.

On the left side of the scheme editor are listed various actions you might perform from the Product menu. Click an action to see its corresponding settings in this scheme. The first action, the Build action, is different from the other actions, because it is common to all of them (the other actions all implicitly involve building); thus the Build action merely determines what target(s) will be built when each of the other actions is performed, and for our simple project this is trivial, because we've only one target and we always need it built. So, now consider the Run action.

When you click the Run action at the left, the editor displays the settings that will be used when you build and run (Figure 6-12). As you can see, the Build Configuration pop-up menu is set to Debug. That explains where the current build configuration comes from. At the moment, whenever you build and run, you're using the Debug build configuration and the build setting values that correspond to it, because you're using this scheme, and that's what this scheme says to do when you build and run.

Now dismiss the scheme editor, and consider how you might proceed if you wanted to build and run using the Release build configuration. (The Debug build configuration settings may affect the behavior of the built app, so you want to test the app as an actual user would experience it.) One way would be to return to the scheme editor and change the build configuration for the Run action for this scheme. Xcode makes this convenient: hold the Option key as you choose Product → Run (or as you click the Run button in the toolbar). The scheme editor appears, containing a Run button. So now you can make any changes you like, such as setting the Build Configuration pop-up menu to Release for the Run action, and proceed directly to build and run the app by clicking Run.

(If you're following along and you did make this change, open the scheme editor again and set the Build Configuration pop-up for the Run action in our Empty Window scheme back to Debug.)

On the other hand, if you were to find yourself often wanting to switch between building and running with the Debug configuration and building and running with the Release configuration, you might create a distinct, additional scheme that uses the Release debug configuration for the Run action. This is easy to do: in the scheme editor, click Duplicate

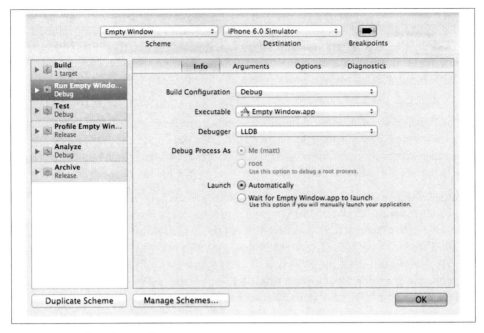

Figure 6-12. The scheme editor

Figure 6-13. The Scheme pop-up menu

Scheme. The name of the new scheme is editable; let's call it Release. Change the Build Configuration pop-up for the Run action in our new scheme to Release, and dismiss the scheme editor.

Now you have two schemes, Empty Window (whose build configuration for running is Debug) and Release (whose build configuration for running is Release). To switch between them easily, you can use the Scheme pop-up menu in the project window toolbar (Figure 6-13) before you build and run.

The Scheme pop-up menu lists each scheme, along with each destination on which you might run your built app. A *destination* is effectively a machine that can run your app. For example, you might want to run the app in the Simulator or on a physical device. There is no configuration of destinations; you are automatically assigned destinations,

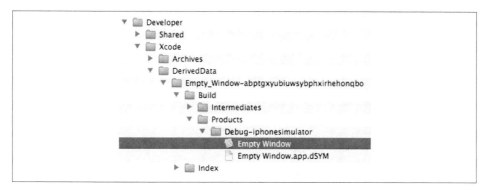

Figure 6-14. The built app, in the Finder

depending on what system your project is set to run on and what devices are connected to your computer.

Destinations and schemes have nothing to do with one another; your app is built the same way regardless of your chosen destination. The presence of destinations in the Scheme pop-up menu is intended as a convenience, allowing you to use this one pop-up menu to choose either a scheme or a destination, or both, in a single move. To switch easily among destinations without changing schemes, click near the right end of the Scheme pop-up menu. To switch among schemes, possibly also determining the destination (as shown in Figure 6-13), click near the left end of the Scheme pop-up menu. You can also switch among schemes or among destinations by using the scheme editor.

From Project to App

An app file is really a special kind of folder called a *package* (and a special kind of package called a *bundle*). The Finder normally disguises a package as a file and does not dive into it to reveal its contents to the user, but you can bypass this protection and investigate an app bundle with the Show Package Contents command. By doing so, you can study the internal structure of your built app bundle.

We'll use the Empty Window app that we built earlier as a sample minimal app to investigate. You'll have to locate it in the Finder; by default, it should be somewhere in your user *Library/Developer/Xcode/DerivedData* folder, as shown in Figure 6-14. (If you're using Mountain Lion, I presume you know how to reveal the user *Library* directory. In theory, you should be able to select the app under Products in Xcode's Navigation pane and choose File → Show in Finder, but there seems to be a long-standing bug preventing this.)

In the Finder, Control-click the Empty Window app, and choose Show Package Contents from the contextual menu.

Figure 6-15. Contents of the app package

Looking inside our minimal app bundle (Figure 6-15), we see that it contains these files:

Default.png and friends
> The three launch image files have been copied to the top level of the bundle, where they can be found for display at launch time.

Empty Window
> Our app's compiled code (the binary). When the app is launched, the binary is linked to the various frameworks, and the code begins to run (starting with the entry point in the main function).

Info.plist
> A configuration file in a strict text format (a *property list* file). It is derived from the project file *Empty Window-Info.plist*. It contains instructions to the system about how to treat and launch the app. For example, if our app had an icon, *Info.plist* would tell the system its name, so that the system could dive into the app bundle, find it, and display it. It also tells the system things like the name of the binary, so that the system can find it and launch the app correctly.

PkgInfo
> A tiny text file reading APPL????, signifying the type and creator codes for this app. The *PkgInfo* file is something of a dinosaur; it isn't really necessary for the functioning of an iOS app and is generated automatically. You'll never need to touch it.

InfoPlist.strings
> A text file intended for text appearing in our *Info.plist* that might need to be translated into different languages. It is copied directly from *InfoPlist.strings* in the project. We haven't edited this file, and our app currently appears only in English, so this file is of no interest at the moment (strings files are discussed in Chapter 9).

ViewController.nib
> Our app's only nib file. It contains instructions for generating the initial contents of our app's main window (currently just a gray rectangle). It is created ("compiled")

from the *ViewController.xib* file in the project; a *.xib* file and a *.nib* file are different forms of the same thing.

In real life, an app bundle will contain more files, but the difference will mostly be one of degree, not kind. For example, our project might have additional nib files, icon image files, and image or sound files. All of these would make their way into the app bundle.

You are now in a position to appreciate, in a general sense, how the components of our project are treated and assembled into an app, and what responsibilities accrue to you, the programmer, in order to ensure that the app is built correctly. The rest of this chapter outlines what goes into the building of an app from a project.

Build Settings

We have already talked about how build settings are determined. Xcode itself, the project, and the target all contribute to the resolved build setting values, some of which may differ depending on the build configuration. Before building, you, the programmer, will have already specified a scheme; the scheme determines the build configuration, the specific set of build setting values that will apply as this build proceeds.

Property List Settings

Your project contains a property list file that will be used to generate the built app's *Info.plist* file. The target knows what file it is because it is specified in the Info.plist File build setting. For example, in our project, the value of the Info.plist File build setting has been set automatically to *Empty Window/Empty Window-Info.plist*. (Take a look at the build settings and see!)

 Because the name of the file in your project from which the built app's *Info.plist* file is generated will vary, depending on the name of the project, I'll refer to it generically as the project's *Info.plist*.

The property list file is a collection of key–value pairs. You can edit it, and you may well need to do so. There are two main ways to edit your project's *Info.plist*:

- Select the *Info.plist* file in the Project navigator and edit in the editor. By default, the key names (and some of the values) are displayed descriptively, in terms of their functionality; for example, it says "Bundle name" instead of the actual key, which is CFBundleName. But you can view the actual keys by choosing Editor → Show Raw Keys & Values (you might have to click in the editor to enable this menu item).

- Edit the target, and click Info at the top of the editor. This pane shows effectively the same information as editing the *Info.plist* in the editor.

For a complete list of the possible keys and their meanings, see Apple's document *Information Property List Key Reference*. I'll talk more in Chapter 9 about property list settings that you're particularly likely to edit.

Nib Files and Storyboard Files

Every app that you write is likely to have at least one nib file (*.xib*) or storyboard file (*.storyboard*), and possibly more.

You edit a nib file to describe graphically some objects that you want instantiated when the nib file loads (Chapter 5). By breaking your interface into multiple nib files, you simplify the relationship between each nib file and your code; also, if nibs that aren't needed when your app launches aren't loaded until they *are* needed, you speed up your app's launch time, and you streamline your app's memory usage (because nib objects are not instantiated until the nib is loaded, and can then be destroyed when they are no longer needed).

A storyboard file is like many nib files in one: in it, you describe graphically the various interfaces (called *scenes*) that you want to appear as the user works with your app. Just as with nib files, a storyboard scene is transformed into actual interface only when it is needed for display, and the memory needed to maintain that interface can be given back when that interface is no longer showing.

The target knows about your nib files and storyboard files because they appear in its Copy Bundle Resources build phase. In the case of a nib file in *.xib* format, the file is not merely copied into the app bundle; Xcode also translates (compiles) it into a smaller *.nib* file (using the `ibtool` tool). Similarly, Xcode translates (compiles) a *.storyboard* file into a smaller *.storyboardc* file in the built app (again, using the `ibtool` tool).

Nib files located inside your app bundle are typically loaded when they are needed as the app runs, usually because code tells them to load. If you elect to use a storyboard as the basis of your main interface, however, it will need to load before any code has a chance to do so. Such a storyboard file is called the *main storyboard file*. This situation is handled through the *Info.plist* file; it contains a key "Main storyboard file base name" (`UIMainStoryboardFile`), and the system sees this and loads the designated storyboard file automatically as the app launches. (Instead of a main storyboard file, it is possible to have a main nib file that loads automatically when the app launches; this was the standard approach for apps created with Xcode 3.2.x and Xcode 4.0, but none of the current Xcode project templates exemplify this approach, so I don't discuss it in this edition of the book.)

A universal app — that is, an app that runs both on the iPad and on the iPhone — typically has nib files or storyboard files in pairs, one to be loaded on the iPad and the other to be loaded on the iPhone. Thus the app can have different basic interfaces on the two different types of device. Naming conventions and *Info.plist* keys allow the runtime to know which nib or storyboard to load depending on the device type. For example, a second *Info.plist* key, "Main storyboard file base name (iPad)" (UIMainStoryboardFile~ipad), specifies the storyboard file to be loaded at launch time on the iPad.

See Chapter 7 for more about editing nib files (and storyboard files) and how they create instances when your code runs. Full details on how nib files and storyboard files are loaded and why — in particular, their relationship to view controllers — appear in Chapter 19.

Other Resources

The three *Default.png* launch image files are examples of resource files. The target knows about them because they appear in its Copy Bundle Resources build phase. Such resources are copied more or less unchanged into the app bundle; I say "more or less" because it turns out that some files, such as *.png* files, may be optimized as they are copied when you build for a device.

In real life, you are likely to add further resources to your project, because you want your running app to be able to fetch them out of its bundle. For example, if your app needs to display a certain image, you'd add the image to your project and make sure it appears in the Copy Bundle Resources build phase. When the app runs, your code (or possibly the code implied by a loaded nib file) reaches into the app bundle, locates the image, and displays it (Chapter 15).

To add a resource to your project, start in the Project navigator and choose File → Add Files to Empty Window (or whatever the name of the project is). Alternatively, drag the resource from the Finder into the Project navigator. Either way, a dialog appears (Figure 6-16) containing a pane in which you make the following settings:

Copy items into destination group's folder (if needed)
> You should almost certainly check this checkbox. Doing so causes the resource to be copied into the project folder. If you leave this checkbox unchecked, your project will be relying on a file that's outside the project folder and that you might delete or change unintentionally. Keeping everything your project needs inside the project folder is far safer.

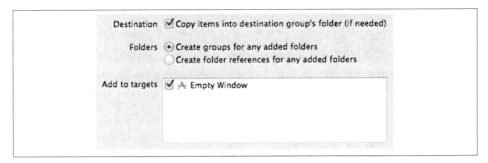

Figure 6-16. Options when adding a resource to a project

Folders

> This choice matters only if what you're adding to the project is a folder. In both cases, whether the folder is copied into the project folder depends on whether you checked the checkbox discussed in the previous paragraph; the difference is in how the project references the folder contents:

> *Create groups for any added folders*
>> The folder is expressed as a group within the Project navigator, but its contents all appear individually in the Copy Bundle Resources build phase, so they will all be copied individually into the app bundle.

> *Create folder references for any added folders*
>> The folder itself is shown in blue in the Project navigator and appears as a folder in the Copy Bundle Resources build phase; thus, the build process will copy the entire folder and its contents into the app bundle. This means that the resources inside the folder won't be at the top level of the bundle, but in a subfolder of it. Such an arrangement can be valuable if you have many resources and you want to separate them into categories (rather than clumping them all at the top level of the app bundle) or if the folder hierarchy among resources is meaningful to your app.

Add to Targets

> Checking this checkbox causes the resource to be added to the target's Copy Bundle Resources build phase. Thus you will almost certainly want to check it; why else would you be adding this resource to the project? But if this checkbox is unchecked and you realize later that a resource listed in the Project navigator needs to be added to the Copy Bundle Resources build phase, you can add it manually, as I described earlier.

An alternative way to copy resources from your project into the app bundle while building is through a custom Copy Files build phase that you add to your target. To make one, edit the target, switch to Build Phases, and click Add Build Phase (at the lower right) and choose Add Copy Files. A Copy Files build phase appears; open its triangle, and you'll find you can specify a custom path within the app bundle. For example, if you leave the Destination pop-up menu set to Resources and type "Pix" in the Subpath field, then any resources you add to this build phase will be copied into a folder called *Pix* in the app bundle.

A custom Copy Files build phase of this sort can be a good way of keeping resources organized by folder inside your app bundle; I frequently use it for this purpose. Bear in mind, however, that it is entirely up to you to make sure that the desired resources are placed inside the appropriate Copy Files build phase (and that they are not placed in the normal Copy Bundle Resources build phase, because if they are, you'll end up with two copies of the resource in your app bundle).

 If you copy resources into a subfolder of your app bundle, either with a folder reference or a custom Copy Files build phase, your code may have to specify that subfolder in order to fetch the resource from inside the app bundle.

Code

Code for two classes, AppDelegate and ViewController, was created for you when the project was created; the implementation files for these classes (*AppDelegate.m* and *ViewController.m*) appear in the target's Compile Sources build phase. If you create any further class files, you'll specify that they should be added to the target, and they too will then have their implementation files listed in the Compile Sources build phase. This (the contents of the Compile Sources build phase) is how your target knows what files to compile to create the app's binary.

The binary that results from compilation of these files is your project's *executable*, and is placed into the app bundle, with its name being by default the same as the name of the target. The system is able to locate the executable inside the app bundle and launch the app because the app bundle's *Info.plist* file has an "Executable file" key (`CFBundle-Executable`) whose value tells the system the name of the binary.

Besides the class code files you create (or that Xcode creates for you), your project contains a *main.m* file. This too is in the Compile Sources build phase; it had better be, because this file contains the all-important `main` function, the entry point to your app's code! Here are the `main` function's contents:

```
int main(int argc, char *argv[])
{
    @autoreleasepool {
        return UIApplicationMain(argc, argv, nil,
                          NSStringFromClass([AppDelegate class]));
    }
}
```

The main function is very simple, but it's crucial. It calls UIApplicationMain, which sets everything else in motion. UIApplicationMain is responsible for solving some tricky problems. As your app starts up, how will any of its code ever run? And how will its starting repertoire of instances ever be generated? UIApplicationMain takes care of these issues. First, your app is a C program, and a C program's main function is always called, to start the program running; thus, UIApplicationMain will in fact be called. Then, UIApplicationMain does the following things:

- It creates your very first instance — the shared application instance, subsequently accessible in code by calling [UIApplication sharedApplication]. The third argument to UIApplicationMain specifies, as a string, what class the shared application instance should be an instance of. If nil, which will usually be the case, the default class is UIApplication; but you can subclass UIApplication and specify that subclass here by substituting something like this (depending on what the subclass is called) as the third argument:

  ```
  NSStringFromClass([MyUIApplicationSubclass class])
  ```

- Optionally, it also creates your second instance — the application instance's *delegate*. Delegation is an important and pervasive Cocoa pattern, described in detail in Chapter 10, but for now let's just say that it is crucial that every app you write have an app delegate instance. The fourth argument to UIApplicationMain specifies, as a string, what class the app delegate instance should be. If this class is specified, as here, UIApplicationMain instantiates that class and ties that instance to the shared application instance as the latter's delegate. If this class is *not* specified (the fourth argument is nil), it is up to you to provide a delegate instance in some other way; since you cannot do this sufficiently early in code, you would have to do it through the loading of the main nib file. (Before iOS 5 and Xcode 4.2, this was in fact the usual way in which the app delegate was instantiated; but Apple has subsequently changed the default pattern so that the app delegate is generated in code by the call to UIApplicationMain.)

- If the *Info.plist* file specifies a main storyboard file or main nib file, UIApplicationMain loads it. (In the latter case, the nib file's owner is the shared application instance.)

- An app delegate instance has now been generated, either because UIApplicationMain instantiated it directly in response to the value of its fourth argument, or because `UIApplicationMain` loaded a main nib file which instantiated it. `UIApplicationMain` now turns to this app delegate instance and starts calling some of its code — in particular, it calls `application:didFinishLaunchingWith-Options:`, which is typically responsible, in turn, for displaying your app's initial interface. (Starting in iOS 6, the sequence of calls to the app delegate's code begins with `application:willFinishLaunchingWithOptions:` if it exists, as I'll explain in Chapter 19).

- The app is now launched and visible to the user. `UIApplicationMain` is still running (like Charlie on the M.T.A., `UIApplicationMain` never returns), and is now just sitting there, watching for the user to do something, maintaining the *event loop*, which will respond to user actions as they occur.

The call to `UIApplicationMain` is wrapped in some memory management functionality (the `@autoreleasepool` curly braces) that I'll explain in Chapter 12.

Finally, notice the file *Empty Window-Prefix.pch* in the Project navigator. This is your project's *precompiled header* file. It isn't listed in the Compile Sources build phase because it is actually compiled *before* that build phase; the target knows about it because it is pointed to by the Prefix Header build setting.

The precompiled header is a device for making compilation go faster. It's a header file; it is compiled once (or at least, very infrequently) and the results are cached (off in the *DerivedData* folder) and are implicitly imported by all your code files. So the precompiled header should consist primarily of `#import` directives for headers that never change (such as the built-in Cocoa headers); it is also a reasonable place to put `#defines` that will never change and that are to be shared by all your code, as I mentioned in Chapter 4.

The default precompiled header file imports `<Foundation/Foundation.h>` (the Core Foundation framework header) and `<UIKit/UIKit.h>` (the Cocoa framework). I'll talk in the next section about what that means.

Frameworks and SDKs

A *framework* is a library of compiled code used by your code. Most of the frameworks you are likely to use will be Apple's built-in frameworks; they are built-in in the sense that they are part of the system on the device where your app will run — they live in */System/Library/Frameworks* on the device, though you can't tell that on an iPhone or iPad because there's no way (normally) to view the file hierarchy directly.

However, your code needs to use these frameworks not only when running on a device but also when building on your computer. It also needs them when running in the Simulator. To make all this possible, part of the device's system — in particular, the part containing its frameworks — is duplicated on your computer, in the Developer folder.

Renaming Things

The name assigned to your project at creation time is used in many places throughout the project, leading beginners to worry that they can never rename a project without breaking something. But fear not! To rename a project, select the project listing at the top of the Project navigator, press Return to make its name editable, type the new name, and press Return again. Xcode presents a dialog proposing to change some other names to match, including the target, the built app, the precompiled header file, and the *Info.plist* — and, by implication, the build settings specifying these. You can check or uncheck any name, and click Rename; your project will continue to work correctly.

You can freely change the target name independently of the project name. It is the target name, not the project name, that is used to derive the name of the product and thus the bundle name, bundle display name, and bundle identifier mentioned earlier in this chapter. Thus, when you settle on a real name for your app, it might be sufficient to change the target name.

Changing the project name (or target name) does not automatically change the scheme name to match. There is no particular need to do so, but you can change a scheme name freely; choose Product → Manage Schemes and click on the scheme name to make it editable.

Changing the project name (or target name) does not automatically change the main group name to match. There is no particular need to do so, but you can freely change the name of a group in the Project navigator, because these names are arbitrary; they have no effect on the build settings or the build process. However, the main group is special, because (as I've already said) it corresponds to a real folder on disk, the folder that sits beside your project file at the top level of the project folder. You can change the group's name (changing the project name does not do this for you automatically), but you should not delete it, and beginners should not change the name of the folder on disk to which it corresponds, as that folder name is hard-coded into several build settings.

You can change the name of the project folder in the Finder at any time, and you can move the project folder in the Finder at will, because all build setting references to file and folder items in the project folder are relative.

This duplicated subset of the device's system is called an *SDK* (for "software development kit").

To use a framework in your code, you must do two things:

Import the framework's header
    A framework has a header file, which provides (usually by importing other header files within the framework) the interface information about classes in that frame-

work. Your code needs this information in order to *compile* successfully. You import the header with an appropriate `#import` directive.

Link to the framework

A framework is a package; you must instruct the build system to associate this package with your app's executable binary, so that your binary's calls to code within that framework can be routed into the framework's compiled code. This is necessary in order for your app to *run* successfully. Such an association is called *linking* the binary with the framework, and this association must be formed when building. You instruct the build system to do this by including the framework in the target's Link Binary With Libraries build phase.

You might think that linkage is impossible because the framework that we ultimately want to use is off on a target device somewhere. But linkage is path-based, and the path is determined relative to the current SDK. When the app launches on the device, there is no SDK, and the path becomes absolute.

So, for example, the linkage to the UIKit framework uses the path *System/Library/Frameworks/UIKit.framework*. This path is relative to the current SDK. Thus:

- When we build for a device, we link to the *System/Library/Frameworks/UIKit.framework* inside the current SDK, which is */Developer/Platforms/iPhoneOS.platform/Developer/SDKs/iPhoneOS6.1.sdk*.
- When we run on a device, there is no SDK, and the established linkage routes our code into the device's top-level */System/Library/Frameworks/UIKit.framework*.

By default, three frameworks are linked into your target:

Foundation

Many basic Cocoa classes, such as NSString and NSArray and others whose names begin with "NS," are part of the Foundation framework. The Foundation framework is imported in the precompiled header file (and, by default, in the headers of new classes that you create). In turn, it imports the Core Foundation headers and loads the Core Foundation framework as a subframework; thus, there is no need for you to import or link explicitly to the Core Foundation framework (which is full of functions and pointer types whose names begin with "CF," such as CFStringRef).

UIKit

Cocoa classes that are specialized for iOS, whose names begin with "UI," are part of the UIKit framework. The UIKit framework is imported in the precompiled header file (and by class code files that constitute the app templates, such as *AppDelegate.h*).

Core Graphics

The Core Graphics framework defines many structs and functions connected with drawing, whose names begin with "CG." It is imported by many UIKit headers, so you don't need to import it explicitly.

You might find that the three default frameworks are sufficient to your needs, or you might find that you need other frameworks to provide additional functionality. How will you know that a class or function you want to use resides outside the three default frameworks? You might get a clue from its name, which won't begin with "NS," "UI," or "CG", but more often, if you're like me, you'll be alerted by banging up against the compiler.

For example, let's say you've just found out about animation (Chapter 17) and you're raring to try it in your app. So, in your code, you create a CABasicAnimation:

```
CABasicAnimation* anim = [CABasicAnimation animation];
```

The next time you try to build your app, the compiler complains that CABasicAnimation is undeclared (and that it therefore can't make sense of `anim` either). That's when you realize you need to import a framework header. Near the start of the CABasicAnimation class documentation is a line announcing that it's in *QuartzCore.framework*. You might guess (correctly) that the way to import the main Quartz Core framework header is to put this line near the start of your implementation file:

```
#import <QuartzCore/QuartzCore.h>
```

This works to quiet the compiler. Remember, though, that using a framework requires two things; we've done only one of them. So your code *still* doesn't build. This time, you get a build error during the link phase of the build process complaining about `_OBJC_CLASS_$_CABasicAnimation` and saying, "Symbol(s) not found." That mysterious-sounding error merely means that you've forgotten to link your target to the Quartz Core framework.

To link your target to a framework, edit the target, click Summary at the top of the editor, and scroll down to the Linked Frameworks and Libraries section. (This is the same information that appears which you click Build Phases at the top of the editor and open the Link Binary with Libraries build phase.) Click the Plus button at the left just below the frameworks. A dialog appears listing the existing frameworks that are part of the active SDK. Select *QuartzCore.framework* and click Add. The Quartz Core framework is added to the target's Link Binary With Libraries build phase. (It also appears in the Project navigator; you might like to drag it manually into the Frameworks group, for the sake of neatness.) Now you can build (and run) your app.

You might wonder why the project isn't linked by default to *all* the frameworks, so that you don't have to go through this process every time you stray beyond the default three frameworks. It's just a matter of time and resources. Importing headers increases the size of your code; linking to frameworks slows down your app's launch time. You should link to only the frameworks needed for your code to run.

Where you import a framework header depends on how you intend to use it. It's simply a matter of scope. If a framework's classes are to be mentioned only within a single implementation file, then you can import it at the start of that implementation file. If you want to subclass one of the framework's classes (or adopt one of its protocols, Chapter 10), you'll need to import it at the start of the interface file that declares the subclass; in that case, every implementation file that imports this interface file imports the framework header, and there's no need to import the framework header separately in the implementation file. Of course, for maximum scope, you can simply import the framework header in the precompiled header file, making that framework available throughout your code.

CHAPTER 7

Nib Management

A *nib file*, or simply *nib*, is a file containing a drawing of a piece of your interface. The term *nib* is not really an English word (it has nothing to do with fountain pens or bits of chocolate); it is based on the file extension *.nib*, which originated as an acronym for "NeXTStep Interface Builder". Nowadays, you will usually develop your interface using a file format whose extension is *.xib*; when your app is built, your target's *.xib* files are translated ("compiled") into *.nib* format (Chapter 6). But a *.xib* file is still referred to as a nib file. I will speak of the same nib file as having either a *.xib* extension (if you're editing it) or a *.nib* extension (if it's in the built app).

You construct your program in two ways — writing code, and drawing the interface. But these are really two ways of accomplishing the same ends; drawing the interface *is* a way of writing code. When the app runs and your drawing of the interface in a nib file is loaded, it is translated into instructions for instantiating and initializing the objects in the nib file. You could equally have instantiated and initialized those same objects in code. (This point is crucial; see "Nib-Based Instantiation" (page 90).) Indeed, deciding whether to create an interface object in code or through a nib file is not always easy; each approach has its advantages. The important thing is to understand how interface objects drawn in a nib file are instantiated and connected to your code when the app runs. That's the subject of this chapter.

(Most of this chapter applies equally to storyboards. Don't skip this chapter on the grounds that you intend to use storyboards instead of nibs! Storyboards do not relieve you of the need to understand nib management. I'll discuss the particular nature and use of storyboards in Chapter 19.)

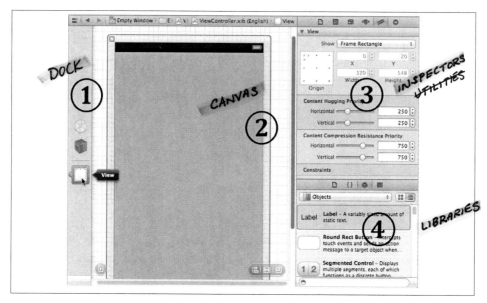

Figure 7-1. Editing a nib file

 Up through Xcode 3.2.x, nib editing was performed in a separate application, Interface Builder. Starting in Xcode 4, the functionality of Interface Builder was rolled into Xcode itself. Nevertheless, the Xcode interface for nib editing is still referred to as Interface Builder.

A Tour of the Nib-Editing Interface

Let's use an actual nib file to explore the Xcode nib-editing interface. In Chapter 6, we created a simple Xcode project, Empty Window; it contains a nib file, so we'll use that. In Xcode, open the Empty Window project, locate the *ViewController.xib* listing in the Project navigator, and click it to edit it.

Figure 7-1 shows the project window after selecting *ViewController.xib* and making some additional adjustments. The Navigator pane is hidden; the Utilities pane is showing. Within the Utilities pane, the Size inspector and the Object library are showing. The interface may be considered in four pieces:

1. At the left of the editor is the *dock*. In Figure 7-1, the dock is collapsed, showing the nib's top-level objects graphically. The dock can be expanded by dragging its right edge or by clicking the right-pointing triangle-in-a-square-in-a-circle at its lower right; then it shows *all* of the nib's objects hierarchically by name.

---

2. The remainder of the editor is devoted to the *canvas,* where you physically design your app's interface. The canvas portrays views in your app's interface and things that can contain views. (A *view* is an interface object, which draws itself into a rectangular area. The phrase "things that can contain views" is my way of including view controllers, which are represented in the canvas even though they are not drawn in your app's interface.)

3. The inspectors in the Utilities pane are where you view and edit details of the currently selected object.

4. The libraries in the Utilities pane, especially the Object library, are your source for interface objects to be added to the nib.

The Dock

The collapsed dock, as I've already said, shows the nib's *top-level objects.* To see what this means, you need first to envision the nib as containing objects. Some of these objects — those that represent views — are arranged in a hierarchy of containment. Objects that are contained by no other object are top-level objects.

A view can contain other views (its *subviews*) and can be contained by another view (its *superview*); for example, if we were to put a button into the view that occupies the canvas in Figure 7-1, the button would be a subview of that view, and that view would be the button's superview. One view can contain many subviews, which might themselves contain subviews. But each view can have only one immediate superview. Thus there is a hierarchical tree of subviews contained by their superviews with a single object at the top. The highest superview of any such hierarchy in the nib is a top-level object and appears in the dock. That's why the view object (labeled View in Figure 7-1) appears in this nib's dock: it is a view contained by no other view.

A top-level object, then, is either a view without a superview or else not a view at all. A nib file can actually portray two types of top-level object:

Placeholders (proxy objects)
  A placeholder, or proxy object, isn't actually in the nib. It represents an object that already exists in your app's code at the time the nib is loaded. Proxy objects are portrayed as top-level objects in a nib file chiefly so that you can provide communication between objects in your app's code and objects instantiated from the nib (by means of connections, discussed later in this chapter). You can't create or delete a proxy object; the dock is populated automatically with them. Proxy objects are shown above the dividing line in the dock.

Figure 7-2. The dock, expanded

Nib objects

A nib object is an object that is instantiated by the nib — that is, the instance it represents will be created when your code runs and the nib loads. You can create new nib objects. Top-level nib objects are shown below the dividing line in the dock.

The dock can be expanded (by clicking the right-pointing triangle-in-a-square-in-a-circle at its lower right); it then portrays objects by name, and shows as an outline the full hierarchy of objects in this nib (Figure 7-2). At present, expanding the dock may seem silly, because there is no hierarchy; all objects in this nib are top-level objects. But when a nib contains many levels of hierarchically arranged objects (plus, starting in iOS 6, their autolayout constraints — see Chapter 14), you're going to be very glad of the ability to survey them all in a nice outline, and to select the one you're after, thanks to the expanded dock. You can also rearrange the hierarchy here; for example, if you've made an object a subview of the wrong view, you can reposition it within this outline by dragging its name.

You can also select objects using the jump bar at the top of the editor. For example, if you click on the canvas background so that no object is selected, and the rightmost jump bar path component reads No Selection, then the entire hierarchy of objects in your nib is shown as a set of hierarchical menus off that path component (Control-6). Again, this may seem like small potatoes now, when your nib contains just three top-level objects and nothing more, but it will be valuable when you've many nib objects in a hierarchy.

The name by which a nib object is designated is its *label*. This name is meaningful to the nib file, not to your code. When the dock is expanded, each object is portrayed by its label, as shown in Figure 7-2. When the dock is collapsed, you can see a top-level object's label by hovering the mouse over it, as shown in Figure 7-1. If you find an object's label unhelpful, you can change it: select the object and edit the Label field in the Document section of the Identity inspector (Command-Option-3). Alternatively, select the object's label in the expanded dock and press Return to make it editable.

Canvas

The canvas provides a graphical representation of a top-level nib object along with its subviews, similar to what you're probably accustomed to in any drawing program. If a

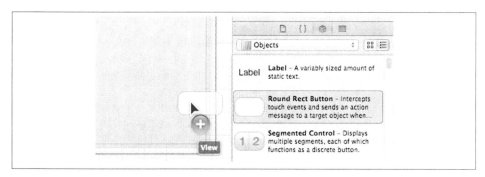

Figure 7-3. Dragging a button into a view

top-level nib object has a graphical representation (not every top-level nib object has one), you can click on it in the dock to display that representation in the canvas.

To remove the canvas representation of a top-level nib object, click the X at its upper left; this merely clears the representation from the canvas — it does not remove the top-level nib object from the dock (or from the nib), and of course you can always bring back the graphical representation by clicking that nib object in the dock again. On the other hand, the canvas is scrollable and automatically accommodates however many graphical representations it contains, so, rather than removing and restoring graphical representations, you can keep many graphical representations open in the canvas and scroll to see each one.

Our simple Empty Window project's *ViewController.xib* contains just one top-level nib object that has a graphical representation — the UIView destined to be the root view of the app's window, called View. The term "root" here implies that the view occupies the entire window. Because this view will be the root view of our app's window, any changes you make here will be reflected in the app's user interface when you run it. To see this, we're going to add a subview to it:

1. Ensure that the View in the dock is being displayed in the canvas.

2. Look at the Object library (Control-Option-Command-3). Click the second button in the segmented control to put the Object library into list view, if it isn't in list view already. Locate the Round Rect Button (you can type "button" into the filter bar at the bottom of the library as a shortcut).

3. Drag the Round Rect Button from the Object library into the View in the canvas (Figure 7-3). Don't accidentally drop the button onto the canvas background, outside of the View! This would cause the button to become a top-level object, which is not what you want. If that happens, select the button in the dock and press Delete, and try again.

A button now appears in the view in the canvas. The move we've just performed — dragging from the Object library into the canvas — is extremely characteristic; you'll do it often as you design your interface. Alternatively, select an object in the Object library and press Return to copy the object into your interface (you might first want to make sure the correct superview is selected in the canvas). Filtering by name with the filter bar also selects, and switching to the Object library with Control-Option-Command-3 also puts focus in the filter bar, so a rapid keyboard-only way to add a button to your interface is to type Control-Option-Command-3, "button", possibly Up or Down arrow to select Round Rect Button, Return.

Take a moment to play around with the button in the view in the canvas. Much as in a drawing program, the nib editor provides features to aid you in designing your interface. Here are some things to try:

- Select it: resizing handles appear.

- Resize it to make it wider: dimension information appears.

- Drag it near the edge of the view: a guideline appears, showing a standard margin space between the edge of the button and the edge of the view. Similarly, drag it near the center of the view: a guideline shows you when the button is centered.

- With the button selected, hold down the Option key and hover the mouse outside the button: arrows and numbers appear showing the distance between the button and the edges of the view. (If you accidentally clicked and dragged while you were holding Option, you'll now have two buttons. That's because Option-dragging an object duplicates it. Select the unwanted button and press Delete to remove it.)

- Shift-Control-click on the button: a menu appears, letting you select the button or whatever's behind it (in this case, the view).

(In Xcode 4.5 and later, you'll also see what look like guidelines or dimension bars when the button is selected and at rest. Those are autolayout constraints, to be discussed in Chapter 14.)

Let's prove that we really are designing our app's interface. We'll run the app to see that its interface has changed.

1. Make sure that the Breakpoints button in the project window toolbar is *not* selected, as we don't want to pause at any breakpoints you may have created while reading the previous chapter.

2. Make sure the destination in the Scheme pop-up menu is the iPhone Simulator.

3. Choose Product → Run (or click the Run button in the toolbar).

After a heart-stopping pause, the iOS Simulator opens, and presto, our empty window is empty no longer (Figure 7-4); it contains a round rect button! You can tap this button

Figure 7-4. The Empty Window app's window is empty no longer

with the mouse, emulating what the user would do with a finger; the button highlights as you tap it.

Inspectors and Libraries

There are four inspectors that appear only when you're editing a nib and apply to whatever object is selected in the dock or canvas:

Identity inspector (Command-Option-3)
> Far and away the most important section of this inspector is the first one, the Custom Class. The selected object's Class setting tells you the object's class, and you can use it to change the object's class. Some situations in which you'll need to change the class of an object in the nib appear later in this chapter.

Attributes inspector (Command-Option-4)
> Settings here correspond to properties and methods that you might use to configure the object in code. For example, changing the setting in the Background pop-up menu in the Attributes inspector for our view corresponds to setting the `backgroundColor` property for the view in code. Similarly, typing a value in the Title

field in the Attributes inspector for our button is like calling the button's set-Title:forState: method.

The Attributes inspector has sections corresponding to the selected object's class inheritance. For example, the UIButton Attributes inspector has three sections, because a UIButton is also a UIControl ("Control" in the inspector) and a UIView ("View" in the inspector).

 The correspondence between Attributes inspector settings and Objective-C methods is mostly a matter of guesswork. The Attributes inspector doesn't always tell you, and there's no way to see the code generated when the nib actually loads.

Size inspector (Command-Option-5)
The X, Y, Width, and Height fields determine the object's frame (its position and size within its superview), corresponding to its frame property in code; you can equally do this in the canvas by dragging and resizing, but numeric precision can be desirable.

What else you see in the Size inspector depends on whether this nib is using autolayout or not. Autolayout, a new iOS 6 feature, may be toggled on or off for a nib at file level: select the nib file in the Project navigator, show the File inspector (Command-Option-1), and check or uncheck Use Autolayout. The default for new nibs in Xcode 4.5 and later, and thus for our Empty Window project, is that autolayout is on. The possibilities for what you'll see in the rest of the Size inspector are:

Autolayout is off
The Size inspector displays an Autosizing box that corresponds to the autoresizingMask property, determining how the object will be repositioned and resized when its superview is resized; a delightful animation demonstrates visually the implications of your settings. The Arrange pop-up menu contains useful commands for positioning the selected object.

Autolayout is on
The Size inspector displays autolayout-related settings: the object's content hugging and content compression resistance priorities, plus any autolayout constraints involving this object. There is no Arrange pop-up menu, but effectively the same menu pops up from the leftmost segment of the little cartouche at the lower right of the canvas.

Connections inspector (Command-Option-6)
I'll discuss this later in this chapter.

There are two libraries that are of particular importance when you're editing a nib:

Object library (Control-Option-Command-3)
> This library, as we've already seen, is your source for objects that you want to add to the nib.

Media library (Control-Option-Command-4)
> This library lists media in your project, such as images that you might want to drag into a UIImageView or directly into your interface (in which case a UIImageView is created for you).

Nib Loading and File's Owner

A nib file is useless until your app runs and the nib file is *loaded*. If a nib is designated by the *Info.plist* key "Main nib file base name" (NSMainNibFile, see Chapter 6), it is loaded automatically as the app launches; but this is an exceptional case, and has now fallen out of favor — there are no automatically loaded main nib files in the current project templates. In general, nibs are loaded explicitly as needed while the app runs. In our Empty Window application, you can actually see where this happens, in *App-Delegate.m*:

```
self.viewController =
    [[ViewController alloc] initWithNibName:@"ViewController" bundle:nil];
```

That line of code does several things, one of which is that (for reasons to be explained more fully in Chapter 19) it causes the nib named @"ViewController" (i.e., the nib file compiled from *ViewController.xib*, the nib file we've been editing) to be loaded, and the resulting views to be put into our app's interface — which is how we were able to obtain the outcome shown in Figure 7-4.

So a nib is not loaded until the app runs and our code decides, at some point in the life of the app, that that nib is needed. This architecture is a source of great efficiency. For example, imagine our app has two complete sets of interface, and the user might never ask to see the second one. It makes obvious sense not to load a nib containing the second set of interface until the user *does* ask to see it. By this strategy, a nib is loaded when its instances are needed, and those instances are destroyed when they are no longer needed. Thus memory usage is kept to a minimum, which is important because memory is at a premium in a mobile device. Also, loading a nib takes time, so loading fewer nibs at launch time makes launching faster.

In order to use nibs (or storyboards, since a storyboard is like a collection of multiple nibs), it is crucial that you understand what happens when a nib loads.

When a nib loads, some already existing instance is designated its owner. A nib cannot load without an owner, and the owner must exist before the nib can load. The nib owner can be an instance of any class; it will often, though not necessarily, be a UIView-Controller instance, because a UIViewController already knows how to load a nib and manage a view that it contains (Chapter 19).

The three most common ways of telling a nib to load are:

`initWithNibName:bundle:`

> This is UIViewController's designated initializer. It tells the UIViewController to which it is sent to prepare to load the named nib *with itself as owner*. (That's what's happening in the line of code from *AppDelegate.m* that I quoted just a moment ago.) The moment of actual loading is automatically postponed until the nib is needed. I'll talk much more about this in Chapter 19.

`loadNibNamed:owner:options:`

> An NSBundle instance method. Usually, you'll direct it to [`NSBundle main-Bundle`]. Observe that the owner is one of the parameters. I'll show an example in the next section of this chapter.

`instantiateWithOwner:options:`

> A UINib instance method. The nib in question was specified when UINib was instantiated. Again, the owner is one of the parameters. An example appears in Chapter 21.

When a nib loads, its nib objects are instantiated, meaning its top-level nib objects and all deeper-level nib objects hierarchically dependent on them. (Proxy objects, by definition, exist before the nib loads; nib loading does not instantiate them.) For example, in our nib, the view is instantiated when the nib loads, bringing with it the button inside it. (Again, see "Nib-Based Instantiation" (page 90); make very sure you understand this point!) This is what nibs are for — to instantiate objects when they load. To put it another way, that is what nib loading is — it is the instantiation of the nib objects described in the nib. At that point, having loaded, the nib's work is done; the nib does not, for example, have to be "unloaded."

 The same nib can be loaded multiple times, generating an entirely new set of instances each time. A frequent beginner question is, "I have a view in a nib; how do I make multiple copies of this view?" The simple solution is to load that nib multiple times. This is common practice. For example, consider table view cells. Every "row" of a table view is a table view cell. Let's say there's a certain look and behavior you want each "row" to have. You design the cell in a nib of its own as a UITableView-Cell. If the table has to display ten rows, you load that nib ten times (Chapter 21).

Making and Loading a Nib

Let's create our own nib-loading code, illustrating at the same time the fact that any instance can be a nib's owner. To do so, we'll need a second nib file in our project.

First, we'll make the nib:

1. Choose File → New → File. The "Choose a template" dialog for files appears.
2. At the left of the dialog, under iOS (not Mac OS X!), choose User Interface, and select View in the main part of the dialog. Click Next.
3. For the Device Family pop-up menu, specify iPhone. Click Next.
4. In the Save dialog, name the file *MyNib*. Make sure you're saving into the Empty Window project folder, that the group is Empty Window, and that the target is Empty Window (and checked); all those things should be true by default. Click Create.

We've now created a nib file, *MyNib.xib*, containing a single top-level nib object, a UI-View. Look at *MyNib.xib* in the editor to see that this is true.

We'll also need an instance to act as the nib's owner. By the time our code will run, we will already have at least one instance we could use (the AppDelegate instance), but to illustrate the procedure fully, we'll create our own class whose sole purpose is to be instantiated so that this instance can act as the owner of the nib file as it loads:

1. In the Empty Window project in Xcode, choose File → New → File. The "Choose a template" dialog for files appears.
2. At the left of the dialog, under iOS (not Mac OS X!), select Cocoa Touch, and select Objective-C Class in the main part of the dialog. Click Next.
3. Name the file *MyClass*. The dialog also offers you a chance to specify what superclass the new class should be a subclass of. Make sure this is NSObject. Click Next.
4. In the Save dialog be sure that you're saving into the Empty Window project folder, that the group is Empty Window, and that the target is Empty Window (and checked); all those things should be true by default. Click Create.

We've now created files *MyClass.h* and *MyClass.m* declaring a class called MyClass.

Next, we'll write code that will load our new nib when the app runs. We need a place in our little app where our code is guaranteed to run: we'll use the AppDelegate instance method `application:didFinishLaunchingWithOptions:` in the file *AppDelegate.m*. Just before or after the call to `makeKeyAndVisible`, insert this code to instantiate MyClass and load *MyNib.nib* with that instance as its owner:

```
MyClass* mc = [MyClass new];
[[NSBundle mainBundle] loadNibNamed:@"MyNib" owner:mc options:nil];
```

Xcode will complain about this, because you can't speak of MyClass without importing its declaration, so after the existing `#import` at the start of this file, add this line:

```
#import "MyClass.h"
```

Now build and run the project. Our new *MyNib.nib* file loads, and its UIView top-level nib object is instantiated. Unfortunately, you can't *see* that this is true! That's because we haven't done anything to obtain the UIView instance that came into existence from the nib loading; in fact, what really happened is that the UIView instance popped into existence and popped right back out again, like a virtual particle in quantum field theory. The next section corrects this, and shows how to obtain visible proof that our nib is loading and that its top-level nib objects are being instantiated.

Outlet Connections

You know how to load a nib file, thus instantiating its top-level nib objects. But those instances are useless to you if you don't know how to get a *reference* to any of them in your code! Doing things with an object such as a label or a button or a text field or whatever (such as setting or getting the text it displays) is easy; but you have to be able to talk *to* the object in the first place, meaning that you need a reference to it, a variable that points to that instance (Chapter 3). Getting a reference to an instance that you created in code is trivial, because you assigned it to a variable at the time you created it (Chapter 5). But there's no such assignment when you load a nib; you just load it and that's the end of that:

```
[[NSBundle mainBundle] loadNibNamed:@"MyNib" owner:mc options:nil];
// no assignment??!! dude, where are my nib-created instances?
```

To refer in code to instances generated from nib objects when the nib loads, you need to have previously set up *an outlet connection from a proxy object in the same nib.*

A *connection* is a named unidirectional linkage from one object in a nib file (the connection's source) to another object in the same nib file (the connection's target). An *outlet* is a connection whose name corresponds to an instance variable in the source object. When the nib loads, and the target object is instantiated, the nib-loading mechanism *assigns the value of the instance variable to be the target object.* Thus the source object winds up with a reference to the target object as the value of one of its instance variables.

Connections can link any two objects in a nib file, but a proxy object as the source of a connection is special because it represents an object that exists before the nib loads. Thus an outlet from a proxy object causes an object that exists *before* the nib loads to end up with a reference to an object that doesn't exist until *after* the nib loads — an object that is in fact instantiated by the loading of the nib.

In the most typical configuration, the proxy object will be the File's Owner. The idea is that the instance that owns the nib has an instance variable, and the File's Owner in the nib has a corresponding outlet to a nib object; the nib loads, and the owner instance ends up with an instance variable that refers to the instance generated from the nib object (Figure 7-5).

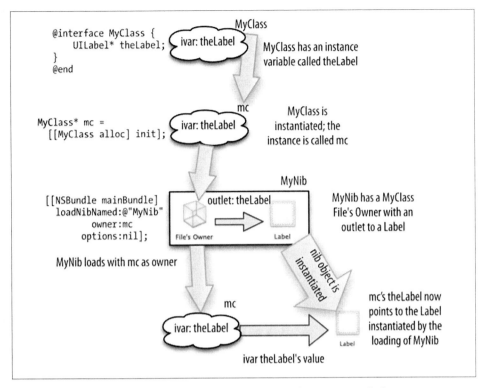

Figure 7-5. How an outlet provides a reference to a nib-instantiated object

The File's Owner top-level object in a nib file is a proxy for the instance that will be the nib's owner when the nib loads. To form a successful connection between this proxy object and a nib object, the nib needs to know the class of that instance. In the nib editor, *you must set the File's Owner's class to match the nib owner's class*. Obviously this means that you must know in advance, while editing the nib, what the class of the nib owner will be when the nib loads. But you do know this, because you (i.e. your code) is what's going to load the nib.

To demonstrate the use of an outlet connection, we'll implement exactly the schema illustrated in Figure 7-5, by making an outlet from the File's Owner to a nib object in *MyNib.xib*.

The nib owner is going to be a MyClass instance when the nib loads. As I've just said, we must tell the nib that this is the case. Let's do that first:

1. In Xcode, click *MyNib.xib* to edit it.

2. In the dock, select the File's Owner proxy object.

3. Show the Identity inspector (Command-Option-3). The Class, under Custom Class, is NSObject. Change this to MyClass. (If you type "My," the word "MyClass" should just appear, as it's the only class Xcode knows about whose name starts with "My." Accept this by pressing Return.)

Next, we need a nib object in *MyNib.xib* to make an outlet to. We already have one — the nib's existing top-level UIView. But this lacks visual impact, so we'll replace the UIView with a top-level UILabel, which will draw some text:

1. In Xcode, click *MyNib.xib* to edit it.

2. In the dock, select the View object and delete it.

3. Drag a Label object (UILabel) from the Object library into the canvas to become a new top-level object. Its graphical representation appears in the canvas.

4. Double-click the word "Label" in the label's graphical representation in the canvas and type "Hello, world!" Hit Return to stop editing; the label resizes to match the size of its text.

Now comes the really crucial part. We need two things, in two different places:

The instance variable
    In its code, MyClass needs an instance variable.

The outlet
    In the nib, the File's Owner proxy, representing a MyClass instance, needs an outlet pointing at the label — an outlet with the same name as the instance variable.

When the app runs and *MyNib.nib* is loaded with a MyClass instance as its owner, as we arranged in the code we've already written, those two pairs of things will be effectively equated:

- The MyClass instance will be equated with the File's Owner proxy in the nib, because it *will* be the nib's owner as it loads.

- MyClass's instance variable will be equated with the File's Owner outlet pointing at the label, because *they have the same name*.

 I'm simplifying. It isn't really the identity of an instance variable's name with that of the outlet that makes the match. It's more complicated than that; the match is made using key–value coding. The rigorous details appear in Chapter 12.

You thus need to work in two places at once: the nib, and MyClass's code. Before Xcode 4, this required working separately in two *different* places, Xcode (where the code was

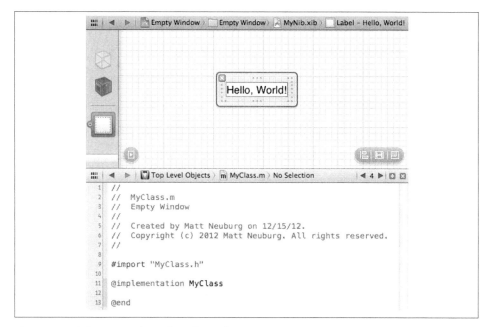

Figure 7-6. Editing a nib, with code in the assistant pane

edited) and Interface Builder (where the nib was edited). Nowadays, Xcode itself edits both the code and the nib, and furthermore you can see the code and the nib *at the same time*, all of which will make creating this pair of things, the instance variable and the outlet, much easier than it once was.

I want you now to arrange to see two things at once: *MyClass.m* (the MyClass implementation file, where we'll declare the instance variable) and *MyNib.xib* (where we'll create the outlet). You could use two project windows if you wanted, but for simplicity, let's use an assistant: while editing *MyNib.xib*, switch to Assistant view (View → Assistant Editor → Show Assistant Editor) as in Figure 7-6. If, when you showed the assistant pane, it didn't appear with MyClass's header file showing, use the jump bar in the assistant pane to make the assistant pane show *MyClass.m*: for example, in the first path component choose Manual → Top Level Objects → MyClass.m. If the assistant pane is beside the nib editor pane rather than below it, choose View → Assistant Editor → All Editors Stacked Vertically.

In *MyClass.m* in the assistant pane, at the start of the implementation section, create curly braces and declare a UILabel instance variable (and save):

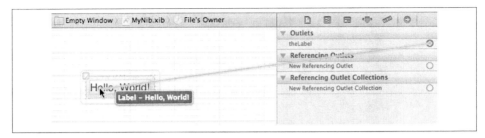

Figure 7-7. Connecting an outlet from the Connections inspector

```
@implementation MyClass
{
    IBOutlet UILabel* theLabel;
}
@end
```

The term `IBOutlet` is linguistically meaningless; it is `#defined` as an empty string, so it is deleted by the preprocessor before the compiler ever sees it. It's purely a hint to Xcode to make it easy for you to create the outlet. Xcode responds by displaying an empty circle in the gutter to the left of the `IBOutlet` line; this indicates that although we're speaking of an outlet in our code, no corresponding outlet connection yet exists in a nib. We'll fix that in a moment.

We have typed the instance variable as a `UILabel*`, because we happen to know that this is the type of object that this instance variable will be pointing to; we could also use `id`, or any superclass of UILabel. If we do not use one of these alternatives (`id`, UILabel, or a superclass of UILabel), we will not be able to form the connection to a UILabel in the nib.

We have accomplished half our task: we've made the instance variable. Now we're ready for the other half, namely, to make the outlet connection. There are several ways to do this, so I'll just pick one for now and demonstrate the others later:

1. Select File's Owner in the nib (which, you remember, represents a MyClass instance) and switch to the Connections inspector (Command-Option-6). Lo and behold, the name of our instance variable, `theLabel`, is listed here! This is the work of the `IBOutlet` hint we created earlier.

2. Click in the empty circle to the right of `theLabel` in the Connections inspector, drag to the Label object in the canvas (Figure 7-7), and release the mouse. (A kind of elastic line follows the mouse as you drag from the circle to show that you're creating a connection.)

With the File's Owner object selected, look again at the Connections inspector; it shows that `theLabel` is connected to the Label nib object, and if you hover the mouse over the filled circle at the right, the label object in the nib is highlighted. And look at the `IBOutlet` line in *MyClass.m*; the circle in the gutter is now filled in, and if you click that filled circle, the label is specified in a pop-up menu next to the circle, and the label object in the nib is highlighted. Mission accomplished! We have made an outlet connection in the nib from the File's Owner proxy (representing a MyClass instance) to the Label object, and this outlet connection has the same name as the instance variable `theLabel` in MyClass's code.

Therefore, when the nib loads and a MyClass instance is the nib's owner, its `theLabel` instance variable will be set to the UILabel object that will be instantiated through the loading of the nib. To prove that this is indeed the case, we'll use that instance variable in our code to do something dramatic. In particular, we'll stick the UILabel into our window, thus making it visible. Its visibility will prove that the nib is loading and that the instance variable is being set by the outlet.

Return to *AppDelegate.m* and modify the nib-loading code like this (you added the first two lines earlier):

```
MyClass* mc = [MyClass new];
[[NSBundle mainBundle] loadNibNamed:@"MyNib" owner:mc options:nil];
UILabel* lab = [mc valueForKey: @"theLabel"];
[self.window.rootViewController.view addSubview: lab];
lab.center = CGPointMake(100,100);
lab.frame = CGRectIntegral(lab.frame);
```

(We haven't written an accessor method in MyClass for `theLabel`, so to save time I used key–value coding.) Build and run the app. The words "Hello, world!" appear! This proves that our outlet worked. We loaded a nib and, using an outlet, we obtained a reference to a nib object and were able to manipulate that object, putting it into our interface.

 Making an instance variable and giving it an `IBOutlet` hint, but forgetting to connect the outlet to anything in the nib, is an unbelievably common beginner (and not-so-beginner) mistake. Had we made this mistake, our code would have run without error, but "Hello, world!" would not appear in the interface because `lab` would be nil. The unfilled circle that appears in the gutter next to an `IBOutlet` line for which no corresponding nib connection exists is your only clue that something's amiss, so watch for it.

More Ways to Create Outlets

I said a moment ago that there were other ways to create the outlet. Let's try some of them. Return to our assistant-paned nib editor, select the File's Owner, switch to the

Figure 7-8. Connecting an outlet by Control-dragging from the source object

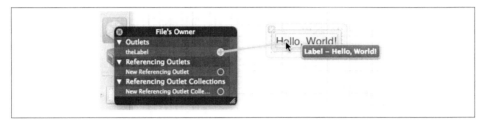

Figure 7-9. Connecting an outlet by dragging from the Connections HUD

Connections inspector, and delete the outlet by clicking the little X to its left. We're going to make this outlet again, a different way:

1. Select the File's Owner in the dock.

2. Hold down the Control key and drag from the File's Owner to the label. An elastic line follows the mouse. Release the mouse.

3. A little window (called a HUD, for "heads-up display") appears, titled Outlets, listing `theLabel` as a possibility (Figure 7-8). Click `theLabel`.

Once again, look at the Connections inspector with the File's Owner selected to confirm that this worked. You can even build and run the project again, to prove it to yourself if you're in any doubt. Now delete the outlet *again*; we're going to make this outlet in yet a *different* way:

1. Select the File's Owner in the dock.

2. Control-click the File's Owner in the dock. A HUD appears, looking a lot like the Connections inspector.

3. Drag from the circle to the right of `theLabel` to the label (Figure 7-9). Release the mouse.

Now delete the outlet *again*; we're going to make this outlet in *another* way. This time, we're going to operate from the point of view of the label. The Connections inspector shows all connections emanating *from* the selected object; it also shows all connections linking *to* the selected object. So, select the label and look at the Connections inspector.

It lists "New Referencing Outlet." This means an outlet *from* something else *to* the thing we're inspecting, the label. So:

1. From the circle at the right of "New Referencing Outlet," drag to the File's Owner. An elastic line follows the mouse. Release the mouse.

2. A HUD saying `theLabel` appears. Click it.

Confirm that, once again, we've made an outlet from the File's Owner to the label. (And we could also have done the same thing by Control-clicking the label to start with, to show its Connections HUD.) Now delete the outlet *again*; we're going to make this outlet in *another* way. This time, we're going to start with the label, but (hold onto your hat) we're going to connect directly to the *code* which is sitting in the assistant pane:

1. Select the label.

2. Make sure that *MyClass.m* is showing in the assistant pane and that you can see the `IBOutlet` line declaring the instance variable `theLabel`.

3. Hold down the Control key and drag from the label in the nib *across the barrier between panes* to that line of code. An elastic line follows the mouse. When you've got the mouse positioned correctly, the words Connect Outlet will appear. Release the mouse.

Yet again, confirm that we've successfully made the desired outlet. And you could also have done the same thing in reverse; starting with the circle at the left of the `IBOutlet` line in the code, you can drag (without holding Control) to the label in the nib.

Now delete the outlet one last time, and (get this) *delete the line of code* declaring the instance variable (but leave the curly braces). We're going to create the outlet and the instance variable declaration, all in a single amazing move:

1. Select the label.

2. Make sure *MyClass.m* is showing in the assistant pane.

3. Hold down the Control key and drag from the label in the nib to the area within the curly braces in the code. An elastic line follows the mouse. The words Insert Outlet or Outlet Collection appear. Release the mouse.

4. A little HUD appears, asking for the name of the instance variable that's about to be created. Call it `theLabel` (and make sure the type is UILabel), and press Return. The `IBOutlet` line declaring the instance variable is created, and the outlet is formed to match it.

Connecting to Code is an Illusion

Making an outlet by connecting directly between code and an interface object in the nib is extremely cool and convenient, but coolness and convenience do not relieve you of the necessity of understanding what an outlet is and how it works. No matter what physical gesture you make in Xcode, and no matter how much Xcode may give you the illusion that you are somehow connecting an object in the nib to the code, that's not really the case. There is no connection between the instance variable in the code and the object in the nib; there is no identity between the instance variable in the code and the outlet connection in the nib. There are always, if an outlet is to work properly, *two distinct and separate things* — an instance variable in a class, and an outlet in the nib, *with the same name* and *coming from an instance of that class*. It is the identity of the names that allows the two to be matched at runtime when the nib loads, so that the instance variable is properly set at that moment. Xcode tries to help you by enforcing this identity of names and by indicating that the connection should work when the code runs, but it is not in fact magically connecting the code to the nib.

More About Outlets

All our examples so far have involved a proxy object, but an outlet connection can connect any two objects in the nib. The only requirement is that the source object be of a class that has an instance variable whose type matches the class of the target object. This class might be your own custom class with an ivar that you gave it, as in our earlier examples, or it might be a built-in Cocoa class with a built-in instance variable that can be used as an outlet.

 Nothing in the documentation for a built-in Cocoa class tells you which of its instance variables are available as outlets. In general, the only way to learn what outlets a built-in class provides is to examine a representative of that class in a nib.

It is also possible to create an *outlet collection*. This is an NSArray instance variable matched by multiple connections to objects of the same type. For example, suppose a class contains this instance variable declaration:

```
IBOutletCollection(UILabel) NSArray* labels;
```

Then it is possible to form multiple `labels` outlets from an instance of that class in a nib, each one to a different UILabel in that nib. When the nib loads, those UILabel instances become the elements of the NSArray `labels`. The order in which the outlets are formed is the order of the elements in the array. This turns out to be particularly useful when forming outlets to autolayout constraints; examples will appear in Chapter 20 and Chapter 23.

Action Connections

Having explored outlet connections, we should also discuss the other kind of connection, action connections.

An *action* is a message emitted automatically by a Cocoa UIControl interface object (a *control*) when the user does something to it, such as tapping the control. The various user behaviors that will cause a control to emit an action message are called *events*. To see a list of possible events, look at the UIControl class documentation, under "Control Events." For example, in the case of a UIButton, the user tapping the button corresponds to the UIControlEventTouchUpInside event. In the case of a UITextField, the user typing or deleting or cutting or pasting corresponds to the UIControlEventEditing-Changed event. A complete list of UIControls and what events they report is provided in Chapter 11, and each type of control is thoroughly dealt with in later chapters, especially Chapter 25.

An action message, then, is a way for your code to respond when the user does something to a control in the interface, such as tapping a button. But your code will not receive an action message from a control unless you explicitly make prior arrangements with that control. You must tell the control what event should trigger an action message, what instance to send the action message to, and what the action message's name should be. There are two ways to make this arrangement: in code, or in a nib.

Either way, we're going to need a method for the action message to call. There are three standard signatures for a method that is to be called through an action message; the most commonly used one takes a single parameter, which will be a reference to the object that emitted the action message. (For full details, see Chapter 11.) So, for example, you could have a method like this (let's agree to put it in the implementation section for ViewController, in *ViewController.m*):

```
- (void) buttonPressed: (id) sender {
    UIAlertView* av = [[UIAlertView alloc] initWithTitle:@"Howdy!"
                                                 message:@"You tapped me."
                                                delegate:nil
                                       cancelButtonTitle:@"Cool"
                                       otherButtonTitles:nil];
    [av show];
}
```

Now, as I mentioned a moment ago, it is possible to arrange in code for `button-Pressed:` to be called when the user taps a button. In particular, if b is a reference to the button, then some ViewController code could say:

```
[b addTarget:self action:@selector(buttonPressed:)
        forControlEvents:UIControlEventTouchUpInside];
```

That code means: "Hey there, button! When the user taps on you (`UIControlEvent-TouchUpInside`), send me (`self`) a `buttonPressed:` message." (See Chapter 3 if you've forgotten about the `@selector` directive.) Of course, such an instruction assumes that this object (`self`) really does implement a `buttonPressed:` method. (If it doesn't, then when the user taps the button, the app will crash.)

However, instead of doing that, we're going to use the existing button in *View-Controller.xib* and arrange *in the nib* for its action message to be `buttonPressed:` and to be sent to a ViewController instance. We're going to form an *action connection* in the nib. We can do this because, as I've already mentioned, a ViewController instance is the owner of *ViewController.nib* when it loads. The template has already set the File's Owner proxy in *ViewController.xib* to be of the ViewController class (look at it and see!). So we can create an action connection in the nib from the button to the File's Owner, as a way of communicating between the button and the ViewController instance that loads the nib when the app runs.

As with outlets, there are several ways to do this; I'll just show you the main ones and leave you to discover the rest. (They are all directly comparable to the many ways of creating an outlet connection.)

1. We need a hint, in our code, that a method with the expected signature exists. This hint involves substituting IBAction for the method's void return type. (The substitution is legal because IBAction is #defined as void; Xcode can see the hint in your code, but the preprocessor will turn IBAction back to void before the compiler ever sees it.) So, in *ViewController.m*, change the first line of our `buttonPressed:` method implementation to look like this (and save the file):

   ```
   - (IBAction) buttonPressed: (id) sender {
   ```

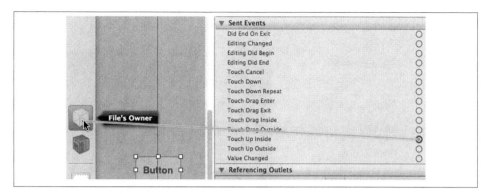

Figure 7-10. Connecting an action from the Connections inspector

This causes an empty circle to appear in the gutter next to the IBAction line.

2. Now edit *ViewController.xib*, select the button in the window, and look at the Connections inspector. The event for which we'd like to send the action message is Touch Up Inside. Drag from its circle to the File's Owner nib object in the dock, which is to receive the message (Figure 7-10). Release the mouse.

3. A little window listing possible ViewController action methods appears; in this case, it lists only buttonPressed:. Click on buttonPressed: to form the connection.

To see that the action connection has been formed, look at the Connections inspector. If you select the button, the Connections inspector reports that the button's Touch Up Inside event is connected to the File's Owner's buttonPressed: method. If you select the File's Owner object, the Connections inspector reports a Received Action where buttonPressed: is called by the Rounded Rect Button's Touch Up Inside event. Finally, look at the code in *ViewController.m*; the circle next to the IBAction line is filled, and you can click it to reveal that the connection is from the button.

Finally, to make assurance doubly sure, you can also build and run the project to confirm that the action connection is working. In the running app, the button inside the window now actually does something when the user taps it! It summons an alert.

As with outlets, we could have formed the action connection by Control-dragging from the button directly to the File's Owner, instead of involving the Connections inspector. If you *just* Control-drag, Interface Builder assumes a default event for you (in this case, it would assume Touch Up Inside). If that isn't what you want, start by Control-clicking on the button to summon a HUD version of the Connections inspector, and drag from the desired event's circle just as you would do from the real Connections inspector.

As with outlets, you can also form the action connection directly from nib to code. (But please reread "Connecting to Code is an Illusion" (page 164); that warning applies

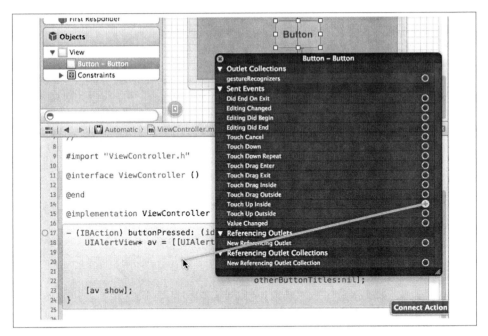

Figure 7-11. Connecting an action to a method implementation

equally to action connections.) In Figure 7-11, we've Control-clicked the button in the nib to summon its Connections HUD, and dragged from the Touch Up Inside circle to the buttonPressed: implementation in code. And we could equally have gone the other way, dragging from the unfilled circle next to the IBAction line in the code to the button in the nib.

But wait, there's more! Instead of writing the action method ahead of time, you can ask Xcode to stub it out for you. To do so, Control-drag from the nib to an empty spot in ViewController's implementation section; the words Insert Action appear, and when you release the mouse, a dialog appears, letting you specify the name of the action method, the number of arguments it should take, and the control event to be used as a trigger. Xcode inserts the method implementation, but doesn't put any code between the curly braces; it's smart, but not smart enough to guess what you want the method to do!

Additional Initialization of Nib-Based Instances

By the time a nib finishes loading, its instances are fully fledged; they have been initialized and configured with all the attributes dictated through the Attributes and Size inspectors, and their outlets have been used to set the values of the corresponding instance variables. Nevertheless, you might want to append your own code to the initialization process as an object is instantiated from a loading nib. Most commonly, to do this, you'll implement awakeFromNib (possibly subclassing a Cocoa class in order to do so). The awakeFromNib message is sent to all nib-instantiated objects just after they are instantiated by the loading of the nib: at the point where this happens, the object has been initialized and configured and its connections are operational.

For example, our Empty Window app is loading *MyNib.xib*, extracting a UILabel from it, and inserting that label into our interface; the result is that the words "Hello, world!" appear in our window. Let's modify the behavior of this UILabel so that it does some additional self-initialization in code. To do that, we will need a class of our own to which our UILabel will belong. Clearly, this needs to be a UILabel subclass. So:

1. In Xcode, choose File → New → File and specify that you want a Cocoa Touch Objective-C class. Click Next.

2. Call the new class MyLabel. Make it a subclass of UILabel. Click Next.

3. Make sure you're saving into the project folder, with the Empty Window group and the Empty Window target (this should be right by default). Click Create.

4. In *MyLabel.m*, somewhere in the implementation section, implement awakeFrom-Nib:

```
- (void) awakeFromNib {
    [super awakeFromNib];
    self.text = @"I initialized myself!";
    [self sizeToFit];
}
```

5. That code won't apply to the label in *MyNib.xib* unless that label *is* a MyLabel, so edit *MyNib.xib* and change the label's class to MyLabel in the Identity inspector.

Now build and run the project. Instead of "Hello, world!" we now see "I initialized myself!" in the window.

Mac OS X Programmer Alert

If you're an experienced Mac OS X programmer, you may be accustomed to rarely or never calling super from awakeFromNib; doing so used to raise an exception, in fact. In iOS, you must always call super in awakeFromNib. Another major difference is that in Mac OS X, a nib owner's awakeFromNib is called when the nib loads, so it's possible for an object to be sent awakeFromNib multiple times; in iOS, awakeFrom-Nib is sent to an object only when that object is itself instantiated from a nib, so it can be sent to an object a maximum of once.

Sometimes, you might need to interfere with a nib object's initialization at an even earlier stage. If this object is a UIView or UIViewController (or a subclass of either), you can implement `initWithCoder:`. In your implementation, be sure to call `super` and return `self` as you would do in any initializer. Your purpose here would typically be to initialize additional instance variables that your subclass has declared, as with any initializer.

Here, for example, is an implementation of MyLabel that declares an instance variable that is an int called _num and manipulates it first in `initWithCoder:` and then in `awakeFromNib`, thus proving that the two are called in that order:

```
@implementation MyLabel
{
    int _num;
}

- (id) initWithCoder:(NSCoder *)aDecoder {
    self = [super initWithCoder:aDecoder];
    if (self) {
        self->_num = 42;
    }
    return self;
}

- (void) awakeFromNib {
    [super awakeFromNib];
    self.text = [NSString stringWithFormat: @"The answer is %i", self->_num];
    [self sizeToFit];
}
@end
```

That's trivial and unnecessary, but it illustrates the principle.

CHAPTER 8

Documentation

> *Knowledge is of two kinds. We know a subject*
> *ourselves, or we know where we can find*
> *information upon it.*
>
> —Samuel Johnson, *Boswell's Life of Johnson*
>
> *You don't remember Cocoa; you look it up!*
>
> —Anonymous programmer, cited by
> Beam and Davidson, *Cocoa in a Nutshell*

No aspect of Cocoa programming is more important than a fluid and nimble relationship with the documentation. There is a huge number of built-in classes, with many methods and properties and other details. Apple's documentation, whatever its flaws, is the definitive official word on how you can expect Cocoa to behave and on the contractual rules incumbent upon you in working with this massive framework whose inner workings you cannot see directly.

The Xcode documentation installed on your machine comes in large chunks called *documentation sets* (or *doc sets*, also called *libraries*). You do not merely install a documentation set; you subscribe to it, so that when Apple releases a documentation update (because a new version of iOS has been released, or because there has been an incremental revision of the documentation), you can obtain the updated version.

When you first install Xcode, the bulk of the documentation is *not* installed on your machine; viewing the documentation in the documentation window (discussed in the next section) requires an Internet connection, so that you can see the online docs at Apple's site. Therefore, you should start up Xcode immediately after installation to let it download and install your initial documentation sets. The process can be monitored, to some extent, in the Downloads pane of the Preferences window (under Documentation); you can also specify here whether you want updates installed automatically or whether you want to click Check and Install Now manually from time to time. This is also where you specify which doc sets you want; I believe that the iOS 6.1 Documentation Set and the Xcode 4.6 Developer Library are all you need for iOS development. You may have to provide your machine's admin password when a doc set is first installed.

The Documentation Window

Your primary access to the documentation is in Xcode, through the Documentation tab of the Organizer window (Window → Organizer and then click Documentation, or Help → Documentation and API Reference). I'll refer to this as the *documentation window*, even though it's really an aspect of the Organizer window.

The documentation window behaves basically as a glorified web browser, because the documentation consists essentially of web pages. Indeed, most of the same pages can be accessed at Apple's developer site, *http://developer.apple.com*. And any page open in the documentation window can be opened instead in your web browser: Control-click for the contextual menu and choose Open Page in Browser. Notice too the contextual menu for links within a documentation window, such as Copy Link and Open Link in Browser. When you're trying to figure something out, the ability to spawn off a page as a secondary window in a browser while you go on searching in the Xcode documentation window can be very useful.

Each doc set has a home page, which you access from the Browse navigator (Editor → Explore Documentation) or from the first component of the jump bar. A typical home page presents a full list of documents, which can be sorted by column and filtered by keyword. Some home pages, such as the iOS 6.1 Documentation Set home page, also have a broad categorical list down the left side, which can similarly be used to filter the document list. In practice I rarely use these home pages, though they can come in handy when you're looking for broad topic introductions (click Guides on the left). The Browse navigator (and the jump bar) can also be used to explore a doc set by category.

When you encounter a documentation page to which you're likely to want to return, make it a bookmark (Editor → Add Bookmark). Bookmarks are accessed through the Bookmarks navigator (Editor → Documentation Bookmarks). Documentation bookmark management is simple but effective: you can rearrange bookmarks or delete a bookmark, and that's all.

My chief way into the documentation — and, I suspect, most users' chief way — is by searching (Editor → Search Documentation). Type a term into the search field (Help → Documentation and API Reference, Shift-Option-Command-?). Click the magnifying glass to choose Show Find Options if they aren't showing. It's important to set these options correctly:

Hits must
> This pop-up menu determines how your search terms are understood. Your choices are "contain search term", "start with search term", and "match search term". It's good

to be nimble about changing this setting as needed. For example, if you are typing the start of the name of a class you want to search for, do a "start with" search, not a "contain" search.

Languages
Check only those languages you're likely to be interested in (probably Objective-C and C).

Doc Sets
Check only those doc sets that interest you; if you're doing iOS development, for example, uncheck any Mac OS X libraries to eliminate inapplicable and duplicate results.

Enter a search term in the search field, and pause. Search results are displayed in categories, in relevance order, in the navigation pane; click a result to view that page. One would like to perform this move — from seeing a list of results in the navigation pane to viewing the page for one of those results — without using the mouse, but I haven't discovered a reliable way to do that.

It's important also to be able to switch nimbly from editing code to consulting the documentation on a term used in that code. Here are two ways:

- Select a term in the editor (or anywhere else that you can select text) and choose Help → Search Documentation for Selected Text (Control-Option-Command-/). This command switches to the documentation window and enters the selected term into the search field, performing the search using the current find options, in a single move.

- Hold Option and hover the mouse over a likely term in code, until the cursor becomes a question mark (and the term turns blue with a dashed underline); then rapidly Option-double-click the term. This, in my opinion, is much the best way, because it bypasses the search field altogether and actually performs the search for the correct term in the correct class in the main documentation display.

  You can perform the same move during code completion (Chapter 9): select one of the terms offered as a completion, and click the More link at the bottom of the pop-up menu.

Don't confuse searching the documentation with finding within the current page. To find within the current documentation page, make sure the focus is within the page itself (probably by clicking in the page), and then use the Edit → Find menu commands. Command-F summons a find bar, as in Safari.

A major difference between the display of a documentation page in Xcode and the display of the same page as a web page at *http://developer.apple.com* is that the latter often shows a Table of Contents column at the left side. In Xcode, this Table of Contents column is suppressed, which saves space, but makes it harder to get a sense for where you are in a document or a set of related documents. The intention is presumably that you should use the jump bar both to get your bearings and to navigate, though personally I find this approach clumsy and frustrating.

Class Documentation Pages

In the vast majority of cases, your target documentation page will be the documentation for a class. I have frequently spoken already of the importance of class documentation pages. A common move on your part will be to search on a class name in the documentation window. If you search on, say, NSString, the search result whose title is *NSString Class Reference* is the class documentation for NSString.

Let's pause to notice the key features of a class documentation page. I'll use UIButton as an example (Figure 8-1):

Inherits from
> Lists, and links to, the chain of superclasses. One of the biggest beginner mistakes is failing to read the documentation up the superclass chain. A class inherits from its superclasses, so the functionality or information you're looking for may be in a superclass. You won't find out about addTarget:action:forControlEvents: from the UIButton class page; that information is in the UIControl class page. You won't find out that a UIButton has a frame property from the UIButton class page; that information is in the UIView class page.

Conforms to
> Lists, and links to, the protocols implemented by this class. Protocols are discussed in Chapter 10.

> Methods injected into a class by a category (Chapter 10) are often *not* listed on that class's documentation page and can be very difficult to discover. For example, awakeFromNib isn't mentioned in the document for UIButton or for any of its superclasses or protocols. This is a major weakness in Apple's organization and display of the documentation. A third-party documentation display application such as AppKiDo can be helpful here (*http://appkido.com*).

Framework
> Tells what framework this class is part of. Your code must link to this framework in order to use this class (see Chapter 6).

Availability
> States the earliest version of the operating system where this class is implemented. For example, EKEventViewController, along with the whole EventKit framework (consisting of classes for querying the user's calendar; see Chapter 32) wasn't

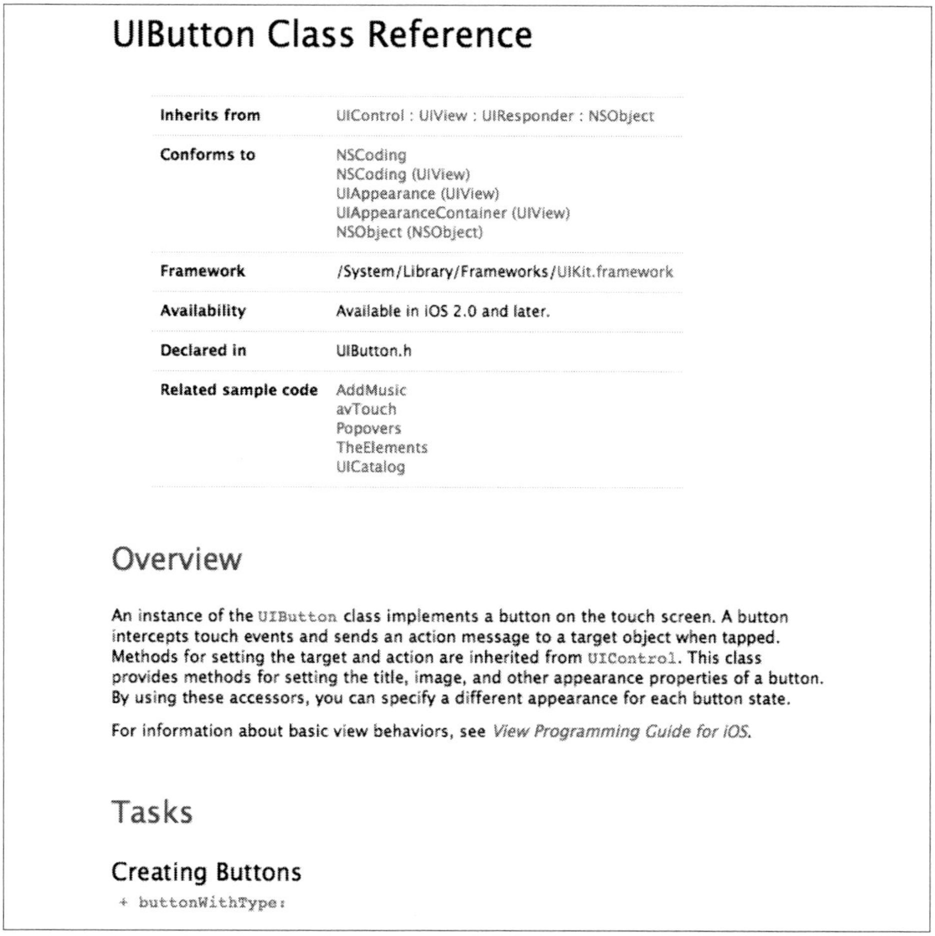

UIButton Class Reference

Inherits from	UIControl : UIView : UIResponder : NSObject
Conforms to	NSCoding NSCoding (UIView) UIAppearance (UIView) UIAppearanceContainer (UIView) NSObject (NSObject)
Framework	/System/Library/Frameworks/UIKit.framework
Availability	Available in iOS 2.0 and later.
Declared in	UIButton.h
Related sample code	AddMusic avTouch Popovers TheElements UICatalog

Overview

An instance of the `UIButton` class implements a button on the touch screen. A button intercepts touch events and sends an action message to a target object when tapped. Methods for setting the target and action are inherited from `UIControl`. This class provides methods for setting the title, image, and other appearance properties of a button. By using these accessors, you can specify a different appearance for each button state.

For information about basic view behaviors, see *View Programming Guide for iOS*.

Tasks

Creating Buttons

```
+ buttonWithType:
```

Figure 8-1. The start of a typical class documentation page

invented until iOS 4.0. So if you want to use this feature in your app, you must make sure either that your app targets only iOS 4.0 or later or that you take precautions not to call into this framework on earlier versions of the operating system. The availability information also confirms that you're looking at the right documentation page; if you're doing iOS programming and this class is available only on Mac OS X, reading this page is pointless. Note that individual methods also have availability information.

Companion guide

If a class documentation page lists a companion guide, you might want to click that link and read that guide. Guides are broad surveys of a topic; they provide important information (including, often, useful code examples), and they can serve to orient your thinking and make you aware of your options. (See the UIView class page for an example.)

Declared in

The header(s) where this class is declared. Unfortunately this is not a link; I have not found any quick way to view a header starting from within the documentation. That's a pity, as it can often be worth looking at the header file, which may contain helpful comments or other details. You can open the header file from your project window, as explained later in this chapter.

Related sample code

If a class documentation page links to sample code, you might want to examine that code. (But see my remarks on sample code in the next section of this chapter.)

Overview

Some class pages provide extremely important introductory information in the Overview section, including links to related guides and further information. (See the UIView class page for an example.)

Tasks

This section lists in categorical order, and links to, the properties and methods that appear later on the page. (Recall from Chapter 5 that a property is a syntactic short-cut for calling an accessor method; the documentation lists the property rather than the accessor.) Often, just looking over this list can give you the hint you're looking for.

Properties, Class Methods, Instance Methods

These sections provide the full documentation for this class's methods. In recent years, this part of the documentation has become quite splendid, with good hyper-links. Note the following subsections:

The property or method name

This name is suitable for copying and pasting into your code (if, for example, you need to enter the name of a selector).

The property or method's purpose

A short summary of what it does.

The formal declaration for the property or method

Read this to learn things like the method's parameters and return type. (Chapter 12 explains how to read a property declaration.) Suitable for copying and pasting into your code in order to enter a call to this method, though you are more likely to use Xcode's code completion feature where possible (see Chapter 9).

Parameters and return value

Precise information on the meaning and purpose of these.

Discussion

Often contains extremely important further details about how this method behaves. Always pay attention to this section!

Availability

An old class can acquire new methods as the operating system advances; if a newer method is crucial to your app, you might want to exclude your app from running on older operating systems that don't implement the method.

See also

Lists and links to related methods. Very helpful for giving you a larger perspective on how this method fits into the overall behavior of this class.

Related sample code

It can sometimes be worth consulting the sample code to see an example of how this particular method is used.

Declared in

The relevant header file.

Constants

Many classes define constants that accompany particular methods. For example, to create a UIButton instance in code, you call the `buttonWithType:` class method; the argument value will be a constant, listed under UIButtonType in the Constants section. (To help you get there, there's a link from the `buttonWithType:` method to the UIButtonType section in Constants.) There's a formal definition of the constant; you won't usually care about this (but do see Chapter 1 if you don't know how to read it). Then each value is explained, and the value name is suitable for copying and pasting into your code.

Sample Code

Apple provides plenty of sample code projects. You can view the code directly in the documentation window; sometimes this will be sufficient, but you can see only one class implementation or header file at a time, so it's difficult to get an overview. The alternative is to open the sample code project in Xcode.

When you look at a sample code page from your browser, there's a button that reads Download Sample Code. In fact, the sample code may already be on your computer. When you look at the same sample code page in the documentation window, the same button will read Open Project. The sample code on your hard disk is zipped, so even if the code is already on your computer, it is first unzipped (into your Downloads folder). This policy of keeping the sample code projects zipped on your hard disk is a good one, as it prevents you from accidentally altering the original, and you are free to experiment with the unzipped copy.

If a sample code project was linked against the frameworks of an older SDK that isn't installed on your computer, the project will be described in the Project navigator with the words "missing base SDK." In earlier versions of Xcode, this situation could prevent you from building and running the project, and features that depend on indexing might not work. In Xcode 4.2 and later, however, the project should build and run regardless. To remove the "missing base SDK" annotation, edit the target, switch to Build Settings, and change the outdated Base SDK setting to Latest iOS.

As a form of documentation, sample code is both good and bad. It can be a superb source of working code that you can often copy and paste and use with very little alteration in your own projects. It is usually heavily commented, because the Apple folks are aware, as they write the code, that it is intended for instructional purposes. Sample code also illustrates concepts that users have difficulty extracting from the documentation. (Users who have not grasped UITouch handling, for instance, often find that the lightbulb goes on when they discover the MoveMe example.) But the logic of a project is often spread over multiple files, and nothing is more difficult to understand than someone else's code (except, perhaps, your own code). Moreover, what learners most need is not the fait accompli of a fully written project but the reasoning process that constructed the project, which no amount of commentary can provide.

My own assessment is that Apple's sample code is generally very thoughtful and instructive and definitely a major component of the documentation, and that it deserves more appreciation and usage than it seems to get. But it is most useful, I think, after you've reached a certain level of competence and comfort.

Other Resources

Here is a survey of other useful resources that supplement the documentation.

Quick Help

Quick Help is a condensed rendering of the documentation on some single topic, usually a symbol name (a class or method). It appears with regard to the current selection or insertion point automatically in the Quick Help inspector (Option-Command-2) if the inspector is showing. Thus, for example, if you're editing code and the insertion point or selection is within the term `CGPointMake`, documentation for `CGPointMake` appears in the Quick Help inspector if it is visible.

Quick Help is also available in the Quick Help inspector for interface objects selected while editing a nib, for build settings while editing a project or target, and so forth.

A slightly reduced version of the same Quick Help documentation can be displayed as a small floating window, without the Quick Help inspector. Select a term and choose Help → Quick Help for Selected Item (Shift-Control-Command-?). Alternatively, hold down Option and hover the mouse over a term until the cursor becomes a question mark (and the term turns blue with a dashed underline); then Option-click the term.

The Quick Help documentation contains links. For example, click the Reference link to open the full documentation in the documentation window; click the header link to open the appropriate header file.

Symbols

A *symbol* is a nonlocally defined term, such as the name of a class, method, or instance variable. If you can see the name of a symbol in your code in an editor in Xcode, you can jump quickly to the definition of the symbol. Select text and choose Navigate → Jump to Definition (Control-Command-J). Alternatively, hold down Command and hover the mouse over a prospective term, until the cursor becomes a pointing finger (and the term becomes blue with a solid underline); Command-click the term to jump to the definition for that symbol.

If the symbol is defined in a Cocoa framework, you jump to the declaration in the header file. If the symbol is defined in your code, you jump to the class or method definition; this can be very helpful not only for understanding your code but also for navigating it.

The precise meaning of the notion "jump" depends upon the modifier keys you use in addition to the Command key, and on your settings in the General pane of Xcode's preferences. For example, if you haven't changed these settings from the default, Command-click jumps in the same editor, Command-Option-click jumps in an assistant pane, and Command-double-click jumps in a new window. Similarly, Control-Option-Command-J jumps in an assistant pane to the definition of the selected term.

Another way to see a list of your project's symbols, and navigate to a symbol definition, is through the Symbol navigator (Chapter 6).

An important and often neglected way to jump to a method or class definition whose name you know, even if you can't see the name in the code before you, is to choose File → Open Quickly (Shift-Command-O). In the search field, type key letters from the name, which will be interpreted intelligently; for example, to search for `application-DidFinishLaunching:`, you might type "appdid". Header file declarations are intermingled with your definitions; for example, for `applicationDidFinishLaunching:` the first listing is this method's declaration in the Cocoa header file *UIApplication.h*, while the second listing is your own AppDelegate class's implementation of this method.

Header Files

Sometimes a header file can be a useful form of documentation. It compactly summarizes a class's instance variables and methods and may contain comments and other helpful information — information that might be documented nowhere else. A single header file can contain declarations for multiple class interfaces and protocols. So it can be an excellent quick reference.

There are various ways to see a header file from an Xcode editor:

- If the class is your own and you're in the implementation file, choose Navigate → Jump to Next Counterpart (Control-Command-Up).
- Click the Related Files button at the left of the jump bar (Control-1). The menu lets you jump to any header files imported in the current file (as well as any files that import the current file) and to the header files of the current class file's superclasses and subclasses and so forth. Hold Option to jump in an assistant pane.
- Select text and choose File → Open Quickly (Shift-Command-O). This command brings up a dialog listing all source and header files containing a given symbol, as I mentioned in the previous section.
- Command-click a symbol, choose Navigate → Jump to Definition, or pass through Quick Help, as described in the previous sections.
- Use the Symbol navigator (Chapter 6).

All of these approaches require that a project window be open; File → Open Quickly requires an active SDK for effective operation, and the others all operate on specific windows or words in an open project. An alternative that works under all circumstances, even when no project is open, is to switch to the Terminal and use the open -h command to open a header file in Xcode. The argument may represent part of a header file's name. The command is interactive if there's an ambiguity; for example, open -h NSString proposes to open *NSString.h* or *NSStringDrawing.h* (or both, or neither). I wish this command were built into Xcode itself.

Internet Resources

Programming has become a lot easier since the Internet came along and Google started indexing it. It's amazing what you can find out with a Google search. Your problem is very likely one that someone else has faced, solved, and written about on the Internet. Often you'll find sample code that you can paste into your project and adapt.

Apple's documentation resources are available at *http://developer.apple.com*. These resources are updated before the changes are rolled into your doc sets for download. There are also some materials here that aren't part of the Xcode documentation on your computer. As a registered iOS developer, you have access to iTunes videos, including the videos for all WWDC 2012 sessions (as well as for some earlier years), and to Apple's developer forums (*https://devforums.apple.com*). Also, much of Apple's documentation comes in an alternative PDF format, convenient for storing and viewing on an iPad. Even better, Ole Zorn's Docsets app will let you download and browse entire docsets on an iPad or iPhone; it isn't freeware, but it's open source (*https://github.com/omz/DocSets-for-iOS*), so it's free if you're willing to build it yourself.

Apple maintains some public mailing lists (*http://lists.apple.com/mailman/listinfo*). I have long subscribed to the Xcode-users group (for questions about use of the Xcode tools) and the Cocoa-dev group (for questions about programming Cocoa). Cocoa-dev does permit iOS questions, but it is not heavily used for these. The lists are searchable, but Apple's own search doesn't work very well; you're better off using Google with a `site:lists.apple.com` term, or *http://www.cocoabuilder.com*, which archives the lists. Apple has not added a mailing list devoted to iOS programming; that's what the developer forums are supposed to be for, but the interface for these is extraordinarily clunky, and this — plus the lack of openness (to Google and to the world in general) — has limited their usefulness.

Other online resources, such as forums, have sprung up spontaneously as iOS programming has become more popular, and lots of iOS and Cocoa programmers blog about their experiences. I am particularly fond of Stack Overflow (*http://www.stackoverflow.com*); it isn't devoted exclusively to iOS programming, of course, but lots of iOS programmers hang out there, questions are answered succinctly and correctly, and the interface lets you focus on the right answer quickly and easily.

CHAPTER 9

Life Cycle of a Project

This chapter surveys some of the main stages in the life cycle of an Xcode project, from inception to submission at the App Store. This survey will provide an opportunity to discuss some additional features of the Xcode development environment. You already know how to create a project, define a class, and link to a framework (Chapter 6), as well as how to create and edit a nib (Chapter 7) and how to use the documentation (Chapter 8).

Device Architecture and Conditional Code

As you create a project (File → New → Project), after you pick a project template, in the screen where you name your project, the Devices pop-up menu offers a choice of iPad, iPhone, or Universal (meaning an app that runs on both iPhone and iPad natively, typically with a different interface on each type of device).

You are not tied forever to your initial decision, but your life will be simpler if you decide correctly from the outset. The iPhone and iPad differ in their physical characteristics as well as their programming interfaces. The iPad has a larger screen size, along with some built-in interface features that don't exist on the iPhone, such as split views and popovers (Chapter 22); thus an iPad project's nib files and some other resources will typically differ from those of an iPhone project.

Your choice in the Devices pop-up menu affects the details of the template on which your new project will be based. It also affects your project's Targeted Device Family build setting:

iPad
> The app will run only on an iPad.

Additional Simulator SDKs

When the Deployment Target is set to a system earlier than 6.0, earlier Simulator SDK versions may become available as destinations in the Scheme pop-up menu. Exactly what versions appear depends on the contents of */Developer/Platforms/iPhoneSimulator.platform/Developer/SDKs/*. Xcode 4.6 includes only the iOS 6.1 Simulator SDK, but you can download and install the iOS 6.0 and iOS 5.1/5.0 Simulator SDKs from the Downloads pane of the Preferences window (under Components).

---

iPhone
> The app will run on an iPhone or iPod touch; it can also run on an iPad, but not as a native iPad app (it runs in a reduced enlargeable window, which I call the *iPhone Emulator*; Apple sometimes refers to this as "compatibility mode").

iPhone/iPad
> The app will run natively on both kinds of device, and should be structured as a universal app.

Two additional build settings determine what systems your device will run on:

Base SDK
> The *latest* system your app can run on. As of this writing, in Xcode 4.6, you have just two choices, iOS 6.1 and Latest iOS — but Latest iOS means iOS 6.1, so what's the difference? It's that, if you update Xcode to develop for a subsequent system, any existing projects that are already set to Latest iOS will use that newer system's SDK as their Base SDK automatically, without your also having to update their Base SDK setting. Latest iOS is the default when you create a new project.
>
> For example, while I was writing this book, iOS 6.1 was released, so the current iOS version changed from iOS 6.0 to iOS 6.1. All my existing projects automatically started using the iOS 6.1 SDK as their Base SDK, because Latest iOS, which had been interpreted previously as meaning iOS 6.0, was now interpreted as meaning iOS 6.1.

iOS Deployment Target
> The *earliest* system your app can run on: in Xcode 4.5 and later, this can be any major iOS system number from the current system all the way back to 4.3. You can change the iOS Deployment Target setting easily by editing your project or your target: the project's Info tab has an iOS Deployment Target pop-up menu, and the target's Summary tab has a Deployment Target pop-up menu. These both represent the iOS Deployment Target build setting; you will probably want to edit the target, because if you edit the project only, the target setting will override it.

Writing an app whose Deployment Target differs from its Base SDK is something of a challenge. There are two chief problems:

Unsupported features

 With each new system, Apple adds new features. Xcode will happily allow you to compile using any features of the Base SDK, even if they don't exist on the Deployment Target system; but your app will crash if execution encounters features not supported by the system (device or Simulator) on which it is actually running. Thus, if you were to set the target's Deployment Target to iOS 5, it would be able to compile and run on an iOS 5 device even if it contained iOS 6–only features, but it would crash on the iOS 5 device if any of those features were actually encountered.

 Our Empty Window project is a case in point. Install the iOS 5.1 Simulator SDK, change the Empty Window target's Deployment Target to 5.1, set the destination in the Scheme pop-up menu to iPhone 5.1 Simulator, and run the project. Crash! Why? Because, by default, a new project's nibs use autolayout, and any interface widgets they contain — such as the button in our *ViewController.xib* — use autolayout constraints, which are instances of NSLayoutConstraint. But there is no NSLayoutConstraint class in iOS 5.1 or before.

Changed behavior

 With each new system, Apple permits itself to change the way some features work. The result is that such features work differently on different systems, and will thus require two different sets of code. Sometimes these two sets of code can live side by side; sometimes you will have to write conditional code, so that one set of code executes when running on one system, another when running on another.

 Interface rotation is an obvious case in point; this UIViewController feature (Chapter 19) was completely revised between iOS 5 and iOS 6. If your app launches into portrait orientation, the UIViewController methods called are totally different on the two different systems; code that launches your app correctly and successfully on iOS 5 might end up displaying a blank screen on iOS 6 (guess how I know that?). More insidiously, text is drawn differently on iOS 6 from how it was drawn on iOS 5; the very same code might thus display text in a certain position on iOS 5, but in a different position on iOS 6 (guess how I know that?).

How can you guard against such problems? Backwards compatibility isn't easy, and it gets harder the further backwards you want to be compatible. Xcode 4.5 and later doesn't support a Deployment Target earlier than 4.3; to compile for an earlier system, you'll need an earlier version of Xcode. Xcode 4.5 and later doesn't support a Simulator SDK earlier than 5.0; to test on an earlier version of the Simulator, you'll need an earlier version of Xcode. But writing code compatible with an earlier version of Xcode is itself not easy; many of the modern Objective-C features used in this book won't work in Xcode 4.2 or earlier. Moreover, testing in the Simulator is not enough; a physical device is essential for testing, implying that you need to maintain an arsenal of old iOS devices, in order to discover compatibility issues before your app is let loose upon a world of users. Personally, I adopt wherever possible the Dr. Kronkheit Defense (look it up on Wikipedia): Don't do that. Once I've rewritten one of my apps for iOS 6, it usually runs only on iOS 6 or later.

Even if you can afford the luxury of not attempting backwards compatibility, however, you *still* might need to grapple with the problem of conditional code — if you want to write a universal app. Although you'll probably want to reduce duplication by sharing some code between the iPhone and the iPad version of the app, nevertheless some code will likely have to be kept separate, because your app will need to behave differently on the different types of device. As I already mentioned, you can't summon a popover on an iPhone; and the complexities can run considerably deeper, because the overall interfaces might be quite different, and might behave very differently — tapping a table cell on the iPhone might summon an entire new screenful of stuff, whereas on the larger iPad, it might only alter what appears in one region of the screen.

Various programming devices help govern dynamically what code is encountered, based on what system or device type the app is running on; thus you can steer your code away from a crash or from undesirable behavior based on the runtime environment (see also Example 29-1):

- The UIDevice class lets you query the current device to learn its system version (`systemVersion`) and type (`userInterfaceIdiom`, either `UIUserInterfaceIdiom-Phone` or `UIUserInterfaceIdiomPad`):

```
if ([UIDevice currentDevice].userInterfaceIdiom == UIUserInterfaceIdiomPhone)
{
    // do things appropriate to iPhone
} else {
    // do things appropriate to iPad
}
```

  For an actual example, make a Universal project from the Master–Detail Application template and look in *AppDelegate.m*. You'll see code that configures the initial interface differently depending on the device type we're running on.

- Certain *Info.plist* settings apply only to one device type or the other. Again, a Universal project based on the Master–Detail Application template is a case in point. You'll see that the *Info.plist* contains two sets of "Supported interface orientations" settings, a general set and an iPad-only set that overrides the general case when the app launches on an iPad.

  Similarly, if you create your Master-Detail Application Universal project with Use Storyboards checked, the project contains two storyboards, one containing the interface for running on an iPhone, the other for an iPad. The choice between them is made through the *Info.plist* setting "Main storyboard file base name", which appears twice, once for the general case and once for iPad only, the latter overriding the former when the app launches on an iPad. (If you create your Master-Detail Application Universal project *without* Use Storyboards checked, the project contains two pairs of nibs, and the choice of which ones to load as the app launches is made in code, in App Delegate's `application:didFinishLaunchingWith-Options:`, using the `userInterfaceIdiom` technique from the previous paragraph.)

- Many calls that load resources by name from your app's bundle will automatically select an alternative resource whose name (before the extension) ends with `~iphone` or `~ipad` as appropriate to the device type — if there is such an alternative resource. This relieves your code from using conditionals. For example, UIImage's `image-Named:` method, if you specify the image name as `@"linen.png"`, will load an image called *linen~ipad.png* if it finds one and if we're running on an iPad. We'll see in Chapter 15 that the same sort of naming convention will also help you automatically load a double-resolution image on a device with a double-resolution screen.

- If your app is linked to a framework and tries to run on a system that lacks that framework, it will crash at launch time. The solution is to link to that framework optionally, by changing the Required pop-up menu item in its listing in the target's Linked Frameworks and Libraries to Optional; this is technically referred to as *weak-linking* the framework.

- You can test for the existence of a method using `respondsToSelector:` and related NSObject calls:

```
if ([UIButton respondsToSelector: @selector(appearance)]) {
    // ok to call appearance class method
} else {
    // don't call appearance class method
}
```

- You can test for the existence of a class using the `NSClassFromString` function, which yields nil if the class doesn't exist. Also, if the Base SDK is 5.0 or later, and if the class's framework is present or weak-linked, you can send the class any message (such as `[CIFilter class]`) and test the result for nil; this works because classes are themselves weak-linked starting in iOS 5:

```
// assume Core Image framework is weak-linked
if ([CIFilter class]) { // ok to do things with CIFilter
```

- You can test for the existence of a constant name, including the name of a C function, by taking the name's address and testing against zero. For example:

```
if (&UIApplicationWillEnterForegroundNotification) {
    // OK to refer to UIApplicationWillEnterForegroundNotification
```

Localization

A device can be set by the user to prefer a certain language as its primary language. You might like the text in your app's interface to respond to this situation by appearing in that language. This is achieved by *localizing* the app for that language.

Localization operates through localization folders in your project and in the built app bundle. Let's say that a resource in one of these localization folders has a counterpart in the other localization folders. Then, when your app goes to load such a resource, it automatically loads the one appropriate to the user's preferred language.

For example, if there's a copy of *InfoPlist.strings* in the English localization folder and a copy of *InfoPlist.strings* in the French localization folder, the latter will be used when the app needs a copy of *InfoPlist.strings* on a device on which French is the preferred language. Not for nothing have I used *InfoPlist.strings* as my example. This is a file that's present by default in your project — for example, it appears in our Empty Window example project — but its purpose wasn't discussed in Chapter 6, so presumably you've been on tenterhooks since then, wondering what it was for. Well, it's a *.strings* file; the purpose of a *.strings* file is to be localized.

The purpose of this particular *.strings* file, *InfoPlist.strings*, is to store localized versions of *Info.plist* key values. So, for example, the value of the `CFBundleDisplayName` key, as set in your project's *Info.plist* file, appears under your app's icon on the user's device. We might want to change this name depending the user's primary language setting. For example, on a French language device, we might like our Empty Window app to be called Fenêtre Vide.

As an example of localization, let's arrange for that very thing to happen. First we must set up our app for localization to French; then we must localize *InfoPlist.strings*.

1. Edit the project. Under Info, the Localizations table lists our app's localizations.

2. Click the Plus button under the Localizations table. From the pop-up menu that appears, choose French.

3. A dialog appears, listing files that are currently localized for English (because they came that way as part of the app template). We're dealing here with just *Info-Plist.strings*, so leave it checked but uncheck any other files that appear here. Click Finish.

We have now set up *InfoPlist.strings* to be localized for both English and French. This fact is reflected in two ways:

- In the Project navigator, the listing for *InfoPlist.strings* has acquired a flippy triangle. Open the triangle to reveal that our project now contains *two* copies of *Info-

Figure 9-1. How a localized strings file is represented in Xcode

Plist.strings, one for English and one for French (Figure 9-1). Thus we can now edit either one individually.

- In the Empty Window project folder on disk, there is now both an *en.lproj* folder and a *fr.lproj* folder. The former contains the copy of *InfoPlist.strings* destined for English language users; the latter contains the copy of *InfoPlist.strings* destined for French language users. Moreover, when we build, this folder structure is copied into the built app.

Now let's edit our *InfoPlist.strings* files. A *.strings* file is simply a collection of key–value pairs in the following format:

```
/* Optional comments are C-style comments */
"key" = "value";
```

In the case of *InfoPlist.strings*, the key is simply the key name from *Info.plist* — the raw key name, not the English-like name. So the English *InfoPlist.strings* should look like this:

```
"CFBundleDisplayName" = "Empty Window";
```

The French *InfoPlist.strings* should look like this:

```
"CFBundleDisplayName" = "Fenêtre Vide";
```

Now let's try it!

1. Build and run Empty Window on the iPhone Simulator.

2. In Xcode, stop the running project. In the Simulator, the home screen is revealed.

3. Examine the name of our app, as displayed in the Simulator home screen. It is Empty Window (truncated to "Empty…ndow").

4. In the Simulator, launch the Settings app and change the language to French (General → International → Language → Français). Our app's name is now displayed as Fenêtre Vide.

Is this fun or what? When you're done marveling at your own cosmopolitanism, change the Simulator's language back to English.

Now let's talk about nib files (and storyboard files). Before Xcode 4.5 and iOS 6, the case of a nib file (or storyboard file) was similar to what we just did with *InfoPlist.strings*: it was necessary to localize the entire nib (or storyboard). So, for example, you would have selected *ViewController.xib* in the Project navigator, switched to the File inspector, and checked French in the Localization table. This would cause you to end up with two copies of *ViewController.xib*, and you would edit each one so that any text displayed in the interface, such as button titles, appeared in the appropriate language.

Starting in Xcode 4.5 and iOS 6, however, there's a better way:

1. Edit the project again, and below the Localization table, check Use Base Internationalization.

2. A dialog appears, listing nib and storyboard files that are currently localized only for English. At present, it lists just *ViewController.xib*, and it is checked. That's good! Click Finish.

3. Back in the Project navigator, select *ViewController.xib*. Look in the File inspector. The Localization table now contains three entries: Base, English, and French. Base is already checked. Check French.

4. Clean the build folder (hold Option and choose Product → Clean Build Folder)! Omitting this step will probably cause your app to misbehave in future.

In the Project navigator, the result is that *ViewController.xib* has a flippy triangle. Open it to reveal that *ViewController.xib* is now split into two different types of file:

- If the user's device is not localized for French, the Base file will be used. That's the nib file itself, which has been moved on disk into a new *Base.lproj* folder. Thus we can continue to edit the nib file, *ViewController.xib*, using English as the default language.

- If the user's device is localized for French, a *.strings* file will be used — *ViewController.strings*, located on disk inside the *fr.lproj* folder. This file, including the keys and initial values, has been generated for us automatically based on the content of *ViewController.xib*.

So, at the moment the French *ViewController.strings* file contains this line:

```
"38.normalTitle" = "Button";
```

Let's change that to French. *Don't change the key!* It's meaningless to you and out of your control (though if you're really determined you can pretty easily work out how it is derived), and you don't want to break the connection between this string and the button to which it applies. Change only the value:

```
"38.normalTitle" = "Bouton";
```

Build and run the app in the Simulator and switch languages as before to see the effects of your work.

Finally, what about strings that appear in your app's interface but whose value is generated in code? (In the Empty Window app as we've developed it so far, examples include the modified text of the UILabel, or the content of the alert summoned by tapping the button.) The approach is the same — a *strings* file — but your code must be modified to use it explicitly. There are various ways to do this, but the simplest is to use the NSLocalizedString macro (which calls an NSBundle instance method, localizedStringForKey:table:). So, for example, we might modify our buttonPressed: method to look like this:

```
UIAlertView* av = [[UIAlertView alloc]
                initWithTitle:NSLocalizedString(@"AlertGreeting", nil)
                message:NSLocalizedString(@"YouTappedMe", nil)
                delegate:nil
                cancelButtonTitle:NSLocalizedString(@"Cool", nil)
                otherButtonTitles:nil];
```

The string provided as the first argument to NSLocalizedString is the key in a *strings* file. Our code is now broken, however, as there is no corresponding *strings* file. By default, the *strings* file expected here is called *Localizable.strings*. But no such file exists. There's no error, but these keys have no value either — so the key itself is used when the alert appears, which is not what we want. You'll need to create the required *strings* file:

1. Choose File → New → File.
2. The "choose a template" dialog appears. On the left, under iOS, select Resource. On the right, select Strings File. Click Next.
3. Name the file *Localizable.strings*. Pick an appropriate Group, and make sure this file is part of our Empty Window target. Click Create.
4. Now we must localize the new file. In the Project navigator, select *Localizable.strings*. In the File inspector, under Localization, click the "Make localized" button. A dialog offers to move the existing file into the English localization, which is exactly what you want.
5. In the File inspector, you can now add localizations as desired. For example, you could check French.

You must now also provide our *Localizable.strings* files with content, in accordance with the localizable string keys specified in your code. What? We have to comb through our code, looking for calls to NSLocalizedString, and copying out the keys into our *strings* files? This sounds like a royal pain, not to mention being an invitation to make some careless mistake. Fortunately, the genstrings command-line tool will do the work for you, seeking out the NSLocalizedString calls and generating the initial contents of a *strings* file (using the keys as default values). So, for example, on my machine I would now say, in the Terminal:

```
$ genstrings /Users/matt/Desktop/Empty\ Window/Empty\ Window/ViewController.m
```

The result is a file *Localizable.strings* in the current directory, reading as follows:

```
/* No comment provided by engineer. */
"AlertGreeting" = "AlertGreeting";

/* No comment provided by engineer. */
"Cool" = "Cool";

/* No comment provided by engineer. */
"YouTappedMe" = "YouTappedMe";
```

We are now waving our hands; completing the localization of our Empty Window project is left as an exercise for the reader. For a full if somewhat outdated discussion of localization, see Apple's *Internationalization Programming Topics*.

Editing Your Code

Many aspects of Xcode's editing environment can be modified to suit your tastes. Your first step should be to pick a font face and size you like in the Fonts & Colors preference pane. Nothing is so important as being able to read and write code comfortably! I like a largish size (13, 14 or even 16) and a pleasant monospaced font such as Monaco, Menlo, or Consolas (or the freeware Inconsolata).

Xcode has some formatting, autotyping, and text selection features adapted for Objective-C. Exactly how these behave depends upon your settings in the Editing and Indentation tabs of Xcode's Text Editing preference pane. I'm not going to describe these settings in detail, but I urge you to take advantage of them. Under Editing, I like to check just about everything, including Line Numbers; visible line numbers are useful when debugging. Under Indentation, I like to have just about everything checked too; I find the way Xcode lays out Objective-C code to be excellent with these settings. A sound approach might be to check everything initially and then, when you've some experience editing with Xcode, switch off features you don't prefer.

If you like Xcode's smart syntax-aware indenting, but you find that once in a while a line of code isn't indenting itself correctly, try choosing Editor → Structure → Re-Indent (Control-I), which autoindents the current line. (Autoindent problems can also be caused by incorrect syntax earlier in the file, so hunt for that too.)

Under Editing, notice "Automatically balance brackets in Objective-C method calls." If this option is checked, then when you type a closing square bracket after some text, Xcode intelligently inserts the opening square bracket before the text. I like this feature, as it allows me to type nested square brackets without planning ahead. For example, I type this:

```
UIAlertView* av = [UIAlertView alloc
```

I now type the right square bracket *twice*. The first right square bracket closes the open left square bracket (which highlights to indicate this). The second right square bracket also inserts a space before itself, plus the missing left square bracket:

```
UIAlertView* av = [[UIAlertView alloc] ]
//          insertion point is here: ^
```

The insertion point is positioned before the second right square bracket, ready for me to type `init`.

With "Enable type-over completions" checked, Xcode goes even further. As I start to type that same line of code:

```
UIAlertView* av = [U
```

Xcode automatically appends the closing right square bracket, with the insertion point still positioned before it:

```
UIAlertView* av = [U]
```

That closing right square bracket, however, is tentative; it's in gray. When I finish typing the first nested method call:

```
UIAlertView* av = [UIAlertView alloc]
```

I can now confirm the closing right square bracket in any of several ways. I can actually type a right square bracket; or I can type Tab or Right arrow. The tentative right square bracket is replaced by a real right square bracket, and the insertion point is now positioned after it, ready for me to continue typing. With practice, you'll quickly get used to this feature, which has greatly increased my own fluidity in typing code.

Autocompletion

As you write code, you'll take advantage of Xcode's autocompletion feature. Objective-C is a verbose language, and whatever reduces your time and effort typing will be a relief. However, I personally do *not* check "Suggest completions while typing" under Editing; instead, I check "Use Escape key to show completion suggestions", and when I want autocompletion to happen, I ask for it manually, by pressing Esc.

For example, suppose my code is as displayed in the previous example, with the insertion point before the second right square bracket. I now type `init` and then press Esc, and a little menu pops up, listing the four `init` methods appropriate to a UIAlertView (Figure 9-2). You can navigate this menu, dismiss it, or accept the selection, using only the keyboard. So, if it were not already selected by default, I would navigate to `initWith-Title:...` and press Return to accept the selected choice.

Alternatively, I might press Control-Period instead of Esc. Pressing Control-Period repeatedly cycles through the alternatives. Again, press Return to accept the selected choice. Another possibility is to press Tab, which performs a partial completion without

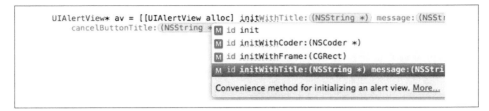

Figure 9-2. The autocompletion menu

dismissing the autocompletion menu; in Figure 9-2, if I were to press Tab at this moment, `initWith` would be completed in my code — that's what the dashed underlines are telling me — and bare `init`, no longer an eligible completion, would be eliminated from the menu.

Observe also that there is a reduced form of Quick Help at the bottom of the autocompletion menu; click the More link to view (in the documentation window) the full documentation for the currently selected method (Chapter 8).

When I choose an alternative from the autocompletion menu, the template for the correct method call is entered in my code (I've broken it manually into multiple lines to show it here):

```
[[UIAlertView alloc] initWithTitle:<#(NSString *)#>
                           message:<#(NSString *)#>
                          delegate:<#(id)#>
                 cancelButtonTitle:<#(NSString *)#>
                 otherButtonTitles:<#(NSString *), ...#>, nil]
```

The expressions in `<#...#>` are *placeholders*, showing the type of each parameter; you can select the next placeholder with Tab (if the insertion point precedes a placeholder) or by choosing Navigate → Jump to Next Placeholder (Control-Slash). Thus I can select a placeholder and type in its place the actual argument I wish to pass, select the next placeholder and type that argument, and so forth.

Placeholders are delimited by `<#...#>` behind the scenes, but they appear in Xcode as "text tokens" to prevent them from being edited accidentally. To convert a placeholder to a normal string without the delimiters, select it and press Return, or double-click it.

Autocompletion also works for method declarations. You don't have to know or enter a method's return type beforehand. Just type the initial - or + (to indicate an instance method or a class method) followed by the first few letters of the method's name. For example, in my app delegate I might type:

```
- appli
```

If I then press Esc, I see a list of methods such as `application:didChangeStatusBar-`
`Frame:`; these are methods that might be sent to my app delegate (by virtue of its being
the app delegate, as discussed in Chapter 11). When I choose one, the declaration is
filled in for me, including the return type and the parameter names:

```
- (void)application:(UIApplication *)application
    didChangeStatusBarFrame:(CGRect)oldStatusBarFrame
```

At this point I'm ready to type the left curly brace, followed by a Return character; this
causes the matching right curly brace to appear, with the insertion point positioned
between them, ready for me to start typing the body of this method.

Snippets

Code autocompletion is supplemented by code snippets. A code snippet is a bit of text
with an abbreviation. Code snippets are kept in the Code Snippet library (Control-
Option-Command-2), but a code snippet's abbreviation is globally available, so you can
use it without showing the library. You type the abbreviation and the snippet's name is
included among the possible completions.

For example, to enter an `if` block, I would type `if` and press Esc, to get autocompletion,
and select "If Statement". When I press Return, the `if` block appears in my code, and
the condition area (between the parentheses) and statements area (between the curly
braces) are placeholders.

To learn a snippet's abbreviation, you must open its editing window — double-click the
snippet in the Code Snippet library — and click Edit. If learning a snippet's abbreviation
is too much trouble, simply drag it from the Code Snippet library into your text.

You can add your own snippets, which will be categorized as User snippets; the easiest
way is to drag text into the Code Snippet library. Edit to suit your taste, providing a
name, a description, and an abbreviation; use the <#...#> construct to form any desired
placeholders.

Fix-it and Live Syntax Checking

Xcode's extremely cool Fix-it feature can actually make *and implement* positive suggestions on how to avert a problem. To summon it, click on an issue badge in the gutter.
Such an issue badge will appear after compilation if there's a problem.

For instance, in Figure 9-3 I've accidentally omitted the @ before an Objective-C
NSString literal, and the compiler is warning (because what I've typed is a C string literal,
a very different thing). By clicking on the warning badge in the gutter, I've summoned
a little dialog that not only describes the mistake but tells me how to fix it. Not only that:
it has tentatively (in grey) implemented that solution; it has inserted the missing @ into

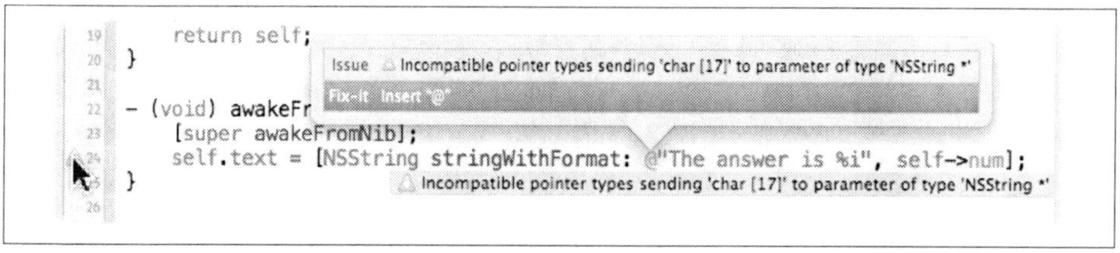

```
19        return self;
20    }
21
22 - (void) awakeFr
23      [super awakeFromNib];
24      self.text = [NSString stringWithFormat: @"The answer is %i", self->num];
25    }
26
```

Issue ⚠ Incompatible pointer types sending 'char [17]' to parameter of type 'NSString *'

Fix-it Insert "@"

⚠ Incompatible pointer types sending 'char [17]' to parameter of type 'NSString *'

Figure 9-3. A warning with a Fix-it suggestion

my code. Not only *that*: if I press Return, or double-click the "Fix-it" button in the dialog, Xcode *really* inserts the missing @ into my code — and the warning vanishes, because the problem is solved. If I'm confident that Xcode will do the right thing, I can choose Editor → Fix All in Scope (Control-Option-Command-F), and Xcode will implement *all* nearby Fix-it suggestions without my even having to show the dialog.

Live syntax checking is like a form of constant compilation. Even if you don't compile or even save, live syntax checking can detect the presence of a problem, and can suggest the solution with Fix-it. This feature can be toggled on or off using the "Show live issues" checkbox in the General preference pane. Personally, I keep it turned off, as I find it intrusive. My code is almost never valid while I'm typing, because the terms and parentheses are always half-finished; that's what it means to be typing. For example, merely typing a left parenthesis will instantly cause the syntax checker to complain of a parse error (until I type the corresponding right parenthesis).

Navigating Your Code

Developing an Xcode project involves editing code in many files at once. Xcode provides numerous ways to navigate your code. Many of these have been mentioned in previous chapters. Most navigation methods can be tweaked with the Option key to navigate in an assistant pane instead of the main editor, or with Shift-Option to bring up the navigation window.

The Project navigator
> If you know something about the name of a file, you can find it quickly in the Project navigator (Command-1) by typing into the search field in the filter bar at the bottom of the navigator (Edit → Filter → Filter in Navigator, Command-Option-J). For example, type xib to see just your nib files. Moreover, after using the filter bar, you can press Tab and then the Up or Down arrow key to navigate the Project navigator. Thus you can reach the desired file with the keyboard alone.

The Symbol navigator
> If you highlight the first two icons in the filter bar (the first two are dark, the third is light), the Symbol navigator lists your project's classes and their methods. Now

you can navigate to a desired method. As with the Project navigator, the filter bar's search field can quickly get you where you want to go.

The jump bar

Every path component of the jump bar is a menu:

The bottom level

At the bottom level (farthest right) in the jump bar is a list of your file's method and function declarations and definitions, in the order in which they appear (hold Command while choosing the menu to see them in alphabetical order); choose one to navigate to it. Start typing while the menu is open to filter what the menu displays.

You can add section titles to this bottom-level menu using the `#pragma mark` directive. For example, try modifying *ViewController.m* in our Empty Window project:

```
#pragma mark - View lifecycle

- (void)viewDidLoad
{
    [super viewDidLoad];
    // Do any additional setup after loading the view...
}
```

The result is that the "viewDidLoad" item in the bottom-level menu falls within a "View lifecycle" section. (But only if a method definition precedes the `#pragma` line. I regard this limitation as a bug.)

To make a section divider line in the menu, type a `#pragma mark` directive whose value is a hyphen; in the preceding example, both a hyphen (to make a section divider line) and a title (to make a bold section title) are used. Similarly, comments outside of any method and starting with `TODO:`, `FIXME:`, `???:`, or `!!!:` will appear in the bottom-level menu.

Higher levels

Higher-level path components are hierarchical menus; thus you can use any of them to work your way down the file hierarchy.

History

Each editor pane remembers the names of files you've edited in it. The Back and Forward triangles are both buttons and pop-up menus (or choose Navigate → Go Back and Navigate → Go Forward, Control-Command-Left and Control-Command-Right).

Related items

The leftmost button in the jump bar summons a hierarchical menu of files related to the current file, such as counterparts, superclasses, and included files.

New in Xcode 4.5 and later, this list even includes methods that call or are called by the currently selected method.

The Assistant pane

The Assistant lets you be in two places at once. Hold Option while navigating to open something in an Assistant pane instead of the primary editor pane.

The first path component in an Assistant pane's jump bar sets its automatic relationship to the main pane (*tracking*). This is effectively the same hierarchical menu of related items I mentioned a moment ago, applied to the main pane. If the chosen relationship involves multiple files, triangle buttons appear at the right end of the jump bar, letting you navigate between them; or choose from the second path component's pop-up menu (Control-5). For example, show *AppDelegate.m* in the main pane and switch the assistant pane's related items pop-up menu to Includes; the triangle buttons at the right end of the jump bar then navigate between different files #imported by *AppDelegate.m*.

You can also be in two places at once by opening a tab or a separate window.

Jump to definition

Navigate → Jump to Definition (Control-Command-J) lets you jump to the declaration or definition of the symbol already selected in your code.

Open quickly

File → Open Quickly (Shift-Command-O) searches in a dialog for a symbol in your code and the Cocoa headers. You can type the symbol in the search field, or, if a symbol is selected when you summon the dialog, it will be entered in the search field for you. You can navigate the dialog entirely with the keyboard.

Breakpoints

The Breakpoint navigator lists all breakpoints in your code. Xcode lacks code bookmarks, but you can misuse a disabled breakpoint as a bookmark. Breakpoints are discussed later in this chapter.

Finding

Finding is a form of navigation. Xcode has both a global find (Edit → Find → Find in Workspace, Shift-Command-F, which is the same as using the Search navigator) and an editor-level find (Edit → Find → Find, Command-F); don't confuse them.

Find options are all-important. Both sorts of find have options that you can summon by clicking the magnifying glass. The global find options (Figure 6-3) allow you to specify the scope of a search (which files will be searched) in sophisticated ways: choose Custom in the "Find in" pop-up menu to create a scope. The global find search bar also pops down a menu automatically as you type if the find options aren't showing, letting you switch among the most important options. You can also find using regular expressions. There's a lot of power lurking here.

To replace text, click on the word Find at the left end of the search bar to summon the pop-up menu, and choose Replace. (It may be necessary to perform a global find first, before a global replace on the same search term will work.) You can replace all occurrences, or select particular find results in the Search navigator and replace only those (click Replace instead of Replace All). The Search navigator's Preview button summons a dialog that shows you the effect of each possible replacement, and lets you check or uncheck particular replacements in advance of performing the replacement. For editor-level find, hold Option before clicking Replace All, to find-and-replace within only the current selection.

A sophisticated form of editor-level find is Editor → Edit All In Scope, which finds simultaneously all occurrences of the currently selected term (usually a variable name) within the current set of curly braces; you can use this to change a variable's name throughout its scope, or just to survey how the name is used.

 To change a symbol's name throughout your code, as well as for auto-mated, intelligent assistance in performing various code rearrangements that commonly arise in Objective-C programming, use Xcode's Refactoring feature (see "Make Projectwide Changes" in the *Xcode 4 User Guide*).

Debugging

Debugging is the art of figuring out what's wrong with the behavior of your app as it runs. I divide this art into two main techniques: caveman debugging and pausing your running app.

Caveman Debugging

Caveman debugging consists of altering your code, usually temporarily, typically by adding code to dump informative messages into the console.

The standard command for sending a message to the console is NSLog. It's a C function, and it takes an NSString which operates as a format string, followed by the format arguments.

A *format string* is a string (here, an NSString) containing symbols called *format specifiers*, for which values (the format arguments) will be substituted at runtime. All format specifiers begin with a percent sign (%), so the only way to enter a literal percent sign in a format string is as a double percent sign (%%). The character(s) following the percent sign specify the type of value that will be supplied at runtime. The most common format specifiers are %@ (an object reference), %i (an integer), %f (a float), and %p (a pointer, usually an object reference, shown as the address in memory pointed to, useful for making certain that two references refer to the same instance). For example:

```
NSLog(@"the window: %@", self.window);
```

In that example, self.window is the first (and only) format argument, so its value will be substituted for the first (and only) format specifier, %@, when the format string is printed in the console. Thus the console output looks something like this:

```
the window: <UIWindow: 0x6a08140; frame = (0 0; 320 480);
            layer = <UIWindowLayer: 0x6a08230>>
```

This nice display of information is due to UIWindow's implementation of the description method: an object's description method is called when that object is used with the %@ format specifier. For this reason, you will probably want to implement description in your own classes, so that you can investigate an instance with a simple NSLog call.

For the complete repertory of format specifiers available in a format string, read Apple's document *String Format Specifiers*. The format specifiers are largely based on those of the C printf standard library function; see K&R B1.2, the sprintf man page, and the IEEE printf specification linked from the documentation.

 If an object reference has been set to nil, NSLog will report it as (null). But if an object reference is uninitialized, an NSLog call referring to it will probably fail silently, or even crash the debugger. This is very frustrating, especially since the fact that this object reference is uninitialized is probably just what you were trying to debug. Fortunately, if you use ARC (Chapter 12), an object reference is autoinitialized to nil if you don't initialize it explicitly.

The main ways to go wrong with NSLog (or any format string) are to supply a different number of format arguments from the number of format specifiers in the string, or to supply an argument value different from the type declared by the corresponding format specifier. I often see beginners claim that logging shows a certain value to be nonsense, when in fact it is their NSLog call that is nonsense; for example, a format specifier was %i but the value of the corresponding argument was a float. Fortunately, recent versions of the compiler will try to help you with warnings.

C structs are not objects, so to see a struct's value with NSLog you must somehow deconstruct or translate the struct. Common Cocoa structs usually supply convenience functions for this purpose. For example:

```
NSLog(@"%@", NSStringFromCGRect(self.window.frame)); // {{0, 0}, {320, 480}}
```

Purists may scoff at caveman debugging, but I use it heavily: it's easy, informative, and lightweight. And sometimes it's the only way. Unlike the debugger, NSLog works with any build configuration (Debug or Release) and wherever your app runs (in the Simulator or on a device). It works when pausing is impossible (because of threading issues, for example). It even works on someone else's device, such as a tester to whom you've distributed your app. It's a little tricky for a tester to get a look at the console so as to be able to report back to you, but it can be done: the tester can connect the device to a computer and view its log in Xcode's Organizer window or with Apple's iPhone Configuration Utility; there's also a free utility app called Console that displays the log right on the device.

Remember to remove or comment out NSLog calls before shipping your app, as you probably don't want your finished app to dump lots of messages into the console. A useful trick (shamelessly stolen from Jens Alfke) is to call MyLog instead of NSLog, and define MyLog like this in your precompiled header (and when it's time to stop logging, change the 0 to 1):

```
#define MyLog if(0); else NSLog
```

A useful fact when logging is that the variable name _cmd holds the selector for the current method. Thus a single form of statement can signal where you are:

```
NSLog(@"Logging %@ in %@", NSStringFromSelector(_cmd), self);
```

(Similarly, in a C function, NSLog(@"%s", __FUNCTION__) logs the name of the function.)

Another sort of call with which you can pepper your code is *asserts*. Asserts are conditions that you claim (assert) are true at that moment — and you feel so strongly about this that you want your app to crash if you're wrong. Asserts are a very good way to confirm that the situation matches your expectations, not just now as you write your code, but in the future as the app develops.

The simplest form of assert is the C function (actually it's a macro) assert, to which you pass one argument, a condition — something that can be evaluated as false (0) or true (some other value). If it's false, your app will crash when this line is encountered, along with a nice explanation in the log. For example, suppose we assert NO, which is false and will certainly cause a crash. Then when this line is encountered we crash with this log message:

```
Assertion failed: (NO),
function -[AppDelegate application:didFinishLaunchingWithOptions:],
file /Users/mattleopard/Desktop/testing/testing/AppDelegate.m, line 20.
```

That's plenty for us to track down the assertion failure: we know the assertion condition, the method in which the assertion occurred, the file containing that method, and the line number.

For higher-level asserts, look at NSAssert (used in Objective-C methods) and NSCAssert (used in C functions). They allow you to form your own log message, which is to appear in the console in addition to the native `assert` logging; the log message can be a format string followed by values corresponding to the format specifiers, as with NSLog.

Some developers think that asserts should be allowed to remain in your code even when your app is finished. By default, however, higher-level asserts are disabled in a Release build, thanks to the Other C Flags build setting, which is set to `-DNS_BLOCK_ASSERTIONS=1` in Apple's project templates; the effect of this setting is to `#define` the preprocessor macro `NS_BLOCK_ASSERTIONS`, which in turn is the signal for asserts to be effectively neutered at precompile time. To keep asserts working in a Release build, clear that value from the Other C Flags build setting in your target.

The Xcode Debugger

When you're building and running in Xcode, you can pause in the debugger and use Xcode's debugging facilities. There isn't a strong difference between running and debugging in Xcode; the main distinction is whether breakpoints are effective or ignored. The effectiveness of breakpoints can be toggled at two levels:

Globally
> Breakpoints as a whole are either active or inactive. If breakpoints are inactive, we won't pause at any breakpoints.

Individually
> A given breakpoint is either enabled or disabled. Even if breakpoints are active, we won't pause at this one if it is disabled. Disabling a breakpoint allows you to leave in place a breakpoint that you might need later without pausing at it every time it's encountered.

A breakpoint, then, is ignored if it is disabled or if breakpoints as a whole are inactive.

The important thing, if you want to use the debugger, is that the app should be built with the Debug build configuration. The debugger is not very helpful against an app built with the Release build configuration, not least because compiler optimizations can destroy the correspondence between steps in the compiled code and lines in your code. Trying to debug a Release build is a common beginner error (though it's less likely to occur accidentally in Xcode 4, in which by default a scheme's Run action uses the Debug build configuration).

To create a breakpoint (Figure 9-4), select in the editor the line where you want to pause, and choose Product → Debug → Add Breakpoint at Current Line (Command-Backslash). This keyboard shortcut toggles between adding and removing a breakpoint for the current line. The breakpoint is symbolized by an arrow in the gutter. Alternatively, a simple click in the gutter adds a breakpoint; to remove a breakpoint gesturally, drag it out of the gutter.

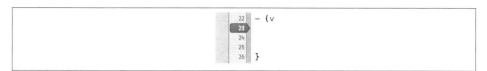

Figure 9-4. A breakpoint

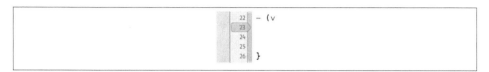

Figure 9-5. A disabled breakpoint

To disable a breakpoint at the current line, click on the breakpoint in the gutter to toggle its enabled status. Alternatively, Control-click on the breakpoint and choose Disable Breakpoint in the contextual menu. A dark breakpoint is enabled; a light breakpoint is disabled (Figure 9-5).

Once you have some breakpoints in your code, you'll want to survey and manage them. That's what the Breakpoint navigator is for. Here you can navigate to a breakpoint, enable or disable a breakpoint by clicking on its arrow in the navigator, and delete a breakpoint.

You can also edit a breakpoint's behavior. Control-click on the breakpoint, in the gutter or in the Breakpoint navigator, and choose Edit Breakpoint; or Command-Option-click the breakpoint. This is a very powerful facility: you can have a breakpoint pause only under a certain condition or after it has been encountered a certain number of times, and you can have a breakpoint perform one or more actions when it is encountered, such as issuing a debugger command, logging, playing a sound, speaking text, or running a script.

A breakpoint can be configured to continue automatically after performing its action when it is encountered. This can be an excellent alternative to caveman debugging: instead of inserting an NSLog call, which must be compiled into your code and later removed when the app is released, you can set a breakpoint that logs and continues; by definition, such a breakpoint operates only when you're debugging.

In the Breakpoint navigator, you can create two kinds of breakpoint that you can't create in the code editor: exception breakpoints and symbolic breakpoints. Click the Plus button at the bottom of the navigator and choose from its pop-up menu.

Exception breakpoint
    An exception breakpoint causes your app to pause at the time an exception is thrown or caught, without regard to whether the exception would crash your app later. I recommend that you create an exception breakpoint to pause on all exceptions

Figure 9-6. Paused at a breakpoint

when they are thrown, because this gives the best view of the call stack and variable values at the moment of the exception (rather than later when the crash actually occurs); you can see where you are in your code, and you can examine variable values, which may help you understand the cause of the problem. If you do create such an exception breakpoint, I also suggest that you use the contextual menu to say Move Breakpoint To → User, which makes this breakpoint permanent and global to all your projects.

Symbolic breakpoint

A symbolic breakpoint causes your app to pause when a certain method or function is called, regardless of what object called it or to what object the message is sent. The method or function name may be specified directly; a method may alternatively be specified using the instance method or class method symbol (- or +) followed by square brackets containing the class name and the method name. For example, to learn where in my app the `beginReceivingRemoteControlEvents` message was being sent to my shared application instance, I configured a symbolic breakpoint like this:

```
-[UIApplication beginReceivingRemoteControlEvents]
```

To toggle the active status of breakpoints as a whole, click the Breakpoints button in the project window toolbar, or choose Product → Debug → Activate/Deactivate Breakpoints (Command-Y). The active status of breakpoints as a whole doesn't affect the enabled or disabled status of any breakpoints; if breakpoints are inactive, they are simply ignored en masse, and no pausing at breakpoints takes place. Breakpoint arrows are blue if breakpoints are active, gray if they are inactive.

When the app runs with breakpoints active and an enabled breakpoint is encountered (and assuming its conditions are met, and so on), the app pauses. In the active project window, the editor shows the file containing the point of execution, which will usually be the file containing the breakpoint. The point of execution is shown as a green arrow; this is the line that is *about* to be executed (Figure 9-6). Depending on the settings for Running → Pauses in the Behaviors preference pane, the Debug navigator and the Debug pane will also appear.

Here are some things you might like to do while paused at a breakpoint:

See where you are

One common reason for setting a breakpoint is to make sure that the path of execution is passing through a certain line. You can see where you are in any of your methods by clicking on the method name in the call stack, shown in the Debug navigator.

Methods listed in the call stack with a User icon, with the text in black, are yours; click one to see where you are paused in that method. Other methods, with the text in gray, are methods for which you have no source code, so there would be little point clicking one unless you know something about assembly language. The slider in the filter bar hides chunks of the call chain, to save space, starting with the methods for which you have no source.

You can also navigate the call stack using the jump bar at the top of the Debug pane.

Study variable values

This is a very common reason for pausing. In the Debug pane, variable values for the current scope (corresponding to what's selected in the call stack) are visible in the variables list. You can see additional object features, such as collection elements, instance variables, and even some private information, by opening triangles.

Switch the pop-up menu above the variables list to Auto to see only those variables that Xcode thinks will interest you (because their value has been recently changed, for instance); if you're after completeness, Local will probably be the best setting. You can use the search field to filter variables by name or value.

In some cases, toggling Show Summmaries in the contextual menu can give a faster or more reliable display of variables. Even with formatted summaries turned off, you can send `description` to an object variable and view the output: choose Print Description of [Variable] from the contextual menu.

Set a watchpoint

A watchpoint is like a breakpoint, but instead of depending on a certain line of code it depends on a variable's value: the debugger pauses whenever the variable's value changes. You can set a watchpoint only while paused in the debugger. Control-click on the variable in the variables list and choose Watch [Variable]. Watchpoints, once created, are listed and managed in the Breakpoint navigator.

Manage expressions

An expression is code to be added to the variables list and evaluated every time we pause. Choose Add Expression from the contextual menu in the variables list. The expression is evaluated within the current context in your code, so be careful of side effects! Using `expr` in the console or as a breakpoint's Debugger Command action (see the next paragraph) would be less of a blunt instrument.

Talk to the debugger

You can communicate verbally with the debugger in the console. Xcode's debugger is a front end to an underlying command-line debugger tool (GDB or LLDB). Thus, by talking directly to that command-line tool you can do everything that you can do through the Xcode debugger interface, and more.

A common command is po (for "print object") followed by an object variable's name or a method call that returns an object; it calls the object's `description` method, just like NSLog. Another valuable command is `expr`, which evaluates an Objective-C expression in the current context — meaning, among other things, that you can call a method, or change the value of a variable in scope! Any such command is also eligible to be used as a breakpoint's Debugger Command action, meaning that a breakpoint can issue the command automatically.

For a good list of other things you're likely to say, see *http://lldb.llvm.org/lldb-gdb.html*.

Fiddle with breakpoints

You are free to create, destroy, enable and disable, and otherwise manage breakpoints dynamically even though your app is running, which is useful because where you'd like to pause next might depend on what you learn while you're paused here.

Indeed, this is one of the main advantages of breakpoints over caveman debugging. To change your caveman debugging, you have to stop the app, edit it, rebuild it, and start running the app all over again. But to fiddle with breakpoints, you don't have to be stopped; you don't even have to be paused! An operation that went wrong, if it doesn't crash your app, can probably be repeated in real time; so you can just add a breakpoint and try again. For example, if tapping a button produces the wrong results, you can add a breakpoint and tap the button again; this time through the same code, you can work out what the trouble is.

Step or continue

To proceed with your paused app, you can either resume running until the next breakpoint is encountered (Product → Debug → Continue) or take one step and pause again. Also, if you hover the mouse over the gutter, a green Continue to Here button appears; pressing this, or alternatively choosing Product → Debug → Continue to Current Line (or Continue to Here in the contextual menu), effectively sets a breakpoint at the chosen line, continues, and removes the breakpoint.

The stepping commands (under Product → Debug) are:

Step Over
> Pause at the next line.

Step Into
> Pause in your method that the current line calls, if there is one; otherwise, pause at the next line.

Step Out
> Pause when we return from the current method.

You can access these commands through convenient buttons at the top of the Debug pane. Even if the Debug pane is collapsed, the part containing the buttons appears while running.

You can also float the project window over everything else on your computer while debugging by choosing Product → Debug Workflow → Xcode Always In Front; after you then switch to the Simulator, you can interact with the Xcode window without giving it focus. If you do want to give it focus, to type in a filter bar for instance, click Focus in the toolbar. This mode of working could be useful while you're interacting with the Simulator, so as not to have to keep switching between the Simulator and Xcode. To return the project window to its normal state, choose Standard Windowing from the Debugging pop-up menu in the window toolbar (or click Stop in the toolbar to kill the running app).

Start over, or abort
> To kill the running app, click Stop in the toolbar (Product → Stop, Command-Period). To kill the running app and relaunch it without rebuilding it, Control-click Run in the toolbar (Product → Perform Action → Run Without Building, Control-Command-R).

You can make changes to your code while the app is running or paused, but those changes are not magically communicated to the running app; there are languages and programming milieus where that sort of thing is possible, but Xcode and Objective-C are not among them. You must stop the app and run in the normal way (which includes building) to see your changes in action.

 Clicking the Home button in the Simulator or on the device does *not* stop the running app in the multitasking world of iOS 4 and later.

Unit Testing

Another way of verifying the correctness of your code is through unit tests. A unit test is basically a suite of methods that call methods of your app's code and use asserts to describe what should happen. Typically, unit tests are constructed so as to confirm not only that the app behaves as expected under normal conditions, but also that incorrect or extreme inputs are handled properly. There's even a school of thought that suggests you should write unit tests *before* writing the real code.

The easiest way to attach unit tests to your app is at the time you create the project: in the second dialog, check Include Unit Tests. Xcode endows your project with a secondary target, which is a Unit Testing Bundle consisting of the test code and linked to the SenTestingKit framework. The unit testing target has a *dependency* on the normal target; thus, if you build the normal target, you build your app normally, but if you build the unit testing target, you build your app along with the unit testing bundle.

To run unit tests against your app, you choose Product → Test. The project's scheme specifies that this means to build the unit testing target, and lists the test methods that are to be run; to specify particular test methods, edit the scheme.

You can subsequently add another Unit Testing Bundle target to your project if you like. When you do, an additional scheme is created. So, to run the tests in an added unit testing target, you'd change the scheme selection in the Scheme pop-up menu to specify that target, and choose Product → Test. However, adding such targets may require further work on your part: you might have to set up the necessary target dependency, edit the scheme, and adjust the target membership of your app's class files. The details can be tricky: see Setting Up Application Unit Tests in Apple's *Xcode Unit Testing Guide*.

For more information about unit testing, see Apple's *Xcode Unit Testing Guide*. The appendix to that document lists the SenTestingKit assert functions (actually macros) that you can use.

Static Analyzer

From time to time, you should use the static analyzer to look for possible sources of error in your code; choose Product → Analyze (Shift-Command-B). This command causes your code to be compiled, and the static analyzer studies it and reports its findings in the Issue navigator and in your code.

The static analyzer is static (it's analyzing your code, not debugging in real time), but it is remarkably intelligent and may well alert you to potential problems that could otherwise escape your notice. You might think that the compiler — including ARC, if you're using it — knows all there is to know about your code; and it is certainly true that one of the main reasons for using the static analyzer, namely, to assist with manual memory management of Objective-C instances, is essentially gone if you're using ARC. Still, the static analyzer actually studies the possible values and paths of execution in your code, and can detect potential sources of trouble in your program's *logic* that no mere compiler would worry about. For example, in this code, the static analyzer knows that i in the second line is uninitialized:

```
int i;
if (i) NSLog(@"here");
```

In this code, the static analyzer knows that the second line throws away the existing value of i without that value ever having been read:

```
int i=0;
i=1;
```

Those are tiny problems, but they illustrate how, in a complex program, the static analyzer is capable of noticing possible sources of trouble and bringing them to your attention. For more about the static analyzer, see *http://clang-analyzer.llvm.org*.

Clean

From time to time, during repeated testing and debugging, and before making a different sort of build (switching from Debug to Release, or running on a device instead of the Simulator), it is a good idea to *clean* your target. This means that existing builds will be removed and caches will be cleared, so that all code will be considered to be in need of compilation and the next build will build your app from scratch.

The first build of your app after you clean will take longer than usual. But it's worth it, because cleaning removes the cruft, quite literally. For example, suppose you have been including a certain resource in your app, and you decide it is no longer needed. You can remove it from the Copy Bundle Resources build phase (or from your project as a whole), but that doesn't remove it from your built app. Only cleaning will do that, because it removes the built app completely.

To clean, choose Product → Clean. For more complete cleaning, hold Option to get Product → Clean Build Folder.

In addition, Xcode stores builds and project indexes in *~/Library/Developer/Xcode/DerivedData*. From time to time, with Xcode not running, I like to move the contents of that folder to the trash. This is effectively a massive and even more complete clean of every project that you've opened recently. Alternatively, to trash the folder in *Derived-Data* for a single project from within Xcode, switch to the Projects tab of the Organizer window (Window → Organizer), select the project at the left, and click the Delete button next to the Derived Data listing at the top of the window. A project will take longer to open for the first time afterward, because its index must be rebuilt, and it will take longer to build, because its build information has been removed. But the space savings on your hard disk can be significant, and forcing the index to rebuild itself can actually ward off certain problems.

You should also from time to time remove all versions of your built app from the Simulator cache. Choose iOS Simulator → Reset Content and Settings. Alternatively, you can clean the Simulator cache by hand. To do so, first quit the Simulator if it's running. Then find the cache in ~/Library/Application Support/iPhone Simulator, followed by the system version of the SDK (for example, there might be a folder called 6.1); within this, find the Applications folder, and move the contents of that folder to the trash. If there are multiple system version folders here, you might want to jettison the contents of the Applications folders of all of them.

Running in the Simulator

When you build and run with the Simulator as the destination, you run in the iOS Simulator application. The Simulator window represents a device. If your app runs on either iPhone or iPad (natively or in the iPhone emulator), you can choose which device is simulated as you choose your destination; similarly, if your app runs on multiple system versions, you can choose the system version of the simulated device as you choose your destination. (See Chapter 6 on destinations, and the first section of this chapter on device architectures and the Deployment Target build setting.)

You can also switch device types by choosing Hardware → Device in the Simulator. This quits your app running in the Simulator; you can relaunch it by building and running in Xcode again, or by clicking your app's icon in the Simulator. In the latter case there is no longer any connection to Xcode (you aren't using the debugger, so you won't stop at breakpoints, and log messages won't be relayed to the Xcode console); still, you might do this just to check quickly on how your app looks or behaves on a different device.

The one key choice you can make using Hardware → Device in the Simulator that you *can't* make by choosing a destination in Xcode is between iPad and iPad (Retina), or between iPhone, iPhone (Retina 3.5-inch), and iPhone (Retina 4-inch):

- The Retina display is a double-resolution screen, so it can be displayed at double size, with each pixel of the Retina display corresponding to a pixel of your computer's monitor.

- The Retina 4-inch display is the size of the iPhone 5 and 5th-generation iPod touch screen, as opposed to the Retina 3.5-inch screen, which is the size of the iPhone 4 and 4S, as well as the 4th-generation iPod touch. The Retina 3.5-inch screen is the double-resolution version of the screens of all earlier single-resolution iPhones and iPod touches.

Changing this setting quits your app running in the Simulator, but your choice will stick if you return to Xcode and build and run on iPhone again.

The Simulator window can be displayed at half, three-quarter, or full size (choose from Window → Scale). This is a matter of display merely, comparable to zooming the window, so your app running in the Simulator does not quit when you change this setting. For example, you might run a Retina device in the Simulator at full size to see every double-resolution pixel, or at half size to save space.

You can interact with the Simulator in some of the same basic ways as you would a device. Using the mouse, you can tap on the device's screen; hold Option to make the mouse represent two fingers and Option-Shift to move those fingers in parallel. Some Simulator representations display a Home button, which you click with the mouse, but the most reliable way to click the Home button is to choose Hardware → Home (Shift-Command-H). Menu items also let you perform hardware gestures such as rotating the device, shaking it, and locking its screen; you can also test your app by simulating certain rare events, such as a low-memory situation (and this is a useful thing to do from time to time; I'll talk more about it in Chapter 19).

The Debug menu in the Simulator is useful for detecting problems with animations and drawing. You can choose from this menu while your app is running in the Simulator, without causing the app to quit. Toggle Slow Animations is unique to the Simulator; it makes animations unfold in slow motion so that you can see just what's happening (animation is discussed in Chapter 17). The other four menu items represent features that were previously available only when running on a device using Instruments (mentioned later in this chapter), under the Core Animation instrument; now they are rolled directly into the Simulator as well.

I'll return to the specifics of what these menu items do when discussing drawing (Chapter 15) and layers (Chapter 16); but here's an example you can try immediately. Return to the Empty Window project developed in Chapter 7. In *AppDelegate.m*, we are pulling a label out of a nib and putting it into our interface by setting its center, like this:

```
[self.window.rootViewController.view addSubview: lab];
lab.center = CGPointMake(100,100);
lab.frame = CGRectIntegral(lab.frame);
```

If you comment out that last line, run the project in the Simulator with the device set to iPhone — not iPhone (Retina) — and toggle on Debug → Color Misaligned Images, you may see the label painted with a magenta overlay. That's because, without the call to CGRectIntegral, the label is misaligned; by default, the label is 21 points high, which is an odd number, so setting its center to an integral point value has caused its vertical position to be halfway between two integer pixel values on the device. The effect of this misalignment is actually visible to the naked eye if you know what to look for: the text looks fuzzy or bold. Using Debug → Color Misaligned Images alerts you to the issue; calling CGRectIntegral fixes it.

The Debug menu also contains some items that are useful when you're testing an app that uses Core Location (discussed in Chapter 35).

Running on a Device

Sooner or later, you're going to want to switch from running and testing and debugging in the Simulator to running and testing and debugging on a real device. The Simulator is nice, but it's only a simulation; there are many differences between the Simulator and a real device. The Simulator is really your computer, which is fast and has lots of memory, so problems with memory management and speed won't be exposed until you run on a device. User interaction with the Simulator is limited to what can be done with a mouse: you can click, you can drag, you can hold Option to simulate use of two fingers, but more elaborate gestures can be performed only on an actual device. And many iOS facilities, such as the accelerometer and access to the music library, are not present on the Simulator at all, so that testing an app that uses them is possible *only* on a device.

 Don't even think of developing an app without testing it on a device. You have no idea how your app *really* looks and behaves until you run it on a device. Submitting to the App Store an app that you have not run on a device is asking for trouble.

Before you can run your app on a device, even just to test, you must join the iOS Developer Program by paying the annual fee. (Yes, this is infuriating. Now get over it.) Only in this way can you obtain and provide to Xcode the credentials for running on a device. Once you have joined the iOS Developer Program, obtaining these credentials involves use of the iOS Provisioning Portal, which is accessed online, through your web browser (or, for certain actions, through Xcode itself).

 To reach the iOS Provisioning Portal in your browser (once you're an iOS Developer Program member), go to *http://developer.apple.com/devcenter/ios*. Click Log In to log in, and then click iOS Provisioning Portal at the upper right.

You will need to perform the following initial steps once:

1. Join the iOS Developer Program (*http://developer.apple.com/programs/ios*). This requires filling out a form and paying the annual fee. Unless you have multiple developers, all of whom might need to build and run on their own devices, the Individual program is sufficient. The Company program costs no more, but adds the ability to privilege additional developers in various roles. (You do *not* need the Company program just in order to distribute your built app to other users for testing.)

2. Obtain a *development certificate* that identifies and authorizes your computer. This is the computer to which you'll be attaching the device so you can run on it. Basically,

this certificate matches the person who uses your computer to the person interacting with the iOS Provisioning Portal. The certificate will be stored in your computer's keychain, where Xcode will be able to see it automatically.

The certificate depends upon a private–public key pair. The private key will live in your keychain; the public key will be handed over to the iOS Provisioning Portal, to be built into the certificate. The way you give the Portal your public key is through a *request* for the certificate. So, you generate the private–public key pair; your keychain keeps the private key; the public key goes into the certificate request; you submit the request, containing the public key, to the Portal; and the Portal sends back the certificate, also containing the public key, which also goes into your keychain, where it is matched with the private key, thus ensuring that you are you.

Detailed instructions for generating the private–public key pair and the certificate request are available once you've joined the iOS Developer Program and have logged in at Apple's developer site. (The process is described at *http://developer.apple.com/ios/ manage/certificates/team/howto.action*. A video review of the steps involved is available to anyone at *http://developer.apple.com/ios/videos/popupcerts.action*.) Basically, you start up Keychain Access and choose Keychain Access → Certificate Assistant → Request a Certificate from a Certificate Authority. Using your name and email address as identifiers, you generate and save to disk a 2048-bit RSA certificate request file. Your private key is stored in your keychain then and there; the certificate request contains your public key.

You then go to the iOS Provisioning Portal in your browser. At the Portal, upload the certificate request file using the Development (not Distribution!) tab of the Certificates section. You may have to approve your own request, and you may have to refresh that web page to see the Download button.

 If this is your very, very first time obtaining any certificate from the Portal, you will need *another* certificate: the WWDR Intermediate Certificate. This is the certificate that certifies that certificates issued by WWDR (the Apple Worldwide Developer Relations Certification Authority) are to be trusted. (You can't make this stuff up.) You'll see a link for this intermediate certificate; click it to download the intermediate certificate. Double-click the intermediate certificate file; it is imported by your keychain. You can then throw the file away.

When the development certificate itself is ready, you download it and double-click it; Keychain Access automatically imports the certificate and stores it in your keychain. You do not need to keep the certificate request file or the development certificate file; your keychain now contains all the needed credentials. If this has worked, you can see

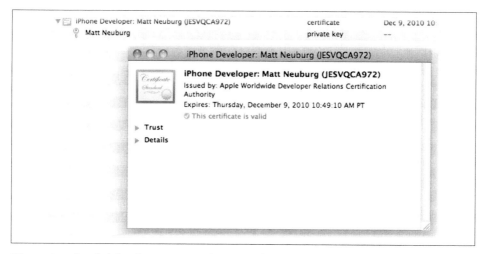

Figure 9-7. A valid development certificate, as shown in Keychain Access

the certificate in your keychain, read its details, and observe that it is valid and linked to your private key (Figure 9-7).

With your development certificate in place, you need to register a device for development use, meaning that you'll be able to build and run from Xcode onto that device rather than the Simulator. This can be done entirely from within Xcode. Open the Organizer window (Window → Organizer) and switch to the Devices tab. Select Provisioning Profiles under Library at the left, and make sure Automatic Device Provisioning is checked at the bottom of the window. Attach your device to the computer; the device name appears at the left under Devices. Select it, and click Use For Development. You'll be asked for your Portal username and password. Xcode connects to the Portal via the Internet and does two things:

- It registers your device at the Portal by its name and unique identifier number. You could have done this yourself in your browser (at the Portal, under Devices), but this way it is done for you.

- It creates and downloads from the Portal a universal development provisioning profile (referred to as a *team provisioning profile*) for development on this device. This is something you can't do at the Portal yourself. A development provisioning profile created manually at the Portal applies to a single app; in the past, when the Portal was the only way to obtain a development provisioning profile, you had to generate a new development provisioning profile for each app you wanted to test on a device, which was very inconvenient. But the team provisioning profile generated by Xcode applies to all apps. The team provisioning profile appears in the Organizer, under Provisioning Profiles; you can identify it because it is called iOS

Team Provisioning Profile and has an app identifier consisting of just a key and an asterisk, like this: B398E68A3D.*.

If your device is already registered at the Portal but Use For Development doesn't appear in Xcode and you've no team provisioning profile, go back to Provisioning Profiles under Library and click Refresh at the bottom right of the window. The team provisioning profile will be regenerated. If you later add further devices for development (Use for Development) and you already have a team provisioning profile, they will be added to it automatically, within Xcode.

 If you develop an app that uses certain specialized features, such as push notifications (Chapter 37), iCloud (Chapter 36), or in-app purchases, you must generate a development provisioning profile the old way, manually at the Portal, in order to obtain the necessary entitlements. To do so, first enter your app by name and bundle id in the App IDs section of the Portal. Now go to Provisioning and the Development section and generate a new provisioning profile, specifying that app and your device(s). You can then download the provisioning profile in the Organizer window, under Provisioning Profiles, by clicking the Refresh button.

You now have a development provisioning profile in Xcode (the team provisioning profile). You can install this provisioning profile onto your device manually in the Organizer window by dragging its listing (under Provisioning Profiles) onto the device's name (under Devices) when the device is connected. Alternatively, you can just start building and running on the device. Start with a project window. With the device attached to the computer, pick the destination in the Scheme pop-up menu corresponding to your device; then build and run. If Xcode complains that your device doesn't contain a copy of the provisioning profile, and offers to install it for you, accept that offer.

The app is built, loaded onto your device, and runs. As long as you launch the app from Xcode, everything is just as when running in the Simulator: you can run, or you can debug, and the running app is in communication with Xcode, so that you can stop at breakpoints, read messages in the console, and so on. The outward difference is that to interact physically with the app, you use the device (attached to your computer), not the Simulator.

Profile and Device Management

Your central location for surveying provisioning profiles, identities (certificates) and devices is the Devices tab of the Organizer window (Window → Organizer). Under

Library, select Provisioning Profiles for a list of profiles. Under Teams, you'll see a list of your developer identities and their associated certificates.

As someone with more than one computer, I find the coolest feature of this interface to be the Export button at the bottom of the window. When you click it, you're asked for a password (twice), which can be anything you like; it outputs a *.developerprofile* file. On another computer, run Xcode and double-click that *.developerprofile* file in the Finder. Xcode asks for a password. Enter the same password you gave previously, and like magic the entire suite of teams and identities and certificates and provisioning profiles springs to life in that other copy of Xcode, including the entries in your keychain.

When a device is attached to the computer, it is listed with a green dot under Devices. Click its name to access information on the device. You can see the device's unique identifier. You can see provisioning profiles that have been installed on the device. You can view the device's console log in real time, just as if you were running the Console application to view your computer's logs. You can see log reports for crashes that took place on the device. And you can take screenshots that image your device's screen; you'll need to do this for your app when you submit it to the App Store. Device logs and screenshots are also available under Library.

Version Control

Various systems of *version control* exist for taking periodic snapshots (technically called *commits*) of your project. The value of such a system to you will depend on what system you use and how you use it; for example, you might use version control because it lets you store your commits in a repository offsite, so that your code isn't lost in case of a local computer glitch or some equivalent "hit by a bus" scenario, or because it allows multiple developers to access the same code.

To me, personally, the chief value of version control is *freedom from fear*. Having version control actually changes the way I program. A project is a complicated thing, consisting of numerous files. Often, changes must be made in many files before a new feature can be tested. Thus it is all too easy to start down some virtual road involving creating or editing multiple files, only to find yourself at the end of a blind alley and needing to retrace your steps. Version control means that I can easily retrace my steps; I have but to say, in the language of some version control system I've been using, "Forget everything I just did and return the whole project to where it was at such-and-such a commit." I rarely, if ever, *in fact* retrace my steps, but the knowledge that I *could* do so gives me the courage to try some programming strategy whose outcome may not be apparent until after many days of effort. Also, I can ask a version control system, "What the heck are all the changes I've made since the last commit?" In short, without version control I'd be lost, confused, hesitant, rooted to the spot, paralyzed with uncertainty; with it, I forge boldly ahead and get things done. For this reason, my current personal favorite version

Figure 9-8. Version comparison

control system is git (*http://git-scm.com*), whose agile facilities for managing branches give me tremendous license to experiment.

Xcode provides various version control facilities. Starting with Xcode 4, those facilities concentrate on git and Subversion (*http://subversion.apache.org*). This doesn't mean you can't use any other version control system with your projects! It means only that you can't use any other version control system in an integrated fashion from inside Xcode. Personally, I don't find that to be any kind of restriction. For years I've used Subversion, and more recently git, on my Xcode projects from the command line in Terminal, or through specialized third-party GUI front ends such as svnX for Subversion (*http://www.lachoseinteractive.net/en/products*) or SourceTree for git (*http://www.sourcetreeapp.com*). I'm comfortable and nimble at the command line, and access to version control from within Xcode itself is not a priority for me.

At the same time, version control integration in Xcode 4 is greatly improved and far more extensive than previously:

Automatic git repository creation
 When you create a new project, the Save dialog includes a checkbox that offers to place a git repository into your project folder from the outset.

Automatic repository detection
 When you open an existing project, if that project is already managed with Subversion or git, Xcode detects this and is ready instantly to display version control information in its interface.

Version comparison
 The Version editor (View → Version Editor → Show Version Editor, or click the third button in the Editor segmented control in the project window toolbar) includes a view similar to that of the File Merge utility, graphically displaying the differences between versions of a file. For example, in Figure 9-8, I can see that in the more recent version of this file (on the left) I've changed `representative-Item` to `items[0]`. The Version editor also includes various ways to survey and navigate versions and commit logs. For example, if I switch to Blame view I can see my own commit message explaining the change I just mentioned: "Stop using `representativeItem`, in order to avoid nasty log messages (reported to Apple)."

Without minimizing these features, I don't rely on them exclusively or even primarily (although I certainly take advantage of them where convenient). I find version control management through the command line far easier and clearer for many purposes, and Xcode doesn't come close to the command line's power, especially for managing branches; Xcode has nothing like the visual branch representation of git's own gitk tool; and Xcode's repository management in the Organizer window is downright crude. In addition, as of this writing, Xcode's git integration is fundamentally flawed: if I create a new file in a git-controlled project, Xcode adds it to the staging area (the git index) rather than letting me compose the commit in my own way, so that I typically have to switch to the command line and say git reset to fend off Xcode's interference.

Version control in general is a large and complicated topic. Use and configuration of any version control system can be tricky and scary at first and always requires some care. So I'm deliberately not going to say anything specific about it; I'm mentioning it at all only because version control of some sort is in fact likely, sooner or later, to play a role in the life cycle of your projects. When it does, you'll want to read up on the use of your chosen version control system, along with "Save and Revert Changes to Projects" in the *Xcode 4 User Guide.* You'll find Xcode's integrated version control facilities in three chief locations:

The File menu
> The relevant menu items are all under File → Source Control. The most frequently used commands are Add and Commit on the one hand, and Discard Changes on the other. You can go a very long way with elementary use of git through just those three menu items.

The Version editor
> Choose View → Version Editor → Show Version Editor, or click the third button in the Editor segmented control in the project window toolbar.

The Organizer
> The Repositories tab of the Organizer window lists known repositories and branches for each project, along with their commit logs. Also, use the Plus button at the bottom of the navigator to enter data about a remote repository, so that you can obtain a copy of its contents.

Xcode also contains its own way of taking and storing a snapshot of your project as a whole; this is done using File → Create Snapshot (and, according to your settings, some mass operations such as find-and-replace or refactoring may offer to take a snapshot first). Snapshots themselves are managed in the Projects tab of the Organizer window. Although these snapshots are not to be treated as full-fledged version control, they are in fact maintained as git repositories, and can certainly serve the purpose of giving confidence in advance of performing some change that might subsequently engender regret. You can manage snapshots in the Projects tab of the Organizer window; here you export a snapshot, thus resurrecting an earlier state of your project folder.

Instruments

As your app approaches completion, you may wish to fine-tune it for memory usage, speed, and other real-time behavior. Xcode provides a sophisticated and powerful utility application, Instruments, that lets you collect profiling data on your app as it runs. The graphical display and detailed data provided by Instruments may give you the clues you need to optimize your app.

You can use Instruments on the Simulator or the device. The device is where you'll do your ultimate testing, and certain instruments (such as Core Animation) are available only for the device; on the other hand, certain other instruments (such as Zombies) are available only in the Simulator.

To get started with Instruments, set the desired destination in the Scheme pop-up menu in the project window toolbar, and choose Product → Profile. (For memory usage, your destination can be the Simulator, but for most other forms of analysis, you'll want to run on a device to achieve maximum verisimilitude.) Your app builds using the Profile action for your scheme; by default, this uses the Release build configuration, which is probably what you want. If you're running on a device, you may see some some validation warnings, but you can safely ignore them. Instruments launches; if your scheme's Instrument pop-up menu for the Profile action is set to Ask on Launch (the default), Instruments presents a dialog where you choose a trace template. If you're running on the Simulator, you might have to pass through an authorization dialog the first time you use Instruments. With Instruments running, you should interact with your app like a user; Instruments will record its statistics. Once Instruments is running, it can be further customized to profile the kind of data that particularly interests you, and you can save the structure of the Instruments window as a custom template.

Use of Instruments is an advanced topic and beyond the scope of this book. Indeed, an entire book could (and really should) be written about Instruments alone. For proper information, you should read Apple's documents, especially the *Instruments User Reference* and *Instruments User Guide*. Also, many WWDC videos from current and prior years are about Instruments; look for sessions with "Instruments" or "Performance" in their names. Here, I'll just demonstrate, without much explanation, the sort of thing Instruments can do.

I'll start by charting the memory usage of my TidBITS News app as it starts up and the user proceeds to work with it. Memory is a scarce resource on a mobile device, so it's important to be certain that we're not hogging too much of it. I'll set the destination to the Simulator and choose Product → Profile; Instruments launches, and I'll choose the Allocations trace template and click Profile. My app starts running in the Simulator, and I work with it for a while and then pause Instruments, which meanwhile has charted my memory usage (Figure 9-9). Examining the chart, I find there are a couple of spikes early on, first as the app launches and then as the app downloads and parses an RSS

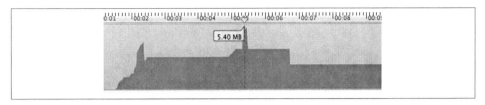

Figure 9-9. Instruments graphs memory usage over time

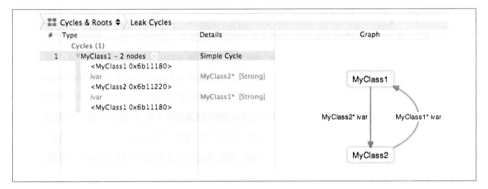

Figure 9-10. Instruments describes a leak

feed; but it's only 5.40 MB at its maximum, and the app settles down to use slightly over 2 MB pretty steadily thereafter. These are very gentle memory usage figures, so I'm happy.

Another field of Instruments expertise is the ability to detect memory leaks. Memory leaks, discussed further in Chapter 12, remain possible even under ARC. In this trivial example, I have two classes, MyClass1 and MyClass2; MyClass1 has an ivar property which is a MyClass2 instance, and MyClass2 has an ivar property which is a MyClass1 instance. The app runs this code:

```
MyClass1* m1 = [MyClass1 new];
MyClass2* m2 = [MyClass2 new];
m1.ivar = m2;
m2.ivar = m1;
```

There are steps I could have taken to prevent this from being a memory leak, as I'll explain in Chapter 12; but I haven't taken those steps, so it *is* a memory leak. I'll set the destination to the Simulator and choose Product → Profile; Instruments launches, and I'll choose the Leaks trace template and click Profile. My app starts running in the Simulator, and after about 10 seconds (the default interval at which Instruments runs its leak analysis), a leak is detected. After some appropriate button-pushing, I'm actually shown a diagram of the mistake that's causing this leak (Figure 9-10)!

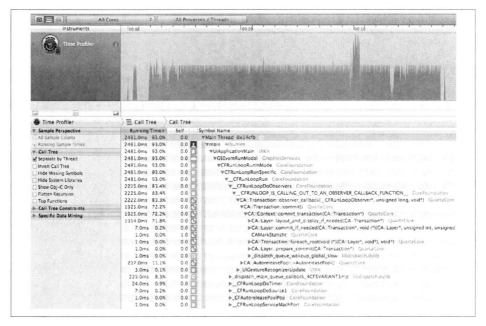

Figure 9-11. A time profile in Instruments

In this final example, I'm concerned with what's taking my Albumen app so long to switch from master view to detail view. I'll set the destination to a device, because that's where speed matters and needs to be measured, and choose Product → Profile; Instruments launches, and I'll choose the Time Profiler trace template and click Profile. The master view appears; I'll tap a cell in the table view, and after a significant delay, the detail view appears. Now I'll pause Instruments and look at what it's telling me.

As we can see from Figure 9-11, this transition is taking nearly three seconds. Opening the triangles in the lower portion of the window, it turns out that much of this is spent in something described as `CA::Layer::layout_and_display_if_needed`. That's not my code; it's deep inside Cocoa. But by clicking the little arrow that appears to the right of that line when I hover the mouse over it, I can see the call stack and discover how my code is involved in this call (Figure 9-12).

One line of my code is involved in this call: `tableView:heightForRowAtIndexPath:`. This is where we work out the heights of the table view cells to be shown in the detail view. By double-clicking the listing of that line, I can see my own code, time-profiled (Figure 9-13).

This is really useful information. It's also fairly depressing. The bulk of the time is being spent in Cocoa's `systemLayoutSizeFittingSize:`. That call is how I calculate the height

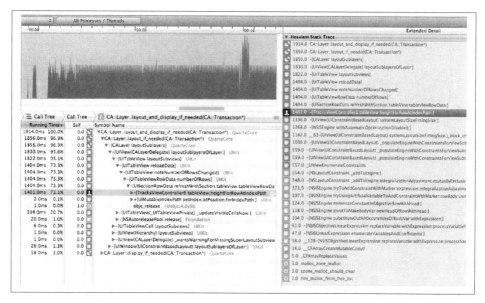

Figure 9-12. Drilling down into the time profile

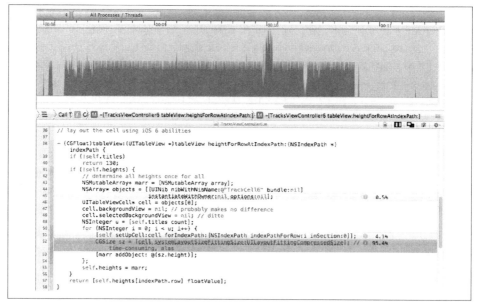

Figure 9-13. My code, time-profiled

of the table view cell using iOS 6's new autolayout feature (Chapter 21). This approach is working perfectly, but clearly it is relatively expensive.

It is a programming proverb that one should not optimize prematurely; equally, one should not spend time optimizing when the resulting savings will make no perceptible difference to the user. I know how I used to calculate the table view cell height before iOS 6; it was much less elegant, but it was faster — and I can prove this quantitatively through further measurement, analysis, and experimentation. That's exactly the value of Instruments: for guesswork and impressions, it substitutes actual numbers and facts. Unfortunately, Instruments can't tell me how to make the trade-off between the increased speed of the old approach and the greater elegance and reliability of the new approach.

Distribution

By *distribution* is meant providing your app to others who are not developers on your team. There are two kinds of distribution:

Ad Hoc distribution
> You are providing a copy of your app to a limited set of known users so that they can try it on their devices and report bugs, make suggestions, and so forth.

App Store distribution
> You are providing the app to the App Store so that anyone can download it (possibly for a fee) and run it.

 The Portal imposes a registration limit of 100 devices per year per developer (not per app), which limits your number of Ad Hoc testers. Your own devices used for development are counted against this limit.

To perform any kind of distribution, you will need a *distribution certificate*, which is different from the development certificate discussed earlier in this chapter. Like the development certificate, you need only one distribution certificate; it identifies you as you. Obtaining a distribution certificate is exactly like obtaining a development certificate, except that, at the iOS Provisioning Portal, under Certificates, you use the Distribution tab instead of the Development tab.

You will also need a *distribution profile* specifically for this app, which is different from the development profile you obtained earlier. You can't obtain a distribution profile from within Xcode; you must get it at the Portal in your browser. You might need *two* distribution profiles, because the profile for an Ad Hoc distribution is different from the profile for an App Store distribution. Remember, you will need a separate set of distribution profiles for each app you plan to distribute.

When you build for distribution, you'll use the Product → Archive command. Indeed, you can think of *archive* as meaning "build for distribution." However, you have some preparation to do before you can archive in such a way as to make an app you can actually distribute. If you look at the Archive action in your default scheme, you'll discover that it is set to use the Release distribution configuration. But if you examine the Code Signing Identity build setting for your project, you'll see that by default it uses a development profile (most likely the team development profile). This won't do; when you intend to distribute a copy of your app, you want to use a distribution profile. The solution I recommend is to create a third build configuration called Distribution; you can then set the Archive action in your scheme to use the Distribution build configuration, and set the Code Signing Identity build setting to use the distribution profile when the Distribution build configuration is in force.

First, here are the steps for obtaining a distribution profile:

1. To obtain an Ad Hoc distribution profile, collect the unique identifiers of all the devices where this build is to run, and add each of the device identifiers at the Portal under Devices. (For an App Store profile, omit this step.)

2. In the Portal, in the Distribution (not Development!) tab of the Provisioning section, ask for a New Profile. In the New Profile form, ask for an Ad Hoc profile or an App Store profile, depending on which you're after.

3. Describe the profile, giving it a name, and specifying your distribution certificate and this app. For an Ad Hoc profile, also specify all the devices you want the app to run on. Be careful about the profile's name, as you will need to be able to identify it later from within Xcode! My own practice is to assign a name containing both the name of the app and the term "adhoc" or "appstore".

4. Click Submit to generate the profile; you might then have to refresh the browser window to see the Download button next to your new profile. Download the profile and drag it onto Xcode's icon in the Dock. You can now throw the profile away in the Finder; Xcode has kept a copy (which should appear in the Organizer window).

Now here are the steps to create and use a Distribution build configuration for your project:

1. Edit the project. In the Info tab, click the Plus button below the list of configurations, and duplicate the Release configuration. Name the new configuration Distribution.

2. Edit the project (still). In the Build Settings tab, locate the Code Signing Identity entry. The Distribution build setting is now listed here, with a subentry Any iOS SDK. Set the value of this subentry to the appropriate distribution profile for this app.

3. Edit the scheme, and switch to the Archive action. Change the build configuration to Distribution, and click OK.

The result is that from now on, when you choose Build → Archive, you'll use a distribution profile associated with this app. That means you'll be able to distribute the archived app.

Ad Hoc Distribution

To create and distribute an Ad Hoc distribution build, first switch to the iOS Device destination in the Scheme pop-up menu in the project window toolbar. Until you do this, the Product → Archive menu item will be disabled. You do *not* have to have a device connected; you are not building to run on a particular device, but to save an archive.

Apple's docs say that an Ad Hoc distribution build should include an icon that will appear in iTunes, but my experience is that this step is unnecessary. If you want to include this icon, it should be a PNG or JPEG file, 512×512 pixels in size, and its name should be *iTunesArtwork*, with *no file extension*. Make sure the icon is included in the build, being present in the Copy Bundle Resources build phase.

Now choose Product → Archive. The build is created and copied into a date folder within *~/Library/Developer/Xcode/Archives*; it also appears in the Organizer window in the Archives tab. Locate the archive in the Organizer window. You can add a comment here; you can also change the archive's name (this won't affect the name of the app).

 If Xcode refuses to build because of a Code Sign error, it may help to close the project window and delete this project's entire build folder from the DerivedData directory, as described earlier in this chapter. When you reopen the project, after Xcode has finished reindexing it, check the build settings for your Distribution configuration; it may help to set once again the value of Any iOS SDK for the Distribution configuration under Code Signing Identity. See also Apple's tech note TN2250, "Understanding and Resolving Code Signing Issues."

Select the archive and press the Distribute button at the upper right of the window. A dialog appears. Here, you are to specify a procedure; choose Save for Enterprise or Ad-Hoc Deployment. You are now asked to choose a code signing identity; specify the identity associated with the Ad Hoc distribution profile for this app. Click Next.

After a while, a Save dialog appears. Give the file a useful name; this won't affect the name of the app. Save the file to disk. It will have the suffix *.ipa* ("iPhone app").

Locate in the Finder the file you just saved. Provide this file to your users with instructions. A user should copy the *.ipa* file to a safe location, such as the Desktop, and then launch iTunes and drag the *.ipa* file from the Finder onto the iTunes icon in the Dock. Then the user should connect the device to the computer, make certain the app is present *and checked* in the list of apps for this device, and sync the device to cause the app to be copied to it. (If this isn't the first version of your app that you've distributed to your ad hoc testers, the user might need to delete the current version from the device beforehand; otherwise, the new version might not be copied to the device when syncing.)

If you listed your own device as one of the devices for which this Ad Hoc distribution profile was to be enabled, you can obey these instructions yourself to make sure the Ad Hoc distribution is working as expected. First, remove from your device any previous copies of this app (such as development copies) and any profiles that might be associated with this app (in the Settings app, under General → Profiles). Then copy the app onto your device by syncing with iTunes as just described. The app should run on your device, and you should see the Ad Hoc distribution profile on your device (in the Settings app). Because you are not privileged over your other Ad Hoc testers, what works for you should work for them.

Final App Preparations

As the big day approaches when you're thinking of submitting your app to the App Store, don't let the prospect of huge fame or massive profits hasten you past the all-important final stages of app preparation. Apple has a lot of requirements for your app, such as icons and launch images, and failure to meet them can cause your app to be rejected. Take your time. Make a checklist and go through it carefully. See the *iOS Application Programming Guide* for full details.

At various stages, you can obtain validation of your app to confirm that you haven't omitted certain requirements. For example, by default, a new project's Release build configuration has the Validate Build Product build setting set to Yes. Thus, when I do a build of the Empty Window app we've developed in previous chapters, if that build uses the Release build configuration (or the Distribution build configuration duplicated from it), Xcode warns that the app has no icon. When you submit your app to the App Store, it will be subjected to even more rigorous validation.

Icons in the App

An icon file must be a PNG file, without alpha transparency. It should be a full square, without shading (the "shine" effect that you see in the upper part of icons on your device); the rounding of the corners and shine will be added for you. You can prevent the shine effect from being added to the icon for your App Store build by defining and checking the "Icon already includes gloss and bevel effects" key (UIPrerenderedIcon) in your *Info.plist*.

On a device, the system uses the "Icon files" key in your app's *Info.plist* file to locate your icons, and it decides which icon to use under what circumstances by examining their sizes. Therefore, these sizes must be exactly correct. The required sizes for current systems and devices are as follows:

- For an iPhone app, there should be two primary app icons, one 57×57 pixels, the other 114×114 pixels (for use on the double-resolution Retina display).

- For an iPad app, there should be two primary app icons, one 72×72 pixels, the other 144×144 pixels (for use on the double-resolution Retina display).

A double-resolution variant of an icon should have the same name as the single-resolution variant, except for the addition of @2x to its name. A universal app will need all four icons.

To add your icons, edit the target and drag-and-drop each icon into the appropriate space in the Summary tab. Xcode will incorporate the icons into the project and the target and configure your *Info.plist* for you. For example, if I drop a 57×57 PNG file called *myDumbIcon.png* onto the first iPhone icon space, it is copied into the project and added to the target. In my *Info.plist*, the result is a structure as follows:

```
Icon files (iOS 5)  (Dictionary)
    Primary Icon    (Dictionary)
      Icon files    (Array)
        Item 0      myDumbIcon.png
```

Other icons can be added to the "Icon files" array. (The reason for this rather convoluted structure is so that Newsstand apps can include a separate Newsstand icon.) Alternatively, you can specify the icon file(s) manually. You will then have to take upon yourself the responsibility for making sure that each icon file is part of the target and the Copy Bundle Resources build phase, and you'll have to edit *Info.plist* yourself.

Optionally, you may elect to include smaller versions of your icon to appear when the user does a search on the device, as well as in the Settings app, if you include a settings bundle (Chapter 36). The smaller icon sizes are 29×29 (and 58×58 pixels for its double-resolution partner) for iPhone search results and the Settings bundle, and 50×50 (and 100×100 for its double-resolution partner) for iPad search results. Follow the instructions in the previous paragraph for specifying these icon files manually. However, I never include these icons, and no ill consequences have accrued.

 The difficulty of getting the required icon sizes right is greatly increased by the proliferation of outdated information throughout Apple's own documentation. The "App-Related Resources" chapter of the *iOS App Programming Guide* appears to be the best source of information at the moment. See also "Custom Icon and Image Creation Guidelines" in Apple's *iOS Human Interface Guidelines*.

Other Icons

When you submit the app to the App Store, you will be asked to supply a 1024×1024 PNG, JPEG, or TIFF icon to be displayed at the App Store. Have this icon ready before submission. Apple's guidelines say that it should not merely be a scaled-up version of your app's icon, but it must not differ perceptibly from your app's icon, either, or your app will be rejected (I know this from experience).

The App Store icon does *not* need to be built into your app; indeed, it should not be, as it will merely swell the built app's size unnecessarily (remember that space is at a premium on a device, and that your app must be downloaded from the App Store, so users appreciate your keeping your app as small as possible). On the other hand, you will probably want to keep it in your project (and in your project folder) so that you can find and maintain it easily. So I recommend that you import it into your project and copy it into your project folder, but do *not* add it to any target.

If you created a 512×512 icon file for Ad Hoc distribution, you may wish to delete it from the Copy Bundle Resources build phase now so that it doesn't swell the final app's size unnecessarily.

Launch Images

There is a delay between the moment when the user taps your app's icon to launch it and the moment when your app is up and running and displaying its initial window. To cover this delay and give the user the sense that something is happening, you must provide a launch image to be displayed during that interval.

The launch image might be just a blank depiction of the main elements or regions of the app's interface, so that when the actual window appears, those elements or regions will seem to be filled in. The best way to create such a launch image is to start with a screenshot of your app's actual initial interface. That way, all you have to do is blank out the details. Typically, I add some temporary code to my app such that it will launch into a blank version of its normal interface; I then take a screenshot of that, and remove the temporary code. Taking screenshots is covered in the next section.

You do not need to blank out the status bar. On an iPhone (or iPad touch), the status bar area of your launch image will be covered by the real status bar. For an iPad, you must trim the status bar area off your launch image entirely. (I use the shareware GraphicConverter, *http://www.lemkesoft.com*, to do this easily and precisely.)

Starting with the advent of the iPhone 5 (and fifth-generation iPod touch), whose screen has a longer height dimension, the runtime now uses the launch image for a second purpose — namely, to determine whether your app is to run "natively" on these devices. The rule is that if your app contains a launch image specifically targeted to this elongated screen size, your app will occupy the entire screen; if not, it will be displayed letterboxed, at the size of the iPhone 4 screen, with black bars at the top and bottom.

Don't add an iPhone 5 launch image to your app unless it *can* run natively on the iPhone 5! Your app must be able to respond to the fact that it might appear in the iPhone 4's shorter screen dimensions or in the iPhone 5's longer screen dimensions. This will require adjustment of the interface in real time. The best way to perform such adjustment is through autolayout constraints (Chapter 14), but of course there's a backwards-compatibility trade-off here, because (as I mentioned earlier in this chapter) you can't use autolayout constraints in an app running on iOS 5 or earlier.

A launch image must be a PNG file, and must be named *Default.png* with the addition of appropriate name qualifiers. An iPhone app will typically have a single initial launch orientation, but an iPad app is supposed to launch into either portrait or landscape orientation and thus requires a launch image for each orientation. A minimally full set of launch images must therefore have the following names and sizes:

- *Default.png*, 320×480 pixels
- *Default@2x.png*, 640×960 pixels (Retina)
- *Default-568h@2x.png*, 640×1136 pixels (iPhone 5)
- *Default-Portrait~ipad.png*, 768×1004 pixels
- *Default-Landscape~ipad.png*, 1004×768 pixels
- *Default-Portrait@2x~ipad.png*, 1536×2008 pixels (Retina)
- *Default-Landscape@2x~ipad.png*, 2008×1536 pixels (Retina)

The current versions of the Xcode app templates include initial all-black versions of the three iPhone launch images. This is a courtesy that permits you to run your app on the iPhone 5, including the Simulator, at native size from the outset. You'll need to replace these with real launch images before submission to the App Store.

 Annoyingly, initial all-black versions of the four iPad launch images are *not* included in the app templates — and the consequence is that, for a universal app, the iPhone launch images are wrongly used on the iPad! I have submitted a bug to Apple regarding this, and my impression is that I'm not the only one.

In Xcode 4.5 and later, adding launch images is easy. Delete the existing launch images first. Now edit the target and drag-and-drop each launch image onto the appropriate area of the Summary tab. Xcode will copy and rename the image for you, and include it in your target and the Copy Bundle Resources build phase. For example, if I drop a 320×480 PNG file called *myLaunchImage.png* onto the first iPhone launch image space for our Empty Window project, it is copied into the project and added to the target, and the copy is renamed *Default.png*.

In theory, you can use the orientation suffixes in the names of launch images on the iPhone as well. To distinguish between a launch image to be used on the iPhone and a launch image with the same orientation suffix to be used on the iPad, use additional suffixes ~ipad and ~iphone. Thus you can end up with file names like *Default-Portrait@2x~iphone.png*. In addition, you can replace *Default* with some other base name by creating the "Launch image" key in your *Info.plist* file and setting its value appropriately; but I've never done that.

For further details, see the "App-Related Resources" chapter of the *iOS App Programming Guide*, and "Custom Icon and Image Creation Guidelines" in Apple's *iOS Human Interface Guidelines*.

Screenshots

When you submit the app to the App Store, you will be asked for one or more screenshots of your app in action to be displayed at the App Store. You should take these screenshots beforehand and be prepared to provide them during the app submission process.

The required screenshot sizes are listed in Apple's *iTunes Connect Developer Guide*, under "Adding New Apps"; look for Table 7-3, "Icon and screenshot field descriptions". The dimensions of a screenshot depend on its orientation, the screen size, and whether this is a full-screen app — if it isn't, you must trim the status bar off the screenshot. You must provide at least one screenshot corresponding to the screen size of every device on which your app can run, except that all screenshots must be double-resolution — not because the target device will necessarily be double-resolution, but because there's a chance that this screenshot will be viewed on a double-resolution device. Typical screenshot dimensions for an app that displays the status bar are thus 640×920 or 960×600 (iPhone), 640×1096 or 1136×600 (iPhone 5), and 1536×2008 or 2048×1496 (iPad).

You can obtain screenshots either from the Simulator or from a device connected to the computer. The Simulator is a particularly good approach when you need a double-resolution launch image and you don't have a double-resolution device.

If you're going to use the Simulator, configure it to the correct device with the Hardware → Device menu. Run the app and get it into the desired state. Then:

Simulator
 In the Simulator application, choose File → Save Screen Shot.

Device
 In Xcode, in the Organizer window, locate your device under Devices and click Screenshots. Click New Screenshot, at the lower right of the window.

To make screenshots available for upload, select each one in the left side of the Devices tab of the Organizer window and click Export to save it with a nice filename into the Finder. Trim off the status bar if necessary. You may need to rotate a screenshot to get it into the correct orientation.

If a screenshot is listed in the Organizer window, you can turn it directly into a launch image (see the previous section): select it and click Save as Launch Image. A dialog will ask what name to assign to it and what open project to add it to.

Property List Settings

A number of settings in *Info.plist* are crucial to the proper behavior of your app. You should peruse Apple's *Information Property List Key Reference* for full information. Most of the required keys are created as part of the template, and are given reasonable default values, but you should check them anyway. The following are particularly worthy of attention:

Bundle display name (`CFBundleDisplayName`)
> The name that appears under your app's icon on the device screen; this name needs to be short in order to avoid truncation.

Status bar style (`UIStatusBarStyle`)
> On the iPhone and iPod touch, the look of the status bar. (On the iPad, the status bar is always black opaque.) In Xcode 4.5 and later, you can set this value using the Style pop-up menu in the Summary tab when you edit your target. Your choices are Default ("Gray style", `UIStatusBarStyleDefault`), Black Translucent ("Transparent black style", `UIStatusBarStyleBlackTranslucent`), and Black Opaque ("Opaque black style", `UIStatusBarStyleBlackOpaque`). This setting will be used in conjunction with your launch image, even before the app is actually running.
>
> However, in iOS 6 the old default status bar style ("Gray style") won't appear when the app runs. Instead, the default status bar is black opaque, and if your Style choice is Default, the Tinting pop-up menu comes into play. The reason is that, in iOS 6 on an iPhone, whenever there is a navigation bar at the top of the screen (Chapter 25), the status bar is automatically tinted to match it. *You cannot prevent this behavior.* Therefore, if there is a navigation bar at the top of your app's initial interface, you might like the status bar that appears during launch to match the running app's initial status bar. (Otherwise, the status bar will appear to change color during launch — which is no terrible thing, and in my experience Apple won't reject your app for it.) To arrange that, you must describe your initial navigation bar in your *Info.plist*:
>
> - If your initial navigation bar has a standard color style (Default, Black Translucent, or Black Opaque), use that style here.

- If your initial navigation bar has a tint color, use Custom Color and set the tint color in the color well.
- If your initial navigation bar has a custom background image, use Custom Image and choose that image. (If your app draws a custom image from scratch at runtime, run in the Simulator to show the interface, use Custom Color, show the color picker, click the magnifying glass icon, and sample the color of a pixel near the *bottom* of your running app's navigation bar.)
- If there is no initial navigation bar, use Disabled; the status bar will be black opaque during launch.

If your Tinting choice is not Disabled, the "Status bar tinting parameters" key (`UIStatusBarTintParameters`) is set to a "Navigation bar" dictionary describing the navigation bar.

If the status bar is to be hidden initially, set "Status bar is initially hidden" (`UIStatusBarHidden`) instead.

Supported interface orientations (`UISupportedInterfaceOrientations`)
In iOS 6, this key designates the totality of orientations in which the app is ever permitted to appear (Chapter 19). *This is a major change from iOS 5 and before.* You can perform this setting graphically in the Summary tab when editing your target. But you may also need to edit the *Info.plist* manually to rearrange the order of possible orientations, because on an iPhone the *first* orientation listed is the one into which the app will actually launch.

Required device capabilities (`UIRequiredDeviceCapabilities`)
You should set this key if the app requires capabilities that are not present on all devices. Be sure to look over the list of possible values. Don't use this key unless it makes no sense for your app to run *at all* on a device lacking the specified capabilities.

(The current project templates include `armv7` in the list of required device capabilities. This may prove troublesome for backwards compatibility.)

Property list settings can adopt different values depending on what device type you're running on. To specify that a property list setting applies only on a particular type of device, you add to its key the suffix `~iphone`, `~ipod`, or `~ipad`. This feature is typically useful in a universal app, as I described earlier in this chapter.

Your app also needs a version number. Edit the Target and click Summary at the top of the page; enter a version string in the Version text field. Things are a little confusing here because there is both a Version field and a Bundle field; the former corresponds to "Bundle versions string, short" (`CFBundleShortVersionString`), while the latter corresponds to "Bundle version" (`CFBundleVersion`). As far as I can determine, Apple will pay attention to the former if it is set, and otherwise will fall back on the latter. In general

I play it safe and set both to the same value when submitting to the App Store. The value needs to be a version string, such as "1.0". This version number will appear at the App Store. Failure to increment the version string when submitting an update will cause the update to be rejected.

Submission to the App Store

Before submitting your app to the App Store, build it (Product → Archive) and test it as an Ad Hoc build. The archived build that appears in the Organizer window can be used to generate either an Ad Hoc build or an App Store build. You can't test an App Store build, so you use this archived build to generate an Ad Hoc build and test with that. When you generate the App Store build, you use this same archived build; it is the exact same binary, so you are guaranteed that its behavior will be exactly the same as the build you tested. (That is one of the purposes of archiving.)

When you're satisfied that your app works well, and you've installed or collected all the necessary resources, you're ready to submit your app to the App Store for distribution. To do so, you'll need to make preparations at the iTunes Connect website. You can find a link to it on the iOS developer pages when you've logged in at Apple's site. You can go directly to *http://itunesconnect.apple.com*, but you'll still need to log in with your iOS Developer username and password.

 The first time you visit iTunes Connect, you should go to the Contracts section and complete submission of your contract. You can't offer any apps for sale until you do, and even free apps require completion of a contractual form.

I'm not going to recite all the steps you have to go through to tell iTunes Connect about your app, as these are described thoroughly in Apple's *iTunes Connect Developer Guide*, which is the final word on such matters. But I'll just mention the main pieces of information you will have to supply:

Your app's name
> This is the name that will appear at the App Store; it need not be identical to the short name that will appear under the app's icon on the device, dictated by the Bundle Display Name setting in your *Info.plist* file. This name can be up to 255 characters long, though Apple recommends that you limit it to fewer than 70 and ideally to fewer than 35 characters. You can get a rude shock when you submit your app's information to iTunes Connect and discover that the name you wanted is already taken. There is no reliable way to learn this in advance, and such a discovery can require a certain amount of scrambling on your part: you might have to Build

and Archive your app yet again with a new name and possibly other last-minute changes.

Description

You must supply a description of fewer than 4,000 characters; Apple recommends fewer than 580 characters, and the first paragraph is the most important, because this may be all that users see at first when they visit the App Store. It must be pure text, without HTML and without character styling.

Keywords

This is a comma-separated list shorter than 100 characters. These keywords will be used, in addition to your app's name, to help users discover your app through the Search feature of the App Store.

Support

This the URL of a website where users can find more information about your app; it's good to have the site ready in advance.

Copyright

Do not include a copyright symbol in this string; it will be added for you at the App Store.

SKU number

This is unimportant, so don't get nervous about it. It's just a unique identifier, unique within the world of your own apps. It's convenient if it has something to do with your app's name. It needn't be a number; it can actually be any string.

Price

You don't get to make up a price. You have to choose from a list of pricing "tiers."

Availability Date

There's an option to make the app available as soon as it is approved, and this will typically be your choice. Alternatively, Apple will send you an email when the app is approved, and you can then return to iTunes Connect and make the app available manually.

When you've submitted the information for your app, you can do a final validation check: return to the Organizer window, select the archived build, and click Validate. (This feature has not worked well for me in the past, however.)

Finally, when you're ready to upload the app for which you've already submitted the information at iTunes Connect, and when the iTunes Connect status for your app is "Waiting for Upload," you can perform the upload using Xcode. Select the archived build in the Organizer and click Distribute. In the dialog, choose "Submit to the iOS App Store." You'll be asked to provide your developer username and password, so that Xcode can make sure that this app really is waiting for upload at iTunes Connect. You'll then specify your identity as contained in the App Store distribution profile, and Xcode will proceed to upload the app. Some validation will then be performed at the far end.

Alternatively, you can use Application Loader. Export the archive as an *.ipa* file, as for an Ad Hoc distribution, but use the App Store distribution profile. Launch Application Loader by choosing Xcode → Open Developer Tool → Application Loader, and hand it the *.ipa* file.

You will subsequently receive emails from Apple informing you of your app's status as it passes through various stages: "Waiting For Review," "In Review," and finally, if all has gone well, "Ready For Sale" (even if it's a free app). Your app will then appear at the App Store.

When Your Certificate Expires

When one of your certificates expires, as will happen after a year, all profiles dependent upon it will become invalid. I have never figured out what Apple expects you to do at this point; certainly none of the courses of action suggested in Apple's documentation have worked for me. The only thing that ever *has* worked for me is to delete *everything* (except the WWDR certificate, which remains good for several years) and start over from scratch:

1. Before you even begin to make yourself a new certificate, *quit Xcode*. This step is crucial. Xcode has a nasty habit of unexpectedly downloading fresh copies of your profiles from the Portal. But your existing profiles are part of the problem: they are expiring. Moreover, when this happens, Xcode has an even nastier habit of installing the certificates contained in these profiles into your keychain. But those certificates are *heart* of the problem: they are expiring. Moreover, Xcode will balk if it finds two versions of a certificate in your keychain — even if Xcode itself installed them! Therefore you must take Xcode out of the picture before you begin.

2. Go the Portal in your browser and delete all development and distribution profiles. That's because they depend on your old certificates. You don't want them in the Portal, because if they are still there when you next run Xcode, Xcode might download them (see the previous step).

3. Now launch Xcode. You are safe to do so: Xcode cannot now download fresh copies of your profiles from the Portal, because there are no profiles at the Portal! So proceed to delete all development and distribution profiles from the Provisioning Profiles section of the Devices tab of the Organizer window. Just to be on the safe side, it might be a good idea at this point to delete all development and distribution profiles from each of your test devices as well.

4. Delete the development and distribution certificates from your keychain.

5. Everything is now gone, and it's safe to begin recreating it all from scratch. First, repeat the process of obtaining fresh development and distribution certificates, downloading them, and installing them in your keychain.

6. At the Portal, create any actively needed distribution profiles, and any development profiles with special entitlements. Your app ID and device information is still at the Portal, and your certificates are now fresh, so this won't present any difficulties. Download and install the profiles.

7. Finally, you need to prod Xcode into recreating the team development profile. To do so, connect one of your development devices to the computer and ask Xcode to add it at the Portal (even though it has already been added to the Portal previously). This in turn will cause Xcode to ask the Portal for a new team development profile.

PART III

Cocoa

When you program for iOS, you take advantage of a suite of frameworks provided by Apple. These frameworks, taken together, constitute *Cocoa*; the brand of Cocoa that provides the API for programming iOS is *Cocoa Touch*. Cocoa thus plays an important and fundamental role in iOS programming; your code will ultimately be almost entirely about communicating with Cocoa — interacting with the frameworks provided by Apple, in order to make an app that does what you want it to do.

The Cocoa Touch frameworks are a huge boon to you, the programmer, because they provide the underlying functionality that any iOS app needs to have. Your app can put up a window, show the interface containing a button, respond to that button being tapped by the user, and so forth, because Cocoa knows how to do those things. But with the great advantages of working with a framework come great responsibilities. You have to think the way the framework thinks, put your code where the framework expects it, and fulfill many obligations imposed on you by the framework.

- Chapter 10 picks up where Chapter 5 left off, describing some Objective-C linguistic features used by Cocoa, such as categories and protocols; it also surveys some important fundamental classes.

- Chapter 11 describes Cocoa's event-driven model, along with its major design patterns. An *event* is a message sent by Cocoa to your code. Cocoa is event-based; if Cocoa doesn't send your code an event, your code doesn't run. Getting your code to run at the appropriate moment is all about knowing what events you can expect Cocoa to send you and when.

- Chapter 12 describes your responsibilities for making your instances nicely encapsulated and good memory-management citizens in the world of Cocoa objects.

- Chapter 13 surveys some answers to the question of how your objects are going to see and communicate with one another within the Cocoa-based world.

CHAPTER 10

Cocoa Classes

Using the Cocoa frameworks requires an understanding of how those frameworks organize their classes. Cocoa class organization depends upon certain Objective-C language features that are introduced in this chapter. The chapter also surveys some commonly used Cocoa utility classes, along with a discussion of the Cocoa root class.

Subclassing

Cocoa effectively hands you a large repertory of objects that already know how to behave in certain desirable ways. A UIButton, for example, knows how to draw itself and how to respond when the user taps it; a UITextField knows how to display editable text, how to summon the keyboard when the user taps in it, and how to accept keyboard input.

Often, the default behavior or appearance of an object supplied by Cocoa won't be quite what you're after, and you'll want to customize it. Cocoa classes are heavily endowed with methods that you can call and properties that you can set for precisely this purpose, and these will be your first resort. Always study the documentation for a Cocoa class to see whether instances can already be made to do what you want. For example, the class documentation for UILabel (Chapter 27) shows that you can set the font, size, color, line-breaking behavior, and horizontal alignment of its text, among other things.

Nevertheless, sometimes setting properties and calling methods won't suffice to customize an instance the way you want to. In such cases, Cocoa may provide methods that are called internally as an instance does its thing, and whose behavior you can customize by subclassing and overriding (Chapter 4). You don't have the code to any of Cocoa's built-in classes, but you can still subclass them, creating a new class that acts just like a built-in class except for the modifications you provide.

Oddly enough, however (and you might be particularly surprised by this if you've used another object-oriented application framework), subclassing is probably one of the less important ways in which your code will relate to Cocoa. Knowing or deciding when to subclass can be somewhat tricky, but the general rule is that you probably shouldn't subclass unless you're invited to.

A common case is a UIView that is to be drawn in some custom manner. You don't actually draw a UIView; rather, when a UIView needs drawing, its `drawRect:` method is called so that the view can draw itself. So the way to draw a UIView in some completely custom manner is to subclass UIView and implement `drawRect:` in the subclass. As the documentation says, "Subclasses override this method if they actually draw their views." That's a pretty strong hint that you *need* to subclass UIView in this situation.

For example, suppose we want our window to contain a horizontal line. There is no horizontal line interface widget built into Cocoa, so we'll just have to roll our own — a UIView that draws itself as a horizontal line. Let's try it:

1. In our Empty Window example project, choose File → New → File and specify a Cocoa Touch Objective-C class, and in particular a subclass of UIView. Call it *MyHorizLine*. Xcode creates *MyHorizLine.m* and *MyHorizLine.h*.

2. In *MyHorizLine.m*, replace the contents of the implementation section with this (without further explanation; you'll know all about this after you read Chapter 15):

```
- (id)initWithCoder:(NSCoder *)decoder {
    self = [super initWithCoder:decoder];
    if (self) {
        self.backgroundColor = [UIColor clearColor];
    }
    return self;
}

- (void)drawRect:(CGRect)rect {
    CGContextRef c = UIGraphicsGetCurrentContext();
    CGContextMoveToPoint(c, 0, 0);
    CGContextAddLineToPoint(c, self.bounds.size.width, 0);
    CGContextStrokePath(c);
}
```

3. Edit *ViewController.xib*. Find UIView in the Object library, and drag it into the View object in the canvas. You may resize it to be less tall.

4. With the UIView that you just dragged into the canvas still selected, use the Identity inspector to change its class to MyHorizLine.

Build and run the app in the Simulator. You'll see a horizontal line corresponding to the location of the top of the MyHorizLine instance in the window. Our view has drawn itself as a horizontal line, because we subclassed it to do so.

In that example, we started with a bare UIView that had no drawing functionality of its own. That's why there was no need to call super; the default implementation of UIView's `drawRect:` does nothing. But you might also be able to subclass a built-in UIView subclass to modify the way it already draws itself. Again using UILabel as an example, the documentation shows that two methods are present for exactly this purpose. Both drawTextInRect: and textRectForBounds:limitedToNumberOfLines: explicitly tell us: "You should not call this method directly. This method should only be overridden by subclasses." The implication is that these are methods that will be called for us, automatically, by Cocoa, as a label draws itself; thus, we can subclass UILabel and implement them in our subclass to modify how a particular type of label draws itself.

Here's an example from one of my own apps, in which I subclass UILabel to make a label that draws its own rectangular border and has its content inset somewhat from that border, by overriding drawTextInRect:. As the documentation tells us: "In your overridden method, you can configure the current [graphics] context further and then invoke super to do the actual drawing [of the text]." Let's try it:

1. In the Empty Window project, make a new class file, a UILabel subclass this time; call it *MyBoundedLabel*.

2. In *MyBoundedLabel.m*, insert this code into the implementation section:

```
- (void)drawTextInRect:(CGRect)rect {
    CGContextRef context = UIGraphicsGetCurrentContext();
    CGContextStrokeRect(context, CGRectInset(self.bounds, 1.0, 1.0));
    [super drawTextInRect:CGRectInset(rect, 5.0, 5.0)];
}
```

3. In *MyNib.xib*, select the UILabel and change its class in the Identity inspector to MyBoundedLabel.

Build and run the app, and you'll see how the rectangle is drawn and the label's text is inset within it.

Similarly, in a table view (a UITableView) you might very well be able to avoid subclassing the table view cell (UITableViewCell), because it provides so many properties through which you can customize its appearance. If you want text to appear in the cell using a certain font, the built-in cell styles and the ability to access and modify the cell's labels might be quite sufficient. You can directly replace a cell's background or put a checkmark at the right end of the cell. All of that is simply a matter of setting the cell's built-in properties. But if you want a table view cell that doesn't look or behave like any of the built-in cell styles, then you'll probably subclass UITableViewCell. (We'll go deeply into this in Chapter 21.)

You wouldn't subclass UIApplication (the class of the singleton shared application instance) just in order to respond when the application has finished launching, because the delegate mechanism (Chapter 11) provides a way to do that (application:didFinishLaunchingWithOptions:). On the other hand, if you need to perform certain tricky customizations of your app's fundamental event messaging behavior, you might subclass UIApplication in order to override sendEvent:. The documentation does tell you this, and it also tells you, rightly, that needing to do this would be fairly rare (though I have had occasion to do it).

> If you do subclass UIApplication, you'll need to change the third argument in the call to UIApplicationMain in *main.m* from nil to the NSString name of your subclass. Otherwise your UIApplication subclass won't be instantiated as the shared application instance.

Another class that's commonly subclassed is UIViewController (Chapter 19). And any class you write will naturally need to be a subclass of NSObject, if nothing else. You definitely want your class to inherit all of NSObject's yummy goodness, including alloc and init, which make it possible to instantiate your class in the first place (see "The Secret Life of NSObject" (page 266)).

Categories

A *category* is an Objective-C language feature that allows you to reach right into an existing class and define additional methods. You can do this even if you don't have the code for the class, as with Cocoa's classes. Your instance methods can refer to self, and this will mean the instance to which the message was originally sent, as usual. A category, unlike a subclass, cannot define additional instance variables; it can override methods, but you should probably not take advantage of this ability.

Defining a category is just like defining the class on which the category is being defined: you need an interface section and an implementation section, and you'll typically distribute them into the standard *.h* and *.m* class file pair. At the start of both the interface section and the implementation section, where you give the class's name, you add a category name in parentheses. The *.h* file will probably need to import the header for the original class (or the header of the framework that defines it), and the *.m* file will, as usual, import the *.h* file, as will any *.m* file that wants to call one of your additional methods.

The easiest way to set up your *.h* and *.m* class file pair as a category is to ask Xcode to do it for you. Choose File → New → File, and in the "Choose a template" dialog, among the iOS Cocoa Touch file types, pick "Objective-C category". You'll be asked to give a name for the category and the class on which you're defining this category.

For example, in one of my apps I found myself performing a bunch of string transformations in order to derive the path to various resource files inside the app bundle based on the resource's name and purpose. I ended up with half a dozen utility methods. Given that these methods all operated on an NSString, it was appropriate to implement them as a category of NSString, thus allowing *any* NSString, anywhere in my code, to respond to them.

The code was structured like this (I'll show just one of the methods):

```
// StringCategories.h:
#import <Foundation/Foundation.h>

@interface NSString (MyStringCategories)
- (NSString*) basePictureName;
@end

// StringCategories.m:
#import "StringCategories.h"

@implementation NSString (MyStringCategories)
- (NSString*) basePictureName {
    return [self stringByAppendingString:@"IO"];
}
@end
```

If basePictureName had been implemented as a utility method within some other class, it would need to take a parameter — we'd have to pass an NSString to it — and, it were an instance method, we'd need to go to the extra trouble of obtaining a reference to an instance of that class. A category is neater and more compact. We've extended NSString *itself* to have basePictureName as an instance method, so, in any *.m* file that imports *StringCategories.h*, we can send the basePictureName message directly *to* any NSString we want to transform:

```
NSString* aName = [someString basePictureName];
```

A category is particularly appropriate in the case of a class like NSString, because the documentation warns us that subclassing NSString is a bad idea. That's because NSString is part of a complex of classes called a *class cluster*, which means that an NSString object's real class might actually be some other class. A category is a much better way to modify a class within a class cluster than subclassing.

A method defined through a category can equally be a class method. Thus you can inject utility methods into any appropriate class and call those methods without the overhead of instantiating anything at all. Classes are globally available, so your method becomes, in effect, a global method (see Chapter 13).

Splitting a Class

A category can be used to split a class over multiple *.h/.m* file pairs. If a class threatens to become long and unwieldy, yet it clearly needs to be a single class, you can define the basic part of it (including instance variables) in one file pair, and then add another file pair defining a category on your own class to contain further methods.

Cocoa itself does this. A good example is NSString. NSString is defined as part of the Foundation framework, and its basic methods are declared in *NSString.h*. Here we find that NSString itself, with no category, has just two methods, length and characterAt-

Index:, because these are regarded as the minimum that a string needs to do in order to be a string. Additional methods (those that create a string, deal with a string's encoding, split a string, search in a string, and so on) are clumped into categories. The interface for many of these categories appears in this same file, *NSString.h*. But a string may serve as a file pathname, so we also find a category on NSString in *NSPath-Utilities.h*, where methods are declared for splitting a pathname string into its constituents and the like. Then, in *NSURL.h*, there's another NSString category, declaring a couple of methods for dealing with percent-escaping in a URL string. Finally, off in a completely different framework (UIKit), *UIStringDrawing.h* adds yet another NSString category, with methods for drawing a string in a graphics context.

This organization won't matter to you as a programmer, because an NSString is an NSString, no matter how it acquires its methods, but it can matter when you consult the documentation. The NSString methods declared in *NSString.h*, *NSPathUtilities.h*, and *NSURL.h* are documented in the NSString class documentation page, but the NSString methods declared in *UIStringDrawing.h* are not, presumably because they originate in a different framework. Instead, they appear in a separate document, *NSString UIKit Additions Reference*. As a result, the string drawing methods can be difficult to discover, especially as the NSString class documentation doesn't link to the other document. I regard this as a major flaw in the structure of the Cocoa documentation. A third-party utility such as AppKiDo can be helpful here.

Class Extensions

A *class extension* is a nameless category that exists solely as an interface section, like this:

```
@interface MyClass ()
// stuff goes here
@end
```

Typically, the only classes that will be permitted to "see" a class extension will be the class that's being extended or a subclass of that class. If only the former is the case, the class extension will usually appear directly in the class's *implementation file*, like this:

```
// MyClass.m:

@interface MyClass ()
// stuff goes here
@end

@implementation MyClass {
    // ivars
}
// methods
@end
```

That's such a common arrangement that Xcode's project template files actually give you a class extension in certain classes. For example, our Empty Window project comes with a class extension at the start of *ViewController.m* — take a look and see!

I'm sure you're leaping out of your chair with eagerness to know what on earth sort of "stuff" could possibly go into a class extension to make it so useful that it appears in a template file. Unfortunately, in modern Objective-C the answer has mostly to do with property declarations, which I don't discuss until Chapter 12. So your curiosity will have to remain unsatisfied until then.

A class extension *used* to be the standard solution to the problem of method definition order. One method in an implementation section couldn't call another method in that same implementation section unless either the definition or a method declaration for that other method preceded it. It's finicky work trying to arrange all the method definitions in the right order, so the obvious solution is a method declaration. A method declaration can go only into an interface section. But to put a method declaration into the interface section in this class's header file is annoying — it means we must switch to another file — and, even worse, it makes that method public; any class that imports that header file can now see and call this method. That's fine if this method is supposed to be public; but what if we wanted to keep it private? The solution: a class extension at the start of this class's implementation file. Put the method declarations into that class extension; all the methods in the implementation section can now see those method declarations and can call one another, but no other class can see them.

However, since LLVM compiler version 3.1 (Xcode 4.3) that trick has been unnecessary: methods (and functions) in a class implementation can see and call one another regardless of order.

Protocols

Every reasonably sophisticated object-oriented language must face the fact that the hierarchy of subclasses and superclasses is insufficient to express the desired relationships between classes. For example, a Bee object and a Bird object might need to have certain features in common by virtue of the fact that both a bee and a bird can fly. But Bee might inherit from Insect, and not every insect can fly, so how can Bee acquire the aspects of a Flier in a way that isn't completely independent of how Bird acquires them?

Some object-oriented languages solve this problem through *mixin* classes. For example, in Ruby you could define a Flier module, complete with method definitions, and incorporate it into both Bee and Bird. Objective-C uses a simpler, lighter-weight approach — the *protocol*. Cocoa makes heavy use of protocols.

A protocol is just a named list of method declarations, with no implementation. A class may formally declare that it *conforms* to (or *adopts*) a protocol; such conformance is inherited by subclasses. This declaration satisfies the compiler when you try to send a corresponding message. If a protocol declares an instance method myCoolMethod, and if MyClass declares conformance to that protocol, then you can send the myCool-Method message to a MyClass instance and the compiler won't complain.

Actually implementing the methods declared in a protocol is up to the class that conforms to it. A protocol method may be required or optional. If a protocol method is required, then if a class conforms to that protocol, the compiler will warn if that class fails to implement that method. Implementing optional methods, on the other hand, is optional. (Of course, that's just the compiler's point of view; at runtime, if a message is sent to an object with no implementation for the corresponding method, a crash can result; see Chapter 3.)

Here's an example of how Cocoa uses a protocol. Some objects can be copied; some can't. This has nothing to do with an object's class heritage. Yet we would like a uniform method to which any object that *can* be copied will respond. So Cocoa defines a protocol named NSCopying, which declares just one method, copyWithZone: (required). A class that explicitly conforms to NSCopying is promising that it implements copyWithZone:.

Here's how the NSCopying protocol is defined (in *NSObject.h*, where your code can see it):

```
@protocol NSCopying
- (id)copyWithZone:(NSZone *)zone;
@end
```

That's all there is to defining a protocol. The definition uses the @protocol compiler directive; it states the name of the protocol; it consists entirely of method declarations; and it is terminated by the @end compiler directive. A protocol definition will typically appear in a header file, so that classes that need to know about it, in order to adopt it or call its methods, can import it. A protocol section of a header file is not inside any other section (such as an interface section). Any optional methods must be preceded by the @optional directive. A protocol definition may state that the protocol incorporates other protocols; these constitute a comma-separated list in angle brackets after the protocol's name, like this example from Apple's own code (*UIAlertView.h*):

```
@protocol UIAlertViewDelegate <NSObject>
@optional
- (void)alertView:(UIAlertView *)alertView
    clickedButtonAtIndex:(NSInteger)buttonIndex;
// ... more optional method declarations ...
@end
```

The NSCopying protocol definition in *NSObject.h* is just a definition; it is not a statement that NSObject conforms to NSCopying. Indeed, NSObject does *not* conform to NSCopying. To see this, try sending the copyWithZone: method to your own subclass of NSObject:

```
MyClass* mc = [MyClass new];
MyClass* mc2 = [mc copyWithZone: [mc zone]];
```

The compiler warns that a MyClass instance may not respond to copyWithZone:; under ARC, this code won't compile at all.

To conform formally to a protocol, a class's interface section appends the name of the protocol, in angle brackets, after the name of the superclass (or, if this is a category declaration, after the parentheses). This will necessitate importing the header file that declares the protocol (or some header file that imports that header file). To state that a class conforms to multiple protocols, put multiple protocol names in the angle brackets, separated by comma.

Let's see what happens if you conform formally to the NSCopying protocol. Modify the first line of the interface section of your class as follows:

```
@interface MyClass : NSObject <NSCopying>
```

Now the compiler warns that MyClass fails to implement copyWithZone: and thus does not fully implement the NSCopying protocol (because copyWithZone: is a required method of the NSCopying protocol).

The name of a protocol may also be used when specifying an object type. Most often, the object will be typed as an id, but with the accompanying proviso that it conforms to a protocol, whose name appears in angle brackets.

To illustrate, let's look at another typical example of how Cocoa uses protocols, namely in connection with a table (UITableView). A UITableView has a dataSource property, declared like this:

```
@property (nonatomic, assign) id<UITableViewDataSource> dataSource
```

This property represents an instance variable whose type is id <UITableViewData-Source>. This means "I don't care what class my data source belongs to, but whatever it is, it should conform to the UITableViewDataSource protocol." Such conformance constitutes a promise that the data source will implement at least the required instance methods tableView:numberOfRowsInSection: and tableView:cellForRowAtIndex-Path:, which the table view will call when it needs to know what data to display.

If you attempt to set a table view's dataSource property to an object that does *not* conform to UITableViewDataSource, you'll get a warning from the compiler. So, for example:

```
MyClass* mc = [MyClass new];
UITableView* tv = [UITableView new];
tv.dataSource = mc; // compiler warns
```

Under ARC, this warning is couched in rather confusing terms, along these lines: "Passing 'MyClass *const __strong' to parameter of incompatible type 'id<UITableViewDataSource>."

To quiet the compiler, MyClass's declaration should state that it conforms to UITableViewDataSource. Once it does so, MyClass *is* an id <UITableViewDataSource>, and the third line no longer generates a warning. Of course, you must also supply implementations of `tableView:numberOfRowsInSection:` and `tableView:cellForRowAtIndexPath:` in MyClass to avoid the other warning, namely that you're not fully implementing a protocol you've claimed to conform to.

In a very large percentage of cases, the object that you want to assign where conformity to a protocol is expected is `self`. In this situation, you can declare this class's conformity to the protocol in the implementation file as part of a class extension, like this:

```
// MyClass.m:
@interface MyClass () <UITableViewDataSource>
@end

@implementation MyClass
- (void) someMethod {
    UITableView* tv = [UITableView new];
    tv.dataSource = self;
}
@end
```

I prefer this architecture, because it means that the declaration of conformity to the protocol is right there in the same implementation file that uses the protocol, and because the header defining the protocol can be imported in the implementation file, rather than in the class's header file where it will be unnecessarily shared with any other classes that import the same header file.

A prevalent use of protocols in Cocoa is in connection with delegate objects. We'll talk in detail about delegates in Chapter 11, but you can readily see that many classes have a `delegate` property and that the class of this property is often id <SomeProtocol>. For example, in our Empty Window project, the AppDelegate class provided by the project template is declared like this:

```
@interface AppDelegate : UIResponder <UIApplicationDelegate>
```

The reason is that AppDelegate's purpose on earth is to serve as the shared application's delegate. The shared application object is a UIApplication, and a UIApplication's `delegate` property is typed as an id <UIApplicationDelegate>. So AppDelegate announces its role by explicitly conforming to UIApplicationDelegate.

As a programmer, Cocoa's use of protocols will matter to you in two ways:

Conformity

As I've just been saying, if an object value that you wish to assign or pass as an argument is typed as id <SomeProtocol>, you must make sure that that object's class does indeed conform to SomeProtocol (and implements any methods required by that protocol).

Using the documentation

A protocol has its own documentation page. When the UIApplication class documentation tells you that a UIApplication's delegate property is typed as an id <UIApplicationDelegate>, it's implicitly telling you that if you want to know what messages a UIApplication's delegate might receive, you need to look in the UIApplicationDelegate protocol documentation.

Similarly, when a class's documentation mentions that the class conforms to a protocol, don't forget to examine that protocol's documentation, because the latter might contain important information about how the class behaves. To learn what messages can be sent to an object, you need to look upward through the superclass inheritance chain (Chapter 8); you also need to look at any protocols that this object's class conforms to.

You will probably not have frequent cause to define a protocol yourself. But protocols effectively allow one class to declare a method that another class is to implement, and there are certain situations where that's exactly the problem you need to solve; so a protocol will be the solution.

For example, in one of my apps I present a view where the user can move three sliders to choose a color. Appropriately, its code is in a class called ColorPickerController. When the user taps Done or Cancel, the view should be dismissed; but first, the code that presented this view needs to hear about what color the user chose. So I need to send a message from the ColorPickerController instance back to the instance that presented it. Here is the declaration for that message:

```
- (void) colorPicker:(ColorPickerController*)picker
     didSetColorNamed:(NSString*)theName
              toColor:(UIColor*)theColor;
```

The question is: where should this declaration go?

Now, it happens that in my app I know the class of the instance that will present the ColorPickerController's view: it is a SettingsController. So I could simply declare this method in the interface section of SettingsController's header file. But this feels wrong:

- It should not be up to SettingsController to declare a method that it is implementing only in deference to ColorPickerController.

- If SettingsController declares this message in its header file, ColorPickerController will have to import that header file in order to send the message; but this means that ColorPickerController now knows all about SettingsController, whereas the *only* thing it needs to know about SettingsController is that it implements this one method.

- It is merely a contingent fact that the instance being sent this message *is* a Settings-Controller; it should be open to *any* class to present and dismiss a ColorPicker-Controller's view, and thus to be eligible to receive this message.

Therefore we want ColorPickerController *itself* to declare the method that *it itself is going to send*; and we want it to send the message blindly to some receiver, without regard to the class of that receiver. Thus there needs to be a linkage, as it were, between the declaration of this method in ColorPickerController and the implementation of this method in the receiver. That linkage is precisely what a protocol creates! The solution, then, is for ColorPickerController to define a protocol in its header file, with this method as part of that protocol, and for the class that presents a ColorPickerController's view to conform to that protocol.

If you create a project from Xcode's own Utility Application template, you will see that this is exactly the architecture it exemplifies. We start with a MainViewController. It eventually creates a FlipsideViewController. When the FlipsideViewController is ready to go out of existence, it is going to want to send the `flipsideViewControllerDid-Finish:` message back to whoever created it. So FlipsideViewController defines a FlipsideViewControllerDelegate protocol requiring the `flipsideViewControllerDid-Finish:` method, along with a `delegate` property typed as `id <FlipsideView-ControllerDelegate>`. When a MainViewController instance creates a FlipsideView-Controller instance, it specifies that it itself, the MainViewController instance, is the FlipsideViewController's `delegate`; and it can do this, because MainViewController does in fact adopt the FlipsideViewControllerDelegate protocol! Problem solved, mission accomplished.

Optional Methods

A protocol can explicitly designate some or all of its methods as optional. The question thus arises: How, in practice, is such an optional method feasible? We know that if a message is sent to an object and the object can't handle that message, an exception is raised (and your app will likely crash). But a method declaration is a contract suggesting that the object *can* handle that message. If we subvert that contract by declaring a method that might or might not be implemented, aren't we inviting crashes?

The answer is that Objective-C is not only dynamic but also introspective. You can ask an object whether it can deal with a message without actually sending it that message. This makes optional methods quite safe, provided you know that a method is optional.

The key method here is NSObject's respondsToSelector:, which takes a selector parameter and returns a BOOL. With it, you can send a message to an object only if it would be safe to do so:

```
MyClass* mc = [MyClass new];
if ([mc respondsToSelector:@selector(woohoo)]) {
    [mc woohoo];
}
```

You wouldn't want to do this before sending just any old message, because it isn't necessary except for optional methods, and it slows things down a little. But Cocoa does in fact call respondsToSelector: on your objects as a matter of course. To see that this is true, implement respondsToSelector: on AppDelegate in our Empty Window project and instrument it with logging:

```
- (BOOL) respondsToSelector: (SEL) sel {
    NSLog(@"%@", NSStringFromSelector(sel));
    return [super respondsToSelector:(sel)];
}
```

The output on my machine, as the Empty Window app launches, includes the following (I'm omitting private methods and multiple calls to the same method):

```
application:handleOpenURL:
application:openURL:sourceApplication:annotation:
applicationDidReceiveMemoryWarning:
applicationWillTerminate:
applicationSignificantTimeChange:
application:willChangeStatusBarOrientation:duration:
application:didChangeStatusBarOrientation:
application:willChangeStatusBarFrame:
```

```
application:didChangeStatusBarFrame:
application:deviceAccelerated:
application:deviceChangedOrientation:
applicationDidBecomeActive:
applicationWillResignActive:
applicationDidEnterBackground:
applicationWillEnterForeground:
applicationWillSuspend:
application:didResumeWithOptions:
application:shouldSaveApplicationState:
application:supportedInterfaceOrientationsForWindow:
application:willFinishLaunchingWithOptions:
application:didFinishLaunchingWithOptions:
```

That's Cocoa, checking to see which of the optional UIApplicationDelegate protocol methods (including a couple of undocumented methods) are actually implemented by our AppDelegate instance — which, because it is the UIApplication object's delegate and formally conforms to the UIApplicationDelegate protocol, has explicitly agreed that it *might* be willing to respond to any of those messages. The entire delegate pattern (Chapter 11) depends upon this technique. Observe the policy followed here by Cocoa: it checks all the optional protocol methods once, when it first meets the object in question, and presumably stores the results; thus, the app is slowed a tiny bit by this one-time initial bombardment of respondsToSelector: calls, but now Cocoa knows all the answers and won't have to perform any of these same checks on the same object later on.

Some Foundation Classes

The Foundation classes of Cocoa provide basic data types and utilities that will form the basis of much that you do in Cocoa. Obviously I can't list all of them, let alone describe them fully, but I can survey a few that I use frequently and that you'll probably want to be aware of before writing even the simplest Cocoa program. For more information, start with Apple's list of the Foundation classes in the *Foundation Framework Reference*.

Useful Structs and Constants

NSRange is a struct of importance in dealing with some of the classes I'm about to discuss. Its components are integers (NSUInteger), location and length. For example, a range whose location is 1 starts at the second element of something (because element counting is always zero-based), and if its length is 2 it designates this element and the next. Cocoa also supplies various convenience methods for dealing with a range; you'll use NSMakeRange frequently. (Note that the name, NSMakeRange, is backward compared to names like CGPointMake and CGRectMake.)

NSNotFound is a constant integer indicating that some requested element was not found. For example, if you ask for the index of a certain object in an NSArray and the object isn't present in the array, the result is NSNotFound. The result could not be 0 to indicate the absence of the object, because 0 would indicate the first element of the array. Nor could it be nil, because nil is 0 (and in any case is not appropriate when an integer is expected). The true numeric value of NSNotFound is of no concern to you; always compare against NSNotFound itself, to learn whether a result is a meaningful index.

If a search returns a range and the thing sought is not present, the location component of the resulting NSRange will be NSNotFound.

NSString and Friends

NSString, which has already been used rather liberally in examples earlier in this book, is the Cocoa object version of a string. You can create an NSString through a number of class methods and initializers, or by using the NSString literal notation @"...", which is really a compiler directive. Particularly important is stringWithFormat:, which lets you convert numbers to strings and combine strings; see Chapter 9, where I discussed format strings in connection with NSLog. Here are some strings in action:

```
int x = 5;
NSString* s = @"widgets";
NSString* s2 = [NSString stringWithFormat:@"You have %i %@.", x, s];
```

NSString has a modern, Unicode-based idea of what a string can consist of. A string's "elements" are its characters, whose count is its length. These are not bytes, because the numeric representation of a Unicode character could be multiple bytes, depending on the encoding. Nor are they glyphs, because a composed character sequence that prints as a single "letter" can consist of multiple characters. Thus the length of an NSRange indicating a single "character" might be greater than 1.

An NSString can be searched using various rangeOf... methods, which return an NSRange. In addition, NSScanner lets you walk through a string looking for pieces that fit certain criteria; for example, with NSScanner (and NSCharacterSet) you can skip past everything in a string that precedes a number and then extract the number. The rangeOfString: family of search methods lets you look for a substring; it can specify an option NSRegularExpressionSearch, which lets you search using a regular expression, and regular expressions are also supported as a separate class, NSRegular-Expression (which uses NSTextCheckingResult to describe match results).

In this example from one of my apps, the user has tapped a button whose title is something like "5 by 4" or "4 by 3". I want to know both numbers; one tells me how many rows the layout is to have, the other how many columns. I use an NSScanner to locate the two numbers in the title:

```
NSString* s = [as buttonTitleAtIndex:ix];
NSScanner* sc = [NSScanner scannerWithString:s];
int rows, cols;
[sc scanInt:&rows];
[sc scanUpToCharactersFromSet:[NSCharacterSet decimalDigitCharacterSet]
                    intoString:nil];
[sc scanInt:&cols];
```

Here's how I might do the same thing using a regular expression:

```
NSString* s = [as buttonTitleAtIndex:ix];
int rowcol[2]; int* prowcol = rowcol;
NSError* err = nil;
NSRegularExpression* r =
    [NSRegularExpression regularExpressionWithPattern:@"\\d"
                                              options:0
                                                error:&err];
// error-checking omitted
for (NSTextCheckingResult* match in
    [r matchesInString:s options:0 range:NSMakeRange(0, [s length])])
        *prowcol++ = [[s substringWithRange: [match range]] intValue];
```

The syntax seems oddly tortured, though, because we must convert each match from an NSTextCheckingResult to a range, then to a substring of our original string, and finally to an integer.

More sophisticated automated textual analysis is supported by some additional classes, such as NSDataDetector, an NSRegularExpression subclass that efficiently finds certain types of string expression such as a URL or a phone number, and NSLinguisticTagger, which actually attempts to analyze text into its grammatical parts of speech.

An NSString object's string is immutable. You can use a string to generate another string in various ways, such as by appending another string or by extracting a substring, but you can't alter the string *itself*. For that, you need NSString's subclass, NSMutableString.

NSString has convenience utilities for working with a file path string, and is often used in conjunction with NSURL, which is another Foundation class worth looking into. NSString and some other classes discussed in this section provide methods for writing out to a file's contents or reading in a file's contents; when they do, the file can be specified either as an NSString file path or as an NSURL (Chapter 36).

An NSString carries no font and size information. Interface objects that display strings (such as UILabel) have a font property that is a UIFont; but this determines the *single* font and size in which the string will display. Before iOS 6, display of styled text — where different runs of text have different style attributes (size, font, color, and so forth) — was quite challenging. The NSAttributedString class, embodying a string along with style runs, required the use of Core Text (Chapter 23), and you had to lay out the styled text by drawing it yourself; you couldn't display styled text in any standard interface object.

Starting in iOS 6, however, NSAttributedString is a full-fledged Objective-C class, with methods and supporting classes that allow you to style text and paragraphs easily in sophisticated ways — and the built-in interface objects that display text can display styled text. This is a major improvement.

String drawing in a graphics context can be performed with methods provided through the UIStringDrawing category on NSString (see the *String UIKit Additions Reference*) and the NSStringDrawing category on NSAttributedString (see the *NSAttributedString UIKit Additions Reference*, new in iOS 6).

NSAttributedString, along with its supporting classes (NSMutableAttributedString, NSParagraphStyle, NSMutableParagraphStyle) and its drawing commands, is discussed in Chapter 23.

NSDate and Friends

An NSDate is a date and time, represented internally as a number of seconds (NSTime-Interval) since some reference date. Calling [`NSDate date`] gives you a date object for the current date and time; other date operations may involve NSDateComponents and NSCalendar and can be a bit tricky because calendars are complicated (see the *Date and Time Programming Guide*; NSDateComponents examples appear in Chapter 25 and Chapter 32).

You will also likely be concerned with dates represented as strings. Creation and parsing of date strings involves NSDateFormatter, which uses a format string similar to NSString's `stringWithFormat`. A complication is added by the fact that the exact string representation of a date component or format can depend upon the user's locale, con-sisting of language, region format, and calendar settings. (Actually, locale considerations can also play a role in NSString format strings.)

In this example from one of my apps, I prepare the content of a UILabel reporting the date and time when our data was last updated. The app is not localized — the word "at" appearing in the string is always going to be in English — so I want complete control of the presentation of the date and time components as well. To get it, I have to insist upon a particular locale:

```
NSDateFormatter *df = [NSDateFormatter new];
if ([[NSLocale availableLocaleIdentifiers] indexOfObject:@"en_US"]
        != NSNotFound) {
    NSLocale* loc = [[NSLocale alloc] initWithLocaleIdentifier:@"en_US"];
    [df setLocale:loc]; // English month name and time zone name if possible
}
[df setDateFormat:@"'Updated' d MMMM yyyy 'at' h:mm a z"];
[self setRefreshControlTitle:[df stringFromDate: [NSDate date]]]; // just now
```

Locales are an interesting and complicated topic; to learn more, consult in your browser the documentation for ICU (International Components for Unicode), from which the iOS support for creating and parsing date strings is derived. To study what locales exist, use the locale explorer at *http://demo.icu-project.org/icu-bin/locexp*.

NSNumber

An NSNumber is an object that wraps a numeric value (including BOOL). Thus, you can use it to store and pass a number where an object is expected. An NSNumber is formed from an actual number with a method that specifies the numeric type; for example, you can call `numberWithInt:` to form a number from an int:

```
[[NSUserDefaults standardUserDefaults] registerDefaults:
    [NSDictionary dictionaryWithObjectsAndKeys:
        [NSNumber numberWithInt: 4],
        @"cardMatrixRows",
        [NSNumber numberWithInt: 3],
        @"cardMatrixColumns",
        nil]];
```

As I mentioned in Chapter 5, LLVM compiler version 4.0 (Xcode 4.4) brought with it a new syntax for forming a new NSNumber instance:

- Precede a literal number (or BOOL) with @. To specify further the numeric type, follow the literal number with U (unsigned integer), L (long integer), LL (long long integer), or F (float). (There is no NSNumber wrapper for an unsigned long.) For example, @3.1415 is equivalent to [NSNumber numberWithDouble:3.1415]; @YES is equivalent to [NSNumber numberWithBool:YES].

- If an expression yields a number, wrap it in parentheses and precede the left parenthesis with @. For example, if height and width are floats, @(height/width) is equivalent to [NSNumber numberWithFloat: height/width].

Thus, the preceding example can be rewritten like this:

```
[[NSUserDefaults standardUserDefaults] registerDefaults:
    [NSDictionary dictionaryWithObjectsAndKeys:
        @4,
        @"cardMatrixRows",
        @3,
        @"cardMatrixColumns",
        nil]];
```

(There is also a new NSDictionary literal syntax, so it will turn out, a few pages from now, that we can rewrite that code even more compactly.)

An NSNumber is not itself a number, however, so you still can't use it in calculations or where an actual number is expected. Instead, you must explicitly extract the number from its NSNumber wrapper using the inverse of the method that wrapped the number to begin with. Knowing what that method was is up to you. So, for example, if an NSNumber wraps an int, you can call `intValue` to extract the int:

```
NSUserDefaults* ud = [NSUserDefaults standardUserDefaults];
int therows = [[ud objectForKey:@"cardMatrixRows"] intValue];
int thecols = [[ud objectForKey:@"cardMatrixColumns"] intValue];
```

Actually, this is such a common transformation when communicating with NSUser-Defaults that it provides convenience methods. So I could have written the same thing this way:

```
NSUserDefaults* ud = [NSUserDefaults standardUserDefaults];
int therows = [ud integerForKey:@"cardMatrixRows"];
int thecols = [ud integerForKey:@"cardMatrixColumns"];
```

An NSNumber subclass, NSDecimalNumber, *can* be used in calculations, thanks to a bunch of arithmetic methods (or their C equivalent functions, which are faster). This is useful particularly for rounding, because there's a handy way to specify exactly the desired rounding behavior.

NSValue

NSValue is NSNumber's superclass. Use it for wrapping nonnumeric C values such as structs. Convenience methods provided through the NSValueUIGeometryExtensions category on NSValue (see the *NSValue UIKit Additions Reference*) allow easy wrapping and unwrapping of CGPoint, CGSize, CGRect, CGAffineTransform, UIEdgeInsets, and UIOffset; additional categories allow easy wrapping and unwrapping of CATransform3D, CMTime, CMTimeMapping, CMTimeRange, MKCoordinate, and MKCoordinateSpan.

You are unlikely to need to store any other kind of C value in an NSValue, but you can if you need to.

NSData

NSData is a general sequence of bytes; basically, it's just a buffer, a chunk of memory. It is immutable; the mutable version is its subclass NSMutableData.

In practice, NSData tends to arise in two main ways:

- When downloading data from the Internet. For example, the NSURLConnection class supplies whatever it retrieves from the Internet as NSData. Transforming it from there into (let's say) a string, specifying the correct encoding, would then be up to you.

- When storing an object as a file or in user preferences. For example, you can't store a UIColor value directly into user preferences. So if the user has made a color choice and you need to save it, you transform the UIColor into an NSData (using NSKeyedArchiver) and save that:

```
[[NSUserDefaults standardUserDefaults] registerDefaults:
    [NSDictionary dictionaryWithObjectsAndKeys:
        [NSKeyedArchiver archivedDataWithRootObject:[UIColor blueColor]],
        @"myColor",
        nil]];
```

The use of NSKeyedArchiver, and its reversal with NSKeyedUnarchiver, is discussed further in Chapter 19 and Chapter 36.

Equality and Comparison

The foregoing types will quickly come to seem to you like basic data types, but of course they are actually object types — which means that they are pointers (Chapter 3) Therefore you cannot compare them using the C operators for testing equality as you would with actual numbers. That's because, in the case of object types, the C operators compare the pointers, not the object content of the instances. For example:

```
NSString* s1 = [NSString stringWithFormat:@"%@, %@", @"Hello", @"world"];
NSString* s2 = [NSString stringWithFormat:@"%@, %@", @"Hello", @"world"];
if (s1 == s2) // false
    // ...
```

The two strings are equivalent (@"Hello, world") but are not the same object. (The example is deliberately elaborate because Cocoa's efficient management of string literals sees to it that two strings initialized directly as @"Hello, world" *are* the same object, which wouldn't illustrate the point I'm making.) It is up to individual classes to implement a test for equality. The general test, isEqual:, is inherited from NSObject and overridden, but some classes also define more specific and efficient tests. Thus, the correct way to perform the above test is like this:

```
if ([s1 isEqualToString: s2])
```

Similarly, it is up to individual classes to supply ordered comparison methods. The standard method is called compare:, and returns one of three constants: NSOrdered-Ascending (the receiver is less than the argument), NSOrderedSame (the receiver is equal to the argument), or NSOrderedDescending (the receiver is greater than the argument); for an example, see Example 3-2.

NSIndexSet

NSIndexSet expresses a collection of unique whole numbers; its purpose is to express element numbers of an ordered collection, such as an NSArray. Thus, for instance, to retrieve multiple objects simultaneously from an array, you specify the desired indexes as an NSIndexSet. It is also used with other things that are array-like; for example, you pass an NSIndexSet to a UITableView to indicate what sections to insert or delete.

To take a specific example, let's say you want to speak of elements 1, 2, 3, 4, 8, 9, and 10 of an NSArray. NSIndexSet expresses this notion in some compact implementation that can be readily queried. The actual implementation is opaque, but you can imagine that in this case the set might consist of two NSRange structs, {1,4} and {8,3}, and NSIndexSet's methods actually invite you to think of an NSIndexSet as composed of ranges.

An NSIndexSet is immutable; its mutable subclass is NSMutableIndexSet. You can form a simple NSIndexSet consisting of just one contiguous range directly, by passing an NSRange to `indexSetWithIndexesInRange:`; but to form a more complex index set you'll need to use NSMutableIndexSet so that you can append additional ranges.

To walk through (enumerate) the index values or ranges specified by an NSIndexSet, call `enumerateIndexesUsingBlock:` or `enumerateRangesUsingBlock:` or their variants.

NSArray and NSMutableArray

An NSArray is an ordered collection of objects. Its length is its `count`, and a particular object can be obtained by index number using `objectAtIndex:`. The index of the first object is zero, so the index of the last object is `count` minus one.

Starting with LLVM compiler version 4.0 (Xcode 4.5), it is no longer necessary to call `objectAtIndex:`; instead, you can use a notation reminiscent of C and other languages that have arrays, namely, append square brackets containing the index number to the array reference (*subscripting*).

So, for example, if pep contains @"Manny", @"Moe", and @"Jack", then pep[2] yields @"Jack"; it is equivalent to [pep objectAtIndex:2]. Okay, I lied; actually, pep[2] is equivalent to [pep objectAtIndexedSubscript:2]. That's because the subscripting notation causes *any* reference to which the subscript is appended to be sent `objectAt-IndexedSubscript:`. This in turn means that *any* class can implement `objectAt-IndexedSubscript:` and become eligible for subscripting notation — including your classes. Note that this method must be publicly declared for the compiler to permit the subscripting notation.

You can form an NSArray in various ways, but typically you'll start by supplying a list of the objects it is to contain. As I mentioned in Chapter 3, a new Objective-C literal syntax (starting with LLVM compiler version 4.0, Xcode 4.4 or later) lets you wrap this list in @[...] as a way of generating the NSArray:

```
NSArray* pep = @[@"Manny", @"Moe", @"Jack"];
```

An NSArray is immutable. This doesn't mean you can't mutate any of the objects it contains; it means that once the NSArray is formed you can't remove an object from it, insert an object into it, or replace an object at a given index. To do those things, you can derive a new array consisting of the original array plus or minus some objects, or use NSArray's subclass, NSMutableArray.

NSMutableArray's `addObject:` and `replaceObjectAtIndex:withObject:` are supplemented by the same subscripting notation that applies to NSArray. In this case, though, the subscripted reference is an lvalue — you're assigning to it:

```
pep[3] = @"Zelda";
```

That causes the NSMutableArray to be sent `setObject:atIndexedSubscript:`. The way NSMutableArray implements this, if `pep` has three elements, `pep[3] = @"Zelda"` is equivalent to `addObject:` (you're appending to the end of the array); if `pep` has more than three elements, it's equivalent to `replaceObjectAtIndex:withObject:`. (If `pep` has fewer than three elements, an exception is thrown.)

You can walk through (enumerate) every object in an array with the `for...in` construct described in Chapter 1. (You'll get an exception if you try to mutate an array while enumerating it.)

You can seek an object within an array with `indexOfObject:` or `indexOfObject-IdenticalTo:`; the former's idea of equality is to call `isEqual:`, whereas the latter uses pointer equality.

Those familiar with other languages may miss such utility array functions as `map`, which builds a new array of the results of calling a method on each object in the array. (`make-ObjectsPerformSelector:` requires a selector that returns no value, and `enumerate-ObjectsUsingBlock:` requires a block function that returns no value.) The usual workaround is to make an empty mutable array and then enumerate the original array, calling a method and appending each result to the mutable array (Example 10-1). It is also sometimes possible to use key–value coding as a `map` substitute (see Chapter 12).

Example 10-1. Building an array by enumerating another array

```
NSMutableArray* marr = [NSMutableArray array];
for (id obj in myArray) {
    id result = [obj doSomething];
    [marr addObject: result];
}
```

You can filter an array to produce a new array consisting of just those objects meeting a test that can be described as an NSPredicate:

```
NSArray* pep = @[@"Manny", @"Moe", @"Jack"];
NSPredicate* p = [NSPredicate predicateWithFormat:@"self BEGINSWITH[cd] 'm'"];
NSArray* ems = [pep filteredArrayUsingPredicate:p];
```

To search or filter an array on a more customized test, you can walk through the array applying the test and adding those that meet it to an NSMutableArray (similar to

Example 10-1). And there are many methods that give you the ability to search or filter an array using a block:

```
NSArray* pep = @[@"Manny", @"Moe", @"Jack"];
NSArray* ems =
    [pep objectsAtIndexes: [pep indexesOfObjectsPassingTest:
     ^BOOL(id obj, NSUInteger idx, BOOL *stop) {
        return ([(NSString*)obj rangeOfString:@"m"
            options:NSCaseInsensitiveSearch].location == 0);
    }]];
```

You can derive a sorted version of the array, supplying the sorting rules in various ways, or if it's a mutable array, you can sort it directly; see Example 3-1 and Example 3-2.

> Forming a new array from some or all of the elements of an existing array is *not* an expensive operation. The objects constituting the elements of the first array are not copied; the new array consists merely of a new set of pointers to the already existing objects. The same is true for the other collection types I'm about to discuss.

NSSet and Friends

An NSSet is an unordered collection of distinct objects. "Distinct" means that no two objects in a set can return YES when they are compared using isEqual:. Learning whether an object is present in a set is much more efficient than seeking it in an array, and you can ask whether one set is a subset of, or intersects, another set. You can walk through (enumerate) a set with the for...in construct, though the order is of course undefined. You can filter a set, as you can an array. Indeed, much of what you can do with a set is parallel to what you can do with an array, except that of course you can't do anything with a set that involves the notion of ordering.

To escape even that restriction, you can use an ordered set. An ordered set (NSOrdered-Set) is *very* like an array, and the methods for working with it are very similar to the methods for working with an array — NSOrderedSet even implements objectAt-IndexedSubscript:, so you can fetch an element by subscripting. But an ordered set's elements must be distinct. Handing an array over to an ordered set *uniques* the array, meaning that order is maintained but only the first occurrence of an equal object is moved to the set. An ordered set provides many of the advantages of sets: for example, as with an NSSet, learning whether an object is present in an ordered set is much more efficient than for an array, and you can readily take the union, intersection, or difference with another set. Since the distinctness restriction will often prove no restriction at all (because the elements were going to be distinct anyway), it is likely that programmers will want to get into the habit of using NSOrderedSet instead of NSArray wherever possible.

An NSSet is immutable. You can derive one NSSet from another by adding or removing elements, or you can use its subclass, NSMutableSet. Similarly, NSOrderedSet has its mutable counterpart, NSMutableOrderedSet (which implements setObject:at-IndexedSubscript:). There is no penalty for adding to, or inserting into, a mutable set an object that the set already contains; nothing is added (and so the distinctness rule is enforced), but there's no error.

NSCountedSet, a subclass of NSMutableSet, is a mutable unordered collection of objects that are *not* necessarily distinct (this concept is usually referred to as a *bag*). It is implemented as a set plus a count of how many times each element has been added.

NSDictionary and NSMutableDictionary

An NSDictionary is an unordered collection of key–value pairs. The key is usually an NSString, though it doesn't have to be. The value can be any object. An NSDictionary is immutable; its mutable subclass is NSMutableDictionary.

The keys of a dictionary are distinct (using isEqual: for comparison). If you add a key–value pair to an NSMutableDictionary, then if that key is not already present, the pair is simply added, but if the key is already present, then the corresponding value is replaced.

The fundamental use of an NSDictionary is to request an entry's value by key (using objectForKey:); if no such key exists, the result is nil, so this is also the way to find out whether a key is present. A dictionary is thus an easy, flexible data storage device, an object-based analogue to a struct. Cocoa often uses a dictionary to provide you with an extra packet of named values, as in the userInfo of an NSNotification, the options parameter of application:didFinishLaunchingWithOptions:, and so on.

The same Objective-C modernizations that brought us array literals and subscripting have brought us dictionary literals and subscripting. In addition to forming a dictionary from an array of objects and an array of keys (dictionaryWithObjects:forKeys:) or as a nil-terminated list of alternating objects and keys (dictionaryWithObjectsAnd-Keys:), a dictionary may be formed literally as a comma-separated list of key–value pairs, each key followed by a colon and the value, and wrapped in @{...}. Thus, recall our earlier NSUserDefaults example:

```
[[NSUserDefaults standardUserDefaults] registerDefaults:
    [NSDictionary dictionaryWithObjectsAndKeys:
        @4,
        @"cardMatrixRows",
        @3,
        @"cardMatrixColumns",
        nil]];
```

That can be rewritten like this:

```
[[NSUserDefaults standardUserDefaults] registerDefaults:
    @{@"cardMatrixRows":@4, @"cardMatrixColumns":@3}];
```

To fetch a value from a dictionary by its key, instead of calling `objectForKey:`, you can now subscript the key in square brackets to the dictionary reference: `dict[key]`. Similarly, to add a key–value pair to an NSMutableDictionary, instead of calling `setObject:forKey:`, you can assign to the subscripted dictionary reference. Parallel to NSArray, this is accomplished behind the scenes by calling `objectForKeyedSubscript:` and `setObject:forKeyedSubscript:`, and your own classes can declare these methods and be eligible for keyed subscripting notation.

Data structures such as an array of dictionaries, a dictionary of dictionaries, and so forth, are extremely common, and will often lie at the heart of an app's functionality. Here's an example from one of my own apps. The app bundle contains a text file laid out like this:

```
chapterNumber [tab] pictureName [return]
chapterNumber [tab] pictureName [return]
```

As the app launches, I load this text file and parse it into a dictionary, each entry of which has the following structure:

```
key: (chapterNumber, as an NSNumber)
value: [Mutable Array]
    (pictureName)
    (pictureName)
    ...
```

Thus, as we walk the text file, we end up with all pictures for a chapter collected under the number of that chapter. This makes it easy for me later to present all the pictures for a given chapter. For each line of the text file, if the dictionary entry for that chapter number doesn't exist, we create it, with an empty mutable array as its value. Whether that dictionary entry existed or not, it does now, and its value is a mutable array, so we append the picture name to that mutable array. Observe how this single typical example (Example 10-2) brings together many of the Foundation classes discussed in this section.

Example 10-2. Parsing a file with Foundation classes

```
NSString* f = [[NSBundle mainBundle] pathForResource:@"index" ofType:@"txt"];
NSError* err = nil;
NSString* s = [NSString stringWithContentsOfFile:f
                                        encoding:NSUTF8StringEncoding
                                           error:&err];
// error-checking omitted
NSMutableDictionary* d = [NSMutableDictionary dictionary];
for (NSString* line in [s componentsSeparatedByString:@"\n"]) {
    NSArray* items = [line componentsSeparatedByString:@"\t"];
    NSInteger chnum = [items[0] integerValue];
    NSNumber* key = @(chnum);
    NSMutableArray* marr = d[key];
```

```
    if (!marr) { // no such key, create key-value pair
        marr = [NSMutableArray array];
        d[key] = marr;
    }
    // marr is now a mutable array, empty or otherwise
    NSString* picname = items[1];
    [marr addObject: picname];
}
```

You can get from an NSDictionary a list of keys, a sorted list of keys, or a list of values. You can walk through (enumerate) a dictionary by its keys with the for...in construct, though the order is of course undefined. A dictionary also supplies an object-Enumerator, which you can use with the for...in construct to walk through just the values. You can also walk through the key–value pairs together using a block, and you can even filter an NSDictionary by some test against its values.

Migrating to Modern Objective-C
If you have old code that you'd like to convert to use the modern NSNumber, NSArray, and NSDictionary literal Objective-C syntax, and to use array and dictionary subscripting, you can do so with no work whatever. Simply choose Edit → Refactor → Convert to Modern Objective-C Syntax.

NSNull

NSNull does nothing but supply a pointer to a singleton object, [NSNull null]. Use this singleton object to stand for nil in situations where an actual object is required and nil is not permitted. For example, you can't use nil as the value of an element of a collection (such as NSArray, NSSet, or NSDictionary), so you'd use [NSNull null] instead.

Despite what I said earlier about equality, you can test an object against [NSNull null] using the C equality operator, because this is a singleton instance and therefore pointer comparison works.

Immutable and Mutable

Beginners sometimes have difficulty with the Foundation's immutable/mutable class pairs, so here are some hints.

The documentation may not make it completely obvious that the mutable classes obey and, if appropriate, override the methods of the immutable classes. Thus, for example, [NSArray array] generates an immutable array, but [NSMutableArray array] generates a mutable array. (You will look in vain for the expected [NSMutableArray mutable-

Array].) The same is true of all the initializers and convenience class methods for instantiation: they may all have "array" in their name, but when sent to NSMutableArray, they yield a mutable array.

That fact also answers the question of how to make an immutable array mutable, and *vice versa*. If `arrayWithArray:`, sent to the NSArray class, yields a new immutable array containing the same objects in the same order as the original array, then the same method, `arrayWithArray:`, sent to the NSMutableArray class, yields a *mutable* array containing the same objects in the same order as the original. Thus this single method can transform an array between immutable and mutable in either direction. You can also use `copy` (produces an immutable copy) and `mutableCopy` (produces a mutable copy).

All of the above applies equally, of course, to the other immutable/mutable class pairs. You will often want to work internally and temporarily with a mutable instance but then store (and possibly vend, as an instance variable) an immutable instance, thus protecting the value from being changed accidentally or behind your own back. What matters is not a variable's declared class but what class the instance really is (polymorphism; see Chapter 5), so it's good that you can easily switch between an immutable and a mutable version of the same data.

To test whether an instance is mutable or immutable, do *not* ask for its `class`. These immutable/mutable class pairs are all implemented as *class clusters*, which means that Cocoa uses a secret class, different from the documented class you work with. This secret class is subject to change without notice, because it's none of your business and you should never have looked at it in the first place. Thus, code of this form is subject to breakage:

```
if ([NSStringFromClass([n class]) isEqualToString: @"NSCFArray"]) // wrong!
```

Instead, to learn whether an object is mutable, ask it whether it responds to a mutability method:

```
if ([n respondsToSelector:@selector(addObject:)]) // right
```

 Here's a reminder: just because a collection class is immutable doesn't mean that the objects it collects are immutable. They are still objects and do not lose any of their normal behavior merely because they are pointed to by an immutable collection.

Property Lists

A *property list* is a string (XML) representation of data. The Foundation classes NSString, NSData, NSArray, and NSDictionary are the only classes that can be converted into a property list. Moreover, an NSArray or NSDictionary can be converted into a property list only if the only classes it collects are these classes, along with NSDate and NSNumber. (This is why, as mentioned earlier, you must convert a UIColor into an NSData in order to store it in user defaults; the user defaults is a property list.)

The primary use of a property list is to store data as a file. NSArray and NSDictionary provide convenience methods `writeToFile:atomically:` and `writeTo-URL:atomically:` that generate property list files given a pathname or file URL, respectively; they also provide inverse convenience methods that initialize an NSArray object or an NSDictionary object based on the property list contents of a given file. For this very reason, you are likely to start with one of these classes when you want to create a property list. (NSString and NSData, with their methods `writeToFile:...` and `write-ToURL:...`, just write the data out as a file directly, not as a property list.)

When you initialize an NSArray or NSDictionary from a property list file in this way, the objects in the collection are all immutable. If you want them to be mutable, or if you want to convert an instance of one of the other property list classes to a property list, you'll use the NSPropertyListSerialization class (see the *Property List Programming Guide*).

The Secret Life of NSObject

Because every class inherits from NSObject, it's worth taking some time to investigate and understand NSObject. NSObject is constructed in a rather elaborate way:

- It defines some native class methods and instance methods having mostly to do with the basics of instantiation and of method sending and resolution. (See the *NSObject Class Reference*.)

- It adopts the NSObject protocol. This protocol declares instance methods having mostly to do with memory management, the relationship between an instance and its class, and introspection. Because all the NSObject protocol methods are required, the NSObject class implements them all. (See the *NSObject Protocol Reference*.) This architecture is what permits NSProxy to be a root class; it, too, adopts the NSObject protocol.

- It implements convenience methods related to the NSCopying, NSMutable-Copying, and NSCoding protocols, without formally adopting those protocols. NSObject intentionally doesn't adopt these protocols because this would cause all other classes to adopt them, which would be wrong. But thanks to this architecture, if a class does adopt one of these protocols, you can call the corresponding convenience method. For example, NSObject implements the copy instance method, so you can call copy on any instance, but you'll crash unless the instance's class adopts the NSCopying protocol and implements copyWithZone:.

- A large number of methods are injected into NSObject by more than two dozen categories on NSObject, scattered among various header files. For example, `awakeFromNib` (see Chapter 7) comes from the UINibLoadingAdditions category on NSObject, declared in *UINibLoading.h*. And `performSelector:withObject:afterDelay:`, discussed in Chapter 11, comes from the NSDelayedPerforming category on NSObject, declared in *NSRunLoop.h*.

- A class object, as explained in Chapter 4, is an object. Therefore all classes, which are objects of type Class, inherit from NSObject. Therefore, *any method defined as an instance method by NSObject can be called on a class object as a class method!* For example, `respondsToSelector:` is defined as an instance method by NSObject, but it can (therefore) be treated also as a class method and sent to a class object.

The problem for the programmer is that Apple's documentation is rather rigid about classification. When you're trying to work out what you can say to an object, you don't care where that object's methods come from; you just care what you can say. But Apple differentiates methods by where they come from. Even though NSObject is the root class, the most important class, from which all other classes inherit, *no single page of the documentation provides a conspectus of all its methods.* Instead, you have to look at both the *NSObject Class Reference* and the *NSObject Protocol Reference* simultaneously, plus the pages documenting the NSCopying, NSMutableCopying, and NSCoding protocols (in order to understand how they interact with methods defined by NSObject), plus you have to supply mentally a class method version of every NSObject instance method!

Of the methods injected into NSObject by categories, many are delegate methods used in restricted situations (so that these are really informal protocols), and do not need centralized documentation; for example, `animationDidStart:` is documented under the CAAnimation class, quite rightly, because you need to know about it only and exactly when you're working with CAAnimation. Others that are general in nature are documented on the NSObject class documentation page itself; for example, `cancelPreviousPerformRequestsWithTarget:` comes from a category declared in *NSRunLoop.h*, but it is documented under NSObject, quite rightly, since this is a class method, and therefore effectively a global method, that you might want to send at any time. However, every object responds to `awakeFromNib`, and it's likely to be crucial to every app you write; yet you must learn about it outside of the NSObject documentation, sitting all by itself in the *NSObject UIKit Additions Reference* page, where you're extremely unlikely to discover it! The same goes, it might be argued, for all the key–value coding methods (Chapter 12) and key–value observing methods (Chapter 13).

Once you've collected, by hook or by crook, all the NSObject methods, you can see that they fall into a certain natural classification, much as outlined in Apple's documentation (see also "The Root Class" in the "Cocoa Objects" section of the *Cocoa Fundamentals Guide*):

Creation, destruction, and memory management

Methods for creating an instance, such as alloc and copy, along with methods that you might override in order to learn when something is happening in the lifetime of an object, such as initialize (see Chapter 11) and dealloc (see Chapter 12), plus methods that manage memory (see Chapter 12).

Class relationships

Methods for learning an object's class and inheritance, such as class, superclass, isKindOfClass:, and isMemberOfClass:.

To check the class of an instance (or class), use methods such as isKindOfClass: and isMemberOfClass:. Direct comparison of two class objects, as in [someObject class] == [otherObject class], is rarely advisable, especially because a Cocoa instance's class might be a private, undocumented subclass of the class you expect. I mentioned this already in connection with class clusters, and it can happen in other cases.

Object introspection and comparison

Methods for asking what would happen if an object were sent a certain message, such as respondsToSelector:; for representing an object as a string (description, used in debugging; see Chapter 9); and for comparing objects (isEqual:).

Message response

Methods for meddling with what does happen when an object is sent a certain message, such as doesNotRecognizeSelector:. If you're curious, see the *Objective-C Runtime Programming Guide*. An example appears in Chapter 25.

Message sending

Methods for sending a message indirectly. For example, performSelector: takes a selector as parameter, and sending it to an object tells that object to perform that selector. This might seem identical to just sending that message to that object, but what if you don't know what message to send until runtime? Moreover, variants on performSelector: allow you send a message on a specified thread (Chapter 38), or send a message after a certain amount of time has passed (performSelector:withObject:afterDelay: and similar).

CHAPTER 11

Cocoa Events

None of your code runs until Cocoa calls it. The art of Cocoa programming consists largely of knowing when and why Cocoa will call your code. If you know this, you can put your code in the correct place, with the correct method name, so that your code runs at the correct moment, and your app behaves the way you intend.

In Chapter 7, for example, we wrote a method to be called when the user taps a certain button in our interface, and we also arranged things so that that method *would* be called when the user taps that button:

```
- (void) buttonPressed: (id) sender {
    // ... react to the button being pressed
}
```

This architecture typifies the underpinnings of a Cocoa program. Your code itself is like a panel of buttons, waiting for Cocoa to press one. If something happens that Cocoa feels your code needs to know about and respond to, it presses the right button — if the right button is there. You organize your code with Cocoa's behavior in mind. Cocoa makes certain promises about how and when it will dispatch messages to your code. These are Cocoa's *events*. You know what these events are, and you arrange for your code to be ready when Cocoa delivers them.

Thus, to program for Cocoa, you must, in a sense, surrender control. Your code never gets to run just whenever it feels like it. It can run *only* in response to some kind of event. Something happens, such as the user making a gesture on the screen, or some specific stage arriving in the lifetime of your app, and Cocoa dispatches an event to your code — if your code is prepared to receive it. So you don't write just any old code you want to and put it in any old place. You use the framework, by letting the framework use you. You submit to Cocoa's rules and promises and expectations, so that your code will be called at the right time and in the right way.

The specific events that you can receive are listed in the documentation. The overall architecture of how and when events are dispatched and the ways in which your code arranges to receive them is the subject of this chapter.

Reasons for Events

Broadly speaking, the reasons you might receive an event may be divided informally into four categories. These categories are not official; I made them up. Often it isn't completely clear which of these categories an event fits into; an event may well appear to fit two categories. But they are still generally useful for visualizing how and why Cocoa interacts with your code:

User events
> The user does something interactive, and an event is triggered directly. Obvious examples are events that you get when the user taps or swipes the screen, or types a key on the keyboard.

Lifetime events
> These are events notifying you of the arrival of a stage in the life of the app, such as the fact that the app is starting up or is about to go into the background, or of a component of the app, such as the fact that a UIViewController's view has just loaded or is about to be removed from the screen.

Functional events
> Cocoa is about to do something, and turns to you in case you want to supply additional functionality. I would put into this category things like UIView's `draw-Rect:` (your chance to have a view draw itself) and UILabel's `drawTextInRect:` (your chance to modify the look of a label), with which we experimented in Chapter 10.

Query events
> Cocoa turns to you to ask a question; its behavior will depend upon your answer. For example, the way data appears in a table (a UITableView) is that whenever Cocoa needs a cell for a row of the table, it turns to you and asks for the cell.

Subclassing

A built-in Cocoa class may define methods that Cocoa itself will call and that you are invited (or required) to override in a subclass, so that your custom behavior, and not (merely) the default behavior, will take place.

An example I gave in Chapter 10 was UIView's `drawRect:`. This is what I call a functional event. By overriding `drawRect:` in a UIView subclass, you dictate the full procedure by which a view draws itself. You don't know exactly when this method will be called, and you don't care; when it is, you draw, and this guarantees that the view will always appear the way you want it to. (You never call `drawRect:` yourself; if some underlying condition has changed and you want the view to be redrawn, you call `setNeedsDisplay` and let Cocoa call `drawRect:` in response.)

Built-in UIView subclasses may have other functional event methods you'll want to customize through subclassing. Typically this will be in order to change the way the view is drawn, without taking command of the entire drawing procedure yourself. In Chapter 10 I gave an example involving UILabel and its `drawTextInRect:`. Another example is UISlider, which lets you customize the position and size of the slider's "thumb" by overriding `thumbRectForBounds:trackRect:value:` (Chapter 25).

UIViewController (Chapter 19) is a good example of a class meant for subclassing. Of the methods listed in the UIViewController class documentation, just about all are methods you might have reason to override. If you create a UIViewController subclass in Xcode, you'll see that the template already includes a few methods to get you started; these are all method overrides. For example, `viewDidLoad` is called to let you know that your view controller's view has loaded, so you can perform initializations; it's an obvious example of a lifetime event.

A UIViewController method like `supportedInterfaceOrientations` is what I call a query event. Your job is to return a bitmask telling Cocoa what orientations your view can appear in at this moment — whenever that may be. You don't know exactly when this method will be called, and you don't care; you trust Cocoa to call it at the appropriate moments, so that if the user rotates the device, your app will or won't be rotated to compensate, depending on what value you return.

When looking for events that you can receive through subclassing, be sure to look upward though the inheritance hierarchy. For example, if you're wondering how to be notified when your custom UILabel subclass is embedded into another view, you won't find the answer in the UILabel class documentation; a UILabel receives the appropriate event by virtue of being a UIView. In the UIView class documentation, you'll learn that you can override `didMoveToSuperview` to be informed when this happens.

Even further up the inheritance hierarchy, you'll find things like NSObject's `initialize` class method. Before any class is sent its first class message (including instantiation), it is sent the `initialize` message. Thus, `initialize` can be overridden in order to run code extremely early in a class's lifetime (before it even has an instance). Your project's application delegate class (such as AppDelegate in our Empty Window project) is instantiated very early in the app's lifetime, so its `initialize` can be a good place to perform very early app initializations, such as setting default values for any user preferences. When implementing `initialize`, we must test, as a matter of course, whether `self` really is the class in question (and this is one of the few situations in which we will compare two classes directly against one another); otherwise there is a chance that `initialize` will be called again (and our code will run again) if a subclass of this class is used:

```
// MyClass.m:
+ (void)initialize {
    if (self == [MyClass class]) {
        // do stuff
    }
}
```

Notifications

Cocoa provides your app with a single instance of NSNotificationCenter, informally called the *notification center*, and available as `[NSNotificationCenter default-Center]`. This instance is the basis of a mechanism for sending messages called *notifications*. A notification includes an instance of NSNotification (a *notification object*). The idea is that any object can be registered with the notification center to receive certain notifications. Another object can hand the notification center a notification object to send out (this is called *posting* the notification). The notification center will then send that notification object, in a notification, to all objects that are registered to receive it.

The notification mechanism is often described as a dispatching or broadcasting mechanism, and with good reason. It lets an object send a message without knowing or caring what object or how many objects receive it. This relieves your app's architecture from the formal responsibility of somehow hooking up instances just so a message can pass from one to the other (which can sometimes be quite tricky or onerous, as discussed in Chapter 13). When objects are conceptually "distant" from one another, notifications can be a fairly lightweight way of permitting one to message the other.

An NSNotification object has three pieces of information associated with it, which can be retrieved by instance methods:

`name`
An NSString which specifies the notification's meaning.

`object`
An instance associated with the notification; typically, the instance that posted it.

`userInfo`
Not every notification has a `userInfo`; it is an NSDictionary, and can contain additional information associated with the notification. What information this NSDictionary will contain, and under what keys, depends on the particular notification; you have to consult the documentation. For example, the documentation tells us that UIApplication's `UIApplicationDidChangeStatusBarFrameNotification` includes a `userInfo` dictionary with a key `UIApplicationStatusBarFrameUserInfoKey` whose value is the status bar's frame. When you post a no-

tification yourself, you can put anything you like into the userInfo for the notification's recipient(s) to retrieve.

Receiving a Built-In Notification

Cocoa itself posts notifications through the notification center, and your code can register to receive them. You'll find a separate Notifications section in the documentation for a class that provides them.

To register for a notification, you send one of two messages to the notification center. One is addObserver:selector:name:object:. The parameters are as follows:

addObserver:
> The instance to which the notification is to be sent. This will typically be self; it isn't usual for one instance to register a different instance as the receiver of a notification.

selector:
> The message to be sent to the observer instance when the notification occurs. The designated method should return void and should take one parameter, which will be the NSNotification object (so the parameter should be typed as NSNotification* or id). Don't forget to implement this method! If the notification center sends a notification by sending the message specified as the selector: here, and there is no method implemented to receive this message, your app will crash. Failing to specify the selector: accurately is a common beginner mistake (and the compiler doesn't save you from yourself).

name:
> The NSString name of the notification you'd like to receive. If this parameter is nil, you're asking to receive *all* notifications sent by the object designated in the object: parameter. A built-in Cocoa notification's name is usually a constant. As I explained in Chapter 1, this is helpful, because if you flub the name of a constant, the compiler will complain, whereas if you enter the name of the notification directly as an NSString literal and you get it wrong, the compiler won't complain but you will mysteriously fail to get any notifications (because no notification has the name you actually entered) — a very difficult sort of mistake to track down.

object:
> The object of the notification you're interested in, which will usually be the object that posted it. If this is nil, you're asking to receive *all* notifications with the name designated in the name parameter. (If both the name: and object: parameters are nil, you're asking to receive all notifications!)

For example, in one of my apps I need to respond, by changing my interface, if the device's music player starts playing a different song. The API for the device's built-in music player belongs to the MPMusicPlayerController class (Chapter 29); this class provides a notification to tell me when the built-in music player changes its playing state, listed under Notifications in the MPMusicPlayerController's class documentation as `MPMusicPlayerControllerNowPlayingItemDidChangeNotification`.

It turns out, looking at the documentation, that this notification won't be posted at all unless I call MPMusicPlayerController's `beginGeneratingPlaybackNotifications` instance method. This architecture is not uncommon; Cocoa saves itself some time and effort by not sending out certain notifications unless they are switched on, as it were. So my first job is to get an instance of MPMusicPlayerController and call this method:

```
MPMusicPlayerController* mp = [MPMusicPlayerController iPodMusicPlayer];
[mp beginGeneratingPlaybackNotifications];
```

Now I register myself to receive the desired playback notification:

```
[[NSNotificationCenter defaultCenter] addObserver:self
        selector:@selector(nowPlayingItemChanged:)
            name:MPMusicPlayerControllerNowPlayingItemDidChangeNotification
        object:nil];
```

So now, whenever an `MPMusicPlayerControllerNowPlayingItemDidChange-Notification` is posted, my `nowPlayingItemChanged:` method will be called:

```
- (void) nowPlayingItemChanged: (NSNotification*) n {
    MPMusicPlayerController* mp = [MPMusicPlayerController iPodMusicPlayer];
    self->_nowPlayingItem = mp.nowPlayingItem;
    // ... and so on ...
}
```

The other way to register to receive a notification is by calling `addObserverFor-Name:object:queue:usingBlock:`. Its `name:` and `object:` parameters are just like those of `addObserver:selector:name:object:`, but it doesn't specify an observer and it doesn't specify a selector. Instead, you provide a block — the actual code to be executed when the notification fires. There is no need to specify an observer, and there is no `user-Info:` parameter, because you're providing a block: the code that will be called is this block, right here, and there can be no difficulty providing the block's code with whatever values it needs. (This method also returns a value, whose purpose I'll explain in a moment.)

This way of registering for a notification has some tremendous advantages. For `add-Observer:selector:name:object:` to work properly, you must get the selector right and make sure you implement the corresponding method. With a block, there is no selector and there is no separate method; everything happens right there in the block, like this:

```
MPMusicPlayerController* mp = [MPMusicPlayerController iPodMusicPlayer];
[mp beginGeneratingPlaybackNotifications];
id ob = [[NSNotificationCenter defaultCenter]
 addObserverForName:MPMusicPlayerControllerNowPlayingItemDidChangeNotification
 object:nil queue:nil usingBlock:^(NSNotification *n) {
        self->_nowPlayingItem = mp.nowPlayingItem;
        // ... and so on ...
    }
}];
```

Consider how maintainable and understandable that code is. Heavy use of add-Observer:selector:name:object: means that your code ends up peppered with methods that exist solely in order to be called by the notification center. But there is nothing about these methods that tells you what they are for — you will probably want to use explicit comments in order to remind yourself — and the methods are separate from the registration call, all of which makes your code very method-heavy and confusing. With a block, on the other hand, the whole purpose of the registration is crystal-clear, because the block accompanies it. And notice how, in the block, I don't have to redefine mp as I did in the separate method nowPlayingItemChanged:; it is still in scope from where it was defined a couple of lines earlier. Blocks are so convenient!

Unregistering

It is up to you, for every object that you register as a recipient of notifications, to unregister that object before it goes out of existence. If you fail to do this, and if the object does go out of existence, and if a notification for which that object is registered is posted, the notification center will attempt to send the appropriate message to that object, which is now missing in action. The result will be a crash at best, and chaos at worst.

To unregister an object as a recipient of notifications, send the notification center the removeObserver: message. (Alternatively, you can unregister an object for just a specific set of notifications with removeObserver:name:object:.) The object passed as the observer: argument is the object that is no longer to receive notifications. What object that is depends on how you registered in the first place:

You called addObserver:...
    You supplied an observer originally; that is the observer you must now unregister.

You called addObserverForName:...
    The call returned an observer token object, which you captured as an id variable (its real class and nature are no concern of yours); that is the observer you must now unregister.

The trick is finding the right moment to do this. The fallback solution is the registered instance's dealloc method, this being the last lifetime event an instance is sent before it goes out of existence. If you're using ARC and addObserverForName:..., there are memory management implications that I'll talk about in Chapter 12.

Keep it simple, because complicated logic for registering and unregistering for notifications can be difficult to debug, especially as NSNotificationCenter provides no kind of introspection: you cannot ask an NSNotificationCenter what objects are registered with it as notification recipients. I once had a devil of a time understanding why one of my instances was not receiving a notification for which it was registered. Caveman debugging didn't help. Eventually I realized that some code I'd forgotten about was unregistering my instance.

If you're calling addObserverForName:... multiple times from the same class, you're going to end up receiving from the notification center multiple observer tokens, which you need to preserve so that you can unregister by handing them back to the notification center. If your plan is to unregister everything at once, one way to handle this situation is through an instance variable that is a mutable collection. So, for example, I might have an NSMutableSet instance variable called _observers. Early on, I initialize it to an empty set:

```
self->_observers = [NSMutableSet set];
```

Each time I register for a notification using a block, I capture the result and add it to the set:

```
id ob = [[NSNotificationCenter defaultCenter]
    addObserverForName:@"whatever" object:nil queue:nil
    usingBlock:^(NSNotification *note) {
        // ... whatever ...
    }];
[self->_observers addObject:ob];
```

Ultimately, I unregister by enumerating the set:

```
for (id ob in self->_observers)
    [[NSNotificationCenter defaultCenter] removeObserver:ob];
```

The tedium of doing all that is a price worth paying in order to take advantage of blocks when using notifications.

 I am skipping over some other aspects of notifications that you probably won't need to know about. Read Apple's *Notification Programming Topics for Cocoa* if you want the gory details.

NSTimer

A timer (NSTimer) is not, strictly speaking, a notification; but it behaves very similarly. It is an object that gives off a signal (*fires*) after the lapse of a certain time interval. The signal is a message to one of your instances. Thus you can arrange to be notified when a certain time has elapsed. The timing is not perfectly accurate, but it's pretty good.

Timer management is not exactly tricky, but it is a little unusual. A timer that is actively watching the clock is said to be *scheduled*. A timer may fire once, or it may be a *repeating* timer. To make a timer go out of existence, it must be *invalidated*. A timer that is set to fire once is invalidated automatically after it fires; a repeating timer repeats until *you* invalidate it by sending it the `invalidate` message. An invalidated timer should be regarded as off-limits: you cannot revive it or use it for anything further, and you should probably not send any messages to it.

The straightforward way to create a timer is with the NSTimer class method `scheduled-TimerWithTimeInterval:target:selector:userInfo:repeats:`. This creates the timer and schedules it, so that it begins watching the clock immediately. The target and selector determine what message will be sent to what object when the timer fires; the method in question should take one parameter, which will be a reference to the timer. The `userInfo` is just like the `userInfo` of a notification.

For example, one of my apps is a game with a score; I want to penalize the user, by diminishing the score, for every ten seconds after each move that elapses without the user making a further move. So each time the user makes a move, I create a repeating timer whose time interval is ten seconds (and I also invalidate any existing timer); in the method that the timer calls, I diminish the score.

Timers have some memory management implications that I'll discuss in Chapter 12.

Delegation

Delegation is an object-oriented design pattern, a relationship between two objects, in which the first object's behavior is customized or assisted by the second. The second object is the first object's *delegate*. No subclassing is involved, and indeed the first object is agnostic about the second object's class.

As implemented by Cocoa, here's how delegation works. A built-in Cocoa class has an instance variable, usually called `delegate` (it will certainly have `delegate` in its name). For some instance of that Cocoa class, you set the value of this instance variable to an instance of one of *your* classes. At certain moments in its activity, the Cocoa class promises to turn to its delegate for instructions by sending it a certain message: if the Cocoa instance finds that its delegate is not nil, and that its delegate is prepared to receive that message (see Chapter 10 on `respondsToSelector:`), the Cocoa instance sends the message to the delegate.

Recall the discussion of protocols from Chapter 10. Delegation is one of Cocoa's main uses of protocols. In the old days, delegate methods were listed in the Cocoa class's documentation, and their method signatures were made known to the compiler through an informal protocol (a category on NSObject). Now, though, a class's delegate methods are usually listed in a genuine protocol with its own documentation. There are over 70

Cocoa delegate protocols, showing how heavily Cocoa relies on delegation. Most delegate methods are optional, but in a few cases you'll discover some that are required.

To customize a Cocoa instance's behavior through delegation, you start with one of your classes, which, if necessary, declares conformance to the relevant delegate protocol. When the app runs, you set the Cocoa instance's delegate ivar (or whatever its name is) to an instance of your class. You might do this in code, usually through a property; you might do it in a nib, by connecting an instance's delegate outlet (or whatever it's called) to an appropriate instance that is to serve as delegate. Your delegate class will probably do other things besides serving as this instance's delegate. Indeed, one of the nice things about delegation is that it leaves you free to slot delegate code into your class architecture however you like. For example, if a view has a controller (a UIView-Controller), it will often make sense for the controller to serve also as the delegate of that view, and even of its subviews.

Here's a simple example, involving UIAlertView. If a UIAlertView has no delegate, then when its Cancel button is tapped, the alert view is dismissed. But if you want to *do* something in response to the alert view being dismissed, you need to give it a delegate so that you can receive an event telling you that the alert view *was* dismissed. It's so common to give a UIAlertView a delegate that its designated initializer allows you to supply one; typically, the delegate will be the instance that summoned the alert view in the first place:

```
- (void) gameWon {
    UIAlertView* av =
        [[UIAlertView alloc] initWithTitle:@"Congratulations!"
                              message:@"You won the game. Another game?"
                              delegate:self
                          cancelButtonTitle:@"No, thanks."
                          otherButtonTitles:@"Sure!", nil];
    [av show];
}

- (void) alertView:(UIAlertView*) av
        didDismissWithButtonIndex: (NSInteger) ix {
    if (ix == 1) { // user said "Sure!"
        [self newGame];
    }
}
```

The delegation mechanism is the last piece of the puzzle needed to explain the built-in bootstrapping procedure of a minimal app like our Empty Window project. Recall, from Chapter 6, that the fourth argument to UIApplicationMain is the string name of the class of the shared application instance's delegate. So, having instantiated the class of the shared application (usually UIApplication), UIApplicationMain instantiates the class nominated in its fourth argument — in this case, AppDelegate; there is now, therefore, before much of anything has happened, an AppDelegate instance. Moreover,

`UIApplicationMain` sets the shared application's `delegate` property to this AppDelegate instance. UIApplication's delegate is typed as `id <UIApplicationDelegate>` — and, by golly, AppDelegate is declared as conforming to the UIApplicationDelegate protocol.

This, as we saw in Chapter 10, causes the shared application instance to bombard this AppDelegate instance with `respondsToSelector:` messages, to find out exactly which UIApplicationDelegate methods AppDelegate actually implements. One such method that it does implement is `application:didFinishLaunchingWithOptions:`. So the UIApplication instance now actually sends `application:didFinishLaunchingWith-Options:` to its delegate, the AppDelegate instance. That is why, in some earlier examples, we put code into the implementation of that method: this is code that is guaranteed, thanks to the UIApplication's contract with its delegate, to run very early in the app's lifetime. We know the `application:didFinishLaunchingWithOptions:` message will be sent, we know *when* it will be sent (early in our app's lifetime), and we know to *whom* it will be sent (the application's delegate object); so we've put appropriate code there, waiting to be called. Moreover, there is already boilerplate code in the project template's implementation of this method that does some very important things, such as making our app's window and showing it:

```
self.window = [[UIWindow alloc] initWithFrame:[[UIScreen mainScreen] bounds]];
[self.window makeKeyAndVisible];
```

 The UIApplication delegate methods are also provided as notifications. This lets an instance other than the app delegate hear conveniently about application lifetime events, by registering for them. A few other classes provide duplicate events similarly; for example, UITableView's delegate method `tableView:didSelectRowAtIndexPath:` is matched by a notification `UITableViewSelectionDidChangeNotification`.

By convention, many Cocoa delegate method names contain the modal verbs `should`, `will`, or `did`. A `will` message is sent to the delegate just before something happens; a `did` message is sent to the delegate just after something happens. A `should` method is special: it returns a BOOL, and you are expected to respond with YES to permit something or NO to prevent it. The documentation tells you what the default response is; you don't have to implement a `should` method if the default response is always acceptable.

In many cases, a property will control the overall behavior; the delegate message lets you pick and choose the behavior based on circumstances at runtime. For example, whether the user can tap the status bar to make a scroll view scroll quickly to the top is governed by the scroll view's `scrollsToTop` property; but even if this property's value is YES, you can prevent this behavior for a particular tap by returning NO from the delegate's `scrollViewShouldScrollToTop:`.

When you're searching the documentation for how you can be notified of a certain event, be sure to consult the corresponding delegate protocol, if there is one. (And don't forget to consult the class's superclasses to see if one of *them* has a corresponding delegate protocol.) You'd like to know when the user taps in a UITextField to start editing it? You won't find anything relevant in the UITextField class documentation; what you're after is `textFieldDidBeginEditing:` in the UITextFieldDelegate protocol. You want to respond when the user rearranges items on your tab bar? Look in UITabBarController-Delegate. You want to know how to make a UITextView zoomable (through the user making a pinch gesture)? A UITextView is a UIScrollView; a scroll view is not zoomable unless its delegate returns a view from `viewForZoomingInScrollView:`, documented under UIScrollViewDelegate.

Data Sources

A *data source* is like a delegate, except that its methods supply the data for another object to display. The chief Cocoa classes with data sources are UITableView, UICollection-View, UIPickerView, and UIPageViewController. In each case, the data source must formally conform to a protocol with required methods.

It comes as a surprise to some beginners that a data source is necessary at all. Why isn't a table's data just part of the table? Or why isn't there at least some fixed data structure that contains the data? The reason is that such policies would violate generality. Use of a data source separates the object that displays the data from the object that manages the data, and leaves the latter free to store and obtain that data however it likes (see on model–view–controller in Chapter 13). The only requirement is that the data source must be able to supply information quickly, because it will be asked for it in real time when the data needs displaying.

Another surprise is that the data source is different from the delegate. But this again is only for generality; it's an option, not a requirement. There is no reason why the data source and the delegate should not be the same object, and most of the time they probably will be.

In this simple example, we implement a UIPickerView that allows the user to select by name a day of the week (the Gregorian week, using English day names). The first two methods are UIPickerView data source methods; the third method is a UIPickerView delegate method:

```
- (NSInteger) numberOfComponentsInPickerView: (UIPickerView*) pickerView {
    return 1;
}

- (NSInteger) pickerView: (UIPickerView*) pickerView
        numberOfRowsInComponent: (NSInteger) component {
    return 7;
}
```

```
- (NSString*) pickerView:(UIPickerView*)pickerView
             titleForRow:(NSInteger)row
           forComponent:(NSInteger)component {
    NSArray* arr = @[@"Sunday",
                     @"Monday",
                     @"Tuesday",
                     @"Wednesday",
                     @"Thursday",
                     @"Friday",
                     @"Saturday"];
    return arr[row];
}
```

Actions

Recall the discussion of actions in Chapter 7. An *action* is a message emitted by an instance of a UIControl subclass (a *control*) reporting a significant user event taking place in that control. The UIControl subclasses (Chapter 25) are all simple interface objects that the user can interact with directly, like a button (UIButton), a switch (UISwitch), a segmented control (UISegmentedControl), a slider (UISlider), or a text field (UITextField).

The significant user events (*control events*) are listed under UIControlEvents in the Constants section of the UIControl class documentation. See Chapter 25 for a list of which controls implement which control events.

The way you hear about a control event is through an action message. A control maintains an internal dispatch table: for each control event, there is some number of target–action pairs, of which the *action* is a selector (the name of a method) and the *target* is the object to which that message is to be sent. When a control event occurs, the control consults its dispatch table, finds all the target–action pairs associated with that control event, and sends each action message to the corresponding target. This architecture is reminiscent of a notification (Figure 11-1).

There are two ways to manipulate a control's action dispatch table: you can configure an action connection in a nib (as explained in Chapter 7), or you can use code. To use code, you send the control the message addTarget:action:forControlEvents:, where the target: is an object, the action: is a selector, and the controlEvents: are designated by a bitmask (see Chapter 1 if you've forgotten how to construct a bitmask). Unlike a notification center, a control also has methods for introspecting the dispatch table (Chapter 25).

Recall the example from Chapter 7 (where b is a reference to a UIButton):

```
[b addTarget:self action:@selector(buttonPressed:)
    forControlEvents:UIControlEventTouchUpInside];
```

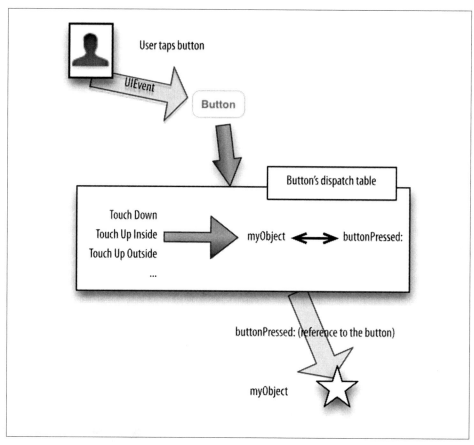

Figure 11-1. The target–action architecture

After that, whenever the user taps in the button, our `buttonPressed:` method will be called. It might, again as in Chapter 7, look like this:

```
- (void) buttonPressed: (id) sender {
    UIAlertView* av = [[UIAlertView alloc] initWithTitle:@"Howdy!"
                                                 message:@"You tapped me."
                                                delegate:nil
                                       cancelButtonTitle:@"Cool"
                                       otherButtonTitles:nil];
    [av show];
}
```

The signature for the action selector can be in any of three forms. The fullest form takes two parameters:

- The control, usually typed as `id`.

- The UIEvent that generated the control event.

A shorter form (the most commonly used form) omits the second parameter; a still shorter form omits both parameters.

Mac OS X Programmer Alert

If you're an experienced Mac OS X Cocoa developer, you'll note that there are some major differences between the Mac OS X implementation of actions and the iOS implementation. In Mac OS X, a control has just one action; in iOS, a control may respond to multiple control events. In Mac OS X, an action has just one target; in iOS, a single event can trigger multiple action messages to multiple targets. In Mac OS X, an action message selector comes in just one form; in iOS, there are three possible forms.

What is the UIEvent, and what is it for? Well, a *touch event* is generated whenever the user does something with a finger (sets it down on the screen, moves it, raises it from the screen). UIEvents are the lowest-level objects charged with communication of touch events to your app. A UIEvent is basically a timestamp (a double) along with a collection (NSSet) of touch events (UITouch). The action mechanism deliberately shields you from the complexities of touch events, but by electing to receive the UIEvent, you can still deal with those complexities if you want to. (See Chapter 18 for full details.)

Curiously, none of the action selector parameters provide any way to learn *which* control event triggered the current action selector call! Thus, for example, to distinguish a Touch Up Inside control event from a Touch Up Outside control event, their corresponding target–action pairs must specify two different action handlers; if you dispatch them to the same action handler, that handler cannot discover which control event occurred.

The Responder Chain

A *responder* is an object that knows how to receive UIEvents directly (see the previous section). It knows this because it is an instance of UIResponder or a UIResponder subclass. If you examine the Cocoa class hierarchy, you'll find that just about any class that has anything to do with display on the screen is a responder. A UIView is a responder. A UIWindow is a responder. A UIViewController is a responder. Even a UIApplication is a responder. In iOS 5 and later, the app delegate is a responder.

If you look in the documentation for the UIResponder class, you'll find that it implements four low-level methods for receiving touch-related UIEvents: touches-Began:withEvent:, touchesMoved:withEvent:, touchesEnded:withEvent: and touchesCancelled:withEvent:. These are called to notify a responder of a touch event. No matter how your code ultimately hears about a user-related touch event — indeed, even if your code *never* hears about a touch event (because Cocoa reacted in some automatic way to the touch, without your code's intervention) — the touch was initially communicated to a responder through one of these methods.

The mechanism for this communication starts by deciding which responder the user touched. The UIView methods `hitTest:withEvent:` and `pointInside:withEvent:` are called until the correct view (the *hit-test view*) is located. Then UIApplication's `sendEvent:` method is called, which calls UIWindow's `sendEvent:`, which calls the correct method of the hit-test view (a responder). I'll cover all this again in full detail in Chapter 18.

The responders in your app participate in a *responder chain*, which essentially links them up through the view hierarchy. A UIView can sit inside another UIView, its *superview*, and so on until we reach the app's UIWindow (a UIView that has no superview). The responder chain, from bottom to top, looks like this:

1. The UIView that we start with (here, the hit-test view).
2. The UIViewController that controls that UIView, if there is one.
3. The UIView's superview, and then *its* UIViewController if there is one. Repeat this step, moving up the superview hierarchy one superview at a time, until we reach…
4. The UIWindow.
5. The UIApplication.
6. The UIApplication's delegate.

Deferring Responsibility

The responder chain can be used to let a responder defer responsibility for handling a touch event. If a responder receives a touch event and can't handle it, the event can be passed up the responder chain to look for a responder that *can* handle it. This can happen in two main ways: (1) the responder doesn't implement the relevant method; (2) the responder implements the relevant method to call `super`.

For example, a plain vanilla UIView has no native implementation of the touch event methods. Thus, by default, even if a UIView is the hit-test view, the touch event effectively falls through the UIView and travels up the responder chain, looking for someone to respond to it. If this UIView is an instance of your own subclass, you might implement the touch event methods in that subclass to catch touch events in the UIView itself; but if the UIView is controlled by a UIViewController, you have already subclassed UIView-Controller, and that subclass is probably where the interface behavior logic for this UIView is already situated, so you might well prefer to implement the touch event methods there instead. You are thus taking advantage of the responder chain to defer responsibility for handling touch events from the UIView to its UIViewController, in a natural and completely automatic way.

Again, I'll come back to this in Chapter 18; don't worry about it for now. I'm actually telling you about the responder chain chiefly in order to discuss nil-targeted actions, which is the subject of the next section.

Nil-Targeted Actions

A *nil-targeted action* is a target–action pair in which the target is nil. There is no designated target object, so the following rule is used: starting with the hit-test view (the view with which the user is interacting), Cocoa looks up the responder chain for an object that can respond to the action message.

Suppose, for example, we have a UIButton inside a UIView. And suppose we run this code early in the button's lifetime, where b is the button:

```
[b addTarget:nil action:@selector(doButton:)
    forControlEvents:UIControlEventTouchUpInside];
```

That's a nil-targeted action. So what happens when the user taps the button? First, Cocoa looks in the UIButton itself to see whether it responds to doButton:. If not, then it looks in the UIView that is its superview. And so on, up the responder chain. If a responder is found that handles doButton:, the action message is sent to that object; otherwise, the message goes unhandled.

Thus, suppose the UIView containing the UIButton is an instance of your own UIView subclass. Let's call it MyView. If MyView implements doButton:, then when the user taps the button, it is MyView's doButton: that will be called.

To create a nil-targeted action in a nib, you form a connection to the First Responder proxy object (in the dock). This is what the First Responder proxy object is for! The First Responder isn't a real object with a known class, so before you can connect an action to it, you have to define the action message within the First Responder proxy object, like this:

1. Select the First Responder proxy in the nib, and switch to the Attributes inspector.

2. You'll see a table (probably empty) of user-defined nil-targeted First Responder actions. Click the Plus button and give the new action a signature; it must take a single parameter (so that its name will end with a colon).

3. Now you can Control-drag from a control, such as a UIButton, to the First Responder proxy to specify a nil-targeted action with the signature you specified.

Swamped by Events

Your code runs only because Cocoa sends an event and you had previously set up a method ready to receive it. Cocoa has the potential to send lots of events, telling you what the user has done, informing you of each stage in the lifetime of your app and its objects, asking for your input on how to proceed. To receive the events that you need to hear about, your code is peppered with methods that are *entry points* — methods that you have written with just the right name and in just the right class so that they can be called by Cocoa through events. In fact, it is easy to imagine that in many cases your code for a class will consist almost entirely of entry points.

That fact is one of your primary challenges as an iOS programmer. You know what you want to do, but you have to divide it up and allocate it according to when Cocoa is going to call into your code. Before you've written a single line of your own code, the skeleton structure of a class is likely to have been largely mapped out for you by the need to be prepared to receive the events that Cocoa is going to want to send you.

Suppose, for example, that your iPhone app contains a screen that effectively consists entirely of a table view. (This is in fact an extremely probable scenario.) You're most like to have a corresponding UITableViewController subclass; UITableViewController is a built-in UIViewController subclass, plus you'll probably use this same class as the table view's data source and delegate. In this single class, then, you're likely to want to implement *at a minimum* the following methods:

`initWithCoder:` *or* `initWithNibName:bundle:`
  UIViewController lifetime method, where you perform custom instance initializations.

`viewDidLoad:`

UIViewController lifetime method, where you perform view-related initializations.

`viewWillAppear:`

UIViewController lifetime method, where you set up states that need to apply only while your view is onscreen. For example, if you're going to register for a notification or set up a timer, this is a likely place to do it.

`viewDidDisappear:`

UIViewController lifetime method, where you reverse what you did in `viewWill-Appear:`. For example, this would be a likely place to unregister for a notification or invalidate a repeating timer that you set up in `viewWillAppear:`.

`supportedInterfaceOrientations`

UIViewController query method, where you specify what device orientations are allowed for this view.

`numberOfSectionsInTableView:`
`tableView:numberOfRowsInSection:`
`tableView:cellForRowAtIndexPath:`

UITableView data source query methods, where you specify the contents of the table.

`tableView:didSelectRowAtIndexPath:`

UITableView delegate user action method, where you respond when the user taps a row of the table.

`dealloc`

NSObject lifetime method, where you perform end-of-life cleanup. (If you're not using ARC, you will have memory management tasks to perform here.)

Suppose, further, that you did in fact use `viewWillAppear:` to register for a notification and to set up a timer. Then that notification has a selector (unless you used a block), and the timer has a selector; you must therefore also implement the methods described by those selectors.

We already have, then, about a dozen methods whose presence is effectively a matter of boilerplate. These are not *your* methods; *you* are never going to call them. They are *Cocoa's* methods, which you have placed here so that each can be called at the appropriate moment in the life story of your app.

(Don't try to learn any of those method names now! I'll talk in detail about these matters in Chapter 19 and Chapter 21. At the moment I'm just showing you that a major portion of the structure of this class is likely to be dictated to you by the event-driven nature of a Cocoa app.)

The logic of a program laid out in this fashion is by no means easy to understand! I'm not criticizing Cocoa here — indeed, it's hard to imagine how else an application framework could work — but, purely as an objective matter of fact, the result is that a Cocoa program, even your own program, even *while you're developing it*, is hard to read, because it consists of numerous disconnected entry points, each with its own meaning, each called at its own set moment which is not in any way obvious from looking at the program. To understand what our hypothetical class does, you have to know *already* such things as when viewWillAppear: is called and how it is typically used; otherwise, you don't even know where to look to find the program's logic and behavior, let alone how to interpret what you see when you do look there. And this difficulty is greatly compounded when you try to read someone else's code (this is one reason why, as I mentioned in Chapter 8, sample code is not all that helpful to a beginner).

Looking at the code of an iOS program — even your own code — your eyes can easily glaze over at the sight of all these methods called automatically by Cocoa under various circumstances. To be sure, experience will teach you about such things as the overridden UIViewController methods and the table view delegate and data source methods. On the other hand, no amount of experience will tell you that a certain method is called as a button's action or through a notification. Comments really help, and I strongly advise you, as you develop any iOS app, to comment every method, quite heavily if need be, saying what that method does and under what circumstances you expect it to be called — especially if it is an entry point, where it is Cocoa itself that will do the calling.

Perhaps the most common kind of mistake in writing a Cocoa app is not that there's a bug in your code itself, but that you've put the code in the wrong place. Your code isn't running, or it's running at the wrong time, or the pieces are running in the wrong order. I see questions about this sort of thing all the time on the various online user forums (these are all actual examples that appeared over the course of just two days):

- "There's a delay between the time when my view appears and when my button takes on its correct title." That's because you put the code that sets the button's title in viewDidAppear:. That's *too late*; your code needs to run earlier, perhaps in viewWillAppear:.

- "My subviews are positioned in code and they're turning out all wrong." That's because you put the code that positions your subviews in viewDidLoad. That's *too early*; your code needs to run later, when your view's dimensions have been determined.

- "My view is rotating even though my view controller's supportedInterfaceOrientations says not to." That's because you implemented supportedInterfaceOrientations in the *wrong class*; it needs to be implemented in the UINavigationController that contains your view controller.

- "I set up an action connection for Value Changed on a text field, but my code isn't being called when the user edits." That's because you connected the *wrong action*; a text field emits Editing Changed, not Value Changed.

Adding to your challenges is that fact that you can't really know precisely when an entry point will be called. The documentation may give you a general sense, but in most cases it doesn't guarantee anything about *precisely* when events will arrive and in what order. What you think is going to happen, and even what the documentation leads you to believe is going to happen, might not be quite what really does happen. Your own code can trigger unintended events. The documentation might not make it clear just when a notification will be sent. There could even be a bug in Cocoa such that events are called in a way that seems to contradict the documentation. And you have no access to the Cocoa source code, so you can't work out the underlying details. Therefore I also recommend that as you develop your app, you instrument your code heavily with caveman debugging (NSLog; see Chapter 9). As you test your code, keep an eye on the console output and check whether the messages make sense. You may be surprised at what you discover.

For example, in one app that I was developing, I suddenly found that in a UIViewController subclass, `viewDidLoad` was being called twice as the app started up, which should be impossible. Fortunately, my code was heavily instrumented with NSLog calls, or I would never have discovered this problem. Adding even more NSLog calls, I found that `viewDidLoad` was being called while I was still in the middle of executing `awakeFromNib`, which should *really* be impossible. The reason turned out to be my own mistake: I was referring to my class's `view` property during `awakeFromNib`, which was causing `viewDidLoad` to be called. The problem went away when I corrected my mistake.

Delayed Performance

Some of your code tells Cocoa what to do. But Cocoa is a black box, so what Cocoa actually will do, and precisely when it will do it, is out of your control. Your code was executed in response to some event; but your code in turn may trigger a new event or chain of events. Sometimes this causes bad things to happen: there might be a crash, or Cocoa might appear not to have done what you said to do. One of the chief causes of these difficulties is the chain of triggered events itself. Sometimes you just need to step outside that chain for a moment and wait for everything to settle down before proceeding.

The technique for doing this is called *delayed performance*. You tell Cocoa to do something not right this moment, but in a little while, when things have settled down. Your purpose might be a matter of simple timing, such as when you want to do something different depending whether the user taps twice in quick succession or only once; basically, when the user first taps, you respond using delayed performance, to give the user time to tap again if two taps are intended (Chapter 18). Or perhaps you need only a very short delay, possibly even as short as zero seconds, just to let Cocoa finish doing something, such as laying out interface. Technically, you're allowing the current run loop to finish, completing and unwinding the entire current method call stack, before proceeding further with your own code.

You're likely to be using delayed performance a lot more than you might expect. With experience, you'll develop a kind of sixth sense for when delayed performance might be the solution to your difficulties. There are three chief implementations of delayed performance that I use in my own code:

performSelector:withObject:afterDelay:
I mentioned this NSObject method at the end of Chapter 10. It limits you as to the signature of the selector — it must take one parameter or none — so you might have to restructure your own code slightly.

dispatch_after
I mentioned this in Chapter 3. It takes a block, not a selector, which can result in more direct and readable code.

dispatch_async
Often, the delay you're after doesn't need to be more than zero. What you're trying to do is postpone the next step until the consequences of the previous step have worked themselves out. So it suffices to wait until nothing is happening. You can do this with a call to dispatch_async onto the same queue where everything is happening now, namely the main queue (dispatch_get_main_queue, Chapter 38).

In all three cases, what you propose to do will be done later on; you're deliberately breaking out of your own code's line-by-line sequence of execution. So a delayed performance call will be the last call in its method (or block), and cannot return any value.

In this example from one of my own apps, the user has tapped a row of a table, and my code responds by creating and showing a new view controller:

```
- (void) tableView:(UITableView *)tableView
      didSelectRowAtIndexPath:(NSIndexPath *)indexPath {
    TracksViewController *t =
        [[TracksViewController alloc]
         initWithMediaItemCollection:(self.albums)[indexPath.row]];
    [self.navigationController pushViewController:t animated:YES];
}
```

Unfortunately, the innocent-looking call to my TracksViewController method init-WithMediaItemCollection: can take a moment to complete, so the app comes to a stop with the table row highlighted — very briefly, but just long enough to startle the user. To cover this delay with a sense of activity, I've rigged my UITableViewCell subclass to show a spinning activity indicator when it's selected:

```
- (void)setSelected:(BOOL)selected animated:(BOOL)animated {
    if (selected) {
        [self.activityIndicator startAnimating]; // appear and spin
    } else {
        [self.activityIndicator stopAnimating]; // disappear
    }
    [super setSelected:selected animated:animated];
}
```

However, the spinning activity indicator never appears and never spins. The reason is that the events are stumbling over one another here. UITableViewCell's set-Selected:animated: isn't called until the UITableView delegate method table-View:didSelectRowAtIndexPath: has finished. But the delay we're trying to paper over is *during* tableView:didSelectRowAtIndexPath:; the whole problem is that it *doesn't* finish fast enough. Delayed performance to the rescue! I'll rewrite tableView:did-SelectRowAtIndexPath: so that it finishes immediately — thus triggering set-Selected:animated: immediately and causing the activity indicator to appear and spin — and call initWithMediaItemCollection: later on, when the interface has ironed itself out:

```
- (void) tableView:(UITableView *)tableView
        didSelectRowAtIndexPath:(NSIndexPath *)indexPath {
    // tiny delay to allow spinner to start spinning
    double delayInSeconds = 0.1;
    dispatch_time_t popTime =
        dispatch_time(DISPATCH_TIME_NOW, delayInSeconds * NSEC_PER_SEC);
    dispatch_after(popTime, dispatch_get_main_queue(), ^(void){
        TracksViewController *t =
            [[TracksViewController alloc]
             initWithMediaItemCollection:(self.albums)[indexPath.row]];
        [self.navigationController pushViewController:t animated:YES];
    });
}
```

Here's an example that I came across on the Internet, involving a crash. The developer has a table view each of whose rows contains a text field. If the user deletes everything in one of those text fields, the table row containing it should be deleted. The code is an implementation of one of the text field's delegate methods:

```
- (void)textFieldEditingDidEnd:(UITextField *)textField {
    NSIndexPath *indexPath = // Index path of the row in the table view
    if ([textField.text length] == 0) {
        // Delete the cell from the table view
        [self.tableView deleteRowsAtIndexPaths:@[indexPath]
            withRowAnimation:UITableViewRowAnimationAutomatic];
    }
}
```

This was crashing. My suggestion — which worked — was to call deleteRowsAtIndex-Paths:withRowAnimation: using delayed performance. The reason is that, as things stand, we are trying to delete the row containing the text field while the text field is still busy reporting to its delegate that editing is ending. With delayed performance, we allow Cocoa's call to this delegate method to finish, and *then* we delete the row.

There will be many more examples of delayed performance later in this book.

Application Lifetime Events

As I explained in Chapter 6, your app's one and only application object (a UIApplication instance, or on rare occasions a UIApplication subclass instance) is created for you as the shared application object by UIApplicationMain, along with its delegate; in the Xcode project templates, this is an instance of the AppDelegate class. As I've discussed earlier in this chapter, the application immediately starts reporting lifetime events through method calls to its delegate; subsequently, your other instances can also register to receive these same events as notifications. I can't think of a better place in this book to describe these events, so I'm going to do so here and now.

What application lifetime events you can receive depends on whether or not your app participates in *multitasking*. In the old days, before iOS 4, there was no multitasking. If the user pressed the Home button while running your app, your app was terminated. The next time the user launched your app by tapping its icon, your app launched from scratch. Even under iOS 4 and later, your app can opt out of multitasking and behave like a pre–iOS 4 app, if you set the "Application does not run in background" key (UIApplicationExitsOnSuspend) in your *Info.plist*. For some apps, such as certain games, this might be a reasonable thing to do.

The suite of basic application lifetime events received by the app delegate in a nonmultitasking app is pretty simple:

application:didFinishLaunchingWithOptions:
> The app has started up. This, as we have already seen, is the earliest opportunity for your code to configure the interface by creating and showing the app's window, and it's fair to assume that every app you ever write will do exactly that. If you don't show your app's interface, the user won't see anything! (In an app with a main storyboard, however, the storyboard loading mechanism creates the window for you.) Of course you can and will perform other early initializations here.

 Starting in iOS 6, there's a new event, application:willFinish-LaunchingWithOptions:, that arrives even earlier than application:didFinishLaunchingWithOptions:. Its purpose is to allow your app to participate in the new mechanism for saving and restoring state. Since view controllers are the primary basis of this mechanism, I'll discuss it in Chapter 19.

`applicationDidBecomeActive:`

The app has started up; received after `application:didFinishLaunchingWith-Options:`. Also received after the end of the situation that caused the app delegate to receive `applicationWillResignActive:`.

`applicationWillResignActive:`

Something has blocked the app's interface. The most common cause is that the screen has been locked. An alert dialog from outside your app, or an incoming phone call whose interface takes over the screen, could also cause this event. When this situation ends, the app delegate will receive `applicationDidBecomeActive:`.

`applicationWillTerminate:`

The app is about to quit. This is your last signal to preserve state (typically, by storing information with NSUserDefaults) and perform other final cleanup tasks.

If your app participates in multitasking, as it almost certainly will, `applicationWill-Terminate:` is virtually a dead letter. The Home button doesn't terminate your app; it backgrounds and suspends it. This means that your app is essentially freeze-dried in the background; its process still exists, but it isn't actively running, and it isn't getting any events — though notifications can be stored by the system for later delivery if your app comes to the front once again. Your app is terminated, not because the user switches away from it, but because the system has killed it while it was suspended (for example, because it needed to reclaim the memory your suspended app was using). Thus you'll probably *never* get `applicationWillTerminate:`, because when your app is terminated by the system, it was already suspended and incapable of receiving events.

 Under highly specialized circumstances (discussed, for instance, in Chapter 27 and Chapter 35), your app can be backgrounded without being suspended. Nevertheless, throughout this section I'll speak as if backgrounding and suspension are one and the same.

In the multitasking world, you have to worry about what will happen when the app is suspended and when it returns from being suspended (`applicationDidEnter-Background:` and `applicationWillEnterForeground:`, and their corresponding notifications), and the notion of the application becoming inactive or active also takes on increased importance (`applicationWillResignActive:` and `applicationDidBecome-Active:`, and their notifications). These notifications all take on a wide range of meaning — indeed, in my opinion, the information your app is given is unfortunately too coarse-grained — so they are best understood by examining some typical scenarios:

The app launches freshly

Your app delegate receives these messages (just as in the premultitasking world):

- `application:didFinishLaunchingWithOptions:`
- `applicationDidBecomeActive:`

The user clicks the Home button
If your app is frontmost, it is suspended, and your app delegate receives these messages:

- `applicationWillResignActive:`
- `applicationDidEnterBackground:`

The user summons your suspended app to the front
Your app delegate receives these messages:

- `applicationWillEnterForeground:`
- `applicationDidBecomeActive:`

 If the user summons your suspended app to the front indirectly, another delegate message may be sent between these two calls. For example, if the user asks another app to hand a file off to your app (Chapter 36), your app receives `application:handleOpenURL:` between `applicationWillEnterForeground:` and `applicationDidBecome-Active:`. If the user taps a local notification alert belonging to your app (Chapter 26), your app receives `application:didReceiveLocal-Notification:` between `applicationWillEnterForeground:` and `applicationDidBecomeActive:`.

The user double-clicks the Home button
The user can now work in the app switcher. If your app is frontmost, your app delegate receives this message:

- `applicationWillResignActive:`

The user, in the app switcher, taps on your app's window
Your app delegate receives this message:

- `applicationDidBecomeActive:`

The user, in the app switcher, chooses another app
If your app is frontmost, your app delegate receives this message:

- `applicationDidEnterBackground:`

A local notification alert (Chapter 26) from another app appears
If your app is frontmost, your app delegate receives this message:

- `applicationWillResignActive:`

From a local notification alert, the user launches the other app
Your app delegate receives these messages:

- `applicationDidBecomeActive:`

- `applicationWillResignActive:`

- `applicationDidEnterBackground:`

The screen is locked
If your app is frontmost, your app delegate receives these messages:

- `applicationWillResignActive:`

- `applicationDidEnterBackground:`

The screen is unlocked
If your app is frontmost, your app delegate receives these messages:

- `applicationWillEnterForeground:`

- `applicationDidBecomeActive:`

The user holds the screen-lock button down
The device offers to shut itself down. If your app is frontmost, your app delegate receives this message:

- `applicationWillResignActive:`

The user, as the device offers to shut itself down, cancels
If your app is frontmost, your app delegate receives this message:

- `applicationDidBecomeActive:`

The user, as the device offers to shut itself down, accepts
If your app is frontmost, your app delegate receives these messages:

- `applicationDidEnterBackground:`

- `applicationWillTerminate:` (probably the only way a normal app will receive this message in a multitasking world)

You can see what I mean when I say that this repertory of events is rather coarse-grained. `applicationWillResignActive:`, for example, could mean that the user is summoning the app switcher, or that another application's local notification alert has appeared in front of your app, or that the user is locking the screen, or that the user has single-clicked the Home button to leave your app altogether, or that a phone call has arrived while your app was frontmost. But you can't distinguish *which* of these things is happening.

Of all the tasks with which you'll concern yourself over your app's lifetime, probably the most important is saving state. If the user has done or specified things that the app needs to preserve, it must do so before it is terminated. Since a multitasking app is probably never going to be notified by `applicationWillTerminate:`, you'll need to find an appropriate earlier moment. Unless your app is killed by the system outright, before the user's eyes, for committing some crime (such as hogging the main thread for too long at a stretch), you'll surely receive `applicationDidEnterBackground:` before being terminated, and indeed this might well be the last event your app ever receives; so it is clearly the default signal that you should save state. (You are given a little time to do this before your app is actually suspended; Chapter 38 discusses what to do if you think a little time might not be enough.)

In iOS 6, as I've already mentioned, there's a new mechanism for helping you save state. It's quite possible that your app, if it adopts this new mechanism, won't need to save state in `applicationDidEnterBackground:` after all. (See Chapter 19.) On the other hand, you still might want to respond to `applicationDidEnterBackground:` by saving information that doesn't qualify as state. For instance, your app stands a better chance of not being terminated while suspended, the less memory resources it uses; you might therefore take `applicationDidEnterBackground:` as a signal to release whatever large memory resources you can, perhaps writing them out to disk and recovering them when your app receives `applicationWillEnterForeground:`. (In addition, while running in the foreground, your app will be sent the delegate message `applicationDidReceive-MemoryWarning:` to inform you of a low memory situation. I'll return to this topic in Chapter 19 as well.)

CHAPTER 12

Accessors and Memory Management

An *accessor* is a method for getting or setting the value of an instance variable. An accessor that gets the instance variable's value is called a *getter*; an accessor that sets the instance variable's value is called a *setter*.

Accessors are important in part because instance variables, by default, are protected (Chapter 5), whereas publicly declared methods are public; without public accessor methods, a protected instance variable can't be accessed by any object whose class (or superclass) isn't the one that declares the instance variable. You might be tempted to conclude from this that you needn't bother making an accessor for an instance variable that isn't intended for public access, and to some extent this is a reasonable conclusion. But here are some counterarguments:

- Cocoa often uses the string name of an instance variable to derive the name of the accessor and call it if it exists. Thus there needs to be an accessor so that Cocoa can find it.

- If your app doesn't use ARC, and if your instance variable is an object, there are going to be memory management tasks to worry about every time you get and (especially) set that value; the best way to ensure that you're carrying out those tasks reliably and consistently is to pass through an accessor.

- Even if your app does use ARC, there may be additional tasks that need to be performed every time the instance variable's value is touched; an accessor, acting as a gateway to the instance variable, ensures that these tasks are performed consistently.

- Making accessors is no bother, as you usually won't have to write the code for an accessor; Objective-C can write your accessors for you.

This chapter will discuss all of those points in depth.

There are naming conventions for accessors, and you should obey them. The conventions are simple:

The setter

A setter's name should start with set, followed by a capitalized version of the instance variable's name (without an initial underscore if the instance variable has one). The setter should take one parameter — the new value to be assigned to the instance variable. Thus, the instance variable is named myVar (or _myVar), the setter should be named setMyVar:.

The getter

A getter should have the same name as the instance variable (without an initial underscore if the instance variable has one). This will not cause you or the compiler any confusion, because variable names and method names are used in completely different contexts. Thus, if the instance variable is named myVar (or _myVar), the getter should be named myVar.

If the instance variable's value is a BOOL, you may optionally start the getter's name with is (for example, an ivar showing or _showing can have a getter isShowing), though in fact I never do this.

Although I keep saying that the names of the accessor methods use the name of the instance variable, there is no law requiring that they use the name of a *real* instance variable. Quite the contrary: you might deliberately have methods myVar and setMyVar: when in fact there is no myVar (or _myVar) instance variable. Perhaps the accessors are masking the real name of the instance variable, or perhaps there is no instance variable at all, and these accessors are really doing something quite different behind the scenes. Accessors effectively present a façade, as if there were a certain instance variable, shielding the caller from any knowledge of the underlying details.

Key–Value Coding

Cocoa derives the name of an accessor from a string name through a mechanism called *key–value coding,* or simply *KVC.* (See also Chapter 5, where I introduced key–value coding.) The *key* is a string (an NSString) that names the value to be accessed. The basis for key–value coding is the NSKeyValueCoding protocol, an informal protocol (it is actually a category) to which NSObject (and therefore every object) conforms. Key–value coding is a big subject; see the *Key-Value Coding Programming Guide* for full information.

The fundamental key–value coding methods are valueForKey: and setValue:forKey:. When one of these methods is called on an object, the object is introspected. In simplified terms, first the appropriate accessor is sought; if it doesn't exist, the instance variable is accessed directly.

So, for example, suppose the call is this:

```
[myObject setValue:@"Hello" forKey:@"greeting"];
```

First, a method `setGreeting:` is sought in `myObject`; if it exists, it is called, passing `@"Hello"` as its argument. If that fails, but if `myObject` has an instance variable called `greeting` (or `_greeting`), the value `@"Hello"` is assigned directly to that ivar.

 The key–value coding mechanism can bypass completely the privacy of an instance variable! Cocoa knows that you might not want to allow that, so a class method `accessInstanceVariablesDirectly` is supplied, which you can override to return NO (the default is YES).

Both `valueForKey:` and `setValue:forKey:` require an object as the value. Your accessor's signature (or, if there is no accessor, the instance variable itself) might not use an object as the value, so the key–value coding mechanism converts for you. Numeric types (including BOOL) are expressed as an NSNumber; other types (such as CGRect and CGPoint) are expressed as an NSValue.

 A class is *key–value coding compliant* (or *KVC compliant*) on a given key if it implements the methods, or possesses the instance variable, required for access via that key.

Another useful pair of methods is `dictionaryWithValuesForKeys:` and `setValuesForKeysWithDictionary:`, which allow you to get and set multiple key–value pairs by way of an NSDictionary with a single command.

KVC is extremely dynamic. It allows you, in effect, to decide at runtime what instance variable to access; you obtain the instance variable's name as an NSString and pass that to `valueForKey:` or `setValue:forKey:`. Thus, by using an NSString instead of an instance variable or method name, you're throwing away compile-time checking as to the message you're sending. Moreover, key–value coding is agnostic about the actual class of the object you're talking to; you can send `valueForKey:` to *any* object and successfully get a result, provided the class of that object is key–value coding compliant for that key, so you're throwing away compile-time checking as to the object you're sending the message to. These are both strong advantages of key–value coding, and I often find myself using it because of them.

Here's an example of key–value coding used in my own code on my own object. In a flashcard app, I have a class Term, representing a Latin term, that defines many instance variables. Each card displays one term, with its instance variables shown in different text fields. If the user taps any of three text fields, I want the interface to change from the term that's currently showing to the next term whose value is different for the instance variable that this text field represents. Thus this code is the same for all three text fields; the only difference is what instance variable to consider as we hunt for the term to be displayed. By far the simplest way to express this is through key–value coding:

```
NSInteger tag = g.view.tag; // the tag tells us which text field was tapped
NSString* key = nil;
switch (tag) {
    case 1: key = @"lesson"; break;
    case 2: key = @"lessonSection"; break;
    case 3: key = @"lessonSectionPartFirstWord"; break;
}
// get current value of corresponding instance variable
NSString* curValue = [[self currentCardController].term valueForKey: key];
// ...
```

A number of built-in Cocoa classes permit you to use key–value coding in a special way. For example:

- If you send `valueForKey:` to an NSArray, it sends `valueForKey:` to each of its elements and returns a new array consisting of the results, an elegant shorthand (and a kind of poor man's `map`). NSSet behaves similarly.

- NSSortDescriptor sorts an NSArray by sending `valueForKey:` to each of its elements.

- NSDictionary implements `valueForKey:` as an alternative to `objectForKey:` (useful particularly if you have an NSArray of dictionaries). Similarly, NSMutable-Dictionary treats `setValue:forKey:` as a synonym for `setObject:forKey:`, except that `value:` can be nil, in which case `removeObject:forKey:` is called.

- CALayer (Chapter 16) and CAAnimation (Chapter 17) permit you to use key–value coding to define and retrieve the values for arbitrary keys, as if they were a kind of dictionary; this is useful for attaching identifying and configuration information to one of these instances.

- NSManagedObject, used in conjunction with Core Data (Chapter 36), is guaranteed to be key–value coding compliant for attributes you've configured in the entity model. Therefore, it's common to access those attributes with `valueForKey:` and `setValue:forKey:`.

KVC and Outlets

Key–value coding lies at the basis of how outlet connections work. I said in Chapter 7 that the name of the outlet in the nib is matched to the name of an instance variable, but I waved my hands over how this matching is performed. The truth is that key–value coding is used. The name of the outlet in the nib is a string. Key–value coding turns the string into a hunt for appropriate accessors.

Suppose you have a class MyClass with an instance variable myVar, and you've drawn a myVar outlet from that class's representative in the nib to an OtherClass nib object. When the nib loads, the outlet name myVar is translated to the method name setMyVar:, and your MyClass instance's setMyVar: method, if it exists, is called with the OtherClass instance as its parameter, thus setting the value of your MyClass instance's instance variable to the OtherClass instance (Figure 7-5).

By the same token, you should *not* use accessor names for methods that aren't accessors! For example, you probably would *not* want MyClass to have a method called setMy-Var: if it is *not* the accessor for myVar. If it did have such a method, it would be called when the nib loads, the OtherClass instance would be passed to it, and the OtherClass instance would *not* be assigned to the myVar instance variable! As a result, references in your code to myVar would be references to nil.

On the other hand, an attempt to access a nonexistent key through key–value coding will result, by default, in a crash at runtime, with an error message of this form: "This class is not key value coding-compliant for the key myKey." The lack of quotation marks around the word after "the key" has misled many a beginner, so remember: the last word in that error message is the name of the key that gave Cocoa trouble. A common way to encounter this error message is to change the name of an instance variable so that the name of an outlet in a nib no longer matches it; at runtime, when the nib loads, Cocoa will attempt to use key–value coding to set a value in your object based on the name of the outlet, will fail (because there is no longer an instance variable or accessor by that name), and will generate this error.

Key Paths and Array Accessors

A *key path* allows you to chain keys in a single expression. If an object is key–value coding compliant for a certain key, and if the value of that key is itself an object that is key–value coding compliant for another key, you can chain those keys by calling value-ForKeyPath: and setValue:forKeyPath:. A key path string looks like a succession of key names joined with a dot (.). For example, valueForKeyPath:@"key1.key2" effectively calls valueForKey: on the message receiver, with @"key1" as the key, and then takes the object returned from that call and calls valueForKey: on that object, with @"key2" as the key.

To illustrate this shorthand, imagine that our object myObject has an instance variable theData which is an array of dictionaries such that each dictionary has a name key and a description key. I'll show you the actual value of theData as displayed by NSLog:

```
(
    {
        description = "The one with glasses.";
        name = Manny;
    },
```

```
        {
            description = "Looks a little like Governor Dewey.";
            name = Moe;
        },
        {
            description = "The one without a mustache.";
            name = Jack;
        }
    )
```

Then [myObject valueForKeyPath: @"theData.name"] returns an array consisting of the strings @"Manny", @"Moe", and @"Jack". If you don't understand why, review what I said a few paragraphs ago about how NSArray and NSDictionary implement valueForKey:.

Key–value coding also allows an object to implement a key as if its value were an array (or a set), even if it isn't. This is similar to what I said earlier about how accessors function as a façade, putting an instance variable name in front of hidden complexities. To illustrate, I'll add these methods to the class of our object myObject:

```
- (NSUInteger) countOfPepBoys {
    return [self.theData count];
}

- (id) objectInPepBoysAtIndex: (NSUInteger) ix {
    return (self.theData)[ix];
}
```

By implementing countOf... and objectIn...AtIndex:, I'm telling the key–value coding system to act as if the given key (@"pepBoys" in this case) existed and were an array. An attempt to fetch the value of the key @"pepBoys" by way of key–value coding will succeed, and will return an object that can be treated as an array, though in fact it is a proxy object (an NSKeyValueArray). Thus we can now say [myObject valueForKey: @"pepBoys"] to obtain this array proxy, and we can say [myObject valueForKeyPath: @"pepBoys.name"] to get the same array of strings as before. This particular example may seem a little silly because the underlying implementation is already an array instance variable, but you can imagine an implementation whereby the result of objectInPepBoysAtIndex: is obtained through some completely different sort of operation.

The proxy object returned through this sort of façade behaves like an NSArray, not like an NSMutableArray. If you want the caller to be able to manipulate the proxy object provided by a KVC façade as if it were a mutable array, you must implement two more methods, and you must obtain a different proxy object by calling mutableArrayValueForKey:. So, for example:

```
- (void) insertObject: (id) val inPepBoysAtIndex: (NSUInteger) ix {
    [self.theData insertObject:val atIndex:ix];
}

- (void) removeObjectFromPepBoysAtIndex: (NSUInteger) ix {
    [self.theData removeObjectAtIndex: ix];
}
```

Now you can call [myObject mutableArrayValueForKey: @"pepBoys"] to obtain something that acts like a mutable array. (The true usefulness of mutableArrayValue-ForKey: will be clearer when we talk about key–value observing in Chapter 13.)

A complication for the programmer is that none of these methods can be looked up directly in the documentation, because they involve key names that are specific to your object. You can't find out from the documentation what removeObjectFromPepBoysAt-Index: is for; you have to know, in some other way, that it is part of the implementation of key–value coding compliance for a key @"pepBoys" that can be obtained as a mutable array. Be sure to comment your code so that you'll be able to understand it later. Another complication, of course, is that getting a method name wrong can cause your object *not* to be key–value coding compliant. Figuring out why things aren't working as expected in a case like that can be tricky.

Memory Management

It comes as a surprise to many beginning Cocoa coders that the programmer has an important role to play in the explicit management of memory. What's more, managing memory incorrectly is probably the most frequent cause of crashes — or, inversely, of memory leakage, whereby your app's use of memory increases relentlessly until, in the worst-case scenario, there's no memory left.

Fortunately, if your app uses ARC, your explicit memory management responsibilities can be greatly reduced, which is a tremendous relief, as you are far less likely to make a mistake, and more of your time is liberated to concentrate on what your app actually does instead of dealing with memory management concerns. But even with ARC it is still possible to make a memory management mistake (I speak from personal experience), so you still need to understand Cocoa memory management, so that you know what ARC is doing for you, and so that you know how to interface with ARC in situations where it needs your assistance. Do not, therefore, suppose that you don't need to read this section on the grounds that you're going to be using ARC.

Principles of Cocoa Memory Management

The reason why memory must be managed at all is that object references are pointers. As I explained in Chapter 1, the pointers themselves are simple C values (basically they are just integers) and are managed automatically, whereas what an object pointer points to is a hunk of memory that must explicitly be set aside when the object is brought into existence and that must explicitly be freed up when the object goes out of existence. We already know how the memory is set aside — that is what `alloc` does. But how is this memory to be freed up, and when should it happen?

At the very least, an object should certainly go out of existence when no other objects exist that have a pointer to it. An object without a pointer to it is useless; it is occupying memory, but no other object has, or can ever get, a reference to it. This is a *memory leak*. Many computer languages solve this problem through a policy called *garbage collection*. Simply put, the language prevents memory leaks by periodically sweeping through a central list of all objects and destroying those to which no pointer exists. But affixing a form of garbage collection to Objective-C would be an inappropriately expensive strategy on an iOS device, where memory is strictly limited and the processor is relatively slow (and may have only a single core). Thus, memory in iOS must be managed more or less manually.

But manual memory management is no piece of cake, because an object must go out existence neither too late nor too soon. Suppose we endow the language with the ability for one object to command that another object go out of existence now, this instant. But multiple objects can have a pointer (a reference) to the very same object. If both the object Manny and the object Moe have a pointer to the object Jack, and if Manny tells Jack to go out of existence now, poor old Moe is left with a pointer to nothing (or worse, to garbage). A pointer whose object has been destroyed behind the pointer's back is a *dangling pointer*. If Moe subsequently uses that dangling pointer to send a message to the object that it thinks is there, the app will crash.

To prevent both dangling pointers and memory leakage, Objective-C and Cocoa implement a policy of manual memory management based on a number, maintained by every object, called its *retain count*. Other objects can increment or decrement an object's retain count. As long as an object's retain count is positive, the object will persist. No object has the direct power to tell another object to be destroyed; rather, as soon as an object's retain count is decremented to zero, it is destroyed automatically.

By this policy, every object that needs Jack to persist should increment Jack's retain count, and should decrement it once again when it no longer needs Jack to persist. As long as all objects are well-behaved in accordance with this policy, the problem of manual memory management is effectively solved:

- There cannot be any dangling pointers, because any object that has a pointer to Jack has incremented Jack's retain count, thus ensuring that Jack persists.
- There cannot be any memory leaks, because any object that no longer needs Jack decrements Jack's retain count, thus ensuring that eventually Jack will go out of

Debugging Memory Management Mistakes

Memory management mistakes are among the most common pitfalls for beginners and even for experienced Cocoa programmers. Though far less likely to occur under ARC, they still *can* occur under ARC, especially because a programmer using ARC is prone to suppose (wrongly) that they can't. What experience really teaches is to use every tool at your disposal to ferret out possible mistakes. Here are some of those tools (and see Chapter 9):

- The static analyzer (Product → Analyze) knows a lot about memory management and can help call potential memory management mistakes to your attention.

- Instruments has excellent tools for noticing leaks and tracking memory management of individual objects (Product → Profile).

- Good old caveman debugging can help confirm that your objects are behaving as you want them to. Implement `dealloc` with an NSLog call. If it isn't called, your object is not going out of existence. This technique can reveal problems that neither the static analyzer nor Instruments will directly expose.

- Dangling pointers are particularly difficult to track down, but they can often be located by "turning on zombies." This is easy in Instruments with the Zombies template, but unfortunately it doesn't work on a device. For a device, edit the Run action in your scheme, switch to the Diagnostics tab, and check Enable Zombie Objects. The result is that no object ever goes out of existence; instead, it is replaced by a "zombie" that will report to the console if a message is sent to it ("message sent to deallocated instance"). Be sure to turn zombies back off when you've finished tracking down your dangling pointers.

existence (when the retain count reaches zero, indicating that no object needs Jack any longer).

Obviously, all of this depends upon all objects cooperating in obedience to this memory management policy. Cocoa's objects (objects that are instances of built-in Cocoa classes) are well-behaved in this regard, but *you* must make sure *your* objects are well-behaved. Before ARC, ensuring that your objects were well-behaved was entirely up to you and your explicit code; under ARC, your objects will be well-behaved more or less automatically, provided you understand how to cooperate with ARC's automated behavior.

The Golden Rules of Memory Management

An object is well-behaved with respect to memory management as long as it adheres to certain very simple rules in conformity with the basic concepts of memory management outlined in the previous section.

Before I tell you the rules, it may help if I remind you (because this is confusing to beginners) that a variable name, including an instance variable, is just a pointer. When you send a message to that pointer, you are really sending a message *through* that pointer, to the object to which it points. The rules for memory management are rules about objects, not names, references, or pointers. You cannot increment or decrement the retain count of a pointer; there is no such thing. The memory occupied by the pointer is managed automatically (and is tiny). Memory management is concerned with the object to which the pointer points.

(That is why I've referred to my example objects by proper names — Manny, Moe, and Jack — and not by variable names. The question of who has retained Jack has nothing to do with the *name* by which any particular object *refers* to Jack.)

The two things are easily confused, especially because — as I've often pointed out in earlier chapters — the variable name pointing to an object is so often treated as the object that there is a tendency to think that it *is* the object. It's clumsy, in fact, to distinguish the name from the object it points to. But in discussing memory management, I'll try to maintain that distinction.

Here, then, are the golden rules of Cocoa memory management:

- To increment the retain count of any object, send it the `retain` message. This is called *retaining* the object. The object is now guaranteed to persist at least until its retain count is decremented once more. To make this a little more convenient, a `retain` call returns as its value the retained object — that is, `[myObject retain]` returns the object pointed to by `myObject`, but with its retain count incremented.

- When you (meaning a certain object) say `alloc` to a class — or `new`, which is a way of saying `alloc` — the resulting instance comes into the world with its retain count already incremented. You do *not* need to retain an object you've just instantiated by saying `alloc` or `new` (and you should not). Similarly, when you say `copy` to an instance, the resulting new object (the copy) comes into the world with its retain count already incremented. You do *not* need to retain an object you've just instantiated by saying `copy` (and you should not).

- To decrement the retain count of any object, send it the `release` message. This is called *releasing* the object. If you (meaning a certain object) obtained an object by saying `alloc` or `copy`, or if you said `retain` to an object, you (meaning the same object) should balance this eventually by saying `release` to that object, *once*. You should assume that thereafter the object no longer exists.

A general way of understanding the golden rules of Cocoa memory management is to think in terms of *ownership*. If Manny has said `alloc`, `retain`, or `copy` with regard to Jack, Manny has asserted ownership of Jack. More than one object can own Jack at once, but each such object is responsible only for managing its own ownership of Jack correctly. It is the responsibility of an owner of Jack eventually to release Jack, and a non-owner of Jack must *never* release Jack. As long as all objects that ever take ownership of Jack behave this way, Jack will not leak nor will any pointer to Jack be left dangling.

Now, under ARC, as I shall explain presently in more detail, these rules remain exactly the same, but they are obeyed for you in an automated fashion by the compiler. In an ARC-based app, you *never* say `retain` or `release` — in fact, you're not allowed to. Instead, the compiler says `retain` or `release` for you, using exactly the principles you would have had to use if you *had* said them (the golden rules of Cocoa memory management)! Since the compiler is smarter (or at least more ruthlessly tenacious) than you are about this sort of nit-picky rule-based behavior, it won't make any of the mistakes you might have made due to carelessness or confusion.

The moment an object is released, there is a chance it will be destroyed. Before ARC, this fact was a big worry for programmers. In a non-ARC program, you must take care not to send any messages subsequently through any pointer to an object that has been destroyed — including the pointer you just used to release the object. In effect, you've just turned your *own* pointer into a possible dangling pointer! If there is any danger that you might accidentally attempt to use this dangling pointer, a wise policy is to *nilify* the pointer — that is, to set the pointer itself to nil. A message to nil has no effect, so if you do send a message through that pointer, it won't do any good, but at least it won't do any harm (kind of like chicken soup).

In an ARC-based program, this policy, too, is strictly followed: ARC will nilify for you any pointer to whose object it has just sent the last balancing `release` message (meaning that the object might now have gone out of existence). Since, as I mentioned in Chapter 3, ARC also sets an instance pointer to nil when you declare it (if you don't initialize it yourself, there and then, to point to an actual instance), there follows as the night the day the following delightful corollary: *under ARC, every instance pointer either points to an actual instance or is nil.* This fact alone should send you rushing to convert all your existing non-ARC apps to ARC if you possibly can.

What ARC Is and What It Does

When you create a new Xcode project and choose an application template, a checkbox in the second dialog lets you elect to Use Automatic Reference Counting. Automatic Reference Counting is ARC. If this checkbox is checked, then (among other things):

- The LLVM compiler build setting Objective-C Automatic Reference Counting (`CLANG_ENABLE_OBJC_ARC`) for your project is set to YES.
- Any `retain` or `release` statements that would have been present in the non-ARC version of any of the project template's *.m* files are stripped out.

- Any code that Xcode subsequently inserts automatically, such as a property generated by Control-dragging from a nib into code, will conform to ARC conventions.

It is also possible to convert an existing non-ARC project to ARC; choose Edit → Refactor → Convert to Objective-C ARC for assistance with the necessary code changes. You do not have to adopt ARC for an entire project; if you have old non-ARC code, possibly written by someone else, you may wish to incorporate that code into your ARC-based project without substantially altering the non-ARC code. To do so, confine all non-ARC code to its own files, and for each of those files, edit the target, switch to the Build Phases tab, and in the Compile Sources section, double-click the non-ARC file's listing and type `-fno-objc-arc` in the box (to enter it in the Compiler Flags column).

 ARC is actually a feature of LLVM 3.0 and later, and is one of the main purposes for which the LLVM compiler was developed. For full technical information, see *http://clang.llvm.org/docs/AutomaticReference Counting.html*.

When you compile an ARC-based project, the compiler will treat any explicit `retain` or `release` commands as an error, and will instead, behind the scenes, insert its own commands that effectively do the exact same work as `retain` and `release` commands. Your code is thus manually memory-managed, in conformity with the principles and golden rules of manual memory management that I've already described, but the author of the manual memory-management code is the compiler (and the memory-management code itself is invisible, unless you feel like reading assembly language).

ARC does its work of inserting `retain` and `release` commands in two stages:

1. It behaves very, very conservatively; basically, if in doubt, it retains — and of course it later releases. In effect, ARC retains at every juncture that might have the slightest implications for memory management: it retains when an object is received as an argument, it retains when an object is assigned to a variable, and so forth. It may even insert temporary variables to enable it to refer sufficiently early to an object so that it can retain it. But of course it also releases to match. This means that at the end of the first stage, memory management is technically correct; there may be far more retains and releases on a single object than you would have put if you were writing those commands yourself, but at least you can be confident that no pointer will dangle and no object will leak.

2. It optimizes, removing as many `retain` and `release` pairs from each object as it possibly can while still ensuring safety with regard to the program's actual behavior. This means that at the end of the second stage, memory management is still technically correct, and it is also efficient.

So, for example, consider the following code:

```
- (void) myMethod {
    NSArray* myArray = [NSArray array];
    NSArray* myOtherArray = myArray;
}
```

Now, in actual fact, no additional memory management code is needed here (for reasons that I'll clarify in the next section). But in its first pass, we may imagine that ARC will behave very, very conservatively: it will ensure that every variable is nil or points to an object, and it will retain every value as it is assigned to a variable, at the same time releasing the value previously pointed to by the variable being assigned to, on the assumption that it previously retained *that* value when assigning it to that variable as well. So we may imagine (though this is unlikely to be exactly correct) a scenario where ARC compiles that code at first into the equivalent of Example 12-1.

Example 12-1. Imaginary scenario: ARC's conservative memory management

```
- (void) myMethod {
    // create all new object pointers as nil
    NSArray* myArray = nil;
    // retain as you assign, release the previous value
    id temp1 = myArray;
    myArray = [NSArray array];
    [myArray retain];
    [temp1 release]; // (no effect, it's nil)
    // create all new object pointers as nil
    NSArray* myOtherArray = nil;
    // retain as you assign, release the previous value
    id temp2 = myOtherArray;
    myOtherArray = myArray;
    [myOtherArray retain];
    [temp2 release]; // (no effect, it's nil)
    // method is ending, balance out retains on local variables
    [myArray release];
    myArray = nil;
    [myOtherArray release];
    myOtherArray = nil;
}
```

The ARC optimizer will then come along and reduce the amount of work being done here. For example, it may observe that myArray and myOtherArray turn out to be pointers to the same object, so it may therefore remove some of the intermediate retains and releases. And it may observe that there's no need to send release to nil. But retains and releases are so efficient under ARC that it wouldn't much matter if the optimizer didn't remove any of the intermediate retains and releases.

But there's more to the manual memory management balancing act than matching retain and release: in particular, I said earlier that alloc and copy yielded objects whose retain count had already been incremented, so that they, too, must be balanced by `release`. In order to obey this part of the golden rules of Cocoa memory management, ARC resorts to *assumptions about how methods are named*. This means that *you* had better conform, in your code, to the same assumptions about how methods are named, or you can accidentally cause ARC to do the wrong things (although, as it turns out, there are ways out of this predicament if you have a wrongly-named method whose name you absolutely can't change).

In particular, when your code receives an object as the returned value of a method call, ARC looks at the opening word (or words) of the camelCased method name. (The term *camelCased* describes a compound word whose individual words are demarcated by internal capitalization, like the words "camel" and "Cased" in the word "camelCased.") If the opening word of the name of that method is `alloc`, `init`, `new`, `copy`, or `mutable-Copy`, ARC assumes that the object it returns comes with an incremented retain count that will need to be balanced with a corresponding `release`.

So, in the preceding example, if the array had been received from a call to `[NSArray new]` instead of `[NSArray array]`, ARC would know that an extra `release` will be needed, to balance the incremented retain count of the object returned from a method whose name begins with `new`.

Your own responsibility in this regard, then, is *not* to name any of your methods inappropriately in such a way as to set off that sort of alarm bell in ARC's head. The easiest approach is not to start any of your own method names with `alloc`, `init` (unless you're writing an initializer, of course), `new`, `copy`, or `mutableCopy`. Doing so might not cause any damage, but it is better not to take the risk: obey the ARC naming conventions if you possibly can.

How Cocoa Objects Manage Memory

Built-in Cocoa objects will take ownership of objects you hand them, by retaining them, if it makes sense for them to do so. (Indeed, this is so generally true that if a Cocoa object is *not* going to retain an object you hand it, there will be a note to that effect in the documentation.) Thus, you don't need to worry about managing memory for an object if the only thing you're going to do with it is hand it over to a Cocoa object.

A good example is an NSArray. Consider the following minimal example:

```
NSString* s = [[NSDate date] description];
NSArray* arr = [NSArray arrayWithObject: s];
```

When you hand the string to the array, the array retains the string. As long as the array exists and the string is in the array, the string will exist. When the array goes out of existence, if the string is still in the array, the array will also release the string; if no other object is retaining the string, the string will then go out of existence in good order, without leaking, and all will be well. All of this is right and proper; the array could hardly "contain" the string without taking ownership of it.

An NSMutableArray works the same way, with additions. When you add an object to an NSMutableArray, the array retains it. When you remove an object from an NSMutableArray, the array releases it. Again, the array is always doing the right thing.

Thus you should stay out of, and not worry yourself about, memory management for objects you don't own; the right thing will happen all by itself. For instance, look back at Example 10-2. Here it is again:

```
NSString* f = [[NSBundle mainBundle] pathForResource:@"index" ofType:@"txt"];
NSError* err = nil;
NSString* s = [NSString stringWithContentsOfFile:f
                                        encoding:NSUTF8StringEncoding
                                           error:&err];
// error-checking omitted
NSMutableDictionary* d = [NSMutableDictionary dictionary];
for (NSString* line in [s componentsSeparatedByString:@"\n"]) {
    NSArray* items = [line componentsSeparatedByString:@"\t"];
    NSInteger chnum = [items[0] integerValue];
    NSNumber* key = @(chnum);
    NSMutableArray* marr = d[key];
    if (!marr) { // no such key, create key-value pair
        marr = [NSMutableArray array];
        d[key] = marr;
    }
    // marr is now a mutable array, empty or otherwise
    NSString* picname = items[1];
    [marr addObject: picname];
}
```

No explicit memory management is happening here, and no additional memory management needs to happen (even if you aren't using ARC). We're generating a lot of objects, but never do we say alloc (or copy), so we have no ownership, and memory management is therefore not our concern. Moreover, no bad thing is going to happen between one line and the next while this code is running. The mutable dictionary d, for example, generated by calling [NSMutableDictionary dictionary], is not going to vanish mysteriously before we can finish adding objects to it. (I'll say a bit more, later in this chapter, about why I'm so confident of this.)

On the other hand, it is possible (if you aren't using ARC) to be tripped up by how Cocoa objects manage memory. Consider the following:

```
NSString* s = myMutableArray[0];
[myMutableArray removeObjectAtIndex: 0]; // bad idea! (but just fine under ARC)
```

Here we remove a string from an array, keeping a reference to it ourselves as s. But, as I just said, when you remove an object from an NSMutableArray, the array releases it. So the commented line of code in the previous example involves an implicit release of the string in question, and if this reduces the string's retain count to zero, it will be destroyed. In effect, we've just done the thing I warned you about earlier: we've turned our own pointer s into a possible dangling pointer, and a crash may be in our future when we try to use it as if it were a string.

The way to ensure against such possible destruction in non-ARC code is to retain the object before doing anything that might destroy it (Example 12-2).

Example 12-2. How non-ARC code ensures a collection element's persistence

```
NSString* s = myMutableArray[0];
[s retain]; // this is non-ARC code
[myMutableArray removeObjectAtIndex: 0];
```

Of course, now you have made management of this object your business; you have asserted ownership of it, and must make sure that this retain is eventually balanced by a subsequent release, or the string object may leak.

However, the very same code works perfectly under ARC:

```
NSString* s = myMutableArray[0];
[myMutableArray removeObjectAtIndex: 0]; // Just fine under ARC
```

The reason is that, as I mentioned earlier, ARC is insanely conservative at the outset. Just as in Example 12-1, ARC retains on assignment, so we may imagine that ARC will operate according to something like the imaginary scenario shown in Example 12-3.

Example 12-3. Imaginary scenario: ARC ensures a collection element's persistence

```
NSString* s = nil;
// retain as you assign, release the previous value
id temp = s;
s = myMutableArray[0];
[s retain];
[temp release]; // (no effect, it's nil)
// and now this move is safe
[myMutableArray removeObjectAtIndex: 0];
// ... and later ...
[s release];
s = nil;
```

This turns out to be exactly the right thing to do! When the call to removeObjectAt-Index: comes along, the retain count of the object received from the array is still incremented, exactly as in our non-ARC Example 12-2.

Autorelease

When you call a method and receive as a result what Chapter 5 calls a ready-made instance, how does memory management work? Consider, for example, this code:

```
NSArray* myArray = [NSArray array];
```

According to the golden rules of memory management, the object now pointed to by myArray doesn't need memory management. You didn't say alloc in order to get it, so you haven't claimed ownership of it and you don't need to release it (and shouldn't do so). But how is this possible? How is the NSArray class able to vend an array that you don't have to release without also leaking that object?

If you don't see why this is mysterious, pretend that *you* are NSArray. How would you implement the array method so as to generate an array that the caller doesn't have to memory-manage? Don't say that you'd just call some *other* NSArray method that vends a ready-made instance; that merely pushes the same problem back one level. You *are* NSArray. Sooner or later, *you* must somehow supply this magical instance. Ultimately you will have to generate the instance from scratch, and then how will you manage its memory? You can't do it like this:

```
- (NSArray*) array {
    NSArray* arr = [[NSArray alloc] init];
    return arr; // hmmm, not so fast...
}
```

This, it appears, can't work. On the one hand, we generated arr's value by saying alloc. This means we must release the object pointed to by arr. On the other hand, when are we going to do this? If we do it just *before* returning arr, arr will be pointing to garbage and we will be vending garbage. We cannot do it just *after* returning arr, because our method exits when we say return. This is a puzzle. It is our job, if we are to be a good Cocoa citizen and follow the golden rules of memory management, to decrement the retain count of this object. We need a way to vend this object without decrementing its retain count *now* (so that it stays in existence long enough for the caller to receive and work with it), yet ensure that we *will* decrement its retain count (to balance our alloc call and fulfill our own management of this object's memory).

The solution, which is explicit in pre-ARC code, is autorelease:

```
- (NSArray*) array {
    NSArray* arr = [[NSArray alloc] init];
    [arr autorelease];
    return arr;
}
```

Or, because autorelease returns the object to which it sent, we can condense that:

```
- (NSArray*) array {
    NSArray* arr = [[NSArray alloc] init];
    return [arr autorelease];
}
```

Here's how autorelease works. Your code runs in the presence of something called an *autorelease pool*. (If you look in *main.m*, you can actually see an autorelease pool being created.) When you send autorelease to an object, that object is placed in the autorelease pool, and a number is incremented saying how many times this object has been placed in this autorelease pool. From time to time, when nothing else is going on, the autorelease pool is automatically *drained*. This means that the autorelease pool sends release to each of its objects, the same number of times as that object was placed in this autorelease pool, and empties itself of all objects. If that causes an object's retain count to be zero, fine; the object is destroyed in the usual way. So autorelease is just like release — effectively, it *is* a form of release — but with a proviso, "later, not right this second."

You don't need to know exactly when the current autorelease pool will be drained; indeed, you can't know (unless you force it, as we shall see). The important thing is that in a case like our method array, there will be plenty of time for whoever called array to retain the vended object if desired.

The vended object in a case like our method array is called an *autoreleased object*. The object that is doing the vending has in fact completed its memory management of the vended object. The vended object thus potentially has a zero retain count. But it doesn't have a zero retain count just yet. The vended object is not going to vanish right this second, just after your call to [NSArray array], because *your code is still running and so the autorelease pool is not going to be drained right this second*. The recipient of such an object needs to bear in mind that this object may be autoreleased. The object won't vanish while the code that called the method that vended the object is running, but if the receiving object wants to be sure that the vended object will persist later on, it should retain it.

This explains why there's no explicit memory management in Example 10-2 (cited earlier in this chapter): we don't madly retain every object we obtain in that code, even in non-ARC code, because those objects will all persist long enough for our code to finish. This fits with the golden rules of memory management. An object you receive by means *other* than those listed among the golden rules as asserting ownership (alloc or copy) isn't under your ownership. The object will either be owned and retained by some other persistent object, in which case it won't vanish while the other object persists, or it will be independent but autoreleased, in which case it will at least persist while your code continues to run. If you want it to persist and you're afraid it might not, you should take ownership of it by retaining it.

Under ARC, as you might expect, all the right things happen of their own accord. You don't have to say autorelease, and indeed you cannot. Instead, ARC will say it for you. And it says it in accordance with the method naming rule I described earlier. A method called array, for example, does not start with a camelCase unit new, init, alloc, copy, or mutableCopy. Therefore it must return an object whose memory management is balanced, using autorelease for the last release. ARC will see to it that this is indeed the case. On the other side of the ledger, the method that called array and received an array in return must assume that this object is autoreleased and could go out of existence if we don't retain it. That's exactly what ARC does assume.

Sometimes you may wish to drain the autorelease pool immediately. Consider the following:

```
for (NSString* aWord in myArray) {
    NSString* lowerAndShorter = [[aWord lowercaseString] substringFromIndex:1];
    [myMutableArray addObject: lowerAndShorter];
}
```

Every time through that loop, two objects are added to the autorelease pool: the lowercase version of the string we start with, and the shortened version of that. The first object, the lowercase version of the string, is purely an *intermediate object*: as the current iteration of the loop ends, no one except the autorelease pool has a pointer to it. If this loop had very many repetitions, or if these intermediate objects were themselves very large in size, this could add up to a lot of memory. These intermediate objects will all be released when the autorelease pool drains, so they are not leaking; nevertheless, they are accumulating in memory, and in certain cases there could be a danger that we will run out of memory before the autorelease pool drains. The problem can be even more acute than you know, because you might repeatedly call a built-in Cocoa method that itself accumulates a lot of intermediate objects.

The solution is to intervene in the autorelease pool mechanism by supplying your own autorelease pool. This works because the autorelease pool used to store an autoreleased object is the most recently created pool. So you can just create an autorelease pool at the top of the loop and drain it at the bottom of the loop, each time through the loop. In modern Objective-C, the notation for doing this is to surround the code that is to run under its own autorelease pool with the directive @autoreleasepool{}, like this:

```
for (NSString* aWord in myArray) {
    @autoreleasepool {
        NSString* lowerAndShorter =
            [[aWord lowercaseString] substringFromIndex:1];
        [myMutableArray addObject: lowerAndShorter];
    }
}
```

Many classes provide the programmer with two equivalent ways to obtain an object: either an autoreleased object or an object that you create yourself with alloc and some form of init. So, for example, NSArray supplies both the class method arrayWithObjects: and the instance method initWithObjects:. Which should you use? Before ARC, Apple stated that they would prefer you to lean toward initWithObjects:. In general, where you can generate an object with alloc and some form of init, they'd like you to do so. That way, you are in charge of releasing the object. This policy prevents your objects from hanging around in the autorelease pool and keeps your use of memory as low as possible. Under ARC, I still tend to adhere to this policy from force of habit, but in fact the ARC autorelease pool architecture is so efficient that the old policy may no longer provide any advantage.

Memory Management of Instance Variables (Non-ARC)

Before ARC, the main place for the programmer to make a memory management mistake was with respect to instance variables. Memory management of temporary variables within a single method is pretty easy; you can see the whole method at once, so now just follow the golden rules of memory management, balancing every `retain`, `alloc`, or `copy` with a `release` (or, if you're returning an object with an incremented retain count, `autorelease`). But instance variables make things complicated, for many reasons:

- Instance variables are persistent. Your own instance variables will persist when this method is over and your code has stopped running and the autorelease pool has been drained. So if you want an object value pointed to by an instance variable not to vanish in a puff of smoke, leaving you with a dangling pointer, you'd better retain it as you assign it to the instance variable.

- Instance variables are managed from different places in your code. This means that memory management can be spread out over several different methods, making it difficult to get right and difficult to debug if you get it wrong. For example, if you retained a value assigned to an instance variable, you'll later need to release it, conforming with the golden rules of memory management, to prevent a leak — but in some other method.

- Instance variables might not belong to you. You will often assign to or get a value from an instance variable belonging to another object. You are now sharing access to a value with some other persistent object. If that other object were to go out of existence and release its instance variables, and you have a pointer to the instance variable value coming from that other object and you haven't asserted your own ownership by retaining that value, you can wind up with a dangling pointer.

To see what I mean, return once more to Example 10-2. As I have already explained, there was no need to worry about memory management during this code, even without ARC. We have a mutable dictionary d, which we acquired as a ready-made instance by calling [NSMutableDictionary dictionary], and it isn't going to vanish while we're working with it. Now, however, suppose that in the *next* line we propose to assign d to an instance variable of ours:

```
self->_theData = d; // in non-ARC code this would be a bad idea!
```

Before ARC, that code constituted a serious potential mistake. If our code now comes to a stop, we're left with a persistent pointer to an object over which we have never asserted ownership; it might vanish, leaving us with a dangling pointer. The solution, obviously, is to retain this object as we assign it to our instance variable. You could do it like this:

```
[d retain];
self->_theData = d;
```

Or you could do it like this:

```
self->_theData = d;
[self->_theData retain];
```

Or, because `retain` returns the object to which it sent, you could actually do it like this:

```
self->_theData = [d retain];
```

So which should you use? Probably none of them. Consider what a lot of trouble it will be if you ever want to assign a *different* value to `self->_theData`. You're going to have to remember to release the object already pointed to (to balance the retain you've used here), and you're going to have to remember to retain the next value as well. It would be much better to encapsulate memory management for this instance variable in an accessor (a setter). That way, as long as you always pass through the accessor, memory will be managed correctly. A standard template for such an accessor might look like Example 12-4.

Example 12-4. A simple retaining setter

```
- (void) setTheData: (NSMutableArray*) value {
    if (self->_theData != value) {
        [self->_theData release];
        self->_theData = [value retain];
    }
}
```

In Example 12-4, we release the object currently pointed to by our instance variable (and if that object is nil, no harm done) and retain the incoming value before assigning it to our instance variable (and if that value is nil, no harm done either). The test for whether the incoming value is the very same object already pointed to by our instance variable is not just to save a step; it's because if we were to release that object, it could vanish then and there, instantly turning `value` into a dangling pointer — which we would then, horribly, assign to `self->_theData`.

The setter accessor now manages memory correctly for us; provided we always use it to set our instance variable, all will be well. This is one of the main reasons why accessors are so important! So the assignment to the instance variable in our original code should now look like this:

```
[self setTheData: d];
```

Observe that we can also use this setter subsequently to release the value of the instance variable and nilify the instance variable itself, thus preventing a dangling pointer, all in a single easy step:

```
[self setTheData: nil];
```

So there's yet another benefit of using an accessor to manage memory.

Our memory management for this instance variable is still incomplete, however. We (meaning the object whose instance variable this is) must also remember to release the object pointed to by this instance variable at the last minute before we ourselves go out of existence. Otherwise, if this instance variable points to a retained object, there will be a memory leak. The "last minute" is typically dealloc, the NSObject method (Chapter 10) that is called as an object goes out of existence.

In dealloc, there is no need to use accessors to refer to an instance variable, and in fact it's not a good idea to do so, because you never know what other side effects an accessor might have. And (under non-ARC code) you must always call super last of all. So here's our implementation of this object's dealloc:

```
- (void) dealloc {
    [self->_theData release];
    [super dealloc];
}
```

That completes the memory management for one instance variable. In general, if you are not using ARC, you will need to make sure that *every* object of yours has a dealloc that releases *every* instance variable whose value has been retained. This, obviously, is one more very good opportunity for you to make a mistake.

 Never, never call dealloc in your code, except to call super last of all in your override of dealloc. Under ARC, you *can't* call dealloc — yet another example of how ARC saves you from yourself.

Just as it's not a good idea to use your own accessors to refer to your own instance variable in dealloc, so you should not use your own accessors to refer to your own instance variables in an initializer (see Chapter 5). The reason is in part that the object is not yet fully formed, and in part that an accessor can have other side effects. Instead, you will set your instance variables directly, but you must also remember to manage memory.

To illustrate, I'll rewrite the example initializer from Chapter 5 (Example 5-3). This time I'll allow our object (a Dog) to be initialized with a name. The reason I didn't discuss this possibility in Chapter 5 is that a string is an object whose memory must be managed! So, imagine now that we have an instance variable _name whose value is an NSString, and we want an initializer that allows the caller to pass in a value for this instance variable. It might look like Example 12-5.

Example 12-5. A simple initializer that retains an ivar

```
- (id) initWithName: (NSString*) s {
    self = [super init];
    if (self) {
        self->_name = [s retain];
    }
    return self;
}
```

Actually, it is more likely in the case of an NSString that you would copy it rather than merely retain it. The reason is that NSString has a mutable subclass NSMutableString, so some other object might call initWithName: and hand you a mutable string to which it still holds a reference — and then mutate it, thus changing this Dog's name behind your back. So the initializer would look like Example 12-6.

Example 12-6. A simple initializer that copies an ivar

```
- (id) initWithName: (NSString*) s {
    self = [super init];
    if (self) {
        self->_name = [s copy];
    }
    return self;
}
```

In Example 12-6, we don't bother to release the existing value of _name; it is certainly not pointing to any *previous* value (because there is no previous value), so there's no point.

Thus, memory management for an instance variable may take place in as many as three places: the initializer, the setter, and dealloc. This is a common architecture. It is a lot of work, and a common source of error, having to look in multiple places to check that you are managing memory consistently and correctly, but that's what you must do if you aren't using ARC (though, as I'll point out later in this chapter, Objective-C has the ability to write your accessors for you).

Earlier, I mentioned that KVC will set an instance variable directly if it can't find a setter corresponding to the key. When it does this, *it retains the incoming value*. This fact is little-known and poorly documented — and scary. The last thing you want, in non-ARC code, is implicit memory management. This is one more reason to provide accessors. On the other hand, if you're using ARC, this is not such a worry, since ARC is already providing implicit memory management.

Memory Management of Instance Variables (ARC)

If you're using ARC, ARC will manage your instance variable memory for you; you needn't (and, by and large, you can't) do it for yourself. By default, ARC will treat an instance variable the same way it treats any variable: on assignment to that instance variable, it creates a temporary variable, retains the assigned value in it, releases the current value of the instance variable, and performs the assignment. Thus, you write this code:

```
self->_theData = d; // an NSMutableDictionary
```

ARC, in effect, in accordance with its rule that it retains on assignment and releases the old value, substitutes something like this scenario:

```
// imaginary scenario: retain on assignment, release the previous value
id temp = self->_theData;
self->_theData = d;
[self->_theData retain];
[temp release];
```

This is exactly the right thing to have happened; in fact, it will not have escaped your attention that it is virtually the same code you would have written for a formal accessor such as Example 12-4. So much for worrying about release and retain on assignment! If you did want to write a setter, it might consist of no more than a direct assignment:

```
- (void) setTheData: (NSMutableArray*) value {
    self->_theData = value;
}
```

Moreover, when your object goes out of existence, ARC releases its retained instance variable values. So much for worrying about releasing in dealloc! You may still need, under ARC, to implement dealloc for other reasons — for example, it could still be the right place to unregister for a notification (Chapter 11) — but you won't call release on any instance variables there, and you won't call super. At the time dealloc is called, your instance variables have not yet been released, so it's fine to refer to them in dealloc.

At this point you may be imagining that, under ARC, you might be able to live without any accessors at all: instead, you can just assign directly to your instance variables and all the right memory-management things will happen, so who needs a formal setter? However, a formal accessor, as I'll explain later, can do things above and beyond ARC's automated insertion of release-and-retain, such as copying instead of retaining, dealing with multithreading, and adding your own custom behaviors. Also, obviously, accessors can be made public and so available to other objects, whereas an instance variable is not public.

In the absence of a release call, which is forbidden under ARC, what happens if you want to release an instance variable's value manually? The solution is simple: set the instance variable to nil. When you nilify a variable, ARC releases its existing value for you by default.

You may be wondering about ARC's implications for the way you'll write an initializer that involves setting object instance variable values, as in Example 12-5 and Example 12-6. The code for these initializers will be just the same under ARC as under non-ARC, except that you needn't (and can't) say retain. So Example 12-5 under ARC would look like Example 12-7.

Example 12-7. A simple initializer that retains an ivar under ARC

```
- (id) initWithName: (NSString*) s {
    self = [super init];
    if (self) {
        self->_name = s;
    }
    return self;
}
```

Example 12-6 under ARC will be unchanged, as shown in Example 12-8; you can still say copy under ARC, and ARC understands how to manage the memory of an object returned from a method whose camelCased name starts with (or simply is) copy.

Example 12-8. A simple initializer that copies an ivar under ARC

```
- (id) initWithName: (NSString*) s {
    self = [super init];
    if (self) {
        self->_name = [s copy];
    }
    return self;
}
```

Retain Cycles and Weak References

ARC's behavior is automatic and mindless; it knows nothing of the logic of the relationships between objects in your app. Sometimes, you have to provide ARC with further instructions to prevent it from doing something detrimental. Typically, this detrimental thing will be the creation of a retain cycle.

A *retain cycle* is a situation in which object A and object B are each retaining one another. This can arise quite innocently, because relationships in an object graph can run both ways. For example, in a system of orders and items, an order needs to know what its items are and an item might need to know what orders it is a part of, so you might be tempted to let it be the case *both* that an order retains its items *and* that an item retains its orders. That's a retain cycle, with object A (an order) retaining object B (an item) and *vice versa*. Such a situation, if allowed to persist, will result in a leak of both objects, as neither object's retain count can decrement to zero. Another way of looking it is to say that object A, by retaining object B, is also retaining itself, and thus preventing its own destruction.

To illustrate the problem, I'll suppose a simple class MyClass with a single ivar _thing and a single public setter setThing:, with logging in dealloc, like this:

```
@implementation MyClass {
    id _thing;
}

- (void) setThing: (id) what {
    self->_thing = what;
}

-(void)dealloc {
    NSLog(@"%@", @"dealloc");
}
@end
```

We now run this code:

```
MyClass* m1 = [MyClass new];
MyClass* m2 = [MyClass new];
m1.thing = m2;
m2.thing = m1;
```

Under ARC, unless you take steps to the contrary, this will be a retain cycle; by default, m1 and m2 are now retaining one another, because by default, ARC retains on assignment. When the code runs, dealloc is never called for either of our MyClass instances. They have leaked.

You can prevent an instance variable from retaining the object assigned to it by specifying that the instance variable should be a *weak reference*. You can do this with the __weak qualifier in the instance variable's declaration:

```
@implementation MyClass {
    __weak id _thing;
}
```

Now there is no retain cycle. In our example, since both m1 and m2 exist only as automatic variables in the scope of the code that creates them, they will both go out of existence instantly when that code comes to an end and ARC releases them both (to balance the new calls that created them).

In ARC, a reference not explicitly declared weak is a *strong reference*. Thus, a strong reference is one where ARC retains as it assigns. There is in fact a __strong qualifier, but in practice you'll never use it, as it is the default. (There are also two additional qualifiers, __unsafe_unretained and __autoreleasing, but they are rarely needed and I don't talk about them in this book.)

In real life, a weak reference is most commonly used to connect an object to its delegate (Chapter 11). A delegate is an independent entity; there is usually no reason why an object needs to claim ownership of its delegate. The object should have no role in the persistence of its delegate; and it could even be that the delegate might for some reason retain the object, causing a retain cycle. Therefore, most delegates should be declared as weak references. For example, in an ARC project created from Xcode's Utility Application project template, you'll find this line:

```
@property (weak, nonatomic) id <FlipsideViewControllerDelegate> delegate;
```

(The delegate may also be tagged as an IBOutlet.) The keyword weak in the property declaration, as I'll explain more fully later in this chapter, is equivalent to declaring the _delegate instance variable as __weak.

In non-ARC code, a reference can be prevented from causing a retain cycle merely by not retaining when assigning to that reference; the reference isn't memory-managed at all. You will see this referred to as a weak reference; it is not, however, quite the same thing as an ARC weak reference. A non-ARC weak reference risks turning into a dangling pointer when the instance to which it points is released. Thus it is possible for the reference to be non-nil and pointing to garbage, so that a message sent to it can have mysteriously disastrous consequences. Amazingly, however, this cannot happen with an ARC weak reference: the instance to which it points can be released and have its retain count reach zero and vanish, but when it does, any ARC weak reference that was pointing to it is set to nil! This amazing feat is accomplished by some behind-the-scenes bookkeeping: when an object is assigned to a weak reference, ARC in effect notes this fact on a scratchpad list. When the object is released, ARC consults the scratchpad list and discovers the existence of the weak reference to it, and assigns nil to that weak reference. This is yet *another* reason for preferring to use ARC wherever possible! ARC sometimes refers to non-ARC weak references, disdainfully but accurately, as "unsafe." (Non-ARC weak references are in fact the __unsafe_unretained references I mentioned a moment ago.)

Unfortunately, large parts of Cocoa don't use ARC. Most properties of built-in Cocoa classes that keep weak references are non-ARC weak references (because they are old and backwards-compatible, whereas ARC is new). Such properties are declared using the keyword assign. For example, UINavigationController's delegate property is declared like this:

```
@property(nonatomic, assign) id<UINavigationControllerDelegate> delegate
```

This means that if you assign some object to a UINavigationController as its delegate, and if that object is about to go out of existence at a time when this UINavigation-Controller still exists, you have a duty (regardless of whether you're using ARC) to set that UINavigationController's `delegate` property to some other object, or to nil; otherwise, it might try to send a message to its delegate at some future time, when the object no longer exists and its `delegate` property is a dangling pointer, and the app will then crash — and, since this happens at some future time, figuring out the cause of the crash can be quite difficult. (This is the sort of situation in which you might need to turn on zombies in order to debug, as described earlier in this chapter.)

 New in iOS 6 are collections whose memory management policy is up to you. NSPointerArray, NSHashTable, and NSMapTable are similar respectively to NSMutableArray, NSMutableSet, and NSMutable-Dictionary. But an NSHashTable, say, created with the class method `weakObjectsHashTable` maintains weak references to its elements. Under ARC, these are weak references in the ARC sense: they are replaced by nil if the retain count of the object to which they were pointing has dropped to zero. You may find uses for these classes as a way of avoiding retain cycles.

Unusual Memory Management Situations

NSNotificationCenter presents some curious memory management features. As you are likely to want to use notifications (Chapter 11), you'll need to know about these.

If you registered with the notification center using `addObserver:selector:name:object:`, you handed the notification center a reference to yourself as the first argument; the notification center's reference to you is a non-ARC weak reference, and there is a danger that after you go out of existence the notification center will try to send a notification to whatever is referred to, which, if it isn't you (because you no longer exist), will be garbage. That is why you must unregister yourself before you go out of existence. By unregistering yourself, you remove the notification center's reference to you, so there's no chance it will ever again try to send you a notification. This is similar to the situation with delegates that I was talking about a moment ago.

If you registered with the notification center using `addObserverForName:object:queue:usingBlock:`, memory management can be quite tricky, under ARC in particular. Here are the key facts to know:

- The observer token returned from the call to `addObserverFor-Name:object:queue:usingBlock:` is retained by the notification center until you unregister it.

- The observer token may also be retaining you through the block. If so, then until you unregister the observer token from the notification center, the notification center is retaining you. This means that you will leak until you unregister. But you cannot unregister from the notification center in dealloc, because dealloc isn't going to be called so long as you are registered.

- In addition, if you also retain the observer token, then if the observer token is retaining you, you have a retain cycle on your hands.

Consider, for example, this code, in which we register for a fictitious notification:

```
self->_observer = [[NSNotificationCenter defaultCenter]
    addObserverForName:@"heyho"
    object:nil queue:nil usingBlock:^(NSNotification *n) {
        NSLog(@"%@", self);
    }];
```

Our intention is eventually to unregister the observer; that's why we're keeping a reference to it:

```
[[NSNotificationCenter defaultCenter] removeObserver:self->_observer];
```

But there are two problems:

The notification center is retaining us (self)
The rule is that if self is mentioned in a block, then if the block is copied, self is retained. This is a situation where the block *is* copied. Thus the block retains self, the observer token retains the copied block, and the notification center retains the observer. Therefore we won't be sent dealloc so long as the observer token remains registered.

There's a potential retain cycle
Because self is mentioned in the block, the observer token is retaining us. But we are also retaining the observer token, through the assignment to an instance variable.

How do we know that the block is copied and that self is retained? The NSNotificationCenter class documentation on addObserverFor-Name:object:queue:usingBlock: says so: "The block is copied by the notification center and (the copy) held until the observer registration is removed." Under ARC, a copied block retains self if self is referred to, even indirectly (that is, even if what is referred to is an instance variable).

In effect, we have retained ourselves twice, once by virtue of being registered with the notification center, and again by virtue of retaining the observer token. I will present three solutions to this problem, in what I take to be the order of increasing goodness:

Unregister the observer and release the observer

Since `dealloc` won't be called until after we unregister, you'll have to set up some earlier code that *will* be called. If this is a view controller, for example, `viewDidDisappear:` can be a good place. Unregister the observer, thus causing the notification center to release the observer token. Then set `_observer` to nil, thus causing ourselves to release the observer token. Now no one is retaining the observer token. The observer token goes out of existence, releasing `self` as it does so, and we won't leak.

Unregister the observer and don't retain the observer in the first place

Make `_observer` a weak reference. Now the assignment to `self->_observer` doesn't retain the observer token. `dealloc` still won't be called until after we unregister, so we still have to find earlier code that will be called. Unregister the observer, thus causing the notification center to release the observer token; no one else is retaining it, so it goes out of existence, releasing `self` as it does so, and we won't leak.

Don't let the block retain `self` in the first place

If the block doesn't retain `self`, *none* of these problems arises. `dealloc` *will* be called even if the observer is still registered. In `dealloc`, unregister the observer.

How can you prevent the block from retaining `self`? You use a technique demonstrated in Apple's WWDC 2011 videos, commonly called "the weak–strong dance" (Example 12-9).

Example 12-9. The weak–strong dance prevents a copied block from retaining `self`

```
__weak MyClass* wself = self; ❶
self->observer = [[NSNotificationCenter defaultCenter]
    addObserverForName:@"heyho"
    object:nil queue:nil usingBlock:^(NSNotification *n) {
        MyClass* sself = wself; ❷
        if (sself) {
            NSLog(@"%@", sself); ❸
        }
}];
```

The weak–strong dance works like this:

❶   We form a local weak reference to self, outside the block but where the block can see it. It is this weak reference that will pass into the block.

❷   Inside the block, we form from that weak reference a normal strong reference. This step may seem unnecessary, but in a multithreaded situation, there is a chance that a weak reference, even a weak reference to `self`, may vanish out from under us between one line of code and the next. Assigning to a strong reference retains `self` throughout the rest of the block.

❸   We use that normal strong reference in place of any references to `self` inside the block. The nil test is because, in a multithreaded situation, our weak reference to `self` may have vanished out from under us before the previous step; it would then be nil, because it's an ARC weak reference, and in that case there would be no point continuing.

The weak–strong dance may seem elaborate, but it's worth learning to do. It is, as I said, the *only* one of the three proposed solutions that allows `dealloc` to be called *before* you unregister the observer. Thus, it is the only solution that allows you to unregister the observer *in* your `dealloc` implementation, which is typically just where you'd prefer to do it.

> If you expect the notification to be posted and the block to be called *only once*, there's another solution: unregister *in the block*. I'll show how to do that in Chapter 38.

Another unusual case is NSTimer (Chapter 10). The NSTimer class documentation says that "run loops retain their timers"; it then says of `scheduledTimerWithTimeInterval:target:selector:userInfo:repeats:` that "The target object is retained by the timer and released when the timer is invalidated." This means that as long as a repeating timer has not been invalidated, the target is being retained by the run loop; the only way to stop this is to send the `invalidate` message to the timer. (With a non-repeating timer, the problem doesn't arise, because the timer invalidates itself immediately after firing.)

When you called `scheduledTimerWithTimeInterval:target:selector:userInfo:repeats:`, you probably supplied `self` as the `target:` argument. This means that you (`self`) are being retained, and cannot go out of existence until you invalidate the timer. You can't do this in your `dealloc` implementation, because as long as the timer is repeating and has not been sent the `invalidate` message, `dealloc` won't be called. You therefore need to find another appropriate moment for sending `invalidate` to the timer. There's no good way out of this situation; you simply have to find such a moment, and that's that.

A block-based alternative to a timer is available through GCD. The timer "object" is a `dispatch_source_t`, and must be retained, typically as an instance variable (which ARC will manage for you, even though it's a pseudo-object). The timer will fire repeatedly after you initially "resume" it, and will stop firing when it is released, typically by nilifying the instance variable. But you must *still* take precautions to prevent the timer's block from retaining self and causing a retain cycle, just as with notification observers. Here's some typical skeleton code:

```
@implementation OtherViewController {
    dispatch_source_t _timer; // ARC will manage this pseudo-object
}

- (IBAction)doStart:(id)sender {
    self->_timer = dispatch_source_create(
        DISPATCH_SOURCE_TYPE_TIMER,0,0,dispatch_get_main_queue());
    dispatch_source_set_timer(
        self->_timer, dispatch_walltime(NULL, 0),
        1 * NSEC_PER_SEC, 0.1 * NSEC_PER_SEC);
    dispatch_source_set_event_handler(self->_timer, ^{
        NSLog(@"%@", self); // retain cycle
    });
    dispatch_resume(self->_timer);
}

- (IBAction)doStop:(id)sender {
    self->_timer = nil;
}

-(void)viewWillDisappear:(BOOL)animated {
    [super viewWillDisappear:animated];
    self->_timer = nil; // break retain cycle
}
@end
```

In general, you must be on the lookout for Cocoa objects with unusual memory management behavior. Such behavior will usually be called out clearly in the documentation. For example, the UIWebView documentation warns: "Before releasing an instance of UIWebView for which you have set a delegate, you must first set its delegate property to nil." And a CAAnimation object *retains its delegate*; this is exceptional and can cause trouble if you're not conscious of it.

There are also situations where the documentation fails to warn of any special memory management considerations, but ARC itself will warn of a possible retain cycle due to the use of self in a block. Again, the weak–strong dance is likely to be your best defense. An example is the completion handler of UIPageViewController's instance method setViewControllers:direction:animated:completion:, where the compiler will warn, "Capturing 'self' strongly in this block is likely to lead to a retain cycle." Using the weak–strong dance, you capture self weakly instead.

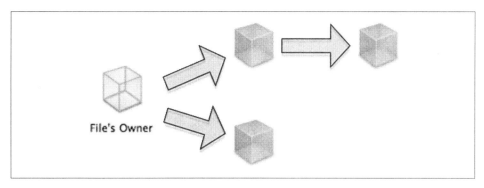

Figure 12-1. An outlet graph with retain

Nib Loading and Memory Management

On iOS, when a nib loads, the top-level nib objects that it instantiates are autoreleased. So if someone doesn't retain them, they'll quickly vanish in a puff of smoke. There are two primary strategies for preventing that from happening:

Outlet graph with retain

A memory management graph is formed: every top-level object is retained by another top-level object (without retain cycles, of course), with the File's Owner as the start of the graph. So, the File's Owner proxy has an outlet to a top-level object; when the nib loads and the top-level object is assigned to the corresponding instance variable of the actual nib owner instance (Chapter 7), it is retained. If you arrange the chain of retains correctly, all objects that need to be retained will be (Figure 12-1). This is the strategy you'll typically use when loading a nib.

You can see this strategy being used, for example, in a project made from the Single View Application template. The ViewController class is a UIViewController subclass; UIViewController has a `view` property which retains the value assigned to it. Inside the nib, an outlet called `view` runs from the File's Owner, which is a ViewController, to the top-level UIView (called View) in the nib. Thus this view is assigned to the ViewController's `view` property when the nib loads; therefore it is retained and doesn't vanish in a puff of smoke.

Mass retain

The call to NSBundle's `loadNibNamed:owner:options:` (Chapter 7) returns an NSArray of the top-level objects instantiated from the nib; retain this NSArray. This is the strategy used by `UIApplicationMain` when it loads the app's main nib, if there is one. Similarly, UINib's `instantiateWithOwner:options:` returns an array of the top-level objects instantiated from the nib. In Chapter 21 I'll show an example.

Objects in the nib that are *not* top-level objects are already part of a memory management object graph, so there's no need for you to retain them directly. For example, if you have a top-level UIView in the nib, and it contains a UIButton, the UIButton is the UIView's subview — and a view retains its subviews and takes ownership of them. Thus, it is sufficient to manage the UIView's memory and to let the UIView manage the UIButton. If you have an outlet to this button, you typically don't have to retain the button, because it is retained by the UIView as long as the UIButton is inside it (though you would want to retain the button in the rare case where you are planning at some point in your code to remove the button from its superview while keeping it on hand for later use).

Mac OS X Programmer Alert
Memory management for nib-loaded instances is different on iOS than on Mac OS X. On Mac OS X, nib-loaded instances are not autoreleased, so they don't have to be retained, and memory management is usually automatic in any case because the file's owner is usually an NSWindowController, which takes care of these things for you. On iOS, memory management of top-level nib objects is up to you. On Mac OS X, an outlet to a non-top-level object does not cause an extra retain if there is no accessor for the corresponding ivar; on iOS, it does.

Memory Management of Global Variables

In C, and therefore in Objective-C, it is permitted to declare a variable outside of any method. K&R (Chapter 1) calls this an *external variable* (see K&R 4.3); I call it a *global variable*. It is common practice, though not strictly required, to qualify such a variable's declaration as `static`; such qualification is a technical matter of scope and has no effect on the variable's persistence or its global nature.

Global variables are a C variable type, defined at file level; they know nothing of instances. Insofar as they have any relation to object-based programming, they may be defined in a class file so they are effectively class-level variables.

In Objective-C code, a global variable is not uncommonly used as a constant. You can sometimes initialize it as you declare it:

```
NSString* g_myString = @"my string";
```

If the value you want to assign to a global isn't itself a constant, you'll have to assign the value in actual code; the question is then where to put that code. Since a global variable is effectively a class-level variable, it makes sense to initialize it early in the lifetime of the class, namely in `initialize` (see Chapter 11).

The upshot is that a global variable is a class-level value and thus persists for the lifetime of the program. It has no memory management connected with instances, because it itself is not connected with instances. Thus in some sense it leaks, but deliberately so, in the same innocuous sense that a class object leaks.

On the other hand, you might have to use a tiny bit of explicit memory management in order to initialize a global variable in the first place. For example, suppose you're not using ARC and you initialize a global variable in `initialize` to an autoreleased value. Clearly you'll have to retain it, or it will just vanish out from under you. But you'll never bother to release it; there's no need, and no place where it would make sense to do so.

Memory Management of Pointer-to-Void Context Info

A number of Cocoa methods take an optional parameter typed as `void*`, and often called `context:`. You might think that `void*`, the universal pointer type, would be the same as `id`, the universal object type, because a reference to an object is a pointer. But an `id` is a universal *object* type; `void*` is just a C pointer. This means that Cocoa won't treat this value as an object. So the use of the `void*` type is a clue to you that Cocoa won't do any memory management on this value. Thus, making sure that it persists long enough to be useful is up to you.

The big change wrought by ARC in this regard has to do, not with memory management, but with "crossing the bridge" between an `id` and a `void*`. Before ARC, these two types were treated as equivalent, in the sense that you could supply one where the other was expected. But ARC is not so sanguine. ARC manages memory for objects only. Thus, it manages memory for something typed as `id`, but *not* for something typed as `void*`. Therefore, if you want to use an object where a `void*` is expected, or a `void*` where an object is expected, you must reassure ARC that you know what you're doing.

When an object comes into existence by instantiation under ARC, it is memory-managed by ARC from birth to death, as it were. But when an object is cast to a `void*`, it passes out of the realm of ARC memory management, and ARC will not let go without more information, because it doesn't understand what its memory management responsibilities should be at this moment. Similarly, when a non-object (a `void*`) is cast to an object type, it passes ready-made into the realm of ARC memory management, and ARC will not accept it without more information.

When you pass value in as a `context:` argument, your purpose is to get it back out again later; it's an identifier, or a carrier of extra information or data. For example, when you pass a `context:` value as you send `addObserver:forKeyPath:options:context:` to some object (see on key–value observing in Chapter 13), this is so that you can obtain that same value when Cocoa later sends `observeValueForKeyPath:ofObject:change:context:` back to you. Cocoa isn't going to retain the value for you, but on the other hand the value needs to exist only as long as you are likely to be called back in this way.

Thus it will make the most sense if you simply keep a reference to that value and manage its memory through that reference. The `context:` value itself is just a pointer. As a result, as the `context:` argument passes out of ARC's purview, and later as it passes back in again, ARC has *no* memory management responsibilities: you just want ARC to permit the cast. The way to indicate this is to cast the value explicitly, with a `__bridge` qualifier.

For example, let's say that you write this:

```
[someObject addObserver:self forKeyPath:@"yoho"
    options:0 context:myContext];
```

Before ARC, that code was legal. Under ARC, it isn't; the compiler will stop you in your tracks with this complaint: "Implicit conversion of Objective-C pointer type 'id' to C pointer type 'void *' requires a bridged cast." So you supply the bridged cast:

```
[someObject addObserver:self forKeyPath:@"yoho"
    options:0 context:(__bridge void*) myContext];
```

Later, when the context comes back to you in a callback, you'll cast it back to a `__bridge` id so that ARC will accept it and you can continue treating it as an object.

This leaves only the question of how to manage the memory of the object that's being handed back and forth as the `context:` argument. All this is happening in different methods, and the object must persist through all of them. Clearly the most sensible solution is to maintain the object through an instance variable. Under ARC, in particular, this is a lightweight approach; the object will be memory-managed with no particular effort on your part. It may persist even after it is no longer needed, but it won't actually leak. The situation is only slightly more complicated if you've more than one context object to manage simultaneously; for example, you could store them all in a collection, such as an NSMutableSet instance variable.

Considerations of this sort do not apply to parameters that are typed as objects. For instance, when you call `postNotificationName:object:userInfo:`, the `userInfo` is typed as an NSDictionary and is retained for you by the notification center (and released after the notification is posted); its memory management behind the scenes is not your concern.

Memory Management of CFTypeRefs

A CFTypeRef (see Chapter 3) is a value obtained through a C function that is a pointer to a struct; its type name will usually end in "Ref". It is a kind of object, even though it isn't a full-fledged Cocoa Objective-C object, and it must be managed in much the same way as a Cocoa object. *ARC is irrelevant to this fact.* ARC manages Objective-C objects; it has no concern with CFTypeRefs. You must manage the memory of CFTypeRefs manually, even if you're using ARC. Indeed, as I shall explain, the fact that you are using ARC actually *increases* the degree of your memory management responsibility.

I will divide the discussion into two halves: memory management of CFTypeRefs on their own, and what happens when you "cross the bridge" between a CFTypeRef and a full-fledged Objective-C object type.

Just as, in the Objective-C world of objects, certain method names (`alloc`, `copy`, and `retain`) alert you to your memory management responsibilities, so too in the world of CFTypeRefs. The golden rule here is that if you obtained such an object through a function whose name contains the word `Create` or `Copy`, you are responsible for releasing it. In the case of a Core Foundation object (its type name begins with `CF`), you'll release it with the `CFRelease` function; other object creation functions are paired with their own object release functions.

 An Objective-C object can be sent messages even if it is nil. But `CFRelease` cannot take a nil argument. Be sure that a CFTypeRef variable is not nil before releasing it.

The matter is not a complicated one; it's much simpler than memory management of Cocoa objects, and the documentation will usually give you a hint about your memory management responsibilities. As an example, here (without further explanation) is some actual code from one of my apps, strongly modeled on Apple's own example code, in which I set up a base pattern color space (for drawing with a pattern):

```
- (void) addPattern: (CGContextRef) context color: (CGColorRef) incolor {
    CGColorSpaceRef baseSpace = CGColorSpaceCreateDeviceRGB();
    CGColorSpaceRef patternSpace = CGColorSpaceCreatePattern(baseSpace);
    CGContextSetFillColorSpace(context, patternSpace);
    CGColorSpaceRelease(patternSpace);
    CGColorSpaceRelease(baseSpace);
    // ...
}
```

Never mind exactly what that code does; the important thing here is that the values for `baseSpace` and `patternSpace` are a CFTypeRef (in particular, a CGColorSpaceRef) obtained through functions with `Create` in their name, so after we're done using them, we release them with the corresponding release function (here, `CGColorSpaceRelease`).

Similarly, you can retain a Core Foundation object, if you are afraid that it might go out of existence while you still need it, with the `CFRetain` function, and you are then, once again, responsible for releasing it with the `CFRelease` function.

We now come to the business of "crossing the bridge." As I explained in Chapter 3, many Core Foundation object types are toll-free bridged with a corresponding Cocoa object type. Now, from a theoretical point of view, memory management is memory management: it makes no difference whether you use Core Foundation memory management or Cocoa memory management. Thus, if you obtain a CFStringRef through a `Create` or `Copy` function and assign it to an NSString variable, sending `release` to it through the NSString variable is just as good as calling `CFRelease` on it as a CFStringRef. And before ARC, that was the end of the matter.

Under ARC, however, we face the same problem I described in the preceding section. ARC manages memory for Objective-C objects; it knows nothing of CFTypeRefs. Therefore, ARC is not going to let you hand an object into or out of its memory-management purview without explicit information about how to manage its memory. This means a little extra thought for you, but it's a good thing, because it means you can tell ARC to do automatically what you would have done manually.

For example, a moment ago I said that, before ARC, you might obtain a CFStringRef through a `Create` or `Copy` function, cast it to an NSString, and later send `release` to it through the NSString. Under ARC, you can't say `release`, but you can arrange for ARC to do exactly the same thing: as you "cross the bridge", you pass the CFString through the `CFBridgingRelease` function. The result is an `id` that can be assigned to an NSString variable, and that ARC will release to balance out the incremented retain count generated by the original `Create` or `Copy` function.

You have three choices as you cross the toll-free bridge:

`__bridge` *cast*
> As illustrated in the previous section, you cast explicitly to the across-the-bridge type and qualify the cast with `__bridge`. This means that memory management responsibilities are independent on either side of the bridge. You're telling ARC that you're going to be performing complete and correct memory management on the CFTypeRef side of the bridge.

`CFBridgingRelease` *function*
> You're crossing the bridge from the CFTypeRef side to the object side. You're telling ARC that memory management for this object is incomplete: it has a raised retain count on the CFTypeRef side (probably because you generated it with a `Create` or `Copy` function, or called `CFRetain` on it), and it will be up to ARC to perform the corresponding release on the object side. (Alternatively, you can do a `__bridge_transfer` cast.) Here's an artificial but correct example:

```
CFArrayRef arr_ref = CFLocaleCopyISOCountryCodes(); // note "copy"
NSArray* arr = CFBridgingRelease(arr_ref); // memory management complete
// ARC will manage this array correctly from here on
```

`CFBridgingRetain` *function*
> You're crossing the bridge from the object side to the CFTypeRef side. You're telling ARC that it should leave memory management for this object incomplete: you're aware of the raised retain count on the object side, and you intend to call `CFRelease` on it yourself on the CFTypeRef side. (Alternatively, you can do a `__bridge_retained` cast.)

You may see `__bridge_transfer` and `__bridge_retained` in code written by other people, but I strongly recommend that you stick to `CFBridgingRelease` and `CFBridging-Retain` in your own code, as they are eminently clearer (and better named). Note that it is perfectly possible to pass an object out of the object world with `CFBridging-Retain` and back into it later with `CFBridgingRelease`.

Properties

A *property* (see Chapter 5) is syntactic sugar for calling an accessor by using dot-notation. For instance, in an example earlier in this chapter we had an object with an NSMutableArray instance variable and a setter, which we called like this:

```
[self setTheData: d];
```

We could equally have said this:

```
self.theData = d;
```

The effect would be exactly the same, because setting a property is just a shorthand for calling the setter method. Similarly, suppose we were to say this:

```
NSMutableArray* arr = self.theData;
```

That is exactly the same as calling the getter method, `[self theData]`.

In those examples, we are presuming the existence of the getter and setter methods. The declaration of an accessor method is what permits us to use the corresponding notation: the declaration of the setter lets us use property notation in an lvalue (to assign to the property), and the declaration of the getter lets us use property notation otherwise (to fetch the property's value).

It is also possible to declare a property explicitly, *instead* of declaring the getter and setter methods. Declaring a property is thus a shorthand for declaring accessors, just as using a property is shorthand for calling an accessor. But declaring a property can do much more for you and your code than that. How much more it can do has increased historically, depending on what system and what version of Xcode you're using; here's a list of the powers of property declaration, roughly in order of increasing power, which is also roughly the order in which those powers were introduced historically:

- A property declaration saves you from having to declare accessor methods. It is simpler to declare one property than to declare two accessor methods.

- A property declaration includes a statement of the setter's *memory management policy*. This lets you, the programmer, know easily, just by glancing at a property declaration, how the incoming value will be treated. You could find this out otherwise only by looking at the setter's code — which, if this is a built-in Cocoa type, you cannot do (and even in the case of your own code, it's a pain having to locate and consult the setter directly).

- With a property declaration, you can optionally *omit writing one or both accessors*. The compiler will write them for you! To get the compiler to do this, you include a `@synthesize` directive in your class's implementation section. Such an automatically constructed accessor is called, naturally enough, a *synthesized accessor*.

  Writing accessors is boring and error-prone. It can also be hard! In a multithreading situation, it is doubtful that you would even know how to write a thread-safe accessor; a synthesized accessor is thread-safe by default. Any time correct code is written for you automatically, it's a major benefit. Moreover, your class is now key–value coding compliant for the accessor name, with no effort on your part.

  Furthermore, your setter memory management policy, as specified in the property declaration, is followed by the synthesized setter. Your wish is Cocoa's command!

- With a synthesized accessor, you don't have to declare the corresponding instance variable that the accessor gets or sets. It is implicitly declared for you! Automatic implicit declaration of instance variables was introduced as part of a major advance in Objective-C: the documentation refers to the earlier period (when you still had to declare instance variables yourself, even with a declared property and a synthesized accessor) as "the legacy runtimes", and the later period (automatic implicit declaration of instance variables) as "the modern runtimes".

  As part of the `@synthesize` directive, you can specify the name of the instance variable that is to be implicitly declared for you.

- The ultimate convenience is the most recent (starting in LLVM compiler version 4.0, Xcode 4.4): you can omit the `@synthesize` directive! The compiler automatically inserts it for you, implicitly. This is called *autosynthesis*.

  The only downside to taking advantage of autosynthesis is that, because the `@synthesize` directive is omitted, you have no place to specify the name of the automatically declared instance variable. That isn't much of a disadvantage; the name is supplied according to a simple rule, and the vast majority of the time you'll be perfectly happy with it.

Thanks to autosynthesis, the mere presence of the property declaration — one line of code — is sufficient to trigger the entire stack of automatic behaviors: it equates to declaration of the accessors, and the accessors are written for you (in accordance with your declared memory management policy), and the instance variable is implicitly declared for you.

Property Memory Management Policies

The possible memory management policies correspond simply to what has already been said in this chapter about the ARC reference types and how a setter might behave:

`strong, retain`

> Under ARC, the instance variable itself will be a normal (strong) reference, so when ARC assigns the incoming value to it, it will retain the incoming value and release the existing value of the instance variable. Under non-ARC, the setter method will retain the incoming value and release the existing value of the instance variable. The terms are pure synonyms of one another and can be used in ARC or non-ARC code; `retain` is the term inherited, as it were, from pre-ARC days.

`copy`

> The same as `strong` or `retain`, except that the incoming value is copied (by sending `copy` to it) and the copy, which has an increased retain count already, is assigned to the instance variable. This is appropriate particularly when a nonmutable class has a mutable subclass (such as NSString and NSMutableString, or NSArray and NSMutableArray), to prevent the setter's caller from passing in an object of the mutable subclass; it is legal for the setter's caller to do so, because (in accordance with polymorphism, Chapter 5) where an instance of a class is expected, an instance of its subclass can be passed, but the `copy` call creates an instance of the nonmutable class (Chapter 10).

`weak`

> Under ARC, the instance variable will be a weak reference. ARC will assign the incoming value to it without retaining it. ARC will also magically nilify the instance variable if the instance to which it points goes out of existence. This is useful, as already explained earlier in this chapter, for breaking a potential retain cycle and for declining to retain inappropriately, and to reduce overhead where it is known that no memory management is needed, as with an interface object that is already retained by its superview. The setter method can be synthesized only under ARC; using weak in non-ARC code is not strictly impossible but probably makes no sense.

`assign` *(the default)*

> This policy is inherited from pre-ARC days; it is used in the same ways as weak. The setter does not manage memory; the incoming value is assigned directly to the instance variable. The instance variable is *not* an ARC weak reference and will *not* be nilified automatically if the instance to which it points goes out of existence; it is a non-ARC weak reference (`__unsafe_unretained`) and can become a dangling pointer.

As I've already said, a property's declared memory management policy is an instruction to the compiler if the setter is synthesized. If the setter is *not* synthesized, the declared memory management policy is "purely conventional" (as the LLVM documentation puts it), meaning that if you write your own setter, you'd better make that setter behave the way you declared you would, but nothing is going to force you to do so.

Property Declaration Syntax

We come now to the formal syntax for declaring a property. A property is declared in the same part of a class's interface section where you would declare methods. Its syntax schema is as follows:

```
@property (attribute, attribute, ...) type name;
```

Here's a real example, for the NSMutableArray instance variable we were talking about a moment ago:

```
@property (nonatomic, strong) NSMutableArray* theData;
```

The *type* and *name* will usually match the type and name of an instance variable, but what you're really indicating here are the name of the property (as used in dot-notation) and the default names of the setter (here, `setTheData:`) and getter (here, `theData`), and the type of value to be passed to the setter and obtained from the getter.

If this property will be represented by an outlet in a nib, you can say `IBOutlet` before the *type*. This is a hint to Xcode and has no formal meaning.

The *type* doesn't have to be an object type; it can be a simple type such as BOOL, CGFloat, or CGSize. Of course in that case no memory management is performed (as none is needed), and no memory management policy should be declared; but the advantages of using a property remain — the accessors can be synthesized and the instance variable declared automatically.

The possible *attribute* values are:

A memory management policy
I listed the names of these a few paragraphs ago. You will supply exactly one; under ARC this will usually be `strong`. The default if you omit any memory management policy is `assign`, but such omission is dangerous and you'll get a warning from the compiler.

`nonatomic`
If omitted, the synthesized accessors will use locking to ensure correct operation if your app is multithreaded. This will rarely be a concern, and locking slows down the operation of the accessors, so you'll probably specify `nonatomic` most of the time. It's a pity that `nonatomic` isn't the default, but such is life.

`readwrite` *or* `readonly`
If omitted, the default is `readwrite`. If you say `readonly`, any attempt to use the property as a setter will cause a compile error (a useful feature), and if the accessors are to be synthesized, no setter is synthesized.

`getter=`*gname,* `setter=`*sname:*

> By default, the property name is used to derive the names of the getter and setter methods that will be called when the property is used. If the property is named `myProp`, the default getter method name is `myProp` and the default setter name is `setMyProp:`. You can use either or both of these attributes to change that. If you say `getter=getALife`, you're saying that the getter method corresponding to this property is called `getALife` (and if the accessors are synthesized, the getter will be given this name). Users of the property won't be affected, but calling an accessor method explicitly under a nonexistent name is a compile error.

To *make a property declaration private*, put it in a class extension (Chapter 10). Most commonly, the class extension will be at the top of the implementation (*.m*) file, before the implementation section. As a result, this class can use the property or call the accessors but other classes cannot (Example 12-10).

Example 12-10. A private property

```
// MyClass.m:
@interface MyClass ()
@property (nonatomic, strong) NSMutableArray* theData; // private
@end

@implementation MyClass
// other code goes here
@end
```

Being able to declare private properties is so useful that I find myself routinely adding a class extension to the top of any new class files (if the Xcode project template hasn't done it for me), to make it easy to add private properties later if I need to. Note that knowledge of private properties is not inherited by subclasses; an elegant solution is to move the class extension interface section off into an isolated *.h* file of its own and import that into the implementation files of both the superclass and the subclass.

Another reason to put a property declaration in a class extension is so as to *redeclare* the property. For example, we might want our property to be `readonly` as far as the rest of the world knows, but `readwrite` for code within our class. To implement this, declare the property `readonly` in the interface section in the header file, which the rest of the world sees, and then redeclare it, *not* as `readonly` (in which case it will be `readwrite` by default), in the class extension in the implementation file, which only this class sees. All other attributes must match between both declarations.

A property declaration can also appear in a protocol or category declaration. This makes sense because, with a property declaration, you're really just declaring accessor methods, and these are places where method declarations can go.

Property Accessor Synthesis

To request explicitly that the accessors be synthesized for you, use the @synthesize directive. It appears anywhere inside the class's implementation section, any number of times, and takes a comma-separated list of property names. The behavior and names of the synthesized accessors will accord with the property declaration attributes I've just talked about. You can state that the synthesized accessors should access an instance variable whose name differs from the property name by using the syntax *property-Name=ivarName* in the property name list; otherwise, the instance variable will have *the same name as the property*. As I mentioned earlier, you don't have to declare the instance variable; it will be declared for you automatically as part of accessor synthesis.

 An instance variable declared automatically through accessor synthesis is strictly private, meaning that it is not inherited by subclasses. This fact will rarely prove troublesome, but if it does, simply declare the instance variable explicitly.

Thus, having declared a property theData, to request explicitly that accessors be synthesized, you'd say this in the implementation section:

```
@synthesize theData;
```

The result is that any accessors you don't write (theData and setTheData:, unless you changed these names in the property declaration) will be written for you behind the scenes, and if you didn't declare an instance variable theData, it will be declared for you.

The name of the automatically declared instance variable is likely to be important to you, because you're probably going to need to access the instance variable directly, especially in an initializer (and in dealloc if you're not using ARC), as well as in any accessors that you write yourself.

Starting in the Xcode 4.2 application templates, Apple began following a convention where a synthesized accessor would take advantage of the *propertyName=ivarName* syntax to give the instance variable a name different from that of the property in that the former was prefixed with an underscore. For example, the AppDelegate class's implementation section contained this line:

```
@synthesize window = _window;
```

The evident value of following this naming convention is that we can refer in our code to the property explicitly as self.window, but if we were accidentally to refer to the instance variable directly as window, we'd get a compilation error, because there is no instance variable window (it's called _window). The convention thus prevents accidental direct access to the instance variable without passing through the accessors, as well as just distinguishing clearly in code which names are instance variables — they're the ones prefixed with an underscore. Moreover, this policy frees up the property name (here, `window`) to be used as a local variable in a method, without getting a warning from the compiler that we're overshadowing the name of an instance variable.

Autosynthesis follows the same naming policy. If you omit the `@synthesize` directive, the automatically generated name of the automatically declared instance variable is the name of the property prefixed with an underscore. For example, a declared property called `theData` will result in an instance variable called `_theData`. If for some reason that isn't what you want, then use the `@synthesize` directive explicitly. Remember, if you do so, that if you don't specify the instance variable name explicitly, the default instance variable name will be the same as the property name, *without* any underscore.

Regardless of whether you explicitly include a `@synthesize` directive or you take advantage of autosynthesis, you are permitted to write one or both accessors yourself. Synthesis means that any accessors you *don't* provide will be provided for you. If you use autosynthesis (no `@synthesize` directive) and you provide *both* accessors, *you won't get any automatically declared instance variable.* This is a very sensible policy: you've surrendered your chance to dictate the instance variable's name in the `@synthesize` directive, but you're also taking complete manual control of your accessors, so you're given complete manual control of your instance variable as well.

A useful trick is to take advantage of the `@synthesize` syntax *propertyName=ivarName* to override the synthesized accessor without losing any of its functionality. What I mean is this. Suppose you want the setter for `_myIvar` to do more than just set `_myIvar`. One possibility is to write your own setter; however, writing a setter from scratch is tedious and error-prone, whereas a synthesized setter does the job correctly and writing it is no work at all. The solution is to declare a property `myIvar` along with a corresponding private property (Example 12-10) — let's call it `myIvarAlias` — and synthesize the private property `myIvarAlias` to access the `_myIvar` instance variable. You must then write the accessors for `myIvar` by hand, but all they need to do, at a minimum, is use the `myIvarAlias` properties to set and get the value of `_myIvar` respectively. The key point is that you can also do *other* stuff in those accessors (Example 12-11); whoever gets or sets the property `myIvar` will be doing that other stuff.

Example 12-11. Overriding synthesized accessors

```
// In the header file:
@interface MyClass : NSObject
@property (nonatomic, strong) NSNumber* myIvar;
@end

// In the implementation file:
@interface MyClass ()
@property (nonatomic, strong) NSNumber* myIvarAlias;
@end
```

```
@implementation MyClass
@synthesize myIvarAlias=_myIvar;
- (void) setMyIvar: (NSNumber*) num {
    // do other stuff here
    self.myIvarAlias = num;
}
- (NSNumber*) myIvar {
    // do other stuff here
    return self.myIvarAlias;
}
@end
```

Dynamic Accessors

Instead of writing your own accessors or providing a @synthesize directive or using autosynthesis, you can accompany a property declaration with a @dynamic directive (in the implementation section). This tells the compiler that even though it doesn't see any implementation of any accessors for this property, and even though it isn't going to provide the accessors for you, it should permit the property declaration anyway, on the grounds that at runtime, when a call to one of the accessors arrives, your code will somehow magically handle it in some way that the compiler can't grasp. Basically, you're suppressing the compiler's warning system; it just gives up and stands aside, and leaves you to hang yourself at runtime.

This is a rare but not unheard-of thing to do. It arises chiefly in two contexts: when defining your own animatable view property (Chapter 17), and when using managed object properties in Core Data (Chapter 36). In both of those situations, you harness the power of Cocoa to perform the magic handling of the accessor calls; you don't know precisely *how* Cocoa performs this magic, and you don't care.

But what if you wanted to perform this magic yourself? To put it another way, what sort of magic might Cocoa be using in those two limited situations? The answer lies in the power of Objective-C's dynamic messaging. This is an advanced topic, but it's so cool that I'll show you an example anyway.

I propose to write a class that declares properties name (an NSString) and number (an NSNumber) but that has no accessor methods for name or number and that doesn't use accessor synthesis. Instead, in our interface section we declare these properties dynamic. Since we're not getting any help from synthesis, we must also declare the instance variables ourselves:

```
// the interface section declares properties "name" and "number"
@implementation MyClass {
    NSString* _name;
    NSNumber* _number;
```

```
}
@dynamic name, number;
// ...insert magic here...
@end
```

I can think of a couple of ways to concoct the necessary magic; in this example, I'm going to take advantage of a little-known NSObject class method called resolve-InstanceMethod:. Recall that sending a message to an object is not the same as calling that method in that object; there are some additional steps, if that method is not found in that object, to resolve the method. One of the first of these steps, the *first* time a given message arrives and is found to have no corresponding method in the object's class, is that the runtime looks for an implementation of resolveInstanceMethod in that class. If it finds it, it calls it, handing it the selector for the message that is giving us difficulty. resolveInstanceMethod: then returns a BOOL; a YES answer means, "Don't worry, I've got it covered; go ahead and call that method."

How can resolveInstanceMethod: possibly say this? What could it do, if the method doesn't exist, to make it possible to call that method? Well, it could *create that method*. Objective-C is so dynamic that there's a way to do this. And remember, resolve-InstanceMethod: is called just once per method, so once it has created a method and returned YES, the problem is solved forever after for that method.

To create a method in real time, we call the class_addMethod function. (This will require importing <objc/runtime.h>.) It takes four parameters:

- The class to which the method is to be added.
- The selector for the method that is being added (basically, this is the name of the method).
- The IMP for the method. What's an IMP? It's the *function that backs this method*. Behind every Objective-C method lies a C function. This function takes the same parameters as the Objective-C method, with the addition of two extra parameters, which come at the start: the object that acts as self within this function, and the selector for the method that this function is backing.
- A C string describing, in a special code, the type of the function's returned value (which is also the type of the method's returned value) and the argument types of the function. When I say "type" I mean little more than C type; every object type is considered the same.

In our example we have four methods to cover (the two accessors for the two dynamic properties) — name, setName:, number, and setNumber:. So in order to call class_add-Method in resolveInstanceMethod:, we will also have to have written C functions to act as the IMP for each of those methods. Now, we could just write four C functions — but that would be pointless! If we were going to do that, why are we going to all the trouble of using a dynamic accessor? Instead, I propose to write just two C functions, one to handle *any* getter that we may care to direct at it, and one to handle *any* setter that we may care to direct at it.

Let's take the getter first, as it is much the simpler case. What must a generalized getter do? It must access the corresponding instance variable. And what's the name of the corresponding instance variable? Well, the way we've set things up, it's the name of the method with an underscore prefixed to it. So, we grab the name of the method (which we can do because it has arrived as the selector, the second parameter to this function), stick an underscore on the front, and return the value of the instance variable whose name we've just derived. To make life simple, I'll obtain the value of that instance variable using key–value coding; the presence of the underscore means that this won't result in any circularity (that is, our function won't end up calling itself in an infinite recursion):

```
id callValueForKey(id self, SEL _cmd) {
    NSString* key = NSStringFromSelector(_cmd);
    key = [@"_" stringByAppendingString:key];
    return [self valueForKey:key];
}
```

Now that we've done that, we can see how to write the setter. It's just a matter of doing a slightly more elaborate manipulation of the selector's name in order to get the name of the instance variable. We must pull the set off the front and the colon off the end, and make sure the first letter is lowercase — and then we prefix the underscore, just as before:

```
void callSetValueForKey(id self, SEL _cmd, id value) {
    NSString* key = NSStringFromSelector(_cmd);
    key = [key substringWithRange:NSMakeRange(3, [key length]-4)];
    NSString* firstCharLower =
        [[key substringWithRange:NSMakeRange(0,1)] lowercaseString];
    key = [key stringByReplacingCharactersInRange:NSMakeRange(0,1)
                                       withString:firstCharLower];
    key = [@"_" stringByAppendingString:key];
    [self setValue:value forKey:key];
}
```

Finally, we're ready to write resolveInstanceMethod:. In my implementation, I've used this method as a gatekeeper, explicitly checking that the method to be called is an accessor for one of our dynamic properties:

```
+ (BOOL) resolveInstanceMethod: (SEL) sel {
    // this method will be called
    if (sel == @selector(setName:) || sel == @selector(setNumber:)) {
        class_addMethod([self class], sel, (IMP) callSetValueForKey, "v@:@");
        return YES;
    }
    if (sel == @selector(name) || sel == @selector(number)) {
        class_addMethod([self class], sel, (IMP) callValueForKey, "@@:");
```

```
        return YES;
    }
    return [super resolveInstanceMethod:sel];
}
```

You'll just have to trust me on the encoded C string in the fourth argument to class_add-Method; if you don't, read the documentation to see what it means. My overall implementation here is simple-minded — in particular, my use of key–value coding is sort of an easy way out, and I've failed to grapple with the need for copy semantics in the NSString setter — but it's quite general, and gives you a peek under the Objective-C hood.

CHAPTER 13

Data Communication

As soon as an app grows to more than a few objects, puzzling questions can arise about how to send a message or communicate data between one object and another. The problem is essentially one of architecture. Constructing your code so that all the pieces fit together and key information can be shared is something of an art. But it isn't difficult. This chapter presents some general considerations that may provide the needed clue.

Model–View–Controller

In Apple's documentation and elsewhere, you'll find references to the term *model–view–controller*, or *MVC*. This refers to an architectural goal of maintaining a distinction between three functional aspects of a program that displays information to the user and permits the user to alter that information. The notion goes back to the days of Smalltalk, and much has been written about it since then, but informally, here's what the terms mean:

Model
> The data and its management, often referred to as the program's "business logic," the hard-core stuff that the program is really all about.

View
> What the user sees and interacts with.

Controller
> The mediation between the model and the view.

Consider, for example, a game where the current score is displayed to the user:

- A UILabel that shows the user the current score for the game in progress is *view*; it is effectively nothing but a pixel-maker, and its business is to know how to draw itself. The knowledge of *what* it should draw — the score, and the fact that this *is* a

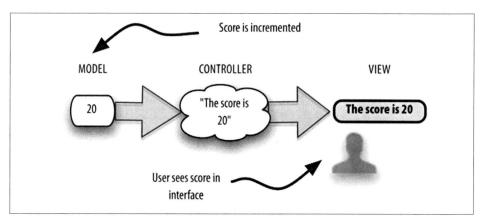

Figure 13-1. Model–view–controller

score — lies elsewhere. A rookie programmer might try to use the score displayed by the UILabel as the actual score: to increment the score, read the UILabel's string, turn that string into a number, increment the number, turn the number back into a string, and present that string in place of the previous string. That is a gross violation of the MVC philosophy. The view presented to the user should *reflect* the score; it should not *store* the score.

- The score is data being maintained internally; it is *model*. It could be as simple as an instance variable along with a public increment method or as complicated as a Score object with a raft of methods. The score is numeric, whereas a UILabel displays a string; this alone is enough to show that the view and the model are naturally different.

- Telling the score when to change, and seeing that this fact is reflected in the user interface, is the work of the *controller*. This will be particularly clear if we imagine that the model's numeric score needs to be transformed in some way for presentation to the user. For example, suppose the UILabel that presents the score reads: "Your current score is 20". The model is presumably storing and providing the number 20, so what's the source of the phrase "Your current score is…"? Whoever is deciding that this phrase should precede the score in the presentation of the score to the user, and is making it so, is a controller.

Even this simplistic example (Figure 13-1) illustrates very well the advantages of MVC. By separating powers in this way, we allow the aspects of the program to evolve with a great degree of independence. Do you want a different font and size in the presentation of the score? Change the view; the model and controller need know nothing about it, but will just go on working exactly as they did before. Do you want to change the phrase that precedes the score? Change the controller; the model and view are unchanged.

Adherence to MVC is particularly appropriate in a Cocoa app, because Cocoa itself adheres to it. The very names of Cocoa classes reveal the MVC philosophy that underlies them. A UIView is a view. A UIViewController is a controller; its purpose is to embody the logic that tells the view what to display. In Chapter 11 we saw that a UIPickerView does not hold the data it displays; it gets that data from a data source. So the UIPicker-View is a view; the data source is model.

A further distinction, found in Apple's documentation, is this: true model material and true view material should be quite reusable, in the sense that they can be transferred wholesale into some other app; controller material is generally not reusable, because it is concerned with how *this* app mediates between the model and the view.

In one of my own apps, for example, we download an XML (RSS) news feed and present the article titles to the user as a table. The storage and parsing of the XML are pure model material, and are so reusable that I didn't even write this part of the code (I used some code called FeedParser, by Kevin Ballard). The table is a UITableView, which is obviously reusable, seeing as I obtained it directly from Cocoa. But when the UITableView turns to me and asks what I'd like to display in this cell, and I turn to the XML and ask for the title of the article corresponding to this row of the table, that's controller logic.

By keeping the MVC architectural philosophy in mind as you develop your app, you'll implicitly solve one data communication problem. The data will live in the model, the view will be purely presentational in nature, and the communication between them will be handled by your own deliberately written controller code. You'll be communicating between the view and the model because controller code is *about* communicating between the view and model.

Instance Visibility

The problem of communication often comes down to one object being able to see another: object Manny needs to be able to find object Jack repeatedly and reliably over the long term so as to be able to send Jack messages. (This is the same problem I spoke of in Chapter 2 as getting a *reference* to an object.)

An obvious solution is an instance variable of Manny whose value is Jack. This is appropriate particularly when Manny and Jack share certain responsibilities or supplement one another's functionality, and when they will both persist, especially when they will both persist together. The application object and its delegate, a table view and its data source, a view controller and the view that it controls — these are cases where the former must have an instance variable pointing at the latter.

With instance variables comes the question of memory management policy (Chapter 12). Should Manny, which has an instance variable pointing to Jack, also retain Jack? Basically, it depends on how closely allied the objects are. An object does not typically retain its delegate or its data source; it can exist without a delegate or a data source, and the delegate and data source have lives of their own — it is none of this object's business to say whether its delegate or data source should be allowed to go out of existence. This object is therefore always prepared for the possibility that its delegate or data source may be nil. Similarly, an object that implements the target–action pattern, such as a UIControl, does not retain its target. On the other hand, a view controller is useless without a view to control; its very job is to be coterminous with its view, and to release its view when it itself goes out of existence. Similarly, an object that owns a nib as the nib loads rules the lifetimes of that nib's top-level objects.

Even when two objects go together closely, it will not necessarily be the case that each holds an instance variable pointing at the other. When each *does* point to the other, you must of course be careful not to let each *retain* the other; that's a retain cycle, and will cause both objects to leak. But if one object is the instigator of communication between the two, it can simply pass along a reference to itself as a method argument, if it thinks the second object might need this in order to send back a message later on.

This behavior is conventional in a delegate message, for example. The parameter of the delegate message `textFieldShouldBeginEditing:` is a reference to the UITextField that sent the message. The same policy is followed by target–action messages in their fuller forms; the first parameter is a reference to the sender. You can follow a similar policy.

Visibility by Instantiation

The real question is how one object is to be introduced to the other in the first place. Much of the art of Cocoa programming (and of object-oriented programming generally) lies in getting a reference to a desired object. Every case is different and must be solved separately, but a major clue comes from the fact that every instance comes from somewhere. This means that some object commanded this instance to come into existence in the first place. That object therefore has a reference to the instance at that moment. That fact is always the starting point for establishment of future communication.

When Manny instantiates Jack, Manny has a reference to Jack, and can keep that reference if it will be needed later. Moreover, if Manny knows that Jack is going to need a reference to itself (Manny) or to some piece of data, Manny can hand Jack that reference early in Jack's lifetime. Indeed, you might write Jack with an initializer that will take this reference as a parameter, so that Jack will possess it from the moment it comes into existence. (Compare the approach taken, for example, by UIActionSheet and UIAlert-View, where the delegate is one of the initializer's parameters, or by UIBarButtonItem, where the target is one of the initializer's parameters.)

This example, from one of my apps, is from a table view controller. The user has tapped a row of the table. We create a secondary table view controller, a TrackViewController instance, handing it the data it will need, and display the secondary table view. I deliberately devised TrackViewController to have a designated initializer `initWithMedia-`

ItemCollection: to make it virtually obligatory for a TrackViewController to have access to the data it needs:

```
- (void)showItemsForRow: (NSIndexPath*) indexPath {
    // create subtable of tracks and go there
    TrackViewController *t =
        [[TrackViewController alloc] initWithMediaItemCollection:
            (self.albums)[indexPath.row]];
    [self.navigationController pushViewController:t animated:YES];
}
```

The loading of a nib is also a case of visibility by instantiation. As I explained at length in Chapter 7, you will want to prepare your nib objects, including some proxy object such as the File's Owner, with outlets corresponding to instance variables or accessors in that object's class; as the nib loads, the object pointed to by each outlet will be handed to the corresponding instance variable as its value, or the setter as its argument, so that each instance that will need a reference to an object instantiated from the nib will in fact now have it and will be able to communicate as needed with the nib-instantiated object (Figure 7-5).

But what if two objects are conceptually distant from each other? A common case in point is when objects are going to be instantiated from *different* nibs. How can an instance from one nib get a reference to an instance from another nib? True, you can't draw a connection between an object in nib A and an object in nib B (see "Connections Between Nibs" (page 165)). But someone (Manny) is going to be the file's owner when nib A loads, and someone (Jack) is going to be the file's owner when nib B loads. Those two file's owners might be able to see each other; if so, the problem is solved. Perhaps they are the same object. Perhaps Manny instantiated Jack in the first place. Perhaps they are both instantiated by some third object, which provides a communication path for them.

Visibility by Relationship

Objects may acquire the ability to see one another automatically by virtue of their position in a containing structure. Before worrying about how to supply one object with a reference to another, consider whether there may *already* be a chain of references leading from one to another.

For example, a subview can see its superview, through its superview property. A superview can see all its subviews, through its subviews property, and can pick out a specific subview through that subview's tag property, by calling viewWithTag:. A subview in a window can see its window, through its window property. (There will be more about all that in Chapter 14.) A responder (Chapter 11) can see the next responder in the responder chain, through the nextResponder method — which also means, because of the structure of the responder chain, that a view can see the view controller that manages it.

Similarly, view controllers are part of a containment hierarchy (Chapter 19) and therefore can see one another. If a view controller is currently presenting a view through a second view controller, the latter is the former's presentedViewController, and the former is the latter's presentingViewController. If a view controller is contained by a UINavigationController, the latter is its navigationController. A UINavigation-Controller's visible view is controlled by its visibleViewController. And from any of these, you can reach the view controller's view through its view property, and so forth.

All of these relationships are public. So if you can get a reference to just one object within any of these structures or a similar structure, you can effectively navigate the whole structure through a chain of references and lay your hands on any other object within the structure.

Global Visibility

Some objects are globally visible (that is, visible to all other objects). In general, these are singletons vended by a class method. Some of these objects have properties pointing to other objects, making those other objects likewise globally visible.

For example, any object can see the singleton UIApplication instance by calling [UIApplication sharedApplication]. So any object can also see the app's primary window, because that is its keyWindow property, and any object can see the app delegate, because that is its delegate property. And the chain continues: any object can see the app's root view controller, because that is the primary window's rootViewController — and from there, as I said in the previous section, we can navigate the view controller hierarchy and the view hierarchy. You can take advantage of this to make objects globally visible by attaching them to a globally visible object. A public property of the app delegate, which you are free to create, is globally visible by virtue of the app delegate being globally visible (by virtue of the shared application being globally visible).

Another globally visible object is the shared defaults object obtained by calling [NSUser-Defaults standardUserDefaults]. This object is the gateway to storage and retrieval of user defaults, which is similar to a dictionary (a collection of values named by keys). The user defaults are automatically saved when your application quits and are automatically available when your application is launched again later, so they are one of the ways in which your app maintains state between launches. But, being globally visible, they are also a conduit for communicating values within your app.

For example, in one of my apps there's a setting I call @"hazyStripy". This determines whether a certain visible interface object is drawn with a hazy fill or a stripy fill. This is a setting that the user can change, so there is a preferences interface allowing the user to make this change. When the user displays this preferences interface, I examine the @"hazyStripy" setting in the user defaults to configure the interface to reflect it; if the

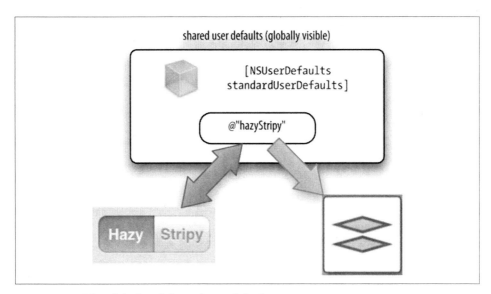

Figure 13-2. The global visibility of user defaults

user interacts with the preferences interface to change the @"hazyStripy" setting, I respond by changing the actual @"hazyStripy" setting in the user defaults.

But the preferences interface is not the only object that uses the @"hazyStripy" setting in the user defaults; the drawing code that actually draws the hazy-or-stripy-filled object also uses it, so as to know which way to draw itself. Thus there is no need for the object that draws the hazy-or-stripy-filled object and the object that manages the preferences interface to be able to see one another! They can both see this common object, the @"hazyStripy" user default (Figure 13-2). Indeed, it is not uncommon to "misuse" the user defaults storage to hold information that is *not* used to maintain state between runs of the app, but is placed there just because this is a location globally visible to all objects.

Notifications

Notifications (Chapter 11) can be a way to communicate between objects that are conceptually distant from one another without bothering to provide *any* way for one to see the other. All they really need to have in common is a knowledge of the name of the notification. Using a notification in this way may seem lazy, an evasion of your responsibility to architect your objects sensibly. But sometimes one object doesn't need to know, and indeed shouldn't know, what object (or objects) it is sending a message to.

For example, in one of my apps, the app delegate may detect a need to tear down the interface and built it back up again from scratch. If this is to happen without causing memory leaks (and all sorts of other havoc), every view controller that is currently running a repeating NSTimer needs to invalidate that timer (Chapter 12). Rather than my having to work out what view controllers those might be, and endowing every view controller with a method that can be called, I simply have the app delegate shout "Everybody stop timers!" — by posting a notification. My view controllers that run timers have all registered for this notification, and they know what to do when they receive it.

Key–Value Observing

Key–value observing, or *KVO*, is a mechanism somewhat similar to the target–action mechanism, except that it is not limited to controls. (The KVO mechanism is provided through an informal protocol, NSKeyValueObserving, which is actually a set of categories on NSObject and other classes.) The similarity is that objects register with a particular object to be notified when something happens. The "something" is that a certain value in that object is changed.

Mac OS X Programmer Alert
Mac OS X bindings don't exist on iOS, but you can sometimes use KVO to achieve similar aims.

KVO can be broken down into three stages:

Registration
> To hear about a change in a value belonging to object A, object B must be registered with object A.

Change
> The change takes place in the value belonging to object A, and it must take place in a special way — a KVO compliant way.

Notification
> Object B is automatically notified that the value in object A has changed and can respond as desired.

Here's a simple complete example — a rather silly example, but sufficient to demonstrate the KVO mechanism in action. We have a class MyClass1; this will be the class of object A. We also have a class MyClass2; this will be the class of object B. Finally, we have code that creates a MyClass1 instance called objectA and a MyClass2 instance called objectB; this code registers objectB to hear about changes in an instance variable of objectA called value, and then changes value, and sure enough, objectB is automatically notified of the change:

```
// MyClass1.h:
@interface MyClass1 : NSObject
@property (nonatomic, copy) NSString* value;
@end

// MyClass2.m:
- (void) observeValueForKeyPath:(NSString *)keyPath
                       ofObject:(id)object
                         change:(NSDictionary *)change
                        context:(void *)context {
    NSLog(@"I heard about the change!");
}

// Somewhere else entirely:
MyClass1* objectA = [MyClass1 new];
MyClass2* objectB = [MyClass2 new];
// register for KVO
[objectA addObserver:objectB forKeyPath:@"value" options:0 context:nil]; ❶
// change the value in a KVO compliant way
objectA.value = @"Hello, world!"; ❷
// result: objectB's observeValueForKeyPath:... is called ❸
```

❶ We call addObserver:forKeyPath:options:context: to register objectB to hear about changes in objectA's value. We didn't use the options: or context: parameters for anything; I'll talk about the options: parameter in a moment. (The context: parameter is for handing in a value to be provided as part of the notification; see Chapter 12.)

❷ We change objectA's value, and we do it in a KVO compliant way, namely, by passing through the setter (because setting a property is equivalent to passing through the setter). This is another reason why, as I said in Chapter 12, accessors (and properties) are a good thing: they help you guarantee KVO compliance when changing a value.

❸ When we change objectA's value, the third stage takes place automatically: a call is made to objectB's observeValueForKeyPath:.... We have implemented this method in MyClass2 in order to receive the notification. In this simple example, we expect to receive only one notification, so we just log to indicate that we did indeed receive it. In real life, where a single object might be registered to receive more than one KVO notification, you'd use the incoming parameters to distinguish between different notifications and decide what to do.

At the very least, you'll probably want to know, when observeValueForKeyPath:... is called, what the new value is. We can find that out easily, because we are handed a reference to the object that changed, along with the key path for the value within that object. Thus we can use KVC to query the changed object in the most general way:

```
- (void) observeValueForKeyPath:(NSString *)keyPath
                       ofObject:(id)object
                         change:(NSDictionary *)change
                        context:(void *)context {
    id newValue = [object valueForKeyPath:keyPath];
    NSLog(@"The key path %@ changed to %@", keyPath, newValue);
}
```

It is also possible to request that the new value be included as part of the notification. This depends upon the `options` passed with the original registration. Here, we'll request that both the old and new values be included with the notification:

```
objectA.value = @"Hello";
[objectA addObserver:objectB forKeyPath:@"value"
    options: NSKeyValueObservingOptionNew | NSKeyValueObservingOptionOld
    context: nil];
objectA.value = @"Goodbye"; // notification is triggered
```

When we receive the notification, we fetch the old and new values out of the `change` dictionary:

```
- (void) observeValueForKeyPath:(NSString *)keyPath
                       ofObject:(id)object
                         change:(NSDictionary *)change
                        context:(void *)context {
    id newValue = change[NSKeyValueChangeNewKey];
    id oldValue = change[NSKeyValueChangeOldKey];
    NSLog(@"The key path %@ changed from %@ to %@",
        keyPath, oldValue, newValue);
}
```

No memory management happens as part of the registration process, so it is incumbent upon you to unregister object B before it is destroyed. Otherwise, object A may later attempt to send a notification to a dangling pointer (see Chapter 12). This is done by sending object A the `removeObserver:forKeyPath:` message; you must explicitly unregister the observer for every key path for which it is registered; you can't use nil as the second argument to mean "all key paths".

 The runtime will send you a nice warning in the log if an object *being observed* under KVO goes out of existence. But you get no warning if an *observer* object goes out of existence. It is crucial that the observer should be unregistered with the observed as the observer goes out of existence, to prevent the observed from trying to send it any notifications later. In real life, where an object will typically register itself as an observer, it will usually unregister itself in its `dealloc` implementation (and this could be yet another reason to implement `dealloc` under ARC).

Beginners are often confused about how to use KVO to observe changes to a mutable array, to be notified when an object is added to, removed from, or replaced within the array. You can't add an observer to an array itself; you have to observe through an object that has a key path to the array (through accessors, for example). The simple-minded solution is then to access the array using `mutableArrayValueForKey:`, which provides an observable proxy object.

For example, as in Chapter 12, let's posit an object with a property `theData` which is an array of dictionaries:

```
(
        {
        description = "The one with glasses.";
        name = Manny;
    },
        {
        description = "Looks a little like Governor Dewey.";
        name = Moe;
    },
        {
        description = "The one without a mustache.";
        name = Jack;
    }
)
```

Suppose this is an NSMutableArray. Then we can register with our object to observe the key path `@"theData"`:

```
[objectA addObserver:objectB forKeyPath:@"theData" options:0 context:nil];
```

Now object B will be notified of changes to this mutable array, but only if those changes are performed through the `mutableArrayValueForKey:` proxy object:

```
[[objectA mutableArrayValueForKeyPath:@"theData"] removeObjectAtIndex:0];
// notification is triggered
```

But it seems onerous to require clients to know that they must call `mutableArrayValueForKey:`. The simple solution is for our object A itself to provide a getter that calls `mutableArrayValueForKey:`. Here's a possible implementation:

```
// MyClass1.h:
@interface MyClass1 : NSObject
@property (nonatomic, strong, getter=theDataGetter) NSMutableArray* theData;
@end

// MyClass1.m:
- (NSMutableArray*) theDataGetter {
    return [self mutableArrayValueForKey:@"theData"];
}
```

The result is that, as far as any client knows, this object has a key @"theData" and a property theData, and we can register to observe with the key and then access the mutable array through the property:

```
[objectA addObserver:objectB forKeyPath:@"theData"
    options: NSKeyValueObservingOptionNew | NSKeyValueObservingOptionOld
    context:nil];
[objectA.theData removeObjectAtIndex:0]; // notification is triggered
```

If you're going to take this approach, you should really also implement (in MyClass1) the four KVC compliance methods for a mutable array façade (see Chapter 12). Although things will appear to work just fine without them, and although they appear trivial (they are merely delegating to self->_theData the equivalent calls), they will be called by the vended proxy object, which increases its efficiency (and, some would argue, its safety). Without these methods, the proxy object resorts to setting the instance variable directly, replacing the entire mutable array, every time a client changes the mutable array:

```
- (NSUInteger) countOfTheData {
    return [self->_theData count];
}

- (id) objectInTheDataAtIndex: (NSUInteger) ix {
    return self->_theData[ix];
}

- (void) insertObject: (id) val inTheDataAtIndex: (NSUInteger) ix {
    [self->_theData insertObject:val atIndex:ix];
}

- (void) removeObjectFromTheDataAtIndex: (NSUInteger) ix {
    [self->_theData removeObjectAtIndex: ix];
}
```

If what you want to observe are mutations within an individual element of an array, things are more complicated. Suppose our array of dictionaries is an array of mutable dictionaries. To observe changes to the value of the @"description" key of any dictionary in the array, you'd need to register for that key with *each* dictionary in the array, separately. You can do that efficiently with NSArray's instance method addObserver:to-ObjectsAtIndexes:forKeyPath:options:context:, but if the array *itself* is mutable then you're also going to have to register for that key with any *new* dictionaries that are subsequently added to the array (and unregister when a dictionary is removed from the array). This is doable but daunting, and I'm not going to go into the details here.

Key–value observing is a deep mechanism; consult Apple's *Key-Value Observing Guide* for full information. It does have some unfortunate shortcomings — for one thing, it's a pity that all notifications arrive by calling the same bottleneck method, observe-

`ValueForKeyPath:...` — but in general, KVO is useful for keeping values coordinated in different objects.

 The properties of Apple's built-in classes are typically KVO compliant. Indeed, so are many classes that don't use properties per se; for example, NSUserDefaults is KVO compliant. Unfortunately, Apple warns that undocumented KVO compliance can't necessarily be counted on.

PART IV

Views

This part of the book is about the things that appear in an app's interface. All such things are, ultimately, *views*. A view is a unit of your app that knows how to draw itself. A view also knows how to sense that the user has touched it. Views are what your user sees on the screen, and what your user interacts with by touching the screen. Thus, views are the primary constituent of an app's visible, touchable manifestation. They *are* your app's interface. So it's going to be crucial to know how views work.

- Chapter 14 discusses views in their most general aspect — their hierarchy, visibility, and position, including an explanation of autolayout, a way of positioning views that's new in iOS 6.

- Chapter 15 is about drawing. A view knows how to draw itself; this chapter explains how to tell a view what you want it to draw, from simply displaying an already existing image to constructing a drawing line by line.

- Chapter 16 explains about layers. The drawing power of a view comes ultimately from its layer. To put it another way, a layer is effectively the aspect of a view that knows how to draw — with even more power.

- Chapter 17 tells about animation. An iOS app's interface isn't generally static; it's lively. Much of that liveliness comes from animation. iOS gives you great power to animate your interface with remarkable ease; that power resides ultimately in layers.

- Chapter 18 is about touches. A view knows how to draw itself; it also knows how to sense that the user is touching it. This chapter explains the iOS view-based mechanisms for sensing and responding to touches, with details on how touches are routed to the appropriate view and how you can customize that routing.

CHAPTER 14

Views

A *view* (an object whose class is UIView or a subclass of UIView) knows how to draw itself into a rectangular area of the interface. Your app has a visible interface thanks to views. Creating and configuring a view can be extremely simple: "Set it and forget it." You've already seen that you can drag an interface widget, such as a UIButton, into a view in the nib; when the app runs, the button appears, and works properly. But you can also manipulate views in powerful ways, in real time. Your code can do some or all of the view's drawing of itself; it can make the view appear and disappear, move, resize itself, and display many other physical changes, possibly with animation.

A view is also a *responder* (UIView is a subclass of UIResponder). This means that a view is subject to user interactions, such as taps and swipes. Thus, views are the basis not only of the interface that the user sees, but also of the interface that the user touches. Organizing your views so that the correct view reacts to a given touch allows you to allocate your code neatly and efficiently.

The *view hierarchy* is the chief mode of view organization. A view can have subviews; a subview has exactly one immediate superview. Thus there is a tree of views. This hierarchy allows views to come and go together. If a view is removed from the interface, its subviews are removed; if a view is hidden (made invisible), its subviews are hidden; if a view is moved, its subviews move with it; and other changes in a view are likewise shared with its subviews. The view hierarchy is also the basis of, though it is not identical to, the responder chain (Chapter 11).

A view may come from a nib, or you can create it in code. On balance, neither approach is to be preferred over the other; it depends on your needs and inclinations and on the overall architecture of your app.

The Window

The top of the view hierarchy is the app's window. It is an instance of UIWindow (or your own subclass thereof), which is a UIView subclass. Your app should have exactly one main window. It occupies the entire screen and forms the background to, and is the ultimate superview of, all your other visible views. Other views are visible by virtue of being subviews, at some depth, of your app's window. (If your app can display views on an external screen, you'll create an additional UIWindow to contain those views; but in this chapter I'll behave as if there were just one screen, the device's own screen, and just one window.)

The Xcode project templates all generate your app's window for you. The technique used, in a nonstoryboard app, is to create the window explicitly in code, in the app delegate's `application:didFinishLaunchingWithOptions:`. The window must persist for the lifetime of the app, so the app delegate has a `window` property that retains it:

```
self.window = [[UIWindow alloc] initWithFrame:[[UIScreen mainScreen] bounds]];
```

The window's designated initializer is `initWithFrame:`; I'll explain in a moment what "frame" and "bounds" are, but the effect is to make the window the same size as the screen. In the template, the comment, "Override point for customization after application launch," comes *after* that line of code, because any code customizing what's in the window will need the window to exist first. The various templates adopt various strategies for giving the window some content; this generally involves setting the window's `rootViewController` to a UIViewController, whose `view` thus automatically becomes the window's single primary subview. (I will refer to this as the window's *root view*.)

For example, in the Single View Application project template, the ViewController class is instantiated, and the resulting instance is set to the window's `rootViewController`. This sets in motion a further train of events automatically. The nib *ViewController.xib* loads with the ViewController instance as its owner; the UIView pointed to by the File's Owner's `view` outlet in the nib is instantiated, and the ViewController instance's `view` property is set by the nib-loading process to that UIView; and the window makes that view its single primary subview. Finally, the template code sends the window instance the `makeKeyAndVisible` message in order to make your app's interface appear.

If you choose the Storyboard option as you specify a template, the process works a little differently. The app is given a main storyboard, pointed to by the *Info.plist* key "Main storyboard file base name" (UIMainStoryboardFile). After UIApplicationMain instantiates the app delegate class (Chapter 6), it asks the app delegate for the value of its `window` property; if that value is nil, the window is created and assigned to the app delegate's `window` property. The storyboard's initial view controller is then instantiated and assigned to the window's `rootViewController` property, with the result that its view is placed in the window as its root view; the window is then sent the makeKeyAnd-

Visible message. All of that is done behind the scenes by UIApplicationMain, with no visible code whatever. That is why, in a storyboard template, the application:did-FinishLaunchingWithOptions: implementation is empty.

An app whose main window has no rootViewController is not strictly illegal, but it is strongly discouraged by a warning from the runtime as the app launches. The Single View Application template supplies a minimal root view controller for you. The Empty Application template does not; if you use it as is, it generates the warning. To experiment with code that populates the interface with views, you can use the Empty Application template and put your code in its application:didFinishLaunchingWithOptions:, but if you want to avoid the warning, you'll need to create a minimal root view controller and add the views to its view, like this:

```
self.window = [[UIWindow alloc] initWithFrame:[[UIScreen mainScreen] bounds]];
// Override point for customization after application launch.
self.window.rootViewController = [UIViewController new];
UIView* v = [[UIView alloc] initWithFrame:CGRectMake(100,100,50,50)];
v.backgroundColor = [UIColor redColor]; // small red square
// add it to the root view controller's view
[self.window.rootViewController.view addSubview: v];
self.window.backgroundColor = [UIColor whiteColor];
[self.window makeKeyAndVisible];
return YES;
```

Alternatively, use the Single View Application template. In that case, any code that adds views should appear in View Controller's viewDidLoad implementation, and the views should be added to self.view:

```
[super viewDidLoad];
// Do any additional setup after loading the view, typically from a nib.
UIView* v = [[UIView alloc] initWithFrame:CGRectMake(100,100,50,50)];
v.backgroundColor = [UIColor redColor]; // small red square
// add it to this view controller's view
[self.view addSubview: v];
```

To experiment with views created in a nib, start with the Single View Application project template, as we did with our earlier Empty Window example. The view supplied in the nib will become the window's root view, and whatever you drag into it in the nib will appear in the window when the app runs.

It is improbable that you would want to subclass UIWindow and substitute an instance of your subclass as the app's main window, but you can certainly do so. If the window is generated explicitly in code, you would obviously substitute the name of your window subclass as the class to be instantiated and assigned to the app delegate's window property in application:didFinishLaunchingWithOptions:, in the template code I quoted a moment ago. If you're using a main storyboard, however, application:didFinish-LaunchingWithOptions: is too late; you'll have to perform the substitution when UIApplicationMain asks for the app delegate's window property, by implementing the app delegate's `window` getter to create the window and set the `window` property exactly once:

```
- (UIWindow*) window {
    UIWindow* w = self->_window;
    if (!w) {
        w = [[MyWindow alloc] initWithFrame:[[UIScreen mainScreen] bounds]];
        self->_window = w;
    }
    return w;
}
```

Once the app is up and running, the app delegate points to the window as the value of its `window` property; so any code in the app delegate class can refer to the window as `self.window`. Code elsewhere can get a reference to the app delegate, so it can also get a reference to the app's window:

```
UIWindow* theWindow = [[[UIApplication sharedApplication] delegate] window];
```

That code is unusual, though, and may require typecasting to quiet the compiler (because the class of the application's `delegate` property is otherwise unknown). You'd be more likely to use the application's `keyWindow` property:

```
UIWindow* theWindow = [[UIApplication sharedApplication] keyWindow];
```

Perhaps the most typical way to get a reference to your app's window would be through a subview of the window, at any depth of the hierarchy. You are very likely to have a reference to at least one such subview, and its `window` property points to the window that contains it, which is the app's window. You can also use a UIView's `window` property as a way of asking whether it is ultimately embedded in a window; if it isn't, its `window` property is nil. A UIView whose `window` property is nil cannot be visible to the user.

Although your app will have exactly one primary window, it may generate other windows of which you are not conscious. For example, if you put up an alert view (UIAlert-View), it is displayed in a secondary window that lies on top of your app's window; at that moment, this secondary window is the application's `keyWindow`. You would not be conscious of this fact, however, unless you needed a reference to your app's window while an alert was showing, which is unlikely.

The window's `backgroundColor` property, which it inherits from UIView, affects the appearance of the app if the window is visible behind its subviews. However, you are likely to give your window a primary subview that occupies the entire window and blocks it from sight; the window's `backgroundColor` would then make no visible difference. The window would function solely as a container for the app's visible views.

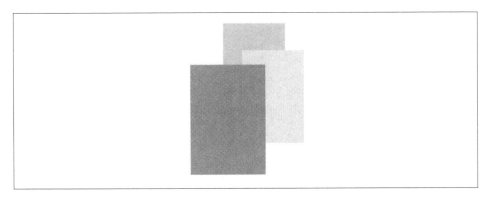

Figure 14-1. Overlapping views

Subview and Superview

Once upon a time, and not so very long ago, a view owned precisely its rectangular area. No part of any view that was not a subview of this view could appear inside it, because when this view redrew its rectangle, it would erase the overlapping portion of the other view. No part of any subview of this view could appear outside it, because the view took responsibility for its own rectangle and no more.

Those rules, however, were gradually relaxed, and starting in Mac OS X 10.5 Apple introduced an entirely new architecture for view drawing that lifted those restrictions completely. iOS view drawing is based on this revised architecture. So now some or all of a subview can appear outside its superview, and a view can overlap another view and can be drawn partially or totally in front of it without being its subview.

So, for example, Figure 14-1 shows three overlapping views. All three views have a background color, so each is completely represented by a colored rectangle. You have no way of knowing, from this visual representation, exactly how the views are related within the view hierarchy. In actual fact, the view in the middle (horizontally) is a sibling view of the view on the left (they are both direct subviews of the root view), and the view on the right is a subview of the middle view.

When views are created in the nib, you can examine the view hierarchy in the expanded dock to learn their actual relationship (Figure 14-2). When views are created in code, you know their hierarchical relationship because you created that hierarchy. But the visible interface doesn't tell you, because view overlapping is so flexible.

Nevertheless, a view's position in the view hierarchy does affect how it is drawn. Most important, a view's position in the view hierarchy dictates the *order* in which it is drawn. Sibling subviews of the same superview have a layering order: one is "further back" than the other. This will make no visible difference if there is no overlap, but the subview that is "further back" is drawn first, so if there *is* overlap, it will appear to be behind its sibling.

Figure 14-2. A view hierarchy as displayed in the nib

Similarly, a superview is "further back" than its subviews; the superview is drawn first, so it will appear to be behind its subviews.

You can see this illustrated in Figure 14-1. The view on the right is a subview of the view in the middle and is drawn on top of it. The view on the left is a sibling of the view in the middle, but it is a later sibling, so it is drawn on top of the view in the middle and on top of the view on the right. The view on the left *cannot* appear behind the view on the right but in front of the view in the middle, because those views are subview and superview and are drawn together — both are drawn either before or after the view on the left, depending on the "further back" ordering of the siblings.

This layering order can be governed in the nib by arranging the views in the expanded dock. (If you click in the canvas, you may be able to use the menu items of the Editor → Arrange menu instead — Send to Front, Send to Back, Send Forward, Send Backward.) In code, there are methods for arranging the sibling order of views, which we'll come to in a moment.

Here are some other effects of the view hierarchy:

- If a view is removed from or moved within its superview, its subviews go with it.
- If a view's size is changed, its subviews can be resized automatically.
- A view's degree of transparency is inherited by its subviews.
- A view can optionally limit the drawing of its subviews so that any parts of them outside the view are not shown. This is called *clipping* and is set with the view's clipsToBounds property.
- A superview *owns* its subviews, in the memory-management sense, much as an NSArray owns its elements; it retains them and is responsible for releasing a subview when that subview ceases to be its subview (it is removed from the collection of this view's subviews) or when it itself goes out of existence.

A UIView has a superview property (a UIView) and a subviews property (an NSArray of UIViews, in back-to-front order), allowing you to trace the view hierarchy in code. There is also a method isDescendantOfView: letting you check whether one view is a subview of another at any depth. If you need a reference to a particular view, you will probably arrange this beforehand as an instance variable, perhaps through an outlet.

Alternatively, a view can have a numeric tag (its `tag` property), and can then be referred to by sending any view higher up the view hierarchy the `viewWithTag:` message. Seeing that all tags of interest are unique within their region of the hierarchy is up to you.

Manipulating the view hierarchy in code is easy. This is part of what gives iOS apps their dynamic quality, and it compensates for the fact that there is basically just a single window. It is perfectly reasonable for your code to rip an entire hierarchy of views out of the superview and substitute another. Such behavior can be implemented elegantly by using a UIViewController, a subject to which we'll return later (Chapter 19). But you can do it directly, too. The method `addSubview:` makes one view a subview of another; `removeFromSuperview` takes a subview out of its superview's view hierarchy. In both cases, if the superview is part of the visible interface, the subview will appear or disappear; and of course this view may itself have subviews that accompany it. Just remember that removing a subview from its superview releases it; if you intend to reuse that subview later on, you will wish to retain it first. This is often taken care of through a property with a retain policy.

Events inform a view of these dynamic changes. To respond to these events requires subclassing. Then you'll be able to override any of `didAddSubview:` and `willRemoveSubview:`, `didMoveToSuperview` and `willMoveToSuperview:`, `didMoveToWindow` and `willMoveToWindow:`.

When `addSubview:` is called, the view is placed last among its superview's subviews; thus it is drawn last, meaning that it appears frontmost. A view's subviews are indexed, starting at 0, which is rearmost. There are additional methods for inserting a subview at a given index (`insertSubview:atIndex:`), or below (behind) or above (in front of) a specific view (`insertSubview:belowSubview:`, `insertSubview:aboveSubview:`); for swapping two sibling views by index (`exchangeSubviewAtIndex:withSubviewAtIndex:`); and for moving a subview all the way to the front or back among its siblings (`bringSubviewToFront:`, `sendSubviewToBack:`).

Oddly, there is no command for removing all of a view's subviews at once. However, a view's `subviews` array is an immutable copy of the internal list of subviews, so it is legal to cycle through it and remove each subview one at a time:

```
for (UIView* v in view.subviews)
    [v removeFromSuperview];
```

Visibility and Opacity

A view can be made invisible by setting its `hidden` property to YES, and visible again by setting it to NO. This takes it (and its subviews, of course) out of the visible interface without the overhead of actually removing it from the view hierarchy. A hidden view does not (normally) receive touch events, so to the user it really is as if the view weren't there. But it is there, so it can still be manipulated in code.

A view can be assigned a background color through its `backgroundColor` property. A color is a UIColor; this is not a difficult class to use, and I'm not going to go into details. A view whose background color is nil (the default) has a transparent background. It is perfectly reasonable for a view to have a transparent background and to do no additional drawing of its own, just so that it can act as a convenient superview to other views, making them behave together.

A view can be made partially or completely transparent through its `alpha` property: `1.0` means opaque, `0.0` means transparent, and a value may be anywhere between them, inclusive. This affects subviews: if a superview has an `alpha` of `0.5`, none of its subviews can have an *apparent* opacity of more than `0.5`, because whatever `alpha` value they have will be drawn relative to `0.5`. (Just to make matters more complicated, colors have an alpha value as well. So, for example, a view can have an `alpha` of `1.0` but still have a transparent background because its `backgroundColor` has an alpha less than `1.0`.) A view that is completely transparent (or very close to it) is like a view whose `hidden` is YES: it is invisible, along with its subviews, and cannot (normally) be touched.

A view's `alpha` property value affects the apparent transparency of its background color and the apparent transparency of its contents separately. For example, if a view displays an image and has a background color and its `alpha` is less than 1, the background color will seep through the image (and whatever is behind the view will seep through both).

A view's **opaque** property, on the other hand, is a horse of a different color; changing it has no effect on the view's appearance. Rather, this property is a hint to the drawing system. If a view completely fills its bounds with ultimately opaque material and its `alpha` is `1.0`, so that the view has no effective transparency, then it can be drawn more efficiently (with less drag on performance) if you inform the drawing system of this fact by setting its **opaque** to YES. Otherwise, you should set its **opaque** to NO. The opaque value is *not* changed for you when you set a view's `backgroundColor` or `alpha`! Setting it correctly is entirely up to you; the default, perhaps surprisingly, is YES.

Frame

A view's `frame` property, a CGRect, is the position of its rectangle within its superview, *in the superview's coordinate system.* By default, the superview's coordinate system will have the origin at its top left, with the x-coordinate growing positively rightward and the y-coordinate growing positively downward.

Setting a view's frame to a different CGRect value repositions the view, or resizes it, or both. If the view is visible, this change will be visibly reflected in the interface. On the other hand, you can also set a view's frame when the view is not visible — for example, when you create the view in code. In that case, the frame describes where the view *will* be positioned within its superview when it is given a superview. UIView's designated initializer is initWithFrame:, and you'll often assign a frame this way, especially because the default frame might otherwise be {{0,0},{0,0}}, which is rarely what you want.

 Forgetting to assign a view a frame when creating it in code, and then wondering why it isn't appearing when added to a superview, is a common beginner mistake. A view with a zero-size frame is effectively invisible. If a view has a standard size that you want it to adopt, especially in relation to its contents (like a UIButton in relation to its title), an alternative is to send it the sizeToFit message.

Knowing this, we can generate programmatically the interface displayed in Figure 14-1. This code might appear in the application:didFinishLaunchingWith-Options: method of the app delegate in an Empty Application template-based app (as I suggested earlier):

```
UIView* v1 = [[UIView alloc] initWithFrame:CGRectMake(113, 111, 132, 194)];
v1.backgroundColor = [UIColor colorWithRed:1 green:.4 blue:1 alpha:1];
UIView* v2 = [[UIView alloc] initWithFrame:CGRectMake(41, 56, 132, 194)];
v2.backgroundColor = [UIColor colorWithRed:.5 green:1 blue:0 alpha:1];
UIView* v3 = [[UIView alloc] initWithFrame:CGRectMake(43, 197, 160, 230)];
v3.backgroundColor = [UIColor colorWithRed:1 green:0 blue:0 alpha:1];
[self.window.rootViewController.view addSubview: v1];
[v1 addSubview: v2];
[self.window.rootViewController.view addSubview: v3];
```

In that code, we determined the layering order of v1 and v3 (the middle and left views, which are sibling subviews of the window) by the order in which we inserted them into the view hierarchy with addSubview:.

Bounds and Center

Suppose we wish to give a view a subview inset by 10 points, as in Figure 14-3. The utility function CGRectInset makes it easy to derive one rectangle as an inset from another, but *what* rectangle should we use as a basis? Not the superview's frame; the frame represents a view's position within *its* superview, and in that superview's coordinates. What we're after is a CGRect describing our superview's rectangle in its *own* coordinates, because those are the coordinates in which the subview's frame is to be expressed. That CGRect, describing a view's rectangle in its own coordinates, is the view's bounds property.

So, the code to generate Figure 14-3 looks like this:

Figure 14-3. A subview inset from its superview

```
UIView* v1 = [[UIView alloc] initWithFrame:CGRectMake(113, 111, 132, 194)];
v1.backgroundColor = [UIColor colorWithRed:1 green:.4 blue:1 alpha:1];
UIView* v2 = [[UIView alloc] initWithFrame:CGRectInset(v1.bounds, 10, 10)];
v2.backgroundColor = [UIColor colorWithRed:.5 green:1 blue:0 alpha:1];
[self.window.rootViewController.view addSubview: v1];
[v1 addSubview: v2];
```

You'll very often use a view's bounds in this way. When you need coordinates for drawing inside a view, whether drawing manually or placing a subview, you'll often refer to the view's bounds.

Interesting things happen when you set a view's bounds. If you change a view's bounds *size*, you change its *frame*. The change in the view's frame takes place around its *center*, which remains unchanged. So, for example:

```
UIView* v1 = [[UIView alloc] initWithFrame:CGRectMake(113, 111, 132, 194)];
v1.backgroundColor = [UIColor colorWithRed:1 green:.4 blue:1 alpha:1];
UIView* v2 = [[UIView alloc] initWithFrame:CGRectInset(v1.bounds, 10, 10)];
v2.backgroundColor = [UIColor colorWithRed:.5 green:1 blue:0 alpha:1];
[self.window.rootViewController.view addSubview: v1];
[v1 addSubview: v2];
CGRect f = v2.bounds;
f.size.height += 20;
f.size.width += 20;
v2.bounds = f;
```

What appears is a single rectangle; the subview completely and exactly covers its superview, its frame being the same as the superview's bounds. The call to CGRectInset started with the superview's bounds and shaved 10 points off the left, right, top, and bottom to set the subview's frame (Figure 14-3). But then we added 20 points to the subview's bounds height and width, and thus added 20 points to the subview's frame height and width as well (Figure 14-4). The center didn't move, so we effectively put the 10 points back onto the left, right, top, and bottom of the subview's frame.

Figure 14-4. A subview exactly covering its superview

When you create a UIView, its bounds coordinate system's {0,0} point is at its top left. If you change a view's bounds *origin*, you move the *origin of its internal coordinate system*. Because a subview is positioned in its superview with respect to its superview's coordinate system, a change in the bounds origin of the superview will change the apparent position of a subview. To illustrate, we start with our subview inset evenly within its superview, and then change the bounds origin of the superview:

```
UIView* v1 = [[UIView alloc] initWithFrame:CGRectMake(113, 111, 132, 194)];
v1.backgroundColor = [UIColor colorWithRed:1 green:.4 blue:1 alpha:1];
UIView* v2 = [[UIView alloc] initWithFrame:CGRectInset(v1.bounds, 10, 10)];
v2.backgroundColor = [UIColor colorWithRed:.5 green:1 blue:0 alpha:1];
[self.window.rootViewController.view addSubview: v1];
[v1 addSubview: v2];
CGRect f = v1.bounds;
f.origin.x += 10;
f.origin.y += 10;
v1.bounds = f;
```

Nothing happens to the superview's size or position. But the subview has moved up and to the left so that it is flush with its superview's top-left corner (Figure 14-5). Basically, what we've done is to say to the superview, "Instead of calling the point at your upper left {0,0}, call that point {10,10}." Because the subview's frame origin is itself at {10,10}, the subview now touches the superview's top-left corner. The effect of changing a view's bounds origin may seem directionally backward — we increased the superview's origin in the positive direction, but the subview moved in the negative direction — but think of it this way: a view's bounds origin point coincides with its frame's top left.

We have seen that changing a view's bounds size affects its frame size. The converse is also true: changing a view's frame size affects its bounds size. What is *not* affected by changing a view's bounds size is the view's center. This property, like the frame property, represents the view's position within its superview, in the superview's coordinates, but it is the position of the bounds center, the point derived from the bounds like this:

Figure 14-5. The superview's bounds origin has been shifted

```
CGPoint c = CGPointMake(CGRectGetMidX(theView.bounds),
                        CGRectGetMidY(theView.bounds));
```

A view's center is thus a single point establishing the positional relationship between a view's bounds and its superview's bounds. Changing a view's bounds does not change its center (we already saw that when we increased a view's bounds size, its frame expanded around a stationary center); changing a view's center does not change its bounds.

Thus, a view's bounds and center are orthogonal (independent), and describe (among other things) both the view's size and its position within its superview. The view's frame is therefore superfluous! In fact, the frame property is merely a convenient expression of the center and bounds values. In most cases, this won't matter to you; you'll use the frame property anyway. When you first create a view from scratch, the designated initializer is initWithFrame:. You can change the frame, and the bounds size and center will change to match. You can change the bounds size or the center, and the frame will change to match. Nevertheless, the proper and most reliable way to position and size a view within its superview is to use its bounds and center, not its frame; there are some situations in which the frame is meaningless (or will at least behave very oddly), but the bounds and center will always work.

We have seen that every view has its own coordinate system, expressed by its bounds, and that a view's coordinate system has a clear relationship to its superview's coordinate system, expressed by its center. This is true of every view in a window, so it is possible to convert between the coordinates of any two views in the same window. Convenience methods are supplied to perform this conversion both for a CGPoint and for a CGRect: convertPoint:fromView:, convertPoint:toView:, convertRect:fromView:, and convertRect:toView:. If the second parameter is nil, it is taken to be the window.

For example, if v2 is a subview of v1, then to center v2 within v1 you could say:

```
v2.center = [v1 convertPoint:v1.center fromView:v1.superview];
```

When setting a view's position by setting its center, if the height or width of the view is not an even integer, the view can end up *misaligned* (on a single-resolution screen): its point values in one or both dimensions are located between the screen pixels. This can cause the view to be displayed incorrectly; for example, if the view contains text, the text may be blurry. You can detect this situation in the Simulator by checking Debug → Color Misaligned Images. A simple solution is to set the view's frame, after positioning it, to the `CGRectIntegral` of its frame.

Transform

A view's `transform` property alters how the view is drawn — it may, for example, change the view's perceived size and orientation — without affecting its bounds and center. A transformed view continues to behave correctly: a rotated button, for example, is still a button, and can be tapped in its apparent location and orientation.

A transform value is a CGAffineTransform, which is a struct representing six of the nine values of a 3×3 transformation matrix (the other three values are constants, so there's no point representing them in the struct). You may have forgotten your high-school linear algebra, so you may not recall what a transformation matrix is. For the details, which are quite simple really, see the "Transforms" chapter of Apple's *Quartz 2D Programming Guide*, especially the section called "The Math Behind the Matrices." But you don't really need to know those details, because convenience functions, whose names start with CGAffineTransformMake..., are provided for creating three of the basic types of transform: rotation, scaling, and translation (i.e., changing the view's apparent position). A fourth basic transform type, skewing or shearing, has no convenience function.

By default, a view's transformation matrix is CGAffineTransformIdentity, the identity transform. It has no visible effect, so you're unaware of it. Any transform that you do apply takes place around the view's center, which is held constant.

Here's some code to illustrate use of a transform:

```
UIView* v1 = [[UIView alloc] initWithFrame:CGRectMake(113, 111, 132, 194)];
v1.backgroundColor = [UIColor colorWithRed:1 green:.4 blue:1 alpha:1];
UIView* v2 = [[UIView alloc] initWithFrame:CGRectInset(v1.bounds, 10, 10)];
v2.backgroundColor = [UIColor colorWithRed:.5 green:1 blue:0 alpha:1];
[self.window.rootViewController.view addSubview: v1];
[v1 addSubview: v2];
v1.transform = CGAffineTransformMakeRotation(45 * M_PI/180.0);
```

The transform property of the view v1 is set to a rotation transform. The result (Figure 14-6) is that the view appears to be rocked 45 degrees clockwise. (I think in degrees, but Core Graphics thinks in radians, so my code has to convert.) Observe that the view's center property is unaffected, so that the rotation seems to have occurred around the view's center. Moreover, the view's bounds property is unaffected; the internal coordinate system is unchanged, so the subview is drawn in the same place relative to its superview. The view's frame, however, is now useless, as no mere rectangle can describe the region of the superview apparently occupied by the view; the frame's actual value, {{63.7416, 92.7416}, {230.517, 230.517}}, describes the minimal bounding rectangle surrounding the view's apparent position. The rule is that if a view's transform is not the identity transform, you should not set its frame; also, automatic resizing of a subview, discussed later in this chapter, requires that the superview's transform be the identity transform.

Suppose, instead of CGAffineTransformMakeRotation, we call CGAffineTransform-MakeScale, like this:

```
v1.transform = CGAffineTransformMakeScale(1.8, 1);
```

The bounds property of the view v1 is still unaffected, so the subview is still drawn in the same place relative to its superview; this means that the two views seem to have

Figure 14-6. A rotation transform

Figure 14-7. A scale transform

stretched horizontally together (Figure 14-7). No bounds or centers were harmed by the application of this transform!

Transformation matrices can be chained. There are convenience functions for applying one transform to another. Their names do *not* contain "Make." These functions are not commutative; that is, order matters. If you start with a transform that translates a view to the right and then apply a rotation of 45 degrees, the rotated view appears to the right of its original position; on the other hand, if you start with a transform that rotates a view 45 degrees and then apply a translation to the right, the meaning of "right" has changed, so the rotated view appears 45 degrees down from its original position. To demonstrate the difference, I'll start with a subview that exactly overlaps its superview:

```
UIView* v1 = [[UIView alloc] initWithFrame:CGRectMake(20, 111, 132, 194)];
v1.backgroundColor = [UIColor colorWithRed:1 green:.4 blue:1 alpha:1];
UIView* v2 = [[UIView alloc] initWithFrame:v1.bounds];
v2.backgroundColor = [UIColor colorWithRed:.5 green:1 blue:0 alpha:1];
[self.window.rootViewController.view addSubview: v1];
[v1 addSubview: v2];
```

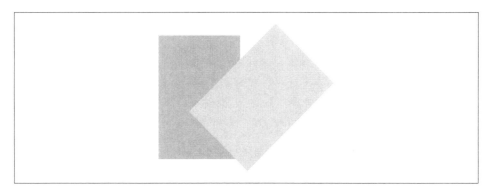

Figure 14-8. Translation, then rotation

Figure 14-9. Rotation, then translation

Then I'll apply two successive transforms to the subview, leaving the superview to show where the subview was originally. In this example, I translate and then rotate (Figure 14-8):

```
v2.transform = CGAffineTransformMakeTranslation(100, 0);
v2.transform = CGAffineTransformRotate(v2.transform, 45 * M_PI/180.0);
```

In this example, I rotate and then translate (Figure 14-9):

```
v2.transform = CGAffineTransformMakeRotation(45 * M_PI/180.0);
v2.transform = CGAffineTransformTranslate(v2.transform, 100, 0);
```

The function `CGAffineTransformConcat` concatenates two transform matrices using matrix multiplication. Again, this operation is not commutative. The order is the *opposite* of the order when using convenience functions for applying one transform to another. For example, this gives the same result as Figure 14-9:

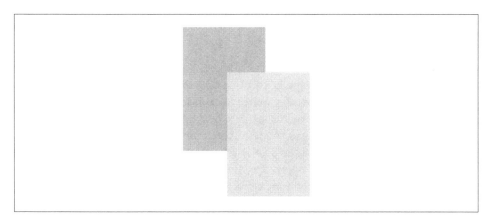

Figure 14-10. Rotation, then translation, then inversion of the rotation

Figure 14-11. Skew (shear)

```
CGAffineTransform r = CGAffineTransformMakeRotation(45 * M_PI/180.0);
CGAffineTransform t = CGAffineTransformMakeTranslation(100, 0);
v2.transform = CGAffineTransformConcat(t,r); // not r,t
```

To remove a transform from a combination of transforms, apply its inverse. A convenience function lets you obtain the inverse of a given affine transform. Again, order matters. In this example, I rotate the subview and shift it to its "right," and then remove the rotation (Figure 14-10):

```
CGAffineTransform r = CGAffineTransformMakeRotation(45 * M_PI/180.0);
CGAffineTransform t = CGAffineTransformMakeTranslation(100, 0);
v2.transform = CGAffineTransformConcat(t,r);
v2.transform =
    CGAffineTransformConcat(CGAffineTransformInvert(r), v2.transform);
```

Finally, as there are no convenience methods for creating a skew (shear) transform, I'll illustrate by creating one manually, without further explanation (Figure 14-11):

```
v1.transform = CGAffineTransformMake(1, 0, -0.2, 1, 0, 0);
```

Transforms are useful particularly as temporary visual indicators. For example, you might call attention to a view by applying a transform that scales it up slightly, and then applying the identity transform to restore it to its original size, and animating those changes (Chapter 17).

The transform property lies at the heart of an iOS app's ability to rotate its interface. The window's frame and bounds, as I've already said, are invariant, locked to the screen; but the root view's frame and bounds are not. Suppose the user rotates the device 90 degrees and the app interface is to rotate to compensate. How is this done? The root view's frame is adjusted to match the new applicationFrame, so that it continues to fill the window except for the part covered by the status bar. In addition, a 90-degree rotation transform is applied to the root view, so that its {0,0} point moves to what the user now sees as the top left of the view. The root view's subviews have their frame in the root view's bounds coordinate system, so they are effectively rotated.

But what about the *position* of the root view's subviews? Consider, for example, a subview located at the bottom right of the screen when the device is in portrait orientation. If the device is rotated 90 degrees, the screen is now considerably shorter vertically, and if a 90-degree rotation transform is applied to the root view to compensate for the device rotation, the root view's bounds width and bounds height are effectively swapped, with what was the longer dimension becoming the shorter dimension and *vice versa*. So that poor old subview will now be off the screen — unless something further is done. That's the subject of the next section.

Layout

We have seen that a subview moves when its superview's bounds *origin* is changed. But what happens to a subview when its superview's bounds *size* is changed? (And remember, this includes changing the superview's frame size.)

Of its own accord, nothing happens. The subview's bounds and center haven't changed, and the superview's bounds origin hasn't moved, so the subview stays in the same position relative to the top left of its superview. In real life, however, that often won't be what you want. You'll want subviews to be resized and repositioned when their superview's bounds size is changed. This is called *layout*.

The need for layout is obvious in a context such as Mac OS X, where the user can freely resize a window, potentially disturbing your interface. For example, you'd want an OK button near the lower-right corner to stay in the lower-right corner as the window grows, while a text field at the top of the window should stay at the top of the window, but perhaps should widen as the window widens.

There are no user-resizable windows on an iOS device, but still, a superview might be resized dynamically. For example, you might respond to the user rotating the device 90 degrees by swapping the width and height values of a view; now its subviews should shift to compensate. Or you might want to provide a reusable complex view, such as a table view cell containing several subviews, without knowing its precise final dimensions in advance. And the introduction of the iPhone 5, with its taller screen, means that one and the same app might launch into portrait orientation on an iPhone 4 and on an iPhone 5, with different height dimensions, which may call for some adjustment of the interface.

Layout is performed in three primary ways in iOS 6:

Manual layout

> The superview is sent the `layoutSubviews` message whenever it is resized; so, to lay out subviews manually, provide your own subclass and override `layout-Subviews`. Clearly this could turn out to be a lot of work, but it means you can do anything you like.

Autoresizing

> Autoresizing is the pre-iOS 6 way of performing layout automatically. It depends ultimately on the superview's `autoresizesSubviews` property. To turn off a view's automatic resizing altogether, set this property to NO. If it is YES, then a subview will respond automatically to its superview's being resized, in accordance with the rules prescribed by the subview's `autoresizingMask` property value. Autoresizing is performed before `layoutSubviews` is called.

Autolayout

> Autolayout, introduced in iOS 6, depends on the *constraints* of views. A constraint (an instance of NSLayoutConstraint) is much more sophisticated than the `autoresizingMask`; it's a full-fledged object with numeric values, and can describe a relationship between *any* two views (not just a subview and its superview).

> Autolayout is an opt-in technology (though it is the default for new nibs created in Xcode 4.5 and later), and is incompatible with systems before iOS 6. You can implement it on a view by view basis; for example, you might lay out a superview using autoresizing but its subviews using autolayout. Autolayout replaces not only autoresizing but also the use of a view's frame (or bounds and center) to position that view; once you choose to use autolayout for a view, you should use only autolayout for that view, both to set its position and to determine what should happen if there's a change in another view to which this one is bound by a constraint.

Autoresizing

Autoresizing is a matter of conceptually assigning a subview "springs and struts." A spring can stretch; a strut can't. Springs and struts can be assigned internally or externally. Thus you can specify (using *internal* springs and struts) whether and how the view can be resized, and (using *external* springs and struts) whether and how the view can be repositioned. For example:

- Imagine a subview that is centered in its superview and is to stay centered, but is to resize itself as the superview is resized. It would have struts externally and springs internally.

- Imagine a subview that is centered in its superview and is to stay centered, and is *not* to resize itself as the superview is resized. It would have springs externally and struts internally.

- Imagine an OK button that is to stay in the lower right of its superview. It would have struts internally, struts externally to its right and bottom, and springs externally to its top and left.

- Imagine a text field that is to stay at the top of its superview. It is to widen as the superview widens. It would have struts externally; internally it would have a vertical strut and a horizontal spring.

To experiment with autoresizing in a nib, you'll need autolayout to be turned off for that nib. By default, autolayout is turned on for a new nib created in Xcode 4.5 and later. To turn it off, select the nib in the Project navigator and show the File inspector: uncheck "Use autolayout."

When editing a nib file with autolayout turned off, you can assign a view springs and struts in the Size inspector (Autosizing). A solid line externally represents a strut; a solid line internally represents a spring. A helpful animation shows you the effect on your view's position as its superview is resized.

In code, a combination of springs and struts is set through a view's autoresizing-Mask property. It's a bitmask, so you use logical-or to combine options (Chapter 1). The options, with names that start with UIViewAutoresizingFlexible..., represent springs; whatever isn't specified is a strut. The default is UIViewAutoresizingNone, meaning all struts — but of course it can't really be *all* struts, because if the superview is resized, *something* needs to change; in reality, UIViewAutoresizingNone is the same as UIViewAutoresizingFlexibleRightMargin together with UIViewAutoresizing-FlexibleBottomMargin.

To demonstrate autoresizing, I'll start with a view and two subviews, one stretched across the top, the other confined to the lower right (Figure 14-12):

```
UIView* v1 = [[UIView alloc] initWithFrame:CGRectMake(100, 111, 132, 194)];
v1.backgroundColor = [UIColor colorWithRed:1 green:.4 blue:1 alpha:1];
UIView* v2 = [[UIView alloc] initWithFrame:CGRectMake(0, 0, 132, 10)];
v2.backgroundColor = [UIColor colorWithRed:.5 green:1 blue:0 alpha:1];
UIView* v3 = [[UIView alloc] initWithFrame:CGRectMake(v1.bounds.size.width-20,
                                                      v1.bounds.size.height-20,
                                                      20, 20)];
```

Figure 14-12. Before autoresizing

Figure 14-13. After autoresizing

```
v3.backgroundColor = [UIColor colorWithRed:1 green:0 blue:0 alpha:1];
[self.window.rootViewController.view addSubview: v1];
[v1 addSubview: v2];
[v1 addSubview: v3];
```

To that example, I'll add code applying springs and struts to the two subviews to make them behave like the text field and the OK button I was hypothesizing earlier:

```
v2.autoresizingMask = UIViewAutoresizingFlexibleWidth;
v3.autoresizingMask = UIViewAutoresizingFlexibleTopMargin |
                      UIViewAutoresizingFlexibleLeftMargin;
```

Now I'll resize the superview, thus bringing autoresizing into play; as you can see (Figure 14-13), the subviews remain pinned in their correct relative positions:

```
CGRect f = v1.bounds;
f.size.width += 40;
f.size.height -= 50;
v1.bounds = f;
```

Autolayout

Autolayout is an opt-in technology. By default, as your app launches, autolayout is switched off, and the system behaves as in iOS 5 and before. But if, at any time while your app runs, the system sees an autolayout constraint (generated in code or by the loading of a nib that has "Use autolayout" checked), the autolayout system is switched on, and from then on you're running under autolayout.

 A common place to create constraints is in a view's update-Constraints implementation (discussed later in this chapter). However, if there are no constraints to start with, updateConstraints won't be called. So you might need a way to bootstrap autolayout. That way is to implement the UIView class method requiresConstraintBasedLayout to return YES in some UIView subclass.

An autolayout constraint, or simply *constraint*, is an NSLayoutConstraint instance, and describes either the absolute width or height of a view or a relationship between an attribute of one view and an attribute of another view. In the latter case, the attributes don't have to be the same attribute, and the two views don't have to be siblings (subviews of the same superview) or parent and child (superview and subview) — the only requirement is that they share a common ancestor (a superview at some height up the view hierarchy).

Here are the chief properties of an NSLayoutConstraint:

firstItem
firstAttribute
secondItem
secondAttribute

The two views and their respective attributes involved in this constraint. If the constraint is describing a view's absolute height or width, the second view will be nil and the second attribute will be NSLayoutAttributeNotAnAttribute (which you'll probably write as 0). Additional attribute types are:

- NSLayoutAttributeLeft
- NSLayoutAttributeRight
- NSLayoutAttributeTop
- NSLayoutAttributeBottom
- NSLayoutAttributeLeading
- NSLayoutAttributeTrailing
- NSLayoutAttributeWidth
- NSLayoutAttributeHeight
- NSLayoutAttributeCenterX
- NSLayoutAttributeCenterY

- NSLayoutAttributeBaseline

The meanings of the attributes are intuitively obvious, except that you might be wondering about what "leading" and "trailing" mean: they are the international equivalent of "left" and "right", automatically reversing their meaning on systems whose language is written right-to-left (making it easy, say, to align the beginnings of several labels of different lengths, irrespective of localization).

multiplier
constant

Numbers to be applied to the second attribute's value to determine the first attribute's value. The multiplier is multiplied by the second attribute's value; the constant is added to that product. (The name *constant* is a very poor choice, as this value isn't constant; have the Apple folks never heard the term *addend*?) Basically, you're writing an equation of the form $a_1 = ma_2 + c$, where a_1 and a_2 are the two attributes, and m and c are the multiplier and the constant. Thus, in the most degenerate case, when the first attribute's value is to equal the second attribute's value, the multiplier will be 1 and the constant will be 0.

relation

How the two attribute values are to be related to one another, as modified by the multiplier and the constant. This is the operator that goes in the spot where I put the equal sign in the equation in the preceding paragraph. It might be an equal sign (NSLayoutRelationEqual, which you'll probably write as 0), but then again it might not; inequalities are also permitted (NSLayoutRelationLessThanOrEqual, NSLayoutRelationGreaterThanOrEqual).

priority

Priority values range from 1000 (required) down to 1, and certain standard behaviors have standard priorities. Constraints can have different priorities, determining the order in which they are applied. Constraints are permitted to conflict with one another provided they have different priorities.

A constraint belongs to a view. A view can have many constraints: a UIView has a constraints property, along with instance methods addConstraint:, addConstraints:, removeConstraint, and removeConstraints:.

The question then is *which* view a given constraint should belong to. The answer is absolute: it is the *closest superview* of both views involved in a constraint. Thus, for example, if the constraint dictates a view's absolute width, it belongs to that view; if it aligns the tops of two sibling views, it belongs to their superview; if it sets the top of a view in relation to the top of its superview, it belongs to the superview. The runtime may permit you to cheat and add a constraint at too high a level, but adding a constraint that refers to a view outside the subview hierarchy of the view to which you add it will cause a crash (with a helpful error message).

Both views involved in a constraint must be present in the view hierarchy before the constraint can be added.

NSLayoutConstraint properties are read-only, except for `priority` and `constant`. In Chapter 17, it will turn out that changing a constraint's `constant` in real time is a good way to animate a view. If you want to change anything else about a constraint, you must remove the constraint and add a new one.

If you use constraints, and if a view is created either in code or in a nib where "Use autolayout" is unchecked, that view's `autoresizingMask` is automatically translated into constraint form and applied in addition to any constraints you apply. It isn't one of the view's `constraints`, but it's operating as a set of constraints anyway. If that isn't what you want — that is, if *only* the constraints you apply are to be treated as constraints — you must explicitly turn off this behavior by setting the view's `translatesAutoresizing-MaskIntoConstraints` property to NO, because the default is YES.

 It may seem inconvenient to have to keep turning off `translates-AutoresizingMaskIntoConstraints`; why is the default YES? For a very good reason: that's what allows you to use autolayout for some views and autoresizing for others. If a minimum of just one view has a minimum of just one explicit constraint, the *entire* autolayout system springs to life throughout your entire interface. This doesn't cause havoc, because all the views without explicit constraints have `translates-AutoresizingMaskIntoConstraints` turned on by default, so their autoresizing masks are implicitly translated into constraints (hence the name!) and the layout dictated by those autoresizing masks continues to work.

We are now ready to write some code involving constraints! I'll generate the same views and subviews and layout behavior as in Figure 14-12 and Figure 14-13, but using constraints:

```
UIView* v1 = [[UIView alloc] initWithFrame:CGRectMake(100, 111, 132, 194)];
v1.backgroundColor = [UIColor colorWithRed:1 green:.4 blue:1 alpha:1];
UIView* v2 = [UIView new];
UIView* v3 = [UIView new];
v2.backgroundColor = [UIColor colorWithRed:.5 green:1 blue:0 alpha:1];
v3.backgroundColor = [UIColor colorWithRed:1 green:0 blue:0 alpha:1];
[self.window.rootViewController.view addSubview: v1];
[v1 addSubview: v2];
[v1 addSubview: v3];

v2.translatesAutoresizingMaskIntoConstraints = NO;
v3.translatesAutoresizingMaskIntoConstraints = NO;
[v1 addConstraint:
 [NSLayoutConstraint
```

```
    constraintWithItem:v2 attribute:NSLayoutAttributeLeft
    relatedBy:0
    toItem:v1 attribute:NSLayoutAttributeLeft
    multiplier:1 constant:0]];
[v1 addConstraint:
 [NSLayoutConstraint
  constraintWithItem:v2 attribute:NSLayoutAttributeRight
  relatedBy:0
  toItem:v1 attribute:NSLayoutAttributeRight
  multiplier:1 constant:0]];
[v1 addConstraint:
 [NSLayoutConstraint
  constraintWithItem:v2 attribute:NSLayoutAttributeTop
  relatedBy:0
  toItem:v1 attribute:NSLayoutAttributeTop
  multiplier:1 constant:0]];
[v2 addConstraint:
 [NSLayoutConstraint
  constraintWithItem:v2 attribute:NSLayoutAttributeHeight
  relatedBy:0
  toItem:nil attribute:0
  multiplier:1 constant:10]];
[v3 addConstraint:
 [NSLayoutConstraint
  constraintWithItem:v3 attribute:NSLayoutAttributeWidth
  relatedBy:0
  toItem:nil attribute:0
  multiplier:1 constant:20]];
[v3 addConstraint:
 [NSLayoutConstraint
  constraintWithItem:v3 attribute:NSLayoutAttributeHeight
  relatedBy:0
  toItem:nil attribute:0
  multiplier:1 constant:20]];
[v1 addConstraint:
 [NSLayoutConstraint
  constraintWithItem:v3 attribute:NSLayoutAttributeRight
  relatedBy:0
  toItem:v1 attribute:NSLayoutAttributeRight
  multiplier:1 constant:0]];
[v1 addConstraint:
 [NSLayoutConstraint
  constraintWithItem:v3 attribute:NSLayoutAttributeBottom
  relatedBy:0
  toItem:v1 attribute:NSLayoutAttributeBottom
  multiplier:1 constant:0]];
```

Now, I know what you're thinking. You're thinking: "What are you, nuts? That is a boatload of code!" (Except that you probably used another four-letter word instead of "boat".) But that's something of an illusion. I'd argue that what we're doing here is actually *simpler* than the code with which we created Figure 14-12 through autoresizing:

- We create eight constraints in eight commands; I've broken each command into multiple lines, but that's just a matter of formatting. They're verbose, but they are the same command repeated with different parameters, so creating them is just a matter of copy-and-paste.

- It looks as though just two commands (setting the autoresizing masks of the two subviews) have been replaced by eight commands. But we're getting more bang for our buck than that: we're no longer assigning v2 and v3 an initial frame! The constraints describe the positions of those views from the outset, and this, in constraint terms, remains their position *even as their superview is resized*. So constraints replace *both* setting a view's autoresizing mask *and* setting its frame (or bounds and center) as a way of describing its layout.

- Constraints are a far clearer expression of what's supposed to happen than setting the autoresizing mask.

- Constraints are also a far clearer expression of a subview's position than setting its frame! For example, in describing v3's position, we don't have to use any math to place its frame origin. Recall what we had to say before:

```
v3 = [[UIView alloc] initWithFrame:CGRectMake(v1.bounds.size.width-20,
                                              v1.bounds.size.height-20,
                                              20, 20)];
```

That business of subtracting the view's height and width from its superview's bounds height and width in order to place the view is skanky and error-prone. With constraints, we can speak the truth directly; our code says, plainly and simply, "v3 is 20 points wide and 20 points high and it's flush with the bottom right corner of v1".

In addition, constraints can express things that autoresizing can't. For example, instead of applying an absolute height to v2, we could require that its height be exactly one-tenth of v1's height, regardless of how v1 is resized. That sort of thing is utterly impossible without constraints (unless you implement layoutSubviews and enforce it manually, in code).

If you really find our code too verbose, it may be possible to condense it somewhat. Instead of creating each constraint individually, we can sometimes describe multiple constraints simultaneously through a sort of text-based shorthand, called a *visual format*. The shorthand is best understood by example:

```
@"V:|[v2(10)]"
```

In that expression, V: means that the vertical dimension is under discussion; the alternative is H:, which is also the default (so it is permitted to specify no dimension). A view's name appears in square brackets, and a pipe (|) signifies the superview, so here we're describing v2's top edge as butting up against its superview's top edge. Numeric dimensions appear in parentheses, and a numeric dimension accompanying a view's name sets that dimension of that view, so here we're also taking advantage of this specification of the vertical dimension to set v2's height to 10.

To use a visual format, you have to provide a dictionary mapping the string name of each view mentioned to the actual view. For example, the dictionary accompanying the preceding expression might be @{@"v2":v2}. We can form this dictionary automatically with a macro, NSDictionaryOfVariableBindings, which takes a list of variable names. So here's another way of expressing of the preceding code example, using the visual format shorthand throughout:

```
UIView* v1 = [[UIView alloc] initWithFrame:CGRectMake(100, 111, 132, 194)];
v1.backgroundColor = [UIColor colorWithRed:1 green:.4 blue:1 alpha:1];
UIView* v2 = [UIView new];
UIView* v3 = [UIView new];
v2.backgroundColor = [UIColor colorWithRed:.5 green:1 blue:0 alpha:1];
v3.backgroundColor = [UIColor colorWithRed:1 green:0 blue:0 alpha:1];
[self.window.rootViewController.view addSubview: v1];
[v1 addSubview: v2];
[v1 addSubview: v3];

NSDictionary *vs = NSDictionaryOfVariableBindings(v2,v3);
v2.translatesAutoresizingMaskIntoConstraints = NO;
v3.translatesAutoresizingMaskIntoConstraints = NO;
[v1 addConstraints:
 [NSLayoutConstraint
  constraintsWithVisualFormat:@"H:|[v2]|"
  options:0 metrics:nil views:vs]];
[v1 addConstraints:
 [NSLayoutConstraint
  constraintsWithVisualFormat:@"V:|[v2(10)]"
  options:0 metrics:nil views:vs]];
[v1 addConstraints:
 [NSLayoutConstraint
  constraintsWithVisualFormat:@"H:[v3(20)]|"
  options:0 metrics:nil views:vs]];
[v1 addConstraints:
 [NSLayoutConstraint
  constraintsWithVisualFormat:@"V:[v3(20)]|"
  options:0 metrics:nil views:vs]];
```

That example creates the same constraints as the previous example, but in four commands instead of eight.

The visual format syntax shows itself to best advantage when multiple views are laid out in relation to one another along the same dimension; in that situation, you get a lot of bang for your buck (many constraints generated by one visual format string). The syntax, however, is somewhat limited in what constraints it can express; it conceals the number and exact nature of the constraints that it produces; and personally I find it easier to make a mistake with the visual format syntax than with the complete expression of each constraint. Still, you'll want to become familiar with it, not least because console messages describing a constraint sometimes use it.

Here are some further things to know when generating constraints with the visual format syntax:

- The metrics: parameter is a dictionary of NSNumber values. This lets you use a name in the visual format string where a numeric value needs to go.

- The options: parameter is a bitmask letting you do things like add alignments. The alignments you specify are applied to all the views mentioned in the visual format string.

- To specify the distance between two successive views, use hyphens surrounding the numeric value, like this: @"[v1]-20-[v2]". The numeric value may optionally be surrounded by parentheses. A single hyphen means that a default distance should be used.

- A numeric value in parentheses may be preceded by an equality or inequality operator, and may be followed by an at sign with a priority. Multiple numeric values, separated by comma, may appear in parentheses together. For example: @"[v1(>=20@400,<=30)]".

You can make two major kinds of mistake with constraints:

Conflict
> You can apply constraints that can't be satisfied simultaneously. This will be reported in the console (at great length). Only required constraints (priority 1000) can contribute to a conflict, as the runtime is free to ignore lower-priority constraints that it can't satisfy. For example, to the previous code, append this line:

```
[v1 addConstraints:
 [NSLayoutConstraint
  constraintsWithVisualFormat:@"V:[v3(10)]|"
  options:0 metrics:nil views:vs]];
```

> The height of v3 can't be both 10 (as here) and 20 (as in the preceding line). The runtime reports the conflict, and tells you which constraints are causing it.

Underdetermination (ambiguity)
> You haven't supplied sufficient information to determine the size and position of some view. This is a far more insidious problem, because nothing bad may seem to happen, so you might not discover it until much later. If you're lucky, the view will at least fail to appear, or will appear in an undesirable place, alerting you to the problem. For example, in the last line of the previous code, we set the height of v3 to 20; suppose we remove that specification:

```
[v1 addConstraints:
 [NSLayoutConstraint
  constraintsWithVisualFormat:@"V:[v3]|"
  options:0 metrics:nil views:vs]];
```

Fortunately, v3 fails to appear in the interface, so we know we've made a mistake.

To help you analyze ambiguity, log a view's hasAmbiguousLayout property (a BOOL); be sure to remove that call before submitting your app to the App Store. Alternatively, pause the running app and ask the debugger for the key window's _autolayoutTrace; ambiguously laid out views are clearly marked:

```
(lldb) po [[UIWindow keyWindow] _autolayoutTrace]
(id) $1 = 0x074a41a0
*<UIWindow:0x749b890>
|   *<UIView:0x749ccb0>
|   |   *<UIView:0x749c280>
|   |   |   *<UIView:0x749c790>
|   |   |   *<UIView:0x749c930> - AMBIGUOUS LAYOUT
```

I find it useful to set up a category on NSLayoutConstraint with a method that lets me check a view and all its subviews at any depth for ambiguity:

```
@implementation NSLayoutConstraint (Ambiguity)
+ (void) reportAmbiguity:(UIView*) v {
    if (nil == v)
        v = [[UIApplication sharedApplication] keyWindow];
    for (UIView* vv in v.subviews) {
        NSLog(@"%@ %i", vv, vv.hasAmbiguousLayout);
        if (vv.subviews.count)
            [self reportAmbiguity:vv];
    }
}
@end
```

Given the notions of conflict and ambiguity, we can understand what priorities are for. Imagine that all constraints have been placed in boxes, where each box is a priority value, in descending order. The first box (1000) contains all the required constraints, so all required constraints are obeyed first. (If they conflict, that's bad, and a report appears in the log; meanwhile, the system implicitly lowers the priority of one of the conflicting constraints, so that it doesn't have to obey it and can continue with layout by satisfying the remaining required constraints.) If there still isn't enough information to perform unambiguous layout given the required priorities alone, we pull the constraints out of the next box and try to obey them. If we can, consistently with what we've already done, fine; if we can't, or if ambiguity remains, we look in the *next* box — and so on. For a box after the first, we don't care about obeying exactly the constraints it contains; if an ambiguity remains, we can use a lower-priority constraint value to give us something to aim at, resolving the ambiguity, without fully obeying the lower-priority constraint's desires. For example, an inequality is an ambiguity, because an infinite number of values will satisfy it; a lower-priority equality can tell us what value to prefer, resolving the ambiguity, but there's no conflict even if we can't fully achieve that preferred value.

Some built-in interface objects have an inherent size in one or both dimensions, so they are not ambiguously laid out even if no explicit NSLayoutConstraint dictates their size. Rather, the inherent size is used to generate constraints implicitly. For example, a button has a standard height, and its width is determined by its title. This inherent size is the object's *intrinsic content size*. You can supply an intrinsic size in your own custom UI-View subclass by implementing `intrinsicContentSize`. If you need the runtime to call `intrinsicContentSize` again, because that size has changed and the view needs to be laid out afresh, send your view the `invalidateIntrinsicContentSize` message.

The tendency of an interface object to size itself to its intrinsic content size can conflict with its tendency to obey explicit constraints. For example, we wouldn't want a UILabel to extend out of its superview, no matter how long its text may be; if the text isn't permitted to wrap, it should be truncated. Therefore these tendencies have a priority:

`contentHuggingPriorityForAxis:`
> The tendency of a view to refuse to grow larger than its intrinsic size in this dimension. The default is 250 (also known as `UILayoutPriorityDefaultLow`).

`contentCompressionResistancePriorityForAxis:`
> The tendency of a view to refuse to shrink smaller than its intrinsic size in this dimension. The default is 750 (also known as `UILayoutPriorityDefaultHigh`).

(The dimensions are `UILayoutConstraintAxisHorizontal` and `UILayoutConstraint-AxisVertical`.) Those methods are getters; there are corresponding setters. You're unlikely, however, to change the priorities for these tendencies — at least, you're unlikely to change them by much. A situation where you *would* possibly need to change them is when two views with an intrinsic content size are pinned to one another. This can result in an ambiguity. Of two adjacent labels, which should be truncated if the superview gets narrower? To dictate the answer, it suffices to raise the compression resistance priority of one of the labels by a single point.

Another common situation is where you'll want to lower the priority of some other constraint, to allow intrinsic content size to predominate. An example that Apple gives is a label to the left of a centered button: the button's bottom is pinned to the superview's bottom, and the label and button are pinned to one another with their baselines aligned, and the button's horizontal center is pinned to its superview's horizontal center. If the label's text grows longer (or the superview's width grows narrower), the label should not stretch leftward past the left side of its superview, so it has an inequality constraint pinning its left at a guaranteed minimum distance from the superview's left. But the text should not then be truncated if it doesn't have to be, so the priority with which the button is horizontally centered is made lower than the label's compression resistance priority:

```
self.button.translatesAutoresizingMaskIntoConstraints = NO;
self.label.translatesAutoresizingMaskIntoConstraints = NO;
id button = self.button;
id label = self.label;

NSDictionary* d = NSDictionaryOfVariableBindings(button,label);
[self.view addConstraints:
 [NSLayoutConstraint
  constraintsWithVisualFormat:@"V:[button]-|"
  options:0 metrics:nil views:d]];
[self.view addConstraints:
 [NSLayoutConstraint
  constraintsWithVisualFormat:@"H:|-(>=10)-[label]-[button]-(>=10)-|"
  options:NSLayoutFormatAlignAllBaseline metrics:nil views:d]];
NSLayoutConstraint* con =
 [NSLayoutConstraint
  constraintWithItem:button attribute:NSLayoutAttributeCenterX
  relatedBy:0
  toItem:self.view attribute:NSLayoutAttributeCenterX
  multiplier:1 constant:0];
con.priority = 700;
[self.view addConstraint:con];
```

Behind the scenes, compression resistance and content hugging work like this: Suppose the view's intrinsic width is 100 points. Then two implicit constraints are generated, an inequality saying that the view's width should be greater than or equal to 100 points, but with a priority of 750, and an inequality saying that the view's width should be less than or equal to 100 points, but with a priority of 250. All other things being equal, the view's width will be exactly 100 points, as this satisfies both inequalities unambiguously. But higher-priority constraints could cause the width to be less or greater. In the preceding example, as the label's text becomes longer, its intrinsic width grows. The first inequality says we may make the label's width greater than its intrinsic width, at a priority of 750, but the button's tenacity to hold its position in the center is even less, at a priority of 700, so the label adopts its intrinsic width and the button shifts right to obey the spacing constraint between them (which is required). But there is also an inequality spacing constraint on the button's right side (which is also required); eventually the button moves so far to the right that it can move no further without violating that constraint, which is impossible. At that point, since the first inequality cannot be satisfied, the second inequality is consulted; it permits the label to be narrower than its intrinsic content, the label stops growing to match its growing intrinsic width, and its text is truncated instead.

Constraints in the Nib

In a nib where "Use autolayout" is checked, when you add a view to a superview or move or resize it within its superview, the nib editor adds constraints. A constraint is an object, so these are nib objects. Constraints in the nib are visible in three places:

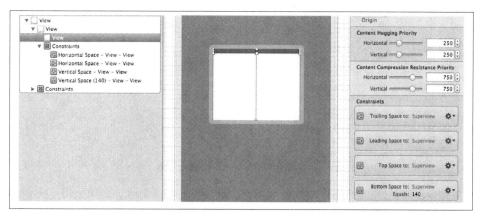

Figure 14-14. A view's constraints displayed in the nib

In the expanded dock

Constraints are listed in a special category, "Constraints", under the view to which they belong. You'll have a much easier time distinguishing these constraints if you give your views meaningful labels! (See Chapter 7.) Select a constraint and show the Attributes inspector to view its numeric value, its priority, and so on.

In the canvas

Constraints appear graphically as dimension lines. Select a constraint and show the Attributes inspector to view its numeric value, its priority, and so on.

In the Size inspector

When a view involved in any constraints is selected, the Size inspector displays those constraints, along with the view's content hugging priority and compression resistance priority in each dimension. For example, in Figure 14-14, I've started to set up a view and a subview like v1 and v2 in the earlier code example; the subview is selected, so its constraints are shown in the Size inspector.

The nib editor's automatic creation of constraints in the nib is clever, but it presents two major challenges:

- It doesn't know what you really intend to have happen if a view's superview is resized at runtime.

- It won't let you create, even temporarily, an ambiguous or conflicted layout — but it *will* let you create a layout that could generate a conflict if a superview is resized at runtime.

As a result, you'll often find yourself trying to correct a misapprehension on the nib editor's part, and you'll find that this can be quite tricky. Figure 14-14 shows a case in point. Of the automatically generated constraints affecting the subview, three are correct

— the left, right, and top space between the subview and its superview — but the fourth is not. Xcode has created a constraint describing the space between the bottom of the subview and the bottom of the superview; I want that space free to change. Instead, I want to fix the subview's height (at 10 points). But Xcode won't let me delete the unwanted constraint, because that would cause ambiguous layout.

The solution is to create the new constraint first. To do so, select the affected view(s) and choose from the Editor → Align or Editor → Pin menu (or use the first or second pop-up menu in the floating cartouche at the lower right of the canvas). In this case, we want to constrain the subview's height to its current height, so we select the subview and choose Editor → Pin → Height.

This generates an additional constraint. Unfortunately we now have a potential conflict. Our subview has a height constraint of 10 points; meanwhile, its top is still pinned to the top of its superview, and its bottom is still pinned to the bottom of its superview. Xcode permits this situation because it is legal *now*, but if the superview's height changes at runtime, it won't be possible to satisfy all of those constraints; something needs to give. In this situation, you can do one of three things:

Delete the unwanted constraint
> In this case, that's the simplest solution. We can select the constraint that pins the bottom of the subview to the bottom of its superview and delete it. In more complicated situations, though, the nib editor might not permit that.

Lower the priority of the unwanted constraint
> If the unwanted constraint has a low enough priority, it will have no effect on the layout. You can lower the constraint's priority by selecting the constraint and adjusting the Priority slider in the Attributes inspector.

Remove the unwanted constraint in code
> If you're really desperate, you can make an outlet to the unwanted constraint and use this to remove the constraint in code after the nib loads (but before layout actually takes place). I've found myself in situations so complex that this was my only recourse; I simply couldn't bully the nib editor into letting me do what I wanted, even though that wouldn't have resulted in an ambiguous layout.

Another maddening feature of the nib editor is its tendency to change what's selected. For example, when you select the subview and choose Editor → Pin → Height, the newly created constraint is selected instead of the subview. If what you're trying to do is create several constraints having to do with a certain view, Xcode keeps deselecting the view and you have to keep reselecting it.

The nib editor, like the visual format syntax, can't specify every possible constraint. For example, you can't express a multiplier, or a relationship between one view and another that isn't its sibling or superview. Sometimes there's no alternative to adding or adjusting a constraint in code after the nib loads.

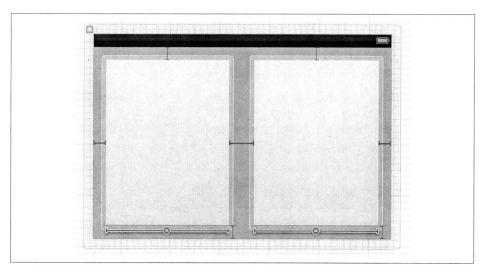

Figure 14-15. An equal widths constraint configured in the nib

Still, once you get used to it, you'll find that being able to set up constraints in the nib is really nice. It's quite easy to construct an interface that keeps working correctly when the app launches on the iPhone 5 (with its taller screen) vs. the iPhone 4, or when the app is rotated. Figure 14-15 shows two subviews with their superview margins set and configured to have their widths equal to one another. This was easily attained by selecting both views and choosing Editor → Pin → Widths Equally. The result, which looks great both on the iPhone 5 and on the iPhone 4, requires no code; without constraints, only manual layout (in `layoutSubviews`) could have achieved the same thing.

Here's how to achieve in code the constraints created by the nib in Figure 14-15 (in the view controller's `viewDidLoad`). Presume that we are starting with a nib where "Use autolayout" is unchecked, so it contains no constraints; and presume we have outlets to the two subviews, `v1` and `v2`:

```
UIView* sup = self.view;
v1.translatesAutoresizingMaskIntoConstraints = NO;
v2.translatesAutoresizingMaskIntoConstraints = NO;
NSDictionary* d = NSDictionaryOfVariableBindings(sup, v1, v2);
[sup addConstraints:
 [NSLayoutConstraint
  constraintsWithVisualFormat:@"|-[v1]-(40)-[v2(==v1)]-|"
  options:0 metrics:0 views:d]];
[sup addConstraints:
 [NSLayoutConstraint
  constraintsWithVisualFormat:@"V:|-[v1]-|"
  options:0 metrics:0 views:d]];
```

```
[sup addConstraints:
 [NSLayoutConstraint
  constraintsWithVisualFormat:@"V:|-[v2]-|"
  options:0 metrics:0 views:d]];
```

I'll modify that same code to illustrate the notion of removing and adding constraints in code after the nib loads. Presume this time that our nib's "Use autolayout" is checked. But let's pretend that we can't set up the horizontal spacing and width constraints in the nib; instead, both subviews have all four edges pinned to the corresponding edge of the superview. We already have outlets v1 and v2 to the two subviews; in addition, we create outlets cons1 and cons2 to the two unwanted constraints — the left subview's right constraint and the right subview's left constraint. Then, in the view controller's viewDid-Load, we simply remove those constraints and replace them with what we really want:

```
UIView* sup = self.view;
[sup removeConstraints:@[cons1, cons2]];
NSDictionary* d = NSDictionaryOfVariableBindings(sup, v1, v2);
[sup addConstraints:
 [NSLayoutConstraint
  constraintsWithVisualFormat:@"|-[v1]-(40)-[v2(==v1)]-|"
  options:0 metrics:0 views:d]];
```

Another situation in which the nib editor may misunderstand what you intend is when a view has an intrinsic size. Should a label or a button, for example, be assigned an explicit width constraint, or should its width be governed by its intrinsic size? Xcode tries to guess which you want, based on the signals you give it; so it helps to know what signals Xcode is watching for. If you set a view's size explicitly, Xcode will probably assume that you want an explicit size constraint. If you select a view and choose Editor → Size to Fit Content, Xcode will remove the view's explicit size constraints, letting the intrinsic size predominate.

You can't turn off autolayout for just part of a nib. Either all views have constraints or all views use autoresizing. There's no nib equivalent to the translatesAutoresizingMaskIntoConstraints property for an individual view. A workaround, if you're bent on generating different parts of your interface in nibs, one part with autoresizing, another part with autolayout, is to separate those parts into different nibs and then combine them at runtime.

If a nib's "Use autolayout" is checked, do not load it on any system earlier than iOS 6. If you do, your app will crash, because you're using a class, NSLayoutConstraint, that doesn't exist before iOS 6. Unfortunately, "Use autolayout" *is* checked, by default, in all nibs created in Xcode 4.5 and later.

Order of Layout Events

When the moment comes to lay out a view, the following events take place:

1. The view and its subviews are sent `updateConstraints`, starting at the *bottom* of the hierarchy (the deepest subview) and working up to the top (the view itself, possibly the root view). This event may be omitted for a view if its constraints have not changed.

   You can override `updateConstraints` in a subclass. You might do this, for example, if your subclass is capable of altering its own constraints and you need a signal that now is the time to do so. You must call `super` or the app will crash (with a helpful error message). You should never call `updateConstraints`; to trigger an immediate call to `updateConstraints`, send a view the `updateConstraintsIfNeeded` message.

   If you're not using autolayout, `updateConstraints` by default won't be sent to your view as part of the layout process. If you want it to be sent, send `setNeedsUpdateConstraints` to the view. You'll then get `updateConstraints` events from then on, whenever layout is to be performed.

2. The view and its subviews are sent `layoutSubviews`, starting at the *top* of the hierarchy (the view itself, possibly the root view) and working down to the bottom (the deepest subview).

   You can override `layoutSubviews` in a subclass in order to take a hand in the layout process. If you're not using autolayout, `layoutSubviews` does nothing by default; `layoutSubviews` is your opportunity to perform manual layout after autoresizing has taken place. If you are using autolayout, you must call `super` or the app will crash (with a helpful error message). You should never call `layoutSubviews`; to trigger an immediate call to `layoutSubviews`, send a view the `layoutIfNeeded` message (which may cause layout of the entire view tree, not only below but also above this view), or send `setNeedsLayout` to trigger a call to `layoutSubviews` later on, after your code finishes running, when layout would normally take place.

When you're using autolayout, what happens in `layoutSubviews`? The runtime examines all the constraints affecting this view's subviews, works out values for their frames, and assigns those views those frames. In other words, `layoutSubviews` performs manual layout! The constraints are merely instructions attached to the views; `layoutSubviews` reads them and responds accordingly, setting frames in the good old-fashioned way.

Knowing this, you might override `layoutSubviews` when you're using autolayout, in order to tweak the outcome. First you call `super`, causing all the subviews to adopt their new frames. Then you examine those frames. If you don't like the outcome, you can change the situation, removing subviews, adding or removing constraints, and so on — and then you call super again, to get a new layout outcome.

Unless you explicitly demand immediate layout, layout isn't performed until your code finishes running (and then only if needed). Moreover, ambiguous layout isn't ambiguous until layout actually takes place. Thus, for example, it's perfectly reasonable to cause an ambiguous layout temporarily, provided you resolve the ambiguity before layout-Subviews is called. (Your last best opportunity to do this is in updateConstraints!) That's why it was legal for me, in the code at the end of the preceding section, to remove two constraints before adding some new ones; there was briefly an ambiguous layout situation, but no layout took place during that time.

On the other hand, a conflicting constraint conflicts the instant it is added. This code may cause a conflict report to appear in the log:

```
NSDictionary* d = NSDictionaryOfVariableBindings(sup, v1, v2);
[sup addConstraints:
 [NSLayoutConstraint
  constraintsWithVisualFormat:@"|-[v1]-(40)-[v2(==v1)]-|"
  options:0 metrics:0 views:d]];
[sup removeConstraints:@[cons1, cons2]];
```

If you try it and no conflict report appears, that's only because this code is in the view controller's viewDidLoad, which is called when the views in question are not yet part of the visible interface. If that same code were postponed to run at a later time, the add-Constraints: call would generate the conflict report. The moral is clear: remove constraints that need to be removed before adding new ones that need to be added.

It is also possible to *simulate* layout of a view in accordance with its constraints and those of its subviews. This is useful for discovering ahead of time what the view's size would be if layout were performed at this moment. Send the view the systemLayout-SizeFittingSize: message. The system will attempt to reach or at least approach the size you specify, at a very low priority; mostly likely you'll specify either UILayout-FittingCompressedSize or UILayoutFittingExpandedSize, depending on whether what you're after is the smallest or largest size the view can legally attain. I'll show an example in Chapter 21.

Autolayout and View Transforms

Suppose I apply to a view a transform that shrinks it to half its size:

```
v.transform = CGAffineTransformMakeScale(0.5,0.5);
```

I expect the view to shrink in both dimensions, toward its center. Instead, under auto-layout, I might see it shrink just its height, while its width holds steady, and instead of shrinking toward its center, it shrinks toward its bottom; and this could turn out to be because its width and bottom are determined by constraints.

The fact is that autolayout does not play well with view transforms. The reason, apparently, is that (as I explained in the preceding section) autolayout works by treating the constraints as a to-do list and obeying them in layoutSubviews by applying manual layout. If a constraint describes a view's frame by pinning one of its edges, then autolayout will set that view's frame. But setting a view's frame is exactly what you're *not* supposed to do when a view has a nonidentity transform.

 A further problem is that applying a transform to a view triggers layout immediately. This feels like a bug.

One possible solution is this: if a view is to be given a transform, then take it out of autolayout's influence altogether. In this code, I prepare to apply a transform to a view (self.otherView) by removing its constraints and any constraints of its superview (self.view) that affect it:

```
NSMutableArray* cons = [NSMutableArray array];
for (NSLayoutConstraint* con in self.view.constraints)
    if (con.firstItem == self.otherView || con.secondItem == self.otherView)
        [cons addObject:con];
[self.view removeConstraints:cons];
[self.otherView removeConstraints:self.otherView.constraints];
```

Unfortunately, this won't quite do, as otherView vanishes from the screen. The reason is that we are still using autolayout, and now otherView has no constraints whatever, so it has neither size nor position! To complete our code, we must prevent autolayout from using constraints as a way of positioning otherView, which we can do by bringing its autoresizing mask back into play:

```
self.otherView.translatesAutoresizingMaskIntoConstraints = YES;
```

The result is that otherView is now treated exactly as it was before autolayout existed, and a transform applied to it works correctly.

Perhaps, however, that approach seems too drastic, as we have completely lost the benefit of being able to position our view through constraints. An alternative might be to use only constraints that don't conflict with the transform we intend to apply. For example, if a view with an internally fixed width and height is positioned solely by pinning its center, then we can freely apply scale and rotation transforms to it, as these are applied around the view's center and thus don't conflict with the constraints that position it. Unfortunately, you probably won't be able to arrange that in a nib, so you'll have to use code to remove the existing constraints and then apply new ones:

```
// remove constraints affecting otherView's edges
NSMutableArray* cons = [NSMutableArray array];
for (NSLayoutConstraint* con in self.view.constraints)
    if (con.firstItem == self.otherView || con.secondItem == self.otherView)
```

```
        [cons addObject:con];
    [self.view removeConstraints:cons];
    // add constraints positioning otherView by its center
    [self.view addConstraint:
     [NSLayoutConstraint
      constraintWithItem:self.otherView attribute:NSLayoutAttributeCenterX
      relatedBy:0
      toItem:self.view attribute:NSLayoutAttributeLeft
      multiplier:1 constant:self.otherView.center.x]];
    [self.view addConstraint:
     [NSLayoutConstraint
      constraintWithItem:self.otherView attribute:NSLayoutAttributeCenterY
      relatedBy:0 toItem:self.view attribute:NSLayoutAttributeTop
      multiplier:1 constant:self.otherView.center.y]];
```

A further variant would be to use a host view and a subview. The host view is positioned by constraints, in the normal way: you can use the host view's edges as part of the overall constraint-based layout. But the host view is also invisible. Now we can apply either of the preceding two solutions to the host view's subview, which is visible. Either the subview has a fixed width and height, and is pinned by its center to the host view's center, in which case scale and rotation transforms can be applied to it, or else we take the subview out of the influence of autolayout altogether, in which case any transform can be applied to it.

Still another solution is to use a layer transform (Chapter 16) instead of a view transform, since applying a layer transform doesn't trigger layout.

CHAPTER 15

Drawing

Many UIView subclasses, such as a UIButton or a UITextField, know how to draw themselves; sooner or later, though, you're going to want to do some drawing of your own. A class like UIImageView will display a static image; you can generate that image dynamically by drawing it in code. And a pure UIView does little or no drawing of its own; you can draw its appearance.

Drawing is not difficult, but it is a very large topic. This chapter will make you comfortable with the basic principles, so that you can consult and understand Apple's documentation when you need further details.

UIImage and UIImageView

The basic general UIKit image class is UIImage. UIImage can read a file from disk, so if an image does not need to be created dynamically, but has already been created before your app runs, then drawing may be as simple as providing an image file as a resource in your app's bundle. The system knows how to work with many standard image file types, such as TIFF, JPEG, GIF, and PNG. You can also obtain image data in some other way, such as by downloading it, and transform this into a UIImage. Conversely, you can draw your own image for display in your interface or for saving to disk (image file output is discussed in Chapter 36).

In the very simplest case, an image file in your app's bundle can be obtained through the UIImage class method `imageNamed:`. This method looks at the top level of your app's bundle for an image file with the supplied name, including the file extension, and reads it as a UIImage instance. A nice thing about this approach is that memory management is handled for you: the image data may be cached in memory, and if you ask for the same image by calling `imageNamed:` again later, the cached data may be supplied immediately. You can also read an image file from anywhere in your app's bundle using the class method `imageWithContentsOfFile:` or the instance method `initWith-`

`ContentsOfFile:`, both of which expect a pathname string; you can get a reference to your app's bundle with [`NSBundle mainBundle`], and NSBundle then provides instance methods for getting the pathname of a file within the bundle, such as `pathForResource:ofType:`.

Many built-in Cocoa interface objects will accept a UIImage as part of how they draw themselves; for example, a UIButton can display an image, and a UINavigationBar or a UITabBar can have a background image. I'll discuss those in Chapter 25. But when you simply want an image to appear in your interface, you'll probably hand it to a UIImageView, which has the most knowledge and flexibility with regard to displaying images and is intended for this purpose. If a UIImageView instance begins life in a nib and is to display a UIImage from a file in your app's bundle, you won't even need any code; the UIImageView can be set to that file directly in the nib. (This mechanism works most easily if the file will be at the top level of the app's bundle.)

A UIImageView can actually have *two* images, one assigned to its `image` property and the other assigned to its `highlightedImage` property; the value of the UIImageView's `highlighted` property dictates which of the two is displayed. A UIImageView does not automatically highlight itself, the way a button does, for example, merely because the user taps it. However, there are certain situations where a UIImageView will respond to the highlighting of its surroundings; for example, within a table view cell, a UIImageView will show its highlighted image when the cell is highlighted. You can, of course, also use the notion of UIImageView highlighting yourself however you like.

When an image is obtained by name from the bundle, as with `imageNamed:` or the name you enter in the nib for a UIImageView's image, a file with the same name extended by `~ipad` will automatically be used if the app is running on an iPad. You can use this in a universal app to supply different images automatically depending on whether the app runs on an iPhone or iPod touch, on the one hand, or on an iPad, on the other. This is true not just for images but for *any* resource obtained by name from the bundle. See Apple's *Resource Programming Guide*.

Similarly, on a device with a double-resolution screen, when an image is obtained by name from the bundle, a file with the same name extended by `@2x`, if there is one, will be used automatically, with the resulting UIImage marked as double-resolution by assigning it a `scale` property value of `2.0`. In this way, your app can contain both a single-resolution and a double-resolution version of an image file; on the double-resolution display device, the double-resolution version of the image is used, and is drawn at the same size as the single-resolution image. Thus, on the double-resolution screen, your code continues to work without change, but your images look sharper.

A UIImageView is a UIView, so it can have a background color in addition to its image, it can have an alpha (transparency) value, and so forth (see Chapter 14). A UIImageView without a background color is invisible except for its image, so the image simply appears

Figure 15-1. Mars appears in my interface

in the interface, without the user being aware that it resides in a rectangular host. An image may have areas that are transparent, and a UIImageView will respect this; thus an image of any shape can appear. A UIImageView without an image and without a background color is invisible, so you could start with an empty UIImageView in the place where you will later need an image and subsequently assign the image in code. You can assign a new image to substitute one image for another.

How a UIImageView draws its image depends upon the setting of its `contentMode` property. (The `contentMode` property is inherited from UIView; I'll discuss its more general purpose later in this chapter.) For example, `UIViewContentModeScaleToFill` means the image's width and height are set to the width and height of the view, thus filling the view completely even if this alters the image's aspect ratio; `UIViewContent-ModeCenter` means the image is drawn centered in the view without altering its size. The best way to get a feel for the meanings of the various `contentMode` settings is to assign a UIImageView a small image in a nib and then, in the Attributes inspector, change the Mode pop-up menu, and see where and how the image draws itself.

When creating a UIImageView in code, you can take advantage of a convenience initializer, `initWithImage:` (or `initWithImage:highlightedImage:`). The default `contentMode` is `UIViewContentModeScaleToFill`, but the image is not initially scaled; rather, the view itself is sized to match to the image. You will still probably need to position the UIImageView correctly in its superview. In this example, I'll put a picture of the planet Mars in the center of the app's interface (Figure 15-1):

```
UIImageView* iv =
    [[UIImageView alloc] initWithImage:[UIImage imageNamed:@"Mars.png"]];
[self.window.rootViewController.view addSubview: iv];
iv.center = CGPointMake(CGRectGetMidX(iv.superview.bounds),
                        CGRectGetMidY(iv.superview.bounds));
iv.frame = CGRectIntegral(iv.frame);
```

If we have a second image file called *Mars@2x.png*, it will be used on a double-resolution device.

Under autolayout (Chapter 14), the size of an image assigned to a UIImageView becomes that UIImageView's `intrinsicContentSize` — even if the UIImageView already exists. This can lead to new behavior if your code adopts autolayout. Previously, assigning an image to an existing UIImageView (as opposed to creating the UIImageView with `initWithImage:`) had no effect on the UIImageView's bounds; under autolayout, it calls `setNeedsLayout` and, at layout time, the UIImageView's bounds are changed. Thus, this code, too, will display Mars in the center of the interface:

```
UIImageView* iv = [UIImageView new];
[self.window.rootViewController.view addSubview: iv];
iv.translatesAutoresizingMaskIntoConstraints = NO;
[iv.superview addConstraint:
 [NSLayoutConstraint
  constraintWithItem:iv attribute:NSLayoutAttributeCenterX
  relatedBy:0
  toItem:iv.superview attribute:NSLayoutAttributeCenterX
  multiplier:1 constant:0]];
[iv.superview addConstraint:
 [NSLayoutConstraint
  constraintWithItem:iv attribute:NSLayoutAttributeCenterY
  relatedBy:0
  toItem:iv.superview attribute:NSLayoutAttributeCenterY
  multiplier:1 constant:0]];
iv.image = [UIImage imageNamed:@"Mars.png"];
```

(If a UIImageView is assigned both an `image` and a `highlightedImage`, and if they are of different sizes, the view's `intrinsicContentSize` adopts the size of `image`.)

A UIImage can be transformed into a *resizable image*, by sending it the `resizableImageWithCapInsets:resizingMode:` message. (This method is new in iOS 6, superseding the less flexible `resizableImageWithCapInsets:` introduced in iOS 5 — which itself superseded the notion of a stretchable image from previous system versions.) The `capInsets:` argument is a UIEdgeInsets, a struct consisting of four floats representing inset values starting at the top and moving *counterclockwise* — top, left, bottom, right. They represent distances inwards from the edges of the image. In a context (such as a UIImageView) larger than the image, a resizable image can behave in one of two ways, depending on the `resizingMode:` value:

UIImageResizingModeTile
> The interior rectangle of the inset area is tiled (repeated) in the interior; each edge is formed by tiling the corresponding edge rectangle outside the inset area. The four corner rectangles outside the inset area are shown unchanged at the four corners.

UIImageResizingModeStretch
> The interior rectangle of the inset area is stretched *once* to fill the interior; each edge is formed by stretching the corresponding edge rectangle outside the inset area *once*. The four corner rectangles outside the inset area are shown unchanged at the four corners.

Resizable images may seem like a curiosity at first, but in fact they are extremely useful. Some places in the interface require them; for example, a custom image that serves as

Figure 15-2. Tiling the entire image of Mars

the background of a slider or progress view (Chapter 25) must be resizable, so that it can fill a space of any length. And there can frequently be situations where you want to fill a background by tiling a texture or by extending an existing image.

First, I'll illustrate tiling:

```
UIImage* mars = [UIImage imageNamed:@"Mars.png"];
UIImage* marsTiled = [mars resizableImageWithCapInsets:UIEdgeInsetsZero
                    resizingMode: UIImageResizingModeTile];
UIImageView* iv = [[UIImageView alloc] initWithFrame:
                    CGRectMake(20,5,mars.size.width*2,mars.size.height*4)];
iv.image = marsTiled;
```

The image view is eight times the size of the Mars image, and the inset area is the entire image, so we see eight complete copies of the Mars image (Figure 15-2).

Now we'll tile the interior of the image, changing the `capInsets:` argument from the previous code (Figure 15-3):

```
UIImage* marsTiled = [mars resizableImageWithCapInsets:
                    UIEdgeInsetsMake(mars.size.height/4.0,
                                mars.size.width/4.0,
                                mars.size.height/4.0,
                                mars.size.width/4.0)
                resizingMode: UIImageResizingModeTile];
```

Next, I'll illustrate stretching. We'll start by changing just the `resizingMode:` from the previous code (Figure 15-4):

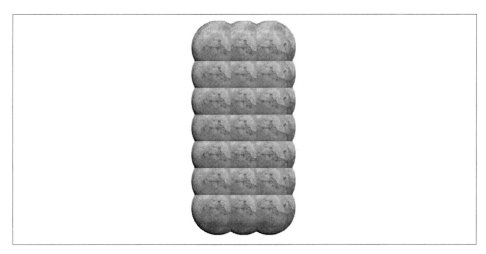

Figure 15-3. Tiling the interior of Mars

Figure 15-4. Stretching the interior of Mars

```
UIImage* marsTiled = [mars resizableImageWithCapInsets:
                UIEdgeInsetsMake(mars.size.height/4.0,
                                 mars.size.width/4.0,
                                 mars.size.height/4.0,
                                 mars.size.width/4.0)
                resizingMode: UIImageResizingModeStretch];
```

A common stretching strategy is to make almost half the original image serve as a cap inset, leaving just a pixel or two in the center to fill the entire interior of the resulting

Figure 15-5. Stretching a single pixel at the interior of Mars

image (Figure 15-5); this generates a stretched border whose corners are the corners of
the original image:

```
UIImage* marsTiled = [mars resizableImageWithCapInsets:
                      UIEdgeInsetsMake(mars.size.height/2.0 - 1,
                                       mars.size.width/2.0 - 1,
                                       mars.size.height/2.0 - 1,
                                       mars.size.width/2.0 - 1)
                  resizingMode: UIImageResizingModeStretch];
```

Graphics Contexts

UIImageView draws an image for you and takes care of all the details; in many cases, it
will be all you'll need. Eventually, though, you may want to create some drawing yourself,
directly, in code. To do so, you will always need a *graphics context.*

A graphics context is basically a place you can draw. Conversely, you can't draw in code
unless you've got a graphics context. There are several ways in which you might obtain
a graphics context; in this chapter I will concentrate on two, which have proven in my
experience to be far and away the most common:

You create an image context

The function UIGraphicsBeginImageContextWithOptions creates a graphics context suitable for use as an image. You then draw into this context to generate the
image. When you've done that, you call UIGraphicsGetImageFromCurrentImage
Context to turn the context into a UIImage, and then UIGraphicsEndImage
Context to dismiss the context. Now you have a UIImage that you can display in
your interface or draw into some other graphics context or save as a file.

Cocoa hands you a graphics context

You subclass UIView and implement `drawRect:`. At the time your `drawRect:` implementation is called, Cocoa has already created a graphics context and is asking you to draw into it, right now; whatever you draw is what the UIView will display. (A slight variant of this situation is that you subclass a CALayer and implement `drawInContext:`, or make some object the delegate of a layer and implement `drawLayer:inContext:`; layers are discussed in Chapter 16.)

Moreover, at any given moment there either is or is not a *current graphics context*:

- `UIGraphicsBeginImageContextWithOptions` not only creates an image context, it also makes that context the current graphics context.

- When `drawRect:` is called, the UIView's drawing context is already the current graphics context.

- Callbacks with a `context:` argument have *not* made any context the current graphics context; rather, that argument is a reference to a graphics context.

What beginners find most confusing about drawing is that there are two separate sets of tools with which you can draw, and they take different attitudes towards the context in which they will draw:

UIKit

Various Objective-C classes know how to draw themselves; these include UIImage, NSString (for drawing text), UIBezierPath (for drawing shapes), and UIColor. Some of these classes provide convenience methods with limited abilities; others are extremely powerful. In many cases, UIKit will be all you'll need.

With UIKit, you can draw *only into the current context*. So if you're in a `UIGraphics-BeginImageContextWithOptions` or `drawRect:` situation, you can use the UIKit convenience methods directly; there is a current context and it's the one you want to draw into. If you've been handed a `context:` argument, on the other hand, then if you want to use the UIKit convenience methods, you'll have to make that context the current context; you do this by calling `UIGraphicsPushContext` (and be sure to restore things with `UIGraphicsPopContext` later).

Core Graphics

This is the full drawing API. Core Graphics, often referred to as Quartz, or Quartz 2D, is the drawing system that underlies all iOS drawing — UIKit drawing is built on top of it — so it is low-level and consists of C functions. There are a lot of them! This chapter will familiarize you with the fundamentals; for complete information, you'll want to study Apple's *Quartz 2D Programming Guide*.

With Core Graphics, you must *specify a graphics context* (a CGContextRef) to draw into, explicitly, in every function call. If you've been handed a `context:` argument, then, hey presto, you have a graphics context, and it's probably the graphics context you want to draw into. But in a `UIGraphicsBeginImageContextWithOptions` or `drawRect:` situation, you have no reference to a context; to use Core Graphics, you need to get such a reference. Since the context you want to draw into is the current graphics context, you call `UIGraphicsGetCurrentContext` to get the needed reference.

So we have two sets of tools and three ways in which a context might be supplied; that makes six ways of drawing, and in case you're confused, I'll now demonstrate all six of them. Without worrying just yet about the actual drawing commands, focus your attention on how the context is specified and on whether we're using UIKit or Core Graphics. First, I'll draw a blue circle by implementing a UIView subclass's `drawRect:`, using UIKit to draw into the current context, which Cocoa has already prepared for me:

```
- (void) drawRect: (CGRect) rect {
    UIBezierPath* p =
        [UIBezierPath bezierPathWithOvalInRect:CGRectMake(0,0,100,100)];
    [[UIColor blueColor] setFill];
    [p fill];
}
```

Now I'll do the same thing with Core Graphics; this will require that I first get a reference to the current context:

```
- (void) drawRect: (CGRect) rect {
    CGContextRef con = UIGraphicsGetCurrentContext();
    CGContextAddEllipseInRect(con, CGRectMake(0,0,100,100));
    CGContextSetFillColorWithColor(con, [UIColor blueColor].CGColor);
    CGContextFillPath(con);
}
```

Next, I'll implement a UIView subclass's `drawLayer:inContext:`. In this case, we're handed a reference to a context, but it isn't the current context. So I have to make it the current context in order to use UIKit:

```
- (void)drawLayer:(CALayer*)lay inContext:(CGContextRef)con {
    UIGraphicsPushContext(con);
    UIBezierPath* p =
        [UIBezierPath bezierPathWithOvalInRect:CGRectMake(0,0,100,100)];
    [[UIColor blueColor] setFill];
    [p fill];
    UIGraphicsPopContext();
}
```

To use Core Graphics in `drawLayer:inContext:`, I simply keep referring to the context I was handed:

```
- (void)drawLayer:(CALayer*)lay inContext:(CGContextRef)con {
    CGContextAddEllipseInRect(con, CGRectMake(0,0,100,100));
    CGContextSetFillColorWithColor(con, [UIColor blueColor].CGColor);
    CGContextFillPath(con);
}
```

Finally, for the sake of completeness, let's make a UIImage of a blue circle. We can do this at any time (we don't need to wait for some particular method to be called) and in any class (we don't need to be in a UIView subclass). First, I'll use UIKit:

```
UIGraphicsBeginImageContextWithOptions(CGSizeMake(100,100), NO, 0);
UIBezierPath* p =
    [UIBezierPath bezierPathWithOvalInRect:CGRectMake(0,0,100,100)];
[[UIColor blueColor] setFill];
[p fill];
UIImage* im = UIGraphicsGetImageFromCurrentImageContext();
UIGraphicsEndImageContext();
// im is the blue circle image, do something with it here ...
```

Here's the same thing using Core Graphics:

```
UIGraphicsBeginImageContextWithOptions(CGSizeMake(100,100), NO, 0);
CGContextRef con = UIGraphicsGetCurrentContext();
CGContextAddEllipseInRect(con, CGRectMake(0,0,100,100));
CGContextSetFillColorWithColor(con, [UIColor blueColor].CGColor);
CGContextFillPath(con);
UIImage* im = UIGraphicsGetImageFromCurrentImageContext();
UIGraphicsEndImageContext();
// im is the blue circle image, do something with it here ...
```

You may be wondering about the arguments to `UIGraphicsBeginImageContextWith-Options`. The first argument is obviously the size of the image to be created. The second argument declares whether the image should be opaque; if I had passed YES instead of NO here, my image would have a black background, which I don't want. The third argument specifies the image scale, corresponding to the UIImage `scale` property I discussed earlier; by passing 0, I'm telling the system to set the scale for me in accordance with the main screen resolution, so my image will look good on both single-resolution and double-resolution devices.

You don't have to use UIKit or Core Graphics exclusively; on the contrary, you can intermingle UIKit calls and Core Graphics calls to operate on the same graphics context. They merely represent two different ways of talking about the same graphics context.

UIImage Drawing

A UIImage provides methods for drawing itself into the current context. We now know how to obtain an image context and make it the current context, so we can experiment with these methods. Here, I'll make a UIImage consisting of two pictures of Mars side by side:

Figure 15-6. Two images of Mars combined side by side

```
UIImage* mars = [UIImage imageNamed:@"Mars.png"];
CGSize sz = [mars size];
UIGraphicsBeginImageContextWithOptions(
    CGSizeMake(sz.width*2, sz.height), NO, 0);
[mars drawAtPoint:CGPointMake(0,0)];
[mars drawAtPoint:CGPointMake(sz.width,0)];
UIImage* im = UIGraphicsGetImageFromCurrentImageContext();
UIGraphicsEndImageContext();
```

The resulting UIImage im is suitable anywhere you would use a UIImage. For instance, you could hand it over to a visible UIImageView, thus causing the image to appear onscreen (Figure 15-6).

Additional UIImage methods let you scale an image into a desired rectangle as you draw, and specify the compositing (blend) mode whereby the image should combine with whatever is already present. To illustrate, I'll create an image showing Mars centered in another image of Mars that's twice as large, using the Multiply blend mode (Figure 15-7):

```
UIImage* mars = [UIImage imageNamed:@"Mars.png"];
CGSize sz = [mars size];
UIGraphicsBeginImageContextWithOptions(
    CGSizeMake(sz.width*2, sz.height*2), NO, 0);
[mars drawInRect:CGRectMake(0,0,sz.width*2,sz.height*2)];
[mars drawInRect:CGRectMake(sz.width/2.0, sz.height/2.0, sz.width, sz.height)
        blendMode:kCGBlendModeMultiply alpha:1.0];
UIImage* im = UIGraphicsGetImageFromCurrentImageContext();
UIGraphicsEndImageContext();
```

There is no UIImage drawing method for specifying the source rectangle — that is, for specifying that you want to extract a smaller region of the original image. You can work around this by specifying a smaller graphics context and positioning the image drawing so that the desired region falls into it. For example, to obtain an image of the right half of Mars, you'd make a graphics context half the width of the mars image, and then draw mars shifted left, so that only its right half intersects the graphics context. There is no harm in doing this, and it's a perfectly standard device; the left half of mars simply isn't drawn (Figure 15-8):

Figure 15-7. Two images of Mars in different sizes, composited

Figure 15-8. Half the original image of Mars

```
UIImage* mars = [UIImage imageNamed:@"Mars.png"];
CGSize sz = [mars size];
UIGraphicsBeginImageContextWithOptions(
    CGSizeMake(sz.width/2.0, sz.height), NO, 0);
[mars drawAtPoint:CGPointMake(-sz.width/2.0, 0)];
UIImage* im = UIGraphicsGetImageFromCurrentImageContext();
UIGraphicsEndImageContext();
```

CGImage Drawing

The Core Graphics version of UIImage is CGImage (actually a CGImageRef). They are easily converted to one another: a UIImage has a `CGImage` property that accesses its Quartz image data, and you can make a UIImage from a CGImage using `imageWith-CGImage:` or `initWithCGImage:` (in real life, you are likely to use their more configurable siblings, `imageWithCGImage:scale:orientation:` and `initWithCGImage:scale:orientation:`).

A CGImage lets you create a new image directly from a rectangular region of the original image, which you can't do with UIImage. (A CGImage has other powers a UIImage doesn't have; for example, you can apply an image mask to a CGImage.) I'll demonstrate by splitting the image of Mars in half and drawing the two halves separately

Figure 15-9. Image of Mars split in half

(Figure 15-9). Observe that we are now operating in the CFTypeRef world and must take care to manage memory manually; ARC won't help us here (Chapter 12):

```
UIImage* mars = [UIImage imageNamed:@"Mars.png"];
// extract each half as a CGImage
CGSize sz = [mars size];
CGImageRef marsLeft = CGImageCreateWithImageInRect([mars CGImage],
                      CGRectMake(0,0,sz.width/2.0,sz.height));
CGImageRef marsRight = CGImageCreateWithImageInRect([mars CGImage],
                      CGRectMake(sz.width/2.0,0,sz.width/2.0,sz.height));
// draw each CGImage into an image context
UIGraphicsBeginImageContextWithOptions(
    CGSizeMake(sz.width*1.5, sz.height), NO, 0);
CGContextRef con = UIGraphicsGetCurrentContext();
CGContextDrawImage(con,
                   CGRectMake(0,0,sz.width/2.0,sz.height), marsLeft);
CGContextDrawImage(con,
                   CGRectMake(sz.width,0,sz.width/2.0,sz.height), marsRight);
UIImage* im = UIGraphicsGetImageFromCurrentImageContext();
UIGraphicsEndImageContext();
CGImageRelease(marsLeft); CGImageRelease(marsRight);
```

But there's a problem with that example: the drawing is upside-down! It isn't rotated; it's mirrored top to bottom, or, to use the technical term, *flipped*. This phenomenon can arise when you create a CGImage and then draw it with `CGContextDrawImage`, and is due to a mismatch in the native coordinate systems of the source and target contexts.

There are various ways of compensating for this mismatch between the coordinate systems. One is to draw the CGImage into an intermediate UIImage and extract *another* CGImage from that. Example 15-1 presents a utility function for doing this.

Example 15-1. Utility for flipping an image drawing

```
CGImageRef flip (CGImageRef im) {
    CGSize sz = CGSizeMake(CGImageGetWidth(im), CGImageGetHeight(im));
    UIGraphicsBeginImageContextWithOptions(sz, NO, 0);
    CGContextDrawImage(UIGraphicsGetCurrentContext(),
                       CGRectMake(0, 0, sz.width, sz.height), im);
```

```
    CGImageRef result = [UIGraphicsGetImageFromCurrentImageContext() CGImage];
    UIGraphicsEndImageContext();
    return result;
}
```

Armed with the utility function from Example 15-1, we can now draw the halves of Mars the right way up in the previous example:

```
CGContextDrawImage(con, CGRectMake(0,0,sz.width/2.0,sz.height),
                   flip(marsLeft));
CGContextDrawImage(con, CGRectMake(sz.width,0,sz.width/2.0,sz.height),
                   flip(marsRight));
```

However, we've *still* got a problem: on a double-resolution device, if there is a high-resolution (@2x) version of our image file, the drawing comes out all wrong. The reason is that we are loading our starting Mars image using `imageNamed:`, which automatically substitutes the high-resolution version of the image on the high-resolution device. The UIImage compensates for the doubled size of the image by setting its own `scale` property to match. But a CGImage doesn't have a `scale` property, and knows nothing of the fact that the image dimensions are doubled!

When you call a UIImage's `CGImage` method, therefore, you can't assume that the resulting CGImage is the same size as the original UIImage; a UIImage's `size` property is the same for a single-resolution image and its double-resolution counterpart, because the `scale` tells it how to compensate, but the CGImage of a double-resolution UIImage is twice as large in both dimensions as the CGImage of the corresponding single-resolution image.

So, in extracting a desired piece of the CGImage, we must either multiply all appropriate values by the scale or express ourselves in terms of the CGImage's dimensions. In this case, as we are extracting the left and right halves of the image, the latter is obviously the simpler course. So here's a version of our original code that draws correctly on either a single-resolution or a double-resolution device, and compensates for flipping:

```
UIImage* mars = [UIImage imageNamed:@"Mars.png"];
CGSize sz = [mars size];
// Derive CGImage and use its dimensions to extract its halves
CGImageRef marsCG = [mars CGImage];
CGSize szCG = CGSizeMake(CGImageGetWidth(marsCG), CGImageGetHeight(marsCG));
CGImageRef marsLeft =
    CGImageCreateWithImageInRect(
        marsCG, CGRectMake(0,0,szCG.width/2.0,szCG.height));
CGImageRef marsRight =
    CGImageCreateWithImageInRect(
        marsCG, CGRectMake(szCG.width/2.0,0,szCG.width/2.0,szCG.height));
UIGraphicsBeginImageContextWithOptions(
    CGSizeMake(sz.width*1.5, sz.height), NO, 0);
// The rest is as before, calling flip() to compensate for flipping
CGContextRef con = UIGraphicsGetCurrentContext();
```

```
CGContextDrawImage(con, CGRectMake(0,0,sz.width/2.0,sz.height),
                   flip(marsLeft));
CGContextDrawImage(con, CGRectMake(sz.width,0,sz.width/2.0,sz.height),
                   flip(marsRight));
UIImage* im = UIGraphicsGetImageFromCurrentImageContext();
UIGraphicsEndImageContext();
CGImageRelease(marsLeft); CGImageRelease(marsRight);
```

If this is starting to look rather clumsy and involved, don't worry; I have up my sleeve another flipping solution that simplifies things considerably. Instead of calling our flip utility, you can wrap your CGImage in a UIImage before drawing. This has two big advantages:

- The UIImage compensates for flipping automatically as it draws.

- The UIImage can be formed in such a way as to compensate for scale: call image-WithCGImage:scale:orientation: as you form the UIImage from the CGImage.

So here's a self-contained approach that deals with both flipping and scale:

```
UIImage* mars = [UIImage imageNamed:@"Mars.png"];
CGSize sz = [mars size];
// Derive CGImage and use its dimensions to extract its halves
CGImageRef marsCG = [mars CGImage];
CGSize szCG = CGSizeMake(CGImageGetWidth(marsCG), CGImageGetHeight(marsCG));
CGImageRef marsLeft =
    CGImageCreateWithImageInRect(
        marsCG, CGRectMake(0,0,szCG.width/2.0,szCG.height));
CGImageRef marsRight =
    CGImageCreateWithImageInRect(
        marsCG, CGRectMake(szCG.width/2.0,0,szCG.width/2.0,szCG.height));
UIGraphicsBeginImageContextWithOptions(
    CGSizeMake(sz.width*1.5, sz.height), NO, 0);
[[UIImage imageWithCGImage:marsLeft
                     scale:[mars scale]
               orientation:UIImageOrientationUp]
 drawAtPoint:CGPointMake(0,0)];
[[UIImage imageWithCGImage:marsRight
                     scale:[mars scale]
               orientation:UIImageOrientationUp]
 drawAtPoint:CGPointMake(sz.width,0)];
UIImage* im = UIGraphicsGetImageFromCurrentImageContext();
UIGraphicsEndImageContext();
CGImageRelease(marsLeft); CGImageRelease(marsRight);
```

Yet another solution to flipping is to apply a transform to the graphics context before drawing the CGImage, effectively flipping the context's internal coordinate system. This is elegant, but can be confusing if there are other transforms in play. I'll talk more about graphics context transforms later in this chapter.

CIFilter and CIImage

The "CI" in CIFilter and CIImage stands for Core Image, a technology for transforming images through mathematical filters. Core Image started life on the desktop (Mac OS X), and migrated initially to iOS 5, bringing only a limited subset of the desktop filters, as iOS devices are not suitable for certain heavily intensive mathematical operations. In iOS 6, many more filters are provided; of about 140 filters available on the desktop, only about 40 are absent from iOS 6. To use Core Image, you'll have to link your target to *CoreImage.framework*.

A filter is a CIFilter. The available filters fall naturally into several categories:

Patterns and gradients
> These filters create CIImages that can then be combined with other CIImages, such as a single color, a checkerboard, stripes, or a gradient.

Compositing
> These filters combine one image with another, using compositing blend modes familiar from image processing programs such as Photoshop.

Color
> These filters adjust or otherwise modify the colors of an image. Thus you can alter an image's saturation, hue, brightness, contrast, gamma and white point, exposure, shadows and highlights, and so on.

Geometric
> These filters perform basic geometric transformations on an image, such as scaling, rotation, and cropping.

Transformation
> These filters distort, blur, or stylize an image. They are the most intensive filters, so relatively few of them are available on iOS.

Transition

> These filters provide a frame of a transition between one image and another; by asking for frames in sequence, you can animate the full transition.

The basic use of a CIFilter is quite simple; it essentially works as if a filter were a kind of dictionary consisting of keys and values. You create the filter by supplying the string name of a filter; to learn what these names are, consult Apple's *Core Image Filter Reference*, or call the CIFilter class method `filterNamesInCategories:` with a nil argument. Each filter has a small number of keys and values that determine its behavior; for each key that you're interested in, you supply a key–value pair, either by calling `setValue:forKey:` or by supplying all the keys and values as you specify the filter name. In supplying values, a number must be wrapped up as an NSNumber, and there are a few supporting classes such as CIVector (like CGPoint and CGRect combined) and CIColor, whose use is easy to grasp.

A CIFilter's keys include any image or images on which the filter is to operate; such an image must be a CIImage. You can obtain a CIImage from a CGImage with `initWithCGImage:`; we already know how to obtain a CGImage from a UIImage. You can also obtain a CGImage as the output of a filter; thus filters can be chained together.

As you build a chain of filters, nothing actually happens. The only calculation-intensive move comes at the very end, when you produce the result of the entire chain as a CGImage. You do this by creating a CIContext (by calling `contextWithOptions:`) and then calling `createCGImage:fromRect:`. The only mildly tricky thing here is that a CIImage doesn't have a frame or bounds; it has an `extent`. You will often use this as the second argument to `createCGImage:fromRect:`. The final output CGImage is ready for any purpose, such as for display in your app, for transformation into a UIImage, or for use in further drawing.

To illustrate, I'll start with an ordinary photo of myself (it's true I'm wearing a motorcycle helmet, but it's still ordinary) and create a circular vignette effect. We start by generating a clear color. Then we make a radial gradient. Finally, we treat the radial gradient as a mask for blending between the photo of me and the clear color: where the radial gradient is white (everything inside the gradient's inner radius) we see just me, and where the radial gradient is black (everything outside the gradient's outer radius) we see just the clear color, with a gradation in between, so that the image fades away in the circular band between the gradient's radii. The result is the UIImage `moi4`; displaying it an an image view (Figure 15-10), we see behind it the image view's background color — or, if the image view's background is clear, whatever is behind the image view:

```
CIFilter* col = [CIFilter filterWithName:@"CIConstantColorGenerator"];
CIColor* cicol = [[CIColor alloc] initWithColor:[UIColor clearColor]];
[col setValue:cicol forKey:@"inputColor"];
CIImage* colorimage = [col valueForKey: @"outputImage"];
```

Figure 15-10. A photo of me, vignetted

```
CIFilter* grad = [CIFilter filterWithName:@"CIRadialGradient"];
CIVector* center = [CIVector vectorWithX:moi.size.width/2.0
                                       Y:moi.size.height/2.0];
[grad setValue:center forKey:@"inputCenter"];
[grad setValue:@85 forKey:@"inputRadius0"];
[grad setValue:@100 forKey:@"inputRadius1"];
CIImage *gradimage = [grad valueForKey: @"outputImage"];

CIFilter* blend = [CIFilter filterWithName:@"CIBlendWithMask"];
[blend setValue:moi2 forKey:@"inputImage"];
[blend setValue:colorimage forKey:@"inputBackgroundImage"];
[blend setValue:gradimage forKey:@"inputMaskImage"];

CGImageRef moi3 = [[CIContext contextWithOptions:nil]
                    createCGImage:blend.outputImage
                    fromRect:moi2.extent];
moi4 = [UIImage imageWithCGImage:moi3];
CGImageRelease(moi3);
```

In this example, we use the same image of me to generate a kaleidoscopic tile effect
(Figure 15-11):

```
CIFilter* tile = [CIFilter filterWithName:@"CIFourfoldRotatedTile"];
[tile setValue:moi2 forKey:@"inputImage"];
CIVector* center = [CIVector vectorWithX:moi.size.width/2.0-60
                                       Y:moi.size.height/2.0-70];
[tile setValue:center forKey:@"inputCenter"];
[tile setValue:@50 forKey:@"inputWidth"];

CGImageRef moi3 = [[CIContext contextWithOptions:nil]
                    createCGImage:tile.outputImage
                    fromRect:moi2.extent];
moi4 = [UIImage imageWithCGImage:moi3];
CGImageRelease(moi3);
```

Figure 15-11. A photo of me, tiled

It is also possible to draw a filter's output directly into an OpenGL context, but OpenGL is outside the scope of this book. Core Image can also perform automatic face detection in an image.

Drawing a UIView

The most flexible way to draw a UIView is to draw it yourself. As I've already said, you don't actually draw a UIView; you subclass UIView and endow the subclass with the ability to draw itself. When a UIView needs drawing, its `drawRect:` method is called. Overriding that method is your chance to draw. At the time that `drawRect:` is called, the current graphics context has already been set to the view's own graphics context. You can use Core Graphics functions or UIKit convenience methods to draw into that context. Thus, everything I did earlier generating a UIImage and displaying it somehow in the interface could have been done instead by putting into my interface a UIView subclass that knows how to display itself as desired.

 You should *never* call `drawRect:` yourself! If a view needs updating and you want its `drawRect:` called, send the view the `setNeeds-Display` message. This will cause `drawRect:` to be called at the next proper moment. Also, don't override `drawRect:` unless you are assured that this is legal. For example, it is not legal to override `draw-Rect:` in a subclass of UIImageView; you cannot combine your drawing with that of the UIImageView.

So, for example, let's say we have a UIView subclass called MyView. How this class gets instantiated, and how the instance gets into our view hierarchy, isn't important. One possibility would be to drag a UIView into a view in the nib and set its class to MyView in the identity inspector; another would be to create the MyView instance and put it into the interface in code.

Let's suppose that MyView's job is to draw the two halves of Mars, one at each end of the view. We can readily adapt the earlier example of doing this. There is no need for an image context; we just draw directly into the current context, which is the view's own graphics context:

```
- (void)drawRect:(CGRect)rect {
    CGRect b = self.bounds;
    UIImage* mars = [UIImage imageNamed:@"Mars.png"];
    CGSize sz = [mars size];
    CGImageRef marsCG = [mars CGImage];
    CGSize szCG =
        CGSizeMake(CGImageGetWidth(marsCG), CGImageGetHeight(marsCG));
    CGImageRef marsLeft =
        CGImageCreateWithImageInRect(
            marsCG, CGRectMake(0,0,szCG.width/2.0,szCG.height));
    CGImageRef marsRight =
        CGImageCreateWithImageInRect(
            marsCG, CGRectMake(szCG.width/2.0,0,szCG.width/2.0,szCG.height));
    [[UIImage imageWithCGImage:marsLeft
                        scale:[mars scale]
                  orientation:UIImageOrientationUp]
      drawAtPoint:CGPointMake(0,0)];
    [[UIImage imageWithCGImage:marsRight
                        scale:[mars scale]
                  orientation:UIImageOrientationUp]
      drawAtPoint:CGPointMake(b.size.width-sz.width/2.0,0)];
    CGImageRelease(marsLeft); CGImageRelease(marsRight);
}
```

There is no need to call super, because the superclass here is UIView, whose drawRect: does nothing.

The need to draw in real time, on demand, surprises some beginners, who worry that drawing may be a time-consuming operation. Where drawing is extensive and can be compartmentalized into sections, you may be able to gain some efficiency by paying attention to the rect parameter passed into drawRect:. It designates the region of the view's bounds that needs refreshing. Normally, this is the view's entire bounds; but if you called setNeedsDisplayInRect:, it will be the CGRect that you passed in as argument. You could respond by drawing only what goes into those bounds; but even if you don't, your drawing will be clipped to those bounds, so, while you may not spend less time drawing, the system will draw more efficiently.

In general, however, you should not optimize prematurely. The code for a drawing operation may appear verbose and yet be extremely fast. Moreover, the iOS drawing system is efficient; it doesn't call drawRect: unless it has to (or is told to, through a call to setNeedsDisplay), and once a view has drawn itself, the result is cached so that the cached drawing can be reused instead of repeating the drawing operation from scratch. (Apple refers to this cached drawing as the view's *bitmap backing store*.) You can readily satisfy yourself of this fact with some caveman debugging, logging in your `drawRect:` implementation; you may be amazed to discover that your code is called only once in the entire lifetime of the app! In fact, moving code to `drawRect:` is a common way to *increase* efficiency. This is because it is more efficient for the drawing engine to render directly onto the screen than for it to render offscreen and then copy those pixels onto the screen.

When creating a custom UIView subclass instance in code, you may be surprised and annoyed to find that the view has a black background. This can be frustrating if what you expected and wanted was a transparent background; this is a source of considerable confusion among beginners. The black background arises when two things are true:

- The view's `backgroundColor` is nil.
- The view's `opaque` is YES.

Unfortunately, when creating a UIView in code, both those things *are* true by default! So if you don't want the black background, you must do something about one or the other of them (or both). For example, you might eliminate the black background by setting the view's `backgroundColor` to `[UIColor clearColor]`. But then you should *still* set its `opaque` to NO, because the view isn't opaque, and it's up to you to tell the drawing system this.

With a UIView created in the nib, on the other hand, the black background problem doesn't arise. This is because such a UIView's `backgroundColor` is not nil. The nib assigns it *some* actual background color, even if that color is `[UIColor clearColor]`.

Of course, if a view fills its rectangle with opaque drawing or has an opaque background color, you can leave `opaque` set to YES and gain some drawing efficiency (see Chapter 14).

Graphics Context Settings

When you draw in a graphics context, the drawing obeys the context's current settings. Thus, the procedure is always to configure the context's settings first, and then draw. For example, to draw a red line followed by a blue line, you would first set the context's line color to red, and then draw the first line; then you'd set the context's line color to blue, and then draw the second line. To the eye, it appears that the redness and blueness are properties of the individual lines, but in fact, at the time you draw each line, line color is a feature of the entire graphics context. This is true regardless of whether you use UIKit methods or Core Graphics functions.

A graphics context thus has, at every moment, a *state*, which is the sum total of all its settings; the way a piece of drawing looks is the result of what the graphics context's state was at the moment that piece of drawing was performed. To help you manipulate entire states, the graphics context provides a *stack* for holding states. Every time you call CGContextSaveGState, the context pushes the entire current state onto the stack; every time you call CGContextRestoreGState, the context retrieves the state from the top of the stack (the state that was most recently pushed) and sets itself to that state.

Thus, a common pattern is: call CGContextSaveGState; manipulate the context's settings, thus changing its state; draw; call CGContextRestoreGState to restore the state and the settings to what they were before you manipulated them. You do not have to do this before *every* manipulation of a context's settings, however, because settings don't necessarily conflict with one another or with past settings. You can set the context's line color to red and then later to blue without any difficulty. But in certain situations you do want your manipulation of settings to be undoable, and I'll point out several such situations later in this chapter.

Many of the settings that constitute a graphics context's state, and that determine the behavior and appearance of drawing performed at that moment, are similar to those of any drawing application. Here are some of them, along with some of the commands that determine them; I provide Core Graphics functions here, but keep in mind that UIKit commands are actually calling these same functions and manipulating the context's state in the same ways:

Line thickness and dash style
> CGContextSetLineWidth, CGContextSetLineDash

Line end-cap style and join style
> CGContextSetLineCap, CGContextSetLineJoin, CGContextSetMiterLimit

Line color or pattern
> CGContextSetRGBStrokeColor, CGContextSetGrayStrokeColor, CGContextSet-StrokeColorWithColor, CGContextSetStrokePattern

Fill color or pattern
> CGContextSetRGBFillColor, CGContextSetGrayFillColor, CGContextSetFill-ColorWithColor, CGContextSetFillPattern

Shadow
> CGContextSetShadow, CGContextSetShadowWithColor

Blend mode
> CGContextSetBlendMode (this determines how drawing that you do now will be composited with drawing already present)

Overall transparency
> CGContextSetAlpha (individual colors also have an alpha component)

Text features
> CGContextSelectFont, CGContextSetFont, CGContextSetFontSize, CGContext-SetTextDrawingMode, CGContextSetCharacterSpacing

Whether anti-aliasing and font smoothing are in effect
> CGContextSetShouldAntialias, CGContextSetShouldSmoothFonts

Additional settings include:

Clipping area
> Drawing outside the clipping area is not physically drawn.

Transform (or "CTM," for "current transform matrix")
> Changes how points that you specify in subsequent drawing commands are mapped onto the physical space of the canvas.

Many (but not all) of these settings will be illustrated by examples later in this chapter.

Paths and Drawing

By issuing a series of instructions for moving an imaginary pen, you trace out a *path*. Such a path does *not* constitute drawing! First you provide a path; *then* you draw. Drawing can mean stroking the path or filling the path, or both. Again, this should be a familiar notion from certain drawing applications.

A path is constructed by tracing it out from point to point. Think of the drawing system as holding a pen. Then you must first tell that pen where to position itself, setting the current point; after that, you issue a series of commands telling it how to trace out each subsequent piece of the path. Each additional piece of the path starts at the current point; its end becomes the new current point.

Here are some path-drawing commands you're likely to give:

Position the current point
> CGContextMoveToPoint

Trace a line
> CGContextAddLineToPoint, CGContextAddLines

Trace a rectangle
> CGContextAddRect, CGContextAddRects

Trace an ellipse or circle
> CGContextAddEllipseInRect

Trace an arc

CGContextAddArcToPoint, CGContextAddArc

Trace a Bezier curve with one or two control points

CGContextAddQuadCurveToPoint, CGContextAddCurveToPoint

Close the current path

CGContextClosePath. This appends a line from the last point of the path to the first point. There's no need to do this if you're about to fill the path, since it's done for you.

Stroke or fill the current path

CGContextStrokePath, CGContextFillPath, CGContextEOFillPath, CGContext-DrawPath. Stroking or filling the current path *clears the path*. Use CGContextDraw-Path if you want both to fill and to stroke the path in a single command, because if you merely stroke it first with CGContextStrokePath, the path is cleared and you can no longer fill it.

There are also a lot of convenience functions that create a path and stroke or fill it all in a single move: CGContextStrokeLineSegments, CGContextStrokeRect, CGContextStrokeRectWithWidth, CGContextFillRect, CGContextFillRects, CGContextStrokeEllipseInRect, CGContextFillEllipseInRect.

A path can be compound, meaning that it consists of multiple independent pieces. For example, a single path might consist of two separate closed shapes: a rectangle and a circle. When you call CGContextMoveToPoint in the middle of constructing a path (that is, after tracing out a path and without clearing it by filling, stroking, or calling CGContextBeginPath), you pick up the imaginary pen and move it to a new location without tracing a segment, thus preparing to start an independent piece of the same path. If you're worried, as you begin to trace out a path, that there might be an existing path and that your new path might be seen as a compound part of that existing path, you can call CGContextBeginPath to specify that this is a different path; many of Apple's examples do this, but in practice I usually do not find it necessary.

There is also a function for erasing an area: CGContextClearRect. This erases all existing drawing in a rectangle; combined with clipping, though, it can erase an area of any shape. The result can "punch a hole" through all existing drawing.

The behavior of CGContextClearRect depends on whether the context is transparent or opaque. This is particularly obvious and intuitive when drawing into an image context. If the image context is transparent — the second argument to UIGraphicsBegin-ImageContextWithOptions is NO — CGContextClearRect erases to transparent; otherwise it erases to black.

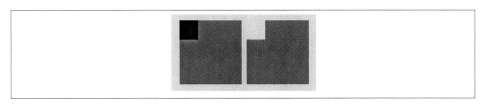

Figure 15-12. The very strange behavior of CGContextClearRect

When drawing directly into a view (as with `drawRect:` or `drawLayer:inContext:`), if the view's background color is nil or a color with even a tiny bit of transparency, the result of `CGContextClearRect` will appear to be transparent, punching a hole right through the view including its background color; if the background color is completely opaque, the result of `CGContextClearRect` will be black. This is because *the view's background color determines whether the view's graphics context is transparent or opaque*; thus, this is essentially the same behavior that I described in the preceding paragraph.

Figure 15-12 illustrates; the blue square on the left has been partly cut away to black, while the blue square on the right has been partly cut away to transparency. Yet these are instances of the same UIView subclass, drawn with exactly the same code! The difference between the views is that the `backgroundColor` of the first view is set in the nib to solid red with an alpha of 1, while the `backgroundColor` of the second view is set in the nib to solid red with an alpha of 0.99. This difference is utterly imperceptible to the eye (not to mention that the red color never appears, as it is covered with a blue fill), but it completely changes the effect of `CGContextClearRect`. The UIView subclass's `drawRect:` looks like this:

```
CGContextRef con = UIGraphicsGetCurrentContext();
CGContextSetFillColorWithColor(con, [UIColor blueColor].CGColor);
CGContextFillRect(con, rect);
CGContextClearRect(con, CGRectMake(0,0,30,30));
```

To illustrate the typical use of path-drawing commands, I'll generate the up-pointing arrow shown in Figure 15-13. This might not be the best way to create the arrow, and I'm deliberately avoiding use of the convenience functions, but it's clear and shows a nice basic variety of typical commands:

```
// obtain the current graphics context
CGContextRef con = UIGraphicsGetCurrentContext();

// draw a black (by default) vertical line, the shaft of the arrow
CGContextMoveToPoint(con, 100, 100);
CGContextAddLineToPoint(con, 100, 19);
CGContextSetLineWidth(con, 20);
CGContextStrokePath(con);

// draw a red triangle, the point of the arrow
```

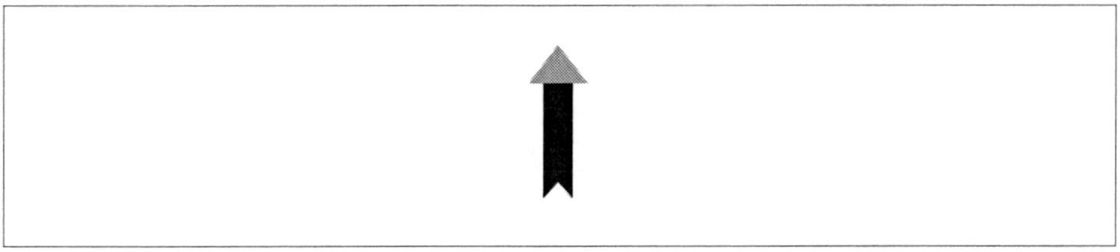

Figure 15-13. A simple path drawing

```
CGContextSetFillColorWithColor(con, [[UIColor redColor] CGColor]);
CGContextMoveToPoint(con, 80, 25);
CGContextAddLineToPoint(con, 100, 0);
CGContextAddLineToPoint(con, 120, 25);
CGContextFillPath(con);

// snip a triangle out of the shaft by drawing in Clear blend mode
CGContextMoveToPoint(con, 90, 101);
CGContextAddLineToPoint(con, 100, 90);
CGContextAddLineToPoint(con, 110, 101);
CGContextSetBlendMode(con, kCGBlendModeClear);
CGContextFillPath(con);
```

Properly speaking, we should probably surround our drawing code with calls to CGContextSaveGState and CGContextRestoreGState, just in case. It probably wouldn't make any difference in this particular example, as the context does not persist between calls to drawRect:, but it can't hurt.

If a path needs to be reused or shared, you can encapsulate it as a CGPath, which is actually a CGPathRef. You can either create a new CGMutablePathRef and construct the path using various CGPath functions that parallel the graphics path-construction functions, or you can copy the graphics context's current path using CGContextCopy-Path. There are also a number of CGPath functions for creating a path based on simple geometry (CGPathCreateWithRect, CGPathCreateWithEllipseInRect) or based on an existing path (CGPathCreateCopyByStrokingPath, CGPathCreateCopyByDashing-Path, CGPathCreateCopyByTransformingPath).

A UIKit class, UIBezierPath, wraps CGPath. It provides methods for drawing certain path shapes, as well as for stroking, filling, and for accessing certain settings of the current graphics context state. Similarly, UIColor provides methods for setting the current graphics context's stroke and fill colors. Thus we could rewrite our arrow-drawing routine like this:

```
UIBezierPath* p = [UIBezierPath bezierPath];
[p moveToPoint:CGPointMake(100,100)];
[p addLineToPoint:CGPointMake(100, 19)];
[p setLineWidth:20];
[p stroke];
```

```
[[UIColor redColor] set];
[p removeAllPoints];
[p moveToPoint:CGPointMake(80,25)];
[p addLineToPoint:CGPointMake(100, 0)];
[p addLineToPoint:CGPointMake(120, 25)];
[p fill];

[p removeAllPoints];
[p moveToPoint:CGPointMake(90,101)];
[p addLineToPoint:CGPointMake(100, 90)];
[p addLineToPoint:CGPointMake(110, 101)];
[p fillWithBlendMode:kCGBlendModeClear alpha:1.0];
```

There's no savings of code in this particular case, but UIBezierPath still might be useful if you need object features, and it does offer one convenience method, bezierPathWith-RoundedRect:cornerRadius:, that is particularly attractive; drawing a rectangle with rounded corners using only Core Graphics functions is rather tedious.

Clipping

Another use of a path is to mask out areas, protecting them from future drawing. This is called *clipping*. By default, a graphics context's clipping region is the entire graphics context: you can draw anywhere within the context.

The clipping area is a feature of the context as a whole, and any new clipping area is applied by intersecting it with the existing clipping area; so if you apply your own clipping region, the way to remove it from the graphics context later is to plan ahead and wrap things with calls to CGContextSaveGState and CGContextRestoreGState.

To illustrate, I'll rewrite the code that generated our original arrow (Figure 15-13) to use clipping instead of a blend mode to "punch out" the triangular notch in the tail of the arrow. This is a little tricky, because what we want to clip to is not the region inside the triangle but the region outside it. To express this, we'll use a compound path consisting of more than one closed area — the triangle, and the drawing area as a whole (which we can obtain with CGContextGetClipBoundingBox).

Both when filling a compound path and when using it to express a clipping region, the system follows one of two rules:

Winding rule
    The fill or clipping area is denoted by an alternation in the direction (clockwise or counterclockwise) of the path demarcating each region.

Even-odd rule (EO)
    The fill or clipping area is denoted by a simple count of the paths demarcating each region.

> ## How Big Is My Context?
>
> At first blush, it appears that there's no way to learn a graphics context's size. Typically, this doesn't matter, because either you created the graphics context or it's the graphics context of some object whose size you know, such as a UIView. But in fact, because the default clipping region of a graphics context is the entire context, you can use `CGContext-GetClipBoundingBox` to learn the context's "bounds" (before changing the clipping region, of course).

Our situation is extremely simple, so it's easier to use the even-odd rule. So we set up the clipping area using `CGContextEOClip` and then draw the arrow:

```
// obtain the current graphics context
CGContextRef con = UIGraphicsGetCurrentContext();

// punch triangular hole in context clipping region
CGContextMoveToPoint(con, 90, 100);
CGContextAddLineToPoint(con, 100, 90);
CGContextAddLineToPoint(con, 110, 100);
CGContextClosePath(con);
CGContextAddRect(con, CGContextGetClipBoundingBox(con));
CGContextEOClip(con);

// draw the vertical line
CGContextMoveToPoint(con, 100, 100);
CGContextAddLineToPoint(con, 100, 19);
CGContextSetLineWidth(con, 20);
CGContextStrokePath(con);

// draw the red triangle, the point of the arrow
CGContextSetFillColorWithColor(con, [[UIColor redColor] CGColor]);
CGContextMoveToPoint(con, 80, 25);
CGContextAddLineToPoint(con, 100, 0);
CGContextAddLineToPoint(con, 120, 25);
CGContextFillPath(con);
```

Gradients

Gradients can range from the simple to the complex. A simple gradient (which is all I'll describe here) is determined by a color at one endpoint along with a color at the other endpoint, plus (optionally) colors at intermediate points; the gradient is then painted either linearly between two points in the context or radially between two circles in the context.

You can't use a gradient as a path's fill color, but you can restrict a gradient to a path's shape by clipping, which amounts to the same thing.

To illustrate, I'll redraw our arrow, using a linear gradient as the "shaft" of the arrow (Figure 15-14):

```
// obtain the current graphics context
CGContextRef con = UIGraphicsGetCurrentContext();
CGContextSaveGState(con);

// punch triangular hole in context clipping region
CGContextMoveToPoint(con, 90, 100);
CGContextAddLineToPoint(con, 100, 90);
CGContextAddLineToPoint(con, 110, 100);
CGContextClosePath(con);
CGContextAddRect(con, CGContextGetClipBoundingBox(con));
CGContextEOClip(con);

// draw the vertical line, add its shape to the clipping region
CGContextMoveToPoint(con, 100, 100);
CGContextAddLineToPoint(con, 100, 19);
CGContextSetLineWidth(con, 20);
CGContextReplacePathWithStrokedPath(con);
CGContextClip(con);

// draw the gradient
CGFloat locs[3] = { 0.0, 0.5, 1.0 };
CGFloat colors[12] = {
    0.3,0.3,0.3,0.8, // starting color, transparent gray
    0.0,0.0,0.0,1.0, // intermediate color, black
    0.3,0.3,0.3,0.8 // ending color, transparent gray
};
CGColorSpaceRef sp = CGColorSpaceCreateDeviceGray();
CGGradientRef grad =
    CGGradientCreateWithColorComponents (sp, colors, locs, 3);
CGContextDrawLinearGradient (
    con, grad, CGPointMake(89,0), CGPointMake(111,0), 0);
CGColorSpaceRelease(sp);
CGGradientRelease(grad);

CGContextRestoreGState(con); // done clipping

// draw the red triangle, the point of the arrow
CGContextSetFillColorWithColor(con, [[UIColor redColor] CGColor]);
CGContextMoveToPoint(con, 80, 25);
CGContextAddLineToPoint(con, 100, 0);
CGContextAddLineToPoint(con, 120, 25);
CGContextFillPath(con);
```

The call to `CGContextReplacePathWithStrokedPath` pretends to stroke the current path, using the current line width and other line-related context state settings, but then creates a new path representing the outside of that stroked path. Thus, instead of a thick line we have a rectangular region that we can use as the clip region.

Figure 15-14. Drawing with a gradient

Figure 15-15. A patterned fill

We then create the gradient and paint it. The procedure is verbose but simple; everything is boilerplate. We describe the gradient as a set of locations on the continuum between one endpoint (0.0) and the other endpoint (1.0), along with the colors corresponding to each location; in this case, I want the gradient to be lighter at the edges and darker in the middle, so I use three locations, with the dark one at 0.5. We must also supply a color space in order to create the gradient. Finally, we create the gradient, paint it into place, and release the color space and the gradient.

Colors and Patterns

A color is a CGColor (actually a CGColorRef). CGColor is not difficult to work with, and is bridged to UIColor through UIColor's colorWithCGColor: and CGColor methods.

A pattern, on the other hand, is a CGPattern (actually a CGPatternRef). You can create a pattern and stroke or fill with it. The process is rather elaborate. As an extremely simple example, I'll replace the red triangular arrowhead with a red-and-blue striped triangle (Figure 15-15). To do so, remove this line:

```
CGContextSetFillColorWithColor(con, [[UIColor redColor] CGColor]);
```

In its place, put the following:

```
CGColorSpaceRef sp2 = CGColorSpaceCreatePattern(nil);
CGContextSetFillColorSpace (con, sp2);
CGColorSpaceRelease (sp2);
CGPatternCallbacks callback = {
    0, drawStripes, nil
};
```

```
CGAffineTransform tr = CGAffineTransformIdentity;
CGPatternRef patt = CGPatternCreate(nil,
                     CGRectMake(0,0,4,4),
                     tr,
                     4, 4,
                     kCGPatternTilingConstantSpacingMinimalDistortion,
                     true,
                     &callback);
CGFloat alph = 1.0;
CGContextSetFillPattern(con, patt, &alph);
CGPatternRelease(patt);
```

That code is verbose, but it is almost entirely boilerplate. To understand it, it almost helps to read it backward. What we're leading up to is the call to `CGContextSetFill-Pattern`; instead of setting a fill color, we're setting a fill pattern, to be used the next time we fill a path (in this case, the triangular arrowhead). The third parameter to `CGContextSetFillPattern` is a pointer to a CGFloat, so we have to set up the CGFloat itself beforehand. The second parameter to `CGContextSetFillPattern` is a CGPattern-Ref, so we have to create that CGPatternRef beforehand (and release it afterward).

So now let's talk about the call to `CGPatternCreate`. A pattern is a drawing in a rectangular "cell"; we have to state both the size of the cell (the second argument) and the spacing between origin points of cells (the fourth and fifth arguments). In this case, the cell is 4×4, and every cell exactly touches its neighbors both horizontally and vertically. We have to supply a transform to be applied to the cell (the third argument); in this case, we're not doing anything with this transform, so we supply the identity transform. We supply a tiling rule (the sixth argument). We have to state whether this is a color pattern or a stencil pattern; it's a color pattern, so the seventh argument is `true`. And we have to supply a pointer to a callback function that actually draws the pattern into its cell (the eighth argument).

Except that that's *not* what we have to supply as the eighth argument. To make matters more complicated, what we actually have to supply here is a pointer to a CGPattern-Callbacks struct. This struct consists of the number 0 and pointers to *two* functions, one called to draw the pattern into its cell, the other called when the pattern is released. We're not specifying the second function, however; it is for memory management, and we don't need it in this simple example.

We have almost worked our way backward to the start of the code. It turns out that before you can call `CGContextSetFillPattern` with a colored pattern, you have to set the context's fill color space to a pattern color space. If you neglect to do this, you'll get an error when you call `CGContextSetFillPattern`. So we create the color space, set it as the context's fill color space, and release it.

But we are *still* not finished, because I haven't shown you the function that actually draws the pattern cell! This is the function whose address is taken as drawStripes in our code. Here it is:

```
void drawStripes (void *info, CGContextRef con) {
    // assume 4 x 4 cell
    CGContextSetFillColorWithColor(con, [[UIColor redColor] CGColor]);
    CGContextFillRect(con, CGRectMake(0,0,4,4));
    CGContextSetFillColorWithColor(con, [[UIColor blueColor] CGColor]);
    CGContextFillRect(con, CGRectMake(0,0,4,2));
}
```

As you can see, the actual pattern-drawing code is very simple. The only tricky issue is that the call to CGPatternCreate must be in agreement with the pattern-drawing function as to the size of a cell, or the pattern won't come out the way you expect. We know in this case that the cell is 4×4. So we fill it with red, and then fill its lower half with blue. When these cells are tiled touching each other horizontally and vertically, we get the stripes that you see in Figure 15-15.

Note, finally, that the code as presented has left the graphics context in an undesirable state, with its fill color space set to a pattern color space. This would cause trouble if we were later to try to set the fill color to a normal color. The solution, as usual, is to wrap the code in calls to CGContextSaveGState and CGContextRestoreGState.

You may have observed in Figure 15-15 that the stripes do not fit neatly inside the triangle of the arrow-head: the bottommost stripe is something like half a blue stripe. This is because a pattern is positioned not with respect to the shape you are filling (or stroking), but with respect to the graphics context as a whole. We could shift the pattern position by calling CGContextSetPatternPhase before drawing.

Graphics Context Transforms

Just as a UIView can have a transform, so can a graphics context. However, applying a transform to a graphics context has no effect on the drawing that's already in it; it affects only the drawing that takes place after it is applied, altering the way the coordinates you provide are mapped onto the graphics context's area. A graphics context's transform is called its CTM, for "current transformation matrix."

It is quite usual to take full advantage of a graphics context's CTM to save yourself from performing even simple calculations. You can multiply the current transform by any CGAffineTransform using CGContextConcatCTM; there are also convenience functions for applying a translate, scale, or rotate transform to the current transform.

The base transform for a graphics context is already set for you when you obtain the context; this is how the system is able to map context drawing coordinates onto screen coordinates. Whatever transforms you apply are applied to the current transform, so the base transform remains in effect and drawing continues to work. You can return to the base transform after applying your own transforms by wrapping your code in calls to CGContextSaveGState and CGContextRestoreGState.

For example, we have hitherto been drawing our upward-pointing arrow with code that knows how to place that arrow at only one location: the top left of its rectangle is hard-coded at {80,0}. This is silly. It makes the code hard to understand, as well as inflexible and difficult to reuse. Surely the sensible thing would be to draw the arrow at {0,0}, by subtracting 80 from all the x-values in our existing code. Now it is easy to draw the arrow at *any* position, simply by applying a translate transform beforehand, mapping {0,0} to the desired top-left corner of the arrow. So, to draw it at {80,0}, we would say:

```
CGContextTranslateCTM(con, 80, 0);
// now draw the arrow at (0,0)
```

A rotate transform is particularly useful, allowing you to draw in a rotated orientation without any nasty trigonometry. However, it's a bit tricky because the point around which the rotation takes place is the origin. This is rarely what you want, so you have to apply a translate transform first, to map the origin to the point around which you really want to rotate. But then, after rotating, in order to figure out where to draw you will probably have to reverse your translate transform.

To illustrate, here's code to draw our arrow repeatedly at several angles, pivoting around the end of its tail (Figure 15-16). First, we'll encapsulate the drawing of the arrow as a UIImage. Then we simply draw that UIImage repeatedly:

```
UIGraphicsBeginImageContextWithOptions(CGSizeMake(40,100), NO, 0.0);
CGContextRef con = UIGraphicsGetCurrentContext();

// draw the arrow into the image context
// draw it at (0,0)! adjust all x-values by subtracting 80
// ... actual code omitted ...

UIImage* im = UIGraphicsGetImageFromCurrentImageContext();
UIGraphicsEndImageContext();

con = UIGraphicsGetCurrentContext();

[im drawAtPoint:CGPointMake(0,0)];
for (int i=0; i<3; i++) {
    CGContextTranslateCTM(con, 20, 100);
    CGContextRotateCTM(con, 30 * M_PI/180.0);
    CGContextTranslateCTM(con, -20, -100);
    [im drawAtPoint:CGPointMake(0,0)];
}
```

A transform is also one more solution for the "flip" problem we encountered earlier with CGContextDrawImage. Instead of reversing the drawing, we can reverse the context into which we draw it. Essentially, we apply a "flip" transform to the context's coordinate

Figure 15-16. Drawing rotated with a CTM

system. You move the context's top downward, and then reverse the direction of the y-coordinate by applying a scale transform whose y-multiplier is -1:

```
CGContextTranslateCTM(con, 0, theHeight);
CGContextScaleCTM(con, 1.0, -1.0);
```

How far down you move the context's top depends on how you intend to draw the image. So, for example, we could draw the two halves of Mars (from the example earlier in this chapter) without flipping, like this:

```
CGContextTranslateCTM(con, 0, sz.height); // sz is [mars size]
CGContextScaleCTM(con, 1.0, -1.0);
CGContextDrawImage(con,
    CGRectMake(0,0,sz.width/2.0,sz.height),
    marsLeft);
CGContextDrawImage(con,
    CGRectMake(b.size.width-sz.width/2.0, 0, sz.width/2.0, sz.height),
    marsRight);
```

Shadows

To add a shadow to a drawing, give the context a shadow value before drawing. The shadow position is expressed as a CGSize, where the positive direction for both values indicates down and to the right. The blur value is an open-ended positive number; Apple doesn't explain how the scale works, but experimentation shows that 12 is nice and blurry, 99 is so blurry as to be shapeless, and higher values become problematic.

Figure 15-17 shows the result of the same code that generated Figure 15-16, except that before we start drawing the arrow repeatedly, we give the context a shadow:

```
con = UIGraphicsGetCurrentContext();
CGContextSetShadow(con, CGSizeMake(7, 7), 12);
[im drawAtPoint:CGPointMake(0,0)]; // ... and so on
```

However, there's a subtle cosmetic problem with this approach. It may not be evident from Figure 15-17, but we are adding a shadow each time we draw. Thus the arrows are able to cast shadows on one another. What we want, however, is for all the arrows to cast a single shadow collectively. The way to achieve this is with a *transparency layer*;

Figure 15-17. Drawing with a shadow

this is basically a subcontext that accumulates all drawing and then adds the shadow. Our code for drawing the shadowed arrows would thus look like this:

```
CGContextSetShadow(con, CGSizeMake(7, 7), 12);
CGContextBeginTransparencyLayer(con, nil);
[im drawAtPoint:CGPointMake(0,0)];
for (int i=0; i<3; i++) {
    CGContextTranslateCTM(con, 20, 100);
    CGContextRotateCTM(con, 30 * M_PI/180.0);
    CGContextTranslateCTM(con, -20, -100);
    [im drawAtPoint:CGPointMake(0,0)];
}
CGContextEndTransparencyLayer(con);
```

Points and Pixels

A point is a dimensionless location described by an x-coordinate and a y-coordinate. When you draw in a graphics context, you specify the points at which to draw, and this works regardless of the device's resolution, because Core Graphics maps your drawing nicely onto the physical output (using the base CTM, along with any anti-aliasing and smoothing). Therefore, throughout this chapter I've concerned myself with graphics context points, disregarding their relationship to screen pixels.

However, pixels do exist. A pixel is a physical, integral, dimensioned unit of display in the real world. Whole-numbered points effectively lie between pixels, and this can matter if you're fussy, especially on a single-resolution device. For example, if a vertical path with whole-number coordinates is stroked with a line width of 1, half the line falls on each side of the path, and the drawn line on the screen of a single-resolution device will seem to be 2 pixels wide (because the device can't illuminate half a pixel).

You will sometimes encounter advice suggesting that if this effect is objectionable, you should try shifting the line's position by 0.5, to center it in its pixels. This advice may appear to work, but it makes some simple-minded assumptions. A more sophisticated approach is to obtain the UIView's contentScaleFactor property. This value will be either 1.0 or 2.0, so you can divide by it to convert from pixels to points. Consider also that the most accurate way to draw a vertical or horizontal line is not to stroke a path

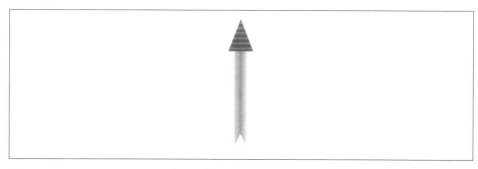

Figure 15-18. Automatic stretching of content

but to fill a rectangle. So this UIView subclass code will draw a perfect 1-pixel-wide vertical line on any device:

```
CGContextFillRect(con, CGRectMake(100,0,1.0/self.contentScaleFactor,100));
```

Content Mode

A view that draws something within itself, as opposed to merely having a background color and subviews (as in the previous chapter), has *content*. This means that its content-Mode property becomes important whenever the view is resized. As I mentioned earlier, the drawing system will avoid asking a view to redraw itself from scratch if possible; instead, it will use the cached result of the previous drawing operation (the bitmap backing store). So, if the view is resized, the system may simply stretch or shrink or reposition the cached drawing, if your contentMode setting instructs it to do so.

It's a little tricky to illustrate this point, because I have to arrange for the view to be resized without also causing it to be redrawn (that is, without triggering a call to draw-Rect:). Here's how I'll do that. As the app starts up, I'll create an instance of a UIView subclass that knows how to draw our arrow. Then I'll use delayed performance to resize the instance after the window has shown and the interface has been initially displayed:

```
void (^resize) (void) = ^{
    CGRect f = mv.bounds; // mv is the MyView instance
    f.size.height *= 2;
    mv.bounds = f;
};
dispatch_time_t popTime = dispatch_time(DISPATCH_TIME_NOW, NSEC_PER_SEC);
dispatch_after(popTime, dispatch_get_main_queue(), resize);
```

We double the height of the view without causing drawRect: to be called. The result is that the view's drawing appears at double its correct height. For example, if our view's drawRect: code is the same as the code that generated Figure 15-14, we get Figure 15-18.

This, however, is almost certainly not what we want. Sooner or later `drawRect:` will be called, and the drawing will be refreshed in accordance with our code. Our code doesn't say to draw the arrow at a height that is relative to the height of the view's bounds; it draws the arrow at a fixed height. Thus, not only has the arrow stretched, but at some future time, it will snap back to its original size.

The moral is that our view's `contentMode` property needs to be in agreement with how the view draws itself. For example, our `drawRect:` code dictates the size and position of the arrow relative to the view's bounds origin, its top left. So we could set its `contentMode` to `UIViewContentModeTopLeft`. Alternatively, and more likely, we could set it to `UIViewContentModeRedraw`; this will cause automatic scaling and repositioning of the cached content to be turned off, and instead the view's `setNeedsDisplay` method will be called, ultimately triggering `drawRect:` to redraw the content.

On the other hand, if a view might be resized only *momentarily* — say, as part of an animation — then stretching behavior might be exactly what you want. Suppose we're going to animate the view by making it get a little larger for a moment and then returning it to its original size, perhaps as a way of attracting the user's attention. Then presumably we do want the view's content to stretch and shrink as the view stretches and shrinks; that's the whole point of the animation. This is precisely what the default `contentMode` value, `UIViewContentModeScaleToFill`, does for us. And remember, it does it efficiently; what's being stretched and shrunk is just a cached image of our view's content.

CHAPTER 16

Layers

The tale told in Chapter 14 and Chapter 15 of how a UIView works and how it draws itself is only half the story. A UIView has a partner called its *layer*, a CALayer. A UIView does not actually draw itself onto the screen; it draws itself into its layer, and it is the layer that is portrayed on the screen. As I've already mentioned, a view is not redrawn frequently; instead, its drawing is cached, and the cached version of the drawing (the bitmap backing store) is used where possible. The cached version is, in fact, the layer. What I spoke of in Chapter 15 as the view's graphics context is actually the layer's graphics context.

This might seem like a mere implementation detail, but layers are important and interesting. To understand layers is to understand views more deeply; layers extend the power of views. In particular:

Layers have properties that affect drawing.
> Layers have drawing-related properties beyond those of a UIView. Because a layer is the recipient and presenter of a view's drawing, you can modify how a view is drawn on the screen by accessing the layer's properties. In other words, by reaching down to the level of its layer, you can make a view do things you can't do through UIView methods alone.

Layers can be combined within a single view.
> A UIView's partner layer can contain additional layers. Since the purpose of layers is to draw, portraying visible material on the screen, this allows a UIView's drawing to be composited of multiple distinct pieces. This can make drawing easier, with the constituents of a drawing being treated as objects.

Layers are the basis of animation.
> Animation allows you to add clarity, emphasis, and just plain coolness to your interface. Layers are made to be animated (the "CA" in "CALayer" stands for "Core

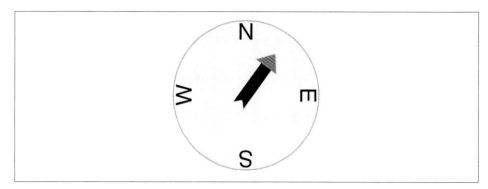

Figure 16-1. A compass, composed of layers

Animation"). Animation is the subject of Chapter 17; understanding layers is a prerequisite for reading that chapter.

For example, suppose we want to add a compass indicator to our app's interface. Figure 16-1 portrays a simple version of such a compass. It takes advantage of the arrow that we figured out how to draw in Chapter 15; the arrow is drawn into a layer of its own. The other parts of the compass are layers too: the circle is a layer, and each of the cardinal point letters is a layer. The drawing is thus easy to composite in code (and later in this chapter, that's exactly what we'll do); even more intriguing, the pieces can be repositioned and animated separately, so it's easy to rotate the arrow without moving the circle (and in Chapter 17, that's exactly what we'll do).

The documentation discusses layers chiefly in connection with animation (in particular, in the *Core Animation Programming Guide*). This categorization gives the impression that layers are of interest only if you intend to animate. That's misleading. Layers are the basis of animation, but they are also the basis of view drawing, and are useful and important even if you don't use them for animation.

CALayer is not part of UIKit. It's part of the Quartz Core framework, which is not linked by default into the project template. If your app contains code that refers to CALayer or related classes, you must link your target to *QuartzCore.framework*, and you must import <QuartzCore/QuartzCore.h> into any file containing such code.

View and Layer

A UIView instance has an accompanying CALayer instance, accessible as the view's layer property. This layer has a special status: it is partnered with this view to embody all of the view's drawing. The layer has no corresponding view property, but the view is the layer's delegate. The documentation sometimes speaks of this layer as the view's "underlying layer."

By default, when a UIView is instantiated, its layer is an instance of CALayer. But if you subclass UIView and you want your subclass's underlying layer to be an instance of a CALayer subclass (built-in or your own), implement the UIView subclass's layer-Class class method.

That, for example, is how the compass in Figure 16-1 is created. We have a UIView subclass, CompassView, and a CALayer subclass, CompassLayer. CompassView contains these lines:

```
+ (Class) layerClass {
    return [CompassLayer class];
}
```

Thus, when CompassView is instantiated, its underlying layer is a CompassLayer. In this example, there is no drawing in CompassView; its job is to give CompassLayer a place in the visible interface, because a layer cannot appear without a view.

Because every view has an underlying layer, there is a tight integration between the two. The layer portrays all the view's drawing; if the view draws, it does so by contributing to the layer's drawing. The view is the layer's delegate. And the view's properties are often merely a convenience for accessing the layer's properties. For example, when you set the view's backgroundColor, you are really setting the layer's backgroundColor, and if you set the layer's backgroundColor directly, the view's backgroundColor is set to match. Similarly, the view's frame is really the layer's frame and *vice versa*.

 A CALayer's delegate property is settable, but you must never set the delegate property of a UIView's underlying layer. To do so would be to break the integration between them, thereby causing drawing to stop working correctly. A UIView *must* be the delegate of its underlying layer; moreover, it must *not* be the delegate of any *other* layer. *Don't do anything to mess this up.*

The view draws into its layer, and the layer caches that drawing; the layer can then be manipulated, changing the view's appearance, without necessarily asking the view to redraw itself. This is a source of great efficiency in the drawing system. It also explains such phenomena as the content stretching that we encountered in the last section of Chapter 15: when the view's bounds size changes, the drawing system, by default, simply stretches or repositions the cached layer image, until such time as the view is told to generate a new drawing of itself (drawRect:) to replace the layer's content.

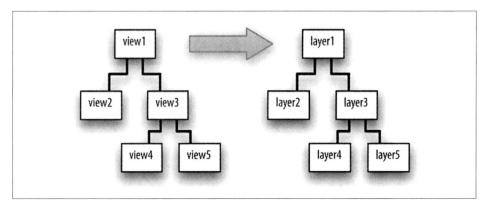

Figure 16-2. A hierarchy of views and the hierarchy of layers underlying it

Mac OS X Programmer Alert

On Mac OS X, NSView existed long before CALayer was introduced, so today a view might have no layer, or, if it does have a layer, it might relate to it in various ways. You may be accustomed to terms like *layer-backed view* or *layer-hosting view*. On iOS, layers were incorporated from the outset: every UIView has an underlying layer and relates to it in the same way.

Layers and Sublayers

A layer can have sublayers, and a layer has at most one superlayer. Thus there is a tree of layers. This is similar and parallel to the tree of views (Chapter 14). In fact, so tight is the integration between a view and its underlying layer that these hierarchies are effectively the same hierarchy. Given a view and its underlying layer, that layer's superlayer is the view's superview's underlying layer, and that layer has as sublayers all the underlying layers of all the view's subviews. Indeed, because the layers are how the views actually get drawn, one might say that the view hierarchy really *is* a layer hierarchy (Figure 16-2).

At the same time, the layer hierarchy can go beyond the view hierarchy. A view has exactly one underlying layer, but a layer can have sublayers that are not the underlying layers of any view. So the hierarchy of layers that underlie views exactly matches the hierarchy of views (Figure 16-2), but the total layer tree may be a superset of that hierarchy. In Figure 16-3, we see the same view-and-layer hierarchy as in Figure 16-2, but two of the layers have additional sublayers that are theirs alone (that is, sublayers that are not any view's underlying layers).

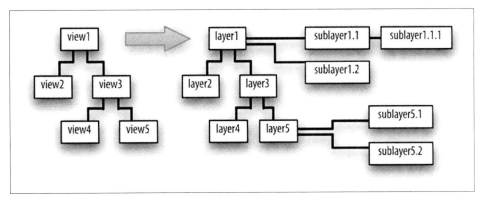

Figure 16-3. Layers that have sublayers of their own

From a visual standpoint, there may be nothing to distinguish a hierarchy of views from a hierarchy of layers. For example, in Chapter 14 we drew three overlapping rectangles using a hierarchy of views (Figure 14-1). This code gives exactly the same visible display by manipulating layers:

```
UIView* v = self.window.rootViewController.view;
CALayer* lay1 = [CALayer new];
lay1.frame = CGRectMake(113, 111, 132, 194);
lay1.backgroundColor =
    [[UIColor colorWithRed:1 green:.4 blue:1 alpha:1] CGColor];
[v.layer addSublayer:lay1];
CALayer* lay2 = [CALayer new];
lay2.backgroundColor =
    [[UIColor colorWithRed:.5 green:1 blue:0 alpha:1] CGColor];
lay2.frame = CGRectMake(41, 56, 132, 194);
[lay1 addSublayer:lay2];
CALayer* lay3 = [CALayer new];
lay3.backgroundColor =
    [[UIColor colorWithRed:1 green:0 blue:0 alpha:1] CGColor];
lay3.frame = CGRectMake(43, 197, 160, 230);
[v.layer addSublayer:lay3];
```

There are, indeed, situations in which it is not clear whether a piece of interface should be constructed as a view hierarchy or a layer hierarchy. Several of my apps have an interface that is a rectangular grid of objects of the same type; in some cases, I implement these as layers, in some cases I implement them as views, and sometimes it isn't clear to me that my choice is much more than arbitrary. A layer on its own is more lightweight than a view; on the other hand, a view is a UIResponder, so it can respond to touches, and layers lack any form of automatic layout.

Manipulating the Layer Hierarchy

Layers come with a full set of methods for reading and manipulating the layer hierarchy, parallel to the methods for reading and manipulating the view hierarchy. A layer has a superlayer property and a sublayers property; there are methods addSublayer:, insertSublayer:atIndex:, insertSublayer:below:, insertSublayer:above:, replaceSublayer:with:, and removeFromSuperlayer.

Unlike a view's subviews property, a layer's sublayers property is writable; thus, you can give a layer multiple sublayers in a single move, by assigning to its sublayers property. To remove all of a layer's sublayers, set its sublayers property to nil.

Although a layer's sublayers have an order, reflected in the sublayers order and regulated with the methods I've just mentioned, this is not necessarily the same as their back-to-front drawing order. By default, it is, but a layer also has a zPosition property, a CGFloat, and this also determines drawing order. The rule is that all sublayers with the same zPosition are drawn in the order they are listed among their sublayers siblings, but lower zPosition siblings are drawn before higher zPosition siblings. (The default zPosition is 0.)

Sometimes, the zPosition property is a more convenient way of dictating drawing order than sibling order is. For example, if layers represent playing cards laid out in a solitaire game, it will likely be a lot easier and more flexible to determine how the cards overlap by setting their zPosition than by rearranging their sibling order.

Methods are also provided for converting between the coordinate systems of layers within the same layer hierarchy: convertPoint:fromLayer:, convertPoint:to-Layer:, convertRect:fromLayer:, and convertRect:toLayer:.

Positioning a Sublayer

Layer coordinate systems and positioning are similar to those of views. A layer's own internal coordinate system is expressed by its bounds, just like a view; its size is its bounds size, and its bounds origin is the internal coordinate at its top left.

However, a sublayer's position within its superlayer is not described by its center, like a view; a layer does not have a center. Instead, a sublayer's position within its superlayer is defined by a combination of two properties, its position and its anchorPoint. Think of the sublayer as pinned to its superlayer; then you have to say both where the pin passes through the sublayer and where it passes through the superlayer. (I didn't make up that analogy, but it's pretty apt.)

position
    A point expressed in the superlayer's coordinate system.

anchorPoint

> Where the `position` point is with respect to the layer's own bounds. It is a pair of floating-point numbers (a CGPoint) describing a fraction (or multiple) of the layer's own bounds width and bounds height. Thus, for example, `{0,0}` is the layer's top left, and `{1,1}` is its bottom right.

If the `anchorPoint` is `{0.5,0.5}` (the default), the `position` property works like a view's center property. A view's `center` is thus a special case of a layer's `position`. This is quite typical of the relationship between view properties and layer properties; the view properties are often a simpler, more convenient, and less powerful version of the layer properties.

A layer's `position` and `anchorPoint` are orthogonal (independent); changing one does not change the other. Therefore, changing either of them without changing the other changes where the layer is drawn within its superlayer.

For example, in Figure 16-1, the most important point in the circle is its center; all the other objects need to be positioned with respect to it. Therefore they all have the same `position`: the center of the circle. But they differ in their `anchorPoint`. For example, the arrow's `anchorPoint` is `{0.5,0.8}`, the middle of the shaft, near the end. On the other hand, the `anchorPoint` of a cardinal point letter is more like `{0.5,3}`, well outside the letter's bounds, so as to place the letter near the edge of the circle.

A layer's `frame` is a purely derived property. When you get the `frame`, it is calculated from the bounds size along with the `position` and `anchorPoint`. When you set the `frame`, you set the bounds size and `position`. In general, you should regard the `frame` as a convenient façade and no more. Nevertheless, it is convenient! For example, to position a sublayer so that it exactly overlaps its superlayer, you can just set the sublayer's `frame` to the superlayer's bounds.

 A layer created in code (as opposed to a view's underlying layer) has a `frame` and bounds of `{{0,0},{0,0}}` and will not be visible on the screen even when you add it to a superlayer that is on the screen. Be sure to give your layer a nonzero width and height if you want to be able to see it.

CAScrollLayer

If you're going to be moving a layer's bounds origin as a way of repositioning its sublayers *en masse*, you might like to make the layer a CAScrollLayer, a CALayer subclass that provides convenience methods for this sort of thing. (Despite the name, a CAScrollLayer provides no scrolling interface; the user can't scroll it by dragging, for example.) By default, a CAScrollLayer's `masksToBounds` property is YES; thus, the CAScrollLayer acts like a window through which you see can only what is within its bounds. (You can set its masksToBounds to NO, but this would be an odd thing to do, as it somewhat defeats the purpose.)

To move the CAScrollLayer's bounds, you can talk either to it or to a sublayer (at any depth):

Talking to the CAScrollLayer
scrollToPoint:
> Changes the CAScrollLayer's bounds origin to that point.

scrollToRect:
> Changes the CAScrollLayer's bounds origin minimally so that the given portion of the bounds rect is visible.

Talking to a sublayer
scrollPoint:
> Changes the CAScrollLayer's bounds origin so that the given point *of the sublayer* is at the top left of the CAScrollLayer.

scrollRectToVisible:
> Changes the CAScrollLayer's bounds origin so that the given rect *of the sublayer's bounds* is within the CAScrollLayer's bounds area. You can also ask the sublayer for its visibleRect, the part of this sublayer now within the CAScrollLayer's bounds.

Layout of Sublayers

The view hierarchy is actually a layer hierarchy (Figure 16-2). The positioning of a view within its superview is actually the positioning of its layer within its superlayer (the superview's layer). It follows as the night the day that what I described in Chapter 14 as layout of views is actually layout of layers. Whether a view is positioned manually (by setting its frame or bounds and center) or automatically through its autoresizing-Mask or automatically through autolayout based on its constraints, what's really being laid out is a layer.

But what about a sublayer that isn't any view's underlying layer (Figure 16-3)? The system obviously keeps such a sublayer at the same position with respect to its superlayer's bounds; but that's all it does, and it doesn't really count as layout. The only option for layout of such sublayers is manual layout that you perform in code.

When a layer needs layout, either because its bounds have changed or because you called setNeedsLayout, you can respond in either of two ways:

- The layer's layoutSublayers method is called; to respond, override layout-Sublayers in your CALayer subclass.

- Alternatively, implement `layoutSublayersOfLayer:` in the layer's delegate. (Remember, if the layer is a view's underlying layer, the view is its delegate.)

To do effective manual layout of sublayers, you'll probably need a way to identify or refer to the sublayers. There is no layer equivalent of `viewWithTag:`, so such identification and reference is entirely up to you. Key–value coding can be helpful here; layers implement key–value coding in a special way, discussed at the end of this chapter.

Mac OS X Programmer Alert
On Mac OS X, layers have extensive layout support, including both constraints and custom layout managers. But iOS lacks all of this.

For a view's underlying layer, `layoutSublayers` or `layoutSublayersOfLayer:` is called after the view's `layoutSubviews`. Under autolayout, you must call `super` or else autolayout will break. Moreover, these methods may be called more than once during the course of autolayout; if you're looking for an automatically generated signal that it's time to do manual layout of sublayers (because the device has been rotated, for example), the view's `layoutSubviews` might be a better choice.

Drawing in a Layer

There are various ways to make a layer display something (apart from having a partnered view draw into it, as discussed in Chapter 15).

The simplest way to make something appear in a layer is through its `contents` property. This is parallel to the `image` in a UIImageView (Chapter 15). It is expected to be a CGImageRef (or nil, signifying no image). A CGImageRef is not an object type, but the `contents` property is typed as an `id`; in order to quiet the compiler, you'll have to typecast your CGImageRef to an `id` as you assign it, like this:

```
layer.contents = (id)[im CGImage];
```

You may be wondering why, under ARC, we don't also have to "cross the bridge" from the CFTypeRef world of a CGImageRef to the object world of an `id` by supplying a `__bridge` cast, as discussed in Chapter 12. It's because the `CGImage` method is a Cocoa method and supplies ARC with the memory management information it needs. Coming back the other way, though, we would need an explicit `__bridge` cast:

```
CGImageRef imref = (__bridge CGImageRef)layer.contents;
```

Setting a layer's contents to a UIImage, rather than a CGImage, will fail silently — the image doesn't appear, but there is no error either. This is absolutely maddening, and I wish I had a nickel for every time I've done it and then wasted hours figuring out why my layer isn't appearing.

There are also four methods that can be implemented to provide or draw a layer's content on demand, similar to a UIView's `drawRect:`. A layer is very conservative about calling these methods (and you must not call any of them directly). When a layer *does* call these methods, I will say that the layer *redisplays itself*. Here is how a layer can be caused to redisplay itself:

- If the layer's `needsDisplayOnBoundsChange` property is NO (the default), then the only way to cause the layer to redisplay itself is by calling `setNeedsDisplay` (or `setNeedsDisplayInRect:`). Even this might not cause these methods to be called right away; if that's crucial, then you will also call `displayIfNeeded`.

- If the layer's `needsDisplayOnBoundsChange` property is YES, then the layer will also redisplay itself when the layer's bounds change (rather like a UIView's `UIViewContentModeRedraw`).

Here are the four methods that can be called when a layer redisplays itself; pick one to implement (don't try to combine them, you'll just confuse things):

`display` *in a subclass*
> Your CALayer subclass can override `display`. There's no graphics context at this point, so `display` is pretty much limited to setting the `contents` image.

`displayLayer:` *in the delegate*
> You can set the CALayer's `delegate` property and implement `displayLayer:` in the delegate. As with `display`, there's no graphics context, so you'll just be setting the `contents` image.

`drawInContext:` *in a subclass*
> Your CALayer subclass can override `drawInContext:`. The parameter is a graphics context into which you can draw directly; it is *not* automatically made the current context.

`drawLayer:inContext:` *in the delegate*
> You can set the CALayer's `delegate` property and implement `drawLayer:inContext:`. The second parameter is a graphics context into which you can draw directly; it is *not* automatically made the current context.

Remember, you must not set the `delegate` property of a view's underlying layer! The view is its delegate and must remain its delegate. This restriction is not as onerous as it

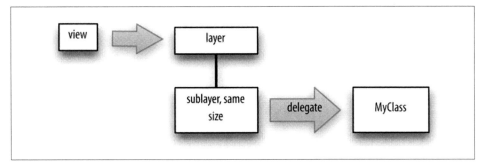

Figure 16-4. A view and a layer delegate that draws into it

seems; there's generally an easy architectural way to draw into a layer by way of some other delegate if that's what you want to do.

For example, in one of my apps there's an overlay view, sitting on top of everything else on the screen; the user is unaware of this, because the view is transparent and usually does no drawing, and the view ignores touches, which fall through to the visible views, as if the overlay were not there at all. But every once in a while I want the overlay view to display something (this is its purpose). I don't want the overhead of making an image, and my app has a main controller, which already knows what needs drawing, so I want to draw *using this controller as a layer delegate*. But it can't be the delegate of the overlay view's underlying layer, so I give that layer a sublayer and make my main controller *that* sublayer's delegate. Thus we have a view and its underlying layer that do nothing, except to serve as a host for this sublayer (Figure 16-4) — and there's nothing wrong with that.

Assigning a layer a `contents` image and drawing directly into the layer are, in effect, mutually exclusive. So:

- If a layer's `contents` is assigned an image, this image is shown immediately and replaces whatever drawing may have been displayed in the layer.
- If a layer redisplays itself and `drawInContext:` or `drawLayer:inContext:` draws into the layer, the drawing replaces whatever image may have been displayed in the layer.
- If a layer redisplays itself and none of the `display` methods provides content (perhaps because you didn't override any of them), the layer will be empty of content.

A layer has a scale, its `contentsScale`, which maps point distances in the layer's graphics context to pixel distances on the device. A layer that's managed by Cocoa, if it has contents, will adjust its `contentsScale` automatically as needed; for example, if a UIImageView has a double-resolution image (its `scale` is 2), and if we're running on a device with a double-resolution screen, then the image view's underlying layer is assigned a `contentsScale` of 2. A layer that you are creating and managing yourself, however, has no such automatic behavior; it's up to you, if you plan to draw into the layer, to set its `contentsScale` appropriately. Content drawn into a layer with a `contentsScale` of 1 may appear pixellated or fuzzy on a double-resolution screen.

Three layer properties strongly affect what the layer displays, in ways that can be baffling to beginners: its `backgroundColor` property, its `opaque` property, and its `opacity` property. Here's what you need to know:

- Think of the `backgroundColor` as separate from the layer's own drawing, and as painted *behind* the layer's own drawing. It is equivalent to a view's `backgroundColor` (and if this layer is a view's underlying layer, it *is* the view's `backgroundColor`). Changing the `backgroundColor` takes effect immediately.

- The `opaque` property determines whether the layer's *graphics context is opaque.* An opaque graphics context is black; you can draw on top of that blackness, but the blackness is still there. A non-opaque graphics context is clear; where no drawing is, it is completely transparent. Changing the `opaque` property has no effect until the layer redisplays itself.

  If a layer is a view's underlying layer, then setting the view's `backgroundColor` to an opaque color (alpha component of 1) sets the layer's `opaque`, though not the view's `opaque`, to YES. I regard this as extremely weird. (It is the reason behind the strange behavior of `CGContextClearRect` described in Chapter 15.)

- The `opacity` property affects the overall apparent transparency of the layer. It is equivalent to a view's `alpha` (and if this layer is a view's underlying layer, it *is* the view's `alpha`). It affects the apparent transparency of the layer's sublayers as well. It affects the apparent transparency of the background color and the apparent transparency of the layer's content separately (just as with a view's `alpha`). Changing the `opacity` property takes effect immediately.

When drawing directly into a layer, the behavior of `GCContextClearRect` differs from what was described in Chapter 15: instead of punching a hole through the background color, it effectively paints with the layer's background color. (This can have curious side effects.)

Content Resizing and Positioning

Once a layer has content, regardless of whether this content came from an image (setting the `contents` property) or from direct drawing into its context (`drawInContext:`, `drawLayer:inContext:`), various properties dictate how the content should be drawn in relation to the layer's bounds. It is as if the cached content is itself treated as an image, which can then be resized, repositioned, cropped, and so on. These properties are:

contentsGravity

> This property, a string, is parallel to a UIView's `contentMode` property, and describes how the content should be positioned or stretched in relation to the bounds. For example, `kCAGravityCenter` means the content is centered in the bounds without resizing; `kCAGravityResize` (the default) means the content is sized to fit the bounds, even if this means distorting its aspect; and so forth.

> For historical reasons, the terms "bottom" and "top" in the names of the `contentsGravity` settings have the opposite of their expected meanings.

contentsRect

> A CGRect expressing the proportion of the content that is to be displayed. The default is `{{0,0},{1,1}}`, meaning the entire content is displayed. The specified part of the content is sized and positioned in relation to the bounds in accordance with the `contentsGravity`. Thus, for example, you can scale up part of the content to fill the bounds, or slide part of a larger image into view without redrawing or changing the `contents` image.

> You can also use the `contentsRect` to scale down the content, by specifying a larger `contentsRect` such as `{{-.5, -.5}, {1.5, 1.5}}`; but any content pixels that touch the edge of the `contentsRect` will then be extended outwards to the edge of the layer (to prevent this, make sure that the outermost pixels of the content are all empty).

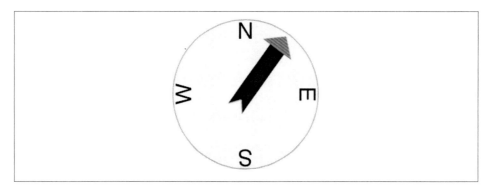

Figure 16-5. One way of resizing the compass arrow

contentsCenter

> A CGRect expressing the central region of nine rectangular regions of the contents-
> Rect that are variously allowed to stretch if the contentsGravity calls for stretch-
> ing. The central region (the actual value of the contentsCenter) stretches in both
> directions. Of the other eight regions (inferred from the value you provide), the
> four corner regions don't stretch, and the four side regions stretch in one direction.
> (This should remind you of how a resizable image stretches.)

If you're drawing directly into the layer's graphics context (e.g., with drawLayer:in-
Context:), and the contentsRect is the entire content, then if the layer redisplays itself,
the contentsGravity won't matter, because the graphics context fills the layer. But if
the layer's bounds are resized when needsDisplayOnBoundsChange is NO, then its
cached content from the last time you drew is treated as an image. By a judicious combination of settings, you can attain some fairly sophisticated automatic behavior, with
no need to redraw the content yourself. For example, Figure 16-5 shows the result of
the following settings:

```
arrow.needsDisplayOnBoundsChange = NO;
arrow.contentsCenter = CGRectMake(0.0, 0.4, 1.0, 0.6);
arrow.contentsGravity = kCAGravityResizeAspect;
arrow.bounds = CGRectInset(arrow.bounds, -20, -20);
```

Because needsDisplayOnBoundsChange is NO, the content is not redisplayed when the
arrow's bounds are increased; instead, the cached content is used. The contents-
Gravity setting tells us to resize proportionally; therefore, the arrow is both longer and
wider than in Figure 16-1, but not in such a way as to distort its proportions. However,
notice that although the triangular arrowhead is wider, it is not longer; the increase in
length is due entirely to the stretching of the shaft. That's because the contents-
Center region is restricted to the shaft of the arrow.

If the content is larger than the bounds of the layer (which can easily happen if you're assigning a `contents` image), and if the `contentsGravity` and `contentsRect` do not resize the content to fit the bounds, then by default the content will be drawn larger than the layer; the layer does not automatically clip its content to its bounds (just as it does not automatically clip its sublayers to its bounds). To get such clipping, for both content and sublayers, set the layer's `masksToBounds` property to YES.

 The value of a layer's bounds origin does not affect where its content is drawn. It affects only where its sublayers are drawn.

Layers that Draw Themselves

A few built-in CALayer subclasses provide some basic but extremely helpful self-drawing ability:

CATextLayer

A CATextLayer has a `string` property, which can be an NSString or NSAttributedString, along with other text formatting properties; it draws its `string`. The default text color, the `foregroundColor` property, is white, which is unlikely to be what you want. The text is different from the `contents` and is mutually exclusive with it: either the contents image or the text will be drawn, but not both, so in general you should not give a CATextLayer any contents image. In Figure 16-1, the cardinal point letters are CATextLayer instances.

 Text drawing has changed in iOS 6. If you were using CATextLayer in iOS 5 or before, you may find that your text appears differently in iOS 6 (for example, its position may be shifted).

CAShapeLayer

A CAShapeLayer has a `path` property, which is a CGPath. It fills or strokes this path, or both, depending on its `fillColor` and `strokeColor` values, and displays the result; the default is a `fillColor` of black and no `strokeColor`. A CAShapeLayer may also have `contents`; the shape is displayed on top of the contents image, but there is no property permitting you to specify a compositing mode. In Figure 16-1, the background circle is a CAShapeLayer instance, stroked with gray and filled with a lighter, slightly transparent gray.

CAGradientLayer

A CAGradientLayer covers its background with a simple linear gradient; thus, it's an easy way to composite a gradient into your interface (and if you need something more elaborate you can always draw with Core Graphics instead). The gradient is

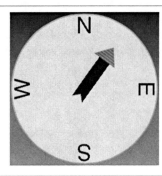

Figure 16-6. A gradient drawn behind the compass

defined much as in the Core Graphics gradient example in Chapter 15, an array of locations and an array of corresponding colors (except that these are NSArrays, not C arrays), along with a start and end point. To clip the gradient, you can add a mask to the CAGradientLayer (masks are discussed later in this chapter). A CAGradient-Layer's contents are not displayed.

The colors array requires CGColors, not UIColors. But CGColorRef is not an object type, whereas NSArray expects objects, so to quiet the compiler you'll need to typecast (to id).

Figure 16-6 shows our compass drawn with an extra CAGradientLayer behind it.

Transforms

The way a layer is drawn on the screen can be modified though a transform. This is not surprising, because a view can have a transform (see Chapter 14), and a view is drawn on the screen by its layer. As with the bounds and other properties, a view and its underlying layer are tightly linked; when you change the transform of one, you are changing the transform of the other. But, as so often happens, the layer's transform is more powerful than the view's transform. Thus, you can use the transform of the underlying layer to accomplish things with a view that you can't accomplish with the view's transform alone.

In the simplest cases, when a transform is two-dimensional, you can use the setAffine-Transform: and affineTransform methods. The value is a CGAffineTransform, familiar from Chapter 14 and Chapter 15. The transform is applied around the anchor-Point. Thus, the anchorPoint has a second purpose that I didn't tell you about when discussing it earlier.

You now know everything you need to know in order to understand the code that generated Figure 16-6, so here is that code. Notice how the four cardinal point letters are drawn by a CATextLayer and placed using a transform. They are drawn at the same coordinates, but they have different rotation transforms. Moreover, even though the CATextLayers are small (just 40 by 40) and appear near the perimeter of the circle, they are anchored, and so their rotation is centered, at the center of the circle. In this code, self is the CompassLayer; it does no drawing of its own, but merely assembles and configures its sublayers. To generate the arrow, we make ourselves the arrow layer's delegate and call setNeedsDisplay; this causes drawLayer:inContext: to be called in CompassLayer (that code is just the same code we developed for drawing the arrow into a context in Chapter 15, and is not repeated here):

```
// the gradient
CAGradientLayer* g = [CAGradientLayer new];
g.contentsScale = [UIScreen mainScreen].scale;
g.frame = self.bounds;
g.colors = @[(id)[[UIColor blackColor] CGColor],
             (id)[[UIColor redColor] CGColor]];
g.locations = @[@0.0f,
                @1.0f];
[self addSublayer:g];

// the circle
CAShapeLayer* circle = [CAShapeLayer new];
circle.contentsScale = [UIScreen mainScreen].scale;
circle.lineWidth = 2.0;
circle.fillColor =
[[UIColor colorWithRed:0.9 green:0.95 blue:0.93 alpha:0.9] CGColor];
circle.strokeColor = [[UIColor grayColor] CGColor];
CGMutablePathRef p = CGPathCreateMutable();
CGPathAddEllipseInRect(p, nil, CGRectInset(self.bounds, 3, 3));
circle.path = p;
[self addSublayer:circle];
circle.bounds = self.bounds;
circle.position = CGPointMake(CGRectGetMidX(self.bounds),
                             CGRectGetMidY(self.bounds));

// the four cardinal points
NSArray* pts = @[@"N", @"E", @"S", @"W"];
for (int i = 0; i < 4; i++) {
    CATextLayer* t = [CATextLayer new];
    t.contentsScale = [UIScreen mainScreen].scale;
    t.string = pts[i];
    t.bounds = CGRectMake(0,0,40,40);
    t.position = CGPointMake(CGRectGetMidX(circle.bounds),
                            CGRectGetMidY(circle.bounds));
    CGFloat vert = CGRectGetMidY(circle.bounds) / CGRectGetHeight(t.bounds);
    t.anchorPoint = CGPointMake(0.5, vert);
    t.alignmentMode = kCAAlignmentCenter;
    t.foregroundColor = [[UIColor blackColor] CGColor];
```

```
        [t setAffineTransform:CGAffineTransformMakeRotation(i*M_PI/2.0)];
        [circle addSublayer:t];
    }

    // the arrow
    CALayer* arrow = [CALayer new];
    arrow.contentsScale = [UIScreen mainScreen].scale;
    arrow.bounds = CGRectMake(0, 0, 40, 100);
    arrow.position = CGPointMake(CGRectGetMidX(self.bounds),
                                 CGRectGetMidY(self.bounds));
    arrow.anchorPoint = CGPointMake(0.5, 0.8);
    arrow.delegate = self;
    [arrow setAffineTransform:CGAffineTransformMakeRotation(M_PI/5.0)];
    [self addSublayer:arrow];
    [arrow setNeedsDisplay];
```

A full-fledged layer transform, the value of the transform property, takes place in three-dimensional space; its description includes a z-axis, perpendicular to both the x-axis and y-axis. (By default, the positive z-axis points out of the screen, toward the viewer's face.) Layers do not magically give you realistic three-dimensional rendering — for that you would use OpenGL, which is beyond the scope of this discussion. Layers are two-dimensional objects, and they are designed for speed and simplicity. Nevertheless, they do operate in three dimensions, quite sufficiently to give a cartoonish but effective sense of reality, especially when performing an animation. We've all seen the screen image flip like turning over a piece of paper to reveal what's on the back; that's a rotation in three dimensions.

A three-dimensional transform takes place around a three-dimensional extension of the anchorPoint, whose z-component is supplied by the anchorPointZ property. Thus, in the reduced default case where anchorPointZ is 0, the anchorPoint is sufficient, as we've already seen in using CGAffineTransform.

The transform itself is described mathematically by a struct called a CATransform3D. The *Core Animation Function Reference* lists the functions for working with these transforms. They are a lot like the CGAffineTransform functions, except they've got a third dimension. For example, here's the declaration of the function for making a 2D scale transform:

```
CGAffineTransform CGAffineTransformMakeScale (
    CGFloat sx,
    CGFloat sy
);
```

And here's the declaration of the function for making a 3D scale transform:

```
CATransform3D CATransform3DMakeScale (
    CGFloat sx,
    CGFloat sy,
    CGFloat sz
);
```

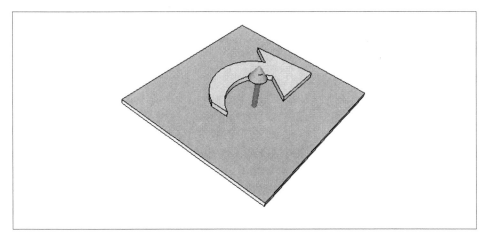

Figure 16-7. An anchor point plus a vector defines a rotation plane

The rotation 3D transform is a little more complicated. In addition to the angle, you also have to supply three coordinates describing the vector around which the rotation takes place. Perhaps you've forgotten from your high-school math what a vector is, or perhaps trying to visualize three dimensions boggles your mind, so think of it this way.

Pretend for purposes of discussion that the anchor point is the origin, {0,0,0}. Now imagine an arrow emanating from the anchor point; its other end, the pointy end, is described by the three coordinates you provide. Now imagine a plane that intersects the anchor point, perpendicular to the arrow. That is the plane in which the rotation will take place; a positive angle is a clockwise rotation, as seen from the side of the plane with the arrow (Figure 16-7). In effect, the three points you supply describe, relative to the anchor point, where your eye would have to be to see this rotation as an old-fashioned two-dimensional rotation.

The three values you give specify a direction, not a point. Thus it makes no difference on what scale you give them: {1,1,1} means the same thing as {10,10,10}. If the three values are {0,0,1}, with all other things being equal, the case is collapsed to a simple CGAffineTransform, because the rotational plane is the screen. On the other hand, if the three values are {0,0,-1}, it's a backward CGAffineTransform, so that a positive angle looks counterclockwise (because we are looking at the "back side" of the rotational plane).

A layer can itself be rotated in such a way that its "back" is showing. For example, the following rotation flips a layer around its y-axis:

```
someLayer.transform = CATransform3DMakeRotation(M_PI, 0, 1, 0);
```

By default, the layer is considered double-sided, so when it is flipped to show its "back," what's drawn is an appropriately reversed version of the content of the layer (along with its sublayers, which by default are still drawn in front of the layer, but reversed and positioned in accordance with the layer's transformed coordinate system). But if the layer's doubleSided property is NO, then when it is flipped to show its "back," the layer disappears (along with its sublayers); its "back" is transparent and empty.

Depth

There are two ways to place layers at different nominal depths with respect to their siblings. One is through the z-component of their position, which is the zPosition property. Thus the zPosition, too, has a second purpose that I didn't tell you about earlier. The other is to apply a transform that translates the layer's position in the z-direction. These two values (the z-component of a layer's position and the z-component of its translation transform) are related; in some sense, the zPosition is a shorthand for a translation transform in the z-direction. (If you provide both a zPosition and a z-direction translation, you can rapidly confuse yourself.)

In the real world, changing an object's zPosition would make it appear larger or smaller, as it is positioned closer or further away; but this, by default, is not the case in the world of layer drawing. There is no attempt to portray perspective; the layer planes are drawn at their actual size and flattened onto one another, with no illusion of distance. (This is called *orthographic projection*, and is the way blueprints are often drawn to display an object from one side.)

However, there's a widely used trick for introducing a quality of perspective into the way layers are drawn: make them sublayers of a layer whose sublayerTransform property maps all points onto a "distant" plane. (This is probably just about the only thing the sublayerTransform property is ever used for.) Combined with orthographic projection, the effect is to apply one-point perspective to the drawing, so that things do get perceptibly smaller in the negative z-direction.

For example, let's try applying a sort of "page-turn" rotation to our compass: we'll anchor it at its right side and then rotate it around the y-axis. For purposes of the example, the sublayer we're actually rotating is accessed through a property, rotationLayer:

```
self.rotationLayer.anchorPoint = CGPointMake(1,0.5);
self.rotationLayer.position =
    CGPointMake(CGRectGetMaxX(self.bounds), CGRectGetMidY(self.bounds));
self.rotationLayer.transform = CATransform3DMakeRotation(M_PI/4.0, 0, 1, 0);
```

The results are disappointing (Figure 16-8); the compass looks more squashed than rotated. Now, however, we'll also apply the distance-mapping transform. The superlayer here is self:

```
CATransform3D transform = CATransform3DIdentity;
transform.m34 = -1.0/1000.0;
self.sublayerTransform = transform;
```

Figure 16-8. A disappointing page-turn rotation

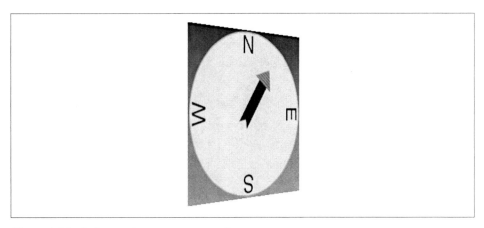

Figure 16-9. A dramatic page-turn rotation

The results (shown in Figure 16-9) are better, and you can experiment with values to replace 1000.0; for example, 500.0 gives an even more exaggerated effect. Also, the zPosition of the rotationLayer will now affect how large it is.

Another way to draw layers with depth is to use CATransformLayer. This CALayer subclass doesn't do any drawing of its own; it is intended solely as a host for other layers. It has the remarkable feature that you can apply a transform to it and it will maintain the depth relationships among its own sublayers. For example:

```
// lay1 is a layer, f is a CGRect
CALayer* lay2 = [CALayer layer];
lay2.frame = f;
lay2.backgroundColor = [UIColor blueColor].CGColor;
[lay1 addSublayer:lay2];
CALayer* lay3 = [CALayer layer];
lay3.frame = CGRectOffset(f, 20, 30);
```

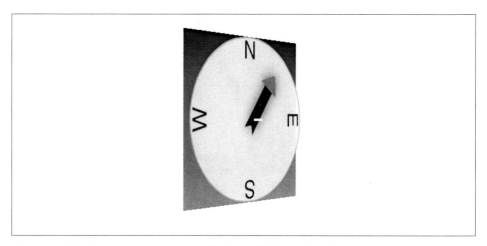

Figure 16-10. Page-turn rotation applied to a CATransformLayer

```
lay3.backgroundColor = [UIColor greenColor].CGColor;
lay3.zPosition = 10;
[lay1 addSublayer:lay3];
lay1.transform = CATransform3DMakeRotation(M_PI, 0, 1, 0);
```

In that code, the superlayer lay1 is flipped like a page being turned by setting its transform. Normally, as I mentioned earlier, the sublayer drawing order doesn't change; the green layer is drawn in front of the blue layer, even after the transform is applied. But if lay1 is a CATransformLayer, the green layer is drawn *behind* the blue layer after the transform; they are both sublayers of lay1, so their depth relationship is maintained.

Figure 16-10 shows our page-turn rotation yet again, still with the sublayer-Transform applied to self, but this time the only sublayer of self is a CATransform-Layer. The CATransformLayer, to which the page-turn transform is applied, holds the gradient layer, the circle layer, and the arrow layer. Those three layers are at different depths (using different zPosition settings), and you can see that the circle layer floats in front of the gradient layer. (This is clear from its apparent offset, but I wish you could see this page-turn as an animation, which makes the circle jump right out from the gradient as the rotation proceeds.) I've also tried to emphasize the arrow's separation from the circle by adding a shadow.

Even more remarkable, note the little white peg sticking through the arrow and running into the circle. It is a CAShapeLayer, rotated to be perpendicular to the CATransform-Layer. Normally, it runs straight out of the circle toward the viewer, so it is seen end-on, and because a layer has no thickness, it is invisible. But as the CATransformLayer pivots forward in our page-turn rotation, the peg maintains its orientation relative to the circle, and comes into view.

There is, I think, a slight additional gain in realism if the same `sublayerTransform` is applied also to the CATransformLayer, but I have not done so here.

Shadows, Borders, and More

A CALayer has many additional properties that affect details of how it is drawn. Once again, all of these drawing details can, of course, be applied equally to a UIView; changing these properties of the UIView's underlying layer changes how the view is drawn. Thus, these are effectively view features as well.

A CALayer can have a shadow, defined by its `shadowColor`, `shadowOpacity`, `shadow-Radius`, and `shadowOffset` properties. To make the layer draw a shadow, set the `shadow-Opacity` to a nonzero value. The shadow is normally based on the shape of the layer's nontransparent region, but deriving this shape can be calculation-intensive (so much so that in early versions of iOS, layer shadows weren't implemented). You can vastly improve performance by defining the shape yourself and assigning this shape as a CGPath to the `shadowPath` property.

A CALayer can have a border (`borderWidth`, `borderColor`); the `borderWidth` is drawn inward from the bounds, potentially covering some of the content unless you compensate.

A CALayer can be bounded by a rounded rectangle, by giving it a `cornerRadius` greater than zero. If the layer has a border, the border has rounded corners too. If the layer has a `backgroundColor`, that background is clipped to the shape of the rounded rectangle. If the layer's `masksToBounds` is YES, the layer's content and its sublayers are clipped by the rounded corners.

Like a UIView, a CALayer has a `hidden` property that can be set to take it and its sublayers out of the visible interface without actually removing it from its superlayer.

A CALayer can have a mask. This is itself a layer, whose content must be provided somehow. The transparency of the mask's content in a particular spot becomes (all other things being equal) the transparency of the layer at that spot. The hues in the mask's colors are irrelevant; only transparency matters. To position the mask, pretend it's a sublayer.

For example, Figure 16-11 shows our arrow layer, with the gray circle layer behind it, and a mask applied to the arrow layer. The mask is silly, but it illustrates very well how masks work: it's an ellipse, with an opaque fill and a thick, semitransparent stroke. Here's the code that generates and applies the mask:

```
CAShapeLayer* mask = [CAShapeLayer new];
mask.frame = arrow.bounds;
CGMutablePathRef p2 = CGPathCreateMutable();
CGPathAddEllipseInRect(p2, nil, CGRectInset(mask.bounds, 10, 10));
```

Figure 16-11. A layer with a mask

```
mask.strokeColor = [[UIColor colorWithWhite:0.0 alpha:0.5] CGColor];
mask.lineWidth = 20;
mask.path = p2;
arrow.mask = mask;
CGPathRelease(p2);
```

Using a mask, we can do manually and in a more general way what the `cornerRadius` and `masksToBounds` properties do, clipping all our content drawing and our sublayers (and, if this layer is a view's underlying layer, the view's subviews) to a desired path. Here's a utility method that generates a CALayer suitable for use as a rounded rectangle mask:

```
- (CALayer*) maskOfSize:(CGSize)sz roundingCorners:(CGFloat)rad {
    CGRect r = (CGRect){CGPointZero, sz};
    UIGraphicsBeginImageContextWithOptions(r.size, NO, 0);
    CGContextRef con = UIGraphicsGetCurrentContext();
    CGContextSetFillColorWithColor(
        con,[UIColor colorWithWhite:0 alpha:0].CGColor);
    CGContextFillRect(con, r);
    CGContextSetFillColorWithColor(
        con,[UIColor colorWithWhite:0 alpha:1].CGColor);
    UIBezierPath* p =
        [UIBezierPath bezierPathWithRoundedRect:r cornerRadius:rad];
    [p fill];
    UIImage* im = UIGraphicsGetImageFromCurrentImageContext();
    UIGraphicsEndImageContext();
    CALayer* mask = [CALayer layer];
    mask.frame = r;
    mask.contents = (id)im.CGImage;
    return mask;
}
```

Layer Efficiency

By now, you're probably envisioning all sorts of compositing fun, with layers masking sublayers and laid semitransparently over other layers. There's nothing wrong with that, but when an iOS device is asked to animate the movement of its drawing from place to place, the animation may stutter because the device lacks the necessary computing power to composite repeatedly and rapidly. This sort of issue is likely to emerge particularly when your code performs an animation (Chapter 17) or when the user is able to animate drawing through touch, as when scrolling a table view (Chapter 21). You may be able to detect these problems by eye, and you can quantify them on a device by using the Core Animation template in Instruments, which shows the frame rate achieved during animation. Also, both the Core Animation template and the Simulator's Debug menu let you summon colored overlays that provide clues as to possible sources of inefficient drawing which can lead to such problems.

In general, opaque drawing is most efficient. (Nonopaque drawing is what Instruments marks in red as "blended layers.") If a layer will always be shown over a background consisting of a single color, you can give the layer its own background of that same color; when additional layer content is supplied, the visual effect will be the same as if that additional layer content were composited over a transparent background. For example, instead of an image masked to a rounded rectangle (with a layer's `cornerRadius` or `mask` property), you could use Core Graphics to clip the drawing of that image into the graphics context of a layer whose background color is the same as that of the destination in front of which the drawing will be shown. Here's an example from a view's `draw-Rect:` in one of my own apps:

```
// clip to rounded rect
CGRect r = CGRectInset(rect, 1, 1);
[[UIBezierPath bezierPathWithRoundedRect:r cornerRadius:6] addClip];
// draw image
UIImage* im = [UIImage imageNamed: @"linen.jpg"];
// simulate UIViewContentModeScaleAspectFill
// make widths the same, image height will be too tall
CGFloat scale = im.size.width/rect.size.width;
CGFloat y = (im.size.height/scale - rect.size.height) / 2.0;
CGRect r2 = CGRectMake(0,-y,im.size.width/scale, im.size.height/scale);
r2 = CGRectIntegral(r2); // looks a whole lot better if we do this
[im drawInRect:r2];
```

Another way to gain some efficiency is by "freezing" the entirety of the layer's drawing as a bitmap. In effect, you're drawing everything in the layer to a secondary cache and using the cache to draw to the screen. Copying from a cache is less efficient than drawing directly to the screen, but this inefficiency may be more than compensated for, if there's a deep or complex layer tree, by not having to composite that tree every time we render. To do this, set the layer's `shouldRasterize` to YES and its `rasterizationScale` to some sensible value (probably `[UIScreen mainScreen].scale`). You can always turn rasterization off again by setting `shouldRasterize` to NO, so it's easy to rasterize just before some massive or sluggish rearrangement of the screen and then unrasterize afterward. (In addition, you can get some cool "out of focus" effects by setting the `rasterization-Scale` to around `0.3`.)

New in iOS 6 is a layer property `drawsAsynchronously`. The default is NO. If set to YES, the layer's graphics context accumulates drawing commands and obeys them later on a background thread. Your drawing commands thus run very quickly, because they are not in fact being obeyed at the time you give them. I haven't had occasion to use this, but presumably there could be situations where it keeps your app responsive when drawing would otherwise be time-consuming.

Layers and Key–Value Coding

All of a layer's properties are accessible through key–value coding by way of keys with the same name as the property. Thus, to apply a mask to a layer, instead of saying this:

```
layer.mask = mask;
```

we could have said:

```
[layer setValue: mask forKey: @"mask"];
```

In addition, CATransform3D and CGAffineTransform values can be expressed through key–value coding and key paths. For example, instead of writing this earlier:

```
self.rotationLayer.transform = CATransform3DMakeRotation(M_PI/4.0, 0, 1, 0);
```

we could have written this:

```
[self.rotationLayer setValue:[NSNumber numberWithFloat:M_PI/4.0]
                  forKeyPath:@"transform.rotation.y"];
```

This notation is possible because CATransform3D is key–value coding compliant for a repertoire of keys and key paths. These are not properties, however; a CATransform3D doesn't have a `rotation` property. It doesn't have *any* properties, because it isn't even an object. You cannot say:

```
self.rotationLayer.transform.rotation.y = //... No, sorry
```

The transform key paths you'll use most often are `rotation.x`, `rotation.y`, `rotation.z`, `rotation` (same as `rotation.z`), `scale.x`, `scale.y`, `scale.z`, `translation.x`, `translation.y`, `translation.z`, and `translation` (two-dimensional, a CGSize).

The Quartz Core framework also injects KVC compliance into CGPoint, CGSize, and CGRect, allowing you to use keys and key paths matching their struct component names. For a complete list of KVC compliant classes related to CALayer, along with the keys and key paths they implement, plus rules for how to wrap nonobject values as objects, see "Core Animation Extensions to Key-Value Coding" in the *Core Animation Programming Guide*.

Moreover, you can treat a CALayer as a kind of NSDictionary, and get and set the value for *any* key. This is tremendously useful, because it means you can attach arbitrary information to an individual layer instance and retrieve it later. For example, earlier I mentioned that to apply manual layout to a layer's sublayers, you will need a way of identifying those sublayers. This feature could provide a way of doing that. For example:

```
[myLayer1 setValue:@"Manny" forKey:@"name"];
[myLayer2 setValue:@"Moe" forKey:@"name"];
```

A layer doesn't have a name property; the @"name" key is something I'm attaching to these layers arbitrarily. Now I can identify these layers later by getting the value of their respective @"name" keys.

Also, CALayer has a defaultValueForKey: class method; to implement it, you'll need to subclass and override. In the case of keys whose value you want to provide a default for, return that value; otherwise, return the value that comes from calling super. Thus, even if a value for a particular key has never been explicitly provided, it can have a non-nil value.

The truth is that this feature, though delightful (and I often wish that all classes behaved like this), is not put there for your convenience and enjoyment. It's there to serve as the basis for animation, which is the subject of the next chapter.

CHAPTER 17

Animation

Animation is the visible change of an attribute over time. The changing attribute might be positional, but not necessarily. For example, a view's background color might change from red to green, not instantly, but perceptibly fading from one to the other. Or a view's opacity might change from opaque to transparent, not instantly, but perceptibly fading away.

Without help, most of us would find animation beyond our reach. There are just too many complications — complications of calculation, of timing, of screen refresh, of threading, and many more. Fortunately, help is provided. You don't perform an animation yourself; you describe it, you order it, and it is performed for you. You get *animation on demand*.

Asking for an animation can be as simple as setting a property value; under some circumstances, a single line of code will result in animation:

```
myLayer.backgroundColor = [[UIColor redColor] CGColor]; // animate to red
```

And this is no coincidence. Apple wants to facilitate your use of animation. Animation is crucial to the character of the iOS interface. It isn't just cool and fun; it clarifies that something is changing or responding. For example, one of my first apps was based on a Mac OS X game in which the user clicks cards to select them. In the Mac OS X version, a card was highlighted to show it was selected, and the computer would beep to indicate a click on an ineligible card. On iOS, these indications were insufficient: the highlighting felt weak, and you can't use a sound warning in an environment where the user might have the volume turned off or be listening to music. So in the iOS version, animation is the indicator for card selection (a selected card waggles eagerly) and for tapping on an ineligible card (the whole interface shudders, as if to shrug off the tap).

Recall from Chapter 16 that CALayer requires the Quartz Core framework; so do the other "CA" (Core Animation) classes discussed here, such as CAAnimation. To use them, you'll link your target to *QuartzCore.framework* and import `<QuartzCore/QuartzCore.h>`.

 The Simulator's Debug → Toggle Slow Animations menu item helps you inspect animations by making them run more slowly.

Drawing, Animation, and Threading

When you change a visible view property, even *without* animation, that change does *not* visibly take place there and then. Rather, the system records that this is a change you would like to make, and marks the view as needing to be redrawn. You can change many visible view properties, but these changes are all just accumulated for later. Later, when all your code has run to completion and the system has, as it were, a free moment, then it redraws all views that need redrawing, applying their new visible property features. Let's call this the *redraw moment*. (I'll explain what the redraw moment really is later in this chapter.)

You can see that this is true simply by changing some visible aspect of a view and changing it back again, in the same code: on the screen, nothing happens. For example, suppose a view's background color is green. Suppose your code changes it to red, and then later changes it back to green:

```
// view starts out green
view.backgroundColor = [UIColor redColor];
// ... time-consuming code goes here ...
view.backgroundColor = [UIColor greenColor];
// code ends, redraw moment arrives
```

The system accumulates all the desired changes until the redraw moment happens, and the redraw moment doesn't happen until after your code has finished, so when the redraw moment does happen, the last accumulated change in the view's color is to green — which is its color already. Thus, no matter how much time-consuming code lies between the change from green to red and the change from red to green, the user won't see any color change at all.

That's why you don't order a view to be redrawn; rather, you tell it that it *needs* redrawing — `setNeedsDisplay` — at the next redraw moment. It's also why I used delayed performance in the `contentMode` example in Chapter 15: by calling `dispatch_after`, I give the redraw moment a chance to happen, thus giving the view some content, *before* resizing the view. This use of delayed performance to let a redraw moment happen is quite common; later in this chapter I'll suggest another way of accomplishing the same goal.

Similarly, when you ask for an animation to be performed, the animation doesn't start happening on the screen until the next redraw moment. (You can force an animation to be performed immediately, but this is unusual.)

While the animation lasts, it is effectively in charge of the screen. Pretend that the animation is a kind of movie, a cartoon, interposed between the user and the "real" screen. When the animation is finished, this movie is removed, revealing the state of the "real" screen behind it. The user is unaware of this, because (if you've done things correctly) at the time that it starts, the movie's first frame looks just like the state of the "real" screen at that moment, and at the time that it ends, the movie's last frame looks just like the state of the "real" screen at *that* moment.

So, when you reposition a view from position 1 to position 2 with animation, you can envision a typical sequence of events like this:

1. The view is set to position 2, but there has been no redraw moment, so it is still portrayed at position 1.

2. The rest of your code runs to completion.

3. The redraw moment arrives. If there were no animation, the view would now be portrayed at position 2. But there *is* an animation, and it (the "animation movie") starts with the view portrayed at position 1, so that is still what the user sees.

4. The animation proceeds, portraying the view at intermediate positions between position 1 and position 2. The documentation describes the animation as now *in-flight*.

5. The animation ends, portraying the view ending up at position 2.

6. The "animation movie" is removed, revealing the view indeed at position 2.

Animation takes place on an independent thread. Multithreading is generally rather tricky and complicated, but the system makes it easy in this case. Nevertheless, you can't completely ignore the threaded nature of animation. Awareness of threading issues, and having a mental picture of how animation is performed, will help you to ask yourself the right questions and thus to avoid confusion and surprises. For example:

1. *The time when an animation starts is somewhat indefinite (because you don't know exactly when the next redraw moment will be). The time when an animation ends is also somewhat indefinite (because the animation happens on another thread, so your code cannot just wait for it to end). So what if your code needs to do something in response to an animation beginning or ending?*

   The Powers That Be have anticipated these needs. Most ways of animating allow you to arrange to be sent a message before or after the animation ends, and there's a general way of being sent a message when all animations end.

2. *Since animation happens on its own thread, something might cause code of yours to start running while an animation is still in-flight. What happens if your code now changes a property that is currently being animated? What happens if your code asks for another animation?*

If you ask for an animation when an animation is already scheduled for the next redraw moment or already in-flight, there might be no problem; both animations can take place simultaneously. But if both animations attempt to animate *the same property*, the first animation may be forced to end instantly. Similarly, changing a property directly (without animation) while that property is being animated might kill the animation. You might do this intentionally as a way of effectively canceling an in-flight animation. To chain animations, you can wait until one animation ends before ordering the next one, or you can create a single animation combining multiple changes starting at different times. There is also a way to "blend" a new animation with an existing animation.

3. *While an animation is in-flight, if your code is not running, the interface is responsive to the user. What happens if the user tries to touch a view whose position is currently being animated?*

It's your job to prevent the user from doing that. During animation, a view is not really where it appears to be on the screen, so the user can easily touch the wrong thing. The usual solution is to turn off the app's responsiveness to touches, or at least an animated view's responsiveness to touches, while an animation is in-flight. (I'll talk more in Chapter 18 about restricting user touches, as well as how to let the user touch a view while it's in animated motion; it's a difficult problem to solve.)

4. *In a multitasking world, the user can suspend my app without quitting it. What happens if an animation is in-flight at that moment?*

If your app is suspended (Chapter 11) during animation, the animation is removed. This simply means that the "animation movie" is cancelled. Any animation, whether in-flight or scheduled, is simply a slowed-down visualization of a property change; that property is still changed, and indeed was probably changed before the animation even started. If your app is resumed, therefore, no animations will be running, and properties that were changed remain changed, and are shown as changed.

UIImageView and UIImage Animation

UIImageView provides a form of animation that is so simple and crude as to be scarcely deserving of the name. Nevertheless, sometimes this form of animation is all you need — a trivial solution to what might otherwise be a tricky problem. Supply the UIImage-View with an array of UIImages, as the value of its `animationImages` or `highlighted-AnimationImages` property; this causes the `image` or `highlightedImage` to be hidden. This array represents the "frames" of a simple cartoon; when you send the `start-`

`Animating` message, the images are displayed in turn, at a frame rate determined by the `animationDuration` property, repeating as many times as specified by the `animation-RepeatCount` property (the default is 0, meaning to repeat forever, or until the `stop-Animating` message is received).

For example, suppose we want an image of Mars to appear out of nowhere and flash three times on the screen. This might seem to require some sort of NSTimer-based solution (see Chapter 11), but it's far simpler to use an animating UIImageView:

```
UIImage* mars = [UIImage imageNamed: @"mars.png"];
UIGraphicsBeginImageContextWithOptions(mars.size, NO, 0);
UIImage* empty = UIGraphicsGetImageFromCurrentImageContext();
UIGraphicsEndImageContext();
NSArray* arr = @[mars, empty, mars, empty, mars];
UIImageView* iv =
    [[UIImageView alloc] initWithFrame:CGRectMake(56, 63, 208, 208)];
[self.window.rootViewController.view addSubview: iv];
iv.animationImages = arr;
iv.animationDuration = 2;
iv.animationRepeatCount = 1;
[iv startAnimating];
```

You can combine UIImageView animation with other kinds of animation. For example, you could flash the image of Mars while at the same time sliding the UIImageView rightward, using view animation as described in the next section.

In addition, UIImage supplies a simple form of animation parallel to what UIImageView provides. An image can itself be an *animated image*. Just as with UIImageView, this really means that you've multiple images that form a sequence serving as the "frames" of a simple cartoon. You can designate an image as an animated image with one of two UIImage class methods:

animatedImageWithImages:duration:

As with UIImageView's animationImages, you supply an array of UIImages. You also supply the duration for the whole animation.

animatedImageNamed:duration:

You supply the name of a single image file at the top level of your app bundle, as with imageNamed: — except that you omit the file extension, and the system does not look for an image file by this name. Instead, it appends @"0" to the name you supply (and then, I presume, several different possible file extensions) and looks for *that* image file, and makes it the first image in the animation sequence. Then it appends @"1" to the name you supply and looks for *that* image file. And so on, until it fails to find any more image files with any of these constructed names, up through @"1024". It is fine if image files for some constructed names don't exist; for example, animatedImageNamed:@"moi" works even if the only "moi" image files are *moi101.png* and *moi293.png*.

A third method, animatedResizableImageNamed:capInsets:resizing-Mode:duration:, combines an animated image with a resizable image (Chapter 15).

You do not tell an animated image to start animating, nor are you able to tell it how long you want the animation to repeat. Rather, an animated image is *always animating*, so long as it appears in your interface; to control the animation, add the image to your interface or remove it from the interface, possibly exchanging it for a similar image that isn't animated. Moreover, an animated image can appear in the interface *anywhere a UIImage can appear* as a property of some interface object. So, it can appear in a UIImageView, but it can also appear as the background of a UIButton or a UINavigation-Bar, and so forth.

In this example, I construct a sequence of red circles of different sizes, in code, and build an animated image which I then display in a UIButton to the left of its title:

```
NSMutableArray* arr = [NSMutableArray array];
float w = 18;
for (int i = 0; i < 6; i++) {
    UIGraphicsBeginImageContextWithOptions(CGSizeMake(w,w), NO, 0);
    CGContextRef con = UIGraphicsGetCurrentContext();
    CGContextSetFillColorWithColor(con, [UIColor redColor].CGColor);
    CGContextAddEllipseInRect(con, CGRectMake(0+i,0+i,w-i*2,w-i*2));
    CGContextFillPath(con);
    UIImage* im = UIGraphicsGetImageFromCurrentImageContext();
    UIGraphicsEndImageContext();
    [arr addObject:im];
}
UIImage* im = [UIImage animatedImageWithImages:arr duration:0.5];
UIButton* b = [UIButton buttonWithType:UIButtonTypeRoundedRect];
```

```
[b setTitle:@"Howdy" forState:UIControlStateNormal];
[b setImage:im forState:UIControlStateNormal];
b.center = CGPointMake(100,100);
[b sizeToFit];
[self.window.rootViewController.view addSubview:b];
```

But please, use your mighty powers for good, not evil. I do *not* want to see any apps that overuse animated images!

View Animation

Animation is ultimately layer animation. However, for a limited range of attributes, you can animate a UIView directly: these are its `alpha`, `backgroundColor`, `bounds`, `center`, `frame`, and `transform`. You can also animate a UIView's change of contents. Despite the brevity of the list, UIView animation is an excellent way to become acquainted with animation and to experiment with the various parameters you can use to determine how an animation behaves; in many cases it will prove quite sufficient.

There are actually two ways to ask for UIView animation: the old way using animation blocks (before iOS 4.0, and still available), and the new way using Objective-C blocks (Chapter 3). I'll describe the old way first; the documentation describes this approach as "discouraged," but it is not officially deprecated and it does still work, and it may offer some advantages over the newer block-based animation.

Animation Blocks

To animate a change to an animatable UIView property the old way, wrap the change in calls to the UIView class methods `beginAnimations:context:` and `commit-Animations`. The region between these calls is referred to as an *animation block*, even though it is *not* a block in the syntactical Objective-C sense.

So, animating a change to a view's background color could be as simple as this:

```
[UIView beginAnimations:nil context:nil];
v.backgroundColor = [UIColor yellowColor];
[UIView commitAnimations];
```

Any animatable change made within an animation block will be animated, so we can animate a change both to the view's color and its position simultaneously:

```
[UIView beginAnimations:nil context:nil];
v.backgroundColor = [UIColor yellowColor];
CGPoint p = v.center;
p.y -= 100;
v.center = p;
[UIView commitAnimations];
```

We can also animate changes to multiple views. For example, suppose we want to make one view dissolve into another. We start with the second view present in the view hierarchy, but with an `alpha` of 0, so that it is invisible. Then we animate the change of the first view's `alpha` to 0 and the second view's `alpha` to 1, simultaneously. This might be a way, for example, to make the text of a label or the title of a button appear to dissolve while changing.

The two parameters to `beginAnimations:context:` are an NSString and a pointer-to-void that are completely up to you; the idea is that an animation can have a delegate (so that you can be notified when the animation starts and ends), and you can supply values here that will be passed along in the delegate messages, helping you identify the animation and so forth. (On memory management of a pointer-to-void `context:` value, see Chapter 12.)

Modifying an Animation Block

An animation has various characteristics that you can modify, and an animation block provides a way to make such modifications: within the animation block, you call a UIView class method whose name begins with `setAnimation...`.

> Some of the `setAnimation...` method calls are oddly picky as to whether they precede or follow the actual property value changes within the animation block. If a call seems to be having no effect, try moving it to the beginning or end of the animation block. I find that in general these calls work best if they *precede* the value changes.

Animation blocks can be nested. The result is a single animation, whose description is not complete until the outermost animation block is terminated with `commit-Animations`. Therefore, by using `setAnimation...` method calls in the different nested animation blocks, you can give the parts of the animation different characteristics. Within each animation block, the animation for any property changes will have the default characteristics unless you change them.

> Nested animation blocks are different from successive top-level animation blocks; successive top-level animation blocks are different animations, which, as I mentioned earlier, can have undesirable effects, possibly causing the earlier animation to be cancelled abruptly.

Here are the `setAnimation...` UIView class methods:

`setAnimationDuration:`
Sets the "speed" of the animation, by dictating (in seconds) how long it takes to run from start to finish. Obviously, if two views are told to move different distances in the same time, the one that must move further must move faster.

`setAnimationRepeatAutoreverses:`
> If YES, the animation will run from start to finish (in the given duration time), and will then run from finish to start (also in the given duration time).

`setAnimationRepeatCount:`
> Sets how many times the animation should be repeated. Unless the animation also autoreverses, the animation will "jump" from its end to its start to begin the next repetition. The value is a float, so it is possible to end the repetition at some midpoint of the animation.

`setAnimationCurve:`
> Describes how the animation changes speed during its course. Your options are:
>
> - `UIViewAnimationCurveEaseInOut` (the default)
> - `UIViewAnimationCurveEaseIn`
> - `UIViewAnimationCurveEaseOut`
> - `UIViewAnimationCurveLinear`
>
> The term "ease" means that there is a gradual acceleration or deceleration between the animation's central speed and the zero speed at its start or end.

`setAnimationDelay:`
> Postpones the start of the animation. (An alternative method, `setAnimationStartDate:`, is and always has been broken, as far as I can tell.)

`setAnimationDelegate:`
> Arranges for your code to be notified as the animation starts or ends; the methods to be called on the delegate are specified as follows:
>
> `setAnimationWillStartSelector:`
> > The "start" method must take two parameters; these are the values passed into `beginAnimations:context:`, namely an identifying NSString and a pointer-to-void. This method is not called unless something within the animation block triggers an actual animation.
>
> `setAnimationDidStopSelector:`
> > The "stop" method must take three parameters: the second parameter is a BOOL wrapped as an NSNumber, indicating whether the animation completed successfully, and the other two are like the "start" method parameters. This method is called, with the second parameter representing YES, even if nothing within the animation block triggers any animations.

`setAnimationsEnabled:`
> Call this with a NO argument to perform subsequent animatable property changes within the animation block without making them part of the animation.

`setAnimationBeginsFromCurrentState:`

If YES, and if this animation animates a property already being animated by an animation that is previously ordered or in-flight, then instead of canceling the previous animation (completing the requested change instantly), this animation will use the presentation layer to decide where to start, and will "blend" its animation with the previous animation if possible.

If an animation autoreverses, and if, when the animation ends, the view's actual property is still at the finish value, the view will appear to jump as the "animation movie" is removed. So, for example, suppose we want a view to animate its position to the right and then back to its original position. This code causes the view to animate right, animate left, and then (unfortunately) jump right:

```
[UIView beginAnimations:nil context:nil];
[UIView setAnimationRepeatAutoreverses:YES];
CGPoint p = v.center;
p.x += 100;
v.center = p;
[UIView commitAnimations];
```

How can we prevent this? We want the view to stay at the start value after the animation reverses and ends. If we try to eliminate the jump at the end by setting the view's position back to its starting point after the animation block, there is no animation at all (because when the redraw moment arrives, there is no property change):

```
[UIView beginAnimations:nil context:nil];
[UIView setAnimationRepeatAutoreverses:YES];
CGPoint p = v.center;
p.x += 100;
v.center = p;
[UIView commitAnimations];
p = v.center;
p.x -= 100;
v.center = p;
```

The coherent solution is to use the "stop" delegate method to set the view's position back to its starting point when the animation ends:

```
[UIView beginAnimations:nil context:nil];
[UIView setAnimationRepeatAutoreverses:YES];
[UIView setAnimationDelegate:self];
[UIView setAnimationDidStopSelector:@selector(stopped:fin:context:)];
CGPoint p = v.center;
p.x += 100;
v.center = p;
[UIView commitAnimations];

// ...
```

```
- (void) stopped:(NSString *)anim fin:(NSNumber*)fin context:(void *)context {
    CGPoint p = v.center;
    p.x -= 100;
    v.center = p;
}
```

In that example, we happened to know how the animation had changed the view's position, so we could hard-code the instructions for reversing the change. To be more general, we could take advantage of our ability to pass information into the animation block and retrieve this same information in the delegate method. Or, we could store the view's original position in its layer (recall that a CALayer is a dictionary-like container):

```
[UIView beginAnimations:nil context:nil];
[UIView setAnimationRepeatAutoreverses:YES];
[UIView setAnimationDelegate:self];
[UIView setAnimationDidStopSelector:@selector(stopped:fin:context:)];
CGPoint p = v.center;
[v.layer setValue:[NSValue valueWithCGPoint:p] forKey:@"origCenter"];
p.x += 100;
v.center = p;
[UIView commitAnimations];
// ...
- (void) stopped:(NSString *)anim fin:(NSNumber*)fin context:(void *)context {
    v.center = [[v.layer valueForKey:@"origCenter"] CGPointValue];
}
```

Here's an example to illustrate use of the "stop" delegate method parameters. We pop a view out of existence by shrinking it as we remove it from its superview. The removal from the superview needs to come after the animation, so we put it in the "stop" delegate method. We can generalize this by using the context: parameter to say which view to remove:

```
[UIView beginAnimations:@"removeThisView" context:(__bridge void*)v];
[UIView setAnimationDelegate:self];
[UIView setAnimationDidStopSelector:@selector(stopped:fin:context:)];
v.transform = CGAffineTransformMakeScale(0,0);
[UIView commitAnimations];
// ...
-(void)stopped:(NSString*)identifier fin:(BOOL)fin context:(void*) context {
    if ([identifier isEqualToString:@"removeThisView"]) {
        UIView* v = (__bridge id)context;
        [v removeFromSuperview];
    }
}
```

To illustrate setAnimationBeginsFromCurrentState:, consider the following:

```
[UIView beginAnimations:nil context:nil];
[UIView setAnimationDuration:1];
CGPoint p = v.center;
p.x += 100;
v.center = p;
```

```
[UIView commitAnimations];

[UIView beginAnimations:nil context:nil];
// uncomment the next line to fix the problem
//[UIView setAnimationBeginsFromCurrentState:YES];
[UIView setAnimationDuration:1];
CGPoint p2 = v.center;
p2.x = 0;
v.center = p2;
[UIView commitAnimations];
```

The result is that the view jumps 100 points rightward, and then animates leftward. That's because the second animation caused the first animation to be thrown away; the move 100 points rightward was performed instantly, instead of being animated. But if we uncomment the call to setAnimationBeginsFromCurrentState:, the result is that the view animates leftward from its current position, with no jump.

Even more interesting is what happens when we change x to y in the second animation. If we uncomment the call to setAnimationBeginsFromCurrentState:, both the x-component and the y-component of the view's position are animated together, as if we had ordered one animation instead of two.

Transition Animations

A *transition* is a sort of animated redrawing of a view. The usual reason for a transition animation is that you are making some change in the view's appearance, and you want to emphasize this by animating the view. To order a transition animation using an animation block, call setAnimationTransition:forView:cache:.

- The first parameter describes how the animation should behave; your choices are:
  - — UIViewAnimationTransitionFlipFromLeft
  - — UIViewAnimationTransitionFlipFromRight
  - — UIViewAnimationTransitionCurlUp
  - — UIViewAnimationTransitionCurlDown
- The second parameter is the view.
- The third parameter is whether to cache the view's contents right now, effectively taking a "snapshot" of those contents at the moment and as they will be after the contents change, and using these snapshots throughout the transition. The alternative is to redraw the contents repeatedly throughout the transition. You'll want to say YES wherever possible.

Here's a simple example that flips a UIImageView while changing its image. The result is that the UIImageView appears to flip over, like a piece of paper being rotated to show its reverse side — a piece of paper with Mars on its front and Saturn on its back:

```
[UIView beginAnimations:nil context:nil];
[UIView setAnimationTransition:UIViewAnimationTransitionFlipFromLeft
                       forView:iv cache:YES];
// iv is a UIImageView whose image is Mars.png
iv.image = [UIImage imageNamed:@"Saturn.gif"];
[UIView commitAnimations];
```

The example is a little misleading, because the change in the image does not necessarily have to be inside the animation block. The animation described by setAnimation-Transition:... will be performed in any case. The change of image will be performed in any case as well. They will both happen at the redraw moment, so they are performed together. Thus, we could have written the same example this way:

```
iv.image = [UIImage imageNamed:@"Saturn.gif"];
[UIView beginAnimations:nil context:nil];
[UIView setAnimationTransition:UIViewAnimationTransitionFlipFromLeft
                       forView:iv cache:YES];
[UIView commitAnimations];
```

Nevertheless, it is customary to order the changes in the view from inside the animation block, and I'll continue to do so in subsequent examples.

You can do the same sort of thing with any built-in view subclass. Here's a button that seems to be labeled "Start" on one side and "Stop" on the other:

```
[UIView beginAnimations:nil context:nil];
// b is a UIButton; _stopped is a BOOL ivar
[UIView setAnimationTransition:UIViewAnimationTransitionFlipFromLeft
                       forView:b cache:YES];
[b setTitle:(_stopped ? @"Start" : @"Stop") forState:UIControlStateNormal];
[UIView commitAnimations];
```

To do the same thing with a custom UIView subclass that knows how to draw itself in its drawRect:, call setNeedsDisplay to cause a redraw. For example, imagine a UIView subclass with a reverse BOOL property, which draws an ellipse if reverse is YES and a square if reverse is NO. Then we can animate the square flipping over and becoming an ellipse (or *vice versa*):

```
v.reverse = !v.reverse;
[UIView beginAnimations:nil context:nil];
[UIView setAnimationTransition:UIViewAnimationTransitionFlipFromLeft
                       forView:v cache:YES];
[v setNeedsDisplay];
[UIView commitAnimations];
```

Block-Based View Animation

A UIView can also be animated using a syntax involving Objective-C blocks. This is intended to replace the old animation block syntax I've just been describing. In the new syntax:

- The behavior to be animated is a block.

- The code to be run when the animation ends is also a block. Thus, there is no need for the two-part structure involving an animation block and a separate delegate method.

- Options describing the animation are part of the original animation method call, not separate calls as with an animation block.

- Transition animations have more options than with animation blocks.

- User touch interactions with an animated view are disabled, by default. This is not the case with an animation block (or with layer-based animation, described later in this chapter). The option `UIViewAnimationOptionAllowUserInteraction` permits user touch interaction with the animated view.

The basis of the new syntax is the UIView class method `animateWith-Duration:delay:options:animations:completion:`. There are also two reduced calls, the first letting you omit the `delay:` and `options:` parameters and the second letting you also omit the `completion:` parameter. The parameters of the full form are:

`duration`
  The duration of the animation.

`delay`
  The delay before the animation starts. The default, in the reduced forms, is no delay.

`options`
  A bitmask stating additional options. The default is `UIViewAnimationOptionCurve-EaseInOut` (which is also the default animation curve for animation blocks). For an ordinary animation (not a transition), the chief options are:

  Animation curve
    Your choices are:

    - `UIViewAnimationOptionCurveEaseInOut`

    - `UIViewAnimationOptionCurveEaseIn`

    - `UIViewAnimationOptionCurveEaseOut`

    - `UIViewAnimationOptionCurveLinear`

  Repetition and autoreverse
    Your options are:

    - `UIViewAnimationOptionRepeat`

    - `UIViewAnimationOptionAutoreverse`

There is no way to specify a certain number of repetitions; you either repeat forever or not at all. This feels like an oversight (a serious oversight); I'll suggest a workaround in a moment. The documentation's claim that you can autoreverse only if you also repeat is incorrect; you can use either or both (or neither).

animations

> The block containing view property changes to be animated.

completion

> The block to run when the animation ends. It takes one BOOL parameter indicating whether the animation ran to completion. (There is no way to specify a notification when the animation starts, but this should not be needed, as the animation code is itself a block.) It's fine for this block to order a further animation. The block is called, with a parameter indicating YES, even if nothing in the animations: block triggers any animations.

Here's an example, recasting an earlier example to use Objective-C blocks instead of animation blocks. We move a view rightward and reverse it back into place. With animation blocks, we used a delegate so that we could set the view back to its original position, and we stored that position in the layer so as to be able to retrieve it in the delegate method. With blocks, however, the original position can live in a variable that remains in scope, so things are much simpler (to increase readability, I've expressed the blocks and the options as named variables):

```
CGPoint p = v.center;
CGPoint pOrig = p;
p.x += 100;
void (^anim) (void) = ^{
    v.center = p;
};
void (^after) (BOOL) = ^(BOOL f) {
    v.center = pOrig;
};
NSUInteger opts = UIViewAnimationOptionAutoreverse;
[UIView animateWithDuration:1 delay:0 options:opts
                animations:anim completion:after];
```

Working around the inability to specify a finite number of repetitions is not easy. Here's one approach using recursion:

```
- (void) animate: (int) count {
    CGPoint p = v.center;
    CGPoint pOrig = p;
    p.x += 100;
    void (^anim) (void) = ^{
        v.center = p;
    };
    void (^after) (BOOL) = ^(BOOL f) {
        v.center = pOrig;
```

```
        if (count)
            [self animate: count-1];
    };
    NSUInteger opts = UIViewAnimationOptionAutoreverse;
    [UIView animateWithDuration:1 delay:0 options:opts
                animations:anim completion:after];
}
```

If we call the `animate:` method with an argument of 2, our animation takes place three times and stops. There is always a danger, with recursion, of filling up the stack and running out of memory, but I think we're safe if we start with a small `count` value.

There are also some options saying what should happen if another animation is already ordered or in-flight:

`UIViewAnimationOptionBeginFromCurrentState`
> Similar to `setAnimationBeginsFromCurrentState:`.

`UIViewAnimationOptionOverrideInheritedDuration`
> Prevents inheriting the duration from an already ordered or in-flight animation (the default is to inherit it).

`UIViewAnimationOptionOverrideInheritedCurve`
> Prevents inheriting the animation curve from an already ordered or in-flight animation (the default is to inherit it).

A widely used technique for canceling a repeating animation is to start another animation of the same property of the same view. (Reread the first section of this chapter if you don't understand why that would work.) This example builds on our previous examples; we have an autoreversing animation of our view's `center` that repeats, nominally infinitely. To stop it, we animate the same `center` property of the same view back to its original position. This is a great opportunity to use `UIViewAnimationOptionBeginFromCurrentState`; without it, the animation ends abruptly. Two different methods need access to the view's original `center`, so I've put it in an instance variable:

```
- (void) animate {
    CGPoint p = v.center;
    self->_pOrig = p;
    p.x += 100;
    void (^anim) (void) = ^{
        v.center = p;
    };
    void (^after) (BOOL) = ^(BOOL f) {
        v.center = self->_pOrig;
    };
    NSUInteger opts = UIViewAnimationOptionAutoreverse |
                      UIViewAnimationOptionRepeat;
    [UIView animateWithDuration:1 delay:0 options:opts
                animations:anim completion:after];
}
```

```
- (void) cancelAnimation {
    void (^anim) (void) = ^{
        v.center = self->_pOrig;
    };
    NSUInteger opts = UIViewAnimationOptionBeginFromCurrentState;
    [UIView animateWithDuration:0.2 delay:0 options:opts
                     animations:anim completion:nil];
}
```

There is also a layout option, UIViewAnimationOptionLayoutSubviews. This is useful if the view that you are about to animate does its layout manually through an override of layoutSubviews (Chapter 14). In that case, if you supply this option, layout-Subviews is called while we are still within the animation block; the changes ordered by your layoutSubviews implementation will thus be part of the animation. If you don't supply this option, the changes ordered by your layoutSubviews implementation will appear as a sudden jump as the animation begins.

Transitions are ordered using one of two methods. The one that's parallel to set-AnimationTransition..., described earlier in connection with animation blocks, is transitionWithView:duration:options:animations:completion:. The transition animation types are expressed as part of the options: bitmask; the last three have no parallel in the older animation block syntax:

- UIViewAnimationOptionTransitionFlipFromLeft

- UIViewAnimationOptionTransitionFlipFromRight

- UIViewAnimationOptionTransitionCurlUp

- UIViewAnimationOptionTransitionCurlDown

- UIViewAnimationOptionTransitionCrossDissolve

- UIViewAnimationOptionTransitionFlipFromBottom

- UIViewAnimationOptionTransitionFlipFromTop

Here's a recasting, using transitionWithView..., of the earlier example where we flip a rectangle into an ellipse by means of a custom UIView subclass whose drawRect: behavior depends on its reverse property:

```
v.reverse = !v.reverse;
void (^anim) (void) = ^{
    [v setNeedsDisplay];
};
NSUInteger opts = UIViewAnimationOptionTransitionFlipFromLeft;
[UIView transitionWithView:v duration:1 options:opts
                animations:anim completion:nil];
```

During a transition, by default, a snapshot of the view's final appearance is used; this is parallel to what happens when you supply YES as the `cache:` argument to `setAnimation-Transition:forView:cache:`. If that isn't what you want, use `UIViewAnimationOption-AllowAnimatedContent` in the `options` bitmask. For example, suppose v is the view to be animated using a transition, and v2 is a subview of v that currently occupies part of its width. In this block, to be used as the animation during the transition, we increase the width of v2 to occupy the entire width of v:

```
void (^anim) (void) = ^{
    CGRect f = v2.frame;
    f.size.width = v.frame.size.width;
    f.origin.x = 0;
    v2.frame = f;
};
```

Without `UIViewAnimationOptionAllowAnimatedContent`, that change in the frame of v2 takes place in a jump after the transition is over. With `UIViewAnimationOptionAllow-AnimatedContent`, it is seen to happen smoothly as part of the transition animation.

The second transition method is `transitionFromView:toView:duration:options:completion:`. It names two views; the first is replaced by the second, while their superview undergoes the transition animation. This has no parallel in the older animation block syntax. There are actually two possible configurations, depending on the options you provide:

Remove one subview, add the other

If `UIViewAnimationOptionShowHideTransitionViews` is *not* one of the options, then the second subview is not in the view hierarchy when we start; the transition removes the first subview from its superview and adds the second subview to that same superview.

Hide one subview, show the other

If `UIViewAnimationOptionShowHideTransitionViews` *is* one of the options, then both subviews are in the view hierarchy when we start; the `hidden` of the first is NO, the `hidden` of the second is YES, and the transition reverses these values.

So, for example, this code causes the superview of v1 to rotate like a piece of paper being turned over, while at the same v1 is removed from it and v2 is added to it:

```
NSUInteger opts = UIViewAnimationOptionTransitionFlipFromLeft;
[UIView transitionFromView:v1 toView:v2
            duration:1 options:opts completion:nil];
```

It's up to you to make sure beforehand that v2 has the desired position, so that it will appear in the right place in its superview.

Implicit Layer Animation

If a layer is not a view's underlying layer, animating it can be as simple as setting a property. A change in what the documentation calls an *animatable property* is automatically interpreted as a request to animate that change. In other words, animation of layer property changes is the default! Multiple property changes are considered part of the same animation. This mechanism is called *implicit animation.*

 You cannot use implicit animation on the underlying layer of a UIView. You can animate a UIView's underlying layer directly, but you must use explicit layer animation (discussed later in this chapter).

For example, in Chapter 16 we constructed a compass out of layers. The compass itself is a CompassView that does no drawing of its own; its underlying layer is a CompassLayer that also does no drawing, serving only as a superlayer for the layers that constitute the drawing. None of the layers that constitute the actual drawing is the underlying layer of a view, so a property change to any of them is animated automatically.

So, presume that we have a reference to the arrow layer, a property arrow of the CompassLayer, and also a reference to the CompassView, a property compass of the app delegate, which is self. If we rotate the arrow by changing its transform property, that rotation is animated:

```
CompassLayer* c = (CompassLayer*)self.compass.layer;
// the next line is an implicit animation
c.arrow.transform = CATransform3DRotate(c.arrow.transform, M_PI/4.0, 0, 0, 1);
```

CALayer properties listed in the documentation as animatable in this way are anchorPoint and anchorPointZ, backgroundColor, borderColor, borderWidth, bounds, contents, contentsCenter, contentsRect, cornerRadius, doubleSided, hidden, masksToBounds, opacity, position and zPosition, rasterizationScale and shouldRasterize, shadowColor, shadowOffset, shadowOpacity, shadowRadius, and sublayerTransform and transform (but *not* affineTransform!). In addition, a CAShapeLayer's path, fillColor, strokeColor, lineWidth, lineDashPhase, and miterLimit are animatable; so are a CATextLayer's fontSize and foregroundColor. (See Chapter 16 for discussion of those properties.)

Basically, a property is animatable because there's some sensible way to interpolate the intermediate values between one value and another. The nature of the animation attached to each property is therefore just what you would intuitively expect. When you change a layer's hidden property, it fades out of view (or into view). When you change a layer's contents, the old contents are dissolved into the new contents. And so forth.

Observe that I didn't say `frame` was an animatable property. That's because it isn't an animatable property! To animate the changing of a layer's frame, you'll change other properties such as its `bounds` and `position`. Trying to animate a layer's frame is a common beginner error. This is a feature, not a bug; a CALayer's frame is a purely derived value, and in any case there needs to be a way to position or resize a layer without triggering implicit animation, and `frame` is it.

Animation Transactions

Implicit animation operates with respect to a *transaction* (a CATransaction), which groups animation requests into a single animation. Every animation request takes place in the context of a transaction. You can make this explicit by wrapping your animation requests in calls to the CATransaction class methods `begin` and `commit`; the result is a *transaction block*. But additionally there is already an *implicit transaction* surrounding all your code, and you can operate on this implicit transaction without any `begin` and `commit`.

To modify the characteristics of an implicit animation, you modify its transaction. Typically, you'll use these CATransaction class methods:

`setAnimationDuration:`
    The duration of the animation.

`setAnimationTimingFunction:`
    A CAMediaTimingFunction; timing functions are discussed in the next section.

`setCompletionBlock:`
    A block to be called when the animation ends. The block takes no parameters. The block is called even if no animation is triggered during this transaction.

By nesting transaction blocks, you can apply different animation characteristics to different elements of an animation. But you can also use transaction commands outside of any transaction block to modify the implicit transaction.

So, in our previous example, we could slow down the animation of the arrow like this:

```
CompassLayer* c = (CompassLayer*)self.compass.layer;
[CATransaction setAnimationDuration:0.8];
c.arrow.transform = CATransform3DRotate(c.arrow.transform, M_PI/4.0, 0, 0, 1);
```

Another useful feature of animation transactions is to turn implicit animation *off*. It's important to be able to do this, because implicit animation is the default, and can be unwanted (and a performance drag). To do so, call the CATransaction class method `setDisableActions:` with argument YES. There are other ways to turn off implicit animation (discussed later in this chapter), but this is the simplest.

The Truth About Transactions

All my hand-waving in this and earlier chapters about when drawing, layout, layer property settings, and animation take place is resolved now that you know about transactions. You ask to draw; `drawRect:` is called "later." You ask for layout; layout happens "later." You order an animation; the animation happens "later." This later time — the redraw moment — is the end of the current transaction. Your code runs within an implicit transaction. Your code comes to an end, and the transaction commits itself. It is as part of the transaction commit procedure that everything happens in relation to what appears on the screen: first layout, then drawing, then obedience to layer property changes, then the start of any animations. The transaction then continues onto a background thread while any animations are performed, and finally calls its completion block, if any, when the animations are over.

`setCompletionBlock:` is an extraordinarily useful and probably underutilized tool. The transaction's completion block signals the end, not only of the implicit layer property animations you yourself have ordered as part of this transaction, but of *all* animations ordered during this transaction, including Cocoa's own animations. For example, consider what happens when you explicitly dismiss a popover with animation:

```
[myPopoverController dismissPopoverAnimated: YES];
```

There's no completion block, and this isn't your animation, so how can you learn when the animation is over and the popover is well and truly gone? A transaction completion block solves the problem.

CATransaction implements KVC to allow you set and retrieve a value for an arbitrary key, similar to CALayer. An example appears later in this chapter.

 An explicit transaction block that orders an animation to a layer, if the block is *not preceded by any other changes to the layer*, can cause animation to begin immediately when the CATransaction class method `commit` is called, without waiting for the redraw moment, while your code continues running. In my experience, this can cause confusion (for example, animation delegate messages cannot arrive, and the presentation layer can't be queried properly) and should be avoided.

Media Timing Functions

The CATransaction class method `setAnimationTimingFunction:` takes as its parameter a media timing function (CAMediaTimingFunction). This class is the general expression of the animation curves we have already met (ease-in-out, ease-in, ease-out, and linear); in fact, you are most likely to use it with those very same predefined curves, by calling the CAMediaTimingFunction class method `functionWithName:` with one of these parameters:

- `kCAMediaTimingFunctionLinear`
- `kCAMediaTimingFunctionEaseIn`
- `kCAMediaTimingFunctionEaseOut`
- `kCAMediaTimingFunctionEaseInEaseOut`
- `kCAMediaTimingFunctionDefault`

In reality, a media timing function is a Bézier curve defined by two points. The curve graphs the fraction of the animation's time that has elapsed (the x-axis) against the fraction of the animation's change that has occurred (the y-axis); its endpoints are therefore at {0,0} and {1,1}, because at the beginning of the animation there has been no elapsed time and no change, and at the end of the animation all the time has elapsed and all the change has occurred.

The curve's defining points are its endpoints, and each endpoint needs only one Bézier control point to define the tangent to the curve. And because the curve's endpoints are known, defining the two control points is sufficient to describe the entire curve. And because a point is a pair of floating-point values, a media timing function can be expressed as four floating-point values. That is, in fact, how it is expressed.

So, for example, the ease-in-out timing function is expressed as the four values `0.42`, `0.0`, `0.58`, `1.0`. That defines a Bézier curve with one endpoint at {0,0}, whose control point is {0.42,0}, and the other endpoint at {1,1}, whose control point is {0.58,1} (Figure 17-1).

If you want to define your own media timing function, you can supply the coordinates of the two control points by calling `functionWithControlPoints::::` or `initWithControlPoints:::::`; this is one of those rare cases, mentioned in Chapter 3, where the parameters of an Objective-C method have no name. (It helps to design the curve in a standard drawing program first so that you can visualize how the placement of the control points shapes the curve.) For example, here's a media timing function that starts out quite slowly and then whips quickly into place after about two-thirds of the time has elapsed. I call this the "clunk" timing function, and it looks great with the compass arrow:

```
CAMediaTimingFunction* clunk =
    [CAMediaTimingFunction functionWithControlPoints:.9 :.1 :.7 :.9];
[CATransaction setAnimationTimingFunction: clunk];
c.arrow.transform = CATransform3DRotate(c.arrow.transform, M_PI/4.0, 0, 0, 1);
```

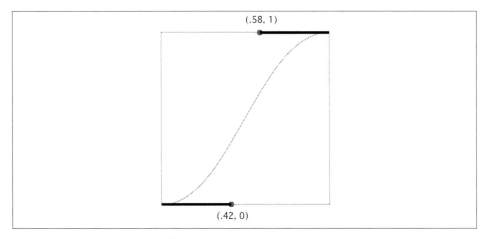

Figure 17-1. An ease-in-out Bézier curve

Core Animation

Core Animation is the fundamental underlying iOS animation technology. View animation and implicit layer animation are merely convenient façades for Core Animation. Core Animation is *explicit layer animation,* and revolves primarily around the CAAnimation class and its subclasses, which allow you to create far more elaborate specifications of an animation than anything we've encountered so far.

You may never program at the level of Core Animation, but you should read this section anyway, if only to learn how animation really works and to get a sense of the mighty powers you would acquire if you *did* elect to use Core Animation directly. In particular, Core Animation:

- Works even on a view's underlying layer. Thus, Core Animation is the *only* way to apply full-on layer property animation to a view.
- Provides fine control over the intermediate values and timing of an animation.
- Allows animations to be grouped into complex combinations.
- Adds transition animation effects that aren't available otherwise, such as new content "pushing" the previous content out of a layer.

CABasicAnimation and Its Inheritance

The simplest way to animate a property with Core Animation is with a CABasic-Animation object. CABasicAnimation derives much of its power through its inheritance, so I'm going to describe that inheritance as well as CABasicAnimation itself. You will readily see that all the property animation features we have met so far are embodied in a CABasicAnimation instance.

CAAnimation

CAAnimation is an abstract class, meaning that you'll only ever use a subclass of it. Some of CAAnimation's powers come from its implementation of the CAMedia-Timing protocol.

`animation`

A class method, a convenient way of creating an animation object.

`delegate`

The delegate messages are `animationDidStart:` and `animationDid-Stop:finished:`, which should sound familiar from the analogous UIView animation delegate messages. A CAAnimation instance *retains its delegate*; this is very unusual behavior and can cause trouble if you're not conscious of it (I'm speaking from experience).

`duration, timingFunction`

The length of the animation, and its timing function (a CAMediaTiming-Function). A duration of 0 (the default) means .25 seconds unless overridden by the transaction.

`autoreverses, repeatCount, repeatDuration, cumulative`

The first two are familiar from UIView animation. The `repeatDuration` property is a different way to govern repetition, specifying how long the repetition should continue rather than how many repetitions should occur; don't specify both a `repeatCount` and a `repeatDuration`. If `cumulative` is YES, a repeating animation starts each repetition where the previous repetition ended (rather than jumping back to the start value).

`beginTime`

The delay before the animation starts. To delay an animation with respect to now, call `CACurrentMediaTime` and add the desired delay in seconds. The delay does not eat into the animation's duration.

`timeOffset`

A shift in the animation's overall timing; looked at another way, specifies the starting frame of the "animation movie," which is treated as a loop. For example, an animation with a duration of 8 and a time offset of 4 plays its second half followed by its first half.

CAAnimation, along with all its subclasses, implements KVC to allow you set and retrieve a value for an arbitrary key, similar to CALayer (Chapter 16) and CATransaction.

CAPropertyAnimation

CAPropertyAnimation is a subclass of CAAnimation. It too is abstract, and adds the following:

keyPath

The all-important string specifying the CALayer key that is to be animated. Recall from Chapter 16 that CALayer properties are accessible through KVC keys; now we are using those keys! A CAPropertyAnimation convenience class method `animationWithKeyPath:` creates the instance and assigns it a `keyPath`.

additive

If YES, the values supplied by the animation are added to the current presentation layer value.

valueFunction

Converts a simple scalar value that you supply into a transform.

 There is no animatable CALayer key called @"frame" (because `frame` is not an animatable layer property).

CABasicAnimation

CABasicAnimation is a subclass (not abstract!) of CAPropertyAnimation. It adds the following:

fromValue, toValue

The starting and ending values for the animation. These values must be objects, so numbers and structs will have to be wrapped accordingly, using NSNumber and NSValue. If neither `fromValue` nor `toValue` is provided, the former and current values of the property are used. If just one of `fromValue` or `toValue` is provided, the other uses the current value of the property.

byValue

Expresses one of the endpoint values as a *difference* from the other rather than in absolute terms. So you would supply a byValue instead of a `fromValue` or instead of a `toValue`, and the actual `fromValue` or `toValue` would be calculated for you by subtraction or addition with respect to the other value. If you supply *only* a byValue, the `fromValue` is the property's current value.

Using a CABasicAnimation

Having constructed and configured a CABasicAnimation, the way you order it to be performed is to *add it to a layer*. This is done with the CALayer instance method `add-Animation:forKey:`. (I'll discuss the purpose of the `forKey:` parameter later; it's fine to ignore it and use nil, as I do in the examples that follow.)

However, there's a slight twist. A CAAnimation is *merely* an animation; all it does is describe the hoops that the presentation layer is to jump through, the "animation movie" that is to be presented. It has no effect on the layer *itself*. Thus, if you naively create a CABasicAnimation and add it to a layer with `addAnimation:forKey:`, the animation happens and then the "animation movie" is whipped away to reveal the layer sitting there in exactly the same state as before. It is up to *you* to change the layer to match what the animation will ultimately portray.

This requirement may seem odd, but keep in mind that we are now in a much more fundamental, flexible world than the automatic, convenient worlds of view animation and implicit layer animation. Using explicit animation is more work, but you get more power. The converse, as we shall see, is that you *don't* have to change the layer if it *doesn't* change as a result of the animation.

To assure good results, we'll start by taking a plodding, formulaic approach to the use of CABasicAnimation, like this:

1. Capture the start and end values for the layer property you're going to change, because you're likely to need these values in what follows.

2. Change the layer property to its end value, first calling `setDisableActions:` to prevent implicit animation.

3. Construct the explicit animation, using the start and end values you captured earlier, and with its `keyPath` corresponding to the layer property you just changed.

4. Add the explicit animation to the layer.

Here's how you'd use this approach to animate our compass arrow rotation:

```
CompassLayer* c = (CompassLayer*)self.compass.layer;
// capture the start and end values
CATransform3D startValue = c.arrow.transform;
CATransform3D endValue = CATransform3DRotate(startValue, M_PI/4.0, 0, 0, 1);
// change the layer, without implicit animation
[CATransaction setDisableActions:YES];
c.arrow.transform = endValue;
// construct the explicit animation
CABasicAnimation* anim = [CABasicAnimation animationWithKeyPath:@"transform"];
anim.duration = 0.8;
CAMediaTimingFunction* clunk =
    [CAMediaTimingFunction functionWithControlPoints:.9 :.1 :.7 :.9];
anim.timingFunction = clunk;
anim.fromValue = [NSValue valueWithCATransform3D:startValue];
anim.toValue = [NSValue valueWithCATransform3D:endValue];
// ask for the explicit animation
[c.arrow addAnimation:anim forKey:nil];
```

Once you know the full form, you will find that in many cases it can be condensed. For example, when `fromValue` and `toValue` are not set, the former and current values of the property are used automatically. (This magic is possible because the presentation layer still has the former value of the property, while the layer itself has the new value.) Thus, in this case there was no need to set them, and so there was no need to capture the start and end values beforehand either. Here's the condensed version:

```
CompassLayer* c = (CompassLayer*)self.compass.layer;
[CATransaction setDisableActions:YES];
c.arrow.transform = CATransform3DRotate(c.arrow.transform, M_PI/4.0, 0, 0, 1);
CABasicAnimation* anim = [CABasicAnimation animationWithKeyPath:@"transform"];
anim.duration = 0.8;
CAMediaTimingFunction* clunk =
    [CAMediaTimingFunction functionWithControlPoints:.9 :.1 :.7 :.9];
anim.timingFunction = clunk;
[c.arrow addAnimation:anim forKey:nil];
```

As I mentioned earlier, you will omit changing the layer if it doesn't change as a result of the animation. For example, let's make the compass arrow appear to vibrate rapidly, without ultimately changing its current orientation. To do this, we'll waggle it back and forth, using a repeated animation, between slightly clockwise from its current position and slightly counterclockwise from its current position. The "animation movie" neither starts nor stops at the current position of the arrow, but for this animation it doesn't matter, because it all happens so quickly as to appear perfectly natural:

```
CompassLayer* c = (CompassLayer*)self.compass.layer;
// capture the start and end values
CATransform3D nowValue = c.arrow.transform;
CATransform3D startValue = CATransform3DRotate(nowValue, M_PI/40.0, 0, 0, 1);
CATransform3D endValue = CATransform3DRotate(nowValue, -M_PI/40.0, 0, 0, 1);
// construct the explicit animation
CABasicAnimation* anim = [CABasicAnimation animationWithKeyPath:@"transform"];
anim.duration = 0.05;
anim.timingFunction =
    [CAMediaTimingFunction functionWithName:kCAMediaTimingFunctionLinear];
anim.repeatCount = 3;
anim.autoreverses = YES;
anim.fromValue = [NSValue valueWithCATransform3D:startValue];
anim.toValue = [NSValue valueWithCATransform3D:endValue];
// ask for the explicit animation
[c.arrow addAnimation:anim forKey:nil];
```

That code, too, can be shortened considerably from its full form. We can eliminate the need to calculate the new rotation values based on the arrow's current transform by setting our animation's `additive` property to YES; this means that the animation's property values are added to the existing property value for us, so that they are relative, not absolute. For a transform, "added" means "matrix-multiplied," so we can describe the waggle without any dependence on the arrow's current rotation. Moreover, because our rotation is so simple (around a cardinal axis), we can take advantage of CAProperty-Animation's `valueFunction`; the animation's property values can then be simple scalars (in this case, angles), because the `valueFunction` tells the animation to interpret these as rotations around the z-axis:

```
CompassLayer* c = (CompassLayer*)self.compass.layer;
CABasicAnimation* anim = [CABasicAnimation animationWithKeyPath:@"transform"];
anim.duration = 0.05;
anim.timingFunction =
    [CAMediaTimingFunction functionWithName:kCAMediaTimingFunctionLinear];
anim.repeatCount = 3;
anim.autoreverses = YES;
anim.additive = YES;
anim.valueFunction =
    [CAValueFunction functionWithName:kCAValueFunctionRotateZ];
anim.fromValue = @(M_PI/40);
anim.toValue = @(-M_PI/40);
[c.arrow addAnimation:anim forKey:nil];
```

 Instead of using a `valueFunction`, we could have achieved the same effect by setting the animation's key path to `@"transform.rotation.z"`. However, Apple advises against this, as it can result in mathematical trouble when there is more than one rotation.

Remember that there is no `@"frame"` key. To animate a layer's frame, if both its `position` and bounds are to change, you must animate both. Recall this earlier example, using block-based animation (where v is v2's superview):

```
void (^anim) (void) = ^{
    CGRect f = v2.frame;
    f.size.width = v.frame.size.width;
    f.origin.x = 0;
    v2.frame = f;
};
```

Here's how to do that with Core Animation:

```
CABasicAnimation* anim1 = [CABasicAnimation animationWithKeyPath:@"bounds"];
CGRect f = v2.layer.bounds;
f.size.width = v.layer.bounds.size.width;
v2.layer.bounds = f;
[v2.layer addAnimation: anim1 forKey: nil];
CABasicAnimation* anim2 = [CABasicAnimation animationWithKeyPath:@"position"];
CGPoint p = v2.layer.position;
p.x = CGRectGetMidX(v.layer.bounds);
v2.layer.position = p;
[v2.layer addAnimation:anim2 forKey: nil];
```

Keyframe Animation

Keyframe animation (CAKeyframeAnimation) is an alternative to basic animation (CABasicAnimation); they are both subclasses of CAPropertyAnimation and they are used in identical ways. The difference is that a keyframe animation, in addition to specifying a starting and ending value, also specifies multiple values through which the animation should pass on the way, the stages (*frames*) of the animation. This can be as simple as setting the animation's `values` property (an NSArray).

Here's a more sophisticated version of our animation for waggling the compass arrow: the animation includes both the start and end states, and the degree of waggle gets progressively smaller:

```
CompassLayer* c = (CompassLayer*)self.compass.layer;
NSMutableArray* values = [NSMutableArray array];
[values addObject: @0.0f];
int direction = 1;
for (int i = 20; i < 60; i += 5, direction *= -1) { // alternate directions
    [values addObject: @(direction*M_PI/(float)i)];
}
[values addObject: @0.0f];
CAKeyframeAnimation* anim =
    [CAKeyframeAnimation animationWithKeyPath:@"transform"];
anim.values = values;
anim.additive = YES;
anim.valueFunction =
    [CAValueFunction functionWithName: kCAValueFunctionRotateZ];
[c.arrow addAnimation:anim forKey:nil];
```

Here are some CAKeyframeAnimation properties:

values
> The array of values the animation is to adopt, including the starting and ending value.

timingFunctions
> An array of timing functions, one for each stage of the animation (so that this array will be one element shorter than the `values` array).

keyTimes
> An array of times to accompany the array of values, defining when each value should be reached. The times start at 0 and are expressed as increasing fractions of 1, ending at 1.

calculationMode
> Describes how the `values` are treated to create *all* the values through which the animation must pass.

- The default is kCAAnimationLinear, a simple straight-line interpolation from value to value.

- kCAAnimationCubic constructs a single smooth curve passing through all the values (and additional advanced properties, tensionValues, continuity-Values, and biasValues, allow you to refine the curve).

- kCAAnimationPaced and kCAAnimationCubicPaced means the timing functions and key times are ignored, and the velocity is made constant through the whole animation.

- kCAAnimationDiscrete means no interpolation: we jump directly to each value at the corresponding key time.

path

When you're animating a property whose values are pairs of floats (CGPoints), this is an alternative way of describing the values; instead of a values array, which must be interpolated to arrive at the intermediate values along the way, you supply the entire interpolation as a single CGPathRef. The points used to draw the path are the keyframe values, so you can still apply timing functions and key times. If you're animating a position, the rotationMode property lets you ask the animated object to rotate so as to remain perpendicular to the path.

Making a Property Animatable

So far, we've been animating built-in animatable properties. If you define your own property on a CALayer subclass, you can make that property animatable through a CAPropertyAnimation (a CABasicAnimation or a CAKeyframeAnimation). You do this by declaring the property @dynamic (so that Core Animation can create its accessors) and returning YES from the class method needsDisplayForKey:, where the key is the string name of the property.

For example, here we'll start writing the code for a layer class MyLayer with an animatable thickness property:

```
// MyLayer.h:
@interface MyLayer : CALayer
@property (nonatomic) CGFloat thickness;
@end

// MyLayer.m:
@implementation MyLayer
@dynamic thickness;

+ (BOOL) needsDisplayForKey:(NSString *)key {
    if ([key isEqualToString: @"thickness"])
        return YES;
```

```
        return [super needsDisplayForKey:key];
    }

    @end
```

Returning YES from needsDisplayForKey: causes this layer to be redisplayed repeatedly as the thickness property changes. So if we want to *see* the animation, this layer also needs to draw itself in some way that depends on the thickness property. Here, I'll implement the layer's drawInContext: to make thickness the thickness of the black border around a red rectangle:

```
- (void) drawInContext:(CGContextRef)con {
    CGRect r = CGRectInset(self.bounds, 20, 20);
    CGContextSetFillColorWithColor(con, [UIColor redColor].CGColor);
    CGContextFillRect(con, r);
    CGContextSetLineWidth(con, self.thickness);
    CGContextStrokeRect(con, r);
}
```

Now we can animate the rectangle's thickness using explicit animation (lay points to a MyLayer instance):

```
CABasicAnimation* ba = [CABasicAnimation animationWithKeyPath:@"thickness"];
ba.toValue = @10.0f;
ba.autoreverses = YES;
[lay addAnimation:ba forKey:nil];
```

At every step of the animation, drawInContext: is called, and because the thickness value differs at each step, it is animated.

Grouped Animations

A grouped animation (CAAnimationGroup) combines multiple animations into one, by means of its animations property (an NSArray of animations). By delaying and timing the various component animations, complex effects can be achieved.

A CAAnimationGroup is itself an animation; it is a CAAnimation subclass, so it has a duration and other animation features. Think of the CAAnimationGroup as the parent and its animations as its children. Then *the children inherit default values from their parent.* Thus, for example, if you don't set a child's duration explicitly, it will inherit the parent's duration. Also, make sure the parent's duration is sufficient to include all parts of the child animations that you want displayed.

For example, we can form a sequence where the compass arrow rotates and then waggles. Very little change is required. We express the first animation in its full form, with explicit fromValue and toValue. We postpone the second animation using its beginTime property; notice that we express this in relative terms, as a number of seconds into the parent's duration, not with respect to CACurrentMediaTime. Finally, we set the overall parent duration to the sum of the child durations, so that it can embrace both of them:

```
CompassLayer* c = (CompassLayer*)self.compass.layer;
// capture current value, set final value
CGFloat rot = M_PI/4.0;
[CATransaction setDisableActions:YES];
CGFloat current =
    [[c.arrow valueForKeyPath:@"transform.rotation.z"] floatValue];
[c.arrow setValue: @(current + rot)
      forKeyPath:@"transform.rotation.z"];

// first animation (rotate and clunk)
CABasicAnimation* anim1 = [CABasicAnimation animationWithKeyPath:@"transform"];
anim1.duration = 0.8;
CAMediaTimingFunction* clunk =
    [CAMediaTimingFunction functionWithControlPoints:.9 :.1 :.7 :.9];
anim1.timingFunction = clunk;
anim1.fromValue = @(current);
anim1.toValue = @(current + rot);
anim1.valueFunction =
    [CAValueFunction functionWithName:kCAValueFunctionRotateZ];

// second animation (waggle)
NSMutableArray* values = [NSMutableArray array];
[values addObject: @0.0f];
int direction = 1;
for (int i = 20; i < 60; i += 5, direction *= -1) { // alternate directions
    [values addObject: @(direction*M_PI/(float)i)];
}
[values addObject: @0.0f];
CAKeyframeAnimation* anim2 =
    [CAKeyframeAnimation animationWithKeyPath:@"transform"];
anim2.values = values;
anim2.duration = 0.25;
anim2.beginTime = anim1.duration;
anim2.additive = YES;
anim2.valueFunction =
    [CAValueFunction functionWithName:kCAValueFunctionRotateZ];

// group
CAAnimationGroup* group = [CAAnimationGroup animation];
group.animations = @[anim1, anim2];
group.duration = anim1.duration + anim2.duration;
[c.arrow addAnimation:group forKey:nil];
```

In that example, I grouped two animations that animated the same property sequentially. Now let's go to the other extreme and group some animations that animate different properties simultaneously. I have a small view (about 56×38), located near the top-right corner of the screen, whose layer contents are a picture of a sailboat facing to the left. I'll "sail" the boat in a curving path, both down the screen and left and right across the screen, like an extended letter "S" (Figure 17-2). Each time the boat comes to a vertex of the curve, changing direction across the screen, I'll turn the boat picture so that it

Figure 17-2. A boat and the course she'll sail

faces the way it's about to move. At the same time, I'll constantly rock the boat, so that it always appears to be pitching a little on the waves.

Here's the first animation, the movement of the boat along its curving path. It illustrates the use of a CAKeyframeAnimation with a CGPath; the calculationMode of kCAAnimationPaced ensures an even speed over the whole path. We don't set an explicit duration because we want to adopt the duration of the group:

```
CGFloat h = 200;
CGFloat v = 75;
CGMutablePathRef path = CGPathCreateMutable();
int leftright = 1;
CGPoint next = self.view.layer.position;
CGPoint pos;
CGPathMoveToPoint(path, nil, next.x, next.y);
for (int i = 0; i < 4; i++) {
    pos = next;
    leftright *= -1;
    next = CGPointMake(pos.x+h*leftright, pos.y+v);
    CGPathAddCurveToPoint(path, nil, pos.x, pos.y+30, next.x, next.y-30,
                          next.x, next.y);
}
CAKeyframeAnimation* anim1 =
    [CAKeyframeAnimation animationWithKeyPath:@"position"];
anim1.path = path;
anim1.calculationMode = kCAAnimationPaced;
```

Here's the second animation, the reversal of the direction the boat is facing. This is simply a rotation around the y-axis. We make no attempt at visually animating this reversal, so we set the calculationMode to kCAAnimationDiscrete (the boat image reversal is a sudden change). There is one fewer value than the number of points in our first animation's path, and the first animation has an even speed, so the reversals take place at each curve apex with no further effort on our part. (If the pacing were more complicated, we could give both the first and the second animation identical key-Times arrays, to coordinate them.) Once again, we don't set an explicit duration:

```
NSArray* revs = @[@0.0f, @M_PI, @0.0f, @M_PI];
CAKeyframeAnimation* anim2 =
    [CAKeyframeAnimation animationWithKeyPath:@"transform"];
anim2.values = revs;
anim2.valueFunction =
    [CAValueFunction functionWithName:kCAValueFunctionRotateY];
anim2.calculationMode = kCAAnimationDiscrete;
```

Here's the third animation, the rocking of the boat. It has a short duration, and repeats indefinitely (by giving its `repeatCount` an immense value):

```
NSArray* pitches = @[@0.0f, @(M_PI/60.0), @0.0f, @(-M_PI/60.0), @0.0f];
CAKeyframeAnimation* anim3 =
    [CAKeyframeAnimation animationWithKeyPath:@"transform"];
anim3.values = pitches;
anim3.repeatCount = HUGE_VALF;
anim3.duration = 0.5;
anim3.additive = YES;
anim3.valueFunction =
    [CAValueFunction functionWithName:kCAValueFunctionRotateZ];
```

Finally, we combine the three animations, assigning the group an explicit duration that will be adopted by the first two animations. As we hand the animation over to the layer displaying the boat, we also change the layer's position to match the final position from the first animation, so that the boat won't jump back to its original position afterward:

```
CAAnimationGroup* group = [CAAnimationGroup animation];
group.animations = @[anim1, anim2, anim3];
group.duration = 8;
[view.layer addAnimation:group forKey:nil];
[CATransaction setDisableActions:YES];
view.layer.position = next;
```

Here are some further CAAnimation properties (from the CAMediaTiming protocol) that come into play especially when animations are grouped:

speed

The ratio between a child's timescale and the parent's timescale. For example, if a parent and child have the same duration, but the child's speed is 1.5, its animation runs one-and-a-half times as fast as the parent.

fillMode

Suppose the child animation begins after the parent animation, or ends before the parent animation, or both. What should happen to the appearance of the property being animated, outside the child animation's boundaries? The answer depends on the child's fillMode:

- kCAFillModeRemoved means the child animation is removed, revealing the layer property at its actual current value whenever the child is not running.

- kCAFillModeForwards means the final presentation layer value of the child animation remains afterward.

- kCAFillModeBackwards means the initial presentation layer value of the child animation appears right from the start.

- kCAFillModeBoth combines the previous two.

 CALayer adopts the CAMediaTiming protocol, in the sense that a layer can have a speed. This will affect any animation attached to it. A CALayer with a speed of 2 will play a 10-second animation in 5 seconds.

Transitions

A layer transition is an animation involving two "copies" of a single layer, in which the second "copy" appears to replace the first. It is described by an instance of CATransition (a CAAnimation subclass), which has these chief properties describing the animation:

type
Your choices are:

- kCATransitionFade

- kCATransitionMoveIn

- kCATransitionPush

- kCATransitionReveal

subtype
If the type is not kCATransitionFade, your choices are:

- kCATransitionFromRight

- kCATransitionFromLeft

- kCATransitionFromTop

- kCATransitionFromBottom

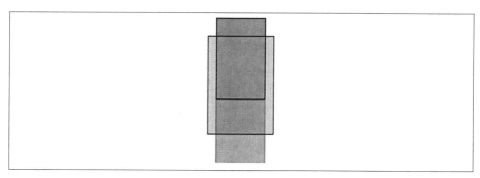

Figure 17-3. A push transition

For historical reasons, the terms "bottom" and "top" in the names of the subtype settings have the opposite of their expected meanings.

To understand the nature of a transition animation, the best approach is to try one, without doing anything else. For example:

```
CATransition* t = [CATransition animation];
t.type = kCATransitionPush;
t.subtype = kCATransitionFromBottom;
[layer addAnimation: t forKey: nil];
```

It will help if the layer's frame is visible (give it a borderWidth, perhaps). What you'll see, then, is that the entire layer exits moving down from its original place, and another "copy" of the same layer enters moving down from above. In Figure 17-3, the green layer (the wider rectangle) is the superlayer of the red layer (the narrower rectangle, which appears twice). The red layer is normally centered in the green layer, but I've managed to freeze the red layer in the middle of a transition.

You can use a layer's superlayer to help restrict the visible part of the layer's transition. If the superlayer's masksToBounds is NO, the user can see the entire transition; its movements will have the whole screen as their visible boundaries. But if the superlayer's masksToBounds is YES, then the visible part of the transition movement is restricted to the superlayer's bounds: it's as if you're seeing the movements through a window that is the superlayer. In Figure 17-3, for example, if the green layer's masksToBounds were YES, we wouldn't see any of the part of the transition animation outside its boundaries. A common device is to have the layer that is to be transitioned live inside a superlayer that is exactly the same size and whose masksToBounds is YES. This confines the visible transition to the bounds of the layer itself.

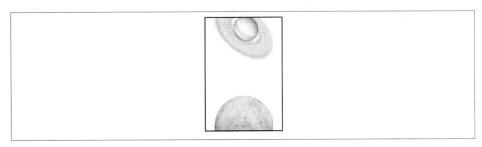

Figure 17-4. Another push transition

Our example appears silly, because there was no motivation for this animation; the two "copies" of the layer are identical. A typical motivation would be that you're changing the contents of a layer and you want to dramatize this. Here, we change the example so that an image of Saturn replaces an image of Mars by pushing it away from above (Figure 17-4). We get a slide effect, as if one layer were being replaced by another; but in fact there is just one layer that holds first one picture, then the other:

```
CATransition* t = [CATransition animation];
t.type = kCATransitionPush;
t.subtype = kCATransitionFromBottom;
[CATransaction setDisableActions:YES];
layer.contents = (id)[[UIImage imageNamed: @"Saturn.gif"] CGImage];
[layer addAnimation: t forKey: nil];
```

A transition on a superlayer can happen simultaneously with animation of a sublayer. The animation will be seen to occur on the second "copy" of the layer as it moves into position. This is analogous to what we achieved earlier with the `UIViewAnimation-OptionAllowAnimatedContent` option using block-based view animation.

The Animations List

The method that asks for an explicit animation to happen is CALayer's `add-Animation:forKey:`. To understand how this method actually works (and what the "key" is), you need to know about a layer's *animations list*.

An animation is an object (a CAAnimation) that modifies how a layer is drawn. It does this merely by being attached to the layer; the layer's drawing mechanism does the rest. A layer maintains a list of animations that are currently in force. To add an animation to this list, you call `addAnimation:forKey:`. When the time comes to draw itself, the layer looks through its animations list and draws itself in accordance with any animations it finds there. (The list of things the layer must do in order to draw itself is sometimes referred to by the documentation as the *render tree*.)

The animations list is maintained in a curious way. The list is not exactly a dictionary, but it behaves somewhat like a dictionary. An animation has a key — the `forKey:`

parameter in `addAnimation:forKey:`. If an animation with a certain key is added to the list, and an animation with that key is already in the list, the one that is already in the list is removed. Thus a rule is maintained that *only one animation with a given key* can be in the list at a time (the *exclusivity rule*). This explains why sometimes ordering an animation can cancel an animation already ordered or in-flight: the two animations had the same key, so the first one was removed. It is also possible to add an animation with *no key* (the key is nil); it is then *not* subject to the exclusivity rule (that is, there can be more than one animation in the list with no key). The order in which animations were added to the list is the order in which they are applied.

The `forKey:` parameter in `addAnimation:forKey:` is thus *not a property name*. It *could* be a property name, but it can be any arbitrary value. Its purpose is to enforce the exclusivity rule. It does *not* have any meaning with regard to what property a CAPropertyAnimation animates; that is the job of the animation's `keyPath`. (Apple's use of the term "key" in `addAnimation:forKey:` is thus unfortunate and misleading; I wish they had named this method `addAnimation:withIdentifier:` or something like that.)

 Actually, there *is* a relationship between the "key" in `addAnimation:forKey:` and a CAPropertyAnimation's `keyPath` — if a CAPropertyAnimation's `keyPath` is nil at the time that it is added to a layer with `addAnimation:forKey:`, *that keyPath is set to the forKey: value*. Thus, you can *misuse* the `forKey:` parameter in `addAnimation:forKey:` as a way of specifying what `keyPath` an animation animates. (This fact is not documented, so far as I know, but it's easily verified experimentally, and it should remain reliably true, as implicit animation crucially depends on it.) I have seen many prominent but misleading examples that use this technique, apparently in the mistaken belief that the "key" in `addAnimation:forKey:` is the way you are *supposed* to specify what property to animate. *This is wrong.* Set the CAPropertyAnimation's `keyPath` explicitly (as do all my examples); that's what it's for.

You can use the exclusivity rule to your own advantage, to keep your code from stepping on its own feet. Some code of yours might add an animation to the list using a certain key; then later, some other code might come along and correct this, removing that animation and replacing it with another. By using the same key, the second code is easily able to override the first: "You may have been given some other animation with this key, but throw it away; play this one instead."

In some cases, the key you supply is ignored and a different key is substituted. In particular, the key with which a CATransition is added to the list is always `kCATransition` (which happens to be `@"transition"`); thus there can be only one transition animation in the list.

You can't access the entire animations list directly. You can access the key names of the animations in the list, with animationKeys; and you can obtain or remove an animation with a certain key, with animationForKey: and removeAnimationForKey:; but animations with a nil key are inaccessible. You can, however, remove all animations, including animations with a nil key, using removeAllAnimations. In the multitasking world, when the app is suspended (Chapter 11), removeAllAnimations is called on all layers for you.

If an animation is in-flight when you remove it from the animations list manually, by calling removeAllAnimations or removeAnimationForKey:, it will stop; however, that doesn't happen until the next redraw moment. You might be able to work around this, if you need an animation to be removed immediately, by wrapping the remove... call in a transaction block.

You can think of an animation in a layer's animations list as being the "animation movie" I spoke of at the start of this chapter. As long as an animation is in the list, the movie is present, either waiting to be played or actually playing. An animation that has finished playing is, in general, pointless; the animation should now be removed from the list. Therefore, an animation has a removedOnCompletion property, which defaults to YES: when the "movie" is over, the animation removes itself from the list.

You can, if desired, set removedOnCompletion to NO. However, even the presence in the list of an animation that has already played might make no difference to the layer's appearance, because an animation's fillMode is kCAFillModeRemoved, which removes the animation from the layer's drawing when the movie is over. Thus, it can usually do no harm to leave an animation in the list after it has played, but it's not a great idea either, because this is just one more thing for the drawing system to worry about. Typically, you'll leave removedOnCompletion set at YES.

 You may encounter examples that set removedOnCompletion to NO and set the animation's fillMode to kCAFillModeForwards or kCAFillMode-Both, as a way of causing the layer to keep the appearance of the last frame of the "animation movie" even after the animation is over, and preventing a property from apparently jumping back to its initial value when the animation ends. *This is wrong.* The correct approach, as I have explained, is to change the property value to match the final frame of the animation. The chief use of kCAFillModeForwards is in connection with grouped animations, as explained earlier.

Animation and Autolayout

The interplay between animation and autolayout can be tricky (see Chapter 14). An animation may appear to work perfectly, but there can be a hidden trap waiting to be sprung. The reason is that animation and layout are two different things. As part of an animation, you may well be directly changing a view's frame (or bounds, or center). You're really not supposed to do that to position a view when you're using autolayout; but no penalty is incurred, because no layout has happened. However, it is entirely possible that layout *will* happen. And at that moment, what's going to matter, as we know very well, are the constraints. If the constraints that the system finds in place don't resolve to the size and position that a view has at that moment, the view will jump as the constraints are obeyed. This is almost certainly not what you want.

To persuade yourself that this can be a problem, just animate a view and then ask for immediate layout by calling layoutIfNeeded, like this:

```
CGPoint p = v.center;
p.x += 100;
[UIView animateWithDuration:1 animations:^{
    v.center = p;
} completion:^(BOOL b){
    [v layoutIfNeeded]; // prove that we are in trouble
}];
```

If we're using autolayout, the view slides to the right and then jumps back to the left. This is bad. It's up to us to keep the constraints synchronized with the reality, so that when layout comes along in the natural course of things, our views don't jump into undesirable states. This is no more than a natural extension of the fact that the last frame of the "animation movie" should be matched by the reality that's revealed when the movie is ripped away. That reality now includes not only the frames of the views but also the constraints that determine those frames.

The details of what you will do to the constraints will depend, clearly, on what the constraints were to start with. In the preceding example, let's say that the view v has a fixed width and height, and is positioned by a constraint pinning its left side at a certain distance from its superview's left side, and its top at a certain distance from its superview's top. Our animation moves the view 100 points to the right, so the value by which the view's left is pinned to its superview's left needs to be increased by 100. If we've planned far ahead, we might have an outlet or other reference to that constraint; but if not, we can find it by walking through the superview's constraints, looking for the one whose firstItem is v and whose firstAttribute is NSLayoutAttributeLeading. We'll remove that constraint and replace it with one whose constant matches the position of v (sup is the superview of v):

```
CGPoint p = v.center;
p.x += 100;
[UIView animateWithDuration:1 animations:^{
    v.center = p;
    NSArray* cons = sup.constraints;
    NSUInteger ix =
    [cons indexOfObjectPassingTest:^BOOL(id obj, NSUInteger idx, BOOL *stop) {
        NSLayoutConstraint* con = obj;
        return ((con.firstItem == v) &&
```

```
                (con.firstAttribute == NSLayoutAttributeLeading));
  }];
  NSLayoutConstraint* con = cons[ix];
  [sup removeConstraint:con];
  [sup addConstraint:
   [NSLayoutConstraint
    constraintWithItem:con.firstItem attribute:con.firstAttribute
    relatedBy:con.relation
    toItem:con.secondItem attribute:con.secondAttribute
    multiplier:1 constant:v.frame.origin.x]];
}];
```

Changing a constraint causes layout to take place, so you'll know immediately that this has worked correctly.

But in this case there is no need for such radical surgery. Recall that a constraint's constant is one of its few writable properties. We are allowed to change our constraint's constant *in place*, like this:

```
CGPoint p = v.center;
p.x += 100;
[UIView animateWithDuration:1 animations:^{
    v.center = p;
    NSArray* cons = sup.constraints;
    NSUInteger ix =
    [cons indexOfObjectPassingTest:^BOOL(id obj, NSUInteger idx, BOOL *stop) {
        NSLayoutConstraint* con = obj;
        return ((con.firstItem == v) &&
                (con.firstAttribute == NSLayoutAttributeLeading));
    }];
    NSLayoutConstraint* con = cons[ix];
    con.constant = v.frame.origin.x;
}];
```

For our very simple case, this suggests an even more compact implementation: instead of animating the view's position and then compensating by changing the constraint that positions it, *animate the change in the constraint that positions the view*. To do so, we set the constraint's constant to its new value, and animate the act of layout:

```
NSArray* cons = sup.constraints;
NSUInteger ix =
[cons indexOfObjectPassingTest:^BOOL(id obj, NSUInteger idx, BOOL *stop) {
    NSLayoutConstraint* con = obj;
    return ((con.firstItem == v) &&
            (con.firstAttribute == NSLayoutAttributeLeading));
}];
NSLayoutConstraint* con = cons[ix];
con.constant += 100;
[UIView animateWithDuration:1 animations:^{
    [v layoutIfNeeded];
}];
```

Another issue has to do with view transforms. As I said at the end of Chapter 14, applying a view transform triggers layout, and constraints then take a hand in positioning the view. Thus an animation involving a view transform will likely misbehave under autolayout.

For example, you would expect a simple autoreversing animation that waggles a view, or scales it up and back down, to work under autolayout. After all, we're not ultimately changing anything's frame. But, alas, that's not true. Even this simple "throb" animation can break under autolayout:

```
[UIView animateWithDuration:0.3 delay:0
                 options:UIViewAnimationOptionAutoreverse
             animations:^{
    v.transform = CGAffineTransformMakeScale(1.1, 1.1);
} completion:^(BOOL finished) {
    v.transform = CGAffineTransformIdentity;
}];
```

The solution in this case is to use Core Animation instead:

```
CABasicAnimation* ba = [CABasicAnimation animationWithKeyPath:@"transform"];
ba.autoreverses = YES;
ba.duration = 0.3;
ba.toValue =
    [NSValue valueWithCATransform3D:CATransform3DMakeScale(1.1, 1.1, 1)];
[v.layer addAnimation:ba forKey:nil];
```

Another useful trick is to take advantage of the fact that the "animation movie" masks the reality. In this example from one of my apps, I apparently shrink a view (english) down to nothingness:

```
CABasicAnimation* ba = [CABasicAnimation animationWithKeyPath:@"opacity"];
self.english.layer.opacity = 0;
ba.duration = 0.2;
[self.english.layer addAnimation:ba forKey:nil];
CABasicAnimation* ba2 = [CABasicAnimation animationWithKeyPath:@"bounds"];
ba2.duration = 0.2;
ba2.toValue = [NSValue valueWithCGRect:self.english.layer.bounds];
[self.english.layer addAnimation:ba2 forKey:nil];
```

This doesn't break under autolayout. Why not? Well, the "animation movie" *portrays* the view as shrinking to nothingness, and also as fading away. But the view's actual bounds were never changed, so there's no conflict with constraints. And by the time the "animation movie" is ripped away, the view is invisible (its opacity is 0), so the user doesn't see that it's actually still at its full size.

Actions

For the sake of completeness, I will now explain how implicit animation works — that is, how implicit animation is turned into explicit animation behind the scenes. The basis of implicit animation is the *action mechanism*.

What an Action Is

An *action* is an object that adopts the CAAction protocol. This means simply that it implements `runActionForKey:object:arguments:`.

The action object could do *anything* in response to this message. The notion of an action is completely general. However, in real life, the only class that adopts the CAAction protocol is CAAnimation. So, an animation is a special case of an action, but in fact it is also the *only* case of an action.

What an animation does when it receives `runActionForKey:object:arguments:` is to assume that the second parameter, the `object:`, is a layer, and to add itself to that layer's animations list. Thus, for an animation, receiving the `runActionForKey:object:arguments:` message is like being told: "Play yourself!"

You would never send `runActionForKey:object:arguments:` to an animation directly. Rather, this message is sent to an animation for you, as the basis of implicit animation.

The Action Search

When you set a property of a layer and trigger an implicit animation, you are actually triggering the *action search*. This basically means that the layer searches for an *action object* to which it can send the `runActionForKey:object:arguments:` message; because that action object will be an animation, and because it will respond to this message by adding itself to the layer's animations list, this is the same as saying that the layer searches for an animation to play itself with respect to the layer. The procedure by which the layer searches for this animation is quite elaborate.

The search for an action object begins because you do something that causes the layer to be sent the `actionForKey:` message. Let us presume that what you do is to change the value of an animatable property. (Other things can cause the `actionForKey:` message to be sent, as I'll show later.) The action mechanism then treats the name of the property as a key, and the layer receives `actionForKey:` with that key — and the action search begins.

At each stage of the action search, the following rules are obeyed regarding what is returned from that stage of the search:

An action object

> If an action object (an animation) is produced, that is the end of the search. The action mechanism sends that animation the `runActionForKey:object:arguments:` message; the animation responds by adding itself to the layer's animations list.

`[NSNull null]`

> If `[NSNull null]` is produced, that is the end of the search. There will be no implicit animation; `[NSNull null]` means, "Do nothing and stop searching."

nil

> If nil is produced, the search continues to the next stage.

The action search proceeds by stages, as follows:

1. The layer's `actionForKey:` might terminate the search before it even starts. For example, the layer will do this if it is the underlying layer of a view, or if a property is set to the same value it already has. In such a case, there should be no implicit animation, so the whole mechanism is nipped in the bud. (This stage is special in that a returned value of nil ends the search and no animation takes place.)

2. If the layer has a delegate that implements `actionForLayer:forKey:`, that message is sent to the delegate, with this layer as the layer and the property name as the key. If an animation or `[NSNull null]` is returned, the search ends.

3. The layer has a property called `actions`, which is a dictionary. If there is an entry in this dictionary with the given key, that value is used, and the search ends.

4. The layer has a property called `style`, which is a dictionary. If there is an entry in this dictionary with the key `actions`, it is assumed to be a dictionary; if this `actions` dictionary has an entry with the given key, that value is used, and the search ends. Otherwise, if there is an entry in the `style` dictionary called `style`, the same search is performed within it, and so on recursively until either an `actions` entry with the given key is found (the search ends) or there are no more `style` entries (the search continues).

   (If the `style` dictionary sounds profoundly weird, that's because it is profoundly weird. It is actually a special case of a larger, separate mechanism, which is also profoundly weird, having to do not with actions, but with a CALayer's implementation of KVC. When you call `valueForKey:` on a layer, if the key is undefined by the layer itself, the `style` dictionary is consulted. I have never written or seen code that uses this mechanism for anything, and I'll say no more about it.)

5. The layer's class is sent `defaultActionForKey:`, with the property name as the key. If an animation or `[NSNull null]` is returned, the search ends.

6. If the search reaches this last stage, a default animation is supplied, as appropriate. For a property animation, this is a plain vanilla CABasicAnimation.

Both the delegate's `actionForLayer:forKey:` and the subclass's `defaultActionFor-Key:` are declared as returning an `id<CAAction>`. To return `[NSNull null]`, therefore, you'll need to typecast it to `id<CAAction>` to quiet the compiler; you're lying (NSNull does not adopt the CAAction protocol), but it doesn't matter.

Hooking Into the Action Search

You can affect the action search at various stages to modify what happens when the search is triggered. Perhaps the most common real-life case is to turn off implicit animation altogether for some particular property. This is done by returning nil from `actionForKey:` itself, in a CALayer subclass; this suppresses the action search altogether. Here's the code from a CALayer subclass that doesn't animate its `position` property (but does animate its other properties normally):

```
-(id<CAAction>)actionForKey:(NSString *)event {
    if ([event isEqualToString:@"position"])
        return nil;
    return [super actionForKey:event];
}
```

Assuming that the action search is permitted, you could cause some stage of the search to produce an animation; that animation will then be used. Assuming that the search is triggered by setting an animatable layer property, you would then be affecting how implicit animation behaves.

You will probably want your animation to be fairly minimal. You may have no way of knowing the former and current values of the property that is being changed, so it would then be pointless (and very strange) to set a CABasicAnimation's `fromValue` or `toValue`. Moreover, although animation properties that you don't set can be set through CATransaction, in the usual manner for implicit property animation, animation properties that you *do* set can *not* be overridden through CATransaction. For example, if you set the duration of the animation that you produce at some stage of the action search, a call to CATransaction's `setAnimationDuration:` cannot change it.

Let's say we want a certain layer's duration for an implicit `position` animation to be 5 seconds. We can achieve this with a minimally configured animation, like this:

```
CABasicAnimation* ba = [CABasicAnimation animation];
ba.duration = 5;
```

The idea now is to situate this animation, `ba`, where it will be produced by the action search when implicit animation is triggered on the `position` property of our layer. We could, for instance, put it into the layer's `actions` dictionary:

```
layer.actions = @{@"position": ba};
```

The result is that when we set that layer's `position`, if an implicit animation results, its duration is 5 seconds, even if we try to change it through CATransaction:

```
[CATransaction setAnimationDuration:1];
layer.position = CGPointMake(100,200); // animation takes 5 seconds
```

Let's use that example to tease apart how the action mechanism makes implicit animation work:

1. You set the value of the layer's `position` property.

2. If your setting does not represent a change in the `position` value, or if this layer is a view's underlying layer, the layer's `actionForKey:` returns nil, and that's the end of the story; there is no implicit property animation.

3. Otherwise, the action search continues. There is no delegate in this case, so the search proceeds to the next stage, the `actions` dictionary.

4. There is an entry under the key `@"position"` in the `actions` dictionary (because we put it there), and it is an animation. That animation is the action, and that is the end of the search.

5. The animation is sent `runActionForKey:object:arguments:`.

6. The animation responds by calling `[object addAnimation:self for-Key:@"position"]`. The animation's keyPath was nil, *so this call also sets the key-Path to the same key!* Thus, there is now an animation in the layer's animations list that animates its `position`, because its `keyPath` is `@"position"`. Moreover, we didn't set the `fromValue` or `toValue`, so the property's previous and new values are used. The animation therefore shows the layer moving from its current position to `{100,200}`.

Using the layer's `actions` dictionary to set default animations is a somewhat inflexible way to hook into the action search, however. It has the disadvantage in general that you must write your animation beforehand. By contrast, if you set the layer's delegate to an instance that responds to `actionForLayer:forKey:`, your code runs at the time the animation is needed, and you have access to the layer that is to be animated. So you can create the animation on the fly, possibly modifying it in response to current circumstances.

Recall also that CATransaction implements KVC to allow you to set and retrieve the value of arbitrary keys. We can take advantage of this fact to pass an additional message from the code that sets the property value, and triggers the action search, to the code that supplies the action. This works because they both take place within the same transaction.

In this example, we use the layer delegate to change the default `position` animation so that instead of being a straight line, the path has a slight waggle. To do this, the delegate constructs a keyframe animation. The animation depends on the old `position` value and the new `position` value; the delegate can get the former direct from the layer, but the latter must be handed to the delegate somehow. Here, a CATransaction key `@"newP"` is used to communicate this information. When we set the layer's `position`, we put its future value where the delegate can retrieve it, like this:

```
CGPoint newP = CGPointMake(200,300);
[CATransaction setValue: [NSValue valueWithCGPoint: newP] forKey: @"newP"];
layer.position = newP; // the delegate will waggle the layer into place
```

The delegate is called by the action search and constructs the animation:

```
- (id < CAAction >)actionForLayer:(CALayer *)layer forKey:(NSString *)key {
    if ([key isEqualToString: @"position"]) {
        CGPoint oldP = layer.position;
        CGPoint newP = [[CATransaction valueForKey: @"newP"] CGPointValue];
        CGFloat d = sqrt(pow(oldP.x - newP.x, 2) + pow(oldP.y - newP.y, 2));
        CGFloat r = d/3.0;
        CGFloat theta = atan2(newP.y - oldP.y, newP.x - oldP.x);
        CGFloat wag = 10*M_PI/180.0;
        CGPoint p1 = CGPointMake(oldP.x + r*cos(theta+wag),
                                 oldP.y + r*sin(theta+wag));
        CGPoint p2 = CGPointMake(oldP.x + r*2*cos(theta-wag),
                                 oldP.y + r*2*sin(theta-wag));
        CAKeyframeAnimation* anim = [CAKeyframeAnimation animation];
        anim.values = @[
                        [NSValue valueWithCGPoint:oldP],
                        [NSValue valueWithCGPoint:p1],
                        [NSValue valueWithCGPoint:p2],
                        [NSValue valueWithCGPoint:newP]
                        ];
        anim.calculationMode = kCAAnimationCubic;
        return anim;
    }
    return nil;
}
```

Finally, I'll demonstrate overriding `defaultActionForKey:`. This code would go into a CALayer subclass where setting its `contents` is to trigger a push transition from the left:

```
+ (id < CAAction >)defaultActionForKey:(NSString *)aKey {
    if ([aKey isEqualToString:@"contents"]) {
        CATransition* tr = [CATransition animation];
        tr.type = kCATransitionPush;
        tr.subtype = kCATransitionFromLeft;
        return tr;
    }
    return [super defaultActionForKey: aKey];
}
```

Nonproperty Actions

Changing a property is not the only way to trigger a search for an action; an action search is also triggered when a layer is added to a superlayer (key kCAOnOrderIn) and when a layer's sublayers are changed by adding or removing a sublayer (key @"sublayers"). We can watch for these keys in the delegate and return an animation.

 These triggers and their keys are incorrectly described in Apple's documentation, and there are additional triggers and keys that are not mentioned there.

In this example, we use our layer's delegate so that when our layer is added to a superlayer, it will "pop" into view. We implement this by fading the layer quickly in from an opacity of 0 and at the same time scaling the layer's transform to make it momentarily appear a little larger:

```
- (id < CAAction >)actionForLayer:(CALayer *)lay forKey:(NSString *)key {
    if ([key isEqualToString:kCAOnOrderIn]) {
        CABasicAnimation* anim1 =
            [CABasicAnimation animationWithKeyPath:@"opacity"];
        anim1.fromValue = @0.0f;
        anim1.toValue = @(lay.opacity);
        CABasicAnimation* anim2 =
            [CABasicAnimation animationWithKeyPath:@"transform"];
        anim2.toValue = [NSValue valueWithCATransform3D:
                        CATransform3DScale(lay.transform, 1.1, 1.1, 1.0)];
        anim2.autoreverses = YES;
        anim2.duration = 0.1;
        CAAnimationGroup* group = [CAAnimationGroup animation];
        group.animations = @[anim1, anim2];
        group.duration = 0.2;
        return group;
    }
}
```

The documentation says that when a layer is removed from a superlayer, an action is sought under the key kCAOnOrderOut. This is true but useless, because by the time the action is sought, the layer has already been removed from the superlayer, so returning an animation has no visible effect. Similarly, an animation returned as an action when a layer's hidden is set to YES is never played. Apple has admitted that this is a bug. A possible workaround is to trigger the animation via the opacity property, perhaps in conjunction with a CATransaction key, and remove the layer afterward:

```
[CATransaction setCompletionBlock: ^{
    [layer removeFromSuperlayer];
}];
[CATransaction setValue:@"" forKey:@"byebye"];
layer.opacity = 0;
```

Now `actionForLayer:forKey:` can test for the incoming key `@"opacity"` and the CA-Transaction key `@"byebye"`, and return the animation appropriate to removal from the superlayer. Here's a possible implementation:

```
if ([key isEqualToString:@"opacity"]) {
    if ([CATransaction valueForKey:@"byebye"]) {
        CABasicAnimation* anim1 =
        [CABasicAnimation animationWithKeyPath:@"opacity"];
        anim1.fromValue = @(layer.opacity);
        anim1.toValue = @0.0f;
        CABasicAnimation* anim2 =
        [CABasicAnimation animationWithKeyPath:@"transform"];
        anim2.toValue = [NSValue valueWithCATransform3D:
                            CATransform3DScale(layer.transform, 0.1, 0.1, 1.0)];
        CAAnimationGroup* group = [CAAnimationGroup animation];
        group.animations = @[anim1, anim2];
        group.duration = 0.2;
        return group;
    }
}
```

Emitter Layers

Emitter layers (CAEmitterLayer) are, to some extent, on a par with animated images: once you've set up an emitter layer, it just sits there animating all by itself. The nature of this animation is rather narrow: an emitter layer emits particles, which are CAEmitterCell instances. However, by clever setting of the properties of an emitter layer and its emitter cells, you can achieve some astonishing effects. Moreover, the animation is itself animatable using Core Animation.

It is easiest to understand emitter layers and emitter cells if you start with some stupid settings to achieve a boring effect. Let's start with the emitter cells. Here are some useful basic properties of a CAEmitterCell:

contents, contentsRect
> These are modeled after the eponymous CALayer properties, although CAEmitter-Layer is not a CALayer subclass; so, respectively, an image (a CGImageRef) and a CGRect defining a region of that image. They define the image that a cell will portray.

birthrate, lifetime
> How many cells per second should be emitted, and how many seconds each cell should live before vanishing, respectively.

velocity
> The speed at which a cell moves. The unit of measurement is not documented; perhaps it's points per second.

`emissionLatitude`, `emissionLongitude`

> The angle at which the cell is emitted from the emitter, as a variation from the perpendicular. Longitude is an angle within the plane; latitude is an angle out of the plane.

So, here's code to create a very elementary emitter cell:

```
UIGraphicsBeginImageContextWithOptions(CGSizeMake(10,10), NO, 0);
CGContextRef con = UIGraphicsGetCurrentContext();
CGContextAddEllipseInRect(con, CGRectMake(0,0,10,10));
CGContextSetFillColorWithColor(con, [UIColor blackColor].CGColor);
CGContextFillPath(con);
UIImage* im = UIGraphicsGetImageFromCurrentImageContext();
UIGraphicsEndImageContext();

CAEmitterCell* cell = [CAEmitterCell emitterCell];
emit.emitterCells = @[cell];
cell.birthRate = 5;
cell.lifetime = 1;
cell.velocity = 100;
cell.contents = (id)im.CGImage;
```

The result is that little black circles should be emitted slowly and steadily, five per second, each one vanishing in five seconds. Now we need an emitter layer from which these circles are to be emitted. Here are some basic CAEmitterLayer properties (beyond those it inherits from CALayer); these define an imaginary object, an emitter, that will be producing the emitter cells:

`emitterPosition`

> The point at which the emitter should located, in superlayer coordinates. You can optionally add a third dimension to this point, `emitterZPosition`.

`emitterSize`

> The size of the emitter.

`emitterShape`

> The shape of the emitter. The dimensions of the shape depend on the emitter's size; the cuboid shape depends also on a third size dimension, `emitterDepth`. Your choices are:
>
> - `kCAEmitterLayerPoint`
> - `kCAEmitterLayerLine`
> - `kCAEmitterLayerRectangle`
> - `kCAEmitterLayerCuboid`
> - `kCAEmitterLayerCircle`
> - `kCAEmitterLayerSphere`

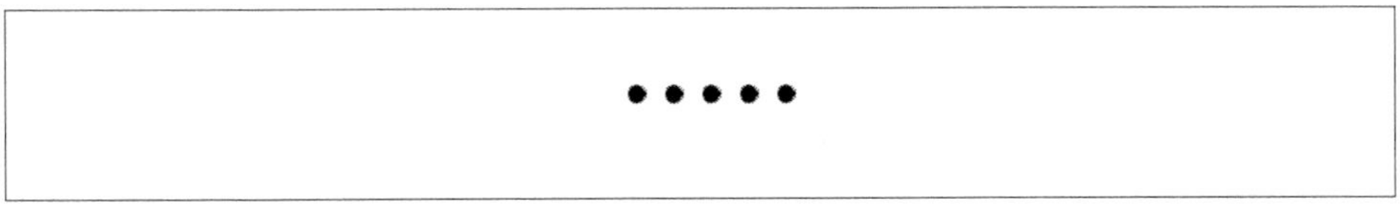

Figure 17-5. A really boring emitter layer

`emitterMode`
 The region of the shape from which cells should be emitted. Your choices are:

- `kCAEmitterLayerPoints`
- `kCAEmitterLayerOutline`
- `kCAEmitterLayerSurface`
- `kCAEmitterLayerVolume`

Let's start with the simplest possible case, a single point emitter:

```
CAEmitterLayer* emit = [CAEmitterLayer new];
emit.emitterPosition = CGPointMake(30,100);
emit.emitterShape = kCAEmitterLayerPoint;
emit.emitterMode = kCAEmitterLayerPoints;
```

We tell the emitter what types of cell to emit by assigning those cells to its `emitter-Cells` property (an array of CAEmitterCell). We have only one type of cell. We then add the emitter to our interface, and presto, it starts emitting:

```
emit.emitterCells = @[cell];
[self.window.rootViewController.view.layer addSublayer:emit];
```

The result is a constant stream of black circles emitted from the point {30,100}, each circle marching steadily to the right and vanishing after one second (Figure 17-5).

Now that we've succeeded in creating a boring emitter layer, we can start to vary some parameters. The `emissionRange` defines a cone in which cells will be emitted; if we increase the `birthRate` and widen the `emissionRange`, we get something that looks like a stream coming from a water hose:

```
cell.birthRate = 100;
cell.lifetime = 1;
cell.velocity = 100;
cell.emissionRange = M_PI/10;
```

As the cell moves, it can be made to accelerate (or decelerate) in each dimension, using its `xAcceleration`, `yAcceleration`, and `zAcceleration` properties. Here, we turn the stream into a falling cascade, like a waterfall coming from the left:

```
cell.birthRate = 100;
cell.lifetime = 1.5;
cell.velocity = 100;
cell.emissionRange = M_PI/10;
cell.xAcceleration = -40;
cell.yAcceleration = 200;
```

All aspects of cell behavior can be made to vary, using the following CAEmitterCell properties:

lifetimeRange, velocityRange

> How much the lifetime and velocity values are allowed to vary randomly for different cells.

scale

scaleRange, scaleSpeed

> The scale alters the size of the cell; the range and speed determine how far and how rapidly this size alteration is allowed to change over the lifetime of each cell.

color

redRange, greenRange, blueRange, alphaRange

redSpeed, greenSpeed, blueSpeed, alphaSpeed

> The color is painted in accordance with the opacity of the cell's contents image; it combines with the image's color, so if we want the color stated here to appear in full purity, our contents image should use only white. The range and speed determine how far and how rapidly each color component is to change.

spin, spinRange

> The spin is a rotational speed (in radians per second); its range determines how far this speed is allowed to change over the lifetime of each cell.

Here we apply some variation so that the circles behave a little more independently of one another. Some live longer than others, some come out of the emitter faster than others. And they all start out a shade of blue, but change to a shade of green about halfway through the stream (Figure 17-6):

```
cell.birthRate = 100;
cell.lifetime = 1.5;
cell.lifetimeRange = .4;
cell.velocity = 100;
cell.velocityRange = 20;
cell.emissionRange = M_PI/5;
cell.scale = 1;
cell.scaleRange = .2;
cell.scaleSpeed = .2;
cell.xAcceleration = -40;
cell.yAcceleration = 200;
cell.color = [UIColor blueColor].CGColor;
cell.greenRange = .5;
cell.greenSpeed = .75;
```

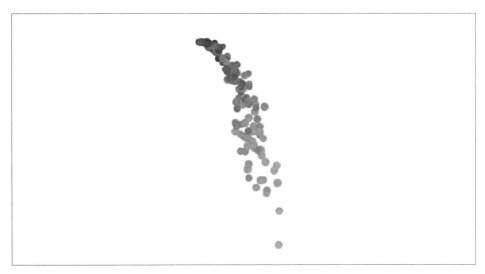

Figure 17-6. An emitter layer that makes a sort of waterfall

But wait, there's more! Once the emitter layer is in place and animating, you can change its parameters and the parameters of its emitter cells. To do so, use KVC on the emitter layer. You can access the emitter cells through the emitter layer's @"emitterCells" key path; to specify a cell type, use its name property (which you'll have to have assigned earlier) as the next piece of the key path. For example, suppose we've set cell.name to @"circle"; now we'll change the cell's greenSpeed so that each cell changes from blue to green much earlier in its lifetime:

```
[emit setValue:@3.0f
    forKeyPath:@"emitterCells.circle.greenSpeed"];
```

But wait, there's *still* more: such changes can themselves be animated! Here, we'll attach to the emitter layer a repeating animation that causes our cell's greenSpeed to move back and forth between two values. The result is that the stream is sometimes mostly blue and sometimes mostly green:

```
CABasicAnimation* ba =
    [CABasicAnimation animationWithKeyPath:@"emitterCells.circle.greenSpeed"];
ba.fromValue = @-1.0f;
ba.toValue = @3.0f;
ba.duration = 4;
ba.autoreverses = YES;
ba.repeatCount = HUGE_VALF;
[emit addAnimation:ba forKey:nil];
```

But wait, there's *still* still more! A CAEmitterCell can itself function as an emitter — that is, it can have cells of its own. Both CAEmitterLayer and CAEmitterCell conform to the CAMediaTiming protocol, and their beginTime and duration properties can be

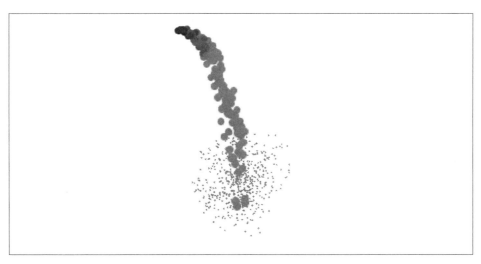

Figure 17-7. The waterfall makes a kind of splash

used to govern their times of operation, much as in a grouped animation. For example, this code causes our existing waterfall to spray tiny droplets in the region of the "nozzle" (the emitter):

```
CAEmitterCell* cell2 = [CAEmitterCell emitterCell];
cell.emitterCells = @[cell2];
cell2.contents = (id)im.CGImage;
cell2.emissionRange = M_PI;
cell2.birthRate = 200;
cell2.lifetime = 0.4;
cell2.velocity = 200;
cell2.scale = 0.2;
cell2.beginTime = .04;
cell2.duration = .2;
```

But if we change the beginTime to be larger (hence later), the tiny droplets happen near the bottom of the cascade. We must also increase the duration, or stop setting it altogether, since if the duration is less than the beginTime, no emission takes place at all (Figure 17-7):

```
cell2.beginTime = .7;
cell2.duration = .8;
```

Of course we can also completely change the picture by changing the behavior of the emitter itself. This change turns the emitter into a line, so that our cascade becomes broader:

Figure 17-8. Midway through a starburst transition

```
emit.emitterPosition = CGPointMake(100,25);
emit.emitterSize = CGSizeMake(100,100);
emit.emitterShape = kCAEmitterLayerLine;
emit.emitterMode = kCAEmitterLayerOutline;
cell.emissionLongitude = 3*M_PI/4;
```

There remains more to know about emitter layers and emitter cells, but at this point you know enough to understand Apple's sample code examples, one portraying fire and smoke, and the other simulating fireworks, and you can explore further on your own.

CIFilter Transitions

New in iOS 6, Core Image filters include transitions. You supply two images and a frame time between 0 and 1; the filter supplies the corresponding frame of a one-second animation transitioning from the first image to the second. For example, Figure 17-8 shows the frame at frame time .75 for a starburst transition from a solid red image to a photo of me. (You don't see the photo of me, because this transition, by default, "explodes" the first image to white first, and then quickly fades to the second image.)

What Core Image transition filters do *not* do for you is animate: that's up to you. Thus we need a way of rapidly calling the same method repeatedly; in that method, we'll request and draw subsequent frames of the transition. This could be a job for an NSTimer (Chapter 11), but an even better way is to use a *display link* (CADisplayLink), a form of timer that's highly efficient, especially when repeated drawing is involved, because it is linked directly to the refreshing of the display (hence the name). The display refresh rate is typically about one-sixtieth of a second; the actual value is given as the display link's duration, and will undergo slight fluctuations. Like a timer, the display link calls a designated method of ours every time it fires. We can slow the rate of calls by an integral amount by setting the display link's frameInterval; for example, a display link with a frameInterval of 2 will call us about every one-thirtieth of a second. We can learn the exact time when the display link last fired by querying its timestamp.

In this simple example, we start by initializing the CIFilter, and we store it in an instance variable; the last thing we want to do is waste time on each frame creating the CIFilter repeatedly from scratch! We also store as instance variables all the other values needed to render the final image — the image's extent and the CIContext used for rendering — as these are time-consuming to generate. We then create the display link, setting it to call into our nextFrame: method, and set it going by adding it to the run loop, which retains it:

```
UIImage* moi = [UIImage imageNamed:@"moi.jpg"];
CIImage* moi2 = [[CIImage alloc] initWithCGImage:moi.CGImage];
self->_moiextent = moi2.extent;
self->_con = [CIContext contextWithOptions:nil];

CIFilter* col = [CIFilter filterWithName:@"CIConstantColorGenerator"];
CIColor* cicol = [[CIColor alloc] initWithColor:[UIColor redColor]];
[col setValue:cicol forKey:@"inputColor"];
CIImage* colorimage = [col valueForKey: @"outputImage"];

CIFilter* tran = [CIFilter filterWithName:@"CIFlashTransition"];
[tran setValue:colorimage forKey:@"inputImage"];
[tran setValue:moi2 forKey:@"inputTargetImage"];
CIVector* center = [CIVector vectorWithX:self->_moiextent.size.width/2.0
                                        Y:self->_moiextent.size.height/2.0];
[tran setValue:center forKey:@"inputCenter"];
self->_tran = tran;

CADisplayLink* link = [CADisplayLink displayLinkWithTarget:self
                              selector:@selector(nextFrame:)];
[link addToRunLoop:[NSRunLoop mainRunLoop] forMode:NSDefaultRunLoopMode];
```

Our nextFrame: method is called with the display link as parameter (sender). We store the initial timestamp in an instance variable, and use the difference between that and each successive timestamp value to calculate our desired frame. We ask the filter for the corresponding image and display it. When the frame value exceeds 1, the animation is over and we invalidate the display link (just like a repeating timer), which releases it from the run loop:

```
if (self->_timestamp < 0.01) { // pick up and store first timestamp
    self->_timestamp = sender.timestamp;
    self->_frame = 0.0;
} else { // calculate frame
    self->_frame = sender.timestamp - self->_timestamp;
}
sender.paused = YES; // defend against frame loss

[_tran setValue:@(self->_frame) forKey:@"inputTime"];
CGImageRef moi3 = [self->_con createCGImage:_tran.outputImage
                                   fromRect:_moiextent];
self->_iv.image = [UIImage imageWithCGImage:moi3];
CGImageRelease(moi3);
```

```
    if (self->_frame > 1.0) {
        [sender invalidate];
        self->_frame = 0.0;
        self->_timestamp = 0.0;
    }
    sender.paused = NO;
```

I have surrounded the time-consuming calculation and drawing of the image with calls to the display link's paused property, in case the calculation time exceeds the time between screen refreshes; perhaps this isn't necessary, but it can't hurt. Our animation occupies one second; changing that value is merely a matter of multiplying by a scale value when we set our _frame instance variable. If you experiment with this code, run on the device, as display links do not work well in the Simulator.

Touches

A *touch* is an instance of the user putting a finger on the screen. The system and the hardware, working together, know *when* a finger contacts the screen and *where* it is. Fingers are fat, but the system and the hardware cleverly reduce the finger's location to a single appropriate point.

A UIView, by virtue of being a UIResponder, is the visible locus of touches. There are other UIResponder subclasses, but none of them is visible on the screen. What the user sees are views; what the user is touching are views. (The user may also see layers, but a layer is not a UIResponder and is not involved with touches. I'll talk later about how to make it seem as if the user can touch a layer.)

It would make sense, therefore, if every touch were reported directly to the view in which it occurred. However, what the system "sees" is not particular views but an app as a whole. So a touch is represented as an object (a UITouch instance) which is bundled up in an envelope (a UIEvent) which the system delivers to your app. It is then up to your app to deliver the envelope to an appropriate UIView. In the vast majority of cases, this will happen automatically the way you expect, and you will respond to a touch by way of the view in which the touch occurred.

In fact, usually you won't concern yourself with UIEvents and UITouches at all. Most built-in interface views deal with these low-level touch reports themselves, and notify your code at a higher level. When a UIButton emits an action message to report a control event such as Touch Up Inside (Chapter 11), it has already performed a reduction of a complex sequence of touches ("the user put a finger down inside me and then, possibly with some dragging hither and yon, raised it when it was still reasonably close to me").

A UITextField reports touches on the keyboard as changes in its own text. A UITable-View reports that the user selected a cell. A UIScrollView, when dragged, reports that it scrolled; when pinched outward, it reports that it zoomed.

Nevertheless, it is useful to know how to respond to touches directly, so that you can implement your own touchable views, and so that you understand what Cocoa's built-in views are actually doing. This chapter discusses touch detection and response by views (and other UIResponders) at their lowest level, along with a slightly higher-level mechanism, gesture recognizers, that categorizes touches into gesture types for you; then it deconstructs the touch-delivery architecture by which touches are reported to your views in the first place.

Touch Events and Views

Imagine a screen that the user is not touching at all: the screen is "finger-free." Now the user touches the screen with one or more fingers. From that moment to the time the screen is once again finger-free, all touches and finger movements together constitute what Apple calls a single *multitouch sequence*.

The system reports to your app, during a given multitouch sequence, every change in finger configuration, so that your app can figure out what the user is doing. Every such report is a UIEvent. In fact, every report having to do with the same multitouch sequence is *the same UIEvent instance*, arriving repeatedly, each time there's a change in finger configuration.

Every UIEvent reporting a change in the user's finger configuration contains one or more UITouch objects. Each UITouch object corresponds to a single finger; conversely, every finger touching the screen is represented in the UIEvent by a UITouch object. Once a certain UITouch instance has been created to represent a finger that has touched the screen, *the same UITouch instance* is used to represent that finger throughout this multitouch sequence until the finger leaves the screen.

Now, it might sound as if the system has to bombard the app with huge numbers of reports constantly during a multitouch sequence. But that's not really true. The system needs to report only *changes* in the finger configuration. For a given UITouch object (representing, remember, a specific finger), only four things can happen. These are called *touch phases*, and are described by a UITouch instance's phase property:

UITouchPhaseBegan
    The finger touched the screen for the first time; this UITouch instance has just been created. This is always the first phase, and arrives only once.

UITouchPhaseMoved
    The finger moved upon the screen.

UITouchPhaseStationary

The finger remained on the screen without moving. Why is it necessary to report this? Well, remember, once a UITouch instance has been created, it must be present every time the UIEvent arrives. So if the UIEvent arrives because something *else* happened (e.g., a new finger touched the screen), we must report what *this* finger has been doing, even if it has been doing nothing.

UITouchPhaseEnded

The finger left the screen. Like UITouchPhaseBegan, this phase arrives only once. The UITouch instance will now be destroyed and will no longer appear in UIEvents for this multitouch sequence.

Those four phases are sufficient to describe everything that a finger can do. Actually, there is one more possible phase:

UITouchPhaseCancelled

The system has aborted this multitouch sequence because something interrupted it.

What might interrupt a multitouch sequence? There are many possibilities. Perhaps the user clicked the Home button or the screen lock button in the middle of the sequence. A local notification alert may have appeared (Chapter 26); on an actual iPhone, a call might have come in. (As we shall see, a gesture recognizer recognizing its gesture may also trigger touch cancellation.) The point is, if you're dealing with touches yourself, you cannot afford to ignore touch cancellation; they are your opportunity to get things into a coherent state when the sequence is interrupted.

When a UITouch first appears (UITouchPhaseBegan), your app works out which UIView it is associated with. (I'll give full details, later in this chapter, as to how it does that.) This view is then set as the touch's view property; from then on, this UITouch is *always* associated with this view. In other words, *a touch's view is that touch's view forever* (until that finger leaves the screen).

The same UIEvent containing the same UITouches can be sent to multiple views; after all, these are programmatic objects, not real-world envelopes containing actual fingers. Accordingly, a UIEvent is distributed to *all the views of all the UITouches it contains.* Conversely, if a view is sent a UIEvent, it's because that UIEvent contains at least one UITouch whose view is this view.

If every UITouch in a UIEvent associated with a certain UIView has the phase UITouchPhaseStationary, that UIEvent is *not* sent to that UIView. There's no point, because as far as that view is concerned, nothing happened.

Receiving Touches

A UIResponder, and therefore a UIView, has four methods corresponding to the four UITouch phases that require UIEvent delivery. A UIEvent is delivered to a view by calling one or more of these four methods (the *touches... methods*):

touchesBegan:withEvent:
> A finger touched the screen, creating a UITouch.

touchesMoved:withEvent:
> A finger previously reported to this view with touchesBegan:withEvent: has moved.

touchesEnded:withEvent:
> A finger previously reported to this view with touchesBegan:withEvent: has left the screen.

touchesCancelled:withEvent:
> We are bailing out on a finger previously reported to this view with touches-Began:withEvent:.

The parameters of these methods are:

The relevant touches
> These are the event's touches whose phase corresponds to the name of the method and (normally) whose view is this view. They arrive as an NSSet (Chapter 10). If you know for a fact that there is only one touch in the set, or that any touch in the set will do, you can retrieve it with anyObject (an NSSet doesn't implement last-Object because a set is unordered).

The event
> This is the UIEvent instance. It contains its touches as an NSSet, which you can retrieve with the allTouches message. This means *all* the event's touches, including but not necessarily limited to those in the first parameter; there might be touches in a different phase or intended for some other view. You can call touchesFor-View: or touchesForWindow: to ask for the set of touches associated with a particular view or window.

A UITouch has some useful methods and properties:

locationInView:, previousLocationInView:
> The current and previous location of this touch with respect to the coordinate system of a given view. The view you'll be interested in will often be self or self.superview; supply nil to get the location with respect to the window. The previous location will be of interest only if the phase is UITouchPhaseMoved.

timestamp
> When the touch last changed. A touch is timestamped when it is created (UITouch-PhaseBegan) and each time it moves (UITouchPhaseMoved).

tapCount
> If two touches are in roughly the same place in quick succession, and the first one is brief, the second one may be characterized as a repeat of the first. They are different touch objects, but the second will be assigned a tapCount one larger than the previous one. The default is 1, so if (for example) a touch's tapCount is 3, then this is the third tap in quick succession in roughly the same spot.

view
> The view with which this touch is associated.

Here are some additional UIEvent properties:

type
> This will be UIEventTypeTouches. There are other event types, but you're not going to receive any of them this way.

timestamp
> When the event occurred.

So, when we say that a certain view *is receiving a touch*, that is a shorthand expression meaning that it is being sent a UIEvent containing this UITouch, over and over, by calling one of its touches... methods, corresponding to the phase this touch is in, from the time the touch is created until the time it is destroyed.

Restricting Touches

Touch events can be turned off entirely at the application level with UIApplication's beginIgnoringInteractionEvents. It is quite common to do this during animations and other lengthy operations during which responding to a touch could cause undesirable results. This call should be balanced by endIgnoringInteractionEvents. Pairs can be nested, in which case interactivity won't be restored until the outermost endIgnoringInteractionEvents has been reached.

A number of UIView properties also restrict the delivery of touches to particular views:

userInteractionEnabled
> If set to NO, this view (along with its subviews) is excluded from receiving touches. Touches on this view or one of its subviews "fall through" to a view behind it.

`opacity`

> If set to `0.0` (or extremely close to it), this view (along with its subviews) is excluded from receiving touches. Touches on this view or one of its subviews "fall through" to a view behind it.

`hidden`

> If set to YES, this view (along with its subviews) is excluded from receiving touches. This makes sense, since from the user's standpoint, the view and its subviews are not even present.

`multipleTouchEnabled`

> If set to NO, this view never receives more than one touch simultaneously; once it receives a touch, it doesn't receive any other touches until that first touch has ended.

`exclusiveTouch`

> This is the only one of these properties that can't be set in the nib. An `exclusiveTouch` view receives a touch only if no other views in the same window have touches associated with them; once an `exclusiveTouch` view has received a touch, then while that touch exists no other view in the same window receives any touches.

 A UIWindow ignores `multipleTouchEnabled`; it always receives multiple touches. Moreover, a UIWindow's behavior with respect to `exclusiveTouch` is unreliable, presumably because it is not itself a view in the window. In general this should not be an issue, since you'll always have a root view covering the window anyway.

Interpreting Touches

Thanks to the existence of gesture recognizers (discussed later in this chapter), in most cases you won't have to interpret touches at all; you'll let a gesture recognizer do most of that work. Even so, it is beneficial to be conversant with the nature of touch interpretation; this will help you interact with a gesture recognizer, write your own gesture recognizer, or subclass an existing one. Furthermore, not every touch sequence can be codified through a gesture recognizer; sometimes, directly interpreting touches is the best approach.

To figure out what's going on as touches are received by a view, your code must essentially function as a kind of state machine. You'll receive various `touches...` method calls, and your response will partly depend upon what happened previously, so you'll have to record somehow, such as in instance variables, the information that you'll need in order to decide what to do when the next `touches...` method is called. Such an architecture can make writing and maintaining touch-analysis code quite tricky. Moreover, although you can distinguish a particular UITouch or UIEvent object over time by keeping a reference to it, you mustn't retain that reference; it doesn't belong to you.

To illustrate the business of interpreting touches, we'll start with a view that can be dragged with the user's finger. For simplicity, I'll assume that this view receives only a single touch at a time. (This assumption is easy to enforce by setting the view's multiple-TouchEnabled to NO, which is the default.)

The trick to making a view follow the user's finger is to realize that a view is positioned by its center, which is in superview coordinates, but the user's finger might not be at the center of the view. So at every stage of the drag we must change the view's center by the change in the user's finger position in superview coordinates:

```
- (void) touchesMoved:(NSSet *)touches withEvent:(UIEvent *)event {
    CGPoint loc =
        [[touches anyObject] locationInView: self.superview];
    CGPoint oldP =
        [[touches anyObject] previousLocationInView: self.superview];
    CGFloat deltaX = loc.x - oldP.x;
    CGFloat deltaY = loc.y - oldP.y;
    CGPoint c = self.center;
    c.x += deltaX;
    c.y += deltaY;
    self.center = c;
}
```

Next, let's add a restriction that the view can be dragged only vertically or horizontally. All we have to do is hold one coordinate steady; but which coordinate? Everything seems to depend on what the user does initially. So we'll do a one-time test the first time we receive touchesMoved:withEvent:. Now we're maintaining two state variables, _decided and _horiz:

```
- (void) touchesBegan:(NSSet *)touches withEvent:(UIEvent *)event {
    self->_decided = NO;
}

- (void) touchesMoved:(NSSet *)touches withEvent:(UIEvent *)event {
    if (!self->_decided) {
        self->_decided = YES;
        CGPoint then = [[touches anyObject] previousLocationInView: self];
        CGPoint now = [[touches anyObject] locationInView: self];
        CGFloat deltaX = fabs(then.x - now.x);
        CGFloat deltaY = fabs(then.y - now.y);
        self->_horiz = (deltaX >= deltaY);
    }
    CGPoint loc =
        [[touches anyObject] locationInView: self.superview];
    CGPoint oldP =
        [[touches anyObject] previousLocationInView: self.superview];
    CGFloat deltaX = loc.x - oldP.x;
    CGFloat deltaY = loc.y - oldP.y;
```

```
        CGPoint c = self.center;
        if (self->_horiz)
            c.x += deltaX;
        else
            c.y += deltaY;
        self.center = c;
    }
```

Look at how things are trending. We are maintaining state variables, which we are managing across multiple methods, and we are subdividing a touches... method implementation into tests depending on the state of our state machine. Our state machine is very simple, involving just two state variables, but already our code is becoming difficult to read and to maintain. Things only become more messy as we try to make our view's behavior more sophisticated.

Another area in which manual touch handling can rapidly prove overwhelming is when it comes to distinguishing between different gestures that the user is to be permitted to perform on a view. Imagine, for example, a view that distinguishes between a finger tapping briefly and a finger remaining down for a longer time. We can't know how long a tap is until it's over, so one approach might be to wait until then before deciding:

```
    - (void) touchesBegan:(NSSet *)touches withEvent:(UIEvent *)event {
        self->_time = [[touches anyObject] timestamp];
    }

    - (void) touchesEnded:(NSSet *)touches withEvent:(UIEvent *)event {
        NSTimeInterval diff = event.timestamp - self->_time;
        if (diff < 0.4)
            NSLog(@"short");
        else
            NSLog(@"long");
    }
```

On the other hand, one might argue that if a tap hasn't ended after some set time (here, 0.4 seconds), we know that it is long, and so we could begin responding to it without waiting for it to end. The problem is that we don't automatically get an event after 0.4 seconds. So we'll create one, using delayed performance:

```
    - (void) touchesBegan:(NSSet *)touches withEvent:(UIEvent *)event {
        self->_time = [[touches anyObject] timestamp];
        [self performSelector:@selector(touchWasLong)
                   withObject:nil afterDelay:0.4];
    }

    - (void) touchesEnded:(NSSet *)touches withEvent:(UIEvent *)event {
        NSTimeInterval diff = event.timestamp - self->_time;
        if (diff < 0.4)
            NSLog(@"short");
    }
```

```
- (void) touchWasLong {
    NSLog(@"long");
}
```

But there's a bug. If the tap is short, we report that it was short, but we *also* report that it was long. That's because the delayed call to touchWasLong arrives anyway. We could use some sort of boolean flag to tell us when to ignore that call, but there's a better way: NSObject has a class method that lets us cancel any pending delayed performance calls. So:

```
- (void) touchesBegan:(NSSet *)touches withEvent:(UIEvent *)event {
    self->_time = [[touches anyObject] timestamp];
    [self performSelector:@selector(touchWasLong)
            withObject:nil afterDelay:0.4];
}

- (void) touchesEnded:(NSSet *)touches withEvent:(UIEvent *)event {
    NSTimeInterval diff = event.timestamp - self->_time;
    if (diff < 0.4) {
        NSLog(@"short");
        [NSObject cancelPreviousPerformRequestsWithTarget:self
                               selector:@selector(touchWasLong)
                                 object:nil];
    }
}

- (void) touchWasLong {
    NSLog(@"long");
}
```

Here's another use of the same technique. We'll distinguish between a single tap and a double tap. The UITouch tapCount property already makes this distinction, but that, by itself, is not enough to help us react differently to the two. What we must do, having received a tap whose tapCount is 1, is to delay responding to it long enough to give a second tap a chance to arrive. This is unfortunate, because it means that if the user intends a single tap, some time will elapse before anything happens in response to it; however, there's nothing we can easily do about that.

Distributing our various tasks correctly is a bit tricky. We *know* when we have a double tap as early as touchesBegan:withEvent:, so that's when we cancel our delayed response to a single tap, but we *respond* to the double tap in touchesEnded:withEvent:. We don't start our delayed response to a single tap until touchesEnded:withEvent:, because what matters is the time between the taps as a whole, not between the starts of the taps. This code is adapted from Apple's own example:

```
- (void) touchesBegan:(NSSet *)touches withEvent:(UIEvent *)event {
    int ct = [[touches anyObject] tapCount];
    if (ct == 2) {
        [NSObject cancelPreviousPerformRequestsWithTarget:self
```

```
                                         selector:@selector(singleTap)
                                         object:nil];
        }
    }

    - (void) touchesEnded:(NSSet *)touches withEvent:(UIEvent *)event {
        int ct = [[touches anyObject] tapCount];
        if (ct == 1)
            [self performSelector:@selector(singleTap)
                        withObject:nil afterDelay:0.3];
        if (ct == 2)
            NSLog(@"double tap");
    }

    - (void) singleTap {
        NSLog(@"single tap");
    }
```

Now let's consider combining our detection for a single or double tap with our earlier code for dragging a view horizontally or vertically. This is to be a view that can detect four kinds of gesture: a single tap, a double tap, a horizontal drag, and a vertical drag. We must include the code for all possibilities and make sure they don't interfere with each other. The result is rather horrifying, a forced join between two already complicated sets of code, along with an additional pair of state variables to track the decision between the tap gestures on the one hand and the drag gestures on the other:

```
    - (void) touchesBegan:(NSSet *)touches withEvent:(UIEvent *)event {
        // be undecided
        self->_decidedTapOrDrag = NO;
        // prepare for a tap
        int ct = [[touches anyObject] tapCount];
        if (ct == 2) {
            [NSObject cancelPreviousPerformRequestsWithTarget:self
                                         selector:@selector(singleTap)
                                         object:nil];
            self->_decidedTapOrDrag = YES;
            self->_drag = NO;
            return;
        }
        // prepare for a drag
        self->_decidedDirection = NO;
    }

    - (void) touchesMoved:(NSSet *)touches withEvent:(UIEvent *)event {
        if (self->_decidedTapOrDrag && !self->_drag)
            return;
        self->_decidedTapOrDrag = YES;
        self->_drag = YES;
        if (!self->_decidedDirection) {
            self->_decidedDirection = YES;
            CGPoint then = [[touches anyObject] previousLocationInView: self];
            CGPoint now = [[touches anyObject] locationInView: self];
```

```
        CGFloat deltaX = fabs(then.x - now.x);
        CGFloat deltaY = fabs(then.y - now.y);
        self->_horiz = (deltaX >= deltaY);
    }
    CGPoint loc =
        [[touches anyObject] locationInView: self.superview];
    CGPoint oldP =
        [[touches anyObject] previousLocationInView: self.superview];
    CGFloat deltaX = loc.x - oldP.x;
    CGFloat deltaY = loc.y - oldP.y;
    CGPoint c = self.center;
    if (self->_horiz)
        c.x += deltaX;
    else
        c.y += deltaY;
    self.center = c;
}

- (void) touchesEnded:(NSSet *)touches withEvent:(UIEvent *)event {
    if (!self->_decidedTapOrDrag || !self->_drag) {
        // end for a tap
        int ct = [[touches anyObject] tapCount];
        if (ct == 1)
            [self performSelector:@selector(singleTap) withObject:nil
                    afterDelay:0.3];
        if (ct == 2)
            NSLog(@"double tap");
        return;
    }
}

- (void) singleTap {
    NSLog(@"single tap");
}
```

That code seems to work, but it's hard to say whether it covers all possibilities coherently; it's barely legible and the logic borders on the mysterious. This is the kind of situation for which gesture recognizers were devised.

Gesture Recognizers

Writing and maintaining a state machine that interprets touches across a combination of three or four touches... methods is hard enough when a view confines itself to expecting only one kind of gesture, such as dragging. It becomes even more involved when a view wants to accept and respond differently to different kinds of gesture. Furthermore, many types of gesture are conventional and standard; it seems insane to require developers to implement independently the elements that constitute what is, in effect, a universal vocabulary.

The solution is gesture recognizers, which standardize common gestures and allow the code for different gestures to be separated and encapsulated into different objects.

Gesture Recognizer Classes

A *gesture recognizer* (a subclass of UIGestureRecognizer) is an object attached to a UI-View, which has for this purpose methods `addGestureRecognizer:` and `removeGesture-Recognizer:`, and a `gestureRecognizers` property. A UIGestureRecognizer implements the four `touches...` handlers, but it is not a responder (a UIResponder), so it does not participate in the responder chain.

If a new touch is going to be delivered to a view, it is also associated with and delivered to that view's gesture recognizers if it has any, and that view's superview's gesture recognizers if it has any, and so on up the view hierarchy. Thus, the place of a gesture recognizer in the view hierarchy matters, even though it isn't part of the responder chain.

UITouch and UIEvent provide complementary ways of learning how touches and gesture recognizers are associated. UITouch's `gestureRecognizers` lists the gesture recognizers that are currently handling this touch. UIEvent's `touchesForGesture-Recognizer:` lists the touches that are currently being handled by a particular gesture recognizer.

Each gesture recognizer maintains its own state as touch events arrive, building up evidence as to what kind of gesture this is. When one of them decides that it has recognized its own type of gesture, it emits either a single message (to indicate, for example, that a finger has tapped) or a series of messages (to indicate, for example, that a finger is moving); the distinction here is between a *discrete* and a *continuous* gesture. What message a gesture recognizer emits, and to what object it sends it, is set through a target–action dispatch table attached to the gesture recognizer; a gesture recognizer is rather like a UIControl (Chapter 11) in this regard. Indeed, one might say that a gesture recognizer simplifies the touch handling of *any* view to be like that of a control. The difference is that one control may report several different control events, whereas each gesture recognizer reports only one gesture type, with different gestures being reported by different gesture recognizers. This architecture implies that it is unnecessary to subclass UIView merely in order to implement touch analysis.

UIGestureRecognizer itself is abstract, providing methods and properties to its subclasses. Among these are:

`initWithTarget:action:`
> The designated initializer. Each message emitted by a UIGestureRecognizer is simply a matter of sending the action message to the target. Further target–action pairs may be added with `addTarget:action:` and removed with `remove-Target:action:`.

Two forms of selector are possible: either there is no parameter, or there is a single parameter which will be the gesture recognizer. Most commonly, you'll use the second form, so that the target can identify and query the gesture recognizer; moreover, using the second form also gives the target a reference to the view, because the gesture recognizer provides a reference to its view as the `view` property.

`locationOfTouch:inView:`
The touch is specified by an index number. The `numberOfTouches` property provides a count of current touches; the touches themselves are inaccessible from outside the gesture recognizer.

`enabled`
A convenient way to turn a gesture recognizer off without having to remove it from its view.

`state, view`
I'll discuss state later on. The view is the view to which this gesture recognizer is attached.

Built-in UIGestureRecognizer subclasses are provided for six common gesture types: tap, pinch, pan (drag), swipe, rotate, and long press. These embody properties and methods likely to be needed for each type of gesture, either in order to configure the gesture recognizer beforehand or in order to query it as to the state of an ongoing gesture:

UITapGestureRecognizer (discrete)
Configuration: `numberOfTapsRequired`, `numberOfTouchesRequired` ("touches" means simultaneous fingers).

UIPinchGestureRecognizer (continuous)
State: `scale`, `velocity`.

UIRotationGestureRecognizer (continuous)
State: `rotation`, `velocity`.

UISwipeGestureRecognizer (discrete)
Configuration: `direction` (meaning permitted directions, a bitmask), `numberOfTouchesRequired`.

UIPanGestureRecognizer (continuous)
Configuration: `minimumNumberOfTouches`, `maximumNumberOfTouches`.

State: `translationInView:`, `setTranslation:inView:`, and `velocityInView:`; the coordinate system of the specified view is used, so to follow a finger you'll use the superview of the view being dragged, just as we did in the examples earlier.

UILongPressGestureRecognizer (continuous)

Configuration: `numberOfTapsRequired`, `numberOfTouchesRequired`, `minimum-PressDuration`, `allowableMovement`. The `numberOfTapsRequired` is the count of taps *before* the tap that stays down; so it can be 0 (the default). The `allowable-Movement` setting lets you compensate for the fact that the user's finger is unlikely to remain steady during an extended press; thus we need to provide some limit before deciding that this gesture is, say, a drag, and not a long press after all. On the other hand, once the long press is recognized, the finger is permitted to drag.

UIGestureRecognizer also provides a `locationInView:` method. This is a single point, even if there are multiple touches. The subclasses implement this variously. For example, for UIPanGestureRecognizer, the location is where the touch is if there's a single touch, but it's a sort of midpoint ("centroid") if there are multiple touches.

We already know enough to implement, using a gesture recognizer, a view that responds to a single tap, or a view that responds to a double tap. We don't yet know quite enough to implement a view that lets itself be dragged around, or a view that can respond to more than one gesture; we'll come to that. Meanwhile, here's code that implements a view that responds to a single tap:

```
UITapGestureRecognizer* t = [[UITapGestureRecognizer alloc]
                            initWithTarget:self
                            action:@selector(singleTap)];
[v addGestureRecognizer:t];
// ...
- (void) singleTap {
    NSLog(@"single");
}
```

And here's code that implements a view that responds to a double tap:

```
UITapGestureRecognizer* t = [[UITapGestureRecognizer alloc]
                            initWithTarget:self
                            action:@selector(doubleTap)];
t.numberOfTapsRequired = 2;
[v addGestureRecognizer:t];
// ...
- (void) doubleTap {
    NSLog(@"double");
}
```

For a continuous gesture like dragging, we need to know both when the gesture is in progress and when the gesture ends. This brings us to the subject of a gesture recognizer's state.

A gesture recognizer implements a notion of *states* (the `state` property); it passes through these states in a definite progression. The gesture recognizer remains in the Possible state until it can make a decision one way or the other as to whether this is in fact the correct gesture. The documentation neatly lays out the possible progressions:

Wrong gesture
Possible → Failed. No action message is sent.

Discrete gesture (like a tap), recognized
Possible → Ended. One action message is sent, when the state changes to Ended.

Continuous gesture (like a drag), recognized
Possible → Began → Changed (repeatedly) → Ended. Action messages are sent once for Began, as many times as necessary for Changed, and once for Ended.

Continuous gesture, recognized but later cancelled
Possible → Began → Changed (repeatedly) → Cancelled. Action messages are sent once for Began, as many times as necessary for Changed, and once for Cancelled.

The actual state names are `UIGestureRecognizerStatePossible` and so forth. The name `UIGestureRecognizerStateRecognized` is actually a synonym for the Ended state; I find this unnecessary and confusing and I'll ignore it in my discussion.

We now know enough to implement, using a gesture recognizer, a view that lets itself be dragged around in any direction by a single finger. Our maintenance of state is greatly simplified, because a UIPanGestureRecognizer maintains a delta (translation) for us. This delta, available using `translationInView:`, is reckoned from the touch's initial position. So we need to store our center only once:

```
UIPanGestureRecognizer* p =
    [[UIPanGestureRecognizer alloc] initWithTarget:self
                                    action:@selector(dragging:)];
[v addGestureRecognizer:p];
// ...
- (void) dragging: (UIPanGestureRecognizer*) p {
    UIView* vv = p.view;
    if (p.state == UIGestureRecognizerStateBegan)
        self->_origC = vv.center;
    CGPoint delta = [p translationInView: vv.superview];
    CGPoint c = self->_origC;
    c.x += delta.x; c.y += delta.y;
    vv.center = c;
}
```

Actually, it's possible to write that code without maintaining any state at all, because we are allowed to reset the UIPanGestureRecognizer's delta, using `setTranslation:in-View:`. So:

```
- (void) dragging: (UIPanGestureRecognizer*) p {
    UIView* vv = p.view;
    if (p.state == UIGestureRecognizerStateBegan ||
            p.state == UIGestureRecognizerStateChanged) {
        CGPoint delta = [p translationInView: vv.superview];
        CGPoint c = vv.center;
        c.x += delta.x; c.y += delta.y;
```

```
            vv.center = c;
            [p setTranslation: CGPointZero inView: vv.superview];
        }
    }
```

A gesture recognizer also works, as I've already mentioned, if it is attached to the superview (or further up the hierarchy) of the view in which the user gestures. For example, if a tap gesture recognizer is attached to the window's root view, the user can tap on any other view, and the tap will be recognized; the other view's mere presence does not "block" the root view's gesture recognizer from recognizing the gesture, even if it is a UIControl that responds autonomously to touches.

This behavior comes as a surprise to beginners, but it makes sense, because if it were not the case, certain gestures would be impossible. Imagine, for example, a pair of views on each of which the user can tap individually, but which the user can also touch simultaneously (one finger on each view) and rotate together around their mutual centroid. Neither view can detect the rotation *qua* rotation, because neither view receives both touches; only the superview can detect it, so the fact that the views themselves respond to touches must not prevent the superview's gesture recognizer from operating.

Suppose, then, that your window's root view has a UITapGestureRecognizer attached to it (perhaps because you want to be able to recognize taps on the background), but there is also a UIButton within it. How is that gesture recognizer to ignore a tap on the button? A UIView instance method introduced in iOS 6 solves the problem: `gesture-RecognizerShouldBegin:`. Its parameter is a gesture recognizer belonging to this view or to a view further up the view hierarchy. That gesture recognizer has recognized its gesture as taking place in this view; but by returning NO, the view can tell the gesture recognizer to bow out and do nothing, not sending any action messages, and permitting this view to respond to the touch as if the gesture recognizer weren't there.

Thus, for example, a UIButton could return NO for a single tap UITapGesture-Recognizer; a single tap on the button would then trigger the button's action message, not the gesture recognizer's action message. And in fact a UIButton, by default, *does* return NO for a single tap UITapGestureRecognizer whose view is not the UIButton itself. (If the gesture recognizer is for some gesture other than a tap, then the problem never arises, because a tap on the button won't cause the gesture recognizer to recognize in the first place.) Other built-in controls may also implement `gestureRecognizer-ShouldBegin:` in such a way as to prevent accidental interaction with a gesture recognizer; the documentation says that a UISlider implements it in such a way that a UISwipeGestureRecognizer won't prevent the user from sliding the "thumb," and there may be other cases that aren't documented explicitly. Naturally, you can take advantage of this feature in your own UIView subclasses.

Remember that this automatic behavior of built-in controls is new in iOS 6. If you write code intended to be backwards-compatible to iOS 5 or before, beware of unexpected interactions between gesture recognizers and controls.

Another way of resolving possible conflicts between a control and a gesture recognizer is through the gesture recognizer's delegate, which I'll discuss later in this chapter.

Multiple Gesture Recognizers

The question naturally arises of what happens when multiple gesture recognizers are in play. This isn't a matter merely of multiple recognizers attached to a single view, because, as I have just said, if a view is touched, not only its own gesture recognizers but any gesture recognizers attached to views further up the view hierarchy are also in play, simultaneously. I like to think of a view as surrounded by a swarm of gesture recognizers — its own and those of its superview (and so on). In reality, it is a touch that has a swarm of gesture recognizers; that's why a UITouch has a `gestureRecognizers` property, in the plural.

In general, once a gesture recognizer succeeds in recognizing its gesture, any *other* gesture recognizers associated with its touches are *forced into the Failed state*, and whatever touches were associated with those gesture recognizers are no longer sent to them; in effect, the first gesture recognizer in a swarm that recognizes its gesture owns the gesture, and those touches, from then on.

In many cases, this behavior alone will correctly eliminate conflicts. For example, we can add *both* our UITapGestureRecognizer for a single tap *and* our UIPanGesture-Recognizer to a view and everything will just work.

What happens if we also add the UITapGestureRecognizer for a double tap? Dragging works, and single tap works; double tap works too, but without preventing the single tap from working. So, on a double tap, both the single tap action handler and the double tap action handler are called.

If that isn't what we want, we don't have to use delayed performance, as we did earlier. Instead, we can create a *dependency* between one gesture recognizer and another, telling the first to suspend judgement until the second has decided whether this is its gesture, by sending the first the `requireGestureRecognizerToFail:` message. This message doesn't mean "force this other recognizer to fail"; it means, "you can't succeed until this other recognizer fails."

So our view is now configured as follows:

```
UITapGestureRecognizer* t2 = [[UITapGestureRecognizer alloc]
                             initWithTarget:self
                             action:@selector(doubleTap)];
t2.numberOfTapsRequired = 2;
[v addGestureRecognizer:t2];

UITapGestureRecognizer* t1 = [[UITapGestureRecognizer alloc]
                             initWithTarget:self
                             action:@selector(singleTap)];
[t1 requireGestureRecognizerToFail:t2];
[v addGestureRecognizer:t1];

UIPanGestureRecognizer* p = [[UIPanGestureRecognizer alloc]
                            initWithTarget:self
                            action:@selector(dragging:)];
[v addGestureRecognizer:p];
```

 Apple would prefer, if you're going to have a view respond both to single tap and double tap, that you *not* make the former wait upon the latter (because this delays your response after the single tap). Rather, they would like you to arrange things so that it doesn't matter that you respond to a single tap that is the first tap of a double tap. This isn't always feasible, of course; Apple's own Mobile Safari is a clear counterexample.

Subclassing Gesture Recognizers

To subclass a built-in gesture recognizer subclass, you must do the following things:

- At the start of the implementation file, import <UIKit/UIGestureRecognizer-Subclass.h>. This file contains a category on UIGestureRecognizer that allows you to set the gesture recognizer's state (which is otherwise read-only), along with declarations for the methods you may need to override.

- Override any touches... methods you need to (as if the gesture recognizer were a UIResponder); you will almost certainly call super so as to take advantage of the built-in behavior. In overriding a touches... method, you need to think like a gesture recognizer. As these methods are called, a gesture recognizer is setting its state; you must interact with that process.

To illustrate, we will subclass UIPanGestureRecognizer so as to implement a view that can be moved only horizontally or vertically. Our strategy will be to make *two* UIPan-GestureRecognizer subclasses — one that allows only horizontal movement, and another that allows only vertical movement. They will make their recognition decisions in a mutually exclusive manner, so we can attach an instance of each to our view. This separates the decision-making logic in a gorgeously encapsulated object-oriented manner — a far cry from the spaghetti code we wrote earlier to do this same task.

I will show only the code for the horizontal drag gesture recognizer, because the vertical recognizer is symmetrically identical. We maintain just one instance variable, _orig-Loc, which we will use once to determine whether the user's initial movement is horizontal. We override touchesBegan:withEvent: to set our instance variable with the first touch's location:

```
- (void) touchesBegan:(NSSet *)touches withEvent:(UIEvent *)event {
    self->_origLoc = [[touches anyObject] locationInView:self.view.superview];
    [super touchesBegan: touches withEvent: event];
}
```

We then override touchesMoved:withEvent:; all the recognition logic is here. This method will be called for the first time with the state still at Possible. At that moment, we look to see if the user's movement is more horizontal than vertical. If it isn't, we set the state to Failed. But if it is, we just step back and let the superclass do its thing:

```
- (void) touchesMoved:(NSSet *)touches withEvent:(UIEvent *)event {
    if (self.state == UIGestureRecognizerStatePossible) {
        CGPoint loc = [[touches anyObject] locationInView:self.view.superview];
        CGFloat deltaX = fabs(loc.x - self->_origLoc.x);
        CGFloat deltaY = fabs(loc.y - self->_origLoc.y);
        if (deltaY >= deltaX)
            self.state = UIGestureRecognizerStateFailed;
    }
    [super touchesMoved: touches withEvent:event];
}
```

We now have a view that moves only if the user's initial gesture is horizontal. But that isn't the entirety of what we want; we want a view that, itself, moves horizontally only. To implement this, we'll simply lie to our client about where the user's finger is, by overriding translationInView::

```
- (CGPoint)translationInView:(UIView *)v {
    CGPoint proposedTranslation = [super translationInView:v];
    proposedTranslation.y = 0;
    return proposedTranslation;
}
```

That example was simple, because we subclassed a fully functional built-in UIGesture-Recognizer subclass. If you were to write your own UIGestureRecognizer subclass entirely from scratch, there would be more work to do:

- You should definitely implement all four touches... handlers. Their job, at a minimum, is to advance the gesture recognizer through the canonical progression of its states. When the first touch arrives at a gesture recognizer, its state will be Possible; you never explicitly set the recognizer's state to Possible yourself. As soon as you know this can't be our gesture, you set the state to Failed (Apple says that a gesture recognizer should "fail early, fail often"). If the gesture gets past all the failure tests, you set the state instead either to Ended (for a discrete gesture) or to Began (for a continuous gesture); if Began, then you might set it to Changed, and ultimately you must set it to Ended. Action messages will be sent automatically at the appropriate moments.

- You should probably implement reset. This is called after you reach the end of the progression of states to notify you that the gesture recognizer's state is about to be set back to Possible; it is your chance to return your state machine to its starting configuration (resetting instance variables, for example).

Keep in mind that your gesture recognizer might stop receiving touches without notice. Just because it gets a touchesBegan:withEvent: call for a particular touch doesn't mean it will ever get touchesEnded:withEvent: for that touch. If your gesture recognizer fails to recognize its gesture, either because it declares failure or because it is still in the Possible state when another gesture recognizer recognizes, it won't get any more touches... calls for any of the touches that were being sent to it. This is why reset is so important; it's the one reliable signal that it's time to clean up and get ready to receive the beginning of another possible gesture.

Gesture Recognizer Delegate

A gesture recognizer can have a delegate, which can perform two types of task:

Block a gesture recognizer's operation
> gestureRecognizerShouldBegin: is sent to the delegate before the gesture recognizer passes out of the Possible state; return NO to force the gesture recognizer to proceed to the Failed state. (This happens *after* gestureRecognizerShould-Begin: has been sent to the view in which the touch took place. That view must not have returned NO, or we wouldn't have reached this stage.)

> gestureRecognizer:shouldReceiveTouch: is sent to the delegate before a touch is sent to the gesture recognizer's touchesBegan:... method; return NO to prevent that touch from ever being sent to the gesture recognizer.

Mediate simultaneous gesture recognition
> When a gesture recognizer is about to declare that it recognizes its gesture, gesture-Recognizer:shouldRecognizeSimultaneouslyWithGestureRecognizer: is sent to the delegate of that gesture recognizer, if this declaration would force the failure of another gesture recognizer, and to the delegate of a gesture recognizer whose failure would be forced. Return YES to prevent that failure, thus allowing both gesture recognizers to operate simultaneously. For example, a view could respond to both a two-fingered pinch and a two-fingered pan, the one applying a scale transform, the other changing the view's center.

As an example, we will use delegate messages to combine a UILongPressGesture-Recognizer and a UIPanGestureRecognizer, as follows: the user must perform a tap-

and-a-half (tap and hold) to "get the view's attention," which we will indicate by a pulsing animation on the view; then (and only then) the user can drag the view.

In keeping with encapsulation, the UILongPressGestureRecognizer's handler will take care of starting and stopping the animation, and the UIPanGestureRecognizer's handler will take care of the drag in the familiar manner:

```
- (void) longPress: (UILongPressGestureRecognizer*) lp {
    if (lp.state == UIGestureRecognizerStateBegan) {
        CABasicAnimation* anim =
            [CABasicAnimation animationWithKeyPath: @"transform"];
        anim.toValue =
            [NSValue valueWithCATransform3D:
                CATransform3DMakeScale(1.1, 1.1, 1)];
        anim.fromValue =
            [NSValue valueWithCATransform3D:CATransform3DIdentity];
        anim.repeatCount = HUGE_VALF;
        anim.autoreverses = YES;
        [lp.view.layer addAnimation:anim forKey:nil];
    }
    if (lp.state == UIGestureRecognizerStateEnded ||
        lp.state == UIGestureRecognizerStateCancelled) {
        [lp.view.layer removeAllAnimations];
    }
}

- (void) panning: (UIPanGestureRecognizer*) p {
    UIView* vv = p.view;
    if (p.state == UIGestureRecognizerStateBegan)
        self->_origC = vv.center;
    CGPoint delta = [p translationInView: vv.superview];
    CGPoint c = self->_origC;
    c.x += delta.x; c.y += delta.y;
    vv.center = c;
}
```

As we created our gesture recognizers, we kept a reference to the UILongPressGesture-Recognizer (longPresser), and we made ourself the UIPanGestureRecognizer's delegate. So we will receive delegate messages. If the UIPanGestureRecognizer tries to declare success while the UILongPressGestureRecognizer's state is Failed or still at Possible, we prevent it. If the UILongPressGestureRecognizer succeeds, we permit the UIPanGestureRecognizer to operate as well:

```
- (BOOL) gestureRecognizerShouldBegin: (UIGestureRecognizer*) g {
    if (self.longPresser.state == UIGestureRecognizerStatePossible ||
        self.longPresser.state == UIGestureRecognizerStateFailed)
        return NO;
    return YES;
}
```

```
- (BOOL)gestureRecognizer: (UIGestureRecognizer*) g1
        shouldRecognizeSimultaneouslyWithGestureRecognizer:
            (UIGestureRecognizer*) g2 {
    return YES;
}
```

The result is that the view can be dragged only if it is pulsing; in effect, what we've done is to compensate, using delegate methods, for the fact that UIGestureRecognizer has no requireGestureRecognizerToSucceed: method.

You might object that that example is a bit artificial, because a UILongPressGesture-Recognizer can implement draggability all on its own. Its Changed state indicates a drag; it lacks the convenient translationInView: method, but we know how to work around that. So here, for completeness, is the same behavior implemented using a single gesture recognizer and a single handler; although this is doable, I find the previous implementation more elegant and readable:

```
- (void) longPress: (UILongPressGestureRecognizer*) lp {
    UIView* vv = lp.view;
    if (lp.state == UIGestureRecognizerStateBegan) {
        CABasicAnimation* anim =
            [CABasicAnimation animationWithKeyPath: @"transform"];
        anim.toValue =
            [NSValue valueWithCATransform3D:
                CATransform3DMakeScale(1.1, 1.1, 1)];
        anim.fromValue =
            [NSValue valueWithCATransform3D:CATransform3DIdentity];
        anim.repeatCount = HUGE_VALF;
        anim.autoreverses = YES;
        [vv.layer addAnimation:anim forKey:nil];
        self->_origOffset =
            CGPointMake(CGRectGetMidX(vv.bounds) - [lp locationInView:vv].x,
                CGRectGetMidY(vv.bounds) - [lp locationInView:vv].y);
    }
    if (lp.state == UIGestureRecognizerStateChanged) {
        CGPoint c = [lp locationInView: vv.superview];
        c.x += self->_origOffset.x;
        c.y += self->_origOffset.y;
        vv.center = c;
    }
    if (lp.state == UIGestureRecognizerStateEnded ||
        lp.state == UIGestureRecognizerStateCancelled) {
        [vv.layer removeAllAnimations];
    }
}
```

If you are subclassing a gesture recognizer class, you can incorporate delegate-like behavior into the subclass. By overriding canPreventGestureRecognizer: and canBe-PreventedByGestureRecognizer:, you can mediate simultaneous gesture recognition at the class level. The built-in gesture recognizer subclasses already do this; that is why, for example, a single tap UITapGestureRecognizer does not, by recognizing its gesture, cause the failure of a double tap UITapGestureRecognizer.

You can also, in a gesture recognizer subclass, send `ignoreTouch:forEvent:` directly to a gesture recognizer (typically, to `self`). This has the same effect as the delegate method `gestureRecognizer:shouldReceiveTouch:` returning NO, blocking delivery of that touch to the gesture recognizer for as long as it exists. For example, if you're in the middle of an already recognized gesture and a new touch arrives, you might well elect to ignore it.

Gesture Recognizers in the Nib

Instead of instantiating a gesture recognizer in code, you can create and configure it in a nib or storyboard. (I'm a bit hazy on what version of Xcode introduced this feature; I first noticed it in Xcode 4.5.) Drag a gesture recognizer from the Object library into the canvas. It becomes a top-level nib object. You can configure the gesture recognizer's properties in the Attributes inspector. Control-drag from a view object (meaning an object whose class is UIView or any UIView subclass) to a gesture recognizer to make that gesture recognizer belong to that view; the view's `gestureRecognizers` property is an array, so its `gestureRecognizers` outlet is an outlet collection (see Chapter 7) and you can add more than one gesture recognizer to a view in the nib.

A gesture recognizer's target–action pair can be configured in the nib as well. This works just like configuring a target–action pair for a control (Chapter 7). As a hint to Xcode, the action method's signature should return IBAction, and it should take a single parameter, which will be a reference to the gesture recognizer. You can then drag from the gesture recognizer, or from its Sent Actions "selector" listing in the Connections inspector, to that method in code in an assistant pane — or, if this method is in a known object's class, such as the File's Owner, you can drag directly to that object within the nib. (However, although a gesture recognizer has a full-fledged target–action dispatch table, only one target–action pair can be configured in the nib. This seems like a bug; after all, control configuration is not restricted in this way.)

A gesture recognizer in the nib also has a `delegate` outlet, which can be hooked to any object.

A view retains its gesture recognizers, so there will usually be no need for memory management on a gesture recognizer in the nib. It's a full-fledged nib object, so you can make an outlet to it; you would do this, for instance, if you needed to send a `require-GestureRecognizerToFail:` message to a gesture recognizer early in its lifetime, as we did previously in order to mediate between a single tap recognizer and a double tap recognizer.

Touch Delivery

Let's now return to the very beginning of the touch reporting process, when the system sends the app a UIEvent containing touches, and tease apart in full detail the entire procedure by which a touch is delivered to views and gesture recognizers:

1. Whenever a new touch appears, the application calls the UIView instance method `hitTest:withEvent:` on the window, which returns the view (called, appropriately, the *hit-test view*) that will be permanently associated with this touch. This method uses the UIView instance method `pointInside:withEvent:` along with `hit-Test:withEvent:` recursively down the view hierarchy to find the frontmost view containing the touch's location and capable of receiving a touch. The logic of how a view's `userInteractionEnabled`, `hidden`, and `opacity` affect its touchability is implemented at this stage.

2. Each time the touch situation changes, the application calls its own `sendEvent:`, which in turn calls the window's `sendEvent:`. The window delivers each of an event's touches by calling the appropriate `touches...` method(s), as follows:

   a. As a touch first appears, it is initially delivered to the hit-test view's swarm of gesture recognizers. It is then also delivered to that view. The logic of withholding touches in obedience to `multipleTouchEnabled` and `exclusiveTouch` is also implemented at this stage. For example, additional touches won't be delivered to a view if that view currently has a touch and has `multipleTouchEnabled` set to NO.

   b. If a gesture is recognized by a gesture recognizer, then for any touch associated with this gesture recognizer:

      i. `touchesCancelled:forEvent:` is sent to the touch's view, and the touch is no longer delivered to its view.

      ii. If that touch was associated with any other gesture recognizer, that gesture recognizer is forced to fail.

   c. If a gesture recognizer fails, either because it declares failure or because it is forced to fail, its touches are no longer delivered to it, but (except as already specified) they continue to be delivered to their view.

   d. If a touch would be delivered to a view, but that view does not respond to the appropriate `touches...` method, a responder further up the responder chain (Chapter 11) is sought that does respond to it, and the touch is delivered there.

The rest of this chapter elaborates on each stage of this standard procedure, nearly every bit of which can be customized to some extent.

Hit-Testing

Hit-testing is the determination of what view the user touched. View hit-testing uses the UIView instance method `hitTest:withEvent:`, which returns either a view (the hit-test view) or nil. The idea is to find the frontmost view containing the touch point. This method uses an elegant recursive algorithm, as follows:

1. A view's `hitTest:withEvent:` first calls the same method on its own subviews, if it has any, because a subview is considered to be in front of its superview. The subviews are queried in reverse order, because that's front-to-back order (Chapter 14): thus, if two sibling views overlap, the one in front reports the hit first.

2. If, as a view hit-tests its subviews, any of those subviews responds by returning a view, it stops querying its subviews and immediately returns the view that was returned to it. Thus, the very first view to declare itself the hit-test view immediately percolates all the way to the top of the call chain and *is* the hit-test view.

3. If, on the other hand, a view has no subviews, or if all of its subviews return nil (indicating that neither they nor their subviews was hit), then the view calls `pointInside:withEvent:` on itself. If this call reveals that the touch was inside this view, the view returns itself, declaring itself the hit-test view; otherwise it returns nil.

   No problem arises if a view has a transform, because `pointInside:withEvent:` takes the transform into account. That's why a rotated button continues to work correctly.

It is also up to `hitTest:withEvent:` to implement the logic of touch restrictions exclusive to a view. If a view's `userInteractionEnabled` is NO, or its `hidden` is YES, or its `opacity` is close to `0.0`, it returns nil without hit-testing any of its subviews and without calling `pointInside:withEvent:`. Thus these restrictions do not, of themselves, exclude a view from being hit-tested; on the contrary, they operate precisely by modifying a view's hit-test result.

However, hit-testing knows nothing about `multipleTouchEnabled` (which involves multiple touches) or `exclusiveTouch` (which involves multiple views). The logic of obedience to these properties is implemented at a later stage of the story.

You can use hit-testing yourself at any moment where it might prove useful. In calling `hitTest:withEvent:`, supply a point *in the coordinates of the view to which the message is sent*. The second parameter can be nil if you have no event.

For example, suppose we have a UIView with two UIImageView subviews. We want to detect a tap in either UIImageView, but we want to handle this at the level of the UIView. We can attach a UITapGestureRecognizer to the UIView, but how will we know which subview, if any, the tap was in?

Our first step must be to set userInteractionEnabled to YES for both UIImageViews. (This step is crucial; UIImageView is one of the few built-in view classes where this is NO by default, and a view whose userInteractionEnabled is NO won't normally be the result of a call to hitTest:withEvent:.) Now, when our gesture recognizer's action handler is called, the view can use hit-testing to determine where the tap was:

```
CGPoint p = [g locationOfTouch:0 inView:self]; // g is the gesture recognizer
UIView* v = [self hitTest:p withEvent:nil];
```

You can also override hitTest:withEvent: in a view subclass, to alter its results during touch delivery, thus customizing the touch delivery mechanism. I call this *hit-test munging*. Hit-test munging can be used selectively as a way of turning user interaction on or off in an area of the interface. In this way, some unusual effects can be produced.

For example, an important use of hit-test munging is to permit the touching of parts of subviews outside the bounds of their superview. If a view's clipsToBounds is NO, a paradox arises: the user can *see* the regions of its subviews that are outside its bounds, but the user can't *touch* them. This can be confusing and seems wrong. The solution is for the view to override hitTest:withEvent: as follows:

```
-(UIView *)hitTest:(CGPoint)point withEvent:(UIEvent *)event {
    UIView* result = [super hitTest:point withEvent:event];
    if (result)
        return result;
    for (UIView* sub in [self.subviews reverseObjectEnumerator]) {
        CGPoint pt = [self convertPoint:point toView:sub];
        result = [sub hitTest:pt withEvent:event];
        if (result)
            return result;
    }
    return nil;
}
```

Here are some further possible uses of hit-test munging, just to stimulate your imagination:

- If a superview contains a UIButton but doesn't return that UIButton from hitTest:withEvent:, that button can't be tapped.

- You might override hitTest:withEvent: to return the result from super most of the time, but to return self under certain conditions, effectively making all subviews untouchable without making the superview itself untouchable (as setting its userInteractionEnabled to NO would do).

- A view whose userInteractionEnabled is NO can break the normal rules and return itself from hit-testing and can thus end up as the hit-test view.

Hit-testing for layers

There is also hit-testing for layers. It doesn't happen automatically, as part of send-Event: or anything else; it's up to you. It's just a convenient way of finding out which layer would receive a touch at a point, if layers received touches. To hit-test layers, call hitTest: on a layer, with a point *in superlayer coordinates.*

Keep in mind, though, that layers do *not* receive touches. A touch is reported to a view, not a layer. A layer, except insofar as it is a view's underlying layer and gets touch reporting because of its view, is completely untouchable; from the point of view of touches and touch reporting, it's as if the layer weren't on the screen at all. No matter where a layer may appear to be, a touch falls right through the layer to whatever view is behind it.

In the case of the layer that is a view's underlying layer, you don't need hit-testing. It is the view's drawing; where it appears is where the view is. So a touch in that layer is equivalent to a touch in its view. Indeed, one might say that this is what views are actually for: to provide layers with touchability.

The only layers on which you'd need special hit-testing, then, would presumably be layers that are not themselves any view's underlying layer, because those are the only ones you don't find out about by normal view hit-testing. However, all layers, including a layer that is its view's underlying layer, are part of the layer hierarchy, and can participate in layer hit-testing. So the most comprehensive way to hit-test layers is to start with the topmost layer, the window's layer. In this example, we subclass UIWindow and override its hitTest:withEvent: so as to get layer hit-testing every time there is view hit-testing:

```
- (UIView*) hitTest:(CGPoint)point withEvent:(UIEvent *)event {
    CALayer* lay = [self.layer hitTest:point];
    // ... possibly do something with that information ...
    return [super hitTest:point withEvent:event];
}
```

Because this is the window, the view hit-test point works as the layer hit-test point; window bounds are screen bounds (Chapter 14). But usually you'll have to convert to superlayer coordinates. In this example, we return to the CompassView developed in Chapter 16, in which all the parts of the compass are layers; we want to know whether the user tapped on the arrow layer. For simplicity, we've given the CompassView a UITapGestureRecognizer, and this is its action handler, in the CompassView itself. We convert to our superview's coordinates, because these are also our layer's superlayer coordinates:

```
// self is the CompassView
CGPoint p = [t locationOfTouch: 0 inView: self.superview];
CALayer* hitLayer = [self.layer hitTest:p];
if (hitLayer == ((CompassLayer*)self.layer).arrow) // ...
```

Layer hit-testing works by calling `containsPoint:`. However, `containsPoint:` takes a point in the layer's coordinates, so to hand it a point that arrives through `hitTest:` you must first convert from superlayer coordinates:

```
BOOL hit =
    [lay containsPoint: [lay convertPoint:point fromLayer:lay.superlayer]];
```

Layer hit-testing knows nothing of the restrictions on touch delivery; it just reports on every sublayer, even those whose view has `userInteractionEnabled` set to NO.

 The documentation warns that `hitTest:` must not be called on a CATransformLayer.

Hit-testing for drawings

The preceding example (letting the user tap on the compass arrow) worked, but we might complain that it is reporting a hit on the arrow even if the hit misses the *drawing* of the arrow. That's true for view hit-testing as well. A hit is reported if we are within the view or layer as a whole; hit-testing knows nothing of drawing, transparent areas, and so forth.

If you know how the region is drawn and can reproduce the edge of that drawing as a CGPath, you can test whether a point is inside it with `CGPathContainsPoint`. So, for a layer, you could override `hitTest` along these lines:

```
- (CALayer*) hitTest:(CGPoint)p {
    CGPoint pt = [self convertPoint:p fromLayer:self.superlayer];
    CGMutablePathRef path = CGPathCreateMutable();
    // ... draw path here ...
    CALayer* result = CGPathContainsPoint(path, nil, pt, true) ? self : nil;
    CGPathRelease(path);
    return result;
}
```

Alternatively, it might be the case that if a pixel of the drawing is transparent, it's outside the drawn region, so that it suffices to detect whether the pixel tapped is transparent. Unfortunately, there's no way to ask a drawing (or a view, or a layer) for the color of a pixel; you have to make a bitmap and copy the drawing into it, and then ask the bitmap for the color of a pixel. If you can reproduce the content as an image, and all you care about is transparency, you can make a one-pixel alpha-only bitmap, draw the image in such a way that the pixel you want to test is the pixel drawn into the bitmap, and examine the transparency of the resulting pixel:

```
// assume im is a UIImage, point is the CGPoint to test
unsigned char pixel[1] = {0};
CGContextRef context = CGBitmapContextCreate(pixel,
                                             1, 1, 8, 1, nil,
                                             kCGImageAlphaOnly);
```

```
UIGraphicsPushContext(context);
[im drawAtPoint:CGPointMake(-point.x, -point.y)];
UIGraphicsPopContext();
CGContextRelease(context);
CGFloat alpha = pixel[0]/255.0;
BOOL transparent = alpha < 0.01;
```

However, there can be complications; for example, there may not be a one-to-one relationship between the pixels of the underlying drawing and the points of the drawing as portrayed on the screen (because the drawing is stretched, for example). It's a tricky problem, but in many cases, the CALayer method `renderInContext:` can be helpful here. This method allows you to copy a layer's actual drawing into a context of your choice. If that context is, say, an image context created with `UIGraphicsBeginImage-ContextWithOptions`, you can now use the resulting image as `im` in the code above.

Hit-testing during animation

If user interaction is allowed during an animation that moves a view from one place to another, then if the user taps on the animated view, the tap might mysteriously fail because the view in the model layer is elsewhere; conversely, the user might accidentally tap where the view actually is in the model layer, and the tap will hit the animated view even though it appears to be elsewhere. If the position of a view or layer is being animated and you want the user to be able to tap on it, therefore, you'll need to hit-test the presentation layer (see Chapter 17).

In this simple example, we have a superview containing a subview. To allow the user to tap on the subview even when it is being animated, we implement hit-test munging in the superview:

```
- (UIView*) hitTest:(CGPoint)point withEvent:(UIEvent *)event {
    // v is the animated subview
    CALayer* lay = [v.layer presentationLayer];
    CALayer* hitLayer = [lay hitTest: point];
    if (hitLayer == lay)
        return v;
    UIView* hitView = [super hitTest:point withEvent:event];
    if (hitView == v)
        return self;
    return hitView;
}
```

If the user taps outside the presentation layer, we cannot simply call `super`, because the user might tap at the spot to which the subview has in reality already moved (behind the "animation movie"), in which case `super` will report that it hit the subview. So if `super` does report this, we return `self` (assuming that we are what's behind the animated subview at its new location).

However, as Apple puts it in the WWDC 2011 videos, the animated view "swallows the touch." For example, suppose the view in motion is a button. Although our hit-test munging makes it possible for the user to tap the button as it is being animated, and although the user sees the button highlight in response, the button's action message is not sent in response to this highlighting if the animation is in-flight when the tap takes place. This behavior seems unfortunate, but it's generally possible to work around it (for instance, with a gesture recognizer).

Initial Touch Event Delivery

When the touch situation changes, an event containing all touches is handed to the UIApplication instance by calling its sendEvent:, and the UIApplication in turn hands it to the relevant UIWindow by calling *its* sendEvent:. The UIWindow then performs the complicated logic of examining, for every touch, the hit-test view and its superviews and their gesture recognizers and deciding which of them should be sent a touches... message, and does so.

These are delicate and crucial maneuvers, and you wouldn't want to lame your application by interfering with them. Nevertheless, you can override sendEvent: in a subclass, and there are situations where you might wish to do so. This is just about the *only* case in which you might subclass UIApplication; if you do, remember to change the third argument in the call to UIApplicationMain in your *main.m* file to the string name of your UIApplication subclass so that your subclass is used to generate the app's singleton UIApplication instance. If you subclass UIWindow, remember to change the window's class in the app delegate code that instantiates the window.

Now that gesture recognizers exist, it is unlikely that you will need to resort to such measures. A typical case, in the past, was that you needed to detect touches directed to an object of some built-in interface class in a way that subclassing it wouldn't permit. For example, you want to know when the user swipes a UIWebView; you're not allowed to subclass UIWebView, and in any case it eats the touch. The solution used to be to subclass UIWindow and override sendEvent:; you would then work out whether this was a swipe on the UIWebView and respond accordingly, or else call super. Now, however, you can attach a UISwipeGestureRecognizer to the UIWebView.

Gesture Recognizer and View

When a touch first appears and is delivered to a gesture recognizer, it is also delivered to its hit-test view, the same touches... method being called on both. This comes as a surprise to beginners, but it is the most reasonable approach, as it means that touch interpretation by a view isn't jettisoned just because gesture recognizers are in the picture. Later on in the multitouch sequence, if all the gesture recognizers in a view's swarm declare failure to recognize their gesture, that view's internal touch interpretation just proceeds as if gesture recognizers had never been invented.

However, if a gesture recognizer in a view's swarm recognizes its gesture, that view is sent `touchesCancelled:withEvent:` for any touches that went to that gesture recognizer and were hit-tested to that view, and subsequently the view no longer receives those touches.

This behavior can be changed by setting a gesture recognizer's `cancelsTouchesInView` property to NO. If this is the case for every gesture recognizer in a view's swarm, the view will receive touch events more or less as if no gesture recognizers were in the picture. Making this change, however, alters delivery logic rather drastically; it seems unlikely that you'd want to do that.

If a gesture recognizer happens to be ignoring a touch (because it was told to do so by `ignoreTouch:forEvent:`), then `touchesCancelled:withEvent:` *won't* be sent to the view for that touch when the gesture recognizer recognizes its gesture. Thus, a gesture recognizer's ignoring a touch is the same as simply letting it fall through to the view, as if the gesture recognizer weren't there.

Gesture recognizers can also *delay* the delivery of touches to a view, and by default they do. The UIGestureRecognizer property `delaysTouchesEnded` is YES by default, meaning that when a touch reaches `UITouchPhaseEnded` and the gesture recognizer's `touchesEnded:withEvent:` is called, if the gesture recognizer is still allowing touches to be delivered to the view because its state is still Possible, it doesn't deliver this touch until it has resolved the gesture. When it does, either it will recognize the gesture, in which case the view will have `touchesCancelled:withEvent:` called instead (as already explained), or it will declare failure and *now* the view will have `touchesEnded:withEvent:` called.

The reason for this behavior is most obvious with a gesture where multiple taps are required. The first tap ends, but this is insufficient for the gesture recognizer to declare success or failure, so it withholds that touch from the view. In this way, the gesture recognizer gets the proper priority. In particular, if there is a second tap, the gesture recognizer should succeed and send `touchesCancelled:withEvent:` to the view — but it can't do that if the view has already been sent `touchesEnded:withEvent:`.

It is also possible to delay the entire suite of `touches...` methods from being called on a view, by setting a gesture recognizer's `delaysTouchesBegan` property to YES. Again, this delay would be until the gesture recognizer can resolve the gesture: either it will recognize it, in which case the view will have `touchesCancelled:withEvent:` called, or it will declare failure, in which case the view will receive `touchesBegan:withEvent:` plus any further `touches...` calls that were withheld — except that it will receive *at most* one `touchesMoved:withEvent:` call, the last one, because if a lot of these were withheld, to queue them all up and send them all at once now would be simply insane.

It is unlikely that you'll change a gesture recognizer's delaysTouchesBegan property to YES, however. You might do so, for example, if you have an elaborate touch analysis within a view that simply cannot operate simultaneously with a gesture recognizer, but this is improbable, and the latency involved may look strange to your user.

When touches are delayed and then delivered, what's delivered is the original touch with the original event, which still have their original timestamps. Because of the delay, these timestamps may differ significantly from now. For this reason (and many others), Apple warns that touch analysis that is concerned with timing should always look at the timestamp, not the clock.

Touch Exclusion Logic

It is up to the UIWindow's sendEvent: to implement the logic of multipleTouch-Enabled and exclusiveTouch.

If a new touch is hit-tested to a view whose multipleTouchEnabled is NO and which already has an existing touch hit-tested to it, then sendEvent: never delivers the new touch to that view. However, that touch *is* delivered to the view's swarm of gesture recognizers.

Similarly, if there's an exclusiveTouch view in the window, then sendEvent: must decide whether a particular touch should be delivered, as already described. If a touch is not delivered to a view because of exclusiveTouch restrictions, it is not delivered to its swarm of gesture recognizers either. (This behavior with regard to gesture recognizers has changed in a confusing and possibly buggy way from system to system, but I believe I'm describing it correctly for iOS 5 and later. The statement in Apple's *SimpleGesture-Recognizers* sample code that "Recognizers ignore the exclusive touch setting for views" now appears to be false.)

Recognition

When a gesture recognizer recognizes its gesture, everything changes. As we've already seen, the touches for this gesture recognizer are sent to their hit-test views as a touches-Cancelled:forEvent: message, and then no longer arrive at those views (unless the gesture recognizer's cancelsTouchesInView is NO). Moreover, all other gesture recognizers pending with regard to these touches are made to fail, and then are no longer sent the touches they were receiving either.

If the very same event would cause more than one gesture recognizer to recognize, there's an algorithm for picking the one that will succeed and make the others fail: a gesture recognizer lower down the view hierarchy (closer to the hit-test view) prevails over one higher up the hierarchy, and a gesture recognizer more recently added to its view prevails over one less recently added.

There are various means for modifying this "first past the post, winner takes all" behavior. One is by telling a gesture recognizer, in effect, that being first isn't good enough:

- `requireGestureRecognizerToFail:` institutes a dependency order, possibly causing the gesture recognizer to which it is sent to be put on hold when it tries to transition from the Possible state to the Began (continuous) or Ended (discrete) state; only if a certain other gesture recognizer fails is this one permitted to perform that transition. Apple says that in a dependency like this, the gesture recognizer that fails first is not sent `reset` (and won't receive any touches) until the second finishes its state sequence and is sent `reset`, so that they resume recognizing together.

- The UIView method `gestureRecognizerShouldBegin:`, sent to the hit-test view, or the delegate method `gestureRecognizerShouldBegin:`, by returning NO, turns success into failure; at the moment when the gesture recognizer is about to declare that it recognizes its gesture, transitioning from the Possible state to the Began (continuous) or Ended (discrete) state, it is forced to fail instead.

Another approach is to permit simultaneous recognition; a gesture recognizer succeeds, but some other gesture recognizer is *not* forced to fail. There are two ways to achieve this:

- A subclass can implement `canPreventGestureRecognizer:` or `canBePreventedBy-GestureRecognizer:` (or both). Here, "prevent" means "by succeeding, you force failure upon this other," and "be prevented" means "by succeeding, this other forces failure upon you."

  These two methods work together as follows. `canPreventGestureRecognizer:` is called first; if it returns NO, that's the end of the story for that gesture recognizer, and `canPreventGestureRecognizer:` is called on the other gesture recognizer. But if `canPreventGestureRecognizer:` returns YES when it is first called, the other gesture recognizer is sent `canBePreventedByGestureRecognizer:`. If it returns YES, that's the end of the story; if it returns NO, the process starts over the other way around, sending `canPreventGestureRecognizer:` to the second gesture recognizer, and so forth. In this way, conflicting answers are resolved without the device exploding: prevention is regarded as exceptional (even though it is in fact the norm) and will happen only if it is acquiesced to by everyone involved.

- The delegate method `gestureRecognizer:shouldRecognizeSimultaneously-WithGestureRecognizer:` can return YES to permit one gesture recognizer to succeed without forcing the other to fail.

Touches and the Responder Chain

A UIView is a responder, and participates in the responder chain (Chapter 11). In particular, if a touch is to be delivered to a UIView (because, for example, it's the hit-test view) and that view doesn't implement the relevant `touches...` method, a walk up the responder chain is performed, looking for a responder that *does* implement it; if such a responder is found, the touch is delivered to that responder. Moreover, the default implementation of the `touches...` methods — the behavior that you get if you call `super` — is to perform the same walk up the responder chain, starting with the next responder in the chain.

The relationship between touch delivery and the responder chain can be useful, but you must be careful not to allow it to develop into an incoherency. For example, if `touches-Began:withEvent:` is implemented in a superview but not in a subview, then a touch to the subview will result in the superview's `touchesBegan:withEvent:` being called, with the first parameter (the touches) containing a touch whose `view` is the subview. But most UIView implementations of the `touches...` methods rely upon the assumption that the first parameter consists of all and only touches whose `view` is `self`; built-in UIView subclasses certainly assume this.

Again, if `touchesBegan:withEvent:` is implemented in both a superview and a subview, and you call `super` in the subview's implementation, passing along the same arguments that came in, then the same touch delivered to the subview will trigger both the subview's `touchesBegan:withEvent:` and the superview's `touchesBegan:withEvent:` (and once again the first parameter to the superview's `touchesBegan:withEvent:` will contain a touch whose `view` is the subview).

The solution is to behave rationally, as follows:

- If all the responders in the affected part of the responder chain are instances of your own subclass of UIView itself or of your own subclass of UIViewController, you will generally want to follow the simplest possible rule: implement *all* the `touches...` events together in one class, so that touches arrive at an instance either because it was the hit-test view or because it is up the responder chain from the hit-test view, and do *not* call `super` in any of them. In this way, "the buck stops here" — the touch handling for this object or for objects below it in the responder chain is bottlenecked into one well-defined place.

- If you subclass a built-in UIView subclass and you override its touch handling, you don't have to override every single `touches...` event, but you *do* need to call `super` so that the built-in touch handling can occur.

- Don't allow touches to arrive from lower down the responder chain at an instance of a built-in UIView subclass that implements built-in touch handling, because such a class is completely unprepared for the first parameter of a `touches...` method containing a touch not intended for itself. Judicious use of userInteraction-Enabled or hit-test munging can be a big help here.

I'm not saying, however, that you have to block all touches from percolating up the responder chain; it's normal for unhandled touches to arrive at the UIWindow or UIApplication, for example, because these classes do not (by default) do any touch handling — so those touches will remain unhandled and will percolate right off the end of the responder chain, which is perfectly fine.

- Never call a touches... method directly (except to call super).

 Apple's documentation has some discussion of a technique called *event forwarding* where you *do* call touches... methods directly. But you are far less likely to need this now that gesture recognizers exist, and it can be extremely tricky and even downright dangerous to implement, so I won't give an example here, and I suggest that you not use it.

PART V

Interface

The previous part of the book introduced views. This part of the book is about the particular kinds of view provided by the Cocoa framework — the built-in "widgets" with which you'll construct an app's interface. These are surprising few, but impressively powerful.

- Chapter 19 is about view controllers. View controllers are a brilliant mechanism for allowing an entire interface to be replaced by another; this ability is especially crucial on the iPhone's small screen. They are also the basis of an app's ability to compensate when the user rotates the device. In real life, every app you write will have its interface managed by view controllers. This chapter also discusses storyboards and segues (including unwind segues, new in iOS 6), and describes iOS 6's new built-in mechanism for letting you save and restore the state of your view controllers between launches of your app.

- Chapter 20 is about scroll views, the iOS mechanism for letting the user scroll and zoom the interface.

- Chapter 21 explains table views, an extremely important and powerful type of scroll view that lets the user navigate through any amount of data, along with collection views, a generalization of table views new in iOS 6.

- Chapter 22 is about two forms of interface unique to, and characteristic of, the iPad — popovers and split views.

- Chapter 23 describes several ways of presenting text (including styled text) in an app's interface — labels, text fields, text views, and text drawn manually with Core Text.

- Chapter 24 discusses web views. A web view is a easy-to-use interface widget backed by the power of a full-fledged web browser. It can also be used to present a PDF and various other forms of data.

- Chapter 25 describes all the remaining built-in iOS (UIKit) interface widgets.

- Chapter 26 is about the forms of modal dialog that can appear in front of an app's interface.

CHAPTER 19

View Controllers

An iOS app's interface is dynamic, and with good reason. On the desktop, an application's windows can be big, and there can be more than one of them, so there's room for lots of interface. With iOS, everything needs to fit on a single display consisting of a single window, which in the case of the iPhone is almost forbiddingly tiny. The iOS solution to this is to swap out interface and replace it with other interface, as needed. Thus, entire regions of interface material — often the entire contents of the screen — must come and go in an agile fashion that is understandable to the user. Animation is often used to emphasize and clarify the replacement of one view by another.

Management of this task resides in a *view controller*, an instance of UIViewController. Actually, a view controller is most likely to be an instance of a UIViewController sub-class. The UIViewController class is designed to be subclassed. You are very unlikely to use a plain vanilla UIViewController object. You might write your own UIView-Controller subclass; you might use a built-in UIViewController subclass such as UINavigationController or UITabBarController; or you might subclass a built-in UIViewController subclass such as UITableViewController (Chapter 21).

(You are less likely to subclass other built-in UIViewController subclasses such as UINavigationController or UITabBarController — except for very specific and limited purposes, such as to customize rotation settings.)

A view controller manages a single view (which can, of course, have subviews); its `view` property points to the view it manages. The view has no explicit pointer to the view controller that manages it, but a view controller is a UIResponder and is in the responder chain just above its view (Chapter 11), so it is the view's `nextResponder`.

The chief concepts involved in the use of view controllers are as follows:

Rotation
> The user can rotate the device, and you might like the interface to rotate in response, to compensate. A window is effectively pinned to the physical display (window

bounds are screen bounds and do not change), but a view can be given a transform so that its top moves to the current top of the display. A UIViewController responds to device rotation by applying this transform.

Root view controller

Every real-life iOS app should have a single view controller that acts as the root view controller for the whole app. Its job is to supply the view that covers the entire window and acts as the superview for all other interface (Chapter 7, Chapter 14). The user will never see the window (except, perhaps, in a glimpse as view controllers are swapped along with animation of their views). The user may never see or be conscious of the root view, either, as it may be completely covered by its subviews, but it still has an important function: it is automatically sized for the app's orientation and the position of the status bar, and allows the entire interface to rotate in response to device rotation.

Prior to iOS 5 it was theoretically possible for an iOS app to lack a root view controller. It's still theoretically possible, but it's strongly discouraged; the runtime issues a warning if the app launches without a root view controller ("Applications are expected to have a root view controller at the end of application launch"). That is why our Empty Window project (Chapter 6 and following) was based on the Single View Application project template: this is the minimal current template that supplies a root view controller along with a nib containing its view.

Parentage

A view controller can *contain* another view controller. The containing view controller is the *parent* of the contained view controller; the contained view controller is a *child* of the containing view controller. This containment relationship of the view controllers is reflected in their views: the child view controller's view is a subview of the parent view controller's view. ("Subview" here may mean "subview at some depth," but most often it means a direct subview.)

Replacement of one view with another often involves a parent view controller managing its children. For example, Figure 19-1 shows the TidBITS News app displaying a typical iPhone interface, consisting of a list of story headlines and summaries; if the user taps an entry in the list, the whole list will slide away to the left and the text of the actual story will slide in from the right. This is done by a parent view controller (a UINavigationController) adding a new child view controller; the parent view controller, meanwhile, stays put (as the app's root view controller, in this case).

In iOS 4 and before, only built-in view controllers such as UITabBarController, UINavigationController, and UISplitViewController could act as parent view controllers. Nowadays, you are free to write your own view controller subclasses that act as parent view controllers (and the support for doing this is even better in iOS 6 than it was in iOS 5).

Figure 19-1. The TidBITS News app

Presentation

In iOS 4 and before, there was a notion of a *modal view controller*, whose view effectively replaced the entire interface. In iOS 5 and later, this has evolved into the notion of a *presented* view controller. One view controller *presents* another view controller; this means that the first view controller, the *presenting* view controller, remains in place, but the presented view controller's view has replaced the presenting view controller's view.

This relationship between view controllers is different from the parent–child relationship. A presenting view controller is *not* the parent view controller of the view controller it presents — it is its presenting view controller.

Animation

The act of swapping views by manipulating child view controllers or presenting a view controller is very frequently accompanied by animation. Certain animation types are built-in and conventional. For example, as I mentioned a moment ago, in Figure 19-1, tapping a story listing will cause the list to slide out to the left while the new view slides in from the right; this is the default behavior of a UINavigation-Controller when it adds a new view controller and makes its view appear. Similarly, as a view controller is presented, the new view can slide in from below, flip into place like a piece of paper being flipped over, and so forth.

Customization

A view controller has properties and methods that are used to customize the interface and its behavior when its view is showing. For example, when a UINavigationController substitutes another view controller's view into its interface (by adding the view controller as a child), it also seeks that view controller's `navigationItem.titleView` property, which is yet another view; if it finds it, it puts that view into the navigation bar at the top of the interface. That is how the TidBITS logo in Figure 19-1 appears in the navigation bar — it's because it is a view controller's `navigationItem.titleView`. Similarly, if a view controller is to be presented, it has properties that allow it to dictate the style of animation that should be used as its view appears.

State saving

View controllers can work together to save state automatically. By taking advantage of this feature (new in iOS 6), you can ensure that if your app is terminated in the background and subsequently relaunched, it will quickly resume displaying the same interface that was showing when the user last saw it.

The View Controller Hierarchy

Because of containment and presentation, there is a hierarchy of view controllers. In a properly constructed iOS app, there should be exactly one root view controller, and it is the *only* view controller that has neither a parent view controller nor a presenting view controller. Any other view controller, if its view is to appear in the interface, must be a child view controller (of some parent view controller) or a presented view controller (of some presenting view controller).

At the same time, at any given moment, the actual views of the interface form a hierarchy dictated by and parallel to some portion of the view controller hierarchy. Every view visible in the interface owes its presence either to the fact that it is a view controller's view or to the fact that it is, at some depth, a subview of a view controller's view. Moreover, a child view controller's view is, at some depth, its parent view controller's view's subview.

The place of a view controller's view in the view hierarchy will most often be *automatic*, by virtue of the view controller's place in the view controller hierarchy. You might never need to put a UIViewController's view into the view hierarchy manually (and it would be wrong to do so, except in specialized circumstances that I'll talk about in a moment).

For example, in Figure 19-1, we see three interface elements (from top to bottom):

- The navigation bar, containing the TidBITS logo.
- Some text, which is actually a UILabel, stating when the list of stories was last updated.

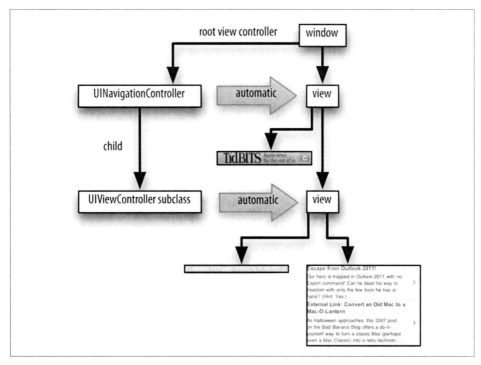

Figure 19-2. The TidBITS News app's initial view controller and view hierarchy

- The list of stories, which is actually a UITableView.

I will describe how all of this comes to appear on the screen through the view controller hierarchy and the view hierarchy (Figure 19-2). The app's root view controller is a UINavigationController; the UINavigationController's view, which is never seen in isolation, is the window's sole immediate subview (the root view), and the navigation bar is a subview of that view. The UINavigationController contains a second UIViewController — a parent–child relationship. The child is a custom UIViewController subclass; *its* view is what occupies the rest of the window, as another subview of the UINavigationController's view. That view contains the UILabel and the UITableView as subviews. This architecture means that when the user taps a story listing in the UITableView, the whole label-and-table complex will slide out, to be replaced by the view of a different UIViewController, while the navigation bar stays.

In Figure 19-2, notice the word "automatic" in the two large right-pointing arrows associating a view controller with its view. This is intended to tell you how the view controller's view became part of the view hierarchy. The UINavigationController's view became the window's subview automatically, by virtue of the UINavigationController being the window's rootViewController. The custom UIViewController's view became

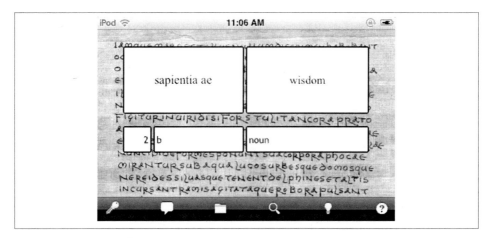

Figure 19-3. A Latin flashcard app

the UINavigationController's view's second subview automatically, by virtue of the UIViewController being the UINavigationController's child.

Now, as I said a moment ago, there is an exception to this rule about views taking their place in the view hierarchy automatically — namely, when you write *your own parent view controller class*. In that case, you will need to put a child view controller's view into the interface *manually*, as a subview (at some level) of the parent view controller's view, if you want it to appear in the interface. (Conversely, you should *not* put a view controller's view into the interface manually under any *other* circumstances.)

I'll illustrate with another app of mine (Figure 19-3). The interface displays a flashcard containing information about a Latin word, along with a toolbar (the black area at the bottom) where the user can tap an icon to choose additional functionality.

Again, I will describe how the interface shown in Figure 19-3 comes to appear on the screen through the view controller hierarchy and the view hierarchy (Figure 19-4). The app actually contains over a thousand of these Latin words, and I want the user to be able to navigate between flashcards to see the next or previous word; there is an excellent built-in view controller for this purpose, the UIPageViewController. However, that's just for the card; the toolbar at the bottom stays there, so it can't be inside the UIPageView-Controller's view. Therefore the app's root view controller is my own UIViewController subclass, which I call RootViewController; its view contains the toolbar and the UIPage-ViewController's view. In accordance with the rules I've just enunciated, this means that I *must* make the UIPageViewController a child view controller of RootViewController, and I must put the UIPageViewController's view manually into the interface as a subview of the RootViewController's view.

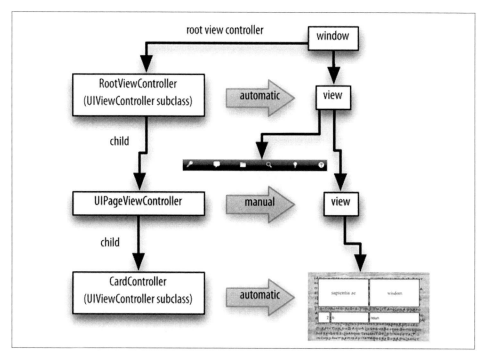

Figure 19-4. The Latin flashcard app's initial view controller and view hierarchy

In Figure 19-4, then, my RootViewController's view becomes the window's subview (the root view) automatically, by virtue of the RootViewController's being the window's root-ViewController. But then, because I want to put a UIPageViewController's view into my RootViewController's view, it is up to me to make RootViewController function as a parent view controller; I must make the UIPageViewController the RootView-Controller's child, and I must put the UIPageViewController's view *manually* into my RootViewController's view. Finally, the way UIPageViewController works as it replaces one view with another is by swapping out a child view controller; so I hand the UIPage-ViewController an instance of my CardController class (another UIViewController subclass) as its child, and the UIPageViewController displays the CardController's view automatically.

Finally, here's an example of a presented view controller. My Latin flashcard app has a second mode, where the user is drilled on a subset of the cards in random order; the interface looks very much like the first mode's interface (Figure 19-5), but it behaves completely differently.

To implement this, I have another UIViewController subclass, DrillViewController; it is structured very much like RootViewController. When the user is in drill mode, a DrillViewController is being *presented* by the RootViewController, meaning that the

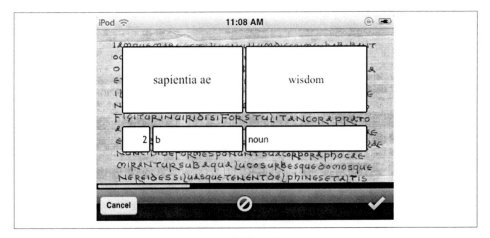

Figure 19-5. The Latin flashcard app, in drill mode

DrillViewController's interface takes over the screen automatically: the DrillView-Controller's view, and its whole subview hierarchy, replaces the RootViewController's view and *its* whole subview hierarchy. The RootViewController and its hierarchy of child view controllers remains in place, but the corresponding view hierarchy is not in the interface; it will be returned to the interface automatically when we leave drill mode (because the presented DrillViewController is dismissed), and the situation will look like Figure 19-4 once again.

For any app that you write, you should be able to construct a diagram showing the hierarchy of view controllers and charting how each view controller's view fits into the view hierarchy. The diagram should be similar to mine! The view hierarchy should run neatly parallel with the view controller hierarchy; there should be no crossed wires or orphan views. And every view controller's view should be placed automatically into the view hierarchy, unless (and only unless) you have written your own parent view controller.

View Controller and View Creation

On the whole, a view controller is created exactly like any other object. A view controller instance comes into existence because you instantiate a view controller class, either in code or by loading a nib (Chapter 5). But the instantiation of a view controller introduces some additional considerations:

- How will the view controller persist?
- How will the view controller's view get into the interface?

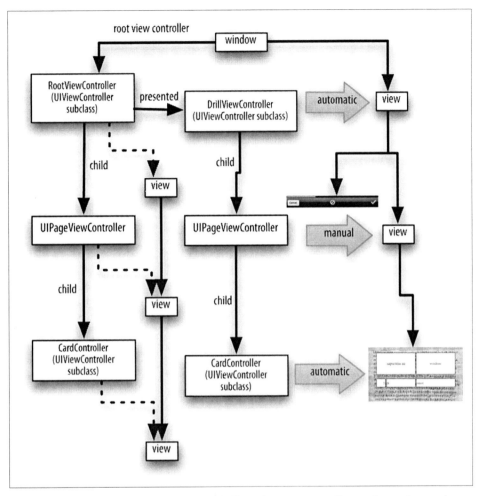

Figure 19-6. The Latin flashcard app's drill mode view controller and view hierarchy

- Where will the view controller's view come from?

We begin with the issue of *persistence*. Even if you're using ARC, memory must be managed somehow (Chapter 12). A view controller instance, once brought into existence, can eventually go right back out of existence if it is not retained; indeed, under ARC this danger is greater, because ARC won't permit an object to leak accidentally. The distinction between a view controller and its view can add to the confusion. It is possible, if things are mismanaged, for a view controller's view to get into the interface while the view controller itself is allowed to go out of existence. *This must not be permitted.* If it does, at the very least the view will apparently misbehave, failing to perform its intended functionality, because that functionality is embodied by the view controller, which no longer exists. (I've made this mistake, so I speak from experience here.)

Fortunately, Cocoa follows a simple rule: if you hand a view controller to some other object whose job is to use that view controller somehow, the other object retains the view controller. For example, assigning a view controller to a window's `rootView-Controller` property retains it. Making a view controller another view controller's child, or presenting a view controller from another view controller, retains it. Passing a view controller as the argument to UIPopoverController's `initWithContentView-Controller:` retains it. (There is then the problem of who will retain the UIPopover-Controller; this will cause much gnashing of teeth in Chapter 22.) And so on.

This means that if you construct the view controller hierarchy correctly, the persistence problem will be largely solved.

Now let's talk about how the view controller's view will get *into the interface*. As I've already said in the preceding section, and emphasized in the diagrams there, this will nearly always happen automatically, and for the very same reason I just gave: if you hand a view controller to some other object whose job is to use that view controller somehow, the other object manages its view. The other object is already managing a view of its own, and it puts the view controller's view into its own view, and otherwise manages it in relation to its own view, automatically.

Thus, when a view controller is assigned to the window's `rootViewController` property, the view controller's view is made the window's subview (the root view), with a correctly maintained frame, automatically. Similarly, built-in view controllers are responsible for displaying the views of their child view controllers in their own views; in Figure 19-2, the UINavigationController puts its child view controller's view into its own view, displaying that view and its subviews (the label and the table view). And a presented view controller's view automatically replaces in the interface the view of the presenting view controller, as in Figure 19-6.

The exceptional case, as I've already mentioned, is when your custom UIViewController subclass is acting as a parent view controller. In that case, it will be up to your code, in the custom UIViewController subclass, to perform that management manually (and in a highly prescribed manner), putting a child view controller's view into its own view, as appropriate. I'll return to this issue and demonstrate with actual code later in this chapter.

Finally, we have the issue of *where a view controller's view comes from*. For a built-in view controller class that you don't subclass, this is not a problem; in fact, you may not even be particularly conscious of the view controller's view. In Figure 19-1 and Figure 19-2, the UINavigationController's view is barely a player. Even though it is in fact the app's root view, it is never seen in the interface as a distinct entity, and there is never any need to speak of it in code. You assign the UINavigationController to the window's `rootViewController` property, and you assign a child view controller to the UINavigationController, and the child view controller's view appears in the interface — and that's the end of that. The UINavigationController created its own view automatically and put both the navigation bar and its child's view into it automatically, and the window put the UINavigationController's view into the interface automatically; the UINavigationController's view functions as a kind of intermediary that you aren't concerned with, containing the interface that you *are* concerned with. The question of its origin never even arises.

When you write a UIViewController subclass, however, the question of where its view is to come from is an extremely important question. It is *crucial* that you understand the answer to this question, which quite possibly causes more confusion to beginners than any other matter connected with iOS programming. The answer is rather involved, though, because there are several different options. The rest of this section treats those options one by one. To anticipate, the alternatives are as follows:

- The view may be created in code, manually.
- The view may be created as an empty generic view, automatically.
- The view may be created in its own separate nib.
- The view may be created in a nib, which is the same nib from which the view controller itself is instantiated.

Before we proceed, here's a caveat: distinguish between *creating* a view and *populating* that view. With a view controller, these are very clearly two different operations. Once the view controller has its view, your UIViewController subclass code will get plenty of further opportunities to customize what's in that view. I'll talk about that, of course, but the primary question with which we're concerned just now is how the UIViewController instance obtains its actual view in the first place, the view that can be accessed as its `view` property.

Manual View

To supply a UIViewController's view manually, in code, implement its `loadView` method. Your job here is to obtain an instance of UIView (or a subclass of UIView) and *assign it to `self.view`.* You must *not* call `super` (for reasons that I'll make clear later on).

Let's try it. Start with a project made from the Empty Application project template (not the Single View Application template; our purpose here is to do all the work ourselves):

1. We need a UIViewController subclass, so choose File → New → File; specify an iOS Cocoa Touch Objective-C class. Click Next.

2. Name the class *RootViewController*, and specify that it is to be a UIViewController subclass. *Uncheck both checkboxes.* Click Next.

3. Confirm that we're saving into the appropriate folder and group, as part of the target. Click Create.

We now have a RootViewController class, and we proceed to edit its code. In *RootViewController.m*, we'll implement `loadView`. To convince ourselves that the example is working correctly, we'll give the view an identifiable color, and we'll put some interface inside it, namely a "Hello, World" label:

```
- (void) loadView {
    UIView* v = [UIView new];
    v.backgroundColor = [UIColor greenColor];
    self.view = v;
    UILabel* label = [UILabel new];
    [v addSubview:label];
    label.text = @"Hello, World!";
    label.autoresizingMask = (
                            UIViewAutoresizingFlexibleTopMargin |
                            UIViewAutoresizingFlexibleLeftMargin |
                            UIViewAutoresizingFlexibleBottomMargin |
                            UIViewAutoresizingFlexibleRightMargin
                            );
    [label sizeToFit];
    label.center = CGPointMake(CGRectGetMidX(v.bounds),
                                CGRectGetMidY(v.bounds));
    label.frame = CGRectIntegral(label.frame);
}
```

We have not yet given a RootViewController instance a place in our view controller hierarchy — in fact, we have no RootViewController instance (and no view controller hierarchy). Let's make one. To do so, we turn to *AppDelegate.m*. (It's a little frustrating having to set things up in two different places before our labors can bear any visible fruit, but such is life.)

In *AppDelegate.m*, add the line `#import "RootViewController.h"` at the start, so that our code can speak of the RootViewController class. Then modify the implementation of `application:didFinishLaunchingWithOptions:` to create a RootViewController instance and make it the window's `rootViewController`. Observe that we must do this *after* our window property actually has a UIWindow as its value! That's why the template's comment, "Override point for customization after application launch," comes *after* the line that creates the UIWindow:

```
self.window = [[UIWindow alloc] initWithFrame:[[UIScreen mainScreen] bounds]];
// Override point for customization after application launch.
RootViewController* theRVC = [RootViewController new];
self.window.rootViewController = theRVC;
// ... and the rest is as in the template
```

Build and run the app. Sure enough, there's our green background and our "Hello, world" label!

We have proved that we can create a view controller and get its view into the interface. But perhaps you're not persuaded that the view controller is *managing* that view in an interesting way. To prove this, let's rotate our interface. (Our app is automatically rotatable, with no need for any code; this is a major change in iOS 6 from iOS 5. I'll talk more about rotation later in this chapter.) While our app is running in the simulator, choose Hardware → Rotate Left or Hardware → Rotate Right. Observe that both the app, as indicated by the orientation of the status bar, and the view, as indicated by the orientation of the "Hello, World" label, automatically rotate to compensate; that's the work of the view controller. We were careful to give the label an appropriate `autoresizingMask`, to keep it centered in the view even when the view's bounds are changed to fit the rotated window.

Perhaps you would prefer that we had used constraints (autolayout, Chapter 14) instead of an autoresizing mask to position the label. Here's a rewrite of `loadView` that does that:

```
UIView* v = [UIView new];
v.backgroundColor = [UIColor greenColor];
self.view = v;
UILabel* label = [UILabel new];
[v addSubview:label];
label.text = @"Hello, World!";

label.translatesAutoresizingMaskIntoConstraints = NO;
[self.view addConstraint:
 [NSLayoutConstraint
  constraintWithItem:label attribute:NSLayoutAttributeCenterX
  relatedBy:0
  toItem:self.view attribute:NSLayoutAttributeCenterX
  multiplier:1 constant:0]];
[self.view addConstraint:
 [NSLayoutConstraint
  constraintWithItem:label attribute:NSLayoutAttributeCenterY
  relatedBy:0
  toItem:self.view attribute:NSLayoutAttributeCenterY
  multiplier:1 constant:0]];
```

We have not bothered to give our view (`self.view`) a reasonable frame. This is because we are relying on someone else to frame the view appropriately. In this case, the "someone else" is the window, which responds to having its `rootViewController` property set to a view controller by framing the view controller's view appropriately as the root view before putting it into the window as a subview. To be precise, the root view's frame as it goes into the window in an iPhone app is {{0, 20}, {320, 460}} — that is, the root view fills the part of the window not covered by the status bar. The window easily accomplishes this magic by setting the root view's frame to [[UIScreen mainScreen] applicationFrame].

If there is no status bar — for example, if "Status bar is initially hidden" is YES in our *Info.plist*, a possibility that I mentioned in Chapter 9 — the call to [[UIScreen main-

Screen] `applicationFrame]` will return the entire bounds of the window, and our root view will fill the screen, which is still a correct result.

If the status bar is present but its status bar style is set to "Transparent black style," then by default our root view's frame fills only the part of the window not covered by the status bar. If you want the root view to underlap the transparent status bar, you'll set the view controller's `wantsFullScreenLayout` to YES. You could do that in the app delegate:

```
RootViewController* theRVC = [RootViewController new];
theRVC.wantsFullScreenLayout = YES;
self.window.rootViewController = theRVC;
```

Alternatively, if you feel that it is the view controller's job to know that its view should underlap the status bar, you could do the same thing at some early point in the life of the view controller, such as `loadView`:

```
- (void) loadView {
    self.wantsFullScreenLayout = YES;
    // ... and so on ...
```

Generic Automatic View

Earlier, I said that we should distinguish between creating a view and populating it. The preceding example fails to draw this distinction. The lines that create our RootView-Controller's view are merely these:

```
UIView* v = [UIView new];
self.view = v;
```

Everything else configures and populates the view, turning it green and putting a label in it. A more appropriate place to populate a view controller's view is in its `viewDid-Load` implementation, which is called after the view exists (so that it can be referred to as `self.view`). We could therefore rewrite the preceding example like this:

```
- (void) loadView {
    UIView* v = [UIView new];
    self.view = v;
}

- (void)viewDidLoad {
    [super viewDidLoad];
    UIView* v = self.view;
    v.backgroundColor = [UIColor greenColor];
    UILabel* label = [UILabel new];
    [v addSubview:label];
    label.text = @"Hello, World!";
    label.autoresizingMask = (
                            UIViewAutoresizingFlexibleTopMargin |
                            UIViewAutoresizingFlexibleLeftMargin |
                            UIViewAutoresizingFlexibleBottomMargin |
                            UIViewAutoresizingFlexibleRightMargin
```

```
                                    );
    [label sizeToFit];
    label.center = CGPointMake(CGRectGetMidX(v.bounds),
                               CGRectGetMidY(v.bounds));
    label.frame = CGRectIntegral(label.frame);
}
```

But if we're going to do that, we can go even further and remove our implementation of `loadView` altogether! If you don't implement `loadView`, and if no view is supplied in any other way, then UIViewController's implementation of `loadView` will do exactly what we are already doing in code: it creates a generic UIView object and assigns it to `self.view`. If we needed our view controller's view to be a particular UIView subclass, that wouldn't be acceptable; but in this case, our view controller's view *is* a generic UIView object, so it *is* acceptable. Comment out or delete the `loadView` implementation from the preceding code, and build and run the app; our example still works!

View in a Separate Nib

A view controller's view can be supplied from a nib file. This approach gives you the convenience of configuring and populating the view through the nib editor interface (Chapter 7). For this to work, it is necessary to prepare the nib file, as follows:

1. The File's Owner class must be set to the appropriate view controller class.
2. Performing the preceding step causes the File's Owner proxy in the nib to have a `view` outlet, corresponding to a UIViewController's `view` property. This outlet must be connected to the view.

Do you see where this is heading? We will then load the nib file *with the view controller instance as its owner*. The view controller's class matches the File's Owner class, the view controller's `view` property is set via the `view` outlet in the nib to the view object, and presto, our view controller has a view. (If you don't understand what I just said, reread Chapter 7! It is *crucial* that you comprehend how this technique works.)

Now let's try it. We can start with the example we've already developed, with our Root-ViewController class. Begin by deleting the implementation of `loadView` and `viewDid-Load` from *RootViewController.m*, because we want the view to come from a nib and we're going to populate it in the nib. Then:

1. Choose File → New → File and specify an iOS User Interface View nib file. Click Next.
2. In the Device Family pop-up menu, choose iPhone. Click Next.
3. Name the file *MyNib*. Confirm the appropriate folder, group, and target membership. Click Create.

4. Edit *MyNib.xib* in the way I described a moment ago: set the File's Owner class to RootViewController (in the Identity inspector), and connect the File's Owner view outlet to the View object.

5. Design the view. To make it clear that this is not the same view we were creating previously, perhaps you should give the view a red background color (in the Attributes inspector). Drag a UILabel into the middle of the view and give it some text, such as "Hello, World!"

Back in *AppDelegate.m*, where we create our RootViewController instance, we must load *MyNib.xib* with the RootViewController instance as its owner. It is, in fact, possible to do this using the technique described back in Chapter 7, though one shouldn't:

```
// shouldn't do this!
RootViewController* theRVC = [RootViewController new];
[[NSBundle mainBundle] loadNibNamed:@"MyNib" owner:theRVC options:nil];
self.window.rootViewController = theRVC;
```

The correct approach is to instantiate the view controller and tell it what nib it is *eventually* to load as owner, but let it load the nib when it needs to. The view controller then manages the loading of the nib and all the associated housekeeping correctly. This technique involves initializing the view controller using initWithNibName:bundle: (which is actually UIViewController's designated initializer), like this:

```
RootViewController* theRVC =
    [[RootViewController alloc] initWithNibName:@"MyNib" bundle:nil];
self.window.rootViewController = theRVC;
```

That works, and you can run the project to prove it. (The nil argument to the bundle: parameter specifies the main bundle, which is almost certainly what you want.)

Now I'm going to show you a shortcut. It turns out that if the nib name passed to initWithNibName:bundle: is nil, a nib will be sought automatically *with the same name as the view controller's class*. This means, in effect, that we can return to using init (or new) to initialize the view controller; the designated initializer is initWithNibName:bundle:, so UIViewController's init actually calls initWithNibName:bundle:, passing nil for both arguments.

Let's try it. Rename *MyNib.xib* to *RootViewController.xib*, and change the code that instantiates and initializes our RootViewController back to what it was before, like this:

```
RootViewController* theRVC = [RootViewController new];
self.window.rootViewController = theRVC;
```

The project still works!

Recall from Chapter 9 that when an image file is sought by name in the app's bundle, naming conventions allow different files to be loaded under different runtime conditions. The same is true for nib files. A nib file named *RootViewController~ipad* will be loaded on an iPad when the name @"RootViewController" is specified, regardless of whether it is specified explicitly (as the first argument to initWithNib-Name:bundle:) or implicitly (because the view controller class is RootViewController, and the first argument to initWithNibName:bundle: is nil). This principle will greatly simplify your life when you're writing a universal app.

But wait, there's more! It seems ridiculous that we should end up with a nib that has "Controller" in its name merely because our view controller, as is so often the case, has "Controller" in *its* name. A nib, after all, is not a controller. Well, there's an additional aspect to the shortcut: the runtime, in looking for a view controller's corresponding nib, will in fact try stripping "Controller" off the end of the view controller class's name. (This feature is undocumented, but it works reliably and I can't believe it would ever be retracted.) Thus, we can name our nib file *RootView.xib* instead of *RootView-Controller.xib*, and it will *still* be properly associated with our RootViewController instance when we initialize that instance using init (or new).

When you create the files for a UIViewController subclass, the Xcode dialog has a checkbox (which we unchecked earlier) offering to create an eponymous *.xib* file at the same time ("With XIB for user interface"). If you accept that option, the nib is created with the File's Owner's class already set to the view controller's class and with its view outlet already hooked up to the view. This automatically created *.xib* file does *not* have "Controller" stripped off the end of its name; you can rename it manually later (I generally do) if the default name bothers you.

You are now in a position to understand how the built-in Xcode project templates work! Take, for example, the Single View Application template. You already know that, using this template, you can design the initial interface in a nib file and have it appear in the running app. And now you also know why. In addition to the AppDelegate class, there's a ViewController class along with a nib file called *ViewController.xib*. The app delegate's application:didFinishLaunchingWithOptions: instantiates ViewController, associating it with its nib, and makes that instance the window's rootViewController:

```
self.window = [[UIWindow alloc] initWithFrame:[[UIScreen mainScreen] bounds]];
// Override point for customization after application launch.
self.viewController =
    [[ViewController alloc] initWithNibName:@"ViewController" bundle:nil];
self.window.rootViewController = self.viewController;
```

That code can be considerably abbreviated. There is no need to assign the view controller instance to a property, as it will be retained and available through the window's root-

When Is the View Loaded?

A UIViewController's `view` property is set "lazily": rather than setting it when the UIViewController itself is instantiated, the `view` property isn't set until it's needed — namely, when someone tries to fetch its value for the first time. At that moment, `load-View` is called. Thus, if the view is to come from a nib, the nib isn't loaded until then. This architecture has several advantages, but it can also trap you: I already mentioned (in Chapter 11) how I made the mistake of mentioning a UIViewController's `view` in its `awakeFromNib` and caused the view to be loaded twice. So don't mention a view controller's view until it's time to load it! The `isViewLoaded` method reports whether the view has in fact been loaded, without mentioning it in a way that will also cause it to be loaded accidentally.

`ViewController` property. And there is no need to specify the `nibName:` argument, because the nib file has the same name as the view controller. So we could have said this:

```
self.window = [[UIWindow alloc] initWithFrame:[[UIScreen mainScreen] bounds]];
// Override point for customization after application launch.
self.window.rootViewController = [ViewController new];
```

In addition, that code works even if we change the name of the nib file to *View.xib*.

A moment ago, I had you delete `viewDidLoad` from RootViewController's code. This was because I wanted you to see clearly that the view was being created and configured in the nib. In real life, however, it is perfectly acceptable, and quite common, to load a view controller's view from a nib file *and* proceed to further configurations and initializations in `viewDidLoad`. By the time `viewDidLoad` is called, we are guaranteed that the view has been loaded from the nib and that we can access it via `self.view`.

On the other hand, if a view controller's view is to come from a nib, you should *not* implement `loadView`. You'll just confuse yourself if you do. The truth is that `load-View` is *always* called when the view controller first decides that it needs its view. If we override `loadView`, we supply and set the `view` in code. If we don't override `loadView`, the default implementation is to load the view controller's associated nib, whose job is to set the `view` through an outlet. (That is why, if we do override `loadView`, we must *not* call `super` — that would cause us to get *both* behaviors.) If we don't override `load-View` and there is no associated nib (because the nib name was nil in `initWithNib-Name:bundle:` and there is no nib whose name matches the name of the view controller class), the default implementation of `loadView` creates a generic UIView as discussed in the previous section.

Nib-Instantiated View Controller

Like any other object, a view controller can be represented by a nib object, to be instantiated through the loading of the nib. In the nib editor, the Object library contains a View Controller (UIViewController) as well as several built-in UIViewController subclasses. Any of these can be dragged into the nib. This way of creating a view controller is particularly useful when what's being created are multiple related view controllers, such as a UINavigationController and its initial child view controller, or a UITabBarController and its multiple child view controllers; it is also the basis of how storyboards work.

To illustrate, let's modify our existing example so as to instantiate RootViewController from a nib. Our first step will be to create an extra nib for no other purpose than to instantiate RootViewController:

1. Choose File → New → File and specify an iOS User Interface Empty nib file. Click Next.

2. In the Device Family pop-up menu, specify iPhone.

3. Name the nib file *RVC* and create it in the usual fashion.

4. Edit the newly created *RVC.xib*. Drag a View Controller into the canvas. In the Attributes inspector, specify that this is a RootViewController instance.

5. We'll need an appropriate File's Owner object with an outlet pointing to our Root-ViewController instance. At the earliest stage of our application's launch process, there's really only one candidate — the app delegate. So select the File's Owner proxy and specify in the Attributes inspector that this is an AppDelegate.

6. We still need that outlet, and we can't make it without a corresponding instance variable in AppDelegate. Option-click *AppDelegate.m* in the Project navigator so that *RVC.xib* is being edited in the main pane of the editor and *AppDelegate.m* is being edited in the assistant pane. Create a place to put an instance variable by adding curly braces after the @implementation line:

   ```
   @implementation AppDelegate {

   }
   ```

   Control-drag from the Root View Controller object in the nib into the curly braces. You're offered the chance to create an outlet; call it vc and change the type (class) to UIViewController. The result is this line of code:

   ```
   IBOutlet UIViewController *vc;
   ```

Now we're ready to tell AppDelegate to load *RVC.xib* with itself as owner and extract the RootViewController instance and use it as the window's rootViewController. Return to *AppDelegate.m* and change the start of `application:didFinishLaunchingWith-Options:` to look like this:

```
self.window = [[UIWindow alloc] initWithFrame:[[UIScreen mainScreen] bounds]];
// Override point for customization after application launch.
[[NSBundle mainBundle] loadNibNamed:@"RVC" owner:self options:nil];
self.window.rootViewController = self->vc;
```

Build and run the app. It works, displaying the interface from *RootViewController.xib* (or *RootView.xib*, if you renamed it)! Do you see why? Nothing has changed from our examples in the previous section except the way we instantiated RootViewController. It comes into existence from the loading of the nib *RVC.xib*, but the runtime then performs the very same search as before for a nib with the same name as the view controller class — and finds it.

But what if the nib had a different name? How would we tell this RootViewController instance about that? We can't call `initWithNibName:bundle:`, because we aren't creating the RootViewController instance in code. Edit *RVC.xib*, select the Root View Controller, and examine its Attributes inspector. You'll find there's a NIB Name field. At the moment it's empty, signifying the equivalent of a nil `nibName:` argument in the initializer. But you could type (or use the combo box to choose) the name of a different nib file, just as you could supply a string argument in a call to `initWithNibName:bundle:`. Thus, everything that was possible in the previous sections, where we instantiated the view controller in code, remains possible now that we're instantiating it from a nib file.

When I say "everything remains possible," I mean it. We can supply this view controller's view in *any* of the ways discussed earlier in this section. The mere fact that this view controller is instantiated from a nib, rather than using code, changes nothing. You can associate a nib file explicitly with this view controller, to set its `view` through the loading of that nib; you can associate a same-named nib file implicitly with this view controller, to set its `view` through the loading of that nib; you can implement `loadView` in this view controller's class, to create its view and set `self.view` in code; or you can do none of those things, and permit a generic view to be created automatically. Moreover, no matter where the view comes from, you can configure it further or do any other initial tasks in the view controller class's `viewDidLoad`.

Additionally, there's a completely new alternative: we can supply the view and design the interface *right here in the same nib file* as the view controller (that is, in *RVC.xib*). In fact, we can design the interface *in the view controller itself*. Notice that the canvas representation of the view controller is the size of an iPhone screen, even though a view controller is not a view object. That's so that the view controller can accommodate a screen-sized view object, to serve as its `view`.

Let's try it! Drag a generic View object from the Object library right into the Root View Controller object in the nib editor canvas. This will now be the view controller's view, and you can now proceed to design the interface within this view. For example, you can make its background color yellow (to distinguish it from all the other interfaces we've been designing) and drag a different label into it (perhaps you could make it say "Howdy, Universe" for a change).

Build and run the project. The yellow background and the "Howdy, Universe" label appear! The view inside the view controller in the nib has become the view controller's view. This way of supplying a view controller's view takes priority, so our *RootView-Controller.xib* (or *RootView.xib*) is ignored.

A view controller's Attributes inspector provides ways to set some further options that would otherwise be set in code. For example, the Wants Full Screen checkbox is our friend the wantsFullScreenLayout property, and the Resize View From NIB checkbox sets the view controller's view's frame to applicationFrame. The meanings of the other options will become evident as this chapter proceeds.

 Like any other nib object, when a view controller is instantiated from a nib or storyboard, its designated initializer in *your* code (initWithNib-Name:bundle:) is *not* called. If your UIViewController subclass needs very early access in code to the view controller instance, it can override initWithCoder: or awakeFromNib (Chapter 7, Chapter 11).

Storyboard-Instantiated View Controller

A *storyboard* is, in effect, a single file representing a collection of things that are rather like nib files, where each nib file contains a view controller nib object (similar to *RVC.xib* in the preceding section). Thus we can also regard a storyboard as a collection of potential view controllers. Unlike an actual nib file containing multiple view controllers, a storyboard is not a nib and its view controllers are not nib objects, so they are not all instantiated when the storyboard is loaded. Instead, the view controllers inside a storyboard are instantiated individually, when needed.

A storyboard might contain just one view controller. It might contain several unrelated view controllers. Typically, it will contain several *related* view controllers, such as a UINavigationController and its initial child view controller. Even more typically, it will contain several related view controllers that won't all be needed simultaneously, such as a UINavigationController and all the child view controllers it will ever have over the course of the app's lifetime. In fact, it isn't uncommon for a single storyboard to be the source of *every view controller that your app will ever instantiate.*

The mechanism for instantiating a view controller from a storyboard is different from the nib-loading mechanism. Before I talk about that, however, I want to stress once again that what I'm about to say about where the view controller comes from changes nothing about where the view comes from. A view controller instantiated from a storyboard is just like a view controller instantiated from a nib, as regards the source of its view. You can give the view controller a view right there in the storyboard, and design that view using the nib editor interface (actually the storyboard editor interface); most often, that's probably what you'll do. But you could equally well let the runtime find the nib based on the view controller class's name, or implement loadView in the view controller's class and create the view in code, or *not* implement loadView and let a generic view be created. And no matter where the view comes from, you can configure it further or do any other initial tasks in the view controller class's viewDidLoad.

 I didn't say you could specify a nib name associated with a view controller by means of the NIB Name field in the view controller's Attributes inspector. That's because this field, present in the nib editor, is missing from the storyboard editor.

A storyboard, like a nib, is an actual file in your project (a *.storyboard* file); it is compiled into your app's bundle. In code, a running app can refer to a storyboard by calling the UIStoryboard class method storyboardWithName:bundle:. Once we have a reference to a storyboard, a view controller can be instantiated from that storyboard in one of four ways:

- At most one view controller in the storyboard is designated the storyboard's *initial view controller*. Typically, this will be the view controller to be used as the app's root view controller at launch. The storyboard is sent instantiateInitialViewController, and returns an instance of the initial view controller's class, configured in accordance with your edits in the storyboard. If your app has a main storyboard, this happens automatically.

- A view controller in a storyboard can be assigned an arbitrary string identifier using the storyboard editor. It is then possible to instantiate that view controller by sending instantiateViewControllerWithIdentifier: to the storyboard; an instance of the view controller's class is returned, configured in accordance with your edits in the storyboard.

- If a parent view controller in a storyboard has immediate children, such as a UINavigationController and its initial child view controller, then when the parent is instantiated, the initial children are instantiated automatically.

- If a view controller in a storyboard has a *future* child view controller or a *future* presented view controller, then that child/presented view controller may be instantiated through a *segue*. A segue is an actual object in the storyboard connecting two view controllers, and when triggered, it takes charge of instantiating the new view controller and handing that instance over to the parent/presenting view controller as its child/presented view controller.

A key feature of segues is that they can be triggered automatically. Thus, if your app has a main storyboard, *all* the view controllers the app will *ever* need can be instantiated, as needed, automatically: the initial view controller (and any immediate children) are instantiated as the app launches through an automatic call to `instantiateInitialViewController`, and view controllers needed after that are instantiated when a segue is triggered.

Let's rewrite our example app so as to generate its initial view controller and its view through a storyboard. It's not worth trying to recast the existing project; we'll use a completely new project. This project should be based on the Single View application template, *with Use Storyboard checked*. The resulting project consists of an AppDelegate class and a ViewController class, and a storyboard (called *MainStoryboard.storyboard*) instead of a nib.

Look in *AppDelegate.m* and you'll discover that `application:didFinishLaunching-WithOptions:` contains no code at all — not to load the storyboard file, nor even to generate the window and display it. That's because `UIApplicationMain` does all the work behind the scenes. Here's how:

1. As I explained in Chapter 6, *MainStoryboard.storyboard* is designated the main storyboard file in our *Info.plist*, using the key "Main storyboard file base name" (`UIMainStoryboardFile`). So now `UIApplicationMain` can call `storyboardWith-Name:bundle:` to get a reference to that storyboard.

2. As I explained in Chapter 14, `UIApplicationMain` instantiates the app delegate class, and now it needs a window instance. It asks the app delegate for the value of its `window` property. If the app delegate returns a UIWindow (or subclass) instance, that's the window instance; otherwise, if the `window` property was nil, `UIApplicationMain` itself creates an instance of UIWindow (and assigns it to the app delegate's `window` property).

3. As I explained earlier in this section, `UIApplicationMain` now sends `instantiate-InitialViewController` to the main storyboard. The result is a view controller instance, which is to serve as the app's root view controller.

4. `UIApplicationMain` assigns that view controller instance to the window's `rootView-Controller` property — which, as you know, means that that view controller's view will become the window's sole subview, the app's root view.

5. Finally, `UIApplicationMain` calls `makeKeyAndVisible` on the window. Therefore, at the next redraw moment, the app's interface appears.

To prove that this works, edit *MainStoryboard.storyboard*. It contains a single view controller object, with several important features already configured:

- It is already designated as the storyboard's initial view controller.
- Its class is already specified as ViewController.
- It already contains a view that will function as its `view`.

So now you can give this view a background color, put a label into it, and build and run the project — and your view appears. *Be sure you understand why*. Storyboards are not magic, and a view controller instantiated from a storyboard is just a normal view controller, and gets its view in normal ways.

Take a moment to study the storyboard editing interface a little. In the expanded dock, a view controller is wrapped in a "scene." The scene contains the view controller object itself, along with its view and any subviews, and two top-level proxy objects associated with it: the First Responder proxy object, which is also present in a nib file (Chapter 11), and the Exit proxy object, which is used for creating unwind segues (discussed later in this chapter). You can add further top-level objects; for example, you could add a gesture recognizer (Chapter 18). Any top-level objects in a scene are also displayed in a black bar in the canvas, below the view controller. There's no File's Owner because this isn't a nib and it doesn't have an owner; the storyboard is loaded without an owner, and when a view controller is instantiated, that instance is returned directly through the call that performed the instantiation.

Rotation

A major part of a view controller's job is to know how to rotate the view. The user will experience this as rotation of the app itself: the top of the app shifts so that it is oriented against a different side of the device's display. There are two complementary uses for rotation:

Compensatory rotation
> The app rotates to compensate for the orientation of the device, so that the app appears right way up with respect to how the user is holding the device. The challenge of compensatory rotation stems, quite simply, from the fact that the screen is not square. This means that if the app rotates 90 degrees, the interface no longer fits the screen, and must be changed to compensate.

Forced rotation
> The app rotates when a particular view appears in the interface, or when the app launches, to indicate that the user needs to rotate the device in order to view the app the right way up. This is typically because the interface has been specifically designed, in the face of the fact that the screen is not square, to appear in one particular mode (portrait or landscape).

In the case of the iPhone, no law says that your app has to perform compensatory rotation. Most of my iPhone apps do not do so; indeed, I have no compunction about doing just the opposite, forcing the user to rotate the device differently depending on what view is being displayed. The iPhone is small and easily reoriented with a twist of the user's wrist, and it has a natural right way up, especially because it's a phone. (The iPod touch isn't a phone, but the same argument works by analogy.) On the other hand, Apple would prefer iPad apps to rotate to at least two opposed orientations (such as landscape with the button on the right and landscape with the button on the left), and preferably to all four possible orientations, so that the user isn't restricted in how the device is held.

It's fairly trivial to let your app rotate to two opposed orientations, because once the app is set up to work in one of them, it can work with no change in the other. But allowing a single interface to rotate between two orientations that are 90 degrees apart is trickier, because its dimensions must change — roughly speaking, its height and width are swapped — and this may require a change of layout and might even call for more substantial alterations, such as removal or addition of part of the interface. A good example is the behavior of Apple's Mail app on the iPad: in landscape mode, the master pane and the detail pane appear side by side, but in portrait mode, the detail pane is removed and must be summoned using a button or by swiping, at which point the user can work only in the detail pane until the detail pane is dismissed.

In iOS 5 and before, coordinating view controllers to support rotation could be quite tricky. Each view controller in the view controller hierarchy could submit its own preference as to how the interface should be permitted to rotate, and these preferences could conflict. Built-in parent view controller classes, such as UINavigationController, might consult the rotation preferences of their children and attempt to mediate among them. Each view controller was forced to submit its rotation preference once and for all; that preference could not readily be dynamically revised, based on the current situation.

In iOS 6, the architecture of view controller rotation support has been completely overhauled. This is one of the most radical and far-reaching API changes Apple has ever instituted in iOS, and may well create serious challenges for a developer whose app is to support both iOS 6 and some earlier system. On the other hand, the new rotation support architecture is extremely simple and sensible, and one could argue that Apple has merely recognized the fact that the earlier rotation architecture, which gave developers so much trouble, was wrong all along.

The iOS 6 architecture for view controller support is top-down, starting with the app itself, and stopping with the top-level view controller. It works like this:

- The app itself, in its *Info.plist*, may declare once and for all every orientation the interface will ever be permitted to assume. It does this under the "Supported interface orientations" key, `UISupportedInterfaceOrientations` (supplemented, for a universal app, by "Supported interface orientations (iPad)", `UISupportedInterfaceOrientations~ipad`). You don't usually have to meddle directly with the *Info.plist* file, though; these keys are set through the graphical interface when you edit the target, in the Summary tab.

- The app delegate may implement `application:supportedInterface-OrientationsForWindow:`, returning a bitmask listing every orientation the interface is permitted to assume. This list *overrides* the *Info.plist* settings. Thus, the app delegate can do dynamically what the *Info.plist* can do only statically. `application:supportedInterfaceOrientationsForWindow:` is called at least once every time the device rotates.

- The top-level view controller may implement `supportedInterface-Orientations`, returning a bitmask listing a set of orientations that *intersects* the set of orientations permitted by the app or the app delegate. The resulting intersection will then be the set of permitted orientations. The resulting intersection must not be empty; if it is, your app will crash. `supportedInterface-Orientations` is called at least once every time the device rotates.

  The top-level view controller has a second way to interfere with the app's permitted orientations: it can implement `shouldAutorotate`. This method returns a BOOL, and the default is YES. `shouldAutorotate` is called at least once every time the device rotates; if it returns NO, the interface will not rotate to compensate for this device orientation. This can be a simpler way than `supportedInterface-Orientations` to veto the app's rotation. If `shouldAutorotate` is implemented and returns NO, `supportedInterfaceOrientations` is not called.

A UIViewController class method `attemptRotationToDeviceOrientation` (introduced in iOS 5) prompts the runtime to do immediately what it would do if the user were to rotate the device, namely to walk the three levels I've just described and, if the results permit rotation of the interface to match the current device orientation, to rotate the interface. This would be useful if, say, your top-level view controller had returned NO from `shouldAutorotate`, so that the interface does not match the current device orientation, but is now for some reason prepared to return YES and wants to be asked again, immediately.

The bitmask you return from `application:supportedInterfaceOrientationsFor-Window:` or `supportedInterfaceOrientations` may be one of these values, or multiple values combined with logical-or (Chapter 1):

- `UIInterfaceOrientationMaskPortrait`
- `UIInterfaceOrientationMaskLandscapeLeft`
- `UIInterfaceOrientationMaskLandscapeRight`
- `UIInterfaceOrientationMaskPortraitUpsideDown`

- `UIInterfaceOrientationMaskLandscape` (a convenient combination of `Left` and `Right`)

- `UIInterfaceOrientationMaskAll` (a convenient combination of `Portrait`, `UpsideDown`, `Left`, and `Right`)

- `UIInterfaceOrientationMaskAllButUpsideDown` (a convenient combination of `Portrait`, `Left`, and `Right`)

If nobody declares or implements anything — no supported interface orientations listed in the *Info.plist* and no implementation of `application:supportedInterface-OrientationsForWindow:` or `supportedInterfaceOrientations` — then the defaults are `UIInterfaceOrientationMaskAllButUpsideDown` on the iPhone and `UIInterface-OrientationMaskAll` on the iPad. But that's an edge case; it's probably not something you should actually do.

On the iPhone, `UIInterfaceOrientationMaskPortraitUpsideDown` is frowned on. The runtime enforces this at the application level; you can approve all four orientations in the app's *Info.plist* or the app delegate's `application:supportedInterface-OrientationsForWindow:`, but the interface will not rotate to compensate when the iPhone is held upside down. However, if you then also return from the top-level view controller's `supportedInterfaceOrientations` a value whose meaning includes `UIInterfaceOrientationMaskPortraitUpsideDown`, the interface *will* rotate to compensate when the iPhone is held upside down.

We can now see why the test project we created at the start of this chapter was able to rotate its interface. We started with the Empty Application project template. In that template, the app's *Info.plist* is set to permit rotation to portrait, landscape left, and landscape right. We didn't change that, and we never added any code to contradict it, so the app *was* permitted to rotate to those orientations.

If your code needs to know the current orientation of the device, it can ask the device, by calling `[UIDevice currentDevice].orientation`. Possible results are `UIDevice-OrientationUnknown`, `UIDeviceOrientationPortrait`, and so on. Convenience macros `UIDeviceOrientationIsPortrait` and `UIDeviceOrientationIsLandscape` let you test a given orientation for whether it falls into that category. By the time you get a rotation-related query event — `application:supportedInterfaceOrientationsFor-Window:`, `supportedInterfaceOrientations`, or `shouldAutorotate` — the device's orientation has already changed.

The current orientation of the interface is available as a view controller's `interface-Orientation` property. Never ask for this value if the device's `orientation` is `UIDevice-OrientationUnknown`.

What Rotates?

We say that your app rotates, and you'll think of it as rotating, but what really rotates is the status bar's position. When the device rotates, a `UIDeviceOrientationDidChange-Notification` is emitted by the UIDevice, and if the app's interface is to rotate to match, the UIApplication instance is sent the `setStatusBarOrientation:animated:` message. A transform is applied so that the window's root view appears "right way up," and in a 90-degree rotation, the window's root view has its width and height dimensions swapped. Moreover, this is all accompanied by animation, so it really looks to the user as if the app is rotating. But the window *itself* doesn't budge; it remains "pinned" to the screen (window bounds are screen bounds). It is taller than it is wide, and its top is at the top of the device (away from the home button). As for the root view, its *bounds* are wider than tall in a landscape orientation, but its *frame* remains taller than wide (though you really shouldn't be referring to the root view's frame in this situation, because it has a transform applied; see Chapter 14).

The interface orientation mask values that you return from `application:supportedInterfaceOrientationsForWindow:` or `supportedInterfaceOrientations` are not the same as the orientation values used by UIDevice to report the current device orientation and by UIViewController to report the current interface orientation. Do not accidentally return a device orientation or interface orientation value where an interface orientation *mask* value is expected!

Rotation and Layout Events

Your UIViewController subclass can override any of the following methods (which are called in the order shown) to be alerted in connection with interface rotation:

`willRotateToInterfaceOrientation:duration:`
> The first parameter is the new orientation; `self.interfaceOrientation` is the old orientation, and the view's bounds are the old bounds.

`willAnimateRotationToInterfaceOrientation:duration:`
> The first parameter is the new orientation; `self.interfaceOrientation` is the new orientation, and the view's bounds are the new bounds. The call is wrapped by an animation block, so changes to animatable view properties are animated.

`didRotateFromInterfaceOrientation:`
> The parameter is the old orientation; `self.interfaceOrientation` is the new orientation, and the view's bounds are the new bounds.

You might take advantage of these events to perform manual layout in response to interface rotation. Imagine, for example, that our app displays a black rectangle at the left side of the screen if the device is in landscape orientation, but not if the device is in portrait orientation. We could implement that as follows:

```
- (UIView*) blackRect { // property getter
    if (!self->_blackRect) {
        if (UIInterfaceOrientationIsPortrait(self.interfaceOrientation))
            return nil;
        CGRect f = self.view.bounds;
        f.size.width /= 3.0;
        f.origin.x = -f.size.width;
        UIView* br = [[UIView alloc] initWithFrame:f];
        br.backgroundColor = [UIColor blackColor];
        self.blackRect = br;
    }
    return self->_blackRect;
}


-(void)willAnimateRotationToInterfaceOrientation:(UIInterfaceOrientation)io
                                duration:(NSTimeInterval)duration {
    UIView* v = self.blackRect;
    if (UIInterfaceOrientationIsLandscape(io)) {
        if (!v.superview) {
            [self.view addSubview:v];
            CGRect f = v.frame;
            f.origin.x = 0;
            v.frame = f;
        }
    } else {
        if (v.superview) {
            CGRect f = v.frame;
            f.origin.x -= f.size.width;
            v.frame = f;
        }
    }
}

- (void) didRotateFromInterfaceOrientation:(UIInterfaceOrientation)io {
    if (UIInterfaceOrientationIsPortrait(self.interfaceOrientation))
        [self.blackRect removeFromSuperview];
}
```

We have a UIView property, blackRect, to retain the black rectangle; we implement its getter to create the black rectangle if it hasn't been created already, but only if we are in landscape orientation, since otherwise we cannot set the rectangle's dimensions properly. The implementation of willAnimateRotationToInterfaceOrientation: duration: slides the black rectangle in from the left as part of the rotation animation if we have ended up in a landscape orientation, but only if it isn't in the interface already; after all, the user might rotate the device 180 degrees, from one landscape orientation to the other. Similarly, it slides the black rectangle out to the left if we have ended up in a portrait orientation, but only if it *is* in the interface already. Finally, didRotateFrom-

InterfaceOrientation:, called after the rotation animation is over, makes sure the rectangle is removed from its superview if we have ended up in a portrait orientation.

However, we can do this in a better way. Recall from Chapter 14 that when a view's bounds change, it is asked to update its constraints (if necessary) with a call to update-Constraints, and then to perform layout with a call to layoutSubviews. Well, when the interface rotates, the top-level UIViewController's view's bounds do change. Moreover, the UIViewController itself is notified just before the view's constraints are updated, with updateViewConstraints, and before and after view layout, with viewWill-LayoutSubviews and viewDidLayoutSubviews. The sequence is:

- willRotateToInterfaceOrientation:duration:
- updateViewConstraints (and you must call super!)
- updateConstraints (to the view)
- viewWillLayoutSubviews
- layoutSubviews (to the view)
- viewDidLayoutSubviews
- willAnimateRotationToInterfaceOrientation:duration:
- didRotateFromInterfaceOrientation:

These UIViewController events allow your view controller to take a hand in its view's layout, without your having to subclass UIView and implement updateConstraints and layoutSubviews directly. Our problem is a layout problem, so it seems more elegant to implement it through layout events. Here's a two-part solution involving constraints. I won't bother to remove the black rectangle from the interface; I'll add it once and for all as I configure the view, and just slide it onscreen and offscreen as needed. In view-DidLoad, then, we add the black rectangle to our interface, and then we prepare two sets of constraints, one describing the black rectangle's position onscreen (within our view bounds) and one describing its position offscreen (to the left of our view bounds):

```
-(void)viewDidLoad {
    UIView* br = [UIView new];
    br.translatesAutoresizingMaskIntoConstraints = NO;
    br.backgroundColor = [UIColor blackColor];
    [self.view addSubview:br];

    // "b.r. is pinned to top and bottom of superview"
    [self.view addConstraints:
     [NSLayoutConstraint
      constraintsWithVisualFormat:@"V:|[br]|"
      options:0 metrics:nil views:@{@"br":br}]];

    // "b.r. is 1/3 the width of superview"
```

```
[self.view addConstraint:
 [NSLayoutConstraint
  constraintWithItem:br attribute:NSLayoutAttributeWidth
  relatedBy:0
  toItem:self.view attribute:NSLayoutAttributeWidth
  multiplier:1.0/3.0 constant:0]];

// "onscreen, b.r.'s left is pinned to superview's left"
NSArray* marrOn =
[NSLayoutConstraint
 constraintsWithVisualFormat:@"H:|[br]"
 options:0 metrics:nil views:@{@"br":br}];

// "offscreen, b.r.'s right is pinned to superview's left"
NSArray* marrOff = @[
[NSLayoutConstraint
 constraintWithItem:br attribute:NSLayoutAttributeRight
 relatedBy:NSLayoutRelationEqual
 toItem:self.view attribute:NSLayoutAttributeLeft
 multiplier:1 constant:0]
];

self.blackRectConstraintsOnscreen = marrOn;
self.blackRectConstraintsOffscreen = marrOff;
}
```

That's a lot of preparation, but the payoff is that responding to a request for layout is simple and clear; we simply swap in the constraints appropriate to the new interface orientation (`self.interfaceOrientation` at layout time):

```
-(void)updateViewConstraints {
    [self.view removeConstraints:self.blackRectConstraintsOnscreen];
    [self.view removeConstraints:self.blackRectConstraintsOffscreen];
    if (UIInterfaceOrientationIsLandscape(self.interfaceOrientation))
        [self.view addConstraints:self.blackRectConstraintsOnscreen];
    else
        [self.view addConstraints:self.blackRectConstraintsOffscreen];
    [super updateViewConstraints];
}
```

The movement of the black rectangle is animated as the interface rotates, because *any* constraint-based layout performed as the interface rotates is animated. We change the constraints, and the runtime animates the act of layout as it animates the rotation of the interface.

Initial Orientation

The basic way to dictate your app's initial orientation, as the user will see it when launching, is to use your app's *Info.plist* settings. The reason is that the system can consult those settings during launch, before any of your code runs:

On the iPhone

The app will launch, preferentially, into the *first* orientation listed in the *Info.plist* in the "Supported interface orientations" array (`UISupportedInterface-Orientations`). In Xcode, edit the *Info.plist*; the editor lets you drag the elements of the array to reorder them.

On the iPad

iPad apps are supposed to be more or less orientation-agnostic, so the order of orientations listed in the *Info.plist* in the "Supported interface orientations" array (`UISupportedInterfaceOrientations`) or "Supported interface orientations (iPad)" (`UISupportedInterfaceOrientations~ipad`) is ignored. Instead, the app will launch into whatever permitted orientation is closest to the device's current orientation.

If you really want to, you *can* force an iPad app to launch into a specific orientation, even if it is permitted to adopt further orientations later on: limit the "Supported interface orientations (iPad)" array to a *single* orientation, and use the app delegate's `application:supportedInterfaceOrientationsForWindow:` to supply the full range of possible orientations. But this seems an unlikely thing to do.

If your initial top-level view controller (the root view controller) limits the supported interface orientations, you should probably order the "Supported interface orientations" entries to agree with it — especially on the iPhone, where this order matters. For example, suppose your app as a whole supports portrait, landscape left, and landscape right, but your initial root view controller supports only landscape left and landscape right. Then you should put "Landscape (right home button)" and "Landscape (left home button)" before "Portrait" in the *Info.plist* "Supported interface orientations" array. Otherwise, if "Portrait" comes first, the app will try to launch into portrait orientation, only to discover, as your code finally starts running and your root view controller's `supportedInterfaceOrientations` can be called, that this is wrong.

The fact is, however, that no matter what initial orientation the user sees, *all apps launch into portrait mode initially*. This is because the window goes only one way, with its top at the top of the device (away from the home button) — window bounds are screen bounds (see "What Rotates?" (page 592)). If the app's initial visible orientation is not portrait, there must then be an initial rotation to that initial visible orientation. The user won't necessarily *see* this initial rotation; it may have happened by the time the user sees the app's actual interface. But it will happen. Thus, an app whose initial orientation is landscape mode *must be configured to rotate from portrait to landscape* even if it doesn't support rotation after that.

The initial setup of such an app's interface can be surprisingly tricky, because the interface takes on portrait dimensions before it takes on landscape dimensions. The usual way to encounter trouble in this regard is to try to work with the interface dimensions in your code *too soon*, before the rotation has taken place. From your point of view, it will appear that the width and height values of your interface bounds are the reverse of what you expect.

For example, let's say that our iPhone app's *Info.plist* has its "Supported interface orientations" ordered with "Landscape (right home button)" first, and our root view controller's viewDidLoad code places a small black square at the top center of the interface, like this:

```
- (void) viewDidLoad {
    [super viewDidLoad];
    UIView* square = [[UIView alloc] initWithFrame:CGRectMake(0,0,10,10)];
    square.backgroundColor = [UIColor blackColor];
    square.center =
        CGPointMake(CGRectGetMidX(self.view.bounds),5); // top center?
    [self.view addSubview:square];
}
```

The app launches into landscape orientation; the user must hold the device with the home button at the right to see it correctly. That's good. But where's the little black square? *Not* at the top center of the screen! The square appears at the top of the screen, but only about a third of the way across. The trouble is that in order to calculate the x-coordinate of the square's center we examined the view's bounds *too soon*, at a time when the view's x-dimension (its width dimension) was still its shorter dimension.

One solution is to use delayed performance. It suffices to wait until after your app's first redraw moment:

```
- (void) viewDidLoad {
    [super viewDidLoad];
    dispatch_async(dispatch_get_main_queue(), ^{
        UIView* square = [[UIView alloc] initWithFrame:CGRectMake(0,0,10,10)];
        square.backgroundColor = [UIColor blackColor];
        square.center = CGPointMake(CGRectGetMidX(self.view.bounds),5);
        [self.view addSubview:square];
    });
}
```

It could be argued, though, that this is somewhat perverse. The problem is that viewDidLoad itself is too early, so a more correct solution is to find a more appropriate event to trigger our code.

In iOS 5 and before, a possible solution was to override one of the rotation events discussed in the previous section, such as didRotateFromInterfaceOrientation:, and complete the configuration of your view there. In iOS 6, however, that won't work, because *rotation events are no longer sent* in conjunction with the initial rotation of your app's interface.

On the other hand, iOS 6 does give us a splendid new layout event, viewWillLayout-Subviews. This seems perfectly appropriate, since layout is exactly what we're doing. We must take care to run our code only once, the very first time viewWillLayout-Subviews is called; a BOOL instance variable solves that problem:

```
- (void) viewWillLayoutSubviews {
    if (!self->_viewInitializationDone) {
        self->_viewInitializationDone = YES;
        UIView* square = [[UIView alloc] initWithFrame:CGRectMake(0,0,10,10)];
        square.backgroundColor = [UIColor blackColor];
        square.center = CGPointMake(CGRectGetMidX(self.view.bounds),5);
        [self.view addSubview:square];
    }
}
```

The best solution of all, I think, is to use autolayout if at all possible, positioning our black square through constraints instead of its frame. The beauty of constraints is that you describe your layout conceptually rather than numerically; those concepts continue to apply through any future rotation. We don't need delayed performance, we don't need a BOOL instance variable, and we can put our code back into viewDidLoad:

```
- (void) viewDidLoad {
    UIView* square = [UIView new];
    square.backgroundColor = [UIColor blackColor];
    [self.view addSubview:square];
    square.translatesAutoresizingMaskIntoConstraints = NO;
    CGFloat side = 10;
    [square addConstraint:
     [NSLayoutConstraint
      constraintWithItem:square attribute:NSLayoutAttributeWidth
      relatedBy:0
      toItem:nil attribute:0
      multiplier:1 constant:side]];
    [self.view addConstraints:
     [NSLayoutConstraint
      constraintsWithVisualFormat:@"V:|[square(side)]"
      options:0 metrics:@{@"side":@(side)}
      views:@{@"square":square}]];
    [self.view addConstraint:
     [NSLayoutConstraint
      constraintWithItem:square attribute:NSLayoutAttributeCenterX
      relatedBy:0
      toItem:self.view attribute:NSLayoutAttributeCenterX
      multiplier:1 constant:0]];
}
```

When designing in the nib, don't be misled by the fact that you can rotate the interface. You can select a top-level view or view controller and choose Landscape in the Orientation pop-up menu in the Simulated Metrics section of the Attributes inspector. But you aren't causing the app's interface to rotate; you're merely swapping a view's apparent height and width values, for convenience while editing the nib. The rotation of the interface is still up to your app and the top-level view controller, and the final disposition of your subviews will still probably be decided through autoresizing or autolayout.

Presented View Controller

The chief purpose of view controllers is to make views come and go coherently in the interface. The simplest way of making a view come and go is through a *presented view controller*. Most often, the view that comes and goes will be fullscreen; while present, it will take over the entire interface. (On the iPhone, this is *always* the case.)

There is a temptation to think of a presented view controller as secondary or temporary. This is often true, but such a conception misses the full power of a presented view controller, which is, quite simply, that it changes the interface. A presented view controller's view may have a complex interface; it might have child view controllers (Figure 19-6); it might present yet another view controller; it might take over the interface permanently. You, the programmer, may be conscious that the presented view controller's view is in some sense covering the previous interface; but the user might or might not experience the interface that way.

For example, in Apple's Music app, the two alternating views that appear when you view the currently playing song are equal partners (Figure 19-7); there's no implication that one is secondary to the other. Yet it's likely that one of them (probably the second one) is a presented view controller.

To make a view controller present another view controller, you send the first view controller `presentViewController:animated:completion:`, handing it the second view controller, which you will probably instantiate for this very purpose. (The first view controller is very typically `self`.) We now have two view controllers that stand in the relationship of `presentingViewController` and `presentedViewController`, and the latter is retained. The presented view controller's view effectively replaces (or covers) the presenting view controller's view in the interface.

This state of affairs persists until the presenting view controller is sent `dismissViewControllerAnimated:completion:`. The presented view controller's view is then removed from the interface, and the presented view controller is released; it will thereupon typically go out of existence together with its view, its child view controllers and *their* views, and so on.

Figure 19-7. Two views that are equal partners

As the view of the presented view controller appears, and again when it is dismissed, there's an option for animation as the transition takes place (the `animated:` argument). The `completion:` parameter lets you supply a block of code to be run after the transition (including the animation) has occurred.

The presenting view controller (the presented view controller's `presentingView-Controller`) is not necessarily the view controller to which you sent `presentView-Controller:animated:completion:`. It will help if we distinguish *three* roles that view controllers can play in presenting a view controller:

- The view controller to which `presentViewController:animated:completion:` was sent. I will call this the *original presenter*.

- The second view controller, the one specified as the first argument to `presentView-Controller:animated:completion:`. This is the *presented view controller*.

  The presented view controller is set as the original presenter's `presentedView-Controller`.

- The view controller whose view is replaced (or covered) by the presented view controller's view. This is the *presenting view controller*. It might be the same as the original presenter, but often it won't be. By default on the iPad, and *always* on the iPhone, the presenting view controller is *the view controller whose view is the entire interface* — namely, either the root view controller or an already existing presented view controller.

The presenting view controller is set as the presented view controller's `presenting-ViewController`, and the presented view controller is set as the presenting view controller's `presentedViewController`. (Yes, this means that the presented view controller might be the `presentedViewController` of two different view controllers.)

The receiver of `dismissViewControllerAnimated:completion:` may be *any* of those three objects; the runtime will use the linkages between them to transmit the necessary messages up the chain on your behalf to the `presentingViewController`.

A view controller can have at most one `presentedViewController`. If you send `present-ViewController:animated:completion:` to a view controller whose `presentedView-Controller` isn't nil, nothing will happen (and you'll get a warning from the runtime). However, a presented view controller can itself present a view controller, so there can be a chain of presented view controllers.

Conversely, you can test for a nil `presentedViewController` or `presentingView-Controller` to learn whether view presentation is occurring. For example, a view controller whose `presentingViewController` is nil is not a presented view controller at this moment.

Let's make one view controller present another. We already have an example project, from earlier in this chapter, containing an AppDelegate class and a RootViewController class. Let's modify it to add a second view controller class, and make RootViewController present it (don't use the project containing a storyboard; I'll talk about storyboards and presented view controllers later):

1. Choose File → New → File and make a new iOS Cocoa Touch Objective-C class. Click Next.

2. Name the class SecondViewController, make sure it is a subclass of UIView-Controller, and check the checkbox "With XIB for user interface" so that we can design this view controller's view quickly and easily in a nib. Click Next.

3. Confirm the folder, group, and target membership, and click Create.

4. Edit *SecondViewController.xib*, and do something there to make the view distinctive, so that you'll recognize it when it appears.

5. We need a way to trigger the presentation of SecondViewController. In RootView-Controller's view's interface, add a button. Connect that button to an action method in *RootViewController.m*; let's call it `doPresent:`.

Now we'll write the code for doPresent:. First, import "SecondViewController.h" at the top of *RootViewController.m*, so that we can speak of SecondViewController. Here's the code:

```
- (IBAction)doPresent:(id)sender {
    [self presentViewController:[SecondViewController new]
                       animated:YES completion:nil];
}
```

Run the project. In RootViewController's view, tap the button. SecondViewController's view slides into place over RootViewController's view.

In our lust for instant gratification, we have neglected to provide a way to dismiss the presented view controller. If you'd like to do that, put a button into SecondView-Controller's view and connect it to an action method in *SecondViewController.m*:

```
- (IBAction)doDismiss:(id)sender {
    [self.presentingViewController dismissViewControllerAnimated:YES
                                                      completion:nil];
}
```

Run the project. You can now alternate between RootViewController's view and Second-ViewController's view.

In real life, it is quite probable that both presentation and dismissal will be a little more involved. Someone, typically the original presenter, will very likely have additional information to impart to the presented view controller as the latter is created and presented. Here's a typical example from one of my apps (this is in fact the transition that engenders Figure 19-6):

```
DrillViewController* dvc =
    [[DrillViewController alloc] initWithData:drillTerms];
[self presentViewController:dvc animated:YES completion:nil];
```

I've given DrillViewController a designated initializer initWithData: precisely so that whoever creates it can pass it the data it will need to do its job while it exists.

The presented view controller, too, will very likely have additional information to pass back to the original presenter. The user is interacting with the presented view controller's view, so it is the presented view controller that knows when it should be dismissed and what happened while it was in existence. To tell the original presenter about this, handing it any needed data and so forth, the presented view controller may need to call some method in the original presenter, before it itself goes out of existence. The presented view controller may thus need a reference to the original presenter and a knowledge of some of its methods.

A standard architecture that solves this problem is for the presented view controller to define a protocol to which the original presenter conforms. The original presenter then hands the presented view controller a (weak!) reference to itself as it creates the presented view controller; we can call this the presented view controller's delegate. In this way the presented view controller is the one that specifies what the communication callbacks will be, and it remains agnostic about the actual class of its delegate. This is the architecture, exemplified by the Utility Application project template, that I discussed in Chapter 10.

To implement this architecture in our existing example with RootViewController and SecondViewController, you'd modify SecondViewController to look like this:

```
// SecondViewController.h:
@protocol SecondViewControllerDelegate
- (void) dismissSecondViewControllerWithData: (id) data;
@end
@interface SecondViewController : UIViewController
@property (nonatomic, weak) id<SecondViewControllerDelegate> delegate;
@end

// SecondViewController.m:
- (IBAction)doDismiss:(id)sender {
    [self.delegate dismissSecondViewControllerWithData:nil];
}
```

RootViewController will need to declare itself as adopting SecondViewController-Delegate; I like to do this with a class extension in the implementation file (*RootView-Controller.m*):

```
@interface RootViewController () <SecondViewControllerDelegate>
@end
```

RootViewController could then present and dismiss SecondViewController like this:

```
- (IBAction)doPresent:(id)sender {
    SecondViewController* svc = [SecondViewController new];
    svc.delegate = self;
    // ... provide any needed data here ...
    [self presentViewController:svc animated:YES completion:nil];
}
- (void)dismissSecondViewControllerWithData:(id)data {
    // ... do something with the data here ...
    [self dismissViewControllerAnimated:YES completion:nil];
}
```

Configuring this architecture involves considerable work, and I know from experience that there is a strong temptation to be lazy and avoid it. It may indeed be possible to get by with a simplified solution. For example, SecondViewController might know that it will be presented only by a RootViewController, and can thus import "RootView-Controller.h", cast its presentingViewController to a RootViewController, and call any RootViewController method. Or SecondViewController could post a notification for which RootViewController has registered. Nevertheless, a protocol is the fullest and most correct architecture for a presented view controller to communicate back to its original presenter.

(I am not saying that another solution would never be possible or justifiable. Perhaps there is a chain of presented view controllers, where different user actions should cause dismissal at different levels up the chain; a notification might then be perfectly reasonable. This is all part of the larger topic of getting a reference, discussed in Chapter 13. No one size fits all.)

Presented View Animation

When a view is presented and later when it is dismissed, an animation can be performed, according to whether the `animated:` parameter of the corresponding method is YES. The possible animation styles (whose names preserve the legacy "modal" designation) are:

`UIModalTransitionStyleCoverVertical` *(the default)*
> The presented view slides up from the bottom to cover the presenting view on presentation and down to reveal the presenting view on dismissal. ("Bottom" is defined differently depending on the orientation of the device and the orientations the view controllers support.)

`UIModalTransitionStyleFlipHorizontal`
> The view flips on the vertical axis as if the two views were the front and back of a piece of paper. (The "vertical axis" is the device's long axis, regardless of the app's orientation.)

`UIModalTransitionStyleCrossDissolve`
> The views remain stationary, and one fades into the other.

`UIModalTransitionStylePartialCurl`
> The first view curls up like a page in a notepad to expose most of the second view, but remains covering the top-left region of the second view. Thus there must not be any important interface in that region, as the user will not be able to see or touch it.

You do not pass the animation style as a parameter when presenting or dismissing a view controller; rather, it is attached beforehand to a view controller as its `modalTransitionStyle` property. (It is legal, but not common, for the `modalTransitionStyle` value to differ at the time of dismissal from its value at the time of presentation. Reversing on dismissal with the same animation style that was used on presentation is a subtle cue to the user that we're returning to a previous state.) The view controller that should have this `modalTransitionStyle` property set will generally be the *presented view controller* (I'll talk about the exception to this rule in a moment). There are three typical ways in which this happens:

- The original presenter sets the presented view controller's `modalTransitionStyle` property.
- The presented view controller sets its own `modalTransitionStyle` property early in its lifetime; for example, it might override `initWithNibName:bundle:`.
- The presented view controller is instantiated in a nib; there's a Transition Style pop-up menu in the nib editor.

Presentation Styles

On the iPhone, the presented view controller's view always occupies the entire interface. On the iPad, there are additional options. These options are expressed through the presented view controller's `modalPresentationStyle` property. Your choices (which display more legacy "modal" names) are:

`UIModalPresentationFullScreen`
The default. The presenting view controller is the root view controller (or a fullscreen presented view controller), and its view — meaning the entire interface — is replaced.

On the iPhone, although it is not illegal to set the `modalPresentationStyle` to another value, a presented view controller will always behave as if it were `UIModalPresentationFullScreen`.

(This is the only mode in which `UIModalTransitionStylePartialCurl` is legal.)

`UIModalPresentationPageSheet`
In a portrait orientation, basically indistinguishable from fullscreen mode. But in a landscape orientation, the presented view has the width of the portrait-oriented screen, so the previous interface remains partially visible behind the presented view, but dimmed so that the user can't interact with it. Thus this mode is very like a modal dialog on Mac OS X.

`UIModalPresentationFormSheet`

Similar to `UIModalPresentationPageSheet`, but the presented view is smaller. As the name implies, this is intended to allow the user to fill out a form (Apple describes this as "gathering structured information from the user").

`UIModalPresentationCurrentContext`

The presented view replaces a view which, although it is a view controller's view, does *not* occupy the whole screen. The replaced view might be contained in a popover, for instance (see Chapter 22), or it might be a child view controller's view that occupies only a portion of the screen.

On the iPad, when the presented view controller's `modalPresentationStyle` is `UIModalPresentationCurrentContext`, a decision has to be made as to what view controller should be the presented view controller's `presentingViewController`. This will determine what view will be replaced by the presented view controller's view. This decision involves another UIViewController property, `definesPresentationContext` (a BOOL). Starting with the view controller to which `presentViewController:animated:completion:` was sent, we walk up the chain of parent view controllers, looking for one whose `definesPresentationContext` property is YES. If we find one, that's the one; it will be the `presentingViewController`, and its view will be replaced by the presented view controller's view. If we *don't* find one, things work as if the presented view controller's `modalPresentationStyle` had been `UIModalPresentationFullScreen`.

Moreover, if, during the search just described, we *do* find a view controller whose `definesPresentationContext` property is YES, we look to see if that view controller's `providesPresentationContextTransitionStyle` property is *also* YES. If so, that view controller's `modalTransitionStyle` is used for this transition animation, instead of using the presented view controller's `modalTransitionStyle`.

To illustrate, I need a parent–child view controller arrangement to work with. This chapter hasn't yet discussed any parent view controllers in detail, but the simplest is UITabBarController, which I discuss in the next section, and it's easy to create a working app with a UITabBarController-based interface, so that's the example I'll use.

Start with an iPad version of the Tabbed Application project template (not using a storyboard). Make a new view controller class and an accompanying nib file to use as a presented view controller; let's call it ExtraViewController. Put a button in the first view controller's view (in *FirstViewController.xib*) and connect it to an action method in the first view controller (*FirstViewController.m*) that summons the new view controller as a presented view controller:

```
- (IBAction)doPresent:(id)sender {
    UIViewController* vc = [ExtraViewController new];
    [self presentViewController:vc animated:YES completion:nil];
}
```

You'll also need to import "ExtraViewController.h" at the top of that file, obviously. Run the project and tap the button. Observe that the presented view controller's view occupies the *entire* interface, covering even the tab bar; it replaces the root view.

Now change the code to look like this:

```
- (IBAction)doPresent:(id)sender {
    UIViewController* vc = [ExtraViewController new];
    self.definesPresentationContext = YES;
    vc.modalPresentationStyle = UIModalPresentationCurrentContext;
    [self presentViewController:vc animated:YES completion:nil];
}
```

Run the project and tap the button. This time, the presented view controller replaces only the first view controller's view; the tab bar remains. That's because the presented view controller's modalPresentationStyle is UIModalPresentationCurrentContext, and when presentViewController:animated:completion: is sent to self, the definesPresentationContext property of self is YES. The search for a context stops, and the presented view replaces the first view controller's view instead of the root view.

The difference is even more dramatic if we change the transition animation. We can do this through the modalTransitionStyle property of the presenting view controller, self. Add two more lines, like this:

```
- (IBAction)doPresent:(id)sender {
    UIViewController* vc = [ExtraViewController new];
    self.definesPresentationContext = YES;
    self.providesPresentationContextTransitionStyle = YES;
    self.modalTransitionStyle = UIModalTransitionStyleFlipHorizontal;
    vc.modalPresentationStyle = UIModalPresentationCurrentContext;
    [self presentViewController:vc animated:YES completion:nil];
}
```

Now the transition uses the flip horizontal animation; the presenting view controller is able to override the transition animation of the presented view controller.

Observe also that you can still switch between the first and second tabbed views, even while the presented view is occupying the place of the first tabbed view. Clearly, very powerful and interesting interfaces can be constructed using this technique.

It's helpful to experiment with the above code, commenting out individual lines to see what effect they have on the overall result. Also, set up a parallel iPhone project, and observe that none of this works; the presented view takes over the whole screen. The UIModalPresentationCurrentContext presentation style, on which this entire behavior depends, is an iPad-only feature.

Rotation of a Presented View

No law requires that every "scene" of your interface should appear in the same orientation. On the iPhone especially, where the user can easily rotate the device while working with an app, it is reasonable and common for one scene to appear in portrait orientation and another to appear in landscape orientation.

One easy way to achieve this is to implement `supportedInterfaceOrientations` differently for a presented view controller. In iOS 6, a simple rule is followed (indeed, the simplicity of this rule is one of the benefits of the overhauled rotation architecture I alluded to earlier): if a presented view controller's view takes over the whole screen, then its `supportedInterfaceOrientations` is consulted and honored.

For example, in my flashcard app pictured in Figure 19-3, the flashcards are viewed only in landscape orientation. But there is also an option to display a list (a UITableView) of all flashcards, a total vocabulary list. This list is far better viewed in portrait orientation, so as to accommodate the greatest possible number of items on the screen at once; therefore, it is permitted to assume portrait orientation only. The user must rotate the device with the hand holding the iPhone, but this is not objectionable; in fact, it quickly becomes automatic and subconscious.

Here's how this is achieved. The app as a whole, as dictated by its *Info.plist*, supports three orientations, in this order: "Landscape (right home button)," "Landscape (left home button)," and "Portrait." My app's RootViewController implements `supported-InterfaceOrientations` to return `UIInterfaceOrientationMaskLandscape`; a card, as shown in Figure 19-3, appears only in landscape. But the view controller whose view contains the total vocabulary list implements `supportedInterfaceOrientations` to return `UIInterfaceOrientationMaskPortrait`; when the total vocabulary list is presented, the app rotates to portrait orientation (and the user must rotate the device to match), and when it is dismissed, the app rotates to landscape orientation (and the user must rotate the device to match).

In addition, iOS 6 introduces a new view controller instance method, `preferred-InterfaceOrientationForPresentation`. For a presented view controller, this method is called before `supportedInterfaceOrientations`: to learn which orientation it would like to appear in *initially*. A single interface orientation (*not* a mask) should be returned. For example:

```
-(UIInterfaceOrientation)preferredInterfaceOrientationForPresentation {
    return UIInterfaceOrientationPortrait;
}

-(NSUInteger)supportedInterfaceOrientations {
    return UIInterfaceOrientationMaskAll;
}
```

That says, "When I am summoned initially as a presented view controller, the app should be rotated to portrait orientation. After that, the app can rotate to compensate for any orientation of the device."

The presented view controller's `supportedInterfaceOrientations` (preceded by its `preferredInterfaceOrientationForPresentation` if implemented) is consulted when the presented view controller is first summoned. Subsequently, both the presenting and presented view controllers' `supportedInterfaceOrientations` are called on each rotation of the device, and the presenting view controller's `supportedInterfaceOrientations` is called when the presented view controller is dismissed. Both view controllers get layout events both when the presented view controller is summoned and when it is dismissed.

Presenting a View in Response to Rotation

An interesting alternative to performing complex layout on rotation, as in "Rotation and Layout Events" (page 592), might be to summon a presented view controller instead. We detect the rotation of the device directly, and replace our view with a presented view suited to the new orientation. To give the proper illusion of rotation, we call the UIApplication instance method `setStatusBarOrientation:animated:`. In iOS 6, that call doesn't give us any actual animation unless `supportedInterfaceOrientations` returns a largely undocumented value, 0. This value forbids automatic rotation of the interface and leaves management of the app's orientation entirely up to us.

In this example, we have two view controllers, RootViewController and LandscapeViewController. In LandscapeViewController, `supportedInterfaceOrientations` allows the interface to rotate automatically if the user switches from one landscape orientation to the other, but returns 0 if we're rotating back to portrait:

```
-(NSUInteger)supportedInterfaceOrientations {
    if ([UIDevice currentDevice].orientation == UIDeviceOrientationPortrait)
        return 0;
    return UIInterfaceOrientationMaskLandscape;
}
```

And here's RootViewController:

```
-(NSUInteger)supportedInterfaceOrientations {
    return 0;
}

- (void) viewDidLoad {
    [super viewDidLoad];
    [[UIDevice currentDevice] beginGeneratingDeviceOrientationNotifications];
    [[NSNotificationCenter defaultCenter]
        addObserver:self selector:@selector(screenRotated:)
        name:UIDeviceOrientationDidChangeNotification object:nil];
}
```

```
- (void)screenRotated:(NSNotification *)n {
    UIDeviceOrientation rot = [UIDevice currentDevice].orientation;
    if (UIDeviceOrientationIsLandscape(rot) & !self.presentedViewController) {
        [[UIApplication sharedApplication]
         setStatusBarOrientation:rot animated:YES];
        UIViewController* vc = [LandscapeViewController new];
        vc.modalTransitionStyle = UIModalTransitionStyleCrossDissolve;
        [self presentViewController:vc animated:YES completion:nil];
    } else if (UIDeviceOrientationPortrait == rot) {
        [[UIApplication sharedApplication]
         setStatusBarOrientation:rot animated:YES];
        [self dismissViewControllerAnimated:YES completion:nil];
    }
}
```

Tab Bar Controllers

A *tab bar* (UITabBar, see also Chapter 25) is a horizontal bar containing items. Each item (a UITabBarItem) displays, by default, an image and a title. At all times, exactly one of these items is selected (highlighted); when the user taps an item, it becomes the selected item.

If there are too many items to fit on a tab bar, the excess items are automatically subsumed into a final More item. When the user taps the More item, a list of the excess items appears, and the user can select one; the user can also be permitted to edit the tab bar, determining which items appear in the tab bar itself and which ones spill over into the More list.

A tab bar is an independent interface object, but it is most commonly used in conjunction with a *tab bar controller* (UITabBarController, a subclass of UIViewController) to form a tab bar interface. The tab bar controller displays the tab bar at the bottom of its own view. From the user's standpoint, the tab bar items correspond to views; when the user selects a tab bar item, the corresponding view appears. The user is thus employing the tab bar to choose an entire area of your app's functionality. In reality, the UITab-BarController is a parent view controller; you give it child view controllers, which the tab bar controller then contains, and the views summoned by tapping the tab bar items are the views of those child view controllers.

Familiar examples of a tab bar interface on the iPhone are Apple's Clock app, which has four tab bar items, and Apple's Music app, which has four tab bar items plus a More item that reveals a list of five more.

You can get a reference to the tab bar controller's tab bar through its `tabBar` property. In general, you won't need this. When using a tab bar interface by way of a UITabBar-Controller, you do not interact (as a programmer) with the tab bar itself; you don't create it or set its delegate. You provide the UITabBarController with children, and it does the rest; when the UITabBarController's view is displayed, there's the tab bar along with the view of the selected item. You can, however, customize the *look* of the tab bar (see Chapter 25 for details).

As discussed earlier in this chapter, your app's automatic rotation depends on the interplay between the app (represented by the *Info.plist* and the app delegate) and the top-level view controller. If a UITabBarController is the top-level view controller, it will help determine your app's automatic rotation, through its implementation of supportedInterfaceOrientations. By default, a UITabBarController does not implement supportedInterfaceOrientations, so your interface will be free to rotate to any orientation permitted by the app as a whole. If that isn't what you want, you'll have to subclass UITabBarController for the sole purpose of implementing supportedInterfaceOrientations. (This seems very silly; why doesn't the API embody this functionality in a settable property?)

Tab Bar Items

For each view controller you assign as a tab bar controller's child, you're going to need a *tab bar item*, which will appear in the tab bar. This tab bar item will be your child view controller's tabBarItem. A tab bar item is a UITabBarItem; this is a subclass of UIBarItem, an abstract class that provides some of its most important properties, such as title, image, and enabled.

There are two ways to make a tab bar item:

By borrowing it from the system
> Instantiate UITabBarItem using initWithTabBarSystemItem:tag:, and assign the instance to your child view controller's tabBarItem. Consult the documentation for the list of available system items. Unfortunately you can't customize a system tab bar item's title; you must accept the title the system hands you. (You can't work around this annoying restriction by somehow copying a system tab bar item's image.)

By making your own
> Instantiate UITabBarItem using initWithTitle:image:tag: and assign the instance to your child view controller's tabBarItem. Alternatively, use the view controller's existing tabBarItem and set its image and title. Instead of setting the title of the tabBarItem, you can set the title property of the view controller itself; setting a view controller's title automatically sets the title of its current tabBarItem (unless the tab bar item is a system tab bar item), but the converse is not true.

The image for a tab bar item should be a 30×30 PNG; if it is larger, it will be scaled down as needed. It should be a *transparency mask*; that is, it should consist of transparent pixels and opaque pixels (possibly including semiopaque pixels). Color is of no consequence and will be ignored; all that matters is the degree of transparency of each pixel. The runtime itself will tint the image, adding a shine effect.

Alternatively, you can provide a normal image by calling `setFinishedSelected-Image:withFinishedUnselectedImage:`; the runtime will not modify this image in any way, and getting the size right is up to you. The selected and unselected image can be the same, but the runtime will not tint the selected image (as it does for an `image`), so you'll probably want two different images, to differentiate the two states. (You can use Core Image, discussed in Chapter 15, to tint or desaturate an image.)

You can also give a tab bar item a badge (see the documentation on the `badgeValue` property). Other ways in which you can customize the look of a tab bar item are discussed in Chapter 25. For example, you can control the font and style of the title, or you can give it an empty title and offset the image.

Configuring a Tab Bar Controller

As I've already said, you configure a tab bar controller by handing it the view controllers that will be its children. To do so, collect those view controllers into an array and set the UITabBarController's `viewControllers` property to that array. The view controllers in the array are now the tab bar controller's child view controllers; the tab bar controller is the `parentViewController` of the view controllers in the array. The tab bar controller is also the `tabBarController` of the view controllers in the array and of all their children; thus a child view controller at any depth can learn that it is contained by a tab bar controller and can get a reference to that tab bar controller. The tab bar controller retains the array, and the array retains the child view controllers.

The tab bar controller's tab bar will automatically display the `tabBarItem` of each child view controller. The order of the tab bar items is the order of the view controllers in the tab bar controller's `viewControllers` array. Thus, the child view controllers will probably want to configure their `tabBarItem` property very early in their lifetime, so that the `tabBarItem` is ready by the time the view controller is handed as a child to the tab bar controller. It is common to override `initWithNibName:bundle:` for this purpose.

Here's a simple example excerpted from the app delegate's `application:didFinish-LaunchingWithOptions:` of one of my apps, in which I construct a tab bar interface and display it:

```
UITabBarController* tbc = [UITabBarController new];
// create tabs
UIViewController* b = [GameBoardController new];
// some code omitted here... never mind what "s" is in the next line
UINavigationController* n =
    [[UINavigationController alloc] initWithRootViewController:s];
```

```
// load up with tab views
tbc.viewControllers = @[b, n];
// configure window
self.window.rootViewController = tbc;
```

You'll notice that I don't configure the contained view controllers' tab bar items. That's because those view controllers configure themselves early in their lifetimes. For example:

```
// GameBoardController.m:

- (id) initWithNibName:(NSString *)nibName bundle:(NSBundle *)nibBundle {
    self = [super initWithNibName:nibName bundle:nibBundle];
    if (self) {
        // we will be embedded in a tab bar interface, configure
        self.tabBarItem.image = [UIImage imageNamed:@"game.png"];
        self.title = @"Game";
    }
    return self;
}
```

If you change the tab bar controller's view controllers array later in its lifetime and you want the corresponding change in the tab bar items to be animated, call setView-Controllers:animated:.

When a child view controller's view is displayed, it is resized to fit the region of the tab bar controller's view above the tab bar. Keep that fact in mind when designing your view. Autoresizing settings or constraints can help here, if you don't want an interface object near the bottom of your view to be left behind and disappear from the interface when the view is resized. Also, when editing your view in the nib editor, you can shrink the view to the size at which it will be displayed in the tab bar interface, thus helping you judiciously situate your interface items; to do so, choose Tab Bar in the Bottom Bar pop-up menu of the Simulated Metrics section of the Attributes inspector.

Initially, by default, the first child view controller's tab bar item is selected and its view is displayed. To tell the tab bar controller which tab bar item should be selected, you can couch your choice in terms of the contained view controller, by setting the selected-ViewController property, or by index number in the array, by setting the selected-Index property. The same properties also tell you what view controller's view the user has displayed by tapping in the tab bar.

You can also set the UITabBarController's delegate; the delegate should adopt the UITabBarControllerDelegate protocol. The delegate gets messages allowing it to prevent a given tab bar item from being selected, and notifying it when a tab bar item is selected and when the user is customizing the tab bar from the More item.

If the tab bar contains few enough items that it doesn't need a More item, there won't be one and the tab bar won't be user-customizable. If there *is* a More item, you can exclude some tab bar items from being customizable by setting the `customizableView-Controllers` property to an array that lacks them; setting this property to nil means that the user can see the More list but can't rearrange the items. Setting the `view-Controllers` property sets the `customizableViewControllers` property to the same value, so if you're going to set the `customizableViewControllers` property, do it *after* setting the `viewControllers` property. The `moreNavigationController` property can be compared with the `selectedViewController` property to learn whether the user is currently viewing the More list; apart from this, the More interface is mostly out of your control, but I'll discuss some sneaky ways of customizing it in Chapter 25.

(If you allow the user to rearrange items, you would presumably want to save the new arrangement and restore it the next time the app runs. You might use NSUserDefaults for this; alternatively, you could take advantage of iOS 6's new automatic state saving and restoration facilities, discussed later in this chapter.)

You can also configure a UITabBarController in a nib or storyboard. The nib editor interface is quite clever about this. The UITabBarController's contained view controllers can be set directly in the nib or storyboard, and are instantiated together with the tab bar controller. Moreover, each contained view controller contains a Tab Bar Item; you can select this and set its title and image directly in the nib. (If a view controller in a nib *doesn't* have a Tab Bar Item and you want to configure this view controller for use in a tab bar interface, drag a Tab Bar Item from the Object library onto the view controller.) The UITabBarController itself has a `delegate` outlet. Thus, it is possible to create a fully configured tab bar interface with essentially no code at all.

Navigation Controllers

A *navigation bar* (UINavigationBar, see also Chapter 25) is a horizontal bar displaying, at its simplest, a center title and a right button. When the user taps the right button, the navigation bar animates, sliding its interface out to the left and replacing it with a new interface that enters from the right, displaying a back button at the left side, and a new center title — and possibly a new right button. Thus the user can now either go further forward (to the right), tapping the right button to proceed to yet another center title, or else go back (to the left), tapping the back button to return to the first center title and the first right button.

There's a computer science name for the architecture I'm describing — a stack. Conceptually, a navigation bar represents a stack. Under the hood, a navigation bar really *is* a stack. A navigation bar holds an internal stack of navigation items (UINavigation-Item). It starts out with one navigation item (the *root* or *bottom item*); you can then push another navigation item onto the stack, and from there you can either pop that navigation item to remove it from the stack or push yet another navigation item onto the stack.

At any moment, therefore, some navigation item is the *top item* on the stack, the most recently pushed item still present on the stack (the topItem). Furthermore, unless the top item is also the root item (because it is the only item in the stack), some navigation item is the *back item* (the backItem), the item that would be top item if we were now to pop the top item.

The state of the stack is reflected in the navigation bar's interface. The navigation bar's center title comes automatically from the top item, and its back button comes from the back item. (See Chapter 25 for a complete description.) Thus, typically, the center shows the user what item is current, and the left side is a button telling the user what item we would return to if the user were to tap that button. The animations reinforce this notion of directionality, giving the user a sense of position within a chain of items. When a navigation item is pushed onto the stack, the new interface slides in from the right; when an item is popped from the stack, the new interface slides in from the left.

A navigation bar is an independent interface object, but it is most commonly used in conjunction with a *navigation controller* (UINavigationController, a subclass of UIViewController) to form a navigation interface. Just as there is a stack of navigation items in the navigation bar, there is a stack of view controllers in the navigation controller. These view controllers are the navigation controller's children, and the navigation items each belong a view controller; each navigation item is, in fact, a view controller's navigationItem. Whatever view controller is at the top of the navigation controller's stack, that is the view controller whose navigationItem is displayed in the navigation bar, and whose view is displayed in the interface. The animation in the navigation bar is matched by an animation of the interface as a whole: a view controller's view slides into the main interface from the left or right just as its navigation item slides into the navigation bar from the left or right.

Your code can control the overall navigation, so in real life, the user may well navigate to the right, not by tapping the right button in the navigation bar, but by tapping something inside the main interface, such as a listing in a table view. (Figure 19-1 is a navigation interface that works this way.) In this situation, your code is deciding in real time what the next view should be; typically, you won't even create the next view controller until the user asks to navigate to the right. The navigation interface thus becomes a *master–detail interface*.

Conversely, you might put a view controller inside a navigation controller just to get the convenience of the navigation bar, with its title and buttons, even when no actual push-and-pop navigation is going to take place. This has always been common practice on the iPhone, and Apple has started adopting it on the iPad as well: for example, by default, the child views of a split view controller now work this way (see Chapter 22).

You can get a reference to the navigation controller's navigation bar through its navigationBar property. In general, you won't need this. When using a navigation interface by way of a UINavigationController, you do not interact (as a programmer) with the navigation bar itself; you don't create it or set its delegate. You provide the UINavigationController with children, and it does the rest, handing each child view controller's navigationItem to the navigation bar for display and showing the child view controller's view each time navigation occurs. You can, however, customize the *look* of the navigation bar (see Chapter 25 for details) — and on the iPhone, in iOS 6, this will affect the color of the status bar.

A navigation interface may also optionally display a toolbar at the bottom. A toolbar (UIToolbar) is a horizontal view displaying a row of items, any of which the user can tap. The tapped item may highlight momentarily but is not selected; it represents the initiation of an action, not a state or a mode, and should be thought of as (and may in fact look like) a button. You can get a reference to a UINavigationController's toolbar through its toolbar property. The look of the toolbar can be customized (Chapter 25).

 A UIToolbar can be used independently, and often is. It then typically appears at the bottom on an iPhone — Figure 19-3 has a toolbar at the bottom — but often appears at the top on an iPad, where it plays something of the role that the menu bar plays on the desktop. When a toolbar is displayed by a navigation controller, though, it always appears at the bottom.

In a navigation interface, the contents of the toolbar are linked to the view controller that is currently the top item in the stack: they are its toolbarItems. The toolbar can also readily be hidden or shown as a certain view controller becomes the top item.

A familiar example of a navigation interface is Apple's Mail app (Figure 19-8), a master–detail interface with the navigation bar at the top and the toolbar displaying additional options and information at the bottom.

As discussed earlier in this chapter, your app's automatic rotation depends on the interplay between the app (represented by the *Info.plist* and the app delegate) and the top-level view controller. If a UINavigationController is the top-level view controller, it will help determine your app's automatic rotation, through its implementation of supportedInterfaceOrientations. By default, a UINavigationController does not implement supportedInterfaceOrientations, so your interface will be free to rotate to any orientation permitted by the app as a whole. If that isn't what you want, you'll have to subclass UINavigationController for the sole purpose of implementing supportedInterfaceOrientations.

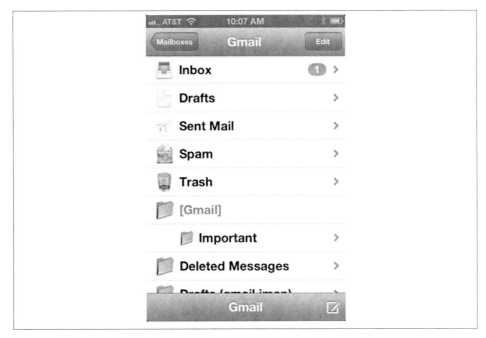

Figure 19-8. A familiar navigation interface

Bar Button Items

The buttons in a UIToolbar or a UINavigationBar are bar button items (UIBarButton-Item, a subclass of UIBarItem). A bar button item comes in one of two broadly different flavors:

Basic bar button item
> The bar button item looks and behaves like a simple button. A bar button item is not, however, the same as a UIButton; it has some button-like qualities, but it does not inherit from UIButton, from UIControl, or even from UIView. (It doesn't even have a frame.)

Custom view
> The bar button item is assigned, and appears as, a `customView`. The `customView` *is* a UIView — *any* kind of UIView. Thus, a bar button item can put *any* sort of view into a toolbar or navigation bar, including a real UIButton or anything else (and implementing any button behavior would then be the responsibility of that view).

Let's start with the basic bar button item (no custom view). A bar button item, like a tab bar item, inherits from UIBarItem the `title`, `image`, and `enabled` properties. A basic bar button item can have a title or an image, but generally not both; assigning an image removes the title if the bar button item is used in a navigation bar, but in a toolbar the title appears below the image. The image should usually be quite small (20×20 pixels is a good size).

A bar button item also has `target` and `action` properties. These give it its button-like behavior: tapping a bar button item can trigger an action method elsewhere (Chapter 11).

The overall look of a basic bar button item is determined by its `style` property; the choices are:

`UIBarButtonItemStyleBordered`

Looks like a button, with a round rectangular border around the image or title.

`UIBarButtonItemStylePlain`

In a toolbar, the bare title or image (or both) is displayed; if just a title, the text size is much larger by default than with a `UIBarButtonItemStyleBordered` button, but you can change that. Like a tab bar item's `image`, a bar button item's `image` must be a transparency mask when used with `UIBarButtonItemStylePlain` in a toolbar. In a navigation bar, `UIBarButtonItemStylePlain` is portrayed as if it were `UIBarButtonItemStyleBordered`.

`UIBarButtonItemStyleDone`

Bordered, and with a blue fill. As the name implies, this is suitable for a Done button in a temporary view.

The look of a basic bar button item can be customized. It can have a tint color or a background image, and, as with a tab bar item, you can control the font and style of the title. Full details appear in Chapter 25.

There are three ways to make a bar button item:

By borrowing it from the system

Instantiate UIBarButtonItem using `initWithBarButtonSystemItem:target:action:`. Consult the documentation for the list of available system items; they are not the same as for a tab bar item. You can't assign a title or change the image. (But you can change the tint color or assign a background image.)

By making your own basic bar button item

Instantiate UIBarButtonItem using `initWithTitle:style:target:action:` or `initWithImage:style:target:action:`.

An additional method, `initWithImage:landscapeImagePhone:style:target:action:`, lets you supply two images, one for portrait orientation, the other for landscape orientation; this is because by default the bar's height might change when the interface is rotated.

By making a custom view bar button item

Instantiate UIBarButtonItem using `initWithCustomView:`, supplying a UIView that the bar button item is to display. The bar button item has no action and target; the UIView itself must somehow implement button behavior if that's what you want. For example, the `customView` might be a UISegmentedButton, but then it is the UISegmentedButton's target and action that give it button behavior.

Bar button items in a toolbar are positioned automatically by the system. You can provide hints to help with this positioning. If you know that you'll be changing an item's title dynamically, you'll probably want its width to accommodate the longest possible title right from the start; to arrange that, set the `possibleTitles` property to an NSSet of strings that includes the longest title. Alternatively, you can supply an absolute `width`. Also, you can incorporate spacers into the toolbar; these are created with `initWithBarButtonSystemItem:target:action:`, but they have no visible appearance, and cannot be tapped. The `UIBarButtonSystemItemFlexibleSpace` is the one most frequently used; place these between the visible items to distribute the visible items equally across the width of the toolbar. There is also a `UIBarButtonSystemItemFixedSpace` whose `width` lets you insert a space of defined size.

Navigation Items

What appears in a navigation bar (UINavigationBar) depends upon the navigation items (UINavigationItem) in its stack. In a navigation interface, the navigation controller will manage the navigation bar's stack for you, but you must still configure each navigation item, which you do by setting properties of the `navigationItem` of each child view controller. The properties are as follows (see also Chapter 25):

`title` *or* `titleView`

Determines what is to appear in the center of the navigation bar when this navigation item is at the top of the stack.

The `title` is a string. Instead of setting `navigationItem.title`, however, you will usually set the view controller's `title` property instead; setting this property sets the `title` of the `navigationItem` automatically.

The `titleView` can be any kind of UIView; if set, it will be displayed instead of the `title`. The `titleView` can implement further UIView functionality; for example, it can be tappable. Even if you are using a `titleView`, you should still give your view controller a `title`, as it will be needed for the back button when a view controller is pushed onto the stack on top of this one.

Figure 19-1 shows the TidBITS News master view, with the navigation bar displaying a `titleView` which is a (tappable) image view; the master view's `title` is therefore not displayed. In the TidBITS News detail view controller, the `titleView` is a

Figure 19-9. A segmented control in the center of a navigation bar

segmented control providing a Previous and Next button, and the back button displays the master view controller's `title` (Figure 19-9).

prompt
> An optional string to appear centered above everything else in the navigation bar. The navigation bar's height will be increased to accommodate it.

rightBarButtonItem *or* rightBarButtonItems
> A bar button item or, respectively, an array of bar button items to appear at the right side of the navigation bar; the first item in the array will be rightmost.
>
> In Figure 19-1, the refresh button is a right bar button item; it has nothing to do with navigation, but is placed here merely because space is at a premium on the small iPhone screen. Similarly, in Figure 19-9, the text size button is a right bar button item, placed here for the same reason.

backBarButtonItem
> When a view controller is pushed on top of this view controller, the navigation bar will display at its left a button pointing to the left, whose title is this view controller's `title`. That button is *this* view controller's navigation item's `barBarButtonItem`. That's right: the back button displayed in the navigation bar belongs, not to the top item (the `navigationItem` of the current view controller), but to the back item (the `navigationItem` of the view controller that is one level down in the stack). In Figure 19-9, the back button in the detail view is the master view controller's default back button, displaying its `title`.
>
> The vast majority of the time, the default behavior is the behavior you'll want, and you'll leave the back button alone. If you wish, though, you can customize the back button by setting a view controller's `navigationItem.backBarButtonItem` so that it contains an image, or a title differing from the view controller's `title`. The best technique is to provide a new UIBarButtonItem whose target and action are nil (its style doesn't matter); the runtime will provide a correct target and action, so as to create a working back button:
>
> ```
> UIBarButtonItem* b =
>     [[UIBarButtonItem alloc] initWithTitle:@"Go Back"
>         style:UIBarButtonItemStylePlain target:nil action:nil];
> self.navigationItem.backBarButtonItem = b;
> ```

A BOOL property, hidesBackButton, allows the top navigation item to suppress display of the back item's back bar button item. Obviously, if you set this to YES, you'll need to consider providing some other means of letting the user navigate back.

leftBarButtonItem *or* leftBarButtonItems

A bar button item or, respectively, an array of bar button items to appear at the left side of the navigation bar; the first item in the array will be leftmost. The leftItems-SupplementBackButton property, if set to YES, allows both the back button and one or more left bar button items to appear.

Here's the view controller code that configures its navigation item to generate the navigation bar shown in Figure 19-1:

```
// title for back button in detail view
self.title = @"TidBITS";
// image to display in navigation bar
UIImageView* imv = [[UIImageView alloc] initWithImage:
    [UIImage imageNamed:@"tb_iphone_banner.png"]];
self.navigationItem.titleView = imv;
// reload button for navigation bar
UIBarButtonItem* b = [[UIBarButtonItem alloc]
    initWithBarButtonSystemItem:UIBarButtonSystemItemRefresh
    target:self action:@selector(doRefresh:)];
self.navigationItem.rightBarButtonItem = b;
```

A view controller's navigation item can have its properties set at any time while being displayed in the navigation bar. This (and not direct manipulation of the navigation bar) is the way to change the navigation bar's contents dynamically. For example, in one of my apps, the titleView is a progress view (UIProgressView, Chapter 25) that needs updating every second, and the right bar button should be either the system Play button or the system Pause button, depending on whether music from the library is playing, paused, or stopped (Figure 19-10). So I have a timer that periodically checks the state of the music player:

```
// change the progress view
if (self->_nowPlayingItem) {
    MPMediaItem* item = self->_nowPlayingItem;
    NSTimeInterval current = self.mp.currentPlaybackTime;
    NSTimeInterval total =
        [[item valueForProperty:MPMediaItemPropertyPlaybackDuration]
            doubleValue];
    self.prog.progress = current / total;
} else {
    self.prog.progress = 0;
}
// change the bar button
int whichButton = -1;
if ([self.mp playbackState] == MPMusicPlaybackStatePlaying)
    whichButton = UIBarButtonSystemItemPause;
```

Figure 19-10. A highly dynamic navigation bar

```
else if ([self.mp playbackState] == MPMusicPlaybackStatePaused ||
        [self.mp playbackState] == MPMusicPlaybackStateStopped)
    whichButton = UIBarButtonSystemItemPlay;
if (whichButton == -1)
    self.navigationItem.rightBarButtonItem = nil;
else {
    UIBarButtonItem* bb =
        [[UIBarButtonItem alloc]
            initWithBarButtonSystemItem:whichButton
            target:self action:@selector(doPlayPause:)];
    self.navigationItem.rightBarButtonItem = bb;
}
```

Toolbar Items

Each view controller to be pushed onto the navigation controller's stack is responsible for supplying the items to appear in the navigation interface's toolbar, if there is one. This is done by setting the view controller's `toolbarItems` property to an array of UIBarButtonItem instances. You can change the toolbar items even while the view controller's view and current `toolbarItems` are showing, optionally with animation, by sending `setToolbarItems:animated:` to the view controller.

A view controller has the power to specify that the navigation interface's toolbar should be hidden whenever it (the view controller) is on the stack. To do so, set the view controller's `hidesBottomBarWhenPushed` property to YES. The trick is that you must do this early enough, namely before the view loads. (The view controller's `viewDidLoad` is too late; its designated initializer is a good place.) The toolbar remains hidden from the time this view controller is pushed to the time it is popped, even if other view controllers are pushed and popped on top of it in the meantime. For more flexibility, you can call the UINavigationController's `setToolbarHidden:animated:` at any time.

Configuring a Navigation Controller

You configure a navigation controller by manipulating its stack of view controllers. If a view controller is in the stack, it is a child view controller of the navigation controller; the navigation controller is its `parentViewController`, and it is also the `navigation-Controller` of this view controller and its child view controllers at any depth. Thus a child view controller at any depth can learn that it is contained by a navigation controller and can get a reference to that navigation controller. The navigation controller retains the view controller as long as the view controller is on its stack; when the view controller is removed from the stack, the navigation controller releases the view controller, which is usually permitted to go out of existence at that point.

The normal way to manipulate a navigation controller's stack is one view controller at a time. When the navigation controller is instantiated, it is usually initialized with `init-WithRootViewController:`; this assigns the navigation controller a single root view controller, the view controller that goes at the bottom of the stack, whose view the navigation controller will initially display:

```
FirstViewController* fvc = [FirstViewController new];
UINavigationController* nav =
    [[UINavigationController alloc] initWithRootViewController:fvc];
self.window.rootViewController = nav;
```

Later, when the user asks to navigate to the right, you obtain the next view controller (typically by creating it) and push it onto the stack by calling `pushView-Controller:animated:` on the navigation controller, and the navigation controller displays its view:

```
// FirstViewController.m:
SecondViewController* svc = [SecondViewController new];
[self.navigationController pushViewController:svc animated:YES];
```

Typically, that's all there is to it! When the user taps the back button to navigate back to the left, the runtime will call `popViewControllerAnimated:` for you.

Instead of `initWithRootViewController:`, you might choose to create the navigation controller with `initWithNavigationBarClass:toolbarClass:`, in which case you'll have to set its root view controller in a subsequent line of code. The reason for wanting to set the navigation bar and toolbar class has to do with customization of the appearance of the navigation bar and toolbar; sometimes you'll create, say, a UIToolbar subclass for no other reason than to mark this kind of toolbar as needing a certain appearance. I'll explain about that in Chapter 25.

You can also set the UINavigationController's delegate; the delegate should adopt the UINavigationControllerDelegate protocol. The delegate receives an event before and after the navigation controller changes what view controller's view is displayed.

You can manipulate the stack more directly if you wish. You can call `popViewController-Animated:` yourself; to pop multiple items so as to leave a particular view controller at the top of the stack, call `popToViewController:animated:`, or to pop all the items down to the root view controller, call `popToRootViewControllerAnimated:`. All of these methods return the popped view controller (or view controllers, as an array), in case you want to do something with them.

To set the entire stack at once, call `setViewControllers:animated:`. You can access the stack through the `viewControllers` property. Manipulating the stack directly is the only way, for instance, to delete or insert a view controller in the middle of the stack.

The view controller at the top of the stack is the `topViewController`; the view controller whose view is displayed is the `visibleViewController`. Those will normally be the same view controller, but they needn't be, as the top view controller might be presenting a view controller. Other view controllers can be accessed through the `viewControllers` array by index number. The root item is at index `0`; if the array's `count` is c, the back item is at index `c-2`.

You'll notice that in the preceding code examples I didn't configure a view controller's `navigationItem` as I pushed it onto the stack. Sometimes, the code that creates a view controller may configure that view controller's `navigationItem`, but it is most common for a view controller to configure its own `navigationItem`. A view controller will be concerned to do this sufficiently early in its own lifetime. The earliest such point is an override of the designated initializer. Other possibilities are:

The view controller's `awakeFromNib`
> Obviously, this choice is possible only in cases where the view controller instance comes from a nib.

The view controller's `viewDidLoad` *(or* `loadView`*)*
> This seems an obvious choice, but Apple warns (in the UIViewController class reference, under `navigationItem`) that configuring a view controller's navigation item in conjunction with the creation of its view is not a good idea, because the circumstances under which the view is needed are not identical to the circumstances under which the navigation item is needed. However, Apple's own code examples often violate this warning.

When a child view controller's view is displayed, it is resized to fit the display area. The size of this area will depend on whether the navigation controller is showing a navigation bar or a toolbar or both (or neither). You should design your view in such a way as to be prepared for such resizing. Autoresizing settings or constraints can help here. Also, when editing your view in the nib editor, you can shrink the view to the size at which it will be displayed in the navigation interface, thus helping you judiciously situate your interface items; to do so, choose appropriately from the Top Bar and Bottom Bar pop-up menus of the Simulated Metrics section of the Attributes inspector.

A navigation controller's navigation bar can be hidden and shown with `setNavigationBarHidden:animated:`, and the toolbar can be hidden and shown with `setToolbarHidden:animated:`. The current view controller's view will be resized then and there; be sure to design your view to accommodate such dynamic resizing, if needed.

You can also configure a UINavigationController or any view controller that is to serve in a navigation interface in a nib or storyboard. In the Attributes inspector, use a navigation controller's Bar Visibility checkboxes to determine the presence of the navigation bar and toolbar. The navigation bar and toolbar are themselves subviews of the navigation controller, and you can configure them with the Attributes inspector as well. The root view controller can be specified; in a storyboard, it will be instantiated together with the navigation controller. Moreover, a view controller has a Navigation Item where you can specify its title, its prompt, and the text of its back button. (If a view controller in a nib or storyboard *doesn't* have a Navigation Item and you want to configure this view controller for use in a navigation interface, drag a Navigation Item from the Object library onto the view controller.) You can drag Bar Button Items into a view controller navigation bar in the canvas to set the left button and right button of its `navigationItem`. Moreover, the Navigation Item has outlets, one of which permits you to set its `titleView`. Plus, you can give a view controller Bar Button Items that will appear in the toolbar. Thus the configuration of a navigation view controller, its root view controller, and any other view controllers that will be pushed onto its stack can be performed to a certain degree in a nib or storyboard. (There are some things you can't do in a nib or storyboard, however; for example, you can't assign a navigation item multiple `rightBarButtonItems` or `leftBarButtonItems`.)

Page View Controller

A page view controller (UIPageViewController) has one or two child view controllers whose view(s) it displays within its own view. The user can then make a gesture (such as dragging) to navigate, revealing the view of a different view controller or pair of view controllers, analogously to the pages of a book.

Page view controllers were introduced in iOS 5, and are a great addition to the repertoire of built-in view controllers. Before iOS 5, I was accomplishing the same sort of thing in my flashcard apps by means of a scroll view (Chapter 20); the code was complex and tricky. With a page view controller, I was able to make my app's code far simpler.

To create a UIPageViewController, initialize it with `initWithTransitionStyle:navigationOrientation:options:`. Here's what the parameters mean:

`transitionStyle:`
    Your choices are:

  - `UIPageViewControllerTransitionStylePageCurl` (the old page curls off of, or onto, the new page)

  - `UIPageViewControllerTransitionStyleScroll` (the new page slides into view while the old page slides out).

`navigationOrientation:`
Your choices are:

- `UIPageViewControllerNavigationOrientationHorizontal`

- `UIPageViewControllerNavigationOrientationVertical`

`options:`
A dictionary. Possible keys are:

`UIPageViewControllerOptionSpineLocationKey`
The position of the spine (the pivot line around which page curl transitions rotate); relevant only if you're using the page curl transition. The value is an NSNumber wrapping one of the following:

- `UIPageViewControllerSpineLocationMin` (left or top)

- `UIPageViewControllerSpineLocationMid` (middle; two pages are shown at once)

- `UIPageViewControllerSpineLocationMax` (right or bottom)

`UIPageViewControllerOptionInterPageSpacingKey`
The spacing between successive pages; relevant only if you're using the scroll transition. The value is an NSNumber wrapping a float.

You then assign the page view controller a `dataSource`, which should conform to the UIPageViewControllerDataSource protocol, and configure the page view controller's initial content by handing it its initial child view controller(s). You do that by calling `setViewControllers:direction:animated:completion:`. Here are the parameters:

- The view controllers are an array of one or two view controllers — one if you're using the scroll transition or if the spine is `min` or `max`, two if the spine is `mid`.

- The direction can be `UIPageViewControllerNavigationDirectionForward` or `UIPageViewControllerNavigationDirectionBackward`; which you specify probably won't matter when you're assigning the page view controller its initial content.

- When you're assigning the page view controller its initial content, you probably won't want any animation.

Here's a minimal example. First I need to explain where my pages come from. I've got a UIViewController subclass called Pep and a data model consisting of an array (`self.pep`) of the names of the Pep Boys, along with eponymous image files in my app bundle portraying each Pep Boy. I initialize a Pep object by calling `initWithPep-Boy:nib:bundle:`, supplying the name of a Pep Boy from the array; Pep's `viewDid-Load` then fetches the corresponding image from the app bundle and assigns it as the image to a UIImageView within its own view. Thus, a page in the page view controller portrays an image of a named Pep Boy.

Here, then, is how I create the page view controller, in the app delegate's application:didFinishLaunchingWithOptions::

```
// make a page view controller
UIPageViewController* pvc =
    [[UIPageViewController alloc]
     initWithTransitionStyle: UIPageViewControllerTransitionStylePageCurl
     navigationOrientation: UIPageViewControllerNavigationOrientationHorizontal
     options: nil];
// give it an initial page
Pep* page = [[Pep alloc] initWithPepBoy: self.pep[0]  nib: nil bundle: nil];
[pvc setViewControllers: @[page]
            direction: UIPageViewControllerNavigationDirectionForward
             animated: NO completion: nil];
// give it a data source
pvc.dataSource = self;
// stick it in the window, retain the page view controller
self.window.rootViewController = pvc;
```

Just as with a navigation controller, you don't supply (or even create) the next page until the user tries to navigate to it. When that happens, the data source's pageView-Controller:viewControllerAfterViewController: or pageViewController:view-ControllerBeforeViewController: will be called; its job is to return the requested view controller. You'll need a strategy for doing that; the strategy you devise will depend on your model, that is, on how you're maintaining your data.

My data is an array of unique strings, so all I have to do is find the previous name or the next name in the array. Here's one of my data source methods:

```
-(UIViewController *)pageViewController:(UIPageViewController *)pvc
        viewControllerAfterViewController:(UIViewController *)viewController {
    NSString* boy = [(Pep*)viewController boy]; // string name of this Pep Boy
    NSUInteger ix = [self.pep indexOfObject:boy]; // find it in the data model
    ix++;
    if (ix >= [self.pep count])
        return nil; // there is no next page
    return [[Pep alloc] initWithPepBoy: self.pep[ix] nib: nil bundle: nil];
} // and "before" is similar
```

You can also call setViewControllers:direction:animated:completion: to change programmatically what page is being displayed, possibly with animation. I do so in my Latin flashcard app during drill mode (Figure 19-5), to advance to the next term in the current drill:

```
[self.terms shuffle];
Term* whichTerm = self.terms[0];
CardController* cdc = [[CardController alloc] initWithTerm:whichTerm];
[self.pvc setViewControllers:@[cdc]
               direction:UIPageViewControllerNavigationDirectionForward
               animated:YES completion:nil];
```

If you refer to `self` in the `completion` block of `setViewControllers:direction:`
`animated:completion:`, ARC will warn of a possible retain cycle. I don't know why
there would be a retain cycle, but I take no chances: I do the weak–strong dance described in Chapter 13.

As of this writing, the scroll transition style has a bug that the page curl transition style
doesn't have. In order to be ready with the next or previous page as the user starts to
scroll, the page view controller caches the next or previous view controller in the sequence. If you navigate manually with `setViewControllers:direction:animated:`
`completion:` to a view controller that isn't the next or previous in the sequence, and if
`animated:` is YES, this cache is not refreshed, and so if the user now navigates with a
scroll gesture, the wrong view controller is shown. I have developed a gut-wrenchingly
horrible workaround: in the `completion:` handler, perform the same navigation again
without animation. This requires doing the weak–strong dance and using delayed performance:

```
__weak UIPageViewController* pvcw = pvc;
[pvc setViewControllers:@[page]
    direction:UIPageViewControllerNavigationDirectionForward
    animated:YES completion:^(BOOL finished) {
        UIPageViewController* pvcs = pvcw;
        if (!pvcs) return;
        dispatch_async(dispatch_get_main_queue(), ^{
            [pvcs setViewControllers:@[page]
                direction:UIPageViewControllerNavigationDirectionForward
                animated:NO completion:nil];
        });
    }];
```

If you're using the scroll style, the page view controller will optionally display a page
indicator (a UIPageControl, see Chapter 25). The user can look at this to get a sense of
what page we're on, and can tap to the left or right of it to navigate. To get the page
indicator, you must implement two more data source methods; they are consulted once
in response to `setViewControllers:direction:animated:completion:`, which we
called initially to configure the page view controller, but if we never call it again, these
data source methods won't be called again either, as the page view controller can keep
track of the current index on its own. Here's my implementation for the Pep Boy example:

```
-(NSInteger)presentationCountForPageViewController:(UIPageViewController*)pvc {
    return [self.pep count];
}

-(NSInteger)presentationIndexForPageViewController:(UIPageViewController*)pvc {
    Pep* page = [pvc viewControllers][0];
    NSString* boy = page.boy;
    return [self.pep indexOfObject:boy];
}
```

It is also possible to assign a page view controller a delegate, which adopts the UIPage-ViewControllerDelegate protocol. You get an event when the user starts turning the page and when the user finishes turning the page, and you get a chance to change the spine location dynamically in response to a change in device orientation.

If you've assigned the page view controller the page curl transition, the user can ask for navigation by tapping at either edge of the view or by dragging across the view. These gestures are detected through two gesture recognizers, which you can access through the page view controller's gestureRecognizers property. The documentation suggests that you might change where the user can tap or drag by attaching them to a different view, and other customizations are possible as well. In this code, I change the page view controller's behavior so that the user must double tap to request navigation:

```
for (UIGestureRecognizer* g in pvc.gestureRecognizers)
    if ([g isKindOfClass: [UITapGestureRecognizer class]])
        ((UITapGestureRecognizer*)g).numberOfTapsRequired = 2;
```

Of course you are also free to add to the user's stock of gestures for requesting navigation. You can supply any controls or gesture recognizers that make sense for your app, and respond by calling setViewControllers:direction:animated:completion:. For example, if you're using the scroll transition style, there's no tap gesture recognizer, so the user can't tap at either edge of the page view controller's view to request navigation. Let's change that. I've added invisible views at either edge of my Pep view controller's view, with tap gesture recognizers attached. When the user taps, the tap gesture recognizer fires, and the action handler posts a notification whose object is the tap gesture recognizer. I receive this notification, use the tap gesture recognizer's view's tag to learn which view it is, and navigate accordingly:

```
[[NSNotificationCenter defaultCenter] addObserverForName:@"tap"
        object:nil queue:nil usingBlock:^(NSNotification *note) {
    UIGestureRecognizer* g = note.object;
    int which = g.view.tag;
    UIViewController* vc =
        which == 0 ?
        [self pageViewController:pvc
            viewControllerBeforeViewController:pvc.viewControllers[0]] :
        [self pageViewController:pvc
            viewControllerAfterViewController:pvc.viewControllers[0]];
    if (!vc) return;
```

```
    UIPageViewControllerNavigationDirection dir =
        which == 0 ?
        UIPageViewControllerNavigationDirectionReverse :
        UIPageViewControllerNavigationDirectionForward;
    [pvc setViewControllers:@[vc] direction:dir animated:YES completion:nil];
}];
```

One further bit of configuration, if you're using the page curl transition, is performed through the doubleSided property. If it is YES, the next page occupies the back of the previous page. The default is NO, unless the spine is in the middle, in which case it's YES and can't be changed. Your only option here, therefore, is to set it to YES when the spine isn't in the middle, and in that case the back of each page would be a sort of throwaway page, glimpsed by the user during the page curl animation. For example, you might make every other page a solid white view.

Container View Controllers

Built-in view controller subclasses such as UITabBarController, UINavigation-Controller, and UIPageViewController are parent view controllers: they accept and maintain child view controllers and manage swapping their views into and out of the interface. Such abilities and behaviors are formalized and generalized into the notion of a *container view controller*, so that your own custom UIViewController subclasses can do the same thing.

A UIViewController has a childViewControllers array, which is maintained for you. To act as a parent view controller, your UIViewController subclass must fulfill certain responsibilities.

When a view controller is to *become your view controller's child*, your view controller must do these things, in this order:

- Send addChildViewController: to itself, with the child as argument. The child is automatically added to your childViewControllers array and is retained.
- Get the child view controller's view into the interface (as a subview of your view controller's view), if that's what adding a child view controller means.
- Send didMoveToParentViewController: to the child with your view controller as its argument.

When a view controller is to *cease being your view controller's child*, your view controller must do these things, in this order:

- Send willMoveToParentViewController: to the child with a nil argument.
- Remove the child view controller's view from your interface.

- Send `removeFromParentViewController` to the child. The child is automatically removed from your `childViewControllers` array and is released.

This is a clumsy and rather poorly designed dance. The underlying reason for it is that a child view controller must always receive `willMoveToParentViewController:` followed by `didMoveToParentViewController:` (and your own child view controllers can take advantage of these events however you like). Well, it turns out that `addChildView-Controller:` sends `willMoveToParentViewController:` for you, and that `removeFrom-ParentViewController` sends `didMoveToParentViewController:` for you; so in each case you must send manually the *other* message, the one that adding or removing a child view controller *doesn't* send for you — and of course you must send it so that everything happens in the correct order, as dictated by the rules I just listed.

I'll illustrate two versions of the dance. First, we'll simply obtain a new child view controller and put its view into the interface, where no child view controller's view was previously:

```
UIViewController* vc = // whatever; this the initial child view controller
[self addChildViewController:vc]; // "will" is called for us
[self.view addSubview: vc.view];
// when we call "add", we must call "did" afterwards
[vc didMoveToParentViewController:self];
vc.view.frame = // whatever, or use constraints
```

This could very well be all you need to do. For example, consider Figure 19-3 and Figure 19-4. My view controller's view contains a UIPageViewController's view *as one of its subviews*. The only to achieve this legally and coherently is for my view controller — in this case, it's the app's root view controller — to act as the UIPageViewController's parent view controller. Here's the actual code as the root view controller configures its interface:

```
// create the page view controller
UIPageViewController* pvc =
[[UIPageViewController alloc]
 initWithTransitionStyle:UIPageViewControllerTransitionStylePageCurl
 navigationOrientation:UIPageViewControllerNavigationOrientationHorizontal
 options: @{UIPageViewControllerOptionSpineLocationKey:
            @(UIPageViewControllerSpineLocationMin)}
];
self.pvc = pvc;
pvc.delegate = self;
pvc.dataSource = self;

// add its view to the interface
[self addChildViewController:pvc];
[self.view addSubview:pvc.view];
[pvc didMoveToParentViewController:self];

// configure the view
```

```
pvc.view.translatesAutoresizingMaskIntoConstraints = NO;
[self.view addConstraints:
 [NSLayoutConstraint
  constraintsWithVisualFormat:@"|[pvc]|"
  options:0 metrics:nil views:@{@"pvc":pvc.view}]];
[self.view addConstraints:
 [NSLayoutConstraint
  constraintsWithVisualFormat:@"V:|[pvc]|"
  options:0 metrics:nil views:@{@"pvc":pvc.view}]];
```

Next, we'll replace one child view controller's view with another. The key is that the parent view controller sends itself `transitionFromViewController:toView-Controller:duration:options:animations:completion:`. The `options:` argument is a bitmask comprising the same possible options that apply to any block-based view transition (see "Block-Based View Animation" (page 481); these are the options whose names start with `UIViewAnimationOption...`). The `animations:` block is for *additional* view animations, as with any transition.

The `completion:` block will be important if this transition is part of removing or adding a child view controller. At the time `transitionFromViewController:...` is called, both view controllers involved must be children of the parent view controller; so if you're going to remove one of the view controllers as a child, you'll do it in the `completion:` block. Similarly, if you owe a new child view controller a `didMoveToParentView-Controller:` call, you'll use the `completion:` block to fulfill that debt.

To keep things simple, suppose that our view controller has one child view controller at a time, and displays the view of that child view controller within its own view. And let's say that when our view controller is handed a new child view controller, it substitutes that new child view controller for the old child view controller and replaces the old child view controller's view with the new child view controller's view. The two view controllers are called `fromvc` and `tovc`:

```
// set up the new view controller's view's frame
tovc.view.frame = // ... whatever
// must have both as children before we can transition between them
[self addChildViewController:tovc]; // "will" is called for us
// when we call "remove", we must call "will" (with nil) beforehand
[fromvc willMoveToParentViewController:nil];
[self transitionFromViewController:fromvc
                  toViewController:tovc
                          duration:0.4
                           options:UIViewAnimationOptionTransitionFlipFromLeft
                        animations:nil
                        completion:^(BOOL done){
                            // we called "add"; we must call "did" afterwards
                            [tovc didMoveToParentViewController:self];
                            [fromvc removeFromParentViewController];
                            // "did" is called for us
                        }];
```

If we're using constraints to position the new child view controller's view, where will we set up those constraints? Before `transitionFromViewController:...` is too soon, as the new child view controller's view is not yet in the interface. The `completion:` block is too late, as the animation has already taken place; unless we also want to set up the view's `frame` beforehand, the view will be added with no constraints and will have no size or position, so the animation will be performed and then the view will suddenly seem to pop into existence as we provide its constraints. The `animations:` block turns out to be a very good place:

```
tovc.view.translatesAutoresizingMaskIntoConstraints = NO;
// must have both as children before we can transition between them
[self addChildViewController:tovc]; // "will" called for us
// when we call remove, we must call "will" (with nil) beforehand
[fromvc willMoveToParentViewController:nil];
[self transitionFromViewController:fromvc
                  toViewController:tovc
                          duration:0.4
                           options:UIViewAnimationOptionTransitionFlipFromLeft
                        animations:^{
                            [self.panel addConstraints:
                             [NSLayoutConstraint
                              constraintsWithVisualFormat:@"H:|[v]|"
                              options:0 metrics:nil views:@{@"v":tovc.view}]];
                            [self.panel addConstraints:
                             [NSLayoutConstraint
                              constraintsWithVisualFormat:@"V:|[v]|"
                              options:0 metrics:nil views:@{@"v":tovc.view}]];
                        }
                        completion:^(BOOL done){
                            // when we call add, we must call "did" afterwards
                            [tovc didMoveToParentViewController:self];
                            [fromvc removeFromParentViewController];
                            // "did" is called for us
                        }];
```

Storyboards

A storyboard (see "Storyboard-Instantiated View Controller" (page 585)) collects, in a single file, multiple view controllers — both parent and children, both presenter and presented. Each view controller is part of a *scene*, analogous to a nib containing that view controller and any related top-level objects. Special connections are drawn between view controllers; these are of two kinds:

Relationship

If view controller A has view controller B as its child *from the outset* (as with a navigation controller and its root view controller, or a tab bar controller and its child view controllers), the connection is a *relationship* emanating from view controller A. View controllers connected by a relationship are instantiated together:

---

when view controller A is instantiated, view controller B is instantiated along with it, because it is needed immediately.

To draw a relationship in a storyboard, Control-drag from a parent view controller to another view controller. If this is a built-in parent view controller type, the little HUD that appears lets you specify a "Relationship segue." (This name is misleading, as a parent–child relationship is in no sense a segue.)

Segue

If view controller B's view is to be replaced by view controller C's view *at some future time* (as with an original presenter and a presented view controller, or a navigation controller's child and a view controller that will later be pushed onto the stack on top of it), the connection is a *segue*. View controller C won't be instantiated until the segue is triggered; at that time, view controller C will be handed over to the appropriate view controller as its child, just as you would have done if you had created it in code.

The segue may emanate from view controller B itself, in which case it will be up to your code to trigger the segue. Often, though, you'll take advantage of a shortcut and have the segue emanate from some interface object in view controller B's view; the idea of the shortcut is that the segue can be triggered automatically when the user taps that interface object.

A segue is directional; it has a source view controller and a destination view controller (view controllers B and C in our hypothetical example). A segue in a storyboard is a full-fledged object, an instance of UIStoryboardSegue (or your custom subclass thereof). It can be assigned a string identifier (in its Attributes inspector); you will just about always want to do this.

To draw a segue in a storyboard, Control-drag from a view controller or a triggering interface object in its view to another view controller. The little HUD calls a segue an "Action segue," and lets you specify a style, which you can change later; I'll explain about segue styles in a moment.

A view controller instantiated from a storyboard has a non-nil `storyboard` property pointing to the storyboard that it comes from; this provides an additional way (besides `storyboardWithName:bundle:`) of getting a reference to a storyboard.

A storyboard might very well contain all the view controller instances your app will ever need over the course of its lifetime. Not only that: the storyboard effectively maps out or diagrams the way those instances will relate, and thus tells the story (hence the name!) of how your app's interface will evolve. It is this concentration of all view controller creation into a single diagrammatic locus that makes storyboards so attractive — and not, I hasten to stress, that a storyboard reduces the amount of code you'll have to write, which might not be the case at all.

Segues

Here are the primary concerns in using and configuring segues in a storyboard:

How to trigger a segue

Wherever possible, you'll probably draw the segue as a connection from the interface object that is to trigger it. The segue will then be triggered automatically. For example, when a button is to trigger the segue, you draw the connection from the button to the destination view controller; the runtime assumes that you want the segue to be triggered in response to the button's Touch Up Inside event. When a table view cell is to trigger the segue, you draw the connection from the cell to the destination view controller; the runtime assumes that you want the segue to be triggered in response to the user selecting the cell.

If that sort of behavior doesn't cover your needs, you can trigger the segue yourself, in code, by calling `performSegueWithIdentifier:sender:` on the source view controller.

New in iOS 6, the source view controller can also *prevent* a segue from being triggered automatically by a user action. Implement `shouldPerformSegueWithIdentifier:sender:` and return NO if you don't want this segue triggered on this occasion.

How to customize the transition performed by a segue

A segue is a nib object with an Attributes inspector. Here, the Style pop-up menu lets you specify the segue as a navigation controller ("Push") segue or as a presenting ("Modal") segue. (It's odd that the storyboard editor perpetuates the term "Modal" just when the rest of Cocoa is trying to deprecate it.) If you choose "Modal," you can use the Transition pop-up menu to specify the transition type. A checkbox (new in iOS 6) lets you turn off transition animation altogether.

If the default transitions don't cover your needs, you can make a custom UIStoryboardSegue subclass. In the storyboard editor, you'll set the segue's Style pop-up menu to "Custom" and type the name of your UIStoryboardSegue subclass in the Segue Class field. In your UIStoryboardSegue subclass, you'll implement `perform`, calling the appropriate transition method, just as you would have done if you weren't using a storyboard. For example, for a custom transition when presenting a view controller, you'd implement `perform` to call `presentViewController:animated:completion:`. Your code can work out what segue is being triggered by examining the segue's `identifier`, `sourceViewController`, and `destinationViewController` properties.

How to configure a view controller before a segue to it

Before a segue is performed, the source view controller is sent `prepareForSegue:sender:`. The view controller can work out what segue is being triggered by examining the segue's `identifier` and `destinationViewController` properties, and the `sender` is the interface object that was tapped to trigger to the segue (or, if `performSegueWithIdentifier:sender:` was called in code, whatever object was supplied as the `sender:` argument). This is the moment when the source view controller and the destination view controller meet; the source view controller can thus perform configurations on the destination view controller, hand it data, and so forth.

The obvious example is a presented view controller. As I said earlier in this chapter, you'll very likely have data to pass along to a presented view controller as you create it; I gave the example of my Latin's app's DrillViewController, which has an `initWithData:` method exactly so that it can be handed the data it needs in order to operate. With a storyboard, where you're not in charge of instantiating the presented view controller, you'll need to hand it its data in some other way and at some other time. That's what `prepareForSegue:sender:` lets you do.

This is the part of storyboard usage that I like least. `prepareForSegue:sender:` feels like a blunt instrument: the `destinationViewController` arrives typed as a generic `id`, and it is up to your code to cast it to its actual type and configure it. Moreover, if more than one segue emanates from a view controller, they are all bottlenecked through the same `prepareForSegue:sender:` implementation, which thus devolves into a series of conditions in order to distinguish them.

How to reverse the transition performed by a segue
In broadest terms, this is easy, because the involvement of the storyboard makes no difference whatever. A pushed view controller in a navigation interface, of course, might be popped automatically through its back button. But to pop a pushed view controller in code, or to dismiss a presented view controller, you can just do in code whatever you would have done without the storyboard. However, this seems inelegant and clumsy, so iOS 6 introduces the notion of an *unwind segue*, which is the subject of the next section.

As I explained earlier in this chapter, a storyboard invites you to design a view controller's view directly inside the view controller's representation in the canvas (though this is not the only way a view controller can get its view, as you know). You can easily construct most of the view controller architectures discussed so far in this chapter, especially if you start with the storyboard version of an Xcode project template:

- Your app has a main storyboard, which is pointed to by the *Info.plist* and is loaded automatically by `UIApplicationMain` (as discussed earlier in this chapter, "Storyboard-Instantiated View Controller" (page 585)). A universal app typically has *two* main storyboards, both pointed to by the *Info.plist*.

- Your app's root view controller will be the main storyboard's initial view controller, and will automatically be instantiated and assigned to the window's `rootView-`

`Controller` by `UIApplicationMain`. The Single View Application template storyboard demonstrates; it consists of *only* an initial view controller.

- To signify a future transition from a view controller to a presented view controller, draw a segue from the first view controller — typically from a triggering button inside its view — to the second view controller and configure it as "Modal." The Utility Application template storyboard for iPhone demonstrates, setting the presented view controller's delegate in `prepareForSegue:sender:`.

- To configure a tab bar controller with its child view controllers, draw relationships from the tab bar controller to the other view controllers. The Tabbed Application template demonstrates.

- To configure a navigation controller with its initial root view controller, draw a relationship from the navigation controller to a view controller. To signify a future push transition, where a subsequent view controller will be pushed on top of this one in the navigation stack, draw a segue from the navigation controller's root view controller to the new view controller and configure it as "Push." The Master–Detail Application template for iPhone demonstrates.

- To configure a page view controller with its initial child view controller, use code. A storyboard doesn't let you draw a relationship from a page view controller! In the Page-Based Application template, the page view controller is created and configured in code.

Custom container view controllers in a storyboard are discussed in a later section.

Unwind Segues

The purpose of an unwind segue (new in iOS 6) is to help solve the problem of reverting from the current view controller, which was summoned through a normal segue, back to an earlier view controller — at the same time possibly communicating data back to that earlier view controller. For example, an unwind segue would be a way to communicate from a presented view controller back to its original presenter (or some other view controller) before it itself goes out of existence. Earlier in this chapter, I showed how to use a protocol and a delegate architecture to accomplish this. An unwind segue is the storyboard-based way to accomplish the same sort of backward communication linkage. Also, an unwind segue actually takes the current view controller out of existence; to take down a presented view controller without an unwind segue, you'd have to call `dismissViewControllerAnimated:completion:` yourself.

An unwind segue can't possibly work like a normal segue. A normal segue emanates from its source view controller and points to its destination view controller; when the segue is triggered, the segue instantiates the destination view controller. But when we're about to get rid of view controller B which was originally presented by a segue from view controller A, the instance of view controller A already exists. The current view controller must not create a new view controller A instance as it goes out of existence; it must go out of existence but send a message first to a certain existing view controller A instance. Thus, in order for an unwind segue to work, the storyboard needs a way to specify not merely a class of view controller but a particular already existing instance. But from the storyboard's point of view, there aren't yet any particular existing instances, so how can this be done?

Apple's solution is frankly ingenious. Somewhere, in the class of a view controller that appears in the storyboard *earlier* in the chain of segues leading to the current view controller, you implement an *unwind method*; this must be a method returning an IBAction (as a hint to the storyboard editor) and taking a single parameter, a UIStoryboardSegue. This causes the Exit proxy object in the storyboard editor to spring to life. You can now draw a segue from a triggering interface object in the current view controller's scene (or the view controller itself) to the Exit proxy object *in the same scene*. The storyboard editor looks back along the chain of segues, sees the unwind method, and allows you to form a kind of action connection to the Exit proxy object. This connection is an unwind segue, whose sourceViewController is the current view controller.

That, however, is only half the story. I have not yet told you what will actually happen when the app runs and the user taps the triggering interface object in the current view controller's interface (or if you trigger the unwind segue yourself, in code). To understand what happens, envision a *view controller chain* leading all the way back from the current view controller, up the view controller hierarchy, to the app's root view controller:

- If a view controller was instantiated by the triggering of a segue, the next view controller up the chain is the view controller from which that segue emanates, its sourceViewController. (The runtime uses some clever record-keeping when a segue is triggered to ensure that the segue trail will be reversible.)
- If a view controller was *not* instantiated by the triggering of a segue, then it has either a parentViewController or a presentingViewController. The next view controller up the chain is that view controller.

A little thought will show that this covers every possibility leading all the way up to the root view controller.

(In fact, it keeps working even if we run out of segues completely. The app's entire view controller hierarchy might not come from a storyboard. The view controller hierarchy could, for example, start out with a root view controller instantiated manually in code, and then proceed to a view controller instantiated from a storyboard through instantiateInitialViewController or instantiateViewControllerWith-Identifier:. That doesn't matter; there is still a well-defined chain and it still leads all the way up to the root view controller.)

Now we're ready to see what happens when an unwind segue is triggered. The basic scenario is as follows:

1. The runtime walks the view controller chain upward from the current view controller instance toward the root view controller, looking for a view controller that implements the unwind method named by the action connection to the Exit proxy object.

2. Let's say that it finds one. Let's call it the *target view controller*. Then the runtime completes the configuration of the unwind segue with the target view controller as its `destinationViewController`. (The unwind segue's `sourceViewController` is the current view controller, the one we started in.)

3. The current view controller's `prepareForSegue:identifier:` is called (preceded by its `shouldPerformSegueWithIdentifier:sender:`, which can stop the whole process dead at this point by returning NO). The two view controllers are thus already in contact, since the target view controller is the segue's `destinationViewController`. This is an opportunity for the current view controller to hand information back before it is destroyed.

4. The target view controller's unwind method is called. Its parameter is a segue which can be identified through its `identifier` property, having the current view controller as its `sourceViewController`. Thus the two view controllers are in contact again. This is an opportunity for the target view controller to grab information from the current view controller before the latter is destroyed.

5. The entire chain from the current view controller to the target view controller is unwound: the current view controller, and all the view controllers in the chain between it and the target view controller, go out of existence! (The animation will be the reverse of the segue that brought the current view controller into existence.)

The point of this procedure is that an unwind segue can unwind *as far as you like* up the view controller chain. Consider, for example, the following storyboard architecture:

- A navigation controller.
- Its root view controller, connected by a relationship from the navigation controller. (This might be the master controller in a master–detail architecture.)
- A second view controller, connected by a push segue from the navigation controller's root view controller. (This might be the detail controller in a master–detail architecture.)
- An extra view controller, connected by a modal segue from the second view controller.

Now the user summons all of these view controllers' views in succession: in the navigation interface, the user moves from the master view to the detail view, and in the detail view, summons the extra view, which appears as a presented view covering everything. In the presented view there's a Done button, which happens to be connected to the extra view controller's Exit proxy object. The user taps the Done button. What happens?

The answer depends on where the unwind method is found. If the unwind method is found in the detail view controller, the presented view just goes away, and we're left back in the detail view. But if the unwind method is found in the master view controller, the presented view goes away *and the detail view is popped from the navigation interface*, and we're left in the master view.

This raises all sorts of possibilities for dictating dynamically, in code, on particular occasions, what unwind method should be executed in what view controller. Apple has thought of this, and has added some extensions and modifications to the process whereby the runtime searches for an unwind method.

A view controller that implements the unwind method we're looking for can shrug off the runtime, during its walk up the view controller chain, by implementing `canPerform-UnwindSegueAction:fromViewController:withSender:` to return NO. In that case, the runtime will ignore this view controller, and will continue walking up the chain of view controllers.

If a view controller was not instantiated by a segue but has a parent view controller, the runtime gives precedence to that parent. Regardless of what the child view controller implements or returns, the runtime looks to see whether the parent implements `view-ControllerForUnwindSegueAction:fromViewController:withSender:`. The parent may do one of the following things:

- It may return itself or (more likely) one of its children as the one whose unwind method should be called.
- It may call `super` and return the result to let the runtime do what it would have done if this method hadn't been implemented.
- It may return nil to tell the runtime to proceed up the chain from here.

For example, let's return to our architecture of a navigation controller, its master view controller child, its detail view controller child, and an extra presented view controller. Suppose that both the master view controller and the detail view controller implement the unwind method, but the detail view controller returns NO from `canPerformUnwind-SegueAction:...`. So the runtime's walk up the chain proceeds to the master view controller. Even if the master view controller returns YES from `canPerformUnwindSegue-Action:...`, the runtime does *not* simply call the master view controller's unwind method. The master view controller is the end of a chain of segues and has a parent, so the runtime consults the parent, the navigation controller.

If the navigation controller implements viewControllerForUnwindSegueAction:fromViewController:withSender:, it can return either the master view controller or the detail view controller. The unwind method in that controller will then be called, regardless of what that view controller returns from canPerformUnwindSegueAction:....

Alternatively, if the navigation controller calls super and returns the result, the runtime returns to where it was in the walk, namely the master view controller. If the master view controller doesn't return NO from canPerformUnwindSegueAction:..., its unwind method is called. Otherwise, the walk continues up through the navigation controller.

(Whatever view controller is returned from viewControllerForUnwindSegueAction:fromViewController:withSender: had better implement the unwind method we're looking for. Otherwise, we'll crash when that message is sent to that view controller!)

In addition, a parent view controller can completely take charge of this unwind segue by substituting a different segue. It does this by implementing segueForUnwindingToViewController:fromViewController:identifier:. The idea is to return an instance of a custom segue class whose perform method dictates the entire transition.

For example, consider once again our sequence of a navigation controller, its master view controller, its detail view controller, and a presented extra view controller. By default, if we unwind directly from the presented view controller to the master view controller, we get only the reverse of the presented view controller's original animation. That's not very clear to the user, since in fact we're going back two steps. To improve things, the navigation controller can substitute a different segue:

```
-(UIStoryboardSegue*)segueForUnwindingToViewController:(UIViewController*)tvc
        fromViewController:(UIViewController*)fvc identifier:(NSString*)ident {
    return [[MyAmazingSegue alloc] initWithIdentifier:@"amazing"
                                    source:fvc
                                    destination:self.viewControllers[0]];
}
```

And that segue would then perform the two-stage transition:

```
-(void)perform {
    UIViewController* vc1 = self.sourceViewController;
    UIViewController* vc2 = vc1.presentingViewController;
    [vc1 dismissViewControllerAnimated:YES completion:^{
        [(UINavigationController*)vc2 popToRootViewControllerAnimated:YES];
    }];
}
```

Storyboards and Custom Container View Controllers

Another new iOS 6 storyboard feature is the ability to represent custom view controller containment. This done using a *container view* and an embed segue.

A container view is a view object in the Object library. Its job is to define where a child view controller's view is to go. You drag the container view into a custom parent view controller's view. The storyboard provides another view controller, with a segue from the container view to that view controller; the segue is automatically an embed segue. This means: "Make this other view controller a child of the first view controller, and put its view inside the container view."

That might be all you need to do. The embed segue, unless you prevent it, is triggered automatically when the parent view controller is instantiated. It acts like a normal segue in the sense that prepareForSegue: is called on the parent view controller, and it then proceeds to instantiate the child view controller. But it does more; it makes the child view controller the parent view controller's child, and puts its view into the interface. By default, this has already happened by the time the parent view controller's viewDid-Load is called!

Now let's go further. Draw a "modal" segue emanating from the child view controller to yet another view controller. Just as you would expect, this sets up the second view controller as a future presented view controller. And if this is an iPad app, you can specify that the second view controller's modalPresentationStyle is UIModalPresentation-CurrentContext — you'll have to set that up in prepareForSegue:..., as there's no way to do it in the storyboard — and that the embedded view controller defines the context, and sure enough, when you run the app, the presented view appears in place of the child view inside your main view!

Other configurations are more complicated — but they are possible. For example, suppose you start with the child view controller, and your goal is to cause this child view controller's view to be replaced by another child view controller's view. You can do it, but you'll have to write a custom segue subclass and do all the work yourself. When the segue from the first child view controller is triggered, it will be up to you to add the second view controller as a child and call transitionFromViewController:... just as you would have done if a storyboard weren't involved (as I described earlier in this chapter).

View Controller Lifetime Events

As views come and go, driven by view controllers and the actions of the user, events arrive that give your view controller the opportunity to respond to the various stages of its existence. By overriding these methods, your UIViewController subclass can perform appropriate tasks. Most commonly, you'll override viewWillAppear:, viewDid-

Appear:, viewWillDisappear:, or viewDidDisappear:. Note that *you must call super* in your override of any of these four methods.

Let's take the case of a UIViewController pushed onto the stack of a navigation controller. It receives, in this order, the following messages:

- willMoveToParentViewController:
- viewWillAppear:
- updateViewConstraints
- viewWillLayoutSubviews
- viewDidLayoutSubviews
- viewDidAppear:
- didMoveToParentViewController:

When this same UIViewController is popped off the stack of the navigation controller, it receives, in this order, the following messages:

- willMoveToParentViewController: (with argument nil)
- viewWillDisappear:
- viewDidDisappear:
- didMoveToParentViewController: (with argument nil)

In these names, the notions "appear" and "disappear" reflect the view's insertion into and removal from the interface. A view that has appeared (or has not yet disappeared) is in the window; it is part of your app's active view hierarchy. A view that has disappeared (or has not yet appeared) is not.

Disappearance can happen because the UIViewController itself is taken out of commission, but it can also happen because another UIViewController supersedes it. For example, let's take the case of the UIViewController functioning as the root view controller of a navigation controller. When another view controller is pushed on top of it, the root view controller gets these messages:

- viewWillDisappear:
- viewDidDisappear:

By the same token, appearance can happen because this UIViewController has been brought into play, but it can also happen because some other UIViewController is no longer superseding it. For example, when a view controller is popped from a navigation controller, the view controller that was below it in the stack receives these events:

- `viewWillAppear:`

- `viewWillLayoutSubviews`

- `viewDidLayoutSubviews`

- `viewDidAppear:`

You may well want a way to distinguish these cases — that is, to find out precisely *why* your view is appearing or disappearing. You can find out, from within the four "appear"/ "disappear" methods, more about why they are being called, by calling these methods on `self`:

- `isBeingPresented`

- `isBeingDismissed`

- `isMovingToParentViewController`

- `isMovingFromParentViewController`

Here are some examples of how these events are used in my own apps:

- A certain view in a navigation controller needs the toolbar, whereas other views do not. In its `viewDidAppear:` and `viewWillDisappear:`, the view controller calls the navigation controller to show and hide the toolbar.

- In a master–detail interface, the root view in a navigation interface displays a table. The data displayed by the root view's table might change while the user is working in a detail view, so I reload the root view table's data in the view controller's `view-WillAppear:`.

- A view that can be pushed onto a navigation controller's stack contains a progress view that is periodically updated through a repeating timer. This timer needs to be in existence and running only when this view is in the interface. So I create the timer in the view controller's `viewWillAppear:` and invalidate and destroy it in `viewDid-Disappear:`. This architecture also allows me to avoid the retain cycle that could result if I waited to invalidate the timer in a `dealloc` that might never come (Chapter 12).

- A certain view that can be shown by switching tab views must reflect the current state of certain user defaults. I refresh the view's interface in its `viewWillAppear:`, so that whenever it does appear, it is current.

- In a master–detail interface, the detail is a long scrollable text. Whenever the user returns to a previously read detail view, I want to scroll it to wherever it was previously scrolled to. So I save the scroll position for this detail view into the user defaults in its `viewWillDisappear:`.

In the multitasking world, `viewWillDisappear:` and `viewDidDisappear:` are *not* called when the app is suspended into the background. Moreover, once suspended, your app might never return to life; it could be terminated in the background. Some of your functionality performed in `viewWillDisappear:` and `viewDidDisappear:` may have to be duplicated in response to an application lifetime event (Chapter 11), such as `applicationDidEnterBackground:`, if you are to cover every case.

A custom parent view controller, as I explained earlier, must effectively send `willMove-ToParentViewController:` and `didMoveToParentViewController:` to its children manually. But other lifetime events, such as the appear events and rotation events, are normally passed along automatically. Alternatively, you can take charge of calling these events manually, by implementing these methods:

`shouldAutomaticallyForwardRotationMethods`
  If you override this method to return YES, you are responsible for calling these methods on your view controller's children:

  - `willRotateToInterfaceOrientation:duration:`
  - `willAnimateRotationToInterfaceOrientation:duration:`
  - `didRotateFromInterfaceOrientation:`

  I have no idea how common it is to take charge of sending these events manually; I've never done it.

`shouldAutomaticallyForwardAppearanceMethods`
  If you override this method to return YES, you are responsible for seeing that these methods on your view controller's children are called:

  - `viewWillAppear:`
  - `viewDidAppear:`
  - `viewWillDisappear:`
  - `viewDidDisappear:`

  In iOS 6, however, you do *not* do this by calling these methods directly. The reason is that you have no access to the correct moment for sending them. Instead, you call these two methods on your child view controller:

  - `beginAppearanceTransition:animated:`; the first parameter is a BOOL saying whether this view controller's view is about to appear (YES) or disappear (NO)
  - `endAppearanceTransition`

Here's an example of a parent view controller swapping one child view controller and its view for another, while taking charge of notifying the child view controllers of the appearance and disappearance of their views (I've put asterisks to call attention to the additional method calls):

```
[self addChildViewController:tovc];
[fromvc willMoveToParentViewController:nil];
[fromvc beginAppearanceTransition:NO animated:YES]; // *
[tovc beginAppearanceTransition:YES animated:YES]; // *
[UIView transitionFromView:fromvc.view
                  toView:tovc.view
              duration:0.4
               options:UIViewAnimationOptionTransitionFlipFromLeft
            completion:^(BOOL finished) {
                [tovc endAppearanceTransition]; // *
                [fromvc endAppearanceTransition]; // *
                [tovc didMoveToParentViewController:self];
                [fromvc removeFromParentViewController];
            }];
```

The key thing to notice about that code is that we do *not* call transitionFromView-Controller:toViewController:...! The reason is that it takes charge of sending the "appear"/"disappear" calls to the children itself. To work around this, we perform the transition animation directly.

View Controller Memory Management

Memory is at a premium on a mobile device. Thus you want to minimize your use of memory — especially when the memory-hogging objects you're retaining are not needed at this moment. Because a view controller is the basis of so much of your application's architecture, it is likely to be the main place where you'll concern yourself with releasing unneeded memory.

The object of releasing memory, in the multitasking world, is partly altruistic and partly selfish. You want to keep your memory usage as low as possible so that other apps can be launched and so that the user can switch between numerous backgrounded apps, bringing each one to the front and finding it in the state in which it was suspended. You also want to prevent your app from being terminated. If your app is backgrounded and is considered a memory hog, it may be terminated when memory runs short; hence you want to reduce your memory usage at the time the app goes into the background. If your app is warned that memory is running short and it doesn't take appropriate action to reduce its memory usage, your app may be killed even while running in the foreground!

The runtime helps you keep your view controller's memory usage as low as possible by managing its memory for you in a special way. A view controller itself is usually lightweight, but a view is memory-intensive. A view controller can persist without its view being visible to the user — for example, because a presented view has replaced its view, or because it is in a tab interface but is not currently selected, or because it is in a navigation interface but is not at the top of the stack. In such a situation, if memory is getting short, then even though the view controller itself persists, the runtime may release its view's backing store (the cached bitmap representing the view's drawn contents). The view will then be redrawn when and if it is shown again later.

 Before iOS 6, when your view's backing store was to be released, your view controller received an event, viewDidUnload, and was expected to respond by releasing other retained interface objects; and your view controller had to be prepared for the possibility that viewDidLoad would later be called again, and its view would have be reconfigured from scratch. In iOS 5, another event was added, viewWillUnload. In iOS 6, Apple has reversed direction completely; the entire view-releasing mechanism has been declared a failure, and your view controller will *never* receive viewWillUnload or viewDidUnload (and should not implement them). viewDidLoad is now called only once in your view controller's lifetime.

In addition, if memory runs low, your view controller may be sent didReceiveMemoryWarning. This call will have been preceded by a call to the app delegate's applicationDidReceiveMemoryWarning:, together with a UIApplicationDidReceiveMemoryWarningNotification posted to any registered objects. You are invited to respond by releasing any data that you can do without. Do not release data that you can't readily and quickly recreate! The documentation advises that you should call super.

If you're going to release data in didReceiveMemoryWarning, you must concern yourself with how you're going to get it back. A simple and reliable mechanism is *lazy loading* — a getter that reconstructs or fetches the data if it is nil.

In this example, in didReceiveMemoryWarning we write myBigData out as a file to disk (Chapter 36) and release it from memory. At the same time, we override the synthesized accessors for myBigData (using the technique shown in Example 12-11) so that if we subsequently try to get myBigData and it's nil, we then try to fetch it from disk and, if we succeed, we delete it from disk (to prevent stale data) and set myBigData before returning it. The result is that myBigData is released when there's low memory, reducing our memory overhead until we actually *need* myBigData, at which time asking for its value (through the getter or property) restores it:

```
@interface ViewController ()
@property (nonatomic, strong) NSData* myBigDataAlias;
@property (nonatomic, strong) NSData* myBigData;
@end
```

```
@implementation ViewController
@synthesize myBigDataAlias = _myBigData;

- (void) setMyBigData: (NSData*) data {
    self.myBigDataAlias = data;
}

- (NSData*) myBigData {
    if (!self.myBigDataAlias) {
        NSFileManager* fm = [NSFileManager new];
        NSString* f = [NSTemporaryDirectory()
                            stringByAppendingPathComponent:@"myBigData"];
        BOOL fExists = [fm fileExistsAtPath:f];
        if (fExists) {
            NSData* data = [NSData dataWithContentsOfFile:f];
            self.myBigDataAlias = data;
            NSError* err = nil;
            BOOL ok = [fm removeItemAtPath:f error:&err];
            NSAssert(ok, @"Couldn't remove temp file");
        }
    }
    return self.myBigDataAlias;
}

- (void)didReceiveMemoryWarning {
    [super didReceiveMemoryWarning];
    if (self->_myBigData) {
        NSString* f = [NSTemporaryDirectory()
                            stringByAppendingPathComponent:@"myBigData"];
        [_myBigData writeToFile:f atomically:NO];
        self.myBigData = nil;
    }
}
@end
```

Xcode gives you a way to test low-memory circumstances artificially. Run your app in the Simulator; in the Simulator, choose Hardware → Simulate Memory Warning. I don't believe this has any actual effect on memory, but a memory warning of sufficient severity is sent to your app, so you can see the results of triggering your low-memory response code, including the app delegate's applicationDidReceiveMemoryWarning: and your view controller's didReceiveMemoryWarning.

On the device, the equivalent is to call an undocumented method:

```
[[UIApplication sharedApplication]
    performSelector:@selector(_performMemoryWarning)];
```

That's helpful if your app won't run on the Simulator (because it uses device-only features), and you can use it in the Simulator as well; basically it's the code equivalent of Hardware → Simulate Memory Warning. (And remember to remove this code when it is no longer needed, as the App Store won't accept an app that calls an undocumented method.)

You might also wish to concern yourself with releasing memory when your app is about to be suspended. To do so, you'll probably want your view controller to be registered with the shared application to receive `UIApplicationDidEnterBackground-Notification`. When this notification arrives, you might like to release any easily restored memory-hogging objects, so that your app won't be terminated in the background if memory runs tight. For example, this would be another opportunity for me to write out `myBigData` to disk and nilify it, just as in the previous example.

Testing how your app's memory behaves in the background isn't easy. In a WWDC 2011 video, an interesting technique is demonstrated. The app is run under Instruments on the device, using the virtual memory instrument, and is then backgrounded by pressing the Home button, thus revealing how much memory it voluntarily relinquishes at that time. Then a special memory-hogging app is launched on the device: its interface loads and displays a very large image in a UIImageView. Even though your app is backgrounded and suspended, the virtual memory instrument continues to track its memory usage, and you can see whether further memory is reclaimed under pressure from the demands of the memory-hogging app in the foreground.

State Restoration

In the multitasking world, when the user leaves your app and then later returns to it, one of two things might have happened in the meantime (Chapter 11):

Your app was suspended
> Your app was suspended in the background, and remained suspended while the user did something else. When the user returns to your app, the system simply unfreezes your app, and there it is, looking just as it did when the user left it.

Your app was terminated
> Your app was suspended in the background, and then, as the user worked with other apps, a moment came where the system decided it needed the resources (such as memory) being held by your suspended app. Therefore it terminated your app. When the user returns to your app, the app launches from scratch.

For most apps, a general goal should be to make those two situations more or less indistinguishable to the user. It should always feel to the user as if the app is being resumed from where it left off the last time it was in the foreground, even if in fact the app was terminated while suspended in the background. This goal is *state restoration*. Your app has a state at every moment: some view controller's view is occupying the screen, and views within it are displaying certain values (for example, a certain switch is set to ON, or a certain table view is scrolled to a certain position). The idea of state restoration is to save that information when the app goes into the background, and use it to make all those things true again if the app is subsequently launched from scratch.

Prior to iOS 6, this was quite a difficult problem, and most apps probably solved it only partially, if at all. It was hard to know exactly what information to save, in what form to save it, or even where to save it — a typical approach was to misuse user preferences (NSUserDefaults) to store something that wasn't really a user preference at all. And the effort involved was a sad expenditure of developer ingenuity, given that state restoration was a near-universal goal, yet had to be reinvented and implemented freshly for every app. Moreover, most solutions were not at all general, making maintainability a nightmare: a small change in an app's interface over the course of its development might well cost hours of time working out its implications for state restoration.

Starting in iOS 6, Apple provides, as part of the system, a general solution to the problem of state restoration. The system takes care of storing and interpreting the saved state: your code doesn't have to worry about the exact format, or even the location, of this saved material. But I'll tell you anyway where it's saved: it's in a folder called Saved Application State in your app's sandboxed Library (see Chapter 36 for more about the app's sandbox).

The solution is centered around UIViewController. This makes sense, since view controllers are the heart of the problem. At the time the app was terminated, some view controller was in charge of the interface, and various other view controllers may have existed; the goal of state restoration must therefore be to reconstruct *all existing view controllers*, initializing each one into the state it previously had.

In taking advantage of iOS 6 state saving and restoration, keep in mind what state isn't. It isn't preferences, and it isn't data. If you were writing apps for iOS 5 and before, you may have been misusing NSUserDefaults to store view controller state and view state, and the new iOS 6 state saving and restoration mechanism is definitely an opportunity to stop doing that. But you should still use NSUserDefaults to store user defaults! If something is a preference, make it a preference. Similarly, if something is data (for example, the underlying model on which your app's functionality is based), don't misuse either NSUserDefaults or the built-in restoration mechanism to store it; keep it in a file (Chapter 36).

The reason for this is not only conceptual; it's because saved state can be lost. For example, suppose the user kills your app outright by double-clicking the Home button to show the app switcher interface, holds down a finger to get the icons into "jiggly mode," and taps the Minus button on your app's icon. The next time your app runs, it will launch from the beginning, making a clean start. In the same way, if your app crashes, the system will throw away its state. And that's not bad; it's good. There could be good reason to throw away state and start your app over from the beginning. It's only state! Your app still works fine if the interface happens to start over from the beginning. But losing the app's saved data, or the user's saved preferences, could be a disaster. So don't store data or preferences as part of your state.

 As of this writing, iOS 6 treats a restart of the device like an app crash. Thus, if the user leaves your app and returns to it, you will get state restoration even if the app was terminated in the background, but *not* if the user switched the device off and on again. This might mean that you have to rely on your own state restoration in addition to, or instead of, the built-in state restoration.

Participating in State Restoration

Built-in state restoration operates more or less automatically. All you have to do is tell the system that you want to participate in it. To do so, you take three basic steps:

Implement app delegate methods
    The app delegate must implement `application:shouldSaveApplicationState:` and `application:shouldRestoreApplicationState:` to return YES. (Naturally, your code can instead return NO to prevent state from being saved or restored on some particular occasion.)

Implement `application:willFinishLaunchingWithOptions:`
    The earliest moment when your code is called in iOS 5 and before, `application:didFinishLaunchingWithOptions:`, is too late for state restoration. Your app needs its basic interface before state restoration begins. The solution is a new iOS 6 app delegate method, `application:willFinishLaunchingWith-Options:`. If implemented, it is called absolutely first, before *any* other code of yours runs, including state restoration. Typically, if you don't care about supporting any earlier system, you can just move all your `application:didFinishLaunchingWith-Options:` code unchanged into `application:willFinishLaunchingWith-Options:`.

Provide restoration IDs
    Both UIViewController and UIView have a `restorationIdentifier` property, which is a string. Setting this string to a non-nil value is your signal to the system that you want this view controller (or view) to participate in state restoration. If a view controller's `restorationIdentifier` is nil, neither it nor any subsequent view controllers down the chain — neither its children nor its presented view controller, if any — will be saved or restored. (A nice feature of this architecture is that it lets you participate *partially* in state restoration, omitting selected view controllers by not assigning them a restoration identifier.)

    You can set the `restorationIdentifier` manually, in code; typically you'll do that early in a view controller's lifetime. If the view controller is instantiated from a nib or storyboard, you'll want to set it there; the Identity inspector has a Restoration ID field for this purpose. (It's a good idea, in general, to make a view controller's restoration ID in the storyboard the same as its storyboard ID, the string used to identify the view controller in a call to `instantiateViewControllerWith-Identifier:`; in fact, it's such a good idea that the storyboard editor provides a checkbox, "Use Storyboard ID," that makes the one value automatically the same as the other.)

In the case of a simple storyboard-based app, where each needed view controller instance can be reconstructed directly from the storyboard, those steps alone can be sufficient to bring state restoration to life, operating correctly at the view controller level. Let's test it. Start with a storyboard-based app with a navigation architecture very similar to the one I posited in an earlier section:

- A navigation controller.
- Its root view controller, connected by a relationship from the navigation controller. This might be the master controller in a master–detail architecture, so call its class MasterViewController.
  — An extra view controller, connected by a modal segue from the root view controller. Call its class ExtraViewController.
- A second view controller, connected by a push segue from the navigation controller's root view controller. This might be the detail controller in a master–detail architecture, so call its class DetailViewController.
  — The very same extra view controller (ExtraViewController), also connected by a modal segue from the second view controller.

This storyboard-based app runs perfectly with just about no code at all; all we need is an empty implementation of an unwind method in MasterViewController and DetailViewController so that we have a way to get back from the presented ExtraViewController instance to either of these.

We will now make this app implement state restoration:

1. Change the name of `application:didFinishLaunchingWithOptions:` in the app delegate to `application:willFinishLaunchingWithOptions:`.
2. Implement `application:shouldSaveApplicationState:` and `application:shouldRestoreApplicationState:` to return YES.
3. Give all four view controller instances in the storyboard restoration IDs: let's call them `@"nav"`, `@"master"`, `@"detail"`, and `@"extra"`.

That's all! The app now saves and restores state.

How to Test State Restoration

To work with state restoration, you need to know how to test. Here's what to do. Run the app as usual, in the Simulator or on a device. At some point, in the Simulator or on the device, click the Home button. This causes the app to be suspended in good order, and state is saved. Now, back in Xcode, stop the running project (Product → Stop) and run the project again. If there is saved state, it is restored. (To test the app's behavior from a truly cold start, delete it from the Simulator or device. You might need to do this after changing something about the underlying save-and-restore model.)

Restoration ID and Restoration Class

The previous example, while entertaining and easy, wasn't very informative or realistic. Having everything done for us by the storyboard reveals nothing about what's really happening. To learn more, let's rewrite the example without a storyboard. Throw away the storyboard (and delete the Main Storyboard entry from the *Info.plist*) and implement the same architecture using code alone:

```
// AppDelegate.m:
- (BOOL)application:(UIApplication *)application
        didFinishLaunchingWithOptions:(NSDictionary *)launchOptions
{
    self.window =
        [[UIWindow alloc] initWithFrame:[[UIScreen mainScreen] bounds]];
    // Override point for customization after application launch.
    MasterViewController* mvc = [MasterViewController new];
    UINavigationController* nav =
        [[UINavigationController alloc] initWithRootViewController:mvc];
    self.window.rootViewController = nav;
    self.window.backgroundColor = [UIColor whiteColor];
    [self.window makeKeyAndVisible];
    return YES;
}

// MasterViewController.m:
-(id)initWithNibName:(NSString*)nibNameOrNil bundle:(NSBundle*)bundleOrNil {
    self = [super initWithNibName:nibNameOrNil bundle:bundleOrNil];
    if (self) {
        self.navigationItem.title = @"Master";
    }
    return self;
}

-(void)viewDidLoad {
    [super viewDidLoad];
    UIBarButtonItem* b =
        [[UIBarButtonItem alloc] initWithTitle:@"Detail"
```

```
                style:UIBarButtonItemStylePlain
                target:self action:@selector(doDetail:)];
        self.navigationItem.rightBarButtonItem = b;
        UIButton* button = [UIButton buttonWithType:UIButtonTypeRoundedRect];
        [button setTitle:@"Extra" forState:UIControlStateNormal];
        [button addTarget:self
            action:@selector(doPresent:)
            forControlEvents:UIControlEventTouchUpInside];
        [button sizeToFit];
        button.center = self.view.center;
        [self.view addSubview:button];
    }

    -(void)doPresent:(id)sender {
        ExtraViewController* evc = [ExtraViewController new];
        [self presentViewController:evc animated:YES completion:nil];
    }

    -(void)doDetail:(id)sender {
        DetailViewController* dvc = [DetailViewController new];
        [self.navigationController pushViewController:dvc animated:YES];
    }

    // DetailViewController.m:
    -(id)initWithNibName:(NSString*)nibNameOrNil bundle:(NSBundle*)bundleOrNil {
        self = [super initWithNibName:nibNameOrNil bundle:bundleOrNil];
        if (self) {
            self.navigationItem.title = @"Detail";
        }
        return self;
    }

    -(void)viewDidLoad {
        [super viewDidLoad];
        UIButton* button = [UIButton buttonWithType:UIButtonTypeRoundedRect];
        [button setTitle:@"Extra" forState:UIControlStateNormal];
        [button addTarget:self
            action:@selector(doPresent:)
            forControlEvents:UIControlEventTouchUpInside];
        [button sizeToFit];
        button.center = self.view.center;
        [self.view addSubview:button];
    }

    -(void)doPresent:(id)sender {
        ExtraViewController* evc = [ExtraViewController new];
        [self presentViewController:evc animated:YES completion:nil];
    }

    // ExtraViewController.m:
    -(void)viewDidLoad {
        [super viewDidLoad];
```

```
    self.view.backgroundColor = [UIColor greenColor];
    UIButton* button = [UIButton buttonWithType:UIButtonTypeRoundedRect];
    [button setTitle:@"Done" forState:UIControlStateNormal];
    [button addTarget:self
        action:@selector(doDismiss:)
        forControlEvents:UIControlEventTouchUpInside];
    [button sizeToFit];
    button.center = self.view.center;
    [self.view addSubview:button];
}

-(void)doDismiss:(id)sender {
    [self dismissViewControllerAnimated:YES completion:nil];
}
```

Now let's start adding state restoration, just as before:

1. Change the name of `application:didFinishLaunchingWithOptions:` in the app delegate to `application:willFinishLaunchingWithOptions:`.

2. Implement `application:shouldSaveApplicationState:` and `application:shouldRestoreApplicationState:` to return YES.

3. Give all four view controller instances restoration IDs: let's call them `@"nav"`, `@"master"`, `@"detail"`, and `@"extra"`. We'll have to do this in code. We're creating each view controller manually, so we may choose to assign its `restoration-Identifier` in the next line, like this:

   ```
   MasterViewController* mvc = [MasterViewController new];
   mvc.restorationIdentifier = @"master";
   UINavigationController* nav =
       [[UINavigationController alloc] initWithRootViewController:mvc];
   nav.restorationIdentifier = @"nav";
   ```

   And so on.

Run the app. We're getting state saving, but not state restoration. That's because the `restorationIdentifier` alone is not sufficient to tell the state restoration mechanism what to do as the app launches. What the restoration mechanism is *trying* to do is to generate instances of all the view controllers that were in existence when the app was suspended, tied together in the same parent–child and presenter–presented relationships. For our example app, the restoration of the relationships is no problem; the question is how to obtain those instances. In our storyboard example, the storyboard was the source of the instances. Now the instances must come from your code.

The `restorationIdentifier` of each view controller instance is the beginning of the restoration process. It is partly a signal that a view controller should be saved, but it is also a guide during restoration as to what view controller is needed at each point in the view controller hierarchy. Any particular view controller instance, given its position in the tree of parent–child and presenter–presented relationships starting with the root view controller, is uniquely identified by the `restorationIdentifier` values of all the view controllers running down that branch of the hierarchy, including its own.

Those `restorationIdentifier` values, taken together and in sequence, constitute the *identifier path* for any given view controller instance. Each identifier path is, in fact, an array of strings. In effect, the identifier paths are like a trail of breadcrumbs that you left behind as you created each view controller while the app was running, and that will now be used to create each view controller *again* as the app launches.

 A `restorationIdentifier` value thus does not have to be unique across your entire application; it only has to be unique to the specific point where it is used in the hierarchy. For example, a sequence `@[@"root", @"root"]` is no problem — the two view controllers identified as `@"root"` needn't even be the same view controller — provided no *other* view controller called `@"root"` could possibly appear at the first position in the hierarchy, and no *other* view controller called `@"root"` could possibly appear at the second position in the hierarchy given that the first position is occupied by `@"root"`.

The system has already saved the identifier paths and relationships for all the view controllers we're going to need. Now, as the app launches, it tries to match them up with existing view controller instances. In our storyboard example, the app succeeded in doing this for every saved identifier path. Suppose that, at the time the app was suspended, the detail view controller's view was showing. The process then went something like this:

1. The first path is `@[@"nav"]`. My first view controller is the initial view controller in the storyboard, which I've already made root view controller of the whole app. Is its restoration identifier `@"nav"`? Why, yes! That's our first problem solved.

2. The next path is `@[@"nav", @"master"]`, and it's a parent–child relationship. Do I have in the storyboard a child of my `@"nav"` view controller whose restoration identifier is `@"master"`? Yes, I do.

3. The next path is `@[@"nav", @"detail"]`, and it's a parent–child relationship. Do I have in the storyboard a child of my `@"nav"` view controller whose restoration identifier is `@"detail"`? Yes, I do.

The identifier paths reflect relationships, not history. Thus, in our example, the third path is @[@"nav", @"detail"], not @[@"nav", @"master", @"detail"] — because the DetailViewController is to be a child of the navigation view controller. The fact that in our app a MasterViewController instance originally summoned this DetailViewController instance is irrelevant to the structure of the identifier path; each view controller's identifier path is the shortest path based purely on parent–child or presenter–presented relationships.

Now, however, there is no storyboard. Again, suppose that, at the time the app was suspended, the detail view controller's view was showing. Bear in mind that state restoration begins *after* application:willFinishLaunchingWithOptions:. Therefore the navigation controller, acting as root view controller of the app, and its first child, the master view controller, already exist. So the process will go something like this:

1. The first path is @[@"nav"]. My first view controller is the root view controller of the whole app. Is its restoration identifier @"nav"? Why, yes! That's our first problem solved.

2. The next path is @[@"nav", @"master"], and it's a parent–child relationship. Is there a child of my @"nav" view controller whose restoration identifier is @"master"? Yes, there is.

3. The next path is @[@"nav", @"detail"], and it's a parent–child relationship. Is there a child of my @"nav" view controller whose restoration identifier is @"detail"? No!

At this moment the restoration mechanism must turn to your code and ask for the view controller whose identifier path is @[@"nav", @"detail"]. But *what* code should it turn to? This is very early in the life of the app, so we have very few instances in existence. But we do have all your app's classes already in existence! Therefore the method in your code to which the restoration mechanism will now turn is a class method. But *what* class? To answer this question, the state saving mechanism has saved a second piece of information about every view controller that was in existence when we were suspended: its *restoration class*. This is a reference to the class that the restoration mechanism should turn to when it wants to reconstruct this view controller instance.

To implement restoration of view controllers in code, then, we perform the following additional modifications for each view controller that has not been restored in application:willFinishLaunchingWithOptions::

- Give the view controller a restorationClass. Typically, this will be the view controller's own class, or the class of the view controller responsible for creating this view controller instance.

- Implement the class method `viewControllerWithRestorationIdentifier-Path:coder:` on the class named by each view controller's `restorationClass` property, returning a view controller instance as specified by the identifier path. Very often, `viewControllerWithRestorationIdentifierPath:coder:` will itself instantiate this view controller.

- Specify formally that each class named as a `restorationClass` implements the UIViewControllerRestoration protocol.

Accordingly, let's make our DetailViewController instance restorable. In our simple example, it is created and configured by the MasterViewController instance, so one possible strategy is for MasterViewController to act as its restoration class. (Another perfectly good strategy would be for DetailViewController to act as its own restoration class.) In its implementation of `viewControllerWithRestorationIdentifier-Path:coder:`, MasterViewController should do for DetailViewController everything that it was doing before we added state restoration to our app — except for putting it into the view controller hierarchy! The state restoration mechanism itself, remember, is responsible for assembling the view controller hierarchy; our job is merely to supply any needed view controller instances.

So MasterViewController now must adopt UIViewControllerRestoration (I like to do this in a class extension inside the implementation file), and will contain this code:

```
-(void)doDetail:(id)sender {
    DetailViewController* dvc = [DetailViewController new];
    dvc.restorationIdentifier = @"detail";
    dvc.restorationClass = [self class]; // *
    [self.navigationController pushViewController:dvc animated:YES];
}

+ (UIViewController*) viewControllerWithRestorationIdentifierPath:(NSArray*)ic
        coder:(NSCoder*)coder {
    if ([[ic lastObject] isEqualToString:@"detail"]) {
        DetailViewController* dvc = [DetailViewController new];
        dvc.restorationIdentifier = @"detail";
        dvc.restorationClass = [self class];
        return dvc;
    }
    return nil;
}
```

In `doDetail:`, MasterViewController is creating a DetailViewController instance and configuring it, prior to pushing it onto the navigation controller's stack; in particular, it is supplying the `restorationIdentifier` and `restorationClass`. Therefore, in `viewControllerWithRestorationIdentifierPath:coder:`, it does all those same things. We thus end up with a DetailViewController instance configured in exactly the same way as before — and that's the point of the exercise.

The result of doing all those same things is, of course, code duplication. We can reduce the amount of code duplication by factoring out the duplicated code into a single method. But remember that doDetail: is an instance method, whereas viewControllerWith-RestorationIdentifierPath:coder: is a class method:

```
+(DetailViewController*) newDetailViewController {
    DetailViewController* dvc = [DetailViewController new];
    dvc.restorationIdentifier = @"detail";
    dvc.restorationClass = [self class];
    return dvc;
}

-(void)doDetail:(id)sender {
    [self.navigationController pushViewController:
        [[self class] newDetailViewController] animated:YES];
}

+ (UIViewController*) viewControllerWithRestorationIdentifierPath:(NSArray*)ic
        coder:(NSCoder*)coder {
    if ([[ic lastObject] isEqualToString:@"detail"]) {
        return [self newDetailViewController];
    }
    return nil;
}
```

The structure of our viewControllerWithRestorationIdentifierPath:coder is typical. We test the identifier path — usually, it's sufficient to examine its last element — and return the corresponding view controller; ultimately, we are also prepared to return nil, in case we are called with an identifier path we can't interpret. viewControllerWith-RestorationIdentifierPath:coder can also return nil deliberately, to tell the restoration mechanism, "Go no further; don't restore the view controller you're asking for here, or any view controller further down the same path."

It should now be obvious how to modify MasterViewController and DetailView-Controller to nominate themselves as, and to function as, the restoration class for the ExtraViewController instance that each creates. (There's no conflict in the notion that both MasterViewController and DetailViewController can fulfill this role, as we're talking about two different ExtraViewController instances.) I'll show the implementation in DetailViewController. *Don't forget to make DetailViewController adopt UIViewControllerRestoration!* Many are the hours I've lost through forgetting that step and then wondering why state restoration wasn't working:

```
+(ExtraViewController*) newExtraViewController {
    ExtraViewController* evc = [ExtraViewController new];
    evc.restorationIdentifier = @"extra";
    evc.restorationClass = [self class];
    return evc;
}
```

```
-(void)doPresent:(id)sender {
    [self presentViewController:
        [[self class] newExtraViewController] animated:YES completion:nil];
}

+ (UIViewController*) viewControllerWithRestorationIdentifierPath:(NSArray*)ic
        coder:(NSCoder*)coder {
    if ([[ic lastObject] isEqualToString:@"extra"]) {
        return [self newExtraViewController];
    }
    return nil;
}
```

In this case, the identifier path will be @[@"nav", @"extra"], because ExtraView-Controller is presented fullscreen and therefore its presentingViewController is the navigation controller, the root view of the app.

It is also permitted *not* to assign a view controller a restorationClass. In that case, if the restoration mechanism can't find a way forward through the sequence, it will call your app delegate's application:viewControllerWithRestorationIdentifier-Path:coder:. If you implement this method, be prepared to receive identifier paths for existing view controllers! For example, if we were to implement application:view-ControllerWithRestorationIdentifierPath:coder: now, it would be called for @[@"nav"] and for @[@"nav", @"master"]. Do not respond by creating a new view controller! These view controllers are already in the view controller hierarchy, because application:willFinishLaunchingWithOptions: has already created them; just return pointers to the existing instances:

```
-(UIViewController *)application:(UIApplication *)application
        viewControllerWithRestorationIdentifierPath:(NSArray *)ic
                                    coder:(NSCoder *)coder {
    if ([[ic lastObject] isEqualToString:@"nav"]) {
        return self.window.rootViewController;
    }
    if ([[ic lastObject] isEqualToString:@"master"]) {
        return [(UINavigationController*)self.window.rootViewController
                viewControllers][0];
    }
    return nil;
}
```

Again, you can return nil on a particular occasion to prevent restoration from continuing down a particular path (if the view controller in question hasn't been created already).

Here's an overview of the order of operations during state restoration:

- application:willFinishLaunchingWithOptions:

- `application:shouldRestoreApplicationState:` (and let's presume the response is YES)
- `viewControllerWithRestorationIdentifierPath:coder:` and `application:viewControllerWithRestorationIdentifierPath:coder:`, as needed, to instantiate all necessary view controllers
- Restoration of individual view controller state, discussed in the next section
- `application:didDecodeRestorableStateWithCoder:`
- `application:didFinishLaunchingWithOptions:`

Restoring View Controller State

Up to now, I've been talking about restoration of the view controller hierarchy. But I haven't yet said anything about restoration of the state of individual view controllers. A view controller might have instance variables, and its view might contain features, whose values need to be saved as we are suspended and restored as part of the state restoration mechanism. And this might need to be done for all the view controller instances in your app, not just the one whose view happens to be showing at restoration time; that, after all, is the overall state of your entire app.

This work is done with the help of a *keyed archiver* (((NSKeyedArchiver)), an NSCoder subclass), as follows:

- When it's time to save state (as the app is about to be suspended), the state saving mechanism sends your app delegate `application:willEncodeRestorableState-WithCoder:`. It then turns to all your existing participating view controller instances and sends them `encodeRestorableStateWithCoder:` (if they implement it). The `coder:` is an NSCoder. If your view controller has state to save, it sends the coder an appropriate encode message with a key, such as `encodeFloat:forKey:` or `encode-Object:forKey:`. Much as in a dictionary, the key is an arbitrary string identifying this value. You should call `super`.

  If an object's class doesn't adopt the NSCoding protocol, you may have to archive it to an NSData object before you can encode it. However, views and view controllers can be handled by this coder, because they are treated as references.

- When it's time to restore this view controller instance and its state, the state restoration mechanism brings back the same coder containing the same keys. Whatever was saved in the coder can be extracted by the reverse operation using the same key, such as `decodeFloatForKey:` or `decodeObjectForKey:`. It is your job to reconfigure the view controller instance so that its state matches that of the instance at the time the app was suspended. The coder is brought back in four places:

— In `application:shouldRestoreApplicationState:`. The coder is the second parameter, and is the same coder that was the second parameter to `application:shouldSaveApplicationState:`.

— In `application:viewControllerWithRestorationIdentifierPath:coder:` or `viewControllerWithRestorationIdentifierPath:coder:`. This is useful if your view controller has an initializer that requires extra data. If that data was saved into the coder, you can now extract it and create the view controller with that data.

— After the view controller instance has been created, it is sent `decodeRestorableStateWithCoder:`. This is your chance to pull out and apply to `self` any material that you didn't pull out for this instance as you created it in `viewControllerWithRestorationIdentifierPath:coder:`. You should call `super`.

— Finally, the app delegate is sent `application:didDecodeRestorableStateWithCoder:`.

I said "the same coder" because there are multiple coders — one for each view controller, and one for the app delegate. This means that you don't have to worry about key names colliding across view controllers; each view controller gets its own coder, so all you have to do is use unique key names with regard to that view controller.

The *UIStateRestoration.h* header file describes three built-in keys that are available from every coder during restoration:

`UIStateRestorationViewControllerStoryboardKey`
A reference to the storyboard from which this view controller came, if any. This could allow your implementation of `viewControllerWithRestorationIdentifierPath:coder:` to extract the same view controller manually from the storyboard, if necessary.

`UIApplicationStateRestorationBundleVersionKey`
Your *Info.plist* `CFBundleVersion` string at the time of state saving. This could allow your implementation of `application:shouldRestoreApplicationState:` to opt out of state restoration after an update.

`UIApplicationStateRestorationUserInterfaceIdiomKey`
An NSNumber wrapping either `UIUserInterfaceIdiomPhone` or `UIUserInterfaceIdiomPad`. This could allow your implementation of `application:shouldRestoreApplicationState:` to opt out of state restoration if the app has been backed up and restored to a different type of device.

In real life, it is very likely that your view controllers will need to implement `encodeRestorableStateWithCoder:` and `decodeRestorableStateWithCoder:`. Even an app whose view controller hierarchy can be completely restored from a storyboard, with no code, will probably also need to restore the state of the individual view controller instances or of views within the view controller's view. `decodeRestorableStateWith-Coder:` is guaranteed to be called *after* `viewDidLoad`, so it is quite typical to update the interface directly from within `decodeRestorableStateWithCoder:`. Here's an example from the TidBITS News app, where we save and restore a feature of the visible user interface:

```
-(void)encodeRestorableStateWithCoder:(NSCoder *)coder {
    [coder encodeObject: self.refreshControl.attributedTitle.string
                forKey:@"lastPubDate"];
    [super encodeRestorableStateWithCoder:coder];
}

-(void)decodeRestorableStateWithCoder:(NSCoder *)coder {
    NSString* s = [coder decodeObjectForKey:@"lastPubDate"];
    if (s)
        [self setRefreshControlTitle:s];
    [super decodeRestorableStateWithCoder:coder];
}
```

As I mentioned a moment ago, it's fine to save a reference to a view controller into the coder. One important reason for doing this is when you have a custom container view controller. The restoration mechanism understands some basic built-in parent view controller types (UINavigationController, UITabBarController), and it understands presented view controllers, but that's all. If you want state restoration for the children of your custom parent view controller, you must save those children into the coder.

As an example, I'll return to the case of a UIPageViewController whose child view controller is an instance of my Pep class, which accepts and stores the name of a Pep Boy and displays his image. The view controller architecture is:

- RootViewController, a custom parent view controller
- pvc, a UIPageViewController, child of RootViewController so that I can display its view inside the RootViewController's view
- Pep, the class of the UIPageViewController's children

RootViewController's `viewDidLoad` creates the interface. It instantiates the UIPageViewController and formally makes that instance, pvc, its own child and puts its view into its own view. It also sets the page view controller's initial child view controller, a Pep instance (displaying Manny, when the app launches for the first time). It also sets itself (the RootViewController) as the page view controller's data source; when a new page is requested, it examines the existing Pep instance to obtain its boy property, works out what Pep Boy is needed now, creates a new Pep and calls its `initWithPep-Boy:nib:bundle:`, and supplies it.

So far so good. Now let's add saving and restoration of state. Here's the problem. We have attached restoration identifiers to the RootViewController, the page view controller, and the Pep instances, but Pep's encodeRestorableStateWithCoder: and decode-RestorableStateWithCoder: are never called; it isn't participating in state saving and restoration. The reason is that the saving and restoration mechanism knows nothing about the structure of our app. It has no innate knowledge of UIPageViewController, and it doesn't know about the parent–child relationship between the RootView-Controller and the UIPageViewController, or between the UIPageViewController and the Pep instance whose view it is displaying. If we want a Pep instance to participate in saving and restoration, we have to show the mechanism a Pep instance.

The way we do this is by saving a Pep instance into the coder. The Pep instance we'll save is, of course, the one that's currently showing in the page view controller. So, in RootViewController:

```
- (void)encodeRestorableStateWithCoder:(NSCoder *)coder {
    UIPageViewController* pvc = self.childViewControllers[0];
    Pep* pep = pvc.viewControllers[0];
    [coder encodeObject:pep forKey:@"pep"];
    [super encodeRestorableStateWithCoder:coder];
}
```

That will cause the state saving mechanism to be aware of the Pep instance. Moreover, the Pep instance has a restoration identifier (which happens to be @"pep"). Therefore it will turn to that Pep instance and send it encodeRestorableStateWithCoder:. So now the Pep instance can record which Pep Boy it's displaying:

```
-(void)encodeRestorableStateWithCoder:(NSCoder *)coder {
    [coder encodeObject:self.boy forKey:@"boy"];
    [super encodeRestorableStateWithCoder:coder];
}
```

Now let's talk about restoration. First, observe that there is no need to give Pep a restoration class. This is just like the case where the app's root view controller is a navigation controller with an initial root view controller; both of those view controllers already exist, so there's no need for the restoration mechanism to hunt for them. In just the same way, there is no need for the restoration mechanism to ask for a Pep instance, because we're going to make a Pep instance in any case, in RootViewController's viewDidLoad. The issue is only to *configure* that Pep instance to correspond to the correct Pep Boy.

I can think of various ways to do that, but the simplest, I think, is to let the Pep instance configure itself. The state restoration mechanism will be able to find and identify this Pep instance, so it's going to be sent decodeRestorableStateWithCoder:, and can extract the boy value that it saved earlier.

But now we have to think about the Pep instance's *interface*. Pep's viewDidLoad configures the interface, based on the boy property:

```
- (void)viewDidLoad {
    [super viewDidLoad];
    self.name.text = self.boy;
    self.pic.image =
        [UIImage imageNamed:
            [NSString stringWithFormat: @"%@.jpg",
            [self.boy lowercaseString]]];
}
```

By the time decodeRestorableStateWithCoder: is called, viewDidLoad has already
been called. In fact, this Pep instance has already been fully configured, thanks to Root-
ViewController's viewDidLoad — but with Manny as its Pep Boy. No problem; all we
have to do is configure it *again*:

```
-(void)decodeRestorableStateWithCoder:(NSCoder *)coder {
    NSString* boy = [coder decodeObjectForKey:@"boy"];
    if (boy) {
        self.boy = boy;
        self.name.text = self.boy;
        self.pic.image =
            [UIImage imageNamed:
                [NSString stringWithFormat: @"%@.jpg",
                [self.boy lowercaseString]]];
    }
    [super decodeRestorableStateWithCoder:coder];
}
```

We are left with some duplicate code; if we don't like that, we can factor it out into a
method that's called by both viewDidLoad and decodeRestorableStateWithCoder:.

The remarkable thing about that example is that RootViewController stored a Pep instance into its coder but never extracted it. It could have done so, but there was no need;
storing the Pep instance was sufficient to switch on state saving and restoration for the
Pep instance itself, which is what we were really after.

I have mentioned more than once that viewDidLoad is called before decodeRestorable-
StateWithCoder:. Not only is this true for each view controller; it's true for all view
controllers collectively. All view controller views exist, and their viewDidLoad has been
called, before decodeRestorableStateWithCoder: is called for any view controller.
When decodeRestorableStateWithCoder: is called, it is called on view controllers
successively from the top down; each view controller's parent or presenter has been
given a chance to configure itself already.

Unfortunately, no similar guarantee can be made for other view-related events. In particular, you can't be sure when decodeRestorableStateWithCoder: will be called with
respect to the various "appear"/"disappear" events. In fact, it's quite easy to write an app
where, if a certain view controller's view was frontmost when the app was suspended,
decodeRestorableStateWithCoder: precedes the "appear"/"disappear" events for each
view controller, but if a different view controller's view was frontmost, decode-

`RestorableStateWithCoder:` follows the "appear"/"disappear" events for each view controller. This is very frustrating, and can make it quite tricky to slot a view controller's state restoration into its other tasks as it comes to life.

We have talked about view controllers, but not about views. A view will participate in automatic saving and restoration of state if its view controller does, and if it itself has a restoration identifier. Some built-in UIView subclasses have built-in restoration abilities. For example, a scroll view that participates in state saving and restoration will automatically return to the point to which it was scrolled previously. You should consult the documentation on each UIView subclass type to see whether it participates usefully in state saving and restoration, and I'll mention a few significant cases when we come to discuss those views in later chapters.

 If your app has additional state restoration work to do on a background thread (Chapter 38), the documentation says you should call UIApplication's `extendStateRestoration` as you begin and `completeStateRestoration` when you've finished. The idea is that if you *don't* call `completeStateRestoration`, the system can assume that something has gone very wrong (like, your app has crashed) and will throw away the saved state information, which may be faulty.

CHAPTER 20

Scroll Views

A scroll view (UIScrollView) is a view whose content is larger than its bounds. To reveal a desired area, the user can scroll the content by dragging or flicking, or you can reposition the content in code.

A scroll view isn't magic. It's really quite an ordinary UIView, taking advantage of ordinary UIView features (Chapter 14). The content is simply the scroll view's subviews. When the scroll view scrolls, what's really changing is the scroll view's own bounds origin; the subviews are positioned with respect to the bounds origin, so they move with it. The scroll view's `clipsToBounds` is usually YES, so any content positioned within the scroll view's bounds width and height is visible and any content positioned outside them is not.

However, a scroll view does bring to the table some nontrivial additional abilities:

- It knows how to shift its bounds origin in response to the user's gestures.
- It provides scroll indicators whose size and position give the user a clue as to the content's size and position.
- It can optionally enforce paging, whereby the user can view only integral portions of the content.
- It can support zooming, so that the user can resize the apparent content by pinching.

Creating a Scroll View

The scroll view's subviews are positioned with respect to its bounds origin. The scroll view knows how far it should be allowed to slide its subviews downward and rightward — the limit is reached when the scroll view's bounds origin is {0,0}. What the scroll view doesn't know is how far it should be allowed to slide its subviews upward and leftward. To tell it, you set the scroll view's `contentSize`. The scroll view uses its `content-Size`, in combination with its own bounds size, to set the limits on how large its bounds origin can become. In effect, the `contentSize` is how large the scrollable content is. If a dimension of the `contentSize` isn't larger than the same dimension of the scroll view's own bounds, the content won't be scrollable in that dimension: there is nothing to scroll, as the entire scrollable content is already showing. A remarkable feature of autolayout (Chapter 14) is that it can calculate the `contentSize` for you based on the constraints of the scroll view's subviews.

To illustrate, I'll start by creating a scroll view and providing it with subviews entirely in code. In the first instance, let's *not* use autolayout. Our project is based on the Empty Application template. Add a UIViewController subclass, ViewController, with no nib. In the app delegate's `application:didFinishLaunchingWithOptions:`, we do the usual dance to get ourselves a root view controller:

```
self.window = [[UIWindow alloc] initWithFrame:
                 [[UIScreen mainScreen] bounds]];
// Override point for customization after application launch.
self.viewController = [ViewController new];
self.window.rootViewController = self.viewController;
[self.window makeKeyAndVisible];
return YES;
```

In the view controller's `loadView` I'll create the scroll view and make it the root view, and populate it with 30 UILabels whose text contains a sequential number so that we can see where we are when we scroll:

```
UIScrollView* sv = [[UIScrollView alloc] initWithFrame:
                     [[UIScreen mainScreen] applicationFrame]];
sv.backgroundColor = [UIColor whiteColor];
self.view = sv;
CGFloat y = 10;
for (int i=0; i<30; i++) {
    UILabel* lab = [UILabel new];
    lab.text = [NSString stringWithFormat:@"This is label %i", i+1];
    [lab sizeToFit];
    CGRect f = lab.frame;
    f.origin = CGPointMake(10,y);
    lab.frame = f;
    [sv addSubview:lab];
    y += lab.bounds.size.height + 10;
}
CGSize sz = sv.bounds.size;
sz.height = y;
sv.contentSize = sz; // This is the crucial line
```

The crucial move, as the comment notes, is that we tell the scroll view how large its content is to be. If we omit this step, the scroll view won't be scrollable; the window will appear to consist of a static column of labels.

There is no rule about the order in which you perform the two operations of setting the contentSize and populating the scroll view with subviews. In this example, we set the contentSize afterward because it is more convenient to track the heights of the subviews as we add them than to calculate their total height in advance. Similarly, you can alter a scroll view's content (subviews) and contentSize dynamically as the app runs.

Any direct subviews of the scroll view may need to have their autoresizing set appropriately in case the scroll view is resized, as would happen, for instance, if our app performs compensatory rotation. To see this, add these lines inside the for loop:

```
lab.backgroundColor = [UIColor redColor]; // make label bounds visible
lab.autoresizingMask = UIViewAutoresizingFlexibleWidth;
```

Run the app, and rotate the device or the Simulator. The labels are wider in portrait orientation because the scroll view itself is wider. (This has nothing to do with the contentSize! The contentSize does not change just because the scroll view's bounds changed, and resizing the contentSize has no effect on the size of the scroll view's subviews; it merely determines the scrolling limit.)

Now I'll rewrite the example to use constraints. The example will be clearer if the scroll view is itself positioned by constraints inside the actual root view. So delete loadView, allowing the root view to be an automatically generated generic UIView, and implement viewDidLoad instead:

```
[super viewDidLoad];
UIScrollView* sv = [UIScrollView new];
sv.backgroundColor = [UIColor whiteColor];
sv.translatesAutoresizingMaskIntoConstraints = NO;
[self.view addSubview:sv];
[self.view addConstraints:
 [NSLayoutConstraint constraintsWithVisualFormat:@"H:|[sv]|"
                                         options:0 metrics:nil
                                           views:@{@"sv":sv}]];
[self.view addConstraints:
 [NSLayoutConstraint constraintsWithVisualFormat:@"V:|[sv]|"
                                         options:0 metrics:nil
                                           views:@{@"sv":sv}]];
UILabel* previousLab = nil;
for (int i=0; i<30; i++) {
    UILabel* lab = [UILabel new];
    lab.translatesAutoresizingMaskIntoConstraints = NO;
    lab.text = [NSString stringWithFormat:@"This is label %i", i+1];
    [sv addSubview:lab];
    [sv addConstraints:
     [NSLayoutConstraint constraintsWithVisualFormat:@"H:|-(10)-[lab]"
                                             options:0 metrics:nil
                                               views:@{@"lab":lab}]];
    if (!previousLab) { // first one, pin to top
        [sv addConstraints:
         [NSLayoutConstraint constraintsWithVisualFormat:@"V:|-(10)-[lab]"
```

```
                                            options:0 metrics:nil
                                            views:@{@"lab":lab}]];
    } else { // all others, pin to previous
        [sv addConstraints:
        [NSLayoutConstraint
         constraintsWithVisualFormat:@"V:[prev]-(10)-[lab]"
                                    options:0 metrics:nil
                                    views:@{@"lab":lab, @"prev":previousLab}]];
    }
    previousLab = lab;
}
// last one, pin to bottom and right, this dictates content size height
[sv addConstraints:
 [NSLayoutConstraint constraintsWithVisualFormat:@"V:[lab]-(10)-|"
                                    options:0 metrics:nil
                                    views:@{@"lab":previousLab}]];
[sv addConstraints:
 [NSLayoutConstraint constraintsWithVisualFormat:@"H:[lab]-(10)-|"
                                    options:0 metrics:nil
                                    views:@{@"lab":previousLab}]];
// look, Ma, no contentSize!
```

As the final comment says, there's no need to set the contentSize. This works because
the constraints of the scroll view's subviews describe completely their relationship to
their superview: besides the tops and bottoms of the subviews being pinned to one
another, the top one is pinned to the top of the superview, the bottom one is pinned to
the bottom of the superview, and the left and right of all of them are pinned to the left
and right of the superview. Consequently, the runtime calculates the contentSize for
us.

(A second strategy for using autolayout inside a scroll view is to provide a single generic
UIView as the sole immediate subview of the scroll view, and position all the other
subviews inside that generic UIView. The generic UIView itself can then keep its
translatesAutoresizingMaskIntoConstraints set to YES and can be given an explicit
size, and the scroll view's contentSize should then be set to match that size.)

Next, I'll design a scroll view in a nib. The example is based on my Zotz! app, where the
user specifies preference settings in a navigation interface inside a tab bar interface. The
problem is that, what with the navigation bar and the tab bar occupying valuable screen
real estate, there isn't enough vertical space for the various interface objects in the preferences view (Figure 20-1). The obvious solution is that the preferences view should be
scrollable. To lay out the preferences view's subviews in code would be painful and
unmaintainable; a nib-based solution is better.

A UIScrollView is available in the nib editor in the Object library, so you can drag it
into a view in the canvas and give it subviews. Alternatively, you can wrap existing views
in the canvas in a UIScrollView as an afterthought: select the views and choose Editor
→ Embed In → Scroll View. The scroll view can't be scrolled in the nib editor, so to

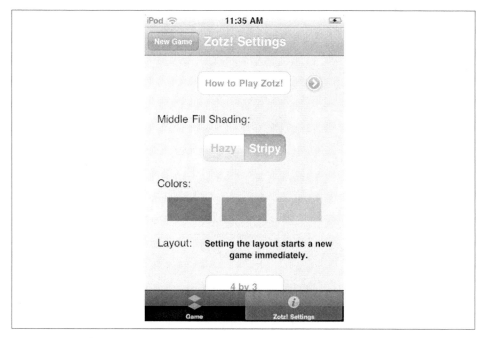

Figure 20-1. The Zotz! settings view

design its subviews, you make the scroll view large enough to accommodate them; if this makes the scroll view too large, you can resize the actual scroll view instance when the nib loads.

Unfortunately, the nib editor provides no way to set the scroll view's contentSize, so you have to do it in code. But what should that contentSize be? In my example, the scroll view doesn't scroll horizontally, so I need to know just the vertical dimension of the contentSize (the horizontal dimension can be 0). Before autolayout, there were two possible solutions to this problem:

- Provide an outlet to the bottommost subview and use its position and height to calculate and set the content size:

```
float width = 0; // sv is the scroll view
// use lowest subview, "lowest", as reference for content height
float height =
    self.lowest.frame.origin.y + self.lowest.frame.size.height + 20.0;
self.sv.contentSize = CGSizeMake(width, height);
```

- Wrap all the scroll view's subviews in a single UIView; that single UIView is the scroll view's sole subview in the nib. Size that UIView correctly to hold all the subviews. When the nib loads, use that UIView's size to set the content size; we don't even need an outlet to the UIView, since we know it is the scroll view's first subview:

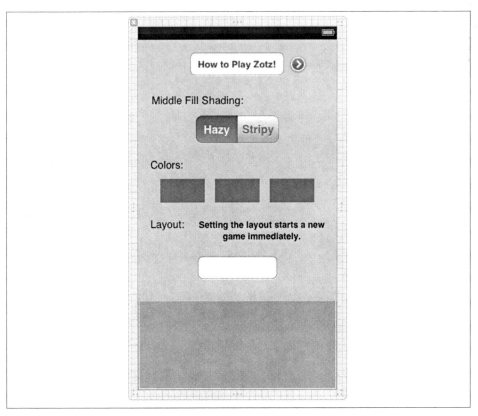

Figure 20-2. The Zotz! settings view, designed in the nib

```
self.sv.contentSize = ((UIView*)self.sv.subviews[0]).bounds.size;
```

If you're using autolayout, you can do something similar to the second solution. We have a scroll view containing a single subview, which itself contains all the other subviews, so that everything can be positioned easily in the nib using constraints (Figure 20-2). The scroll view is pinned to be the same size as its superview, which is the File's Owner's `view` and will be resized to fit the interface when the nib loads. The scroll view's subview is sized correctly to describe the size of the scroll view's content view. We have an outlet to the bottom constraint of the scroll view's subview; when the nib loads, we set that constraint's `constant` to 0. Now our constraints are describing the desired content size correctly, and the scroll view becomes scrollable:

```
- (void)viewDidLoad {
    [super viewDidLoad];
    self.contentViewBottomConstraint.constant = 0;
}
```

Another use of autolayout in connection with a scroll view is to *prevent* a subview of the scroll view from scrolling — that is, from being carried along as the scroll view's bounds origin changes. Use constraints to pin the subview to something *outside* the scroll view. Now this subview will effectively "float" over the scroll view. Before autolayout, this sort of thing was rather tricky to arrange; you had to use a delegate event to respond to every change in the scroll view's bounds origin by shifting the "floating" view's position to compensate, so as to appear to remain fixed. With constraints, you just set up the subview once and that's all.

In this example, I'll pin a small image view to the scroll view's superview. The scroll view's own edges are pinned exactly to those of its superview, so the result is that the image "floats" in the top right corner of the scroll view:

```
UIImageView* iv = [[UIImageView alloc]
                    initWithImage:[UIImage imageNamed:@"smiley.png"]];
iv.translatesAutoresizingMaskIntoConstraints = NO;
[sv addSubview:iv];
UIView* sup = sv.superview;
[sup addConstraint:
 [NSLayoutConstraint
  constraintWithItem:iv attribute:NSLayoutAttributeRight
  relatedBy:0
  toItem:sup attribute:NSLayoutAttributeRight
  multiplier:1 constant:-5]];
[sup addConstraint:
 [NSLayoutConstraint
  constraintWithItem:iv attribute:NSLayoutAttributeTop
  relatedBy:0
  toItem:sup attribute:NSLayoutAttributeTop
  multiplier:1 constant:5]];
```

 Do not assume that the subviews you add to a UIScrollView are its only subviews! The scroll indicators managed by the scroll view, discussed in the next section, are also subviews (they are actually UIImageViews).

Scrolling

For the most part, the purpose of a scroll view will be to let the user scroll. A number of properties affect the user experience with regard to scrolling:

scrollEnabled

If NO, the user can't scroll, but you can still scroll in code (as explained later in this section). You could put a UIScrollView to various creative purposes other than letting the user scroll; for example, scrolling in code to a different region of the content might be a way of replacing one piece of interface by another, possibly with animation.

scrollsToTop

If YES (the default), and assuming scrolling is enabled, the user can tap on the status bar as a way of making the scroll view scroll its content to the top. You can also override this setting dynamically through the scroll view's delegate (discussed later in this chapter).

bounces

If YES (the default), then when the user scrolls to a limit of the content, it is possible to scroll somewhat further (possibly revealing the scroll view's backgroundColor behind the content, if a subview was covering it); the content then snaps back into place when the user releases it. Otherwise, the user experiences the limit as a sudden inability to scroll further in that direction.

alwaysBounceVertical, alwaysBounceHorizontal

If YES, and assuming that bounces is YES, then even if the contentSize in the given dimension isn't larger than the scroll view (so that no scrolling is actually possible in that dimension), the user can nevertheless scroll somewhat and the content then snaps back into place when the user releases it; otherwise, the user experiences a simple inability to scroll in that dimension.

directionalLockEnabled

If YES, and if scrolling is possible in both dimensions (even if only because the appropriate alwaysBounce... is YES), then the user, having begun to scroll in one dimension, can't scroll in the other dimension without ending the gesture and starting over. In other words, the user is constrained to scroll vertically or horizontally but not both at once.

decelerationRate

The rate at which scrolling is damped out, and the content comes to a stop, after a flick gesture. As convenient examples, standard constants UIScrollView-DecelerationRateNormal (0.998) and UIScrollViewDecelerationRateFast (0.99) are provided. Lower values mean faster damping; experimentation suggests that values lower than 0.5 are viable but barely distinguishable from one another. You can also effectively override this value dynamically through the scroll view's delegate (discussed later in this chapter).

showsHorizontalScrollIndicator, showsVerticalScrollIndicator

The scroll indicators are bars that appear only while the user is scrolling in a scrollable dimension (where the content is larger than the scroll view), and serve to indicate both the size of the content in that dimension relative to the scroll view and where the user is within it. The default is YES for both.

Because the user cannot see the scroll indicators except when actively scrolling, there is normally no indication that the view is scrollable. I regard this as somewhat unfortunate, because it makes the possibility of scrolling less discoverable; I'd prefer an option to make the scroll indicators constantly visible. Apple suggests that you call `flashScrollIndicators` when the scroll view appears, to make the scroll indicators visible momentarily.

`indicatorStyle`
The way the scroll indicators are drawn. Your choices are:

- `UIScrollViewIndicatorStyleDefault` (black with a white border)
- `UIScrollViewIndicatorStyleBlack` (black)
- `UIScrollViewIndicatorStyleWhite` (white)

`contentInset`
A UIEdgeInsets struct (four CGFloats in the order `top`, `left`, `bottom`, `right`) specifying margins around the content. A typical use for this would be that your scroll view underlaps an interface element, such as a translucent status bar, navigation bar, or toolbar, and you want your content to be visible even when scrolled to its limit.

For example, suppose that our app with the 30 labels has its *Info.plist* configured with the "Status bar style" key set to "Transparent black style," and that our scroll view's view controller sets its `wantsFullScreenLayout` to YES. The scroll view now underlaps the status bar. This looks cool while scrolling, but at launch time, and if scrolled all the way to the top, the first label is partly covered by the status bar. We can fix this by supplying a `contentInset` whose `top` matches the height of the status bar. We may also have to scroll the content into position at launch time in code so that it looks right:

```
CGFloat top = [[UIApplication sharedApplication] statusBarFrame].size.height;
sv.contentInset = UIEdgeInsetsMake(top,0,0,0);
[sv scrollRectToVisible:CGRectMake(0,0,1,1) animated:NO];
```

If a scroll view participates in state restoration (Chapter 19), its `contentInset` is saved and restored.

`scrollIndicatorInsets`
A UIEdgeInsets struct specifying a shift in the position of the scroll indicators. A typical use is to compensate for the `contentInset`. For example, returning to our scroll view that underlaps the translucent status bar, the content is no longer hidden under the status bar when scrolled to the top, but the top of the vertical scroll indicator is. We can fix this by setting the `scrollIndicatorInsets` to the same value as the `contentInset`.

Here's a trick I've sometimes used: by setting a `scrollIndicator-Insets` component to a negative number and setting the scroll view's `clipsToBounds` to NO, you can make the scroll indicators appear *outside* the scroll view. But because you've turned off `clipsToBounds`, you might have to impose some opaque views on top of the interface to mask off the edges of the scroll view, so that its content isn't visible outside its bounds.

You can scroll in code even if the user can't scroll. The content simply moves to the position you specify, with no bouncing and no exposure of the scroll indicators. You can specify the new position in two ways:

`contentOffset`
> The point (CGPoint) of the content that is located at the scroll view's top left (effectively the same thing as the scroll view's bounds origin). You can get this property to learn the current scroll position, and set it to change the current scroll position. The values normally go up from 0 until the limit dictated by the `contentSize` and the scroll view's own bounds is reached.
>
> To set the `contentOffset` with animation, call `setContentOffset:animated:`. The animation does not cause the scroll indicators to appear; it just slides the content to the desired position.
>
> If a scroll view participates in state restoration (Chapter 19), its `contentOffset` is saved and restored, so when the app is relaunched, the scroll view will reappear scrolled to the same position as before.

`scrollRectToVisible:animated:`
> Adjusts the content so that the specified CGRect of the view is within the scroll view's bounds. This is less precise than setting the `contentOffset`, because you're not saying exactly what the resulting scroll position will be, but sometimes guaranteeing the visibility of a certain portion of the content is exactly what you're after.

If you call a method to scroll with animation and you need to know when the animation ends, implement `scrollViewDidEndScrollingAnimation:` in the scroll view's delegate.

Paging

If its `pagingEnabled` property is YES, the scroll view doesn't let the user scroll freely; instead, the content is considered to consist of sections the size of the scroll view's bounds, and the user can scroll only in such a way as to move to an adjacent section.

For instance, one of Apple's examples consists of a scroll view containing image views. Each image view is the size of the scroll view. This is an appropriate use of `pagingEnabled`. The user can scroll to see the entire next image or the entire previous image.

Figure 20-3. A scroll view coordinated with a page control

The scroll indicator, if it appears, gives the user a sense of how many "pages" constitute the view. Alternatively, you could use delegate messages to coordinate with a UIPage-Control (Chapter 25). Figure 20-3 shows my modification of Apple's Scrolling example, where I've added a UIPageControl below the paging scroll view. Here's the code that updates the page control (pager) when the user scrolls:

```
- (void)scrollViewDidEndDecelerating:(UIScrollView *)scrollView {
    CGFloat x = scrollView.contentOffset.x;
    CGFloat w = scrollView.bounds.size.width;
    self.pager.currentPage = x/w;
}
```

And here's the code that scrolls the scroll view (sv) when the user taps the page control:

```
- (void) userDidPage: (id) sender {
    NSInteger p = self.pager.currentPage;
    CGFloat w = self.sv.bounds.size.width;
    [self.sv setContentOffset:CGPointMake(p*w,0) animated:YES];
}
```

A useful interface is a paging scroll view where you supply pages dynamically as the user scrolls. In this way, you can display a huge number of pages without having to put them all into the scroll view at once. UIPageViewController (Chapter 19) provides exactly that interface. (Prior to iOS 5, before UIPageViewController was introduced, I had written a scroll view that did the same thing; if you're curious about the technique I was using, watch the Advanced Scroll View Techniques video from WWDC 2011, which describes something very similar, calling it "infinite scrolling".)

Tiling

Suppose we have some finite but really big content that we want to display in a scroll view, such as a very large image that the user can inspect, piecemeal, by scrolling. To hold the entire image in memory may be onerous or impossible.

Tiling is one solution to this kind of problem. It takes advantage of the insight that there's really no need to hold the entire image in memory; all we need at any given moment is the part of the image the user is looking at right now. Mentally, divide the content rectangle into a matrix of rectangles; these rectangles are the tiles. In reality, divide the huge image into corresponding rectangles. Then whenever the user scrolls, we look to see whether part of any empty tile has become visible, and if so, we supply its content. At the same time, we can release the content of all tiles that are completely offscreen. Thus, at any given moment, only the tiles that are showing have content. There is some latency associated with this approach (the user scrolls, then any empty newly visible tiles are filled in), but we will have to live with that.

There is actually a built-in CALayer subclass for helping us implement tiling — CATiledLayer. Its tileSize property sets the dimensions of a tile. Its drawLayer:in-Context: is called when content for an empty tile is needed; calling CGContextGetClip-BoundingBox on the context reveals the location of desired tile, and now we can supply that tile's content.

To illustrate, we'll use some tiles already created for us as part of Apple's own Photo-Scroller example. In particular, I'll use the "Shed_1000" images. These all have names of the form *Shed_1000_x_y.png*, where *x* and *y* are integers corresponding to the picture's position within the matrix. The images are 256×256 pixels (except for the ones on the extreme right and bottom edges of the matrix, which are shorter in one dimension).

Once again I'll start with the Empty Application template with an added ViewController class acting as the root view controller. We also have a TiledView class (a UIView subclass). Once again I'll implement loadView to make the root view controller's view a UIScrollView; our scroll view's sole subview will be a TiledView, which exists purely to give our CATiledLayer a place to live. We have just one set of tile images and we want these to appear the same size regardless of the display resolution, so we'll set the CATiledLayer's tile size with respect to its native scale (TILESIZE is defined as 256, to match the image dimensions):

```
UIScrollView* sv = [[UIScrollView alloc] initWithFrame:
                        [[UIScreen mainScreen] applicationFrame]];
sv.backgroundColor = [UIColor whiteColor];
self.view = sv;
CGRect f = CGRectMake(0,0,3*TILESIZE,3*TILESIZE);
TiledView* content = [[TiledView alloc] initWithFrame:f];
float tsz = TILESIZE * content.layer.contentsScale;
[(CATiledLayer*)content.layer setTileSize: CGSizeMake(tsz, tsz)];
[self.view addSubview:content];
[sv setContentSize: f.size];
```

Here's the code for TiledView. The CATiledLayer is our underlying layer; therefore we are its delegate. This means that when drawLayer:inContext: is called, drawRect: is called, and the argument to drawRect: is the same as the result of calling CGContextGet-ClipBoundingBox, namely, it's the rect of the tile we are to draw. As Apple's code points out, we must fetch images with imageWithContentsOfFile: so as to avoid the automatic caching behavior of imageNamed:, because we're doing all this exactly to prevent using more memory than we have to:

```
+ (Class) layerClass {
    return [CATiledLayer class];
}

-(void)drawRect:(CGRect)r {
    CGRect tile = r;
    int x = tile.origin.x/TILESIZE;
    int y = tile.origin.y/TILESIZE;
    NSString *tileName = [NSString stringWithFormat:@"Shed_1000_%i_%i", x, y];
    NSString *path =
        [[NSBundle mainBundle] pathForResource:tileName ofType:@"png"];
    UIImage *image = [UIImage imageWithContentsOfFile:path];
    [image drawAtPoint:tile.origin];
    // uncomment the following to see the tile boundaries
    /*
    UIBezierPath* bp = [UIBezierPath bezierPathWithRect: r];
    [[UIColor whiteColor] setStroke];
    [bp stroke];
    */
}
```

There is no special call for invalidating an offscreen tile. You can call setNeeds-Display or setNeedsDisplayInRect: on the TiledView, but this doesn't erase offscreen tiles. You're just supposed to trust that the CATiledLayer will eventually clear offscreen tiles if needed to conserve memory.

CATiledLayer has a class method fadeDuration that dictates the duration of the animation that fades a new tile into view. You can create a CATiledLayer subclass and override this method to return a value different from the default (0.25), but in general this is probably not worth doing, as the default value is a good one. Returning a smaller value won't make tiles appear faster; it just replaces the nice fade-in with an annoying flash.

Zooming

To implement zooming of a scroll view's content, you set the scroll view's minimumZoom-Scale and maximumZoomScale so that at least one of them isn't 1 (the default). You also implement viewForZoomingInScrollView: in the scroll view's delegate to tell the scroll view which of its subviews is to be the scalable view. The scroll view then zooms by applying a scaling transform (Chapter 14) to this subview. The amount of that transform is the scroll view's zoomScale property. Typically, you'll want the scroll view's entire content to be scalable, so you'll have one direct subview of the scroll view that acts as the scalable view, and anything else inside the scroll view will be a subview of the scalable view, so as to be scaled together with it.

To illustrate, let's return to the first example in this chapter, where we created a scroll view containing 30 labels. To make this scroll view zoomable, we'll need to modify the way we create it. As it stands, the scroll view's subviews are just the 30 labels; there is no single view that we would scale in order to scale all the labels together. This time, as we create the scroll view in our root view controller's loadView implementation, instead of making the 30 labels subviews of the scroll view, we'll make them subviews of a single scalable view and make the scalable view the subview of the scroll view:

```
UIScrollView* sv = [[UIScrollView alloc] initWithFrame:
                        [[UIScreen mainScreen] applicationFrame]];
self.view = sv;
UIView* v = [UIView new];
CGFloat y = 10;
for (int i=0; i<30; i++) {
    UILabel* lab = [UILabel new];
    lab.text = [NSString stringWithFormat:@"This is label %i", i+1];
    [lab sizeToFit];
    CGRect f = lab.frame;
    f.origin = CGPointMake(10,y);
    lab.frame = f;
    [v addSubview:lab];
    y += lab.bounds.size.height + 10;
}
CGSize sz = sv.bounds.size;
sz.height = y;
sv.contentSize = sz;
v.frame = CGRectMake(0,0,sz.width,sz.height);
[sv addSubview:v];
```

So far, nothing has changed; the scroll view works just as before, but it isn't zoomable. To make it zoomable, we add these lines:

```
v.tag = 999;
sv.minimumZoomScale = 1.0;
sv.maximumZoomScale = 2.0;
sv.delegate = self;
```

We have assigned a tag to the view that is to be scaled, so we can find it later. We have set the scale limits for the scroll view. And we have made ourselves the scroll view's delegate. Now all we have to do is implement viewForZoomingInScrollView: and return the scalable view:

```
- (UIView *)viewForZoomingInScrollView:(UIScrollView *)scrollView {
    return [scrollView viewWithTag:999];
}
```

The scroll view now responds to pinch gestures by scaling appropriately! The user can actually scale considerably beyond the limits we set in both directions; when the gesture ends, the scale returns to the limit value. If we wish to confine scaling strictly to our defined limits, we can set the scroll view's bouncesZoom to NO; when the user reaches a limit, scaling will simply stop.

The actual amount of zoom is reflected as the scroll view's current zoomScale. If a scroll view participates in state restoration, its zoomScale is saved and restored, so when the app is relaunched, the scroll view will reappear zoomed by the same amount as before.

 The scroll view zooms by applying a scaling transform to the scalable view; therefore *the frame of the scalable view is scaled as well.* Moreover, the scroll view is concerned to make scrolling continue to work correctly: the limits as the user scrolls should continue to match the limits of the content, and commands like scrollRectToVisible:animated: should continue to work the same way for the same values. Therefore, the scroll view *automatically scales its own contentSize* to match the current zoomScale. (You can actually detect this happening by overriding setContentSize in a UIScrollView subclass: you can see the scroll view adjusting its own content size as you zoom.)

If the minimumZoomScale is less than 1, then when the scalable view becomes smaller than the scroll view, it is pinned to the scroll view's top left. If you don't like this, you can change it by subclassing UIScrollView and overriding layoutSubviews, or by implementing the scroll view delegate method scrollViewDidZoom:. Here's a simple example (drawn from a WWDC 2010 video) demonstrating an override of layoutSubviews that keeps the scalable view centered when it becomes smaller than the scroll view:

```
-(void)layoutSubviews {
    [super layoutSubviews];
    UIView* v = [self.delegate viewForZoomingInScrollView:self];
    CGFloat svw = self.bounds.size.width;
    CGFloat svh = self.bounds.size.height;
    CGFloat vw = v.frame.size.width;
    CGFloat vh = v.frame.size.height;
    CGRect f = v.frame;
    if (vw < svw)
        f.origin.x = (svw - vw) / 2.0;
    else
        f.origin.x = 0;
    if (vh < svh)
        f.origin.y = (svh - vh) / 2.0;
```

```
        else
            f.origin.y = 0;
        v.frame = f;
    }
```

Zooming Programmatically

To zoom programmatically, you have two choices:

`setZoomScale:animated:`
> Zooms in terms of scale value. The `contentOffset` is automatically adjusted to keep the current center centered and the content occupying the entire scroll view.

`zoomToRect:animated:`
> Zooms so that the given rectangle of the content occupies as much as possible of the scroll view's bounds. The `contentOffset` is automatically adjusted to keep the content occupying the entire scroll view.

In this example, I implement double tapping as a zoom gesture. Detecting the double tap is easy thanks to a gesture recognizer attached to the scalable view (Chapter 18). In this implementation of the action handler for the double-tap UITapGestureRecognizer, a double tap means to zoom to maximum scale, minimum scale, or actual size, depending on the current scale value:

```
- (void) tapped: (UIGestureRecognizer*) tap {
    UIView* v = tap.view;
    UIScrollView* sv = (UIScrollView*)v.superview;
    if (sv.zoomScale < 1) {
        [sv setZoomScale:1 animated:YES];
        CGPoint pt =
            CGPointMake((v.bounds.size.width - sv.bounds.size.width)/2.0,0);
        [sv setContentOffset:pt animated:NO];
    }
    else if (sv.zoomScale < sv.maximumZoomScale)
        [sv setZoomScale:sv.maximumZoomScale animated:YES];
    else
        [sv setZoomScale:sv.minimumZoomScale animated:YES];
}
```

Zooming with Detail

By default, when a scroll view zooms, it merely applies a scale transform to the scaled view. The scaled view's drawing is cached beforehand into its layer, so when we zoom in, the bits of the resulting bitmap are drawn larger. This means that a zoomed-in scroll view's content may be fuzzy (pixellated). In some cases this might be acceptable, but in others you might like the content to be redrawn more sharply at its new size.

(On a double-resolution device, this might not be such an issue. For example, if the user is allowed to zoom only up to double scale, you can draw at double scale right from the start; the results will look good at single scale, because the screen has double resolution, as well as at double scale, because that's the scale you drew at.)

One solution is to take advantage of a CATiledLayer feature that I didn't mention earlier. It turns out that CATiledLayer is aware not only of scrolling but also of scaling: you can configure it to ask for tiles to be drawn when the layer is scaled to a new order of magnitude. This approach is extremely easy: your drawing routine is called and you simply draw, the graphics context itself having already been scaled appropriately. In fact, your drawing doesn't even have to involve multiple tiles! Of course it *can* involve tiles; for a large tiled image, you would be forearmed with multiple versions of the image broken into an identical quantity of tiles, each set having double the tile size of the previous set (as in Apple's PhotoScroller example). But you can also just draw directly.

Besides its `tileSize`, you'll need to set two additional CATiledLayer properties:

levelsOfDetail
> The number of different resolutions at which you want to redraw, where each level has twice the resolution of the previous level. So, for example, with two levels of detail we can ask to redraw when zooming to double size (2x) and when zooming back to single size (1x).

levelsOfDetailBias
> The number of levels of detail that are *larger* than single size (1x). For example, if levelsOfDetail is 2, then if we want to redraw when zooming to 2x and when zooming back to 1x, the levelsOfDetailBias is 1, because one of those levels is larger than 1x; if we were to leave levelsOfDetailBias at 0 (the default), we would be saying we want to redraw when zooming to 0.5x and back to 1x — we have two levels of detail but neither is larger than 1x, so one must be smaller than 1x.

The CATiledLayer will ask for a redraw at a higher resolution as soon as the view's size becomes larger than the previous resolution. In other words, if there are two levels of detail with a bias of 1, the layer will be redrawn at 2x as soon as it is zoomed even a little bit larger than 1x. This is an excellent approach, because although a level of detail would look blurry if scaled up, it looks pretty good scaled down.

To illustrate, I'll reuse our previous example, where the root view controller's view is a scroll view whose subview is a TiledView that hosts a CATiledLayer; but this time I'll draw our 30 labels into the CATiledLayer. The tile size is of no particular importance:

```
- (void)loadView {
    UIScrollView* sv = [[UIScrollView alloc] initWithFrame:
                        [[UIScreen mainScreen] applicationFrame]];
    self.view = sv;
    CGRect f = CGRectMake(0, 0, self.view.bounds.size.width,
                          self.view.bounds.size.height * 2);
    TiledView* content = [[TiledView alloc] initWithFrame:f];
    content.tag = 999;
```

```
        CATiledLayer* lay = (CATiledLayer*)content.layer;
        lay.tileSize = f.size;
        lay.levelsOfDetail = 2;
        lay.levelsOfDetailBias = 1;
        [self.view addSubview:content];
        [sv setContentSize: f.size];
        sv.minimumZoomScale = 1.0;
        sv.maximumZoomScale = 2.0;
        sv.delegate = self;
    }


    - (UIView *)viewForZoomingInScrollView:(UIScrollView *)scrollView {
        return [scrollView viewWithTag:999];
    }
```

Here's the code for TiledView. Its `drawRect:` essentially does the work of putting the labels into place that we were previously doing in `loadView`, except that now there are no labels: we're in `drawRect:` so we draw the text directly, with no concern for zooming or scaling:

```
    + (Class) layerClass {
        return [CATiledLayer class];
    }


    -(void)drawRect:(CGRect)r {
        [[UIColor whiteColor] set];
        UIRectFill(self.bounds);
        [[UIColor blackColor] set];
        UIFont* f = [UIFont fontWithName:@"Helvetica" size:18];
        // height consists of 31 spacers with 30 texts between them
        CGFloat viewh = self.bounds.size.height;
        CGFloat spacerh = 10;
        CGFloat texth = (viewh - (31*spacerh))/30.0;
        CGFloat y = spacerh;
        for (int i = 0; i < 30; i++) {
            NSString* s = [NSString stringWithFormat:@"This is label %i", i];
            [s drawAtPoint:CGPointMake(10,y) withFont:f];
            y += texth + spacerh;
        }
        // uncomment the following to see the tiling
        /*
        UIBezierPath* bp = [UIBezierPath bezierPathWithRect:r];
        [[UIColor redColor] setStroke];
        [bp stroke];
        */
    }
```

An alternative and much simpler approach (from a WWDC 2011 video) is to make yourself the scroll view's delegate so that you get an event when the zoom ends, and then change the scalable view's `contentScaleFactor` to match the current zoom scale, compensating for the double-resolution screen at the same time:

```
- (void)scrollViewDidEndZooming:(UIScrollView *)scrollView
                       withView:(UIView *)view
                        atScale:(float)scale {
    view.contentScaleFactor = scale * [UIScreen mainScreen].scale;
}
```

That approach comes with a caveat, however: you mustn't overdo it. If the zoom scale, screen resolution, and scalable view size are high, you will be asking for a very large graphics context to be maintained in memory, which could cause your app to run low on memory or even to be abruptly terminated by the system.

Scroll View Delegate

The scroll view's delegate (adopting the UIScrollViewDelegate protocol) receives lots of messages that can help you track what the scroll view is up to:

scrollViewDidScroll:
> If you scroll in code without animation, you will receive this message *once*. If the user drags or flicks, or uses the scroll-to-top feature, or if you scroll in code with animation, you will receive this message *repeatedly* throughout the scroll, including during the time the scroll view is decelerating after the user's finger has lifted; there are other delegate messages that tell you, in those cases, when the scroll has really ended.

scrollViewDidEndScrollingAnimation:
> If you scroll in code with animation, you will receive this message when the animation ends.

scrollViewWillBeginDragging:
scrollViewWillEndDragging:withVelocity:targetContentOffset:
scrollViewDidEndDragging:willDecelerate:
> If the user scrolls by dragging or flicking, you will receive these messages at the start and end of the user's finger movement. If the user brings the scroll view to a stop before lifting the finger, willDecelerate is NO and the scroll is over. If the user lets go of the scroll view while the finger is moving, or if paging is turned on and the user has not paged perfectly already, willDecelerate is YES and we proceed to the delegate messages reporting deceleration.

> The purpose of scrollViewWillEndDragging:... is to let you customize the outcome of the content's deceleration. The third argument is a pointer to a CGPoint; thus you can use it to set a different CGPoint, specifying the contentOffset value the content should have when the deceleration is over.

`scrollViewWillBeginDecelerating:`
`scrollViewDidEndDecelerating:`

> Sent once each after `scrollViewDidEndDragging:willDecelerate:` arrives with a value of YES. When `scrollViewDidEndDecelerating:` arrives, the scroll is over.

`scrollViewShouldScrollToTop:`
`scrollViewDidScrollToTop:`

> These have to do with the feature where the user can tap the status bar to scroll the scroll view's content to its top. You won't get either of them if `scrollsToTop` is NO, because the scroll-to-top feature is turned off in that case. The first lets you prevent the user from scrolling to the top on this occasion even if `scrollsToTop` is YES. The second tells you that the user has employed this feature and the scroll is over.

In addition, the scroll view has read-only properties reporting its state:

`tracking`

> The user has touched the scroll view, but the scroll view hasn't decided whether this is a scroll or some kind of tap.

`dragging`

> The user is dragging to scroll.

`decelerating`

> The user has scrolled and has lifted the finger, and the scroll is continuing.

So, if you wanted to do something after a scroll ends completely regardless of how the scroll was performed, you'd need to implement many delegate methods:

- `scrollViewDidEndDragging:willDecelerate:` in case the user drags and stops (`willDecelerate` is NO).

- `scrollViewDidEndDecelerating:` in case the user drags and the scroll continues afterward.

- `scrollViewDidScrollToTop:` in case the user uses the scroll-to-top feature.

- `scrollViewDidEndScrollingAnimation:` in case you scroll in code with animation.

You don't need a delegate method to tell you when the scroll is over after you scroll in code without animation: it's over immediately, so if you have work to do after the scroll ends, you can do it in the next line of code.

There are also three delegate messages that report zooming:

`scrollViewWillBeginZooming:withView:`

> If the user zooms or you zoom in code, you will receive this message as the zoom begins.

`scrollViewDidZoom:`

> If you zoom in code, even with animation, you will receive this message *once*. If the user zooms, you will receive this message *repeatedly* as the zoom proceeds. (You will probably also receive `scrollViewDidScroll:`, possibly many times, as the zoom proceeds.)

`scrollViewDidEndZooming:withView:atScale:`

> If the user zooms or you zoom in code, you will receive this message after the last `scrollViewDidZoom:`.

In addition, the scroll view has read-only properties reporting its state during a zoom:

`zooming`

> The scroll view is zooming. It is possible for `dragging` to be true at the same time.

`zoomBouncing`

> The scroll view is returning automatically from having been zoomed outside its minimum or maximum limit. As far as I can tell, you'll get only one `scrollView-DidZoom:` while the scroll view is in this state.

Scroll View Touches

Improvements in the scroll view implementation have eliminated most of the worry once associated with scroll view touches. A scroll view will interpret a drag or a pinch as a command to scroll or zoom, and any other gesture will fall through to the subviews; thus buttons and similar interface objects inside a scroll view work just fine.

You can even put a scroll view inside a scroll view, and this can be quite a useful thing to do, in contexts where you might not think of it at first. A WWDC 2010 video uses as an example Apple's Photos app, where a single photo fills the screen: you can page-scroll from one photo to the next, and you can zoom the current photo with a pinch-out gesture. This, the video demonstrates, can be implemented with a scroll view inside a scroll view: the outer scroll view is for paging between images, and the inner scroll view contains the current image and is for zooming.

Gesture recognizers (Chapter 18) have also greatly simplified the task of adding custom gestures to a scroll view. For instance, some older code in Apple's documentation, showing how to implement a double tap to zoom in and a two-finger tap to zoom out, uses old-fashioned touch handling, but this is no longer necessary. Simply attach to your scroll view's scalable subview any gesture recognizers for these sorts of gesture, and they will mediate automatically among the possibilities.

In the past, making something inside a scroll view draggable required setting the scroll view's `canCancelContentTouches` property to NO. (The reason for the name is that the scroll view, when it realizes that a gesture is a drag or pinch gesture, normally sends touchesCancelled:forEvent: to a subview tracking touches, so that the scroll view and not the subview will be affected.) However, unless you're implementing old-fashioned direct touch handling, you probably won't have to concern yourself with this. Regardless of how canCancelContentTouches is set, a draggable control, such as a UI-Slider, remains draggable inside a scroll view.

On the other hand, something like a UISlider might prove more quickly responsive if you set the scroll view's delaysContentTouches to NO. Without this, the user may have to hold a finger on the slider briefly before it becomes draggable. But even this will be a concern only if the scroll view is scrollable in the same dimension as the slider is oriented; a horizontal slider in a scroll view that can be scrolled only vertically is instantly draggable.

Here's an example of a draggable object inside a scroll view implemented through a gesture recognizer. Suppose we have an image of a map, larger than the screen, and we want the user to be able to scroll it in the normal way to see any part of the map, but we also want the user to be able to drag a flag into a new location on the map. We'll put the map image in an image view and wrap the image view in a scroll view, with the scroll view's contentSize the same as the map image view's size. The flag is a small image view; it's another subview of the scroll view, and it has a UIPanGestureRecognizer:

```
UIScrollView* sv = [UIScrollView new];
self.sv = sv;
[self.view addSubview:sv];
sv.translatesAutoresizingMaskIntoConstraints = NO;
[self.view addConstraints:
 [NSLayoutConstraint
  constraintsWithVisualFormat:@"H:|[sv]|"
  options:0 metrics:nil views:@{@"sv":sv}]];
[self.view addConstraints:
 [NSLayoutConstraint
  constraintsWithVisualFormat:@"V:|[sv]|"
  options:0 metrics:nil views:@{@"sv":sv}]];

UIImageView* imv = [[UIImageView alloc] initWithImage:
                     [UIImage imageNamed:@"map.jpg"]];
[sv addSubview:imv];
imv.translatesAutoresizingMaskIntoConstraints = NO;
// constraints here mean "content view is the size of the map image view"
[self.view addConstraints:
 [NSLayoutConstraint
  constraintsWithVisualFormat:@"H:|[imv]|"
  options:0 metrics:nil views:@{@"imv":imv}]];
[self.view addConstraints:
 [NSLayoutConstraint
  constraintsWithVisualFormat:@"V:|[imv]|"
  options:0 metrics:nil views:@{@"imv":imv}]];

UIImageView* flag = [[UIImageView alloc] initWithImage:
```

```
                        [UIImage imageNamed:@"redflag.png"]];
[sv addSubview: flag];
UIPanGestureRecognizer* pan = [[UIPanGestureRecognizer alloc]
                              initWithTarget:self
                              action:@selector(dragging:)];
[flag addGestureRecognizer:pan];
flag.userInteractionEnabled = YES;
```

The flag image view's UIPanGestureRecognizer has the same dragging: action handler developed in Chapter 18:

```
- (void) dragging: (UIPanGestureRecognizer*) p {
    UIView* v = p.view;
    if (p.state == UIGestureRecognizerStateBegan ||
        p.state == UIGestureRecognizerStateChanged) {
        CGPoint delta = [p translationInView: v.superview];
        CGPoint c = v.center;
        c.x += delta.x; c.y += delta.y;
        v.center = c;
        [p setTranslation: CGPointZero inView: v.superview];
    }
}
```

The user can now drag the map or the flag (Figure 20-4). Dragging the map brings the flag along with it, but dragging the flag doesn't move the map. The state of the scroll view's canCancelContentTouches is irrelevant, because the flag view isn't tracking the touches manually.

An interesting addition to that example would be to implement autoscrolling, meaning that the scroll view scrolls itself when the user drags the flag close to its edge. This, too, is greatly simplified by gesture recognizers; in fact, we can add autoscrolling code directly to the dragging: action handler:

```
- (void) dragging: (UIPanGestureRecognizer*) p {
    UIView* v = p.view;
    if (p.state == UIGestureRecognizerStateBegan ||
        p.state == UIGestureRecognizerStateChanged) {
        CGPoint delta = [p translationInView: v.superview];
        CGPoint c = v.center;
        c.x += delta.x; c.y += delta.y;
        v.center = c;
        [p setTranslation: CGPointZero inView: v.superview];
    }
    // autoscroll
    if (p.state == UIGestureRecognizerStateChanged) {
        CGPoint loc = [p locationInView:self.view.superview];
        CGRect f = self.view.frame;
        UIScrollView* sv = self.sv;
        CGPoint off = sv.contentOffset;
        CGSize sz = sv.contentSize;
        CGPoint c = v.center;
        // to the right
```

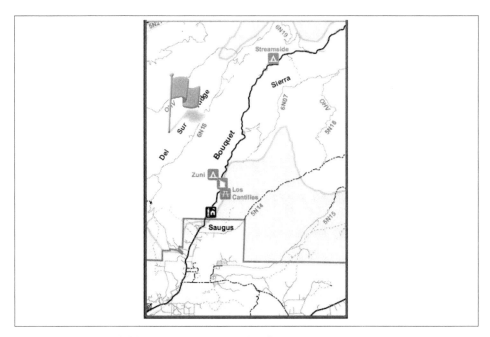

Figure 20-4. A scrollable map with a draggable flag

```
if (loc.x > CGRectGetMaxX(f) - 30) {
    CGFloat margin = sz.width - CGRectGetMaxX(sv.bounds);
    if (margin > 6) {
        off.x += 5;
        sv.contentOffset = off;
        c.x += 5;
        v.center = c;
        [self keepDragging:p];
    }
}
// to the left
if (loc.x < f.origin.x + 30) {
    CGFloat margin = off.x;
    if (margin > 6) {
        // ... omitted ...
    }
}
// to the bottom
if (loc.y > CGRectGetMaxY(f) - 30) {
    CGFloat margin = sz.height - CGRectGetMaxY(sv.bounds);
    if (margin > 6) {
        // ... omitted ...
    }
}
// to the top
```

```
            if (loc.y < f.origin.y + 30) {
                CGFloat margin = off.y;
                if (margin > 6) {
                    // ... omitted ...
                }
            }
        }
    }
}

- (void) keepDragging: (UIPanGestureRecognizer*) p {
    float delay = 0.1;
    dispatch_time_t popTime =
        dispatch_time(DISPATCH_TIME_NOW, delay * NSEC_PER_SEC);
    dispatch_after(popTime, dispatch_get_main_queue(), ^(void){
        [self dragging: p];
    });
}
```

The `delay` in `keepDragging:`, combined with the change in offset, determines the speed of autoscrolling. The material marked as omitted in the second, third, and fourth cases is obviously parallel to the first case, and is left as an exercise for the reader.

A scroll view's touch handling is itself based on gesture recognizers attached to the scroll view, and these are available to your code through the scroll view's `panGesture-Recognizer` and `pinchGestureRecognizer` properties. This means that if you want to customize a scroll view's touch handling, it's easy to add more gesture recognizers and have them interact with those already attached to the scroll view.

To illustrate, I'll build on the previous example. Suppose we want the flag to start out offscreen, and we'd like the user to be able to summon it with a rightward swipe. We can attach a UISwipeGestureRecognizer to our scroll view, but it will never recognize its gesture because the scroll view's own pan gesture recognizer will recognize first. But we have access to the scroll view's pan gesture recognizer, so we can compel it to yield to our swipe gesture recognizer by sending it `requireGestureRecognizerToFail::`:

```
UISwipeGestureRecognizer* swipe =
    [[UISwipeGestureRecognizer alloc]
        initWithTarget:self action:@selector(swiped:)];
[sv addGestureRecognizer:swipe];
[sv.panGestureRecognizer requireGestureRecognizerToFail:swipe];
```

By default, the UISwipeGestureRecognizer will recognize a rightward swipe, which is exactly what we want. Here's my implementation of `swiped:`; we create the flag offscreen and animate it onto the screen:

```
- (void) swiped: (UISwipeGestureRecognizer*) g {
    if (g.state == UIGestureRecognizerStateEnded ||
            g.state == UIGestureRecognizerStateCancelled) {
        UIImageView* flag =
            [[UIImageView alloc] initWithImage:
```

```
                [UIImage imageNamed:@"redflag.png"]];
        UIPanGestureRecognizer* pan = [[UIPanGestureRecognizer alloc]
                                    initWithTarget:self
                                    action:@selector(dragging:)];
        [flag addGestureRecognizer:pan];
        flag.userInteractionEnabled = YES;

        UIScrollView* sv = self.sv;
        CGPoint p = sv.contentOffset;
        CGRect f = flag.frame;
        f.origin = p;
        f.origin.x -= flag.bounds.size.width;
        flag.frame = f;
        [sv addSubview: flag];
        // thanks for the flag, now stop operating altogether
        g.enabled = NO;

        [UIView animateWithDuration:0.25 animations:^{
            CGRect f = flag.frame;
            f.origin.x = p.x;
            flag.frame = f;
        }];
    }
}
```

Scroll View Performance

At several points in earlier chapters I've mentioned performance problems and ways to increase drawing efficiency. Nowhere are you so likely to need these as in connection with a scroll view. As a scroll view scrolls, views must be drawn very rapidly as they appear on the screen. If the view-drawing system can't keep up with the speed of the scroll, the scrolling will visibly stutter.

Performance testing and optimization is a big subject, so I can't tell you exactly what to do if you encounter stuttering while scrolling. But certain general suggestions (mostly extracted from a really great WWDC 2010 video) should come in handy:

- Everything that can be opaque should be opaque: don't force the drawing system to composite transparency, and remember to tell it that an opaque view or layer *is* opaque by setting its opaque property to YES. If you really must composite transparency, keep the size of the nonopaque regions to a minimum; for example, if a large layer is transparent at its edges, break it into five layers — the large central layer, which is opaque, and the four edges, which are not.

- If you're drawing shadows, don't make the drawing system calculate the shadow shape for a layer: supply a shadowPath, or use Core Graphics to create the shadow with a drawing. Similarly, avoid making the drawing system composite the shadow as a transparency against another layer; for example, if the background layer is white, your opaque drawing can itself include a shadow already drawn on a white background.

- Don't make the drawing system scale images for you; supply the images at the target size for the correct resolution.

- In a pinch, you can just eliminate massive swatches of the rendering operation by setting a layer's `shouldRasterize` to YES. You could, for example, do this when scrolling starts and then set it back to NO when scrolling ends.

Apple's documentation also says that setting a view's `clearsContextBeforeDrawing` to NO may make a difference. I can't confirm or deny this; it may be true, but I haven't encountered a case that positively proves it.

As I've already mentioned, Xcode provides tools that will help you detect inefficiencies in the drawing system. In the Simulator, the Debug menu shows you blended layers (where transparency is being composited) and images that are being copied, misaligned, or rendered offscreen. On the device, the Core Animation module of Instruments provides the same functionality, plus it tracks the frame rate for you, allowing you to scroll and measure performance objectively.

CHAPTER 21

Table Views and Collection Views

*I'm gonna ask you the three big questions. — Go
ahead. — Who made you? — You did. — Who
owns the biggest piece of you? — You do. — What
would happen if I dropped you? — I'd go right
down the drain.*

—Dialogue by Garson Kanin and Ruth Gordon,
Pat and Mike

A table view (UITableView) is a scrolling interface (a vertically scrolling UIScrollView,
Chapter 20) for presenting a single column of rectangular cells (UITableViewCell, a
UIView subclass). It is a keystone of Apple's strategy for making the small iPhone screen
useful and powerful, and has three main purposes:

Presentation of information

The cells typically contain text, which the user can read. The cells are usually quite
small, in order to maximize the number of them that appear on the screen at once,
so this text is often condensed, truncated, or otherwise simplified.

Selection

A table view can be used to provide the user with a column of choices. The user
chooses by tapping a cell, which selects the cell; the app responds appropriately to
that choice.

Navigation

The appropriate response to the user's choosing a cell is often navigation to another
interface. This might be done, for example, through a presented view controller or
a navigation interface (Chapter 19). An extremely common configuration is a master–detail interface, in which the master view is (or contains) a table view, often at
the root of a navigation interface; the user taps a listing in the table to navigate to
the details for that choice. This is one reason why truncation of text in a table view
is acceptable: the detail view contains the full information.

In addition to its column of cells, a table view can be extended by a number of other features that make it even more useful and flexible:

- A table can start with a header view at the top and end with a footer view at the bottom.

- The cells can be clumped into sections. Each section can have a header and footer, and these remain visible as long as the section itself occupies the screen, giving the user a clue as to where we are within the table. Moreover, a section index can be provided, in the form of an overlay column of abbreviated section titles, which the user can tap to jump to the start of a section, thus making a long table tractable.

- A table can have a "grouped" format. This is often used for presenting small numbers of related cells.

- Tables can be editable: the user can be permitted to insert, delete, and reorder cells.

Figure 21-1 illustrates four variations of the table view:

1. Apple's Music app lists song titles and artists for a given album in truncated form in a table view within a navigation interface which is itself within a tab bar interface; tapping an album in a table of album titles summons the list of songs within that album, and tapping a song in that list plays it.

2. An app of mine lists Latin words and their definitions in alphabetical order, divided into sections by first letter, with section headers and a section index.

3. Apple's Settings app uses table cells in a grouped format with a header, within a navigation interface, to display a switch and a list of Bluetooth devices; tapping a device name searches for it, while tapping the disclosure button navigates to reveal more information about it.

4. Apple's Music app allows a custom playlist to be edited, with interface for deleting and rearranging cells.

Table cells, too, can be extremely flexible. Some basic table cell formats are provided, such as a text label along with a small image view, but you are free to design your own table cell as you would any other view. There are also some standard interface items that are commonly used in a table cell, such as a checkmark to indicate selection or a right-pointing chevron to indicate that tapping the cell navigates to a detail view.

It would be difficult to overestimate the importance of table views. An iOS app without a table view somewhere in its interface would be a rare thing, especially on the small iPhone screen. I've written apps consisting almost entirely of table views. Indeed, it is not uncommon to use a table view even in situations that have nothing particularly table-like about them, simply because it is so convenient. For example, in one of my apps I want the user to be able to choose between three levels of difficulty. In a desktop application I'd probably use radio buttons; but there are no radio buttons among the

Figure 21-1. Four table view variations

Figure 21-2. A grouped table view as an interface for choosing options

standard iOS interface objects. Instead, I use a grouped table so small that it doesn't even scroll. This gives me a section header, three tappable cells, and a checkmark indicating the current choice (Figure 21-2).

There is a UIViewController subclass, UITableViewController, dedicated to the presentation of a table view. You never really *need* to use a UITableViewController; it's a convenience, but it doesn't do anything that you couldn't do yourself by other means. Here's some of what using a UITableViewController gives you:

- UITableViewController's `initWithStyle:` creates the table view with a plain or grouped format.

- The view controller is automatically made the table view's delegate and data source, unless you specify otherwise.

- The table view is made the view controller's `tableView`. It is also, of course, the view controller's `view`, but the `tableView` property is typed as a UITableView, so you can send table view messages to it without typecasting.

This chapter also discusses collection views (UICollectionView), new in iOS 6. A collection view is a generalization of a table view allowing cells to be laid out and scrolled very flexibly.

Table View Cells

Beginners may be surprised to learn that a table view's structure and contents are not configured in advance. Rather, you supply the table view with a data source and a delegate (which will often be the same object; see Chapter 11), and the table view turns to these in real time, as the app runs, whenever it needs a piece of information about its structure and contents.

This architecture is actually part of a brilliant strategy to conserve resources. Imagine a long table consisting of thousands of rows. It must appear, therefore, to consist of thousands of cells as the user scrolls. But a cell is a UIView and is memory-intensive; to maintain thousands of cells internally would put a terrible strain on memory. Therefore, the table typically maintains only as many cells as are showing simultaneously at any one moment (about ten, let's say). As the user scrolls, the table grabs a cell that is no longer showing on the screen and is therefore no longer needed, and hands it back to you and asks you to configure it as the cell that is about to be scrolled into view. Cells are thus *reused* to minimize the number of actual cells in existence at any one moment.

Therefore your code must be prepared, on demand, to supply the table with pieces of requested data. Of these, the most important is the table cell to be slotted into a given position. A position in the table is specified by means of an index path (NSIndexPath), a class used here to combine a section number with a row number, and is often referred to simply as a *row* of the table. Your data source object may at any moment be sent the message `tableView:cellForRowAtIndexPath:`, and must respond by returning the UITableViewCell to be displayed at that row of the table. And you must return it *fast*: the user is scrolling *now*, so the table needs the next cell *now*.

In this section, then, I'll discuss *what* you're going to be supplying — the table view cell. After that, I'll talk about *how* you supply it.

A table view whose cell contents are known beforehand, such as the one shown in Figure 21-2, *can* in fact be configured in advance, by designing the table's view controller in a storyboard. I'll discuss how to do that later in this chapter.

Built-In Cell Styles

To create a cell using one of the built-in cell styles, call `initWithStyle:reuse-Identifier:`. The `reuseIdentifier` is what allows cells previously assigned to rows that are now longer showing to be reused for cells that are; it will usually be the same for all cells in a table. Your choices of cell style are:

`UITableViewCellStyleDefault`
    The cell has a UILabel (its `textLabel`), with an optional UIImageView (its `imageView`) at the left. If there is no image, the label occupies the entire width of the cell.

`UITableViewCellStyleValue1`
    The cell has two UILabels (its `textLabel` and its `detailTextLabel`), side by side, with an optional UIImageView (its `imageView`) at the left. The first label is left-aligned; the second label is right-aligned. If the first label's text is too long, the second label won't appear.

`UITableViewCellStyleValue2`
    The cell has two UILabels (its `textLabel` and its `detailTextLabel`), side by side. No UIImageView will appear. The first label is right-aligned; the second label is left-aligned. The label sizes are fixed, and the text of either will be truncated if it's too long.

`UITableViewCellStyleSubtitle`
    The cell has two UILabels (its `textLabel` and its `detailTextLabel`), one above the other, with an optional UIImageView (its `imageView`) at the left.

To experiment with the built-in cell styles, do this.

1. Make a new iPhone project from the Empty Application project template.

2. Choose File → New → File and ask for a Cocoa Touch Objective-C class.

3. Make it a UITableViewController subclass called RootViewController. "With XIB for user interface" should be checked, so that Xcode will hook up the table view in the nib correctly.

4. Create the files.

To get our table view into the interface, import "RootViewController.h" into *App-Delegate.m*, and add this line to AppDelegate's `application:didFinishLaunchingWith-Options::`

```
self.window.rootViewController = [RootViewController new];
```

Now modify the RootViewController class (which comes with a lot of templated code), as in Example 21-1.

Example 21-1. The world's simplest table

```
- (NSInteger)numberOfSectionsInTableView:(UITableView *)tableView {
    return 1; ❶
}

- (NSInteger)tableView:(UITableView *)tableView
        numberOfRowsInSection:(NSInteger)section {
    return 20; ❷
}

- (UITableViewCell *)tableView:(UITableView *)tableView
        cellForRowAtIndexPath:(NSIndexPath *)indexPath {
    static NSString *CellIdentifier = @"Cell";
    UITableViewCell *cell =
        [tableView dequeueReusableCellWithIdentifier:CellIdentifier];
    if (cell == nil) {
        cell =
            [[UITableViewCell alloc] initWithStyle:UITableViewCellStyleDefault
                                reuseIdentifier:CellIdentifier]; ❸
        ❹
    }
    cell.textLabel.text = @"Howdy there"; ❺
    return cell;
}
```

The idea is to start by generating a single cell in a built-in cell style and then to examine and experiment with its appearance by tweaking the code and running the app. The key parts of the code are:

❶ Our table will have one section.

❷ Our table will consist of 20 rows. We're going to make our cell without regard to what row it is slotted into; so all 20 rows will be identical. But having multiple rows will give us a sense of how our cell looks when placed next to other cells.

❸ This is where you specify the built-in table cell style you want to experiment with. Change `UITableViewCellStyleDefault` to a different style as desired.

❹ At this point in the code you can modify characteristics of the cell (`cell`) that are to be the same for *every* cell of the table. I'll give an example later.

❺ We now have the cell to be used for *this* row of the table, so at this point in the code you can modify characteristics of the cell (`cell`) that are unique to this row. Of course, that isn't what I've done in the example code; as I just said, all the cells will be identical for now. But that's just because we're only beginners. In real life they'd obviously be likely to have different text, so this is where we put the code that sets the text.

Build and run the app. Behold your table. Now you can start experimenting.

The flexibility of the built-in styles is based mostly on the flexibility of UILabels. Not everything can be customized, because after you return the cell some further configuration takes place, which may override your settings. For example, the size and position of the cell's subviews are not up to you. (I'll explain how to get around that, a little later.) But you get a remarkable degree of freedom. Here are some basic UILabel properties for you to play with (and I'll talk much more about UILabels in Chapter 23):

`text`
> The string shown in the label.

`textColor, highlightedTextColor`
> The color of the text. The `highlightedTextColor` applies when the cell is selected (tap on a cell to select it); if you don't set it, the label may choose its own variant of the `textColor` when the cell is highlighted.

`textAlignment`
> How the text is aligned; some possible choices are `NSTextAlignmentLeft`, `NSTextAlignmentCenter`, and `NSTextAlignmentRight`.

`numberOfLines`
> The maximum number of lines of text to appear in the label. Text that is long but permitted to wrap, or that contains explicit linefeed characters, can appear completely in the label if the label is tall enough and the number of permitted lines is sufficient. `0` means there's no maximum.

`font`
> The label's font. You could reduce the font size as a way of fitting more text into the label. A font name includes its style. For example:
>
> ```
> cell.textLabel.font = [UIFont fontWithName:@"Helvetica-Bold" size:12.0];
> ```

`shadowColor, shadowOffset`
> The text shadow. Adding a little shadow can increase clarity and emphasis for large text.

The image view's frame can't be changed, but you can inset its apparent size by supplying a smaller image and setting the image view's `contentMode` to `UIViewContentModeCenter`. It's probably a good idea in any case, for performance reasons, to supply images at their drawn size and resolution rather than making the drawing system scale them for you (see the last section of Chapter 20). For example:

```
UIImage* im = [UIImage imageNamed:@"pic.png"];
UIGraphicsBeginImageContextWithOptions(CGSizeMake(36,36), YES, 0);
[im drawInRect:CGRectMake(0,0,36,36)];
UIImage* im2 = UIGraphicsGetImageFromCurrentImageContext();
UIGraphicsEndImageContext();
cell.imageView.image = im2;
cell.imageView.contentMode = UIViewContentModeCenter;
```

The cell itself also has some properties you can play with:

accessoryType

A built-in type of accessory view, which appears at the cell's right end. For example:

```
cell.accessoryType = UITableViewCellAccessoryDisclosureIndicator;
```

accessoryView

Your own UIView, which appears at the cell's right end (overriding the accessory-Type). For example:

```
UIButton* b = [UIButton buttonWithType:UIButtonTypeRoundedRect];
[b setTitle:@"Tap Me" forState:UIControlStateNormal];
[b sizeToFit];
// ... also assign button a target and action ...
cell.accessoryView = b;
```

indentationLevel, indentationWidth

These properties give the cell a left margin, useful for suggesting a hierarchy among cells. You can also set a cell's indentation level in real time, with respect to the table row into which it is slotted, by implementing the delegate's table-View:indentationLevelForRowAtIndexPath: method.

selectionStyle

How the background looks when the cell is selected. The default is a blue gradient (UITableViewCellSelectionStyleBlue), or you can choose UITableViewCell-SelectionStyleGray (gray gradient) or UITableViewCellSelectionStyleNone.

backgroundColor
backgroundView
selectedBackgroundView

What's behind everything else drawn in the cell. The selectedBackgroundView is drawn in front of the backgroundView (if any) when the cell is selected, and will appear instead of whatever the selectionStyle dictates. The backgroundColor is behind the backgroundView. (Thus, if both the selectedBackgroundView and the backgroundView have some transparency, both of them and the background-Color can appear composited together when the cell is selected.)

There is no need to set the frame of the backgroundView and selectedBackground-View; they will be resized automatically to fit the cell.

multipleSelectionBackgroundView

If defined (not nil), and if the table's allowsMultipleSelection (or, if editing, allowsMultipleSelectionDuringEditing) is YES, used instead of the selected-BackgroundView when the cell is selected.

Applying a backgroundView or a backgroundColor can be tricky, because:

- The cell's default interface elements, such as the textLabel, automatically adopt the cell's background color as their own background color when the cell is not selected. Thus, they will appear to "punch a hole" through the backgroundView, revealing the background color behind it. (This problem doesn't arise for a selected cell, because when the cell is selected the cell's interface elements automatically switch to a transparent background, allowing the selectionStyle or selected-BackgroundView to show through.) The solution, if you want the background-View to appear behind the interface elements, is to set the backgroundColor of the interface elements to a color with some transparency, possibly [UIColor clear-Color].

- The table's cells automatically take on the same backgroundColor as the table itself, and getting them to stop doing this is not easy. The problem is that tableView:cell-ForRowAtIndexPath: is *too soon*; when you set a cell's backgroundColor here, your command is obeyed, but then the cell's background color reverts to the table's background color as the cell's own setSelected:animated: is called automatically and the cell does various things to its own appearance. One solution is to implement a delegate method, tableView:willDisplayCell:forRowAtIndexPath:, and set the backgroundColor there. Alternatively, don't even try to give a cell a background-Color; instead, give it a colored backgroundView. ·

In this example, we set the backgroundView to display an image with some transparency at the outside edges, so that the backgroundColor shows behind it. We set the selected-BackgroundView to an almost transparent dark rectangle, to darken that image when the cell is selected. And we give the textLabel a clear background color so that the rest of our work shows through (Figure 21-3):

```
UIImageView* v = [UIImageView new];
v.contentMode = UIViewContentModeScaleToFill;
v.image = [UIImage imageNamed:@"linen.png"];
cell.backgroundView = v;
UIView* v2 = [UIView new];
v2.backgroundColor = [UIColor colorWithWhite:0.2 alpha:0.1];
cell.selectedBackgroundView = v2;
cell.textLabel.backgroundColor = [UIColor clearColor];
```

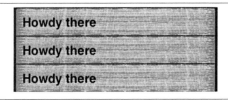

Figure 21-3. A cell with an image background

I'd put that code in the spot numbered 4 in Example 21-1. These features are to be true of every cell ever displayed in the table, and they need to be configured just once for every cell as it first comes into existence. There's no need to waste time doing the same thing all over again when an existing cell is reused.

Finally, there are a few properties of the table view itself worth playing with:

`rowHeight`
> The height of a cell. A taller cell is, among other things, a way to accommodate more text. You can also change this value in the nib file; the table view's row height appears in the Size inspector. The cell's subviews have their autoresizing set so as to compensate correctly. You can also set a cell's height in real time by implementing the delegate's `tableView:heightForRowAtIndexPath:` method; thus a table's cells may differ from one another in height (more about that later in this chapter).

`separatorColor, separatorStyle`
> These can also be set in the nib. The choices of separator style are:
>
> - `UITableViewCellSeparatorStyleNone` (plain style table only)
> - `UITableViewCellSeparatorStyleSingleLine`
> - `UITableViewCellSeparatorStyleSingleLineEtched` (grouped style table only)
>
> Oddly, the separator style names are associated with UITableViewCell even though the separator style itself is a UITableView property.

`backgroundColor, backgroundView`
> What's behind all the cells of the table; this may be seen if the cells have transparency, or if the user bounces the cells beyond their limit. I've already mentioned that cells will, by default, take on the `backgroundColor` of their table. The `backgroundView` is drawn on top of the `backgroundColor`.

`tableHeaderView, tableFooterView`
> Views to be shown before the first row and after the last row, respectively. Their background color is, by default, the background color of the table, but you can change that. The user can, if you like, interact with the views (and their subviews).

You can alter these views dynamically during the lifetime of the app. If you change the height of one of them, you must set the corresponding table view property afresh so that the table view learns what has happened.

Registering a Cell Class

iOS 6 introduces a new way of obtaining a cell in `tableView:cellForRowAtIndexPath:`. Instead of calling `dequeueReusableCellWithIdentifier:` to obtain the cell, you call `dequeueReusableCellWithIdentifier:forIndexPath:`, passing along as the second argument the same `indexPath:` value that you already received. As far as I can tell, however, the `indexPath:` parameter does nothing whatever, except to distinguish the two methods from one another!

The reason for calling this new method is twofold:

The result is never nil
  The value that is returned by `dequeueReusableCellWithIdentifier:forIndexPath:` is never nil. If there is a free reusable cell with the given identifier, it is returned. If there isn't, a new one is created for you. Thus there is no need to check whether the resulting cell is nil and create a new one if it is, as we did at step 3 of Example 21-1.

The identifier is consistent
  A danger with `dequeueReusableCellWithIdentifier:` is that you may accidentally pass an incorrect reuse identifier, or nil, and end up not reusing cells. With `dequeueReusableCellWithIdentifier:forIndexPath:`, that can't happen.

  The way such accidents are prevented is this: before you call `dequeueReusableCellWithIdentifier:forIndexPath:` for the first time, you must register with the table itself. You do this by calling `registerClass:forCellReuseIdentifier:`. This associates a class (which must be UITableViewCell or a subclass thereof) with a string identifier. The specification of the class is how `dequeueReusableCellWithIdentifier:forIndexPath:` knows what class to instantiate when it creates a new cell for you. The only cell types you can obtain are those for which you've registered in this way; if you pass a bad identifier, the app will crash (with a helpful log message).

This is a very elegant mechanism, but it raises some questions:

When should I call `registerClass:forCellReuseIdentifier:`?
  Call it early, before the table view starts generating cells. `viewDidLoad` is a good place.

How do I specify a built-in table cell style?

We are no longer calling `initWithStyle:reuseIdentifier:`, so where do we make our choice of built-in cell style? Well, by default, the cell style will be `UITableView-CellStyleDefault`, so if that's what you were after, the problem is solved. Otherwise, you subclass UITableViewCell and override `initWithStyle:reuse-Identifier:` to substitute the cell style you're after (and pass along the reuse identifier you were handed).

How do I know whether the returned cell is new or reused?

In step 4 of Example 21-1, if the returned cell was nil, we created it and then gave it features that it would need to be assigned only once. For example, if every cell is to have a gray gradient background, there is no point giving every cell returned by `dequeueReusableCellWithIdentifier:forIndexPath:` a gray gradient background; the reused cells already have one. Now, however, no cell is nil. So how will we know which ones need to be given a gray gradient background. It's easy: they are the ones without a gray gradient background! In other words, it's true that you can't check for nil to decide whether this cell needs to be given its initial one-time features, but surely you'll be able to think of something else to check for.

Here's a complete example, also illustrating heavy customization of a table view cell's background and apparent shape. It's a `UITableViewCellStyleValue2` cell (Figure 21-4), and I register a UITableViewCell subclass (MyCell) in order to get it. I draw the cell's background view as a gray gradient, using its layer properties (Chapter 16) to give it a border with rounded corners. My GradientView class is just a UIView whose `layer-Class` is CAGradientLayer, and because MyCell and GradientView are so minimal, and are used only by RootViewController, I've put them into the RootViewController implementation file:

```
@interface MyCell:UITableViewCell
@end
@implementation MyCell
-(id)initWithStyle:(UITableViewCellStyle)style
    reuseIdentifier:(NSString *)reuseIdentifier {
    self = [super initWithStyle:UITableViewCellStyleValue2
                reuseIdentifier:reuseIdentifier];
    return self;
}
@end

@interface GradientView:UIView
@end
@implementation GradientView
+(Class)layerClass { return [CAGradientLayer class]; }
@end
```

```
@implementation RootViewController
-(void)viewDidLoad {
    [super viewDidLoad];
    [self.tableView registerClass:[MyCell class]
          forCellReuseIdentifier:@"Cell"];
}

- (NSInteger)numberOfSectionsInTableView:(UITableView *)tableView {
    return 1;
}

- (NSInteger)tableView:(UITableView *)tableView
        numberOfRowsInSection:(NSInteger)section {
    return 20;
}

- (UITableViewCell *)tableView:(UITableView *)tableView
        cellForRowAtIndexPath:(NSIndexPath *)indexPath {
    UITableViewCell *cell =
        [tableView dequeueReusableCellWithIdentifier:@"Cell"
                                       forIndexPath:indexPath];
    if (cell.backgroundView == nil) { // do one-time configurations
        UIView* v = [UIView new];
        v.backgroundColor = [UIColor blackColor];
        UIView* v2 = [GradientView new];
        CAGradientLayer* lay = (CAGradientLayer*)v2.layer;
        lay.colors = @[(id)[UIColor colorWithWhite:0.6 alpha:1].CGColor,
        (id)([UIColor colorWithWhite:0.4 alpha:1].CGColor)];
        lay.borderWidth = 1;
        lay.borderColor = [UIColor blackColor].CGColor;
        lay.cornerRadius = 5;
        [v addSubview:v2];

        v2.autoresizingMask = UIViewAutoresizingFlexibleHeight |
                              UIViewAutoresizingFlexibleWidth;
        cell.backgroundView = v;
        cell.textLabel.font = [UIFont fontWithName:@"Helvetica-Bold" size:16];
        cell.textLabel.textColor = [UIColor whiteColor];
        cell.textLabel.backgroundColor = [UIColor clearColor];
        cell.detailTextLabel.backgroundColor = [UIColor clearColor];
    }
    cell.textLabel.text = @"Text label";
    cell.detailTextLabel.text = @"Detail text label";
    return cell;
}
@end
```

I'm going to adopt dequeueReusableCellWithIdentifier:forIndexPath: from here on. It isn't backwards-compatible with iOS 5 and before, but it's a great new feature. Also, it's consistent with other ways of generating custom cells, as I'll explain in the next section.

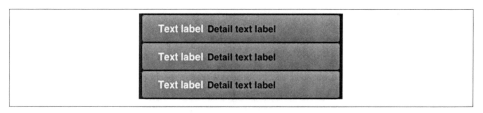

Figure 21-4. A cell with a custom gradient background

Custom Cells

The built-in cell styles give the beginner a leg up in getting started with table views, but there is nothing sacred about them, and sooner or later you'll probably want to go beyond them and put yourself in charge of how a table's cells look and what subviews they contain. There are four possible approaches:

- Supply a UITableViewCell subclass and override `layoutSubviews` to alter the frames of the built-in subviews. The built-in subviews are actually subviews of the cell's `contentView`. The `contentView` is the superview for the cell's subviews, exclusive of things like the `accessoryView`; so by confining your changes to subviews of the `contentView`, you allow the cell to continue working correctly.

- In `tableView:cellForRowAtIndexPath:`, add subviews to each cell's `content-View` as the cell is created. This approach can be combined with the previous one, or you can ignore the built-in subviews and use your own exclusively. As long as the built-in subviews for a particular built-in cell style are not referenced, they are never created or inserted into the cell, so you don't need to remove them if you don't want to use them.

- Design the cell in a nib, and load that nib in `tableView:cellForRowAtIndex-Path:` each time a cell needs to be created.

- Design the cell in a storyboard.

I'll illustrate each approach.

Overriding a cell's subview layout

You can't directly change the frame of a built-in cell style subview in `tableView:cell-ForRowAtIndexPath:` or `tableView:willDisplayCell:forRowAtIndexPath:`, because after your changes, the cell's `layoutSubviews` comes along and overrides them. The workaround is to override the cell's `layoutSubviews`! This is a straightforward solution if your main objection to a built-in style is the frame of an existing subview.

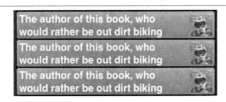

Figure 21-5. A cell with its label and image view swapped

To illustrate, let's modify a `UITableViewCellStyleDefault` cell so that the image is at the right end instead of the left end (Figure 21-5). We'll make a UITableViewCell subclass, MyCell, remembering to register MyCell with the table view, so that `dequeue-ReusableCellWithIdentifier:forIndexPath:` produces a MyCell instance; here is MyCell's `layoutSubviews`:

```
- (void) layoutSubviews {
    [super layoutSubviews];
    CGRect cvb = self.contentView.bounds;
    CGRect imf = self.imageView.frame;
    imf.origin.x = cvb.size.width - imf.size.width;
    self.imageView.frame = imf;
    CGRect tf = self.textLabel.frame;
    tf.origin.x = 5;
    self.textLabel.frame = tf;
}
```

In using this technique, I find it easier to move the subviews using their frame, rather than with constraints. Otherwise, the runtime (which still thinks it owns these subviews) tries to fight us.

Adding subviews in code

Instead of modifying the existing default subviews, you can add completely new views to each UITableViewCell's content view. This has some great advantages over the preceding technique. We won't be fighting the runtime, so we can make our changes in `tableView:cellForRowAtIndexPath:`, and we can assign a frame or constraints. Here are some things to keep in mind:

- The new views must be added when we instantiate a new cell, but not when we reuse a cell (because a reused cell already has them).

- We must never send `addSubview:` to the cell itself — only to its `contentView` (or some subview thereof).

- We should assign the new views an appropriate `autoresizingMask` or constraints, because the cell's content view might be resized.

- Each new view should be assigned a tag so that it can be referred to elsewhere.

I'll rewrite the previous example (Figure 21-5) to use this technique. We are no longer using a UITableViewCell subclass; the registered cell class is UITableViewCell itself:

```
- (UITableViewCell *)tableView:(UITableView *)tableView
        cellForRowAtIndexPath:(NSIndexPath *)indexPath {
    UITableViewCell *cell =
        [tableView dequeueReusableCellWithIdentifier:@"Cell"
                                     forIndexPath:indexPath];
    if (cell.backgroundView == nil) {
        // ... add background view as before ...
        //  now insert our own views into the contentView
        UIImageView* iv = [UIImageView new];
        iv.tag = 1;
        [cell.contentView addSubview:iv];
        UILabel* lab = [UILabel new];
        lab.tag = 2;
        [cell.contentView addSubview:lab];
        // we can use autolayout to lay them out
        NSDictionary* d = NSDictionaryOfVariableBindings(iv, lab);
        iv.translatesAutoresizingMaskIntoConstraints = NO;
        lab.translatesAutoresizingMaskIntoConstraints = NO;
        // image view is vertically centered
        [cell.contentView addConstraint:
         [NSLayoutConstraint
          constraintWithItem:iv attribute:NSLayoutAttributeCenterY
          relatedBy:0
          toItem:cell.contentView attribute:NSLayoutAttributeCenterY
          multiplier:1 constant:0]];
        // it's a square
        [cell.contentView addConstraint:
         [NSLayoutConstraint
          constraintWithItem:iv attribute:NSLayoutAttributeWidth
          relatedBy:0
          toItem:iv attribute:NSLayoutAttributeHeight
          multiplier:1 constant:0]];
        // label has height pinned to superview
        [cell.contentView addConstraints:
         [NSLayoutConstraint
          constraintsWithVisualFormat:@"V:|[lab]|"
          options:0 metrics:nil views:d]];
        // horizontal margins
        [cell.contentView addConstraints:
         [NSLayoutConstraint
          constraintsWithVisualFormat:@"H:|-5-[lab]-10-[iv]-5-|"
          options:0 metrics:nil views:d]];
    }
    UILabel* lab = (UILabel*)[cell viewWithTag: 2];
    // ... set up lab here ...
```

```
            UIImageView* iv = (UIImageView*)[cell viewWithTag: 1];
            // ... set up iv here ...
            return cell;
        }
```

Note how we can refer to the label and the image view, even when we're handed an existing cell for reuse, because we had the foresight to give them tags.

Using our own cell subviews instead of the built-in cell style subviews has some clear advantages; we no longer have to perform an elaborate dance to escape from the restrictions imposed by the runtime. Still, the verbosity of this code is somewhat overwhelming. We can avoid this by designing the cell in a nib.

Designing a cell in a nib

In designing a cell in a nib, we start by creating a nib file that will consist, in effect, solely of this one cell. In Xcode, we create a new iOS User Interface View nib file. Let's call it *MyCell.xib*. In the nib editor, delete the existing View and replace it with a Table View Cell from the Object library.

The cell's design window shows a standard-sized cell; you can resize it as desired, but the actual size of the cell in the interface will be dictated by the table view's width and its rowHeight. The cell's style can be specified in the Style pop-up menu of the Attributes inspector, and this gives you the default subviews, locked in their standard positions; for example, if you choose Basic, the textLabel appears, and if you specify an image in the Image combo box, the imageView appears.

For purposes of the example, let's set the Style pop-up menu to Custom and start with a blank slate. We'll implement, from scratch, the same subviews we've already implemented in the preceding two examples: a UILabel on the left side of the cell, and a UIImageView on the right side. Just as when we add subviews in code, we should set each subview's autoresizing behavior or constraints, and give each subview a tag. The difference is that we now do both those tasks in the nib, not in code. Now, in tableView:cellForRowAtIndexPath:, we'll be able to refer to the label and the image view using viewWithTag:, exactly as in the previous example:

```
            UILabel* lab = (UILabel*)[cell viewWithTag: 2];
            // ... set up lab here ...
            UIImageView* iv = (UIImageView*)[cell viewWithTag: 1];
            // ... set up iv here ...
            return cell;
```

The only remaining question is how to load the cell from the nib. This the Really Cool Part. When we register with the table view, which we're currently doing in viewDidLoad, instead of calling registerClass:forCellReuseIdentifier:, we call registerNib:forCellReuseIdentifier:. To specify the nib, call UINib's class method nibWithNibName:bundle:, like this:

```
[self.tableView registerNib:[UINib nibWithNibName:@"MyCell" bundle:nil]
    forCellReuseIdentifier:@"Cell"];
```

That's all there is to it! In `tableView:cellForRowAtIndexPath:`, when we call `dequeue-ReusableCellWithIdentifier:forIndexPath:`, if the table has no free reusable cell already in existence, the nib will automatically be loaded and the cell will be instantiated from it and returned to us.

You may wonder how that's possible, when we haven't specified a File's Owner class or added an outlet from the File's Owner to the table cell in the nib. The answer is that the nib conforms to a specific format. The UINib instance method `instantiateWith-Owner:options:` (mentioned in Chapter 7) can load a nib with a nil owner; regardless, it returns an NSArray of the nib's instantiated top-level objects. This nib is expected to have exactly one top-level object, and that top-level object is expected to be a UITable-ViewCell; that being so, the cell can easily be extracted from the resulting NSArray, as it is the array's only element. Our nib meets those expectations! Problem solved.

The advantages of this approach should be immediately obvious. Most or all of what we were previously doing in code to configure each newly instantiated cell can now be done in the nib: the label is positioned and configured with a clear background color, its font and text color is set, and so forth. As a result, that code can be deleted.

Some code, unfortunately, is tricky to delete. Suppose, for example, that we want to give our cell a `backgroundView`. The cell in the nib has a `backgroundView` outlet, so we are tempted to drag a view into the canvas and configure that outlet. But if this new view is at the top level of the nib, our nib no longer conforms to the expected format — it has *two* top-level objects — and our app will crash (with a helpful message in the log). This seems an unnecessary restriction; why can't the nib-loader examine the top-level objects and discover the one that's a UITableViewCell? There are workarounds in some cases — you might be able to put the background view *inside* the cell — but in other cases you'll just have to go on using code to add the `backgroundView`.

As I've already mentioned, we are referring to the cell's subviews in code by way of `view-WithTag:`. If you would prefer to use names, simply provide a UITableViewCell subclass with outlet properties, and configure the nib file accordingly:

1. Create the files for a UITableViewCell subclass; let's call it MyCell. Give the class two outlet properties:

    ```
    @property (nonatomic, weak) IBOutlet UILabel* theLabel;
    @property (nonatomic, weal) IBOutlet UIImageView* theImageView;
    ```

2. In the table view cell nib, change the class of the cell to MyCell, and link up the outlets from the cell to the respective subviews.

The result is that in our implementation of `tableView:cellForRowAtIndexPath:`, once we've cast the cell to a MyCell (which will require importing `"MyCell.h"`), the compiler will let us use the property names to access the subviews:

```
MyCell* theCell = (MyCell*)cell;
UILabel* lab = theCell.theLabel;
// ... set up lab here ...
UIImageView* iv = theCell.theImageView;
// ... set up iv here ...
return cell;
```

Designing a cell in a storyboard

If we're using a UITableViewController subclass, its table view's cells can be designed in a storyboard. In the storyboard editor, the UITableViewController comes with a table view. In the Attributes inspector, you set the table view's Content pop-up menu to Dynamic Prototypes, and use the Prototype Cells field to say how many different cell types there are to be — that is, how many different cell identifiers your table view controller's code will be using. In our case (and in most cases) this is 1. The table view in the storyboard editor displays as many table view cells as the Prototype Cells field dictates. Again, in our case that means there's one table view cell.

The prototype cell in the storyboard effectively corresponds to the table view cell in the nib file discussed in the previous section. Just about everything that's true of the cell in the nib file is true of the cell in the storyboard. There's a Style pop-menu. For a Custom cell, you can drag interface objects as subviews into the cell. To refer to those subviews in code, you can assign them tags in the storyboard; alternatively, make a UITableViewCell subclass with outlet properties, specify the prototype cell's class as that subclass, and configure the outlets in the storyboard.

There is one big difference in how you manage the instantiation of the cell from a storyboard. You don't call `registerClass:forCellReuseIdentifier:` or `register-Nib:forCellReuseIdentifier:`. You don't register with the table view at all! Instead, you enter the identifier string directly into the storyboard, in the cell's Identifier field in its Attributes inspector. That way, when you call `dequeueReusableCellWith-Identifier:forIndexPath:`, the runtime knows what prototype cell to load from the storyboard if a new cell needs to be instantiated.

As a final example of generating a cell, I'll obtain Figure 21-5 from a storyboard. I've placed and configured the label and the image view in the storyboard. I've defined a MyCell class with outlet properties `theLabel` and `theImageView`, and I've configured the prototype cell in the storyboard accordingly. To generate the cell's background view, I've created a UIView subclass, MyGradientBackView, consisting of this familiar-looking code:

```
@interface GradientView:UIView
@end
@implementation GradientView
+(Class)layerClass { return [CAGradientLayer class]; }
@end

@implementation MyGradientBackView
- (void) awakeFromNib {
    [super awakeFromNib];
    self.backgroundColor = [UIColor blackColor];
    UIView* v2 = [GradientView new];
    CAGradientLayer* lay = (CAGradientLayer*)v2.layer;
    lay.colors = @[(id)[UIColor colorWithWhite:0.6 alpha:1].CGColor,
    (id)([UIColor colorWithWhite:0.4 alpha:1].CGColor)];
    lay.borderWidth = 1;
    lay.borderColor = [UIColor blackColor].CGColor;
    lay.cornerRadius = 5;
    [self addSubview:v2];
    v2.frame = self.bounds;
    v2.autoresizingMask = UIViewAutoresizingFlexibleHeight |
                          UIViewAutoresizingFlexibleWidth;
}
@end
```

I've dragged a generic UIView into the prototype cell in the storyboard, set its class to
MyGradientBackView, and hooked the cell's backgroundView outlet to it. The cell's
Identifier in the storyboard is @"Cell". Here is the *entire* implementation of my root
view controller:

```
- (NSInteger)numberOfSectionsInTableView:(UITableView *)tableView {
    return 1;
}
- (NSInteger)tableView:(UITableView *)tableView
        numberOfRowsInSection:(NSInteger)section {
    return 20;
}
- (UITableViewCell *)tableView:(UITableView *)tableView
        cellForRowAtIndexPath:(NSIndexPath *)indexPath {
    MyCell *cell =
        (MyCell*)[tableView dequeueReusableCellWithIdentifier:@"Cell"
                                                    forIndexPath:indexPath];
    cell.theLabel.text =
        @"The author of this book, who would rather be out dirt biking";
    UIImage* im = [UIImage imageNamed:@"moi.png"];
    UIGraphicsBeginImageContextWithOptions(CGSizeMake(36,36), YES, 0.0);
    [im drawInRect:CGRectMake(0,0,36,36)];
    UIImage* im2 = UIGraphicsGetImageFromCurrentImageContext();
    UIGraphicsEndImageContext();
    cell.theImageView.image = im2;
    return cell;
}
```

There is no need to perform any one-time configuration on newly instantiated cells; they are completely configured in the nib. There is no need to register with the table view. And I can refer to the cell's subviews using property names. In effect, all the code having to do with the form of the cells has been eliminated. We are left only with code having to do with the content of the table view itself — the actual data that it is intended to display. So far, we have bypassed this issue entirely; we are using a fixed number of table rows, and every cell displays the same content. Displaying real data is the subject of the next section.

Table View Data

The structure and content of the actual data portrayed in a table view comes from the data source, an object pointed to by the table view's `dataSource` property and adopting the UITableViewDataSource protocol. The data source is thus the heart and soul of the table. What surprises beginners is that the data source operates not by *setting* the table view's structure and content, but by *responding on demand*. The data source, *qua* data source, consists of a set of methods that the table view will call when it needs information. This architecture has important consequences for how you write your code, which can be summarized by these simple guidelines:

Be ready
> Your data source cannot know *when* or *how often* any of these methods will be called, so it must be prepared to answer *any question at any time*.

Be fast
> The table view is asking for data in real time; the user is probably scrolling through the table *right now*. So you mustn't gum up the works; you must be ready to supply responses just as fast as you possibly can. (If you can't supply a piece of data fast enough, you may have to skip it, supply a placeholder, and insert the data into the table later. This, however, may involve you in threading issues that I don't want to get into here. I'll give an example in Chapter 37.)

Be consistent
> There are multiple data source methods, and you cannot know *which* one will be called at a given moment. So you must make sure your responses are mutually consistent at *any* moment. For example, a common beginner error is forgetting to take into account, in your data source methods, the possibility that the data might not be ready yet.

This may sound daunting, but you'll be fine as long as you maintain an unswerving adherence to the principles of model–view–controller (Chapter 13). How and when you accumulate the actual data, and how that data is structured, is a *model* concern. Acting as a data source is a *controller* concern. So you can acquire and arrange your data whenever and however you like, just so long as when the table view actually turns to you and asks what to do, you can lay your hands on the relevant data rapidly and consistently. You'll want to design the model in such a way that the controller can access any desired piece of data more or less instantly.

Another source of confusion for beginners is that methods are rather oddly distributed between the data source and the delegate, an object pointed to by the table view's delegate property and adopting the UITableViewDelegate protocol; in some cases, one may seem to be doing the job of the other. This is not usually a cause of any real difficulty, because the object serving as data source will probably also be the object serving as delegate. Nevertheless, it is rather inconvenient when you're consulting the documentation; you'll probably want to keep the data source and delegate documentation pages open simultaneously as you work.

 If a table view's contents are known beforehand, you can design the entire table, *including the contents of individual cells*, in a storyboard. This could be a reason for using a storyboard, even if your app has no main storyboard. I'll give an example later in this chapter.

The Three Big Questions

Like Katherine Hepburn in *Pat and Mike*, the basis of your success (as a data source) is your ability, at any time, to answer the Three Big Questions. The questions the table view will ask you are a little different from the questions Mike asks Pat, but the principle is the same: know the answers, and be able to recite them at any moment. Here they are:

How many sections does this table have?
> The table will call `numberOfSectionsInTableView:`; respond with an integer. In theory you can sometimes omit this method, as the default response is 1, which is often correct. However, I never omit it; for one thing, returning 0 is a good way to say that the table has no data, and will prevent the table view from asking any other questions.

How many rows does this section have?
> The table will call `tableView:numberOfRowsInSection:`. The table supplies a section number — the first section is numbered 0 — and you respond with an integer. In a table with only one section, of course, there is probably no need to examine the incoming section number.

What cell goes in this row of this section?
> The table will call `tableView:cellForRowAtIndexPath:`. The index path is expressed as an NSIndexPath; this is a sophisticated and powerful class, but you don't actually have to know anything about it, because UITableView provides a category on it that adds two read-only properties — `section` and `row`. Using these, you

extract the requested section number and row number, and return a fully configured UITableViewCell, ready for display in the table view. The first row of a section is numbered 0.

I have nothing particular to say about precisely how you're going to fulfill these obligations. It all depends on your data model and what your table is trying to portray. The important thing is to remember that you're going to be receiving an NSIndexPath specifying a section and a row, and you need to be able to lay your hands on the data corresponding to that slot *now* and configure the cell *now*. So construct your model, and your algorithm for consulting it in the Three Big Questions, accordingly.

For example, suppose our table is to list the names of the Pep Boys. Our data model might be an NSArray of string names. Our table has only one section. So our code might look like this:

```
- (NSInteger)numberOfSectionsInTableView:(UITableView *)tableView {
    if (!pep) // data not ready?
        return 0;
    return 1;
}
- (NSInteger)tableView:(UITableView *)tableView
        numberOfRowsInSection:(NSInteger)section {
    return [self.pep count];
}
- (UITableViewCell *)tableView:(UITableView *)tableView
        cellForRowAtIndexPath:(NSIndexPath *)indexPath {
    MyCell *cell =
        (MyCell*)[tableView dequeueReusableCellWithIdentifier:@"Cell"
                                            forIndexPath:indexPath];
    cell.theLabel.text = (self.pep)[indexPath.row];
    return cell;
}
```

At this point you may be feeling some exasperation. You want to object: "But that's trivial!" Exactly so! Your access to the data model *should* be trivial. That's the sign of a data model that's well designed for access by your table view's data source. Your implementation of `tableView:cellForRowAtIndexPath:` might have some interesting work to do in order to configure the *form* of the cell, but accessing the actual *data* should be simple and boring.

For example, consider Figure 19-1. The actual code that fetches the data is trivial:

```
FPItem* item = self.parsedData.items[indexPath.row];
NSString* title = item.title;
NSString* blurb = item.blurbOfItem;
```

That's all there is to it. And the reason why that's all there is to it is that I've structured the data model to be ready for access in exactly this way. However, there then follow about thirty lines of code *formatting* the layout of the text within the cell. The format is elaborate; accessing the data is not.

Another important aspect of tableView:cellForRowAtIndexPath: is that, as I've already illustrated, your strategy will probably be to keep memory usage at a minimum by reusing cells. Once a cell is no longer visible on the screen, it can be slotted into a row that *is* visible — with its portrayed data appropriately modified, of course! — so that no more than the number of simultaneously visible cells need to exist at any given moment. A table view is ready to implement this strategy for you; all you have to do is call dequeueReusableCellWithIdentifier:forIndexPath:. For any given identifier, you'll be handed either a newly minted cell or a reused cell that previously appeared in the table view but is now no longer needed because it has scrolled out of view. The table view can maintain more than one cache of reusable cells; this could be useful if your table view contains more than one type of cell (where the meaning of the concept "type of cell" is pretty much up to you). This why you must *name* each cache, by attaching an identifier string to any cell that can be reused. All the examples in this chapter (and in this book, and in fact in every UITableView I've ever created) use just one cache and just one identifier.

To prove to yourself the efficiency of the cell-caching architecture, do something to differentiate newly instantiated cells from reused cells, and count the newly instantiated cells, like this:

```
- (NSInteger)numberOfSectionsInTableView:(UITableView *)tableView {
    return 1;
}

- (NSInteger)tableView:(UITableView *)tableView
        numberOfRowsInSection:(NSInteger)section {
    return 100;
}

- (UITableViewCell *)tableView:(UITableView *)tableView
        cellForRowAtIndexPath:(NSIndexPath *)indexPath {
    MyCell* cell =
        (MyCell*)[tableView dequeueReusableCellWithIdentifier:@"Cell"
                                            forIndexPath:indexPath];
    if (!cell.backgroundView) {
        cell.backgroundView = [UIView new]
        NSLog(@"creating a new cell");
    }
    UILabel* lab = cell.theLabel;
    lab.text = [NSString stringWithFormat:@"This is row %i of section %i",
                indexPath.row, indexPath.section];
    return cell;
}
```

When we run this code and scroll through the table, every cell is numbered correctly, so there appear to be 100 cells. But the log messages show us that only 11 distinct cells are ever actually created.

If your `tableView:cellForRowAtIndexPath:` code configures the form of newly instantiated cells once (stage 4 in Example 21-1), you have to distinguish whether this cell *is* a newly instantiated cell; the whole idea is to avoid reconfiguring a reused cell. But when you provide a cell's final *individual* configuration (stage 5 in Example 21-1), you do not know or care whether the cell is new or reused. Therefore, you should always configure *everything* about the cell that might need configuring. If you fail to do this, and if the cell is reused, you might be surprised when some aspect of the cell is left over from its previous use; similarly, if you fail to do this, and if the cell is new, you might be surprised when some aspect of the cell isn't configured at all.

For example, in one of my apps that lists article titles in a table, there is a little loudspeaker icon that should appear in the cell only if there is a recording associated with this article. So I initially wrote this code:

```
if (item.enclosures && [item.enclosures count])
    cell.speaker.hidden = NO;
```

This turned out to be a mistake, because when a cell was reused, it had a visible loudspeaker icon if, in a previous incarnation, it had *ever* had a visible loudspeaker icon. The solution was to rewrite the logic to cover all possibilities, like this:

```
cell.speaker.hidden = !(item.enclosures && [item.enclosures count]);
```

You do get a sort of second bite of the cherry: there's a delegate method, `tableView:willDisplayCell:forRowAtIndexPath:`, that is called for every cell just before it appears in the table. This is absolutely the last minute to configure a cell. But don't misuse this method. You're functioning as the delegate here, not the data source; you may set the final details of the cell's appearance — as I mentioned earlier, this is a good place to set a cell's background color if you don't want it to come from the table's background color — but you shouldn't be consulting the data model at this point.

New in iOS 6 is an additional delegate method, `tableView:didEndDisplayingCell:forRowAtIndexPath:`. This tells you that the cell no longer appears in the interface and has become free for reuse. You could take advantage of this to tear down any resource-heavy customization of the cell (I'll give an example in Chapter 37), or simply to prepare it somehow for subsequent reuse. (A UITableViewCell has a `prepareForReuse` method, but you'd need a subclass to override it, and in any case it arrives when the cell is about to be reused, whereas `tableView:didEndDisplayingCell:forRowAtIndexPath:` arrives much earlier, as soon as the cell is no longer being used.)

Table View Sections

Your table data can be expressed as divided into sections. You might clump your data into sections for various reasons (and doubtless there are other reasons beyond these):

- You want to supply section headers (or footers, or both). This can clarify the presentation of your data by dividing the rows into groups. Also, a section header or footer can contain custom views, so it's a place where you might put additional information or functional interface (such as a button the user can tap).

- You want to make navigation of the table easier by supplying an index down the right side. You can't have an index without sections.

- You want to facilitate programmatic rearrangement of the table. For example, it's very easy to hide or move an entire section at once, possibly with animation.

 Don't confuse the section headers and footers with the header and footer of the table as a whole. The latter are view properties of the table view itself and are set through its properties `tableHeaderView` and `tableFooterView`, discussed earlier in this chapter.

The number of sections is determined by your reply to `numberOfSectionsInTableView:`. For each section, the table view will consult your data source and delegate to learn whether this section has a header or a footer, or both, or neither (the default).

The UITableViewHeaderFooterView class, new in iOS 6, is a UIView subclass intended specifically for use as the view of a header or footer; much like a table cell, it is reusable. It has the following properties:

textLabel
Label (UILabel) for displaying the text of the header or footer.

 An additional label, the `detailTextLabel`, appears to be broken. I have never been able to make it appear. I suggest you just ignore it.

contentView
A subview, the size of the header or footer. You can add subviews to it. If you do, you probably should not use the built-in `textLabel`; the `textLabel` is not inside the `contentView` and in a sense doesn't belong to you.

tintColor
The label has, by default, a distinctive gradient. If the `tintColor` is nil, this gradient is gray; setting the `tintColor` lets you change that.

backgroundColor

> You're not supposed to set the header or footer's backgroundColor; instead, set the backgroundColor of its contentView. This overrides the tintColor, removing the gradient.

backgroundView

> Any view you want to assign. The contentView is in front of the backgroundView, so an opaque contentView.backgroundColor will completely obscure the backgroundView.

You can supply a header or footer in two ways:

Header or footer string

> You implement the data source method tableView:titleForHeaderInSection: or tableView:titleForFooterInSection: (or both). Return nil to indicate that the given section has no header (or footer). Return a string to use it as the section's header (or footer).

> Starting in iOS 6, the header or footer view itself is a UITableViewHeaderFooter-View. It is reused (there will be only as many as needed for simultaneous display on the screen). By default, it has the gray gradient tint. The string you supply becomes its textLabel.text.

Header or footer view

> You implement the delegate method tableView:viewForHeaderInSection: or tableView:viewForFooterInSection: (or both). The view you supply is used as the entire header or footer and is automatically resized to the table's width and the section header or footer height. If the view you supply has subviews, be sure to set proper autoresizing or constraints, so that they'll be positioned and sized appropriately when the view itself is resized.

> You are not required to return a UITableViewHeaderFooterView, but you will probably want to, in order to take advantage of reusability. To do so, the procedure is much like making a cell reusable. You register beforehand with the table view by calling registerClass:forHeaderFooterViewReuseIdentifier:. To supply the reusable view, send the table view dequeueReusableHeaderFooterViewWith-Identifier:; the result will be either a newly instantiated view or a reused view. You can then configure this view as desired.

The documentation lists a second way of registering a header or footer view for reuse — `registerNib:forHeaderFooterViewReuse-Identifier:`. Unfortunately, the nib editor's Object library doesn't include a UITableViewHeaderFooterView! This makes `registerNib:for-HeaderFooterViewReuseIdentifier:` pretty much useless, because there's no way to configure the view correctly in the nib.

It is possible to implement *both* `viewFor...` and `titleFor...`. In that case, `viewFor...` is called first, and if it returns a UITableViewHeader-FooterView, `titleFor...` will set its `textLabel.text`.

In addition, two pairs of delegate methods permit you to perform final configurations on your header or footer views:

`tableView:willDisplayHeaderView:forSection:`
`tableView:willDisplayFooterView:forSection:`

> You can perform further configuration here, if desired. A useful possibility is to generate the default UITableViewHeaderFooterView by implementing `title-For...` and then tweak its form slightly here. These delegate methods are new in iOS 6, and are matched by `tableView:didEndDisplayingHeaderView:for-Section:` and `tableView:didEndDisplayingFooterView:forSection:`.

`tableView:heightForHeaderInSection:`
`tableView:heightForFooterInSection:`

> The runtime resizes your header or footer before displaying it. Its width will be the table view's width; this is how you tell the runtime the height. The heights are the table view's `sectionHeaderHeight` and `sectionFooterHeight` (22 by default) if you don't implement these methods; if you do implement these methods and you want to return the height as set by the table view, return `UITableViewAutomatic-Dimension`.

Some lovely effects can be created by modifying a header or footer view, especially because they are further forward than the table cells. For example, a header with transparency shows the table cells as they scroll behind it; a header with a shadow casts that shadow on the adjacent table cell.

A table that is to have section headers or footers (or both) may require some advance planning in the formation of its data model. Just as with a table cell, a section title must be readily available so that it can be supplied quickly in real time. A structure that I commonly use is a pair of parallel arrays: an array of strings containing the section names, and an array of subarrays containing the data for each section.

For example, suppose we intend to display the names of all 50 US states in alphabetical order as the rows of a table view, and that we wish to divide the table into sections according to the first letter of each state's name. I'll prepare the data model by walking through the list of state names, creating a new section name and a new subarray when I encounter a new first letter:

```
NSString* s =
    [NSString stringWithContentsOfFile:
        [[NSBundle mainBundle] pathForResource:@"states" ofType:@"txt"]
                            encoding:NSUTF8StringEncoding error:nil];
NSArray* states = [s componentsSeparatedByString:@"\n"];
self.sectionNames = [NSMutableArray array];
self.sectionData = [NSMutableArray array];
NSString* previous = @"";
for (NSString* aState in states) {
    // get the first letter
    NSString* c = [aState substringToIndex:1];
    // only add a letter to sectionNames when it's a different letter
    if (![c isEqualToString: previous]) {
        previous = c;
        [self.sectionNames addObject: [c uppercaseString]];
        // and in that case, also add a new subarray to our array of subarrays
        NSMutableArray* oneSection = [NSMutableArray array];
        [self.sectionData addObject: oneSection];
    }
    [[self.sectionData lastObject] addObject: aState];
}
```

The value of this preparatory dance is evident when we are bombarded with questions from the table view about cells and headers; supplying the answers is trivial:

```
- (NSInteger)numberOfSectionsInTableView:(UITableView *)tableView {
    return [self.sectionNames count];
}

- (NSInteger)tableView:(UITableView *)tableView
        numberOfRowsInSection:(NSInteger)section {
    return [(self.sectionData)[section] count];
}

- (UITableViewCell *)tableView:(UITableView *)tableView
        cellForRowAtIndexPath:(NSIndexPath *)indexPath {
    UITableViewCell *cell =
        [tableView dequeueReusableCellWithIdentifier:@"Cell"
                                       forIndexPath:indexPath];
    NSString* s = self.sectionData[indexPath.section][indexPath.row];
    cell.textLabel.text = s;
    return cell;
}
```

```
- (NSString *)tableView:(UITableView *)tableView
         titleForHeaderInSection:(NSInteger)section {
    return self.sectionNames[section];
}
```

Let's modify that example to illustrate customization of a header view. I've already reg-istered my header identifier in viewDidLoad:

```
[self.tableView registerClass:[UITableViewHeaderFooterView class]
      forHeaderFooterViewReuseIdentifier:@"Header"];
```

Now, instead of tableView:titleForHeaderInSection:, I'll implement table-View:viewForHeaderInSection:. For completely new views, I'll place my own label and an image view inside the contentView and give them their basic configuration; then I'll perform individual configuration on all views, new or reused, very much like table-View:cellForRowAtIndexPath::

```
- (UIView *)tableView:(UITableView *)tableView
         viewForHeaderInSection:(NSInteger)section {
    UITableViewHeaderFooterView* h =
        [tableView dequeueReusableHeaderFooterViewWithIdentifier:@"Header"];
    if (![h.tintColor isEqual: [UIColor redColor]]) {
        h.tintColor = [UIColor redColor];
        UILabel* lab = [UILabel new];
        lab.tag = 1;
        lab.font = [UIFont fontWithName:@"Georgia-Bold" size:22];
        lab.textColor = [UIColor greenColor];
        lab.backgroundColor = [UIColor clearColor];
        [h.contentView addSubview:lab];
        UIImageView* v = [UIImageView new];
        v.tag = 2;
        v.backgroundColor = [UIColor blackColor];
        v.image = [UIImage imageNamed:@"us_flag_small.gif"];
        [h.contentView addSubview:v];
        lab.translatesAutoresizingMaskIntoConstraints = NO;
        v.translatesAutoresizingMaskIntoConstraints = NO;
        [h.contentView addConstraints:
         [NSLayoutConstraint
          constraintsWithVisualFormat:@"H:|-5-[lab(25)]-10-[v(40)]"
          options:0 metrics:nil views:@{@"v":v, @"lab":lab}]];
        [h.contentView addConstraints:
         [NSLayoutConstraint
          constraintsWithVisualFormat:@"V:|[v]|"
           options:0 metrics:nil views:@{@"v":v}]];
        [h.contentView addConstraints:
         [NSLayoutConstraint
          constraintsWithVisualFormat:@"V:|[lab]|"
           options:0 metrics:nil views:@{@"lab":lab}]];
    }
}
```

```
        UILabel* lab = (UILabel*)[h.contentView viewWithTag:1];
        lab.text = self.sectionNames[section];
        return h;
    }
```

If your table view has the plain style, you can add an index down the right side of the table, which the user can tap to jump to the start of a section — helpful for navigating long tables. To generate the index, implement the data source method `sectionIndex-TitlesForTableView:`, returning an NSArray of string titles to appear as entries in the index. This works even if there are no section headers. The index will appear only if the number of rows exceeds the table view's `sectionIndexMinimumDisplayRowCount` property value; the default is `0` (not `NSIntegerMax` as claimed by the documentation), so the index is always displayed by default. You will want the index entries to be short — preferably just one character — because they will be partially obscuring the right edge of the table; plus, each cell's content view will shrink to compensate, so you're sacrificing some cell real estate.

For our list of state names, that's trivial, as it should be:

```
- (NSArray *)sectionIndexTitlesForTableView:(UITableView *)tableView {
    return self.sectionNames;
}
```

Before iOS 6, there was no official way to modify the index's appearance (such as the color of its entries). New in iOS 6, you can set the table view's `sectionIndexColor` and `sectionIndexTrackingBackgroundColor` (the color that appears behind the index while the user's finger is sliding over it).

Normally, there will be a one-to-one correspondence between the index entries and the sections; when the user taps an index entry, the table jumps to the start of the corresponding section. However, under certain circumstances you may want to customize this correspondence. For example, suppose there are 40 sections, but there isn't room to display 40 index entries comfortably on the iPhone. The index will automatically curtail itself, omitting some index entries and inserting bullets to suggest the omission, but you might prefer to take charge of the situation by supplying a shorter index. In such a case, implement the data source method `tableView:sectionForSectionIndex-Title:atIndex:`, returning the index of the section to jump to for this section index. Both the section index title and its index are passed in, so you can use whichever is convenient.

Apple's documentation elaborates heavily on the details of implementing the model behind a table with an index and suggests that you rely on a class called UILocalized-IndexedCollation. This class is effectively a way of generating an ordered list of letters of the alphabet, with methods for helping to sort an array of strings and separate it into sections. This might be useful if you need your app to be localized, because the notion of the alphabet and its order changes automatically depending on the user's preferred language. But this notion is also fixed; you can't readily use a UILocalizedIndexCollation to implement your own sort order. For example, UILocalizedIndexCollation was of no use to me in writing my Greek and Latin vocabulary apps, in which the Greek words must be sorted, sectioned, and indexed according to the Greek alphabet, and the Latin words use a reduced version of the English alphabet (no initial J, K, or V through Z). Thus I've never actually bothered to use UILocalizedIndexedCollation.

Refreshing Table View Data

The table view has no direct connection to the underlying data. If you want the table view display to change because the underlying data have changed, you have to cause the table view to refresh itself; basically, you're requesting that the Three Big Questions be asked all over again. At first blush, this seems inefficient ("regenerate *all* the data??"); but it isn't. Remember, in a table that caches reusable cells, there are no cells of interest other than those actually showing in the table at this moment. Thus, having worked out the layout of the table through the section header and footer heights and row heights, the table has to regenerate only those cells that are actually visible.

You can cause the table data to be refreshed using any of several methods:

reloadData
> The table view will ask the Three Big Questions all over again, including section headers and footers, and index entries.

reloadRowsAtIndexPaths:withRowAnimation:
> The table view will ask the Three Big Questions all over again, including section headers and footers, but not index entries. The first parameter is an array of index paths; to form an index path, use the NSIndexPath class method indexPathFor-Row:inSection:.

reloadSections:withRowAnimation:
> The table view will ask the Three Big Questions all over again, including section headers and footers, but not index entries. The first parameter is an NSIndexSet (see Chapter 10).

The second two methods can perform animations that cue the user as to what's changing. The withRowAnimation: parameter is one of the following:

UITableViewRowAnimationFade
> The old fades into the new.

UITableViewRowAnimationRight
UITableViewRowAnimationLeft

UITableViewRowAnimationTop
UITableViewRowAnimationBottom
  The old slides out in the stated direction, and is replaced from the opposite direction.

UITableViewRowAnimationNone
  No animation.

UITableViewRowAnimationMiddle
  Hard to describe; it's a sort of venetian blind effect on each cell individually.

UITableViewRowAnimationAutomatic
  The table view just "does the right thing". This is especially useful for grouped style tables, because if you pick the wrong animation, the display can look very funny as it proceeds.

If all you need to do is to refresh the index, call reloadSectionIndexTitles; this calls the data source's sectionIndexTitlesForTableView:.

It is also possible to access and alter a table's individual cells directly. This can be a far more lightweight approach to refreshing the table, plus you can supply your own animation within the cell as it alters its appearance. To do this, you need direct access to the cell you want to change. You'll probably want to make sure the cell is visible within the table view's bounds; if you're taking proper advantage of the table's reusable cell caching mechanism, nonvisible cells don't really exist (except as potential cells waiting in the reuse cache), and there's no point changing them, as they'll be changed when they are scrolled into view, through the usual call to tableView:cellForRowAtIndexPath:. Here are some UITableView methods that mediate between cells, rows, and visibility:

visibleCells
  An array of the cells actually showing within the table's bounds.

indexPathsForVisibleRows
  An array of the rows actually showing within the table's bounds.

cellForRowAtIndexPath:
  Returns a UITableViewCell if the table is maintaining a cell for the given row (typically because this is a visible row); otherwise, returns nil.

indexPathForCell:
  Given a cell obtained from the table view, returns the row into which it is slotted.

It is important to bear in mind that the cells are not the data (view is not model). If you change the content of a cell manually, make sure that you have also changed the model corresponding to it, so that the row will appear correctly if its data is reloaded later.

By the same token, you can get access to the views constituting headers and footers, by calling headerViewForSection: or footerViewForSection: (new in iOS 6). Thus you could modify a view directly. There is no method for learning what header or footer views are visible, but you should assume that if a section is returned by indexPathsFor-VisibleRows, its header or footer might be visible.

 If you just need the table view laid out freshly without reloading *any* cells, send it beginUpdates immediately followed by endUpdates. This fetches the section header and footer titles or views, their heights, and the row heights, and is useful as a way of alerting the table that any of those things have changed. This is a misuse of an updates block; the real use of such a block is discussed later in this chapter. But Apple takes advantage of this trick in the Table View Animations and Gestures example, in which a pinch gesture is used to change a table's row height in real time; so it must be legal.

iOS 6 introduces a new standard interface object for allowing the user to ask that a table view be refreshed — the UIRefreshControl. It is located at the top of the table view (above the table header view, if there is one), and is normally offscreen. To request a refresh, the user scrolls the table view downward to reveal the refresh control and holds there long enough to indicate that this scrolling is deliberate. The refresh control then acknowledges visually that it is refreshing, and remains visible until refreshing is complete. (This interface architecture, known as *pull to refresh*, was invented by Loren Brichter for the Twitter app and has become widespread in various clever implementations; with the UIRefreshControl, Apple is imitating and sanctioning this interface for the first time.)

Oddly, a UIRefreshControl is a property, not of a table view, but of a UITableView-Controller (its refreshControl). It is a control (UIControl, Chapter 25), so it has an action message, emitted for its UIControlEventValueChanged. You can give a table view controller a refresh control in the nib editor, but hooking up its action doesn't work, so you have to do it in code:

```
-(void)viewDidLoad {
    [super viewDidLoad];
    [self.refreshControl addTarget:self action:@selector(doRefresh:)
                  forControlEvents:UIControlEventValueChanged];
}
```

Once a refresh control's action message has fired, the control remains visible and indicates by animation (similar to an activity indicator) that it is refreshing until you send it the endRefreshing message. You can initiate a refresh animation in code with begin-Refreshing, but this does not fire the action message or display the refresh control; to display it, scroll the table view:

```
[self.tableView setContentOffset:CGPointMake(0,-44) animated:YES];
[self.refreshControl beginRefreshing];
// ... now actually do refresh, and later send endRefreshing
```

A refresh control also has a `tintColor` and an `attributedString`, which is displayed as a label below the activity indicator (on attributed strings, see Chapter 23). I use a refresh control and take advantage of its attributed string in the current version of the TidBITS News app to tell the user when the table was last refreshed (and then I scroll the table view just enough to reveal the label):

```
NSString* s = [df stringFromDate: [NSDate date]]; // df is an NSDateFormatter
self.refreshControl.attributedTitle =
    [[NSAttributedString alloc] initWithString:s
        attributes: @{NSForegroundColorAttributeName:[UIColor whiteColor]}];
[self.tableView setContentOffset:CGPointMake(0,-21) animated:YES];
```

Variable Row Heights

Most tables have rows that are all the same height, as set by the table view's `row-Height`. However, the delegate's `tableView:heightForRowAtIndexPath:` can be used to make different rows different heights. You can see this in the TidBITS News app; look at Figure 19-1, where the first cell is shorter than the second cell (because the headline is one line instead of two).

Here are some things to remember when implementing a table whose rows can have different heights:

Avoid performance limits

Variable row heights work best if the table is short and simple (not too many rows). The table view must effectively lay out the entire table in order to load the data and in order at any moment to know the size and offset of the scrolling content. With a table consisting of a large number of rows, this can become too much information for the table to manipulate fast enough as the user scrolls.

Lay out subviews correctly

As a cell is reused, its height may be changed, because the new row into which it is to be slotted is a different height from the old row. Similarly, if the cell comes from a nib, its height in the table view may be changed from its height in the nib. This will expose any weaknesses in your practice for laying out subviews. For example, a mistake in the `autoresizingMask` value of subviews can result in display errors that would not have been exposed if all the rows were the same height. You may have to resort to manual layout (implementing `layoutSubviews` in a UITableView-Cell subclass); alternatively, constraints can be a big help here.

Plan ahead

You (the delegate) are going to be asked for *all* the heights of *all* the rows well before you (the data source) are called upon to provide the data for any individual rows.

You will want to provide this information quickly and accurately. So you will have to plan how the data will appear in *every* row before actually causing the data to appear in *any* row.

This can be a little tricky, because you have to figure out how much room your interface objects will occupy given the contents they'll actually have when they appear in the table. For example, I face this problem in my Albumen app, in a table where each cell displays a song's title (in a label) and the song's artist (in another label). These labels will be displayed one above the other; I want each of them to be just tall enough to contain its content, and the cell to be just tall enough to contain the labels plus some reasonable spacing. What we need is a way to ask a UILabel, "How tall would you be if you contained this text?"

Fortunately there's a way to do that — two ways, actually. We could send a UILabel the sizeThatFits: message, handing it a size that represents its actual maximum width and an excessively tall height. Equivalently, we could send the label's string the sizeWithFont:constrainedToSize: message; this works because we are guaranteed that a UILabel will draw its text the same way that text would draw itself. It happens that I use the latter method.

I start with a utility method, labelHeightsForRow:, that calculates the heights of both labels given their text and font. Note that this method must be able to consult the data model, to learn what the text will be for each label, and it must know in advance the width and font of each label:

```
- (NSArray*) labelHeightsForRow: (NSInteger) row {
    NSString* title = (self.titles)[row];
    NSString* artist = (self.artists)[row];
    // values used in next two lines have been cached as ivars at load time
    CGSize tsz = [title sizeWithFont:self.titleFont
                constrainedToSize:CGSizeMake(_tw, 4000)];
    CGSize asz = [artist sizeWithFont:self.artistFont
                constrainedToSize:CGSizeMake(_aw, 4000)];
    return @[@(tsz.height), @(asz.height)];
}
```

My tableView:heightForRowAtIndexPath: implementation can then call labelHeightsForRow:, using those heights, along with some #defined spacer values, to work out the total height of any requested cell:

```
- (CGFloat)tableView:(UITableView *)tableView
        heightForRowAtIndexPath:(NSIndexPath *)indexPath {
    NSArray* arr = [self labelHeightsForRow: indexPath.row];
    return ([arr[0] floatValue] + [arr[1] floatValue] +
            _topspace + _midspace + _thirdrow + _midspace + _bottomspace);
}
```

My tableView:willDisplayCell:forRowAtIndexPath: implementation calls labelHeightsForRow: *again*, using those same calculated heights *again* and the same

#defined spacer values *again*; the difference is that this time it actually lays out all the subviews of the content view:

```
- (void) tableView:(UITableView *)tableView
      willDisplayCell:(UITableViewCell *)cell
      forRowAtIndexPath:(NSIndexPath *)indexPath {
   // work out heights of views 1 and 2, origin.y of views 1, 2, 3, 4
   CGRect f = cell.frame;
   f.size.height =
      [self tableView: tableView heightForRowAtIndexPath: indexPath];
   cell.frame = f;
   NSArray* arr = [self labelHeightsForRow: indexPath.row];
   //
   CGRect f1 = [cell viewWithTag: 1].frame;
   f1.size.height = [arr[0] floatValue];
   f1.origin.y = _topspace;
   [cell viewWithTag: 1].frame = f1;
   //
   CGRect f2 = [cell viewWithTag: 2].frame;
   f2.size.height = [arr[1] floatValue];
   f2.origin.y = f1.origin.y + f1.size.height + _midspace;
   [cell viewWithTag: 2].frame = f2;
   // ... and so on ...
}
```

This works, but there's something depressing about all that painstakingly calculated layout. When autolayout and constraints came along, I was filled with hope. Instead of calculating the heights myself, surely I could fill a cell with its actual values and let the autolayout system work out the cell's height based on its internal constraints. The key method here is `systemLayoutSizeFittingSize:`; sent to a view, it tells the view to adopt the given size, to the extent that its internal constraints will allow.

So here's my new strategy. I have a new utility method `setUpCell:forIndexPath:` that assigns all labels in my cell their actual values for the given row. I know that `table-View:heightForRowAtIndexPath:` will be called first, so the *first* time it's called, I call my utility method for *all* the cells in the table. For each cell, I thus populate the labels; I then use autolayout to get the height of each resulting cell; and I store those heights in an array, from which I can instantly draw the answer to all subsequent calls to `table-View:heightForRowAtIndexPath::`

```
- (CGFloat)tableView:(UITableView *)tableView
      heightForRowAtIndexPath:(NSIndexPath *)indexPath {
   if (!self.heights) {
      // first time! determine all heights once for all
      NSMutableArray* marr = [NSMutableArray array];
      NSArray* objects = [[UINib nibWithNibName:@"TrackCell" bundle:nil]
                           instantiateWithOwner:nil options:nil];
      UITableViewCell* cell = objects[0];
      NSInteger u = [self.titles count];
      for (NSInteger i = 0; i < u; i++) {
```

```
        [self setUpCell:cell forIndexPath:
            [NSIndexPath indexPathForRow:i inSection:0]];
        CGSize sz = [cell
            systemLayoutSizeFittingSize:UILayoutFittingCompressedSize];
        [marr addObject: @(sz.height)];
    };
    self.heights = marr;
}
return [self.heights[indexPath.row] floatValue];
}
```

In `tableView:cellForRowAtIndexPath:`, I call `setUpCell:forIndexPath:` *again*, secure in the knowledge that the cell height, the label contents, and the constraints will
work exactly the same way as before. This is far more satisfying, but unfortunately the
use of `systemLayoutSizeFittingSize:` makes this approach noticeably slower than
the old manual layout way.

Table View Selection

A table view cell has a normal state, a highlighted state (according to its `highlighted`
property), and a selected state (according to its `selected` property). It is possible
to change these states directly (possibly with animation, using `set-`
`Highlighted:animated:` or `setSelected:animated:`), but you don't want to act behind
the table's back, so you are more likely to manage selection through the table view, letting
the table view manage and track the state of its cells.

These two states are closely related. In particular, when a cell is selected, it propagates
the highlighted state down through its subviews by setting each subview's `highlighted`
property if it has one. That is why a UILabel's `highlightedTextColor` applies when the
cell is selected. Similarly, a UIImageView (such as the cell's `imageView`) can have a
`highlightedImage` that is shown when the cell is selected, and a UIControl (such as a
UIButton) takes on its `highlighted` state when the cell is selected.

One of the chief purposes of your table view is likely to be to let the user select a cell.
This will be possible, provided you have not set the value of the table view's `allows-`
`Selection` property to NO. The user taps a normal cell, and the cell switches to its
selected state. As we've already seen, this will usually mean that the cell is redrawn with
a blue (or gray) background view, but you can change this. If the user taps an already
selected cell, by default it stays selected.

Table views can permit the user to select multiple cells simultaneously. Set the table
view's `allowsMultipleSelection` property to YES. If the user taps an already selected
cell, by default it is deselected.

Your code can also learn and manage the selection through these UITableView instance
methods:

`indexPathForSelectedRow`

`indexPathsForSelectedRows`

These methods report the currently selected row(s), or nil if there is no selection. Don't accidentally call the wrong one. For example, calling `indexPathForSelected-Row` when the table view allows multiple selection gives a result that will have you scratching your head in confusion. (As usual, I speak from experience.)

`selectRowAtIndexPath:animated:scrollPosition:`

The animation involves fading in the selection, but the user may not see this unless the selected row is already visible. The last parameter dictates whether and how the table view should scroll to reveal the newly selected row:

- `UITableViewScrollPositionTop`
- `UITableViewScrollPositionMiddle`
- `UITableViewScrollPositionBottom`
- `UITableViewScrollPositionNone`

For the first three options, the table view scrolls (with animation, if the second parameter is YES) so that the selected row is at the specified position among the visible cells. For `UITableViewScrollPositionNone`, the table view does not scroll; if the selected row is not already visible, it does not become visible.

`deselectRowAtIndexPath:animated:`

Deselects the given row (if it is selected); the optional animation involves fading out the selection. No automatic scrolling takes place. To deselect all currently selected rows, call `selectRowAtIndexPath:animated:scrollPosition:` with a nil index path.

Reloading a cell's data also deselects that cell.

Response to user selection is through the table view's delegate:

- `tableView:shouldHighlightRowAtIndexPath:` (new in iOS 6)
- `tableView:didHighlightRowAtIndexPath:` (new in iOS 6)
- `tableView:didUnhighlightRowAtIndexPath:` (new in iOS 6)
- `tableView:willSelectRowAtIndexPath:`
- `tableView:didSelectRowAtIndexPath:`
- `tableView:willDeselectRowAtIndexPath:`

- `tableView:didDeselectRowAtIndexPath:`

Despite their names, the two "will" methods are actually "should" methods and expect a return value: return nil to prevent the selection (or deselection) from taking place; return the index path handed in as argument to permit the selection (or deselection), or a different index path to cause a different cell to be selected (or deselected). The new "highlight" methods are more sensibly named, and they arrive first, so you can return NO from `tableView:shouldHighlightRowAtIndexPath:` to prevent a cell from being selected.

When the user taps a cell, the cell passes through a complete "highlight" cycle before starting the "select" methods, like this (assuming that all stages are permitted to happen normally):

1. The user's finger goes down. The cell highlights, which propagates to its subviews.

2. There is a redraw moment. Thus, the user will *see* the cell as highlighted, regardless of what happens next.

3. The user lifts the finger. The cell unhighlights, which also propagates to its subviews. But the user doesn't see this, because the next redraw moment hasn't come yet.

4. The cell is selected; the cell is now *not* highlighted, but it manually propagates highlighting down to its subviews anyway.

5. There's another redraw moment. The user now sees the cell as highlighted.

When `tableView:willSelectRowAtIndexPath:` is called because the user taps a cell, and if this table view permits only single cell selection, `tableView:willDeselectRowAtIndexPath:` will be called subsequently for any previously selected cells.

Here's an example of implementing `tableView:willSelectRowAtIndexPath:`. The default behavior for `allowsSelection` (not multiple selection) is that the user can select by tapping, and the cell remains selected; if the user taps a selected row, the selection does not change. We can alter this so that tapping a selected row deselects it:

```
- (NSIndexPath*) tableView:(UITableView*)tv
        willSelectRowAtIndexPath:(NSIndexPath*)ip {
    if ([tv cellForRowAtIndexPath:ip].selected) {
        [tv deselectRowAtIndexPath:ip animated:NO];
        return nil;
    }
    return ip;
}
```

An extremely common response to user selection is navigation. A master–detail architecture is typical: the table view lists things the user can see in more detail, and a tap replaces the table view with the detailed view of the selected thing. Very often the table view will be in a navigation interface, and you will respond to user selection by creating the detail view and pushing it onto the navigation controller's stack. This interface is so common that Xcode's Master–Detail Application project template implements it for you — and in a storyboard, if a segue emanates from a UITableViewCell, the storyboard assumes that you want the segue to be triggered when the user selects a cell.

For example, here's the code from my Albumen app that navigates from the list of albums to the list of songs in the album that the user has tapped:

```
- (void) tableView:(UITableView *)tableView
        didSelectRowAtIndexPath:(NSIndexPath *)indexPath {
    TracksViewController *t =
        [[TracksViewController alloc]
            initWithMediaItemCollection:(self.albums)[indexPath.row]];
    [self.navigationController pushViewController:t animated:YES];
}
```

If you're using a UITableViewController, then by default, whenever the table view appears, the selection is cleared automatically in viewWillAppear: (unless you disable this by setting the table view controller's clearsSelectionOnViewWillAppear to NO), and the scroll indicators are flashed in viewDidAppear:. I sometimes prefer to set clears-SelectionOnViewWillAppear to NO and implement deselection in viewDidAppear:; the effect is that when the user returns to the table, the row is still momentarily selected before it deselects itself:

```
- (void) viewDidAppear:(BOOL)animated {
    // deselect selected row
    [tableView selectRowAtIndexPath:nil animated:NO
        scrollPosition:UITableViewScrollPositionNone];
    [super viewDidAppear:animated];
}
```

By convention, if selecting a table view cell causes navigation, the cell should be given an accessoryType of UITableViewCellAccessoryDisclosureIndicator. This is a plain gray right-pointing chevron at the right end of the cell. The chevron itself doesn't respond to user interaction; it's just a visual cue that we'll "move to the right" if the user taps the cell.

An alternative accessoryType is UITableViewCellAccessoryDetailDisclosure-Button. It *is* a button and *does* respond to user interaction, through your implementation of the table view delegate's tableView:accessoryButtonTappedForRowWithIndex-Path:. The button has a right-pointing chevron, so once again you'd be likely to respond by navigating; in this case, however, you would probably use the button *instead* of selection as a way of letting the user navigate. A common convention is that selecting the cell as a whole does one thing and tapping the disclosure button does something else (involving navigation to the right). For example, in Apple's Phone app, tapping a contact's listing in the Recents table places a call to that contact, but tapping the disclosure button switches to that contact's detail view.

Figure 21-6. Designing a static table in the storyboard editor

Another use of cell selection is to implement a choice among cells, where a section of a table effectively functions as an iOS alternative to Mac OS X radio buttons. The table view usually has the grouped format. An `accessoryType` of `UITableViewCell-AccessoryCheckmark` is typically used to indicate the current choice. Implementing radio-button behavior is up to you.

As an example, I'll implement the interface shown in Figure 21-2. The table view has the grouped style, with two sections. The first section, with a "Size" header, has three mutually exclusive choices: "Easy," "Normal," and "Hard." The second section, with a "Style" header, has two choices: "Animals" or "Snacks."

This is a *static table*; its contents are known beforehand and won't change. This means we can design the entire table, including the headers and the cells, in a storyboard. This requires that a UITableViewController subclass be instantiated from a storyboard. It's worth doing this, even if your app doesn't have a main storyboard, just to take advantage of the ability to design a static table without code! In the storyboard editor, you select the table and set its Content pop-up menu in the Attributes inspector to Static Cells. Then you can construct the entire table, including section header and footer text, and the content of each cell (Figure 21-6).

Even though each cell is designed initially in the storyboard, I can still implement `table-View:cellForRowAtIndexPath:` to call `super` and add further functionality. In this case, that's how I'll add the checkmarks. The user defaults are storing the current choice in each of the two categories; there's a `@"Size"` preference and a `@"Style"` preference, each consisting of a string denoting the title of the chosen cell:

```
- (UITableViewCell *)tableView:(UITableView *)tv
        cellForRowAtIndexPath:(NSIndexPath *)indexPath {
    UITableViewCell* cell =
        [super tableView:tv cellForRowAtIndexPath:indexPath];
    NSUserDefaults* ud = [NSUserDefaults standardUserDefaults];
    cell.accessoryType = UITableViewCellAccessoryNone;
    if ([[ud valueForKey:@"Style"] isEqualToString:cell.textLabel.text] ||
        [[ud valueForKey:@"Size"] isEqualToString:cell.textLabel.text])
        cell.accessoryType = UITableViewCellAccessoryCheckmark;
    return cell;
}
```

When the user taps a cell, the cell is selected. I want the user to see that selection momentarily, as feedback, but then I want to remove that selection and adjust the checkmarks so that that cell is the only one checked in its section. The selection will be visible until the user's finger is lifted, so I can take care of everything in `tableView:didSelect-RowAtIndexPath:`; I set the user defaults, and then I reload the table view's data to remove the selection and adjust the checkmarks:

```
- (void)tableView:(UITableView *)tv
        didSelectRowAtIndexPath:(NSIndexPath *)indexPath {
    NSUserDefaults* ud = [NSUserDefaults standardUserDefaults];
    NSString* setting = [tv cellForRowAtIndexPath:indexPath].textLabel.text;
    NSString* header =
        [self tableView:tv titleForHeaderInSection:indexPath.section];
    [ud setValue:setting forKey:header];
    [tv reloadData]; // deselect all cells, reassign checkmark as needed
}
```

Table View Scrolling and Layout

A UITableView is a UIScrollView, so everything you already know about scroll views is applicable (Chapter 20). In addition, a table view supplies two convenience scrolling methods:

- `scrollToRowAtIndexPath:atScrollPosition:animated:`
- `scrollToNearestSelectedRowAtScrollPosition:animated:`

The `scrollPosition` parameter is as for `selectRowAtIndexPath:...`, discussed earlier in this chapter.

The following UITableView methods mediate between the table's bounds coordinates on the one hand and table structure on the other:

- `indexPathForRowAtPoint:`
- `indexPathsForRowsInRect:`
- `rectForSection:`

- `rectForRowAtIndexPath:`
- `rectForFooterInSection:`
- `rectForHeaderInSection:`

The table's header and footer are views, so their coordinates are given by their frames.

Table View State Restoration

If a UITableView participates in state saving and restoration, the restoration mechanism would like to restore the selection and the scroll position. However, it would prefer not to do this on the basis of mere numbers — the table view's `contentOffset`, or a row number — because what is meaningful in a table is not a number but the data being displayed. There is a possibility that when the app is relaunched, the underlying data may have been rearranged somehow; and the restoration mechanism would like to do the right thing nevertheless.

The problem is that the state saving and restoration mechanism doesn't know anything about the relationship between the table cells and the underlying data. So you have to tell it. You adopt the UIDataSourceModelAssociation protocol and implement two methods:

`modelIdentifierForElementAtIndexPath:inView:`
> Based on the index path, you return some string that you will *later* be able to use to identify uniquely this bit of model data.

`indexPathForElementWithModelIdentifier:inView:`
> Based on the unique identifier you provided earlier, you return the index path at which this bit of model data is displayed in the table *now*.

Devising a system of unique identification and incorporating it into your data model is up to you. In the TidBITS News app, for example, it happens that my bits of data come from a parsed RSS feed and have a `guid` property that is a global unique identifier. So implementing the first method is easy:

```
- (NSString *) modelIdentifierForElementAtIndexPath:(NSIndexPath *)idx
                                           inView:(UIView *)view {
    FPItem* item = self.parsedData.items[idx.row];
    return item.guid;
}
```

Implementing the second method is a little more work; I walk the data model looking for the object whose `guid` matches the identifier in question, and construct its index path:

```
- (NSIndexPath*) indexPathForElementWithModelIdentifier:(NSString *)identifier
                                             inView:(UIView *)view {
    __block NSIndexPath* path = nil;
    [self.parsedData.items
        enumerateObjectsUsingBlock:^(FPItem* item, NSUInteger idx, BOOL *stop)
    {
        if ([item.guid isEqualToString:identifier]) {
            path = [NSIndexPath indexPathForRow:idx inSection:0];
            *stop = YES;
        }
    }];
    return path;
}
```

It is crucial, when the app is relaunched, that the table should have data before that method is called, so I call `reloadData` in my implementation of `decodeRestorable-StateWithCoder:`.

Table View Searching

A table view is a common way to present the results of a search performed through a search field (a UISearchBar; see Chapter 25). This is such a standard interface, in fact, that a class is provided, UISearchDisplayController, to mediate between the search field where the user enters a search term and the table view listing the results of the search. The UISearchDisplayController needs the following things:

A search bar
> A UISearchBar in the interface. This will be the UISearchDisplayController's `searchBar`.

A view controller
> The view controller managing the view in the interface over which the search results are to appear. This will be the UISearchDisplayController's `searchContentsController`.

A results table view
> The table view in which the search results will be presented. This will be the UISearchDisplayController's `searchResultsTableView`. It can already exist, or the UISearchDisplayController will create it.

A data source and delegate for the results table view
> The UISearchDisplayController's `searchResultsDataSource` and `searchResultsDelegate`. They will control the data and structure of the search results table. They are commonly the same object, as for any table view; moreover, they are commonly the view controller.

A delegate

An optional object adopting the UISearchDisplayDelegate protocol. It will be notified of events relating to the display of results. It, too, is commonly the view controller.

Moreover, the UISearchBar itself can also have a delegate, and this, too, is commonly the view controller.

A UISearchDisplayController's `searchContentsController` needn't be a UITableViewController, and the data that the user is searching needn't be the content of an existing table view. But they frequently are! That's because the mental connection between a table and a search is a natural one; when the search results are presented as a table view, the user feels that the search field is effectively filtering the contents of the original table view. A single object may thus be playing all of the following roles:

- The searchable table view's view controller
- The searchable table view's data source
- The searchable table view's delegate
- The view controller for the view over which the search results will appear
- The search results table view's data source
- The search results table view's delegate
- The UISearchDisplayController's delegate
- The UISearchBar's delegate

A common point of confusion among beginners, when using this architecture, is to suppose that the search bar is filtering the original table. It isn't. The search bar and the UISearchDisplayController know nothing of your table. What's being searched is just some data — whatever data you care to search. The fact that this may be the model data for your table is purely secondary. Moreover, there are two distinct tables: yours (the original table view) and the UISearchDisplayController's (the search results table view). You own the former, just as you would if no search were involved; you probably have a view controller that manages it, very likely a UITableViewController whose `tableView` is this table. But the search results table is a completely different table; you do not have a view controller managing it (the UISearchDisplayController does), and in particular it is not your UITableViewController's `tableView`. However, if you wish, you can make it *look* as if these are the same table, by configuring the two tables and their cells the same way — typically, with the same code.

To illustrate, we will implement a table view that is searchable through a UISearchBar and that displays the results of that search in a second table view managed by a UISearchDisplayController.

The first question is how to make the search field appear along with the table view. Apple's own apps, such as the Contacts app, have popularized an interface in which the search field is the table view's header view. Indeed, this is such a common arrangement that the nib editor's Object library contains an object called Search Bar and Search Display Controller; if you drag this onto a UITableView in the nib editor, the search field becomes the table's header view and a UISearchDisplayController is created for you automatically, with all properties hooked up appropriately through outlets, much as I just described. In our example, however, we'll create the UISearchDisplayController and the UISearchBar in code.

Another feature of Apple's standard interface is that the search field isn't initially showing. To implement this, we'll scroll to the first actual row of data when the table view appears.

We're going to start with a table managed by a UITableViewController. In this view controller's `viewDidLoad`, we create the search bar and slot it in as the table's header view; we then load the data and scroll the header view out of sight. We also create the UISearchDisplayController and tie it to the search bar — and to ourselves (the UITableViewController) as the UISearchDisplayController's controller, delegate, search table data source, and search table delegate, as well as making ourselves the UISearchBar delegate. We also retain the UISearchDisplayController by assigning it to a property, so that it doesn't vanish in a puff of smoke before we can use it:

```
[super viewDidLoad];
[self.tableView registerClass:[UITableViewCell class]
        forCellReuseIdentifier:@"Cell"];
UISearchBar* b = [UISearchBar new];
[b sizeToFit];
b.delegate = self;
[self.tableView setTableHeaderView:b];
[self.tableView reloadData];
[self.tableView
    scrollToRowAtIndexPath:[NSIndexPath indexPathForRow:0 inSection:0]
    atScrollPosition:UITableViewScrollPositionTop animated:NO];
UISearchDisplayController* c =
    [[UISearchDisplayController alloc] initWithSearchBar:b
                                    contentsController:self];
self.sbc = c; // retain the UISearchDisplayController
c.delegate = self;
c.searchResultsDataSource = self;
c.searchResultsDelegate = self;
```

When the user initially taps in the search field, the UISearchDisplayController automatically constructs a new interface along with a nice animation. This indicates to the user that the search field is ready to receive input; when the user proceeds to enter characters into the search field, the UISearchDisplayController is ready to display its own search results table view in this interface. The UISearchBar has a Cancel button that the user can tap to dismiss the interface created by the UISearchDisplayController.

As the UISearchDisplayController's table view comes into existence, we get a delegate message. We can take advantage of this to register with this new table for cell reusability:

```
- (void)searchDisplayController:(UISearchDisplayController *)controller
        didLoadSearchResultsTableView:(UITableView *)tableView {
    [tableView registerClass:[UITableViewCell class]
      forCellReuseIdentifier:@"Cell"];
}
```

This is also the place to perform any other initial configurations on the UISearch-DisplayController's table view. For example, if my viewDidLoad is setting my table view's separator style to UITableViewCellSeparatorStyleNone, and if I want the two tables to look identical, this would be the place to set the UISearchDisplayController's table view's separator style to UITableViewCellSeparatorStyleNone as well.

Populating the search results table in response to what the user does in the UISearchBar is up to us. The UITableViewController is both data source and delegate for the original table view, as well as data source and delegate for the search results table. This means that our search is already almost working, because the search results table will automatically have the same data and structure as the original table! Our only additional task, beyond what our code already does, is to check whether the table view that's talking to us is the search results table view (this will be the UISearchDisplayController's search-ResultsTableView) and, if it is, to limit our returned data with respect to the search bar's text. The strategy for doing this should be fairly obvious if we are maintaining our source data in a sensible model.

Let's say, for the sake of simplicity, that our original table is displaying the names of the 50 United States, which it is getting from an array of strings called states:

```
- (NSInteger)numberOfSectionsInTableView:(UITableView *)tableView {
    return 1;
}

- (NSInteger)tableView:(UITableView *)tableView
        numberOfRowsInSection:(NSInteger)section {
    NSArray* model = self.states;
    return [model count];
}

// Customize the appearance of table view cells.
- (UITableViewCell *)tableView:(UITableView *)tableView
        cellForRowAtIndexPath:(NSIndexPath *)indexPath {
    UITableViewCell *cell =
        [tableView dequeueReusableCellWithIdentifier:@"Cell"
                                        forIndexPath:indexPath];
    NSArray* model = self.states;
    cell.textLabel.text = model[indexPath.row];
    return cell;
}
```

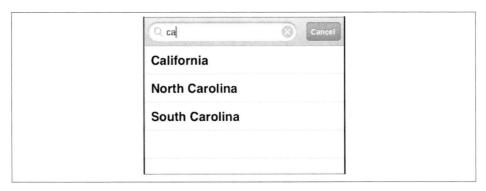

Figure 21-7. Filtering a table with a search bar

To make this work with a UISearchDisplayController, the only needed change is this: Each time we speak of the NSArray called model, we must decide whether it should be self.states, as now, or whether it should be a *different* array that is filtered with respect to the current search — let's call it self.filteredStates. There are two occurrences of this line:

```
NSArray* model = self.states;
```

They are now to be replaced by this:

```
NSArray* model =
    (tableView == self.sbc.searchResultsTableView) ?
    self.filteredStates : self.states;
```

The only remaining question is when and how this filteredStates array should be calculated. An excellent approach, given our small and readily available data set, is to generate a new set of search results every time the user types in the search field, effectively implementing a "live" search (Figure 21-7). We are informed of the user typing through a UISearchBar delegate method, searchBar:textDidChange:, so we implement this to filter the list of states. There is no need to reload the search results table's data, as by default the UISearchDisplayController will do that automatically:

```
- (void)searchBar:(UISearchBar *)searchBar
      textDidChange:(NSString *)searchText {
    NSPredicate* p = [NSPredicate predicateWithBlock:
      ^BOOL(id obj, NSDictionary *d) {
          NSString* s = obj;
          return ([s rangeOfString:searchText
              options:NSCaseInsensitiveSearch].location != NSNotFound);
      }];
    self.filteredStates = [self.states filteredArrayUsingPredicate:p];
}
```

A UISearchBar can also display scope buttons, letting the user alter the meaning of the search. If you add these, then of course you must take them into account when filtering the model data. For example, let's have two scope buttons, "Starts With" and "Contains":

```
UISearchBar* b = [UISearchBar new];
[b sizeToFit];
b.scopeButtonTitles = @[@"Starts With", @"Contains"];
// ...
```

Our filtering routine must now take the state of the scope buttons into account. More-over, the search results table view will reload when the user changes the scope (which we can detect in another UISearchBar delegate method, searchBar:selectedScope-ButtonIndexDidChange:), so if we're doing a live search, we must respond by filtering the data then as well. To prevent repetition, we'll abstract the filtering routine into a method of its own:

```
- (void) filterData {
    NSPredicate* p = [NSPredicate predicateWithBlock:
     ^BOOL(id obj, NSDictionary *d) {
        NSString* s = obj;
        NSStringCompareOptions options = NSCaseInsensitiveSearch;
        if (self.sbc.searchBar.selectedScopeButtonIndex == 0)
            options |= NSAnchoredSearch;
        return ([s rangeOfString:self.sbc.searchBar.text
            options:options].location != NSNotFound);
    }];
    self.filteredStates = [self.states filteredArrayUsingPredicate:p];
}

- (void)searchBar:(UISearchBar *)searchBar
        textDidChange:(NSString *)searchText {
    [self filterData];
}

- (void)searchBar:(UISearchBar *)searchBar
        selectedScopeButtonIndexDidChange:(NSInteger)selectedScope {
    [self filterData];
}
```

Our search bar is initially scrolled out of sight. Let's make it easier for the user to discover its existence and summon it. In an indexed list — one with sections and an index running down the right side — a "magnifying glass" search symbol can be made to appear in the index by including UITableViewIndexSearch (usually as the first item) in the string array returned from sectionIndexTitlesForTableView:. Presume once again that the section names are to be used as index entries and are in an array called sectionNames:

```
- (NSArray *)sectionIndexTitlesForTableView:(UITableView *)tableView {
    return [@[UITableViewIndexSearch]
        arrayByAddingObjectsFromArray:self.sectionNames];
}
```

You'll also need to implement `tableView:sectionForSectionIndexTitle:atIndex:`, because now the correspondence between index entries and sections is off by one. If the user taps the magnifying glass in the index, you scroll to reveal the search field (and you'll also have to return a bogus section number, but there is no penalty for that):

```
- (NSInteger)tableView:(UITableView *)tableView
        sectionForSectionIndexTitle:(NSString *)title
                        atIndex:(NSInteger)index {
    if (index == 0)
        [tableView scrollRectToVisible:tableView.tableHeaderView.frame
                        animated:NO];
    return index-1;
}
```

Here's one final tweak. Whenever the search results table becomes empty (because the search bar is nonempty and `filteredStates` is nil), the words "No Results" appear superimposed on it. I find this incredibly obnoxious, and I can't believe that after all these years Apple still hasn't granted programmers an official way to remove or customize it. Here's an unofficial way:

```
-(BOOL)searchDisplayController:(UISearchDisplayController *)controller
        shouldReloadTableForSearchString:(NSString *)searchString {
    dispatch_async(dispatch_get_main_queue(), ^(void){
        for (UIView* v in self.sbc.searchResultsTableView.subviews) {
            if ([v isKindOfClass: [UILabel class]] &&
                    [[(UILabel*)v text] isEqualToString:@"No Results"]) {
                [(UILabel*)v setText: @""];
                break;
            }
        }
    });
    return YES;
}
```

 A UISearchBar has many properties through which its appearance can be configured; I'll discuss them in Chapter 25. Both the UISearchBar and UISearchDisplayController send their delegate numerous messages that you can take advantage of to customize behavior; consult the documentation. A UISearchBar in a UIToolbar on the iPad can display its results in a popover; I'll talk about that in Chapter 22.

Table View Editing

A table view cell has a normal state and an editing state, according to its `editing` property. The editing state is typically indicated visually by one or more of the following:

Editing controls

At least one editing control will usually appear, such as a minus button (for deletion) at the left side.

Shrinkage

The content of the cell will usually shrink to allow room for an editing control. You can prevent a cell in a grouped-style table from shifting its left end rightward in editing mode by setting its `shouldIndentWhileEditing` to NO, or with the table delegate's `tableView:shouldIndentWhileEditingRowAtIndexPath:`.

Changing accessory view

The cell's accessory view will change automatically in accordance with its `editing-AccessoryType` or `editingAccessoryView`. If you assign neither, so that they are nil, the cell's accessory view will vanish when in editing mode.

As with selection, you could set a cell's `editing` property directly (or use `set-Editing:animated:` to get animation), but you are more likely to let the table view manage editability. Table view editability is controlled through the table view's `editing` property, usually by sending the table the `setEditing:animated:` message. The table is then responsible for putting its cells into edit mode.

 A cell in edit mode can also be selected by the user if the table view's `allowsSelectionDuringEditing` or `allowsMultipleSelection-DuringEditing` is YES. But this would be unusual.

Putting the table into edit mode is usually left up to the user. A typical interface would be an Edit button that the user can tap. In a navigation interface, we might have our view controller supply the button as the navigation item's right button:

```
UIBarButtonItem* bbi =
    [[UIBarButtonItem alloc]
        initWithBarButtonSystemItem:UIBarButtonSystemItemEdit
                          target:self action:@selector(doEdit:)];
self.navigationItem.rightBarButtonItem = bbi;
```

Our action handler will be responsible for putting the table into edit mode, so in its simplest form it might look like this:

```
- (void) doEdit: (id) sender {
    [self.tableView setEditing:YES animated:YES];
}
```

But that does not solve the problem of getting *out* of editing mode. The standard solution is to have the Edit button replace itself by a Done button:

```
- (void) doEdit: (id) sender {
    int which;
    if (![self.tableView isEditing]) {
        [self.tableView setEditing:YES animated:YES];
        which = UIBarButtonSystemItemDone;
    } else {
        [self.tableView setEditing:NO animated:YES];
        which = UIBarButtonSystemItemEdit;
    }
    UIBarButtonItem* bbi = [[UIBarButtonItem alloc]
        initWithBarButtonSystemItem:which
                            target:self action:@selector(doEdit:)];
    self.navigationItem.rightBarButtonItem = bbi;
}
```

However, it turns out that all of this is completely unnecessary if we want standard behavior, as it's already implemented for us! A UIViewController supplies an edit-ButtonItem that calls the UIViewController's setEditing:animated: when tapped, tracks whether we're in edit mode with the UIViewController's editing property, and changes its own title accordingly. Moreover, a UITableViewController's implementation of setEditing:animated: is to call setEditing:animated: on its table view. Thus, if we're using a UITableViewController, we get all of that behavior for free just by inserting the editButtonItem into our interface:

```
self.navigationItem.rightBarButtonItem = self.editButtonItem;
```

When the table view enters edit mode, it consults its data source and delegate about the editability of individual rows:

tableView:canEditRowAtIndexPath: *to the data source*
> The default is YES. The data source can return NO to prevent the given row from entering edit mode.

tableView:editingStyleForRowAtIndexPath: *to the delegate*
> Each standard editing style corresponds to a control that will appear in the cell. The choices are:

UITableViewCellEditingStyleDelete
> The cell shows a minus button at its left end. The user can tap this to summon a Delete button, which the user can then tap to confirm the deletion. This is the default.

UITableViewCellEditingStyleInsert
> The cell shows a plus button at its left end; this is usually taken to be an insert button.

UITableViewCellEditingStyleNone
> No editing control appears.

If the user taps an insert button (the plus button) or a delete button (the Delete button that appears after the user taps the minus button), the data source is sent the `table-View:commitEditingStyle:forRowAtIndexPath:` message and is responsible for obeying it. In your response, you will probably want to alter the structure of the table, and UITableView methods for doing this are provided:

- `insertRowsAtIndexPaths:withRowAnimation:`
- `deleteRowsAtIndexPaths:withRowAnimation:`
- `insertSections:withRowAnimation:`
- `deleteSections:withRowAnimation:`
- `moveSection:toSection:`
- `moveRowAtIndexPath:toIndexPath:`

The row animations here are effectively the same ones discussed earlier in connection with refreshing table data; "left" for an insertion means to slide in from the left, and for a deletion it means to slide out to the left, and so on. The two "move" methods provide animation with no provision for customizing it.

If you're issuing more than one of these commands, you can combine them by surrounding them with `beginUpdates` and `endUpdates`, forming an *updates block*. An updates block combines not just the animations but the requested changes themselves. This relieves you from having to worry about how a command is affected by earlier commands in the same updates block; indeed, order of commands within an updates block doesn't really matter.

For example, if you delete row 1 of a certain section and then (in a separate command) delete row 2 of the same section, you delete two successive rows, just as you would expect; the notion "2" does not change its meaning because you deleted an earlier row first, because you *didn't* delete an earlier row first — the updates block combines the commands for you, interpreting both index paths with respect to the state of the table before any changes are made. If you perform insertions and deletions together in one animation, the deletions are performed first, regardless of the order of your commands, and the insertion row and section numbers refer to the state of the table after the deletions.

An updates block can also include `reloadRows...` and `reloadSections...` commands (but not `reloadData`).

I need hardly emphasize once again (but I will anyway) that view is not model. It is one thing to rearrange the appearance of the table, another to alter the underlying data. It is up to you to make certain you do both together. Do not, even for a moment, permit the data and the view to get out of synch with each other. If you delete a row, remove from the model the datum that it represents. The runtime will try to help you with error messages if you forget to do this, but in the end the responsibility is yours. I'll give examples as we proceed.

Deleting Table Items

Deletion of table items is the default, so there's not much for us to do in order to implement it. If our view controller is a UITableViewController and we've displayed the Edit button as its navigation item's right button, everything happens automatically: the user taps the Edit button, the view controller's setEditing:animated: is called, the table view's setEditing:animated: is called, and the cells all show the minus button at the left end. The user can then tap a minus button; a Delete button appears at the cell's right end. You can customize the Delete button's title with the table delegate method tableView:titleForDeleteConfirmationButtonForRowAtIndexPath:.

What is *not* automatic is the actual response to the Delete button. For that, we need to implement tableView:commitEditingStyle:forRowAtIndexPath:. Typically, you'll remove the corresponding entry from the underlying model data, and you'll call deleteRowsAtIndexPaths:withRowAnimation: or deleteSections:withRowAnimation: to update the appearance of the table. As I said a moment ago, you must delete the row or section in such a way as to keep the table display coordinated with the model's structure. Otherwise, the app may crash (with an extremely helpful error message).

To illustrate, let's suppose once again that the underlying model is a pair of parallel arrays, an array of strings (sectionNames) and an array of arrays (sectionData). These arrays must now be mutable. Our approach will be in two stages:

1. Deal with the model data. We'll delete the requested row; if this empties the section array, we'll also delete that section array and the corresponding section name.

2. Deal with the table's appearance. If we deleted the section array, we'll call deleteSections:withRowAnimation: (and reload the section index if there is one); otherwise, we'll call deleteRowsAtIndexPaths:withRowAnimation::

```
- (void)tableView:(UITableView *)tableView
      commitEditingStyle:(UITableViewCellEditingStyle)editingStyle
       forRowAtIndexPath:(NSIndexPath *)ip {
    [self.sectionData[ip.section] removeObjectAtIndex:ip.row];
    if ([self.sectionData[ip.section] count] == 0) {
        [self.sectionData removeObjectAtIndex: ip.section];
        [self.sectionNames removeObjectAtIndex: ip.section];
        [tableView deleteSections:[NSIndexSet indexSetWithIndex: ip.section]
                withRowAnimation:UITableViewRowAnimationAutomatic];
        [tableView reloadSectionIndexTitles];
    } else {
```

```
            [tableView deleteRowsAtIndexPaths:@[ip]
                        withRowAnimation:UITableViewRowAnimationAutomatic];
        }
    }
```

The user can also delete a row by swiping it to summon its Delete button *without* having explicitly entered edit mode; no other row is editable, and no other editing controls are shown. This feature is implemented "for free" by virtue of our having supplied an implementation of `tableView:commitEditingStyle:forRowAtIndexPath:`. If you're like me, your first response will be: "Thanks for the free functionality, Apple, and now how do I turn this off?" Because the Edit button is already using the UIViewController's `editing` property to track edit mode, we can take advantage of this and refuse to let any cells be edited unless the view controller *is* in edit mode:

```
    - (UITableViewCellEditingStyle)tableView:(UITableView *)aTableView
            editingStyleForRowAtIndexPath:(NSIndexPath *)indexPath {
        return self.editing ?
            UITableViewCellEditingStyleDelete : UITableViewCellEditingStyleNone;
    }
```

Editable Content in Table Items

A table item might have content that the user can edit directly, such as a UITextField (Chapter 23). Because the user is working in the view, you need a way to reflect the user's changes into the model. This will probably involve putting yourself in contact with the interface objects where the user does the editing.

To illustrate, I'll implement a table view cell with a text field that is editable when the cell is in editing mode. Imagine an app that maintains a list of names and phone numbers. A name and phone number are displayed as a grouped-style table, and they become editable when the user taps the Edit button (Figure 21-8).

A UITextField is editable if its `enabled` is YES. To tie this to the cell's `editing` state, it is probably simplest to implement a custom UITableViewCell class. I'll call it MyCell, and I'll design it in the nib, giving it a single UITextField that's pointed to through a property called `textField`. In the code for MyCell, we override `didTransitionTo-State:`, as follows:

```
    - (void) didTransitionToState:(UITableViewCellStateMask)state {
        [super didTransitionToState:state];
        if (state == UITableViewCellStateEditingMask) {
            self.textField.enabled = YES;
        }
        if (state == UITableViewCellStateDefaultMask) {
            self.textField.enabled = NO;
        }
    }
```

Figure 21-8. A simple phone directory app

In the table's data source, we make ourselves the text field's delegate when we create and configure the cell:

```
- (UITableViewCell *)tableView:(UITableView *)tableView
        cellForRowAtIndexPath:(NSIndexPath *)indexPath {
    MyCell* cell =
        (MyCell*)[tableView dequeueReusableCellWithIdentifier:@"Cell"
                                            forIndexPath:indexPath];
    if (indexPath.section == 0)
        cell.textField.text = self.name;
    if (indexPath.section == 1) {
        cell.textField.text = self.numbers[indexPath.row];
        cell.textField.keyboardType = UIKeyboardTypeNumbersAndPunctuation;
    }
    cell.textField.delegate = self;
    return cell;
}
```

We are the UITextField's delegate, so we are responsible for implementing the Return button in the keyboard to dismiss the keyboard:

```
- (BOOL)textFieldShouldReturn:(UITextField *)tf {
    [tf endEditing:YES];
    return NO;
}
```

When a text field stops editing, we are its delegate, so we can hear about it in textField-DidEndEditing:. We work out which cell it belongs to, and update the model accordingly:

```
- (void)textFieldDidEndEditing:(UITextField *)tf {
    // some cell's text field has finished editing; which cell?
    UIView* v = tf;
    do {
```

Figure 21-9. Phone directory app in editing mode

```
        v = v.superview;
    } while (![v isKindOfClass: [UITableViewCell class]]);
    MyCell* cell = (MyCell*)v;
    // update data model to match
    NSIndexPath* ip = [self.tableView indexPathForCell:cell];
    if (ip.section == 1)
        self.numbers[ip.row] = cell.textField.text;
    else if (ip.section == 0)
        self.name = cell.textField.text;
}
```

Inserting Table Items

You are unlikely to attach a plus (insert) button to every row. A more likely interface is that when a table is edited, every row has a minus button except the last row, which has a plus button; this shows the user that a new row can be inserted at the end of the table.

Let's implement this for phone numbers in our name-and-phone-number app, allowing the user to give a person any quantity of phone numbers (Figure 21-9):

```
- (UITableViewCellEditingStyle)tableView:(UITableView *)tableView
        editingStyleForRowAtIndexPath:(NSIndexPath *)indexPath {
    if (indexPath.section == 1) {
        NSInteger ct =
            [self tableView:tableView numberOfRowsInSection:indexPath.section];
```

```
        if (ct-1 == indexPath.row)
            return UITableViewCellEditingStyleInsert;
        return UITableViewCellEditingStyleDelete;
    }
    return UITableViewCellEditingStyleNone;
}
```

The person's name has no editing control (a person must have exactly one name), so we prevent it from indenting in edit mode:

```
- (BOOL)tableView:(UITableView *)tableView
       shouldIndentWhileEditingRowAtIndexPath:(NSIndexPath *)indexPath {
    if (indexPath.section == 1)
        return YES;
    return NO;
}
```

When the user taps an editing control, we must respond. We immediately force our text fields to cease editing: the user have may tapped the editing control while editing, and we want our model to contain the very latest changes, so this is effectively a way of causing our textFieldDidEndEditing: to be called. The model for our phone numbers is a mutable array of strings, numbers. We already know what to do when the tapped control is a delete button; things are similar when it's an insert button, but we've a little more work to do. The new row will be empty, and it will be at the end of the table; so we append an empty string to the numbers model array, and then we insert a corresponding row at the end of the view. But now two successive rows have a plus button; the way to fix that is to reload the first of those rows. Finally, we also show the keyboard for the new, empty phone number, so that the user can start editing it immediately; we do that outside the update block:

```
- (void) tableView:(UITableView *)tableView
       commitEditingStyle:(UITableViewCellEditingStyle)editingStyle
       forRowAtIndexPath:(NSIndexPath *)indexPath {
    [tableView endEditing:YES];
    if (editingStyle == UITableViewCellEditingStyleInsert) {
        [self.numbers addObject: @""];
        NSInteger ct = [self.numbers count];
        [tableView beginUpdates];
        [tableView insertRowsAtIndexPaths:
         @[[NSIndexPath indexPathForRow: ct-1 inSection:1]]
                    withRowAnimation:UITableViewRowAnimationAutomatic];
        [self.tableView reloadRowsAtIndexPaths:
            @[[NSIndexPath indexPathForRow:ct-2 inSection:1]]
                        withRowAnimation:UITableViewRowAnimationAutomatic];
        [tableView endUpdates];
        // crucial that this next bit be *outside* the update block
        UITableViewCell* cell =
            [self.tableView cellForRowAtIndexPath:
                    [NSIndexPath indexPathForRow:ct-1 inSection:1]];
        [((MyCell*)cell).textField becomeFirstResponder];
```

```
    }
    if (editingStyle == UITableViewCellEditingStyleDelete) {
        [self.numbers removeObjectAtIndex:indexPath.row];
        [tableView beginUpdates];
        [tableView deleteRowsAtIndexPaths:@[indexPath]
                    withRowAnimation:UITableViewRowAnimationAutomatic];
        [tableView reloadSections:[NSIndexSet indexSetWithIndex:1]
                withRowAnimation:UITableViewRowAnimationAutomatic];
        [tableView endUpdates];
    }
}
```

Rearranging Table Items

If the data source implements tableView:moveRowAtIndexPath:toIndexPath:, the table displays a reordering control at the right end of each row in editing mode (Figure 21-9), and the user can drag it to rearrange table items. The reordering control can be prevented for individual table items by implementing tableView:canMoveRow-AtIndexPath:. The user is free to move rows that display a reordering control, but the delegate can limit where a row can be moved to by implementing tableView:target-IndexPathForMoveFromRowAtIndexPath:toProposedIndexPath:.

To illustrate, we'll add to our name-and-phone-number app the ability to rearrange phone numbers. There must be multiple phone numbers to rearrange:

```
- (BOOL)tableView:(UITableView *)tableView
        canMoveRowAtIndexPath:(NSIndexPath *)indexPath {
    if (indexPath.section == 1 && [self.numbers count] > 1)
        return YES;
    return NO;
}
```

In our example, a phone number must not be moved out of its section, so we implement the delegate method to prevent this. We also take this opportunity to dismiss the keyboard if it is showing.

```
- (NSIndexPath *)tableView:(UITableView *)tableView
        targetIndexPathForMoveFromRowAtIndexPath:(NSIndexPath*)sourceIndexPath
        toProposedIndexPath:(NSIndexPath*)proposedDestinationIndexPath {
    [tableView endEditing:YES];
    if (proposedDestinationIndexPath.section == 0)
        return [NSIndexPath indexPathForRow:0 inSection:1];
    return proposedDestinationIndexPath;
}
```

After the user moves an item, tableView:moveRowAtIndexPath:toIndexPath: is called, and we trivially update the model to match. We also reload the table, to fix the editing controls:

```
- (void)tableView:(UITableView *)tableView
       moveRowAtIndexPath:(NSIndexPath *)fromIndexPath
            toIndexPath:(NSIndexPath *)toIndexPath {
    NSString* s = self.numbers[fromIndexPath.row];
    [self.numbers removeObjectAtIndex: fromIndexPath.row];
    [self.numbers insertObject:s atIndex: toIndexPath.row];
    [tableView reloadData];
}
```

Dynamic Table Content

We can rearrange a table not just in response to the user working in edit mode, but for some other reason entirely. In this way, many interesting and original interfaces are possible. In this example, we permit the user to double tap on a section header as a way of collapsing or expanding the section — that is, we'll suppress or permit the display of the rows of the section, with a nice animation as the change takes place. (This idea is shamelessly stolen from a WWDC 2010 video.)

Presume that our data model once again consists of the two arrays, sectionNames and sectionData. I've also got an NSMutableSet, hiddenSections, in which I'll list the sections that aren't displaying their rows. That list is all I'll need, since either a section is showing all its rows or it's showing none of them:

```
- (NSInteger)tableView:(UITableView *)tableView
       numberOfRowsInSection:(NSInteger)section {
    if ([self.hiddenSections containsObject:@(section)])
        return 0;
    return [self.sectionData[section] count];
}
```

The section headers are a UITableViewHeaderFooterView with userInteraction-Enabled set to YES and a UITapGestureRecognizer attached, so we can detect a double tap. Here's how we respond to a double tap. We examine the tapped header to learn what section this is, and find out how many rows it has, as we'll need to know that later, regardless of whether we're about to show or hide rows. Then we look for the section number in our hiddenSections set. If it's there, we're about to display the rows, so we remove that section number from hiddenSections; now we work out the index paths of the rows we're about to insert, and we insert them. If it's not there, we're about to hide the rows, so we insert that section number into hiddenSections; again, we work out the index paths of the rows we're about to delete, and we delete them:

```
- (void) tap: (UIGestureRecognizer*) g {
    UITableViewHeaderFooterView* v = (id)g.view;
    NSString* s = v.textLabel.text;
    NSUInteger sec = [self.sectionNames indexOfObject:s];
    NSUInteger ct = [(NSArray*)(self.sectionData)[sec] count];
    NSNumber* secnum = @(sec);
    if ([self.hiddenSections containsObject:secnum]) {
        [self.hiddenSections removeObject:secnum];
```

```
    [self.tableView beginUpdates];
    NSMutableArray* arr = [NSMutableArray array];
    for (int ix = 0; ix < ct; ix ++) {
        NSIndexPath* ip = [NSIndexPath indexPathForRow:ix inSection:sec];
        [arr addObject: ip];
    }
    [self.tableView insertRowsAtIndexPaths:arr
        withRowAnimation:UITableViewRowAnimationAutomatic];
    [self.tableView endUpdates];
    [self.tableView scrollToRowAtIndexPath:[arr lastObject]
                        atScrollPosition:UITableViewScrollPositionNone
                                animated:YES];
} else {
    [self.hiddenSections addObject:secnum];
    [self.tableView beginUpdates];
    NSMutableArray* arr = [NSMutableArray array];
    for (int ix = 0; ix < ct; ix ++) {
        NSIndexPath* ip = [NSIndexPath indexPathForRow:ix inSection:sec];
        [arr addObject: ip];
    }
    [self.tableView deleteRowsAtIndexPaths:arr
        withRowAnimation:UITableViewRowAnimationAutomatic];
    [self.tableView endUpdates];
    }
}
```

Table View Menus

It is possible to display a menu from a table view cell by performing a long press on the cell. A menu, in iOS, is a sort of balloon containing tappable words such as Copy, Cut, and Paste. And as far as I can tell, those are the only words you'll be including in a table view cell's menu; I tried to customize the menu to include other terms, but I failed.

To allow the user to display a menu from a table view's cells, you implement three delegate methods:

tableView:shouldShowMenuForRowAtIndexPath:
:   Return YES if the user is to be permitted to summon a menu by performing a long press on this cell.

tableView:canPerformAction:forRowAtIndexPath:withSender:
:   You'll be called repeatedly with a bunch of selectors for various actions that the system knows about, but as far as I can tell, the only ones worth responding YES to are cut:, copy:, and paste:. Whichever ones you respond YES to will appear in the menu; returning YES, regardless, causes all three menu items to appear in the menu. The menu will now appear unless you return NO to all three actions. The sender is the shared UIMenuController, which I'll discuss more in Chapter 23 and Chapter 39.

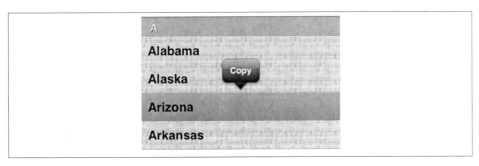

Figure 21-10. A table view cell with a menu

`tableView:performAction:forRowAtIndexPath:withSender:`
The user has tapped one of the menu items; your job is to respond to it somehow.

Here's an example where the user can summon a Copy menu from any cell (Figure 21-10):

```
- (BOOL)tableView:(UITableView *)tableView
        shouldShowMenuForRowAtIndexPath:(NSIndexPath *)indexPath {
    return YES;
}

- (BOOL)tableView:(UITableView *)tableView canPerformAction:(SEL)action
        forRowAtIndexPath:(NSIndexPath *)indexPath withSender:(id)sender {
    return (action == @selector(copy:));
}

- (void)tableView:(UITableView *)tableView performAction:(SEL)action
        forRowAtIndexPath:(NSIndexPath *)indexPath withSender:(id)sender {
    NSString* s = self.sectionData[indexPath.section][indexPath.row];
    if (action == @selector(copy:)) {
        // ... do whatever copying consists of ...
    }
}
```

As Figure 21-10 shows, the long press gesture used to summon a menu also causes the pressed cell to assume its selected state — and hence its selected appearance. Moreover, tapping a menu item to choose it deselects the cell, even if it was previously selected; and tapping elsewhere, to dismiss the menu without choosing any menu item, may then select the cell under that tap. This interweaving of the ability to summon a menu with the cell selection mechanism is unfortunate, especially since Apple has not also provided any properties for detecting that menu display is occurring or for customizing what happens when it is.

Collection Views

A collection view (UICollectionView), new in iOS 6, is a UIScrollView subclass that generalizes the notion of a UITableView. Like a UITableView, you might well manage your collection view through a UIViewController subclass — a subclass of UICollectionViewController. Like a UITableView, a collection view has reusable cells — these are UICollectionViewCell instances, and are extremely minimal. Like a UITableView, you'll make the cells reusable by registering with the collection view, by calling `register-Class:forCellWithReuseIdentifier:` or `registerNib:forCellWithReuse-Identifier:`, or, if you've started with a UICollectionViewController in a storyboard, just assign the reuse identifier in the storyboard. Like a UITableView, a collection view has a data source (UICollectionViewDataSource) and a delegate (UICollectionView-Delegate), and it's going to ask the data source Three Big Questions:

- `numberOfSectionsInCollectionView:`
- `collectionView:numberOfItemsInSection:`
- `collectionView:cellForItemAtIndexPath:`

To answer the third question, you'll supply a cell by calling `dequeueReusableCellWith-ReuseIdentifier:forIndexPath:`.

As the Three Big Questions imply, you can present your data in sections. A section can have a header and footer, though the collection view itself does not call them that; instead, it generalizes its subview types into cells, on the one hand, and supplementary views, on the other, where a supplementary view is just a UICollectionReusableView, which happens to be UICollectionViewCell's superclass. The user can select a cell, or multiple cells. The delegate is notified of highlighting and selection just like a table delegate. Your code can rearrange the cells, inserting, moving, and deleting cells or entire sections. If the delegate permits, the user can long-press a cell to produce a menu (with choices limited to Cut, Copy, and Paste).

In short, knowing about table views, you know a great deal about collection views already.

What you *don't* know about a collection view is how it lays out its cells. A table view lays out its cells in just one way: a vertically scrolling column, where the cells are the width of the table view, the height dictated by the table view or the delegate, and touching one another. A collection view doesn't do that. In fact, a collection view doesn't lay out its cells at all! That job is left to another class, a subclass of UICollectionViewLayout. This class can effectively do anything it wants to do. The WWDC 2012 videos even demonstrate a UICollectionViewLayout that arranges its cells in a circle! The open-ended nature of collection view layout is what makes collection views so general.

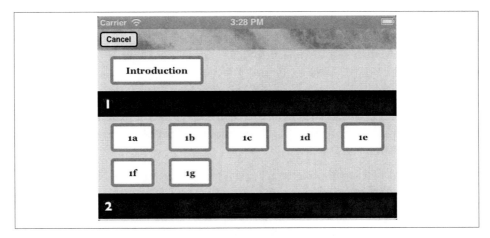

Figure 21-11. A collection view in my Latin flashcard app

To get you started, iOS 6 comes with one built-in UICollectionViewLayout subclass —
UICollectionViewFlowLayout. It arranges its cells in something like a grid. The grid can
be scrolled either horizontally or vertically, so this grid is a series of rows or columns.
Through properties and a delegate (UICollectionViewDelegateFlowLayout), the UI-
CollectionViewFlowLayout instance lets you provide hints about how big the cells are
and how they should be spaced out. UICollectionViewFlowLayout also takes the collection view notion of a supplementary view and hones it to give you the expected
notions of a header and a footer.

Figure 21-11 shows a collection view, laid out with a flow layout, from my Latin flashcard
app. This interface simply lists the chapters and lessons into which the flashcards themselves are divided, and allows the user to jump to a desired lesson by tapping it. Previously, this was a table view; when iOS 6 came along, I instantly adopted a collection view
instead, and you can see why. Instead of a lesson item like "1a" occupying an entire row
that stretches the whole width of a table, it's just a little rectangle; in landscape orientation, the flow layout fits five of these rectangles onto a line for me. So a collection view
is a much more compact and appropriate way to present this interface than a table view.

Here are the classes associated with UICollectionView. This is just a conceptual overview; I don't recite all the properties and methods of each class, which you can learn
from the documentation:

UICollectionViewController

> A UIViewController subclass. Like a table view controller, UICollectionViewCon-
> troller is convenient if a UICollectionView is to be a view controller's view, but is
> not required. It is the delegate and data source of its collectionView by default.
> The initializer, if you create one in code, requires you to supply a layout instance
> for the collection view's designated initializer:

```
RootViewController* rvc =
    [[RootViewController alloc]
        initWithCollectionViewLayout:[UICollectionViewFlowLayout new]];
```

Alternatively, there is a UICollectionViewController nib object.

UICollectionView

A UIScrollView subclass. It has a backgroundColor (because it's a view) and optionally a backgroundView in front of that. Its designated initializer requires you to supply a layout instance, which will be its collectionViewLayout. There is a Collection View nib object.

A collection view's methods are very much parallel to those of a UITableView, only fewer and simpler:

- Where a table view speaks of rows, a collection view speaks of items. UICollectionView even adds a category to NSIndexPath so that you can refer to its item property instead of its row property.

- Where a table view speaks of a header or footer, a collection view speaks of a supplementary view.

- A UICollectionView doesn't do layout, so it is not where things like header and cell size are configured.

- A UICollectionView has no notion of editing.

- A UICollectionView has no section index.

- Where a table view batches updates with beginUpdates and endUpdates, a collection view uses performBatchUpdates:completion:, which takes blocks.

- A collection view performs animation when you insert, delete, or move sections or items, but you don't specify an animation type. (The layout can modify the animation, however.)

Having made those mental adjustments, you can guess correctly all of a UICollectionView's methods, except for layoutAttributesForItemAtIndexPath: and layoutAttributesForSupplementaryElementOfKind:atIndexPath:. To understand what they do, you need to know about UICollectionViewLayoutAttributes.

UICollectionViewLayoutAttributes

A UICollectionViewLayoutAttributes object is basically just a glorified struct, tying together a view's index path within the collection view and the specifications for how it should be drawn — it's frame, center, size, and so forth. It is the mediator between the layout and the collection view, giving the collection view a way to learn from the layout where a particular item should go.

UICollectionViewCell

An extremely minimal view class. It has a `highlighted` property and a `selected` property. It has a `contentView`, a `selectedBackgroundView`, a `backgroundView`, and of course (since it's a view) a `backgroundColor`, layered in that order, just like a table view cell; everything else is up to you.

If you start with a collection view controller in a storyboard, you get prototype cells, just like a table view controller. Otherwise, you obtain cells through registration and dequeuing.

UICollectionReusableView

The superclass of UICollectionViewCell — so it is even more minimal! This is the class of supplementary views such as headers and footers. You obtain reusable views through registration and dequeuing.

UICollectionViewLayout

The layout workhorse class for a collection view. A collection view cannot exist without a layout instance! It manages three types of subview (elements): cells, supplementary views, and decoration views. (A decoration view has no relation to data, which is why a collection view knows nothing of it.) The layout knows how much room all the subviews occupy, and supplies the `collectionViewContentSize` that sets the `contentSize` of the collection view, *qua* scroll view.

The layout's chief task is to answer questions about layout from the collection view. All of these questions are answered with a UICollectionViewLayoutAttributes object, or an NSArray of UICollectionViewLayoutAttributes objects, saying where and how something should be drawn. These questions come in two categories:

Static attributes

The collection view wants to know the layout attributes of an item, supplementary view, or decoration view, specified by index path, or of all elements within a given rect.

Dynamic attributes

The collection view is inserting or removing elements. It asks for the layout attributes that an element, specified by index path, should have before insertion or after removal. The collection view can thus animate between the element's static attributes and these dynamic attributes. For example, if an element's layout attributes `alpha` is 0 after removal, the element will appear to fade away as it is removed.

The collection view also notifies the layout of pending changes through some methods whose names start with "prepare" and "finalize." This is another way for the layout to participate in animations, or to perform other kinds of preparation and cleanup. (One of the "prepare" methods communicates its information through another glorified struct, UICollectionViewUpdateItem, that I don't discuss here.)

UICollectionViewLayout is an abstract class; to use it, you must subclass it, or start with the built-in subclass, UICollectionViewFlowLayout.

UICollectionViewFlowLayout

The included concrete subclass of UICollectionViewLayout; you can use it as is, or you can subclass it. A flow layout is easy to choose and configure as your collection view's layout: a collection view in a nib or storyboard has a Layout pop-up menu that lets you choose a Flow layout, and you can configure the flow layout in the Size inspector (in a storyboard, you can even add and design a header and a footer).

Configuration of a flow layout is very simple. It has a scroll direction, a section-Inset (the margins for a section), an itemSize along with a minimumInterItem-Spacing and minimumLineSpacing, and a headerReferenceSize and footer-ReferenceSize. That's all! At a minimum, if you want to see any section headers, you must assign the flow layout a headerReferenceSize, because the default is CGSizeZero. Otherwise, you get initial defaults that will at least allow you to see something immediately, such as an itemSize of {50,50} and reasonable default spacing between items and lines.

The section margins, item size, item spacing, line spacing, and header and footer size can also be set individually through the flow layout's delegate.

To show that using a collection view is easy, here's how the view shown in Figure 21-11 is created. I have a UICollectionViewController subclass, LessonListController. Every collection view must have a layout, so LessonListController's designated initializer initializes itself with a UICollectionViewFlowLayout:

```
- (id) initWithTerms: (NSArray*) data {
    UICollectionViewFlowLayout* layout = [UICollectionViewFlowLayout new];
    self = [super initWithCollectionViewLayout:layout];
    if (self) {
        // ... perform other self-initializations here ...
    }
    return self;
}
```

In viewDidLoad, we give the flow layout its hints about the sizes of the margins, cells, and headers, as well as registering for cell and header reusability:

```
- (void)viewDidLoad {
    [super viewDidLoad];
    UICollectionViewFlowLayout* layout =
        (id)self.collectionView.collectionViewLayout;
    layout.sectionInset = UIEdgeInsetsMake(10, 20, 10, 20);
    layout.headerReferenceSize = CGSizeMake(0,40); // only height matters
    layout.itemSize = CGSizeMake(70,45);
```

```
[self.collectionView
    registerNib:[UINib nibWithNibName:@"LessonCell" bundle:nil]
    forCellWithReuseIdentifier:@"LessonCell"];
[self.collectionView
    registerClass:[UICollectionReusableView class]
    forSupplementaryViewOfKind:UICollectionElementKindSectionHeader
    withReuseIdentifier:@"LessonHeader"];
self.collectionView.backgroundColor = [UIColor myGolden];
// ...
}
```

The first two of the Three Big Questions to the data source are boring and familiar:

```
-(NSInteger)numberOfSectionsInCollectionView:
        (UICollectionView *)collectionView {
    return [self.sectionNames count];
}

-(NSInteger)collectionView:(UICollectionView *)collectionView
        numberOfItemsInSection:(NSInteger)section {
    return [self.sectionData[section] count];
}
```

The third of the Three Big Questions to the data source creates and configures the cells. In the nib, I've designed the cell with a single subview, a UILabel with tag 1; if the text of the label is still @"Label", that is a sign that it has come freshly minted from the nib and needs further initial configuration. Among other things, I assign each new cell a selectedBackgroundView and give the label a highlightedTextColor, to get an automatic indication of selection:

```
- (UICollectionViewCell *)collectionView:(UICollectionView *)collectionView
        cellForItemAtIndexPath:(NSIndexPath *)indexPath {
    UICollectionViewCell* cell =
        [collectionView dequeueReusableCellWithReuseIdentifier:@"LessonCell"
                                            forIndexPath:indexPath];
    UILabel* lab = (UILabel*)[cell viewWithTag:1];
    if ([lab.text isEqualToString:@"Label"]) {
        lab.highlightedTextColor = [UIColor whiteColor];
        cell.backgroundColor = [UIColor myPaler];
        cell.layer.borderColor = [UIColor brownColor].CGColor;
        cell.layer.borderWidth = 5;
        cell.layer.cornerRadius = 5;
        UIView* v = [UIView new];
        v.backgroundColor = [[UIColor blueColor] colorWithAlphaComponent:0.8];
        cell.selectedBackgroundView = v;
    }
    Term* term = self.sectionData[indexPath.section][indexPath.item];
    lab.text = term.lesson;
    return cell;
}
```

There is also a fourth data source method, asking for the section headers. I haven't bothered to design the header in a nib, so I configure the entire thing in code. Again, I distinguish between newly minted views and reused views; the latter will already have a single subview, a UILabel:

```
-(UICollectionReusableView *)collectionView:(UICollectionView *)collectionView
        viewForSupplementaryElementOfKind:(NSString *)kind
                            atIndexPath:(NSIndexPath *)indexPath {
    UICollectionReusableView* v =
        [collectionView
            dequeueReusableSupplementaryViewOfKind:
                UICollectionElementKindSectionHeader
            withReuseIdentifier:@"LessonHeader"
                forIndexPath:indexPath];
    // either we've already given this one a label or we haven't
    // if we haven't, create it and configure the whole thing
    if ([v.subviews count] == 0) {
        UILabel* lab = [[UILabel alloc] initWithFrame:CGRectMake(10,0,100,40)];
        lab.font = [UIFont fontWithName:@"GillSans-Bold" size:20];
        lab.backgroundColor = [UIColor clearColor];
        [v addSubview:lab];
        v.backgroundColor = [UIColor blackColor];
        lab.textColor = [UIColor myPaler];
    }
    UILabel* lab = (UILabel*)v.subviews[0];
    lab.text = self.sectionNames[indexPath.section];
    return v;
}
```

Two flow layout delegate methods cause the first section to be treated specially —it has no header, and its cell is wider:

```
- (CGSize)collectionView:(UICollectionView *)collectionView
        layout:(UICollectionViewLayout*)collectionViewLayout
        sizeForItemAtIndexPath:(NSIndexPath *)indexPath {
    CGSize sz = ((UICollectionViewFlowLayout*)collectionViewLayout).itemSize;
    if (indexPath.section == 0)
        sz.width = 150;
    return sz;
}

- (CGSize)collectionView:(UICollectionView *)collectionView
        layout:(UICollectionViewLayout*)collectionViewLayout
        referenceSizeForHeaderInSection:(NSInteger)section {
    CGSize sz =
        ((UICollectionViewFlowLayout*)collectionViewLayout).headerReferenceSize;
    if (section == 0)
        sz.height = 0;
    return sz;
}
```

That's all there is to it! When the user taps a cell, I hear about it through the delegate method `collectionView:didSelectItemAtIndexPath:` and respond accordingly.

Without getting deeply into the mechanics of layout, I'll introduce the topic by suggesting a modification of UICollectionViewFlowLayout. By default, the layout wants to full-justify every row of cells horizontally, spacing the cells evenly between the left and right margins, except for the last row, which is left-aligned. Let's say that this isn't what you want — you'd rather that *every* row be left-aligned, with every cell as far to the left as possible given the size of the preceding cell and the minimum spacing between cells.

To achieve this, you'll need to subclass UICollectionViewFlowLayout and override two methods, `layoutAttributesForElementsInRect:` and `layoutAttributesForItemAtIndexPath:`. Fortunately, we're starting with a layout, UICollectionViewFlowLayout, whose answers to these questions are almost right. So we call `super` and make modifications as necessary. The really important method here is `layoutAttributesForItemAtIndexPath:`, which returns a single UICollectionViewLayoutAttributes object. If the index path's `item` is `0`, we have a degenerate case: the answer we got from `super` is right. Alternatively, if this cell is at the start of a row — we can find this out by asking whether the left edge of its frame is close to the margin — we have another degenerate case: the answer we got from `super` is right.

Otherwise, where this cell goes depends on where the previous cell goes, so we obtain the frame of the previous cell recursively; we propose to position our left edge a minimal spacing amount from the right edge of the previous cell. We do that by changing the `frame` of the UICollectionViewLayoutAttributes object. Then we return that object:

```
- (UICollectionViewLayoutAttributes *)layoutAttributesForItemAtIndexPath:
        (NSIndexPath *)indexPath {
    UICollectionViewLayoutAttributes* atts =
        [super layoutAttributesForItemAtIndexPath:indexPath];
    if (indexPath.item == 0) // degenerate case
        return atts;
    if (atts.frame.origin.x - 1 <= self.sectionInset.left) // degenerate case
        return atts;

    NSIndexPath* ipPrev =
        [NSIndexPath indexPathForItem:indexPath.item-1
                            inSection:indexPath.section];
    CGRect fPrev = [self layoutAttributesForItemAtIndexPath:ipPrev].frame;
    CGFloat rightPrev =
        fPrev.origin.x + fPrev.size.width + self.minimumInteritemSpacing;
    CGRect f = atts.frame;
    f.origin.x = rightPrev;
    atts.frame = f;
    return atts;
}
```

The other method, layoutAttributesForElementsInRect:, returns an NSArray of UICollectionViewLayoutAttributes objects for all the cells and supplementary views in a rect. Again we call super and modify the resulting array so that if an element is a cell, its UICollectionViewLayoutAttributes is the result of our layoutAttributesForItemAtIndexPath:::

```
- (NSArray *)layoutAttributesForElementsInRect:(CGRect)rect {
    NSArray* arr = [super layoutAttributesForElementsInRect:rect];
    for (UICollectionViewLayoutAttributes* atts in arr) {
        if (nil == atts.representedElementKind) { // it's a cell
            NSIndexPath* ip = atts.indexPath;
            atts.frame = [self layoutAttributesForItemAtIndexPath:ip].frame;
        }
    }
    return arr;
}
```

Apple supplies some further interesting examples of subclassing UICollectionView-FlowLayout. For instance, the LineLayout example (accompanying the WWDC 2012 videos) implements a single row of horizontally scrolling cells, where a cell grows as it approaches the center of the screen and shrinks as it moves away. To do this, it first of all overrides a UICollectionViewLayout method I didn't mention earlier, should-InvalidateLayoutForBoundsChange:; this causes layout to happen repeatedly while the collection view is scrolled. It then overrides layoutAttributesForElementsIn-Rect: to do the same sort of thing I did a moment ago: it calls super and then modifies, as needed, the transform3D property of UICollectionViewLayoutAttributes for the onscreen cells. (It also overrides another UICollectionViewLayout method I didn't mention, targetContentOffsetForProposedContentOffset:withScrolling-Velocity:, which is like UIScrollViewDelegate's scrollViewWillEndDragging:with-Velocity:targetContentOffset:. This is just a nice touch so that when the user scrolls, a cell always ends up exactly centered on the screen.)

CHAPTER 22

Popovers and Split Views

Popovers and split views are forms of interface that exist only on the iPad.

A *popover* (managed by a UIPopoverController) is a sort of secondary window or dialog: it displays a view layered on top of the main interface. It is usually associated, through a sort of arrow, with a view in the main interface, such as the button that the user tapped to summon the popover. It does not dim out the rest of the screen, like a presented view whose presentation mode is `UIModalPresentationPageSheet` or `UIModal-PresentationFormSheet` (see Chapter 19). It might be effectively modal, preventing the user from working in the rest of the interface; alternatively, it might vanish if the user taps outside it.

A popover, in effect, superimposes a roughly iPhone-sized screen on top of the iPad screen, and is useful in part precisely because it brings to the larger iPad the smaller, more lightweight flavor of the iPhone. For example, in my LinkSame app, both the settings view (where the user configures the game) and the help view (which describes how to play the game) are popovers (Figure 22-1). On the iPhone, both these views would occupy the entire screen; for each, we'd need a way to navigate to it, and then to return to the main interface when the user is finished with it. But with the larger iPad screen, neither view is large enough, or important enough, to occupy the entire screen exclusively. As popovers, these views are shown as what they are: smaller, secondary views which the user summons temporarily and then dismisses.

A *split view* (managed by a UISplitViewController) is a combination of two views, the first having the width of an iPhone screen in portrait orientation. When the iPad is in landscape orientation, the two views appear side by side. When the iPad is in portrait orientation, there are two possibilities:

- Only the second view appears, with an option to summon the first view by tapping a bar button item (or, optionally, by swiping to the right).

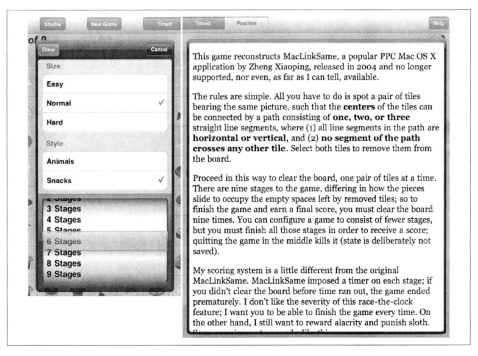

Figure 22-1. Two popovers

- Both views continue to appear side by side; the second view is narrower, because the screen is narrower.

Like popovers, a split view may be regarded as an evolutionary link between the smaller iPhone interface and the larger iPad interface. On the iPhone, you might have a master–detail architecture in a navigation interface, where the master view is a table view, and the detail view is a completely different view pushed onto the navigation stack in place of the master view (Chapter 21). On the iPad, the large screen can accommodate the master view and the detail view *simultaneously*; the split view is a built-in way to do that. It is no coincidence that the Master–Detail Application template in Xcode generates a navigation interface for the iPhone and a split view for the iPad.

Before iOS 5, UISplitViewController was the only legal way in which a single view controller could display the views of two child view controllers side by side. Nowadays, you are free to design your own custom parent view controllers (Chapter 19), so UISplitViewController is of diminished value. Nevertheless, it's built-in and easy to use.

Configuring and Displaying a Popover

To display a popover, you'll need a UIPopoverController, along with a view controller (UIViewController) whose view the popover will contain. UIPopoverController is not itself a UIViewController subclass. The view controller is the UIPopoverController's contentViewController. You'll set this property initially through UIPopover-Controller's designated initializer, initWithContentViewController:. Subsequently, if you like, you can swap out a popover controller's view controller (and hence its contained view) by calling setContentViewController:animated:.

Here's how the UIPopoverController for the first popover in Figure 22-1 is initialized. I have a UIViewController subclass, NewGameController. NewGameController's view contains a grouped table (whose code I showed you in Chapter 21) and a UIPickerView (see Chapter 11 and Chapter 25), and is itself the data source and delegate for both. I instantiate NewGameController and use this instance as the root view controller of a UINavigationController, giving its navigationItem a leftBarButtonItem (Done) and a rightBarButtonItem (Cancel). I don't really intend to do any navigation, but the navigation controller's navigation bar is a convenient way of adding the two buttons to the interface. That UINavigationController then becomes a UIPopoverController's view controller:

```
NewGameController* dlg = [NewGameController new];
UIBarButtonItem* b = [[UIBarButtonItem alloc]
    initWithBarButtonSystemItem: UIBarButtonSystemItemCancel
                         target: self
                         action: @selector(cancelNewGame:)];
dlg.navigationItem.rightBarButtonItem = b;
b = [[UIBarButtonItem alloc]
    initWithBarButtonSystemItem: UIBarButtonSystemItemDone
                         target: self
                         action: @selector(saveNewGame:)];
dlg.navigationItem.leftBarButtonItem = b;
UINavigationController* nav =
    [[UINavigationController alloc] initWithRootViewController:dlg];
UIPopoverController* pop =
    [[UIPopoverController alloc] initWithContentViewController:nav];
```

That code doesn't cause the popover to appear on the screen! I'll come to that in a moment.

The popover controller needs to know the size of the view it is to display, which will be the size of the popover. The default popover size is {320,1100}; Apple would like you to stick to the default width of 320 (the width of an iPhone screen), but a maximum width of 600 is permitted, and the second popover in Figure 22-1 uses it. The popover's height may be shorter than requested if there isn't enough vertical space; the view to be displayed might need to be ready for such resizing.

You can provide the popover size in one of two ways:

UIPopoverController's `popoverContentSize` *property*

This property can be set before the popover appears; it can also be changed while the popover is showing, with `setPopoverContentSize:animated:`.

UIViewController's `contentSizeForViewInPopover` *property*

The UIViewController in question is the UIPopoverController's `contentView-Controller` (or is contained by that view controller, as in a tab bar interface or navigation interface). This approach often makes more sense, because a UIView-Controller will generally know its own view's ideal size. If a view controller is to be instantiated from a nib or storyboard, this value can be set in the Attributes inspector.

In the case of the first popover in Figure 22-1, the NewGameController sets its own `contentSizeForViewInPopover` in `viewDidLoad`; its popover size is simply the size of its view:

```
self.contentSizeForViewInPopover = self.view.bounds.size;
```

The popover itself, however, will need to be somewhat taller, because the NewGame-Controller is embedded in a UINavigationController, whose navigation bar occupies additional vertical space. Delightfully, the UINavigationController takes care of that automatically; its own `contentSizeForViewInPopover` adds the necessary height to that of its child view controller.

If the UIPopoverController and the UIViewController have different settings for their respective content size properties at the time the popover is initially displayed, the UIPopoverController's setting wins. But once the popover is visible, if *either* property is changed, the change is obeyed; for example, if the UIViewController's `contentSize-ForViewInPopover` is changed (not merely set to the value it already has), the UIPopoverController adopts that value as its `popoverContentSize` and the popover's size is adjusted accordingly.

If a popover's `contentViewController` is a UINavigationController, and a view controller is pushed onto or popped off of its stack, then if the current view controller's `contentSizeForViewInPopover` differs from that of the previously displayed view controller, my experiments suggest that the popover's *width* will change to match the new width, but the popover's *height* will change only if the new height is *taller*. This feels like a bug. A workaround is to implement the UINavigationController's delegate method `navigationController:didShowViewController:animated:`, so as to set the navigation controller's `contentSizeForViewInPopover` explicitly:

```
- (void)navigationController:(UINavigationController *)navigationController
        didShowViewController:(UIViewController *)viewController
                    animated:(BOOL)animated {
    navigationController.contentSizeForViewInPopover =
        viewController.contentSizeForViewInPopover;
}
```

(That workaround is not entirely satisfactory from a visual standpoint, as two animations succeed one another, but I tried implementing `willShowViewController...` instead and liked the results even less.)

The popover is made to appear on screen by sending the UIPopoverController one of the following messages (and the UIPopoverController's `popoverVisible` property then becomes YES):

- `presentPopoverFromRect:inView:permittedArrowDirections:animated:`
- `presentPopoverFromBarButtonItem:permittedArrowDirections:animated:`

The popover has a sort of triangular protrusion (called its *arrow*) on one edge, pointing to some region of the existing interface, from which the popover thus appears to emanate and to which it seems to be related. The difference between the two methods lies only in how this region is specified. With the first method, you can provide any CGRect with respect to any visible UIView's coordinate system; for example, to make the popover emanate from a UIButton, you could provide the UIButton's frame with respect to its superview, or (better) the UIButton's bounds with respect to itself. But you can't do that with a UIBarButtonItem, because a UIBarButtonItem isn't a UIView and doesn't have a frame or bounds; hence the second method is provided.

The permitted arrow directions restrict which sides of the popover the arrow can appear on. It's a bitmask, and your choices are:

- `UIPopoverArrowDirectionUp`
- `UIPopoverArrowDirectionDown`
- `UIPopoverArrowDirectionLeft`
- `UIPopoverArrowDirectionRight`
- `UIPopoverArrowDirectionAny`

Usually, you'd specify `UIPopoverArrowDirectionAny`, allowing the runtime to put the arrow on whatever side it feels is appropriate.

Even if you specify a particular arrow direction, you still have no precise control over a popover's location. However, you do get some veto power: set the UIPopoverController's `popoverLayoutMargins` to a UIEdgeInsets stating the margins, with respect to the root view bounds, within which the popover must appear. If an inset that you give is so large that the arrow can no longer touch the presenting rect, it may be ignored, or the arrow may become disconnected from its presenting rect; you probably shouldn't do that.

The first popover in Figure 22-1 has a dark navigation bar even though no such thing was requested when the UINavigationController was created. This is because a popover whose content view controller is a navigation controller likes to take control of its nav-

Figure 22-2. A very silly popover

igation bar's `barStyle` and set it to a special undocumented style, evidently to make it harmonize with the popover's border. If you don't like that, setting the navigation bar's `tintColor` has no effect, but you can change its `backgroundColor` or its background image, and you can customize the position and appearance of its bar button items (Chapter 25).

You can also customize the outside of the popover — that is, the "frame" and the arrow. To do so, you set the UIPopoverController's `popoverBackgroundViewClass` to your subclass of UIPopoverBackgroundView (a UIView subclass) — at which point you can achieve just about anything you want, including the very silly popover shown in Figure 22-2.

Configuring your UIPopoverBackgroundView subclass is a bit tricky, because this single view is responsible for drawing both the arrow and the frame. Thus, in a complete and correct implementation, you'll have to draw differently depending on the arrow direction, which you can learn from the UIPopoverBackgroundView's `arrowDirection` property. I'll give a simplified example in which I cheat by assuming that the arrow direction will be `UIPopoverArrowDirectionUp`. Then drawing the frame is easy: here, I divide the view's overall rect into two areas, the arrow area on top (its height is a `#defined` constant, `ARHEIGHT`) and the frame area on the bottom, and draw the frame into the bottom area as a resizable image (Chapter 15):

```
UIImage* linOrig = [UIImage imageNamed: @"linen.png"];
CGFloat capw = linOrig.size.width / 2.0 - 1;
CGFloat caph = linOrig.size.height / 2.0 - 1;
UIImage* lin = [linOrig
    resizableImageWithCapInsets:UIEdgeInsetsMake(caph, capw, caph, capw)
                 resizingMode:UIImageResizingModeTile];
// ... draw arrow here ...
CGRect arrow;
CGRect body;
CGRectDivide(rect, &arrow, &body, ARHEIGHT, CGRectMinYEdge);
[lin drawInRect:body];
```

I omitted the drawing of the arrow; now let's insert it. The UIPopoverBackgroundView has arrowHeight and arrowBase class methods that you've overridden to describe the arrow dimensions to the runtime. (In my code, their values are provided by two #defined constants, ARHEIGHT and ARBASE; I've set them both to 20.) My arrow will consist simply of a texture-filled isosceles triangle, with an excess base consisting of a rectangle joining it to the frame. The UIPopoverBackgroundView also has an arrowOffset property that the runtime has set to tell you where to draw the arrow: this offset measures the positive distance between the center of the view's edge and the center of the arrow. However, the runtime will have no hesitation in setting the arrowOffset all the way at the edge of the view, or even beyond its bounds (in which case it won't be drawn); to prevent this, I provide a maximum offset limit:

```
CGContextRef con = UIGraphicsGetCurrentContext();
CGContextSaveGState(con);
CGFloat proposedX = self.arrowOffset;
CGFloat limit = 22.0;
CGFloat maxX = rect.size.width/2.0 - limit;
if (proposedX > maxX)
    proposedX = maxX;
if (proposedX < limit)
    proposedX = limit;
CGContextTranslateCTM(con, rect.size.width/2.0 + proposedX - ARBASE/2.0, 0);
CGContextMoveToPoint(con, 0, ARHEIGHT);
CGContextAddLineToPoint(con, ARBASE / 2.0, 0);
CGContextAddLineToPoint(con, ARBASE, ARHEIGHT);
CGContextClosePath(con);
CGContextAddRect(con, CGRectMake(0,ARHEIGHT,ARBASE,15));
CGContextClip(con);
[lin drawAtPoint:CGPointMake(-40,-40)];
CGContextRestoreGState(con);
```

The thickness of the four sides of the frame is dictated by implementing the contentViewInsets class method. New in iOS 6, a class method wantsDefaultContentAppearance can be overridden to return NO if you'd like to turn off the subtle drop shadow cast by the frame on the popover contents.

Managing a Popover

Unlike a presented view controller or a child view controller, a UIPopoverController instance is not automatically retained for you by some presenting view controller or parent view controller; you must retain it yourself. If you fail to do this, then if the UIPopoverController goes out of existence while its popover is on the screen, your app will crash (with a helpful message: "-[UIPopoverController dealloc] reached while popover is still visible"). Also, you might need the retained reference to the UIPopoverController later, when the time comes to dismiss the popover.

There are actually two ways in which a popover can be dismissed: the user can tap outside the popover, or you can explicitly dismiss the popover (as I do with the first popover in Figure 22-1 when the user taps the Done button or the Cancel button). In order to dismiss the popover explicitly, you send its UIPopoverController the `dismissPopover-Animated:` message. Obviously, then, you need a reference to the UIPopoverController.

Even if a popover is normally dismissed automatically by the user tapping outside it, you *still* might want to dismiss it explicitly on certain occasions — so you still might need a reference to the popover controller. For example, in keeping with the transient nature of popovers, I like to dismiss the current popover programmatically when the application undergoes certain strong transitions, such as going into the background or being rotated. (See also Apple's technical note on what to do when the interface rotates while a popover is showing, QA1694, "Handling Popover Controllers During Orientation Changes.") You can listen for the former by registering for `UIApplicationDidEnter-BackgroundNotification`, and for the latter by implementing `willRotateToInterfaceOrientation:duration:`. This policy is not merely aesthetic; some view controllers, especially certain built-in specialized view controllers, recover badly from such transitions when displayed in a popover.

The obvious solution is an instance variable or property with a strong (retain) policy. The question then is how many such instance variables to use if we're going to be displaying more than one popover. We could have an instance variable for *each* popover controller. On the other hand, a well-behaved app, in accordance with Apple's interface guidelines, is probably never going to display more than one popover simultaneously; so a *single* UIPopoverController instance variable (we might call it `currentPop`) should suffice. This one instance variable could be handed a reference to the current popover controller each time we present a popover; using that reference, we would be able later to dismiss the current popover and release its controller.

Dismissing a Popover

An important feature of a popover's configuration is whether and to what extent the user can operate outside it without automatically dismissing it. There are two aspects to this configuration:

UIPopoverController's `passthroughViews` *property*

This is an array of views in the interface behind the popover; the user can interact with these views while the popover is showing. What happens if the user taps a view that is *not* listed in the `passthroughViews` array depends on the `modalInPopover` property.

UIViewController's `modalInPopover` *property*

If this is YES for the popover controller's view controller (or for its current child view controller, as in a tab bar interface or navigation interface), then if the user taps outside the popover on a view not listed in the popover controller's `passthroughViews`, nothing at all happens.

If it is NO (the default), then if the user taps outside the popover on a view not listed in the popover controller's `passthroughViews`, the view tapped on is unaffected, and the popover is dismissed.

 The claim made by the documentation (and by previous editions of this book) that `modalInPopover` prevents *all* user interaction outside a popover is wrong. The user can still interact with a view listed in the `passthroughViews` even if `modalInPopover` is YES.

You should pay attention to the `passthroughViews`, as the default behavior may be undesirable. For example, if a popover is summoned by the user tapping a UIBarButton item in a toolbar using `presentPopoverFromBarButtonItem:...`, the entire toolbar is a passthrough view; this means that the user can tap any button in the toolbar, *including the button that summoned the popover.* The user can thus by default summon the popover *again* while it is still showing, which is certainly not what you want. I like to set the `passthroughViews` to nil; at the very least, while the popover is showing, you should probably disable the UIBarButtonItem that summoned it.

 Setting a UIPopoverController's `passthroughViews` might not have any effect unless the UIPopoverController has already been sent `present-Popover....`

We are now ready for a rigorous specification of the two ways in which a popover can be dismissed:

- The popover controller's view controller's `modalInPopover` is NO, and the user taps outside the popover on a view not listed in the popover controller's `passthroughViews`.

  The UIPopoverController's delegate (adopting the UIPopoverControllerDelegate protocol) is sent `popoverControllerShouldDismissPopover:`; if it doesn't return

NO (which might be because it doesn't implement this method), the popover is dismissed, and the delegate is sent `popoverControllerDidDismissPopover:`.

- The UIPopoverController is sent `dismissPopoverAnimated:` by your code; the delegate methods are *not* sent in that case.

Because a popover can be dismissed in two different ways, if you have a cleanup task to perform as the popover vanishes, you may have to see to it that this task is performed under two different circumstances. That can get tricky.

To illustrate, I'll describe what happens when the first popover in Figure 22-1 is dismissed. Within this popover, the user is interacting with several settings in the user defaults. But if the user taps Cancel, or if the user taps outside the popover (which I take to be equivalent to canceling), I want to revert those defaults to the way they were before the popover was summoned. So, as I initially present the popover, I preserve the relevant current user defaults as an ivar:

```
// save defaults so we can restore them later if user cancels
self.oldDefs =
    [[NSUserDefaults standardUserDefaults]
        dictionaryWithValuesForKeys: @[@"Style", @"Size", @"Stages"]];
```

The user now works within the popover. Any settings that the user changes within the popover are immediately saved into the user defaults. So, if the user then taps Done, the user's settings within the popover have *already* been saved; I explicitly dismiss the popover and proceed to initiate the new game that the user has asked for:

```
- (void) saveNewGame: (id) sender { // done button in New Game popover
    [self.currentPop dismissPopoverAnimated:YES];
    self.currentPop = nil;
    // ... set up new game interface, initialize scores, etc. ...
}
```

On the other hand, if the user taps Cancel, I must revert the user defaults as I dismiss the popover:

```
- (void) cancelNewGame: (id) sender { // cancel button in New Game popover
    [self.currentPop dismissPopoverAnimated:YES];
    self.currentPop = nil;
    [[NSUserDefaults standardUserDefaults]
        setValuesForKeysWithDictionary:self.oldDefs];
}
```

But I must also do the same thing if the user taps outside the popover to dismiss it. Therefore I implement the delegate method to detect this, and revert the user defaults *again*:

```
- (void)popoverControllerDidDismissPopover:(UIPopoverController *)pc {
    [[NSUserDefaults standardUserDefaults]
        setValuesForKeysWithDictionary:self.oldDefs];
    self.currentPop = nil;
}
```

My app, however, has *another* popover (the second popover in Figure 22-1). This popover, too, can be dismissed by the user tapping outside it; in fact, that's the only way
the user can dismiss it. If this same class is also that second popover controller's delegate,
then this same `popoverControllerDidDismissPopover:` will be called. But now we
don't want to call `setValuesForKeysWithDictionary:`; it's the wrong popover, and we
have no preserved defaults to revert. So I must somehow test for *which* popover controller is being passed in as the parameter to `popoverControllerDidDismiss-
Popover:`. But how can I distinguish one popover controller from another? Luckily, my
popover controllers have different types of view controller:

```
- (void)popoverControllerDidDismissPopover:(UIPopoverController *)pc {
    if ([pc.contentViewController isKindOfClass:
            [UINavigationController class]])
        [[NSUserDefaults standardUserDefaults]
            setValuesForKeysWithDictionary:self.oldDefs];
    self.currentPop = nil;
}
```

(If I had two different popovers each of which had a UINavigationController as its view
controller, I'd need some other way of distinguishing them. For example, I might have
to subclass UIPopoverController just so I could tell one popover controller from another
by examining its class.)

I also want to dismiss any currently displayed popover if the interface rotates, or if the
app goes into the background. Clearly this should count as canceling the popover; the
user's changes must not be saved, as the user didn't tap Done. Dismissing a popover
manually doesn't trigger a delegate event, so I must perform all the same tests *again*:

```
-(void)willRotateToInterfaceOrientation:(UIInterfaceOrientation)io
        duration:(NSTimeInterval)duration {
    UIPopoverController* pc = self.currentPop;
    if (pc) {
        if ([pc.contentViewController isKindOfClass:
                [UINavigationController class]])
            [[NSUserDefaults standardUserDefaults]
                setValuesForKeysWithDictionary:self.oldDefs];
        [pc dismissPopoverAnimated:NO];
        self.currentPop = nil;
    }
}

-(void)backgrounding:(id)dummy {
    UIPopoverController* pc = self.currentPop;
    if (pc) {
```

```
    if ([pc.contentViewController isKindOfClass:
            [UINavigationController class]])
        [[NSUserDefaults standardUserDefaults]
            setValuesForKeysWithDictionary:self.oldDefs];
    [pc dismissPopoverAnimated:NO];
    self.currentPop = nil;
}
}
```

The need for all this testing and duplicated functionality, just to display a couple of popovers, suggests to me that the framework's implementation of popover management is flawed. Only one popover is supposed to be showing at a time, so why doesn't the shared application at least maintain a reference to its controller for you, and maybe even (gasp) manage its memory for you? Why do popover controllers come into existence with their passthrough views set to anything but nil? Why doesn't a content view controller have a reference to the popover controller, the way it has a reference to an ancestral navigation controller? Why don't popover controllers have a name or other identifier so you can tell them apart? Don't get me started.

Popovers and Presented Views

A popover can present a view controller internally; you'll specify a modalPresentationStyle of UIModalPresentationCurrentContext, because otherwise the presented view will be fullscreen by default. You'll also specify a transition style of UIModalTransitionStyleCoverVertical — with any other transition style, your app will crash with this message: "Application tried to present inside popover with transition style other than UIModalTransitionStyleCoverVertical." The presented view controller's modalInPopover is automatically set to YES. (You can subvert this by setting the presented view controller's modalInPopover to NO *after* it is presented, but you probably shouldn't.)

If a presented view inside a popover proves troublesome — I've encountered some bugs connected with this arrangement — I suggest trying an alternative interface, such as replacing the popover controller's view controller with a different view controller.

Popover Segues

In an iPad storyboard, a segue can be designated a popover segue, by choosing Popover from the Style pop-up menu in the Attributes inspector. The consequences of doing so are:

- When the segue is triggered, a popover is displayed. The runtime constructs a UIPopoverController and makes the segue's destination view controller the UIPopoverController's content view controller. The popover's "anchor" (the view or bar button item to which its arrow points) is the source object from which you control-drag to form the segue, or it can be set in the Attributes inspector.

- The segue is a UIStoryboardPopoverSegue, a UIStoryboardSegue subclass that adds a single read-only property, `popoverController`. You can use this, for instance, in `prepareForSegue:sender:`, to customize the popover controller.

- An unwind segue from within the popover's content view controller dismisses the popover.

The UIPopoverController created by the triggering of a popover segue is retained behind the scenes; the app does not crash if you fail to retain it explicitly yourself. Nevertheless, you may still wish to retain your own reference to the popover controller, in order to know that a popover is being displayed, in order to dismiss it in code, and so forth. You'll probably obtain that reference in your `prepareForSegue:sender:` implementation.

Popover segues sound tempting, but they do not appreciably reduce the amount of code required to configure and manage a popover. Consider, for example, the code I cited earlier for creating a popover controller whose view controller is a navigation view controller:

```
NewGameController* dlg = [NewGameController new];
UIBarButtonItem* b = [[UIBarButtonItem alloc]
    initWithBarButtonSystemItem: UIBarButtonSystemItemCancel
                         target: self
                         action: @selector(cancelNewGame:)];
dlg.navigationItem.rightBarButtonItem = b;
b = [[UIBarButtonItem alloc]
    initWithBarButtonSystemItem: UIBarButtonSystemItemDone
                         target: self
                         action: @selector(saveNewGame:)];
dlg.navigationItem.leftBarButtonItem = b;
UINavigationController* nav =
    [[UINavigationController alloc] initWithRootViewController:dlg];
UIPopoverController* pop =
    [[UIPopoverController alloc] initWithContentViewController:nav];
```

In a storyboard, you could create a popover segue to a navigation controller whose root view is a NewGameController, and you could create the bar button items in the storyboard. So *that* code has been eliminated. But now how would you hook up the New-GameController's bar button items to make their actions call the correct methods in `self`? You can't do that in the storyboard, because you can't make an action connection from within one scene to something in a different scene. So you'd need some *new* code: in `prepareForSegue:sender:`, you'd have to work your way down from the navigation controller to the NewGameController and its bar button items, and hook up their target and action:

```
UINavigationController* nav = segue.destinationViewController;
UIViewController* vc = nav.childViewControllers[0];
vc.navigationItem.leftBarButtonItem.target = self;
vc.navigationItem.leftBarButtonItem.action = @selector(savePop1:);
vc.navigationItem.rightBarButtonItem.target = self;
vc.navigationItem.rightBarButtonItem.action = @selector(cancelPop1:);
```

Similarly, how would you set a popover controller's `passthroughViews` to nil when the popover controller is generated by a popover segue? You can't do that in the storyboard, so you'd have to do it in `prepareForSegue:sender:`. But `prepareForSegue:sender:` is too soon; you need to do this *after* the popover has been displayed, and you don't get any event notifying you of that. So you'd have to use some form of delayed performance:

```
UIStoryboardPopoverSegue* seg = (id)segue;
UIPopoverController* pop = seg.popoverController;
[CATransaction setCompletionBlock:^{ pop.passthroughViews = nil; }];
```

Finally, as I mentioned earlier, you might still need to maintain a reference to the UIPopoverController (`pop` in the above code), set yourself as its delegate, and configure any other features of the popover controller such as its `popoverLayoutMargins` and `popoverBackgroundViewClass`, just as you would have done if there were no storyboard at all. Personally, I'd rather create the popover controller in code to begin with.

Automatic Popovers

In a few situations, the framework will automatically create and display a popover for you. One such situation is what happens when a search bar (a UISearchBar) tied to a search display controller (UISearchDisplayController) appears in a toolbar (UIToolbar) on the iPad. Recall the search display controller example from Chapter 21, where we search a list of the 50 United States; I'll modify that example to demonstrate. In the nib editor, start with a toolbar at the top of the root view, and drag into it the combined Search Bar and Search Display Controller object from the Object library. This causes a whole bunch of outlets to be configured automatically:

- The search bar's delegate is the File's Owner.
- The File's Owner's `searchDisplayController` is the search display controller. This is a UIViewController property that I didn't mention in Chapter 21, because its worth is not clear when a UISearchDisplayController is created and configured in code. When a UISearchDisplayController is instantiated from a nib, however, this property is an outlet that retains the search display controller, as well as providing access to it in code.
- The search display controller's search bar is the search bar.

- The search display controller's delegate, searchContentsController, search-ResultsDataSource, and searchResultsDelegate are the File's Owner. Of these, only the latter two appear to be of importance in this example.

Now for the code. When our view controller loads its view, we also load the model (the list of states) into an NSArray property called states. We also have an NSArray property called filteredStates. Here is the code for dealing with the search bar and the search display controller's results table:

```
-(void)searchDisplayController:(UISearchDisplayController *)controller
        didLoadSearchResultsTableView:(UITableView *)tableView {
    [tableView registerClass:[UITableViewCell class]
      forCellReuseIdentifier:@"cell"];
}

- (NSInteger)numberOfSectionsInTableView:(UITableView *)tableView {
    return 1;
}

- (NSInteger)tableView:(UITableView *)tableView
        numberOfRowsInSection:(NSInteger)section {
    return [self.filteredStates count];
}

- (UITableViewCell *)tableView:(UITableView *)tableView
          cellForRowAtIndexPath:(NSIndexPath *)indexPath {
    UITableViewCell *cell =
        [tableView dequeueReusableCellWithIdentifier:@"cell"
                                        forIndexPath:indexPath];
    cell.textLabel.text = self.filteredStates[indexPath.row];
    return cell;
}

- (void) filterData {
    NSString* target = self.searchDisplayController.searchBar.text;
    NSPredicate* p = [NSPredicate predicateWithBlock:
     ^(id obj, NSDictionary *d) {
        NSString* s = obj;
        NSStringCompareOptions options = NSCaseInsensitiveSearch;
        BOOL b =
            [s rangeOfString:target options:options].location != NSNotFound;
        return b;
     }];
    self.filteredStates = [states filteredArrayUsingPredicate:p];
}

- (void)searchBar:(UISearchBar *)searchBar
        textDidChange:(NSString *)searchText {
    [self filterData];
}
```

Figure 22-3. An automatically created search results popover

That's all. There is no mention anywhere of a UIPopoverController. Nevertheless, when the user enters text in the search bar, a popover appears, containing a table of search results (Figure 22-3). The "Results" title at the top of the popover can be changed by setting the UISearchDisplayController's searchResultsTitle property; you can also do this in the nib editor. Also, the search bar contains a results list button that summons the popover when tapped, and in that case the popover's top bar contains a Clear button that empties the search bar and dismisses the popover; that behavior is apparently entirely automatic and due to the search display controller. Unfortunately, however, you get no official access to the UIPopoverController itself, so you can't set its passthrough views and so on.

Another example of an automatic popover on the iPad is the alert sheet, discussed in Chapter 26.

Split Views

A split view is implemented through a UISplitViewController (a UIViewController subclass) whose children are the two UIViewControllers whose views are to be displayed in the two regions of the split view. You provide the children through the UISplitView-Controller's viewControllers property (an NSArray); it can be configured in code or in a nib. A UIViewController that is a child, at any depth, of a UISplitViewController has a reference to the UISplitViewController through its splitViewController property.

Figure 22-4. A familiar split view interface

There is very little work for you to do with regard to a split view controller. You can hear about what the split view controller is doing through its delegate (adopting the UISplitViewControllerDelegate protocol), which receives these messages:

`splitViewController:willHideViewController:withBarButtonItem:forPopover-Controller:`

> The split view is rotating to portrait orientation, so it's hiding the first view. The split view controller creates a UIBarButtonItem and hands it to you as the third parameter. The split view controller has already set things up so that if the user taps this bar button item, a popover will be presented through the popover controller

(fourth parameter) displaying the view of the first view controller (second parameter). Your mission, should you decide to accept it, is to put that bar button item into the interface, typically in a toolbar at the top of the second view. You are free to configure the bar button item's appearance as you do so.

It's common practice to keep a reference to the popover controller, in case you need it in order to dismiss the popover later (but don't set its delegate).

If an app with a split view interface launches into portrait orientation, this delegate method is called.

`splitViewController:popoverController:willPresentViewController:`
The user has tapped the bar button item you were handed in the first delegate method, and the popover is about to appear. You probably won't need to implement this method.

`splitViewController:willShowViewController:invalidatingBarButtonItem:`
This is the opposite of the first delegate method: the split view is rotating to landscape orientation, so the split view controller going to break the connection between the bar button item and the popover controller and is going to put the first view back into the interface. You should remove the bar button item from the interface.

Let's focus on the words "put that bar button item into the interface" and "remove the bar button item from the interface." How you do this depends on your interface. The current version of the iPad Master–Detail Application project template, which demonstrates a split view interface, uses a navigation interface in order to get the navigation bar:

```
DetailViewController *detailViewController =
    [[DetailViewController alloc]
        initWithNibName:@"DetailViewController" bundle:nil];
UINavigationController *detailNavigationController =
    [[UINavigationController alloc]
        initWithRootViewController:detailViewController];
```

As a result, the DetailViewController instance, functioning as the UISplitViewController's delegate, gets the bar button item into and out of the interface by setting its own `navigationItem`'s `leftBarButtonItem`:

```
- (void)splitViewController:(UISplitViewController *)splitController
    willHideViewController:(UIViewController *)viewController
        withBarButtonItem:(UIBarButtonItem *)barButtonItem
      forPopoverController:(UIPopoverController *)popoverController
{
    [self.navigationItem setLeftBarButtonItem:barButtonItem animated:YES];
    self.masterPopoverController = popoverController;
}

- (void)splitViewController:(UISplitViewController *)splitController
    willShowViewController:(UIViewController *)viewController
```

```
    invalidatingBarButtonItem:(UIBarButtonItem *)barButtonItem
{
    [self.navigationItem setLeftBarButtonItem:nil animated:YES];
    self.masterPopoverController = nil;
}
```

In addition, you might want to set the bar button item's title in willHide...; by default, it will be the first view controller's title.

If you ask for a main storyboard as you generate your iPad project from the Master–Detail Application project template, you can see how little code is required to implement a working split view. The split view controller is hooked to its child view controllers by relationships in the storyboard; those child view controllers are navigation controllers, and are themselves hooked to their root view controllers by relationships in the storyboard as well. Thus, all five view controllers are instantiated together, automatically, as the app launches.

The only thing that can't be configured in the storyboard is the delegate relationship between the UISplitViewController and the DetailViewController; they are both in the storyboard together, but they're in difference scenes, so no outlet can be drawn between them. To solve this, the template includes the following code in the app delegate's application:didFinishLaunchingWithOptions::

```
UISplitViewController *splitViewController =
    (UISplitViewController *)self.window.rootViewController;
UINavigationController *navigationController =
    [splitViewController.viewControllers lastObject];
splitViewController.delegate = (id)navigationController.topViewController;
```

By the time that code runs, the window's rootViewController has been set and all the view controllers are in place, in their various parent–child relationships; the code is thus able to work its way through the parent–child hierarchy to get references to the two desired view controllers and can make the one the delegate of the other. The Detail-ViewController implements the two UISplitViewControllerDelegate methods to add and remove the UIBarButtonItem in the navigation bar, just as in the nonstoryboard template.

The storyboard editor also provides a Replace segue for use in connection with a split view. This allows either of the split view controller's child view controllers to be swapped out. A typical use is that the user taps something in the left (master) view controller to cause the right (detail) view controller to be replaced by a different view controller. So you'd create a Replace segue leading from the tapped thing in the master view controller to the new view controller, and specify a Destination of Detail Split.

I've been using the word "popover" because that's what the delegate methods call it — and, in iOS 5.0 and before, it really was a popover like any other. Starting in iOS 5.1, however, the interface changed radically. If this is a popover, it's a very strange-looking popover. It has no border and no arrow, and is the height of the screen; when summoned, it slides in from the left, and if the device is rotated it does a smooth animation and becomes the view on the left side of the screen. Apple's Mail application is a familiar example (Figure 22-4).

I suspect that this is a popover in name only. There is a popover controller, and it emits delegate messages; thus, the API remains unchanged, and split view controller code from before iOS 5.1 continues to work. But in reality the popover programming interface is probably a cover for something else entirely. Indeed, in the previous edition of this book, when Apple Mail had introduced the new interface shown in Figure 22-4 but the split view available to programmers through iOS was still using a normal popover, I provided reverse-engineered code showing how to achieve the Mail interface with a custom container controller.

If the UISplitViewController's presentsWithGesture is YES, the second view in portrait orientation will detect a rightward swipe and will respond by summoning the first view (the popover). Otherwise, the bar button item will be the only way to summon the popover in portrait orientation.

It is also possible for a split view interface *not* to hide the first view in portrait orientation. Instead, the left and right view both appear in both orientations; the left view's width is unchanged, while the right view is resized appropriately. (Compare Apple's Settings app on the iPad.) To get that behavior, implement this delegate method:

splitViewController:shouldHideViewController:inOrientation:
> Allows the left view controller to be hidden (return YES) or not (return NO) as the interface rotates to the given orientation. If you return NO, the other delegate methods won't be called in this orientation; there will be no bar button item and no popover.

CHAPTER 23

Text

The high-level text classes are NSString and NSAttributedString. Text can be displayed in various ways:

UILabel

Displays text, possibly consisting of multiple lines; neither scrollable nor editable.

UITextField

Displays a single line of editable text; may have a border, a background image, and overlay views at its right and left end.

UITextView

Displays scrollable text, possibly editable; can use data detectors to display tappable links.

UIWebView

A scrollable view displaying rendered HTML. A good way to show text that includes images and tappable links. Can also display various additional document types, such as PDF, RTF, and *.doc*. Discussed in Chapter 24.

Drawing

There are three main ways to draw text directly:

Core Graphics

Low-level methods for drawing text (not NSStrings). For drawing in general, see Chapter 15.

NSString and NSAttributedString

At a high level, the UIStringDrawing category on NSString and the NSString-Drawing category on NSAttributedString endow strings with the ability to draw themselves, along with metrics methods for learning the dimensions at which a given string will be drawn. Some examples have appeared already in Chapter 12 and Chapter 20.

Core Text
> The underlying low-level technology behind *all* string drawing on iOS. Also provides access to advanced font typographical features.

> An app can include fonts within its bundle; these will be loaded at launch time if the app lists them in its *Info.plist* under the "Fonts provided by application" key (`UIAppFonts`). In this way, your app can use fonts not present by default on the device.

Attributed Strings

Before iOS 6, controls such as UILabel and UITextView could display text only in a *single* font and size. If you wanted styled text — that is, text consisting of multiple style runs, with different font, size, color, and other text features in different parts of the text — you were largely out of luck. You could construct an NSAttributedString to express styled text, by dropping down to the lowest level, Core Text; but to display it in the interface you had to use a CATextLayer or have CoreText draw it, which was a lot of work. Workarounds included using a UIWebView or manipulating multiple UILabels. (For example, that's how the TidBITS News app used to work, as shown in Figure 19-1; the bold headline and the smaller article summary are two different labels.) *Editable* styled text was virtually impossible to achieve.

Starting in iOS 6, however, NSAttributedString is fully integrated. With it, you can draw styled text directly, or you can hand an attributed string to any built-in interface class that understands it, including UILabel, UITextView, and UIButton.

> In general, interface object methods and properties that accept attributed strings stand side by side with their pre-iOS 6 equivalents; the new ones tend to have "attributed" in their name. Thus, you don't *have* to use attributed strings. If a UILabel, for example, is to display text in a single font, size, color, and alignment, it might be easiest to use the pre-iOS 6 plain-old-NSString features of UILabel. If you do decide to use attributed strings with an interface object, it is best not to mix in any of the pre-iOS 6 settings; if you're going to use an attributed string, let it do *all* the work of dictating text style features.

An NSAttributedString consists of an NSString (its `string`) plus the attributes, applied in ranges. For example, if the string "one red word" is blue except for the word "red" which is red, and if these are the only changes over the course of the string, then there are three distinct style runs — everything before the word "red," the word "red" itself, and everything after the word "red." However, we can apply the attributes in two steps, first making the whole string blue, and then making the word "red" red, just as you would expect.

The attributes are described in dictionaries. Each possible attribute has a predefined name, used as a key in these dictionaries:

NSFontAttributeName
> A UIFont, including font family, style, and size.

NSForegroundColorAttributeName
> The text color, a UIColor.

NSBackgroundColorAttributeName
> The color *behind* the text, a UIColor. You could use this to highlight a word, for example.

NSLigatureAttributeName
> An NSNumber wrapping 0 or 1, expressing whether or not you want ligatures used.

NSKernAttributeName
> An NSNumber wrapping the floating-point amount of kerning. A negative value brings a glyph closer to the following glyph; a positive value adds space between them. The special value [NSNull null] turns on inherent autokerning if the font supports it.

NSStrikethroughStyleAttributeName
> An NSNumber wrapping 0 or 1.

NSUnderlineStyleAttributeName
> An NSNumber wrapping 0 or 1.

NSStrokeColorAttributeName
> The stroke color, a UIColor.

NSStrokeWidthAttributeName
> An NSNumber wrapping a float. The stroke width is peculiarly coded. If it isn't zero, it's either a positive or negative float (wrapped in an NSNumber). If it's positive, then the text glyphs are stroked but not filled, giving an outline effect, and the foreground color is used unless the stroke color is defined. If it's negative, then its absolute value is the width of the stroke, and the glyphs are both filled (with the foreground color) and stroked (with the stroke color).

NSShadowAttributeName
> An NSShadow object. An NSShadow is just a glorified struct (what Apple calls a "value object"), combining a shadowOffset, shadowColor, and shadowBlurRadius.

NSParagraphStyleAttributeName

An NSParagraphStyle object. This is basically just a glorified struct, assembling text features that apply properly to paragraphs as a whole, not merely to characters, even if your string consists only of a single paragraph. Here are its most important properties:

- alignment
  — NSTextAlignmentLeft
  — NSTextAlignmentCenter
  — NSTextAlignmentRight
  — NSTextAlignmentJustified (a new facility in iOS 6)
  — NSTextAlignmentNatural (left-aligned or right-aligned depending on the writing direction)

- lineBreakMode (only the two Wrapping options wrap; the others draw a single line)
  — NSLineBreakByWordWrapping
  — NSLineBreakByCharWrapping
  — NSLineBreakByClipping
  — NSLineBreakByTruncatingHead
  — NSLineBreakByTruncatingTail
  — NSLineBreakByTruncatingMiddle

- firstLineHeadIndent, headIndent (left margin), tailIndent (right margin)
- lineHeightMultiple, maximumLineHeight, minimumLineHeight
- lineSpacing
- paragraphSpacing, paragraphSpacingBefore
- hyphenationFactor (a float between 0 and 1)

To construct an NSAttributedString, you can call initWithString:attributes: if the entire string has the same attributes; otherwise, you'll use its mutable subclass NSMutableAttributedString, which lets you set attributes over a range. To construct an NSParagraphStyle, you'll use its mutable subclass NSMutableParagraphStyle. (The properties of NSParagraphStyle itself are all read-only, for historical reasons.) It is sufficient to apply a paragraph style to the first character of a paragraph; to put it another way, the paragraph style of the first character of a paragraph dictates how the whole paragraph is rendered. Both NSAttributedString and NSParagraphStyle come with default values for all attributes, so you only have to set the attributes you care about.

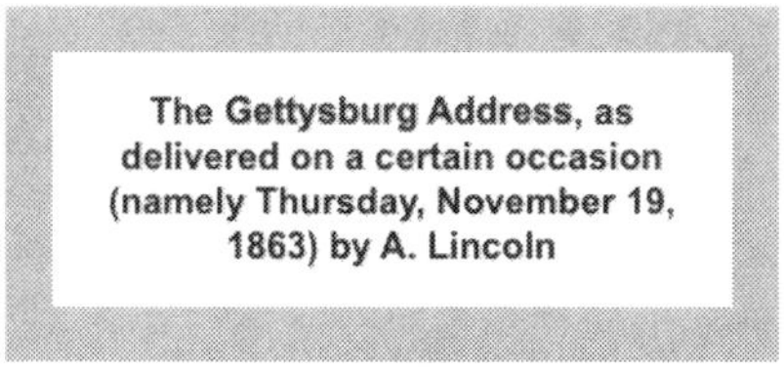

Figure 23-1. A label showing an attributed string

We now know enough for an example! I'll generate the paragraph shown in Figure 23-1. This is a UILabel; its background is white, so you can see its bounds relative to the text. Two words are made extra-bold by stroking in a different color, and the whole paragraph is centered and indented from the edges of the label.

I start by dictating the entire string and the overall style of the text; then I apply the special style to the two stroked words:

```
NSString* s1 = @"The Gettysburg Address, as delivered on a certain occasion "
    @"(namely Thursday, November 19, 1863) by A. Lincoln";
NSMutableAttributedString* content =
    [[NSMutableAttributedString alloc]
     initWithString:s1
     attributes:
        @{
           NSFontAttributeName:
               [UIFont fontWithName:@"Arial-BoldMT" size:15],
           NSForegroundColorAttributeName:
               [UIColor colorWithRed:0.251 green:0.000 blue:0.502 alpha:1]
        }];
NSRange r = [s1 rangeOfString:@"Gettysburg Address"];
[content addAttributes:
    @{
        NSStrokeColorAttributeName:[UIColor redColor],
        NSStrokeWidthAttributeName: @-2.0
    } range:r];
```

Now I create the paragraph style and apply it to the first character. Note how the margins are dictated: the `tailIndent` is negative, to bring the right margin leftward, and the `firstLineHeadIndent` must be set separately, as the `headIndent` does not automatically apply to the first line:

```
NSMutableParagraphStyle* para = [NSMutableParagraphStyle new];
para.headIndent = 10;
para.firstLineHeadIndent = 10;
para.tailIndent = -10;
para.lineBreakMode = NSLineBreakByWordWrapping;
```

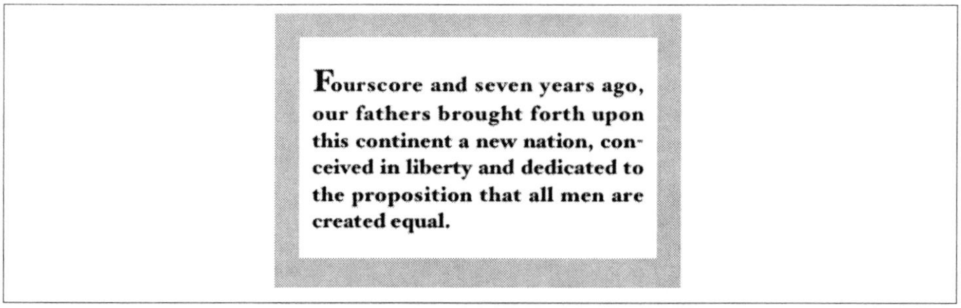

Figure 23-2. A label showing another attributed string

```
para.alignment = NSTextAlignmentCenter;
para.paragraphSpacing = 15;
[content addAttribute:NSParagraphStyleAttributeName
               value:para range:NSMakeRange(0,1)];
```

Now I'll generate the string shown in Figure 23-2. Note the full justification, the automatic hyphenation, and the large initial cap kerned close to the following letter.

Once again, I start by styling the string as a whole; then I style the first letter. There's an obvious but important difference between `setAttributes:` and `addAttributes::`

```
NSString* s2 = @"Fourscore and seven years ago, our fathers brought forth "
    @"upon this continent a new nation, conceived in liberty and dedicated "
    @"to the proposition that all men are created equal.";
NSMutableAttributedString* content2 =
    [[NSMutableAttributedString alloc]
     initWithString:s2
     attributes:
         @{
           NSFontAttributeName:
               [UIFont fontWithName:@"HoeflerText-Black" size:16]
         }];
[content2 setAttributes:
    @{
      NSFontAttributeName:[UIFont fontWithName:@"HoeflerText-Black" size:24]
     } range:NSMakeRange(0,1)];
[content2 addAttributes:
    @{
      NSKernAttributeName:@-4
     } range:NSMakeRange(0,1)];
```

Now I'll construct the paragraph style and add it to the first character:

```
NSMutableParagraphStyle* para2 = [NSMutableParagraphStyle new];
para2.headIndent = 10;
para2.firstLineHeadIndent = 10;
para2.tailIndent = -10;
para2.lineBreakMode = NSLineBreakByWordWrapping;
```

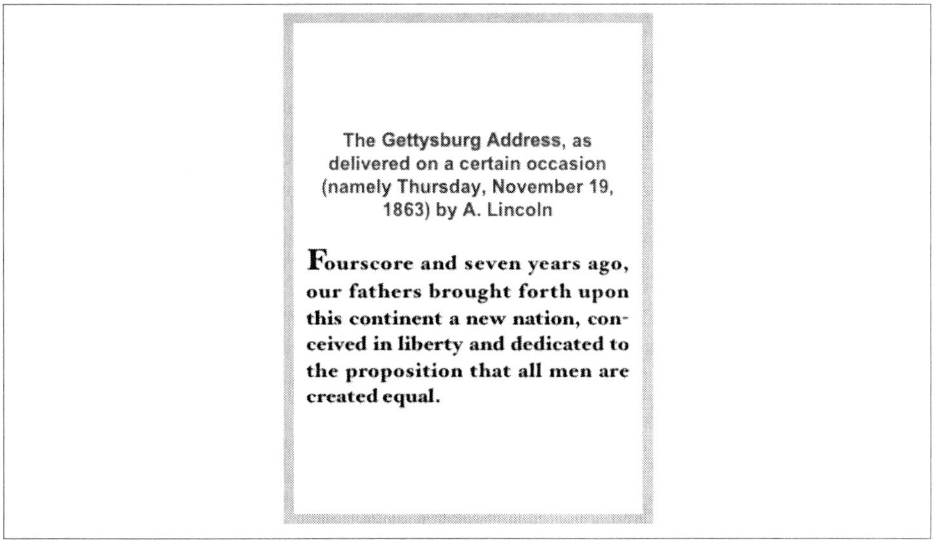

Figure 23-3. A single label containing two differently styled paragraphs

```
para2.alignment = NSTextAlignmentJustified;
para2.lineHeightMultiple = 1.2;
para2.hyphenationFactor = 1.0;
[content2 addAttribute:NSParagraphStyleAttributeName
              value:para2 range:NSMakeRange(0,1)];
```

Now we come to the Really Amazing Part. I can make a *single* attributed string consisting of *both* paragraphs, and a single UILabel can portray it (Figure 23-3):

```
int end = content.length;
[content replaceCharactersInRange:NSMakeRange(end, 0) withString:@"\n"];
[content appendAttributedString:content2];
```

The API for examining and modifying an attributed string invites us to think of style runs as extending over an entire range of characters, but that may be just a convenience. The content of a mutable attributed string may be better envisioned as a sequence of characters, *each* of which has associated attributes. Thus we can coherently modify just the string part of a mutable attributed string. The key method here is `replace-CharactersInRange:withString:`, which can be used to replace characters with a plain string or, using a zero range length, to insert a plain string at the start, middle, or end of an attributed string (as demonstrated in the preceding code). The rule is that if we *replace* characters, the inserted string takes on the attributes of the *first replaced* character. If we *insert* characters, the inserted string takes on the attributes of the character *preceding* the insertion — except that, if we insert at the start, there is no such character, so the inserted string takes on the attributes of the character *following* the insertion.

You can query an attributed string about its attributes one character at a time — asking either about all attributes at once (`attributesAtIndex:effectiveRange:`) or about a particular attribute by name (`attribute:atIndex:effectiveRange:`). The last parameter is a pointer to an NSRange variable, which will be set to the range over which this same attribute value, or set of attribute values, applies:

```
NSRange range;
NSDictionary* d =
    [content attributesAtIndex:content.length-1 effectiveRange:&range];
```

Because style runs are an artifice, however, you might not end up with what you would think of as the *entire* style run. The methods with `longestEffectiveRange:` in their names, at the cost of some efficiency, do work out the full style run for you. Often, however, you don't need the entire range, because you're cycling through ranges, and you want to do that as fast as possible. In this example, I start with the combined two-paragraph attributed string derived in the previous examples, and change all the size 15 material to Arial Bold 20. I explicitly don't care whether I'm handed longest effective ranges; I just want to cycle efficiently:

```
[content enumerateAttribute:NSFontAttributeName
    inRange:NSMakeRange(0,content.length)
    options:NSAttributedStringEnumerationLongestEffectiveRangeNotRequired
    usingBlock:^(id value, NSRange range, BOOL *stop)
{
    UIFont* font = value;
    if (font.pointSize == 15)
        [content addAttribute:NSFontAttributeName
                        value:[UIFont fontWithName: @"Arial-BoldMT" size:20]
                        range:range];
}];
```

You don't need a UILabel to host an attributed string in the interface; you can draw the attributed string directly, and sometimes this will prove to be a more reliable approach. Just as an NSString can be drawn into a rect with `drawInRect:withFont:` and related methods, an NSAttributedString can be drawn with `drawInRect:`. (There's no need to supply a font parameter, because the font is part of the attributed string!) Here, I draw the attributed string into an image:

```
UIGraphicsBeginImageContextWithOptions(rect.size, YES, 0);
[[UIColor whiteColor] setFill];
CGContextFillRect(UIGraphicsGetCurrentContext(), rect);
[self.content drawInRect:rect];
UIImage* im = UIGraphicsGetImageFromCurrentImageContext();
UIGraphicsEndImageContext();
```

That image can then be displayed by an image view, for example. Similarly, you can draw an attributed string directly in a UIView's `drawRect:`. That, in fact, is how the current version of the TidBITS News app works (Figure 23-4). Previously, its table cells contained multiple UILabels, which had to be sized individually to fit their content

Figure 23-4. The TidBITS News app, rewritten for iOS 6

(Chapter 21). Now, each cell is drawn as a *single attributed string* consisting of the article title and the article summary.

I'll describe how that string is drawn. The cell's `contentView` is completely occupied by a custom UIView class that I call StringDrawer; it has an `attributedText` property. In `tableView:cellForRowAtIndexPath:`, I set that property:

```
cell.drawer.attributedText = [self attributedStringForIndexPath: indexPath];
```

StringDrawer's `drawRect:` draws its `attributedText`:

```
- (void)drawRect:(CGRect)rect {
    CGRect r = CGRectOffset(rect, 0, 2); // shoved down a little from top
    [self.attributedText drawWithRect:r
        options:NSStringDrawingTruncatesLastVisibleLine |
                NSStringDrawingUsesLineFragmentOrigin
        context:nil];
}
```

I want an ellipsis at the end of the second paragraph if the whole thing doesn't fit in the given rect (as shown in Figure 23-4). This can't be achieved using `NSLineBreakBy-TruncatingTail`, which truncates the *first line* of the second paragraph. Therefore, I'm using `drawWithRect:options:context:`, instead of simple `drawInRect:`, because it allows me to specify the option `NSStringDrawingTruncatesLastVisibleLine`. However,

I must then also specify NSStringDrawingUsesLineFragmentOrigin; otherwise, the string is drawn with its *baseline* at the rect origin (so that it appears *above* that rect) and it doesn't wrap. The rule is that NSStringDrawingUsesLineFragmentOrigin is the implicit default for simple drawInRect:, but with drawWithRect:options:context: you must specify it explicitly.

To derive the height of the cell, I also *measure* the attributed string beforehand, in tableView:heightForRowAtIndexPath::

```
CGRect r =
    [s boundingRectWithSize:CGSizeMake(320,10000)
        options:NSStringDrawingUsesLineFragmentOrigin context:nil];
CGFloat result = r.size.height;
if (result > 200) // set arbitrary limit on cell heights
    result = 200;
```

Again, the option NSStringDrawingUsesLineFragmentOrigin is crucial; without it, the measured text doesn't wrap and the returned height will be very small.

The context: parameter of drawWithRect:options:context: and boundingRectWithSize:options:context: lets you attach an instance of NSStringDrawingContext. This simple class has properties that let you permit the text to shrink its size and compress its kerning automatically if doing so would allow it to fit in the given space. (This feature works only if the string consists of a single line — that is, a single paragraph whose line break mode doesn't have Wrapping in its name.) It also lets you learn what actually happened. If you set an NSStringDrawingContext instance's minimumScaleFactor (to a positive fraction, such as 0.7) and then draw or measure with this instance as the context: argument, you can then get that instance's actualScaleFactor to learn how much the drawing engine really did shrink the text size. The minimumTrackingAdjustment (a negative fraction, such as -0.7) and actualTrackingAdjustment work similarly.

Additionally, an NSStringDrawingContext instance tells you where you just drew. With a plain NSString, you derive this information from the return value of the drawing command; for example, drawInRect:withFont: returns a CGSize telling you the size of the drawn string. But drawWithRect:options:context: has no return value. Instead, if you attach an NSStringDrawingContext, its totalBounds property tells you, after you draw, the bounds of the drawn string.

Remember CATextLayer from Chapter 16? Its `string` property can be an NSAttributedString. Thus, a CATextLayer is another way to get an attributed string drawn into the interface. If the width of the layer is insufficient to display the entire string, we can get truncation behavior with the `truncationMode` property. If the `wrapped` property is set to YES, the string will wrap. We can also set the alignment with the `alignmentMode` property.

UILabel

UILabel was introduced briefly in Chapter 21 (in "Built-In Cell Styles" (page 699)). If you're configuring a UILabel through a plain NSString, by way of its `text` property, then you are likely also to set its `font`, `textColor`, and `textAlignment` properties, and possibly its `shadowColor` and `shadowOffset` properties. The label's text can have an alternate `highlightedTextColor`, to be used when its `highlighted` property is YES (as happens, for example, when the label is in a selected cell of a table view).

If you're using an NSAttributedString, then you'll set the label's `attributedText` property, and you'll probably want to leave those other properties alone; they do still work, but they're going to change the attributes of your *entire* attributed string, in ways that you might not intend. Setting the `text` of a UILabel that has `attributedText` will basically eliminate the attributes. The `highlightedTextColor` property does *not* work on the `attributedText`.

The nib editor also includes an ingenious interface for letting you set attributes of the text of a label, and of other classes that accept attributed strings in iOS 6; it's not perfect, however, and isn't suitable for dealing with lengthy or complex text.

If a UILabel consists of only one line of text (`numberOfLines` is 1, the default), then if you set its `text`, any line breaks (`@"\n"`) are treated as spaces; but if you set its `attributedText`, line breaks are honored and you won't see whatever follows the first line break.

If a UILabel consists of only one line of text (`numberOfLines` is 1, the default), then you can elect to permit the text to shrink and compress if this would allow the text to fit when otherwise it wouldn't. You can turn on `adjustsFontSizeToFitWidth` and provide a `minimumScaleFactor` (replacing the now-deprecated `minimumFontSize`), or you can turn on `adjustsLetterSpacingToFitWidth`. With plain `text`, you can turn on both; with `attributedText`, you can't (this feels like a bug). If you're using an attributed string, the label's (or attributed string's) line break mode must not have `Wrapping` in its name.

How the text is repositioned when the size shrinks is determined by the label's `baseline-Adjustment` property.

A UILabel may alternatively consist of multiple lines of text, where `numberOfLines` is greater than 1, or `0` to indicate no maximum. This matters even if you're using an attributed string! In Figure 23-3, for example, the full text is shown because I set the label's `numberOfLines` to `0`.

Line breaking (wrapping) and truncation behavior, which applies to both single-line and multiline labels, is determined by its `lineBreakMode`. You can get a feel for line break behavior by experimenting in the nib. Your options are:

`NSLineBreakByWordWrapping`
> Lines break at word-end. This is the default.

`NSLineBreakByClipping`
> Lines break at word-end, but the last line can break in the middle of a word.

`NSLineBreakByCharWrapping`
> All lines can break in the middle of a word.

`NSLineBreakByTruncatingHead`
`NSLineBreakByTruncatingTail`
`NSLineBreakByTruncatingMiddle`
> Lines break at word-end. But now suppose the text is too long for the label. (This might be because a single-line label isn't wide enough, or because the `numberOfLines` is insufficient given the label's width, or because the label isn't tall enough to display the `numberOfLines`.) Then the last line displays an ellipsis at the start, middle, or end respectively, and text is omitted at the point of the ellipsis. Thus, if the `lineBreakMode` is `UILineBreakModeHeadTruncation`, the last line is always displayed, and if the `lineBreakMode` is `UILineBreakModeMiddleTruncation`, the last words are displayed at the end of the last line — preceded, in both cases, by everything that will fit from the start of the text to the ellipsis.

The UILabel line break mode names, which replace the now-deprecated `UILineBreakMode` options, are the same as the NSParagraphStyle line break mode names; but *they do not behave the same way*. All the UILabel line break modes can wrap an NSString, but an NSAttributedString wraps only if its paragraph style's line break mode has `Wrapping` in its name. UILabel will try to wrap and truncate an attributed string the way it wraps and truncates a plain string, but in some cases you will have to help it by setting the label's `lineBreakMode` *in code, after* setting its `attributedText`. (Thanks to Kyle Sluder for discovering this technique.)

If numberOfLines is larger than the number of lines actually needed, the text is vertically centered in the label. This may be undesirable; you might prefer to shrink (or grow) the label to fit its text. In iOS 5 and before, you couldn't use sizeToFit to do this, because the default UILabel implementation of sizeToFit was to make the label the right width to contain all its text on a *single* line. However, in iOS 6 that behavior is completely changed, so that in most simple cases sizeToFit will do exactly the right thing; I suspect that behind the scenes it is just calling boundingRectWithSize:options:context:.

I say "in most simple cases" because there are cases where UILabel's sizeToFit will misbehave. These happen to be exactly the cases where boundingRectWith-Size:options:context: misbehaves. The problem arises particularly with paragraph styles involving margins (headIndent and tailIndent). Take, for example, the label displayed in Figure 23-3. It's too tall for its content, but if we call sizeToFit it becomes too narrow for its content, presumably because boundingRectWith-Size:options:context: ignores the margins. A possible workaround is to call boundingRectWithSize:options:context: and set the width back to the original width, like this:

```
CGRect rect =
    [self.lab.attributedText boundingRectWithSize:self.lab.bounds.size
     options:NSStringDrawingUsesLineFragmentOrigin context:nil];
// width is wrong so we have to widen it again
rect.size.width = self.lab.bounds.size.width;
rect.size.height += 5; // for good measure
CGRect f = self.lab.bounds;
f.size = rect.size;
self.lab.bounds = f;
```

But it turns out there's a better way. Don't forget about constraints! If we're using auto-layout, a UILabel will attempt to configure its own height and width (its intrinsic-ContentSize) to fit its contents. Thus, if the label is left to its own devices, it will set its height correctly for its contents *with no code at all*. Merely configuring the label — setting its text, changing its font, setting its attributed text, and so forth — automatically invalidates its intrinsic content size and causes that size to be recalculated.

However, the label has two dimensions, so we must clearly give it a hint as to how it should mediate between them. One obvious way is to fix the width absolutely — for example, by an internal width constraint, or by pinning both the left and right edges of the label. In that case, assuming that no constraints prevent it, the label's height will automatically adjust to accommodate its contents exactly. (If the label does have a height constraint, it will still adjust its own height, provided that the height constraint's priority is less than its content hugging priority, which is 250.)

An even more flexible approach is to set the label's preferredMaxLayoutWidth. This is the width at which the label, as its contents increase, will stop growing horizontally to accommodate its contents and start growing vertically instead. (This implies that the contents will wrap, so clearly the `numberOfLines` can't be 1.) For example, consider a label containing just a couple of words, whose right edge and top edge are pinned. Thanks to its intrinsic content size, that's sufficient to position and size the label. Now set the label's text to be several sentences long. Assuming that no other constraints intervene, and that the label's `numberOfLines` is not 1, the label's width will increase to its `preferredMaxLayoutWidth` and its height will increase to accommodate its text exactly.

Conversely, you might wish to keep the label's text the same, but make the label narrower and let it grow in height to accommodate its contents. Again, the key here is the `intrinsicContentSize`: we set the label's width and its `intrinsicContentSize` together. For example, suppose we have an outlet to the label and to its width constraint; then this code makes the label narrower horizontally while letting it grow vertically to keep accommodating its contents:

```
self.widthConstraint.constant -= 10;
self.theLabel.preferredMaxLayoutWidth = self.widthConstraint.constant;
```

That's all very well if we are changing the label's width explicitly in code, but what if the label's width is changing automatically in response to its constraints? An obvious example is a label whose left and right are pinned to its superview, and the superview changes size because the interface rotates. The label's height will not change automatically to fit its contents; we must prompt it. For example, the view controller could respond to layout by setting the label's `preferredMaxLayoutWidth` to its new width:

```
-(void)viewDidLayoutSubviews {
    self.lab.preferredMaxLayoutWidth = self.lab.bounds.size.width;
    [self.view layoutSubviews];
}
```

Or we could make the label self-adjusting, by subclassing UILabel and overriding `layoutSubviews`:

```
-(void)layoutSubviews {
    [super layoutSubviews];
    self.preferredMaxLayoutWidth = self.bounds.size.width;
}
```

Methods that you can override in a subclass to modify a label's drawing are `drawTextInRect:` (an example appeared in Chapter 10) and `textRectForBounds:limitedToNumberOfLines:`.

UITextField

A text field portrays just a single line of text (any return characters in its text are treated as spaces); otherwise, it has many of the same properties as a label. So, if you provide it with a plain NSString, it has a `text`, `font`, `textColor`, and `textAlignment`. It has `adjusts-

FontSizeToFitWidth and minimumFontSize properties, although these don't work exactly like a label; a text field won't allow its font size to shrink automatically as small as a label will.

To provide a text field with an attributed string, you set its attributedText. In that case I would suggest that you *not* set its adjustsFontSizeToFitWidth to YES, as this behaves rather badly; it doesn't allow any intermediate sizes, but either shrinks the text absolutely or doesn't; and, if it does shrink it, it will cause your text to appear all in a single font.

Text that is too long for the text field is displayed with an ellipsis at the end. You can change the position of the ellipsis by assigning the text field an attributed string with different truncation behavior, such as NSLineBreakByTruncatingHead. When overly long text is being edited, the text shifts horizontally to show the insertion point. On the whole, though, text that is too long for the text field is probably not a very good idea; the user usually has no arrow keys, as on the desktop, so navigating long text is daunting (the user must select text and stretch the selection into the offscreen part of the text).

Regardless of whether you originally supplied a plain string or an attributed string, if the text field's allowsEditingTextAttributes is YES, the user, when editing in the text field, can summon a menu toggling the selected text's bold, italics, or underline features. (Oddly, there's no way to set this property in a nib.)

A text field has a placeholder property, which is the text that appears faded within the text field when it has no text; the idea is that you can use this to suggest to the user what the text field is for. It has a styled text alternative, attributedPlaceholder.

If a text field's clearsOnBeginEditing property is YES, it automatically deletes its existing text when the user begins editing within it. New in iOS 6, if a text field's clearsOnInsertion property is YES, then when editing begins within it, the entire text is selected, but *invisibly* selected, so that if the user starts typing immediately, the current contents of the text field will be removed.

A text field's border drawing is determined by its borderStyle property. Your options are:

UITextBorderStyleNone
    No border.

UITextBorderStyleLine
    A plain rectangle.

UITextBorderStyleBezel
    A slightly bezeled rectangle: the top and left sides have a very slight, thin shadow.

UITextBorderStyleRoundedRect
    A rounded rectangle; the top and left sides have a stronger shadow, so that the text appears markedly recessed behind the border.

A text field can have a background color (because it is a UIView) or a background image (`background`), possibly along with a second image (`disabledBackground`) to be displayed when the text field's `enabled` property, inherited from UIControl, is NO. The user can't interact with a disabled text field, but without a `disabledBackground` image, the user may lack any visual clue to this fact. (A rounded rectangle text field doesn't display these background images.)

A text field may contain one or two ancillary overlay views, its `leftView` and `rightView`, and possibly a Clear button (a gray circle with a white X). The automatic visibility of each of these is determined by the `leftViewMode`, `rightViewMode`, and `clearViewMode`, respectively. The view mode values are:

`UITextFieldViewModeNever`
> The view never appears.

`UITextFieldViewModeWhileEditing`
> A Clear button appears if there is text in the field and the user is editing. A left or right view appears if there is *no* text in the field and the user is editing.

`UITextFieldViewModeUnlessEditing`
> A Clear button appears if there is text in the field and the user is not editing. A left or right view appears if the user is not editing, or if the user is editing but there is no text in the field.

`UITextFieldViewModeAlways`
> A left or right view always appears; a Clear button appears if there is text in the field.

Depending on what sort of view you use, your `leftView` and `rightView` may have to be sized manually so as not to overwhelm the text view contents. If a right view and a Clear button appear at the same time, the right view may cover the Clear button unless you reposition it. The positions and sizes of *any* of the components of the text field can be set in relation to the text field's bounds by overriding the appropriate method in a subclass:

- `clearButtonRectForBounds:`
- `leftViewRectForBounds:`
- `rightViewRectForBounds:`
- `borderRectForBounds:`
- `textRectForBounds:`
- `placeholderRectForBounds:`
- `editingRectForBounds:`

You should make no assumptions about when or how frequently these methods will be called; the same method might be called several times in quick succession. Also, these methods should all be called with a parameter that is the bounds of the text field, but some are called with a 100×100 bounds; this feels like a bug.

You can also override in a subclass the methods `drawTextInRect:` and `draw-PlaceholderInRect:`. You should either draw the specified text or call `super` to draw it; if you do neither, the text won't appear. Both these methods are called with a parameter whose size is the dimensions of the text field's text area, but whose origin is `{0,0}`. In effect what you've got is a graphics context for just the text area; any drawing you do outside the given rectangle will be clipped.

Summoning and Dismissing the Keyboard

A text field's editing status, as well as the presence or absence of the onscreen simulated keyboard, is intimately tied to its status as the *first responder* (Chapter 11):

- When a text field is first responder, it is being edited and the keyboard is present.

- When a text field is no longer first responder, it is no longer being edited, and if no other text field (or text view) becomes first responder, the keyboard is not present. The keyboard is not dismissed if one text field takes over first responder status from another.

You can programmatically control a text field's editing status, as well as the presence or absence of the keyboard, by way of the text field's first responder status. To make the insertion point appear within a text field and to cause the keyboard to appear, you send `becomeFirstResponder` to that text field; to make a text field stop being edited and to cause the keyboard to disappear, you send `resignFirstResponder` to that text field. Actually, `resignFirstResponder` returns a BOOL, because a responder might return NO to indicate that for some reason it refuses to obey this command. Note also the UIView `endEditing:` method, which can be sent to the first responder *or any superview* (including the window) to ask or compel the first responder to resign first responder status.

In a view presented in the `UIModalPresentationFormSheet` style on the iPad (Chapter 19), the keyboard, by default, does *not* disappear when a text field resigns first responder status. This is apparently because a form sheet is intended primarily for text input, so the keyboard is felt as accompanying the form as a whole, not individual text fields. Optionally, you can prevent this exceptional behavior: in your UIViewController subclass, override `disablesAutomaticKeyboardDismissal` to return NO.

There is no simple way to learn what view is first responder! This is very odd, because a window surely knows what its first responder is — but it won't tell you. There's a method isFirstResponder, but you'd have to send it to every view in a window until you find the first responder. One workaround is to store a reference to the first responder yourself, typically in your implementation of the text field delegate's textFieldDidBeginEditing:. *Do not name this reference firstResponder!* This name is apparently already in use by Cocoa, and a name collision can cause your app to misbehave. (Can you guess how I know that?)

Once the user has tapped in a text field and the keyboard has automatically appeared, how is the user supposed to get rid of it? This is unlikely to be a problem on the iPad, where the keyboard typically contains a special button that dismisses the keyboard. But on the iPhone, it's an oddly tricky issue. You would think that the "return" button in the keyboard would dismiss the keyboard; but, of itself, it doesn't.

One solution is to be the text field's delegate and to implement a text field delegate method, textFieldShouldReturn:. When the user taps the Return key in the keyboard, we hear about it through this method, and we tell the text field to resign its first responder status, which dismisses the keyboard:

```
- (BOOL)textFieldShouldReturn: (UITextField*) tf {
    [tf resignFirstResponder];
    return YES;
}
```

I'll provide a more self-contained, automatic solution later in this chapter.

Keyboard Covers Text Field

The keyboard has a position "docked" at the bottom of the screen. This may cover the text field in which the user wants to type, even if it is first responder. On the iPad, this may not be an issue, because the user can "undock" the keyboard (possibly also splitting and shrinking it) and slide it up and down the screen freely. On the iPhone, you'll typically want to do something to reveal the text field.

To help with this, you can register for keyboard-related notifications:

- UIKeyboardWillShowNotification
- UIKeyboardDidShowNotification
- UIKeyboardWillHideNotification
- UIKeyboardDidHideNotification

Those notifications all have to do with the *docked* position of the keyboard. On the iPhone, keyboard docking and keyboard visibility are equivalent: the keyboard is visible if and only if it is docked. On the iPad, the keyboard is said to "show" if it is being docked, whether that's because it is appearing from offscreen or because the user is docking it; and it is said to "hide" if it is undocked, whether that's because it is moving offscreen or because the user is undocking it.

Two additional notifications are sent *both* when the keyboard enters and leaves the screen *and* (on the iPad) when the user drags it, splits or unsplits it, and docks or undocks it:

- UIKeyboardWillChangeFrameNotification
- UIKeyboardDidChangeFrameNotification

The notification's userInfo dictionary contains information about the keyboard describing what it will do or has done, under these keys:

- UIKeyboardFrameBeginUserInfoKey
- UIKeyboardFrameEndUserInfoKey
- UIKeyboardAnimationDurationUserInfoKey
- UIKeyboardAnimationCurveUserInfoKey

Thus, to a large extent, you can coordinate your actions with those of the keyboard. In particular, by looking at the UIKeyboardFrameEndUserInfoKey, you know what position the keyboard is moving to; if necessary, you can compare this with the screen bounds to learn whether the keyboard will now be on or off the screen.

(In the case of UIKeyboardWillChangeFrameNotification, however, there won't be any UIKeyboardFrameEndUserInfoKey when the user starts dragging the keyboard on the iPad, because the runtime doesn't know where the user will drag the keyboard to. The frame value for the split keyboard on the iPad is the size of the *entire* keyboard, as if it weren't split; but its height is shorter than the height of the normal keyboard, so you may be able to deduce that it is split, if you really need to know that.)

Finding a strategy for dealing with the keyboard's presence depends on the needs of your particular app. It may well be that even on the iPad you can ignore UIKeyboardDidChangeFrameNotification and concern yourself only with the docked position of the keyboard, because, as I mentioned a moment ago, if the keyboard isn't docked, the user is free to move and split it. To illustrate, therefore, I'll concentrate on the most universal case, where the keyboard moves into and out of docked position and we detect this with UIKeyboardWillShowNotification and UIKeyboardWillHideNotification. What should we do if, when the keyboard appears, it covers the text field being edited? I'll describe a couple of basic approaches to get you started.

A natural-looking approach is to slide the entire interface upward as the keyboard appears. To make this easy, you might start with a view hierarchy like this: the root view contains an invisible view that's the same size as the root view; everything else is contained in that invisible view. The invisible view's purpose is to host the rest of the interface; if we slide it upward, the whole interface will slide upward.

Here's an implementation involving constraints. The invisible view, which I'll called the *sliding view*, is pinned by constraints at the top and bottom to its superview with a `constant` of 0, and we have outlets to those constraints. We also have an outlet to the sliding view itself, and we've got a property prepared to hold the first responder:

```
@property (nonatomic, strong)
    IBOutletCollection(NSLayoutConstraint) NSArray* verticalConstraints;
@property (nonatomic, weak) IBOutlet UIView *slidingView;
@property (nonatomic, weak) UIView* fr;
```

In our view controller's `viewDidLoad`, we register for the keyboard notifications:

```
[super viewDidLoad];
[[NSNotificationCenter defaultCenter] addObserver:self
                                    selector:@selector(keyboardShow:)
                                    name:UIKeyboardWillShowNotification
                                    object:nil];
[[NSNotificationCenter defaultCenter] addObserver:self
                                    selector:@selector(keyboardHide:)
                                    name:UIKeyboardWillHideNotification
                                    object:nil];
```

We are the delegate of the various text fields in our interface. When one of them starts editing, we keep a reference to it as first responder:

```
- (void)textFieldDidBeginEditing:(UITextField *)tf {
    self.fr = tf; // keep track of first responder
}
```

As the keyboard threatens to appear, we examine where its top will be. If the keyboard will cover the text field that's about to be edited, we animate the sliding view upward to compensate, by changing the `constant` value of the constraints that pin its top and bottom. Observe that the keyboard's frame comes to us in window/screen coordinates, so it is necessary to convert it to our sliding view's coordinates in order to make sense of it:

```
- (void) keyboardShow: (NSNotification*) n {
    NSDictionary* d = [n userInfo];
    CGRect r = [d[UIKeyboardFrameEndUserInfoKey] CGRectValue];
    r = [self.slidingView convertRect:r fromView:nil];
    CGRect f = self.fr.frame;
    CGFloat y =
        CGRectGetMaxY(f) + r.size.height -
            self.slidingView.bounds.size.height + 5;
    NSNumber* duration = d[UIKeyboardAnimationDurationUserInfoKey];
```

```
        if (r.origin.y < CGRectGetMaxY(f)) {
            [UIView animateWithDuration:[duration floatValue] animations:^{
                for (NSLayoutConstraint* con in self.verticalConstraints) {
                    con.constant = -y;
                }
                [self.view layoutIfNeeded];
            }];
        }
    }
}
```

When the keyboard disappears, we reverse the procedure:

```
- (void) keyboardHide: (NSNotification*) n {
    NSNumber* duration = n.userInfo[UIKeyboardAnimationDurationUserInfoKey];
    [UIView animateWithDuration:[duration floatValue] animations:^{
        for (NSLayoutConstraint* con in self.verticalConstraints) {
            con.constant = 0;
        }
        [self.view layoutIfNeeded];
    }];
}
```

Sometimes, the interface already knows how to slide — because it's a scroll view. In that case, we typically won't move the scroll view; instead, we'll change the behavior of the scroll view so that it operates coherently within the reduced space left by the keyboard. This is a job for contentInset, whose purpose, you will recall (Chapter 20), is precisely to make it possible for the user to view all of the scroll view's content even though part of the scroll view is being covered by something. A nice byproduct of this approach is that the scroll view helps us by scrolling automatically when the first responder changes.

This approach is in fact implemented automatically by a UITableViewController. When a text field inside a table cell is first responder, the table view controller adjusts the table view's contentInset and scrollIndicatorInsets to compensate for the keyboard. The result is that the entire table view is available within the space between the top of the keyboard and the top of the screen.

Let's imitate UITableViewController's behavior with a scroll view containing text fields. In viewDidLoad, we register for keyboard notifications as before. When the keyboard appears, we store the current content offset, content inset, and scroll indicator insets; then we alter them:

```
- (void) keyboardShow: (NSNotification*) n {
    self->_oldContentInset = self.scrollView.contentInset;
    self->_oldIndicatorInset = self.scrollView.scrollIndicatorInsets;
    self->_oldOffset = self.scrollView.contentOffset;
    NSDictionary* d = [n userInfo];
    CGRect r = [[d objectForKey:UIKeyboardFrameEndUserInfoKey] CGRectValue];
    r = [self.scrollView convertRect:r fromView:nil];
    CGRect f = self.fr.frame;
    CGFloat y =
        CGRectGetMaxY(f) + r.size.height -
```

```
                self.scrollView.bounds.size.height + 5;
    if (r.origin.y < CGRectGetMaxY(f))
        [self.scrollView setContentOffset:CGPointMake(0, y) animated:YES];
    UIEdgeInsets insets;
    insets = self.scrollView.contentInset;
    insets.bottom = r.size.height;
    self.scrollView.contentInset = insets;
    insets = self.scrollView.scrollIndicatorInsets;
    insets.bottom = r.size.height;
    self.scrollView.scrollIndicatorInsets = insets;
}
```

When the keyboard disappears, we restore the saved values; this works best if the insets are restored using delayed performance:

```
- (void) keyboardHide: (NSNotification*) n {
    [self.scrollView setContentOffset:self->_oldOffset animated:YES];
    [CATransaction setCompletionBlock:^{
        self.scrollView.scrollIndicatorInsets = self->_oldIndicatorInset;
        self.scrollView.contentInset = self->_oldContentInset;
    }];
}
```

Configuring the Keyboard

A UITextField implements the UITextInputTraits protocol, which defines properties on the UITextField that you can set to determine how the keyboard will look and how typing in the text field will behave. (These properties can also be set in the nib.) For example, you can set the keyboardType to UIKeyboardTypePhonePad to make the keyboard for this text field consist of digits only. You can set the returnKeyType to determine the text of the Return key (if the keyboard is of a type that has one). You can even supply your own keyboard or other input mechanism by setting the text field's inputView. You can turn off autocapitalization (autocapitalizationType) or autocorrection (autocorrectionType), make the Return key disable itself if the text field has no content (enablesReturnKeyAutomatically), and make the text field a password field (secureTextEntry).

 The user's choices in the Settings app with regard to certain text input features, such as autocapitalization or autocorrection, take priority over your configuration of these same features for a particular text field.

You can attach an accessory view to the top of the keyboard by setting the text field's inputAccessoryView. In this example, the accessory view is a UIButton configured in the nib and accessed through an outlet property, buttonView. When editing starts, we configure the keyboard as we store our reference to the text field:

```
- (void)textFieldDidBeginEditing:(UITextField *)tf {
    self.fr = tf; // keep track of first responder
    tf.inputAccessoryView = self.buttonView;
}
```

The button is a Next button. When the user taps it, we use it to move editing to the next text field. In this code, I assume that the order of the text fields as subviews of their superview is the desired "tab" order:

```
- (IBAction)doNextField:(id)sender {
    NSMutableArray* marr = [NSMutableArray array];
    for (UIView* v in self.fr.superview.subviews) {
        if ([v isKindOfClass: [UITextField class]])
            [marr addObject:v];
    }
    NSUInteger ix = [marr indexOfObject:self.fr];
    if (ix == NSNotFound)
        return; // shouldn't happen
    ix++;
    if (ix >= [marr count])
        ix = 0;
    UIView* v = marr[ix];
    [v becomeFirstResponder];
}
```

The user can control the localization of the keyboard character set in the Settings app, either through a choice of the system's base language or by enabling additional "international keyboards." In the latter case, the user can switch among keyboard character sets while the keyboard is showing. But, as far as I can tell, your code can't make this choice, so you can't, for example, have a Russian-teaching app in which a certain text field automatically shows the Cyrillic keyboard. You can ask the user to switch keyboards manually, but if you really want a particular keyboard to appear regardless of the user's settings and behavior, you'll have to create it yourself and provide it as the inputView.

Text Field Delegate and Control Event Messages

As editing begins and proceeds in a text field, a sequence of messages is sent to the text field's delegate. (Some of these are also available as notifications.) Using them, you can customize the text field's behavior during editing:

textFieldShouldBeginEditing:
Return NO to prevent the text field from becoming first responder.

textFieldDidBeginEditing: (and UITextFieldTextDidBeginEditing-Notification)
The text field has become first responder.

textFieldShouldClear:
:   Return NO to prevent the operation of the Clear button or of automatic clearing on entry (clearsOnBeginEditing).

textFieldShouldReturn:
:   The user has tapped the Return button in the keyboard. We have already seen that this can be used as a signal to dismiss the keyboard.

textField:shouldChangeCharactersInRange:replacementString:
:   Sent when the user changes the text in the field by typing or pasting, or by backspacing or cutting (in which case the replacement string will have zero length). Return NO to prevent the proposed change; you can substitute text by changing the text field's **text** directly (there is no circularity, as this delegate method is not called when you do that). In this example, the user can enter only lowercase characters:

    ```
    -(BOOL)textField:(UITextField *)textField
          shouldChangeCharactersInRange:(NSRange)range
          replacementString:(NSString *)string {
        NSString* lc = [string lowercaseString];
        if ([string isEqualToString:lc])
            return YES;
        textField.text =
            [textField.text stringByReplacingCharactersInRange:range
                                            withString:lc];
        return NO;
    }
    ```

Another use of this method is to take advantage of a new iOS 6 text field property, typingAttributes, to set the attributes of the text the user is about to enter. You can also fetch the typingAttributes to find out what the text styling of newly inserted text would otherwise be (following the same rules I enunciated earlier for insertion of text into an attributed string). Not every attribute can be set this way; for example, trying to set underlining will fail, and indeed will cause the typing-Attributes to be completely ineffectual. I'll set the user's text to be red:

```
-(BOOL)textField:(UITextField *)textField
      shouldChangeCharactersInRange:(NSRange)range
      replacementString:(NSString *)string {
    NSDictionary* d = textField.typingAttributes;
    NSMutableDictionary* md = [d mutableCopy];
    [md addEntriesFromDictionary:
        @{NSForegroundColorAttributeName:[UIColor redColor]}];
    textField.typingAttributes = md;
    return YES;
}
```

It is common practice to implement this delegate method as a way of learning that the text has been changed, even if you then always return YES. The UITextField-

`TextDidChangeNotification` corresponds loosely. This method is *not* called when the user changes text styling through the Bold, Italics, or Underline menu items.

`textFieldShouldEndEditing:`
Return NO to prevent the text field from resigning first responder (even if you just sent `resignFirstResponder` to it). You might do this, for example, because the text is invalid or unacceptable in some way. The user will not know why the text field is refusing to end editing, so the usual thing is to put up an alert (Chapter 26) explaining the problem.

`textFieldDidEndEditing:` *(and* `UITextFieldTextDidEndEditingNotification`*)*
The text field has resigned first responder. See Chapter 21 for an example of using `textFieldDidEndEditing:` to fetch the text field's current text and store it in the model.

A text field is also a control. This means you can attach a target–action pair to any of the events that it reports in order to receive a message when that event occurs (see Chapter 11 and Chapter 25):

- The user can touch and drag, triggering Touch Down and the various Touch Drag events.

- If the user touches in such a way that the text field enters editing mode (and the keyboard appears), Editing Did Begin and Touch Cancel are triggered; if the user causes the text field to enter editing mode in some other way (such as by tabbing into it), Editing Did Begin is triggered without any Touch events.

- As the user edits, Editing Changed is triggered. If the user taps while in editing mode, Touch Down (and possibly Touch Down Repeat) and Touch Cancel are triggered.

- Finally, when editing ends, Editing Did End is triggered; if the user stops editing by tapping Return in the keyboard, Did End on Exit is triggered first.

In general, you're more likely to treat a text field as a text field (through its delegate messages) than as a control (through its control events). However, the Did End on Exit event message has an interesting property: it provides an alternative way to dismiss the keyboard when the user taps a text field keyboard's Return button. If there is a Did End on Exit target–action pair for this text field, then if the text field's delegate does not return NO from `textFieldShouldReturn:`, the keyboard will be dismissed *automatically* when the user taps the Return key. (The action handler for Did End on Exit doesn't actually have to *do* anything.)

This suggests the following trick for getting automatic keyboard dismissal *with no code at all.* In the nib, edit the First Responder proxy object in the Attributes inspector, adding a new First Responder Action; let's call it `dummy:`. Now hook the Did End on Exit event of the text field to the `dummy:` action of the First Responder proxy object. That's it! Because the text field's Did End on Exit event now has a target–action pair, the text field automatically dismisses its keyboard when the user taps Return; because there is no penalty for not finding a handler for a message sent up the responder chain, the app doesn't crash even though there is no implementation of `dummy:` anywhere.

Of course, you can implement that trick in code instead:

```
[textField addTarget:nil action:@selector(dummy:)
      forControlEvents:UIControlEventEditingDidEndOnExit];
```

A disabled text field emits no delegate messages or control events.

The Text Field Menu

When the user double-taps or long-presses in a text field, the menu appears. It contains menu items such as Select, Select All, Paste, Copy, Cut, and Suggest; which menu items appear depends on the circumstances.

The menu can be customized, but you've no information about the text field's selection, making it difficult to decide intelligently what menu items should appear or what they should do when chosen. If you still want to alter the menu, the key facts you need to know are these:

- You can add menu items to the menu through the singleton global shared UIMenu-Controller object. Its `menuItems` property is an array of *custom* menu items — that is, menu items that may appear *in addition* to those that the system puts there. A menu item is a UIMenuItem, which is simply a title (which appears in the menu) plus an action selector. The action will be called, nil-targeted (Chapter 11), thus sending it up the responder chain, when the user taps the menu item (and, by default, the menu will be dismissed).

- The actions for the standard menu items are nil-targeted, so they percolate up the responder chain, and you can interfere with their behavior by implementing their actions. Many of the selectors are listed in the UIResponderStandardEditActions informal protocol. Commonly used standard actions are:

  — `cut:`

  — `copy:`

  — `select:`

  — `selectAll:`

  — `paste:`

  — `delete:`

  — `_promptForReplace:`

— _define:

— _showTextStyleOptions:

— toggleBoldface:

— toggleItalics:

— toggleUnderline:

- You govern the presence or absence of *any* menu item by implementing the UIResponder method `canPerformAction:withSender:` in the responder chain.

As an example, we'll devise a text field in which the standard menu is completely replaced by our own menu, which contains a single menu item, Expand. I'm imagining here, for instance, a text field where the user can type a U.S. state two-letter abbreviation (such as "CA") and can then summon the menu and tap Expand to get the state's full name (such as "California"). We'll implement this by means of a UITextField subclass.

At some point before the user can tap in an instance of our UITextField subclass, we modify the global menu; we could do this in the app delegate as the app starts up, for example:

```
UIMenuItem *mi = [[UIMenuItem alloc] initWithTitle:@"Expand"
                                            action:@selector(expand:)];
UIMenuController *mc = [UIMenuController sharedMenuController];
mc.menuItems = @[mi];
```

In our UITextField subclass, we implement `canPerformAction:withSender:` to govern the contents of the menu. The placement of this implementation is crucial. By putting it here, we guarantee that this implementation will be called when an instance of this subclass is first responder, but at no other time. Therefore, every other text field (or any other object that displays a menu) will behave normally, displaying Cut or Select All or whatever's appropriate; only an instance of our subclass will have the special menu, displaying only Expand:

```
- (BOOL) canPerformAction:(SEL)action withSender: (id) sender {
    if (action == @selector(expand:))
        return ([self.text length] == 2); // could be more intelligent here
    return NO;
}
```

When the user chooses the Expand menu item, the `expand:` message is sent up the responder chain. We catch it in our UITextField subclass and obey it. Proceeding to match abbreviations with state names is left as an exercise for the reader:

```
- (void) expand: (id) sender {
    NSString* s = self.text;
    // ... alter s here ...
    self.text = s;
}
```

To demonstrate interference with the standard menu items, we'll modify the example to allow the Copy menu item to appear if it wants to:

```
- (BOOL) canPerformAction:(SEL)action withSender:(id)sender {
    if (action == @selector(expand:))
        return ([self.text length] == 2);
    if (action == @selector(copy:))
        return [super canPerformAction:action withSender:sender];
    return NO;
}
```

Now we'll implement copy: and modify its behavior. First we call super to get standard copying behavior; then we modify what's now on the pasteboard:

```
- (void) copy: (id) sender {
    [super copy: sender];
    UIPasteboard* pb = [UIPasteboard generalPasteboard];
    NSString* s = pb.string;
    // ... alter s here ....
    pb.string = s;
}
```

UITextView

A text view is sort of a scrollable, multiline version of a text field (UITextField, with which it should not be confused). It is a scroll view subclass (UIScrollView, Chapter 20), and thus has (by default) no border; it is *not* a control. Nevertheless, it has many close similarities to a text field. It has text, font, textColor, and textAlignment properties; it can be editable or not, according to its editable property. (You might use a scrollable noneditable text view instead of a UILabel, so as not to be limited to a fixed number of lines of text in a given height.) As with a text field, iOS 6 brings to a text view the attributedText, allowsEditingTextAttributes, and typingAttributes properties, as well as clearsOnInsertion. An editable text view governs its keyboard just as a text field does: when it is first responder, it is being edited and shows the keyboard, and it implements the UITextInput protocol and has inputView and inputAccessoryView properties. Its menu works the same way as a text field's as well.

A thing to watch out for when replacing a UITextView's attributedText is that aspects of its previous attributedText may contaminate the new attributed string. For example:

```
NSAttributedString* s1 =
    [[NSAttributedString alloc] initWithString:@"Hello there!"
        attributes:@{NSForegroundColorAttributeName:[UIColor redColor]}];
NSAttributedString* s2 = [[NSAttributedString alloc] initWithString:@"Howdy"];
self.tv.attributedText = s1;
self.tv.attributedText = s2;
```

The result is that the text view says "Howdy" in red. This is clearly wrong behavior; if you do the same thing with a UILabel, the label says "Howdy" in black. Apparently, setting the text view's `attributedText` the first time also changes its `textColor`, and this color is then allowed to impose itself when you set the text view's `attributed-Text` the second time, presumably because you didn't explicitly set the second attributed string's color. A good workaround is to reset the text view's properties:

```
self.tv.attributedText = s1;
self.tv.text = nil;
self.tv.font = nil;
self.tv.textColor = nil;
self.tv.textAlignment = NSTextAlignmentLeft;
self.tv.attributedText = s2;
```

One big difference, from the programmer's point of view, between a text view and a text field is that a text view gives you information about, and control of, its selection: it has a `selectedRange` property which you can get and set, and it adds a `scrollRangeTo-Visible:` method so that you can scroll in terms of a range of its text. The `selected-Range` is useful especially if the text view is first responder, because the selection is then meaningful and visible, but it does work (invisibly) even if the text view is not first responder.

A text view also has a `dataDetectorTypes` property; this, if the text view is not editable, allows text of certain types (presumably located using NSDataDetector, see Chapter 10) to be rendered as tappable links.

A text view's delegate messages (UITextViewDelegate protocol) and notifications are quite parallel to those of a text field. The big differences are:

- There's a `textViewDidChange:` delegate message (and an accompanying `UIText-ViewTextDidChangeNotification`), whereas a text field has its Editing Changed control event (and notification).

- There's a `textViewDidChangeSelection:` delegate message, whereas a text field is uninformative about the selection.

A text view's `contentSize` is maintained for you, automatically, as the text changes. You can track changes to the content size (in `textViewDidChange:`, for example). A common reason for doing so is to implement a *self-sizing* text view, that is, a text view that adjusts its height automatically to embrace the amount of text it contains.. In this example, we have an outlet to the text view's internal height constraint:

```
- (void)textViewDidChange:(UITextView *)textView {
    self.heightConstraint.constant = textView.contentSize.height;
}
```

A self-sizing text view works best if the text view is not user-scrollable (scroll-Enabled is NO). If it *is* user-scrollable, it might scroll itself as the user enters text, and you might then have to struggle to prevent it from doing so:

```
- (void)scrollViewDidScroll:(UIScrollView *)scrollView {
    scrollView.contentOffset = CGPointZero;
}
```

Dismissing the keyboard for a text view works differently than for a text field. Because a text view is multiline, the Return key is meaningful for character entry; you aren't likely to want to misuse it as a way of dismissing the keyboard, and you don't get a special delegate message for it. On the iPad, the virtual keyboard may contain a button that dismisses the keyboard. On the iPhone, the interface might well consist of a text view and the keyboard, so that instead of dismissing the keyboard, the user dismisses the entire interface. For example, in the Mail app on the iPhone, when the user is composing a message, the keyboard is present the whole time. In the Notes app, a note alternates between being read fullscreen and being edited with the keyboard present; in the latter case, a Done button is provided to dismiss the keyboard. If there's no good place to put a Done button in the interface, you could attach an accessory view to the keyboard itself.

In an interface where the text view occupies more or less the whole screen, the easiest way to deal with the keyboard is to adjust the text view's contentInset, as we did with a scroll view in the previous section. Here's a fairly straightforward implementation; the text view will helpfully scroll to the insertion point automatically after the keyboard appears:

```
-(void)viewDidLoad {
    [[NSNotificationCenter defaultCenter] addObserver:self
        selector:@selector(keyboardShow:)
        name:UIKeyboardWillShowNotification object:nil];
    [[NSNotificationCenter defaultCenter] addObserver:self
        selector:@selector(keyboardHide:)
        name:UIKeyboardWillHideNotification object:nil];
}

- (IBAction)doDone:(id)sender {
    [self.view endEditing:NO];
}

- (void) keyboardShow: (NSNotification*) n {
    NSDictionary* d = [n userInfo];
    CGRect r = [d[UIKeyboardFrameEndUserInfoKey] CGRectValue];
    self.tv.contentInset = UIEdgeInsetsMake(0,0,r.size.height,0);
    self.tv.scrollIndicatorInsets = UIEdgeInsetsMake(0,0,r.size.height,0);
}

- (void) keyboardHide: (NSNotification*) n {
    NSDictionary* d = [n userInfo];
```

```
    NSNumber* curve = d[UIKeyboardAnimationCurveUserInfoKey];
    NSNumber* duration = d[UIKeyboardAnimationDurationUserInfoKey];
    [UIView animateWithDuration:duration.floatValue delay:0
                        options:curve.integerValue << 16
                     animations:
     ^{
         [self.tv setContentOffset:CGPointZero];
     } completion:^(BOOL finished) {
         self.tv.contentInset = UIEdgeInsetsZero;
         self.tv.scrollIndicatorInsets = UIEdgeInsetsZero;
     }];
}
```

Core Text

Underlying all text drawing on iOS is Core Text. Before iOS 6, Core Text was the only way to draw styled text on iOS; now that an NSAttributedString can be drawn directly, or handed to an built-in interface object for it to draw, you may have less need of Core Text. Nevertheless, Core Text can still do some things you can't do in any other way, and it is sitting there under the hood, so you may as well be aware of it. It is implemented by the Core Text framework; to utilize it, your app must link to *CoreText.framework*, and your code must import <CoreText/CoreText.h>. It uses C, not Objective-C, and it's rather verbose, but getting started with it is not difficult.

A good example of the sort of thing Core Text can do that can't be done any other way is to convert between fonts within a font family. Under CoreText, a font is a CTFont (a CTFontRef), a type which is unfortunately *not* bridged to UIFont. In this example, I'll create an attributed string using only Core Text calls. You can use an NSAttributed string or its Core Foundation counterpart, CFAttributedString; they, at least, are toll-free bridged. The Core Text attribute names are listed in Apple's *Core Text String Attributes Reference*, along with their value types.

I'll start with a mutable attributed string:

```
    NSString* s = @"Yo ho ho and a bottle of rum!";
    NSMutableAttributedString* mas =
        [[NSMutableAttributedString alloc] initWithString:s];
```

Now I'll apply some attributes, using Core Text calls exclusively. I'll cycle through the words of the string; to each word I'll apply a slightly larger size of the same font. The name supplied when creating a CTFont must be a PostScript name; a free app, Typefaces, is helpful for learning all the fonts on a device along with their PostScript names:

```
__block CGFloat f = 18.0;
CTFontRef basefont = CTFontCreateWithName((CFStringRef)@"Baskerville", f, nil);
[s enumerateSubstringsInRange:NSMakeRange(0, [s length])
                      options:NSStringEnumerationByWords
                   usingBlock:
 ^(NSString *substring, NSRange substringRange, NSRange encRange, BOOL *stop) {
     f += 3.5;
     CTFontRef font2 = CTFontCreateCopyWithAttributes(basefont, f, nil, nil);
     NSDictionary* d2 =
         @{(NSString*)kCTFontAttributeName: CFBridgingRelease(font2)};
     [mas addAttributes:d2 range:encRange];
 }];
```

Finally, I'll make the last word bold. The easiest way to obtain the range of the last word is to cycle through the words backward and stop after the first one (by setting the incoming BOOL, `stop`, by indirection). Boldness is a font trait; we must obtain a bold variant of the original font. The font we started with, Baskerville, has such a variant, so this will work:

```
[s enumerateSubstringsInRange:NSMakeRange(0, [s length])
                      options: (NSStringEnumerationByWords |
                                NSStringEnumerationReverse)
                   usingBlock:
 ^(NSString *substring, NSRange substringRange, NSRange encRange, BOOL *stop) {
     CTFontRef font2 =
         CTFontCreateCopyWithSymbolicTraits (
             basefont, f, nil, kCTFontBoldTrait, kCTFontBoldTrait);
     NSDictionary* d2 =
         @{(NSString*)kCTFontAttributeName: CFBridgingRelease(font2)};
     [mas addAttributes:d2 range:encRange];
     *stop = YES; // do just once, last word
 }];
```

Finally, let's not forget to complete our memory management:

```
CFRelease(basefont);
```

(And did you notice the cool use of ARC's `CFBridgingRelease`? Recall from Chapter 12 that this is a way of crossing the bridge from a CFTypeRef to an Objective-C object and, at the same time, giving ARC responsibility for completing the memory management that we started by calling a `Create` function.)

You're probably wondering why I seem to ask for the bold variant (`kCTFontBold-Trait`) twice. The first time (the fourth argument in the call to `CTFontCreateCopyWith-SymbolicTraits`) I'm providing a bitmask. The second time (the fifth argument) I'm providing a second bitmask that says which bits of the first bitmask are meaningful. For example, suppose I'm starting with a font that might or might not be italic, and I want to obtain its bold variant — meaning that if it *is* italic, I want a bold italic font. It isn't enough to supply a bitmask whose value is `kCTFontBoldTrait`, because this appears to switch boldness on and everything else off. Thus, the second bitmask says, "Only this

```
```

> Yo ho ho and a bottle of **rum!**

Figure 23-5. A single line of text, drawn by Core Text

one bit is important; leave all other attributes alone." By the same token, to get a nonbold variant of a font that might be bold, you'd supply 0 as the fourth argument and kCTFont-BoldTrait as the fifth argument.

Core Text can also draw into a graphics context. Text will be drawn upside-down unless we flip the graphics context's coordinate system. Positioning the drawing is up to us.

If the string is a single line we can draw it directly into a graphics context with a CTLineRef. The following code, in a custom UIView subclass, draws the attributed string we created a moment ago (Figure 23-5):

```
- (void)drawRect:(CGRect)rect {
    if (!self.text)
        return;
    CGContextRef ctx = UIGraphicsGetCurrentContext();
    // flip context
    CGContextSaveGState(ctx);
    CGContextTranslateCTM(ctx, 0, self.bounds.size.height);
    CGContextScaleCTM(ctx, 1.0, -1.0);
    CTLineRef line =
        CTLineCreateWithAttributedString(
            (__bridge CFAttributedStringRef)self.text);
    CGContextSetTextPosition(ctx, 1, 3);
    CTLineDraw(line, ctx);
    CFRelease(line);
    CGContextRestoreGState(ctx);
}
```

If we want our string to be drawn wrapped, we must use a CTFramesetter. The framesetter requires a frame into which to draw; this is expressed as a CGPath, but don't get all excited about the possibility of drawing wrapped into some interesting shape, such as an ellipse, because on iOS the path must describe a rectangle:

```
- (void)drawRect:(CGRect)rect {
    if (!self.text)
        return;
    CGContextRef ctx = UIGraphicsGetCurrentContext();
    // flip context
    CGContextSaveGState(ctx);
    CGContextTranslateCTM(ctx, 0, self.bounds.size.height);
    CGContextScaleCTM(ctx, 1.0, -1.0);
    CTFramesetterRef fs =
        CTFramesetterCreateWithAttributedString(
            (__bridge CFAttributedStringRef)self.text);
```

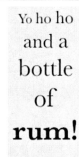

Figure 23-6. Text wrapped and centered, drawn by Core Text

```
    CGMutablePathRef path = CGPathCreateMutable();
    CGPathAddRect(path, nil, rect);
    // range (0,0) means "the whole string"
    CTFrameRef f = CTFramesetterCreateFrame(fs, CFRangeMake(0, 0), path, nil);
    CTFrameDraw(f, ctx);
    CGPathRelease(path);
    CFRelease(f);
    CFRelease(fs);
    CGContextRestoreGState(ctx);
}
```

That code wraps, but the text is left-aligned. Paragraph-level behaviors such as alignment and truncation can be expressed as part of the attributed string itself by applying a CTParagraphStyle. Paragraph styles can also include first-line indent, tab stops, line height, spacing, line break mode, and more. To center our text (which results in a drawing that looks like Figure 23-6), we apply a centered style before drawing it:

```
    NSMutableAttributedString* mas = [self.text mutableCopy];
    NSString* s = [mas string];
    CTTextAlignment centerValue = kCTCenterTextAlignment;
    CTParagraphStyleSetting center =
        {kCTParagraphStyleSpecifierAlignment, sizeof(centerValue), &centerValue};
    CTParagraphStyleSetting pss[1] = {center};
    CTParagraphStyleRef ps = CTParagraphStyleCreate(pss, 1);
    [mas addAttribute:(NSString*)kCTParagraphStyleAttributeName
                value:CFBridgingRelease(ps)
                range:NSMakeRange(0, [s length])];
    self.text = mas;
```

Core Text can also access font typographical features that can't be accessed in any other way, such as the built-in ability of Didot and Hoefler Text to render themselves in small caps. As an example, we'll draw the names of the 50 U.S. states in small caps, centered, in two columns on an iPad (Figure 23-7).

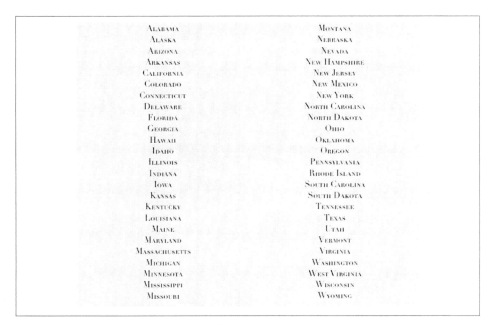

Alabama	Montana
Alaska	Nebraska
Arizona	Nevada
Arkansas	New Hampshire
California	New Jersey
Colorado	New Mexico
Connecticut	New York
Delaware	North Carolina
Florida	North Dakota
Georgia	Ohio
Hawaii	Oklahoma
Idaho	Oregon
Illinois	Pennsylvania
Indiana	Rhode Island
Iowa	South Carolina
Kansas	South Dakota
Kentucky	Tennessee
Louisiana	Texas
Maine	Utah
Maryland	Vermont
Massachusetts	Virginia
Michigan	Washington
Minnesota	West Virginia
Mississippi	Wisconsin
Missouri	Wyoming

Figure 23-7. Two-column text in small caps

As we create the NSAttributedString, we use a convenience function, CTFontDescriptor-CreateCopyWithFeature, to access Didot's small caps variant. I had to log the result of CTFontCopyFeatures to learn how to access this variant of this font (there is also old documentation of font features at *http://developer.apple.com/fonts/registry*). We apply a centered style, as before:

```
NSString* path =
    [[NSBundle mainBundle] pathForResource:@"states" ofType:@"txt"];
NSString* s =
    [NSString stringWithContentsOfFile:path
     encoding:NSUTF8StringEncoding error:nil];
CTFontRef font = CTFontCreateWithName((CFStringRef)@"Didot", 18, nil);
CTFontDescriptorRef fontdesc1 = CTFontCopyFontDescriptor(font);
// names come from SFNTLayoutTypes.h (iOS 6 new feature)
CTFontDescriptorRef fontdesc2 =
CTFontDescriptorCreateCopyWithFeature(fontdesc1,
    (__bridge CFNumberRef)@(kLetterCaseType),
    (__bridge CFNumberRef)@(kSmallCapsSelector));
CTFontRef basefont = CTFontCreateWithFontDescriptor(fontdesc2, 0, nil);
NSDictionary* d =
    @{(NSString*)kCTFontAttributeName: CFBridgingRelease(basefont)};
NSMutableAttributedString* mas =
    [[NSMutableAttributedString alloc] initWithString:s attributes:d];
CTTextAlignment centerValue = kCTCenterTextAlignment;
CTParagraphStyleSetting center =
```

```
        {kCTParagraphStyleSpecifierAlignment, sizeof(centerValue), &centerValue};
    CTParagraphStyleSetting pss[1] = {center};
    CTParagraphStyleRef ps = CTParagraphStyleCreate(pss, 1);
    [mas addAttribute:(NSString*)kCTParagraphStyleAttributeName
            value:CFBridgingRelease(ps)
            range:NSMakeRange(0, [s length])];
    CFRelease(font); CFRelease(fontdesc1); CFRelease(fontdesc2);
```

The two-column arrangement is achieved by drawing into two frames. In our draw-Rect: code, after flipping the context as before (not shown), we draw the entire text into the first frame and then use CTFrameGetVisibleStringRange to learn how much of the text actually fits into it; this tells us where in the attributed string to start drawing into the second frame:

```
    CGRect r1 = rect;
    r1.size.width /= 2.0; // column 1
    CGRect r2 = r1;
    r2.origin.x += r2.size.width; // column 2
    CTFramesetterRef fs =
        CTFramesetterCreateWithAttributedString(
            (__bridge CFAttributedStringRef)self.text);
    // draw column 1
    CGMutablePathRef path = CGPathCreateMutable();
    CGPathAddRect(path, nil, r1);
    CTFrameRef f = CTFramesetterCreateFrame(fs, CFRangeMake(0, 0), path, nil);
    CTFrameDraw(f, ctx);
    CGPathRelease(path);
    CFRange drawnRange = CTFrameGetVisibleStringRange(f);
    CFRelease(f);
    // draw column 2
    path = CGPathCreateMutable();
    CGPathAddRect(path, nil, r2);
    f = CTFramesetterCreateFrame(fs,
            CFRangeMake(drawnRange.location + drawnRange.length, 0), path, nil);
    CTFrameDraw(f, ctx);
    CGPathRelease(path);
    CFRelease(f);
    CFRelease(fs);
```

The result is Figure 23-7. But now let's go further. A frame is itself composed of CTLines describing how each line of text was laid out. To demonstrate, let's turn our two-column list of states into an interactive interface: when the user taps the name of a state, we'll fetch that name, and we'll briefly draw a rectangle around the name to provide feedback (Figure 23-8).

We have two NSMutableArray properties, theLines and theBounds. We initialize them to empty arrays at the start of our drawRect:, and each time we call CTFrameDraw we also call a utility method:

```
    [self appendLinesAndBoundsOfFrame:f context:ctx];
```

Figure 23-8. The user has tapped on California

In `appendLinesAndBoundsOfFrame:context:` we save the CTLines of the frame into `theLines`; we also calculate the drawn bounds of each line and save it into `theBounds`:

```
- (void) appendLinesAndBoundsOfFrame:(CTFrameRef)f context:(CGContextRef)ctx{
    CGAffineTransform t1 =
        CGAffineTransformMakeTranslation(0, self.bounds.size.height);
    CGAffineTransform t2 = CGAffineTransformMakeScale(1, -1);
    CGAffineTransform t = CGAffineTransformConcat(t2, t1);
    CGPathRef p = CTFrameGetPath(f);
    CGRect r = CGPathGetBoundingBox(p); // this is the frame bounds
    NSArray* lines = (__bridge NSArray*)CTFrameGetLines(f);
    [self.theLines addObjectsFromArray:lines];
    CGPoint origins[[lines count]];
    CTFrameGetLineOrigins(f, CFRangeMake(0,0), origins);
    for (int i = 0; i < [lines count]; i++) {
        CTLineRef aLine = (__bridge CTLineRef)lines[i];
        CGRect b = CTLineGetImageBounds((CTLineRef)aLine, ctx);
        // the line origin plus the image bounds size is the bounds we want
        CGRect b2 = { origins[i], b.size };
        // but it is expressed in terms of the frame, so we must compensate
        b2.origin.x += r.origin.x;
        b2.origin.y += r.origin.y;
        // we must also compensate for the flippedness of the graphics context
        b2 = CGRectApplyAffineTransform(b2, t);
        [self.theBounds addObject: [NSValue valueWithCGRect:b2]];
    }
}
```

We have attached a UITapGestureRecognizer to our view; when the user taps, we cycle through the saved bounds to see if any of them contains the tap point. If it does, we fetch the name of the state, and we draw a rectangle around it:

```
- (void) tapped: (UITapGestureRecognizer*) tap {
    CGPoint loc = [tap locationInView:self];
    for (int i = 0; i < [self.theBounds count]; i++) {
        CGRect rect = [self.theBounds[i] CGRectValue];
        if (CGRectContainsPoint(rect, loc)) {
            // draw rectangle for feedback
            CALayer* lay = [CALayer layer];
            lay.frame = CGRectInset(rect, -5, -5);
            lay.borderWidth = 2;
```

```
        [self.layer addSublayer: lay];
        dispatch_time_t popTime =
            dispatch_time(DISPATCH_TIME_NOW, 0.3 * NSEC_PER_SEC);
        dispatch_after(popTime, dispatch_get_main_queue(), ^(void){
            [lay removeFromSuperlayer];
        });
        // fetch the drawn string tapped on
        CTLineRef theLine =
            (__bridge CTLineRef)[self.theLines[i];
        CFRange range = CTLineGetStringRange(theLine);
        CFStringRef s = CFStringCreateWithSubstring(
            nil, (__bridge CFStringRef)[self.text string], range);
        // ... could do something useful with string here ...
        NSLog(@"tapped %@", s);
        CFRelease(s);
        break;
        }
    }
}
```

If we needed to, we could even learn what character the user tapped by going down to the level of glyph runs (CTRun) and glyphs (CTGlyph). We have barely scratched the surface of what Core Text can do. Read Apple's *Core Text Programming Guide* for further information.

CHAPTER 24

Web Views

A web view (UIWebView) is a UIView subclass that acts as a versatile renderer of text in various formats, including:

- HTML
- PDF
- RTF, including *.rtfd* (which must be supplied in a zipped format, *.rtfd.zip*)
- Microsoft Word (*.doc*), Excel (*.xls*), and PowerPoint (*.ppt*)
- Pages, Numbers, and Keynote; before iWork 2009, these must be zipped (e.g., *.key.zip*), but starting with iWork 2009 they must *not* be zipped.

In addition to displaying rendered text, a web view is a web browser. This means that if you ask a web view to display HTML that refers to a resource available on disk or over the Internet, such as an image to be shown as the source of an `<img>` tag, the web view will attempt to fetch it and display it. Similarly, if the user taps, within the web view, on a link that leads to content on disk or over the Internet that the web view can render, the web view by default will attempt to fetch that content and display it. Indeed, a web view is, in effect, a front end for WebKit, the same rendering engine used by Mobile Safari (and by Safari on Mac OS X). A web view can display non-HTML file formats such as PDF, RTF, and so on, precisely because WebKit can display them.

As the user taps links and displays web pages, the web view keeps a Back list and a Forward list, just like a web browser. Two properties, `canGoBack` and `canGoForward`, and two methods, `goBack` and `goForward`, let you interact with this list. Your interface could thus contain Back and Forward buttons, like a miniature web browser.

A web view is scrollable, but UIWebView is *not* a UIScrollView subclass (Chapter 20); it *has* a scroll view, rather than *being* a scroll view. You can access a web view's scroll view as its `scrollView` property. You can use the scroll view to learn and set how far the content is scrolled and zoomed, and you can install a gesture recognizer on it, to detect gestures not intended for the web view itself.

A web view is zoomable if its `scalesToFit` property is YES; in that case, it initially scales its content to fit, and the user can zoom the content (this includes use of the gesture, familiar from Mobile Safari, whereby double-tapping part of a web page zooms to that region of the page). Like a text view (Chapter 23), its `dataDetectorTypes` property lets you set certain types of data to be automatically converted to clickable links. An obvious difference from a text view is that the target of a web page link may be displayed right there in the web view, rather than switching to Mobile Safari.

It is possible to design an entire app that is effectively nothing but a UIWebView — especially if you have control of the server with which the user is interacting. Indeed, before the advent of iOS, an iPhone app *was* a web application. There are still iPhone apps that work this way, but such an approach to app design is outside the scope of this book. (See Apple's *Mobile Safari Web Application Tutorial* if you're curious.)

A web view's most important task is to render HTML content; like any browser, a web view understands HTML, CSS, and JavaScript. In order to construct content for a web view, *you* must know HTML, CSS, and JavaScript. Discussion of those languages is beyond the scope of this book; each would require a book (at least) of its own.

Loading Web View Content

To load a web view with content initially, you're going to need one of three things:

An NSURLRequest
Construct an NSURLRequest and call `loadRequest:`. An NSURLRequest might involve a file URL referring to a file on disk (within your app's bundle, for instance); the web view will deduce the file's type from its extension. But it might also involve the URL of a resource to be fetched across the Internet, in which case you can configure various additional aspects of the request (for example, you can form a POST request). This is the only form of loading that works with `goBack` (because in the other two forms, there is no URL to go back to).

An HTML string
Construct an NSString consisting of valid HTML and call `loadHTMLString:base-URL:`. The `baseURL:` will be used to fetch any resources referred to by a partial (relative) URL in the string. For example, you could cause partial URLs to refer to resources inside your app's bundle.

Data and a MIME type
Obtain an NSData object and call `loadData:MIMEType:textEncodingName:base-URL:`. Obviously, this requires that you know the appropriate MIME type, and that you obtain the content as NSData (or convert it to NSData). Typically, this will be

because the content was itself obtained by fetching it from the Internet (more about that in Chapter 37).

There is often more than one way to load a given piece of content. For instance, one of Apple's own examples suggests that you display a PDF file in your app's bundle by loading it as data, along these lines:

```
NSString *thePath =
    [[NSBundle mainBundle] pathForResource:@"MyPDF" ofType:@"pdf"];
NSData *pdfData = [NSData dataWithContentsOfFile:thePath];
[self.wv loadData:pdfData MIMEType:@"application/pdf"
                textEncodingName:@"utf-8" baseURL:nil];
```

But the same thing can be done with a file URL and loadRequest:, like this:

```
NSURL* url =
    [[NSBundle mainBundle] URLForResource:@"MyPDF" withExtension:@"pdf"];
NSURLRequest* req = [[NSURLRequest alloc] initWithURL:url];
[self.wv loadRequest:req];
```

Similarly, in one of my apps, where the Help screen is a web view (Figure 24-1), the content is an HTML file along with some referenced image files, and I load it like this:

```
NSString* path =
    [[NSBundle mainBundle] pathForResource:@"help" ofType:@"html"];
NSURL* url = [NSURL fileURLWithPath:path];
NSError* err = nil;
NSString* s = [NSString stringWithContentsOfURL:url
                encoding:NSUTF8StringEncoding error:&err];
// error-checking omitted
[view loadHTMLString:s baseURL:url];
```

Observe that I supply both the string contents of the HTML file and the URL reference to the same file, the latter to act as a base URL so that the relative references to the images will work properly. (At the time I wrote that code, the NSBundle method URLFor-Resource:withExtension: didn't yet exist, so I had to form a pathname reference to the file and convert it to a URL.) In this instance, I could have used loadRequest: and the file URL:

```
NSString* path =
    [[NSBundle mainBundle] pathForResource:@"help" ofType:@"html"];
NSURL* url = [NSURL fileURLWithPath:path];
NSURLRequest* req = [[NSURLRequest alloc] initWithURL:url];
[view loadRequest: req];
```

You can use loadHTMLString:baseURL: to form your own web view content dynamically. For example, in the TidBITS News app, the content of an article is displayed in a web view that is loaded using loadHTMLString:baseURL:. The body of the article comes from an RSS feed, but it is wrapped in programmatically supplied material. Thus, in Figure 24-2, the title of the article and the fact that it is a link, the right-aligned author

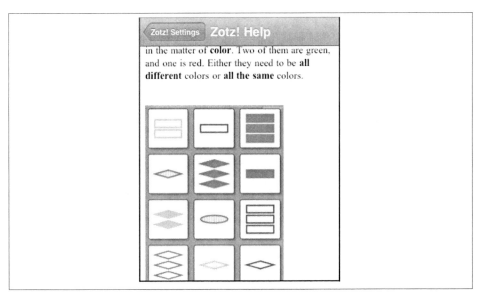

Figure 24-1. A Help screen that's a web view

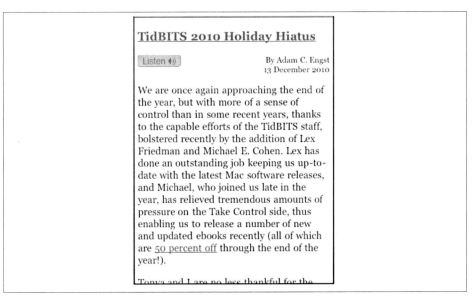

Figure 24-2. A web view with dynamically formed content

byline and publication date, and the Listen button, along with the overall formatting of the text (including the font size), are imposed as the web view appears.

There are many possible strategies for doing this. In the case of the TidBITS News app, I start with a template loaded from disk:

```
<!DOCTYPE HTML PUBLIC "-//W3C//DTD HTML 4.01 Transitional//EN"
"http://www.w3.org/TR/html4/loose.dtd">
<html>
<head>
  <meta http-equiv="content-type" content="text/html; charset=utf-8">
  <meta name="viewport" content="initial-scale=1.0, user-scalable=no">
  <!-- scale images down to fit -->
    <style type="text/css">
      p.inflow_image {
        text-align:center;
      }
      div.indented_image {
        text-align:center;
        margin-left:0;
      }
      img {
        max-width:<maximagewidth>;
        height:auto;
      }
    </style>
  <title>no title</title>
</head>
<body style="font-size:<fontsize>px; font-family:Georgia;
                                     margin:1px <margin>px">
  <!-- title, which is a link to original story at our site -->
  <div style="margin-top: 0px; margin-bottom: 15px">
    <h3><a href="<guid>"><ourtitle></a></h3>
  </div>
  <!-- playbutton or nothing; author and date -->
  <div style="width:100%%">
    <span style="float:left; display:block; vertical-align:middle">
        <playbutton>
    </span>
    <span style="float:right; margin-bottom: 15px;
                 display:block; text-align:right; font-size:80%%;">
      By <author><br><date>
    </span>
  </div>
  <!-- body, from feed -->
  <div style="clear:both; margin:30px 0px;">
    <content>
  </div>
</body>
</html>
```

The template defines the structure of a valid HTML document — the opening and closing tags, the head area (including some CSS styling), and a body consisting of <div>s laying out the parts of the page. But it also includes some tags that are not HTML, some of them appearing in impossible places — <maximagewidth>, <fontsize>, and so on. That's because, when the web view is to be loaded, the template will be read from disk and real values will be substituted for those pseudo-tags:

```
NSString* template =
    [NSString stringWithContentsOfFile:
        [[NSBundle mainBundle] pathForResource:@"htmltemplate" ofType:@"txt"]
                    encoding: NSUTF8StringEncoding error:nil];
NSString* s = template;
s = [s stringByReplacingOccurrencesOfString:@"<maximagewidth>"
                            withString:maxImageWidth];
s = [s stringByReplacingOccurrencesOfString:@"<fontsize>"
                            withString:fontsize.stringValue];
s = [s stringByReplacingOccurrencesOfString:@"<margin>"
                            withString:margin];
s = [s stringByReplacingOccurrencesOfString:@"<guid>"
                            withString:anitem.guid];
s = [s stringByReplacingOccurrencesOfString:@"<ourtitle>"
                            withString:anitem.title];
s = [s stringByReplacingOccurrencesOfString:@"<playbutton>"
                            withString:(canPlay ? playbutton : @"")];
s = [s stringByReplacingOccurrencesOfString:@"<author>"
                            withString:anitem.authorOfItem];
s = [s stringByReplacingOccurrencesOfString:@"<date>"
                            withString:date];
s = [s stringByReplacingOccurrencesOfString:@"<content>"
                            withString:anitem.content];
```

Some of these arguments (such as `anitem.title`, `date`, `anitem.content`) slot values more or less directly from the app's model into the web view. Others are derived from the current circumstances. For example, the local variables `maxImageWidth` and `margin` have been set depending on whether the app is running on the iPhone or on the iPad; `fontsize` comes from the user defaults, because the user is allowed to determine how large the text should be. The result is an HTML string ready for `loadHTMLString:base-URL:`.

Web view content is loaded *asynchronously* (gradually, in a thread of its own), and it might not be loaded at all (because the user might not be connected to the Internet, the server might not respond properly, and so on). If you're loading a resource directly from disk, loading is quick and nothing is going to go wrong; even then, though, rendering the content can take time, and even a resource loaded from disk, or content formed directly as an HTML string, might itself refer to material out on the Internet that takes time to fetch.

Your app's interface is not blocked or frozen while the content is loading. On the contrary, it remains accessible and operative; that's what "asynchronous" means. The web view, in fetching a web page and its linked components, is doing something quite complex, involving both threading and network interaction, but it shields you from this complexity. Your own interaction with the web view stays on the main thread and is straightforward. You ask the web view to load some content, and then you just sit back and let it worry about the details.

Indeed, there's very little you *can* do once you've asked a web view to load content. Your main concerns will probably be to know when loading really starts, when it has finished, and whether it succeeded. To help you with this, a UIWebView's delegate (adopting the UIWebViewDelegate protocol) gets three messages:

- `webViewDidStartLoad:`
- `webViewDidFinishLoad:`
- `webView:didFailLoadWithError:`

In this example from the TidBITS News app, I mask the delay while the content loads by displaying in the center of the interface an activity indicator (a UIActivityIndicator-View, Chapter 25), referred to by a property, `activity`:

```
- (void)webViewDidStartLoad:(UIWebView *)wv {
    [self.view addSubview:self.activity];
    self.activity.center = CGPointMake(CGRectGetMidX(self.view.bounds),
                                       CGRectGetMidY(self.view.bounds));
    [self.activity startAnimating];
    [[UIApplication sharedApplication] beginIgnoringInteractionEvents];
}

- (void)webViewDidFinishLoad:(UIWebView *)webView {
    [self.activity stopAnimating];
    [self.activity removeFromSuperview];
    [[UIApplication sharedApplication] endIgnoringInteractionEvents];
}

- (void)webView:(UIWebView *)webView didFailLoadWithError:(NSError *)error {
    [self.activity stopAnimating];
    [self.activity removeFromSuperview];
    [[UIApplication sharedApplication] endIgnoringInteractionEvents];
}
```

Before designing the HTML to be displayed in a web view, you might want to read up on the brand of HTML native to the mobile WebKit engine. Of course a web view *can* display any valid HTML you throw at it, but the mobile WebKit has certain limitations. For example, mobile WebKit notoriously doesn't use plug-ins, such as Flash; it doesn't implement scrollable frames within framesets; and it imposes limits on the size of resources (such as images) that it can display. On the plus side, it has many special abilities and specifications that you'll want to take advantage of; for example, WebKit is in the forefront of the march towards HTML 5.

A good place to start is Apple's *Safari Web Content Guide*. It contains links to all the other relevant documentation, such as the *Safari CSS Visual Effects Guide*, which describes some things you can do with WebKit's implementation of CSS3 (like animations), and the *Safari HTML5 Audio and Video Guide*, which describes WebKit's audio and video player support.

If nothing else, you'll definitely want to be aware of one important aspect of web page content — the *viewport*. You'll notice that the TidBITS News HTML template I showed a moment ago contains this line within its <head> area:

```
<meta name="viewport" content="initial-scale=1.0, user-scalable=no">
```

Without that line, the HTML string is laid out incorrectly when it is rendered. This is noticeable especially with the iPad version of TidBITS News, where the web view can be rotated when the device is rotated, causing its width to change: in one orientation or the other, the text will be too wide for the web view, and the user has to scroll horizontally to read it. The *Safari Web Content Guide* explains why: if no viewport is specified, the viewport can change when the app rotates. Setting the initial-scale causes the viewport size to adopt correct values in both orientations.

Another important section of the *Safari Web Content Guide* describes how you can use a media attribute in the <link> tag that loads your CSS to load *different* CSS depending on what kind of device your app is running on. For example, you might have one CSS file that lays out your web view's content on an iPhone, and another that lays it out on an iPad.

A web view's loading property tells you whether it is in the process of loading a request. If, at the time a web view is to be destroyed, its loading is YES, it is up to you to cancel the request by sending it the stopLoading message first; actually, it does no harm to send the web view stopLoading in any case. In addition, UIWebView is one of those weird classes I warned you about (in Chapter 12) whose memory management behavior is odd: Apple's documentation warns that if you assign a UIWebView a delegate, you must nilify its delegate property before releasing the web view. Thus, in a controller class whose view contains a web view, I do an extra little dance in dealloc:

```
- (void) dealloc {
    [self.wv stopLoading];
    self.wv.delegate = nil;
}
```

A related problem is that a web view will sometimes leak memory. I've never understood what causes this, but the workaround appears to be to load the empty string into the web view. The TidBITS News app does this in the view controller whose view contains the web view:

```
- (void) viewWillDisappear:(BOOL)animated {
    if (self.isMovingFromParentViewController) {
        [self.wv loadHTMLString: @"" baseURL: nil];
    }
}
```

The suppressesIncrementalRendering property, new in iOS 6, changes nothing about the request-loading process, but it does change what the user *sees*. The default, and the old standard behavior, is NO: the web view assembles its display of a resource incrementally, as it arrives. If this property is YES, the web view does nothing outwardly until the resource has completely arrived and the web view is ready to render the whole thing.

Web View State Restoration

If you provided an HTML string to your web view, then restoring its state when the app is relaunched is up to you. You can use the built-in iOS 6 state saving and restoration to help you, but you'll have to do all the work yourself. The web view has a scroll-View which has a contentOffset, so it's easy to save the scroll position (as an NSValue wrapping a CGPoint) in encodeRestorableStateWithCoder:, and restore it in decode-RestorableStateWithCoder:. What the TidBITS News app does is to restore the scroll position initially into an instance variable:

```
-(void)decodeRestorableStateWithCoder:(NSCoder *)coder {
    // scroll position is a CGPoint wrapped in an NSValue
    self.lastOffset = [coder decodeObjectForKey:@"lastOffset"];
    // ... other stuff ...
    [super decodeRestorableStateWithCoder:coder];
}
```

Then we reload the web view content (manually); when the web view has loaded, we set its scroll position:

```
- (void)webViewDidFinishLoad:(UIWebView *)webView {
    if (self.lastOffset)
        webView.scrollView.contentOffset = self.lastOffset.CGPointValue;
    self.lastOffset = nil;
    // ...
}
```

If, however, a web view participates in state restoration, and if the web view had a URL request (not an HTML string) when the user left the app, the web view will automatically return to life containing that request in its request property, and with its Back and Forward lists intact. Thus, you can use the state restoration mechanism to restore the state of the web view, but you have to perform a little extra dance. This dance is so curious and obscure that initially I was under the impression that a web view's state couldn't really be saved and restored, despite the documentation's assertion that it could.

There are two secrets here; once you know them, you'll understand web view state restoration:

- A restored web view will not automatically load its request; that's up to your code.

- After a restored web view has loaded its request, the first item in its Back list is the same page in the state the user left it (scroll and zoom).

Knowing this, you can easily devise a strategy for web view state restoration. The first thing is to detect that we are restoring state, and raise a flag that says so:

```
-(void)decodeRestorableStateWithCoder:(NSCoder *)coder {
    [super decodeRestorableStateWithCoder:coder];
    self->_didDecode = YES;
}
```

Now we can detect (perhaps in `viewDidAppear:`) that we are restoring state, and that the web view magically contains a request, and load that request:

```
if (self->_didDecode && wv.request)
    [wv loadRequest:wv.request];
```

Now for the tricky part. After the view loads, we immediately "go back." This actually has the effect of restoring the user's previous scroll position (and of removing the extra entry from the top of the Back stack). Then we lower our flag so that we don't make this extra move at any other time:

```
- (void)webViewDidFinishLoad:(UIWebView *)wv {
    if (self->_didDecode && wv.canGoBack)
        [wv goBack];
    self->_didDecode = NO;
}
```

Communicating with a Web View

Having loaded a web view with content, you don't so much configure or command the web view as communicate with it. There are two modes of communication with a web view and its content:

Load requests

When a web view is asked to load content, possibly because the user has tapped a link within it, its delegate is sent the message `webView:shouldStartLoadWith-Request:navigationType:`. This is your opportunity to interfere with the web view's loading behavior; if you return NO, the content won't load.

The second argument is an NSURLRequest, whose URL property you can analyze (very easily, because it's an NSURL). The third argument is a constant describing the type of navigation involved, whose value will be one of the following:

- UIWebViewNavigationTypeLinkClicked

- UIWebViewNavigationTypeFormSubmitted

- UIWebViewNavigationTypeBackForward

- `UIWebViewNavigationTypeReload`

- `UIWebViewNavigationTypeFormResubmitted`

- `UIWebViewNavigationTypeOther` (includes loading the web view with content initially)

JavaScript execution

You can speak JavaScript to a web view's content by sending it the `stringBy-EvaluatingJavaScriptFromString:` message. Thus you can enquire as to the nature and details of that content, and you can alter the content dynamically.

The TidBITS News app uses `webView:shouldStartLoadWithRequest:navigation-Type:` to distinguish between the user tapping an ordinary link and tapping the Listen button (shown in Figure 24-2). The `onclick` script for the `<a>` tag surrounding the Listen button image executes this JavaScript code:

```
document.location='play:me'
```

This causes the web view to attempt to load an NSURLRequest whose URL is `play:me`, which is totally bogus; it's merely an internal signal to ourselves. In the web view's delegate, we intercept the attempt to load this request, examine the NSURLRequest, observe that its URL has a `scheme` called `@"play"`, and prevent the loading from taking place; instead, we head back to the Internet to start playing the online podcast recording associated with this article. Any other load request caused by tapping a link is also prevented and redirected instead to Mobile Safari, because we don't want our web view used as an all-purpose browser. But we do let our web view load a request in the general case, because otherwise it wouldn't even respond to our attempt to load it with HTML content in the first place:

```
- (BOOL)webView:(UIWebView *)webView
      shouldStartLoadWithRequest:(NSURLRequest *)r
      navigationType:(UIWebViewNavigationType)nt {
   if ([r.URL.scheme isEqualToString: @"play"]) {
      [self doPlay:nil];
      return NO;
   }
   if (nt == UIWebViewNavigationTypeLinkClicked) {
      [[UIApplication sharedApplication] openURL:r.URL];
      return NO;
   }
   return YES;
}
```

JavaScript and the document object model (*DOM*) are quite powerful. Event listeners even allow JavaScript code to respond directly to touch and gesture events, so that the user can interact with elements of a web page much as if they were touchable views; it can also take advantage of Core Location facilities to respond to where the user is on earth and how the device is positioned (Chapter 35).

Additional helpful documentation includes Apple's *WebKit DOM Programming Topics*, *WebKit DOM Reference*, and *Safari DOM Additions Reference*.

CHAPTER 25

Controls and Other Views

This chapter discusses all UIView subclasses provided by UIKit that haven't been discussed already (except for the two modal dialog classes, which are described in the next chapter). It's remarkable how few of them there are; UIKit exhibits a noteworthy economy of means in this regard.

Additional UIView subclasses are provided by other frameworks. For example, the Map Kit framework provides the MKMapView (Chapter 34). Also, additional UIView-Controller subclasses are provided by other frameworks as a way of creating interface. For example, the MessageUI framework provides MFMailComposeViewController, which supplies a user interface for composing and sending a mail message (Chapter 33). There will be lots of examples in Part VI.

UIActivityIndicatorView

An activity indicator (UIActivityIndicatorView) appears as the spokes of a small wheel. You set the spokes spinning with `startAnimating`, giving the user a sense that some time-consuming process is taking place. You stop the spinning with `stopAnimating`. If the activity indicator's `hidesWhenStopped` is YES (the default), it is visible only while spinning.

An activity indicator comes in a style, its `activityIndicatorViewStyle`; if it is created in code, you'll set its style with `initWithActivityIndicatorStyle:`. Your choices are:

- `UIActivityIndicatorViewStyleWhiteLarge`
- `UIActivityIndicatorViewStyleWhite`
- `UIActivityIndicatorViewStyleGray`

Figure 25-1. A large activity indicator

An activity indicator has a standard size, which depends on its style. Changing its size in code changes the size of the view, but not the size of the spokes. For bigger spokes, you can resort to a scale transform.

You can assign an activity indicator a color; this overrides the color assigned through the style. An activity indicator is a UIView, so you can set its backgroundColor; a nice effect is to give an activity indicator a contrasting background color and to round its corners by way of the view's layer (Figure 25-1):

```
self.activity.color = [UIColor yellowColor];
self.activity.backgroundColor = [UIColor colorWithWhite:0.2 alpha:0.4];
self.activity.layer.cornerRadius = 10;
CGRect f = self.activity.bounds;
f.size.width += 10;
f.size.height += 10;
self.activity.bounds = f;
```

Here's some code from a UITableViewCell subclass in one of my apps. In this app, it takes some time, after the user taps a cell to select it, for me to construct the next view and navigate to it; to cover the delay, I show a spinning activity indicator in the center of the cell while it's selected:

```
- (void)setSelected:(BOOL)selected animated:(BOOL)animated {
    if (selected) {
        UIActivityIndicatorView* v =
            [[UIActivityIndicatorView alloc] initWithActivityIndicatorStyle:
                UIActivityIndicatorViewStyleWhiteLarge];
        v.center =
            CGPointMake(self.bounds.size.width/2.0,
                        self.bounds.size.height/2.0);
        v.frame = CGRectIntegral(v.frame);
        v.color = [UIColor yellowColor];
        v.tag = 1001;
        [self.contentView addSubview:v];
        [v startAnimating];
    } else {
        [[self.contentView viewWithTag:1001] removeFromSuperview];
        // no harm if non-existent
    }
    [super setSelected:selected animated:animated];
}
```

Figure 25-2. A progress view

If activity involves the network, you might want to set UIApplication's `networkActivity-IndicatorVisible` to YES. This displays a small spinning activity indicator in the status bar. The indicator is not reflecting actual network activity; if it's visible, it's spinning. Be sure to set it back to NO when the activity is over.

An activity indicator is simple and standard, but you can't change the way it's drawn. One obvious alternative would be a UIImageView with an animated image, as described in Chapter 17.

UIProgressView

A progress view (UIProgressView, Figure 25-2) is a "thermometer," graphically displaying a percentage. It is often used to represent a time-consuming process whose percentage of completion is known (if the percentage of completion is unknown, you're more likely to use an activity indicator). But it's good for static percentages too. In one of my apps, I use a progress view to show the current position within the song being played by the built-in music player; in another app, which is a card game, I use a progress view to show how many cards are left in the deck.

A progress view comes in a style, its `progressViewStyle`; if the progress view is created in code, you'll set its style with `initWithProgressViewStyle:`. Your choices are:

- `UIProgressViewStyleDefault`
- `UIProgressViewStyleBar`

The latter is intended for use in a UIBarButtonItem, as the title view of a navigation item, and so on.

The height (the narrow dimension) of a progress view is generally not up to you; it's determined by the progress view's style. Changing a progress view's height has no visible effect on how the thermometer is drawn.

The fullness of the thermometer is the progress view's `progress` property. This is a value between 0 and 1, inclusive; obviously, you'll need to do some elementary arithmetic in order to convert from the actual value you're reflecting to a value within that range. For example, to reflect the number of cards remaining in a deck of 52 cards:

```
prog.progress = [[deck cards] count] / 52.0;
```

You can animate the change from one `progress` value to another by calling `set-Progress:animated:`.

You can customize the colors or images of the parts of the progress view. To customize the colors, set the progress view's `progressTintColor` and `trackTintColor` (the track is the unfilled part of the progress view); this can also be done in the nib. To customize the images, set the progress view's `progressImage` and `trackImage`; these, if set, override the tint colors. The images will be squashed and stretched to fill the appropriate bounds, so a good choice is a resizable image whose height is the progress view's standard height (9 points). In this simple example, the track image and progress image are squares rotated 45 degrees:

```
UIGraphicsBeginImageContextWithOptions(CGSizeMake(9,9), NO, 0);
CGContextRef con = UIGraphicsGetCurrentContext();
CGContextSetFillColorWithColor(con, [UIColor blackColor].CGColor);
CGContextMoveToPoint(con, 0, 4.5);
CGContextAddLineToPoint(con, 4.5, 9);
CGContextAddLineToPoint(con, 9, 4.5);
CGContextAddLineToPoint(con, 4.5, 0);
CGContextClosePath(con);
CGPathRef p = CGContextCopyPath(con);
CGContextFillPath(con);
UIImage* im = UIGraphicsGetImageFromCurrentImageContext();
CGContextSetFillColorWithColor(con, [UIColor whiteColor].CGColor);
CGContextAddPath(con, p);
CGContextFillPath(con);
UIImage* im2 = UIGraphicsGetImageFromCurrentImageContext();
CGPathRelease(p);
UIGraphicsEndImageContext();
im = [im resizableImageWithCapInsets:UIEdgeInsetsMake(4, 4, 4, 4)
                        resizingMode:UIImageResizingModeStretch];
im2 = [im2 resizableImageWithCapInsets:UIEdgeInsetsMake(4, 4, 4, 4)
                          resizingMode:UIImageResizingModeStretch];
prog.trackImage = im;
prog.progressImage = im2;
```

For additional customization — for example, to make a taller progress view — you can design your own UIView subclass that draws something similar to a thermometer. Figure 25-3 shows a simple custom thermometer view; it has a `value` property, and you set this to something between 0 and 1 and call `setNeedsDisplay` to make the view redraw itself. Here's its `drawRect:` code:

```
- (void)drawRect:(CGRect)rect {
    CGContextRef c = UIGraphicsGetCurrentContext();
    [[UIColor whiteColor] set];
    CGFloat ins = 2.0;
    CGRect r = CGRectInset(self.bounds, ins, ins);
    CGFloat radius = r.size.height / 2.0;
    CGMutablePathRef path = CGPathCreateMutable();
    CGPathMoveToPoint(path, nil, CGRectGetMaxX(r)-radius, ins);
```

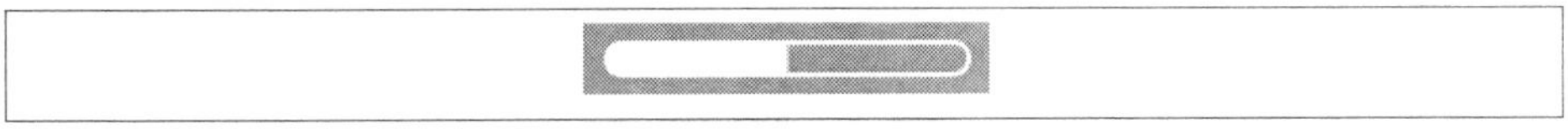

Figure 25-3. A custom progress view

```
CGPathAddArc(path, nil,
    radius+ins, radius+ins, radius, -M_PI/2.0, M_PI/2.0, true);
CGPathAddArc(path, nil,
    CGRectGetMaxX(r)-radius, radius+ins, radius,
    M_PI/2.0, -M_PI/2.0, true);
CGPathCloseSubpath(path);
CGContextAddPath(c, path);
CGContextSetLineWidth(c, 2);
CGContextStrokePath(c);
CGContextAddPath(c, path);
CGContextClip(c);
CGContextFillRect(c, CGRectMake(
    r.origin.x, r.origin.y, r.size.width * self.value, r.size.height));
}
```

UIPickerView

A UIPickerView displays selectable choices using a rotating drum metaphor. It has a standard legal range of possible heights, which is undocumented and must be discovered by trial and error (attempting to set the height outside this range will fail with a warning in the console); its width is largely up to you. Each drum, or column, is called a *component*.

Your code configures the UIPickerView's content through its data source (UIPickerViewDataSource) and delegate (UIPickerViewDelegate), which are usually the same object (see also Chapter 11). Your data source and delegate must answer questions similar to those posed by a UITableView (Chapter 21):

numberOfComponentsInPickerView: *(data source)*
How many components (drums) does this picker view have?

pickerView:numberOfRowsInComponent: *(data source)*
How many rows does this component have? The first component is numbered 0.

pickerView:titleForRow:forComponent:
pickerView:attributedTitleForRow:forComponent: *(new in iOS 6)*
pickerView:viewForRow:forComponent:reusingView: *(delegate)*
What should this row of this component display? The first row is numbered 0. You can supply a simple string, an attributed string (Chapter 23), or an entire view such as a UILabel; but you should supply every row of every component the same way. The reusingView parameter, if not nil, is a view that you supplied for a row now

Figure 25-4. A picker view

no longer visible, giving you a chance to reuse it, much as cells are reused in a table view.

Here's the code for a UIPickerView (Figure 25-4) that displays the names of the 50 U.S. states, stored in an array. We implement `pickerView:viewForRow:forComponent:reusingView:` just because it's the most interesting case; as our views, we supply UILabel instances. The state names appear centered because the labels are centered within the picker view:

```
- (NSInteger)numberOfComponentsInPickerView:(UIPickerView *)pickerView {
    return 1;
}

- (NSInteger)pickerView:(UIPickerView *)pickerView
        numberOfRowsInComponent:(NSInteger)component {
    return 50;
}

- (UIView *)pickerView:(UIPickerView *)pickerView viewForRow:(NSInteger)row
        forComponent:(NSInteger)component reusingView:(UIView *)view {
    UILabel* lab;
    if (view)
        lab = (UILabel*)view; // reuse it
    else
        lab = [UILabel new];
    lab.text = self.states[row];
    lab.backgroundColor = [UIColor clearColor];
    [lab sizeToFit];
    return lab;
}
```

The delegate may further configure the UIPickerView's physical appearance by means of these methods:

- `pickerView:rowHeightForComponent:`

Figure 25-5. A search bar with a search results button

- `pickerView:widthForComponent:`

The delegate may implement `pickerView:didSelectRow:inComponent:` to be notified each time the user spins a drum to a new position. You can also query the picker view directly by sending it `selectedRowInComponent:`.

You can set the value to which any drum is turned using `selectRow:in-Component:animated:`. Other handy picker view methods allow you to request that the data be reloaded, and there are properties and methods to query the picker view's contents (though of course they do not relieve you of responsibility for knowing the data model from which the picker view's contents are supplied):

- `reloadComponent:`
- `reloadAllComponents`
- `numberOfComponents`
- `numberOfRowsInComponent:`
- `viewForRow:forComponent:`

By implementing `pickerView:didSelectRow:inComponent:` and using `reload-Component:` you can make a picker view where the values displayed by one drum depend dynamically on what is selected in another. For example, one can imagine expanding our U.S. states example to include a second drum listing major cities in each state; when the user switches to a different state in the first drum, a different set of major cities appears in the second drum.

UISearchBar

A search bar (UISearchBar) is essentially a wrapper for a text field; it has a text field as one of its subviews, though there is no official access to it. It is displayed by default as a rounded rectangle containing a magnifying glass icon, where the user can enter text (Figure 25-5). It does not, of itself, do any searching or display the results of a search; a common interface involves displaying the results of a search as a table, and the UISearchDisplayController class makes this easy to do (see Chapter 21).

A search bar's current text is its `text` property. It can have a `placeholder`, which appears when there is no text. A `prompt` can be displayed above the search bar to explain its purpose. Delegate methods (UISearchBarDelegate) notify you of editing events; for their use, compare the text field and text view delegate methods discussed in Chapter 23:

- `searchBarShouldBeginEditing:`
- `searchBarTextDidBeginEditing:`
- `searchBar:textDidChange:`
- `searchBar:shouldChangeTextInRange:replacementText:`
- `searchBarShouldEndEditing:`
- `searchBarTextDidEndEditing:`

A search bar has a `barStyle`, for which your choices are `UIBarStyleDefault` or `UIBar-StyleBlack`, and either `translucent` or not. Alternatively, the search bar may have a `tintColor`. The bar style and tint color are the same as for a navigation bar or toolbar (see later in this chapter), and are drawn as a navigation bar or toolbar would draw them; thus, a search bar looks good where a navigation bar or toolbar might go.

A search bar can have a custom `backgroundImage`; this will be treated as a resizable image (that is, it will be either stretched or tiled; see Chapter 15), and overrides the bar style or tint color.

The search field area where the user enters text can be offset with respect to its background with the `searchFieldBackgroundPositionAdjustment` property; you might use this, for example, if you had enlarged the search bar's height and wanted to position the field area within that height. The text can be offset within the field area with the `searchTextPositionAdjustment` property.

You can also replace the image of the search field itself; this is the image that is normally a rounded rectangle. To do so, call `setSearchFieldBackgroundImage:forState:`. According to the documentation, the possible `state:` values are `UIControlStateNormal` and `UIControlStateDisabled`; but the API provides no way in which a search field can be disabled, so what does Apple have in mind here? The only way I've found is to cycle through the search bar's subviews, find the search field, and disable it:

```
for (UIView* v in self.sb.subviews) {
    if ([v isKindOfClass: [UITextField class]]) {
        UITextField* tf = (UITextField*)v;
        tf.enabled = NO;
        break;
    }
}
```

The search field image will be drawn in front of the background and behind the contents of the search field (such as the text); its width will be adjusted for you, but its height will not be — instead, the image is placed vertically centered where the search field needs to go, and choosing an appropriate height, and ensuring a light-colored area in the middle so the user can read the text, is up to you.

A search bar displays an internal cancel button automatically (normally an X in a circle) if there is text in the search field. Internally, at its right end, a search bar may display a search results button (showsSearchResultsButton), which may be selected or not (searchResultsButtonSelected), or a bookmark button (showsBookmarkButton); if you ask to display both, you'll get the search results button. These buttons vanish if text is entered in the search bar so that the cancel button can be displayed. There is also an option to display a Cancel button externally (showsCancelButton, or call setShows-CancelButton:animated:). The internal cancel button works automatically to remove whatever text is in the field; the other buttons do nothing, but delegate methods notify you when they are tapped:

- searchBarResultsListButtonClicked:
- searchBarBookmarkButtonClicked:
- searchBarCancelButtonClicked:

You can customize the images used for the internal left icon (the magnifying glass, by default) and any of the internal right icons (the cancel button, the search results button, and the bookmark button) with setImage:forSearchBarIcon:state:. About 20×20 seems to be a good size for the image. The icons are specified with constants:

- UISearchBarIconSearch
- UISearchBarIconClear
- UISearchBarIconBookmark
- UISearchBarIconResultsList

The documentation says that the possible state: values are UIControlStateNormal and UIControlStateDisabled, but this is wrong; the choices are UIControlState-Normal and UIControlStateHighlighted. The highlighted image appears while the user taps on the icon (except for the left icon, which isn't a button). If you don't supply a normal image, the default image is used; if you supply a normal image but no high-lighted image, the normal image is used for both. Setting searchResultsButton-Selected to YES reverses this button's behavior: it displays the highlighted image, but when the user taps it, it displays the normal image.

The position of an icon can be adjusted with setPositionAdjustment:forSearchBar-Icon:.

A search bar may also display scope buttons (see the example in Chapter 21). These are intended to let the user alter the meaning of the search; precisely how you use them is up to you. To make the scope buttons appear, use the `showsScopeBar` property; the button titles are the `scopeButtonTitles` property, and the currently selected scope button is the `selectedScopeButtonIndex` property. The delegate is notified when the user taps a different scope button:

- `searchBar:selectedScopeButtonIndexDidChange:`

The overall look of the scope bar can be heavily customized. Its background is the `scopeBarBackgroundImage`, which will be stretched or tiled as needed. To set the background of the smaller area constituting the actual buttons, call `setScopeBarButtonBackgroundImage:forState:`; the states are `UIControlStateNormal` and `UIControlStateSelected`. If you don't supply a separate selected image, a darkened version of the normal image is used. If you don't supply a resizable image, the image will be made resizable for you; the runtime decides what region of the image will be stretched behind each button.

The dividers between the buttons are normally vertical lines, but you can customize them as well: call `setScopeBarButtonDividerImage:forLeftSegmentState:rightSegmentState:`. A full complement of dividers consists of three images, one when the buttons on both sides of the divider are normal (unselected) and one each when a button on one side or the other is selected; if you supply an image for just one state combination, it is used for the other two state combinations. The height of the divider image is adjusted for you, but the width is not; you'll normally use an image just a few pixels wide.

The font attributes of the titles of the scope buttons can customized with respect to their font, color, shadow color, and shadow offset; this is done by calling `setScopeBarButtonTitleTextAttributes:forState:`. The `attributes:` argument is a dictionary whose possible keys will be used for several interface objects in this chapter, so I'll call it a *text attributes dictionary*. Don't confuse a text attributes dictionary and its keys with an attributed string attributes dictionary and *its* keys:

- `UITextAttributeFont`, a UIFont; a zero size means "the default size"
- `UITextAttributeTextColor`, a UIColor
- `UITextAttributeTextShadowColor`, a UIColor
- `UITextAttributeTextShadowOffset`, a UIOffset wrapped up as an NSValue

(All the customizing `set...` methods I've mentioned have a corresponding getter, whose name is the same without the "set" prefix.)

It may appear that there is no way to customize the external Cancel button, but in fact, although you've no official direct access to it through the search bar, the Cancel button is a UIBarButtonItem and you can customize it using the UIBarButtonItem appearance proxy, discussed later in this chapter.

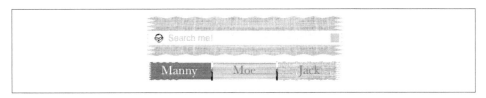

Figure 25-6. A horrible search bar

By combining the various customization possibilities, a completely unrecognizable search bar of inconceivable ugliness can easily be achieved (Figure 25-6). Let's be careful out there.

The problem of allowing the keyboard to appear without hiding the search bar is exactly as for a text field (Chapter 23). Text input properties of the search bar configure its keyboard and typing behavior like a text field as well: `keyboardType`, `autocapitalizationType`, `autocorrectionType`, and `spellCheckingType` (and, new in iOS 6, `inputAccessoryView`). When the user taps the Search key in the keyboard, the delegate is notified, and it is then up to you to dismiss the keyboard (`resignFirst-Responder`) and perform the search:

- `searchBarSearchButtonClicked:`

A common interface on the iPad is to embed a search bar as a bar button item's view in a toolbar at the top of the screen. This approach has its pitfalls; for example, there is no room for a prompt, and scope buttons or an external Cancel button may not appear either. One rather slimy workaround is to layer the search bar over the toolbar rather than having it genuinely live in the toolbar. Another is to have the search bar itself occupy the position of the toolbar at the top of the screen. On the other hand, a search bar in a toolbar that is managed by a UISearchDisplayController will automatically display search results in a popover, which can be a considerable savings of time and effort (though the popover controller is unfortunately out of your hands); see Chapter 22 for an example.

UIControl

UIControl is a subclass of UIView whose chief purpose is to be the superclass of several further built-in classes and to endow them with common behavior. These are classes representing views with which the user can interact (controls).

The most important thing that controls have in common is that they automatically track and analyze touch events (Chapter 18) and report them to your code as significant control events by way of action messages. Each control implements some subset of the possible control events. The full set of control events is listed under UIControlEvents in the Constants section of the UIControl class documentation:

- `UIControlEventTouchDown`
- `UIControlEventTouchDownRepeat`
- `UIControlEventTouchDragInside`
- `UIControlEventTouchDragOutside`
- `UIControlEventTouchDragEnter`
- `UIControlEventTouchDragExit`
- `UIControlEventTouchUpInside`
- `UIControlEventTouchUpOutside`
- `UIControlEventTouchCancel`
- `UIControlEventValueChanged`
- `UIControlEventEditingDidBegin`
- `UIControlEventEditingChanged`
- `UIControlEventEditingDidEnd`
- `UIControlEventEditingDidEndOnExit`
- `UIControlEventAllTouchEvents`
- `UIControlEventAllEditingEvents`
- `UIControlEventAllEvents`

The control events also have informal names that are visible in the Connections inspector when you're editing a nib. I'll mostly use the informal names in the next couple of paragraphs.

Control events fall roughly into three groups: the user has touched the screen (Touch Down, Touch Drag Inside, Touch Up Inside, etc.), edited text (Editing Did Begin, Editing Changed, etc.), or changed the control's value (Value Changed).

Apple's documentation is rather coy about which controls normally emit actions for which control events, so here's a list obtained through experimentation. Keep in mind that Apple's silence on this matter may mean that the details are subject to change:

UIButton
All "Touch" events.

UIDatePicker
Value Changed.

Touch Inside and Touch Outside

There is no explicit "Touch Down Inside" event, because *any* sequence of "Touch" events begins with "Touch Down," which *must* be inside the control. (If it weren't, this sequence of touches would not "belong" to the control, and there would be no control events at all.)

When the user taps within a control and starts dragging, the "Inside" events are triggered even after the drag moves outside the control's bounds. But after a certain distance from the control is exceeded, an invisible boundary is crossed, Touch Drag Exit is triggered, and now "Outside" events are reported until the drag crosses back within the invisible boundary, at which point Touch Drag Enter is triggered and the "Inside" events are reported again. In the case of a UIButton, the crossing of this invisible boundary is exactly when the button automatically unhighlights (as the drag exits). Thus, to catch a legitimate button press, you probably want to consider only Touch Up Inside.

For other controls, there may be some slight complications. For example, a UISwitch will unhighlight when a drag reaches a certain distance from it, but the touch is still considered legitimate and can still change the UISwitch's value; therefore, when the user's finger leaves the screen, the UISwitch reports a Touch Up Inside event, even while reporting Touch Drag Outside events.

UIPageControl
All "Touch" events, Value Changed.

UIRefreshControl
Value Changed.

UISegmentedControl
Value Changed.

UISlider
All "Touch" events, Value Changed.

UISwitch
All "Touch" events, Value Changed.

UIStepper
All "Touch" events, Value Changed.

UITextField
All "Touch" events except the "Up" events, and all "Editing" events (see Chapter 23 for details).

For each control event that you want to hear about automatically, you attach to the control one or more target–action pairs. You can do this in the nib (Chapter 7) or in code (Chapter 11).

For any given control, each control event and its target–action pairs form a dispatch table. The following methods permit you to manipulate and query the dispatch table:

- `addTarget:action:forControlEvents:`
- `removeTarget:action:forControlEvents:`
- `actionsForTarget:forControlEvent:`
- `allTargets`
- `allControlEvents` (a bitmask of control events to which a target–action pair is attached)

An action selector may adopt any of three signatures, whose parameters are:

- The control and the UIEvent
- The control only
- No parameters

The second signature is by far the most common. It's unlikely that you'd want to dispense altogether with the parameter telling you which control sent the control event. On the other hand, it's equally unlikely that you'd want to examine the original UIEvent that triggered this control event, since control events deliberately shield you from dealing with the nitty-gritty of touches — though you might have some reason to examine the UIEvent's `timestamp`.

When a control event occurs, the control consults its dispatch table, finds all the target–action pairs associated with that control event, and reports the control event by sending each action message to the corresponding target.

 The action messaging mechanism is actually more complex than I've just stated. The UIControl does not really send the action message directly; rather, it tells the shared application to send it. When a control wants to send an action message reporting a control event, it calls its own `sendAction:to:forEvent:` method. This in turn calls the shared application instance's `sendAction:to:from:forEvent:`, which actually sends the specified action message to the specified target. In theory, you could call or override either of these methods to customize this aspect of the message-sending architecture, but it is extremely unlikely that you would do so.

To make a control emit its action message to a particular control event right now, in code, call its `sendActionsForControlEvents:` method (which is never called automatically by the framework). For example, suppose you tell a UISwitch programmatically to change its setting from Off to On. This doesn't cause the switch to report a control event, as it would if the user had slid the switch from off to on; if you wanted it to do so, you could use `sendActionsForControlEvents:`, like this:

```
[switch setOn: YES animated: YES];
[switch sendActionsForControlEvents:UIControlEventValueChanged];
```

You might also use `sendActionsForControlEvents:` in a subclass to customize the circumstances under which a control reports control events.

A control has `enabled`, `selected`, and `highlighted` properties; any of these can be YES or NO independently of the others. These correspond to its `state`, which is reported as a bitmask of three possible values:

- `UIControlStateHighlighted`
- `UIControlStateDisabled`
- `UIControlStateSelected`

A fourth state, `UIControlStateNormal`, corresponding to a zero `state` bitmask, means that `enabled`, `selected`, and `highlighted` are all NO.

A control that is not enabled does not respond to user interaction; whether the control also portrays itself differently, to cue the user to this fact, depends upon the control. For example, a disabled UISwitch is faded. But a rounded rect text field, unless you explicitly configure it to display a different background image when disabled (Chapter 23), gives the user no cue that it is disabled. The visual nature of control selection and highlighting, too, depends on the control. Neither highlighting nor selection make any difference to the appearance of a UISwitch, but a highlighted UIButton usually looks quite different from a nonhighlighted UIButton.

A control has `contentHorizontalAlignment` and `contentVerticalAlignment` properties. Again, these matter only if the control has content that can be aligned. You are most likely to use these properties in connection with a UIButton to position its title and internal image.

A text field (UITextField) is a control; see Chapter 23. A refresh control (UIRefresh-Control) is a control; see Chapter 21. The remaining controls are covered here, and then I'll give a simple example of writing your own custom control.

Figure 25-7. A switch in iOS 5

Figure 25-8. A switch in iOS 6, with custom colors

UISwitch

A UISwitch (Figure 25-7) portrays a BOOL value: it looks like a sliding switch whose positions are labeled ON and OFF, and its on property is either YES or NO. The user can slide or tap to toggle the switch's position. When the user changes the switch's position, the switch reports a Value Changed control event. To change the on property's value with accompanying animation, call setOn:animated:.

A switch has only one size (apparently 79×27); any attempt to set its size will be ignored. A switch is not as wide, or drawn the same way, as it was in system versions before iOS 5.

Starting in iOS 5 it became possible to set a switch's onTintColor, and in iOS 6, after years of developer trickery and workarounds, Apple has at last relented and now permits you set a switch's tintColor and thumbTintColor as well. The switch in Figure 25-8 has a black onTintColor and an orange thumbTintColor; it also has a red tintColor, but you can't see that because the switch is ON.

But wait, there's more! iOS 6 also allows you set a switch's onImage and offImage. This means that you can at last legally change the words shown inside the switch. Here's how I drew the "YES" in Figure 25-9:

```
UIGraphicsBeginImageContextWithOptions(CGSizeMake(79,27), NO, 0);
[[UIColor blackColor] setFill];
UIBezierPath* p = [UIBezierPath bezierPathWithRect:CGRectMake(0,0,79,27)];
[p fill];
NSMutableParagraphStyle* para = [NSMutableParagraphStyle new];
para.alignment = NSTextAlignmentCenter;
NSAttributedString* att =
    [[NSAttributedString alloc] initWithString:@"YES" attributes:
        @{
            NSFontAttributeName:[UIFont fontWithName:@"GillSans-Bold" size:16],
            NSForegroundColorAttributeName:[UIColor whiteColor],
            NSParagraphStyleAttributeName:para
        }];
```

Figure 25-9. A switch in iOS 6, with custom words

Figure 25-10. A stepper

```
[att drawInRect:CGRectMake(0,5,79,22)];
UIImage* im = UIGraphicsGetImageFromCurrentImageContext();
UIGraphicsEndImageContext();
self.sw2.onImage = im;
```

> Don't name a UISwitch instance variable or property switch, as this is a reserved word in C.

UIStepper

A stepper (UIStepper, Figure 25-10) lets the user increase or decrease a numeric value: it looks like two buttons side by side, one labeled (by default) with a minus sign, the other with a plus sign. The user can slide a finger from one button to the other as part of the same interaction with the stepper. It has only one size (apparently 94×27). It maintains a numeric value, which is its value. Each time the user increments or decrements the value, it changes by the stepper's stepValue. If the minimumValue or maximumValue is reached, the user can go no further in that direction, and to show this, the corresponding button is disabled — unless the stepper's wraps property is YES, in which case the value goes beyond the maximum by starting again at the minimum, and *vice versa*.

As the user changes the stepper's value, a Value Changed control event is reported. Portraying the numeric value itself is up to you; you might, for example, use a label or (as in this example) a progress view:

```
- (IBAction)doStep:(UIStepper*)step {
    self.prog.progress = step.value / (step.maximumValue - step.minimumValue);
}
```

If a stepper's continuous is YES (the default), a long touch on one of the buttons will update the value repeatedly; the updates start slowly and get faster. If the stepper's autorepeat is NO, the updated value is not reported as a Value Changed control event until the entire interaction with the stepper ends; the default is YES.

Figure 25-11. A customized stepper

Starting in iOS 6, the appearance of a stepper can be customized. You can give it an overall `tintColor` instead of the default gray, and you can dictate the images that constitute its structure with these methods:

- `setDecrementImageForState:`
- `setIncrementImageForState:`
- `setDividerImage:forLeftSegmentState:rightSegmentState:`
- `setBackgroundImage:forState:`

The images work similarly to a search bar and its scope bar (described earlier in this chapter). The background images should probably be resizable (see Chapter 15). They are stretched behind both buttons, half the image being seen as the background of each button. If the button is disabled (because we've reached the value's limit in that direction), it displays the `UIControlStateDisabled` background image; otherwise, it displays the `UIControlStateNormal` background image, except that it displays the `UIControlStateHighlighted` background image while the user is tapping it. You'll probably want to provide all three background images if you're going to provide any; the default (or the tint) is used if a state's background image is nil. You'll probably want to provide three divider images as well, to cover the three combinations normal left and normal right, highlighted left and normal right, and normal left and highlighted right. The increment and decrement images are composited on top of the background image; at a minimum, you'll provide a `UIControlStateNormal` image, which will be adjusted automatically for the other two states, though of course you can provide all three images for each button. Figure 25-10 shows a customized stepper.

UIPageControl

A UIPageControl is a row of dots; each dot is called a *page*, because it is intended to be used in conjunction with some other interface that portrays something analogous to pages, such as a UIScrollView with its `pagingEnabled` set to YES. Coordinating the page control with this other interface is usually up to you; see Chapter 20 for an example and Figure 20-3 for an illustration. A UIPageViewController in scroll style can optionally display a page control that's automatically coordinated with its content (Chapter 19).

The dot colors differentiate the current page, the page control's `currentPage`, from the others; by default, the current page is portrayed as a solid dot, while the others are slightly transparent. Starting in iOS 6, you can customize a page control's `pageIndicatorTint-Color`, the color of the dots in general, and `currentPageIndicatorTintColor`, the color of the current dot.

The number of dots is the page control's `numberOfPages`; this should be small, as the dots need to fit within the page control's bounds. The user can tap to one side or the other of the current page's dot to increment or decrement the current page; the page control then reports a Value Changed control event. You can make the page control wider than the dots to increase the target region on which the user can tap. (You can make the page control taller as well, but only the horizontal component of a tap is taken into account, so this would probably be pointless as well as confusing to the user.) To learn the minimum size required for a given number of pages, call `sizeForNumberOf-Pages:`.

If a page control's `hidesForSinglePage` is YES, the page control becomes invisible when its `numberOfPages` changes to 1.

If a page control's `defersCurrentPageDisplay` is YES, then when the user taps to increment or decrement the page control's value, the display of the current page is not changed. A Value Changed control event is reported, but it is up to your code to handle this action and call `updateCurrentPageDisplay`. A case in point might be if the user's changing the current page starts an animation, but you don't want the current page dot to change until the animation ends.

UIDatePicker

A date picker (UIDatePicker) looks like a UIPickerView (discussed earlier in this chapter), but it is not a UIPickerView subclass; it uses a UIPickerView to draw itself, but it provides no official access to that picker view. Its purpose is to express the notion of a date and time, taking care of the calendrical and numerical complexities so that you don't have to. When the user changes its setting, the date picker reports a Value Changed control event.

A UIDatePicker has one of four modes (`datePickerMode`), determining how it is drawn:

UIDatePickerModeTime
> The date picker displays a time; for example, it has an hour component and a minutes component.

UIDatePickerModeDate
> The date picker displays a date; for example, it has a month component, a day component, and a year component.

`UIDatePickerModeDateAndTime`
> The date picker displays a date and time; for example, it has a component showing day of the week, month, and day, plus an hour component and a minutes component.

`UIDatePickerModeCountDownTimer`
> The date picker displays a number of hours and minutes; for example, it has an hours component and a minutes component.

Exactly what components a date picker displays, and what values they contain, depends by default upon system settings. For example, a U.S. time displays an hour (numbered 1 through 12), minutes, and AM or PM, but a British time displays an hour (numbered 1 through 24) and minutes. If your app contains a date picker displaying a time, and the user changes the system region format on the device from United States to United Kingdom, the date picker's display will change immediately, eliminating the AM/PM component and changing the hour numbers to run from 1 to 24.

A date picker has `calendar` and `timeZone` properties, respectively an NSCalendar and an NSTimeZone; these are nil by default, meaning that the date picker responds to the user's system-level settings. You can also change these values manually; for example, if you live in California and you set a date picker's `timeZone` to GMT, the displayed time is shifted forward by 8 hours, so that 11 AM is displayed as 7 PM (if it is winter).

 Don't change the `timeZone` of a `UIDatePickerModeCountDownTimer` date picker, or the displayed value will be shifted and you will confuse the heck out of yourself and your users.

The minutes component, if there is one, defaults to showing every minute, but you can change this with the `minuteInterval` property. The maximum value is 30, in which case the minutes component values are 0 and 30. An attempt to set a value that doesn't divide evenly into 60 will be silently ignored.

The maximum and minimum values enabled in the date picker are determined by its `maximumDate` and `minimumDate` properties. Values outside this range may appear disabled. There isn't really any practical limit on the range that a date picker can display, because the "drums" representing its components are not physical, and values are added dynamically as the user spins them. In this example, we set the initial minimum and maximum dates of a date picker (dp) to the beginning and end of 1954. We also set the actual `date`, because otherwise the date picker will appear initially set to now, which will be disabled because it isn't within the minimum–maximum range:

```
NSDateComponents* dc = [NSDateComponents new];
[dc setYear:1954];
[dc setMonth:1];
[dc setDay:1];
```

```
NSCalendar* c =
    [[NSCalendar alloc] initWithCalendarIdentifier:NSGregorianCalendar];
NSDate* d = [c dateFromComponents:dc];
dp.minimumDate = d;
dp.date = d;
[dc setYear:1955];
d = [c dateFromComponents:dc];
dp.maximumDate = d;
```

 Don't set the maximumDate and minimumDate properties values for a UIDatePickerModeCountDownTimer date picker, or you might cause a crash with an out-of-range exception.

The date represented by a date picker (unless its mode is UIDatePickerModeCountDown-Timer) is its date property, an NSDate. The default date is now, at the time the date picker is instantiated. For a UIDatePickerModeDate date picker, the time by default is 12 AM (midnight), local time; for a UIDatePickerModeTime date picker, the date by default is today. The internal value is reckoned in the local time zone, so it may be different from the displayed value, if you have changed the date picker's timeZone.

The value represented by a UIDatePickerModeCountDownTimer date picker is its count-DownDuration. The minimum countDownDuration a countdown date picker will report is 1 minute. If the minuteInterval is more than 1, and if the date picker reports 1 minute, you should deduce that the user has set the timer to zero. (This is probably a bug; the user should not be able to set the timer to zero!)

The date picker does not actually do any counting down; you are expected to use some other interface to display the countdown. The Timer tab of Apple's Clock app shows a typical interface; the user configures the date picker to set the countDownDuration initially, but once the counting starts, the date picker is hidden and a label displays the remaining time. The countDownDuration is an NSTimeInterval, which is a double representing a number of seconds; converting to hours and minutes is up to you. You could use the built-in calendrical classes:

```
NSTimeInterval t = datePicker.countDownDuration;
NSDate* d = [NSDate dateWithTimeIntervalSinceReferenceDate:t];
NSCalendar* c =
    [[NSCalendar alloc] initWithCalendarIdentifier:NSGregorianCalendar];
[c setTimeZone: [NSTimeZone timeZoneForSecondsFromGMT:0]]; // normalize
NSUInteger units = NSHourCalendarUnit | NSMinuteCalendarUnit;
NSDateComponents* dc = [c components:units fromDate:d];
NSLog(@"%i hr, %i min", [dc hour], [dc minute]);
```

Similarly, to convert between an NSDate and a string, you'll need an NSDateFormatter (see Chapter 10, and Apple's *Date and Time Programming Guide*):

```
NSDate* d = datePicker.date;
NSDateFormatter* df = [NSDateFormatter new];
[df setTimeStyle:kCFDateFormatterFullStyle];
[df setDateStyle:kCFDateFormatterFullStyle];
NSLog(@"%@", [df stringFromDate:d]);
// "Tuesday, August 10, 1954, 3:16:25 AM GMT-07:00"
```

UISlider

A slider (UISlider) is an expression of a continuously settable value (its `value`) between some minimum and maximum (its `minimumValue` and `maximumValue`; they are 0 and 1 by default). It is portrayed as an object, the *thumb*, positioned along a *track*. As the user changes the thumb's position, the slider reports a Value Changed control event; it may do this continuously as the user presses and drags the thumb (if the slider's `continuous` is YES, the default) or only when the user releases the thumb (if its `continuous` is NO). While the user is pressing on the thumb, the slider is in the `highlighted` state. To change the slider's value with animation, call `setValue:animated:`.

A commonly expressed desire is to modify a slider's behavior so that if the user taps on its track, the slider moves to the spot where the user tapped. Unfortunately, a slider does not, of itself, respond to taps on its track; such a tap doesn't even cause it to report a Touch Up Inside. However, with a gesture recognizer, most things are possible; here's the action handler for a UITapGestureRecognizer attached to a UISlider:

```
- (void) tapped: (UIGestureRecognizer*) g {
    UISlider* s = (UISlider*)g.view;
    if (s.highlighted)
        return; // tap on thumb, let slider deal with it
    CGPoint pt = [g locationInView: s];
    CGRect track = [s trackRectForBounds:s.bounds];
    if (!CGRectContainsPoint(CGRectInset(track, 0, -10), pt))
        return; // not on track, forget it
    CGFloat percentage = pt.x / s.bounds.size.width;
    CGFloat delta = percentage * (s.maximumValue - s.minimumValue);
    CGFloat value = s.minimumValue + delta;
    [s setValue:value animated:YES];
}
```

To customize a slider's appearance, you can change the color of the thumb and the track on either side of it (`thumbTintColor`, `minimumTrackTintColor`, and `maximumTint-Color`), or you can go even further and provide your own thumb image and your own track image, along with images to appear at each end of the track, and you can override in a subclass the methods that position these.

The images at the ends of the track are the slider's `minimumValueImage` and `maximum-ValueImage`, and they are nil by default. If you set them to actual images (which can also be done in the nib), the slider will attempt to position them within its own bounds,

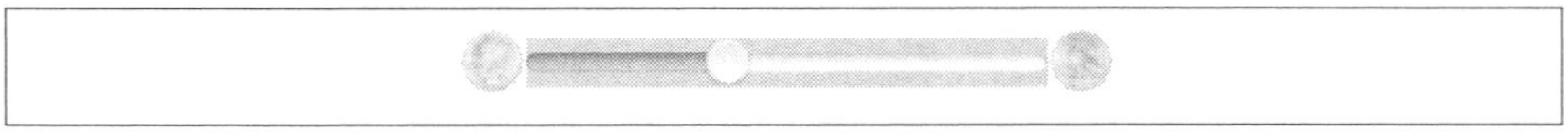

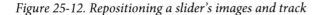

Figure 25-12. Repositioning a slider's images and track

shrinking the drawing of the track to compensate. The slider does not clip its subviews by default, so the images can extend outside the slider's bounds.

For example, suppose the slider's dimensions are 250×23 (the standard height), and suppose the images are 30×30. Then the minimum image is drawn with its origin at {0,-4} — its left edge matches the slider's left edge, and its top is raised so that the center of its height matches the center of the slider's height — and the maximum image is drawn with its origin at {220,-4}. But the track is drawn with a width of only 164 pixels, instead of the normal 246; instead of being nearly the full width of the slider, the track is contracted to allow room for the images.

You can change these dimensions by overriding minimumValueImageRectForBounds:, maximumValueImageRectForBounds:, and trackRectForBounds: in a subclass. The bounds passed in are the slider's bounds. In this example, we expand the track width to the full width of the slider, and draw the images outside the slider's bounds (Figure 25-12; I've given the slider a gray background color so you can see how the track and images are related to its bounds):

```
- (CGRect)maximumValueImageRectForBounds:(CGRect)bounds {
    CGRect result = [super maximumValueImageRectForBounds:bounds];
    result = CGRectOffset(result, 31, 0);
    return result;
}

- (CGRect)minimumValueImageRectForBounds:(CGRect)bounds {
    CGRect result = [super minimumValueImageRectForBounds:bounds];
    result = CGRectOffset(result, -31, 0);
    return result;
}

- (CGRect)trackRectForBounds:(CGRect)bounds {
    CGRect result = [super trackRectForBounds:bounds];
    result.origin.x = 0;
    result.size.width = bounds.size.width;
    return result;
}
```

The thumb is also an image, and you set it with setThumbImage:forState:. There are two chiefly relevant states, UIControlStateNormal and UIControlStateHighlighted, so if you supply images for both, the thumb will change automatically while the user is dragging it. If you supply just an image for the normal state, the thumb image won't change while the user is dragging it. By default, the image will be centered in the track

Figure 25-13. Replacing a slider's thumb

at the point represented by the slider's current value; you can shift this position by overriding `thumbRectForBounds:trackRect:value:` in a subclass. In this example, the image is repositioned upward slightly (Figure 25-13):

```
- (CGRect)thumbRectForBounds:(CGRect)bounds
                    trackRect:(CGRect)rect value:(float)value {
    CGRect result =
        [super thumbRectForBounds:bounds trackRect:rect value:value];
    result = CGRectOffset(result, 0, -7);
    return result;
}
```

Enlarging a slider's thumb can mislead the user as to the area on which it can be tapped to drag it. The slider, not the thumb, is the touchable UIControl; only the part of the thumb that intersects the slider's bounds will be draggable. The user may try to drag the part of the thumb that is drawn outside the slider's bounds, and will fail (and be confused). A solution is to increase the slider's height; you can't do this in the nib editor, but you can do it in code.

The track is two images, one appearing to the left of the thumb, the other to its right. They are set with `setMinimumTrackImage:forState:` and `setMaximumTrackImage:forState:`. If you supply images both for normal state and for highlighted state, the images will change while the user is dragging the thumb.

The images should be resizable (Chapter 15), because that's how the slider cleverly makes it look like the user is dragging the thumb along a single static track. In reality, there are two images; as the user drags the thumb, one image grows horizontally and the other shrinks horizontally. For the left track image, the right end cap inset will be partially or entirely hidden under the thumb; for the right track image, the left end cap inset will be partially or entirely hidden under the thumb. Figure 25-14 shows a track derived from a single 15×15 image of a circular object (a coin):

```
UIImage* coin = [UIImage imageNamed: @"coin.png"];
UIImage* coinEnd = [coin resizableImageWithCapInsets:UIEdgeInsetsMake(0,7,0,7)
                                        resizingMode:UIImageResizingModeStretch];
[slider setMinimumTrackImage:coinEnd forState:UIControlStateNormal];
[slider setMaximumTrackImage:coinEnd forState:UIControlStateNormal];
```

Figure 25-14. Replacing a slider's track

Figure 25-15. A segmented control

UISegmentedControl

A segmented control (UISegmentedControl, Figure 25-15) is a row of tappable segments; a segment is rather like a button. This provides a way for the user to choose among several related options. By default (momentary is NO), the most recently tapped segment remains selected. Alternatively (momentary is YES), the tapped segment is shown as highlighted momentarily (by default, highlighted is indistinguishable from selected, but you can change that); afterward, however, no segment selection is displayed, though internally the tapped segment remains the selected segment.

The selected segment can be retrieved with the selectedSegmentIndex property; it can also be set with the selectedSegmentIndex property, and remains visibly selected (even for a momentary segmented control). A selectedSegmentIndex value of UISegmented-ControlNoSegment means no segment is selected. When the user taps a segment that is not already visibly selected, the segmented control reports a Value Changed event.

A segment can be separately enabled or disabled with setEnabled:forSegmentAt-Index:, and its enabled state can be retrieved with isEnabledForSegmentAtIndex:. A disabled segment, by default, is drawn faded; the user can't tap it, but it can still be selected in code.

A segment has either a title or an image; when one is set, the other becomes nil. The methods for setting and fetching the title and image for existing segments are:

- setTitle:forSegmentAtIndex:
- setImage:forSegmentAtIndex:
- titleForSegmentAtIndex:
- imageForSegmentAtIndex:

You will also want to set the title or image when creating the segment. You can do this in code if you're creating the segmented control from scratch, with initWithItems:, which takes an array each item of which is either a string or an image.

Methods for managing segments dynamically are:

- insertSegmentWithTitle:atIndex:animated:
- insertSegmentWithImage:atIndex:animated:
- removeSegmentAtIndex:animated:
- removeAllSegments

The number of segments can be retrieved with the read-only numberOfSegments property.

A segment's width is adjusted automatically when you create it or call sizeToFit, or you can set it manually with setWidth:forSegmentAtIndex: (and retrieve it with width-ForSegmentAtIndex:). Alternatively, if you set a segment's width to 0, the system will adjust the width for you if the segmented control's apportionsSegmentWidthsBy-Content property is YES. If you're using autolayout (Chapter 14), the segmented control's width constraint (which will exist if the segmented control is created in a nib or storyboard) must have its priority reduced to less than 750 for its width to adjust itself automatically.

You can also change the position of the content (title or image) within a segment. To set this position in code, call setContentOffset:forSegmentAtIndex: (and retrieve it with contentOffsetForSegmentAtIndex:), where the offset is expressed as a CGSize describing how much to move the content from its default centered position.

A segmented control's height is standard in accordance with its style. You can change a segmented control's height in code (if you're using autolayout, this would involve adding a height constraint), but if you later call sizeToFit, it will resume its standard height. A more coherent way to change a segmented control's height is to set its background image, as I'll describe in a moment.

A segmented control comes in a choice of styles (its segmentedControlStyle):

UISegmentedControlStylePlain
: Large default height (44 pixels) and large titles. Deselected segments are gray; the selected segment is blue and has a depressed look.

UISegmentedControlStyleBordered
: Just like UISegmentedControlStylePlain, but a dark border emphasizes the segmented control's outline.

`UISegmentedControlStyleBar`
> Small default height (30 pixels) and small titles. All segments are blue, but you can change this by setting the `tintColor`; the selected segment is slightly darker.

 A fourth style, `UISegmentedControlStyleBezeled`, is deprecated (in the header) and appears to be no longer available. This is a pity, as it was a nice style, with a large default height (44 pixels) and small titles, and could be tinted with the `tintColor`.

Further methods for customizing a segmented control's appearance are parallel to those for setting the look of a stepper or the scope bar portion of a search bar, both described earlier in this chapter. You can set the overall background, the divider image, the text attributes for the segment titles, and the position of segment contents:

- `setBackgroundImage:forState:barMetrics:`
- `setDividerImage:forLeftSegmentState:rightSegmentState:barMetrics:`
- `setTitleTextAttributes:forState:`
- `setContentPositionAdjustment:forSegmentType:barMetrics:`

You don't have to customize for every state, as the segmented control will use the normal state setting for the states you don't specify. As I mentioned a moment ago, setting a background image is a robust way to change a segmented control's height. Here's the code that achieved Figure 25-16; selecting a segment automatically darkens the background image for us (similar to a button's `adjustsImageWhenHighlighted`, described in the next section), so there's no need to specify a separate selected image:

```
// background, set desired height but make width resizable
// sufficient to set for Normal only
UIImage* image = [UIImage imageNamed: @"linen.png"];
CGFloat w = 100;
CGFloat h = 60;
UIGraphicsBeginImageContextWithOptions(CGSizeMake(w,h), NO, 0);
[image drawInRect:CGRectMake(0,0,w,h)];
UIImage* image2 = UIGraphicsGetImageFromCurrentImageContext();
UIGraphicsEndImageContext();
UIImage* image3 =
    [image2 resizableImageWithCapInsets:UIEdgeInsetsMake(0,10,0,10)
                          resizingMode:UIImageResizingModeStretch];
[self.seg setBackgroundImage:image3 forState:UIControlStateNormal
                barMetrics:UIBarMetricsDefault];

// segment images, redraw at final size
NSArray* pep = @[@"manny.jpg", @"moe.jpg", @"jack.jpg"];
for (int i = 0; i < 3; i++) {
    UIImage* image = [UIImage imageNamed: pep[i]];
```

Figure 25-16. A segmented control, customized

```
    UIGraphicsBeginImageContextWithOptions(CGSizeMake(30,30), NO, 0);
    [image drawInRect:CGRectMake(0,0,30,30)];
    UIImage* image2 = UIGraphicsGetImageFromCurrentImageContext();
    UIGraphicsEndImageContext();
    [self.seg setImage:image2 forSegmentAtIndex:i];
}

// divider, set at desired width, sufficient to set for Normal only
UIGraphicsBeginImageContextWithOptions(CGSizeMake(1,10), NO, 0);
[[UIColor whiteColor] set];
CGContextFillRect(UIGraphicsGetCurrentContext(), CGRectMake(0,0,1,10));
UIImage* div = UIGraphicsGetImageFromCurrentImageContext();
UIGraphicsEndImageContext();
[self.seg setDividerImage:div
        forLeftSegmentState:UIControlStateNormal
        rightSegmentState:UIControlStateNormal
               barMetrics:UIBarMetricsDefault];
```

The `segmentType:` parameter in `setContentPositionAdjustment:forSegment-Type:barMetrics:` is needed because, by default, the segments at the two extremes have rounded ends (and, if a segment is the lone segment, both its ends are rounded). The argument allows you distinguish between the various possibilities:

- `UISegmentedControlSegmentAny`

- `UISegmentedControlSegmentLeft`

- `UISegmentedControlSegmentCenter`

- `UISegmentedControlSegmentRight`

- `UISegmentedControlSegmentAlone`

The `barMetrics:` parameter will recur later in this chapter, in the discussion of navigation bars, toolbars, and bar button items; for a segmented control, its value matters only if the segmented control has `UISegmentedControlStyleBar` and only if it is being used inside a navigation bar or toolbar. Otherwise, use `UIBarMetricsDefault`. See "Landscape iPhone Bar Metrics" (page 875) for more information.

UIButton

A button (UIButton) is a fundamental tappable control; its appearance is extremely flexible. It is endowed at creation with a type. The code creation method is a class method, buttonWithType:. The types are:

UIButtonTypeCustom

> Could be completely invisible, if the backgroundColor is clearColor and there's no title or other content. If a backgroundColor is supplied, a thin, subtle rectangular border is also present; you can add more of a border by modifying the button's layer. Alternatively, you can provide a background image, thus making the button appear to be any shape you like (though this does not automatically affect its tappable region).

UIButtonTypeDetailDisclosure
UIButtonTypeContactAdd
UIButtonTypeInfoLight
UIButtonTypeInfoDark

> Basically, these are all UIButtonTypeCustom buttons whose image is set automatically to standard button images: a right-pointing chevron, a plus sign, a light letter "i," and a dark letter "i," respectively.

UIButtonTypeRoundedRect

> A rounded rectangle with a white background and an antialiased gray border. However, supplying a rectangular opaque background image results in a rectangle similar to a UIButtonTypeCustom button. (A rounded rect button is actually an instance of a UIButton subclass, UIRoundedRectButton, but you're probably not supposed to know that.)

> A rounded rect button can have a tintColor which fills the button only while the button is highlighted.

A button has a title, a title color, and a title shadow color. In iOS 6, you can supply instead an attributed title, thus dictating these features and more in a single value through an NSAttributedString (Chapter 23).

Distinguish a button's image from its background image. The background image, if any, is stretched to fit the button's bounds. The image, on the other hand, if smaller than the button, is not resized, and is thus shown internally within the button. The button can have both a title and an image, if the image is small enough; in that case, the image is shown to the left of the title by default.

These six features (title, title color, title shadow color, attributed title, image, and background image) can all be made to vary depending on the button's current state: UIControlStateHighlighted, UIControlStateSelected, UIControlStateDisabled, and UIControlStateNormal. The button can be in more than one state at once, except for `UIControlStateNormal` which effectively means "none of the other states". A state change, whether automatic (the button is highlighted while the user is tapping it) or programmatically imposed, will thus in and of itself alter a button's appearance. To make this possible, the methods for setting these button features all involve specifying a corresponding state — or multiple states, using a bitmask:

- `setTitle:forState:`
- `setTitleColor:forState:` (by default, the title color is white when the button is highlighted)
- `setTitleShadowColor:forState:`
- `setAttributedTitle:forState:`
- `setImage:forState:`
- `setBackgroundImage:forState:`

Similarly, when getting these button features, you must either use a method to specify a single state you're interested in or use a property to ask about the feature as currently displayed:

- `titleForState:`
- `titleColorForState:`
- `titleShadowColorForState:`
- `attributedTitleForState:`
- `imageForState:`
- `backgroundImageForState:`
- `currentTitle`
- `currentTitleColor`
- `currentTitleShadowColor`
- `currentAttributedTitle`
- `currentImage`
- `currentBackgroundImage`

If you don't specify a feature for a particular state, or if the button adopts more than one state at once, an internal heuristic is used to determine what to display. I can't describe all possible combinations, but here are some general observations:

- If you specify a feature for a particular state (highlighted, selected, or disabled), and the button is in *only* that state, that feature will be used.

- If you *don't* specify a feature for a particular state (highlighted, selected, or disabled), and the button is in *only* that state, the normal version of that feature will be used as fallback. (That's why many examples earlier in this book have assigned a title for UIControlStateNormal only; this is sufficient to give the button a title in every state.)

- Combinations of states often cause the button to fall back on the feature for normal state. For example, if a button is both highlighted and selected, the button will display its normal title, even if it has a highlighted title, a selected title, or both.

Don't try to use an attributed title for one state and a plain string title for another state; if you're going to use an attributed title at all, use an attributed title for every state whose title you set. If you set an attributed title for the normal state, you won't automatically get a white version of that title for the highlighted state. This is not surprising, since all of this is being handled by a UILabel (see Chapter 23), the button's titleLabel; I'll talk more about it in a moment.

In this example, we modify an existing button with an image and a title, so as to use an attributed title instead (Figure 25-17). To get the white color when highlighted, we supply a second version of the same string. I'll show how the background image was achieved later in this section:

```
NSMutableAttributedString* mas =
    [[NSMutableAttributedString alloc]
        initWithString:self.button.currentTitle
            attributes: @{
                NSFontAttributeName:
                    self.button.titleLabel.font,
                NSForegroundColorAttributeName:
                    self.button.titleLabel.textColor
            }
    ];
[mas addAttributes:
    @{
        NSStrokeColorAttributeName:[UIColor redColor],
        NSStrokeWidthAttributeName:@(-2.0),
        NSUnderlineStyleAttributeName:@1
    } range:NSMakeRange(4,mas.length-4)];
[self.button setAttributedTitle:mas forState:UIControlStateNormal];

mas = [mas mutableCopy];
[mas setAttributes:
    @{
        NSForegroundColorAttributeName:[UIColor whiteColor]
    } range:NSMakeRange(0,mas.length)];
[self.button setAttributedTitle:mas forState:UIControlStateHighlighted];
```

In addition, a UIButton has some properties determining how it draws itself in various states, which can save you the trouble of specifying different images for different states:

Figure 25-17. A button with an attributed title

Figure 25-18. A button with highlighted glow

showsTouchWhenHighlighted

> If YES, then the button projects a circular white glow when highlighted. If the button has an internal image, the glow is centered behind it (Figure 25-18); thus, this feature is suitable particularly if the button image is small and circular; for example, it's the default behavior for a UIButtonTypeInfoLight or UIButtonTypeInfoDark button. (If the button has no internal image, the glow is centered at the button's center.) The glow is drawn on top of the background image or color, if any.

adjustsImageWhenHighlighted

> If YES (the default), then if there is no separate highlighted image (and if shows-TouchWhenHighlighted is NO), the normal image is darkened when the button is highlighted. This applies equally to the internal image and the background image.

adjustsImageWhenDisabled

> If YES (the default), then if there is no separate disabled image, the normal image is lightened (faded) when the button is disabled. This applies equally to the internal image and the background image.

A button has a natural size in relation to its contents. If you're using autolayout, the button can adopt that size automatically, as its intrinsicContentSize; if not, then if you create a button in code, you'll ultimately want to send sizeToFit to the button (or give it an explicit size), as shown in examples in Chapter 17, Chapter 19, and Chapter 21 — otherwise, the button will have a zero size and you'll be left wondering why your button hasn't appeared in the interface.

The title is a UILabel (Chapter 23), and the label features of the title can be accessed through the button's titleLabel. Thus, for example, you can set the title's font, line-BreakMode, and shadowOffset. If the shadowOffset is not {0,0}, then the title has a shadow, and the title shadow color feature comes into play; the button's reversesTitle-ShadowWhenHighlighted property also applies: if YES, the shadowOffset values are replaced with their additive inverses when the button is highlighted. Similarly, you can manipulate the label's wrapping behavior to make the button's title consist of multiple lines.

The internal image is drawn by a UIImageView (Chapter 15) whose features can be accessed through the button's imageView. Thus, for example, you can change the internal image view's alpha to make the image more transparent.

The internal position of the image and title as a whole are governed by the button's contentVerticalAlignment and contentHorizontalAlignment (inherited from UI-Control). You can also tweak the position of the image and title, together or separately, by setting the button's contentEdgeInsets, titleEdgeInsets, or imageEdgeInsets. Increasing an inset component increases that margin; thus, for example, a positive top component makes the distance between that object and the top of the button larger than normal (where "normal" is where the object would be according to the alignment settings). The titleEdgeInsets or imageEdgeInsets values are added to the overall contentEdgeInsets values. So, for example, if you really wanted to, you could make the internal image appear to the right of the title by decreasing the left titleEdge-Insets and increasing the left imageEdgeInsets.

Four methods also provide access to the button's positioning of its elements:

- titleRectForContentRect:
- imageRectForContentRect:
- contentRectForBounds:
- backgroundRectForBounds:

These methods are called whenever the button is redrawn, including every time it changes state. The content rect is the area in which the title and image are placed. By default, contentRectForBounds: and backgroundRectForBounds: yield the same result.

You can override these methods in a subclass to change the way the button's elements are positioned. In this example, we shrink the button slightly when highlighted (as shown in Figure 25-18) as a way of providing feedback:

```
- (CGRect)backgroundRectForBounds:(CGRect)bounds {
    CGRect result = [super backgroundRectForBounds:bounds];
    if (self.highlighted)
        result = CGRectInset(result, 3, 3);
    return result;
}
```

A button's background image is stretched if the image is smaller, in both dimensions, than the button's backgroundRectForBounds:. You can take advantage of this stretching, for example, to construct a rounded rectangle background for the button by supplying a resizable image. In this example, which generates Figure 25-17 and Figure 25-18, both the internal image and the background image are generated from the same image (which is in fact the same image used to generate the track in Figure 25-14):

```
UIImage* im = [UIImage imageNamed: @"coin2.png"];
CGSize sz = [im size];
UIImage* im2 =
    [im resizableImageWithCapInsets:
        UIEdgeInsetsMake(
            sz.height/2.0, sz.width/2.0, sz.height/2.0, sz.width/2.0)
                    resizingMode:UIImageResizingModeStretch];
[self.button setBackgroundImage: im2 forState: UIControlStateNormal];
self.button.backgroundColor = [UIColor clearColor];
```

Custom Controls

The UIControl class implements several touch-tracking methods that you might override in order to customize a built-in UIControl type or to create your own UIControl subclass, along with properties that tell you whether touch tracking is going on:

- `beginTrackingWithTouch:withEvent:`
- `continueTrackingWithTouch:withEvent:`
- `endTrackingWithTouch:withEvent:`
- `cancelTrackingWithEvent:`
- `tracking` (property)
- `touchInside` (property)

With the advent of gesture recognizers (Chapter 18), such direct involvement with touch tracking is probably less needed than it used to be, especially if your purpose is to modify the behavior of a built-in UIControl subclass. So, to illustrate their use, I'll give a simple example of creating a custom control. The main reason for doing this (rather than using, say, a UIView and gesture recognizers) would probably be to obtain the convenience of control events. Also, the touch-tracking methods, though not as high-level as gesture recognizers, are at least a level up from the UIResponder `touches...` methods (Chapter 18): they track a single touch, and both `beginTracking...` and `continueTracking...` return a BOOL, giving you a chance to stop tracking the current touch.

We'll build a simplified knob control (Figure 25-19). The control starts life at its minimum position, with an internal angle value of 0; it can be rotated clockwise with a single finger as far as its maximum position, with an internal angle value of 5 (radians). To keep things simple, the words "Min" and "Max" appearing in the interface are actually labels; the control just draws the knob, and to rotate it we'll apply a rotation transform.

Figure 25-19. A custom control

Our control is a UIControl subclass, MyKnob. It has a CGFloat `angle` property, and a CGFloat instance variable `_initialAngle` that we'll use internally during rotation. Because a UIControl is a UIView, it can draw itself, which it does with a UIImage included in our app bundle:

```
- (void) drawRect:(CGRect)rect {
    UIImage* knob = [UIImage imageNamed:@"knob.png"];
    [knob drawInRect:rect];
}
```

We'll need a utility function for transforming a touch's Cartesian coordinates into polar coordinates, giving us the angle to be applied as a rotation to the view:

```
static CGFloat pToA (UITouch* touch, UIView* self) {
    CGPoint loc = [touch locationInView: self];
    CGPoint c = CGPointMake(CGRectGetMidX(self.bounds),
                            CGRectGetMidY(self.bounds));
    return atan2(loc.y - c.y, loc.x - c.x);
}
```

Now we're ready to override the tracking methods. `beginTrackingWithTouch:with-Event:` simply notes down the angle of the initial touch location. `continueTracking-WithTouch:withEvent:` uses the difference between the current touch location's angle and the initial touch location's angle to apply a transform to the view, and updates the `angle` property. `endTrackingWithTouch:withEvent:` triggers the Value Changed control event. So our first draft looks like this:

```
- (BOOL) beginTrackingWithTouch:(UITouch*)touch withEvent:(UIEvent*)event {
    self->_initialAngle = pToA(touch, self);
    return YES;
}

- (BOOL) continueTrackingWithTouch:(UITouch*)touch withEvent:(UIEvent*)event {
    CGFloat ang = pToA(touch, self);
    ang -= self->_initialAngle;
    CGFloat absoluteAngle = self->_angle + ang;
    self.transform = CGAffineTransformRotate(self.transform, ang);
    self->_angle = absoluteAngle;
```

```
        return YES;
    }

    - (void) endTrackingWithTouch:(UITouch *)touch withEvent:(UIEvent *)event {
        [self sendActionsForControlEvents:UIControlEventValueChanged];
    }
```

This works: we can put a MyKnob into the interface and hook up its Value Changed control event (this can be done in the nib editor), and sure enough, when we run the app, we can rotate the knob and, when our finger lifts from the knob, the Value Changed action handler is called. However, `continueTrackingWithTouch:withEvent:` needs modification.

First, we need to peg the minimum and maximum rotation at 0 and 5, respectively. For simplicity, we'll just stop tracking, by returning NO, if the rotation goes below 0 or above 5, fixing the angle at the exceeded limit. However, because we're no longer tracking, `end-Tracking...` will never be called, so we also need to trigger the Value Changed control event. (Doubtless you can come up with a more sophisticated way of pegging the knob at its minimum and maximum, but remember, this is only a simple example.) Second, it might be nice to give the programmer the option to have the Value Changed control event reported continuously as `continueTracking...` is called repeatedly. So we'll add a `continuous` BOOL property and obey it.

Here, then, is our revised `continueTracking...` implementation:

```
    - (BOOL) continueTrackingWithTouch:(UITouch*)touch withEvent:(UIEvent*)event {
        CGFloat ang = pToA(touch, self);
        ang -= self->_initialAngle;
        CGFloat absoluteAngle = self->_angle + ang;
        if (absoluteAngle < 0) {
            self.transform = CGAffineTransformIdentity;
            self->_angle = 0;
            [self sendActionsForControlEvents:UIControlEventValueChanged];
            return NO;
        }
        if (absoluteAngle > 5) {
            self.transform = CGAffineTransformMakeRotation(5);
            self->_angle = 5;
            [self sendActionsForControlEvents:UIControlEventValueChanged];
            return NO;
        }
        self.transform = CGAffineTransformRotate(self.transform, ang);
        self->_angle = absoluteAngle;
        if (self->continuous)
            [self sendActionsForControlEvents:UIControlEventValueChanged];
        return YES;
    }
```

Finally, we'll probably want to be able to set the angle programmatically as a way of rotating the knob:

```
- (void) setAngle: (CGFloat) ang {
    if (ang < 0)
        ang = 0;
    if (ang > 5)
        ang = 5;
    self.transform = CGAffineTransformMakeRotation(ang);
    self->_angle = ang;
}
```

This is more work than using a gesture recognizer (which is left as an exercise for the reader), but not much, and it gives a sense of what's involved in creating a custom control.

Bars

As you saw in Chapter 19, the three bar types — UINavigationBar, UIToolbar, and UITabBar — are often used in conjunction with a built-in view controller:

- A UINavigationController has a UINavigationBar.
- A UINavigationController has a UIToolbar.
- A UITabBarController has a UITabBar.

You can also use these bar types independently. You are most likely to do that with a UIToolbar, which is often used as an independent bottom bar. On the iPad, it can also be used as a top bar, adopting a role analogous to a menu bar on the desktop. That's such a common interface, in fact, that certain special automatic behaviors are associated with it; for example, a UISearchBar in a UIToolbar and managed by a UISearchDisplay-Controller will automatically display its search results table in a popover (Chapter 22), which is different from what happens if the UISearchBar is *not* in a UIToolbar.

This section summarizes the facts about the three bar types and the items that populate them.

UINavigationBar

A UINavigationBar is populated by UINavigationItems. The UINavigationBar maintains a stack; UINavigationItems are pushed onto and popped off of this stack. Whatever UINavigationItem is currently topmost in the stack (the UINavigationBar's topItem), in combination with the UINavigationItem just beneath it in the stack (the UINavigationBar's backItem), determines what appears in the navigation bar:

- The title (string) or titleView (UIView) of the topItem appears in the center of the navigation bar.
- The prompt (string) of the topItem appears at the top of the navigation bar.

- The `rightBarButtonItem` and `leftBarButtonItem` appear at the right and left ends of the navigation bar. These are UIBarButtonItems. A UIBarButtonItem can be a system button, a titled button, an image button, or a container for a UIView. A UIBarButtonItem is not itself a UIView, however. I'll discuss bar button items further in a moment (and refer also to the discussion in Chapter 19).

  A UINavigationItem can have multiple right bar button items and multiple left bar button items; its `rightBarButtonItems` and `leftBarButtonItems` properties are arrays (of UIBarButtonItems). The bar button items are displayed from the outside in: that is, the first item in the `leftBarButtonItems` is leftmost, while the first item in the `rightBarButtonItems` is rightmost. Even if there are multiple buttons on a side, you can still speak of that button in the singular: the `rightBarButtonItem` is the first item of the `rightBarButtonItems` array, and the `leftBarButtonItem` is the first item of the `leftBarButtonItems` array.

- The `backBarButtonItem` *of the backItem* appears at the left end of the navigation bar. It typically points to the left, and is automatically configured so that, when tapped, the `topItem` is popped off the stack. If the `backItem` has *no* `backBarButtonItem`, then there is *still* a back button at the left end of the navigation bar, taking its title from the `title` of the `backItem`. However, if the `topItem` has its `hidesBackButton` set to YES, the back button is suppressed. Also, unless the `topItem` has its `leftItemsSupplementBackButton` set to YES, the back button is suppressed if the `topItem` has a `leftBarButtonItem`.

Changes to the navigation bar's buttons can be animated by sending its `topItem` any of these messages:

- `setRightBarButtonItem:animated:`
- `setLeftBarButtonItem:animated:`
- `setRightBarButtonItems:animated:`
- `setLeftBarButtonItems:animated:`
- `setHidesBackButton:animated:`

UINavigationItems are pushed and popped with `pushNavigationItem:animated:` and `popNavigationItemAnimated:`, or you can set all items on the stack at once with `setItems:animated:`.

A UINavigationBar can be styled using its `barStyle`, `translucent`, and `tintColor` properties. Possible `barStyle` values are `UIBarStyleDefault` and `UIBarStyleBlack`; setting a `tintColor` overrides the `barStyle`. For more extensive customization, you can provide a background image (`setBackgroundImage:forBarMetrics:`) and you can set the title's text attributes dictionary (`titleTextAttributes`). You can also shift the title's vertical position by calling `setTitleVerticalPositionAdjustment:forBarMetrics:`.

A bar button item may be instantiated with any of five methods:

- `initWithBarButtonSystemItem:target:action:`
- `initWithTitle:style:target:action:`
- `initWithImage:style:target:action:`
- `initWithImage:landscapeImagePhone:style:target:action:`
- `initWithCustomView:`

The styles are:

- `UIBarButtonItemStyleBordered`
- `UIBarButtonItemStylePlain` (portrayed like `UIBarButtonItemStyleBordered` in a navigation bar)
- `UIBarButtonItemStyleDone` (only in a navigation bar)

In addition to its `title` and `image` (and its `landscapeImagePhone`), a bar button item inherits from UIBarItem the ability to adjust the image position with `imageInsets` (and

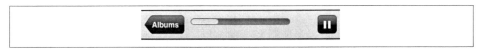

Figure 25-20. A colorful navigation bar

landscapeImagePhoneInsets), plus the enabled and tag properties. Recall from Chapter 19 that you can also set a bar button item's possibleTitles and width properties, to determine its width.

You can also customize the look of a bar button item. It has a tintColor property, or you can give it a background image; and you can apply a text attributes dictionary to its title. These are the customization methods:

- setTitleTextAttributes:forState: (inherited from UIBarItem)
- setTitlePositionAdjustment:forBarMetrics:
- setBackgroundImage:forState:barMetrics:
- setBackgroundVerticalPositionAdjustment:forBarMetrics:

An additional method, setBackgroundImage:forState:style:barMetrics:, is new in iOS 6 and adds further specificity to backgroundImageForState:barMetrics:. Thus, the bar button item can have a different background image depending on what style it is assigned. The value of being able to do this will be obvious when using this method in conjunction with the bar button item appearance proxy, discussed later in this chapter.

In addition, these methods apply only if the bar button item is being used as a back button item:

- setBackButtonTitlePositionAdjustment:forBarMetrics:
- setBackButtonBackgroundImage:forState:barMetrics:
- setBackButtonBackgroundVerticalPositionAdjustment:forBarMetrics:

Figure 19-10 shows how the navigation bar of my Albumen app used to look. When iOS 5 came along, custom colorization became possible, and I jazzed it up a little (Figure 25-20).

When you use a UINavigationBar implicitly as part of a UINavigationController interface, the controller is the navigation bar's delegate. If you were to use a UINavigationBar on its own, you might want to supply your own delegate. The delegate methods are:

- navigationBar:shouldPushItem:
- navigationBar:didPushItem:

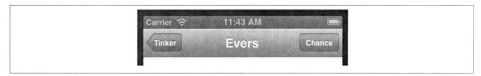

Figure 25-21. A navigation bar

- navigationBar:shouldPopItem:

- navigationBar:didPopItem:

This simple (and silly) example of a stand-alone UINavigationBar (Figure 25-21) implements the legendary baseball combination trio of Tinker to Evers to Chance (see the relevant Wikipedia article if you don't know about them):

```
- (void)viewDidLoad {
    [super viewDidLoad];
    UINavigationItem* ni = [[UINavigationItem alloc] initWithTitle:@"Tinker"];
    UIBarButtonItem* b = [[UIBarButtonItem alloc] initWithTitle:@"Evers"
        style:UIBarButtonItemStyleBordered
        target:self action:@selector(pushNext:)];
    ni.rightBarButtonItem = b;
    self.nav.items = @[ni];
}

- (void) pushNext: (id) sender {
    UIBarButtonItem* oldb = sender;
    NSString* s = oldb.title;
    UINavigationItem* ni = [[UINavigationItem alloc] initWithTitle:s];
    if ([s isEqualToString: @"Evers"]) {
        UIBarButtonItem* b = [[UIBarButtonItem alloc] initWithTitle:@"Chance"
            style:UIBarButtonItemStyleBordered
            target:self action:@selector(pushNext:)];
        ni.rightBarButtonItem = b;
    }
    [self.nav pushNavigationItem:ni animated:YES];
}
```

Notice the subtle shadow at the bottom of the navigation bar in Figure 25-21, cast on whatever is behind it. This effect is new in iOS 6, and can be customized with set-BackgroundImage:forBarMetrics:, if you have also customized the navigation bar's background image. You want a very small image (1×3 is a good size) with some transparency, preferably more transparency at the bottom than at the top; the image will be tiled horizontally across the navigation bar's width. In this way you can harmonize the shadow with your custom background image. The navigation bar's clipsToBounds must be NO, or the shadow won't appear.

Another thing in Figure 25-21 that harmonizes with the navigation bar is the color of the status bar. This behavior is new in iOS 6, confined to the iPhone (and iPod touch). The rule is that if there is a navigation bar at the top of the screen — regardless of whether it is part of a navigation interface — the status bar will derive its color from the color at the *bottom* of the navigation bar. If your interface contains differently customized navigation bars, the status bar will change color in real time to match each one as it appears. This is why, as mentioned in Chapter 9, you must describe your app's initial navigation bar in your *Info.plist* if you want the status bar during launch to adopt the color that it will have when launch is over and the navigation bar has actually appeared.

You can prevent this behavior to some extent by setting the shared application's `status-BarStyle`. For example, this results in a black status bar, regardless of the navigation bar appearance:

```
[[UIApplication sharedApplication]setStatusBarStyle:UIStatusBarStyleDefault];
```

Another trick is to add a *second* navigation bar in front of the real navigation bar. You can prevent this navigation bar from being visible (and keep the user from interacting with it) by setting its `alpha` to 0. I like to make the second navigation bar just 1 pixel high for good measure. For example, this code results in a red status bar, overriding the status bar color that would be derived from the real navigation bar:

```
UINavigationBar* nav =
    [[UINavigationBar alloc] initWithFrame:CGRectMake(0,0,320,1)];
nav.tintColor = [UIColor redColor];
nav.alpha = 0; // prevent visibility
[self.nav.superview addSubview:nav];
```

The same trick can be used in an app that has no visible navigation bar, as a way of coloring the status bar. But you can't obtain what used to be the default status bar; its familiar gray gradient is now a distant fond memory.

UIToolbar

A UIToolbar is intended to appear at the bottom of the screen; on the iPad, it may appear at the top of the screen. It displays a row of UIBarButtonItems, which are its `items`. The items are displayed from left to right in the order in which they appear in the `items` array. You can set the items with animation by calling `setItems:animated:`. You can use the system bar button items `UIBarButtonSystemItemFlexibleSpace` and `UIBar-ButtonSystemItemFixedSpace`, along with the UIBarButtonItem `width` property, to position the items within the toolbar.

See the previous section and Chapter 19 for more about creation and customization of UIBarButtonItems. A bar button item's image, to be used with `UIBarButtonItemStyle-Plain` in a toolbar, must be a transparency mask; colors will be ignored — all that matters is the transparency of the various parts of the image. The color for the image will be supplied by default, or you can customize it with the bar button item's `tintColor`. For `UIBarButtonItemStyleBordered`, on the other hand, the image color does matter, and it is the background of the button that will be colored by the `tintColor`.

A toolbar can be styled using its `barStyle`, `translucent`, and `tintColor` properties. Possible `barStyle` values are `UIBarStyleDefault` and `UIBarStyleBlack`; setting a `tintColor` overrides the `barStyle`. Alternatively, you can provide a background image with `setBackgroundImage:forToolbarPosition:barMetrics:`; the toolbar positions are:

- `UIToolbarPositionAny`
- `UIToolbarPositionBottom`
- `UIToolbarPositionTop` (not supported in the iPhone)

In Figure 19-5, the toolbar has a `UIBarStyleBlack` style, its height is taller than normal to accommodate larger bar button items, and it is populated with three tinted bar button items — a `UIBarButtonSystemItemCancel` bar button item (the tint color tints the button background) and two `UIBarButtonItemStylePlain` bar button items with transparency mask images (the tint color tints the images).

As with a UINavigationBar (see the previous section), a UIToolbar in iOS 6 has a shadow (if its `clipsToBounds` is NO). It normally appears at the top of the toolbar, as a toolbar is expected to be at the bottom of the screen; but on the iPad, where a toolbar at the top of the screen has become standard, the shadow cleverly appears at the bottom of the toolbar in that case. If you've customized the toolbar's background image, you can customize the shadow image as well, with `setShadowImage:forToolbarPosition:`.

UITabBar

A UITabBar displays UITabBarItems (its `items`), each consisting of an image and a name, and maintains a current selection among those items (its `selectedItem`, which is a UITabBarItem, not an index number). To hear about a change of selection, implement `tabBar:didSelectItem:` in the delegate (UITabBarDelegate). To change the items in an animated fashion, call `setItems:animated:`.

The look of a tab bar can be customized. You can set its `tintColor` and `backgroundImage`. The `tintColor` is used to color a tab bar item's image when it is not selected (even if you also set the `backgroundImage`). The tab bar's `selectedImageTintColor` is used to color a tab bar item when it *is* selected. You can also set the image drawn behind the selected tab bar item to indicate that it's selected, the `selectionIndicatorImage`. As with a toolbar (see the previous section), a tab bar in iOS 6 has a shadow, which appears at the top of the tab bar (if its `clipsToBounds` is NO); if you've customized the tab bar's background image, you can customize the shadow image as well, through its `shadowImage` property.

A UITabBarItem is created with one of these two methods:

- `initWithTabBarSystemItem:tag:`
- `initWithTitle:image:tag:`

UITabBarItem is a subclass of UIBarItem, so in addition to its `title` and `image` it inherits the ability to adjust the image position with `imageInsets`, plus the `enabled` and `tag` properties.

A tab bar item's `image` must be a transparency mask; its colors are ignored — only the transparency matters, with tinting applied to the nontransparent areas of the image (the tab bar's `tintColor` and `selectedImageTintColor`). Alternatively, you can call `setFinishedSelectedImage:withFinishedUnselectedImage:` to supply normal images to be shown when the tab bar item is selected and unselected respectively.

You can also customize the look of a tab bar item's title. Call `setTitleTextAttributes:forState:` to apply a text attributes dictionary; and you can adjust the title's position with the `titlePositionAdjustment` property.

The user can be permitted to alter the contents of the tab bar, setting its tab bar items from among a larger repertory of tab bar items. To summon the interface that lets the user do this, call `beginCustomizingItems:`, passing an array of UITabBarItems that may or may not appear in the tab bar. (To prevent the user from removing an item from the tab bar, include it in the tab bar's `items` and *don't* include it in the argument passed to `beginCustomizingItems:`.) A presented view with a Done button appears, behind the tab bar but in front of everything else, displaying the customizable items. The user can then drag an item into the tab bar, replacing an item that's already there. To hear about the customizing view appearing and disappearing, implement delegate methods:

- `tabBar:willBeginCustomizingItems:`
- `tabBar:didBeginCustomizingItems:`
- `tabBar:willEndCustomizingItems:changed:`
- `tabBar:didEndCustomizingItems:changed:`

A UITabBar on its own (outside a UITabBarController) does not provide any automatic access to the user customization interface; it's up to you. In this (silly) example, we populate a UITabBar with four system tab bar items and a More item; we also populate an instance variable array with those same four system tab bar items, plus four more. When the user taps the More item, we show the user customization interface with all eight tab bar items:

```
- (void)viewDidLoad {
    [super viewDidLoad];
    NSMutableArray* arr = [NSMutableArray array];
    for (int ix = 1; ix < 8; ix++) {
        UITabBarItem* tbi =
            [[UITabBarItem alloc] initWithTabBarSystemItem:ix tag:ix];
        [arr addObject: tbi];
    }
    self.items = arr; // copy policy
    [arr removeAllObjects];
    [arr addObjectsFromArray: [self.items subarrayWithRange:NSMakeRange(0,4)]];
    UITabBarItem* tbi =
        [[UITabBarItem alloc] initWithTabBarSystemItem:0 tag:0];
    [arr addObject: tbi]; // More button
    tb.items = arr; // tb is the UITabBar
}

- (void)tabBar:(UITabBar *)tabBar didSelectItem:(UITabBarItem *)item {
    NSLog(@"did select item with tag %i", item.tag);
    if (item.tag == 0) {
        // More button
        tabBar.selectedItem = nil;
        [tabBar beginCustomizingItems:self.items];
    }
}
```

When used in conjunction with a UITabBarController, the customization interface is provided automatically, in an elaborate way. If there are a lot of items, a More item is automatically present, and can be used to access the remaining items in a table view. Here, the user can select any of the excess items, navigating to the corresponding view. Or, the user can switch to the customization interface by tapping the Edit button. (See the iPhone Music app for a familiar example.) Figure 25-22 shows how a More list looks by default.

The way this works is that the automatically provided More item corresponds to a UINavigationController with a root view controller (UIViewController) whose view is a UITableView. Thus, a navigation interface containing this UITableView appears as a tab view when the user taps the More button. When the user selects an item in the table, the corresponding UIViewController is pushed onto the UINavigationController's stack.

You can access this UINavigationController: it is the UITabBarController's more-NavigationController. Through it, you can access the root view controller: it is the first item in the UINavigationController's viewControllers array. And through that, you can access the table view: it is the root view controller's view. This means you can customize what appears when the user taps the More button! For example, let's make the navigation bar black, and let's remove the word More from its title:

Figure 25-22. Automatically generated More list

```
UINavigationController* more = self.tabBarController.moreNavigationController;
UIViewController* list = more.viewControllers[0];
list.title = @"";
UIBarButtonItem* b = [UIBarButtonItem new];
b.title = @"Back";
list.navigationItem.backBarButtonItem = b; // so user can navigate back
more.navigationBar.barStyle = UIBarStyleBlack;
```

We can go even further by supplementing the table view's data source with a data source of our own, thus proceeding to customize the table itself. This is tricky because we have no internal access to the actual data source, and we mustn't accidentally disable it from populating the table. Still, it can be done. I'll start by replacing the table view's data source with an instance of my own MyDataSource, storing a reference to the original data source object in an instance variable of MyDataSource:

```
UITableView* tv = (UITableView*)list.view;
MyDataSource* mds = [MyDataSource new];
self.myDataSource = mds; // retain policy
self.myDataSource.originalDataSource = tv.dataSource;
tv.dataSource = self.myDataSource;
```

Next, I'll use Objective-C's automatic message forwarding mechanism (see the *Objective-C Runtime Programming Guide*) so that MyDataSource acts as a front end for originalDataSource. MyDataSource will magically appear to respond to any message that `originalDataSource` responds to, and any message that arrives that MyDataSource can't handle will be magically forwarded to `originalDataSource`. This way, the insertion of the MyDataSource instance as data source doesn't break whatever the original data source does:

```
- (id)forwardingTargetForSelector:(SEL)aSelector {
    if ([self.originalDataSource respondsToSelector: aSelector])
        return self.originalDataSource;
    return [super forwardingTargetForSelector:aSelector];
}
```

Finally, we'll implement the two Big Questions required by the UITableViewDataSource protocol, to quiet the compiler. In both cases, we first pass the message along to `original-DataSource` (somewhat analogous to calling `super`); then we add our own customizations as desired. Here, I'll remove each cell's disclosure indicator and change its text font:

```
- (NSInteger)tableView:(UITableView *)tv numberOfRowsInSection:(NSInteger)sec {
    // this is just to quiet the compiler
    return [self.originalDataSource tableView:tv numberOfRowsInSection:sec];
}

- (UITableViewCell *)tableView:(UITableView *)tv
        cellForRowAtIndexPath:(NSIndexPath *)ip {
    UITableViewCell* cell =
        [self.originalDataSource tableView:tv cellForRowAtIndexPath:ip];
    cell.accessoryType = UITableViewCellAccessoryNone;
    cell.textLabel.font = [UIFont systemFontOfSize:14];
    return cell;
}
```

The outcome is shown in Figure 25-23:

Appearance Proxy

Instead of sending messages that customize the look of an interface object to the object itself, you can send them to an *appearance proxy* for that object's class. The appearance proxy then passes that same message along to the actual *future* instances of that class. You'll usually configure your appearance proxies very early in the lifetime of the app, and never again. The app delegate's `application:didFinishLaunchingWithOptions:`, before the app's window has been displayed, is the most obvious and common location.

Thus, for example, instead of sending `setTitleTextAttributes:forState:` to a particular UIBarButtonItem, you could send it to a UIBarButtonItem appearance proxy. *All* actual UIBarButtonItems *from then on* would have the text attributes you specified.

This architecture has two chief uses:

Figure 25-23. Customized More list

- It simplifies the task of giving your app a consistent overall appearance. Suppose you want all UIBarButtonItems to have a certain title font. Instead of having to remember to send `setTitleTextAttributes:forState:` to *each* UIBarButtonItem your app ever instantiates, you send it *once* to the appearance proxy and it is sent to those UIBarButtonItems for you.

- It provides access to interface objects that might otherwise be difficult to refer to. For example, you don't get direct access to a search bar's external Cancel button, but it is a UIBarButtonItem and you can customize it through the UIBarButtonItem appearance proxy.

There are two class methods for obtaining an appearance proxy:

`appearance`
Returns a general appearance proxy for that class.

`appearanceWhenContainedIn:`
The argument is a nil-terminated list (not an array!) of classes, arranged in order of containment from inner to outer. The method you send to the appearance proxy returned from this call will be passed on only to instances of the target class that are actually contained in the way you describe. The notion of what "contained"

means is deliberately left vague; basically, it works the way you intuitively expect it to work.

When configuring appearance proxy objects, *specificity trumps generality*. Thus, you could call appearance to say what should happen for *most* instances of some class, and call appearanceWhenContainedIn: to say what should happen *instead* for *certain* instances of that class. Similarly, longer appearanceWhenContainedIn: chains are more specific than shorter ones.

For example, here's some code from my Latin flashcard app (myGolden and myPaler are methods defined by a category on UIColor):

```
[[UIBarButtonItem appearance]
    setTintColor: [UIColor myGolden]]; ❶
[[UIBarButtonItem appearanceWhenContainedIn:
    [UIToolbar class], nil]
        setTintColor: [UIColor myPaler]]; ❷
[[UIBarButtonItem appearanceWhenContainedIn:
    [UIToolbar class], [DrillViewController class], nil]
        setTintColor: [UIColor myGolden]]; ❸
```

That means:

❶   In general, bar button items should be tinted golden.

❷   But bar button items in a toolbar are an exception: they should be paler.

❸   But bar button items in a toolbar in DrillViewController's view are an exception to *that*: they should be golden.

(If you're looking at this book's figures in color, you can see this difference made manifest in Figure 19-3 and Figure 19-5.)

Sometimes, in order to express sufficient specificity, I find myself defining subclasses for no other purpose than to refer to them when obtaining an appearance proxy. For example, here's some more code from my Latin flashcard app:

```
[[UINavigationBar appearance] setBackgroundImage:marble2
                              forBarMetrics:UIBarMetricsDefault];
// counteract the above for the black navigation bar
[[BlackNavigationBar appearance] setBackgroundImage:nil
                              forBarMetrics:UIBarMetricsDefault];
```

In that code, BlackNavigationBar is a UINavigationBar subclass that does nothing whatever. Its sole purpose is to tag one navigation bar in my interface so that I can refer it in that code! Thus, I'm able to say, in effect, "All navigation bars in this app should have marble2 as their background image, unless they are instances of BlackNavigation-Bar."

The ultimate in specificity is, of course, to customize the look of an instance directly. Thus, for example, if you set one particular UIBarButtonItem's `tintColor` property, then `setTintColor:` sent to a UIBarButtonItem appearance proxy will have no effect on that particular bar button item.

You'll want to know which messages can be sent to the appearance proxies for which classes. The best way to find out is to look in the header for that class (or a superclass); any appropriate property or method will be tagged `UI_APPEARANCE_SELECTOR`. For example, here's how the `tintColor` property is declared in *UIBarButtonItem.h*:

```
@property(nonatomic,retain) UIColor *tintColor NS_AVAILABLE_IOS(5_0)
                                        UI_APPEARANCE_SELECTOR;
```

You may also be able to deduce this information from the classification of properties and methods in the documentation, but I find the header to be far more reliable and explicit.

The appearance proxy is an `id`. Therefore, it can be sent *any* message for which a method signature can be found; if you send it a message that isn't tagged `UI_APPEARANCE_SELECTOR` for the class that the proxy represents, the compiler can't stop you, but you'll crash at runtime when the message is actually sent. Also, an `id` has no properties; that's why we must call `setTintColor:` in order to set the UIBarButtonItem's `tintColor` property. A clever workaround for both problems (from a WWDC 2012 video) is to cast the appearance proxy to the class whose proxy you're using. For example, instead of saying this:

```
[[UIBarButtonItem appearance] setTintColor: [UIColor brownColor]];
```

Say this:

```
((UIBarButtonItem*)[UIBarButtonItem appearance]).tintColor =
    [UIColor brownColor];
```

CHAPTER 26

Modal Dialogs

A modal dialog demands attention; while it is present, the user can do nothing other than work within it or dismiss it. You might need to put up a simple modal dialog in order to give the user some information or to ask the user how to proceed. Two UIView subclasses construct and present rudimentary modal dialogs:

UIAlertView

A UIAlertView pops up unexpectedly with an elaborate animation and may be thought of as an attention-getting interruption. An alert is displayed in the center of the screen; it contains a title, a message, and some number of buttons, one of which may be the cancel button, meaning that it does nothing but dismiss the alert. In addition, an alert view may contain a text field, a password field, or both.

Alert views are minimal, but intentionally so; they are intended for simple, quick interaction or display of information. Often there is only a cancel button, the primary purpose of the alert being to show the user the message ("You won the game"); the additional buttons may be used to give the user a choice of how to proceed ("You won the game; would you like to play another?" "Yes," "No," "Replay"). The text field and password field might allow the user to supply login credentials.

UIActionSheet

A UIActionSheet may be considered the iOS equivalent of a menu. An action sheet is displayed arising from the interface: on the iPhone, it slides up from the bottom of the screen; on the iPad, it is typically shown in a popover. It consists of some number of buttons (there can be a title, optionally, but there usually isn't); one may be the cancel button, which appears last, and one may be a "destructive" button, which appears first in red, emphasizing the severity of that option.

Where a UIAlertView is an interruption, a UIActionSheet is a logical branching of what the user is already doing: it typically divides a single piece of interface into multiple possible courses of action. For example, in Apple's Mail app, a single Action button summons an action sheet that lets the user reply to the current message, forward it, or print it (or cancel and do nothing).

One sees occasionally a misuse of the built-in dialogs to include additional interface. For example, a UIActionSheet is a UIView, so in theory you can add a subview to it. I cannot recommend such behavior; it clearly isn't intended, and there's no need for it. If what you want isn't what a built-in dialog normally does, don't use a built-in dialog. I'll suggest some alternatives in the last part of this chapter.

A local notification is an alert that the system presents at a predetermined time on your app's behalf when your app isn't frontmost. This alert can appear as a UIAlertView, so I discuss it in this chapter as well.

New in iOS 6 is the activity view, a modal dialog displaying icons representing possible courses of action, and intended in certain circumstances to replace the action sheet. For example, Mobile Safari now presents an activity view from its Action button; the icons represent external modes of sharing a URL such as Mail, Message, and Twitter, as well as internal actions such as Bookmark and Add to Reading List. I'll discuss activity views at the end of this chapter.

Alert View

The basic method for constructing an alert view (UIAlertView) is `initWith-Title:message:delegate:cancelButtonTitle:otherButtonTitles:`. The method for making a constructed alert view appear onscreen is `show`. The alert is automatically dismissed as soon as the user taps any button. Here's an example (Figure 26-1):

```
UIAlertView* alert = [[UIAlertView alloc] initWithTitle:@"Not So Fast!"
    message:@"Do you really want to do this tremendously destructive thing?"
    delegate:self cancelButtonTitle:@"Yes"
    otherButtonTitles:@"No", @"Maybe", nil];
[alert show];
```

The `otherButtonTitles` parameter is of indefinite length, so it must be either nil or a nil-terminated list (not an array!) of strings. The cancel button needn't be titled "Cancel"; it is drawn darker than the other buttons and comes last in a column of buttons, as you can see from Figure 26-1. If there are more than two `otherButtonTitles` and a nil `cancelButtonTitle`, the last of the `otherButtonTitles` is drawn as if it were a cancel button; this code, too, produces Figure 26-1:

```
UIAlertView* alert = [[UIAlertView alloc] initWithTitle:@"Not So Fast!"
    message:@"Do you really want to do this tremendously destructive thing?"
    delegate:self cancelButtonTitle:nil
    otherButtonTitles:@"No", @"Maybe", @"Yes", nil];
```

If an alert view is to contain a text field, it probably should have at most one or two buttons, with short titles such as "OK" and "Cancel". Otherwise, there might not be

Figure 26-1. An alert view

room on the screen for the alert view and the keyboard. To add a text field to the alert view, modify its alertViewStyle before calling show. Your choices are:

- UIAlertViewStyleDefault, the default (no text fields)
- UIAlertViewStylePlainTextInput, one normal text field
- UIAlertViewStyleSecureTextInput, one secureTextEntry text field
- UIAlertViewStyleLoginAndPasswordInput, one normal text field and one secure-TextEntry text field

You can retrieve the text fields with textFieldAtIndex:; possible arguments are 0 and 1 (where 1 is the password field when the style is UIAlertViewStyleLoginAndPassword-Input). You can treat the text fields as you would any text field (see Chapter 23); for example, you can set the text field's delegate, arrange to receive control events from the text field, determine the text field's keyboard type, and so on:

```
UIAlertView* alert = [[UIAlertView alloc] initWithTitle:@"Enter a number:"
    message:nil delegate:self cancelButtonTitle:@"Cancel"
    otherButtonTitles:@"OK", nil];
alert.alertViewStyle = UIAlertViewStylePlainTextInput;
UITextField* tf = [alert textFieldAtIndex:0];
tf.keyboardType = UIKeyboardTypeNumberPad;
[tf addTarget:self action:@selector(textChanged:)
        forControlEvents:UIControlEventEditingChanged];
[alert show];
```

The alert dialog is modal, but the code that presents it is not: after the alert is shown, your code continues to run. If an alert consists of a single button (the cancel button), you might show it and forget about it, secure in the knowledge that the user must dismiss it sooner or later and that nothing can happen until then. But if you want to respond at the time the user dismisses the alert, or if there are several buttons and you want to know which one the user tapped to dismiss the alert, you'll need to implement at least one of these delegate methods (UIAlertViewDelegate):

- `alertView:clickedButtonAtIndex:`
- `alertView:willDismissWithButtonIndex:`
- `alertView:didDismissWithButtonIndex:`

The cancel button index is usually 0, with the remaining button indexes increasing in the order in which they were defined. If you're in any doubt, or if you need the button title for any other reason, you can call `buttonTitleAtIndex:`. Properties allow you to work out the correspondence between indexes and buttons without making any assumptions:

- `cancelButtonIndex` (-1 if none)
- `firstOtherButtonIndex` (-1 if none)
- `numberOfButtons` (including the cancel button)

You can also dismiss an alert view programmatically, with `dismissWithClickedButton-Index:animated:`. When an alert view is dismissed programmatically, the delegate method `alertView:clickedButtonAtIndex:` is *not* called, because no button was actually clicked by the user. But the button index you specify is still passed along to the two `dismiss` delegate methods. The button index you specify needn't correspond to any existing button; thus, you could use it as a way of telling your delegate method that your code, and not the user, dismissed the alert.

Two additional delegate methods notify you when the alert is initially shown:

- `willPresentAlertView:`
- `didPresentAlertView:`

A further delegate method asks whether the first "other button" should be enabled:

- `alertViewShouldEnableFirstOtherButton:`

The delegate receives that message each time the state of things changes in the alert — in particular, when the alert appears and when the text in a text field changes. In this example, there's a text field, my cancel button says "Cancel", and my other button says "OK"; I enable the OK button only if there is text in the text field:

```
- (BOOL)alertViewShouldEnableFirstOtherButton:(UIAlertView *)alertView {
    UITextField* tf = [alertView textFieldAtIndex:0];
    return [tf.text length] > 0;
}
```

One last delegate method notifies you if the alert is dismissed by the system:

- `alertViewCancel:`

Before iOS 4.0, this could happen because the user quit the app with the alert showing; the system dismissed the alert, and your code had a chance to respond before actually terminating. In the multitasking world, however, if the user clicks the Home button, your app is backgrounded without the system dismissing the alert, and `alertView-Cancel:` may be a dead letter. It would thus be up to your code, as the app is backgrounded, whether to leave the alert there or to dismiss the alert and perhaps take some default action.

Action Sheet

The basic method for constructing an action sheet (UIActionSheet) is `initWith-Title:delegate:cancelButtonTitle:destructiveButtonTitle:otherButton-Titles:`. There are various methods for summoning the actual sheet, depending on what part of the interface you want the sheet to arise from. The following are appropriate on the iPhone, where the sheet typically rises from the bottom of the screen:

`showInView:`
> On the iPhone, far and away the most commonly used method. You will usually specify the root view controller's view. Don't specify a view whose view controller is contained by a view controller that hides the bottom of the interface, such as a tab bar controller or a navigation controller with a toolbar; if you do, some of the buttons may not function (and you get a helpful warning in the console: "Presenting action sheet clipped by its superview"). Instead, specify the tab bar controller's view itself, or the navigation controller's view itself, or use one of the other methods. For example, in my Zotz! app, which has a tab bar interface, the settings view controller summons an action sheet like this (Figure 26-2):
>
> ```
> [sheet showInView: self.tabBarController.view];
> ```

`showFromTabBar:`
`showFromToolbar:`
> On the iPhone, these cause the sheet to rise from the bottom of the screen, just like `showInView:`, because the tab bar or toolbar is at the bottom of the screen; however, they avoid the clipping problem with `showInView:` described earlier.

On the iPad, you are more likely to use one of the following methods, which resemble the methods for presenting a popover (Chapter 22); they do in fact present the action sheet as a popover, with its arrow pointing to the specified part of the interface (Figure 26-3):

- `showFromRect:inView:animated:`

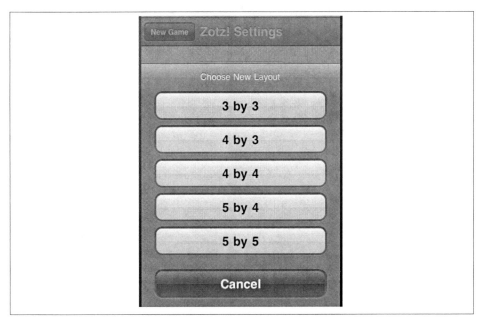

Figure 26-2. An action sheet on the iPhone

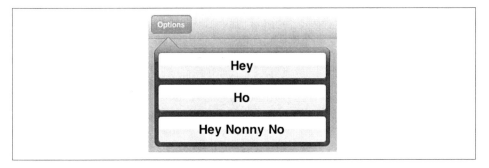

Figure 26-3. An action sheet presented as a popover

- showFromBarButtonItem:animated:

(On the iPhone, those methods should be avoided; they don't cause an error, and they do work — the sheet still ends up at the bottom at the screen — but they can do messy things to the interface.)

On the iPad, there is usually no point including a cancel button title; if the alert sheet is shown as a popover, no cancel button will appear. This is because the popover is

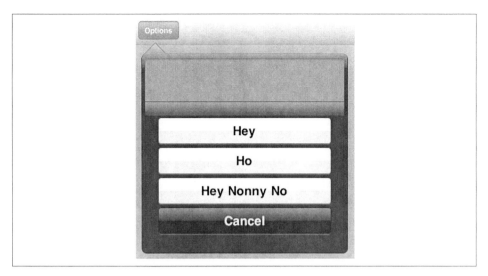

Figure 26-4. An action sheet presented inside a popover

configured to be dismissed when the user taps outside it, which is the same as canceling it.

Alternatively, it is possible on the iPad to show an alert sheet *inside an existing popover*. In this scenario, we are already presenting the popover, and then we summon an action sheet within the popover's view. The action sheet then behaves just as if the popover were an iPhone: you summon it with showInView:, it slides up from the bottom of the popover, and the cancel button, if specified, does appear (Figure 26-4). The action sheet behaves like a presented view inside a popover, where modalInPopover is YES.

An action sheet also has a style, its actionSheetStyle:

- UIActionSheetStyleAutomatic
- UIActionSheetStyleDefault
- UIActionSheetStyleBlackTranslucent
- UIActionSheetStyleBlackOpaque

These values are closely related to the possible styles (barStyle) of a UIToolbar (Chapter 25). However, an action sheet's style depends also on the mode of presentation; my experimentation suggests, for example, that setting the actionSheetStyle of an action sheet that appears as a popover may make no perceptible difference, and that an action sheet that is shown from a tab bar will always be black opaque.

In other respects an action sheet is managed in a manner completely parallel to an alert view. When one of its buttons is tapped, the sheet is dismissed automatically, but you'll probably want to implement a delegate method (UIActionSheetDelegate) in order to learn which button it was:

- `actionSheet:clickedButtonAtIndex:`
- `actionSheet:willDismissWithButtonIndex:`
- `actionSheet:didDismissWithButtonIndex:`

If the action sheet is shown as a popover on the iPad, and if the popover is dismissed by the user tapping outside it, the button index is `-1`.

To respond appropriately to the delegate methods without making assumptions about how the indexes correspond to the buttons, you can use the `buttonTitleAtIndex:` method, and these properties:

- `cancelButtonIndex`
- `destructiveButtonIndex`
- `firstOtherButtonIndex`
- `numberOfButtons`

You can dismiss an action sheet programmatically with `dismissWithClickedButton-Index:animated:`, in which case `actionSheet:clickedButtonAtIndex:` is not called, but the two `dismiss` delegate methods are. Two additional delegate methods notify you when the sheet is initially shown:

- `willPresentActionSheet:`
- `didPresentActionSheet:`

A further delegate method, `actionSheetCancel:`, notifies you if the sheet is dismissed by the system, though in the multitasking world this is unlikely to happen; if your app is backgrounded with an action sheet showing, it's up to you to decide how to proceed.

Here's the code that presents the action sheet shown in Figure 26-2, along with the code that responds to its dismissal:

```
- (void) chooseLayout: (id) sender {
    UIActionSheet* sheet =
        [[UIActionSheet alloc] initWithTitle:@"Choose New Layout"
        delegate:self
        cancelButtonTitle:@"Cancel" destructiveButtonTitle:nil
        otherButtonTitles:@"3 by 3", @"4 by 3", @"4 by 4",
                          @"5 by 4", @"5 by 5", nil];
    [sheet showInView: self.tabBarController.view];
```

```
    }

    - (void)actionSheet:(UIActionSheet *)as clickedButtonAtIndex:(NSInteger)ix {
        if (ix == as.cancelButtonIndex)
            return;
        NSString* s = [as buttonTitleAtIndex:ix];
        // ...
    }
```

On the iPad, an action sheet shown as a popover or inside an existing popover introduces the same issues with regard to the popover's passthroughViews that I enumerated in Chapter 22. When an action sheet is shown as a popover from a bar button item in a toolbar, the toolbar becomes a passthrough view for the popover, and the user can now tap a bar button item without causing the action sheet's popover to be dismissed (possibly even summoning another popover — perhaps even another instance of the same action sheet — simultaneously). You can't solve this problem by adjusting the popover controller's passthroughViews, because you've no access to the popover controller! One workaround is to implement the delegate methods to toggle user interaction with the toolbar:

```
    - (IBAction)doButton:(id)sender { // sender is a bar button item
        UIActionSheet* act = [[UIActionSheet alloc]
            initWithTitle:nil delegate:self cancelButtonTitle:nil
            destructiveButtonTitle:nil
            otherButtonTitles:@"Hey", @"Ho", @"Hey Nonny No", nil];
        [act showFromBarButtonItem:sender animated:YES];
    }

    - (void)didPresentActionSheet:(UIActionSheet *)actionSheet {
        [self.toolbar setUserInteractionEnabled:NO];
    }

    - (void)actionSheet:(UIActionSheet *)actionSheet
            didDismissWithButtonIndex:(NSInteger)buttonIndex {
        [self.toolbar setUserInteractionEnabled:YES];
    }
```

Similarly, an action sheet shown inside a popover causes the popover to behave as if modalInPopover is YES; thus, while the action sheet is showing, the user can't dismiss the popover by tapping anywhere that isn't listed in the popover's passthroughViews. So far, so good. But you must take care that the popover's passthroughViews make sense for this situation; setting the passthroughViews property to nil while the action sheet is present (if it isn't nil already) might be a good idea. But the view controller that presents the action sheet might not have ready access to the popover controller in order to set its passthroughViews! This entire situation is just another maddening consequence of iOS's poor built-in popover management.

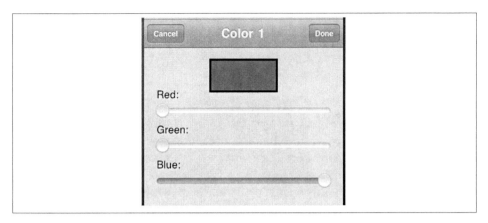

Figure 26-5. A presented view functioning as a modal dialog

Dialog Alternatives

Alert views and actions sheets are limited, inflexible, and inappropriate to any but the simplest cases. In more complex situations, it really isn't that much work to implement an alternative.

On the iPhone, the main alternative is to navigate to a new screenful of interface. This might be by way of a navigation interface, or using a presented view (Chapter 19). For example, in the Zotz! app, in the Settings view, when the user taps a color, I summon a presented view, using a UIViewController subclass of my own, ColorPickerController (Figure 26-5).

On the desktop, the color picker in Figure 26-5 might be presented as a secondary window acting as a dialog. On the small iPhone screen, where there are no secondary windows, the presented view *is* the equivalent of a dialog. Indeed, one might argue that the action sheet shown in Figure 26-2 is not a very appropriate use of an action sheet; it's intrusive and has too many buttons. It might have been better if I'd designed my own presented view. I probably picked an action sheet because it required just a few lines of code; basically, I was being lazy.

On the iPad, a popover is virtually a secondary window, and can be truly modal. An action sheet is usually presented as a popover, but it's limited, and you don't get access to the popover controller; in many cases, you'll probably be better off designing your own view to be presented in a popover. The popovers in Figure 22-1, for example, are effectively modal dialogs. A popover can internally display a secondary presented view or even an action sheet, as we've already seen. Also on the iPad, a presented view can use the UIModalPresentationFormSheet presentation style, which is effectively a dialog window smaller than the screen.

Local Notifications

A *local notification* is an alert to the user that can appear even if your app is not running. In one of its manifestations, it appears as a dialog on top of whatever the user is doing at that moment, which is why it is treated in this chapter. (If a local notification from some other app were to appear as a dialog while *your* app is frontmost, your app would become inactive; see Chapter 11 and the `applicationWillResignActive:` app delegate message.)

 This use of the term *notification* has nothing to do with NSNotification (Chapter 11). The ambiguity is unfortunate.

Your app does not present a local notification alert: indeed, your app *can't* present a local notification alert, because if your app's local notification alert appears, your app *ex hypothesi* isn't frontmost. Rather, your app hands a local notification to the system along with instructions about when the local notification should *fire*. When the specified time arrives, if your app isn't frontmost, the system presents the notification on your behalf.

The user has several choices as to how a notification from your app should be presented. These choices appear in the Settings app, under Notifications. There is a Notification Center, which appears when the user swipes downward from the very top of the screen, and the user can enable or disable your app's notifications appearing there. A notification from your app can also appear as an alert, as a temporary banner at the top of the screen, or not at all. The user can also prohibit your app's alerts from appearing in the lock screen. It is thus perfectly possible for the user to suppress your app's alerts altogether!

No matter the interface whereby a notification presents itself, it generally provides some way for the user to summon your app in response. If the notification is a banner, the user can tap it. If the notification is an alert, the user can tap its action button. If the notification appears in the lock screen, the user can slide the slider at the bottom of the lock screen. If the user does any of these things, your app will be brought to the front, launching it if it isn't already suspended in the background. Your app may need to be concerned with detecting that it has been brought to the front under these special circumstances, and I'll talk in a moment about how it can do that.

To create a local notification, you configure a UILocalNotification object and hand it to the system with UIApplication's `scheduleLocalNotification:`. The UILocalNotification object has properties as follows:

`alertBody`
    The message displayed in the notification.

`alertAction`

This matters only if your notification is displayed as an alert; in that case, this is the text of the action button. If you don't set `alertAction`, the text of the action button will be "Launch."

 According to the documentation, you should be able to set `hasAction` to NO to suppress the action button altogether, but in my testing, doing so has no effect.

`soundName`

The name of a sound file at the top level of your app bundle, to be played when the alert appears. This should be an uncompressed sound (AIFF or WAV). Alternatively, you can specify the default sound, `UILocalNotificationDefaultSound-Name`. If you don't set this property, there won't be a sound. Regardless of the value you supply here, the user can prevent your app's notifications from emitting a sound.

`userInfo`

An optional NSDictionary whose contents are up to you. Your app can retrieve this dictionary later on, if it receives the notification after the notification fires (more about that in a moment).

`fireDate, timeZone`

When you want the local notification to fire. The `fireDate` is an NSDate (see Chapter 10 and Chapter 25 for examples of date manipulation). If you don't include a `timeZone`, the date is measured against universal time; if you *do* include a `time-Zone`, the date is measured against the user's local time zone, even if that time zone changes (because the user travels, for instance).

`repeatInterval, repeatCalendar`

If set, the local notification will recur.

As I've already mentioned, you hand a configured local notification to the system with UIApplication's `scheduleLocalNotification:`. Additional UIApplication methods let you manipulate the list of local notifications you've already scheduled. You can cancel one or all scheduled local notifications (`cancelLocalNotification:`, `cancelAllLocal-Notifications:`); you can also manipulate the list directly by setting UIApplication's `scheduledLocalNotifications`, an NSArray property.

Figure 26-6 shows an alert generated by the firing of a local notification. Here's a simple example of creating and scheduling the local notification that resulted in that alert:

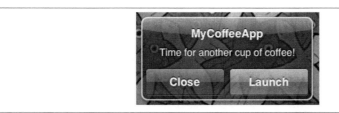

Figure 26-6. An alert posted by the system when a local notification fires

```
UILocalNotification* ln = [UILocalNotification new];
ln.alertBody = @"Time for another cup of coffee!";
ln.fireDate = [NSDate dateWithTimeIntervalSinceNow:15];
ln.soundName = UILocalNotificationDefaultSoundName;
[[UIApplication sharedApplication] scheduleLocalNotification:ln];
```

Now let's talk about what happens when one of your scheduled local notifications fires. There are three possibilities, depending on the state of your app at that moment:

Your app is suspended in the background

If the user summons your app from a notification, your app is brought to the front; your app delegate will then receive `application:didReceiveLocal-Notification:`, where the second parameter is the UILocalNotification, and your application's `applicationState` will be `UIApplicationStateInactive`.

Your app is frontmost

The user won't be informed by the system that the notification has fired (though the notification may be stored in the Notification Center). Your app delegate will receive `application:didReceiveLocalNotification:`, where the second parameter is the UILocalNotification, and your application's `applicationState` will be `UIApplicationStateActive`. The idea is that if your app wants to let the user know that something special is happening, that's your app's business and it can do it in its own way.

Your app isn't running

If the user summons your app from a notification, your app is launched; your app delegate will then receive, *not* `application:didReceiveLocalNotification:`, but rather `application:didFinishLaunchingWithOptions:` with an NSDictionary parameter that includes the `UIApplicationLaunchOptionsLocalNotification-Key`, whose value is the UILocalNotification.

Thus, you should implement `application:didReceiveLocalNotification:` to check the UIApplication's `applicationState`, and you should implement `application:did-FinishLaunchingWithOptions:` to check its second parameter to see whether we are launching in response to a local notification. In this way, you will be able to distinguish the three different possibilities, and you can respond appropriately.

In the first and third cases (your app is suspended in the background, or your app isn't running), you may want to show the user some interface appropriate to the local notification's situation. For example, you might want to push a particular view controller onto your navigation interface or present a particular view controller's view. However, when your app is launched from scratch, the first thing the user sees is its launch image (Chapter 9); and when your app is activated from a suspended state, the first thing the user sees is a screenshot image of your app, taken by the system when your app was suspended. Thus, there may be a mismatch between these images and the interface that you're about to show the user in this special situation; if so, the user will see an odd flash as the image is removed to reveal your app's actual interface. To prevent this flash, you can include in the original UILocalNotification an `alertLaunchImage` to be presented instead of these images. The idea is that this `alertLaunchImage` should be a better match for the interface the user will actually see.

(When your app is launched from scratch by a local notification, if you intend to respond by showing some special interface appropriate to the notification, and if you're using the built-in state saving and restoration mechanism discussed in Chapter 19, you'll want to take steps to prevent inappropriate parts of the interface from being restored automatically in this special situation.)

There is a fourth possibility for what happens when a local notification fires. Under some special circumstances (addressed, for example, in Chapter 27 and Chapter 35), your app might be running, *not* suspended, in the background. In this case, the situation is similar to what happens when your app *is* suspended: the user may be notified, and can summon your app to the front. Your running-in-the-background app can even schedule a notification to fire immediately with the convenience method `presentLocal-NotificationNow:`.

Activity View

An activity view is the view belonging to a UIActivityViewController (new in iOS 6). You start with one or more pieces of data, such as an NSString, that you want the user to have the option of sharing or working with in your app. The activity view contains an icon for every activity (UIActivity) that can work with this type of data. There are nine built-in activities, and your app can provide more. The user may tap an icon in the activity view, and is then perhaps shown additional interface, belonging to the provider of the chosen activity. For example, as I mentioned earlier, the Action button in Mobile Safari presents an activity view (Figure 26-7).

Figure 26-7. An activity view

Don't confuse UIActivityViewController, UIActivity, UIActivity-ItemProvider, and UIActivityItemSource, on the one hand, with UIActivityIndicatorView (Chapter 25) on the other. The similarity of the names is unfortunate.

Presenting an activity view is easy. You instantiate UIActivityViewController by calling `initWithActivityItems:applicationActivities:`, where the first parameter is an NSArray of objects to be shared, such as NSString or UIImage objects. Presumably these are objects associated somehow with the interface the user is looking at right now. You set the controller's `completionHandler` to a block that will be called when the user's interaction with the activity interface ends. Then you present the controller, as a presented controller on the iPhone or as a popover on the iPad. So, for example, on the iPhone:

```
UIActivityViewController* avc =
    [[UIActivityViewController alloc] initWithActivityItems:@[myCoolString]
                                     applicationActivities:nil];
avc.completionHandler = ^(NSString *activityType, BOOL completed) {
    // ...
};
[self presentViewController:avc animated:YES completion:nil];
```

And on the iPad:

```
UIActivityViewController* avc =
    [[UIActivityViewController alloc] initWithActivityItems:@[myCoolString]
                                  applicationActivities:nil];
avc.completionHandler = ^(NSString *activityType, BOOL completed) {
    // ...
};
UIPopoverController* pop =
    [[UIPopoverController alloc] initWithContentViewController:avc];
self.currentPop = pop;
[pop presentPopoverFromBarButtonItem:sender
    permittedArrowDirections:UIPopoverArrowDirectionAny animated:YES];
pop.passthroughViews = nil;
```

There is no Cancel button in the popover presentation of the activity view; the user cancels by tapping outside the popover. If you set a delegate for the UIPopover-Controller, it will be sent popoverControllerDidDismissPopover: if the user cancels, but *not* if the user proceeds to an activity (this feels like a bug).

The activity view is populated automatically with known system-wide activities that can handle any of the types of data you provided as activity items. These activities represent UIActivity types, and are designated by constants:

- UIActivityTypePostToFacebook
- UIActivityTypePostToTwitter
- UIActivityTypePostToWeibo
- UIActivityTypeMessage
- UIActivityTypeMail
- UIActivityTypePrint
- UIActivityTypeCopyToPasteboard
- UIActivityTypeAssignToContact
- UIActivityTypeSaveToCameraRoll

Consult the UIActivity class documentation to learn what types of activity item each of these activities can handle. For example, the UIActivityTypeMail activity will accept an NSString, a UIImage, or a file on disk (such as an image file) designated by an NSURL; it will present a mail composition interface with the activity item in the body of the email.

Since the default is to include all the system-wide activities that can handle the provided data, if you *don't* want a certain system-wide activity included in the activity view, you must exclude it explicitly. You do this by setting the UIActivityViewController's excludedActivityTypes property to an NSArray of any or all of the activity type constants.

The purpose of the applicationActivities: parameter of initWithActivity-Items:applicationActivities: is for you to list any additional activities implemented by your own app, so that their icons will appear as choices in the activity view as well. Each activity will be an instance of one of your own UIActivity subclasses.

To illustrate, I'll create a minimal (and nonsensical) activity called Be Cool that accepts NSString activity items. It is a UIActivity subclass called MyCoolActivity. So, to include Be Cool among the choices presented to the user by a UIActivityViewController, I'd say:

```
UIActivityViewController* avc =
    [[UIActivityViewController alloc]
        initWithActivityItems:@[myCoolString]
        applicationActivities:@[[MyCoolActivity new]]];
```

Now let's implement MyCoolActivity. It has an NSArray property called items, for reasons that will be apparent in a moment. We need to arm ourselves with an image to represent this activity in the activity view; this must be a transparency mask, meaning that colors will be ignored — all that matters is the transparency of the various parts of the image — and should be no larger than 43×43 (55×55 on iPad). It can be smaller, and it needn't be square, as it will be centered in the activity icon automatically.

Here's the preparatory part of the implementation of MyCoolActivity:

```
-(NSString *)activityType {
    return @"com.neuburg.matt.coolActivity"; // make up your own unique string
}

-(NSString *)activityTitle {
    return @"Be Cool";
}

-(UIImage *)activityImage {
    return self.image; // prepared beforehand
}

-(BOOL)canPerformWithActivityItems:(NSArray *)activityItems {
    for (id obj in activityItems) {
        if ([obj isKindOfClass: [NSString class]])
            return YES;
    }
    return NO;
}

-(void)prepareWithActivityItems:(NSArray *)activityItems {
    self.items = activityItems;
}
```

None of these methods actually asks us to perform the activity in question; we haven't yet reached that phase. If we return YES from `canPerformWithActivityItems:`, then an icon for this activity, labeled Be Cool and displaying our `activityImage`, will appear in the activity view. If the user taps our icon, `prepareWithActivityItems:` will be called. We retain the `activityItems` into a property, because they won't be arriving again when we are actually told to perform the activity.

To perform the activity, we implement one of two methods:

`performActivity`
> We simply perform the activity directly, using the activity items we've already retained. If the activity is time-consuming, the activity should be performed on a background thread (Chapter 38) so that we can return immediately; the activity view interface will be taken down and the user will be able to go on interacting with the app.

`activityViewController`
> We have further interface that we'd like to show the user as part of the activity, so we return a UIViewController subclass. The activity view mechanism will present this UIViewController for us in place of the activity view; it is not our job to present or dismiss it. (We may, however, present or dismiss dependent interface. For example, if our UIViewController is a navigation controller with a custom root view controller, we might push another view controller onto its stack while the user is working on the activity.)

No matter which of these two methods we implement, we *must* eventually call this activity instance's `activityDidFinish:`. This is the signal to the activity view mechanism that the activity is over. If the activity view mechanism is still presenting any interface, it will be taken down, and the argument we supply here, a BOOL signifying whether the activity completed successfully, will be passed into the block we supplied earlier as the activity view controller's `completionHandler`. So, for example:

```
-(void)performActivity {
    // ... do something with self.items here ...
    [self activityDidFinish:YES];
}
```

If you're supplying your own view controller from `activityViewController`, you'll want to hand it a reference to `self` before returning it, so that the view controller can call its `activityDidFinish:` when the time comes. For example, suppose our activity involves letting the user draw a mustache on a photo of someone. Our view controller will provide interface for doing that, including some way of letting the user signal completion, such as a Cancel button and a Done button. When the user taps either of those, we'll do whatever else is necessary (such as saving the altered photo somewhere if the user tapped Done) and then call `activityDidFinish:`. Thus, we could implement `activityViewController` like this:

```
-(UIViewController *)activityViewController {
    MustacheViewController* mvc = [MustacheViewController new];
    mvc.activity = self;
    mvc.items = self.items;
    return mvc;
}
```

And then MustacheViewController would have code like this:

```
- (IBAction)doCancel:(id)sender {
    [self.activity activityDidFinish:NO];

}
- (IBAction)doDone:(id)sender {
    [self.activity activityDidFinish:YES];

}
```

Unfortunately, I haven't been able to get `activityViewController` to work properly on the iPad; the view controller is presented fullscreen (contrary to the documentation) and is never dismissed, and logging proves that there are all kinds of memory management issues behind the scenes. This seems to be a major bug. However, it works fine on the iPhone.

PART VI

Some Frameworks

In addition to the basic UIKit and Foundation frameworks, which supply the fundamental interface and utility classes for all apps, Cocoa supplies numerous optional frameworks that you can use if your app has special needs. This part of the book introduces some of these frameworks and their related topics. At the same time, it necessarily exercises some restraint. To explore *all* of the additional iOS frameworks in *full* depth would more than double the size of this book! So this part of the book fully explains the basics, but then stops and leaves you to go further on your own if you need to; it teaches you what you need to know to get started, and it trains you to understand and explore these and related frameworks independently if your app requires a further level of depth and detail.

- Chapter 27 introduces the various iOS means for playing sound files, including audio sessions and playing sounds in the background.

- Chapter 28 describes some basic ways of playing video (movies), along with an introduction to the powerful AV Foundation framework.

- Chapter 29 is about how an app can access the user's music library.

- Chapter 30 is about how an app can access the user's photo library, along with the ability to take photos and capture movies.

- Chapter 31 discusses how an app can access the user's address book.

- Chapter 32 talks about how an app can access the user's calendar data.

- Chapter 33 describes how an app can allow the user to compose and send email and SMS messages and social media posts.

- Chapter 34 explains how an app can display a map, along with custom annotations and overlays. It also talks about how a map can display the user's current location, geocoding, and communicating with the Maps app.

- Chapter 35 is about how an app can learn where the device is located, how it is moving, and how it is oriented.

CHAPTER 27

Audio

iOS provides various means and technologies for allowing your app to produce sound (and even to input it). The topic is a large one, so this chapter can only introduce it. You'll want to read Apple's *Multimedia Programming Guide* and *Core Audio Overview*.

None of the classes discussed in this chapter provide any user interface within your application for allowing the user to stop and start playback of sound. You can create your own such interface, and I'll discuss how you can associate the "remote control" buttons with your application. Also, a web view (Chapter 24) supports the HTML 5 `<audio>` tag; this can be a simple, lightweight way to play audio and to allow the user to control playback. (By default, a web view even allows use of AirPlay.) Alternatively, you could treat the sound as a movie and use the MPMoviePlayerController class discussed in Chapter 28; this can also be a good way to play a sound file located remotely over the Internet.

System Sounds

The simplest form of sound is *system sound*, which is the iOS equivalent of the basic computer "beep." This is implemented through System Sound Services; you'll need to import `<AudioToolbox/AudioToolbox.h>` and link to *AudioToolbox.framework*. You'll be calling one of two C functions, which behave very similarly to one another:

`AudioServicesPlayAlertSound`
> Plays a sound and, on an iPhone, may also vibrate the device, depending on the user's settings.

`AudioServicesPlaySystemSound`
> Plays a short sound of your choice. On an iPhone, there won't be an accompanying vibration, but you can specifically elect to have this "sound" *be* a device vibration (by passing `kSystemSoundID_Vibrate` as the name of the "sound").

The sound file to be played needs to be an uncompressed AIFF or WAV file (or an Apple CAF file wrapping one of these). To hand the sound to these functions, you'll need a SystemSoundID, which you obtain by calling `AudioServicesCreateSystemSoundID` with a CFURLRef (or NSURL) that points to a sound file. In this example, the sound file is in our app bundle:

```
NSURL* sndurl =
    [[NSBundle mainBundle] URLForResource:@"test" withExtension:@"aif"];
SystemSoundID snd;
AudioServicesCreateSystemSoundID ((__bridge CFURLRef)sndurl, &snd);
AudioServicesPlaySystemSound(snd);
```

However, there's a problem with that code: we have failed to exercise proper memory management. We need to call `AudioServicesDisposeSystemSoundID` to release our SystemSoundID. But when shall we do this? `AudioServicesPlaySystemSound` executes asynchronously. So the solution can't be to call `AudioServicesDisposeSystemSound-ID` in the next line of the same snippet, because this would release our sound just as it is about to start playing, resulting in silence. The solution is to implement a sound completion handler, a function that is called when the sound has finished playing. So, our sound-playing snippet now looks like this:

```
NSURL* sndurl =
    [[NSBundle mainBundle] URLForResource:@"test" withExtension:@"aif"];
SystemSoundID snd;
AudioServicesCreateSystemSoundID((__bridge CFURLRef)sndurl, &snd);
AudioServicesAddSystemSoundCompletion(snd, nil, nil, SoundFinished, nil);
AudioServicesPlaySystemSound(snd);
```

And here is our sound completion handler, the `SoundFinished` function referred to in the previous snippet:

```
void SoundFinished (SystemSoundID snd, void* context) {
    AudioServicesRemoveSystemSoundCompletion(snd);
    AudioServicesDisposeSystemSoundID(snd);
}
```

Note that because we are about to release the sound, we first release the sound completion handler information applied to it. The last argument passed to `AudioServicesAdd-SystemSoundCompletion` is a pointer-to-void that comes back as the second parameter of our sound completion handler function; you can use this parameter in any way you like, such as to help identify the sound.

Audio Session

If your app is going to use a more sophisticated way of producing sound, such as an audio player (discussed in the next section), it must specify a *policy* regarding that sound. This policy will answer such questions as: should sound stop when the screen is locked?

Should sound interrupt existing sound (being played, for example, by the Music app) or should it be layered on top of it?

Your policy is declared in an *audio session*, which is a singleton AVAudioSession instance created automatically as your app launches. You'll need to link to *AVFoundation.framework* and import <AVFoundation/AVFoundation.h>. You'll refer to your app's AVAudioSession by way of the class method sharedInstance.

 Before iOS 6, it was also possible, and sometimes necessary, to talk to your audio session in C, by linking to *AudioToolbox.framework* and importing <AudioToolbox/AudioToolbox.h>. In iOS 6, the C API isn't needed, and I don't use it in this edition of the book.

To declare your audio session's policy, you'll set its *category*, by calling setCategory:withOptions:error:. The basic policies for audio playback are:

Ambient (AVAudioSessionCategoryAmbient)
> Your app's audio plays even while Music app music or other background audio is playing, and is silenced by the phone's Silent switch and screen locking.

Solo Ambient (AVAudioSessionCategorySoloAmbient, *the default*)
> Your app stops Music app music or other background audio from playing, and is silenced by the phone's Silent switch and screen locking.

Playback (AVAudioSessionCategoryPlayback)
> Your app stops Music app music or other background audio from playing, and is *not* silenced by the Silent switch. It is silenced by screen locking (in iOS 5 and later) unless it is also configured to play in the background (as explained later in this chapter).

Your audio session's otherAudioPlaying property can tell you whether audio is already playing in some other app, such as the Music app. Apple suggests that you might want your choice of audio session policy, and perhaps what kinds of sound your app plays, to take into account the answer to that question.

Audio session category options (the withOptions: parameter of setCategory:withOptions:error:) allow you to modify the playback policies to some extent. For example:

- You can override the Playback policy so as to allow Music app music or other background audio to play (AVAudioSessionCategoryOptionMixWithOthers). Your sound is then said to be *mixable*. If you don't make your sound mixable, then mixable background audio will still be able to play, but non-mixable background audio won't be able to play.

- You can override a policy that allows Music app music or other background audio to play, so as to *duck* (diminish the volume of) that background audio (`AVAudio-SessionCategoryOptionDuckOthers`). Ducking does *not* depend automatically on whether your app is actively producing any sound; rather, it starts as soon as you turn this override on and remains in place until your audio session is deactivated.

It is common practice to declare your app's initial audio session policy very early in the life of the app, possibly as early as `application:didFinishLaunchingWithOptions:`. You can then, if necessary, change your audio session policy in real time, as your app runs.

Your audio session policy is not in effect, however, unless your audio session is also *active*. By default, it isn't. Thus, asserting your audio session policy is done by a combination of configuring the audio session and activating the audio session. To activate (or deactivate) your audio session, you call `setActive:withOptions:error:`.

The question then is *when* to call `setActive:withOptions:error:`. This is a little tricky because of multitasking. Your audio session can be deactivated automatically if your app is no longer active. So if you want your policy to be obeyed under all circumstances, you must explicitly activate your audio session each time your app becomes active. The best place to do this is in `applicationDidBecomeActive:`, as this is the only method guaranteed to be called every time your app is reactivated under circumstances where your audio session might have been deactivated in the background. (See Chapter 11 for how an app resigns and resumes active status.)

The first parameter to `setActive:withOptions:error:` is a BOOL saying whether we want to activate or deactivate our audio session. There are various reasons why you might deactivate (and perhaps reactivate) your audio session over the lifetime of your app.

One such reason is that you no longer need to hog the device's audio, and you want to yield to other apps to play music in the background. The second parameter to `set-Active:withOptions:error:` lets you supply a single option, `AVAudioSessionSet-ActiveOptionNotifyOthersOnDeactivation` (only when the first parameter is NO). By doing this, you tell the system to allow any audio suspended by the activation of your audio session to resume. After all, enforcing a Playback audio session policy that silences music that was playing in the background is not very nice if your app isn't actively producing any sound *at the moment*; better to activate your Playback audio session only when your app is actively producing sound, and deactivate it when your sound finishes. When you do that along with this option, the effect is one of pausing background audio, playing your audio, and then resuming background audio (if the app providing the background audio responds correctly to this option). I'll give an example later in this chapter.

Another reason for deactivating (and reactivating) your audio session is to bring a change of audio policy into effect. A good example is *ducking*. Let's say that, in general, we don't play any sounds, and we want background sound such as Music app songs to continue playing while our app runs. So we configure our audio session to use the Ambient policy in `application:didFinishLaunchingWithOptions:`, as follows:

```
[[AVAudioSession sharedInstance] setCategory: AVAudioSessionCategoryAmbient
                        withOptions:0 error: nil];
```

We aren't interrupting any other audio with our Ambient policy, so it does no harm to activate our audio session every time our app becomes active, no matter how, in `applicationDidBecomeActive:`, like this:

```
[[AVAudioSession sharedInstance] setActive: YES withOptions: 0 error: nil];
```

That's all it takes to set and enforce your app's overall audio session policy. Now let's say we do *sometimes* play a sound, but it's brief and doesn't require background sound to stop entirely; it suffices for background audio to be quieter momentarily while we're playing our sound. That's ducking! So, just before we play our sound, we duck any external sound by changing the options on our Ambient category:

```
[[AVAudioSession sharedInstance]
    setCategory: AVAudioSessionCategoryAmbient
    withOptions: AVAudioSessionCategoryOptionDuckOthers
        error: nil];
```

When we finish playing our sound, we turn off ducking. This is the tricky part. Not only must we remove the ducking property from our audio session policy, but we must also *deactivate our audio session* to make the change take effect immediately and bring the external sound back to its original level; there is then no harm in reactivating our audio session:

```
[[AVAudioSession sharedInstance] setActive:NO withOptions:0 error:nil];
[[AVAudioSession sharedInstance] setCategory: AVAudioSessionCategoryAmbient
                        withOptions: 0
                            error: nil];
[[AVAudioSession sharedInstance] setActive:YES withOptions: 0 error:nil];
```

Interruptions

Your audio session can be *interrupted*. This could mean that some other app deactivates it: for example, on an iPhone a phone call can arrive or an alarm can go off. In the multitasking world, it could mean that another app asserts its audio session over yours. You can register for a notification to learn of interruptions:

`AVAudioSessionInterruptionNotification`
> To learn whether the interruption began or ended, examine the `AVAudioSession-InterruptionTypeKey` entry in the notification's `userInfo` dictionary; this will be one of the following:

- `AVAudioSessionInterruptionTypeBegan`

- `AVAudioSessionInterruptionTypeEnded`

In the latter case, the `AVAudioSessionInterruptionOptionKey` entry may be present, containing an NSNumber wrapping `AVAudioSessionInterruption-OptionShouldResume`; this is the flip side of `AVAudioSessionSetActiveOption-NotifyOthersOnDeactivation`, which I mentioned earlier: some other app that interrupted you has now deactivated its audio session, and is telling you to feel free to resume your audio.

 Audio session notifications are new in iOS 6. Previously, it was necessary to set an audio session delegate, or install a handler function by way of the C API.

Interruptions are not as intrusive as you might suppose. When your audio session is interrupted, your audio has already stopped and your audio session has been deactivated; you might respond by altering something about your app's user interface to reflect the fact that your audio isn't playing, but apart from this there's no particular work for you to do. When the interruption ends, on the other hand, activating your audio session and possibly resuming playback of your audio might be up to you. Even this may not be necessary, however; if you use an audio player (AVAudioPlayer, discussed in the next section), it activates your audio session for you, and typically resumes playing, when an interruption ends.

In the multitasking world, when your app switches to the background, your audio is paused (unless your app plays audio in the background, as discussed later in this chapter). Various things can happen when your app comes back to the front. Again, if you were playing audio with an AVAudioPlayer, it's possible that the AVAudioPlayer will handle the entire situation: it will automatically reactivate your audio session and resume playing, and you won't get any interruption notifications.

If you're *not* using an AVAudioPlayer, however, it is likely that being moved into the background will count as an interruption of your audio session. You don't get any notifications while you're suspended in the background, so everything happens at once when your app comes back to the front: you'll be notified that the interruption began, then notified that it ended, and then your `applicationDidBecomeActive:` will be called, all in quick succession (and in that order). Make sure that your responses to these events, arriving in a sudden cluster, don't step on each other's toes somehow.

When the user double-taps the Home button to reach the application switcher and uses the Play button to resume the current Music app song, you get a notification that an interruption began; if the user then double-taps the Home button again to return from the application switcher to your app, you get `applicationDidBecomeActive:`, but you do *not* get any notification that the interruption has ended (and an AVAudioPlayer does not automatically resume playing). This seems incoherent.

Routing Changes

Your audio is routed through a particular output (and input). The user can make changes in this routing — for example, by plugging headphones into the device, which causes sound to stop coming out of the speaker and to come out of the headphones instead. By default, your audio continues uninterrupted if any is playing, but your code might like to be notified when routing is changed. You can register for `AVAudioSessionRoute-ChangeNotification` to hear about routing changes.

The notification's `userInfo` dictionary is chock full of useful information about what just happened. You're given a description of the new route and possibly the old route, along with a summation of what changed and why. Here's NSLog's display of the dictionary that results when I detach headphones from the device:

```
AVAudioSessionRouteChangePreviousRouteKey =
    "<AVAudioSessionRouteDescription: 0x1f028840,
        inputs = (null);
        outputs = (
            "<AVAudioSessionPortDescription: 0x1f02af30,
                type = Headphones;
                name = Headphones;
                UID = Wired Headphones;
                channels = (
                    "<AVAudioSessionChannelDescription: 0x1f02af80,
                        name = Headphones Left;
                        number = 1;
                        port UID = Wired Headphones>",
                    "<AVAudioSessionChannelDescription: 0x1f02afa0,
                        name = Headphones Right;
                        number = 2;
                        port UID = Wired Headphones>"
                )>"
        )>";
AVAudioSessionRouteChangeReasonKey = 2;
```

The classes mentioned here — AVAudioSessionRouteDescription, AVAudioSession-PortDescription, AVAudioSessionChannelDescription — are all value classes (glorified structs). For the meaning of the AVAudioSessionRouteChangeReasonKey, see the AVAudioSession class reference; the value here, 2, is `AVAudioSessionRouteChange-ReasonOldDeviceUnavailable` — we stopped using the headphones because there are no headphones any longer. A routing change may not of itself interrupt your sound, but Apple suggests that in this particular situation you might like to respond by stopping your audio deliberately, possibly giving the user the option of resuming it, because otherwise sound may now suddenly be coming out of the speaker in a public place.

Audio Player

An *audio player* is an instance of the AVAudioPlayer class. This is the easiest way to play sounds with any degree of sophistication. A wide range of sound types is acceptable, including MP3, AAC, and ALAC, as well as AIFF and WAV. You can set a sound's volume and stereo pan features, loop a sound, synchronize the playing of multiple sounds simultaneously, change the playing rate, and set playback to begin somewhere in the middle of a sound. New in iOS 6, you can even tell the audio player what output channels of the device to use in producing its sound.

To use an audio player, you'll need to link to *AVFoundation.framework* and import `<AVFoundation/AVFoundation.h>`. An audio player should always be used in conjunction with an audio session; see the previous section.

Not every device type can play a compressed sound format in every degree of compression, and the limits can be difficult or impossible to learn except by experimentation. I encountered this issue when an app of mine worked correctly on an iPod touch 32GB but failed to play its sounds on an iPod touch 8GB (even though the latter was newer). Even more frustrating, the files played just fine in the Music app on *both* devices. The problem appears to be that the compression bit rate of my sound files was too low for AVAudioPlayer on the 8GB device, but not on the 32GB device. But there is no documentation of the limits involved.

An audio player can possess and play only one sound, but it can play that sound repeatedly, and you can have multiple audio players, possibly playing simultaneously. An audio player is initialized with its sound, using a local file URL or NSData. To play the sound, first tell the audio player to `prepareToPlay`, causing it to load buffers and initialize hardware; then tell it to `play`. The audio player's delegate (AVAudioPlayerDelegate) is notified when the sound finishes playing (`audioPlayerDidFinish-Playing:successfully:`); do *not* repeatedly check the audio player's `playing` property to learn its state. Other useful methods include `pause` and `stop`; the chief difference between them is that `pause` doesn't release the buffers and hardware set up by `prepare-ToPlay`, but `stop` does (so you'd want to call `prepareToPlay` again before resuming play). Neither `pause` nor `stop` changes the playhead position (the point in the sound where playback will start if `play` is sent again); for that, use the `currentTime` property.

In a WWDC 2011 video, Apple points out that simultaneously playing multiple sounds that have different sample rates is computationally expensive, and suggests that you prepare your sounds beforehand by converting them to a single sample rate. Also, decoding AAC is faster and less expensive than decoding MP3.

Devising a strategy for instantiating, retaining, and releasing your audio players is up to you. In one of my apps, I use a class called Player, which implements a play: method expecting a string path to a sound file in the app bundle. This method creates a new audio player, stores it as an instance variable, and tells it to play the sound file; it also sets itself up as that audio player's delegate, and emits a notification when the sound finishes playing. In this way, by maintaining a single Player instance, I can play different sounds in succession:

```
- (void) play: (NSString*) path {
    NSURL *fileURL = [[NSURL alloc] initFileURLWithPath: path];
    NSError* err = nil;
    AVAudioPlayer *newPlayer =
        [[AVAudioPlayer alloc] initWithContentsOfURL: fileURL error: &err];
    // error-checking omitted
    self.player = newPlayer; // retain policy
    [self.player prepareToPlay];
    [self.player setDelegate: self];
    [self.player play];
}

- (void)audioPlayerDidFinishPlaying:(AVAudioPlayer *)player // delegate method
                  successfully:(BOOL)flag {
    [[NSNotificationCenter defaultCenter]
        postNotificationName:@"soundFinished" object:nil];
}
```

Here are some useful audio player properties:

pan, volume
:   Stereo positioning and loudness, respectively.

numberOfLoops
:   How many times the sound should repeat after it finishes playing; thus, 0 (the default) means it doesn't repeat. A negative value causes the sound to repeat indefinitely (until told to stop).

duration
:   The length of the sound (read-only).

`currentTime`

The playhead position within the sound. If the sound is paused or stopped, `play` will start at the `currentTime`. You can set this in order to "seek" to a playback position within the sound.

`enableRate, rate`

These properties allow the sound to be played at anywhere from half speed (`0.5`) to double speed (`2.0`). Set `enableRate` to YES *before* calling `prepareToPlay`; you are then free to set the `rate`.

`meteringEnabled`

If YES (the default is NO), you can call `updateMeters` followed by `averagePower-ForChannel:` and/or `peakPowerForChannel:`, periodically, to track how loud the sound is. Presumably this would be so you could provide some sort of graphical representation of this value in your interface.

`settings`

A read-only dictionary describing features of the sound, such as its bit rate (`AVEncoderBitRateKey`), its sample rate (`AVSampleRateKey`), and its data format (`AVFormatIDKey`).

The `playAtTime:` method allows playing to be scheduled to start at a certain time. The time should be described in terms of the audio player's `deviceCurrentTime` property.

As I mentioned in the previous section, an audio player resumes playing when your app comes to the front if it was playing and was forced to stop playing when your app was moved to the background. There are delegate methods `audioPlayerBegin-Interruption:` and `audioPlayerEndInterruption:withOptions:`, but my experience is that the audio player will normally resume playing automatically and the delegate won't be sent these messages at all. In fact, I have yet to discover a situation in which `audioPlayerEndInterruption:withOptions:` is *ever* called when your app is in the foreground (active); it may, however, be called when your app is capable of playing sound in the background, as I'll explain later in this chapter.

Remote Control of Your Sound

Various sorts of signal constitute *remote control*. There is hardware remote control; the user might be using earbuds with buttons, for example. There is also software remote control — for example, the playback controls that you see when you double-click the Home button to view the fast app switcher and then swipe to the right (Figure 27-1). Similarly, the buttons that appear if you double-click the Home button when the screen is locked and sound is playing are a form of software remote control (Figure 27-2).

Figure 27-1. The software remote controls in the app switcher

Figure 27-2. The software remote controls on the locked screen

Your app can arrange to be targeted by *remote control events* reporting that the user has tapped a remote control. This is particularly appropriate in an app that plays sound. Your sound-playing app can respond to the remote play/pause button, for example, by playing or pausing its sound.

Remote control events are a form of UIEvent, and they are sent initially to the first responder. (See Chapter 11 and Chapter 18 on UIResponders and the responder chain.) To arrange to be a recipient of remote control events:

- Your app must contain a UIResponder in its responder chain that returns YES from canBecomeFirstResponder, and that responder must actually be first responder.

- Some UIResponder in the responder chain, at or above the first responder, must implement remoteControlReceivedWithEvent:.

- Your app must call the UIApplication instance method beginReceivingRemote-ControlEvents.

- Your app's audio session's policy must be Playback.

- Your app must emit some sound. The rule is that the running app that is capable of receiving remote control events and that last actually produced sound is the target of remote events. The user can tell what app this is because the icon at the right of the remote control interface (Figure 27-1) is the icon of that app. The remote control event target defaults to the Music app if no other app takes precedence by this rule.

A typical place to put all of this is in your view controller, which is, after all, a UIResponder:

```
- (BOOL)canBecomeFirstResponder {
    return YES;
}

- (void) viewDidAppear:(BOOL)animated {
    [super viewDidAppear: animated];
    [self becomeFirstResponder];
    [[UIApplication sharedApplication] beginReceivingRemoteControlEvents];
}

- (void)remoteControlReceivedWithEvent:(UIEvent *)event {
    // ...
}
```

The question is then how to implement remoteControlReceivedWithEvent:. Your implementation will examine the subtype of the incoming UIEvent to decide what to do. There are many possible subtype values, listed under UIEventSubtype in the UIEvent class documentation; they have names like UIEventSubtypeRemoteControlPlay. A minimal implementation will respond to UIEventSubtypeRemoteControlTogglePlay-Pause. Here's an example in an app where sound is produced by an AVAudioPlayer:

```
- (void)remoteControlReceivedWithEvent:(UIEvent *)event {
    UIEventSubtype type = event.subtype;
    if (type == UIEventSubtypeRemoteControlTogglePlayPause) {
        if ([if self.player isPlaying])
            [self.player pause];
        else
            [self.player play];
    }
}
```

You can also influence what information the user will see in the remote control interface about what's being played. For that, you'll use MPNowPlayingInfoCenter; you'll need to link to *MediaPlayer.framework* and import <MediaPlayer/MediaPlayer.h>. Call the class method defaultCenter and set the resulting instance's nowPlayingInfo property to a dictionary. The relevant keys are listed in the class documentation; they will make more sense after you've read Chapter 29, which discusses the Media Player framework. The code (from my TidBITS News app) that actually produced the interface shown in Figure 27-1 and Figure 27-2 is as follows:

```
MPNowPlayingInfoCenter* mpic = [MPNowPlayingInfoCenter defaultCenter];
mpic.nowPlayingInfo = @{
    MPMediaItemPropertyTitle:self.titleLabel.text,
    MPMediaItemPropertyArtist:self.authorLabel.text
};
```

Playing Sound in the Background

In the multitasking world, when the user switches away from your app to another app, by default, your app is suspended and stops producing sound. But if the business of your app is to play sound, you might like your app to continue playing sound in the background. In earlier sections of this chapter, I've spoken about how your app, in the foreground, relates its sound production to background sound such as the Music app. Now we're talking about how your app can *be* that background sound, possibly playing sound while some other app is in the foreground.

To play sound in the background, your app must do these things:

- In your *Info.plist*, you must include the "Required background modes" key (`UIBackgroundModes`) with a value that includes "App plays audio" (`audio`).
- Your audio session's policy must be Playback (and must be active, of course).

If those things are true, then the sound that your app is playing when the user clicks the Home button and dismisses your application, or switches to another app, will go right on playing.

 When the screen is locked, your app can continue to play sound only if it is capable of playing sound in the background.

Moreover, your app may be able to start playing in the background even if it was *not* playing previously — namely, if it is mixable (`AVAudioSessionCategoryOptionMixWithOthers`, see earlier in this chapter), or if it is capable of being the remote control target. Indeed, an extremely cool feature of playing sound in the background is that remote control events continue to work. Even if your app was not actively playing at the time it was put into the background, it may be the remote control target (because it *was* playing sound earlier, as explained in the preceding section). In that case, if the user causes a remote control event to be sent, your app, if suspended in the background, will be woken up (still in the background) in order to receive the remote control event and can begin playing sound. However, the rules for interruptions still apply; another app can interrupt your app's audio session while your app is in the background, and if that app receives remote control events, then your app is no longer the remote control target.

If your app is the remote control target in the background, then another app can interrupt your app's audio, play some audio of its own, and then deactivate its own audio session with the option telling your app to resume playing. I'll give a minimal example of how this works with an AVAudioPlayer.

Let's call the two apps BackgroundPlayer and Interrupter. Suppose Interrupter has an audio session policy of Ambient. This means that when it comes to the front, background audio doesn't stop. But now Interrupter wants to play a sound of its own, temporarily stopping background audio. To pause the background audio, it sets its own audio session to Playback:

```
[[AVAudioSession sharedInstance] setCategory:AVAudioSessionCategoryPlayback
                                  withOptions:0 error:nil];
[[AVAudioSession sharedInstance] setActive:YES withOptions:0 error:nil];
[self.player setDelegate: self];
[self.player prepareToPlay];
[self.player play];
```

When Interrupter's sound finishes playing, its AVAudioPlayer's delegate is notified. In response, Interrupter deactivates its audio session with the AVAudioSessionSetActive-OptionNotifyOthersOnDeactivation option; then it's fine for it to switch its audio session policy back to Ambient and activate it once again:

```
[[AVAudioSession sharedInstance] setActive:NO
    withOptions:AVAudioSessionSetActiveOptionNotifyOthersOnDeactivation
    error:nil];
[[AVAudioSession sharedInstance] setCategory:AVAudioSessionCategoryAmbient
                                  withOptions:0 error:nil];
[[AVAudioSession sharedInstance] setActive: YES withOptions:0 error:nil];
```

So much for Interrupter. Now let's turn to BackgroundPlayer, which was playing in the background when Interrupter came along and changed its own policy to Playback. When Interrupter changes its own policy to Playback, BackgroundPlayer's sound is interrupted; it stops playing, and its AVAudioPlayer delegate is sent audioPlayerBegin-Interruption:. When Interrupter deactivates its audio session, BackgroundPlayer's AVAudioPlayer delegate is sent audioPlayerEndInterruption:withOptions:. It tests for the resume option and, if it is set, starts playing again:

```
-(void)audioPlayerEndInterruption:(AVAudioPlayer *)p
       withOptions:(NSUInteger)opts {
    if (opts & AVAudioSessionInterruptionOptionShouldResume) {
        [p prepareToPlay];
        [p play];
    }
}
```

An interesting byproduct of your app being capable of playing sound in the background is that while it *is* playing sound, a timer can fire. The timer must have been created and scheduled in the foreground, but after that, it will fire even while your app is in the background, unless your app is currently not playing any sound. This is remarkable, because many sorts of activity are forbidden when your app is running in the background.

Another byproduct of your app playing sound in the background has to do with app delegate events. In Chapter 11, I said that your app delegate will probably never receive the `applicationWillTerminate:` message, because by the time the app terminates, it will already have been suspended and incapable of receiving any events. However, an app that is playing sound in the background is *not* suspended, even though it is in the background. If it is terminated while playing sound in the background, it will receive `applicationDidEnterBackground:`, even though it has *already* received this event previously when it was moved into the background, and then it *will* receive `application-WillTerminate:`.

Further Topics in Sound

iOS is a powerful milieu for production and processing of sound; its sound-related technologies are extensive. This is a big topic, and an entire book could be written about it (in fact, such books do exist). I'll talk in Chapter 29 about accessing sound files in the user's music library. But here are some further topics that there is no room to discuss here:

Other audio session policies

If your app accepts sound input or does audio processing, you'll want to look into additional audio session policies I didn't talk about earlier — Record, Play and Record, and Audio Processing. In addition, if you're using Record or Play and Record, there are modes — voice chat, video recording, and measurement (of the sound being input) — that optimize how sound is routed (for example, what microphone is used) and how it is modified.

Recording sound

To record sound simply, use AVAudioRecorder. Your audio session policy will need to adopt a Record policy before recording begins.

Audio queues

Audio queues implement sound playing and recording through a C API with more granularity than the Objective-C AVAudioPlayer and AVAudioRecorder (though it is still regarded as a high-level API), giving you access to the buffers used to move chunks of sound data between a storage format (a sound file) and sound hardware.

Extended Audio File Services

A C API for reading and writing sound files in chunks. It is useful in connection with technologies such as audio queues.

Audio Converter Services

A C API for converting sound files between formats.

Streaming audio

Audio streamed in real time over the network, such as an Internet radio station, can be played with Audio File Stream Services, in connection with audio queues.

OpenAL

An advanced technology for playing sound with fine control over its stereo stage and directionality.

Audio units

Plug-ins that filter and modify the nature and quality of a sound as it passes through them. See the *Audio Unit Hosting Guide for iOS*.

MIDI

The CoreMIDI framework allows interaction with MIDI devices. The Audio Toolbox framework allows you to play a MIDI file, possibly passing it through an AUGraph that uses the AUSampler audio unit to produce synthesized sound.

CHAPTER 28

Video

Basic video playback is performed in a view owned by an MPMoviePlayerController. You'll need to link to *MediaPlayer.framework* and import `<MediaPlayer/Media-Player.h>`. There are two relevant classes supplied by the Media Player framework:

MPMoviePlayerController
Vends a view that plays a movie, along with controls letting the user regulate playback.

MPMoviePlayerViewController
A UIViewController subclass that owns an MPMoviePlayerController and displays its view, along with controls letting the user regulate playback.

The behavior of MPMoviePlayerController has changed significantly from one system version to the next. It is difficult to use it compatibly with multiple system versions. In this chapter, I describe only its current behavior, with no attempt to discuss earlier differences or to advise you on backward compatibility.

A simple interface for letting the user trim video (UIVideoEditorController) is also supplied.

Sophisticated video playing and editing can be performed through AV Foundation. I'll introduce it at the end of this chapter, describing AVPlayer, an alternative class for playing a movie or a sound, and demonstrating AV Foundation's video- and audio-editing capabilities.

A movie file can be in a standard movie format, such as *.mov* or *.mp4*, but it can also be a sound file. An MPMoviePlayerController or MPMoviePlayerViewController is thus an easy way to play a sound file, including a sound file obtained in real time over the

Internet, along with standard controls for pausing the sound and moving the playhead (unlike AVAudioPlayer, which lacks a user interface: see Chapter 27).

A mobile device does not have unlimited power for decoding and presenting video in real time. A video that plays on your computer might not play at all on an iOS device. See the "Media Layer" chapter of Apple's *iOS Technology Overview* for a list of specifications and limits within which video is eligible for playing.

A web view (Chapter 24) supports the HTML 5 <video> tag. This can be a simple lightweight way to present video and to allow the user to control playback. Both web view video and MPMoviePlayerController support AirPlay.

 If an MPMoviePlayerController or an AVPlayer produces sound, you may need to concern yourself with your application's audio session; see Chapter 27. However, both MPMoviePlayerController and AVPlayer deal gracefully with the app being sent into the background, and will pause when your app is backgrounded and resume when your app comes back to the foreground.

MPMoviePlayerController

An MPMoviePlayerController vends and controls a view, its view property; you assign it a movie described by a URL, its contentURL, which it will present in that view. You are responsible for instantiating and retaining the MPMoviePlayerController, and you'll provide the contentURL in its initializer, initWithContentURL:. The movie URL can be a local file URL, so that the player can show, for example, a movie stored as a file in the app's bundle, or obtained from the Camera Roll / Saved Photos group in the user's photo library (see Chapter 30); or it can be a resource (possibly streamed) to be fetched over the Internet, in which case the MPMoviePlayerController initiates the download automatically as soon as it has the contentURL.

You are also responsible for placing the MPMoviePlayerController's view into your interface. (MPMoviePlayerController is not a UIViewController, so you can put its view *directly* into your interface.) No law says you *have* to put the MPMoviePlayerController's view into your interface, but if you don't, the user won't be able to see the movie or the controls that accompany it by default. An MPMoviePlayerController's view is a real view; you can set its frame, its autoresizingMask, and so forth, and you can give it subviews. An MPMoviePlayerController also has a backgroundView which automatically appears behind its view; you can give the backgroundView subviews as well.

Before you can display a movie in your interface with an MPMoviePlayerController, you must call prepareToPlay, which is part of the MPMediaPlayer protocol, adopted by MPMoviePlayerController.

Things happen slowly with a movie. Even when a movie is a local file, a certain amount of it has to load before the MPMoviePlayerController knows enough about the movie and the movie's specifications to begin playing it. The delay can be perceptible. In the case of a remote resource, this loading process will take even longer. I'll talk in a moment about how you can know when the movie is ready to play.

 If an MPMoviePlayerController fails to load its movie into its view when you're testing your app in the Simulator, this may be due to an All Exceptions breakpoint. Try turning off breakpoints. This seems to be a bug in Xcode's interaction with the Simulator.

If the MPMoviePlayerController's shouldAutoplay property is YES (the default), play will begin as soon as possible, with no further action from you; indeed, play will begin even if you don't put the MPMoviePlayerController's view into your interface! If the movie has sound, the user will then hear it without being able to see it, which could be confusing. To prevent this, put the view into your interface, or set shouldAutoplay to NO (or both).

In this example, we create an MPMoviePlayerController, give it a reference to a movie from our app bundle, retain it through a property, and put its view into our interface:

```
NSURL* m = [[NSBundle mainBundle] URLForResource:@"ElMirage"
                                   withExtension:@"mp4"];
MPMoviePlayerController* mp =
    [[MPMoviePlayerController alloc] initWithContentURL:m];
self.mpc = mp; // retain policy
self.mpc.shouldAutoplay = NO;
[self.mpc prepareToPlay];
self.mpc.view.frame = CGRectMake(10, 10, 300, 250);
self.mpc.backgroundView.backgroundColor = [UIColor redColor];
[self.view addSubview:self.mpc.view];
```

The controls (controlStyle is MPMovieControlStyleEmbedded) include a play/pause button, a slider for changing the current frame of the movie (which may be omitted if the runtime feels the view isn't wide enough to display it), and a fullscreen button (Figure 28-1); there may also be an AirPlay route button, if an appropriate device is found on the network.

The user can tap the view to show or hide the controls at the bottom; the controls may also disappear automatically after play begins.

The controls, when controlStyle is MPMovieControlStyleEmbedded, appear at the bottom of the view. The movie itself is centered and scaled to fill the size of the view in accordance with the MPMoviePlayerController's scalingMode; the default is MPMovie-ScalingModeAspectFit, which scales to fit, keeping the correct aspect ratio, and fills

Figure 28-1. A movie player with controls

Figure 28-2. A movie player when the movie is a sound file

the unfilled dimension with the color of the MPMoviePlayerController's background-View.

That explains why Figure 28-1 doesn't look very good. Our code is not sophisticated about the size of the movie; it just tells the movie's view to adopt a certain size. Within that size, the movie itself is scaled and centered, and the controls appear at the bottom. It would be better to set the size of the view in relation to the size of the movie. You can learn the actual size and aspect ratio of the movie, perhaps so as to eliminate the excess unfilled dimension. To do this, you get the MPMoviePlayerController's naturalSize, but, as I mentioned earlier, it takes time, after the content URL is set and you call prepare-ToPlay, before this value can be determined. I'll show an example in a moment.

If the movie is actually a sound file, the controls are drawn differently: there is a start/ pause button, a slider, and possibly an AirPlay route button, and that's all. The controls are centered in the view (Figure 28-2).

Figure 28-3. A movie player in fullscreen mode, with controls

If the user taps the fullscreen button (or pinches outwards) to enter fullscreen mode, the controls (controlStyle is MPMovieControlStyleFullscreen) at the top include a Done button, a slider, and an increased fullscreen button, and a second set of controls appears at the bottom with a play/pause button and rewind and fast-forward buttons, plus possibly a volume slider and an AirPlay route button. The user can tap to dismiss or summon the controls, double-tap to toggle increased fullscreen mode, and tap Done to stop play and leave fullscreen mode (Figure 28-3).

You can also set the style of the controls (controlStyle) manually, though this would be an odd thing to do, because each style of control goes with a display mode (fullscreen or otherwise); you are most likely to use this feature to make it impossible for the user to summon the controls at all (MPMovieControlStyleNone).

The fullscreen rendering will rotate to compensate for a change in device orientation if the interface in which the MPMoviePlayerController's view is embedded will do so. You can programmatically toggle between fullscreen and not, with set-Fullscreen:animated:. You can set an MPMoviePlayerController to fullscreen programmatically even if the movie is just a sound, whose controller lacks a fullscreen button (Figure 28-4).

The movie can be made to repeat automatically (repeatMode) when it reaches its end. You can get the movie's duration. You can change its initialPlaybackTime and end-PlaybackTime (effectively trimming the start and end off the movie). Further programmatic control over the actual playing of the movie is obtained through the MPMedia-Playback protocol, which (as I mentioned a moment ago) MPMoviePlayerController adopts. This gives you the expected play, pause, and stop methods, as well as commands for seeking quickly forward and backward, and you can get and set the current-PlaybackTime to position the playhead. You can also set the currentPlaybackRate,

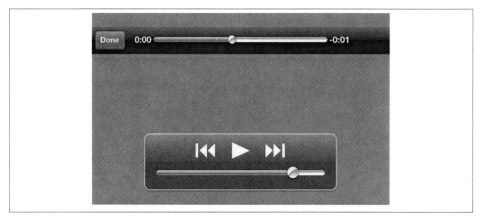

Figure 28-4. A fullscreen movie player when the movie is a sound file

making the movie play slower or faster than normal, and even backward (though in my experience backward play doesn't always work very well; it *skips* backward, playing little forward excerpts, rather than *running* backward as one might have hoped).

An MPMoviePlayerController doesn't have a delegate. Instead, to learn of events as they happen, you must register for notifications. These notifications are how you know when, after assigning a content URL and calling `prepareToPlay`, it is safe for you to query properties of the movie such its `naturalSize` and `duration`. In this example, I'll use a notification to embed the movie view into the interface, at the correct aspect ratio, as soon as the `naturalSize` is known (Figure 28-5):

```
- (void) setUpMPC {
    NSURL* m = [[NSBundle mainBundle] URLForResource:@"ElMirage"
                                       withExtension:@"mp4"];
    // ... the rest as before; do NOT add to view yet ...
    // [self.view addSubview:self.mpc.view];
    [[NSNotificationCenter defaultCenter]
        addObserver:self
          selector:@selector(finishSetup:)
              name:MPMoviePlayerReadyForDisplayDidChangeNotification
            object:self.mpc];
}

- (void) finishSetup: (id) n {
    [[NSNotificationCenter defaultCenter]
        removeObserver:self
                  name:MPMoviePlayerReadyForDisplayDidChangeNotification
                object:self.mpc];
    CGRect f = self.mpc.view.bounds;
    f.size = self.mpc.naturalSize;
    // make width 300, keep ratio
    CGFloat ratio = 300.0/f.size.width;
```

Figure 28-5. A movie player whose view fits its movie

```
        f.size.width *= ratio;
        f.size.height *= ratio;
        self.mpc.view.bounds = f;
        [self.view addSubview:self.mpc.view];
    }
```

 `MPMoviePlayerReadyForDisplayDidChangeNotification` is new in iOS 6, and supersedes `MPMovieNaturalSizeAvailable-Notification` from iOS 5 and before. Unfortunately, it really does supersede it: `MPMovieNaturalSizeAvailableNotification` is no longer sent. No major iOS update has lacked changes to MPMovie-PlayerController that break your existing code; why should iOS 6 be different?

Additional notifications tell such things as when fullscreen mode is entered and exited, and when the movie finishes playing. One of the most important notifications is `MPMovie-PlaybackStateDidChangeNotification`; to learn the actual playback state, query the MPMoviePlayerController's `playbackState`, which will be one of these:

- `MPMoviePlaybackStateStopped`
- `MPMoviePlaybackStatePlaying`
- `MPMoviePlaybackStatePaused`
- `MPMoviePlaybackStateInterrupted`
- `MPMoviePlaybackStateSeekingForward`
- `MPMoviePlaybackStateSeekingBackward`

If the content comes from the Internet, there is of course many a slip possible. Things take time; the Internet might slow down, or go away completely; the resource to be fetched might not exist. You'll want to register for notifications that tell you when things happen, and especially when things go wrong. What I do in the TidBITS News app, where an MPMoviePlayerController is used to play a sound file located remotely across the Internet, is to register for MPMoviePlayerLoadStateDidChangeNotification. When the notification arrives, I check the MPMoviePlayerController's loadState; it's a bitmask, and I look to see whether the MPMovieLoadStatePlaythroughOK bit is set:

```
if (self.mpc.loadState & MPMovieLoadStatePlaythroughOK) { // ...
```

If, on the other hand, the MPMovieLoadStateStalled bit is set, we can assume that the network is in trouble. Play will not stop automatically; the MPMoviePlayerController will keep trying to obtain data. If we want to prevent that, we have to stop it manually (at which point I'd put up an alert informing the user that there's a problem).

Another way to detect a problem is by registering for MPMoviePlayerPlaybackDid-FinishNotification. If there's an error, the userInfo dictionary's MPMoviePlayer-PlaybackDidFinishReasonUserInfoKey will be an NSNumber wrapping MPMovie-FinishReasonPlaybackError, and the dictionary may also have a key called @"error", which will be an NSError; the localizedDescription of this NSError could be suitable for presentation to the user as a statement of the difficulty.

For extended information about the playback of a movie streamed across the Internet, look into MPMoviePlayerController's accessLog and errorLog properties.

There Can Be Only One
Only one MPMoviePlayerController can display a movie in your interface. Judicious use of prepareToPlay can make any MPMoviePlayerController's view the One, but if your interface displays the views of any other MPMoviePlayerControllers, those views may become empty, which doesn't look good and may puzzle the user. To avoid confusion about why one of your MPMoviePlayerControllers is not playing its movie successfully, the simplest solution is to restrict your interface so that it contains only one MPMoviePlayerController's view.

MPMoviePlayerViewController

An MPMoviePlayerViewController is, as its name implies, a view controller (a UIView-Controller subclass). It manages an MPMoviePlayerController (its moviePlayer) and automatically provides a fullscreen presentation of the MPMoviePlayerController's view. Thus, an MPMoviePlayerViewController has some strong advantages of simplicity.

The documentation says that you can use an MPMoviePlayerViewController wherever you would use a UIViewController, such as a child view controller in a tab bar interface or navigation interface, but the MPMoviePlayerViewController's own interface seems to make the most sense when it is a presented view controller. A category on UIView-

Controller even provides a special method for presenting it, presentMoviePlayerView-ControllerAnimated:, which uses a style of animation otherwise unavailable, whereby the current view slides out to reveal the movie view. To remove the view in code, you could then call dismissMoviePlayerViewControllerAnimated. Here's a simple example:

```
NSURL* m = [[NSBundle mainBundle] URLForResource:@"ElMirage"
                                    withExtension:@"mp4"];
MPMoviePlayerViewController* mpvc =
    [[MPMoviePlayerViewController alloc] initWithContentURL: m];
mpvc.moviePlayer.shouldAutoplay = NO; // optional
[self presentMoviePlayerViewControllerAnimated:mpvc];
```

In that code, I've set the MPMoviePlayerViewController's moviePlayer's should-Autoplay property just to show that it can be done; the moviePlayer is an MPMovie-PlayerController, and can be sent the same sorts of message you'd send it if you were using it on its own. For example, you can register for its notifications. You will not, however, need to send it prepareToPlay.

At present, there appears to be a bug where initWithContentURL: on the iPhone triggers a half dozen spurious console log messages complaining of an "invalid context." These messages do no harm, but having them appear in the log is rather unpleasant; a workaround is to wrap that call in a fake graphics context, like this:

```
UIGraphicsBeginImageContext(CGSizeMake(1,1));
MPMoviePlayerViewController* mpvc =
    [[MPMoviePlayerViewController alloc] initWithContentURL: m];
UIGraphicsEndImageContext();
```

You can detect the user pressing the Done button by registering for the MPMoviePlayer-PlaybackDidFinishNotification. If the user tapped Done, the MPMoviePlayer-PlaybackDidFinishReasonUserInfoKey in the notification's userInfo dictionary will be an NSNumber wrapping MPMovieFinishReasonUserExited. If the MPMoviePlayer-ViewController is a presented view controller, it is dismissed automatically when the user taps the Done button or when the movie plays to its end (in which case the MPMovie-PlayerPlaybackDidFinishReasonUserInfoKey is MPMovieFinishReasonPlayback-Ended). If you use the MPMoviePlayerViewController in some other way, the Done button stops play but that's all, and dealing with the interface is up to you.

MPMoviePlayerViewController is a view controller, so if it is used as a presented view controller, it takes charge of whether to rotate in response to a change in the device orientation (Chapter 19). By default, it does nothing, meaning that it will rotate to any orientation permitted by the app and the app delegate. You can subclass MPMovie-PlayerViewController to override supportedInterfaceOrientations if that isn't what you want.

In general, the simplicity of MPMoviePlayerViewController means that a number of choices are made for you, and you may find yourself struggling against them. (For example, when an MPMoviePlayerView-Controller's view is showing, it becomes a recipient of remote control events; see Chapter 27. This feature is convenient, but if it's not what you want, it is not easily overcome; there is no property for turning it off.) A better approach may be to use an MPMoviePlayerController instead. In the current version of the TidBITS News app, I've switched from using MPMoviePlayerViewController to using MPMoviePlayer-Controller and my own view controller, and I'm much happier: with a little more work, I get much more control.

After an MPMoviePlayerViewController's view is dismissed, if your app's revealed interface contains an MPMoviePlayerController's view, that view will be unable to play its movie, because of the rule I stated a moment ago: There Can Be Only One. The MPMoviePlayerViewController's view was the One, so now the MPMoviePlayer-Controller's view is broken. To fix it, send `prepareToPlay` to the MPMoviePlayer-Controller.

UIVideoEditorController

UIVideoEditorController is a view controller that presents an interface where the user can trim video. Its view and internal behavior are outside your control, and you're not supposed to subclass it. You are expected to show the view controller's view as a presented view on the iPhone or in a popover on the iPad, and respond by way of its delegate.

Before summoning a UIVideoEditorController, be sure to call its class method `canEditVideoAtPath:`. Not every video format is editable, and not every device supports video editing. If this call returns NO, don't instantiate UIVideoEditorController to edit the given file. (This call can take some noticeable time to return.) You must also set the UIVideoEditorController instance's `delegate` and `videoPath` before presenting it; the delegate should adopt both UINavigationControllerDelegate and UIVideoEditorControllerDelegate:

```
NSURL* m = [[NSBundle mainBundle] URLForResource:@"ElMirage"
                                   withExtension:@"mp4"];
BOOL can = [UIVideoEditorController canEditVideoAtPath:path];
if (!can) {
    NSLog(@"can't edit this video");
    return;
}
UIVideoEditorController* vc = [UIVideoEditorController new];
vc.delegate = self;
vc.videoPath = path;
if ([[UIDevice currentDevice] userInterfaceIdiom] == UIUserInterfaceIdiomPad) {
```

```
            UIPopoverController* pop =
                [[UIPopoverController alloc] initWithContentViewController:vc];
            pop.delegate = self;
            self.currentPop = pop;
            [pop presentPopoverFromRect:[sender bounds]
                inView:sender permittedArrowDirections:UIPopoverArrowDirectionAny
                                        animated:NO];
    }
    else {
        [self presentViewController:vc animated:YES completion:nil];
    }
```

 In actual fact I have *never* been able to get a UIVideoEditorController to work properly on the iPad! I can summon the interface in a popover, but it is not the correct interface — its title is Choose Video, the right button says Use, and the Cancel button does nothing — and trying to summon the interface as a presented view controller causes a crash. This is a *very* long-standing bug, and I am astounded that Apple has done nothing about it.

The view's interface (on the iPhone) contains Cancel and Save buttons, a trimming box displaying thumbnails from the movie, a Play/Pause button, and the movie itself. The user slides the ends of the trimming box to set the beginning and end of the saved movie. The Cancel and Save buttons do *not* dismiss the presented view; you must do that in your implementation of the delegate methods. There are three of them, and you should implement all three and dismiss the presented view in all of them:

- videoEditorController:didSaveEditedVideoToPath:

- videoEditorControllerDidCancel:

- videoEditorController:didFailWithError:

It's important to implement the didFail... method, because things can go wrong even at this stage.

Saving the trimmed video takes time. When videoEditorController:didSaveEdited-VideoToPath: is called, the trimmed video has already been saved to a file in your app's temporary directory (the same directory returned from a call to NSTemporary-Directory). Doing something useful with the saved file is up to you; if you merely leave it in the temporary directory, you can't rely on it to persist. In this example, I copy the edited movie into the user's Camera Roll photo album (called Saved Photos if the device has no camera). That takes time too, so when I call UISaveVideoAtPathToSavedPhotos-Album, I use the second and third arguments to call a method that dismisses the editor *after* the saving is over:

```
- (void) videoEditorController: (UIVideoEditorController*) editor
        didSaveEditedVideoToPath: (NSString*) editedVideoPath {
    if (UIVideoAtPathIsCompatibleWithSavedPhotosAlbum(editedVideoPath))
        UISaveVideoAtPathToSavedPhotosAlbum(editedVideoPath, self,
            @selector(video:savedWithError:ci:), nil);
    else
        // need to think of something else to do with it
}
```

In our secondary method (here, `video:savedWithError:ci:`), it's important to check for errors, because things can *still* go wrong. In particular, on iOS 6, the user could deny us access to the Photos library (see Chapter 30 for more about that). If that's the case, we'll get an NSError whose `domain` is `ALAssetsLibraryErrorDomain`.

My implementation also has to grapple with the fact that my app's revealed interface, after the presented UIVideoEditorController is dismissed, will contain an MPMovie-PlayerController's view (as described earlier in this chapter). That view will be broken — unable to show its movie — because, as I've already explained, There Can Be Only One. The solution, once again, is to call `prepareToPlay`, but this call won't succeed until the dismissal animation is over and the video editor's movie view has been released; even then, in iOS 6, I have to add an extra delay:

```
-(void)video:(NSString*)path savedWithError:(NSError*)err ci:(void*)ci {
    if (err)
        // ... do something ...
    [self dismissViewControllerAnimated:YES completion:^{
        dispatch_async(dispatch_get_main_queue(), ^{
            [self.mpc prepareToPlay];
        });
    }];
}
```

Introduction to AV Foundation Video

A large suite of AV Foundation classes provides detailed access to media components. To access AV Foundation, you'll need to link to *AVFoundation.framework* (and prob-ably *CoreMedia.framework* as well), and import `<AVFoundation/AVFoundation.h>`. For a list of classes, see the *AV Foundation Framework Reference*. AV Foundation is a huge topic, so there isn't space here to do more than introduce the concepts involved.

The AV Foundation class that performs actual playing of media is AVPlayer. An AV-Player has an AVPlayerItem; this is its media. An AVPlayerItem comprises tracks (AVPlayerItemTrack), which can be individually enabled or disabled. It gets these from its underlying AVAsset; this is the basic media unit, as it were, providing you with access to actual tracks (AVAssetTrack) and metadata. As with an MPMoviePlayerController, you might use an AVPlayer to play a pure sound rather than a full-fledged movie.

An AVPlayer can be an AVQueuePlayer, a subclass that allows multiple AVPlayerItems to be loaded up and then played in sequence; I'll give an example in Chapter 29 of using an AVQueuePlayer to play a series of songs. AVQueuePlayer also has an advanceToNext-Item method, and its list of items can be changed dynamically, so you could use it to give the user access to a set of "chapters."

To display an AVPlayer's movie, you need an AVPlayerLayer (a CALayer subclass). You are unlikely to take this approach unless you need the extended powers of AV Foundation or the sequential playing power of AVQueuePlayer or the flexibility of working directly with a layer and Core Animation. The AVPlayerLayer doesn't even come with controls for letting the user play and pause a movie and visualize its progress; you have to create these yourself. Nevertheless, simply displaying a movie in this way is quite easy:

```
NSURL* m = [[NSBundle mainBundle] URLForResource:@"ElMirage"
                                    withExtension:@"mp4"];
AVPlayer* p = [AVPlayer playerWithURL:m];
self.player = p; // might need a reference later
AVPlayerLayer* lay = [AVPlayerLayer playerLayerWithPlayer:p];
lay.frame = CGRectMake(10,10,300,200);
[self.view.layer addSublayer:lay];
```

To let the user start playing the movie, we might provide a Play button. In this example, the button toggles the playing status of the movie by changing its rate:

```
- (IBAction) doButton: (id) sender {
    CGFloat rate = self.player.rate;
    if (rate < 0.01)
        self.player.rate = 1;
    else
        self.player.rate = 0;
}
```

Another intriguing feature of an AVPlayer is that you can coordinate animation in your interface (Chapter 17) with the playing of the movie. You attach an animation to a layer in more or less the usual way, but the animation takes place in movie playback time: if the movie is stopped, the animation is stopped, and if the movie is run at double rate, the animation runs at double rate. This is done by embedding the layer to be animated in an AVSynchronizedLayer, which is coupled with an AVPlayerItem.

To demonstrate, I'll extend the previous example; after we insert our AVPlayerLayer into the interface, we also create and insert an AVSynchronizedLayer:

```
// create synch layer, put it in the interface
AVPlayerItem* item = p.currentItem;
AVSynchronizedLayer* syncLayer =
    [AVSynchronizedLayer synchronizedLayerWithPlayerItem:item];
syncLayer.frame = CGRectMake(10,220,300,10);
syncLayer.backgroundColor = [[UIColor whiteColor] CGColor];
[self.view.layer addSublayer:syncLayer];
// give synch layer a sublayer
```

Figure 28-6. The black square's position is synchronized to the movie

```
CALayer* subLayer = [CALayer layer];
subLayer.backgroundColor = [[UIColor blackColor] CGColor];
subLayer.frame = CGRectMake(0,0,10,10);
[syncLayer addSublayer:subLayer];
// animate the sublayer
CABasicAnimation* anim = [CABasicAnimation animationWithKeyPath:@"position"];
anim.fromValue = [NSValue valueWithCGPoint: subLayer.position];
anim.toValue = [NSValue valueWithCGPoint: CGPointMake(295,5)];
anim.removedOnCompletion = NO;
anim.beginTime = AVCoreAnimationBeginTimeAtZero; // important trick
anim.duration = CMTimeGetSeconds(item.asset.duration);
[subLayer addAnimation:anim forKey:nil];
```

The result is shown in Figure 28-6. The white rectangle is the AVSynchronizedLayer, tied to our movie. The little black square inside it is its sublayer; when we animate the black square, that animation will be synchronized to the movie, changing its position from the left end of the white rectangle to the right end, starting at the beginning of the movie and with the same duration as the movie. Thus, although we attach this animation to the black square layer in the usual way, the black square *doesn't move* until we tap the button to call doButton: and start the movie playing. Moreover, if we tap the button again to pause the movie, the black square stops. The black square is thus *automatically* representing the current play position within the movie!

For the sake of simplicity, I built the structure in that example from the top down: I started with the AVPlayer and the URL of the media, and extracted the AVPlayerItem and the corresponding AVAsset only when I needed them. That, however, is not typical. In the more general case, you would likely build the structure from the bottom up, starting from the AVAsset, which you can obtain from the URL of the media through a subclass, AVURLAsset. This, then, amounts to the very same thing in bottom-up order:

```
AVURLAsset* asset = [AVURLAsset URLAssetWithURL:m options:nil];
AVPlayerItem* item = [AVPlayerItem playerItemWithAsset:asset];
AVPlayer* p = [AVPlayer playerWithPlayerItem:item];
self.player = p;
AVPlayerLayer* lay = [AVPlayerLayer playerLayerWithPlayer:p];
lay.frame = CGRectMake(10,10,300,200);
[self.view.layer addSublayer:lay];
```

We are now ready to create the synchronized layer. But the synchronization will initially be incorrect unless the AVPlayerLayer is itself ready to display the movie. At that moment, the AVPlayerLayer's `readyForDisplay` property will be YES. To wait for that moment, we use key–value observing (Chapter 13); AV Foundation doesn't generally use notifications, as you're expected to use KVO instead:

```
[lay addObserver:self forKeyPath:@"readyForDisplay" options:0 context:nil];
```

When the AVPlayerLayer is ready for display, we complete the interface by creating the synchronized layer:

```
- (void) observeValueForKeyPath:(NSString *)keyPath ofObject:(id)object
        change:(NSDictionary *)change context:(void *)context {
    if ([keyPath isEqualToString:@"readyForDisplay"]) {
        AVPlayerLayer* lay = (AVPlayerLayer*) object;
        if (lay.readyForDisplay) {
            [lay removeObserver:self forKeyPath:@"readyForDisplay"];
            AVPlayerItem* item = self.player.currentItem;
            AVSynchronizedLayer* syncLayer =
                [AVSynchronizedLayer synchronizedLayerWithPlayerItem:item];
            // ... and the rest is as before ...
```

It takes time for media values to become available. Just as, with MPMoviePlayer-Controller, we couldn't fetch a movie's `naturalSize` immediately, so too, when examining an AVAsset or AVAssetTrack property, you have to wait until that property has been loaded. To do so, you'll call `loadValuesAsynchronouslyForKeys:completion-Handler:`; see the AVAsynchronousKeyValueLoading protocol documentation. I'll give an example in Chapter 29.

AV Foundation also allows you to construct your own media asset in code (AVComposition, an AVAsset subclass, along with *its* subclass, AVMutableComposition). For example, you might combine part of the sound from one asset and part of the video from another into a single movie. In this (oversimplified) example, I extract two five-second snippets from a video file and put them together with a ten-second snippet from an audio file:

```
NSString* type = AVMediaTypeVideo;
NSArray* arr = [myVideoAsset tracksWithMediaType:type];
AVAssetTrack* track = [arr lastObject];

AVMutableComposition* comp = [AVMutableComposition composition];
AVMutableCompositionTrack* comptrack =
```

```
        [comp addMutableTrackWithMediaType:type
            preferredTrackID:kCMPersistentTrackID_Invalid];
    [comptrack insertTimeRange:CMTimeRangeMake(CMTimeMakeWithSeconds(0,1),
                                               CMTimeMakeWithSeconds(5,1))
                ofTrack:track atTime:CMTimeMakeWithSeconds(0,1) error:nil];
    [comptrack insertTimeRange:CMTimeRangeMake(CMTimeMakeWithSeconds(30,1),
                                               CMTimeMakeWithSeconds(5,1))
                ofTrack:track atTime:CMTimeMakeWithSeconds(5,1) error:nil];

    type = AVMediaTypeAudio;
    NSURL* s = [[NSBundle mainBundle] URLForResource:@"snd" withExtension:@"m4a"];
    AVAsset* asset = [AVURLAsset URLAssetWithURL:s options:nil];
    arr = [asset tracksWithMediaType:type];
    track = [arr lastObject];

    comptrack = [comp addMutableTrackWithMediaType:type
                preferredTrackID:kCMPersistentTrackID_Invalid];
    [comptrack insertTimeRange:CMTimeRangeMake(CMTimeMakeWithSeconds(0,1),
                                               CMTimeMakeWithSeconds(10,1))
                ofTrack:track atTime:CMTimeMakeWithSeconds(0,1) error:nil];

    AVPlayerItem* item = [AVPlayerItem playerItemWithAsset:[comp copy]];
```

You can also apply audio volume changes and video opacity and transform changes to the playback of individual tracks. In this example, continuing on from the previous example, we apply a fadeout to the last three seconds of the existing audio:

```
    AVMutableAudioMixInputParameters* params =
        [AVMutableAudioMixInputParameters
            audioMixInputParametersWithTrack:comptrack];
    [params setVolume:1 atTime:CMTimeMakeWithSeconds(0,1)];
    [params setVolumeRampFromStartVolume:1 toEndVolume:0
            timeRange:CMTimeRangeMake(CMTimeMakeWithSeconds(6,1),
                                      CMTimeMakeWithSeconds(2,1))];
    AVMutableAudioMix* mix = [AVMutableAudioMix audioMix];
    mix.inputParameters = [NSArray arrayWithObject: params];

    item.audioMix = mix; // item is our existing AVPlayerItem
```

Here are some other things you can do with AV Foundation:

- Extract single images ("thumbnails") from a movie (AVAssetImageGenerator).

- Export a movie in a different format (AVAssetExportSession), or read/write raw uncompressed data through a buffer to or from a track (AVAssetReader, AVAsset-ReaderOutput, AVAssetWriter, AVAssetWriterInput, and so on).

- Capture audio, video, and stills, on a device that supports it (such as an iPhone, or another device connected to external hardware), including capturing video frames as still images (see Technical Q&A QA1702). I'll say more about this in Chapter 30.

It should be evident from even so brief a summary that you could use AV Foundation to write a movie editor or a sound mixer. To learn more, you'll want to read the *AV Foundation Programming Guide*.

CHAPTER 29

Music Library

An iOS device can be used for the same purpose as the original iPod — to hold and play music and podcasts. These items constitute the device's *music library*; the user can play them with the Music app (formerly called the iPod app on some devices). iOS provides the programmer with various forms of access to the device's music library; you can:

- Explore the music library
- Play an item from the music library
- Learn and control what the Music app's music player is doing
- Present a standard interface for allowing the user to select a music library item

These abilities are provided by the Media Player framework. You'll need to link to *MediaPlayer.framework* and import `<MediaPlayer/MediaPlayer.h>`.

Exploring the Music Library

Everything in the music library, as seen by your code, is an MPMediaEntity. This is an abstract class that endows its subclasses with the ability to describe themselves through key–value pairs called *properties*. (This use of the word "properties" has nothing to do with the Objective-C properties discussed in Chapter 12; these properties are more like entries in an NSDictionary.) The repertoire of properties depends on the sort of entity you're looking at; many of them will be intuitively familiar from your use of iTunes. For example, a media item has a title, an album title, a track number, an artist, a composer, and so on; a playlist has a title, a flag indicating whether it is a "smart" playlist, and so on. The property keys have names like `MPMediaItemPropertyTitle`.

To fetch a property's value, call `valueForProperty:` with its key. You can fetch multiple properties with `enumerateValuesForProperties:usingBlock:`.

An individual item in the music library is an MPMediaItem, an MPMediaEntity subclass. It has a type, according to the value of its `MPMediaItemPropertyMediaType` property: it might, for example, be music, a podcast, an audiobook, or a video. Different types of item have slightly different properties; for example, a podcast, in addition to its normal title, has a podcast title.

An item's artwork image is an instance of the MPMediaItemArtwork class, from which you are supposed to be able to get the image itself scaled to a specified size by calling `imageWithSize:`; my experience is that in reality you'll receive an image of any old size the system cares to give you, so you may have to scale it further yourself. This, for example, is what my Albumen app does:

```
MPMediaItemArtwork* art = //...
UIImage* im = [art imageWithSize:CGSizeMake(36,36)];
// but it probably *isn't* 36 by 36; scale it so that it is
if (im) {
    CGFloat scalew = 36.0/im.size.width;
    CGFloat scaleh = 36.0/im.size.height;
    CGFloat scale = (scalew < scaleh) ? scalew : scaleh;
    CGSize sz = CGSizeMake(im.size.width*scale, im.size.height*scale);
    UIGraphicsBeginImageContextWithOptions(sz, NO, 0);
    [im drawInRect:CGRectMake(0,0,sz.width,sz.height)];
    im = UIGraphicsGetImageFromCurrentImageContext();
    UIGraphicsEndImageContext();
}
```

A playlist is an MPMediaPlaylist. As you would expect, it has `items` and a `count` of those items. It inherits those properties from its superclass, MPMediaItemCollection, which is the other MPMediaEntity subclass. I'll talk more about MPMediaItemCollection in a moment.

Obtaining actual information from the music library requires a *query*, an MPMediaQuery. First, you *form* the query. There are two main ways to do this:

With a convenience constructor
MPMediaQuery provides several class methods that form a query ready to ask the music library for all of its songs, or all of its podcasts, and so on. Here's the complete list:

- `songsQuery`
- `podcastsQuery`
- `audiobooksQuery`
- `playlistsQuery`
- `albumsQuery`
- `artistsQuery`
- `composersQuery`

- `genresQuery`
- `compilationsQuery`

With filter predicates

You can attach to the query one or more MPMediaPropertyPredicate instances, forming a set (NSSet) of predicates. These predicates filter the music library according to criteria you specify; to be included in the result, a media item must successfully pass through all the filters (in other words, the predicates are combined using logical-and). A predicate is a simple comparison. It has two, or possibly three, aspects:

A property

The key to the property you want to compare against. Not every property can be used in a filter predicate; the documentation makes the distinction clear (and you can get additional help from an MPMediaEntity class method, `canFilter-ByProperty:`).

A value

The value that the specified property must have in order to pass through the filter.

A comparison type (optional)

In order to pass through the filter, a media item's property value can either *match* the value you provide (`MPMediaPredicateComparisonEqualTo`, the default) or *contain* the value you provide (`MPMediaPredicateComparison-Contains`).

These two ways of forming a query are actually the same; a convenience constructor is just a quick way of obtaining a query already endowed with a filter predicate.

A query also *groups* its results, according to its `groupingType`. Your choices are:

- `MPMediaGroupingTitle`
- `MPMediaGroupingAlbum`
- `MPMediaGroupingArtist`
- `MPMediaGroupingAlbumArtist`
- `MPMediaGroupingComposer`
- `MPMediaGroupingGenre`
- `MPMediaGroupingPlaylist`
- `MPMediaGroupingPodcastTitle`

The query convenience constructors all supply a groupingType in addition to a filter predicate. Indeed, the grouping is often the salient aspect of the query. For example, an albumsQuery is in fact merely a songsQuery with the added feature that its results are grouped by album.

The groups resulting from a query are *collections*; that is, each is an MPMediaItem-Collection. This class, you will recall, is the superclass of MPMediaPlaylist, and is an MPMediaEntity subclass. So, a collection has properties; it also has items and a count. It also has a representativeItem property, which gives you just one item from the collection. The reason you need this is that properties of a collection are often embodied in its items rather than in the collection itself. For example, an album has no title; rather, its items have album titles that are all the same. So to learn the title of an album, you ask for the album title of a representative item.

 Unfortunately, in iOS 6, asking for a representativeItem can result in some nasty-looking log messages: "Attempting a write transaction on a read-only database," and "BEGIN IMMEDIATE could unexpectedly not be stepped." A possible workaround is to use items[0] instead of representativeItem (even though they are not quite the same thing).

After you form the query, you *perform* the query. You do this simply by asking for the query's results. You can ask either for its collections (if you care about the groups returned from the query) or for its items. Here, I'll discover the titles of all the albums:

```
MPMediaQuery* query = [MPMediaQuery albumsQuery];
NSArray* result = [query collections];
// prove we've performed the query, by logging the album titles
for (MPMediaItemCollection* album in result)
    NSLog(@"%@", [album.representativeItem // or album.items[0]
        valueForProperty:MPMediaItemPropertyAlbumTitle]);
/*
Output starts like this on my device:
Beethoven Concertos
Beethoven Overtures Etc
Beethoven Piano Duet
Beethoven Piano Other
Beethoven Piano Sonatas
...
*/
```

Now let's make our query more elaborate; we'll get the titles of all the albums whose name contains "Sonata". Observe that what we really do is to ask for all songs whose album title contains "Sonata", grouped by album:

```
MPMediaQuery* query = [MPMediaQuery albumsQuery];
MPMediaPropertyPredicate* hasSonata =
    [MPMediaPropertyPredicate predicateWithValue:@"Sonata"
        forProperty:MPMediaItemPropertyAlbumTitle
      comparisonType:MPMediaPredicateComparisonContains];
[query addFilterPredicate:hasSonata];
NSArray* result = [query collections];
for (MPMediaItemCollection* album in result)
    NSLog(@"%@", [album.representativeItem // or album.items[0]
        valueForProperty:MPMediaItemPropertyAlbumTitle]);
/*
Output starts like this on my device:
Beethoven Piano Sonatas
Beethoven Violin Sonatas
Schubert Piano Sonatas
Brahms Sonatas
Mozart Church Sonatas
...
*/
```

Because the results of that query are actually songs (MPMediaItems), we can immediately access any song in any of those albums. Let's modify the output from our previous query to print the titles of all the songs in the first album returned, which happens to be the Beethoven Piano Sonatas album. We don't have to change our query, so I'll start at the point where we perform it:

```
// ... same as before ...
NSArray* result = [query collections];
MPMediaItemCollection* album = result[0];
for (MPMediaItem* song in album.items)
    NSLog(@"%@", [song valueForProperty:MPMediaItemPropertyTitle]);
/*
Output starts like this on my device:
Piano Sonata #1 In F Minor, Op. 2/1 - 1. Allegro
Piano Sonata #1 In F Minor, Op. 2/1 - 2. Adagio
Piano Sonata #1 In F Minor, Op. 2/1 - 3. Menuetto: Allegretto
Piano Sonata #1 In F Minor, Op. 2/1 - 4. Prestissimo
Piano Sonata #2 In A Minor, Op. 2/2 - 1. Allegro Vivace
...
*/
```

One of the properties of an MPMediaEntity is its *persistent ID*, which uniquely identifies this song (MPMediaItemPropertyPersistentID) or playlist (MPMediaPlaylist-PropertyPersistentID). No other means of identification is guaranteed unique; two songs or two playlists can have the same title, for example. Using the persistent ID, you can retrieve again at a later time the same song or playlist you retrieved earlier, even across launches of your app. All sorts of things have persistent IDs — entities in general (MPMediaEntityPropertyPersistentID), albums, artists, composers, and more.

While you are maintaining the results of a search, the contents of the music library may themselves change. For example, the user might connect the device to a computer and add or delete music with iTunes. This can put your results out of date. For this reason, the library's own modified state is available through the MPMediaLibrary class. Call the class method `defaultMediaLibrary` to get the actual library instance; now you can ask it for its `lastModifiedDate`. You can also register to receive a notification, `MPMedia-LibraryDidChangeNotification`, when the music library is modified; this notification is not emitted unless you first send the library `beginGeneratingLibraryChange-Notifications`. You should eventually balance this with `endGeneratingLibrary-ChangeNotifications`.

New in iOS 6, a song has a property `MPMediaItemPropertyIsCloudItem`, allowing you to ask whether it lives in the cloud (thanks to iTunes Match) or on the device. The distinction is clearer in than it was in iOS 5, because a song can now be played from the cloud without downloading it, and the user can manually download a song from the cloud or delete it from the device. Such changes in a song's cloud status do *not* count as a change in the library.

The Music Player

The Media Player framework class for playing an MPMediaItem is MPMusicPlayer-Controller. It comes in two flavors, depending on which class method you use to get an instance:

applicationMusicPlayer
  Plays an MPMediaItem from the music library within your application. The song being played by the `applicationMusicPlayer` can be different from the Music app's current song. This player stops when your app is not in the foreground.

iPodMusicPlayer
  The global music player — the very same player used by the Music app. This might already be playing an item, or might be paused with a current item, at any time while your app runs; you can learn or change what item this is. The global music player continues playing independently of the state of your app, and the user can at any time alter what it is doing.

 An `applicationMusicPlayer` is not really inside your app. It is actually the global music player behaving differently. It has its own audio session. You cannot play its audio when your app is in the background. You cannot make it the target of remote control events. If these limitations prove troublesome, use the `iPodMusicPlayer` (or AVPlayer, discussed later in this chapter).

A music player doesn't merely play an item; it plays from a *queue* of items. This behavior is familiar from iTunes and the Music app. For example, in iTunes, when you switch to a playlist and double-click the first song to start playing, when iTunes comes to the end of that song, it proceeds by default to the next song in the playlist. So at that moment, its queue is the totality of songs in the playlist. The music player behaves the same way; when it reaches the end of a song, it proceeds to the next song in its queue.

Your methods for controlling playback also reflect this queue-based orientation. In addition to the expected play, pause, and stop commands, there's a skipToNextItem and skipToPreviousItem command. Anyone who has ever used iTunes or the Music app (or, for that matter, an old-fashioned iPod) will have an intuitive grasp of this and everything else a music player does. For example, you can also set a music player's repeatMode and shuffleMode, just as in iTunes.

You provide a music player with its queue in one of two ways:

With a query
> You hand the music player an MPMediaQuery. The query's items are the items of the queue.

With a collection
> You hand the music player an MPMediaItemCollection. This might be obtained from a query you performed, but you can also assemble your own collection of MPMediaItems in any way you like, putting them into an array and calling collectionWithItems: or initWithItems:.

In this example, we collect all songs in the library shorter than 30 seconds into a queue and set the queue playing in random order using the application-internal music player:

```
MPMediaQuery* query = [MPMediaQuery songsQuery];
NSMutableArray* marr = [NSMutableArray array];
MPMediaItemCollection* queue = nil;
for (MPMediaItem* song in query.items) {
    NSNumber* dur =
        [song valueForProperty:MPMediaItemPropertyPlaybackDuration];
    if ([dur floatValue] < 30)
        [marr addObject: song];
}
if ([marr count] == 0)
    NSLog(@"No songs that short!");
else
    queue = [MPMediaItemCollection collectionWithItems:marr];
if (queue) {
    MPMusicPlayerController* player =
        [MPMusicPlayerController applicationMusicPlayer];
    [player setQueueWithItemCollection:queue];
    player.shuffleMode = MPMusicShuffleModeSongs;
    [player play];
}
```

If a music player is currently playing, setting its queue will stop it; restarting play is up to you.

You can ask a music player for its nowPlayingItem, and since this is an MPMediaItem, you can learn all about it through its properties. Unfortunately, you can't query a music player as to its queue, but you can keep your own pointer to the MPMediaItemCollection constituting the queue when you hand it to the music player, and you can ask the music player for which song within the queue is currently playing (indexOfNowPlaying-Item). The user can completely change the queue of an iPodMusicPlayer, so if control over the queue is important to you, use the applicationMusicPlayer.

A music player has a playbackState that you can query to learn what it's doing (whether it is playing, paused, stopped, or seeking). It also emits notifications so you can hear about changes in its state:

- MPMusicPlayerControllerPlaybackStateDidChangeNotification
- MPMusicPlayerControllerNowPlayingItemDidChangeNotification
- MPMusicPlayerControllerVolumeDidChangeNotification

These notifications are not emitted until you tell the music player to beginGenerating-PlaybackNotifications. This is an instance method, so you can arrange to receive notifications from just one particular music player if you like. If you do receive notifications from both, you can distinguish them by examining the NSNotification's object and comparing it to each player. You should eventually balance this call with end-GeneratingPlaybackNotifications.

To illustrate, I'll extend the previous example to set a UILabel in our interface every time a different song starts playing. Before we start the player playing, we insert these lines to generate the notifications:

```
[player beginGeneratingPlaybackNotifications];
[[NSNotificationCenter defaultCenter] addObserver:self
    selector:@selector(changed:)
    name:MPMusicPlayerControllerNowPlayingItemDidChangeNotification
    object:player];
self.q = queue; // retain a pointer to the queue
```

And here's how we respond to those notifications:

```
- (void) changed: (NSNotification*) n {
    MPMusicPlayerController* player =
        [MPMusicPlayerController applicationMusicPlayer];
    if ([n object] == player) { // just playing safe
        NSString* title =
            [player.nowPlayingItem valueForProperty:MPMediaItemPropertyTitle];
        NSUInteger ix = player.indexOfNowPlayingItem;
```

```
        [self->label setText: [NSString stringWithFormat:@"%i of %i: %@",
                               ix+1, [self.q count], title]];
    }
}
```

There's no periodic notification as a song plays and the current playhead position advances. To get this information, you'll have to resort to polling. This is not objectionable as long as your polling interval is reasonably sparse; your display may occasionally fall a little behind reality, but this won't usually matter. To illustrate, let's add to our existing example a UIProgressView (p) showing the current percentage of the current song played by the global player. There's no notification, so I'll use an NSTimer and poll the state of the player every 2 seconds:

```
self.timer = [NSTimer scheduledTimerWithTimeInterval:2
                    target:self selector:@selector(timerFired:)
                    userInfo:nil repeats:YES];
```

When the timer fires (timerFired:), the progress view displays the state of the currently playing item:

```
MPMusicPlayerController* mp =
    [MPMusicPlayerController applicationMusicPlayer];
MPMediaItem* item = mp.nowPlayingItem;
if (!item || mp.playbackState == MPMusicPlaybackStateStopped) {
    self.p.hidden = YES;
    return;
}
self.p.hidden = NO;
NSTimeInterval current = mp.currentPlaybackTime;
NSTimeInterval total =
[[item valueForProperty:MPMediaItemPropertyPlaybackDuration] doubleValue];
self.p.progress = current / total;
```

The applicationMusicPlayer has no user interface, unless you count the remote playback controls (Figure 27-1); if you want the user to have controls for playing and stopping a song, you'll have to create them yourself. The iPodMusicPlayer has its own natural interface — the Music app.

The Media Player framework does offer a slider for setting the system output volume, along with an AirPlay route button if appropriate; this is an MPVolumeView. An MPVolumeView works only on a device — not in the Simulator. Starting in iOS 6, it is customizable similarly to a UISlider; you can set the images for the two halves of the track, the thumb, and even the AirPlay route button, for both the Normal and the Highlighted state (while the user is touching the thumb). A nice feature is that you can retrieve the MPVolumeView's default images, so that you can base the modified images upon them. In this example, we make the left half of the track black and the right half red, and we make the thumb larger:

```
CGSize sz = CGSizeMake(20,20);
UIGraphicsBeginImageContextWithOptions(
    CGSizeMake(sz.height,sz.height), NO, 0);
[[UIColor blackColor] setFill];
[[UIBezierPath bezierPathWithOvalInRect:
    CGRectMake(0,0,sz.height,sz.height)] fill];
UIImage* im1 = UIGraphicsGetImageFromCurrentImageContext();
[[UIColor redColor] setFill];
[[UIBezierPath bezierPathWithOvalInRect:
    CGRectMake(0,0,sz.height,sz.height)] fill];
UIImage* im2 = UIGraphicsGetImageFromCurrentImageContext();
UIGraphicsEndImageContext();

[self.vv setMinimumVolumeSliderImage:
    [im1 resizableImageWithCapInsets:UIEdgeInsetsMake(9,9,9,9)
                        resizingMode:UIImageResizingModeStretch]
                        forState:UIControlStateNormal];
[self.vv setMaximumVolumeSliderImage:
    [im2 resizableImageWithCapInsets:UIEdgeInsetsMake(9,9,9,9)
                        resizingMode:UIImageResizingModeStretch]
                        forState:UIControlStateNormal];

UIImage* thumb = [self.vv volumeThumbImageForState:UIControlStateNormal];
sz = thumb.size;
sz.width +=10; sz.height += 10;
UIGraphicsBeginImageContextWithOptions(sz, NO, 0);
[thumb drawInRect:CGRectMake(0,0,sz.width,sz.height)];
UIImage* im3 = UIGraphicsGetImageFromCurrentImageContext();
UIGraphicsEndImageContext();

[self.vv setVolumeThumbImage:im3 forState:UIControlStateNormal];
```

MPMusicPlayerController is convenient and simple, but it's also simple-minded. Its audio session isn't your audio session; the music player doesn't really belong to you. An MPMediaItem, however, has an `MPMediaItemPropertyAssetURL` key whose value is a URL suitable for forming an AVAsset. Thus, another way to play an MPMediaItem is through AV Foundation (Chapter 28). This approach puts playback of the song into your app's audio session and allows you to control it in response to remote control events and to play it while your app is in the background. (Of course, you can do a lot more with AV Foundation than merely to *play* a song from the music library. For example, you could incorporate a song, or part of a song, as the sound track to a movie.)

In this simple example, we start with an array of MPMediaItems and initiate play of those items in an AVQueuePlayer:

```
NSArray* arr = // array of MPMediaItem;
NSMutableArray* assets = [NSMutableArray array];
for (MPMediaItem* item in arr) {
    AVPlayerItem* pi = [[AVPlayerItem alloc] initWithURL:
        [item valueForProperty:MPMediaItemPropertyAssetURL]];
```

```
        [assets addObject:pi];
    }
    self.qp = [AVQueuePlayer queuePlayerWithItems:assets];
    [self.qp play];
```

That's easy enough, but I have the impression, based on something said in one of the WWDC 2011 videos, that it's not what you're supposed to do. Instead of adding a whole batch of AVPlayerItems to an AVQueuePlayer all at once, you should add just a few AVPlayerItems to start with and then add each additional AVPlayerItem when an item finishes playing. So I'll start out by adding just three AVPlayerItems, and use KVO to observe the AVQueuePlayer's @"currentItem" key:

```
    NSArray* arr = // array of MPMediaItem;
    self.assets = [NSMutableArray array];
    for (MPMediaItem* item in arr) {
        AVPlayerItem* pi = [[AVPlayerItem alloc] initWithURL:
            [item valueForProperty:MPMediaItemPropertyAssetURL]];
        [self.assets addObject:pi];
    }
    self->_curnum = 0; // we'll need this later
    self->_total = [self.assets count]; // ditto
    self.qp = [AVQueuePlayer queuePlayerWithItems:
        [self.assets objectsAtIndexes:
            [NSIndexSet indexSetWithIndexesInRange:NSMakeRange(0,3)]]];
    [self.assets removeObjectsAtIndexes:
        [NSIndexSet indexSetWithIndexesInRange:NSMakeRange(0,3)]];
    [self.qp addObserver:self forKeyPath:@"currentItem" options:0 context:nil];
    [self.qp play];
```

The implementation of observeValueForKeyPath:... looks like this:

```
    AVPlayerItem* item = self.qp.currentItem;
    NSArray* arr = item.asset.commonMetadata;
    arr = [AVMetadataItem metadataItemsFromArray:arr
                                withKey:AVMetadataCommonKeyTitle
                             keySpace:AVMetadataKeySpaceCommon];
    AVMetadataItem* met = arr[0];
    [met loadValuesAsynchronouslyForKeys:@[@"value"]
                        completionHandler:^{
        dispatch_async(dispatch_get_main_queue(), ^{
            self.label.text = [NSString stringWithFormat:@"%i of %i: %@",
                            ++self->_curnum, self->_total,
                            [met valueForKey:@"value"]];
        });
    }];
    if (![self.assets count])
        return;
    AVPlayerItem* newItem = self.assets[0];
    [self.qp insertItem:newItem afterItem:[self.qp.items lastObject]];
    [self.assets removeObjectAtIndex:0];
```

That code illustrates how to extract metadata from an AVAsset by way of an AVMetadataItem; in this case, we fetch the AVMetadataCommonKeyTitle and get its value, as the equivalent of fetching an MPMediaItem's MPMediaItemPropertyTitle property in our earlier code. loadValuesAsynchronouslyForKeys:completion-Handler: is the way to retrieve a property from various AV Foundation classes, including AVMetadataItem. There are no guarantees about what thread the completion handler will be called on, so to set the label's text, I step out to the main thread (more about that in Chapter 38).

In the last three lines, we pull an AVPlayerItem off the front of our assets mutable array and add it to the end of the AVQueuePlayer's queue. The AVQueuePlayer itself deletes an item from the start of its queue after playing it, so this way the queue never exceeds three items in length.

Just as in the previous example, where we updated a progress view in response to the firing of a timer to reflect an MPMusicPlayerController's current item's time and duration, we can do the same thing with the currently playing AVPlayerItem. Here's the code that runs when our timer fires:

```
if (self.qp.rate < 0.01)
    self.p.hidden = YES;
else {
    self.p.hidden = NO;
    AVPlayerItem* item = self.qp.currentItem;
    CMTime cur = self.qp.currentTime;
    CMTime dur = item.duration;
    self.p.progress = CMTimeGetSeconds(cur)/CMTimeGetSeconds(dur);
}
```

The Music Picker

The music picker (MPMediaPickerController) is a view controller (UIViewController) whose view is a self-contained navigation interface in which the user can select a media item. This interface looks very much like the Music app. You have no access to the actual view; you are expected to present the view controller (or, on the iPad, to use a popover).

You can limit the type of media items displayed by creating the controller using init-WithMediaTypes:. You can make a prompt appear at the top of the navigation bar (prompt). And you can govern whether the user can choose multiple media items or just one, with the allowsPickingMultipleItems property. New in iOS 6, you can filter out items stored in the cloud (through iTunes Match) by setting showsCloudItems to NO. That's all there is to it.

While the view is showing, you learn what the user is doing through two delegate methods (MPMediaPickerControllerDelegate):

- `mediaPicker:didPickMediaItems:`

- `mediaPickerDidCancel:`

How you use these depends on the value of the controller's `allowsPickingMultiple-Items`:

The controller's `allowsPickingMultipleItems` *is NO (the default)*
Every time the user taps a media item, your `mediaPicker:didPickMediaItems:` is called, handing you an MPMediaItemCollection consisting of all items the user has tapped so far (including the same item multiple times if the user taps the same item more than once). When the user taps Cancel, your `mediaPickerDidCancel:` is called.

The controller's `allowsPickingMultipleItems` *is YES*
The interface has Plus buttons at the right end of every media item, similar to the Music app interface for creating a playlist. When the user taps Done, `media-Picker:didPickMediaItems:` is called, handing you an MPMediaItemCollection consisting of all items for which the user has tapped the Plus button (including the same item multiple times if the user taps the same item's Plus button more than once). Your `mediaPickerDidCancel:` is *never* called.

The view is *not* automatically dismissed; it is up to you to dismiss the presented view controller.

In this example, we put up the music picker, allowing the user to choose one media item; we then play that media item with the application's music player:

```
- (void) presentPicker {
    MPMediaPickerController* picker = [MPMediaPickerController new];
    picker.delegate = self;
    [self presentViewController:picker animated:YES completion:nil];
}

- (void) mediaPicker: (MPMediaPickerController*) mediaPicker
        didPickMediaItems: (MPMediaItemCollection*) mediaItemCollection {
    MPMusicPlayerController* player =
        [MPMusicPlayerController applicationMusicPlayer];
    [player setQueueWithItemCollection:mediaItemCollection];
    [player play];
    [self dismissViewControllerAnimated:YES completion:nil];
}

- (void) mediaPickerDidCancel: (MPMediaPickerController*) mediaPicker {
    [self dismissViewControllerAnimated:YES completion:nil];
}
```

On the iPad, the music picker can be displayed as a presented view, but it also works very well in a popover. I'll use this opportunity to provide a complete example

(Example 29-1) of managing a single view controller as either a presented view or a popover. The presentPicker method is now a button's control event action handler, so that we can point the popover's arrow to the button. How we summon the picker depends on the device; we use UI_USER_INTERFACE_IDIOM to distinguish the two cases. If it's an iPad, we create a popover and set an instance variable to retain it (as discussed in Chapter 22). Two methods dismiss the picker, so that operation is factored out into a utility method (dismissPicker:) that does one thing if there's a popover and another if there's a presented view controller.

Example 29-1. A presented view on the iPhone, a popover on the iPad

```
- (void) presentPicker: (id) sender {
    MPMediaPickerController* picker = [MPMediaPickerController new];
    picker.delegate = self;
    if (UI_USER_INTERFACE_IDIOM() == UIUserInterfaceIdiomPhone)
        [self presentViewController:picker animated:YES completion:nil];
    else {
        UIPopoverController* pop =
            [[UIPopoverController alloc] initWithContentViewController:picker];
        self.currentPop = pop;
        [pop presentPopoverFromRect:[sender bounds] inView:sender
            permittedArrowDirections:UIPopoverArrowDirectionAny animated:YES];
        pop.passthroughViews = nil;
    }
}

- (void) dismissPicker: (MPMediaPickerController*) mediaPicker {
    if (self.currentPop && self.currentPop.popoverVisible) {
        [self.currentPop dismissPopoverAnimated:YES];
    } else {
        [self dismissViewControllerAnimated:YES completion:nil];
    }
}

- (void)mediaPicker: (MPMediaPickerController *)mediaPicker
        didPickMediaItems:(MPMediaItemCollection *)mediaItemCollection {
    MPMusicPlayerController* player =
        [MPMusicPlayerController applicationMusicPlayer];
    [player setQueueWithItemCollection:mediaItemCollection];
    [player play];
    [self dismissPicker: mediaPicker];
}

- (void)mediaPickerDidCancel:(MPMediaPickerController *)mediaPicker {
    [self dismissPicker: mediaPicker];
}

- (void)popoverControllerDidDismissPopover:(UIPopoverController*)popoverController {
    self.currentPop = nil;
}
```

CHAPTER 30

Photo Library and Image Capture

The still photos and movies accessed by the user through the Photos app constitute the *photo library*. Your app can give the user an interface for exploring this library, similar to the Photos app, through the UIImagePickerController class.

In addition, the Assets Library framework lets you access the photo library and its contents programmatically. You'll need to link to *AssetsLibrary.framework* and import `<AssetsLibrary/AssetsLibrary.h>`.

The UIImagePickerController class can also be used to give the user an interface similar to the Camera app, letting the user take photos and videos on devices with the necessary hardware.

At a deeper level, AV Foundation (Chapter 28) provides direct control over the camera hardware. You'll need to link to *AVFoundation.framework* (and probably *Core-Media.framework* as well), and import `<AVFoundation/AVFoundation.h>`

To use constants such as kUTTypeImage, referred to in this chapter, your app must link to *MobileCoreServices.framework* and import `<MobileCoreServices/MobileCore-Services.h>`.

UIImagePickerController

UIImagePickerController is a view controller (UINavigationController) whose view provides a navigation interface, similar to the Photos app, in which the user can choose an item from the photo library. Alternatively, it can provide an interface, similar to the Camera app, for taking a video or still photo if the necessary hardware is present.

How you display the UIImagePickerController depends on what kind of device this is:

On the iPhone

You will typically display the view controller's view as a presented view controller. This presented view controller will appear in portrait orientation, regardless of your app's rotation settings.

On the iPad

If you're letting the user choose an item from the photo library, you'll show it in a popover; attempting to display it as a presented view controller causes a runtime exception. (To see how to structure your universal app code, look at Example 29-1). But if you're letting the user take a video or still photo, you'll probably treat UIImagePickerController as a presented view controller on the iPad, just as on the iPhone.

Choosing from the Photo Library

To let the user choose an item from the photo library, instantiate UIImagePicker-Controller and assign its `sourceType` one of these values:

`UIImagePickerControllerSourceTypeSavedPhotosAlbum`
The user is confined to the contents of the Camera Roll / Saved Photos album.

`UIImagePickerControllerSourceTypePhotoLibrary`
The user is shown a table of all albums, and can navigate into any of them.

You should call the class method `isSourceTypeAvailable:` beforehand; if it doesn't return YES, don't present the controller with that source type.

You'll probably want to specify an array of `mediaTypes` you're interested in. This array will usually contain `kUTTypeImage`, `kUTTypeMovie`, or both; or you can specify all available types by calling the class method `availableMediaTypesForSourceType:`.

After doing all of that, and having supplied a delegate (adopting UIImagePicker-ControllerDelegate and UINavigationControllerDelegate), present the view controller:

```
UIImagePickerControllerSourceType type =
    UIImagePickerControllerSourceTypePhotoLibrary;
BOOL ok = [UIImagePickerController isSourceTypeAvailable:type];
if (!ok) {
    NSLog(@"alas");
    return;
}
UIImagePickerController* picker = [UIImagePickerController new];
picker.sourceType = type;
picker.mediaTypes =
    [UIImagePickerController availableMediaTypesForSourceType:type];
picker.delegate = self;
[self presentViewController:picker animated:YES completion:nil]; // iPhone
```

Figure 30-1. The system prompts for photo library access

New in iOS 6, the very first time you do this, a system alert will appear, prompting the user to grant your app permission to access the photo library (Figure 30-1). You can modify the body of this alert by setting the "Privacy — Photo Library Usage Description" key (`NSPhotoLibraryUsageDescription`) in your app's *Info.plist* to tell the user *why* you want to access the photo library. This is a kind of "elevator pitch"; you need to persuade the user in very few words.

If the user denies your app access, you'll still be able to present the UIImagePicker-Controller, but it will be empty (with a reminder that the user has denied your app access to the photo library) and the user won't be able to do anything but cancel (Figure 30-2). Thus, your code is unaffected. You *can* check beforehand to learn whether your app has access to the photo library — I'll explain how later in this chapter — and opt to do something other than present the UIImagePickerController if access has been denied; but you don't *have* to, because the user will see a coherent interface, and your app will proceed normally afterwards, thinking that the user has cancelled from the picker.

To retest the system alert and other access-related behaviors, go to the Settings app and choose General → Reset → Reset Location & Privacy. This causes the system to forget that it has ever asked about access for any app.

If the user does what Figure 30-2 suggests, switching to the Settings app and enabling access for your app under Privacy → Photos, your app will crash in the background! This is unfortunate, but is probably not a bug; Apple presumably feels that in this situation your app cannot continue coherently and should start over from scratch.

On the iPhone, the delegate will receive one of these messages:

- `imagePickerController:didFinishPickingMediaWithInfo:`

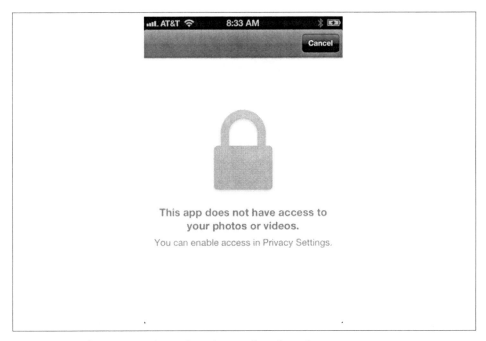

Figure 30-2. The image picker, when the user has denied access

- `imagePickerControllerDidCancel:`

On the iPad, there's no Cancel button, so there's no `imagePickerControllerDid-Cancel:`; you can detect the dismissal of the popover through the popover delegate. On the iPhone, if a UIImagePickerControllerDelegate method is not implemented, the view controller is dismissed automatically; but rather than relying on this, you should implement both delegate methods and dismiss the view controller yourself in each one.

The `didFinish...` method is handed a dictionary of information about the chosen item. The keys in this dictionary depend on the media type.

An image
>   The keys are:
>
>   `UIImagePickerControllerMediaType`
>   A UTI; probably `@"public.image"`, which is the same as `kUTTypeImage`.
>
>   `UIImagePickerControllerOriginalImage`
>   A UIImage.
>
>   `UIImagePickerControllerReferenceURL`
>   An ALAsset URL (discussed later in this chapter).

A movie

The keys are:

`UIImagePickerControllerMediaType`
A UTI; probably @"`public.movie`", which is the same as `kUTTypeMovie`.

`UIImagePickerControllerMediaURL`
A file URL to a copy of the movie saved into a temporary directory. This would be suitable, for example, to display the movie with an MPMoviePlayer-Controller (Chapter 28).

`UIImagePickerControllerReferenceURL`
An ALAsset URL (discussed later in this chapter).

Optionally, you can set the view controller's `allowsEditing` to YES. In the case of an image, the interface then allows the user to scale the image up and to move it so as to be cropped by a preset rectangle; the dictionary will include two additional keys:

`UIImagePickerControllerCropRect`
An NSValue wrapping a CGRect.

`UIImagePickerControllerEditedImage`
A UIImage.

In the case of a movie, if the view controller's `allowsEditing` is YES, the user can trim the movie just as with a UIVideoEditorController (Chapter 28). The dictionary keys are the same as before, but the file URL points to the trimmed copy in the temporary directory.

Because of restrictions on how many movies can play at once (see There Can Be Only One in Chapter 28), if you use a UIImagePickerController to let the user choose a movie and you then want to play that movie in an MPMoviePlayerController, you must destroy the UIImagePickerController first. How you do this depends on how you displayed the UIImagePickerController. If you're using a presented view controller on the iPhone, you can use the completion handler to ensure that the MPMoviePlayerController isn't configured until after the animation dismissing the presented view:

```
-(void)imagePickerController:(UIImagePickerController *)picker
        didFinishPickingMediaWithInfo:(NSDictionary *)info {
    NSURL* url = info[UIImagePickerControllerMediaURL];
    [self dismissViewControllerAnimated:YES completion:^{
        if (url)
            [self showMovie:url];
    }];
}
```

If you're using a popover on the iPad, you can release the UIPopoverController (probably by nilifying the instance variable that's retaining it) after dismissing the popover *without animation*; even then, I find, it is necessary to add a delay before trying to show the movie:

```
-(void)imagePickerController:(UIImagePickerController *)picker
        didFinishPickingMediaWithInfo:(NSDictionary *)info {
    NSURL* url = info[UIImagePickerControllerMediaURL];
    [self.currentPop dismissPopoverAnimated:NO]; // must be NO!
    self.currentPop = nil;
    if (url) {
        [CATransaction setCompletionBlock:^{
            [self showMovie:url];
        }];
    }
}
```

Using the Camera

To prompt the user to take a photo or video in an interface similar to the Camera app, first check `isSourceTypeAvailable:` for `UIImagePickerControllerSourceType-Camera`; it will be NO if the user's device has no camera or the camera is unavailable. If it is YES, call `availableMediaTypesForSourceType:` to learn whether the user can take a still photo (`kUTTypeImage`), a video (`kUTTypeMovie`), or both. Now instantiate UIImagePickerController, set its source type to `UIImagePickerControllerSourceType-Camera`, and set its `mediaTypes` in accordance with which types you just learned are available. Finally, set a delegate (adopting UINavigationControllerDelegate and UIImagePickerControllerDelegate), and present the view controller. In this situation, it is legal (and preferable) to use a presented view controller even on the iPad.

For video, you can also specify the `videoQuality` and `videoMaximumDuration`. Moreover, these additional properties and class methods allow you to discover the camera capabilities:

`isCameraDeviceAvailable:`
Checks to see whether the front or rear camera is available, using one of these parameters:

- `UIImagePickerControllerCameraDeviceFront`
- `UIImagePickerControllerCameraDeviceRear`

`cameraDevice`
Lets you learn and set which camera is being used.

`availableCaptureModesForCameraDevice:`
Checks whether the given camera can capture still images, video, or both. You specify the front or rear camera; returns an NSArray of NSNumbers, from which you can extract the integer value. Possible modes are:

- `UIImagePickerControllerCameraCaptureModePhoto`

- `UIImagePickerControllerCameraCaptureModeVideo`

`cameraCaptureMode`
Lets you learn and set the capture mode (still or video).

`isFlashAvailableForCameraDevice:`
Checks whether flash is available.

`cameraFlashMode`
Lets you learn and set the flash mode (or, for a movie, toggles the LED "torch"). Your choices are:

- `UIImagePickerControllerCameraFlashModeOff`

- `UIImagePickerControllerCameraFlashModeAuto`

- `UIImagePickerControllerCameraFlashModeOn`

 Setting camera-related properties such as `cameraDevice` when there is no camera or when the UIImagePickerController is not set to camera mode can crash your app.

When the view controller appears, the user will see the interface for taking a picture, familiar from the Camera app, possibly including flash button, camera selection button, and digital zoom (if the hardware supports these), still/video switch (if your `media-Types` setting allows both), and Cancel and Shutter buttons. If the user takes a picture, the presented view offers an opportunity to use the picture or to retake it.

Allowing the user to edit the captured image or movie, and handling the outcome with the delegate messages, is the same as I described in the previous section. There won't be any `UIImagePickerControllerReferenceURL` key in the dictionary delivered to the delegate, because the image isn't in the photo library. A still image might report a `UIImage-PickerControllerMediaMetadata` key containing the metadata for the photo. The photo library was not involved in the process of media capture, so no user permission to access the photo library is needed; of course, if you *now* propose to save the media into the photo library (as described later in this chapter), you *will* need permission.

Here's a very simple example in which we offer the user a chance to take a still image; if the user does so, we insert the image into our interface in a UIImageView (`iv`):

```
- (IBAction)doTake:(id)sender {
    BOOL ok = [UIImagePickerController isSourceTypeAvailable:
            UIImagePickerControllerSourceTypeCamera];
    if (!ok) {
        NSLog(@"no camera");
```

```
        return;
    }
    NSArray* arr = [UIImagePickerController availableMediaTypesForSourceType:
                    UIImagePickerControllerSourceTypeCamera];
    if ([arr indexOfObject:(NSString*)kUTTypeImage] == NSNotFound) {
        NSLog(@"no stills");
        return;
    }
    UIImagePickerController* picker = [UIImagePickerController new];
    picker.sourceType = UIImagePickerControllerSourceTypeCamera;
    picker.mediaTypes = @[kUTTypeImage];
    picker.delegate = self;
    [self presentViewController:picker animated:YES completion:nil];
}

- (void)imagePickerControllerDidCancel:(UIImagePickerController *)picker {
    [self dismissViewControllerAnimated:YES completion:nil];
}

- (void)imagePickerController:(UIImagePickerController *)picker
        didFinishPickingMediaWithInfo:(NSDictionary *)info {
    UIImage* im = info[UIImagePickerControllerOriginalImage];
    if (im)
        self.iv.image = im;
    [self dismissViewControllerAnimated:YES completion:nil];
}
```

In the image capture interface, you can hide the standard controls by setting shows-CameraControls to NO, replacing them with your own overlay view, which you supply as the value of the cameraOverlayView. In this case, you're probably going to want some means in your overlay view to allow the user to take a picture! You can do that through these methods:

- takePicture
- startVideoCapture
- stopVideoCapture

You can supply a cameraOverlayView even if you don't set showsCameraControls to NO; but in that case you'll need to negotiate the position of your added controls if you don't want them to cover the existing controls.

The key to customizing the look and behavior of the image capture interface is that a UIImagePickerController is a UINavigationController; the controls shown at the bottom of the default interface are the navigation controller's toolbar. In this example, I'll remove all the default controls and allow the user to double-tap the image in order to take a picture:

```
// ... starts out as before ...
picker.delegate = self;
picker.showsCameraControls = NO;
CGRect f = self.view.window.bounds;
UIView* v = [[UIView alloc] initWithFrame:f];
UITapGestureRecognizer* t =
    [[UITapGestureRecognizer alloc] initWithTarget:self
                                       action:@selector(tap:)];
t.numberOfTapsRequired = 2;
[v addGestureRecognizer:t];
picker.cameraOverlayView = v;
[self presentViewController:picker animated:YES completion:nil];
self.picker = picker;

// ...
- (void) tap: (id) g {
    [self.picker takePicture];
}
```

The interface is marred by a blank area the size of the toolbar at the bottom of the screen,
below the preview image. What are we to do about this? You can zoom or otherwise
transform the preview image by setting the cameraViewTransform property; but this
can be tricky, because different versions of iOS apply your transform differently, and in
any case it's hard to know what values to use. An easier solution is to put your own view
where the blank area will appear; that way, the blank area looks deliberate, not blank:

```
CGFloat h = 53;
UIView* v = [[UIView alloc] initWithFrame:f];
UIView* v2 =
    [[UIView alloc] initWithFrame:
        CGRectMake(0,f.size.height-h,f.size.width,h)];
v2.backgroundColor = [UIColor redColor];
[v addSubview: v2];
UILabel* lab = [UILabel new];
lab.text = @"Double tap to take a picture";
lab.backgroundColor = [UIColor clearColor];
[lab sizeToFit];
lab.center = CGPointMake(CGRectGetMidX(v2.bounds), CGRectGetMidY(v2.bounds));
[v2 addSubview:lab];
```

Another approach is to take advantage of the fact that, because we are the UIImage-
PickerController's delegate, we are not only its UIImagePickerControllerDelegate but
also its UINavigationControllerDelegate. We can therefore get some control over the
navigation controller's interface, and populate its root view controller's toolbar — but
only if we wait until the root view controller's view actually appears. Here, I'll increase
the height of the toolbar to ensure that it covers the blank area, and put a Cancel button
into it:

```
- (void)navigationController:(UINavigationController *)nc
      didShowViewController:(UIViewController *)vc
                  animated:(BOOL)animated {
    [nc setToolbarHidden:NO];
    CGRect f = nc.toolbar.frame;
    CGFloat h = 56; // determined experimentally
    CGFloat diff = h - f.size.height;
    f.size.height = h;
    f.origin.y -= diff;
    nc.toolbar.frame = f;
    UIBarButtonItem* b =
        [[UIBarButtonItem alloc] initWithTitle:@"Cancel"
                                        style:UIBarButtonItemStyleBordered
                                       target:self
                                       action:@selector(doCancel:)];
    UILabel* lab = [UILabel new];
    lab.text = @"Double tap to take a picture";
    lab.backgroundColor = [UIColor clearColor];
    [lab sizeToFit];
    UIBarButtonItem* b2 = [[UIBarButtonItem alloc] initWithCustomView:lab];
    [nc.topViewController setToolbarItems:@[b, b2]];
}
```

When the user double-taps to take a picture, our `didFinishPickingMediaWithInfo` delegate method is called, just as before. We don't automatically get the secondary interface where the user is shown the resulting image and offered an opportunity to use it or retake the image. But we can provide such an interface ourselves, by pushing another view controller onto the navigation controller:

```
- (void)imagePickerController:(UIImagePickerController *)picker
      didFinishPickingMediaWithInfo:(NSDictionary *)info {
    UIImage* im = info[UIImagePickerControllerOriginalImage];
    if (!im)
        return;
    SecondViewController* svc =
        [[SecondViewController alloc] initWithNibName:nil bundle:nil image:im];
    [picker pushViewController:svc animated:YES];
}
```

(Designing the SecondViewController class is left as an exercise for the reader.)

Image Capture With AV Foundation

Instead of using UIImagePickerController, you can control the camera and capture images using the AV Foundation framework (Chapter 28). You get no help with interface (except for displaying in your interface what the camera "sees"), but you get far more detailed control than UIImagePickerController can give you; for example, for stills, you can control focus and exposure directly and independently, and for video, you can determine the quality, size, and frame rate of the resulting movie. You can also capture audio, of course.

The heart of all AV Foundation capture operations is an AVCaptureSession object. You configure this and provide it as desired with inputs (such as a camera) and outputs (such as a file); then you call startRunning to begin the actual capture. You can reconfigure an AVCaptureSession, possibly adding or removing an input or output, while it is running — indeed, doing so is far more efficient than stopping the session and starting it again — but you should wrap your configuration changes in beginConfiguration and commitConfiguration.

As a rock-bottom example, let's start by displaying in our interface, in real time, what the camera sees. This requires an AVCaptureVideoPreviewLayer, a CALayer subclass. This layer is not an AVCaptureSession output; rather, the layer receives its imagery by *owning* the AVCaptureSession:

```
self.sess = [AVCaptureSession new];
AVCaptureDevice* cam =
    [AVCaptureDevice defaultDeviceWithMediaType:AVMediaTypeVideo];
AVCaptureDeviceInput* input =
    [AVCaptureDeviceInput deviceInputWithDevice:cam error:nil];
[self.sess addInput:input];

AVCaptureVideoPreviewLayer* lay =
    [[AVCaptureVideoPreviewLayer alloc] initWithSession:self.sess];
lay.frame = CGRectMake(10,30,300,300);
[self.view.layer addSublayer:lay];
self.previewLayer = lay; // keep a reference so we can remove it later
[self.sess startRunning];
```

Presto! Our interface now contains a window on the world, so to speak. Next, let's permit the user to snap a still photo, which our interface will display instead of the real-time view of what the camera sees. As a first step, we'll need to revise what happens as we create our AVCaptureSession in the previous code. Since this image is to go directly into our interface, we won't need the full eight megapixel size of which the iPhone 4 and 5 cameras are capable, so we'll configure our AVCaptureSession's sessionPreset to ask for a much smaller image. We'll also provide an output for our AVCaptureSession, an AVCaptureStillImageOutput, setting its outputSettings to specify the quality of the JPEG image we're after:

```
self.sess = [AVCaptureSession new];
self.sess.sessionPreset = AVCaptureSessionPreset640x480;
self.snapper = [AVCaptureStillImageOutput new];
self.snapper.outputSettings =
    @{AVVideoCodecKey: AVVideoCodecJPEG, AVVideoQualityKey:@0.6};
[self.sess addOutput:self.snapper];
// ... and the rest is as before ...
```

When the user asks to snap a picture, we send captureStillImageAsynchronouslyFrom-Connection:completionHandler: to our AVCaptureStillImageOutput object. This call requires some preparation. The first argument is an AVCaptureConnection; to find it, we ask the output for its connection that is currently inputting video. The second argument is the block that will be called, possibly on a background thread, when the image data is ready; in the block, we capture the data into a UIImage and, moving onto the main thread (Chapter 38), we construct in the interface a UIImageView containing that image, in place of the AVCaptureVideoPreviewLayer we were displaying previously:

```
AVCaptureConnection *vc =
    [self.snapper connectionWithMediaType:AVMediaTypeVideo];
typedef void(^MyBufBlock)(CMSampleBufferRef, NSError*);
MyBufBlock h = ^(CMSampleBufferRef buf, NSError *err) {
    NSData* data =
        [AVCaptureStillImageOutput jpegStillImageNSDataRepresentation:buf];
    UIImage* im = [UIImage imageWithData:data];
    dispatch_async(dispatch_get_main_queue(), ^{
        UIImageView* iv =
            [[UIImageView alloc] initWithFrame:CGRectMake(10,30,300,300)];
        iv.contentMode = UIViewContentModeScaleAspectFit;
        iv.image = im;
        [self.view addSubview: iv];
        [self.previewLayer removeFromSuperlayer];
        self.previewLayer = nil;
        [self.sess stopRunning];
    });
};
[self.snapper captureStillImageAsynchronouslyFromConnection:vc
                                          completionHandler:h];
```

Our code has not illustrated setting the focus, changing the flash settings, and so forth; doing so is not difficult (see the class documentation on AVCaptureDevice), but note that you should wrap such changes in calls to lockForConfiguration: and unlockForConfiguration. You can turn on the LED "torch" by setting the back camera's torchMode to AVCaptureTorchModeOn, even if no AVCaptureSession is running.

New in iOS 6, you can stop the flow of video data by setting the AVCaptureConnection's enabled to NO, and there are some other new AVCaptureConnection features, mostly involving stabilization of the video image (not relevant to the example, because a preview layer's video isn't stabilized). Plus, AVCaptureVideoPreviewLayer now provides methods for converting between layer coordinates and capture device coordinates; previously, this was a very difficult problem to solve.

AV Foundation's control over the camera, and its ability to process incoming data — especially video data — goes far deeper than there is room to discuss here, so consult the documentation; in particular, see the "Media Capture" chapter of the *AV Foundation Programming Guide*, and the *AV Foundation Release Notes for iOS 5* also contains some useful (and still relevant) hints. There are also excellent WWDC videos on AV Foundation, and some fine sample code; I found Apple's AVCam example very helpful while preparing this discussion.

The Assets Library Framework

The Assets Library framework does for the photo library roughly what the Media Player framework does for the music library (Chapter 29), letting your code explore the library's contents. One obvious use of the Assets Library framework might be to implement your own interface for letting the user choose an image, in a way that transcends the limitations of UIImagePickerController. But you can go further with the photo library than you can with the media library: you can save media into the Camera Roll / Saved Photos album, and you can even create a new album and save media into it.

A photo or video in the photo library is an ALAsset. Like a media entity (Chapter 29), an ALAsset can describe itself through key–value pairs called *properties*. (This use of the word "properties" has nothing to do with the Objective-C properties discussed in Chapter 12.) For example, it can report its type (photo or video), its creation date, its orientation if it is a photo whose metadata contains this information, and its duration if it is a video. You fetch a property value with `valueForProperty:`. The properties have names like `ALAssetPropertyType`.

A photo can provide multiple *representations* (roughly, image file formats). A given photo ALAsset lists these representations as one of its properties, `ALAssetProperty-Representations`, an array of strings giving the UTIs identifying the file formats; a typical UTI might be `@"public.jpeg"` (`kUTTypeJPEG`, if you've linked to *MobileCore-Services.framework*). A representation is an ALAssetRepresentation. You can get a photo's `defaultRepresentation`, or ask for a particular representation by submitting a file format's UTI to `representationForUTI:`.

Once you have an ALAssetRepresentation, you can interrogate it to get the actual image, either as raw data or as a CGImage (see Chapter 15). The simplest way is to ask for its `fullResolutionImage` or its `fullScreenImage` (the latter is more suitable for display in your interface, and is identical to what the Photos app displays); you may then want to derive a UIImage from this using `imageWithCGImage:scale:orientation:`. The original scale and orientation of the image are available as the ALAssetRepresentation's `scale` and `orientation`. Alternatively, if all you need is a small version of the image to display in your interface, you can ask the ALAsset itself for its `aspectRatio-Thumbnail`. An ALAssetRepresentation also has a `url`, which is the unique identifier for the ALAsset.

The photo library itself is an ALAssetsLibrary instance. It is divided into groups (ALAssetsGroup), which have types. For example, the user might have multiple albums; each of these is a group of type `ALAssetsGroupAlbum`. You also have access to the Photo-Stream album. An ALAssetsGroup has properties, such as a name, which you can fetch with `valueForProperty:`; one such property, the group's URL (`ALAssetsGroup-PropertyURL`), is its unique identifier. To fetch assets from the library, you either fetch one specific asset by providing its URL, or you can start with a group, in which case you can then enumerate the group's assets. To obtain a group, you can enumerate the library's groups of a certain type, in which case you are handed each group as an ALAssetsGroup, or you can provide a particular group's URL. Before enumerating a group's assets, you may optionally filter the group using a simple ALAssetsFilter; this limits any subsequent enumeration to photos only, videos only, or both.

The Assets Library framework uses Objective-C blocks for fetching and enumerating assets and groups. These blocks behave in a special way: at the end of the enumeration, they are called one extra time with a nil first parameter. Thus, you must code your block carefully to avoid treating the first parameter as real on that final call. Formerly, I was mystified by this curious block enumeration behavior, but one day the reason for it came to me in a flash: these blocks are all called *asynchronously* (on the main thread), meaning that the rest of your code has already finished running, so you're given an extra pass through the block as your first opportunity to *do* something with the data you've gathered in the previous passes.

As I mentioned earlier in this chapter, the system will ask the user for permission the first time your app tries to access the photo library, and the user can refuse. You can learn directly beforehand whether access has already been enabled:

```
ALAuthorizationStatus stat = [ALAssetsLibrary authorizationStatus];
if (stat == ALAuthorizationStatusDenied ||
    stat == ALAuthorizationStatusRestricted) {
    // in real life, we could put up interface asking for access
    NSLog(@"%@", @"No access");
    return;
}
```

There is, however, no need to do this, because all the block-based methods for accessing the library allow you to supply a failure block; thus, your code will be able to retreat in good order when it discovers that it can't access the library.

We now know enough for an example! I'll fetch the first photo from the album named "mattBestVertical" in my photo library and stick it into a UIImageView in the interface. For readability, I've set up the blocks in my code separately as variables *before* they are used, so it will help to read backward: we enumerate (at the end of the code) using the getGroups block (previously defined), which itself enumerates using the getPix block (defined before that). We must also be prepared with a block that handles the possibility of an error. Here we go:

```
// what I'll do with the assets from the group
ALAssetsGroupEnumerationResultsBlock getPix =
^ (ALAsset *result, NSUInteger index, BOOL *stop) {
    if (!result)
        return;
    ALAssetRepresentation* rep = [result defaultRepresentation];
    CGImageRef im = [rep fullScreenImage];
    UIImage* im2 =
```

```
        [UIImage imageWithCGImage:im scale:0
                    orientation:(UIImageOrientation)rep.orientation];
    self.iv.image = im2; // put image into our UIImageView
    *stop = YES; // got first image, all done
};
// what I'll do with the groups from the library
ALAssetsLibraryGroupsEnumerationResultsBlock getGroups =
^ (ALAssetsGroup *group, BOOL *stop) {
    if (!group)
        return;
    NSString* title = [group valueForProperty: ALAssetsGroupPropertyName];
    if ([title isEqualToString: @"mattBestVertical"]) {
        [group enumerateAssetsUsingBlock:getPix];
        *stop = YES; // got target group, all done
    }
};
// might not be able to access library at all
ALAssetsLibraryAccessFailureBlock oops = ^ (NSError *error) {
    NSLog(@"oops! %@", [error localizedDescription]);
    // e.g., "Global denied access"
};
// and here we go with the actual enumeration!
ALAssetsLibrary* library = [ALAssetsLibrary new];
[library enumerateGroupsWithTypes: ALAssetsGroupAlbum
                    usingBlock: getGroups
                    failureBlock: oops];
```

You can write files into the Camera Roll / Saved Photos album. The basic function for writing an image file to this location is UIImageWriteToSavedPhotosAlbum. Some kinds of video file can also be saved here; in an example in Chapter 28, I checked whether this was true of a certain video file by calling UIVideoAtPathIsCompatibleWithSaved-PhotosAlbum, and I saved the file by calling UISaveVideoAtPathToSavedPhotosAlbum.

The ALAssetsLibrary class extends these abilities by providing five additional methods:

writeImageToSavedPhotosAlbum:orientation:completionBlock:
    Takes a CGImageRef and orientation.

writeImageToSavedPhotosAlbum:metadata:completionBlock:
    Takes a CGImageRef and optional metadata dictionary (such as might arrive through the UIImagePickerControllerMediaMetadata key when the user takes a picture using UIImagePickerController).

writeImageDataToSavedPhotosAlbum:metadata:completionBlock:
    Takes raw image data (NSData) and optional metadata.

videoAtPathIsCompatibleWithSavedPhotosAlbum:
    Takes a file path string. Returns a boolean.

writeVideoAtPathToSavedPhotosAlbum:completionBlock:
    Takes a file path string.

Saving takes time, so a completion block allows you to be notified when it's over. The completion block supplies two parameters: an NSURL and an NSError. If the first parameter is not nil, the write succeeded, and this is the URL of the resulting ALAsset. If the first parameter *is* nil, the write failed, and the second parameter describes the error.

You can create in the Camera Roll / Saved Photos album an image or video that is considered to be a modified version of an existing image or video, by calling an instance method on the original asset:

- `writeModifiedImageDataToSavedPhotosAlbum:metadata:completionBlock:`
- `writeModifiedVideoAtPathToSavedPhotosAlbum:completionBlock:`

Afterwards, you can get from the modified asset to the original asset through the former's `originalAsset` property.

You are also allowed to "edit" an asset — that is, you can replace an image or video in the library with a different image or video — but only if your application created the asset. Check the asset's `editable` property; if it is YES, you can call either of these methods:

- `setImageData:metadata:completionBlock:`
- `setVideoAtPath:completionBlock:`

Finally, you are allowed to create an album:

- `addAssetsGroupAlbumWithName:resultBlock:failureBlock:`

If an album is `editable`, which would be because you created it, you can add an existing asset to it by calling `addAsset:`. This is not the same thing as saving a new asset to an album other than the Camera Roll / Saved Photos album; you can't do that, but once an asset exists, it can belong to more than one album.

CHAPTER 31

Address Book

The user's address book, which the user sees through the Contacts app, is effectively a database that can be accessed directly through a C API provided by the Address Book framework. You'll link to *AddressBook.framework* and import `<AddressBook/Address-Book.h>`.

A user interface for interacting with the address book is also provided, through Objective-C classes, by the Address Book UI framework. You'll link to *AddressBook-UI.framework* and import `<AddressBookUI/AddressBookUI.h>`.

Address Book Database

The address book is an ABAddressBookRef obtained by calling `ABAddressBookCreate-WithOptions`. This method is new in iOS 6. There are in fact no options to pass, so the first parameter is always nil. The important thing is the second parameter, a pointer to a CFErrorRef; if the result is nil, the CFErrorRef describes the error. The reason there can be an error is that the user can now deny your app access to the address book:

```
CFErrorRef err = nil;
ABAddressBookRef adbk = ABAddressBookCreateWithOptions(nil, &err);
if (nil == adbk) {
    NSLog(@"error: %@", err);
    return;
}
```

The very first time your app tries to access the address book, a system alert will appear, prompting the user to grant your app permission to access the user's Contacts. You can modify the body of this alert by setting the "Privacy — Contacts Usage Description" key (`NSContactsUsageDescription`) in your app's *Info.plist* to tell the user *why* you want to access the address book. This is a kind of "elevator pitch"; you need to persuade the user in very few words.

You can learn beforehand whether access has been explicitly denied by calling `ABAddressBookGetAuthorizationStatus`:

```
ABAuthorizationStatus stat = ABAddressBookGetAuthorizationStatus();
if (stat==kABAuthorizationStatusDenied ||
    stat==kABAuthorizationStatusRestricted) {
    NSLog(@"%@", @"no access");
    return;
}
```

If the user *has* denied your app access, you can't make the system alert appear again. You can, of course, use some other interface to request that the user grant access in the Settings app, under Privacy → Contacts.

 To retest the system alert and other access-related behaviors, go to the Settings app and choose General → Reset → Reset Location & Privacy. This causes the system to forget that it has ever asked about access for any app.

 If the user in fact switches to the Settings app and enables access for your app under Privacy → Contacts, your app will crash in the background! This is unfortunate, but is probably not a bug; Apple presumably feels that in this situation your app cannot continue coherently and should start over from scratch.

Another new iOS 6 function, `ABAddressBookRequestAccessWithCompletion`, is pointless, and I don't recommend using it. If the user has already denied your app access, this function won't make the system alert appear again; if the user has already granted your app access, this function is needless; and if the user has never seen the app before, the system alert will appear anyway when you try to access the address book. Thus this function does nothing that you can't accomplish by a combination of `ABAddressBook-GetAuthorizationStatus` and `ABAddressBookCreateWithOptions`.

Assuming that access has been granted, `ABAddressBookCreateWithOptions` returns an actual ABAddressBookRef object. This method's name contains "Create," so you must `CFRelease` the ABAddressBookRef when you're finished with it, as discussed in Chapter 12. (But don't release it until you *are* finished with it!) The address book's data starts out exactly the same as the user's Contacts data. If you make any changes to the data, they are not written through to the user's real address book until you call `ABAddress-BookSave`.

The primary constituent record of the address book database is the ABPerson. You'll typically extract persons from the address book by using these functions:

- `ABAddressBookGetPersonCount`

- `ABAddressBookGetPersonWithRecordID`

- `ABAddressBookCopyPeopleWithName`

- `ABAddressBookCopyArrayOfAllPeople`

The result of the latter two is a CFArrayRef. Their names contain "Copy," so you must `CFRelease` the array when you're finished with it. (I'm going to stop reminding you about memory management from here on.)

An ABPerson doesn't formally exist as a type; it is actually an ABRecord (ABRecordRef), and by virtue of this has an ID, a type, and properties with values. To fetch the value of a property, you'll call `ABRecordCopyValue`, supplying a property identifier to specify the property that interests you. ABPerson properties, as you might expect, include things like first name, last name, and email.

Working with a property value is a little tricky because the way you treat it depends on what type of value it is. You can learn a property value's type dynamically by calling `ABPersonGetTypeOfProperty`, but usually you'll know in advance. Some values are simple, but some are not. For example, a last name is a string, which is straightforward. But a person can have more than one email, so an email value is a "multistring." To work with it, you'll treat it as an ABMultiValue (ABMultiValueRef). This is like an array of values where each value also has a label and an identifier. The label categorizes (for example, a Home email as opposed to a Work email) but is not a unique specifier (because a person might have, say, two or more Work emails); the identifier is the unique specifier.

A person's address is even more involved because not only is it an ABMultiValue (a person can have more than one address), but also a particular address is itself a dictionary (a CFDictionary). Each dictionary may have a key for street, city, state, country, and so on.

There is a lot more to parsing address book information, but that's enough to get you started. We are now ready to illustrate by an example. Assume we have successfully obtained a reference to the address book, `adbk`, as I showed earlier. Now I'll fetch my own record out of the address book database on my device and detect that I've got two email addresses:

```
ABRecordRef moi = nil;
CFArrayRef matts =
    ABAddressBookCopyPeopleWithName(adbk, (CFStringRef)@"Matt");
// might be multiple matts, but let's find the one with last name Neuburg
for (CFIndex ix = 0; ix < CFArrayGetCount(matts); ix++) {
    ABRecordRef matt = CFArrayGetValueAtIndex(matts, ix);
    CFStringRef last = ABRecordCopyValue(matt, kABPersonLastNameProperty);
    if (last && CFStringCompare(last, (CFStringRef)@"Neuburg", 0) == 0)
```

```
        moi = matt;
        if (last) CFRelease(last);
    }
    if (nil == moi) {
        NSLog(@"Couldn't find myself");
        if (matts) CFRelease(matts);
        if (adbk) CFRelease(adbk);
        return;
    }
    // parse my emails
    ABMultiValueRef emails = ABRecordCopyValue(moi, kABPersonEmailProperty);
    for (CFIndex ix = 0; ix < ABMultiValueGetCount(emails); ix++) {
        CFStringRef label = ABMultiValueCopyLabelAtIndex(emails, ix);
        CFStringRef value = ABMultiValueCopyValueAtIndex(emails, ix);
        NSLog(@"I have a %@ address: %@", label, value);
        if (label) CFRelease(label);
        if (value) CFRelease(value);
    }
    if (emails) CFRelease(emails);
    if (matts) CFRelease(matts);
    /*
    output:
    I have a _$!<Home>!$_ address: matt@tidbits.com
    I have a _$!<Work>!$_ address: mattworking@tidbits.com
    */
```

You can also modify an existing record, add a new record (ABAddressBookAddRecord), and delete a record (ABAddressBookRemoveRecord). In this example, I'll create a person called Snidely Whiplash with a Home email snidely@villains.com, add him to the database, and save the database:

```
    ABRecordRef snidely = ABPersonCreate();
    ABRecordSetValue(snidely, kABPersonFirstNameProperty, @"Snidely", nil);
    ABRecordSetValue(snidely, kABPersonLastNameProperty, @"Whiplash", nil);
    ABMutableMultiValueRef addr =
        ABMultiValueCreateMutable(kABStringPropertyType);
    ABMultiValueAddValueAndLabel(addr, @"snidely@villains.com",
                                 kABHomeLabel, nil);
    ABRecordSetValue(snidely, kABPersonEmailProperty, addr, nil);
    ABAddressBookAddRecord(adbk, snidely, nil);
    ABAddressBookSave(adbk, nil);
    if (addr) CFRelease(addr);
    if (snidely) CFRelease(snidely);
```

Sure enough, if we then check the state of the database through the Contacts app, the new person exists (Figure 31-1).

There are also groups (ABGroup); a group, like a person, is a record (ABRecord), so you can add a new group, delete an existing group, add a person to a group, and remove a person from a group (which is more than the Contacts app allows the user to do!). A group doesn't own a person, nor a person a group; they are independent, and a person

Figure 31-1. A contact created programmatically

can be associated with multiple groups just as a group is associated with multiple persons. At an even higher level, there are sources (yet another kind of ABRecord): a person or group might be on the device, but it might instead come from an Exchange server or a CardDAV server. In this case the source really does, in a sense, own the group or person; a person can't belong to two sources. A complicating factor, however, is that the same *real* person might appear in two different sources as two different ABPersons; to deal with this, it is possible for multiple persons to be linked, indicating that they are the same person. For a practical introduction to groups and sources, see Apple's ABUIGroups sample code.

Address Book Interface

The Address Book UI framework puts a user interface, similar to the Contacts app, in front of common tasks involving the address book database. This is a great help, because designing your own interface to do the same thing would be tedious and involved. The framework provides four UIViewController subclasses:

ABPeoplePickerNavigationController
> Presents a navigation interface, effectively the same as the Contacts app but without an Edit button: it lists the people in the database and allows the user to pick one and view the details.

`ABPersonViewController`
> Presents an interface showing the properties of a specific person in the database, possibly editable.

`ABNewPersonViewController`
> Presents an interface showing the editable properties of a new person.

`ABUnknownPersonViewController`
> Presents an interface showing a proposed person with a partial set of noneditable properties.

These view controllers operate coherently with respect to the question of whether your app has access to the address book. For example, if the user has never granted or denied your app access to the address book, attempting to use ABPeoplePickerNavigation-Controller will cause the system alert to appear, requesting access. If the user has denied your app access to the address book, the ABPeoplePickerNavigationController's view will appear, but it will be empty (like Figure 30-2). ABNewPersonViewController, similarly, will lack interface for saving into the database if your app has been denied access, and the user's only option will be to back out of the view controller. On the other hand, you can't even get started usefully with ABPersonViewController if you don't already have access, so if you lack access, you'll discover that fact beforehand.

ABPeoplePickerNavigationController

An ABPeoplePickerNavigationController is a UINavigationController. With it, the user can survey groups, along with the names of all persons in each group. Presenting it can be as simple as instantiating it, assigning it a delegate, and showing it as a presented view controller. On the iPad, you'll probably use a popover; presenting the view controller does work, but a popover looks better. (For the structure of a universal app, see Example 29-1.) Here's the code for an iPhone:

```
ABPeoplePickerNavigationController* picker =
    [ABPeoplePickerNavigationController new];
picker.peoplePickerDelegate = self; // note: not merely "delegate"
[self presentViewController:picker animated:YES completion:nil];
```

You should certainly provide a delegate, because without it the presented view will never be dismissed. This delegate is *not* the controller's `delegate` property! It is the controller's `peoplePickerDelegate` property. You should implement all three delegate methods:

`peoplePickerNavigationController:shouldContinueAfterSelectingPerson:`
> The user has tapped a person in the contacts list, provided to you as an ABRecord-Ref. You have two options:
>
> • Return NO. The user has chosen a person and that's all you wanted done. The selected person remains selected unless the user chooses another person. You are likely to dismiss the picker at this point.

- Return YES (and don't dismiss the picker). The view will navigate to a view of the person's properties. You can limit the set of properties the user will see at this point by setting the ABPeoplePickerNavigationController's displayed-Items. This is an array of NSNumbers wrapping the property identifiers such as kABPersonEmailProperty.

peoplePickerNavigationController:shouldContinueAfterSelecting-
Person:property:identifier:
> The user is viewing a person's properties and has tapped a property. Note that you are not handed the value of this property! You can fetch that yourself if desired, because you have the person and the property; plus, if the property has multiple values, you are handed an identifier so you can pick the correct one out of the array of values by calling ABMultiValueGetIndexForIdentifier and fetching the value at that index. You have two options:
>
> - Return NO. The view is now still sitting there, displaying the person's properties. You are likely to dismiss the picker at this point.
>
> - Return YES. This means that if the property is one that can be displayed in some other app, we will switch to that app. For example, if the user taps an address, it will be displayed in the Maps app; if the user taps an email, we will switch to the Mail app and compose a message addressed to that email.

peoplePickerNavigationControllerDidCancel:
> The user has cancelled; you should dismiss the picker.

In this example, we want the user to pick an email. We have limited the display of properties to emails only:

```
picker.displayedProperties = @[@(kABPersonEmailProperty)];
```

We return YES from the first delegate method. The second delegate method fetches the value of the tapped email and dismisses the picker:

```
- (BOOL)peoplePickerNavigationController:
        (ABPeoplePickerNavigationController *)peoplePicker
        shouldContinueAfterSelectingPerson:(ABRecordRef)person
        property:(ABPropertyID)property
        identifier:(ABMultiValueIdentifier)identifier {
    ABMultiValueRef emails = ABRecordCopyValue(person, property);
    CFIndex ix = ABMultiValueGetIndexForIdentifier(emails, identifier);
    CFStringRef email = ABMultiValueCopyValueAtIndex(emails, ix);
    NSLog(@"%@", email); // do something with the email here
    if (email) CFRelease(email);
    if (emails) CFRelease(emails);
    [self dismissViewControllerAnimated:YES completion:nil];
    return NO;
}
```

ABPersonViewController

An ABPersonViewController is a UIViewController. To use it, instantiate it, set its displayedPerson and personViewDelegate (*not* delegate), and push it onto an existing navigation controller's stack. The user's only way out of the resulting interface will be through the Back button. Presuming that the displayed person is to be someone in the database, you'll need access to the address book in order to get started. For example:

```
CFErrorRef err = nil;
ABAddressBookRef adbk = ABAddressBookCreateWithOptions(nil, &err);
if (nil == adbk) {
    NSLog(@"error: %@", err);
    return;
}
CFArrayRef snides =
    ABAddressBookCopyPeopleWithName(adbk, (CFStringRef)@"Snidely Whiplash");
if (CFArrayGetCount(snides) < 1) {
    NSLog(@"%@", @"No Snidely!");
    return;
}
ABRecordRef snidely = CFArrayGetValueAtIndex(snides, 0);
ABPersonViewController* pvc = [ABPersonViewController new];
pvc.displayedPerson = snidely;
pvc.personViewDelegate = self;
[self.navigationController pushViewController:pvc animated:YES];
if (snides) CFRelease(snides);
if (adbk) CFRelease(adbk);
```

On the iPad, the same interface works, or alternatively you can use a popover. In the latter case you'll probably make the ABPersonViewController the root view of a UINavigationController created on the fly, especially if you intend to set allows-Editing to YES, since without the navigation interface the Edit button won't appear. No Back button is present or needed, because the user can dismiss the popover by tapping outside it.

You can limit the properties to be displayed, as with ABPeoplePickerNavigation-Controller, by setting the displayedProperties. You can highlight a property with set-HighlightedItemForProperty:withIdentifier:.

The delegate is notified when the user taps a property. As with ABPeoplePicker-NavigationController's second delegate method, you'll return YES to allow some other app, such as Maps or Mail, to open the tapped value; return NO to prevent this.

If ABPersonViewController's allowsActions is YES, then buttons such as Send Message, FaceTime, Share Contact, and Add to Favorites appear in the interface. (Exactly what buttons appear depends on what categories of information are displayed.)

If ABPersonViewController's allowsEditing is YES, the right bar button is an Edit button. If the user taps this, the interface is transformed into the same sort of editing interface as `ABNewPersonViewController`. The user can tap Done or Cancel; if Done, the edits are automatically saved into the database. Either way, the user returns to the original display of the person's properties.

Your code is not notified that the user has edited the person, or that the user has returned from the person view controller to the main interface. If that's the kind of thing you need to know, consider one of the next two view controllers.

ABNewPersonViewController

An ABNewPersonController is a UIViewController. To use it, instantiate it, set its `new-PersonViewDelegate` (*not* `delegate`), instantiate a UINavigationController with the ABNewPersonController as its root view, and present the navigation controller:

```
ABNewPersonViewController* npvc = [ABNewPersonViewController new];
npvc.newPersonViewDelegate = self;
UINavigationController* nc =
    [[UINavigationController alloc] initWithRootViewController:npvc];
[self presentViewController:nc animated:YES completion:nil];
```

The presented view controller works on the iPad as well. Alternatively, you can display the UINavigationController in a popover; the resulting popover is effectively modal.

The interface allows the user to fill in all properties of a new contact. You cannot limit the properties displayed. You can provide properties with default values by creating a fresh ABRecordRef representing an ABPerson with `ABPersonCreate`, giving it any property values you like, and assigning it to the `displayedPerson` property.

The delegate has one method, `newPersonViewController:didCompleteWithNew-Person:`, which is responsible for dismissing the presented view or popover. If the new person is nil, the user tapped Cancel. Otherwise, the user tapped Done; the new person is an ABRecordRef and has already been saved into the database.

But what if you don't want the new person saved into the database? What if you were presenting this interface merely because it's such a convenient way of letting the user fill in the property values of an ABPerson? Then simply remove the newly created person from the database, like this:

```
- (void)newPersonViewController:
        (ABNewPersonViewController*)newPersonViewController
    didCompleteWithNewPerson:(ABRecordRef)person {
    if (nil != person) {
        // if we didn't have access, we wouldn't be here!
        ABAddressBookRef adbk = ABAddressBookCreateWithOptions(nil, nil);
        ABAddressBookRemoveRecord(adbk, person, nil);
        ABAddressBookSave(adbk, nil);
        CFStringRef name = ABRecordCopyCompositeName(person);
        NSLog(@"I have a person named %@", name);
        // do something with new person
```

```
            if (name) CFRelease(name);
            if (adbk) CFRelease(adbk);
        }
        [self dismissViewControllerAnimated:YES completion:nil];
    }
```

ABUnknownPersonViewController

An ABUnknownPersonViewController is a UIViewController. It presents, as it were, a proposed partial person. You can set the name displayed as the controller's alternate-Name property, and the text below this as the controller's message property. You can add actual person property values just as for an ABNewPersonViewController, namely, by creating a fresh ABRecordRef representing an ABPerson with ABPersonCreate, giving it some property values, and assigning it to the displayedPerson property.

To use ABUnknownPersonViewController, instantiate it, set the properties listed in the foregoing paragraph, set its unknownPersonViewDelegate (*not* delegate), and push it onto the stack of an existing navigation controller. The user's only way out of the resulting interface will be through the Back button. For example:

```
ABUnknownPersonViewController* unk =
    [ABUnknownPersonViewController new];
unk.alternateName = @"Johnny Appleseed";
unk.message = @"Person who really knows trees";
unk.allowsAddingToAddressBook = YES;
ABRecordRef person = ABPersonCreate();
ABMutableMultiValueRef addr =
    ABMultiValueCreateMutable(kABStringPropertyType);
ABMultiValueAddValueAndLabel(addr, @"johnny@seeds.com",
                             kABHomeLabel, nil);
ABRecordSetValue(person, kABPersonEmailProperty, addr, nil);
unk.displayedPerson = person;
unk.unknownPersonViewDelegate = self;
[self.navigationController pushViewController:unk animated:YES];
if (person) CFRelease(person);
if (addr) CFRelease(addr);
```

On the iPad, make the ABUnknownPersonViewController the root view of a UINavigationController and present the navigation controller as a popover. No Back button is present or needed, because the user can dismiss the popover by tapping outside it.

What the user can do here depends on two other properties:

allowsAddingToAddressBook
> If YES, and if your app has access to the address book, a Create New Contact button and an Add to Existing Contact button appear:
>
> • If the user taps Create New Contact, the editing interface appears (as in ABNewPersonViewController and an editable ABPersonViewController). It is

filled in with the property values of the `displayedPerson`. If the user taps Done, the person is saved into the database.

- If the user taps Add to Existing Contact, a list of all contacts appears (as in the first screen of ABPersonViewController). The user can Cancel or tap a person. If the user taps a person, the properties from the `displayedPerson` are merged into that person's record.

`allowsActions`
>If YES, buttons such as Send Message, FaceTime, and Share Contact appear. (Exactly what buttons appear depends on what categories of information are displayed.)

The delegate has two methods, the first of which is required:

`unknownPersonViewController:didResolveToPerson:`
>Called if `allowsAddingToAddressBook` is YES and the user finishes working in a presented editing view. The editing view has already been dismissed and the user has either cancelled (the second parameter is nil) or has tapped Done (the second parameter is the ABPerson already saved into the database).

`unknownPersonViewController:shouldPerformDefaultActionForPerson:property:`
`identifier:`
>Return NO, as with ABPeoplePickerNavigationController, to prevent a tap on a property value from navigating to another app.

CHAPTER 32

Calendar

The user's calendar information, which the user sees through the Calendar app, is effectively a database. This database can be accessed directly through the Event Kit framework. You'll link to *EventKit.framework* and import `<EventKit/EventKit.h>`. Starting in iOS 6, the calendar database also includes reminders, which the user sees through the Reminders app.

A user interface for interacting with the calendar, similar to the Calendar app, is also provided, through the Event Kit UI framework. You'll link to *EventKitUI.framework* and import `<EventKitUI/EventKitUI.h>`.

Calendar Database

The calendar database is accessed as an instance of the EKEventStore class. This instance is expensive to obtain but lightweight to maintain, so your usual strategy, in an app where you'll be working with the user's calendar database, will be to instantiate EKEventStore (by calling `[EKEventStore new]`) early in the life of the app or of some other appropriate object, such as a view controller, and to maintain that instance in an instance variable until you no longer need it. That's the strategy adopted by the examples in this chapter; my EKEventStore instance is called `self.database` throughout.

New in iOS 6, an attempt to work with the calendar database will fail unless the user has authorized access. You should start by calling `authorizationStatusForEntityType:` with either `EKEntityTypeEvent` (to work with calendar events) or `EKEntityType-Reminder` (to work with reminders). If the returned EKAuthorizationStatus is `EKAuthorizationStatusNotDetermined`, you can call `requestAccessToEntity-Type:completion:`, with a non-nil completion block taking a BOOL and an NSError; this causes a system alert to appear, prompting the user to grant your app permission to access the user's Calendar or Reminders. You can modify the body of this alert by setting the "Privacy — Calendars Usage Description" key (`NSCalendarsUsage-`

Description) or the "Privacy — Reminders Usage Description" key (NSReminders-UsageDescription) in your app's *Info.plist* to tell the user *why* you want to access the database. This is a kind of "elevator pitch"; you need to persuade the user in very few words. Here's an example, showing how I create my EKEventStore reference and check for authorization at the outset:

```
self.database = [EKEventStore new];
EKAuthorizationStatus status =
    [EKEventStore authorizationStatusForEntityType:EKEntityTypeEvent];
if (status == EKAuthorizationStatusNotDetermined)
    // completion block cannot be nil!
    [self.database requestAccessToEntityType:EKEntityTypeEvent
                            completion:^(BOOL granted, NSError *error)
    {
        NSLog(@"%i", granted);
    }];
```

If the user *has* denied your app access, you can't make the system alert appear again. You can, of course, use some other interface to request that the user grant access in the Settings app, under Privacy → Calendars or Privacy → Reminders.

 To retest the system alert and other access-related behaviors, go to the Settings app and choose General → Reset → Reset Location & Privacy. This causes the system to forget that it has ever asked about access for any app.

 If the user in fact switches to the Settings app and enables access for your app under Privacy → Calendars or Privacy → Reminders, your app will crash in the background! This is unfortunate, but is probably not a bug; Apple presumably feels that in this situation your app cannot continue coherently and should start over from scratch.

Starting with an EKEventStore instance, you can obtain two kinds of object:

A calendar

A calendar is a named (title) collection of calendar items (*entities*). It is an instance of EKCalendar. A particular calendar comprises calendar items that are either calendar events or reminders; a calendar's allowedEntityTypes tells you which type(s) of calendar item it comprises. Curiously, an EKCalendar object has no calendar items; to obtain and create calendar items, you work directly with the EKEventStore itself.

Calendars have various types (type), reflecting the nature of their origin: a calendar can be created and maintained by the user locally (EKCalendarTypeLocal), but it might also live remotely on the network (EKCalendarTypeCalDAV, EKCalendarType-

Exchange), possibly being updated by subscription (EKCalendarType-Subscription); the Birthday calendar (EKCalendarTypeBirthday) is generated automatically from information in the address book. The type is supplemented and embraced by the calendar's source, an EKSource whose sourceType can be EKSourceTypeLocal, EKSourceTypeExchange, EKSourceTypeCalDAV (which includes iCloud), and so forth; a source can also have a title, and it has a unique identifier (sourceIdentifier). You can get an array of all sources known to the EKEventStore, or specify a source by its identifier. You'll probably use the source exclusively and ignore the calendar's type property.

There are three ways of requesting a calendar:

- Fetch all calendars comprising a particular calendar item type (EKEntityType-Event or EKEntityTypeReminder) by calling calendarsForEntityType:. You can send this message either to the EKEventStore or to an EKSource.

- Fetch an individual calendar by means of a previously obtained calendar-Identifier by calling calendarWithIdentifier:.

- Fetch the default calendar for a particular calendar item type through the defaultCalendarForNewEvents property or the defaultCalendarForNew-Reminders property; this is appropriate particularly if your intention is to create a new calendar item.

You can also create a calendar, by calling calendarForEntityType:eventStore:. At that point, you can specify the source to which the calendar belongs.

Depending on the source, a calendar will be modifiable in various ways. The calendar might be subscribed. If the calendar is immutable, you can't delete the calendar or change its attributes; but its allowsContentModifications might still be YES, in which case you can add, remove, and alter its events. You can update your copy of the calendar from any remote sources by calling refreshSourcesIf-Necessary.

A calendar item

A calendar item (EKCalendarItem), in iOS 6, is either a calendar event (EKEvent) or a reminder (EKReminder). Think of it as a memorandum describing when something happens. As I mentioned a moment ago, you don't get calendar items from a calendar; rather, a calendar item has a calendar, but you get it from the EKEventStore as a whole. There are two chief ways of doing so:

- Fetch all events or reminders according to a predicate: eventsMatching-Predicate:, enumerateEventsMatchingPredicate:, fetchReminders-MatchingPredicate:completion:. Methods starting with predicate... allow you to form the predicate. The predicate specifies things like the calendar(s) the item is to come from and the item's date range.

- Fetch an individual calendar item by means of a previously obtained `calendar-ItemIdentifier` by calling `calendarItemWithIdentifier:`.

Changes to the database can be atomic. There are two prongs to the implementation of this feature:

- The methods for saving and removing calendar items and calendars have a `commit:` parameter. If you pass NO as the argument, the changes that you're ordering are batched; later, you can call `commit:` (or `reset` if you change your mind). If you pass NO and forget to call `commit:`, your changes will never happen.

- An abstract class, EKObject, functions as the superclass for all the other persistent object types, such as EKCalendar, EKCalendarItem, EKSource, and so on. It endows those classes with methods `isNew` and `hasChanges`, along with `refresh`, `rollback`, and `reset`.

Let's start by creating an events calendar. We need to assign a source; we'll choose EKSourceTypeLocal, meaning that the calendar will be created on the device itself. (To test this on your own device, you might have to unsubscribe from iCloud to give yourself a local source.) Assume that a reference to the database (the EKEventStore) is already stored in `self.database`. We can't ask the database for the local source directly, so we have to cycle through all sources looking for it. When we find it, we make a new calendar called "CoolCal":

```
// check for authorization
EKAuthorizationStatus status =
    [EKEventStore authorizationStatusForEntityType:EKEntityTypeEvent];
if (status == EKAuthorizationStatusDenied ||
    status == EKAuthorizationStatusRestricted) {
    NSLog(@"%@", @"no access");
    return;
}
// obtain local source
EKSource* src = nil;
for (src in self.database.sources)
    if (src.sourceType == EKSourceTypeLocal)
        break;
if (!src) {
    NSLog(@"%@", @"failed to find local source");
    return;
}
// create and configure new calendar
EKCalendar* cal = [EKCalendar calendarForEntityType:EKEntityTypeEvent
                                         eventStore:self.database];
cal.source = src;
```

```
cal.title = @"CoolCal";
// save new calendar into the database
NSError* err;
BOOL ok;
ok = [self.database saveCalendar:cal commit:YES error:&err];
if (!ok) {
    NSLog(@"save calendar %@", err.localizedDescription);
    return;
}
NSLog(@"%@", @"no errors");
```

EKEvent is a subclass of EKCalendarItem, from which it inherits some of its important properties. If you've ever used the Calendar app, or iCal on the Mac, you already have a sense for how an EKEvent can be configured. It has a `title` and optional `notes`. It is associated with a `calendar`, as I've already said. It can have one or more alarms and one or more recurrence rules; I'll talk about both of those in a moment. All of that is inherited from EKCalendarItem. EKEvent itself adds the all-important `startDate` and `endDate` properties; these are NSDates and involve both date and time. If the event's `allDay` property is YES, the time aspect of its dates is ignored; the event is associated with a day or a stretch of days as a whole. If the event's `allDay` property is NO, the time aspect of its dates matters; a typical event will then usually be bounded by two times on the same day.

Making an event is simple, if tedious. You *must* provide a `startDate` and an `endDate`! The simplest way to construct dates is with NSDateComponents. I'll create an event and add it to our new calendar, which I'll locate by its title. We really should be using the `calendarIdentifier` to obtain our calendar; the title isn't reliable, since the user might change it, and since multiple calendars can have the same title. However, it's only an example:

```
// ... assume we've checked for authorization ...
// obtain calendar
EKCalendar* cal = nil;
NSArray* calendars =
    [self.database calendarsForEntityType:EKEntityTypeEvent];
for (cal in calendars) // (should be using identifier)
    if ([cal.title isEqualToString: @"CoolCal"])
        break;
if (!cal) {
    NSLog(@"%@", @"failed to find calendar");
    return;
}
// construct start and end dates
NSCalendar* greg =
    [[NSCalendar alloc] initWithCalendarIdentifier:NSGregorianCalendar];
NSDateComponents* comp = [NSDateComponents new];
comp.year = 2013;
comp.month = 8;
comp.day = 10;
```

```
comp.hour = 15;
NSDate* d1 = [greg dateFromComponents:comp];
comp.hour = comp.hour + 1;
NSDate* d2 = [greg dateFromComponents:comp];
// construct event
EKEvent* ev = [EKEvent eventWithEventStore:self.database];
ev.title = @"Take a nap";
ev.notes = @"You deserve it!";
ev.calendar = cal;
ev.startDate = d1;
ev.endDate = d2;
// save event
NSError* err;
BOOL ok =
    [self.database saveEvent:ev span:EKSpanThisEvent commit:YES error:&err];
if (!ok) {
    NSLog(@"save simple event %@", err.localizedDescription);
    return;
}
NSLog(@"%@", @"no errors");
```

An alarm is an EKAlarm, a very simple class; it can be set to fire either at an absolute
date or at a relative offset from the event time. On an iOS device, an alarm fires through
a local notification (Chapter 26). We could easily have added an alarm to our event as
we were configuring it:

```
EKAlarm* alarm = [EKAlarm alarmWithRelativeOffset:-3600]; // one hour before
[ev addAlarm:alarm];
```

Recurrence is embodied in a recurrence rule (EKRecurrenceRule); a calendar item can
have multiple recurrence rules, which you manipulate through its recurrenceRules
property, along with methods addRecurrenceRule: and removeRecurrenceRule:. A
simple EKRecurrenceRule is described by three properties:

Frequency
> By day, by week, by month, or by year.

Interval
> Fine-tunes the notion "by" in the frequency. A value of 1 means "every." A value of
> 2 means "every other." And so on.

End
> Optional, because the event might recur forever. It is an EKRecurrenceEnd instance,
> describing the limit of the event's recurrence either as an end date or as a maximum
> number of occurrences.

The options for describing a more complex EKRecurrenceRule are best summarized by
its initializer:

```
- (id)initRecurrenceWithFrequency:(EKRecurrenceFrequency)type
                     interval:(NSInteger)interval
                 daysOfTheWeek:(NSArray *)days
                daysOfTheMonth:(NSArray *)monthDays
              monthsOfTheYear:(NSArray *)months
               weeksOfTheYear:(NSArray *)weeksOfTheYear
                 daysOfTheYear:(NSArray *)daysOfTheYear
                  setPositions:(NSArray *)setPositions
                           end:(EKRecurrenceEnd *)end
```

The meanings of all these parameters are mostly obvious from their names. The arrays are mostly of NSNumber, except for daysOfTheWeek, which is an array of EKRecurrenceDayOfWeek, a class that allows specification of a week number as well as a day number so that you can say things like "the fourth Thursday of the month." Many of these values can be negative to indicate counting backwards from the last one. Numbers are all 1-based, not 0-based. The setPositions parameter is an array of numbers filtering the occurrences defined by the rest of the specification against the interval; for example, if daysOfTheWeek is Sunday, -1 means the last Sunday. You can use any valid combination of parameters; the penalty for an invalid combination is a return value of nil.

An EKRecurrenceRule is intended to embody the RRULE event component in the iCalendar standard specification (originally published as RFC 2445 and recently superseded by RFC 5545, *http://datatracker.ietf.org/doc/rfc5545*); in fact, the documentation tells you how each EKRecurrenceRule property corresponds to an RRULE attribute, and if you log an EKRecurrenceRule with NSLog, what you're shown *is* the underlying RRULE. RRULE can describe some amazingly sophisticated recurrence rules, such as this one:

```
RRULE:FREQ=YEARLY;INTERVAL=2;BYMONTH=1;BYDAY=SU
```

That means "every Sunday in January, every other year." Let's form this rule. Observe that we should attach it to an event whose startDate and endDate make sense as an example of the rule — that is, on a Sunday in January. Fortunately, NSDateComponents makes that easy:

```
// ... make sure we have authorization ...
// ... obtain our calendar (cal) ...
// form the rule
EKRecurrenceDayOfWeek* everySunday = [EKRecurrenceDayOfWeek dayOfWeek:1];
NSNumber* january = @1;
EKRecurrenceRule* recur =
    [[EKRecurrenceRule alloc]
     initRecurrenceWithFrequency:EKRecurrenceFrequencyYearly // every year
     interval:2 // no, every *two* years!
     daysOfTheWeek:@[everySunday]
     daysOfTheMonth:nil
     monthsOfTheYear:@[january]
     weeksOfTheYear:nil
     daysOfTheYear:nil
     setPositions: nil
```

```
            end:nil];
    // create event with this rule
    EKEvent* ev = [EKEvent eventWithEventStore:self.database];
    ev.title = @"Mysterious Sunday-in-January ritual";
    [ev addRecurrenceRule: recur];
    ev.calendar = cal;
    // need a start date and end date
    NSCalendar* greg =
        [[NSCalendar alloc] initWithCalendarIdentifier:NSGregorianCalendar];
    NSDateComponents* comp = [NSDateComponents new];
    comp.year = 2013;
    comp.month = 1;
    comp.weekday = 1; // Sunday
    comp.weekdayOrdinal = 1; // *first* Sunday
    comp.hour = 10;
    ev.startDate = [greg dateFromComponents:comp];
    comp.hour = 11;
    ev.endDate = [greg dateFromComponents:comp];
    // save the event
    NSError* err;
    BOOL ok = [self.database saveEvent:ev span:EKSpanFutureEvents
                            commit:YES error:&err];
    if (!ok) {
        NSLog(@"save recurring event %@", err.localizedDescription);
        return;
    }
    NSLog(@"%@", @"no errors");
```

In that code, the event we save into the database is a recurring event. When we save or delete a recurring event, we must specify its span. This is either EKSpanThisEvent or EKSpanFutureEvents, and corresponds exactly to the two buttons the user sees in the Calendar interface when saving or deleting a recurring event (Figure 32-1). The buttons and the span types reflect their meaning exactly: the change affects either this event alone, or this event plus all *future* (not past) recurrences. This choice determines not only how this and future recurrences of the event are affected now, but also how they relate to one another from now on.

An EKEvent can also be used to embody a meeting, with attendees (EKParticipant) and an organizer, but that is not a feature of an event that you can set.

Now let's talk about how to extract an event from the database. One way, as I mentioned earlier, is by its unique identifier. Before iOS 6, this was its eventIdentifier; on iOS 6 there is a more general calendarItemIdentifier. Not only is this identifier a fast and unique way to obtain an event, but also it's just a string, which means that it persists even if the EKEventStore subsequently goes out of existence. Remember to obtain it, though, while the EKEventStore *is* still in existence; an EKEvent drawn from the database loses its meaning and its usability if the EKEventStore instance is destroyed. (Even this unique identifier *might* not survive changes in a calendar between launches of your app.)

Figure 32-1. The user specifies a span

You can also extract events from the database by matching a predicate (NSPredicate). To form this predicate, you specify a start and end date and an array of eligible calendars, and call the EKEventStore method predicateForEventsWithStartDate:end-Date:calendars:. That's the only kind of predicate you can use, so any further filtering of events is then up to you. In this example, I'll gather all events from our "CoolCal" calendar; because I have to specify a date range, I ask for events occurring over the next year. Because enumerateEventsMatchingPredicate: can be time-consuming, it's best to run it on a background thread (Chapter 38):

```
// ... make sure we have authorization ...
// ... obtain our calendar (cal) ...
NSDate* d1 = [NSDate date];
// how to do calendrical arithmetic
NSCalendar* greg =
    [[NSCalendar alloc] initWithCalendarIdentifier:NSGregorianCalendar];
NSDateComponents* comp = [NSDateComponents new];
comp.year = 1; // we're going to add 2 to the year
NSDate* d2 = [greg dateByAddingComponents:comp toDate:d1 options:0];
NSPredicate* pred =
    [self.database predicateForEventsWithStartDate:d1 endDate:d2
                                  calendars:@[cal]];
NSMutableArray* marr = [NSMutableArray array];
dispatch_async(dispatch_get_global_queue(0, 0), ^{
    [self.database enumerateEventsMatchingPredicate:pred usingBlock:
      ^(EKEvent *event, BOOL *stop) {
        [marr addObject: event];
        if ([event.title rangeOfString:@"nap"].location != NSNotFound)
            self.napid = event.calendarItemIdentifier;
    }];
    [marr sortUsingSelector:@selector(compareStartDateWithEvent:)];
    NSLog(@"%@", marr);
});
```

That example shows you what I mean about further filtering of events. I obtain the "nap" event and the "mysterious Sunday-in-January ritual" events, but the "nap" event is the one I really want, so I filter further to find it in the block. In real life, if I weren't also testing this call by collecting all returned events into an array, I would then set `*stop` to YES to end the enumeration. The events are enumerated in no particular order; the convenience method `compareStartDateWithEvent:` is provided as a sort selector to put them in order by start date.

When you extract events from the database, event recurrences are treated as separate events (as happened in the preceding example). Recurrences of the same event will have different start and end dates but the same identifier. When you fetch an event by identifier, you get the *earliest* event with that identifier. This makes sense, because if you're going to make a change affecting this and future recurrences of the event, you need the option to start with the earliest possible recurrence (so that "future" means "all").

New in iOS 6 is support for reminders. A reminder (EKReminder) is very parallel to an event (EKEvent); they both inherit from EKCalendarItem, so a reminder has a calendar (which the Reminders app refers to as a "list"), a title, notes, alarms, recurrence rules, and attendees. Instead of a start date and an end date, it has a start date, a due date, a completion date, and a `completed` property. The start date and due date are expressed directly as NSDateComponents, so you can supply as much detail as you wish: if you don't include any time components, it's an all-day reminder.

To illustrate, I'll make an all-day reminder for today:

```
// specify calendar
EKCalendar* cal = [self.database defaultCalendarForNewReminders];
if (!cal) {
    NSLog(@"%@", @"failed to find calendar");
    return;
}
// create and configure the reminder
EKReminder* rem = [EKReminder reminderWithEventStore:self.database];
rem.title = @"Take a nap";
rem.calendar = cal;
NSDate* today = [NSDate date];
NSCalendar* greg =
    [[NSCalendar alloc] initWithCalendarIdentifier:NSGregorianCalendar];
unsigned comps = NSYearCalendarUnit | NSMonthCalendarUnit |  NSDayCalendarUnit;
rem.dueDateComponents = [greg components:comps fromDate:today];
// save the reminder
NSError* err = nil;
BOOL ok = [self.database saveReminder:rem commit:YES error:&err];
if (!ok) {
    NSLog(@"save calendar %@", err.localizedDescription);
    return;
}
NSLog(@"%@", @"no error");
```

New in iOS 6 are *proximity* alarms, which are triggered by the user's approaching or leaving a certain location (also known as *geofencing*). This is appropriate particularly for reminders: one might wish to be reminded of something when approaching the place where that thing can be accomplished. To form the location, you'll need to use the CLLocation class; you'll link to *CoreLocation.framework* and import <CoreLocation/CoreLocation.h> (and see Chapter 35). If Reminders doesn't have location access, it might ask for it when you create a reminder with a proximity alarm. Here, I'll attach a proximity alarm to a reminder (rem); the alarm will fire when I'm near my local Trader Joe's:

```
EKAlarm* alarm = [EKAlarm new];
EKStructuredLocation *loc =
    [EKStructuredLocation locationWithTitle:@"Trader Joe's"];
loc.geoLocation =
    [[CLLocation alloc] initWithLatitude:34.271848 longitude:-119.247714];
loc.radius = 10*1000; // metres
alarm.structuredLocation = loc;
alarm.proximity = EKAlarmProximityEnter; // "geofence": alarm when *arriving*
[rem addAlarm:alarm];
```

The calendar database is an odd sort of database, because calendars can be maintained in so many ways and places. A calendar can change while your app is running (the user might sync, or the user might edit with the Calendar app), which can put your information out of date. You can register for a single EKEventStore notification, EKEventStoreChangedNotification; if you receive it, you should assume that any calendar-related instances you're holding are invalid. This situation is made relatively painless, though, by the fact that every calendar-related instance can be refreshed with refresh. Keep in mind that refresh returns a Boolean; if it returns NO, this object is *really* invalid and you should stop working with it entirely (it may have been deleted from the database).

Calendar Interface

The graphical interface consists of three views for letting the user work with events and calendars:

EKEventViewController
Shows the description of a single event, possibly editable.

EKEventEditViewController
Allows the user to create or edit an event.

EKCalendarChooser
Allows the user to pick a calendar.

EKEventViewController simply shows the little rounded rectangle containing the event's title, date, and time, familiar from the Calendar app, possibly with additional rounded rectangles describing alarms, notes, and so forth (Figure 32-2). The user can't tap these to do anything (except that a URL, if the event has one, is a tappable hyperlink).

Figure 32-2. The event interface

To use EKEventViewController, instantiate it, give it an event in the database, and push it onto the stack of an existing UINavigationController. The user's only way out will be the Back button.

 Do *not* use EKEventViewController for an event that isn't in the database, or at a time when the database isn't open! It won't function correctly if you do.

So, for example:

```
EKEventViewController* evc = [EKEventViewController new];
evc.event = ev; // must be an event in the database...
// ...and the database must be open (like our retained self.database)
evc.delegate = self;
evc.allowsEditing = YES;
[self.navigationController pushViewController:evc animated:YES];
```

The documentation says that `allowsEditing` is NO by default, but in my testing the default was YES; perhaps you'd best play safe and set it regardless. If it is YES, an Edit button appears in the navigation bar, and by tapping this, the user can edit the various aspects of an event in the same interface as the Calendar app, including the large red Delete button at the bottom. If the user ultimately deletes the event, or edits it and taps Done, the change is saved into the database.

You can assign the EKEventViewController a delegate (EKEventViewDelegate) in order to hear about what the user did. However, the delegate method, `eventView-Controller:didCompleteWithAction:`, is called only if the user deletes an event or accepts an invitation. There is no EKEventViewController delegate method informing you that the user has left the interface; if you want to know what editing the user may have performed on your event, you'll have to examine the event in the database.

On the iPad, you use the EKEventViewController as the root view of a navigation controller created on the fly and set the navigation controller as a popover's view controller. A Done button appears as the right bar button; the delegate method eventView-Controller:didCompleteWithAction: is called if the user taps the Done button, and you'll need to dismiss the popover there. If allowsEditing is YES, the left bar button is the Edit button. Here's a complete example that works both on the iPhone and on the iPad:

```
- (IBAction) showEventUI:(id)sender {
    // ... make sure we have authorization ...
    // get event
    EKEvent* ev =
        (EKEvent*)[self.database calendarItemWithIdentifier:self.napid];
    if (!ev) {
        NSLog(@"failed to retrieve event");
        return;
    }
    // create and configure the controller
    EKEventViewController* evc = [EKEventViewController new];
    evc.event = ev;
    evc.delegate = self;
    evc.allowsEditing = YES;
    // on iPhone, push onto existing navigation interface
    if (UI_USER_INTERFACE_IDIOM() == UIUserInterfaceIdiomPhone)
        [self.navigationController pushViewController:evc animated:YES];
    // on iPad, create navigation interface in popover
    else {
        UINavigationController* nc =
        [[UINavigationController alloc] initWithRootViewController:evc];
        UIPopoverController* pop =
        [[UIPopoverController alloc] initWithContentViewController:nc];
        self.currentPop = pop;
        [pop presentPopoverFromRect:[sender bounds] inView:sender
            permittedArrowDirections:UIPopoverArrowDirectionAny animated:YES];
    }
}

-(void)eventViewController:(EKEventViewController *)controller
        didCompleteWithAction:(EKEventViewAction)action {
    if (self.currentPop && self.currentPop.popoverVisible) {
        [self.currentPop dismissPopoverAnimated:YES];
        self.currentPop = nil;
    }
}
```

EKEventEditViewController (a UINavigationController) presents the interface for editing an event. To use it, set its eventStore and editViewDelegate (EKEventEditView-

Delegate, *not* `delegate`), and optionally its event, and present it as a presented view controller (or, on the iPad, in a popover). The event can be nil for a completely empty new event; it can be an event you've just created (and possibly partially configured) and not stored in the database, or it can be an existing event from the database. If access to the database has been denied, the interface will be empty (like Figure 30-2) and the user will simply cancel.

The delegate method `eventEditViewControllerDefaultCalendarForNewEvents:` may be implemented to specify what calendar a completely new event should be assigned to. If you're partially constructing a new event, you can assign it a calendar then, and of course an event from the database already has a calendar.

You must implement the delegate method `eventEditViewController:didComplete-WithAction:` so that you can dismiss the presented view. Possible actions are that the user cancelled, saved the edited event into the database, or deleted an already existing event from the database. You can get a reference to the edited event as the EKEvent-EditViewController's event.

On the iPad, the presented view works, or you can present the EKEventEditView-Controller as a popover. You'll use `eventEditViewController:didCompleteWith-Action:` to dismiss the popover; the user can also dismiss it by tapping outside it (in which case the user's changes are not saved to the database). Here's a complete example that works on both platforms to let the user create an event from scratch:

```
- (IBAction)editEvent:(id)sender {
    EKEventEditViewController* evc = [EKEventEditViewController new];
    evc.eventStore = self.database;
    evc.editViewDelegate = self;
    if (UI_USER_INTERFACE_IDIOM() == UIUserInterfaceIdiomPhone)
        [self presentViewController:evc animated:YES completion:nil];
    else {
        UIPopoverController* pop =
        [[UIPopoverController alloc] initWithContentViewController:evc];
        self.currentPop = pop;
        [pop presentPopoverFromRect:[sender bounds] inView:sender
            permittedArrowDirections:UIPopoverArrowDirectionAny animated:YES];
    }
}

-(void)eventEditViewController:(EKEventEditViewController *)controller
        didCompleteWithAction:(EKEventEditViewAction)action {
    NSLog(@"%@", controller.event); // could do something with event here
    if (self.currentPop && self.currentPop.popoverVisible) {
        [self.currentPop dismissPopoverAnimated:YES];
        self.currentPop = nil;
    } else if (self.presentedViewController)
        [self dismissViewControllerAnimated:YES completion:nil];
}
```

EKCalendarChooser displays a list of calendars. To use it, call `initWithSelection-Style:displayStyle:entityType:eventStore:`, set a `delegate` (EKCalendar-ChooserDelegate), create a UINavigationController with the EKCalendarChooser as its root view controller, and show the navigation controller as a presented view controller (iPhone) or a popover (iPad). The `selectionStyle` dictates whether the user can pick one or multiple calendars; the `displayStyle` states whether all calendars or only writable calendars will be displayed. If access to the database has been denied, the interface will be empty (like Figure 30-2) and the user will simply cancel.

Two properties, `showsCancelButton` and `showsDoneButton`, determine whether these buttons will appear in the navigation bar. In a presented view controller, you'll certainly show at least one and probably both, because otherwise the user has no way to dismiss the presented view. In a popover, though, the user can dismiss the popover by tapping elsewhere, and your delegate will hear about what the user does in the view, so depending on the circumstances you might not need either button; for example, if your purpose is to let the user change what calendar an existing event belongs to, this might be considered a reversible, nondestructive action, so it wouldn't need the overhead of Cancel and Done buttons.

There are three delegate methods, all of them required:

- `calendarChooserSelectionDidChange:`
- `calendarChooserDidFinish:`
- `calendarChooserDidCancel:`

("Finish" means the user tapped the Done button.) In the Finish and Cancel methods, you'll certainly dismiss the presented view controller or popover. What else you do will depend on the circumstances.

In this example, we implement a potentially destructive action: we offer to delete the selected calendar. Because this is potentially destructive, we pass through a UIAction-Sheet. There is no way to pass context information into a UIActionSheet, so we store the chosen calendar's identifier in an instance variable:

```
- (IBAction)deleteCalendar:(id)sender {
    EKCalendarChooser* choo =
    [[EKCalendarChooser alloc]
     initWithSelectionStyle:EKCalendarChooserSelectionStyleSingle
     displayStyle:EKCalendarChooserDisplayAllCalendars
     entityType:EKEntityTypeEvent
     eventStore:self.database];
    choo.showsDoneButton = YES;
    choo.showsCancelButton = YES;
    choo.delegate = self;
    UINavigationController* nav =
        [[UINavigationController alloc] initWithRootViewController:choo];
```

```
        if (UI_USER_INTERFACE_IDIOM() == UIUserInterfaceIdiomPhone)
            [self presentViewController:nav animated:YES completion:nil];
        // on iPad, create navigation interface in popover
        else {
            UIPopoverController* pop =
            [[UIPopoverController alloc] initWithContentViewController:nav];
            self.currentPop = pop;
            [pop presentPopoverFromRect:[sender bounds] inView:sender
                permittedArrowDirections:UIPopoverArrowDirectionAny animated:YES];
        }
    }

    -(void)calendarChooserDidCancel:(EKCalendarChooser *)calendarChooser {
        NSLog(@"chooser cancel");
        if (self.currentPop && self.currentPop.popoverVisible) {
            [self.currentPop dismissPopoverAnimated:YES];
            self.currentPop = nil;
        } else if (self.presentedViewController)
            [self dismissViewControllerAnimated:YES completion:nil];
    }

    -(void)calendarChooserDidFinish:(EKCalendarChooser *)calendarChooser {
        NSLog(@"chooser finish");
        NSSet* cals = calendarChooser.selectedCalendars;
        if (cals && cals.count) {
            self.calsToDelete = [cals valueForKey:@"calendarIdentifier"];
            UIActionSheet* act =
                [[UIActionSheet alloc] initWithTitle:@"Delete selected calendar?"
                    delegate:self cancelButtonTitle:@"Cancel"
                    destructiveButtonTitle:@"Delete" otherButtonTitles: nil];
            [act showInView:calendarChooser.view];
            return;
        }
        if (self.currentPop && self.currentPop.popoverVisible) {
            [self.currentPop dismissPopoverAnimated:YES];
            self.currentPop = nil;
        } else if (self.presentedViewController)
            [self dismissViewControllerAnimated:YES completion:nil];
    }

    -(void)calendarChooserSelectionDidChange:(EKCalendarChooser*)calendarChooser {
        NSLog(@"chooser change");
    }

    -(void)actionSheet:(UIActionSheet *)actionSheet
            didDismissWithButtonIndex:(NSInteger)buttonIndex {
        NSString* title = [actionSheet buttonTitleAtIndex:buttonIndex];
        if ([title isEqualToString:@"Delete"]) {
            for (id ident in self.calsToDelete) {
                EKCalendar* cal = [self.database calendarWithIdentifier:ident];
                if (cal)
                    [self.database removeCalendar:cal commit:YES error:nil];
```

```
        }
        self.calsToDelete = nil;
    }
    if (self.currentPop && self.currentPop.popoverVisible) {
        [self.currentPop dismissPopoverAnimated:YES];
        self.currentPop = nil;
    } else if (self.presentedViewController)
        [self dismissViewControllerAnimated:YES completion:nil];
}
```

These view controllers automatically listen for changes in the database and, if needed, will automatically call refresh on the information being edited, updating their display to match. If a view controller is displaying an event in the database and the database is deleted while the user is viewing it, the delegate will get the same notification as if the user had deleted it.

CHAPTER 33

Mail and Messages

Your app can present an interface allowing the user to edit and send a mail message or an SMS message. Two view controller classes are provided by the Message UI framework; your app will link to *MessageUI.framework* and import `<MessageUI/MessageUI.h>`. The classes are:

MFMailComposeViewController
    Allows composition and sending of a mail message.

MFMessageComposeViewController
    Allows composition and sending of an SMS message.

New in iOS 6, the Social framework lets you post a message to Twitter or Facebook (or Weibo) on the user's behalf. Link to *Social.framework* and import `<Social/Social.h>`. You can use an SLComposeViewController to give the user an interface to construct and send a message, or prepare and post a message directly using SLRequest.

Also new iOS 6, UIActivityViewController (Chapter 26) provides a unified interface for letting the user choose any of the built-in messaging milieus (mail, SMS, Facebook, Twitter, and Weibo). To give the user a chance to send a message through one of these milieus, with an initial message body or other data that you supply, you should use UIActivityViewController. However, I have not found any way to make UIActivity-ViewController fill in the fields of a proposed mail message. For example, for my users to be able to email me from within one of my apps, I must fill in the To field in the mail composition form. MFMailComposeViewController lets me do that; UIActivityView-Controller doesn't. Thus, the Message UI framework remains important.

Mail Message

The MFMailComposeViewController class, a UINavigationController, allows the user to edit a mail message. The user can attempt to send the message there and then, or can cancel but save a draft, or can cancel completely. Before using this class to present a view, call canSendMail; if the result is NO, go no further, as a negative result means that the device is not configured for sending mail. A positive result does not mean that the device is connected to the network and can send mail right now, only that sending mail is generally possible with this device; actually sending the mail (or storing it as a draft) will be up to the device's internal processes.

To use MFMailComposeViewController, instantiate it, provide a mailCompose-Delegate (*not* delegate), and configure the message to any desired extent. The user can later alter your preset configurations, at which time the message details will be out of your hands. Configuration methods are:

- setSubject:
- setToRecipients:
- setCcRecipients:
- setBccRecipients:
- setMessageBody:isHTML:
- addAttachmentData:mimeType:fileName:

Typically, you'll show the MFMailComposeViewController as a presented view controller. This approach works equally well on the iPad (use UIModalPresentationForm-Sheet if a full-screen presentation feels too overwhelming).

The delegate (MFMailComposeViewControllerDelegate) will receive the message mail-ComposeController:didFinishWithResult:error: describing the user's final action, which might be any of these:

- MFMailComposeResultCancelled
- MFMailComposeResultSaved
- MFMailComposeResultSent
- MFMailComposeResultFailed

Dismissing the presented view is up to you, in the delegate method.

Here's a minimal example:

```
- (IBAction)doMail:(id)sender {
    BOOL ok = [MFMailComposeViewController canSendMail];
    if (!ok) return;
    MFMailComposeViewController* vc = [MFMailComposeViewController new];
    vc.mailComposeDelegate = self;
    [self presentViewController:vc animated:YES completion:nil];
}
```

```
-(void)mailComposeController:(MFMailComposeViewController *)controller
      didFinishWithResult:(MFMailComposeResult)result
      error:(NSError *)error {
    // could do something with result/error
    [self dismissViewControllerAnimated:YES completion:nil];
}
```

Text Message

The MFMessageComposeViewController class is a UINavigationController subclass. Before using this class to present a view, call canSendText; if the result is NO, go no further. The user has no option to save an SMS message as a draft, so even if this device sometimes *can* send text, there's no point proceeding if the device can't send text *now*. However, you can register for the MFMessageComposeViewControllerTextMessage-AvailabilityDidChangeNotification in the hope that the device might later be able to send text; if the notification arrives, check its MFMessageComposeViewController-TextMessageAvailabilityKey.

To use MFMessageComposeViewController, instantiate the class, give it a message-ComposeDelegate, configure it as desired through the recipients (phone number strings) and body properties, and show it as a presented view controller. The user can later alter your preset configurations, at which time the message details will be out of your hands.

The delegate (MFMessageComposeViewControllerDelegate) will receive the message messageComposeViewController:didFinishWithResult: with a description of the user's final action, which might be any of these:

- MessageComposeResultCancelled
- MessageComposeResultSent
- MessageComposeResultFailed

Dismissing the presented view is up to you, in the delegate method.

Here's a minimal example:

```
- (IBAction)doMessage:(id)sender {
    BOOL ok = [MFMessageComposeViewController canSendText];
    if (!ok) return;
    MFMessageComposeViewController* vc = [MFMessageComposeViewController new];
    vc.messageComposeDelegate = self;
    [self presentViewController:vc animated:YES completion:nil];
}
```

```
-(void)messageComposeViewController:(MFMessageComposeViewController*)controller
        didFinishWithResult:(MessageComposeResult)result {
    // could do something with result
    [self dismissViewControllerAnimated:YES completion:nil];
}
```

Twitter Post

In iOS 6, the interface for letting the user construct a Twitter post is SLComposeView-Controller, part of the Social framework (superseding TWTweetComposeViewController and the Twitter framework). Twitter, together with Facebook and Weibo, are represented by constant strings. You'll use a class method to learn whether the desired service is available; if it is, you can instantiate SLComposeViewController for that service and present it as a presented view controller.

Instead of a delegate, SLComposeViewController has a `completionHandler`. Set it to a block taking one parameter, an SLComposeViewControllerResult. In the block, dismiss the view controller.

Here's a minimal example:

```
BOOL ok =
    [SLComposeViewController
        isAvailableForServiceType:SLServiceTypeTwitter];
if (!ok) return;
SLComposeViewController* vc =
    [SLComposeViewController
        composeViewControllerForServiceType:SLServiceTypeTwitter];
if (!vc) return;
vc.completionHandler = ^(SLComposeViewControllerResult result) {
    // could do something with result
    [self dismissViewControllerAnimated:YES completion:nil];
};
[self presentViewController:vc animated:YES completion:nil];
```

You can also, with the user's permission, gain secure access to the user's Twitter account information (or Facebook, or Weibo) through the ACAccountStore class (part of the Accounts framework). Using this, along with the SLRequest class, your app can construct and post a message directly, without passing through the message composition interface; see Apple's Tweeting example. The ACAccountStore class can manipulate accounts in other ways as well.

CHAPTER 34

Maps

Your app can imitate the Maps app, displaying a map interface and placing annotations and overlays on the map. UIView subclasses for displaying the map, along with the programming API, are provided by the Map Kit framework. You'll link to *Map-Kit.framework* and import `<MapKit/MapKit.h>`. You might also need the Core Location framework to express locations by latitude and longitude; you'll link to *Core-Location.framework* and import `<CoreLocation/CoreLocation.h>`.

Displaying a Map

A map is displayed through a UIView subclass, an MKMapView. The map is potentially a map of the entire world; the map view is usually configured to display a particular area. An MKMapView instance can be created in code or through the nib editor. A map has a `type`, which is one of the following:

- `MKMapTypeStandard`
- `MKMapTypeSatellite`
- `MKMapTypeHybrid`

The area displayed on the map is its `region`, an MKCoordinateRegion. This is a struct comprising a location (a CLLocationCoordinate2D), describing the latitude and longitude of the point at the center of the region (the map's `centerCoordinate`), along with a span (an MKCoordinateSpan), describing the quantity of latitude and longitude embraced by the region and hence the scale of the map. Convenience functions help you construct an MKCoordinateRegion.

In this example, I'll initialize the display of an MKMapView (`map`) to show a place where I like to go dirt biking (Figure 34-1):

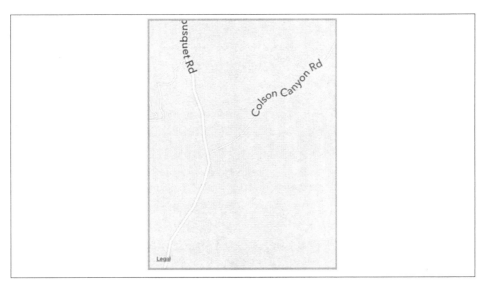

Figure 34-1. A map view showing a happy place

```
CLLocationCoordinate2D loc =
    CLLocationCoordinate2DMake(34.924365,-120.217372);
MKCoordinateSpan span = MKCoordinateSpanMake(.015, .015);
MKCoordinateRegion reg = MKCoordinateRegionMake(loc, span);
self.map.region = reg;
```

An MKCoordinateSpan is described in degrees of latitude and longitude. It may be, however, that what you know is the region's proposed dimensions in meters. To convert, call `MKCoordinateRegionMakeWithDistance`. The ability to perform this conversion is important, because an MKMapView shows the world through a Mercator projection, where longitude lines are parallel and equidistant, and scale increases at higher latitudes. This means, for example, that trying to display an MKCoordinateSpan with a fixed quantity of latitude will require the map to zoom out further at higher latitudes.

I happen to know that the area I want to display is about 1200 meters on a side. Hence, this is another way of displaying approximately the same region:

```
CLLocationCoordinate2D loc =
    CLLocationCoordinate2DMake(34.924365,-120.217372);
MKCoordinateRegionreg = MKCoordinateRegionMakeWithDistance(loc, 1200, 1200);
self.map.region = reg;
```

Another way of describing a map region is MKMapRect, a struct built up from MKMap-Point and MKMapSize. The earth has already been projected onto the map for us, and now we are describing a rectangle of that map, in terms of the units in which the map is drawn. The exact relationship between an MKMapPoint and the corresponding latitude/longitude coordinates is arbitrary and of no interest; what matters is that you can ask for the conversion (`MKMapPointForCoordinate`, `MKCoordinateForMapPoint`), along with the ratio of points to meters (which will vary with latitude: `MKMetersPerMapPoint-AtLatitude`, `MKMapPointsPerMeterAtLatitude`, `MKMetersBetweenMapPoints`). To determine what the map view is showing in MKMapRect terms, use its `visibleMapRect` property. Thus, this is yet another way of displaying approximately the same region:

```
CLLocationCoordinate2D loc =
    CLLocationCoordinate2DMake(34.924365,-120.217372);
MKMapPoint pt = MKMapPointForCoordinate(loc);
double w = MKMapPointsPerMeterAtLatitude(loc.latitude) * 1200;
self.map.visibleMapRect = MKMapRectMake(pt.x - w/2.0, pt.y - w/2.0, w, w);
```

In none of those examples did I bother with the question of the actual dimensions of the map view itself. I simply threw a proposed region at the map view, and it decided how best to portray the corresponding area. Values you assign to the map's `region` and `visibleMapRect` are unlikely to be the exact values the map adopts in any case; that's because the map view will optimize for display without distorting the map's scale. You can perform this same optimization in code by calling these methods:

- `regionThatFits:`
- `mapRectThatFits:`
- `mapRectThatFits:edgePadding:`

By default, the user can zoom and scroll the map with the usual gestures; you can turn this off by setting the map view's `zoomEnabled` and `scrollEnabled` to NO. Usually you will set them both to YES or both to NO. For further customization of an MKMapView's response to touches, use a UIGestureRecognizer (Chapter 18).

You can change programmatically the region displayed, optionally with animation, by calling these methods:

- `setRegion:animated:`
- `setCenterCoordinate:animated:`
- `setVisibleMapRect:animated:`
- `setVisibleMapRect:edgePadding:animated:`

The map view's delegate (MKMapViewDelegate) is notified as the map loads and as the region changes (including changes triggered programmatically):

- `mapViewWillStartLoadingMap:`
- `mapViewDidFinishLoadingMap:`
- `mapViewDidFailLoadingMap:withError:`

- `mapView:regionWillChangeAnimated:`
- `mapView:regionDidChangeAnimated:`

Annotations

An *annotation* is a marker associated with a location on a map. To make an annotation appear on a map, two objects are needed:

The object attached to the MKMapView
> The annotation itself is attached to the MKMapView. It consists of any instance whose class adopts the MKAnnotation protocol, which specifies a coordinate, a title, and a subtitle for the annotation. You might have reason to define your own class to handle this task, or you can use the simple built-in MKPointAnnotation class. The annotation's `coordinate` is its most important property; this says where on earth the annotation should be drawn. The title and subtitle are optional, to be displayed in a callout.

The object that draws the annotation
> An annotation is drawn by an MKAnnotationView, a UIView subclass. This can be extremely simple. In fact, even a nil MKAnnotationView might be perfectly satisfactory: it draws a red pin. If red is not your favorite color, a built-in MKAnnotation-View subclass, MKPinAnnotationView, displays a pin in red, green, or purple; by convention you are supposed to use these colors for different purposes (destination points, starting points, and user-specified points, respectively). For more flexibility, you can provide your own UIImage as the MKAnnotationView's `image` property. And for even *more* flexibility, you can take over the drawing of an MKAnnotation-View by overriding `drawRect:` in a subclass.

Not only does an annotation require two separate objects, but in fact those objects do not initially exist together. An annotation object has no pointer to the annotation view object that will draw it. Rather, it is up to you to supply the annotation view object in real time, on demand, in the MKMapView's delegate. This architecture may sound confusing, but in fact it's a very clever way of reducing the amount of resources needed at any given moment. Think of it this way: an annotation itself is merely a lightweight object that a map can always possess; the corresponding annotation view is a heavyweight object that is needed only so long as that annotation's coordinates are within the visible portion of the map.

Let's add the simplest possible annotation to our map. The point where the annotation is to go has been stored in an instance variable:

```
self.annloc = CLLocationCoordinate2DMake(34.923964,-120.219558);
```

We create the annotation, configure its properties, and add it to the MKMapView:

Figure 34-2. A simple annotation

```
MKPointAnnotation* ann = [MKPointAnnotation new];
ann.coordinate = self.annloc;
ann.title = @"Park here";
ann.subtitle = @"Fun awaits down the road!";
[self.map addAnnotation:ann];
```

That code is sufficient to produce Figure 34-2. I didn't implement any MKMapView delegate methods, so the MKAnnotationView is nil. But a nil MKAnnotationView, as I've already said, produces a red pin. I've also tapped the annotation, to display its callout, containing the annotation's title and subtitle.

This location is a starting point, so by convention the pin should be green. We can easily create a green pin using MKPinAnnotationView, which has a `pinColor` property. To supply the annotation view, we must give the map view a delegate (MKMapView-Delegate) and implement `mapView:viewForAnnotation:`.

The structure of `mapView:viewForAnnotation:` is rather similar to the structure of `tableView:cellForRowAtIndexPath:` (Chapter 21), which is not surprising, considering that they both do the same sort of thing. Recall that the goal of `tableView:cellForRowAtIndexPath:` is to allow the table view to reuse cells, so that at any given moment only as many cells are needed as are *visible* in the table view, regardless of how many rows the table as a whole may consist of. The same thing holds for a map and its annotation views. The map may have a huge number of annotations, but it needs to display annotation views for only those annotations that are within its current `region`. Any extra annotation views that have been scrolled out of view can thus be reused and are held for us by the map view in a cache for exactly this purpose.

So, in mapView:viewForAnnotation:, we start by calling dequeueReusableAnnotation-ViewWithIdentifier: to see whether there's an already existing annotation view that's not currently being displayed and that we might be able to reuse. If there isn't, we create one, attaching to it an appropriate reuse identifier.

Here's our implementation of mapView:viewForAnnotation:. Observe that in creating our green pin, we explicitly set its canShowCallout to YES, as this is not the default:

```
- (MKAnnotationView *)mapView:(MKMapView *)mapView
            viewForAnnotation:(id <MKAnnotation>)annotation {
    MKAnnotationView* v = nil;
    if ([annotation.title isEqualToString:@"Park here"]) { ❶
        static NSString* ident = @"greenPin"; ❷
        v = [mapView dequeueReusableAnnotationViewWithIdentifier:ident];
        if (v == nil) {
            v = [[MKPinAnnotationView alloc] initWithAnnotation:annotation
                                                reuseIdentifier:ident];
            ((MKPinAnnotationView*)v).pinColor = MKPinAnnotationColorGreen;
            v.canShowCallout = YES;
        }
        v.annotation = annotation; ❸
    }
    return v;
}
```

The structure of this implementation of mapView:viewForAnnotation: is typical (though it seems pointlessly elaborate when we have only one annotation in our map):

❶   We might have more than one reusable type of annotation view. (A view can perhaps be reconfigured and thus reused, but cannot be magically converted into a view of a different type.) Here, some of our annotations might be marked with green pins, and other annotations might be marked by a different sort of annotation view altogether. So we must first somehow distinguish these cases, based on something about the incoming annotation. Here, I use the annotation's title as a distinguishing mark; later in this chapter, I'll suggest a much better approach.

❷   After that, for each reusable type, we proceed much as with table view cells. We have an identifier that categorizes this sort of reusable view. We try to dequeue an unused annotation view of the appropriate type, and if we can't, we create one and configure it.

❸   Even if we *can* dequeue an unused annotation view, and even if we have no other configuration to perform, we must associate the annotation view with the incoming annotation by assigning the annotation to this annotation view's annotation property.

MKAnnotationView has one more option of which we might avail ourselves: when it draws the annotation view (the pin), it can animate it into place, dropping it in the manner familiar from the Maps app. All we have to do is add one line of code:

```
((MKPinAnnotationView*)v).animatesDrop = YES;
```

Now let's go further. Instead of a green pin, we'll substitute our own artwork. I'll revise the code at the heart of my mapView:viewForAnnotation: implementation, such that instead of creating an MKPinAnnotationView, I create an instance of its superclass, MKAnnotationView, and give it a custom image showing a dirt bike. The image is too large, so I shrink the view's bounds before returning it; I also move the view up a bit, so that the bottom of the image is at the coordinates on the map (Figure 34-3):

```
- (MKAnnotationView *)mapView:(MKMapView *)mapView
            viewForAnnotation:(id <MKAnnotation>)annotation {
    MKAnnotationView* v = nil;
    if ([annotation.title isEqualToString:@"Park here"]) {
        static NSString* ident = @"greenPin";
        v = [mapView dequeueReusableAnnotationViewWithIdentifier:ident];
        if (v == nil) {
            v = [[MKAnnotationView alloc] initWithAnnotation:annotation
                                            reuseIdentifier:ident];
            v.image = [UIImage imageNamed:@"clipartdirtbike.gif"];
            CGRect f = v.bounds;
            f.size.height /= 3.0;
            f.size.width /= 3.0;
            v.bounds = f;
            v.centerOffset = CGPointMake(0,-20);
            v.canShowCallout = YES;
        }
        v.annotation = annotation;
    }
    return v;
}
```

For more flexibility, we can create our own MKAnnotationView subclass and endow it with the ability to draw itself. At a minimum, such a subclass should override the initializer and assign itself a frame, and should implement drawRect:. Here's the implementation for a class MyAnnotationView that draws a dirt bike:

```
- (id)initWithAnnotation:(id <MKAnnotation>)annotation
        reuseIdentifier:(NSString *)reuseIdentifier {
    self = [super initWithAnnotation:annotation
                    reuseIdentifier:reuseIdentifier];
    if (self) {
        UIImage* im = [UIImage imageNamed:@"clipartdirtbike.gif"];
        self.frame =
            CGRectMake(0, 0, im.size.width/3.0 + 5, im.size.height/3.0 + 5);
        self.centerOffset = CGPointMake(0,-20);
        self.opaque = NO;
    }
```

Figure 34-3. A custom annotation image

```
    return self;
}

- (void) drawRect: (CGRect) rect {
    UIImage* im = [UIImage imageNamed:@"clipartdirtbike.gif"];
    [im drawInRect:CGRectInset(self.bounds, 5, 5)];
}
```

The corresponding implementation of `mapView:viewForAnnotation:` now has much less work to do:

```
- (MKAnnotationView *)mapView:(MKMapView *)mapView
          viewForAnnotation:(id <MKAnnotation>)annotation {
    MKAnnotationView* v = nil;
    if ([annotation.title isEqualToString:@"Park here"]) {
        static NSString* ident = @"bike";
        v = [mapView dequeueReusableAnnotationViewWithIdentifier:ident];
        if (v == nil) {
            v = [[MyAnnotationView alloc] initWithAnnotation:annotation
                                          reuseIdentifier:ident];
            v.canShowCallout = YES;
        }
        v.annotation = annotation;
    }
    return v;
}
```

For ultimate flexibility, we should provide our own annotation class as well. A minimal annotation class will look like this:

```
@interface MyAnnotation : NSObject <MKAnnotation>
@property (nonatomic) CLLocationCoordinate2D coordinate;
@property (nonatomic, copy) NSString *title, *subtitle;
- (id)initWithLocation:(CLLocationCoordinate2D)coord;
@end

@implementation MyAnnotation
- (id)initWithLocation: (CLLocationCoordinate2D) coord {
    self = [super init];
    if (self) {
        self->_coordinate = coord;
    }
    return self;
}
@end
```

Now when we create our annotation and add it to our map, our code looks like this:

```
MyAnnotation* ann = [[MyAnnotation alloc] initWithLocation:loc];
ann.title = @"Park here";
ann.subtitle = @"Fun awaits down the road!";
[self.map addAnnotation:ann];
```

A major advantage of this change appears in our implementation of mapView:viewFor-Annotation:, where we test for the annotation type. Formerly, it wasn't easy to distinguish those annotations that needed to be drawn as a dirt bike; we were rather artificially examining the title:

```
if ([annotation.title isEqualToString:@"Park here"]) {
```

Now, however, we can just look at the class:

```
if ([annotation isKindOfClass:[MyAnnotation class]]) {
```

A further advantage of supplying our own annotation class is that this approach gives our implementation room to grow. For example, at the moment, every MyAnnotation is drawn as a bike, but we could now add another property to MyAnnotation that tells us what drawing to use. We could also give MyAnnotation further properties saying such things as which way the bike should face, what angle it should be drawn at, and so on. Our implementation of mapView:viewForAnnotation:, you'll recall, assigns the annotation to the annotation view's annotation property; thus, MyAnnotationView would be able to read those MyAnnotation properties and draw itself appropriately.

To add our own animation to an annotation view as it appears on the map, analogous to the built-in MKPinAnnotationView pin-drop animation, we implement the map view delegate method mapView:didAddAnnotationViews:. The key fact here is that at the moment this method is called, the annotation view has been added but the redraw moment has not yet arrived (Chapter 17). So if we animate the view, that animation will be performed at the moment the view appears onscreen. Here, I'll animate the opacity of the view so that it fades in, while growing the view from a point to its full size; the only even mildly tricky bit is identifying the view:

```
- (void)mapView:(MKMapView *)mapView didAddAnnotationViews:(NSArray *)views {
    for (MKAnnotationView* aView in views) {
        if ([aView.reuseIdentifier isEqualToString:@"bike"]) {
            aView.transform = CGAffineTransformMakeScale(0, 0);
            aView.alpha = 0;
            [UIView animateWithDuration:0.8 animations:^{
                aView.alpha = 1;
                aView.transform = CGAffineTransformIdentity;
            }];
        }
    }
}
```

The callout is visible in Figure 34-2 and Figure 34-3 because before taking the screenshot, I tapped on the annotation, thus *selecting* it. MKMapView has methods allowing annotations to be selected or deselected programmatically, thus (by default) causing their callouts to appear or disappear. The delegate has methods notifying you when the user selects or deselects an annotation, and you are free to override your custom MKAnnotationView's `setSelected:animated:` if you want to change what happens when the user taps an annotation.

A callout can contain left and right accessory views; these are the MKAnnotationView's `leftCalloutAccessoryView` and `rightCalloutAccessoryView`. They are UIViews, and should be small (less than 32 pixels in height). You can respond to taps on these views as you would any view or control; as a convenience, a delegate method `mapView:annotationView:calloutAccessoryControlTapped:` is called when the user taps an accessory view, provided it is a UIControl.

An MKAnnotationView can optionally be draggable by the user; set its `draggable` property to YES and implement the map view delegate's `mapView:annotationView:didChangeDragState:fromOldState:`. You can also customize changes to the appearance of the view as it is dragged, by implementing your annotation view class's `setDragState:animated:` method. If you're using a custom annotation class, you'll also need to implement its `setCoordinate:` method; in our custom annotation class, MyAnnotation, that's done automatically, as the `coordinate` property is synthesized and is not `readonly`.

Certain annotation properties and annotation view properties are automatically animatable through view animation, provided you've implemented them in a KVO compliant way (Chapter 13). For example, in MyAnnotation, the `coordinate` property is synthesized, so it is KVO compliant; therefore, we are able to animate the shifting of the annotation's position:

```
[UIView animateWithDuration:0.25 animations:^{
    CLLocationCoordinate2D loc = ann.coordinate;
    loc.latitude = loc.latitude + 0.0005;
    loc.longitude = loc.longitude + 0.001;
    ann.coordinate = loc;
}];
```

MKMapView has extensive support for adding and removing annotations.

 Annotation views don't change size as the map is zoomed in and out, so if there are several annotations and they are brought close together by the user zooming out, the display can become crowded. Moreover, if too many annotations are being drawn simultaneously in a map view, scroll and zoom performance can degrade. The only way to prevent this is to respond to changes in the map's visible region (for example, in the delegate method mapView:regionDidChangeAnimated:) by removing and adding annotations dynamically. This is a tricky problem, and it's surprising that the API doesn't give you any assistance with it.

Overlays

An overlay differs from an annotation in being drawn entirely with respect to points on the surface of the earth. Thus, whereas an annotation's size is always the same, an overlay's size is tied to the zoom of the map view.

Overlays are implemented much like annotations. You provide an object that adopts the MKOverlay protocol (which itself conforms to the MKAnnotation protocol) and add it to the map view. When the map view delegate method mapView:viewForOverlay: is called, you provide an MKOverlayView and hand it the overlay object; the overlay view then draws the overlay on demand. As with annotations, this architecture means that the overlay itself is a lightweight object, and the overlay view is needed only if the part of the earth that the overlay covers is actually being displayed in the map view. An MKOverlayView has no reuse identifier.

Some built-in MKShape subclasses adopt the MKOverlay protocol: MKCircle, MKPolygon, and MKPolyline. In parallel to those, MKOverlayView has built-in subclasses MKCircleView, MKPolygonView, and MKPolylineView, ready to draw the corresponding shapes. Thus, as with annotations, you can base your overlay entirely on the power of existing classes.

In this example, I'll use MKPolygonView to draw an overlay triangle pointing up the road from the parking place annotated in our earlier examples (Figure 34-4). We add the MKPolygon as an overlay to our map view, and derive the MKPolygonView from it in our implementation of mapView:viewForOverlay:. First, the MKPolygon overlay:

```
CLLocationCoordinate2D loc = self.annloc;
CGFloat lat = loc.latitude;
CLLocationDistance metersPerPoint = MKMetersPerMapPointAtLatitude(lat);
MKMapPoint c = MKMapPointForCoordinate(loc);
c.x += 150/metersPerPoint;
c.y -= 50/metersPerPoint;
MKMapPoint p1 = MKMapPointMake(c.x, c.y);
p1.y -= 100/metersPerPoint;
MKMapPoint p2 = MKMapPointMake(c.x, c.y);
p2.x += 100/metersPerPoint;
MKMapPoint p3 = MKMapPointMake(c.x, c.y);
p3.x += 300/metersPerPoint;
p3.y -= 400/metersPerPoint;
MKMapPoint pts[3] = {
    p1, p2, p3
};
MKPolygon* tri = [MKPolygon polygonWithPoints:pts count:3];
[self.map addOverlay:tri];
```

Second, the delegate method, where we provide the MKPolygonView:

```
- (MKOverlayView *)mapView:(MKMapView *)mapView
        viewForOverlay:(id <MKOverlay>)overlay {
    MKPolygonView* v = nil;
    if ([overlay isKindOfClass:[MKPolygon class]]) {
        v = [[MKPolygonView alloc] initWithPolygon:(MKPolygon*)overlay];
        v.fillColor = [[UIColor redColor] colorWithAlphaComponent:0.1];
        v.strokeColor = [[UIColor redColor] colorWithAlphaComponent:0.8];
        v.lineWidth = 2;
    }
    return v;
}
```

Now let's go further. The triangle in Figure 34-4 is rather crude; I could draw a better arrow shape using a CGPath (Chapter 15). The built-in MKOverlayView subclass that lets me do that is MKOverlayPathView. To structure my use of MKOverlayView similarly to the preceding example, I'll supply the CGPath when I add the overlay instance to the map view. No built-in class lets me do that, so I'll use a custom class, MyOverlay, that implements the MKOverlay protocol.

A minimal overlay class looks like this:

```
@interface MyOverlay : NSObject <MKOverlay>
@property (nonatomic, readonly) CLLocationCoordinate2D coordinate;
@property (nonatomic, readonly) MKMapRect boundingMapRect;
- (id) initWithRect: (MKMapRect) rect;
@end

@implementation MyOverlay
- (id) initWithRect: (MKMapRect) rect {
    self = [super init];
    if (self) {
        self->_boundingMapRect = rect;
```

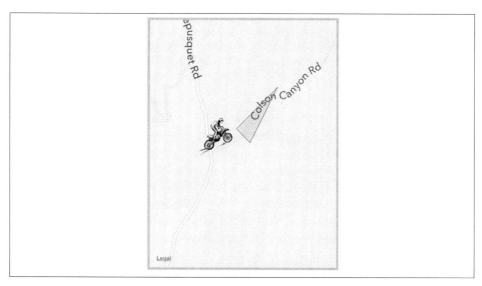

Figure 34-4. An overlay view

```
        }
        return self;
    }
    - (CLLocationCoordinate2D) coordinate {
        MKMapPoint pt = MKMapPointMake(
            MKMapRectGetMidX(self.boundingMapRect),
            MKMapRectGetMidY(self.boundingMapRect));
        return MKCoordinateForMapPoint(pt);
    }
    @end
```

Our actual MyOverlay class will also have a `path` property; this will be a UIBezierPath that holds our CGPath and supplies it to the MKOverlayView.

Just as the `coordinate` property of an annotation tells the map view where on earth the annotation is to be drawn, the `boundingMapRect` property of an overlay tells the map view where on earth the overlay is to be drawn. Whenever any part of the `boundingMap-Rect` is displayed within the map view's bounds, the map view will have to concern itself with drawing the overlay. With MKPolygon, we supplied the points of the polygon in earth coordinates and the `boundingMapRect` was calculated for us. With our custom overlay class, we must supply or calculate it ourselves.

At first it may appear that there is a typological impedance mismatch: the `boundingMap-Rect` is an MKMapRect, whereas a CGPath is defined by CGPoints. However, it turns out that these units are interchangeable: the CGPoints of our CGPath will be translated for us directly into MKMapPoints on the same scale — that is, the *distance* between any two CGPoints will be the distance between the two corresponding MKMapPoints. However, the *origins* are different: the CGPath must be described relative to the top-left corner of the `boundingMapRect` — that is, the `boundingMapRect` is described in earth coordinates, but the top-left corner of the `boundingMapRect` is {0,0} as far as the CGPath is concerned. (You might think of this difference as analogous to the difference between a UIView's frame and its bounds.)

To make life simple, I'll think in meters; actually, I'll think in chunks of 75 meters, because this turns out to be a good unit for positioning and laying out the arrow. In other words, a line one `unit` long would in fact be 75 meters long if I were to arrive at this actual spot on the earth and discover the overlay literally drawn on the ground. Having derived this chunk (`unit`), I use it to lay out the `boundingMapRect`, four units on a side and positioned slightly east and north of the annotation point (because that's where the road is). Then I simply construct the arrow shape within the 4×4-unit square, rotating it so that it points in roughly the same direction as the road:

```
// start with our position and derive a nice unit for drawing
CLLocationCoordinate2D loc = self.annloc;
CGFloat lat = loc.latitude;
CLLocationDistance metersPerPoint = MKMetersPerMapPointAtLatitude(lat);
MKMapPoint c = MKMapPointForCoordinate(loc);
CGFloat unit = 75.0/metersPerPoint;
// size and position the overlay bounds on the earth
CGSize sz = CGSizeMake(4*unit, 4*unit);
MKMapRect mr =
    MKMapRectMake(c.x + 2*unit, c.y - 4.5*unit, sz.width, sz.height);
// describe the arrow as a CGPath
CGMutablePathRef p = CGPathCreateMutable();
CGPoint start = CGPointMake(0, unit*1.5);
CGPoint p1 = CGPointMake(start.x+2*unit, start.y);
CGPoint p2 = CGPointMake(p1.x, p1.y-unit);
CGPoint p3 = CGPointMake(p2.x+unit*2, p2.y+unit*1.5);
CGPoint p4 = CGPointMake(p2.x, p2.y+unit*3);
CGPoint p5 = CGPointMake(p4.x, p4.y-unit);
CGPoint p6 = CGPointMake(p5.x-2*unit, p5.y);
CGPoint points[] = {
    start, p1, p2, p3, p4, p5, p6
};
// rotate the arrow around its center
CGAffineTransform t1 = CGAffineTransformMakeTranslation(unit*2, unit*2);
CGAffineTransform t2 = CGAffineTransformRotate(t1, -M_PI/3.5);
CGAffineTransform t3 = CGAffineTransformTranslate(t2, -unit*2, -unit*2);
CGPathAddLines(p, &t3, points, 7);
CGPathCloseSubpath(p);
// create the overlay and give it the path
MyOverlay* over = [[MyOverlay alloc] initWithRect:mr];
over.path = [UIBezierPath bezierPathWithCGPath:p];
CGPathRelease(p);
// add the overlay to the map
[self.map addOverlay:over];
```

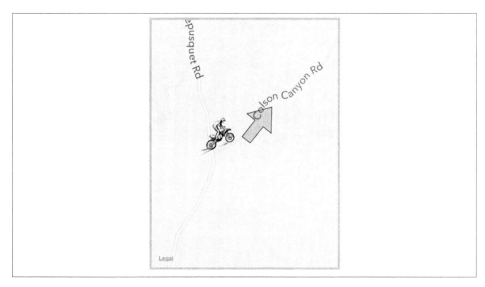

Figure 34-5. A nicer overlay view

The delegate method, where we provide the MKOverlayPathView, is simple. We pull the CGPath out of the MyOverlay instance and hand it to the MKOverlayPathView, also telling the MKOverlayPathView how to stroke and fill that path:

```
- (MKOverlayView*)mapView:(MKMapView*)mapView
        viewForOverlay:(id <MKOverlay>)overlay {
    MKOverlayView* v = nil;
    if ([overlay isKindOfClass: [MyOverlay class]]) {
        v = [[MKOverlayPathView alloc] initWithOverlay:overlay];
        MKOverlayPathView* vv = (MKOverlayPathView*)v;
        vv.path = ((MyOverlay*)overlay).path.CGPath;
        vv.strokeColor = [UIColor blackColor];
        vv.fillColor = [[UIColor redColor] colorWithAlphaComponent:0.2];
        vv.lineWidth = 2;
    }
    return v;
}
```

The result is a much nicer arrow (Figure 34-5), and of course this technique can be generalized to draw an overlay from any CGPath we like.

For full generality, you could define your own MKOverlayView subclass; your subclass must override and implement `drawMapRect:zoomScale:inContext:`. The incoming `mapRect:` parameter describes a tile of the visible map (not the size and position of the overlay). The overlay itself is available through the inherited `overlay` property, and conversion methods such as `rectForMapRect:` are provided for converting between the map's `mapRect:` coordinates and the overlay view's graphics context coordinates.

In our example, we can move the entire functionality for drawing the arrow into an MKOverlayView subclass, which I'll call MyOverlayView. Its initializer takes an angle: parameter, with which I'll set its angle property; now our arrow can point in any direction. Another nice benefit of this architectural change is that we can use the zoomScale: parameter to determine the stroke width. For simplicity, our implementation of drawMapRect:zoomScale:inContext: ignores the incoming mapRect value and just draws the entire arrow every time it is called:

```
- (id) initWithOverlay:(id <MKOverlay>)overlay angle: (CGFloat) ang {
    self = [super initWithOverlay:overlay];
    if (self) {
        self->_angle = ang;
    }
    return self;
}

- (void)drawMapRect:(MKMapRect)mapRect zoomScale:(MKZoomScale)zoomScale
        inContext:(CGContextRef)context {
    NSLog(@"draw this: %@", MKStringFromMapRect(mapRect));
    CGContextSetStrokeColorWithColor(context, [UIColor blackColor].CGColor);
    CGContextSetFillColorWithColor(context,
        [[UIColor redColor] colorWithAlphaComponent:0.2].CGColor);
    CGContextSetLineWidth(context, 1.2/zoomScale);
    CGFloat unit = MKMapRectGetWidth([self.overlay boundingMapRect])/4.0;
    CGMutablePathRef p = CGPathCreateMutable();
    CGPoint start = CGPointMake(0, unit*1.5);
    CGPoint p1 = CGPointMake(start.x+2*unit, start.y);
    CGPoint p2 = CGPointMake(p1.x, p1.y-unit);
    CGPoint p3 = CGPointMake(p2.x+unit*2, p2.y+unit*1.5);
    CGPoint p4 = CGPointMake(p2.x, p2.y+unit*3);
    CGPoint p5 = CGPointMake(p4.x, p4.y-unit);
    CGPoint p6 = CGPointMake(p5.x-2*unit, p5.y);
    CGPoint points[] = {
        start, p1, p2, p3, p4, p5, p6
    };
    // rotate the arrow around its center
    CGAffineTransform t1 = CGAffineTransformMakeTranslation(unit*2, unit*2);
    CGAffineTransform t2 = CGAffineTransformRotate(t1, self.angle);
    CGAffineTransform t3 = CGAffineTransformTranslate(t2, -unit*2, -unit*2);
    CGPathAddLines(p, &t3, points, 7);
    CGPathCloseSubpath(p);
    CGContextAddPath(context, p);
    CGContextDrawPath(context, kCGPathFillStroke);
    CGPathRelease(p);
}
```

To add the overlay to our map, we still must determine its MKMapRect:

```
CLLocationCoordinate2D loc = self.annloc;
CGFloat lat = loc.latitude;
CLLocationDistance metersPerPoint = MKMetersPerMapPointAtLatitude(lat);
MKMapPoint c = MKMapPointForCoordinate(loc);
CGFloat unit = 75.0/metersPerPoint;
// size and position the overlay bounds on the earth
CGSize sz = CGSizeMake(4*unit, 4*unit);
MKMapRect mr =
    MKMapRectMake(c.x + 2*unit, c.y - 4.5*unit, sz.width, sz.height);
MyOverlay* over = [[MyOverlay alloc] initWithRect:mr];
[self.map addOverlay:over];
```

The delegate, providing the overlay view, now has very little work to do; in our implementation, it must supply an angle for the arrow:

```
- (MKOverlayView *)mapView:(MKMapView *)mapView
          viewForOverlay:(id <MKOverlay>)overlay {
    MKOverlayView* v = nil;
    if ([overlay isKindOfClass: [MyOverlay class]]) {
        v = [[MyOverlayView alloc] initWithOverlay: overlay
                                      angle: -M_PI/3.5];
    }
    return v;
}
```

That's not an ideal architecture; the angle really should belong to the overlay and be
passed along with it to the overlay view. But our code does draw the arrow and it does
illustrate the basic use of a MKOverlayView subclass.

Our MyOverlay class, adopting the MKOverlay protocol, also implements the
coordinate getter method to return the center of the boundingMapRect. This is crude,
but it's a good minimal implementation. The purpose of the MKOverlay coordinate
property is to specify the position where you would add an annotation describing the
overlay. For example:

```
// ... create overlay and assign it a path as before ...
[self.map addOverlay:over];
MKPointAnnotation* annot = [MKPointAnnotation new];
annot.coordinate = over.coordinate;
annot.title = @"This way!";
[self.map addAnnotation:annot];
```

The MKOverlay protocol also lets you provide an implementation of intersectsMap-
Rect: to refine your overlay's definition of what constitutes an intersection with itself;
the default is to use the boundingMapRect, but if your overlay is drawn in some non-
rectangular shape, you might want to use its actual shape as the basis for determining
intersection.

Overlays are maintained by the map view as an array and are drawn from back to front
starting at the beginning of the array. MKMapView has extensive support for adding
and removing overlays, and for managing their layering order.

Map Kit and Current Location

A device may have sensors that can determine its current location (Chapter 35). Map Kit provides simple integration with these facilities. Keep in mind that the user can turn off these sensors or can refuse your app access to them (in the Settings app, under Privacy → Location Services), so trying to use these features may fail. Also, determining the device's location can take time.

You can ask an MKMapView in your app to display the device's location just by setting its showsUserLocation property to YES. If your app has not been granted or denied access to Location Services, the system alert requesting authorization will appear. If access is granted, the map automatically puts an annotation at that location.

The userLocation property of the map view is an MKUserLocation, adopting the MKAnnotation protocol. It has a location property, a CLLocation, whose coordinate is a CLLocationCoordinate2D; if the map view's showsUserLocation is YES and the map view has actually worked out the user's location, the coordinate describes that location. It also has title and subtitle properties, plus you can check whether it is currently updating. You are free to supply your own annotation view to be displayed for this annotation, just as for any annotation.

Displaying the appropriate region of the map — that is, actually *showing* the part of the world where the user is located — is the responsibility of the map delegate's mapView:did-UpdateUserLocation: method:

```
- (void)mapView:(MKMapView *)mapView
        didUpdateUserLocation:(MKUserLocation *)userLocation {
    CLLocationCoordinate2D coordinate = userLocation.location.coordinate;
    MKCoordinateRegion reg =
        MKCoordinateRegionMakeWithDistance(coordinate, 600, 600);
    mapView.region = reg;
}
```

You can ask the map view whether the user's location, if known, is in the visible region of the map (isUserLocationVisible).

MKMapView also has a userTrackingMode that you can set to determine how the user's real-world location should be tracked *automatically* by the map display; your options are:

MKUserTrackingModeNone

　　If showsUserLocation is YES, the map gets an annotation at the user's location, but that's all. Deciding whether to set the map's region in mapView:didUpdateUser-Location:, as I've just shown, is up to you.

`MKUserTrackingModeFollow`

Setting this mode sets `showsUserLocation` to YES. The map automatically centers the user's location and scales appropriately. You should *not* set the map's `region` in `mapView:didUpdateUserLocation:`, as you'll be struggling against the tracking mode's attempts to do the same thing.

`MKUserTrackingModeFollowWithHeading`

Like `MKUserTrackingModeFollow`, but the map is also rotated so that the direction the user is facing is up. In this case, the `userLocation` annotation also has a `heading` property, a CLHeading; I'll talk more about headings in Chapter 35.

When the `userTrackingMode` is one of the `follow` modes, if the user is left free to zoom and scroll the map, and if the user scrolls in such a way that the user location annotation is no longer visible, the `userTrackingMode` may be automatically changed back to `MKUserTrackingModeNone` (and the user location annotation may be removed). You'll probably want to provide a way to let the user turn tracking back on again, or to toggle among the three tracking modes.

One way to do that is with an MKUserTrackingBarButtonItem, a UIBarButtonItem subclass. You initialize MKUserTrackingBarButtonItem with a map view, and its behavior is automatic from then on: when the user taps it, it switches the map view to the next tracking mode, and its icon reflects the current tracking mode. (The behavior of MKUserTrackingBarButtonItem is a bit *too* automatic for my taste, however.)

New in iOS 6, you can ask the Maps app to display the device's current location by starting with an MKMapItem returned by the class method `mapItemForCurrent-Location`. This call doesn't attempt to determine the device's location, nor does it contain any location information; it merely generates an MKMapItem which, when sent to the Maps app, will cause *it* to attempt to determine (and display) the device's location:

```
MKMapItem* mi = [MKMapItem mapItemForCurrentLocation];
[mi openInMapsWithLaunchOptions:
    @{MKLaunchOptionsMapTypeKey:@(MKMapTypeStandard)}];
```

Geocoding

The term *geocoding* refers to the translation of an address to a coordinate and *vice versa*. Geocoding functionality is encapsulated in the CLGeocoder class; to use it, you'll need to link to *CoreLocation.framework*. Geocoding takes time and might not succeed at all, as it depends upon network and server availability; moreover, results may be more or less uncertain. Therefore, all geocoding methods take a completion handler which will eventually be called with two arguments:

NSArray* placemark
> An NSArray of CLPlacemark objects. If things went really well, the array will contain exactly one CLPlacemark; if there are multiple placemark objects, the first one is the best guess. If nil, something went wrong.

NSError* error
> If the placemark array was nil, this argument reports the reason things went wrong.

A CLPlacemark can be used to initialize an MKPlacemark, a CLPlacemark subclass that adopts the MKAnnotation protocol, and is therefore suitable to be handed directly over to an MKMapView for display. Here is an (unbelievably simple-minded) example that allows the user to enter an address in a UISearchBar (Chapter 25) to be displayed in an MKMapView:

```
-(void)searchBarSearchButtonClicked:(UISearchBar *)searchBar {
    NSString* s = searchBar.text;
    [searchBar resignFirstResponder];
    CLGeocoder* geo = [CLGeocoder new];
    [geo geocodeAddressString:s
            completionHandler:^(NSArray *placemarks, NSError *error) {
        if (nil == placemarks) {
            NSLog(@"%@", error.localizedDescription);
            return;
        }
        CLPlacemark* p = [placemarks objectAtIndex:0];
        MKPlacemark* mp = [[MKPlacemark alloc] initWithPlacemark:p];
        [self.map removeAnnotations:self.map.annotations];
        [self.map addAnnotation:mp];
        [self.map setRegion: MKCoordinateRegionMakeWithDistance
                                (mp.coordinate, 1000, 1000)
                        animated: YES];
    }];
}
```

By default, the resulting annotation's callout `title` contains a nicely formatted string describing the address.

That example illustrates *forward geocoding*, the conversion of an address to a coordinate. Instead of a string, you can provide a dictionary. Not surprisingly, the keys of this dictionary are exactly the keys you would get by extracting an address from the user's address book (Chapter 31); thus, you can go quite directly from an address book contact to a coordinate.

The converse operation is *reverse geocoding*: you start with a coordinate — actually a CLLocation, which you'll obtain from elsewhere, or construct from a coordinate using `initWithLatitude:longitude:` — and call `reverseGeocodeLocation:completionHandler:` in order to obtain an address. The address is expressed through the CLPlacemark `addressDictionary` property, which is an address in address book format; you can translate it to a string with `ABCreateStringWithAddressDictionary`. Alternatively, you can consult directly various CLPlacemark properties, such as subthoroughfare (such as a house number), thoroughfare (a street name), locality (a town), and administrativeArea (a state). These properties are present in a placemark resulting from forward geocoding as well; thus, one nice byproduct of forward geocoding is that it can format and complete an address, including adding a zip code (postalCode) to the address.

In this example of reverse geocoding, we have an MKMapView that is already tracking the user, and so we have the user's location as the map's userLocation; we ask for the corresponding address:

```
CLGeocoder* geo = [CLGeocoder new];
CLLocation* loc = userLocation.location;
[geo reverseGeocodeLocation:loc
        completionHandler:^(NSArray *placemarks, NSError *error)
  {
      if (placemarks) {
          CLPlacemark* p = [placemarks objectAtIndex:0];
          NSLog(@"%@", p.addressDictionary); // do something with address
      }
  }];
```

Communicating With the Maps App

New in iOS 6, your app can communicate with the Maps app. For example, instead of displaying a point of interest in a map view in our own app, we can ask the Maps app to display it. This is useful because the Maps app can help the user in ways that our app may not be able to; for example, it can give the user turn-by-turn directions to a place, and the user can store a place as a bookmark. The channel of communication between your app and the Maps app is the MKMapItem class.

Here, I'll ask the Maps app to display the same point marked by the annotation in our earlier examples, on a hybrid map portraying the same region of the earth (Figure 34-6):

```
MKPlacemark* p =
    [[MKPlacemark alloc] initWithCoordinate:self.annloc
                          addressDictionary:nil];
MKMapItem* mi = [[MKMapItem alloc] initWithPlacemark: p];
mi.name = @"A Great Place to Dirt Bike"; // label to appear in Maps app
NSValue* span = [NSValue valueWithMKCoordinateSpan:self.map.region.span];
[mi openInMapsWithLaunchOptions:
    @{MKLaunchOptionsMapTypeKey: @(MKMapTypeHybrid),
      MKLaunchOptionsMapSpanKey: span
    }
];
```

New in iOS 6.1, the MKLocalSearch class, along with MKLocalSearchRequest and MKLocalSearchResponse, lets you ask the Maps app to perform a natural language search for you. This is less formal than forward geocoding, described in the previous

Figure 34-6. The Maps app displays our point of interest

section; instead of searching for an address, you can search for a point of interest by name or description. In this example, I'll do a natural language search for the same intersection displayed by our earlier examples, and I'll display it with an annotation in our map view:

```
MKLocalSearchRequest* req = [MKLocalSearchRequest new];
req.naturalLanguageQuery =
    @"Tepusquet Road and Colson Canyon Road, Santa Maria, California";
MKLocalSearch* search = [[MKLocalSearch alloc] initWithRequest:req];
[search startWithCompletionHandler:
 ^(MKLocalSearchResponse *response, NSError *error) {
    MKMapItem* where = response.mapItems[0]; // I'm feeling lucky
    MKPlacemark* place = where.placemark;
    CLLocationCoordinate2D loc = place.location.coordinate;
    MKCoordinateRegion reg =
        MKCoordinateRegionMakeWithDistance(loc, 1200, 1200);
    [self.map setRegion:reg animated:YES];
    [self.map addAnnotation:place];
}];
```

CHAPTER 35

Sensors

A device may contain hardware for sensing the world around itself — where it is located, how it is oriented, how it is moving.

Information about the device's current location and how that location is changing over time, using its Wi-Fi, cellular networking, and GPS capabilities, along with information about the device's orientation relative to north, using its magnetometer, is provided through the Core Location framework. You'll link to *CoreLocation.framework* and import `<CoreLocation/CoreLocation.h>`.

Information about the device's change in speed and attitude using its accelerometer is provided through the UIEvent class (for device shake) and the Core Motion framework, which provides increased accuracy by incorporating the device's gyroscope, if it has one, as well as the magnetometer; you'll link to *CoreMotion.framework* and import `<Core-Motion/CoreMotion.h>`.

One of the major challenges associated with writing code that takes advantage of the sensors is that not all devices have all of this hardware. If you don't want to impose stringent restrictions on what devices your app will run on in the first place (`UIRequired-DeviceCapabilities` in *Info.plist*), your code must be prepared to fail gracefully and possibly provide a subset of its full capabilities when it discovers that the current device lacks certain features. Moreover, certain sensors may experience momentary inadequacy; for example, Core Location might not be able to get a fix on the device's position because it can't see cell towers, GPS satellites, or both. Also, some sensors take time to "warm up," so that the values you'll get from them initially will be invalid. You'll want to respond to such changes in the external circumstances, in order to give the user a decent experience of your application regardless.

Location

Core Location provides facilities for the device to determine and report its location (*location services*). It takes advantage of three sensors:

Wi-Fi

The device (if Wi-Fi is turned on) may scan for nearby Wi-Fi devices and compare these against an online database.

Cell

The device (if it has cell capabilities) may compare nearby telephone cell towers against an online database.

GPS

The device's GPS (if it has one) may be able to obtain a position fix from GPS satellites.

Core Location will automatically use whatever facilities the device does have; all *you* have to do is ask for the device's location. Core Location allows you to specify how accurate a position fix you want; more accurate fixes may require more time.

The notion of a location is encapsulated by the CLLocation class and its properties, which include:

coordinate

A CLLocationCoordinate2D; see Chapter 34.

altitude

A CLLocationDistance, which is a double representing a number of meters.

speed

A CLLocationSpeed, which is a double representing meters per second.

heading

A CLLocationDirection, which is a double representing degrees (*not* radians!) clockwise from north.

horizontalAccuracy

A CLLocationAccuracy, which is a double representing meters.

In addition to the sensor-related considerations I mentioned a moment ago, use of Core Location poses the following challenges:

- Accuracy of a reported location may vary depending on a number of factors. The GPS is the most accurate location sensor, but it takes the longest to get a fix.

- Battery usage due to running the sensors is a serious concern. The GPS in particular is probably the most battery-intensive of all the onboard sensors.

- Behavior of your app may depend on the device's physical location. To help you test, Xcode lets you pretend that the device is at a particular location on earth. The Simulator's Debug → Location menu lets you enter a location; the Scheme editor lets you set a default location (under Options); and the Debug pane lets you switch among locations (using the Location pop-up menu in the bar at the top). You can set a built-in location or supply a standard GPX file containing a waypoint. You can also set the location to None; it's important to test for what happens when no location information is available.

To use Core Location and location services directly, you need a location manager — a CLLocationManager instance. Use of a location manager typically operates along the following lines:

1. You'll confirm that the desired services are available. CLLocationManager class methods let you find out whether the user has switched on the device's location services as a whole (locationServicesEnabled), whether the user has authorized *this* app to use location services (authorizedStatus), and whether a particular service is available.

   If location services are switched off, you can start using a location manager anyway, as a way of getting the runtime to present the dialog asking the user to switch them on. Be prepared, though, for the possibility that the user won't do so. You can modify the body of this alert by setting the "Privacy — Location Usage Description" key (NSLocationUsageDescription) in your app's *Info.plist* (superseding the location manager's pre–iOS 6 purpose property) to tell the user *why* you want to access the database. This is a kind of "elevator pitch"; you need to persuade the user in very few words.

2. You'll instantiate CLLocationManager and retain the instance somewhere, usually an instance variable.

3. You'll set yourself as the location manager's delegate (CLLocationManager-Delegate).

4. You'll configure the location manager. For example, set its desiredAccuracy if you don't need best possible accuracy; it might be sufficient for your purposes to know very quickly but very roughly the device's location (and recall that highest accuracy may also cause the highest battery drain). The accuracy setting is not a filter: the location manager will still send you whatever location information it has, and checking a location's horizontalAccuracy is then up to you.

   The location manager's distanceFilter lets you specify that you don't need a location report unless the device has moved a certain distance since the previous report. This can help keep you from being bombarded with events you don't need. Other configuration settings depend on the particular service you're asking for, as I'll explain later.

5. You'll tell the location manager to begin generating information; for example, you'll call `startUpdatingLocation`. The location manager, in turn, will begin calling the appropriate delegate method repeatedly; in the case of `startUpdatingLocation`, it's `locationManager:didUpdateToLocation:fromLocation:`. Your delegate will also always implement `locationManager:didFailWithError:`, to receive error messages. You'll deal with each delegate method call in turn. Remember to call the corresponding `stop...` method when you no longer need delegate method calls.

As a simple example, we'll turn on location services manually, just long enough to see if we can determine our position. We begin by ascertaining that location services are in fact available and that we have or can get authorization. If all is well, we instantiate CLLocationManager, set ourselves as the delegate, configure the location manager, set some instance variables so we can track what's happening, and call `startUpdating-Location` to turn on location services:

```
BOOL ok = [CLLocationManager locationServicesEnabled];
if (!ok) {
    NSLog(@"oh well");
    return;
}
CLAuthorizationStatus auth = [CLLocationManager authorizationStatus];
if (auth == kCLAuthorizationStatusRestricted ||
        auth == kCLAuthorizationStatusDenied) {
    NSLog(@"sigh");
    return;
}
CLLocationManager* lm = [CLLocationManager new];
self.locman = lm;
self.locman.delegate = self;
self.locman.desiredAccuracy = kCLLocationAccuracyBest;
self.locman.purpose = @"This app would like to tell you where you are.";
self.startTime = [NSDate date]; // now
self.gotloc = NO;
[self.locman startUpdatingLocation];
```

If something goes wrong, such as the user refusing to authorize this app, we'll just turn location services back off:

```
- (void)locationManager:(CLLocationManager *)manager
        didFailWithError:(NSError *)error {
    NSLog(@"error: %@", [error localizedDescription]);
    // e.g., if user refuses to authorize...
    // ..."The operation couldn't be completed."
    [manager stopUpdatingLocation];
}
```

If things *don't* go wrong, we'll be handed our location as soon as it is determined. In this case, I've decided to demand accuracy better than 70 meters. If I don't get it, I wait for the next location, but I also compare each location's timestamp to the timestamp I created at the outset, so that I won't wait forever for an accuracy that might never arrive. If I get the desired accuracy within the desired time, I turn off location services and am ready to use the location information:

```
- (void)locationManager:(CLLocationManager *)manager
        didUpdateToLocation:(CLLocation *)newLocation
        fromLocation:(CLLocation *)oldLocation {
    if (!self.gotloc &&
        ([newLocation.timestamp timeIntervalSinceDate:self.startTime] > 20))
            {
                NSLog(@"this is just taking too long");
                [self.locman stopUpdatingLocation];
                return;
            }
    CLLocationAccuracy acc = newLocation.horizontalAccuracy;
    NSLog(@"%f", acc);
    if (acc > 70)
        return; // wait for better accuracy
    // if we get here, we have an accurate location
    [manager stopUpdatingLocation];
    self.gotloc = YES;
    // ... and now we could do something with newLocation ...
}
```

The first time that app runs, the log messages chart the increasing accuracy of the location reports. You can see that it was worth waiting a few seconds to get better accuracy:

```
2013-02-09 09:02:29.569 p718p736location[407:707] 45383.659065
2013-02-09 09:02:31.358 p718p736location[407:707] 1413.314191
2013-02-09 09:02:32.154 p718p736location[407:707] 163.886905
2013-02-09 09:02:36.137 p718p736location[407:707] 10.000000
```

Core Location will also use the GPS to determine which way and how quickly the device is moving. This information, if available, is returned automatically as part of a CLLocation object in locationManager:didUpdateToLocation:fromLocation:, through its speed and course properties. For information about the device's heading (which way is north), see the next section.

You can also use Core Location when your app is not in the foreground. There are two quite different ways to do this. The first is that your app can run in the background. Use of Core Location in the background is similar to production and recording of sound in the background (Chapter 27): you set the UIBackgroundModes key of your app's *Info.plist*, giving it a value of location. This tells the system that if you have turned on location services and the user clicks the Home button, your app should not be suspended, the use of location services should continue, and your delegate should keep receiving Core Location events. Background use of location services can cause a power drain, but if you want your app to function as a positional data logger, for instance, it may be the only way; you can also help conserve power by making judicious choices, such as setting a coarse distanceFilter value and not requiring high accuracy. Starting in iOS 6, Core Location can operate in deferred mode (`allowDeferredLocation-UpdatesUntilTraveled:timeout:`) so that your background app doesn't receive updates until the user has moved a specified amount or until a fixed time interval has elapsed; this, too, can help conserve power, as the device may be able to power down some its sensors temporarily.

The second way of using of Core Location without being in the foreground *doesn't even require your app to be running.* You do *not* have to set the `UIBackgroundModes` of your *Info.plist.* You register with the system to receive a certain kind of notification, and when such a notification arrives, your app will be launched if it isn't running. There are two notifications of this kind:

Significant location monitoring

> If `significantLocationChangeMonitoringAvailable` is YES, you can call `start-MonitoringSignificantLocationChanges`. The delegate's `locationManager:did-UpdateToLocation:fromLocation:` will be called when the device's location has changed significantly.

Region monitoring

> If `regionMonitoringAvailable` and `regionMonitoringEnabled` are YES, you can call `startMonitoringForRegion:` or `startMonitoringForRegion:desired-Accuracy:` for each region in which you are interested. Regions are collected as an NSSet, which is the location manager's `monitoredRegions`. A region is a CLRegion, initialized with `initCircularRegionWithCenter:radius:identifier:;` the `identifier` serves as a unique key, so that if you start monitoring for a region whose identifier matches that of a region already in the `monitoredRegions` set, the latter will be ejected from the set. The following delegate methods may be called:

> - `locationManager:didEnterRegion:`
> - `locationManager:didExitRegion:`
> - `locationManager:monitoringDidFailForRegion:withError:`

> For example, a reminder alarm uses region monitoring to notify the user when approaching or leaving a specific place (*geofencing*), as shown in Chapter 32.

Both significant location monitoring and region monitoring use cell tower position to estimate the device's location. Since the cell is probably working anyway — for example, the device is a phone, so the cell is always on and is always concerned with what cell towers are available — little or no additional power is required. Apple says that the system will also take advantage of other clues (requiring no extra battery drain) to decide that there may have been a change in location: for example, the device may observe a change in the available Wi-Fi networks, strongly suggesting that the device has moved.

As I've already mentioned, notifications for location monitoring and region monitoring can arrive even if your app isn't in the foreground. In that case, there are two possible states in which your app might find itself when an event arrives:

Your app is suspended in the background
> Your app is woken up long enough to receive the normal delegate event and do something with it.

Your app is not running at all
> Your app is relaunched (remaining in the background), and your app delegate will be sent `application:didFinishLaunchingWithOptions:` with an NSDictionary containing `UIApplicationLaunchOptionsLocationKey`, thus allowing it to discern the special nature of the situation. At this point you probably have no location manager — your app has just launched from scratch. So you should get yourself a location manager and start up location services for long enough to receive the normal delegate event.

Heading

For appropriately equipped devices, Core Location also supports use of the magnetometer to determine which way the device is facing (its *heading*). Although this information is accessed through a location manager, you do *not* need location services to be turned on, nor your app to be authorized, merely to use the magnetometer to report the device's orientation with respect to *magnetic* north; but you do need those things in order to report *true* north, as this depends on the device's location.

As with location, you'll first check that the desired feature is available (`heading-Available`); then you'll instantiate and configure the location manager, and call `start-UpdatingHeading`. The delegate will be sent `locationManager:didUpdateHeading:`. Heading values are reported as a CLHeading; recall that this involves degrees (*not* radians) clockwise from the reference direction.

In this example, I'll use the device as a compass. The `headingFilter` setting is to prevent us from being bombarded constantly with readings. For best results, the device should probably be held level (like a tabletop, or a compass); the reported heading will be the direction in which the top of the device (the end away from the Home button) is pointing:

```
BOOL ok = [CLLocationManager headingAvailable];
if (!ok) {
    NSLog(@"drat");
    return;
}
CLLocationManager* lm = [CLLocationManager new];
self.locman = lm;
```

```
self.locman.delegate = self;
self.locman.headingFilter = 3;
self.locman.headingOrientation = CLDeviceOrientationPortrait;
[self.locman startUpdatingHeading];
```

In the delegate, I'll display our magnetic heading as a rough cardinal direction in a label in the interface (`lab`):

```
- (void) locationManager:(CLLocationManager *)manager
        didUpdateHeading:(CLHeading *)newHeading {
    CGFloat h = newHeading.magneticHeading;
    __block NSString* dir = @"N";
    NSArray* cards = @[@"N", @"NE", @"E", @"SE",
                       @"S", @"SW", @"W", @"NW"];
    [cards enumerateObjectsUsingBlock:^(id obj, NSUInteger idx, BOOL *stop) {
        if (h < 45.0/2.0 + 45*idx) {
            dir = obj;
            *stop = YES;
        }
    }];
    if (self.lab.hidden)
        self.lab.hidden = NO;
    if (![self.lab.text isEqualToString:dir])
        self.lab.text = dir;
    NSLog(@"%f %@", h, dir);
}
```

In that code, I asked only for the heading's `magneticHeading`. I can freely ask for its `trueHeading`, but the resulting value will be invalid (a negative number) unless we are *also* receiving location updates.

(Combining the magnetometer with the compass interface we developed in Chapter 16 and Chapter 17, so as to simulate a physical compass, is left as an exercise for the reader.)

Acceleration and Attitude

Acceleration results from the application of a force to the device, and is detected through the device's accelerometer, supplemented by the gyroscope if it has one. Gravity is a force, so the accelerometer always has something to measure, even if the user isn't consciously applying a force to the device; thus the device can report its attitude relative to the vertical.

Acceleration information can arrive in two ways:

As a prepackaged UIEvent
You can receive a UIEvent notifying you of a predefined gesture performed by accelerating the device. At present, the only such gesture is the user shaking the device.

With the Core Motion framework

You instantiate CMMotionManager and then obtain information of a desired type. You can ask for accelerometer information, gyroscope information, or device motion information (and you can also use Core Motion to get magnetometer information); device motion combines the gyroscope data with data from the other sensors to give you the best possible description of the device's attitude in space.

Shake Events

A shake event is a UIEvent (Chapter 18). Receiving shake events is rather like receiving remote events (Chapter 27), involving the notion of the first responder. To receive shake events, your app must contain a UIResponder which:

- Returns YES from `canBecomeFirstResponder`
- Is in fact first responder

This responder, or a UIResponder further up the responder chain, should implement some or all of these methods:

`motionBegan:withEvent:`
Something has started to happen that might or might not turn out to be a shake.

`motionEnded:withEvent:`
The motion reported in `motionBegan:withEvent:` is over and has turned out to be a shake.

`motionCancelled:withEvent:`
The motion reported in `motionBegan:withEvent:` wasn't a shake after all.

Thus, it might be sufficient to implement `motionEnded:withEvent:`, because this arrives if and only if the user performs a shake gesture. The first parameter will be the event subtype, but at present this is guaranteed to be `UIEventSubtypeMotionShake`, so testing it is pointless.

The view controller in charge of the current view is a good candidate to receive shake events. Thus, a minimal implementation might look like this:

```
- (BOOL) canBecomeFirstResponder {
    return YES;
}

- (void) viewDidAppear: (BOOL) animated {
    [super viewDidAppear: animated];
    [self becomeFirstResponder];
}
```

```
- (void)motionEnded:(UIEventSubtype)motion withEvent:(UIEvent *)event {
    NSLog(@"hey, you shook me!");
}
```

By default, if the first responder is of a type that supports undo (such as an NSTextField), and if `motionBegan:withEvent:` is sent up the responder chain, and if you have not set the shared UIApplication's `applicationSupportsShakeToEdit` property to NO, a shake will be handled through an Undo or Redo alert. Your view controller might not want to rob any responders in its view of this capability. A simple way to prevent this is to test whether the view controller is itself the first responder; if it isn't, we call `super` to pass the event on up the responder chain:

```
- (void)motionEnded:(UIEventSubtype)motion withEvent:(UIEvent *)event {
    if ([self isFirstResponder])
        NSLog(@"hey, you shook me!");
    else
        [super motionEnded:motion withEvent:event];
}
```

Raw Acceleration

If the device has an accelerometer but no gyroscope, you can learn about the forces being applied to it, but some compromises will be necessary. The chief problem is that, even if the device is completely motionless, its acceleration values will constitute a normalized vector pointing toward the center of the earth, popularly known as *gravity*. The accelerometer is thus constantly reporting a combination of gravity and user-induced acceleration. This is good and bad. It's good because it means that, with certain restrictions, you can use the accelerometer to detect the device's attitude in space. It's bad because gravity values and user-induced acceleration values are mixed together. Fortunately, there are ways to separate these values mathematically:

With a low-pass filter
  A low-pass filter will damp out user acceleration so as to report gravity only.

With a high-pass filter
  A high-pass filter will damp out the effect of gravity so as to detect user acceleration only, reporting a motionless device as having zero acceleration.

In some situations, it is desirable to apply both a low-pass filter and a high-pass filter, so as to learn both the gravity values and the user acceleration values. A common additional technique is to run the output of the high-pass filter itself through a low-pass filter to reduce noise and small twitches. Apple provides some nice sample code for implementing a low-pass or a high-pass filter; see especially the AccelerometerGraph example, which is also very helpful for exploring how the accelerometer behaves.

The technique of applying filters to the accelerometer output has some serious downsides, which are inevitable in a device that lacks a gyroscope:

- It's up to you to apply the filters; you have to implement boilerplate code and hope that you don't make a mistake.

- Filters mean *latency*. Your response to the accelerometer values will lag behind what the device is actually doing; this lag may be noticeable.

There are actually two ways to read the raw accelerometer values: UIAccelerometer and Core Motion. UIAccelerometer is slated for deprecation, and its delegate method is in fact deprecated, so I'll describe how to read the raw accelerometer values with Core Motion. The technique is really a subset of how you read *any* values with Core Motion; in some ways it is similar to how you use Core Location:

1. You start by instantiating CMMotionManager; retain the instance somewhere, typically as an instance variable.

2. Confirm, using instance properties, that the desired hardware is available.

3. Set the interval at which you wish the motion manager to update itself with new sensor readings.

4. Call the appropriate `start` method.

5. Poll the motion manager whenever you want data, asking for the appropriate `data` property. This step is surprising; you probably expected that the motion manager would call into a delegate, but in fact a motion manager has no delegate. The polling interval doesn't have to be the same as the motion manager's update interval; when you poll, you'll obtain the motion manager's *current* data — that is, the data generated by its most recent update, whenever that was.

   If your app's purpose is to collect all the data, then instead of calling a `start` method, you can call a `start...UpdatesToQueue:withHandler:` method and receive callbacks in a block, possibly on a background thread, managed by an NSOperation-Queue (Chapter 38); but this is an advanced technique and you aren't likely to need it, so I'm not going to talk about it.

6. Don't forget to call the corresponding `stop` method when you no longer need data.

In this example, I will simply report whether the device is lying flat on its back. I start by creating and configuring my motion manager, and I launch a repeating timer to trigger polling:

```
self.motman = [CMMotionManager new];
if (!self.motman.accelerometerAvailable) {
    NSLog(@"oh well");
    return;
}
self.motman.accelerometerUpdateInterval = 1.0 / 30.0;
[self.motman startAccelerometerUpdates];
```

```
self.timer =
    [NSTimer
        scheduledTimerWithTimeInterval:self.motman.accelerometerUpdateInterval
        target:self selector:@selector(pollAccel:) userInfo:nil repeats:YES];
```

My pollAccel: method is now being called repeatedly. In pollAccel:, I ask the motion manager for its accelerometer data. This arrives as a CMAccelerometerData, which is a timestamp plus a CMAcceleration; a CMAcceleration is simply a struct of three values, one for each axis of the device, measured in Gs. The positive x-axis points to the right of the device. The positive y-axis points toward the top of the device, away from the Home button. The positive z-axis points out of the screen toward the user.

The two axes orthogonal to gravity, which are the x and y axes when the device is lying more or less on its back, are much more accurate and sensitive to small variation than the axis pointing toward or away from gravity. So our approach is to ask first whether the x and y values are close to zero; only then do we use the z value to learn whether the device is on its back or on its face. To keep from updating our interface constantly, we implement a crude state machine; the state (an instance variable) starts out at -1, and then switches between 0 (device on its back) and 1 (device not on its back), and we update the interface only when there is a state change:

```
CMAccelerometerData* dat = self.motman.accelerometerData;
CMAcceleration acc = dat.acceleration;
CGFloat x = acc.x;
CGFloat y = acc.y;
CGFloat z = acc.z;
CGFloat accu = 0.08; // feel free to experiment with this value
if (fabs(x) < accu && fabs(y) < accu && z < -0.5) {
    if (state == -1 || state == 1) {
        state = 0;
        self.label.text = @"I'm lying on my back... ahhh...";
    }
} else {
    if (state == -1 || state == 0) {
        state = 1;
        self.label.text = @"Hey, put me back down on the table!";
    }
}
```

This works, but it's sensitive to small motions of the device on the table. To damp this sensitivity, we can run our input through a low-pass filter. The low-pass filter code comes straight from Apple's own examples, and involves maintaining the previously filtered reading as a set of instance variables:

```
-(void)addAcceleration:(CMAcceleration)accel {
    double alpha = 0.1;
    self->oldX = accel.x * alpha + self->oldX * (1.0 - alpha);
    self->oldY = accel.y * alpha + self->oldY * (1.0 - alpha);
    self->oldZ = accel.z * alpha + self->oldZ * (1.0 - alpha);
}
```

Our polling code now starts out by passing the data through the filter:

```
CMAccelerometerData* dat = self.motman.accelerometerData;
CMAcceleration acc = dat.acceleration;
[self addAcceleration: acc];
CGFloat x = self->oldX;
CGFloat y = self->oldY;
CGFloat z = self->oldZ;
// ... and the rest is as before ...
```

In this next example, the user is allowed to slap the side of the device against an open hand — perhaps as a way of telling it to go to the next or previous image or whatever it is we're displaying. We pass the acceleration input through a high-pass filter to eliminate gravity (again, the filter code comes straight from Apple's examples):

```
-(void)addAcceleration:(CMAcceleration)accel {
    double alpha = 0.1;
    self->oldX = accel.x - ((accel.x * alpha) + (self->oldX * (1.0 - alpha)));
    self->oldY = accel.y - ((accel.y * alpha) + (self->oldY * (1.0 - alpha)));
    self->oldZ = accel.z - ((accel.z * alpha) + (self->oldZ * (1.0 - alpha)));
}
```

What we're looking for, in our polling routine, is a high positive or negative x value. A single slap is likely to consist of several consecutive readings above our threshold, but we want to report each slap only once, so we take advantage of the timestamp attached to a CMAccelerometerData, maintaining the timestamp of our previous high reading as an instance variable and ignoring readings that are too close to one another in time. Another problem is that a sudden jerk involves both an acceleration (as the user starts the device moving) and a deceleration (as the device stops moving); thus a left slap might be preceded by a high value in the opposite direction, which we might interpret wrongly as a right slap. We can compensate crudely, at the expense of some latency, with delayed performance (the `report:` method simply logs to the console):

```
CMAccelerometerData* dat = self.motman.accelerometerData;
CMAcceleration acc = dat.acceleration;
[self addAcceleration: acc];
CGFloat x = self->oldX;
CGFloat thresh = 1.0;
if ((x < -thresh) || (x > thresh))
    NSLog(@"%f", x);
if (x < -thresh) {
    if (dat.timestamp - self->oldTime > 0.5 || self->lastSlap == 1) {
        self->oldTime = dat.timestamp;
        self->lastSlap = -1;
        [NSObject cancelPreviousPerformRequestsWithTarget:self];
        [self performSelector:@selector(report:)
                withObject:@"left" afterDelay:0.5];
    }
}
if (x > thresh) {
    if (dat.timestamp - self->oldTime > 0.5 || self->lastSlap == -1) {
```

```
            self->oldTime = dat.timestamp;
            self->lastSlap = 1;
            [NSObject cancelPreviousPerformRequestsWithTarget:self];
            [self performSelector:@selector(report:)
                    withObject:@"right" afterDelay:0.5];
        }
    }
```

The gesture we're detecting is a little tricky to make: the user must slap the device into
an open hand *and hold it there*; if the device jumps out of the open hand, that movement
may be detected as the last in the series, resulting in the wrong report (left instead of
right, or *vice versa*). And the latency of our gesture detection is very high; here's a typical
successful detection of a leftward slap:

```
2012-02-13 12:03:18.673 p724p742smackMe[4024:707] -1.204655
2012-02-13 12:03:18.743 p724p742smackMe[4024:707] -1.153451
2012-02-13 12:03:18.775 p724p742smackMe[4024:707] 1.168514
2012-02-13 12:03:18.809 p724p742smackMe[4024:707] -1.426584
2012-02-13 12:03:18.875 p724p742smackMe[4024:707] -1.297352
2012-02-13 12:03:18.942 p724p742smackMe[4024:707] -1.072046
2012-02-13 12:03:19.316 p724p742smackMe[4024:707] left
```

The gesture started with an involuntary shake; then the rapid acceleration to the left
was detected as a positive value; finally, the rapid deceleration was detected as a negative
value, and it took several tenths of a second for our delayed performance to decide that
this was the end of the gesture and report a leftward slap. Of course we might try tweaking some of the magic numbers in this code to improve accuracy and performance, but
a more sophisticated analysis would probably involve storing a stream of all the most
recent CMAccelerometerData objects and studying the entire stream to work out the
overall trend.

Gyroscope

The inclusion of an electronic gyroscope in the panoply of onboard hardware in some
devices has made a huge difference in the accuracy and speed of gravity and attitude
reporting. A gyroscope has the property that its attitude in space remains constant; thus
it can detect any change in the attitude of the containing device. This has two important
consequences for accelerometer measurements:

- The accelerometer can be supplemented by the gyroscope to detect quickly the
  difference between gravity and user-induced acceleration.

- The gyroscope can observe pure rotation, where little or no acceleration is involved
  and so the accelerometer would not have been helpful. The extreme case is constant
  attitudinal rotation around the gravity axis, which the accelerometer alone would
  be completely unable to detect (because there is no user-induced force, and gravity
  remains constant).

It is possible to track the raw gyroscope data: make sure the device has a gyroscope, and then call `startGyroUpdates`. What we get from the motion manager is a CMGyroData object, which combines a timestamp with a CMRotationRate that reports the *rate of rotation* around each axis, measured in radians per second, where a positive value is *counterclockwise* as seen by someone whose eye is pointed to by the positive axis. (This is the opposite of the direction graphed in Figure 16-7.) The problem, however, is that the gyroscope values are *scaled* and *biased*. This means that the values are based on an arbitrary scale and are increasing (or decreasing) at a roughly constant rate. Thus there is very little merit in the exercise of dealing with the raw gyroscope data.

What you are likely to be interested in is a combination of at least the gyroscope and the accelerometer. The mathematics required to combine the data from these sensors can be daunting. Fortunately, there's no need to know anything about that. Core Motion will happily package up the calculated combination of data as a CMDeviceMotion instance, with the effects of the sensors' internal bias and scaling already factored out. CMDeviceMotion consists of the following properties, all of which provide a triple of values corresponding to the device's natural 3D frame (x increasing to the right, y increasing to the top, z increasing out the front):

`gravity`
　　A CMAcceleration expressing a vector with value 1 pointing to the center of the earth, measured in Gs.

`userAcceleration`
　　A CMAcceleration describing user-induced acceleration, with no gravity component, measured in Gs.

`rotationRate`
　　A CMRotationRate describing how the device is rotating around its own center. This is essentially the CMGyroData `rotationRate` with scale and bias accounted for.

`magneticField`
　　A CMCalibratedMagneticField describing (in its `field`) the magnetic forces acting on the device, measured in microteslas. The sensor's internal bias has already been factored out. The CMMagneticField's `accuracy` is one of the following:

- `CMMagneticFieldCalibrationAccuracyUncalibrated`
- `CMMagneticFieldCalibrationAccuracyLow`
- `CMMagneticFieldCalibrationAccuracyMedium`
- `CMMagneticFieldCalibrationAccuracyHigh`

attitude

A CMAttitude, descriptive of the device's instantaneous attitude in space. When you ask the motion manager to start generating updates, you can ask for any of four reference systems for the `attitude` (having first called the class method `available-AttitudeReferenceFrames` to ascertain that the desired reference frame is available on this device):

CMAttitudeReferenceFrameXArbitraryZVertical

The negative z-axis points at the center of the earth, but the x-axis and y-axis, though orthogonal to the other axes, could be pointing anywhere.

CMAttitudeReferenceFrameXArbitraryCorrectedZVertical

The same as in the previous option, but the magnetometer is used to improve accuracy.

CMAttitudeReferenceFrameXMagneticNorthZVertical

The x-axis points toward magnetic north.

CMAttitudeReferenceFrameXTrueNorthZVertical

The x-axis points toward true north. This value will be inaccurate unless you are also using Core Location to obtain the device's location.

The `attitude` value's numbers can be accessed through various CMAttitude properties corresponding to three different systems, each being convenient for a different purpose:

pitch, roll, *and* yaw

The device's angle of offset from the reference frame, in radians, around the device's natural x, y, and z-axis respectively.

rotationMatrix

A CMRotationMatrix struct embodying a 3×3 matrix expressing a rotation in the reference frame.

quaternion

A CMQuaternion describing an attitude. (Quaternions are commonly used in OpenGL.)

In this example, we turn the device into a simple compass/clinometer, merely by asking for its `attitude` with reference to magnetic north and taking its `pitch`, `roll`, and `yaw`. We begin by making the usual preparations; notice the use of the `showsDeviceMovement-Display` property, which will allow the runtime to prompt the user to move the device in a figure-of-eight if the magnetometer needs calibration:

```
self.motman = [CMMotionManager new];
if (!self.motman.deviceMotionAvailable) {
    NSLog(@"oh well");
    return;
```

```
    }
    CMAttitudeReferenceFrame f = CMAttitudeReferenceFrameXMagneticNorthZVertical;
    if (([CMMotionManager availableAttitudeReferenceFrames] & f) == 0) {
        NSLog(@"darn");
        return;
    }
    self.motman.showsDeviceMovementDisplay = YES;
    self.motman.deviceMotionUpdateInterval = 1.0 / 30.0;
    [self.motman startDeviceMotionUpdatesUsingReferenceFrame:f];
    NSTimeInterval t = self.motman.deviceMotionUpdateInterval * 10;
    self.timer =
        [NSTimer scheduledTimerWithTimeInterval:t target:self
        selector:@selector(pollAttitude:) userInfo:nil repeats:YES];
```

In pollAttitude:, we wait until the magnetometer is ready, and then we start taking attitude readings (converted to degrees):

```
    CMDeviceMotion* mot = self.motman.deviceMotion;
    if (mot.magneticField.accuracy <= CMMagneticFieldCalibrationAccuracyLow)
        return; // not ready yet
    CMAttitude* att = mot.attitude;
    CGFloat to_deg = 180.0 / M_PI; // I like degrees
    NSLog(@"%f %f %f", att.pitch * to_deg, att.roll * to_deg, att.yaw * to_deg);
```

The values are all close to zero when the device is level with its top pointing to magnetic north, and each value increases as the device is rotated counterclockwise with respect to an eye that has the corresponding positive axis pointing at it. So, for example, a device held upright (top pointing at the sky) has a pitch approaching 90; a device lying on its right edge has a roll approaching 90; and a device lying on its back with its top pointing west has a yaw approaching 90.

There are some quirks to be aware of in the way that Euler angles operate mathematically:

- roll and yaw increase with counterclockwise rotation from 0 to π (180 degrees) and then jump to $-\pi$ (-180 degrees) and continue to increase to 0 as the rotation completes a circle; but pitch increases to $\pi/2$ (90 degrees) and then decreases to 0, then decreases to $-\pi/2$ (-90 degrees) and increases to 0. This means that attitude alone, if we are exploring it through pitch, roll, and yaw, is insufficient to describe the device's attitude, since a pitch value of, say, $\pi/4$ (45 degrees) could mean two different things. To distinguish those two things, we can supplement attitude with the z-component of gravity:

    ```
    NSLog(@"%f %f %f", att.pitch * to_deg, att.roll * to_deg, att.yaw * to_deg);
    CMAcceleration g = mot.gravity;
    NSLog(@"pitch is tilted %@", g.z > 0 ? @"forward" : @"back");
    ```

- Values become inaccurate in certain orientations. In particular, when pitch is ±90 degrees (the device is upright or inverted), roll and yaw become erratic. (You may see this effect referred to as the "singularity" or as "gimbal lock.") I believe that, depending on what you are trying to accomplish, you can solve this by using a different expression of the attitude, such as the `rotationMatrix`, which does not suffer from this limitation.

This next (simple and very silly) example illustrates a use of CMAttitude's `rotation-Matrix` property. Our goal is to make a CALayer rotate in response to the current attitude of the device. We start as before, except that our reference frame is `CMAttitude-ReferenceFrameXArbitraryZVertical`; we are interested in how the device moves from its initial attitude, without reference to any particular fixed external direction such as magnetic north. In `pollAttitude`, our first step is to store the device's current attitude in a CMAttitude instance variable, `ref`:

```
CMDeviceMotion* mot = self.motman.deviceMotion;
CMAttitude* att = mot.attitude;
if (!self.ref) {
    self.ref = att;
    return;
}
```

That code works correctly because on the first few polls, as the attitude-detection hardware warms up, `att` is nil, so we don't get past the `return` call until we have a valid initial attitude. Our next step is highly characteristic of how CMAttitude is used: we call the CMAttitude method `multiplyByInverseOfAttitude:`, which transforms our attitude so that it is relative *to the stored initial attitude*:

```
[att multiplyByInverseOfAttitude:self.ref];
```

Finally, we apply the attitude's rotation matrix directly to a layer in our interface as a transform. Well, not quite directly: a rotation matrix is a 3×3 matrix, whereas a CA-Transform3D, which is what we need in order to set a layer's `transform`, is a 4×4 matrix. However, it happens that the top left nine entries in a CATransform3D's 4×4 matrix constitute its rotation component, so we start with an identity matrix and set those entries directly:

```
CMRotationMatrix r = att.rotationMatrix;
CATransform3D t = CATransform3DIdentity;
t.m11 = r.m11;
t.m12 = r.m12;
t.m13 = r.m13;
t.m21 = r.m21;
t.m22 = r.m22;
t.m23 = r.m23;
t.m31 = r.m31;
t.m32 = r.m32;
t.m33 = r.m33;
CALayer* lay = // whatever;
[CATransaction setDisableActions:YES];
lay.transform = t;
```

The result is that the layer apparently tries to hold itself still as the device rotates. The example is rather crude because we aren't using OpenGL to draw a three-dimensional object, but it illustrates the principle well enough.

There is a quirk to be aware of in this case as well: over time, the transform has a tendency to drift. Thus, even if we leave the device stationary, the layer will gradually rotate. That is the sort of effect that CMAttitudeReferenceFrameXArbitraryCorrectedZVertical is designed to help mitigate, by bringing the magnetometer into play.

Here are some additional considerations to be aware of when using Core Motion:

- The documentation warns that your app should create only one CMMotion-Manager instance. This is not a terribly onerous restriction, but it's rather odd that, if this is important, the API doesn't provide a shared singleton instance accessed through a class method.

- Use of Core Motion is legal while your app is running the background. To take advantage of this, your app would need to be running in the background for some *other* reason; there is no Core Motion UIBackgroundModes setting in an *Info.plist*. For example, you might run in the background because you're using Core Location, and take advantage of this to employ Core Motion as well.

- Core Motion requires that various sensors be turned on, such as the magnetometer and the gyroscope. This can result in some increased battery drain, so try not to use any sensors you don't have to, and remember to stop generating updates as soon as you no longer need them.

PART VII

Final Topics

This part of the book is a miscellany of topics.

- Chapter 36 is about files. It explains how your app can store data on disk to be retrieved the next time the app runs (including both standalone files and user defaults). It also discusses sharing files with the user through iTunes and with other apps, plus the document architecture and iCloud, and concludes with a survey of how iOS can work with some common file formats (XML, SQLite, Core Data, and image files).

- Chapter 37 introduces networking, with an emphasis on HTTP downloading of data, and giving a nod to other aspects of networks (such as Bonjour and push notifications) that you can explore independently if your app requires them.

- Chapter 38 is about threads. Making your code multithreaded can introduce great complexity and is not a beginner topic, but you still might need to understand the basic concepts of multithreading, either in order to prevent a lengthy task from blocking user interaction with your app, or because some framework explicitly relies on it. Special attention is paid to the advantages of NSOperation and (especially) Grand Central Dispatch.

- Chapter 39 describes how iOS supports Undo in your app.

- Chapter 40 lists additional frameworks and facilities that were found to be beyond the scope of this book. You are now a proud graduate of this book's school of iOS programming fundamentals. You are fully prepared to proceed independently. Your mission, should you decide to accept it, is to explore further if and when you need to. iOS is huge; you'll never stop learning and experimenting. Good hunting!

CHAPTER 36

Persistent Storage

The device on which your app runs contains flash memory that functions as the equivalent of a hard disk, holding files that survive the device's being powered down (*persistent storage*). Apps can store files to, and retrieve them from, this virtual hard disk. Apps can also define document types in which they specialize and can hand such documents to one another; apps can also share documents into the cloud (iCloud), so that multiple copies of the same app can retrieve them on different devices.

User preferences can be maintained in NSUserDefaults (Chapter 13), and visible state can be maintained through the iOS 6 state saving and restoration mechanism (Chapter 19), but the data that constitutes your app's model in the model–view–controller architecture is neither preferences nor state, so if your app has such data, and if that data is to persist between uses, your app will probably save the data to disk as a file or files. At a minimum, you'll probably save your data to disk when your app goes into the background (Chapter 11), so that if your app is terminated in the background, you can load your data from disk when your app launches. More proactively, you might save your data to disk more often, for extra safety, and, if your data is large, you might also release it when your app goes into the background, so as to use less memory in the background and reduce your chances of being terminated while suspended; in that case, you'll load your data from disk whenever your app comes to the foreground. (I described a possible strategy for loading your data "lazily," whenever your app finds that it has no reference to the data, in "View Controller Memory Management" (page 646).)

Settling on a structure or format for your data on disk is up to you; this chapter concludes with some examples of how to manipulate some important file formats, but only you can decide what suits your app's particular needs.

The Sandbox

The hard disk as a whole is not open to your app's view. A limited portion of the hard disk is dedicated to your app alone: this is your app's *sandbox*. The idea is that every app, seeing only its own sandbox, is hindered from spying or impinging on the files belonging to other apps, and in turn is protected from having its own files spied or impinged on by other apps. Your app's sandbox is thus a safe place for you to store your data. Your sandbox, and hence your data, will be deleted if the user deletes your app; otherwise, it should reliably persist. (Your app can also see some higher-level directories owned by the system as a whole, but cannot write to them.)

The sandbox contains some standard directories. For example, suppose you want a reference to the Documents directory. Here's one way to access it:

```
NSString* docs = [NSSearchPathForDirectoriesInDomains(
        NSDocumentDirectory, NSUserDomainMask, YES) lastObject];
```

That code returns a path string for the Documents directory. The preferred way to refer to a file or directory, however, is with a URL. You can obtain this from an NSFileManager instance:

```
NSFileManager* fm = [NSFileManager new];
NSError* err = nil;
NSURL* docsurl =
    [fm URLForDirectory:NSDocumentDirectory
                inDomain:NSUserDomainMask appropriateForURL:nil
                   create:YES error:&err];
// error-checking omitted
```

A question that will immediately occur to you is: *where* should I put files and folders that I want to save now and read later? The Documents directory can be a good place. But if your app supports file sharing (discussed later in this chapter), the user can see and modify your app's Documents directory through iTunes, so you might not want to put things there that the user isn't supposed to see and change.

Personally, I favor the Application Support directory for most purposes. On a Mac, this directory is shared by multiple applications, each of which must confine itself to an individual subfolder, but on iOS each app has its own private Application Support directory in its own sandbox, so you can safely put files anywhere within it. This directory may not exist initially, so you can obtain it and create it at the same time:

```
NSURL* suppurl =
    [fm URLForDirectory:NSApplicationSupportDirectory
                inDomain:NSUserDomainMask appropriateForURL:nil
                   create:YES error:&err];
```

See also "Where You Should Put Your App's Files" in the "File System Basics" chapter of Apple's *File System Programming Guide*, which talks about the implications of various file storage locations when the user syncs or backs up the device. The advice given there, however, fails to grapple with the fact that file sharing makes the Documents directory directly modifiable by the user.

Although URLs are the favored way of referring to files and folders, they are a more recent innovation than path strings, and there are some operations that still require a string. To derive a path string from an NSURL, send it the `path` message.

Basic File Operations

Let's say we intend to create folder *MyFolder* inside the Documents directory. Assume that we have an NSFileManager instance `fm` and an NSURL `docsurl` pointing at the Documents directory, as shown in the previous section. We can then generate a reference to *MyFolder*; we can then ask our NSFileManager instance to create the folder if it doesn't exist already:

```
NSURL* myfolder = [docsurl URLByAppendingPathComponent:@"MyFolder"];
NSError* err = nil;
BOOL ok =
    [fm createDirectoryAtURL:myfolder
        withIntermediateDirectories:YES attributes:nil error:nil];
// ... error-checking omitted
```

To learn what files and folders exist within a directory, you can ask for an array of the directory's contents:

```
NSError* err = nil;
NSArray* arr =
    [fm contentsOfDirectoryAtURL:docsurl
        includingPropertiesForKeys:nil options:0 error:&err];
// ... error-checking omitted
NSLog(@"%@", [arr valueForKey:@"lastPathComponent"]);
/*
MyFolder
*/
```

The array resulting from `contentsOfDirectoryAtURL:...` lists full URLs of the directory's *immediate* contents; it is shallow. For a deep array, which might be very big, you can enumerate the directory, so that you are handed only one file reference at a time:

```
NSDirectoryEnumerator* dir =
    [fm enumeratorAtURL:docsurl
        includingPropertiesForKeys:nil options:0 errorHandler:nil];
for (NSURL* f in dir)
    if ([[f pathExtension] isEqualToString: @"txt"])
        NSLog(@"%@", [f lastPathComponent]);
/*
file1.txt
file2.txt
*/
```

A directory enumerator also permits you to decline to dive into a particular subdirectory (`skipDescendants`), so you can make your traversal even more efficient; I'll give an example later in this chapter.

Consult the NSFileManager class documentation for more about what you can do with files, and see also Apple's *Low-Level File Management Programming Topics*.

Saving and Reading Files

To save or read a simple file, you are likely to use one of the convenience methods for the class appropriate to the file's contents. NSString, NSData, NSArray, and NSDictionary provide `writeToURL...` and `initWithContentsOfURL...` methods.

NSString and NSData objects map directly between their own contents and the contents of the file. Here, I'll generate a text file from a string:

```
NSError* err = nil;
BOOL ok =
    [@"howdy" writeToURL:[myfolder URLByAppendingPathComponent:@"file1.txt"]
                atomically:YES encoding:NSUTF8StringEncoding error:&err];
// error-checking omitted
```

NSArray and NSDictionary files are actually property lists (Chapter 10), and will work only if all the contents of the array or dictionary are property list types (NSString, NSData, NSDate, NSNumber, NSArray, and NSDictionary).

So how do you save to a file an object of some other class? Well, if an object's class adopts the NSCoding protocol, you can convert it to an NSData and back again using NSKeyed-Archiver and NSKeyedUnarchiver; an NSData can then be saved as a file or in a property list. An example of doing this with a UIColor object appears in Chapter 10.

You can make your own class adopt the NSCoding protocol. This can become somewhat complicated because an object can refer (through an instance variable) to another object, which may also adopt the NSCoding protocol, and thus you can end up saving an entire graph of interconnected objects if you wish. However, I'll confine myself to illustrating a simple case (and you can read the *Archives and Serializations Programming Guide* for more information).

Let's say, then, that we have a simple Person class with a `firstName` property and a `last-Name` property. We'll declare that it adopts the NSCoding protocol:

```
@interface Person : NSObject <NSCoding>
```

To make this class actually conform to NSCoding, we must implement `encodeWith-Coder:` (to archive the object) and `initWithCoder:` (to unarchive the object). In `encode-WithCoder:`, we must first call `super` if the superclass adopts NSCoding, and then call the appropriate `encode...` method for each instance variable we want preserved:

```
- (void)encodeWithCoder:(NSCoder *)encoder {
    //[super encodeWithCoder: encoder]; // not in this case
    [encoder encodeObject:self.lastName forKey:@"last"];
    [encoder encodeObject:self.firstName forKey:@"first"];
}
```

In `initWithCoder`, we must call `super`, using either `initWithCoder:` if the superclass adopts the NSCoding protocol or the designated initializer if not, and then call the appropriate `decode...` method for each instance variable stored earlier, finally return-ing `self`; memory management is up to us (but under ARC there will probably be no need to think about that):

```
- (id) initWithCoder:(NSCoder *)decoder {
    //self = [super initWithCoder: decoder]; // not in this case
    self = [super init];
    self->_lastName = [decoder decodeObjectForKey:@"last"];
    self->_firstName = [decoder decodeObjectForKey:@"first"];
    return self;
}
```

We can test our code by creating, configuring, and saving a Person instance as a file:

```
Person* moi = [Person new];
moi.firstName = @"Matt";
moi.lastName = @"Neuburg";
NSData* moidata = [NSKeyedArchiver archivedDataWithRootObject:moi];
NSURL* moifile = [docsurl URLByAppendingPathComponent:@"moi.txt"];
[moidata writeToURL:moifile atomically:NO];
```

We can retrieve the saved Person at a later time:

```
NSData* persondata = [[NSData alloc] initWithContentsOfURL:moifile];
Person* person = [NSKeyedUnarchiver unarchiveObjectWithData:persondata];
NSLog(@"%@ %@", person.firstName, person.lastName); // Matt Neuburg
```

If the NSData object is itself the entire content of the file, as here, then instead of using `archivedDataWithRootObject:` and `unarchiveObjectWithData:`, you can skip the intermediate NSData object and use `archiveRootObject:toFile:` and `unarchiveObjectWithFile:`.

Saving a single Person as an archive may seem like overkill; why didn't we just make a text file consisting of the first and last names? But imagine that a Person has a lot more properties, or that we have an array of hundreds of Persons, or an array of hundreds of dictionaries where one value in each dictionary is a Person; now the power of an archivable Person is evident. Even though Person now adopts the NSCoding protocol, an NSArray containing a Person object still cannot be written to disk using NSArray's `writeToFile...` or `writeToURL...`, because Person is still not a property list type. But the array can be archived and written to disk with NSKeyedArchiver.

User Defaults

User defaults (NSUserDefaults), which have often been referred to earlier in this book (see especially Chapter 10 and Chapter 13), are intended as the persistent storage of the user's preferences. They are little more, really, than a special case of an NSDictionary property list file. You talk to the NSUserDefaults `standardUserDefaults` object much as if it were a dictionary; it has keys and values. And the only legal values are property list values (see the preceding section); thus, for example, to store a Person in user defaults, you'd have to archive it first to an NSData object. Unlike NSDictionary, NSUserDefaults provides convenience methods for converting between a simple data type such as a float or a BOOL and the object that is stored in the defaults (`setFloat:forKey:`, `floatForKey:`, and so forth). But the defaults themselves are still a dictionary.

Meanwhile, somewhere on disk, this dictionary is being saved for you automatically as a property list file — though you don't concern yourself with that. You simply set or retrieve values from the dictionary by way of their keys, secure in the knowledge that the file is being read into memory or written to disk as needed. Your chief concern is to make sure that you've written everything needful into user defaults before your app terminates; as we saw in Chapter 11, in a multitasking world this will usually mean when the app delegate receives `applicationDidEnterBackground:` at the latest. If you're worried that your app might crash, you can tell the `standardUserDefaults` object to `synchronize` as a way of forcing it to save right now, but this is rarely necessary.

To provide the value for a key before the user has had a chance to do so — the default default, as it were — use `registerDefaults:`. What you're supplying here is a dictionary whose key–value pairs will each be written into the defaults, but only if there is no such key already. Recall this example from Chapter 10:

```
[[NSUserDefaults standardUserDefaults] registerDefaults:
    @{@"cardMatrixRows":@4, @"cardMatrixColumns":@3}];
```

The idea is that we call `registerDefaults:` extremely early as the app launches. Either the app has run at some time previously and the user has set these preferences, in which case this call has no effect and does no harm, or not, in which case we now have initial values for these preferences with which to get started. So, in the game app from which that code comes, we start out with a 4×3 game layout, but the user can change this at any time.

This leaves only the question of how the user is to interact with the defaults. One way is that your app provides some kind of interface. For example, in the TidBITS News app, there's a single button for setting the size of text, and that's the only preference with which the user ever interacts directly.

The game app from which the previous code comes has a tab bar interface; the second tab is where the user sets preferences (Figure 20-1). The app is compiled for iOS 5, and hence doesn't participate in the iOS 6 built-in state saving and restoration. So it uses (or misuses) the user defaults to store state information. It records the state of the game board and the card deck into user defaults every time these change, so that if the app is terminated and then launched again later, we can restore the game as it was when the user left off. One might argue that, while the current card layout may be state, the card deck itself is data — and so I am also misusing the user defaults to store data. However, while purists may grumble, it's a very small amount of data and I don't think the distinction is terribly significant in this case. (See also Chapter 13 on user defaults as a locus of global values.)

Alternatively, you can provide a *settings bundle*, consisting mostly of one or more property list files describing an interface and the corresponding user default keys and their initial values; the Settings app is then responsible for translating your instructions into an actual interface, and for presenting it to the user.

Using a settings bundle has some obvious disadvantages: the user may not think to look in the Settings app; the user has to leave your app to access preferences; and you don't get the kind of control over the interface that you have within your own app. Also, in a multitasking world, this means that the user can set preferences while your app is backgrounded; you'll need to register for `NSUserDefaultsDidChangeNotification` in order to hear about this.

In some situations, though, a settings bundle has some clear advantages. Keeping the preferences interface out of your app can make your app's own interface cleaner and simpler. You don't have to write any of the "glue" code that coordinates the preferences

Figure 36-1. The iTunes file sharing interface

interface with the user default values. And it may be appropriate for the user to be able to set preferences for your app even when your app isn't running.

Writing a settings bundle is described in the "Implementing Application Preferences" chapter of Apple's *iOS Application Programming Guide*, along with the *Settings Application Schema Reference*.

File Sharing

If your app supports file sharing, its Documents directory becomes available to the user through iTunes (Figure 36-1). The user can add files to your app's Documents directory, and can save files and folders from your app's Documents directory to the computer, as well as renaming and deleting files and folders. This could be appropriate, for example, if your app works with common types of file that the user might obtain elsewhere, such as PDFs or JPEGs.

To support file sharing, set the *Info.plist* key "Application supports iTunes file sharing" (`UIFileSharingEnabled`).

Once your entire Documents directory is exposed to the user this way, you are suddenly not so likely to use the Documents directory to store private files. As I mentioned earlier, I like to use the Application Support directory instead.

Your app doesn't get any notification when the user has altered the contents of the Documents directory. Noticing that the situation has changed and responding appropriately is entirely up to you.

Document Types

Your app can declare itself willing to open documents of a certain type. In this way, if another app obtains a document of this type, it can propose to hand the document off to your app. For example, the user might download the document with Mobile Safari, or receive it in a mail message with the Mail app; now we need a way to get it from Safari or Mail to you.

To let the system know that your app is a candidate for opening a certain kind of document, you will configure the "Document types" (CFBundleDocumentTypes) key in your *Info.plist*. This is an array, where each entry will be a dictionary specifying a document type by using keys such as "Document Content Type UTIs" (LSItemContentTypes), "Document Type Name" (CFBundleTypeName), CFBundleTypeIconFiles, and LSHandlerRank. Far and away the simplest method for configuring the *Info.plist* is through the interface available in the Info tab when you edit the target.

For example, suppose I want to declare that my app opens PDFs. My *Info.plist* could contain this simple entry (as seen in the standard editor):

```
Document types                         (1 item)
    Item 0                             (1 item)
        Document Type Name             PDF
        Document Content Type UTIs     (1 item)
            Item 0                     com.adobe.pdf
```

Now suppose the user receives a PDF in an email message. The Mail app can display this PDF, but the user can also tap the Action button to bring up an activity view offering, among other things, to open the file in my app. (The interface will resemble Figure 36-2, with my app listed as one of the buttons.)

Next, suppose the user actually *taps* the button that hands the PDF off to my app. For this to work, my app delegate must implement application:handleOpenURL:. When that method is called, my app has been brought to the front, either by launching it from scratch or by reviving it from background suspension; its job is now to handle the opening of the document whose URL has arrived as the second parameter. To prevent me from peeking into another app's sandbox, the system has already copied the document into my sandbox, into the Inbox directory, which is created for exactly this purpose.

 The Inbox directory is created in your Documents folder. Thus, if your app implements file sharing, the user can see the Inbox folder; you may wish to delete the Inbox folder, therefore, as soon as you're done retrieving files from it.

In this simple example, my app has just one view controller, which has an outlet to a UIWebView where we will display any PDFs that arrive in this fashion. So my app delegate contains this code:

```
- (BOOL)application:(UIApplication *)application handleOpenURL:(NSURL *)url {
    [self.viewController displayPDF:url];
    return YES;
}
```

And my view controller contains this code:

```
- (void) displayPDF: (NSURL*) url {
    NSURLRequest* req = [NSURLRequest requestWithURL:url];
    [self.wv loadRequest:req];
}
```

In real life, things might be more complicated. Our implementation of `application:handleOpenURL:` might check to see whether this really *is* a PDF, and return NO if it isn't. Also, our app might be in the middle of something else, possibly displaying a completely different view controller's view; because `application:handleOpenURL:` can arrive at any time, we may have to be prepared to drop whatever we were doing and showing previously and display the incoming document instead.

If our app is launched from scratch by the arrival of this URL, `application:didFinishLaunchingWithOptions:` will be sent to our app delegate as usual. The options dictionary (the second parameter) will contain the `UIApplicationLaunchOptionsURLKey`, and we can take into account, if we like, the fact that we are being launched specifically to open a document. The usual thing, however, is to ignore this key and launch in the normal way; `application:handleOpenURL:` will then arrive in good order after our interface has been set up, and we can handle it just as we would if we had already been running.

Your app delegate can also implement `application:openURL:sourceApplication:annotation:` in order to receive more information about the incoming URL. If implemented, this will be called in preference to `application:handleOpenURL:`.

The example I've been discussing assumes that the UTI for the document type is standard and well-known. It is also possible that your app will operate on a new document type, that is, a type of document that the app itself defines. In that case, you'll also want to add this UTI to your app's list of Exported UTIs in the *Info.plist*. I'll give an example later in this chapter.

Handing Off a Document

The converse of the situation discussed in the previous section is this: your app has somehow acquired a document and wants to let the user hand off a copy of it to whatever app can deal with it. This is done through the UIDocumentInteractionController class.

Figure 36-2. The document Open In activity view

This class operates asynchronously, so retaining an instance of it is up to you; typically, you'll store it in an instance variable with a retain setter policy.

For example, let's say our app has a PDF sitting in its Documents directory. Assuming we have an NSURL pointing to this document, presenting the interface for handing the document off to some other application (Figure 36-2) could be as simple as this (`sender` is a button that the user has just tapped):

```
self.dic =
    [UIDocumentInteractionController interactionControllerWithURL:url];
BOOL y =
    [self.dic presentOpenInMenuFromRect:[sender bounds]
                               inView:sender animated:YES];
```

Starting in iOS 6, this interface is an activity view (Chapter 26); formerly, it was an action sheet. There are actually two activity views available:

`presentOpenInMenuFromRect:inView:animated:`
`presentOpenInMenuFromBarButtonItem:animated:`
> Presents an activity view listing apps in which the document can be opened.

`presentOptionsMenuFromRect:inView:animated:`
`presentOptionsMenuFromBarButtonItem:animated:`
> Presents an activity view listing apps in which the document can be opened, along with other possible actions, such as Print, Copy, and Mail.

These methods work on both iPhone and iPad interfaces; on the iPad, the buttons appear in a popover.

Your app can't learn *which* other applications are capable of accepting the document! Indeed, it can't even learn in advance whether *any* other applications are capable of accepting the document; your only clue is that the returned BOOL value afterward will be NO if UIDocumentInteractionController couldn't present the requested interface.

UIDocumentInteractionController can, however, be interrogated for *some* information about the document type. In this example, we configure a button in our interface to make its image the icon of the document type:

```
self.dic =
    [UIDocumentInteractionController interactionControllerWithURL:url];
UIImage* icon = self.dic.icons[0];
[self.b setImage:icon forState:UIControlStateNormal];
```

A UIDocumentInteractionController can also present a preview of the document, if the document is of a type for which preview is enabled. You must give the UIDocument-InteractionController a delegate (UIDocumentInteractionControllerDelegate), and the delegate must implement documentInteractionControllerViewControllerFor-Preview:, returning an existing view controller that will contain the preview's view controller. So, here we ask for the preview:

```
self.dic =
    [UIDocumentInteractionController interactionControllerWithURL:url];
self.dic.delegate = self;
[self.dic presentPreviewAnimated:YES];
```

In the delegate, we supply the view controller; it happens that, in my code, this delegate *is* a view controller — in fact, it's the very view controller that is presenting the UIDocumentInteractionController — so it simply returns self:

```
- (UIViewController *) documentInteractionControllerViewControllerForPreview:
        (UIDocumentInteractionController *) controller {
    return self;
}
```

If the view controller returned were a UINavigationController, the preview's view controller would be pushed onto it. In this case it isn't, so the preview's view controller is a presented view controller with a Done button. The preview interface also contains an Action button that lets the user summon the Options activity view. In fact, this preview interface is exactly the same interface already familiar from the Mail app.

Delegate methods allow you to track what's happening in the interface presented by the UIDocumentInteractionController. Probably most important are those that inform you that key stages of the interaction are ending:

- documentInteractionControllerDidDismissOptionsMenu:

- documentInteractionControllerDidDismissOpenInMenu:

- documentInteractionControllerDidEndPreview:

- documentInteractionController:didEndSendingToApplication:

Previews are actually provided through the Quick Look framework, and you can skip the UIDocumentInteractionController and present the preview yourself through a

QLPreviewController; you'll link to *QuickLook.framework* and import `<QuickLook/QuickLook.h>`. It's a view controller, so to display the preview you show it as a presented view controller or push it onto a navigation controller's stack, just as UIDocument-InteractionController would have done. A nice feature of QLPreviewController is that you can give it more than one document to preview; the user can move between these, within the preview, using arrow buttons that appear at the bottom of the interface. Apart from this, the interface looks just like the interface presented by the UIDocument-InteractionController.

In this example, I have in my Documents directory several PDF documents. I acquire a list of their URLs and present a preview for them:

```
// obtain URLs of PDFs as an array
NSFileManager* fm = [NSFileManager new];
NSURL* docsurl =
    [fm URLForDirectory:NSDocumentDirectory inDomain:NSUserDomainMask
        appropriateForURL:nil create:NO error:nil];
NSDirectoryEnumerator* dir =
    [fm enumeratorAtURL:[docsurl URLByAppendingPathComponent:@"Inbox"]
        includingPropertiesForKeys:nil options:0 errorHandler:nil];
if (!dir)
    return; // proper error-checking omitted
NSMutableArray* marr = [NSMutableArray array];
for (NSURL* f in dir) {
    [dir skipDescendants];
    if ([[f pathExtension] isEqualToString: @"pdf"])
        [marr addObject: f];
}
self.pdfs = marr; // retain policy
if (![self.pdfs count])
    return;
// show preview interface
QLPreviewController* preview = [QLPreviewController new];
preview.dataSource = self;
[self presentViewController:preview animated:YES completion:nil];
```

You'll notice that I haven't told the QLPreviewController what documents to preview. That is the job of QLPreviewController's data source. In my code, this very same view controller is also the data source. It simply fetches the requested information from the list of URLs, which was previously saved into an instance variable:

```
- (NSInteger) numberOfPreviewItemsInPreviewController:
        (QLPreviewController *) controller {
    return [self.pdfs count];
}

- (id <QLPreviewItem>) previewController: (QLPreviewController *) controller
                    previewItemAtIndex: (NSInteger) index {
    return self.pdfs[index];
}
```

The second data source method requires us to return an object that adopts the QLPreviewItem protocol. By a wildly improbable coincidence, NSURL *does* adopt this protocol, so the example works.

The Document Architecture

If your app opens and saves documents of a type peculiar to itself, you may want to take advantage of the *document architecture*. This architecture revolves around a class, UIDocument, that takes care of a number of pesky issues, such as the fact that loading or writing your data might take some time. Plus, UIDocument provides autosaving behavior, so that your data is written out automatically whenever it changes. Moreover, UIDocument is your gateway to allowing your documents to participate in iCloud, so your app's documents on one of the user's devices will automatically be mirrored onto another of the user's devices.

Getting started with UIDocument is not difficult. You'll start with a UIDocument subclass, and you'll override two methods:

`loadFromContents:ofType:error:`
Called when it's time to open a document from disk. You are expected to convert the `contents` value into a model object that your app can use, store that model object, and return YES. (If there was a problem, you'll set the `error:` by indirection and return NO.)

`contentsForType:error:`
Called when it's time to save a document to disk. You are expected to convert the app's model object into an NSData instance (or, if your document is a package, an NSFileWrapper) and return it. (If there was a problem, you'll set the `error:` by indirection and return nil.)

Your UIDocument subclass, then, in addition to its implementation of those two methods, will need a place to store and retrieve the data model object. Obviously, this might be an instance variable. However, your UIDocument instance will probably be partnered in some way with a view controller instance, and that view controller will need access to the data, so a more sophisticated solution might be to set up a delegate relationship between the view controller and the UIDocument and allow the UIDocument to call methods that set and retrieve a property of the view controller.

To instantiate a UIDocument, call its designated initializer, `initWithFileURL:`. This sets the UIDocument's `fileURL` property, and associates the UIDocument with this file on disk, typically for the remainder of its lifetime.

In my description of the two key UIDocument methods that your subclass will override, I used the phrase, "when it's time" (to open or save the document). This raises the question of how your UIDocument instance will know when to open and save a document. There are three circumstances to distinguish:

Make a new document

> The `fileURL:` points to a nonexistent file. Immediately after instantiating the UIDocument, you send it `saveToURL:forSaveOperation:completionHandler:`, where the second argument is `UIDocumentSaveForCreating`. (The first argument will be the UIDocument's own `fileURL`.) This in turn causes `contentsForType:error:` to be called, and the contents of an empty document are saved out to disk. This implies that your UIDocument subclass should know of some default value that represents the model data when there is no data.

Open an existing document

> Send the UIDocument instance `openWithCompletionHandler:`. This in turn causes `loadFromContents:ofType:error:` to be called.

Save an existing document

> There are two approaches to saving an existing document:

> *Autosave*

>> Usually, you'll mark the document as "dirty" by calling `updateChangeCount:`. From time to time, the UIDocument will notice this situation and will save the document to disk, calling `contentsForType:error:` in the process.

> *Manual save*

>> On certain occasions, waiting for autosave won't be appropriate. We've already seen an example of such an occasion — when the file itself needs to be created on the spot. Another is when the app is going into the background; we will want to preserve our document there and then, in case the app is terminated. You'll call `saveToURL:forSaveOperation:completionHandler:`; if the file is not being created for the first time, the second argument will be `UIDocumentSaveForOverwriting`. Alternatively, if you know you're finished with the document (perhaps the interface displaying the document is about to be torn down) you can call `closeWithCompletionHandler:`.

The `open...`, `close...`, and `saveTo...` methods have a `completionHandler:` argument. This is UIDocument's solution to the fact that reading and saving may take time. The file operations themselves take place on a background thread; the `completionHandler:` block is then called on the main thread.

We now know enough for an example! I'll reuse my Person class from earlier in this chapter. Imagine a document effectively consisting of multiple Person instances; I'll call it each document a *people group*. Our app, People Groups, will list all people groups in the user's Documents folder; it will also open any people group from disk and display its contents, allowing the user to edit any Person's `firstName` or `lastName` (Figure 36-3).

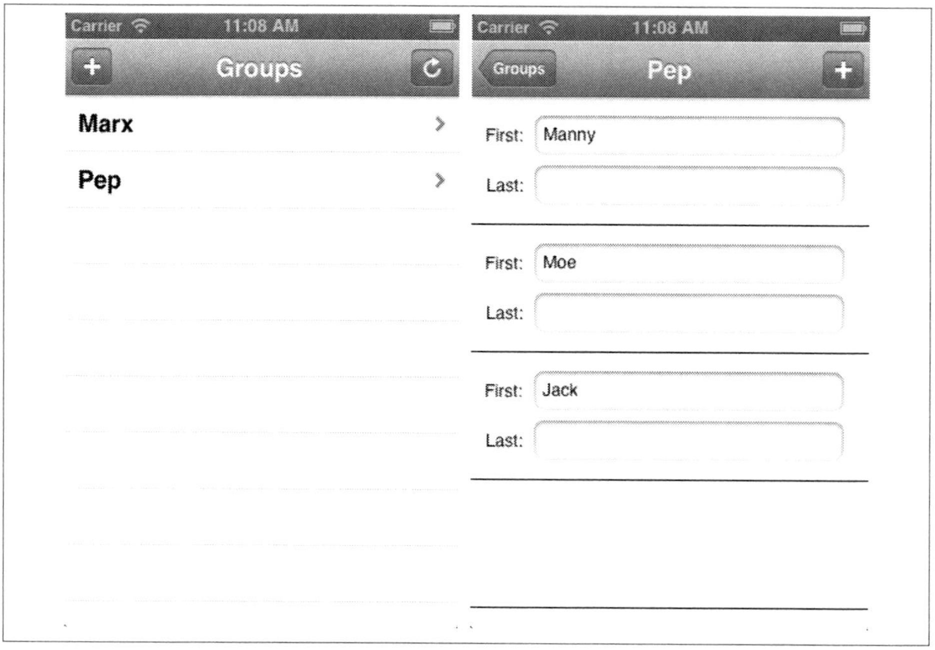

Figure 36-3. The People Groups interface

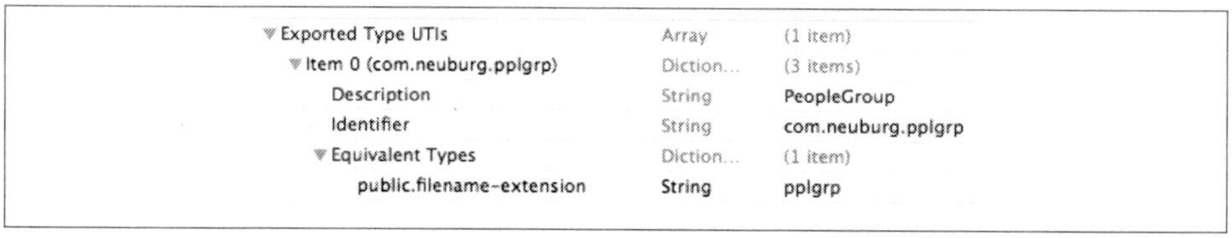

▼ Exported Type UTIs	Array	(1 item)
▼ Item 0 (com.neuburg.pplgrp)	Diction...	(3 items)
Description	String	PeopleGroup
Identifier	String	com.neuburg.pplgrp
▼ Equivalent Types	Diction...	(1 item)
public.filename-extension	String	pplgrp

Figure 36-4. Defining a custom UTI

My first step is to define a custom UTI in my app's *Info.plist*, associating a file type (`com.neuburg.pplgrp`) with a file extension (`@"pplgrp"`), as shown in Figure 36-4. I then also define a document type that uses this UTI, as shown earlier in this chapter.

A document consists of multiple Persons, so a natural model implementation is an NSArray of Persons. Moreover, as I mentioned earlier, since Person implements NSCoding, an NSArray of Persons can be archived directly into an NSData. Thus, assuming that our UIDocument subclass (which I'll call PeopleDocument) has a `people` property, it can be implemented like this:

```
-(id)initWithFileURL:(NSURL *)url {
    self = [super initWithFileURL:url];
    if (self) {
        self->_people = [NSMutableArray array];
```

```
    }
    return self;
}

- (BOOL)loadFromContents:(id)contents ofType:(NSString *)typeName
                    error:(NSError **)outError {
    NSArray* arr = [NSKeyedUnarchiver unarchiveObjectWithData:contents];
    self.people = [NSMutableArray arrayWithArray:arr];
    return YES;
}

- (id)contentsForType:(NSString *)typeName error:(NSError **)outError {
    NSData* data = [NSKeyedArchiver archivedDataWithRootObject:self.people];
    return data;
}
```

We override initWithFileURL: to give ourselves something to save if we are called upon to save a new empty document; we then use NSKeyedUnarchiver and NSKeyed-Archiver exactly as in our earlier examples.

The remaining questions are architectural: when should a PeopleDocument be initialized, where should it be stored, and what should be the nature of communications with it? The first view controller merely lists documents by name, and provides an interface for letting the user create a new group; only the second view controller, the one that displays the first and last names of the people in the group, actually needs to work with PeopleDocument. I'll call this view controller PeopleLister. PeopleLister's designated initializer requires that it be given a fileURL: argument, with which it sets its own fileURL property. In its viewDidLoad implementation, PeopleLister instantiates a People-Document with that same fileURL, and retains it through a property (doc). If the URL points to a nonexistent file, PeopleLister requests that it be created by calling saveTo-URL:forSaveOperation:completionHandler:; otherwise, it requests that the document be read, by calling openWithCompletionHandler:. Either way, the completion handler points PeopleLister's own people property at the PeopleDocument's people property (so that they share the same data model object) and refreshes the interface:

```
NSFileManager* fm = [NSFileManager new];
self.doc = [[PeopleDocument alloc] initWithFileURL:self.fileURL];
void (^listPeople) (BOOL) = ^(BOOL success) {
    if (success) {
        self.people = self.doc.people;
        [self.tableView reloadData];
    }
};
if (![fm fileExistsAtPath:[self.fileURL path]])
    [self.doc saveToURL:doc.fileURL
        forSaveOperation:UIDocumentSaveForCreating
      completionHandler:listPeople];
else
    [self.doc openWithCompletionHandler:listPeople];
```

When the user performs a significant editing maneuver, such as creating or deleting a person or editing a person's first or last name, PeopleLister tells its PeopleDocument that the document is dirty, and allows autosaving to take it from there:

```
[self.doc updateChangeCount:UIDocumentChangeDone];
```

When the app is about to go into the background, or when PeopleLister's own view is disappearing, it forces PeopleDocument to save immediately:

```
- (void) forceSave: (id) n {
    [self.tableView endEditing:YES];
    [self.doc saveToURL:doc.fileURL
        forSaveOperation:UIDocumentSaveForOverwriting
        completionHandler:nil];
}
```

That's all it takes; adding UIDocument support to your app is easy, because UIDocument is merely acting as a supplier and preserver of your app's data model object. UIDocument presents itself in the documentation as a large and complex class, but that's chiefly because it is so heavily customizable both at high and low levels; for the most part, you won't need any of that heavy customization, and use of UIDocument really will be as simple as what I've shown here. You might go further in order to give your UIDocument a more sophisticated understanding of what constitutes a significant change in your data by working with its undo manager; I'll talk about undo managers in Chapter 39. For further details, see Apple's *Document-based App Programming Guide for iOS*.

iCloud

Once your app is operating through UIDocument, iCloud compatibility falls right into your lap. You have just two steps to perform:

Register for iCloud entitlements
> In the Portal (Chapter 9), register your app and configure it to be enabled for iCloud (a simple checkbox); then create a provisioning profile for the app (obviously, while developing, this would be a Development profile), download it, and hand it over to Xcode.

> Back in your project, edit the target; under Summary, check Enable Entitlements in the Entitlements section. This causes the entire entitlements mechanism to spring to life. The entitlements file is added to the project. The Enable iCloud checkbox is enabled; check it if it isn't checked. You'll also need one Ubiquity Container (listed just below the iCloud checkbox); if there isn't one, add one, which will automatically be assigned your app's bundle id.

Obtain an iCloud-compatible directory
> Early in your app's lifetime, call NSFileManager's URLForUbiquityContainer-Identifier: (typically passing nil as the argument), on a background thread, to

obtain the URL of a cloud-shared directory. It will probably be an app-specific directory inside *file://localhost/private/var/mobile/Library/Mobile%20Documents/*; you are given sandbox access to this directory even though strictly speaking it isn't inside your sandbox area. Any documents your app puts here by way of a UIDocument subclass will be automatically shared into the cloud.

Thus, for example, having registered for iCloud entitlements, I was able to make my People Groups app iCloud-compatible with just two code changes. In the app delegate, as my app launches, I step out to background thread (Chapter 38), obtain the cloud-shared directory's URL, and then step back to the main thread and retain the URL through a property, ubiq:

```
dispatch_async(dispatch_get_global_queue(0, 0), ^{
    NSFileManager* fm = [NSFileManager new];
    NSURL* ubiq = [fm URLForUbiquityContainerIdentifier:nil];
    dispatch_async(dispatch_get_main_queue(), ^{
        self.ubiq = ubiq;
    });
});
```

 New in iOS 6, you can precede that code with a call to NSFileManager's ubiquityIdentityToken. You can do that on the main thread, in the normal way, because it returns immediately. If the result is nil, iCloud isn't available, or this user hasn't registered for iCloud, and you might omit any subsequent attempt to work with iCloud. (If it *isn't* nil, it identifies the user's iCloud account; this can be useful, for example, to detect when the user has logged into a different account.)

Then, anywhere in my code that I was specifying the URL for the user's Documents folder as the place to seek and save people groups, I now specify ubiq if it isn't nil:

```
NSURL* docsurl = [fm URLForDirectory:NSDocumentDirectory
                           inDomain:NSUserDomainMask
                 appropriateForURL:nil create:NO error:nil];
NSURL* ubiq =
    [(AppDelegate*)[[UIApplication sharedApplication] delegate] ubiq];
if (ubiq)
    docsurl = ubiq;
```

To test, I ran the app on one device and created a people group with some people in it. I then switched to a different device and ran the app there; presto, there was the same document with the same name containing the same people. It was quite thrilling.

There are a few further refinements that my app probably needs in order to be a good iCloud citizen. For example, my app is not automatically aware that a new document has appeared in the cloud. To be notified of that, I'd want to run an NSMetadataQuery. The usual strategy is: instantiate NSMetadataQuery, configure the search, register for notifications such as `NSMetadataQueryDidFinishGatheringNotification` and `NSMetadataQueryDidUpdateNotification`, start the search, and retain the NSMetadataQuery instance with the search continuing to run for the entire lifetime of the app.

Another concern is that my app should be notified when the currently open document changes on disk because a new version of it was downloaded from the cloud (that is, someone edited the document while I had it open). For that, register for `UIDocument-StateChangedNotification`. To learn the document's state, consult its `document-State` property. A big issue is likely to be what should happen if the document state is `UIDocumentStateInConflict`. You'll want to resolve the conflict in coordination with the NSFileVersion class; for details and example code, see the "Resolving Document Version Conflicts" chapter of Apple's *Document-based App Programming Guide for iOS*.

Yet another issue is the question of what should happen if the availability of iCloud changes in the course of our app's career. The problem here is that the data is stored in two different places (the Documents directory, or `ubiq`). Suppose, for example, that our app starts life without iCloud — because the user hasn't registered for it, or has it turned off for our app — and then suddenly iCloud is available. We could then call NSFile-Manager's `setUbiquitous:itemAtURL:destinationURL:error:` to transfer the document to our ubiquity container directory. However, it is not so obvious what to do if iCloud is switched from on to off, as we can no longer access the ubiquity container directory to rescue the document.

Further iCloud details are outside the scope of this discussion. Getting started is easy; making your app a good iCloud citizen, capable of dealing with the complexities that iCloud may entail, is not. For further details, see the "iCloud Storage" chapter of Apple's *iOS App Programming Guide*.

 Instead of, or in addition to, storing full-fledged documents in the cloud, your app might like to store some key–value pairs, similar to a sort of online NSUserDefaults. To do this, use the NSUbiquitousKeyValue-Store class; get the `defaultStore` shared object and talk to it much as you would talk to NSUserDefaults. The `NSUbiquitousKeyValueStore-DidChangeExternallyNotification` tells you when data is changed in the cloud. Material that you store in the cloud through NSUbiquitous-KeyValueStore does *not* count against the user's iCloud storage limit, but it needs to be kept short and simple.

XML

XML is a highly flexible and widely used general-purpose text file format for storage and retrieval of structured data. You might use it yourself to store data that you'll need to retrieve later, or you could encounter it when obtaining information from elsewhere, such as the Internet.

Mac OS X Cocoa provides a set of classes (NSXMLDocument and so forth) for reading, parsing, maintaining, searching, and modifying XML data in a completely general way, but iOS does *not* include these. I think the reason must be that their tree-based approach is too memory-intensive. Instead, iOS provides NSXMLParser, a much simpler class that walks through an XML document, sending delegate messages as it encounters elements. With this, you can parse an XML document once, but what you do with the pieces as they arrive is up to you. The general assumption here is that you know in advance the structure of the particular XML data you intend to read and that you have provided classes for storage of the same data in object form and for transforming the XML pieces into that storage.

To illustrate, let's return once more to our Person class with a `firstName` and a `last-Name` property. Imagine that as our app starts up, we would like to populate it with Person objects, and that we've stored the data describing these objects as an XML file in our app bundle, like this:

```
<?xml version="1.0" encoding="utf-8"?>
<people>
    <person>
        <firstName>Matt</firstName>
        <lastName>Neuburg</lastName>
    </person>
    <person>
        <firstName>Snidely</firstName>
        <lastName>Whiplash</lastName>
    </person>
    <person>
        <firstName>Dudley</firstName>
        <lastName>Doright</lastName>
    </person>
</people>
```

This data could be mapped to an array of Person objects, each with its `firstName` and `lastName` properties appropriately set. (This is a deliberately easy example, of course; not all XML is so readily expressed as objects.) Let's consider how we might do that.

Using NSXMLParser is not difficult in theory. You create the NSXMLParser, handing it the URL of a local XML file (or an NSData, perhaps downloaded from the Internet), set its delegate, and tell it to `parse`. The delegate starts receiving delegate messages. For simple XML like ours, there are only three delegate messages of interest:

`parser:didStartElement:namespaceURI:qualifiedName:attributes:`
 The parser has encountered an opening element tag. In our document, this would be <people>, <person>, <firstName>, or <lastName>.

`parser:didEndElement:namespaceURI:qualifiedName:`
> The parser has encountered the corresponding closing element tag. In our document this would be `</people>`, `</person>`, `</firstName>`, or `</lastName>`.

`parser:foundCharacters:`
> The parser has encountered some text between the starting and closing tags for the current element. In our document this would be, for example, `Matt` or `Neuburg` and so on.

In practice, responding to these delegate messages poses challenges of maintaining state. If there is just one delegate, it will have to bear in mind at every moment what element it is currently encountering; this could make for a lot of instance variables and a lot of if-statements in the implementation of the delegate methods. To aggravate the issue, `parser:foundCharacters:` can arrive multiple times for a single stretch of text; that is, the text may arrive in pieces, so we have to accumulate it into an instance variable, which is yet another case of maintaining state.

An elegant way to meet these challenges is by resetting the NSXMLParser's delegate to different objects at different stages of the parsing process. We make each delegate responsible for parsing one element; when a child of that element is encountered, we make a new object and make *it* the delegate. The child element delegate is then responsible for making the parent the delegate once again when it finishes parsing its own element. This is slightly counterintuitive because it means `parser:didStartElement...` and `parser:didEndElement...` for the same element are arriving at two different objects. Imagine, for example, what the job of our `<people>` parser will be:

- When `parser:didStartElement...` arrives, the `<people>` parser looks to see if this is a `<person>`. If so, it creates an object that knows how to deal with a `<person>`, handing that object a reference to itself (the `<people>` parser), and makes it the delegate.

- Delegate messages now arrive at this newly created `<person>` parser. If any text is encountered, `parser:foundCharacters:` will be called, and the text must be accumulated into an instance variable.

- Eventually, `parser:didEndElement...` arrives. The `<person>` parser now uses its reference to make the `<people>` parser the delegate once again. Thus, the `<people>` parser is in charge once again, ready if another `<person>` element is encountered (and the old `<person>` parser might now go quietly out of existence).

With this in mind, we can design a simple all-purpose base class for parsing an element (simple especially because we are taking no account of namespaces, attributes, and other complications):

```
@interface MyXMLParserDelegate : NSObject <NSXMLParserDelegate>

@property (nonatomic, copy) NSString* name;
@property (nonatomic, strong) NSMutableString* text;
@property (nonatomic, weak) MyXMLParserDelegate* parent;
@property (nonatomic, strong) MyXMLParserDelegate* child;
- (void) start: (NSString*) elementName parent: (id) parent;
- (void) makeChild: (Class) class
        elementName: (NSString*) elementName
            parser: (NSXMLParser*) parser;
- (void) finishedChild: (NSString*) s;

@end
```

Here's how these properties and methods are intended to work:

name
> The name of the element we are parsing now.

text
> A place for any characters to accumulate as we parse our element.

parent
> The MyXMLParserDelegate who created us and whose child we are.

child
> If we encounter a child element, we'll create a MyXMLParserDelegate and retain it here, making it the delegate.

start:parent:
> When we create a child parser, we'll call this method on the child so that it knows who its parent is. The first parameter is the name of the element the child will be parsing; we know this because we, not the child, received `parser:didStart-Element....` (In a fuller implementation, this method would be more elaborate and we'd hand the child *all* the information we got with `parser:didStart-Element....`)

makeChild:elementName:parser:
> If we encounter a child element, there's a standard dance to do: instantiate some subclass of MyXMLParserDelegate, make it our `child`, make it the parser's delegate, and send it `start:parent:`. This is a utility method that embodies that dance.

finishedChild:
> When a child receives `parser:didEndElement...`, it sends this message to its parent before making its parent the delegate. The parameter is the `text`, but the parent can use this signal to obtain any information it expects from the child before the child goes out of existence.

Now we can sketch in the default implementation for MyXMLParserDelegate:

```
- (void) start: (NSString*) el parent: (id) p {
    self.name = el;
    self.parent = p;
    self.text = [NSMutableString string];
}

- (void) makeChild: (Class) class
        elementName: (NSString*) elementName
            parser: (NSXMLParser*) parser {
    MyXMLParserDelegate* del = [class new];
    self.child = del;
    parser.delegate = del;
    [del start: elementName parent: self];
}

- (void) finishedChild: (NSString*) s { // subclass implements as desired
}

- (void)parser:(NSXMLParser *)parser foundCharacters:(NSString *)string {
    [self.text appendString:string];
}

- (void)parser:(NSXMLParser *)parser didEndElement:(NSString *)elementName
        namespaceURI:(NSString *)namespaceURI qualifiedName:(NSString *)qName {
    if (self.parent) {
        [self.parent finishedChild: [self.text copy]];
        parser.delegate = self.parent;
    }
}
```

We can now create subclasses of MyXMLParserDelegate: one for each kind of element we expect to parse. The chief responsibility of such a subclass, if it encounters a child element in `parser:didStartElement...`, is to create an instance of the appropriate MyXMLParserDelegate subclass, send it `start:parent:`, and make it the delegate; we have already embodied this in the utility method `makeChild:elementName:parser:`. The reverse process is already built into the default implementation of `parser:didEnd-Element...`: we call the parent's `finishedChild:` and make the parent the delegate.

We can now parse our sample XML into an array of Person objects very easily. We start by obtaining the URL of the XML file, handing it to an NSXMLParser, creating our first delegate parser and making it the delegate, and telling the NSXMLParser to start:

```
NSURL* url =
    [[NSBundle mainBundle] URLForResource:@"folks" withExtension:@"xml"];
NSXMLParser* parser = [[NSXMLParser alloc] initWithContentsOfURL:url];
MyPeopleParser* people = [MyPeopleParser new];
[parser setDelegate: people];
[parser parse];
// ... do something with people.people ...
```

Here is MyPeopleParser. It is the top-level parser so it has some extra work to do: when it encounters the `<people>` element, which is the first thing that should happen, it creates the `people` array that will hold the Person objects; this array will be the final result of the entire parsing operation. If it encounters a `<person>` element, it does the standard dance I described earlier, creating a `<person>` parser (MyPersonParser) as its child and making it the delegate; when the `<person>` parser calls back to tell us it's finished, MyPeopleParser expects the `<person>` parser to supply a Person through its `person` property:

```
- (void)parser:(NSXMLParser *)parser didStartElement:(NSString *)elementName
        namespaceURI:(NSString *)namespaceURI
        qualifiedName:(NSString *)qualifiedName
        attributes:(NSDictionary *)attributeDict
{
    if ([elementName isEqualToString: @"people"])
        self.people = [NSMutableArray array];
    if ([elementName isEqualToString: @"person"])
        [self makeChild:[MyPersonParser class] elementName:elementName
                parser:parser];
}

- (void) finishedChild: (NSString*) s {
    [self.people addObject: [(MyPersonParser*)self.child person]];
}
```

MyPersonParser does the same child-making dance when it encounters a `<first-Name>` or a `<lastName>` element; it uses a plain vanilla MyXMLParserDelegate to parse these children, because the built-in ability to accumulate text and hand it back is all that's needed. In `finishedChild:`, it makes sure it has a Person object ready to hand back to its parent through its `person` property; key–value coding is elegantly used to match the name of the element with the name of the Person property to be set:

```
- (void)parser:(NSXMLParser *)parser didStartElement:(NSString *)elementName
        namespaceURI:(NSString *)namespaceURI
        qualifiedName:(NSString *)qualifiedName
        attributes:(NSDictionary *)attributeDict {
    [self makeChild:[MyXMLParserDelegate class] elementName:elementName
            parser:parser];
}

- (void) finishedChild:(NSString *)s {
    if (!self.person) {
        Person* p = [Person new];
        self.person = p; // retain policy
    }
    [self.person setValue: s forKey: self.child.name];
}
```

This may seem like a lot of work to parse such a simple bit of XML, but it is neatly object-oriented and requires very little new code once we've established the MyXMLParser-Delegate superclass, which is of course reusable in many other situations.

On the other hand, if you really want tree-based XML parsing along with XPath and so forth, you can have it, because the libxml2 library is present in the SDK (and on the device). This is a C *dylib* (short for "dynamic library," extension *.dylib*), and Xcode doesn't automatically know during the build process where to find its headers (even though it's part of the SDK), so the instructions for accessing it in your project are a tiny bit more involved than linking to an Objective-C framework:

1. In Xcode, add *libxml2.dylib* to the Link Binary With Libraries build phase for your target, just as you would do with a framework.

2. Now comes the extra step that differs from using a framework; it is needed because, although the Xcode build process automatically looks inside the SDK's */usr/ include/* folder for headers, it doesn't automatically recurse down into folders, so it won't look inside the *libxml2* folder unless you tell it to. Edit the target's build settings and set the Header Search Paths build setting to $SDKROOT/usr/include/ libxml2. (When you close the dialog for adding a search path, this will transform itself into *iphoneos/usr/include/libxml2*.)

3. In your code, import <libxml/tree.h>.

You now have to talk to libxml2 using C. This is no trivial task. Here's an example proving we can do it; we read our XML file, parse it into a tree, and traverse all its elements:

```
NSURL* url =
    [[NSBundle mainBundle] URLForResource:@"folks" withExtension:@"xml"];
NSString* path = [url absoluteString];
const char* filename = [path UTF8String];
xmlDocPtr doc = nil;
xmlNode *root_element = nil;
doc = xmlReadFile(filename, nil, 0);
root_element = xmlDocGetRootElement(doc);
traverse_elements(root_element); // must be previously defined
xmlFreeDoc(doc);
xmlCleanupParser();
```

Here's our definition for traverse_elements; it logs each person and the person's first and last name, just to prove we are traversing successfully:

```
void traverse_elements(xmlNode * a_node) {
    xmlNode *cur_node = nil;
    for (cur_node = a_node; cur_node; cur_node = cur_node->next) {
        if (cur_node->type == XML_ELEMENT_NODE) {
            if (strcmp(cur_node->name, "person") == 0)
                NSLog(@"found a person");
```

```
        if (strcmp(cur_node->name, "firstName") == 0)
            NSLog(@"First name: %s", cur_node->children->content);
        if (strcmp(cur_node->name, "lastName") == 0)
            NSLog(@"Last name: %s", cur_node->children->content);
    }
    traverse_elements(cur_node->children);
    }
}
```

If talking C to libxml2 is too daunting, you can interpose an Objective-C front end by taking advantage of a third-party library. See, for example, *https://github.com/Touch Code/TouchXML*.

Keep in mind, however, that you're really not supposed to do what I just did. Even if you use libxml2, you're supposed to use stream-based parsing, not tree-based parsing. See Apple's XMLPerformance example code.

 A foundation class for constructing and parsing JSON strings is also provided — NSJSONSerialization. It's a very simple class: all its methods are class methods, and eligible structures are required to be an array or dictionary (corresponding to what JSON calls an *object*) whose elements must be a string, number, array, dictionary, or null. NSData is used as the medium of exchange; you'll archive or unarchive as appropriate. JSON arises often as a lightweight way of communicating structured data across the network; for more information, see *http://www.json.org/*.

SQLite

SQLite (*http://www.sqlite.org/docs.html*) is a lightweight, full-featured relational database that you can talk to using SQL, the universal language of databases. This can be an appropriate storage format when your data comes in rows and columns (records and fields) and needs to be rapidly searchable. Also, the database as a whole is never loaded into memory; the data is accessed only as needed. This is valuable in an environment like an iOS device, where memory is at a premium.

In the same way as you can link to libxml2.dylib, you can link to libsqlite3.dylib (and import <sqlite3.h>) to access the power of SQLite. As with libxml2, talking C to sqlite3 may prove annoying. There are a number of lightweight Objective-C front ends. In this example, I use fmdb (*https://github.com/ccgus/fmdb*) to read the names of people out of a previously created database:

```
NSString* docsdir = [NSSearchPathForDirectoriesInDomains(
    NSDocumentDirectory, NSUserDomainMask, YES) lastObject];
NSString* dbpath = [docsdir stringByAppendingPathComponent:@"people.db"];
FMDatabase* db = [FMDatabase databaseWithPath:dbpath];
```

```
if (![db open]) {
    NSLog(@"Ooops");
    return;
}
FMResultSet *rs = [db executeQuery:@"select * from people"];
while ([rs next]) {
    NSLog(@"%@ %@", rs[@"firstname"], rs[@"lastname"]);
}
[db close];
/* output:
Matt Neuburg
Snidely Whiplash
Dudley Doright
*/
```

You can include a previously constructed SQLite file in your app bundle, but you can't write to it there; the solution is to copy it from your app bundle into another location, such as the Documents directory, before you start working with it.

Core Data

The Core Data framework provides a generalized way of expressing objects and properties that form a relational graph; moreover, it has built-in facilities for persisting those objects to disk — typically using SQLite as a storage format — and reading them from disk only when they are needed, thus making efficient use of memory. For example, a person might have not only multiple addresses but also multiple friends who are also persons; expressing persons and addresses as explicit object types, working out how to link them and how to translate between objects in memory and data in storage, and tracking the effects of changes, such as when a person is deleted from the data, can be tedious. Core Data can help.

It is important to stress, however, that Core Data is *not* a beginner-level technology. It is difficult to use and extremely difficult to debug. It expresses itself in a highly verbose, rigid, arcane way. It has its own elaborate way of doing things — everything you already know about how to create, access, alter, or delete an object within an object collection becomes completely irrelevant! — and trying to bend it to your particular needs can be tricky and can have unintended side-effects. Nor should Core Data be seen as a substitute for a true relational database.

Therefore, I have no intention of explaining Core Data; that would require an entire book. Indeed, such books exist, and if Core Data interests you, you should read some of them. See also the *Core Data Programming Guide* and the other resources referred to there. I will, however, illustrate what it's like to work with Core Data.

I will describe the People Groups example from earlier in this chapter as a Core Data app. We will no longer have multiple documents, each representing a single Group of

People; instead, we will now have a single document, maintained for us by Core Data, containing both Groups and People.

A Core Data project is linked to *CoreData.framework* and will import <CoreData/Core-Data.h>, usually in the precompiled header file (*.pch*; see Chapter 4). To construct a Core Data project, you'll specify the Master–Detail Application template (or the Empty Application template) and check Use Core Data in the second screen. This gives you template code in the app delegate implementation file for constructing the Core Data *persistence stack*, a set of objects that work together to fetch and save your data; in most cases there will no reason to alter this template code, and I have not done so for this example.

The app delegate template code gives the app delegate three properties representing the important singleton objects comprising the persistence stack: managedObjectContext, managedObjectModel, and persistentStoreCoordinator. It also supplies "lazy" getters to give these properties their values when first needed. Of these, the managedObject-Context is the most important for other classes to have access to. The managed object context is the world in which your data objects live and move and have their being: to obtain an object, you fetch it from the managed object context; to create an object, you insert it into the managed object context; to save your data, you save the managed object context.

The Master–Detail Application template also gives the Master view controller a managed-ObjectContext property, and the app delegate sets its value when it instantiates the Master view controller. My Master view controller is called GroupLister, so the app delegate's application:didFinishLaunchingWithOptions: contains these lines:

```
GroupLister* gl = [GroupLister new];
gl.managedObjectContext = self.managedObjectContext;
UINavigationController* nav =
    [[UINavigationController alloc] initWithRootViewController:gl];
self.window.rootViewController = nav;
```

To describe the structure and relationships of the objects constituting your data model, you design an object graph in a data model document. Our object graph is very simple; a Group can have multiple Persons (Figure 36-5). The attributes, analogous to object properties, are all strings, except for the timestamps which are dates; the timestamps will be used for determining the sort order in which groups and people will be displayed in the interface — the display order is the order of creation.

Core Data attributes are not quite object properties. Group and Person are not classes; they are entity names. All Core Data model objects are instances of NSManagedObject, and therefore they do not, of themselves, have a name property, a firstName property, a lastName property, and so on. Instead, Core Data model objects make themselves dynamically KVC compliant for attribute names. For example, Core Data knows, thanks to our object graph, that a Person entity is to have a firstName attribute, so you can set

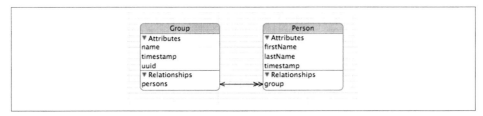

Figure 36-5. The Core Data model for the People Groups app

a Person's firstName attribute using KVC (setValue:forKey:). I find this maddening, so, at the very least, I like to give NSManagedObject the necessary properties through a category:

```
// NSManagedObject+GroupAndPerson.h:
#import <CoreData/CoreData.h>
@interface NSManagedObject (GroupAndPerson)
@property (nonatomic) NSString *firstName, *lastName;
@property (nonatomic) NSString *name, *uuid;
@property (nonatomic) NSDate* timestamp;
@property (nonatomic) NSManagedObject* group;
@end

// NSManagedObject+GroupAndPerson.m:
#import "NSManagedObject+GroupAndPerson.h"
@implementation NSManagedObject (GroupAndPerson)
@dynamic firstName, lastName, name, uuid, timestamp, group;
@end
```

(For the effect of the @dynamic directive, compare the discussion in Chapter 12.) Now we'll be able to use name and firstName and the rest as properties, and CoreData will generate the corresponding accessors for us.

Now let's talk about the first view controller, GroupLister. Its job is to list groups and to allow the user to create a new group (Figure 36-3). The way you ask Core Data for a model object is with a fetch request. In iOS, where Core Data model objects are often the data source for a UITableView, fetch requests are conveniently managed through an NSFetchedResultsController. The template code gives us an NSFetchedResultsController property, along with a "lazy" getter method that generates an NSFetchedResults-Controller if the property is nil, and for GroupLister I've only had to change it a little bit: my entity name is Group and my cache name is Groups, and I've renamed the property itself, frc.

The result is that self.frc is the data model, analogous to an array of Group objects. The implementation of the table view's Three Big Questions to the data source, all pretty much straight from the template code, looks like this:

```
- (NSInteger)numberOfSectionsInTableView:(UITableView *)tableView {
    return [self.frc.sections count];
}

- (NSInteger)tableView:(UITableView *)tableView
        numberOfRowsInSection:(NSInteger)section {
    id<NSFetchedResultsSectionInfo> sectionInfo = self.frc.sections[section];
    return sectionInfo.numberOfObjects;
}

- (UITableViewCell *)tableView:(UITableView *)tableView
        cellForRowAtIndexPath:(NSIndexPath *)indexPath {
    UITableViewCell *cell =
        [tableView dequeueReusableCellWithIdentifier:@"Cell"];
    cell.accessoryType = UITableViewCellAccessoryDisclosureIndicator;
    NSManagedObject *object = [self.frc objectAtIndexPath:indexPath];
    cell.textLabel.text = object.name;
    return cell;
}
```

The only really interesting thing about that code is our ability to speak of
object.name; we can do that because of the category on NSManagedObject that we
created earlier. Otherwise, we'd have to fetch a Group entity's name attribute as value-
ForKey:@"name".

Now let's talk about object creation. GroupLister's table is initially empty because our
app starts out life with no data. When the user asks to create a group, I put up a UIAlert-
View asking for the name of the new group. If the user provides a valid name, I create
a new Group entity and save the managed object context. Again, this is almost boilerplate
code, copied from the template's insertNewObject: method:

```
NSManagedObjectContext *context = self.frc.managedObjectContext;
NSEntityDescription *entity = self.frc.fetchRequest.entity;
NSManagedObject *mo =
    [NSEntityDescription insertNewObjectForEntityForName:entity.name
                                inManagedObjectContext:context];
mo.name = name;
mo.uuid = [[NSUUID UUID] UUIDString]; // new in iOS 6
mo.timestamp = [NSDate date];
// save context
NSError *error = nil;
BOOL ok = [context save:&error];
if (!ok) {
    NSLog(@"%@", error);
    return;
}
```

The second view controller class is PeopleLister (Figure 36-3). It lists all the people in a
particular Group, so I don't want PeopleLister to be instantiated without a Group;
therefore, its designated initializer is initWithNibName:bundle:groupManaged-
Object:, and it looks like this:

```
- (id) initWithNibName:(NSString *)nibNameOrNil
              bundle:(NSBundle *)nibBundleOrNil
        groupManagedObject: (NSManagedObject*) object {
    self = [super initWithNibName:nibNameOrNil bundle:nibBundleOrNil];
    if (self) {
        self->_groupObject = object;
    }
    return self;
}
```

To navigate from the GroupLister view to the PeopleLister view, I instantiate People-Lister and push it onto the navigation controller's stack. For example, here's what happens when the user taps a Group name in the GroupLister table view:

```
- (void)tableView:(UITableView *)tableView
    didSelectRowAtIndexPath:(NSIndexPath *)indexPath {
    PeopleLister* pl =
        [[PeopleLister alloc] initWithNibName:@"PeopleLister" bundle:nil
            groupManagedObject:[self.frc objectAtIndexPath:indexPath]];
    [self.navigationController pushViewController:pl animated:YES];
}
```

PeopleLister, too, has an `frc` property, along with a getter that is almost identical to the template code for generating an NSFetchedResultsController. Almost, but not quite. In the case of GroupLister, we wanted every group; but a PeopleLister instance should list only the People belonging to one particular group, which has been stored as the `groupObject` property. So our implementation of the `frc` getter method contains these lines:

```
NSPredicate* pred =
    [NSPredicate predicateWithFormat:@"group = %@", self.groupObject];
req.predicate = pred; // req is the NSFetchRequest we're configuring
```

As you can see from Figure 36-3, the PeopleLister interface consists of a table of text fields. Populating the table is easy enough:

```
- (UITableViewCell *)tableView:(UITableView *)tableView
    cellForRowAtIndexPath:(NSIndexPath *)indexPath {
    UITableViewCell *cell =
        [tableView dequeueReusableCellWithIdentifier:@"Person"];
    NSManagedObject *object = [self.frc objectAtIndexPath:indexPath];
    UITextField* first = (UITextField*)[cell viewWithTag:1];
    UITextField* last = (UITextField*)[cell viewWithTag:2];
    first.text = object.firstName;
    last.text = object.lastName;
    first.delegate = last.delegate = self;
    return cell;
}
```

When the user edits a text field (the first or last name of a Person), I update the data model and save the managed object context; the first part of this code should be familiar from Chapter 21:

```
-(void)textFieldDidEndEditing:(UITextField *)textField {
    UIView* v = textField.superview;
    while (![v isKindOfClass: [UITableViewCell class]])
        v = v.superview;
    UITableViewCell* cell = (UITableViewCell*)v;
    NSIndexPath* ip = [self.tableView indexPathForCell:cell];
    NSManagedObject* object = [self.frc objectAtIndexPath:ip];
    [object setValue:textField.text
            forKey: ((textField.tag == 1) ? @"firstName" : @"lastName")];
    // save context
    NSError *error = nil;
    BOOL ok = [context save:&error];
    if (!ok) {
      NSLog(@"%@", error);
      return;
    }
}
```

The trickiest part is what happens when the user asks to make a new Person. It starts out analogously to making a new Group: I make a new Person entity, configure its attributes with an empty first name and last name, and save the context. But we must also make this empty Person appear in the table! To do so, we act as the NSFetchedResultsController's delegate (NSFetchedResultsControllerDelegate); the delegate methods are triggered by the change in the managed object context:

```
- (void) doAdd: (id) sender {
    [self.tableView endEditing:YES];
    NSManagedObjectContext *context = self.frc.managedObjectContext;
    NSEntityDescription *entity = self.frc.fetchRequest.entity;
    NSManagedObject *mo =
    [NSEntityDescription insertNewObjectForEntityForName:[entity name]
                                  inManagedObjectContext:context];
    mo.group = self.groupObject;
    mo.lastName = @"";
    mo.firstName = @"";
    mo.timestamp = [NSDate date];
    // save context
    NSError *error = nil;
    BOOL ok = [context save:&error];
    if (!ok) {
        NSLog(@"%@", error);
        return;
    }
}

// delegate methods

-(void)controllerWillChangeContent:(NSFetchedResultsController *)controller {
    [self.tableView beginUpdates];
}

-(void)controllerDidChangeContent:(NSFetchedResultsController *)controller {
```

```
        [self.tableView endUpdates];
    }

    -(void)controller:(NSFetchedResultsController *)controller
      didChangeObject:(id)anObject
          atIndexPath:(NSIndexPath *)indexPath
        forChangeType:(NSFetchedResultsChangeType)type
         newIndexPath:(NSIndexPath *)newIndexPath {
        if (type == NSFetchedResultsChangeInsert) {
            [self.tableView insertRowsAtIndexPaths:@[newIndexPath]
                withRowAnimation:UITableViewRowAnimationAutomatic];
            // wait for interface to settle...
            // ...then start editing first name of new person
            dispatch_async(dispatch_get_main_queue(), ^{
                UITableViewCell* cell =
                    [self.tableView cellForRowAtIndexPath:newIndexPath];
                UITextField* tf = (UITextField*)[cell viewWithTag:1];
                [tf becomeFirstResponder];
            });
        }
    }
}
```

Image File Formats

The Image I/O framework provides a simple, unified way to open image files (from disk
or downloaded from the network, as described in Chapter 37), to save image files, to
convert between image file formats, and to read metadata from standard image file
formats, including EXIF and GPS information from a digital camera. You'll need to link
to *ImageIO.framework* and import <ImageIO/ImageIO.h>.

Obviously, such features were not entirely missing before the Image I/O framework was
introduced (starting in iOS 4). UIImage can read the data from most standard image
formats, and you can convert formats with functions such as UIImage-
JPEGRepresentation and UIImagePNGRepresentation. But you could not, for example,
save an image as a TIFF without the Image I/O framework.

The Image I/O framework introduces the notion of an *image source* (CGImageSource-
Ref). This can be created from the URL of a file on disk or from an NSData object
(actually CFDataRef, to which NSData is toll-free bridged). You can use this to obtain
a CGImage of the source's image (or, if the source format contains multiple images, a
particular image). But you can also obtain metadata from the source *without* transforming the source into a CGImage, thus conserving memory. For example:

```
NSURL* url =
    [[NSBundle mainBundle] URLForResource:@"colson"
                            withExtension:@"jpg"];
CGImageSourceRef src =
    CGImageSourceCreateWithURL((__bridge CFURLRef)url, nil);
```

```
CFDictionaryRef result1 = CGImageSourceCopyPropertiesAtIndex(src, 0, nil);
NSDictionary* result = CFBridgingRelease(result1);
// ... do something with result ...
CFRelease(src);
```

Without having opened the image file as an image, we now have a dictionary full of information about it, including its pixel dimensions (kCGImagePropertyPixelWidth and kCGImagePropertyPixelHeight), its resolution, its color model, its color depth, and its orientation — plus, because this picture originally comes from a digital camera, the EXIF data such as the aperture and exposure at which it was taken, plus the make and model of the camera.

We can obtain the image as a CGImage, with CGImageSourceCreateImageAtIndex. Alternatively, we can request a thumbnail version of the image. This is a very useful thing to do, and the name "thumbnail" doesn't really do it justice. If your purpose in opening this image is to display it in your interface, you don't care about the original image data; a thumbnail is *precisely* what you want, especially because you can specify any size for this "thumbnail" all the way up to the original size of the image! This is tremendously convenient, because to assign a small UIImageView a large image wastes all the memory reflected by the size difference.

To generate a thumbnail at a given size, you start with a dictionary specifying the size along with other instructions, and pass that, together with the image source, to CGImageSourceCreateThumbnailAtIndex. The only pitfall is that, because we are working with a CGImage and specifying actual pixels, we must remember to take account of the scale of our device's screen. So, for example, let's say we want to scale our image so that its largest dimension is no larger than the width of the UIImageView (iv) into which we intend to place it:

```
NSURL* url =
    [[NSBundle mainBundle] URLForResource:@"colson"
                            withExtension:@"jpg"];
CGImageSourceRef src =
    CGImageSourceCreateWithURL((__bridge CFURLRef)url, nil);
CGFloat scale = [UIScreen mainScreen].scale;
CGFloat w = self.iv.bounds.size.width*scale;
NSDictionary* d =
    @{(id)kCGImageSourceShouldAllowFloat: (id)kCFBooleanTrue,
      (id)kCGImageSourceCreateThumbnailWithTransform: (id)kCFBooleanTrue,
      (id)kCGImageSourceCreateThumbnailFromImageAlways: (id)kCFBooleanTrue,
      (id)kCGImageSourceThumbnailMaxPixelSize: @((int)w)};
CGImageRef imref =
    CGImageSourceCreateThumbnailAtIndex(src, 0, (__bridge CFDictionaryRef)d);
UIImage* im =
    [UIImage imageWithCGImage:imref scale:scale
                  orientation:UIImageOrientationUp];
self.iv.image = im;
CFRelease(imref); CFRelease(src);
```

The Image I/O framework also introduces the notion of an *image destination*, used for saving an image into a specified file format. As a final example, I'll show how to save our image as a TIFF. We never open the image as an image! We save directly from the image source to the image destination:

```
NSURL* url =
    [[NSBundle mainBundle] URLForResource:@"colson"
                            withExtension:@"jpg"];
CGImageSourceRef src =
    CGImageSourceCreateWithURL((__bridge CFURLRef)url, nil);
NSFileManager* fm = [NSFileManager new];
NSURL* suppurl = [fm URLForDirectory:NSApplicationSupportDirectory
                           inDomain:NSUserDomainMask
                  appropriateForURL:nil
                             create:YES error:nil];
NSURL* tiff = [suppurl URLByAppendingPathComponent:@"mytiff.tiff"];
CGImageDestinationRef dest =
    CGImageDestinationCreateWithURL((__bridge CFURLRef)tiff,
                                    (CFStringRef)@"public.tiff", 1, nil);
CGImageDestinationAddImageFromSource(dest, src, 0, nil);
bool ok = CGImageDestinationFinalize(dest);
// error-checking omitted
CFRelease(src); CFRelease(dest);
```

CHAPTER 37

Basic Networking

Networking is difficult and complicated, chiefly because it's ultimately out of your control. My motto with regard to the network is, "There's many a slip 'twixt the cup and the lip." You can ask for a resource from across the network, but at that point anything can happen: the resource might not be found (the server is down, perhaps), it might take a while to arrive, it might never arrive, the network itself might vanish after the resource has partially arrived. iOS, however, makes at least the *basics* of networking very easy, so that's what this chapter will deal with.

Many earlier chapters have described interface and frameworks that network for you automatically. Put a UIWebView in your interface (Chapter 24) and poof, you're networking; the UIWebView does all the grunt work, and it does it a lot better than you'd be likely to do it from scratch. The same is true of MPMovieViewController (Chapter 28), MFMailComposeViewController (Chapter 33), and MKMapView (Chapter 37).

HTTP Requests

A simple HTTP request is made through an NSURLConnection object. You hand it an NSURLRequest describing what you'd like to do, and start the download. The actual network operations happen asynchronously (unless you specifically demand that they happen synchronously, which you'd never do); in other words, the NSURLConnection object does all its work in the background. Data received from the network in response to your request will arrive as an NSData object.

For the very simplest cases, you can download a resource asynchronously without using a delegate: call the class method `sendAsynchronousRequest:queue:completion-Handler:`. This creates an NSURLConnection and starts the download immediately. When the download ends, whether in failure or success, the completion handler block is called on the NSOperationQueue you specified, with three parameters: an NSURL-Response, an NSData (which will be the entire download if the download succeeded), and an NSError object. Here's an example of downloading a JPEG image file and displaying it in the interface; I specify the main queue (the queue of the main thread), because my completion handler is going to talk directly to my app's interface (see also Chapter 38):

```
NSString* s = @"http://www.someserver.com/somefolder/someimage.jpg";
NSURL* url = [NSURL URLWithString:s];
NSURLRequest* req = [NSURLRequest requestWithURL:url];
NSOperationQueue* q = [NSOperationQueue mainQueue];
[NSURLConnection sendAsynchronousRequest:req queue:q
    completionHandler:^(NSURLResponse *resp, NSData *d, NSError *err) {
        if (d) {
            UIImage* im = [UIImage imageWithData:d];
            self.iv.image = im;
        }
}];
```

The more formal and comprehensive approach is to specify the NSURLRequest along with a delegate. When the download starts, you stand back and let delegate messages arrive. To obtain and initialize an NSURLConnection object using this approach, call one of the following:

`connectionWithRequest:delegate:`
`initWithRequest:delegate:`
> The download begins immediately.

`initWithRequest:delegate:startImmediately:`
> This is the designated initializer; the other two methods call it. If the last argument is NO, the download does not begin until you send the connection the `start` message. You can specify an NSOperationQueue (Chapter 38) with `setDelegate-Queue:` if you'd like the delegate messages to arrive on a background thread.

The data will arrive piecemeal, so you have to maintain state; in particular, you'll prepare an NSMutableData object (probably as an instance variable, as it needs to persist while different methods refer to it) to which you'll keep appending each new chunk of NSData until you're told that the entire data has arrived — or that the request has failed. (The whole process is somewhat reminiscent of what we did with an NSXMLParser in Chapter 36.)

All the real work happens in four delegate methods:

`connection:didReceiveResponse:`
> The server is responding. We can now hope that our data will start to arrive, so get ready. If you like, you can interrogate the NSURLResponse object that is handed to you, to learn things from the response headers such as the data's expected size and MIME type. You can also ask for the `originalRequest` and the `currentRequest` to learn whether redirects or other forces have altered the NSURLRequest that is now being fulfilled.

`connection:didReceiveData:`
> Some data has arrived. Append it to the NSMutableData object.

`connectiondidFinishLoading:`
> All of the data has arrived; the NSMutableData object presumably contains it. Clean up as needed.

`connection:didFailWithError:`
> Something went wrong. Clean up as needed.

Here's an example of initiating a download of a JPEG image file:

```
self.receivedData = [NSMutableData data];
NSString* s = @"http://www.someserver.com/somefolder/someimage.jpg";
NSURL* url = [NSURL URLWithString:s];
NSURLRequest* req = [NSURLRequest requestWithURL:url];
NSURLConnection* conn =
    [NSURLConnection connectionWithRequest:req delegate:self];
```

Here are the corresponding delegate method implementations:

```
- (void) connection:(NSURLConnection *)connection
        didReceiveResponse:(NSURLResponse *)response {
    // connection is starting, clear buffer
    [self.receivedData setLength:0];
}

- (void) connection:(NSURLConnection *)connection
        didReceiveData:(NSData *)data {
    // data is arriving, add it to the buffer
    [self.receivedData appendData:data];
}

- (void)connection:(NSURLConnection*)connection
        didFailWithError:(NSError *)error {
    // something went wrong, clean up interface as needed
}

- (void)connectionDidFinishLoading:(NSURLConnection *)connection {
    // all done, we are ready to rock and roll
    // do something with self.receivedData
}
```

You should be wondering at this point how memory management works for an NSURL-Connection. We don't retain the NSURLConnection, so how does it live long enough to do any downloading? The answer is that NSURLConnection memory management works like NSTimer memory management (Chapter 12): as the download starts, the run loop retains it (and doesn't release it until the connection fails, finishes, or is canceled). Both `connectionWithRequest:delegate:` and `initWithRequest:delegate:` begin the download immediately, so the connection object that they return is retained by the run loop and doesn't need to be retained elsewhere.

On the other hand, an NSURLConnection initialized with `initWith-Request:delegate:startImmediately:`, as I mentioned earlier, does not start immediately if the third argument is NO, and you'll want to keep a reference to it in order to send it the `start` message later; so, in the general case, we ought to have an NSURL-Connection property with a retain policy. If we're going to do that, we should probably wrap the entire connection process in a dedicated object to hold this instance variable, because otherwise keeping track of multiple simultaneous NSURLConnections would be a nightmare. Here's the complete implementation for such a wrapper object, My-Downloader:

```
// MyDownloader.h:

@interface MyDownloader : NSObject
@property (nonatomic, strong, readonly) NSURLConnection* connection;
@property (nonatomic, strong, readonly) NSData* receivedData;
- (id) initWithRequest: (NSURLRequest*) req;
- (void) cancel;
@end

// MyDownloader.m:

@interface MyDownloader ()
@property (nonatomic, strong, readwrite) NSURLConnection* connection;
@property (nonatomic, copy, readwrite) NSURLRequest* request;
@property (nonatomic, strong, readwrite) NSMutableData* mutableReceivedData;
@end

@implementation MyDownloader

- (NSData*) receivedData {
    return [self.mutableReceivedData copy];
}

- (id) initWithRequest: (NSURLRequest*) req {
    self = [super init];
    if (self) {
        self->_request = [req copy];
        self->_connection =
            [[NSURLConnection alloc] initWithRequest:req
                delegate:self startImmediately:NO];
        self->_mutableReceivedData = [NSMutableData new];
    }
    return self;
}

- (void) connection:(NSURLConnection *)connection
        didReceiveResponse:(NSURLResponse *)response {
    [self.mutableReceivedData setLength:0];
}
```

```
- (void) connection:(NSURLConnection *)connection
        didReceiveData:(NSData *)data {
    [self.mutableReceivedData appendData:data];
}

- (void)connection:(NSURLConnection *)connection
        didFailWithError:(NSError *)error {
    [[NSNotificationCenter defaultCenter]
        postNotificationName:@"connectionFinished"
        object:self userInfo:@{@"error": error}];
}

- (void)connectionDidFinishLoading:(NSURLConnection *)connection {
    [[NSNotificationCenter defaultCenter]
        postNotificationName:@"connectionFinished" object:self];
}

- (void) cancel {
    // cancel download in progress, replace connection, start over
    [self.connection cancel];
    self->_connection =
        [[NSURLConnection alloc] initWithRequest:self->_request
            delegate:self startImmediately:NO];
}
@end
```

The class uses a combination of private and redeclared properties along with an explicit getter to make certain that clients have read-only access to instance variables (and, in the case of our NSMutableData object, access only to an immutable copy). Communication back to the client when the download finishes is through a notification; it is up to the client to register for this notification beforehand.

In the line that creates the NSURLConnection, we have used the designated initializer with a `startImmediately:` argument value of NO. Thus, a MyDownloader object can exist and be ready for action before doing any actual downloading. To set the download into motion, we tell the MyDownloader's `connection` to `start`. (Sending `start` to an NSURLConnection that is already downloading has no effect.) In the past, there have been complaints that sending `start` to an NSURLConnection that does not start immediately can cause a crash. I have not seen this myself, so perhaps it has been fixed in more recent iOS versions, but the solution is to schedule the connection on a run loop explicitly just before starting it:

```
[connection scheduleInRunLoop:[NSRunLoop currentRunLoop]
                      forMode:NSDefaultRunLoopMode];
[connection start];
```

The following sentence in the NSURLConnection header file may cause some concern: "The delegate is retained by the NSURLConnection until a terminal condition is encountered." MyDownloader retains the NSURLConnection and is its delegate, which raises a worry that a retain cycle may be looming in our future. However, in practice this should cause no difficulty; as that sentence implies, the delegate is released when the NSURLConnection is no longer downloading, so one way or another a leak will be avoided with no special action on our part. The delegate is retained for the same reason that an NSTimer's target is retained: if the delegate were to go out of existence while the download is ongoing, the attempt to send it delegate messages could cause a nasty crash. In any case we cannot set an NSURLConnection's delegate to nil, as it has no `delegate` property. If a download needs to be abandoned in midflight, the client should send us the `cancel` message, and the download will be stopped in the background in good order.

An NSURLConnection that has started downloading can be canceled by sending it the `cancel` message, and MyDownloader's implementation of `cancel` does this. However, an NSURLConnection that has been canceled is then good for nothing; it cannot be reused to try to start a connection ever again. Therefore, MyDownloader's `cancel` implementation also replaces its NSURLConnection with a fresh NSURLConnection configured in the same way, in case the client wants to try again later. The same thing is true of an NSURLConnection that has failed or that has finished in good order: it, too, is then good for nothing. However, MyDownloader does not replace its NSURL-Connection in that case, because the client is expected to abandon the MyDownload instance completely at that point.

How would we use MyDownloader if we have several objects to download? We might, for example, keep a mutable array of MyDownloader objects. To initiate a download, we create a MyDownloader object, register for its @"connectionFinished" notification, stuff it into the array, and set its connection going:

```
if (!self.connections)
    self.connections = [NSMutableArray array];
NSString* s = @"http://www.someserver.com/somefolder/someimage.jpg";
NSURL* url = [NSURL URLWithString:s];
NSURLRequest* req = [NSURLRequest requestWithURL:url];
MyDownloader* d = [[MyDownloader alloc] initWithRequest:req];
[self.connections addObject:d];
[[NSNotificationCenter defaultCenter] addObserver:self
    selector:@selector(finished:) name:@"connectionFinished" object:d];
[d.connection start];
```

When the notification arrives, either we've failed with an error or we've finished in good order. In the latter case, we grab the received data; either way, we remove the My-Downloader from the array, thus releasing it, along with its connection and its data:

```
- (void) finished: (NSNotification*) n {
    MyDownloader* d = [n object];
    NSData* data = nil;
    if ([n userInfo]) {
        // ... error of some kind! ...
    } else {
        data = d.receivedData;
        // ... and do something with the data right now ...
```

```
    }
    [[NSNotificationCenter defaultCenter]
        removeObserver:self name:@"connectionFinished" object:d];
    [self.connections removeObject:d];
}
```

In real life, you'd probably subclass MyDownloader to fit some particular task, and incorporate your downloaders directly into your application's model, letting them fetch the data on demand. Suppose, for example, you need to download images to serve as thumbnails in the cells of a UITableView. Let's consider how these images can be supplied lazily on demand. The model, as we saw in Chapter 21, might be an array of dictionaries. In this case, the dictionary might contain some text and a downloader whose job is to supply the image. So what I'm proposing is a model like this:

```
array
    dictionary
        text: @"Manny"
        pic: Downloader whose job is to supply an image of Manny
    dictionary
        text: @"Moe"
        pic: Downloader whose job is to supply an image of Moe
    dictionary
        text: @"Jack"
        pic: Downloader whose job is to supply an image of Jack
    ....
```

When the table turns to the data source for data, the data source will turn to the dictionary corresponding to the requested row, and ask that dictionary's downloader for its image. At that point, either the downloader has an image, in which case it supplies it, or it hasn't, in which case it returns nil (or some placeholder) and begins the download.

Here's the key point. When a downloader succeeds in downloading its image, it notifies the data source. If the corresponding row is visible, the data source immediately tells the table to reload the corresponding row; the table once again asks the data source for the data, the data source once again turns to the dictionary corresponding to the requested row and once again asks that dictionary's downloader for its image, and this time it obtains the image! Moreover, once an image is downloaded, the downloader continues to hold on to it and to supply it on request, so as the user scrolls, previously downloaded images just appear as part of the table.

The downloader we're imagining here is a MyDownloader subclass, MyImageDownloader, with an image property so that the data source can request the image. MyImageDownloader's implementation is straightforward. The data source is *not* going to abandon a MyImageDownloader that has failed — it isn't going to abandon *any* MyImageDownloader, because a MyImageDownloader either knows how to fetch the image or is the vendor of the fetched image — so we override connection:didFailWithError: to replace the now useless NSURLConnection, allowing the download to be attempted again later. We also override `cancel` to do nothing if the download is complete:

```
- (UIImage*) image {
    if (self->_image)
        return self->_image;
    [self.connection start];
    return nil; // or a placeholder
}

- (void)connectionDidFinishLoading:(NSURLConnection *)connection {
    UIImage* im = [UIImage imageWithData:self.receivedData];
    if (im) {
        self.image = im;
        [[NSNotificationCenter defaultCenter]
            postNotificationName:@"imageDownloaded" object:self];
    }
}

- (void)connection:(NSURLConnection *)connection
        didFailWithError:(NSError *)error {
    // prepare to try again
    self.connection =
        [[NSURLConnection alloc] initWithRequest:self.request
            delegate:self startImmediately:NO];
}

- (void) cancel {
    if (!self.image) // no point canceling if we finished the download
        [super cancel];
}
```

The data source looks perfectly normal:

```
- (UITableViewCell *)tableView:(UITableView *)tableView
        cellForRowAtIndexPath:(NSIndexPath *)indexPath {
    UITableViewCell *cell =
        [tableView dequeueReusableCellWithIdentifier:@"Cell"];
    NSDictionary* d = (self.model)[indexPath.row];
    cell.textLabel.text = d[@"text"];
    MyImageDownloader* imd = d[@"pic"];
    cell.imageView.image = imd.image;
    return cell;
}
```

Now for the key point. The data source is also registered for an `@"imageDownloaded"` notification. When such a notification arrives, it works out the table row corresponding to the MyImageDownloader that posted the notification and reloads that row:

```
- (void) imageDownloaded: (NSNotification*) n {
    MyImageDownloader* d = [n object];
    NSUInteger row = [self.model indexOfObjectPassingTest:
                        ^BOOL(id obj, NSUInteger idx, BOOL *stop) {
```

```
                    return (((NSDictionary*)obj)[@"pic"] == d);
            }];
    if (row == NSNotFound) return; // shouldn't happen
    NSIndexPath* ip = [NSIndexPath indexPathForRow:row inSection:0];
    NSArray* ips = [self.tableView indexPathsForVisibleRows];
    if ([ips indexOfObject:ip] != NSNotFound) {
        [self.tableView reloadRowsAtIndexPaths:@[ip]
                        withRowAnimation:UITableViewRowAnimationFade];
    }
}
```

A new feature in iOS 6 is that the table view delegate is notified when a cell scrolls out of view. We can take advantage of this to increase our efficiency and reduce our demands for bandwidth; if that cell's MyImageDownloader was still downloading its image, we can stop it, thus limiting the maximum number of images that will ever be requested simultaneously to the number of visible rows:

```
-(void)tableView:(UITableView *)tableView
        didEndDisplayingCell:(UITableViewCell *)cell
        forRowAtIndexPath:(NSIndexPath *)indexPath {
    NSDictionary* d = (self.model)[indexPath.row];
    MyImageDownloader* imd = d[@"pic"];
    [imd cancel];
}
```

The only missing piece of the puzzle is what should happen when a cell's downloader fails. If the user scrolls the failed cell out of view and later scrolls it back into view, the table will ask the data source for its data and the MyImageDownloader will try again to download its image. But that won't happen for a failed cell that's never scrolled out of view. How you deal with this is up to you; it's a matter of providing the best user experience without having an undue impact upon performance, battery, and so forth. In this instance, because these images are fairly unimportant, I might arrange that when an NSTimer with a fairly large interval fires (every 60 seconds, say), we reload the visible rows; this will cause any failed MyImageDownloader whose corresponding row is visible to try again.

In planning your interface, it is useful to draw a distinction as to whether the user will experience a particular networking session explicitly or implicitly. This changes nothing about *how* you network; it's a matter of presentation. Downloading images to be slotted into the cells of an existing table view would presumably be implicit networking: it happens regardless of whether the user wants it, and it doesn't seriously affect overall functionality, even if some or all of the images fail to arrive. In the TidBITS News app, on the other hand, everything displayed comes from a downloaded RSS feed: no feed, no data. This is explicit networking; the user needs to know when we are using the network, and needs to be informed of failure. The app preserves the previously downloaded feed, so the user has something to read even in the absence of the network, but the feed is explicitly refreshed when the user summons the table's UIRefreshControl, along with the spinning network activity indicator (Chapter 25); if the download fails, we put up an alert.

Bonjour

Bonjour is the ingenious technology, originated at Apple and now becoming a universal standard, for allowing network devices to advertise services they provide and to discover dynamically other devices offering such services. Once an appropriate service is detected, a client device can resolve it to get a network address and can then begin communicating with the server device. Actually communicating is outside the scope of this book, but device discovery via Bonjour is easy.

In this example, we'll look to see whether any device, such as a Mac, is running iTunes with library sharing turned on. We can search for domains or for a particular service; here, we'll pass the empty string as the domain to signify "any domain," and concentrate on the service, which is @"_daap._tcp". We maintain two instance variables, the NSNetServiceBrowser that will look for devices, and a mutable array in which to store any services it discovers:

```
self.services = [NSMutableArray array];
NSNetServiceBrowser* browser = [NSNetServiceBrowser new];
self.nsb = browser;
self.nsb.delegate = self;
[self.nsb searchForServicesOfType:@"_daap._tcp" inDomain:@""];
```

The NSNetServiceBrowser is now searching for devices advertising iTunes sharing and will keep doing so until we destroy it or tell it to stop. It is common to leave the service browser running, because devices can come and go very readily. As they do, the service browser's delegate (NSNetServiceBrowserDelegate) will be informed. For purposes of this example, I'll simply maintain a list of services, and update the app's interface when the situation changes:

```
- (void)netServiceBrowser:(NSNetServiceBrowser *)netServiceBrowser
        didFindService:(NSNetService *)netService
           moreComing:(BOOL)moreServicesComing {
    [self.services addObject:netService];
    if (!moreServicesComing)
        [self updateInterface];
}

- (void)netServiceBrowser:(NSNetServiceBrowser *)netServiceBrowser
        didRemoveService:(NSNetService *)netService
           moreComing:(BOOL)moreServicesComing {
    [self.services removeObject:netService];
    if (!moreServicesComing)
        [self updateInterface];
}
```

The delegate messages very kindly tell me whether they have finished listing a series of changes, so I can wait to update the interface until after a full batch of changes has ended. In this example, I don't really have any interface to update; I'll just log the list of services, each of which is an NSNetService instance:

```
- (void) updateInterface {
    for (NSNetService* service in self.services) {
        if (service.port == -1) {
            NSLog(@"service %@ of type %@, not yet resolved",
                service.name, service.type);
        }
    }
}
```

To connect to a service, we would first need to *resolve* it, thus obtaining an address and other useful information. An unresolved service has port -1, as shown in the previous code. To resolve a service, you tell it to resolve (resolveWithTimeout:); you will probably also set a delegate on the service (NSNetServiceDelegate), so as to be notified when the resolution succeeds (or fails). Here, I'll have the delegate call my update-Interface method again if a resolution succeeds, and I'll extend updateInterface to show the port number for any resolved services:

```
- (void) updateInterface {
    for (NSNetService* service in self.services) {
        if (service.port == -1) {
            NSLog(@"service %@ of type %@, not yet resolved",
                service.name, service.type);
            [service setDelegate:self];
            [service resolveWithTimeout:10];
        } else {
            NSLog(@"service %@ of type %@, port %i, addresses %@",
                service.name, service.type, service.port, service.addresses);
        }
    }
}

- (void)netServiceDidResolveAddress:(NSNetService *)sender {
    [self updateInterface];
}
```

The addresses of a resolved service constitute an array of NSData. Logging an address like this is largely pointless, as it is not human-readable, but it's useful for handing to a CFSocket. In general you'll call the service's getInputStream:outputStream: to start talking over the connection; that's outside the scope of this discussion. See Apple's WiTap example for more.

Push Notifications

If your app uses a server on the network that's under your control, you can arrange for the user to be notified when a significant event takes place on the server. This is called a *push notification* (or *remote notification*). The user interface for a push notification is the same as for a local notification, and the user can disable your app's notifications altogether (Chapter 26).

For example, the TidBITS News app is about news stories on the TidBITS website. The app's data comes from an RSS feed, which is refreshed on the server side whenever something changes on the site, such as a new news story being posted. It might be appropriate (and cool) if we were to add push notifications to the server code that refreshes the RSS feed, so that users could be alerted to the fact that they might like to launch TidBITS News and read a newly posted story.

Implementing push notifications is not trivial, and requires cooperation across the network between your app and your server, and between your server and Apple's push notification server. I've never actually tried this, so I'm just describing what the architecture is like; for details, read Apple's *Local and Push Notification Programming Guide*.

When developing your app, you obtain from the iOS Provisioning Portal (Chapter 9) credentials identifying your app, and allowing communication between your server and Apple's push notification server, and between Apple's push notification server and your app running on the user's device. When your app launches, it calls the UIApplication method `registerForRemoteNotificationTypes:`, which communicates asynchronously with Apple's push notification server to obtain a token identifying this instance of your app. If successful, the token comes back in the app delegate method `application:didRegisterForRemoteNotificationsWithDeviceToken:`. At that point, your app must communicate with your server to provide it with this token.

The server is now maintaining two pieces of information: its credentials and a list of tokens effectively representing users. When an event occurs at your server for which the server wishes to push a notification out to users, the server uses its credentials to connect with Apple's push notification server and — for *every individual user* whom the server wishes to notify — streams a message to Apple's push notification server, providing the user token plus a "payload" that describes the notification, much as a UILocalNotification does (Chapter 26). The payload is written in JSON (Chapter 36).

Meanwhile, the user's device, if it is still on, is (with luck) connected to the network in a low-power mode that allows it to hear from Apple's push notification server. The push notification server sends the message to the user's device, where the system treats it much like a local notification. If the user summons your app through the notification interface, your app can learn what has happened through either the app delegate message `application:didReceiveRemoteNotification:` or (if the app had to be launched from scratch) through `application:didFinishLaunchingWithOptions:`, whose dictionary will contain `UIApplicationLaunchOptionsRemoteNotificationKey`. The notification itself, instead of being a UILocalNotification object, is an NSDictionary corresponding to the original JSON payload.

Beyond Basic Networking

There are many aspects of basic networking that I haven't gone into in this chapter. For example:

- An NSURLRequest has a cache policy, which you can set to determine whether the request might be satisfied without freshly downloading previously downloaded data.
- An NSURLRequest to be handed to an NSURLConnection can specify that it wants to use the FTP, HTTP, or HTTPS scheme, including POST requests.
- An NSURLConnection can handle redirects and authentication.

See the *URL Loading System Programming Guide*.

You can also get as deep into the details of networking as you like; see in particular the *CFNetwork Programming Guide*.

Apple provides a generous amount of sample code. See in particular Simple-URLConnections, AdvancedURLConnections, SimpleNetworkStreams, Simple-FTPSample, and MVCNetworking.

CHAPTER 38

Threads

A *thread* is, simply put, a subprocess of your app that can execute even while other subprocesses are also executing. Such simultaneous execution is called *concurrency*. The iOS frameworks use threads all the time; if they didn't, your app would be less responsive to the user — perhaps even completely unresponsive. The genius of the frameworks, though, is that, for the most part, they use threads precisely so that you don't have to.

For example, suppose your app is downloading something from the network (Chapter 37). This download doesn't happen all by itself; somewhere, someone is running code that interacts with the network and obtains data. Similarly, how does Core Motion work (Chapter 35)? The data from the sensors is being gathered and processed constantly, with extra calculations to separate gravity from user-induced acceleration and to account for bias and scaling in the gyroscope. Yet none of that prevents your code from running; none of that prevents the user from tapping and swiping things in your interface. That's concurrency in action.

It is a testament to the ingenuity of the iOS frameworks that this book has proceeded so far with so little mention of threads. Indeed, it would have been nice to avoid the topic altogether. Threads are difficult and dangerous, and if at all possible you should avoid them. But sometimes that *isn't* possible. So this chapter introduces threads, along with a warning: threads entail complications and subtle pitfalls, and can make your code hard to debug. There is much more to threading, and especially to making your threaded code safe, than this chapter can possibly touch on. For detailed information about the topics introduced in this chapter, read Apple's *Concurrency Programming Guide* and *Threading Programming Guide*.

The Main Thread

You are always using *some* thread. All your code must run somewhere; "somewhere" means a thread. When code calls a method, that method normally runs on the same

What Is Concurrency, Really?

Part of the power of threads is that they implement concurrency without your having to worry about precisely how they do it. On a Mac Pro with eight cores, you could theoretically run eight threads truly *simultaneously*, one on each core. A recent model iPhone or iPad has two cores; but earlier iOS devices have just one core. Nevertheless, an iOS app is multithreaded. How can this be? Basically, the processor performs a little code from one thread, then a little code from another, then a little code from yet another, and so on; it switches its attention between threads so quickly that they seem to run at the same time. But this is still concurrency. Also, all iOS devices have a second processor, the graphics card (or *GPU*); certain graphics-related operations are performed by the GPU, leaving the main processor free.

thread as the code that called it. Your code is called through events (Chapter 11); those events normally call your code on the *main thread*. The main thread has certain special properties:

The main thread automatically has a run loop.
> A *run loop* is a recipient of events. It is how your code is notified that something is happening; without a run loop, a thread can't receive events. Cocoa events normally arrive on the main thread's run loop; that's why your code, called by those events, executes on the main thread.

The main thread is the interface thread.
> When the *user* interacts with the interface, those interactions are reported as events — on the main thread. When *your code* interacts with the interface, it too must do so on the main thread. Of course that will normally happen automatically, because your code normally runs on the main thread.

The main thread thus has a very great deal of work to do. Here's how life goes in your app:

1. An event arrives on the main thread; the user has tapped a button, for example, and this is reported to your app as a UIEvent and to the button through the touch delivery mechanism (Chapter 18) — on the main thread.

2. The control event causes your code (the action handler) to be called — on the main thread. Your code now runs — on the main thread. While your code runs, nothing else can happen on the main thread. Your code might command some changes in the interface; this is safe, because your code is running on the main thread.

3. Your code finishes. The main thread's run loop is now free to report more events, and the user is free to interact with the interface once again.

The bottleneck here is obviously step 2, the running of your code. Your code runs on the main thread. That means the main thread can't do anything else while your code is running. No events can arrive while your code is running. The user can't interact with the interface while your code is running. But this is usually no problem, because:

- Your code executes really fast. It's true that the user can't interact with the interface while your code runs, but this is such a tiny interval of time that the user will probably never even notice.

- Your code, as it runs, blocks the user from interacting with the interface. But that's not bad: it's good! Your code, in response to what the user does, might update the interface; it would be insane if the user could do something else in the interface while you're in the middle of updating it.

On the other hand, as I've already mentioned, the frameworks operate in secondary threads all the time. The reason this doesn't affect you is that they usually talk to *your* code on the *main* thread. You have seen many examples of this in the preceding chapters. For example:

- During an animation (Chapter 17), the interface remains responsive to the user, and it is possible for your code to run. The Core Animation framework is running the animation and updating the presentation layer on a background thread. But your delegate methods or completion blocks are called on the main thread.

- A UIWebView's fetching and loading of its content is asynchronous (Chapter 24); that means the work is done in a background thread. But your delegate methods are called on the main thread. The same is normally true of downloading a resource from the network with NSURLConnection (Chapter 37).

- Sounds are played asynchronously (Chapter 27, Chapter 29). But your delegate methods are called on the main thread. Similarly, loading, preparation, and playing of movies happens asynchronously (Chapter 28). But your delegate methods are called on the main thread.

- Saving a movie file takes time (Chapter 28 and Chapter 30). So the saving takes place on a background thread. Similarly, UIDocument saves and reads on a background thread (Chapter 36). But your delegate methods or completion blocks are called on the main thread.

Thus, you can (and should) usually ignore threads and just keep plugging away on the main thread. However, there are two kinds of situation in which your code will need to be explicitly aware of threading issues:

Your code is called back, but not on the main thread.
Some frameworks explicitly inform you in their documentation that callbacks are not guaranteed to take place on the main thread. For example, the documentation

on CATiledLayer (Chapter 20) warns that `drawLayer:inContext:` is called in a background thread. By implication, our `drawRect:` code, triggered by CATiled-Layer to update tiles, is running in a background thread. Fortunately, the UIKit drawing-related classes are thread-safe, and so is accessing the current context. Nevertheless, we cannot completely ignore the fact that this code is not running on the main thread.

Similarly, the documentation on AV Foundation (Chapter 28, Chapter 30) warns that its blocks and notifications can arrive on a background thread. So if you intend to update the user interface, or use a value that might also be used by your main-thread code, you'll need to be thread-conscious.

Your code takes significant time.

If your code takes significant time to run, you might need to run that code on a background thread, rather than letting it block the main thread and prevent anything else from happening there. For example:

During startup

You want your app to launch as quickly as possible. In Chapter 36, I called `URLForUbiquityContainerIdentifier:` during app launch. The documentation told me to call this method on a background thread, because it can take some time to return; we don't want to block the main thread waiting for it, because the app is trying to launch on the main thread, and the user won't see our interface until the launch process is over.

When the user can see or interact with the app

In Chapter 32, I called `enumerateEventsMatchingPredicate:` on a background thread in order to prevent the user interface from freezing up in case the enumeration took a long time. If I hadn't done this, then when the user taps the button that triggers this call, the button will stay highlighted for a significant amount of time, during which the interface will be completely frozen.

Similarly, when your app is in the process of being suspended into the background, or resumed from the background, your app should not block the main thread for too long; it must act quickly and get out of the way. This isn't just a matter of aesthetics or politeness; the system "watchdog" will summarily kill your app if it discovers that the main thread is blocked for too long.

Why Threading Is Hard

The one certain thing about computer code is that it just clunks along the path of execution, one statement at a time. Lines of code, in effect, are performed in the order in which they appear. With threading, that certainty goes right out the window. If you have code that can be performed on a background thread, then you don't know when it will be performed in relation to the code being performed on any other thread. For example, any line of your background-thread code could be interleaved between any two lines of your main-thread code.

You also might not know *how many times* a piece of your background-thread code might be running simultaneously. Unless you take steps to prevent it, the same code could be spawned off as a thread even while it's already running in a thread. So any line of your background-thread code could be interleaved between any two lines of *itself*.

This situation is particularly threatening with regard to *shared data*. Suppose two threads were to get hold of the same object and change it. Who knows what horrors might result? Objects in general have state, adding up to the state of your app as a whole. If multiple threads are permitted to access your objects, they and your entire app can be put into an indeterminate or nonsensical state.

This problem cannot be solved by simple logic. For example, suppose you try to make data access safe with a condition, as in this pseudo-code:

```
if (no other thread is touching this data)
    do something to the data...
```

Such logic cannot succeed. Suppose the condition succeeds; no other thread is touching this data. But between the time when that condition is evaluated and the time when the next line executes and you start to do something to the data, another thread can come along and start touching the data!

It is possible to request assistance at a deeper level to ensure that a section of code is not run by two threads simultaneously. For example, you can implement a *lock* around a section of code. But locks generate an entirely new level of potential pitfalls. In general, a lock is an invitation to forget to use the lock, or to forget to remove the lock after you've set it. And threads can end up contending for a lock in a way that permits neither thread to proceed.

Another problem is that the lifetime of a thread is independent of the lifetimes of other objects in your app. When an object is about to go out of existence and its `dealloc` has been called and executed, you are guaranteed that none of your code in that object will ever run again. But a thread might still be running, and might try to talk to your object, even after your object has gone out of existence. You cannot solve this problem by having the thread retain your object, because then there is the danger that the thread might be the *last* code retaining your object, so that when the thread releases your object, your object's `dealloc` is called on that thread rather than the main thread, which could be a disaster.

Not only is threaded code hard to get right; it's also hard to test and hard to debug. It introduces indeterminacy, so you can easily make a mistake that never appears in your testing, but that does appear for some user. The real danger is that the user's experience will consist only of distant consequences of your mistake, long after the point where you made it, making the real cause of the problem extraordinarily difficult to track down.

Perhaps you think I'm trying to scare you away from using threads. You're right! For an excellent (and suitably frightening) account of some of the dangers and considerations that threading involves, see Apple's tech note TN2109. If terms like *race condition* and *deadlock* don't strike fear into your veins, look them up on Wikipedia.

 When you call NSLog in your multithreaded code, the output in the console displays a number (in square brackets, after the colon) identifying the thread on which it was called. This is unbelievably helpful.

Three Ways of Threading

Without pretending to completeness or even safety, this section will illustrate three approaches to threading, progressing from worst to best. To give the examples a common base, we envision an app that draws the Mandelbrot set. (The actual code, not all of which is shown here, is adapted from a small open source project I downloaded from the Internet.) All it does is draw the basic Mandelbrot set in black and white, but that's enough crunching of numbers to introduce a significant delay. The idea is then to see how we can get that delay off the main thread.

The app contains a UIView subclass, MyMandelbrotView, which has one instance variable, a CGContextRef called _bitmapContext. Here's the structure of MyMandelbrotView's implementation:

```
// jumping-off point: draw the Mandelbrot set
- (void) drawThatPuppy {
    [self makeBitmapContext: self.bounds.size];
    CGPoint center =
        CGPointMake(CGRectGetMidX(self.bounds), CGRectGetMidY(self.bounds));
    [self drawAtCenter: center zoom: 1];
    [self setNeedsDisplay];
}

// create (and memory manage) instance variable
- (void) makeBitmapContext:(CGSize)size {
    if (self->_bitmapContext)
        CGContextRelease(self->_bitmapContext);
    // ... configure arguments ...
    CGContextRef context = CGBitmapContextCreate(nil, /* ... */);
    self->_bitmapContext = context;
}

// draw pixels of self->_bitmapContext
- (void) drawAtCenter:(CGPoint)center zoom:(CGFloat)zoom {
    // .... do stuff to self->_bitmapContext
```

```
    }

    // turn pixels of self->_bitmapContext into CGImage, draw into ourselves
    - (void) drawRect:(CGRect)rect {
        CGContextRef context = UIGraphicsGetCurrentContext();
        CGImageRef im = CGBitmapContextCreateImage(self->_bitmapContext);
        CGContextDrawImage(context, self.bounds, im);
        CGImageRelease(im);
    }

    // final memory managment
    - (void) dealloc {
        if (self->_bitmapContext)
            CGContextRelease(self->_bitmapContext);
    }
```

(I haven't discussed creating a bitmap context from scratch; see "Graphics Contexts" in the *Quartz 2D Programming Guide* for example code. In this case, we take advantage of a feature that lets us pass nil as the first argument to `CGBitmapContextCreate`, which relieves us of the responsibility for creating and memory-managing a data buffer associated with the graphics context.)

The `drawAtCenter:zoom:` method, which calculates the pixels of the instance variable `_bitmapContext`, is time-consuming, and we can see this by running the app on a device. If the entire process is kicked off by tapping a button whose action handler calls `drawThatPuppy`, there is a significant delay before the Mandelbrot graphic appears in the interface, during which time the button remains highlighted. That is a sure sign that we are blocking the main thread. We will consider three ways of moving this work off onto a background thread: with an old-fashioned manual thread, with NSOperation, and with Grand Central Dispatch.

Manual Threads

The simple way to create a thread manually is to send `performSelectorInBackground:withObject:` to some object containing a method to be performed on a background thread. Even with this simple approach, there is additional work to do:

Pack the arguments.
>   The method designated by the first argument to `performSelectorInBackground:withObject:` can take only one parameter, whose value you supply as the second argument. So, if you want to pass more than one piece of information into the thread, or if the information you want to pass isn't an object, you'll need to pack it into a single object. Typically, this will be an NSDictionary.

Set up an autorelease pool.
>   Secondary threads don't participate in the global autorelease pool. So the first thing you must do in your threaded code is to wrap everything in an autorelease pool.

Otherwise, you'll probably leak memory as autoreleased objects are created behind the scenes and are never released.

We'll rewrite MyMandelbrotView to use manual threading. Our drawAtCenter:zoom: method takes two parameters (and neither is an object), so we'll have to pack the argument that we pass into the thread, as a dictionary. Once inside the thread, we'll set up our autorelease pool and unpack the dictionary. This will all be made much easier if we interpose a trampoline method between drawThatPuppy and drawAtCenter:zoom:. So our implementation now looks like this (ignoring the parts that haven't changed):

```
- (void) drawThatPuppy {
    [self makeBitmapContext: self.bounds.size];
    CGPoint center =
        CGPointMake(CGRectGetMidX(self.bounds), CGRectGetMidY(self.bounds));
    NSDictionary* d =
        @{@"center": [NSValue valueWithCGPoint:center], @"zoom": @1};
    [self performSelectorInBackground:@selector(reallyDraw:) withObject:d];
    // [self setNeedsDisplay];
}

// trampoline, background thread entry point
- (void) reallyDraw: (NSDictionary*) d {
    @autoreleasepool {
        [self drawAtCenter: [d[@"center"] CGPointValue]
                      zoom: [d[@"zoom"] intValue]];
    }
}
```

So far so good, but we haven't yet figured out how to draw our view. We have commented out the call to setNeedsDisplay in drawThatPuppy, because it's too soon; the call to performSelectorInBackground:withObject: launches the thread and returns immediately, so our _bitmapContext instance variable isn't ready yet. Clearly, we need to call setNeedsDisplay *after* drawAtCenter:zoom: finishes generating the pixels of the graphics context. We can do this at the end of our trampoline method reallyDraw:, but we must remember that we're now in a background thread. Because setNeedsDisplay is a form of communication with the interface, we should call it on the main thread. We can do that with easily with performSelectorOnMainThread:withObject:waitUntilDone:. For maximum flexibility, it will probably be best to implement a second trampoline method:

```
// trampoline, background thread entry point
- (void) reallyDraw: (NSDictionary*) d {
    @autoreleasepool {
        [self drawAtCenter: [[d objectForKey:@"center"] CGPointValue]
                      zoom: [[d objectForKey:@"zoom"] intValue]];
        [self performSelectorOnMainThread:@selector(allDone)
                               withObject:nil waitUntilDone:NO];
    }
}
```

```
// called on main thread! background thread exit point
- (void) allDone {
    [self setNeedsDisplay];
}
```

This code is specious; the seeds of nightmare are already sown. We now have a single object, MyMandelbrotView, some of whose methods are to be called on the main thread and some on a background thread; this invites us to become confused at some later time. Even worse, the main thread and the background thread are constantly sharing a piece of data, the instance variable _bitmapContext; what's to stop some other code from coming along and triggering drawRect: while drawAtCenter:zoom: is in the middle of filling _bitmapContext?

To solve these problems, we might need to use locks, and we would probably have to manage the thread more explicitly. For instance, we might use the NSThread class, which lets us retain our thread as an instance and query it from outside (with isExecuting and similar). Such code can become quite elaborate and difficult to understand, even with an extremely basic implementation. It will be easier and safer at this point to use NSOperation, the subject of the next threading approach.

NSOperation

The essence of NSOperation is that it encapsulates a task, not a thread. The operation described by an NSOperation object may be performed on a background thread, but you don't have to concern yourself with that directly. You describe the operation and add the NSOperation to an NSOperationQueue to set it going. When the operation finishes, you are notified, typically by the NSOperation posting a notification. You can query both the queue and its operations from outside with regard to their state.

We'll rewrite MyMandelbrotView to use NSOperation. We need a property, an NSOperationQueue; we'll call it queue. And we have a new class, MyMandelbrotOperation, an NSOperation subclass. It is possible to take advantage of a built-in NSOperation subclass such as NSInvocationOperation or NSBlockOperation, but I'm deliberately illustrating the more general case by subclassing NSOperation itself.

Our implementation of drawThatPuppy makes sure that the queue exists; it then creates an instance of MyMandelbrotOperation, configures it, registers for its notification, and adds it to the queue:

```
- (void) drawThatPuppy {
    CGPoint center =
        CGPointMake(CGRectGetMidX(self.bounds), CGRectGetMidY(self.bounds));
    if (!self.queue) {
        NSOperationQueue* q = [NSOperationQueue new];
        self.queue = q; // retain policy
    }
```

```
MyMandelbrotOperation* op =
    [[MyMandelbrotOperation alloc] initWithSize:self.bounds.size
                                 center:center zoom:1];
[[NSNotificationCenter defaultCenter] addObserver:self
    selector:@selector(operationFinished:)
    name:@"MyMandelbrotOperationFinished"
    object:op];
[self.queue addOperation:op];
}
```

Our time-consuming calculations are performed by MyMandelbrotOperation. An NSOperation subclass, such as MyMandelbrotOperation, will typically have at least two methods:

A designated initializer
> The NSOperation may need some configuration data. Once the NSOperation is added to a queue, it's too late to talk to it, so you'll usually hand it this configuration data as you create it, in its designated initializer.

A main *method*
> This method will be called (with no parameters) automatically by the NSOperation-Queue when it's time for the NSOperation to start.

MyMandelbrotOperation has three instance variables for configuration (_size, _center, and _zoom), to be set in its initializer; it must be told MyMandelbrotView's geometry explicitly because it is completely separate from MyMandelbrotView. My-MandelbrotOperation also has its own CGContextRef instance variable, _bitmap-Context, along with an accessor so MyMandelbrotView can retrieve a reference to this graphics context when the operation has finished. Note that this is different from My-MandelbrotView's _bitmapContext; one of the benefits of using NSOperation is that we are no longer sharing data so promiscuously between threads.

Here's the implementation for MyMandelbrotOperation. All the calculation work has been transferred from MyMandelbrotView to MyMandelbrotOperation without change; the only difference is that _bitmapContext now means MyMandelbrot-Operation's instance variable:

```
- (id) initWithSize: (CGSize) sz center: (CGPoint) c zoom: (CGFloat) z {
    self = [super init];
    if (self) {
        self->_size = sz;
        self->_center = c;
        self->_zoom = z;
    }
    return self;
}

- (void) dealloc {
    if (self->_bitmapContext)
```

```
        CGContextRelease(self->_bitmapContext);
    }

    - (CGContextRef) bitmapContext {
        return self->_bitmapContext;
    }

    - (void)makeBitmapContext:(CGSize)size {
        // ... same as before ...
    }

    - (void)drawAtCenter:(CGPoint)center zoom:(CGFloat)zoom {
        // ... same as before ...
    }

    - (void) main {
        if ([self isCancelled])
            return;
        [self makeBitmapContext: self->_size];
        [self drawAtCenter: self->_center zoom: self->_zoom];
        if (![self isCancelled])
            [[NSNotificationCenter defaultCenter]
                postNotificationName:@"MyMandelbrotOperationFinished" object:self];
    }
```

The only method of interest is `main`. First, we call the NSOperation method `isCancelled` to make sure we haven't been cancelled while sitting in the queue; this is good practice. Then, we do exactly what `drawThatPuppy` used to do, initializing our graphics context and drawing into its pixels.

When the operation is over, we need to notify MyMandelbrotView to come and fetch our data. There are two ways to do this; either `main` can post a notification through the NSNotificationCenter, or MyMandelbrotView can use key–value observing (Chapter 13) to be notified when our `isFinished` key path changes. We've chosen the former approach; observe that we check one more time to make sure we haven't been cancelled.

Now we are back in MyMandelbrotView, hearing that MyMandelbrotOperation has finished. We must immediately pick up any required data, because the NSOperation-Queue is about to release this NSOperation. However, we must be careful; the notification may have been posted on a background thread, in which case our method for responding to it will also be called on a background thread. We are about to set our own graphics context and tell ourselves to redraw; those are things we want to do on the main thread. So we immediately trampoline ourselves out to the main thread:

```
// warning! called on background thread
- (void) operationFinished: (NSNotification*) n {
    [self performSelectorOnMainThread:@selector(redrawWithOperation:)
                        withObject:[n object] waitUntilDone:NO];
}
```

As we set MyMandelbrotView's _bitmapContext by reading MyMandelbrotOperation's
_bitmapContext, we must concern ourselves with the memory management of a
CGContext obtained from an object that may be about to release that context:

```
// now we're back on the main thread
- (void) redrawWithOperation: (MyMandelbrotOperation*) op {
    [[NSNotificationCenter defaultCenter]
        removeObserver:self
        name:@"MyMandelbrotOperationFinished"
        object:op];
    CGContextRef context = [op bitmapContext];
    if (self->_bitmapContext)
        CGContextRelease(self->_bitmapContext);
    self->_bitmapContext = (CGContextRef) context;
    CGContextRetain(self->_bitmapContext);
    [self setNeedsDisplay];
}
```

Using NSOperation instead of manual threading may not seem like any reduction in
work, but it is a tremendous reduction in headaches:

The operation is encapsulated.

Because MyMandelbrotOperation is an object, we've been able to move all the code
having to do with drawing the pixels of the Mandelbrot set into it. No longer does
MyMandelbrotView contain some code to be called on the main thread and some
code to be called on a background thread. The *only* MyMandelbrotView method
that can be called in the background is operationFinished:, and that's a method
we'd never call explicitly ourselves, so we won't misuse it accidentally.

The data sharing is rationalized.

Because MyMandelbrotOperation is an object, it has its own _bitmapContext. The
only moment of data sharing comes in redrawWithOperation:, when we must set
MyMandelbrotView's _bitmapContext to MyMandelbrotOperation's _bitmap-
Context. Even if multiple MyMandelbrotOperation objects are added to the queue,
the moments when we set MyMandelbrotView's _bitmapContext all occur on the
main thread, so they cannot conflict with one another.

The coherence of MyMandelbrotView's _bitmapContext does depend upon our obedience to an implicit contract not to set it or write into it anywhere except a few specific
moments in MyMandelbrotView's code. But this is always a problem with data sharing
in a multithreaded world, and we have done all we can to simplify the situation.

If we are concerned with the possibility that more than one instance of MyMandelbrot-
Operation might be added to the queue and executed concurrently, we have a further
defense — we can set the NSOperationQueue's maximum concurrency level to 1:

```
NSOperationQueue* q = [NSOperationQueue new];
[q setMaxConcurrentOperationCount:1];
self.queue = q;
```

This turns the NSOperationQueue into a true serial queue; every operation on the queue must be completely executed before the next can begin. This might cause an operation added to the queue to take longer to execute, if it must wait for another operation to finish before it can even get started; however, this delay might not be important. What *is* important is that by executing the operations on this queue completely separately, we guarantee that only one operation at a time can do any data sharing. A serial queue is thus a form of data locking.

Because MyMandelbrotView can be destroyed (if, for example, its view controller is destroyed), there is still a risk that it will create an operation that will outlive it and will try to access it after it has been destroyed. We can reduce that risk by canceling all operations in our queue before releasing it:

```
- (void)dealloc {
    // release the bitmap context
    if (self->_bitmapContext)
        CGContextRelease(self->_bitmapContext);
    [self->_queue cancelAllOperations];
}
```

In our code, we are still using the potentially confusing trampoline technique. Our operationFinished: method is called by a notification on what may be a background thread, so it calls redrawWithOperation: on the main thread. By a neat trick involving a block, we can actually eliminate the trampoline and both of those methods.

Recall, from Chapter 11, the NSNotificationCenter method addObserverFor-Name:object:queue:usingBlock:. The queue: argument here is an NSOperation-Queue — the queue on which we'd like our block to be called. I said in Chapter 11 that this will usually be nil, signifying the same thread that posted the notification, which will usually be the main thread. In this case, though, the thread that posted the notification might *not* be the main thread, so we can request *explicitly* that the block be called on the main thread. In other words, NSNotificationCenter will perform the trampolining for us.

As I said in Chapter 12, we have to take precautions to avoid a retain cycle; addObserver-ForName:object:queue:usingBlock: returns an observer which retains us, so we mustn't retain it in turn. We don't want to keep our observer as an instance variable because there might be multiple conflicting simultaneous observers. So we declare it as __weak to prevent the retain cycle, and we declare it as __block so that we can see its future value (the value it will have after the call to addObserverFor-Name:object:queue:usingBlock: returns) inside the block and use it to deregister when the notification arrives:

```
MyMandelbrotOperation* op =
    [[MyMandelbrotOperation alloc] initWithSize:self.bounds.size
                                    center:center zoom:1];
__block __weak id observer = [[NSNotificationCenter defaultCenter]
```

```
addObserverForName:@"MyMandelbrotOperationFinished"
object:op queue:[NSOperationQueue mainQueue]
usingBlock:^(NSNotification *note) {
    MyMandelbrotOperation* op2 = note.object;
    CGContextRef context = [op2 bitmapContext];
    if (self->_bitmapContext)
        CGContextRelease(self->_bitmapContext);
    self->_bitmapContext = (CGContextRef) context;
    CGContextRetain(self->_bitmapContext);
    [self setNeedsDisplay];
    [[NSNotificationCenter defaultCenter]
        removeObserver:observer
        name:@"MyMandelbrotOperationFinished"
        object:op2];
}];
[self.queue addOperation:op];
```

That's pretty elegant, but in the next section we'll go even further — we'll effectively
eliminate data sharing entirely by using Grand Central Dispatch.

 A number of useful methods mentioned earlier in this book expect an
NSOperationQueue argument; see Chapter 35 (`startDeviceMotion-`
`UpdatesToQueue:withHandler:`, and similarly for the other sensors)
and Chapter 37 (`sendAsynchronousRequest:queue:completion-`
`Handler:`).

Grand Central Dispatch

Grand Central Dispatch, or *GCD*, is a sort of low-level analogue to NSOperation and
NSOperationQueue (in fact, NSOperationQueue uses GCD under the hood). When I
say GCD is low-level, I'm not kidding; it's effectively baked into the operating system
kernel. Thus it can be used by any code whatsoever and is tremendously efficient.

Using GCD is like a mixture of the manual threading approach with the NSOperation-
Queue approach. It's like the manual threading approach because code to be executed
on one thread appears together with code to be executed on another; however, you have
a much better chance of keeping the threads and data management straight, because
GCD uses Objective-C blocks. It's like the NSOperationQueue approach because it uses
queues; you express a task and add it to a queue, and the task is executed on a thread as
needed. Moreover, by default these queues are serial queues, with each task on a queue
finishing before the next is started, which, as we've already seen, is a form of data locking.

We'll rewrite MyMandelbrotView to use GCD. The structure of its interface is very
slightly changed from the original, nonthreaded version. Our `makeBitmapContext:`
method now returns a graphics context rather than setting an instance variable directly;
and our `drawAtCenter:zoom:` method now takes an additional parameter, the graphics

context to draw into. Also, we have a new instance variable to hold our queue, which is a *dispatch queue*; a dispatch queue is a lightweight opaque pseudo-object consisting essentially of a list of blocks to be executed:

```
@implementation MyMandelbrotView {
    CGContextRef _bitmapContext;
    dispatch_queue_t _draw_queue;
}
```

In MyMandelbrotView's implementation, we create our dispatch queue as the view is created:

```
- (id)initWithCoder:(NSCoder *)aDecoder {
    self = [super initWithCoder: aDecoder];
    if (self) {
        self->_draw_queue =
            dispatch_queue_create("com.neuburg.mandeldraw", nil);
    }
    return self;
}
```

A call to `dispatch_queue_create` must be balanced by a call to `dispatch_release`. New in iOS 6, however, ARC understands GCD pseudo-objects and will take care of this for us (and in fact calling `dispatch_release` explicitly is forbidden).

Now for the implementation of `drawThatPuppy`. Here it is:

```
- (void) drawThatPuppy {
    CGPoint center = ❶
        CGPointMake(CGRectGetMidX(self.bounds), CGRectGetMidY(self.bounds));
    dispatch_async(self->_draw_queue, ^{ ❷
        CGContextRef bitmap = [self makeBitmapContext: self.bounds.size];
        [self drawAtCenter: center zoom: 1 context:bitmap];
        dispatch_async(dispatch_get_main_queue(), ^{ ❸
            if (self->_bitmapContext)
                CGContextRelease(self->_bitmapContext);
            self->_bitmapContext = bitmap;
            [self setNeedsDisplay];
        });
    });
}
```

That's all there is to it. No trampoline methods. No `performSelector`.... No packing arguments into a dictionary. No autorelease pools. No instance variables. No notifications. And effectively no sharing of data across threads. That's the beauty of blocks.

❶ We begin by calculating our `center`, as before. This value will be visible within the blocks, because blocks can see their surrounding context.

❷ Now comes our task to be performed in a background thread on our queue, _draw_queue. We specify this task with the dispatch_async function. GCD has a lot of functions, but this is the one you'll use 99 percent of the time; it's the most important thing you need to know about GCD. We specify a queue and we provide a block saying what we'd like to do. Thanks to the block, we don't need any trampoline methods. In the block, we begin by declaring bitmap as a variable *local to the block*. We then call makeBitmapContext: to create the graphics context bitmap, and drawAtCenter:zoom:context: to set its pixels; we make these calls *directly*, just as we would do if we weren't threading in the first place.

❸ Now we need to get back onto the main thread. How do we do that? With dispatch_async again! We specify the main queue (which is effectively the main thread) with a function provided for this purpose and describe what we want to do in *another* block. This second block is nested inside the first, so it isn't performed until the preceding commands in the first block have finished; moreover, because the first block is part of the second block's surrounding context, the second block can see our block-local bitmap variable! We set our _bitmapContext instance variable (with no need for further memory management, because makeBitmapContext has returned a retained graphics context), and call setNeedsDisplay.

 I used this same technique in Chapter 36, to call URLForUbiquity-ContainerIdentifier: on a background thread (so as not to block the main thread and the app launch process) and then to set an instance variable on the main thread (so as not to conflict with any other access to that instance variable).

The benefits and elegance of GCD as a form of concurrency management are stunning. The bitmap variable is not shared; it is local to each specific call to drawThatPuppy. The nested blocks are executed in succession, so any instance of bitmap must be completely filled with pixels before being used to set the _bitmapContext instance variable. More-over, the *entire* operation is performed on a serial queue, and _bitmapContext is touched only from code running on the main thread; thus there is no data sharing and no pos-sibility of conflict. Our code is also highly maintainable, because the entire task on all threads is expressed within the single drawThatPuppy method, thanks to the use of blocks; indeed, the code is only very slightly modified from the original, nonthreaded version.

You might object that we still have methods makeBitmapContext: and drawAt-Center:zoom:context: hanging around MyMandelbrotView, and that we must there-fore still be careful not to call them on the main thread, or indeed from anywhere except

from within drawThatPuppy. If that were true, we could at this point destroy makeBitmap-
Context: and drawAtCenter:zoom:context: and move their functionality completely
into drawThatPuppy. But it *isn't* true, because these methods are now *thread-safe*: they
are self-contained utilities that touch no instance variables or persistent objects, so it
doesn't matter what thread they are called on. Still, I'll demonstrate in a moment how
we can intercept an accidental attempt to call a method on the wrong thread.

The two most important GCD functions are:

dispatch_async
> Push a block onto the end of a queue for later execution, and proceed immediately
> with our own code. Thus, we can finish our own execution without waiting for the
> block to execute.
>
> Examples of using dispatch_async as a way of getting back onto the main thread
> (dispatch_get_main_queue) in order to talk to the interface from inside a block
> that might be executed on a background thread have appeared in Chapter 29 and
> Chapter 30. Also, in Chapter 11 I described a technique for using dispatch_async
> to step onto the main thread even though you're already on the main thread, as a
> way of waiting for the run loop to complete and for the interface to settle down —
> a minimal form of delayed performance. I used that technique in Chapter 19,
> Chapter 21, Chapter 28, and Chapter 36.

dispatch_sync
> Push a block onto the end of a queue for later execution, and wait until the block
> has executed before proceeding with our own code — because, for example, you
> intend to use a result that the block is to provide. The purpose of the queue would
> be, once again, as a lightweight, reliable version of a lock, mediating access to a
> shared resource. Here's a case in point, from Apple's own code:
>
> ```
> - (AVAsset*)asset {
>     __block AVAsset *theAsset = nil;
>     dispatch_sync(assetQueue, ^(void) {
>         theAsset = [[self getAssetInternal] copy];
>     });
>     return theAsset;
> }
> ```
>
> Any thread might call the asset method; to avoid problems, we require that only
> blocks run from a particular queue (assetQueue) may touch an AVAsset. But we
> need the result that this block returns; hence the call to dispatch_sync.

Examples in this book have also made use of dispatch_after (Chapter 11, Chapter 15, Chapter 20, Chapter 23) as an alternative to performSelector:with-
Object:afterDelay:.

Another useful GCD function is `dispatch_once`, a thread-safe way of assuring that a block is called only once; it's often used to vend a singleton. I showed an example in Chapter 3.

Besides serial dispatch queues, there are also concurrent dispatch queues. A concurrent queue's blocks are started in the order in which they were submitted to the queue, but a block is allowed to start while another block is still executing. Obviously, you wouldn't want to submit to a concurrent queue a task that touches a shared resource — that would be throwing away the entire point of serial queues. The advantage of concurrent queues is a possible speed boost when you don't care about the order in which multiple tasks are finished — for example, when you want to do something in response to every element of an array. The built-in global queues (available by calling `dispatch_get_global_queue`) are concurrent; you can also create a concurrent queue by passing `DISPATCH_QUEUE_CONCURRENT` as the second argument to `dispatch_queue_create`.

An interesting tweak is that you can queue up a *barrier block* on a concurrent queue; a barrier block has the property that it won't be dequeued until all the blocks preceding it on the queue have been not only dequeued but fully executed, and that no blocks following it in the queue will be dequeued until it itself has fully executed (rather like Benjamin Britten's "curlew sign," signifying that every musician must wait here until all the other musicians have reached the same point).

A frequent use of concurrent queues is with `dispatch_apply`. This function is like `dispatch_sync` (the caller pauses until the block has finished executing), but the block is called multiple times with an iterator argument. Thus, `dispatch_apply` on a concurrent queue is like a for loop whose iterations are multithreaded; on a device with multiple cores, this could result in a speed improvement. (Of course, this technique is applicable only if the iterations do not depend on one another.)

Arbitrary context data can be attached to a queue in the form of key–value pairs (`dispatch_queue_set_specific`) and retrieved by key. The `dispatch_queue_get_specific` function retrieves a key's value for a queue to which we already have a valid reference; `dispatch_get_specific` retrieves a key's value for the *current* queue, the one in whose thread we are actually running. In fact, `dispatch_get_specific` is the *only* valid way to identify the current queue (a function formerly used for this purpose, `dispatch_get_current_queue`, has been shown to be potentially unsafe and is now deprecated).

We can use this technique, for example, to make certain that a method is called only on the correct queue. Recall that in our Mandelbrot-drawing example, we may be concerned that a method such as `makeBitmapContext:` might be called on some other queue than the background queue that we created for this purpose. If this is really a worry, we can attach an identifying key–value pair to that queue when we create it. Both key and value should be pointers, so let's start by defining some static C strings:

```
static char* QKEY = "label";
static char* QVAL = "com.neuburg.mandeldraw";
```

We then create the queue like this:

```
self->_draw_queue = dispatch_queue_create(QVAL, nil);
dispatch_queue_set_specific(self->_draw_queue, QKEY, QVAL, nil);
```

Later, we can examine that identifying key–value pair for the queue on which a particular method is called:

```
- (CGContextRef) makeBitmapContext:(CGSize)size {
    NSAssert(dispatch_get_specific(QKEY) == QVAL, @"Wrong thread");
```

Note that we are comparing the values purely as pointers; the fact that either one of them is a C string is irrelevant. A common device, where threads generated by different instances of the same class need to be distinguished, is to attach to a queue a key–value pair whose value is the instance itself.

Threads and App Backgrounding

When your app is backgrounded and suspended (Chapter 11), a problem arises if your code is running. The system doesn't want to kill your code while it's executing; on the other hand, some other app may need to be given the bulk of the device's resources now. So as your app goes into the background, the system waits a short time for your app to finish doing whatever it may be doing, but it then suspends your app and stops it by force.

This shouldn't be a problem from your main thread's point of view, because your app shouldn't have any time-consuming code on the main thread in the first place; you now know that you can avoid this by using a background thread. On the other hand, it could be a problem for lengthy background operations, including asynchronous tasks performed by the frameworks. You can request time to complete a lengthy task (or at to least abort it yourself, coherently) in case your app is backgrounded, by wrapping it in calls to UIApplication's `beginBackgroundTaskWithExpirationHandler:` and `endBackgroundTask:`.

You call `beginBackgroundTaskWithExpirationHandler:` to announce that a lengthy task is beginning; it returns an identification number. At the end of your lengthy task, you call `endBackgroundTask:`, passing in that same identification number. This tells the application that your lengthy task is over and that, if your app has been backgrounded while the task was in progress, it is now okay to suspend you.

The argument to `beginBackgroundTaskWithExpirationHandler:` is a block, but this block does *not* express the lengthy task. It expresses what you will do *if your extra time expires* before you finish your lengthy task. At the very least, your expiration handler must call endBackgroundTask:, just as your lengthy task would have done; otherwise, your app won't just be suspended — it will be killed.

 If your expiration handler block *is* called, you should make no assumptions about what thread it is running on.

Let's use MyMandelbrotView, from the preceding section, as an example. Let's say that if drawThatPuppy is started, we'd like it to be allowed to finish, even if the app is suspended in the middle of it, so that our _bitmapContext instance variable is updated as requested. To try to ensure this, we call beginBackgroundTaskWithExpiration-Handler: beforehand and call endBackgroundTask: at the end of the innermost block:

```
- (void) drawThatPuppy {
    CGPoint center =
        CGPointMake(CGRectGetMidX(self.bounds), CGRectGetMidY(self.bounds));
    __block UIBackgroundTaskIdentifier bti =
        [[UIApplication sharedApplication]
            beginBackgroundTaskWithExpirationHandler: ^{
                [[UIApplication sharedApplication] endBackgroundTask:bti];
            }];
    if (bti == UIBackgroundTaskInvalid)
        return;
    dispatch_async(self->_draw_queue, ^{
        CGContextRef bitmap = [self makeBitmapContext: self.bounds.size];
        [self drawAtCenter: center zoom: 1 context:bitmap];
        dispatch_async(dispatch_get_main_queue(), ^{
            if (self->_bitmapContext)
                CGContextRelease(self->_bitmapContext);
            self->_bitmapContext = bitmap;
            [self setNeedsDisplay];
            [[UIApplication sharedApplication] endBackgroundTask:bti];
        });
    });
}
```

If our app is backgrounded while drawThatPuppy is in progress, it will (we hope) be given enough time to live that it can run all the way to the end. Thus, the instance variable _bitmapContext will be updated, and setNeedsDisplay will be called, before we are actually suspended. Our drawRect: will not be called until our app is brought back to the front, but there's nothing wrong with that.

The __block qualifier on the declaration of bti is like the __block qualifier in the add-ObserverForName:object:queue:usingBlock: example earlier: it allows us to see, inside the block, the value that bti *will* have when the call to beginBackgroundTaskWith-

`ExpirationHandler:` returns (Chapter 3). The check against `UIBackgroundTask-Invalid` can do no harm, and there may be situations or devices where our request to complete this task in the background will be denied.

It's good policy to use a similar technique when you're notified that your app is being backgrounded. You might respond to the app delegate message `applicationDidEnter-Background:` (or the corresponding `UIApplicationDidEnterBackground-Notification`) by saving data and reducing memory usage, but this can take time, whereas you'd like to return from `applicationDidEnterBackground:` as quickly as possible. A reasonable solution is to implement `applicationDidEnterBackground:` very much like `drawThatPuppy` in the example I just gave: call `beginBackgroundTask-WithExpirationHandler:` and then call `dispatch_async` to get off the main thread, and do your saving and so forth in its block.

What about lengthy asynchronous operations such as networking (Chapter 37)? As far as I can tell, it might not strictly be necessary to use `beginBackgroundTaskWith-ExpirationHandler:` with NSURLConnection; it appears that NSURLConnection has the ability to resume automatically after an interruption when your app is suspended. Still, it might be better not to rely on that behavior (or on an assumption that, just because the network is present now, it will be present when the app awakes from suspension), so you might like to integrate `beginBackgroundTaskWithExpirationHandler:` into your use of NSURLConnection.

Such integration can be just a little tricky, because `beginBackgroundTaskWith-ExpirationHandler:` and `endBackgroundTask:` rely on a shared piece of information, the UIBackgroundTaskIdentifier — but the downloading operation begins in one place (when the NSURLConnection is created, or when it is told to `start`) and ends in one of two other places (the NSURLConnection's delegate is informed that the download has failed or succeeded), so information is not so easily shared. However, with something like our MyDownloader class, an entire single downloading operation is encapsulated, and we can give the class a UIBackgroundTaskIdentifier instance variable. So, we would set this instance variable with a call to `beginBackgroundTaskWithExpiration-Handler:` just before telling the connection to `start`, and then both `connection:did-FailWithError:` and `connectionDidFinishLoading:` would use the value stored in that instance variable to call `endBackgroundTask:` as their last action.

CHAPTER 39

Undo

The ability to undo the most recent action is familiar from Mac OS X. The idea is that, provided the user realizes soon enough that a mistake has been made, that mistake can be reversed. Typically, a Mac application will maintain an internal stack of undoable actions; choosing Edit → Undo or pressing Command-Z will reverse the action at the top of the stack, and will also make that action available for Redo.

Some iOS apps, too, may benefit from at least a limited Undo facility, and this is not difficult to implement. Some built-in views — in particular, those that involve text entry, UITextField and UITextView (Chapter 23) — implement Undo already. And you can add it in other areas of your app.

The Undo Manager

Undo is provided through an instance of NSUndoManager, which basically just maintains a stack of undoable actions, along with a secondary stack of redoable actions. The goal in general is to work with the NSUndoManager so as to handle both Undo and Redo in the standard manner: when the user chooses to undo the most recent action, the action at the top of the Undo stack is popped off and reversed and is pushed onto the top of the Redo stack.

To illustrate, I'll use an artificially simple app in which the user can drag a small square around the screen. We'll start with an instance of a UIView subclass, MyView, to which has been attached a UIPanGestureRecognizer to make it draggable, as described in Chapter 18. The gesture recognizer's action target is the MyView instance itself:

```
- (void) dragging: (UIPanGestureRecognizer*) p {
    if (p.state == UIGestureRecognizerStateBegan ||
            p.state == UIGestureRecognizerStateChanged) {
        CGPoint delta = [p translationInView: self.superview];
        CGPoint c = self.center;
        c.x += delta.x; c.y += delta.y;
```

```
        self.center = c;
        [p setTranslation: CGPointZero inView: self.superview];
    }
}
```

To make dragging of this view undoable, we need an NSUndoManager instance. Let's store this in an instance variable of MyView itself, accessible through a property, undoer.

There are two ways to register an action as undoable. The one we'll use involves the NSUndoManager method `registerUndoWithTarget:selector:object:`. This method uses a target–action architecture: you provide a target, a selector for a method that takes one parameter, and the object value to be passed as argument when the method is called. Then, later, if the NSUndoManager is sent the undo message, it simply sends to that target that action with that argument.

What we want to undo here is the setting of our center property. This can't expressed directly using a target–action architecture: we can call `setCenter:`, but its parameter needs to be a CGPoint, which isn't an object. This means we're going to have to provide a secondary method that *does* take an object parameter. This is neither bad nor unusual; it is quite common for actions to have a special representation just for the purpose of making them undoable.

So, in our `dragging:` method, instead of setting `self.center` to c directly, we now call a secondary method (let's call it `setCenterUndoably:`):

```
[self setCenterUndoably: [NSValue valueWithCGPoint:c]];
```

At a minimum, `setCenterUndoably:` should do the job that setting `self.center` used to do:

```
- (void) setCenterUndoably: (NSValue*) newCenter {
    self.center = [newCenter CGPointValue];
}
```

This works in the sense that the view is draggable exactly as before, but we have not yet made this action undoable. To do so, we must ask ourselves what message the NSUndoManager would need to send in order to undo the action we are about to perform. We would want the NSUndoManager to set `self.center` back to the value it has *now*, before we change it as we are about to do. And what method would NSUndoManager call in order to do that? It would call `setCenterUndoably:`, the very method we are implementing; that's *why* we are implementing it. So:

```
- (void) setCenterUndoably: (NSValue*) newCenter {
    [self.undoer registerUndoWithTarget:self
        selector:@selector(setCenterUndoably:)
            object:[NSValue valueWithCGPoint:self.center]];
    self.center = [newCenter CGPointValue];
}
```

This not only makes our action undoable, it also makes it redoable. Why? Consider what happens when we want to undo this action:

1. We send undo to the NSUndoManager.
2. The NSUndoManager calls setCenterUndoably: with the new value, which is the old value that we passed in earlier when we called registerUndoWith-Target:selector:object:.
3. In our implementation of setCenterUndoably:, we send registerUndoWith-Target:selector:object: to the NSUndoManager — and there's a rule that, if the NSUndoManager is sent this message *while it is undoing*, it puts the target–action information on the Redo stack instead of the Undo stack (because Redo *is* the Undo of an Undo, if you see what I mean). That's one of the chief tricks to working with an NSUndoManager: it will respond differently to registerUndoWith-Target:selector:object: depending on its state.

So far, so good. But our implementation of Undo is very annoying, because we are adding a single object to the Undo stack every time dragging: is called — and it is called many times during the course of a single drag. Thus, undoing merely undoes the tiny increment corresponding to one individual dragging: call. What we'd like, surely, is for undoing to undo an *entire* dragging gesture. We can implement this through *undo grouping*. As the gesture begins, we start a group; when the gesture ends, we end the group:

```
- (void) dragging: (UIPanGestureRecognizer*) p {
    if (p.state == UIGestureRecognizerStateBegan)
        [self.undoer beginUndoGrouping];
    if (p.state == UIGestureRecognizerStateBegan ||
            p.state == UIGestureRecognizerStateChanged) {
        CGPoint delta = [p translationInView: self.superview];
        CGPoint c = self.center;
        c.x += delta.x; c.y += delta.y;
        [self setCenterUndoably: [NSValue valueWithCGPoint:c]];
        [p setTranslation: CGPointZero inView: self.superview];
    }
    if (p.state == UIGestureRecognizerStateEnded ||
            p.state == UIGestureRecognizerStateCancelled)
        [self.undoer endUndoGrouping];
}
```

This works: each complete gesture of dragging MyView, from the time the user's finger contacts the view to the time it leaves, is now undoable (and then redoable) as a single unit.

A further refinement would be to animate the "drag" that the NSUndoManager performs when it undoes or redoes a user drag gesture. To do so, we take advantage of the fact that we, too, can examine the NSUndoManager's state; we animate the center change when the NSUndoManager is "dragging," but not when the user is dragging:

```
- (void) setCenterUndoably: (NSValue*) newCenter {
    [self.undoer registerUndoWithTarget:self
        selector:@selector(setCenterUndoably:)
          object:[NSValue valueWithCGPoint:self.center]];
    if (self.undoer.isUndoing || self.undoer.isRedoing) { // animate
        UIViewAnimationOptions opt =
            UIViewAnimationOptionBeginFromCurrentState;
        [UIView animateWithDuration:0.4 delay:0.1 options:opt animations:^{
            self.center = [newCenter CGPointValue];
        } completion:nil];
    } else { // just do it
        self.center = [newCenter CGPointValue];
    }
}
```

Earlier I said that `registerUndoWithTarget:selector:object:` was one of two ways to register an action as undoable. The other is `prepareWithInvocationTarget:`. In general, the advantage of `prepareWithInvocationTarget:` is that it lets you specify a method with any number of parameters, and those parameters needn't be objects. You provide the target and, *in the same line of code,* send to the object returned from this call the message and arguments you want sent when the NSUndoManager is sent undo (or, if we are undoing now, redo). So, in our example, instead of this line:

```
[self.undoer registerUndoWithTarget:self
    selector:@selector(setCenterUndoably:)
      object:[NSValue valueWithCGPoint:self.center]];
```

You'd say this:

```
[[self.undoer prepareWithInvocationTarget:self]
    setCenterUndoably: [NSValue valueWithCGPoint:self.center]];
```

That code seems impossible: how can we send `setCenterUndoably:` without *calling* `setCenterUndoably:`? Either we are sending it to `self`, in which case it should actually be called at this moment, or we are sending it to some other object that doesn't implement `setCenterUndoably:`, in which case our app should crash. However, under the hood, the NSUndoManager is cleverly using Objective-C's dynamism (similarly to the message-forwarding example in Chapter 25) to capture this call as an NSInvocation object, which it can use later to send the same message with the same arguments to the specified target.

If we're going to use `prepareWithInvocationTarget:`, there's no need to wrap the CGPoint value representing the old and new `center` of our view as an NSNumber. So our complete implementation now looks like this:

```
- (void) setCenterUndoably: (CGPoint) newCenter {
    [[self.undoer prepareWithInvocationTarget:self]
        setCenterUndoably: self.center];
    if (self.undoer.isUndoing || self.undoer.isRedoing) { // animate
        UIViewAnimationOptions opt =
            UIViewAnimationOptionBeginFromCurrentState;
        [UIView animateWithDuration:0.4 delay:0.1 options:opt animations:^{
            self.center = newCenter;
        } completion:nil];
    } else { // just do it
        self.center = newCenter;
    }
}

- (void) dragging: (UIPanGestureRecognizer*) p {
    [self becomeFirstResponder];
    if (p.state == UIGestureRecognizerStateBegan)
        [self.undoer beginUndoGrouping];
    if (p.state == UIGestureRecognizerStateBegan ||
            p.state == UIGestureRecognizerStateChanged) {
        CGPoint delta = [p translationInView: self.superview];
        CGPoint c = self.center;
        c.x += delta.x; c.y += delta.y;
        [self setCenterUndoably: c];
        [p setTranslation: CGPointZero inView: self.superview];
    }
    if (p.state == UIGestureRecognizerStateEnded ||
        p.state == UIGestureRecognizerStateCancelled)
        [self.undoer endUndoGrouping];
}
```

The Undo Interface

We must now decide how to let the user *request* Undo and Redo. In developing the code from the preceding section, I used two buttons: an Undo button that sent undo to the NSUndoManager, and a Redo button that sent redo to the NSUndoManager. This can be a perfectly reasonable interface, but let's talk about some others.

By default, your application supports *shake-to-edit*. This means the user can shake the device to bring up an undo/redo interface. We discussed this briefly in Chapter 35. If you don't turn off this feature by setting the shared UIApplication's application-SupportsShakeToEdit property to NO, then when the user shakes the device, the framework walks up the responder chain, starting with the first responder, looking for a responder whose inherited undoManager property returns an actual NSUndoManager instance. If it finds one, it puts up the undo/redo interface, allowing the user to communicate with that NSUndoManager.

You will recall what it takes for a UIResponder to be first responder in this sense: it must return YES from canBecomeFirstResponder, and it must actually be made first res-

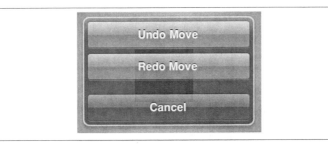

Figure 39-1. The shake-to-edit undo/redo interface

ponder through a call to becomeFirstResponder. Let's make MyView satisfy these requirements. For example, we might call becomeFirstResponder at the end of dragging:, like this:

```
- (BOOL) canBecomeFirstResponder {
    return YES;
}

- (void) dragging: (UIPanGestureRecognizer*) p {
    // ... the rest as before ...
    if (p.state == UIGestureRecognizerStateEnded ||
        p.state == UIGestureRecognizerStateCancelled) {
        [self.undoer endUndoGrouping];
        [self becomeFirstResponder];
    }
}
```

Then, to make shake-to-edit work, we have only to provide a getter for the undoManager property that returns our undo manager, undoer:

```
- (NSUndoManager*) undoManager {
    return self.undoer;
}
```

This works: shaking the device now brings up the undo/redo interface, and its buttons work correctly. However, I don't like the way the buttons are labeled; they just say Undo and Redo. To make them more expressive, we should provide a string describing each undoable action by calling setActionName:. We can appropriately and conveniently do this in setCenterUndoably:, as follows:

```
[[self.undoer prepareWithInvocationTarget:self]
    setCenterUndoably: self.center];
[self.undoer setActionName: @"Move"];
// ... and so on ...
```

Now the buttons say Undo Move and Redo Move, which is a nice touch (Figure 39-1).

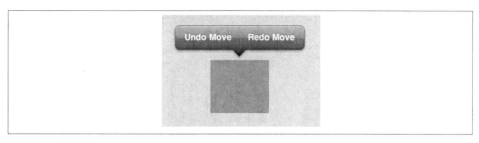

Figure 39-2. The shared menu as an undo/redo interface

Another possible interface is through a menu (Figure 39-2). Personally, I prefer this approach, as I am not fond of shake-to-edit (it seems both violent and unreliable). This is the same menu used by a UITextField or UITextView for displaying the Copy and Paste menu items (Chapter 23). The requirements for summoning this menu are effectively the same as those for shake-to-edit: we need a responder chain with a first responder at the bottom of it. So the code we've just supplied for making MyView first responder remains applicable.

We can make a menu appear, for example, in response to a long press on our MyView instance. So let's attach another gesture recognizer to MyView. This will be a UILong-PressGestureRecognizer, whose action handler is called longPress:. Recall from Chapter 23 how to implement the menu: we get the singleton global UIMenuController object and specify an array of custom UIMenuItems as its menuItems property. We can make the menu appear by sending the UIMenuController the setMenuVisible:animated: message. But a particular menu item will appear in the menu only if we also return YES from canPerformAction:withSender: for that menu item's action:

```
- (void) longPress: (UIGestureRecognizer*) g {
    if (g.state == UIGestureRecognizerStateBegan) {
        UIMenuController *m = [UIMenuController sharedMenuController];
        [m setTargetRect:self.bounds inView:self];
        UIMenuItem *mi1 =
            [[UIMenuItem alloc] initWithTitle:[self.undoer undoMenuItemTitle]
                                        action:@selector(undo:)];
        UIMenuItem *mi2 =
            [[UIMenuItem alloc] initWithTitle:[self.undoer redoMenuItemTitle]
                                        action:@selector(redo:)];
        [m setMenuItems:@[mi1, mi2]];
        [m setMenuVisible:YES animated:YES];
    }
}

- (BOOL)canPerformAction:(SEL)action withSender:(id)sender {
    if (action == @selector(undo:))
        return [self.undoer canUndo];
    if (action == @selector(redo:))
```

```
        return [self.undoer canRedo];
    return [super canPerformAction:action withSender:sender];
}

- (void) undo: (id) dummy {
    [self.undoer undo];
}

- (void) redo: (id) dummy {
    [self.undoer redo];
}
```

Observe how we consult our NSUndoManager throughout. We get the titles for our custom menu items from the NSUndoManager (there might, after all, be more than one undoable kind of action, and therefore more than one title), and we know whether to display the Undo menu item or the Redo menu item (or both, or neither) by calling our NSUndoManager's canUndo and canRedo, which essentially asks whether there's anything on the respective stack.

The Undo Architecture

Implementing basic Undo is not particularly difficult. But maintaining an appropriate Undo stack at the right point (or points) in your responder hierarchy, so that the right thing happens at every moment, can require some planning.

In general, your chief concern will be maintaining a consistent state in your app and in the Undo and Redo stacks of any NSUndoManager instances. You don't want an Undo stack to contain a method call that, if actually sent, would be impossible to obey, or if obeyed, would make nonsense of your app's state, because of things that have happened in the meantime. To prevent this, you have to make sure you are not implementing Undo only partially.

Suppose, for example, your app presents a To-Do list in which the user can add items, edit items, and so forth. And suppose you implemented Undo and Redo for inserting an item but not for editing an item. Then if the user inserted an item and then edited it, and then did an Undo of an item insertion followed by a Redo of that item insertion, this would fail to restore the state of the app, because the editing has been omitted from the Redo.

That is why you typically want each undoable action to pass consistently through a bottleneck method that will register this action with the NSUndoManager. And you will usually want this bottleneck method to be the same method that is registered with the NSUndoManager, so that the Undo and Redo stacks are kept synchronized properly (as with our simple example earlier in this chapter). The sole exception involves independent constructive and destructive actions, such as insertion into a list and deletion from that list; in that case, the Undo method for insertion will be the deletion method, and the Undo method for deletion will be the insertion method. (You can customize the arrangement of bottlenecks further and in more complex ways, but it's easy to become confused.)

Not all aspects of communication with an NSUndoManager need to be performed in the same place, however. We already saw this in the examples earlier in this chapter: setCenterUndoably:, the bottleneck method, knows what method to register with the NSUndoManager, but dragging: knows what a complete gesture is and therefore knows where to place the boundaries of a group. Similarly, it happens that our bottleneck method is the one that called setActionName:, but in real life it will often be some other method that knows best what name should be attached to a particular action. You will thus end up with a single NSUndoManager being bombarded with messages from various places in your code. Indeed, NSUndoManager accomodates exactly this sort of design; this is why it accepts methods describing features of an action *before* that action is actually registered. Also, NSUndoManager emits many notifications for which you can register, to help tie together operations that are performed at disparate locations in your code.

Then there are the larger architectural questions of how many NSUndoManager objects your app needs and how long each one needs to live. There's typically nothing wrong with an iOS app having occasional short-lived, short-depth Undo stacks and no Undo the rest of the time. Apple's SimpleUndo example constructs an app with an Edit interface, where the user makes changes and then taps either Cancel or Save, returning to the main interface. Here, the user can shake to undo what happened during that edit session. And that's all that's undoable within this app. If the user taps Edit again, it would make sense to clear the existing Undo stack; there's no point in letting the user return to an earlier Edit session's state. If the user switches away to a different view controller, it would make sense to release the NSUndoManager completely and start with a clean slate when we come back; if the user had any intention of undoing, the time to do so was before abandoning this part of the interface.

Your architectural decisions will often be closely tied to the actual functionality and nature of your app. For example, consider again the MyView instance that the user can move, and whose movements the user can undo. Suppose our app has *two* MyView instances in the same window. In our earlier examples, we've implemented Undo at the level of the individual MyView instance. Is this right when there are multiple MyView instances, or should we move the implementation to a higher point in the responder chain that effectively contains them both — for example, to the view controller of whose view they are subviews? There's no single right answer. It depends on what makes sense for what our app actually does. If these are fairly independent objects, in terms of the app's functionality and the mental world it creates, then it might make sense to be able to undo a move of either view, independently of the other. But if these are, say, two playing cards in a deck, then obviously it isn't up to an individual card whether it can be put back into the place it was before; the only undoable card is the most recently moved of *all* cards.

In a document based-app, the document itself is the natural locus of Undo: as long as the user is working in a document, it's that document's state that needs to be undoable and redoable. As I mentioned in Chapter 36, UIDocument has an undo manager (its undoManager property), and you can mark a file as dirty by using it. Instead of calling updateChangeCount:, as we did in that chapter, you register undoable actions with the UIDocument's undo manager, as in *this* chapter, and the UIDocument uses this information to know when a file is dirty and needs autosaving. You do not have to use the default NSUndoManager object returned from undoManager; this property is settable, so you can supply your own NSUndoManager subclass if the needs and nature of your document require specialized behaviors. An action can be marked as discardable by sending the NSUndoManager the setActionIsDiscardable: message before registering an action as undoable; the idea, apparently, is that UIDocument might be unable to save the document, and a discardable action is one that can be harmlessly ejected from the stack.

For more about the NSUndoManager class and how to use it, read Apple's *Undo Architecture* as well as the documentation for the class itself.

CHAPTER 40

Epilogue

You may go, for you're at liberty.

—W. S. Gilbert, *The Pirates of Penzance*

This book must come to an end, but your exploration of iOS will go on and on. There's much more to know and to discover. A single book that described completely, or even introduced, every aspect of iOS programming would be immense — many times the size of this one. Inevitably, severe limits have had to be set. Having read this book, you are now in a position to investigate many further areas of iOS that this book hasn't explored in any depth. Some of these areas have been mentioned in individual chapters; here are a few others:

OpenGL

> An open source C library for drawing, including 3D drawing, that takes full advantage of graphics hardware. This is often the most efficient way to draw, especially when animation is involved. iOS incorporates a simplified version of OpenGL called OpenGL ES. See the *OpenGL Programming Guide for iOS*. Open GL interface configuration, texture loading, shading, and calculation are simplified by the GLKit framework; see the *GLKit Framework Reference*.

Accelerate

> Certain computation-intensive processes will benefit from the vector-based Accelerate framework. See the *vDSP Programming Guide*.

Game Kit

> The Game Kit framework covers three areas that can enhance your user's game experience: Wireless or Bluetooth communication directly between devices (peer-to-peer); voice communication across an existing network connection; and Game Center, a networking facility that facilitates these and many other aspects of interplayer communication, such as posting and viewing high scores and setting up

combinations of players who wish to compete. See the *Game Kit Programming Guide*.

Advertising

The iAD framework lets your free app attempt to make money by displaying advertisements provided by Apple. See the *iAD Programming Guide*.

Purchases

Your app can allow the user to buy something, using Apple's App Store to process payments. For example, you could provide a renewable subscription, or offer to unlock advanced app features. See the *In App Purchase Programming Guide*.

Newsstand

Your app may represent a subscription to something like a newspaper or magazine. See the *Newsstand Kit Framework Reference*.

Printing

See the "Printing" chapter of the *Drawing and Printing Guide for iOS*.

Security

This book has not discussed security topics such as keychains, certificates, and encryption. See the *Security Overview* and the Security framework.

Accessibility

VoiceOver assists visually impaired users by describing the interface aloud. To participate, views must be configured to describe themselves usefully. Built-in views already do this to a large extent, and you can extend this functionality. See the *Accessibility Programming Guide for iOS*.

Telephone

The Core Telephony framework lets your app get information about a particular cellular carrier and call.

Pass Kit

New in iOS 6, the Pass Kit framework allows creation of downloadable passes to go into the user's Passbook app. See the *Passbook Programming Guide*.

External accessories

The user can attach an external accessory to the device, either directly via USB or wirelessly via Bluetooth. Your app can communicate with such an accessory. See *External Accessory Programming Topics*.

Index

We'd like to hear your suggestions for improving our indexes. Send email to index@oreilly.com.

About the Author

Matt Neuburg has a PhD in Classics and has taught at many universities and colleges. He has been programming computers since 1968. He has written applications for Mac OS X and iOS, is a former editor of *MacTech Magazine*, and is a long-standing contributing editor for TidBITS. His previous O'Reilly books are *Frontier: The Definitive Guide*, *REALbasic: The Definitive Guide*, and *AppleScript: The Definitive Guide*. He makes a living writing books, articles, and software documentation, as well as by programming, consulting, and training.

Colophon

The animal on the cover of *Programming iOS 6* is a kingbird, one of the 13 species of North American songbirds making up the genus *Tyrannus*. A group of kingbirds is called a "coronation," a "court," or a "tyranny."

Kingbirds eat insects, which they often catch in flight, swooping from a perch to grab the insect midair. They may also supplement their diets with berries and fruits. They have long, pointed wings, and males perform elaborate aerial courtship displays.

Both the genus name (meaning "tyrant" or "despot") and the common name ("kingbird") refer to these birds' aggressive defense of their territories, breeding areas, and mates. They have been documented attacking red-tailed hawks (which are more than twenty times their size), knocking bluejays out of trees, and driving away crows and ravens. (For its habit of standing up to much larger birds, the gray kingbird has been adopted as a Puerto Rican nationalist symbol.)

"Kingbird" most often refers to the Eastern kingbird (*T. tyrannus*), an average-size kingbird (7.5–9 inches long, wingspan 13–15 inches) found all across North America. This common and widespread bird has a dark head and back, with a white throat, chest, and belly. Its red crown patch is rarely seen. Its high-pitched, buzzing, stuttering sounds have been described as resembling "sparks jumping between wires" or an electric fence.

The cover image is from *Cassell's Natural History*. The cover font is Adobe ITC Garamond. The text font is Adobe Minion Pro; the heading font is Adobe Myriad Condensed; and the code font is Dalton Maag's Ubuntu Mono.

Have it your way.